D1529091

THE BELGIAN CONTRIBUTION TO
THE SECOND VATICAN COUNCIL

BIBLIOTHECA
EPHEMERIDUM THEOLOGICARUM LOVANIENSIUM

UNIVERSITÉ CATHOLIQUE DE LOUVAIN
LOUVAIN-LA-NEUVE

KATHOLIEKE UNIVERSITEIT LEUVEN
LEUVEN

BIBLIOTHECA EPHEMERIDUM THEOLOGICARUM LOVANIENSIUM

CCXVI

THE BELGIAN CONTRIBUTION TO THE SECOND VATICAN COUNCIL

INTERNATIONAL RESEARCH CONFERENCE AT MECHELEN, LEUVEN AND LOUVAIN-LA-NEUVE (SEPTEMBER 12-16, 2005)

EDITED BY

D. DONNELLY – J. FAMERÉE – M. LAMBERIGTS – K. SCHELKENS

UITGEVERIJ PEETERS
LEUVEN – PARIS – DUDLEY, MA
2008

A CIP record for this book is available from the Library of Congress.

ISBN 978-90-429-2101-6 (Peeters Leuven)
D/2008/0602/91

© 2008, Peeters, Bondgenotenlaan 153, B-3000 Leuven (Belgium)

PREFACE

Anniversaries are causes for celebration particularly when we gather with friends to recall some event from the past that brims with elation and significance. Such was the occasion in September, 2005, when a community of scholars assembled in Mechelen, Leuven, and Louvain-la-Neuve to consider the influence of the so-called "Squadra Belga" at Vatican Council II (1962-1965).

The timing for a 40th anniversary event (1965-2005) was fitting for at least three reasons. First, supportive relationships existed among its sponsors – The Cardinal Suenens Center at John Carroll University (Cleveland) in the United States, the Center for the Study of Second Vatican Council (Katholieke Universiteit, Leuven) and the Centre Lumen Gentium (Université Catholique de Louvain, Louvain-la-Neuve) in Belgium, and there was a collective wish in these centers to do something to commemorate the anniversary of the Council's close in 1965. Second, while it is indisputably true that much pioneer work had already been done on Belgians and Vatican Council II, it was also true that the recent publication of inventories on private conciliar archives offered an opportunity to consult newly available primary sources, so that the contribution of the Belgians might be re-assessed and studied in its full historical complexity. Third, an energetic and intergenerational team of international scholars from Belgium, Canada, France, Germany, Italy, the Netherlands and the United States guaranteed a balanced appraisal concerning the role of the Belgians. It was the convergence of these three factors that led to the colloquium and subsequently to this volume.

While this volume attests to the critical research undertaken during this five-day conference, leading to a richer and fuller understanding of the Belgian contribution to the Council and of the general historiography of Vatican II, there was also time for conviviality provided through the generous hospitality of Cardinal Godfried Danneels, Aldegonde and Hubert Brenninkmeijer, Peeters Publishers, and Margaret F. Grace. At one celebratory occasion, the Cardinal Suenens Center presented its "Living Water Award" to Giuseppe Alberigo in recognition of his extraordinary commitment to keep alive the vision of Vatican Council II. Professor Alberigo was present with his wife Angelina to accept the award at a dinner in his honor in Leuven at the conclusion of our colloquium. We now mourn the death of Giuseppe Alberigo in June, 2007, at the same time that we recognize our position as beneficiaries of his legacy, not limited to the *History of Vatican II* and the presence of Fondazione per le Scienze Religiose, a world-class research center in Bologna that he led with distinction. We would therefore like to dedicate this volume to the memory of Giuseppe Alberigo.

We gratefully acknowledge the work and expertise of the scholars who contributed to this volume. We also thank Robert Maryks (New York) for his careful editing of the English texts. F.W.O.-Vlaanderen offered financial support in addition to Margaret Grace's generosity and made the 2005 colloquium of Mechelen, Leuven and Louvain-la-Neuve an anniversary to remember. Finally, we extend our appreciation to the Editorial Board of *Bibliotheca Ephemeridum Theologicarum Lovaniensium* for the honour in accepting this volume in its prestigious series.

The editors

TABLE OF CONTENTS

CONTENTS   XI

INTRODUCTION

In accordance with the September 2005 colloquium, the present volume approaches the Belgian activities and influences at the Second Vatican Council from various angles. The many contributions are therefore organized, by logic and convenience, into three sections.

Part I consists of two methodological considerations and one testimony: John Coleman (Los Angeles, USA) provides an analysis of the often unexpected but powerful dynamics of small groups in a large assembly; Leo Kenis (Leuven, Belgium) offers insight concerning private diaries as sources for Vatican II; and thanks to Luc Van Hilst (Mechelen, Belgium), we have an original testimony of Msgr Loris Capovilla (Rome, Italy), secretary to Pope John XXIII.

Part II highlights the influence of Cardinal Suenens at Vatican II. This section is introduced by Mathijs Lamberigts (Leuven, Belgium) and Leo Declerck (Bruges, Belgium), co-authors of a lengthy essay on the role of Cardinal Suenens at the Council. Their essay is followed by studies on important relationships of Cardinal Suenens with other protagonists at Vatican II: Guido Treffler (Munich, Germany) on cardinals Suenens and Döpfner; Dirk Claes (Leuven, Belgium) on cardinals Suenens and Giacomo Lercaro; Giovanni Turbanti (Bologna, Italy) on cardinals Suenens and Lercaro, and Giuseppe Dossetti; Leo Declerck and Toon Osaer (Brussels, Belgium) on cardinals Suenens and Montini/Paul VI; Gilles Routhier (Québec, Canada) on cardinals Suenens and Léger.

Part III focuses on key areas where the influence of the Squadra Belga – its Belgian theologians and bishops – was especially in evidence. In the area of Ecumenism and the document *Unitatis redintegratio*, Emmanuel Lanne (Chevetogne, Belgium) writes on the role of the Chevetogne monastery, and Peter De Mey (Leuven, Belgium) studies the influence of Gustave Thils. In the area of Revelation theology (*Dei verbum*), Karim Schelkens (Leuven, Belgium) clarifies the role of Lucien Cerfaux and the preparations of the Schema *De fontibus revelationis*, while Jared Wicks (Cleveland, USA) and Claude Soetens (Louvain-la-Neuve, Belgium) offer separate studies of the contributions of Charles Moeller (the former on Moeller and the Schema *De revelatione*, the latter on Moeller and *Lumen gentium*). Also in the area of Ecclesiology and especially *Lumen gentium*, Jan Grootaers (Brussels, Belgium) provides a revealing study on the

diversity of tendencies between Giuseppe Dossetti and Gérard Philips;
Joseph Famerée (Louvain-la-Neuve, Belgium) makes available new
insight and research on Gustave Thils and the Schema *De ecclesia*.
Philippe Bordeyne (Paris, France) studies the collaboration of Pierre
Haubtmann with the Belgian *periti* for the drafting of *Gaudium et spes*,
and Mathijs Lamberigts pays due attention to Bishop Calewaert and
Sacrosanctum concilium. On issues of religious liberty and missiology,
Silvia Scatena (Bologna, Italy) furnishes us with a study of Émile-Joseph
De Smedt, John Courtney Murray and *Dignitatis humanae*, while Eddy
Louchez (Louvain-la-Neuve, Belgium) rounds out with a look at the
typology and the strategy of the Belgian missionary bishops.

The last words in the form of summary observations were in the hands
of Michael Fahey (Chestnut Hill, USA) who suggested that we might
consider the 2005 colloquium as the first of two colloquia. There were
still areas to explore, according to Fahey. As a result, plans are in preparation for a next gathering not only to review the contributions of those
Belgian Council participants who remained unconsidered in 2005, but
also, when warranted, to study in greater detail the role of some who
were already considered at the first colloquium.

The Cardinal Suenens Center	D. DONNELLY
Cleveland, OH	
Université Catholique de Louvain	J. FAMERÉE
Louvain-la-Neuve	
Katholieke Universiteit Leuven	M. LAMBERIGTS
Leuven	
Katholieke Universiteit Leuven	K. SCHELKENS
Leuven	

PART I

METHODOLOGICAL ISSUES

VATICAN II AS A SOCIAL MOVEMENT

I title my essay, "Vatican II as a Social Movement". This choice exhibits a decided primarily sociological focus on the Council itself, in its processes and social dynamic more than on how it was at the time or has been since "received" or re-assessed in the church. The church is so often, one-sidedly, viewed as almost entirely an institution that not enough sociological attention is given to the ways and times in which it is also a social movement. Social movement literature in sociology deals precisely with the framing of new issues and symbols in society; how they are contested; who the actors involved in the contestation are; what their resources may be and how *ad hoc* pressure or lobby groups mold sentiments and garner adherents to their cause and sway the non-aligned. Sociologists refer to these actions of "ginger" or lobby groups in social movements as "social mobilization"[1]. Social movements typically emerge when underlying societal issues fester or are not being addressed by institutions and/or when received institutional interpretations or frames no longer garner allegiance. Often, however, social movements do not erupt spontaneously. They need to be evoked by leaders and small groups. In the midst of a social movement, outcomes often remain uncertain, allies not always clear.

I want to preface the substance of this treatment of Vatican II as a social movement with three animadversiones or pre-notes, two of them almost droll anecdotes. When I told several colleagues at my university that I would present a paper at a conference on the role of the Belgium bishops at Vatican Council II, one quipped: "What do you know about the Belgium bishops?" and another snorted: "Well not knowing about something never seems to have stopped you much before!". Mercifully, my task is not to assess, in any close way, the role of the Belgium Bishops during Vatican Council II, although toward the end of my remarks I will

---

1. For an account of social movements see N.J. SMELSER, *Theory of Collective Behavior*, New York, The Free Press, 1962; A. MORRIS – C. MUELLER (eds.), *Frontiers in Social Movement Theory*, New Haven, CT, Yale University Press, 1992; M. ZALD – J. McCARTHY (eds.), *Social Movements in an Organizational Society,* New Brunswick, NJ, Transaction, 1984; J. GOODWIN – J. JASPER (eds.), *Rethinking Social Movements: Structure, Meaning and Emotion,* Lanham, MD, Rowman and Littlefield, 2004; M. GUIGN – D. McADAM – C. TILLY (eds.), *How Social Movements Matter*, Minneapolis, MN, University of Minnesota Press, 1999.

venture a few hypotheses to explain their importance, even pre-eminence, during the Council.

Even the most casual observer of the history of the Council would know the central, even pivotal, role of Leon-Joseph Cardinal Suenens. His many interventions on collegiality, religious freedom, the purposes of marriage, women religious, a married deaconate, priestly formation, the media, the missions, lay apostolic movements, the Church in the Modern World; his key role in insisting that the chapter on the people of God be placed in the document on the Church before the section on the hierarchical principle in the church; his abundant periodic and, usually effective, practical procedural suggestions to cut through voting or deliberation impasses; his formal positions as a member of the Coordinating Commission in the interim between the first and second session of the Council and as a moderator from the second session of the Council onwards – no one can doubt that, without the leadership and acumen of Cardinal Suenens, the Council would have had different outcomes. Sociologists love to quantify things. So, I attempted a trivial counting mechanism using the index of the notable volume, still a much plumbed resource at least in American settings, by Xavier Rynne[2]. No other residential cardinal was as often evoked and cited as Leon Cardinal Suenens (53 index citations). Other important leadership cardinals and bishops (Bernard Cardinal Alfrink, Julius Cardinal Döpfner, Joseph Cardinal Frings, Franz Cardinal Köning, Giacomo Cardinal Lecaro, Paul-Émile Cardinal Léger, Achille Cardinal Liénart) received index notations numbering in the twenties or mid thirties. Only Cardinal Ottaviani (with 70 citations) looms in Rynne's authoritative insiders account anywhere near Suenens.

But Émile-Joseph De Smedt of Brugge, consonant with his position in the newly inaugurated Secretariat for Promoting Christian Unity, also played crucial roles in furthering ecumenism and religious liberty. His interventions at the council on the question of two sources of revelation, on the internationalization of the curia, on the laity and collegiality swayed many. No other speaker during the Council received as prolonged and insistent applause as did De Smedt when, during a difficult and uncertain period of the Council's proceedings, he introduced, as *relator*, the document on Religious Liberty at the third session of the Council[3]. For his part, Bishop André-Marie Charue of Namur, a member of the Theological Commission, also helped expedite the moving forward of Schema

2. X. RYNNE, *Vatican Council II*, Maryknoll, NY, Orbis, 1999.
3. *Ibid.*, p. 420.

13 in a special inter-session meeting in Zurich in the summer of 1964 and had weighty interventions on documents dealing with religious life. More than any one else, at a critical moment in the debates on collegiality, Charue brought forth a scripturally-based coherent account for the concept. Later, during an impasse over the notion of the church and "the world" in Schema 13, Charue clarified various meanings of the term "world" in scripture in order to defend the progressives' desired title, "The Church in the Modern World".

I leave to the church historians in this volume any closer assessment of this Belgian role. My theme is a broader one: how can we look at Vatican II as a social movement and use sociological categories from social movement literature to understand how the progressives and moderates – against all initial expectations – came to predominate at the Council? I will want to step away from the Belgium particularity to look at the entire Council's social dynamic.

The second anecdote came recently to me from an acquaintance who teaches at one of the ecclesial universities in Rome. He asked, in a take-off on the standard joke: "How many cardinals in Rome does it take to change a light bulb?". The answer is not in any preferred number but in the querulous, even whining, exclamation: "Change!!!?" with a question mark looming over it as if it were ridiculous. So, a sociological account which looks to the dynamic of the Second Vatican Council needs to ask: how was it that the Curia cardinals who seemed to control so many more resources in the Council's apparatus ultimately were stymied in their attempts to muffle reform or have the Council merely reiterate older doctrinal positions and avoid new pastoral challenges? What theological and organizational resources did the progressives mobilize to bring about a truly reform council? How did they organize differently than the conservatives to win adherents to their positions?

My third pre-note stresses the precise focus of my essay, its main sources and some preliminary attempt at rendering the audience relatively benevolent for sociological concepts which may not be familiar – even seem far fetched and strange – to a reading audience composed mainly of theologians or historians. I will not be speaking of Vatican II as a social movement in terms of its reception by the wider church and society. Sociologists have been quite clear and relatively unanimous in arguing that the Vatican Council represents the most significant case of institutionalized religious change since the Reformation. A number of important sociological studies attribute great significance to the Council and measure the extensive effects of the Council Reforms on church attitudes and practice[4]. For example, sociologist José Casanova refers to Vatican II as "a collective redefinition that resulted in the transformation of the church from a state-centered to a society centered institution"[5]. Michele Dillon speaks of Vatican II as a "revolutionary event that redefined the church"[6]. Most such studies look mainly at the reception of Vatican II and do little to examine the forces within the Council, itself, which put a final stamp on the character and extent of these changes. They focus more on the impact of the changes than on how change occurred, against expectations. How was it that an entrenched and powerful Roman Curia, at the near zenith of its power, in control of Council preparations, proceedings and agenda did not have more impact on its outcome? Clearly, at the start of the Council, most observers did not expect it to eventuate in such substantive and progressive reforms.

I will rely heavily, in my account, on two sociological studies of the Council's inner social dynamic. Rocco Caporale published his sociological interpretation of his interviews with some 80 Council leaders (both progressive and conservative) in 1964. Caporale's snow-ball sample of bishops and cardinals nominated by fellow bishops as "leaders' at the Council was finished by the end of the first session. These interviews throw light on how bishops saw the Council in its preparatory phases and the dramatic impact of the First Session[7]. Relying on those interviews and further archival data, Melissa Wilde, a sociologist at the University of Indiana in Bloomington, is publishing her new and very original book, *Vatican II: A Sociological Analysis of Religious Change*, shortly with Princeton University Press[8]. She has graciously sent me a manuscript of her book and I draw on it, with her acquiescence, extensively for my remarks. Following Wilde, I will evoke a set of concepts from the literature on social mobilization theory in sociology: Collective effervescence; an historical event; framing an event and divergent organizing strategies within a social movement to try to illuminate the answer to the

4. A. GREELEY, *The Catholic Revolution: New Wine, Old Wine Skins and the Second Vatican Council*, Berkeley, CA, University of California Press, 2004.

5. J. CASANOVA, *Public Religions in the Modern World*, Chicago, IL, University of Chicago Press, 1994, p. 71.

6. M. DILLON, *Catholic Identity: Balancing Reason, Faith and Power*, New York, Cambridge University Press, 1999.

7. R. CAPORALE, *Vatican II: The Last of the Councils*, Baltimore, MD, Helicon Press, 1964.

8. M.J. WILDE, *Vatican II: A Sociological Analysis of Religious Change*, Princeton, NJ, Princeton University Press, 2007.

question why the progressives were able to wrest control of the social dynamic of the Council. When they appear I will try to provide adequate definitions of the concepts and then attempt to show their relevance to the argument of this paper.

Wilde's thesis, to which I subscribe, is that at the beginning of the Council few bishops anticipated much from it. Most thought it would be a rubber-stamp Council. Few said they had, themselves, ever anticipated a Council, although some said they had seen the need for some mechanism of change in the Church. By the end of the First Session of the Council, some, but not all bishops saw it as a collective élan, what Émile Durkheim spoke of as "collective effervescence" and these bishops evoked the symbol of the Holy Spirit to ground their justification for change. They also viewed the Council as an historic event.

In several key battlegrounds of the Council (whether there should be a separate schema on Mary or she should be located in the document of the Church; on the question of two sources for revelation; on religious liberty) the progressives were able to sway the unaligned and not only tap into their natural "sentiment pool" of the like-minded but draw the unaligned or even some conservative bishops into their camp. They could do so more successfully than the conservative Curial cardinals or residential bishops because of differing organizational strategies which allowed the progressives to reach out more widely in communicating in the Council and to get quick feed-back and make compromises. Finally, a competitive market position for the Church (which will be explained later but refers to a position where the Church holds a significant societal presence but does not constitute a majority and faces pluralism) helps to illuminate Council votes on many of these key issues. Moreover, an unspoken force at the Council, which fed into the progressives' sentiment pool and inhibited conservative strategies was the presence of Protestant observers. Where reforms were key to the ecumenical movement, positions congenial to mainline Protestants almost always won the day.

In the following paragraphs and sections I will, then, focus on: (1) The Council at the beginning; (2) The importance of the First Session in creating collective effervescence and an historical event; (3) Differing organizational strategies of the two major lobby or ginger groups: The Domus Mariae Commission of 22 and the ten to sixteen members of a conservative lobby group, *The Coetus Internationalis Patrum*[9]; (4) Some important *caveat*s in using the Social Mobilization Analogy and (5) Finally,

9. The *Domus Mariae* group is presented in M. WILDE, *How Culture Mattered at Vatican II: Collegiality Trumps Authority in the Council's Social Movement*, in *The*

I will address, following Wilde, differing votes among bishops from countries, which experienced internal religious pluralism versus those from more solidly Catholic majoritarian countries, such as Italy, Spain and Columbia. At that point, I will, very briefly, return from my more general concern with the Council as a social movement to the particular role of the Belgium bishops at Vatican Council II.

I. THE COUNCIL AT THE BEGINNING

Rocco Caporale's interviews of 80 key bishops and cardinals, nominated, in a snow-ball sample, by their fellow bishops as leaders or major actors at the Council, were all completed by the end of the second session. Caporale asked his bishop informants whether – prior to John XXIII's surprise announcement of it on January 25, 1958 – they had ever anticipated a Council or thought there would be one. He also asked about their initial expectations for the Council. Eighty-seven percent of his sample responded either that they had never thought of a Council or had not thought one could or would occur.

Archbishop Roberts, a progressive English bishop from India, said to Caporale: "I never even dreamed of a Council and never met anybody who did"[10]. Bishop Marty from France gave this response: "We did not think about the Council because it seemed impossible". No significant differences can be found, in Caporale's interview data, between conservatives or progressives on the questions about whether they had, on their own, envisioned a Council or their initial expectations for such a Council when it had been announced. Few had anticipated the event. Few expected much to come of it. They thought it would be a rubber stamp Council.

Bishop Fares, a conservative Italian put it this way: "At the first session, the majority of our bishops were unprepared. It was a new

---

American Sociological Review (forthcoming). The *Coetus Internationalis Patrum* is treated in G. ALBERIGO – J.A. KOMONCHAK (eds.), *History of Vatican II*. Vol. II: *The Formation of the Council's Identity: First Period and Intersession October 1962 – September 1963*, Maryknoll, NY, Orbis; Leuven, Peeters, 1997, pp. 197-198 and in L. PERRIN, *Il Coetus Internationalis Patrum e la minoranza conciliare*, in M. FATTORI – A. MELLONI (eds.), *L'evento e le decisioni: Studi sulle dinamiche del Concilio Vaticano II* (Testi e ricerche di scienze religiose. Nuova Serie, 20), Bologna, Il Mulino, 1997, 173-187.
10. The direct citations from the Caporale interview sample derive from M. Wilde's book, *Vatican II* (n. 8). Readers will need to read her rich and innovative book for a much denser look at supporting material for her use of social mobilization theory to apply to the groups within the Council. Wilde had access to the entire file of Caporale's field interviews.

experience for us, like running in time. Many bishops thought it would be a rubber stamp Council, something that would be read out to us, to be approved, a few decrees". For his part, Archbishop Roberts also reported minimal expectations for the Council at the outset: "Most bishops were pessimistic when the Council began: they thought that by the time the Council would end we would all be dead!". If even those whom Caporale's informants had nominated as leading figures at the Council seemed taken aback by its announcement and unclear about its likely agenda and purposes, all the more so the majority of bishops who were even less prepared. One difference, however, emerges in Caporale's interviews to distinguish conservatives from progressives. Although progressives had not envisioned a Council, more of them said that they had seen the necessity for change in the church. They entered the Council with sentiments which embraced change.

Speaking about the preliminary *vota* or polling, culled by an Ante-Preparatory Commission created by John XXIII to elicit from the bishops of the world their desires for a concrete agenda for the Council, Bishop Marcus McGrath (a progressive American missionary bishop in Panama) wrote: "I well remember the perfunctory fashion in which our staff answered the first questionnaires sent on what the Council might study. We simply did not take our participation seriously, nor that of most of the outlying Church. We had become so accustomed to the highly centralized doctrinal and jurisdictional operation of the Church in our century, exercised by the Holy Father personally and through his Curia, that we could not awake quickly"[11].

Giuseppe Alberigo and his colleagues, in their multi-volume history of Vatican II, give reasons why the majority of bishops did not have very high expectations for the Council. Studying the bishops' letters in response to the Ante-Preparatory Commission's requests for topics for the Council, Alberigo argues that their cautiousness largely conformed to pre-conciliar expectations and adherence to Vatican protocol[12]. Preliminary work for the Council lay almost entirely in the hands of the Roman Curia, largely conservative, if not reactionary. Curial preparatory commissions wrote preliminary schemas for the Council debate, which did little more than reassert current church doctrine and condemn those who publicly questioned them. As Alberigo, *et al.* summarize this preparatory

---

11. Cited in WILDE, *Vatican II*. Chapter 2: *Collective Effervescence and the Holy Spirit*, p. 14.

12. G. ALBERIGO – J.A. KOMONCHAK (eds.), *History of Vatican II*. Vol. I: *Announcing and Preparing Vatican Council II: Toward a New Era in Catholicism*, Maryknoll, NY, Orbis; Leuven, Peeters, 1995, p. 108.

phase: "The spirit in which the ante-preparatory work was done was one of strengthening the Church's defenses against dangers from outside. The individuals selected for the work, their conceptual frameworks and their working methods led, after considerable effort, to a result that could have been foreseen: an evident Romanization of the plan for the Council, both in the organization of the preparation and in the subjects it would treat"[13].

On the eve of the Council, there was no real social movement yet in the church and little by way of concrete mobilization. Something dramatic clearly happened during the first session to allow the progressive majority to experience the Council as a "collective effervescence" and a "historic event". To that important shift and the sociological meanings and significance of the two terms, collective effervescence and historic event, we now turn.

II. The First Session of Vatican II
Collective Effervescence and an Historical Event

Historians of the Council place great stress on three critical turning points during the first session which exhibited (even to themselves) the power of the progressive forces at the Council and the weaknesses of the Curia. The first such event took place early on, at the very first meeting of the Council, when members were asked to vote for 160 members to staff the ten commissions for the drafting and re-working of Council documents. The Curia had hoped for the automatic re-election of the members of the pre-conciliar commissions and sought earnestly to bring it about. Right after the opening mass, Cardinal Felici, the Secretary General of the Council, mandated a vote on commission membership. Giuseppe Alberigo describes this strategy of the Curia in calling for an early vote, while not allowing any time for debate. "Every father had to vote for 160 of his colleagues and it was not possible for each voter to come up with his own list out of so many possibilities. Given the lack of knowledge of particular bishops, each would have ended up reproducing to a greater or lesser degree the list of men on the pre-conciliar commission"[14].

When Felici called for the vote, notes Alberigo: "There was great bewilderment in the Council hall at the announcement that the election should begin immediately. Some bishops used the master of ceremonies

---

13. *Ibid.*, p. 156.
14. ALBERIGO – KOMONCHAK (eds.), *History of Vatican II*. Vol. II (n. 9), p. 56.

to exchange private messages and to get advice from their colleagues. There was disorder in the hall. The process of writing down 160 names would have taken a great deal of time, certainly more than an hour"[15].

Just as the vote was commencing, amidst the growing hubbub, Cardinal Liénart of France, breaking with precedent, asked to speak. Eugène Cardinal Tisserant, the Council's presiding officer that day, replied that he could not allow Liénart's speech since the program did not provide for any discussion time before the vote. Notwithstanding, Liénart, one of the Council moderators and a revered elderly Cardinal, stood up and asked for a delay in the voting to allow the bishops to get to know each other and for the national Episcopal conferences to confer on the lists. Prolonged and spontaneous applause greeted Liénart's motion, which was, then, seconded by Cardinal Frings. Upon an impromptu deliberation of the Council Presidents, the vote was postponed for several days. As a result, the commissions ultimately elected were more diverse, theologically and by nationality, than they would have been had the preparatory commissions been simply re-elected.

The success of Liénart's tactic demonstrated, at the very outset, that the Curia could be made to yield to the assembly of bishops, that Vatican II need not be a rubber-stamp Council and that Council structures were negotiable. Discussion of two substantive documents dominated this first session. The document on the liturgy was the first major decree to be debated and voted on. Its choice as the first document for discussion was not, simply, a matter of chance. Progressive bishops had intensely lobbied for the document on the liturgy to be the first item addressed by the Council. As we will analyze further, already in the first session, twenty-two progressive and moderate bishops, from a number of countries had, following again upon a suggestion of Cardinal Liénart, begun meeting weekly at the Domus Mariae, a retreat center in Rome, to discuss and reflect on the direction of the Council[16].

Progressives thought the document on the liturgy was the only preparatory schema even worthy of conciliar discussion. In part, the preparatory commission, which drafted the schema on the liturgy was the only commission not dominated by conservatives and the Curia. Very few conservatives had much experience with the issue of liturgy and its reform. Thus, the preliminary commission, which drafted the schema on the

---

15. *Ibid.*, p. 28.

16. Cf. the account of *Domus Mariae* in R. ETCHEGARAY, *Interventi scritti*, in *Paolo VI e la collegialità episcopale. Colloquio internazionale di studio, Brescia 25-26-27 settembre 1992*, Rome, Edizioni Studium, 1985, p. 293.

liturgy had been formed, principally, from experts with extensive experience in the movements for liturgical reform. Despite determined efforts of the conservatives to defeat the schema, it passed with overwhelming support toward the middle of the first session. It was clear from this first substantive vote on a theological issue taken at the Council that a majority of participants were interested or could be swayed to vote for reform.

As actors in what was becoming a social movement where structures yielded to fresh framing of questions, progressives sought to sway what was emerging as a "sentiment pool" of allies or possible converts to their agenda. Actually, the progressives in Caporale's interview sample note that they themselves were somewhat surprised at the lop-sided vote. Preliminary debate had indicated a relatively equal number of conciliar interventions in favor or against the liturgy draft. In retrospect, however, it became clear that more conservatives spoke out in the Council than did progressives (who often allowed others to make their points or serve as their spokesmen). Canadian Bishop Carter told Caporale: "The voting pattern has been surprising at times. While the number of interventions in support of each side seems equal, the voting is overwhelmingly uneven. Probably that may be explained by the fact that the men who disagree feel the need to talk the most". One of Caporale's respondents, Bishop Bogarin from Paraguay, noted the significance of the Council having begun with the schema on the liturgy: "The Constitution on the liturgy is marvelous. It gave the bishops courage to speak because it was easy ground. I don't know if this was planned or by chance. In any case, the Holy Spirit worked".

The other important discussion during the first session focused on the document on Revelation. Conservatives tried to defend the inerrancy of the Bible, impede or relativize the validity of the historical-critical method about layers of pre-existing stories and the various redactions by authors in the Bible, and to affirm that there are two separable sources of revelation, Scripture and Tradition, where Tradition includes Church's interpretation of the Bible. As Alberigo notes, much was at stake in this debate since the theory of two separable sources "involved the very role of the ecclesiastical *magisterium* (or the authority of the Church to interpret Jesus' teachings[17]. Lurking behind this document lay a telling query: was the *magisterium*, itself, under the more pre-eminent norm of the Scriptures?

Progressives, for their part, were more open to historical-critical methods for studying and interpreting the Bible and, for ecumenical reasons,

---

17. ALBERIGO – KOMONCHAK (eds.), *History of Vatican II*. Vol. II (n. 9), p. 233.

toward downplaying the two-source theory. Prior to the Council, progressive theologians (including *periti*) circulated detailed critiques of the original document on Revelation. Indeed, over 1500 copies of a summary of these critiques were handed out to the bishops in three languages (Latin, French, English) as they arrived in Rome for the Council.

Within less than a week of intense debates on the document, the Council moderators intervened asking for a vote on whether to continue the discussion of the document as it existed or to return the document to committee for substantial revisions, since the complaints about its current form were so numerous. 1368 voted for an "interruption" of the proceedings to remand the text back to committee for substantial revision; 668 voted to continue discussion on the text as it existed. This vote was 105 ballots shy of the two-thirds majority required for a binding decision. The Council had come to a kind of stalemate. Alberigo notes: "The Council seemed destined to be plunged into a crisis from which there was no return"[18].

John XXIII intervened to rescue the Council from this impasse. He decided to refer the document to a new mixed commission, which would include some members of the Doctrinal Commission and some from the Secretariat for Promoting Christian Unity. Protestant observers at the first session noted the implications of the Pope's intervention: the reason was that the text proposed would have rendered the ecumenical dialogue sterile on a capital point – the point of the supremacy of Scripture for Christian life and within the Church.

Xavier Rynne comments on the effects of these three events on the progressive majority: "The first session had a decided effect on the collective consciousness of the bishops themselves ... The bishops began to understand that it was not sufficient to wait passively for a charismatic inspiration or to repeat the formulas of scholastic manuals. They must take cognizance of the fact that they were the free instruments used by the Holy Spirit in the spreading of the Christian faith, and that they had been given an immense task which they must accept with humility and courage"[19]. It was becoming clear, by the end of the first session, that the Council had revolutionary potential. An inspection of participants' descriptions of how the first session of the Council affected them, using Caporale's sample, reveals that for some of the bishops the Council was being seen as a collective effervescence and an historical event. Others experienced it differently. Both of these terms are technical sociological

18. *Ibid.*, p. 263.
19. RYNNE, *Vatican Council II* (n. 2), p. 131.

concepts. I want to use them to help us parse Rynne's comments about a new collective consciousness of the bishops themselves and the evocation of the Holy Spirit as a concrete symbol of that new consciousness.

Collective effervescence, a term coined by the sociologist Émile Durkheim, refers to a period of heightened élan, an intense, non-routine set of inter-actions. Durkheim coined the phrase when reflecting on the sort of group frenzy that seemed to accompany ritual gatherings of Australian aborigines[20]. He also claimed to see collective effervescence in outbursts such as the French Revolution or other forms of non-institutionalized collective behavior. Robert Bellah has suggested that Durkheim's notion of collective effervescence is "a concept much like that of the unconscious; it could almost be called a social unconscious"[21]. Durkheim remarks of this intense set of communication, inter-action and breakdown of institutional routines that it is "the state in which men find themselves when they believe they have been swept up into a world entirely different from the one they have before their eyes"[22].

Durkheim notes: "The very act of congregating is an exceptionally powerful stimulant. Once the individuals are gathered together, a sort of electricity is generated from their closeness[23]. The term is a short-hand way of evoking intense and tangible feelings of group cohesion, bondedness and solidarity. For Durkheim, there is a close correlation between collective effervescence and what he termed, "collective representations – dense and pregnant symbols or myths of group cohesion and togetherness. These symbols tap into and, in a sense, through ritualization, invoke and recreate the original sense of intense we-feeling and collective élan.

More recent sociological theory which has drawn on Durkheim's concept of collective effervescence (for example, in studies of ritual, festivities, fiestas, intense group bonding) has tried to tie it to more tangible and measurable variables such as a notable increase, within a collectivity, in the volume and intensity of communication and of alternative channels of communication[24]. The Durkheimian anthropologist, Victor Turner,

20. É. DURKHEIM, *The Elementary Forms of Religious Life*, London, Allen and Unwin, 1954, Vol. II, chapter 7.

21. R.N. BELLAH, *Beyond Belief*, New York, Harper and Row, 1970, p. 239.

22. DURKHEIM, *The Elementary Forms* (n. 20), p. 234.

23. *Ibid.*, p. 217.

24. See P. SLATER, *Microcosm*, New York, John Wiley, 1966. I argue that collective effervescence is best measured by an increase in volume and intensity of communication and an expansion of routinized channels of communication in a section entitled, *The Dutch Pastoral Council as an Expression of Collective Effervescence*, in J.A. COLEMAN, *The Evolution of Dutch Catholicism, 1958-1974*, Berkeley, CA, University of California Press, 1978, 159-167.

turns to a variant of collective effervescence to speak of it as an anti-structural element. For Turner, every collectivity or organization contains two, analytically distinct, faces: structure (the routine and institutional-ized scripts) and *communitas*, the anti-structural break-out from the every day as, for example, in an office Christmas party where ordinary rules of communication determined by status and institutionalized norms get over-turned[25]. Episodes of collective effervescence (as during a natural disas-ter) intensify fellow-feeling and lift up the possibilities of an alternative way of being and acting. In its non-ordinariness and intensity, collective effervescence might be episodic (e.g., a sport event, Mardi Gras) or more prolonged. The more collective effervescence is prolonged, the more alternative ways of structuring every day life and institutions get envi-sioned as possibilities.

"An historical event", a term coined by William Sewell, a student of social mobilization, is defined by Sewell: "(1) A ramified sequence of occurrences that (2) is recognized as notable by contemporaries and thus (3) results in a durable transformation of structures"[26]. For Sewell, an historical event presupposes an experience of collective effervescence but includes, further, actors' awareness that real structural changes could occur as a result of an event in which they are participating. It involves, like collective effervescence, a heightened collective consciousness but adds a telling sense of making history.

In the Caporale interviews, and in other memoirs or accounts of the Council, it is very clear that a large number of those who participated in the Council – as *periti* or bishops – felt such strong surges of solidarity and alternative possibility. They saw the Council as an historical event. Cardinal Suenens, in his interview with Caporale, captures this: "surely, we all have changed considerably between the first and second sessions, very much so. The action of the Holy Spirit was evident. One could almost touch it everywhere".

Caporale's interviews include many respondents who claim to have seen profound conversions and changes in the bishops. The interviewees lifted up the face-to-face contacts they encountered with many and diverse bishops from different nations. Many reflected on experiencing a new sense of church or of vitality in the church. In a profound sense, as the citation from Cardinal Suenens indicates, the evocation of the Holy Spirit

25. V. TURNER, *The Ritual Process: Structure and Anti-Structure*, Chicago, IL, Aldine Press, 1969.
26. W. SEWELL, *Historical Events as Transformations of Structures*, in *Social Forces* 25/6 (1996) 844.

(or, alternatively, some supernatural agency) permeates many of the Caporale interviews. The Holy Spirit serves as a "collective representation" justifying the historical event. Bishop Boudreaux, an American moderate, for example, spoke of his experience of the Council at the end of the first session: "Ever since the first few days, I began to go through a spiritual experience. Feeling God in the Church, pushing us all". Bishop Elchinger, a German, reported: "We can perceive how the Holy Spirit animates the whole Church". Bishop Miranda from Mexico told Caporale: "I am sure I am not the only one to note that we felt the presence of the Holy Spirit very deeply". Canada's Bishop Carter stated: "The direction of the Council by the Holy Spirit is visible". Archbishop Hallinan, an American echoes this sentiment: "The sense of the universality and unity of the Church – you read about it, but here you realize it, as when you are part of a drama. Supernatural forces are at play".

Liberals and moderates in the Caporale sample speak of themselves as having changed, of having a palpable, tangible, if somewhat mysterious, sense of God's inspiration, the Spirit at work. 88% of liberals in the Caporale sample (compared to 54% of conservatives) said they had gotten to know more people through the Council. They were more likely than conservatives to say that they took part in more meetings, outside the Council structure. In response to a question, which asked if the Council exposed them to new ideas, 14 of 15 conservative respondents said no, whereas 61% of the moderates and 51 % of the liberals said yes. One fourth of the liberals and moderates explicitly evoked the Holy Sprit. Clearly, the Holy Spirit was being cited as a resonant symbol to legitimate and indicate approval of and immersion in the collective effervescence of the Council.

In some real sense, only the liberals and moderates experienced the full effervescence of the Council. The collective experience increased their inter-actions with diverse groups, exposed them to new ideas and people. No conservative in the Caporale sample ever mentioned the Holy Spirit or evoked some collective élan of change and transformation of structures. The one exception, Cardinal Siri, called upon the Spirit, not as something he had personally experienced in the Council but as his hope: that in the end the Spirit would finally appear and prevail against what Siri saw as Council excesses and distortion of truths. Interestingly, in the Caporale sample, only the conservatives questioned John XXIII's claim that the Council came to him as a divine inspiration. One remarked: "John said he was inspired but he seemed to be confused. A Council was not needed". Another told Caporale: "John told me the Council was an inspiration, but I am not so certain about this".

By the start of the second session, conservatives and progressives were experiencing different Councils. If in the first session, the liberals mobilized their pre-existing common sentiment pools, by the second they were beginning to "convert" bishops who had never thought about the issues raised or had been previously unsympathetic to the progressive viewpoint. Progressives engaged in what social mobilization theorists refer to as a "frame transformation", such that many of the non-aligned began to see in new lenses or frames. I turn now to alternative models of organizing as a lobby group by the progressives and conservatives at the Council.

III. DIFFERING ORGANIZATIONAL STRATEGIES
DOMUS MARIAE vs. COETUS INTERNATIONALIS PATRUM

Social movements never, simply, auto-generate themselves. Rather, typically, they spawn new, often *ad hoc*, organizational forms – in effect lobby groups – intent on influencing or contesting the direction of the social movement. At the Council, two such lobby groups emerged, respectively, of a progressive and pro-collegiality formation, the Domus Mariae group (hereafter DM) and an anti-collegiality conservative lobby group, the Coetus Intenationalis Patrum (hereafter, CIP)[27].

French theologian and later cardinal Roger Etchegaray who became the secretary of DM renders a retrospective account of its inception: "Cardinal Liénart asked me at the opening of the Council, to make "useful contacts" with bishops of other countries. There had been little mutual contact and meetings were even up to that point discouraged by Rome … Thus, stimulated by the two bishops I met the first evening, I was so bold as to invite a few bishops, as I met them, to meet regularly for an exchange of views on the proceedings"[28].

The DM consisted of 22 core members, representing divergent regions of the world (Africa, North America, Latin America, Asia). Every major European country, with the exception of Italy, was represented, either directly or through close linkages – e.g., the German representative consulted also regularly with contacts in Switzerland and Austria; the representative from Great Britain also made contact with the episcopacy of Ireland. Eastern Europe was only represented by Poland. Two regional groups of bishops (CELAM for Latin America, represented by its two vice

---

27. Cf. citations in n. 9.
28. ETCHEGARAY, *Interventi scritti* (n. 16), p. 293.

Presidents, Brazil's Dom Hélder Câmara, and Manuel Larraín of Chile and The Federation of African Episcopal Conferences) had two representatives apiece. But generally great care was taken, to ensure representativeness that no Episcopal Conference was allowed more than one representative. The DM insisted on the committed regular weekly participation of its core members and kept the group small enough to function well as a kind of nexus of information and consultation across national Episcopal Conferences. Early on in the Council, the DM circulated a petition stating that they saw collegiality as a central priority for the Council and proposing that the schema on collegiality be discussed and decided upon first.

The DM relied heavily on Episcopal Conferences at the Council. Many Episcopal Conferences (e.g., France, Canada, Brazil, the Netherlands, the United States) pre-dated the Council and had long histories of regular meetings among each nation's bishops. During the Council, itself, the number of Episcopal Conferences almost doubled from forty to seventy[29]. The task of the DM representative was two-fold: to communicate within his Episcopal Conference the proceedings and deliberations and thought of the DM (usually consisting of bullet points) and, conversely, to bring back to the DM detailed reports of the deliberations, questions and directions of his own conference. Early on, however, at its second meeting, the DM also appointed a sub-committee to reach out actively to bishops from countries, which lacked an Episcopal Conference.

As a result, within a week or so (the more active Episcopal Conferences met weekly during the Council), the DM was able to be in contact with almost 1800 bishops. The DM group was committed to collegiality, desired an open communication system, sought to report and respond to divergent views from its own and was willing to make compromises. It never referred to itself publicly as a separate group and never claimed any victories. Etchegaray, in a letter to Cardinal Suenens (who was not a member of the DM) stated: "I send you the list of the 22 regular participants. All more of less represent their own episcopacy according to the structure and degree of 'collegial conscience' of their Episcopal Conference. While they are naturally not able to engage their colleagues in debates they, nevertheless, reflect the more general thought of their episcopacy

---

29. This is the estimate in J. BROUWERS, *Vatican II: Derniers préparatifs et première session. Activités conciliaires en coulisses*, in É. FOUILLOUX (éd.), *Vatican II commence: Approches francophones* (Instrumenta Theologica, 12), Leuven, Bibliotheek van de Faculteit der Godgeleerdheid, 1993, 353-368.

and in turn report on all that is said in the meetings of the *Domus Mariae*"[30].

At the end of the first session, the DM opposed having a separate schema on Mary, preferring that her role be incorporated into a schema on the church by re-framing the issue in the following terms, to court opposition votes of those who favored a separate schema on Mary: "It is not possible to speak of the Church without speaking of Mary"[31]. At the beginning of the second session, in what was the closest vote ever of the Council (1114 to 1074), a decision was taken to incorporate the treatment of Mary into the schema on the Church. Bishop Primeau, the American representative to the DM, told Etchegaray that a presentation on the subject of Mariology by four respected theologians at a special session of the United States Episcopal Conference held a day before this crucial vote, had, in Primeau's judgment, swayed at least twenty votes of the American bishops. A switch of twenty votes to the conservative position would have sunk the progressive proposal. During this second session of the Council, the DM worked intensively with the Episcopal Conference structure to help generate suggested lists of bishops to be elected to the commissions[32]. In later sessions, the DM deliberated on best strategies to expedite the documents on religious liberty and the Jews. Most of the literature on social mobilization emphasizes the comparative advantage of groups such as DM, which are flexible, cover multiple bases and seek to forge alliances beyond their own narrower sentiment pools[33].

In contrast to the DM, CIP was a later development, formed only after the second session began. Only with the loss on the vote on a separate schema for Mary and a vote taken a day later than the vote on Mary on collegiality, did conservatives even contemplate a separate lobby group. They realized that their fortress of conservatism in the Curial representation at the Council was being stormed. By the second session, the Curia had fallen into discredit. CIP was a bastion of opposition to collegiality. Its three founders, Italian Bishop Carli, Brazilian Archbishop Sigaud and African Bishop and Former Superior General, Marcel Lefebvre, all spoke

30. Cited in J. GROOTAERS, *De Vatican II à Jean-Paul II: Le grand tournant de l'Église catholique*, Paris, Centurion, 1981, p. 141.

31. RYNNE, *Vatican Council II* (n. 2), p. 158.

32. P. NOEL, *Gli Incontri Delle Conferenze Episcopali Durante il Concilio II: Gruppo della Domus Mariae*, in FATTORI – MELLONI (eds.), *L'evento e le decisioni* (n. 9), 94-133, p. 112.

33. For evidence that a more participatory, flexible network is effective in social mobilization see F. POLLETA, *Freedom is an Endless Meeting: Democracy in American Social Movements*, Chicago, IL, University of Chicago Press, 2002.

publicly and disparagingly of collegiality. They also spoke at the Council against the idea of Episcopal Conferences, fearing them as Trojan horses for fostering and institutionalizing collegiality. Indeed, the minutes of the first CIP meeting show that the group's primary purpose was to bolster "opposition to the idea of collegiality ... adopting as a banner the defense of the rights of the Supreme Pontiff and, secondarily, those of each individual bishop"[34]. At its height, CIP drew about sixteen bishops to its weekly strategy meetings. One of its petitions, circulated during the Fourth session, proposing a conciliar condemnation of Communism, garnered 435 signatures. Indeed, at the beginning of the Council, recognizing that the DM existed and deeming it dangerous, conservatives had sought to ban all informal groups of theologians and bishops from meeting outside the formal Council structure. John XXIII, however, claimed that he would not "interfere with the legitimate right of bishops to inform themselves regarding the issues before the Council"[35].

One drawback to CIP was its inability to communicate effectively with Episcopal Conference structures, the most reliable way to disseminate information at the Council. CIP did not believe in the legitimacy of Episcopal Conferences and, hence, could not utilize this structure to communicate and disseminate their ideas. At the most, they once drew about eighty bishops to a meeting they organized. They tended to communicate with the like-minded and not seek to sway the undecided. They never reported or responded to divergent views (unlike the DM which, although it did not always reach a consensus, sought compromises which might gain wide acceptance)[36]. In effect, CIP resorted to impersonal mailings or circulated petitions, rather than using personal contacts or deliberation, to reach out to potential allies. CIP's founders were actually more reactionaries than mere conservatives and were seen as too closely allied to the dis-credited Curia. CIP's other strategy was to go beyond the Council to appeal for a papal intervention, e.g., an unsuccessful petition from Sigaud to Pope Paul VI to counter-act the loss on the vote on Mary by a papal act consecrating the world to Mary. Because it stayed within a closed circle, CIP actually had few clues about what DM was doing and tended to refer to it as some kind of mysterious, progressive cabal or mafia. As we saw earlier, conservatives were able to block, had it not been for a special intervention of John XXIII, the attempts of DM and

---

34. Cited in PERRIN, *Coetus Internationalis Patrum* (n. 9), p. 177.
35. RYNNE, *Vatican Council II* (n. 2), p. 92.
36. That the DM did not always reach consensus, see GROOTAERS, *De Vatican II à Jean-Paul II* (n. 30), p. 161.

others to oppose the two-sources theory of Revelation. In point of fact, then, CIP does not seem to have marshalled even the full numbers of its own potential conservative sentiment pool. Wilde in her forthcoming book estimates that potential pool at around 44 percent of the Council. But still seeing the Council more as an institution than a social movement CIP did not mobilize as well as their potential suggested.

Clearly, DM was better at reaching and mobilizing a diverse population, even beyond its obvious pre-existing sentiment pool and in re-framing issues than was CIP. Notably, in the Caporale interview sample, three fourths of the members of DM were nominated by fellow bishops as belonging to the most influential leaders at the Council.

IV. The Social Mobilization Analogy for Understanding Vatican II

It may strike a thoughtful reader as a bit precious or fanciful to speak of a "social movement" whose principal agents were bishops and cardinals! I remain convinced of the fruitfulness of employing some key concepts of social mobilization theory in sociology to Vatican II ("collective effervescence"; "sentiment pools"; "re-framing"; alternative models of mobilizing, where flexible mobilization has a comparative advantage over restricted or formalistic forms of mobilization, etc.). Clearly, however, my evidence thus far is a kind of heuristic devise, a still truncated version of how the social mobilization perspective would, eventually, need to be further developed. To do it justice, we would need to expand on its agents, its locale and its time frame. We would also have to consider some of the constraints on the social movement phase by its ecclesial institutional context.

1. Expansion of Agents

Clearly, other actors, besides bishops, got involved in social mobilization or attempts to influence key actors or frame discussions at Vatican II. The *periti* play a key role here. Sometimes, *periti* were merely or mainly subordinate resources for furthering the bishops' purposes at the Council. But in some key documents (especially *Dignitatis humanae* on religious liberty) *periti*, such as Pietro Pavan and John Courtney Murray, were much more active than merely crafting texts. They mobilized and attempted to influence bishops or win over potential opposition from compatible bishops groups (e.g., Pavan and Murray's attempts to overcome the French bishops' initial objections to a mainly juridical treatment of religious liberty)[37]. Moreover, in sheer numbers progressive *periti* (or the-ologians who hung around the Council) seem to have outnumbered more conservative ones. Progressive bishops had more ample resources from *periti* than did the conservatives. Protestant observers at the Council did more than just simply observe. They inter-acted with *periti* and bishops. Journalists who swarmed into Rome to cover the Council had either active inter-actions with the bishops or, minimally, served as a kind of reference point for bishops. These and other actors and their interactions with pro-gressive and/or conservative bishops would need to be mined by histori-ans to probe more deeply Vatican II as a social movement.

2. Expansion of Locales

The Council as a social movement was not restricted to Rome. Bishops returned home to their own countries in inter-session periods and, there, interacted with lower clergy and lay experts. The churches back home (their clientele and expectations) were differentially mobilized and also served as a locus for social movement mobilization. My treatment would need expansion to do justice to this aspect of the Council as a social move-ment. Thus, to take one example, *Pax Christi* as an international movement and The Catholic Worker Movement in the United States actively lobbied individual bishops back home (and not just through the few representatives who went to Rome during Council sessions) to include a vigorous section on peace and the legitimacy of conscientious objection in the document, *The Church in the Modern World*. Differing national Episcopal Confer-ences, as we have seen, were better organized and operational than oth-ers. Similarly, in some national settings (e.g., Canada, the Netherlands) church ginger groups and lobby organizations abounded more or had more access to their bishops. Bishops from countries with such homegrown mobilization were more likely to tilt toward the progressive direction.

3. Time Frames

Time frames are important in understanding social mobilization. Ear-lier mobilized groups may have and retain a comparative advantage, as we saw in the distinctions between the Domus Mariae and Coetus Inter-nationalis Patrum groups. Since social mobilization erupts especially in situations of change or uncertainty and looks toward the eventual new

---

37. L. GRIFFIN, *Dignitatis Humanae*, in K. HIMES, et al. (eds.), *Modern Catholic Social Teaching: Commentaries and Interpretations*, Washington, DC, Georgetown University Press, 2005, 244-265.

institutionalization of new norms, roles and organizations, the trajectory
of the time frame remains important throughout the differing phases of
an organizational re-alignment. Thus, for example, some social mobilizations have relatively short-term aims (e.g., the gaining of an international treaty banning land mines) and, when the aim is achieved, the
mobilization may simply disperse. Other mobilizations continue even
after new institutionalization as an on-going interest group. A key question for historians who might use the social mobilization perspective for
looking at Vatican II entails the full trajectory of the mobilization. Did it
disperse somewhat toward the end of the Council, allowing conservative
voices to regain an upper hand. Were the progressives already a bit com-
placent that their positions would gain an upper hand by the last sessions
of the Council, such that they pulled back somewhat on organizational
efforts and intense networking? It does seem that at the end of the Council the progressive bishops turned their attention more to applying it back
at home and their cross-national networking declined and even dispersed.

Often, too, a social mobilization is able to gain on a given issue (in the
short term) a coalition of allies whose internal differences are papered
over for the moment. Only later do these differences re-emerge and lead
to a kind of splintering, as, for example, within a relatively short time after
the Council the progressives seemed to split into what became *The Concilium* and *The Communio* parties with differing visions about implementing the reforms of the Council[38].

4. Institutional Constraints on Social Mobilization at the Council

Sometimes social movements are almost purely social movements.
No or few institutional restraints or embodiments channel or contain the
initial mobilization. Thus, for example, in the 1960s the nascent envi-
ronmental movement did not have to, greatly, tailor or constrain its activity. But the Council as a social movement was always constrained by
certain elements of the Council as a formal ecclesial institution. The
movement and the Council had to run along somewhat parallel lines. John
Noonan, in recalling the Council, ignores completely the Council as a
social movement and speaks of it simply in its more formal terms:

> What we found [at the Council] in fact was a legislature in action. A legis-
> lature with a right, center and left. A legislature with a variety of commit-
> tees composing legislation, compromising disputes, considering amend-
> ments. A legislature of bishops guided by staffs of experts. A legislature

---

38. *Concilium* and *Communio*, rival international journals for interpreting the Council
and its implementation split what had been a greater unity at the Council.

interacting with the executive power possessed by the pope. A legislature surrounded by lobbyists on every issue[39].

In Noonan's view there is no need to evoke the notion of a social movement since the Council looked pretty straightforwardly like a political legislature (even if its legislation was religious rather than secular and its ethos eschewed formal divisions into parties). Every legislature has lobbyists vying to influence outcomes and differing factions and parties. Why evoke the more strained notion of a social movement? The answer, of course, is that a Council is such a rare phenomenon, entails (for each new Council, often centuries in time apart) new and untried procedures and processes. A Council is so ephemeral that it lacks the solidity of an established on-going legislature. The very constitution of the parties, the lobby groups and the swirl of influence at a Council must be created anew. This calls for the forging for an imperfectly and ephemerally organized institution of a parallel social mobilization.

Briefly, we now turn to a final point: the role of internal societal pluralism and other factors in predicting (statistically) episcopal votes at the Council. In this final section of the essay I return to the particularity of Belgium.

V. Religious Pluralism and Other Sociological Factors Predicting More Progressive Votes at the Council

A large number of sociologists of religion point to religious pluralism as a significant variable in predicting a nation's religious behavior. They often evoke concepts theologians may find a bit crass such as market share, supply-side religion, unregulated religious markets[40]. The heart of the argument of such sociologists is that where religions enjoy a monopoly, they may become lazy or intolerant monopolies, content with government support and regulation of religion. Conversely, religious competition drives innovation, a desire to retain adherents, accommodation with some forms of pluralism. Market share refers to the size of a religious presence to a society. Where a religious group is a very small minority, it may eschew any strategies of larger presence to the societal

---

39. J. NOONAN, *The Lustre of Our Country: The American Experience of Religious Freedom*, Berkeley, CA, University of California Press, 1998, p. 338.

40. For notions of supply-side religion and market share see R. FINKE – R. STARK, *The Churching of America, 1776-2005: Winners and Losers in Our Religious Economy*, New Brunswick, NJ, Rutgers University Press, 2005.

structures. Where a religious group is a decided societal presence, but in a competitive religious environment and without state support for religion, it is likely to want to accommodate to the pluralist situation yet retain a societal influence strategy[41].

In terms of the Council, bishops from religiously competitive countries with a separation of church and state and where the Catholic presence, while sizeable enough to make a difference, was far from a monopoly were, statistically (with, of course, individual exceptions) more likely to support key Council initiatives on ecumenism and religious liberty and to be sensitive to Protestant and not just Catholic concerns. Whether on the question of the two-source theory of revelation, the vote on a separate schema on Mary, the document on religious liberty, or the treatment of Jews, bishops from sizeable Catholic populations in a pluralist and religiously competitive country were statistically more likely to vote with the eventual progressive majority on these issues than were even liberal bishops from less pluralist situations. Indeed, about sixty percent of anti-collegial votes at the Council came from religiously monopolistic countries such as Spain and Italy.

A key tactic of the progressives, for example, in garnering support from Eastern European episcopacies for the document on religious liberty was to argue that those churches own demands for religious liberty from communist regimes would be undercut if the Church in Council did not, credibly, proclaim its own doctrine of liberty of conscience and religious freedom. While Belgium does not have a large presence of either Protestants or Jews, it is a religiously competitive society due to a sizeable proportion (roughly 21 percent) of influential non-churched liberals and socialists. These latter represented – at least in the classic quasi-*verzuiling* or pillarized Belgium institutional life – a religiously competitive environment. From its inception, Belgium – whose rallying cry toward independence had been "a free church in a free state" – institutionalized separation of church and state. Not by chance, then, did Msgr. Gérard Phillips explicitly contact the Belgium, Dutch and German bishops – all parts of religiously pluralist societies – to obtain their approval of his proposal to include the treatment of Mary in the schema on the church[42]. There is also no question that the Protestant observers at the Council were an important reference

41. D. MARTIN, *The Religious and the Secular: Studies in Secularization*, New York, Schoken Books, 1969; the classic argument that religious pluralism for Catholicism leads to revised and accomodationist societal influence strategies is I. VALLIER, *Catholicism, Social Control and Modernization in Latin America*, Englewood Cliffs, NJ, Prentice-Hall, 1970.

42. G. ALBERIGO – J.A. KOMONCHAK (eds.), *History of Vatican II*. Vol. III: *The Mature Council: Second Period and Intersession, September 1963 – September 1964*, Maryknoll NY, Orbis; Leuven, Peeters, 2000, p. 52.

group for many of the bishops from religiously pluralist countries. These
bishops often advanced explicit arguments against the original Curial
schemas that to accept them would inhibit ecumenical dialogue or scan-
dalize Protestants. There is even evidence that the Protestant presence
served as a kind of break on the conservatives. Bishop Carli, one of the
founders of CIP complained that the Protestant presence inhibited his ability to speak candidly on a host of issues: "So many insist that we say
nothing about those doctrines of ours that could possibly offend Protestants. Thus, it seems that we cannot speak of the Blessed Virgin Mary"[43].
Because Protestants were constantly present at the Council (and many
wrote about the debates in the Council for the Protestant press), they served
as an important reference group. Insider Catholics were aware they were
being "observed". Had Protestants not been present as observers the group
dynamic at the Council would have, likely, been very different.

A second statistically significant predictor of bishops voting with the
progressive majority was a background factor in a bishop's career. Bishops
who had had previous careers as professional theologians and scripture
scholars (as opposed to simply having had an advanced degree in theology) were also more likely to vote with the progressive majority. Belgium
had a number of such bishops, most notably Cardinal Suenens who had
taught for many years in Louvain. Again language facility played a role.
Although, surely anachronistically, Latin was the official language of the
Council, in the actual networking at the Council, multi-lingual bishops had
an advantage in bridging national episcopacies. Educated Belgians have
notoriously spoken French, Dutch, English and sometimes German. The
Belgium bishops were well placed to play a key networking role.

In the end, of course, as a Catholic and even something of a theologian
as well as a sociologist, I would like to say that, in fact, the result of the
Council was the palpable and decided work of the Holy Spirit. But seeing the Council through the lens of sociology and social mobilization theory in social movements can help us also to see how even the Holy Spirit
in her grace works through natural societal processes and structures.

Bellarmine College of Liberal Arts   John A. COLEMAN, S.J.
Loyola Marymount University
1 LMU Drive
Los Angeles, CA
90045-2659
USA

---

43. RYNNE, *Vatican Council II* (n. 2), p. 11.

DIARIES

PRIVATE SOURCES FOR A STUDY
OF THE SECOND VATICAN COUNCIL

In the study of the Second Vatican Council, hermeneutics and methodology related matters have regularly been the subject of discussions or
even polemics between scholars. By way of introduction, it may be useful to give a brief outline of some of those discussions and to draw a few
lessons from it, specifically with respect to the subject of this article, the
use of private diaries for studying the Council. In addition to these
methodological considerations, we shall provide information about the
Belgian contribution to the Second Vatican Council. We shall specifically mention the results of scholarly and editorial work with respect to
private sources of Belgians involved with the Council. Finally, we shall
present an example in order to show the possibilities of using these specific sources.

I. THE USE OF DIARIES IN RESEARCH ON VATICAN II

1. Controversies Concerning the Interpretation of the Council

Let us start with some polemic from a recent date. On 17th June 2005,
in the "Pietro da Cortona" room of the Musei Capitolini, Cardinal
Camillo Ruini, the Pope's vicar for the diocese of Rome, introduced a
book written by Agostino Marchetto. The latter is a canonist and church
diplomat, and presently the secretary to the Pontifical Council for the
Pastoral Care of Migrants and Itinerant People[1]. Marchetto's book was
entitled *Il Concilio Ecumenico Vaticano II. Contrappunto per la sua storia*, and consisted of a collection of articles and book reviews written
over the past fifteen years[2].

---

1. See the report by Sandro MAGISTER, *Vatican II: The Real Untold Story*. June 22,
2005. http://www.chiesa.espressonline.it/dettaglio.jsp?id=34283&eng=y (access 18.8.2005).
2. A. MARCHETTO, *Il Concilio Ecumenico Vaticano II: Contrappunto per la sua storia* (Storia e attualità, 17), Vatican City, Libreria Editrice Vaticana, 2005.

Cardinal Ruini considers Marchetto's work a counterpoint because it defends an interpretation of Vatican II being "the polar opposite […] to the interpretation that until now has monopolized Catholic historiography throughout the world", and that is the interpretation underlying the five-volume *History of Vatican II*, published under the direction of Giuseppe Alberigo. The *History* represents the "central thesis" of Alberigo and his "Bologna School", and can be summarized as follows: "the documents produced by Vatican Council II are not its primary elements. The main thing is the event itself. The real Council is the 'spirit' of the Council. It cannot be reduced to the 'letter' of its documents, and is incomparably superior to these"[3].

According to Ruini, the 'spirit' of the Council is identified by Alberigo by pope John XXIII's dream about church renewal, whereas the 'letter' of the Council was typical of pope Paul VI, who promulgated the Council documents. This interpretation is connected with the thesis that the renewal introduced by Vatican II caused a fundamental 'rupture' with what preceded in church history.

Ruini resolutely rejects this interpretation for being historically incorrect and theologically inadmissible. It needs to be countered with an interpretation that puts Vatican II, even in its new orientation, in continuity with tradition. In his conclusion, he announces that Alberigo's *History* project is basically outdated: "The interpretation of the Council as a rupture and a new beginning is coming to an end. This interpretation is very feeble today, and has no real foothold within the body of the Church. It is time for historiography to produce a new reconstruction of Vatican II which will also be, finally, a true story".

It is not our intention to critically discuss Ruini's opinion as far as its correctness and fairness are concerned. However, we found it useful to mention it, if only to show that the historiographical project, in which many of the contributors to this book have been involved for years, is not accepted on a whim, but is indeed subject to criticism. This criticism, however biased and unnuanced it may be, must stimulate us to constantly test the methodological options of our historical-theological approach to the Council and further finetune it[4].

---

3. MAGISTER, *Vatican II* (n. 1).

4. Basically, these options are a further development of the principles outlined by Giuseppe ALBERIGO in well-known programmatic articles such as, *Critères herméneutiques pour une histoire de Vatican II*, in M. LAMBERIGTS – C. SOETENS (eds.), *À la veille du Concile Vatican II: Vota et réactions en Europe et dans le catholicisme oriental* (Instrumenta Theologica, 9), Leuven, Bibliotheek van de Faculteit der Godgeleerdheid, 1992, 12-23; also in J.-P. JOSSUA (ed.), *Interpréter: Mélanges offerts à Claude Geffré*, Paris, Cerf, 1992, 261-275.

In a second step, we now focus on Marchetto's criticism of the method-ological principles of what he too calls the "Bologna School"[5]. What is interesting, in Marchetto's judgment, is the fact that he explicitly directs his critique towards the subject of this article, namely the use of private sources such as diaries for the study of the Council.

2. The Importance of Diaries in the Study of the Council

Diaries are a type of source that have been used regularly in the his-toriography of the councils. In the study of the Second Vatican Council they were 'discovered' relatively late and included into research thanks to the opening up of various local archives[6]. They have not been inte-grated into the *Acta Synodalia* and were flooded for quite some time by the well-known published diaries and chronicles accompanying the Coun-cil. Even though they may be related to the latter[7], they are a proper type of source: given that they are not intended for immediate publication, they are written in more of a subjective style, more open to impressions of events, more personal in content. Their importance for studying the Second Vatican Council was stressed by Alberto Melloni[8], who feels, however, that they do not primarily owe this importance to their proper style. What makes them really indispensable is the fact that, from an insider's point of view, they provide an analysis of the dynamics that were so characteristic of the Council. On the basis of these sources, scholars may now understand the complexity of the factors playing in the Council's decision-making process. They will be able to track down

---

5. By the way, Marchetto directs his criticism not only against Bologna but also against Louvain: with respect to the Council's hermeneutics, he feels there exists "una certa qual 'alleanza'" between "Bologna" and "Louvain". MARCHETTO, *Il Concilio Ecu-menico Vaticano II* (n. 2), p. 376; see also p. 382: both cooperate and show the same line of thought.

6. Here too, the initiatives in the framework of the preparation of the *History of Vati-can II* project led by G. Alberigo must be expressly mentioned.

7. Personal notes might be the (intended) basis for published chronicles. The best example is Yves Congar, who held an extensive diary of the Council (published in 2002: *Mon Journal du Concile*. Présenté et annoté par Éric MAHIEU, 2 vols., Paris, Cerf, 2002) and simultaneously published *Le concile au jour le jour*, 4 vols., Paris, Cerf, 1963-1966.

8. A. MELLONI, *Les journaux privés dans l'histoire de Vatican II*, in M.-D. CHENU, *Notes quotidiennes au Concile: Journal de Vatican II 1962-1963*. Édition critique et intro-duction par A. MELLONI (Histoire à vif), Paris, Cerf, 1995, 7-54; also ID., *L'usage des journaux privés pour l'étude de la participation canadienne à Vatican II*, in G. ROUTHIER (ed.), *L'Église canadienne et Vatican II* (Héritage et projet, 58), Montreal, Fides, 1998, 415-432; more in general: ID., *Tipologia delle fonti per la storia del Vaticano II*, in *Cristianesimo nella Storia* 13 (1992) 493-514.

non-programmed partnerships as well as detect communication and cooperation short-circuits while retrieving the formation of a *communis opinio*
through various channels. Melloni concludes that private diaries may well
serve to help write the history of the Council precisely *as* a council[9].
Without them, you can fill libraries with commentaries, but you will not
be able to write the history of Vatican II[10].

Clearly, Melloni's appreciation of private diaries is linked to his
approach towards the Council as an event, which can only really be
understood if it is interpreted as a dynamic process of its own kind.
Accordingly, Marchetto rejects the importance given to private documents with respect to interpreting the Council[11]. In his view, the sole
basis for interpreting the Council remains with the study of the official
acta and documents. At the most, other sources may only illustrate the
reading of the *acta* and final texts. When researchers, in their prefer-
ential choice of sources, make the "salto mortale" from official to private, they show an unacceptable "ideological partiality". Marchetto has
already read a great number of those particular sources, and says that
he is faced with a certain feeling of despondency every time he is forced
to approach these fragmentary, incomplete, subjective documents with
the criticism required. Thus, for example, his conclusion regarding the
edition of Albert Prignon's *Journal conciliaire* is as follows: in the
end, this type of sources only teaches us the "piccola storia", which at
the most can only illustrate the official texts and add some flavor to
them[12].

"Piccola storia" or "indispensable sources": the following will clearly
show in what sense we appreciate the study of private diaries. We shall
first discuss a few attempts at the classification of diaries and mention
some methodological criteria for their use. Then we will provide an
overview of the Belgian diaries available, and finally utilize an example
to show the significance of this type of sources.

---

9. "La fonction infrangible des journaux [...] est de faire prendre conscience au
chercheur de la complexité des facteurs en jeu, de l'instauration au sein de l'assemblée de
partnerships non programmées et de coordinations lacunaires, de la formation d'une *opinio
communis* par des canaux très différenciés – en somme, ils servent à faire l'histoire du concile et tant que concile", MELLONI, *Les journaux privés* (n. 8), p. 11, n. 2.

10. "... les journaux proprement dits, ceux sans lesquels on peut certes écrire des
bibliothèques de commentaires, mais pas l'histoire de Vatican II" (*ibid.*, p. 13).

11. MARCHETTO, *Il Concilio Ecumenico Vaticano II* (n. 2), esp. pp. 297-299, 316-317,
370-387.

12. *Ibid.*, p. 317: it ultimately concerns the "piccola storia nei confronti di quella
grande"; this is a quotation from Congar's diary: CONGAR, *Mon journal du Concile* (n. 7),
vol. II, p. 72. On Prignon's diary, see below, n. 34.

II. Private Diaries:
A Typology and Some Methodological Criteria

Besides Melloni, Joseph Famerée also developed a typology of private diaries. Furthermore, diaries were integrated into the overview of conciliar sources, produced by Massimo Faggioli and Giovanni Turbanti[13]. These rather tentative classifications can be integrated and further specified in a simple overview.

1. Typology of Diaries

A typology of diaries as a principle of classification and a basis for interpretation has primarily an orientating function. Indeed, the affinity, the mixture of genre and characteristics of the diaries discussed, demand that the different sorts be approached with the flexibility required. A strict or fine-tuned typological distinction is not easy to be made, nor does it seem to be absolutely necessary for an adequate appreciation of the sources[14]. Therefore, some major distinctive features of private diaries may suffice to provide the basis for their interpretation.

The private character of diaries, which self-evidently distinguishes them from public documents, appears to be important for identification. Public texts are primarily intended for a general audience of contemporaries, whom the author wishes to inform or convince via a public medium (such as chronicles in periodicals or newspapers, or memoirs published as books). As such, they presuppose, on the author's side, a discourse that differs substantially from those used in private texts. Consequently, they need to be interpreted on the basis of other assessment criteria. Private texts are not directly intended for a general audience of contemporaries[15]. This means, among other things, that they may have a rather direct, 'unmediated', less reflective relationship with the subject.

---

13. See, besides Melloni's studies mentioned in n. 8, J. FAMERÉE, *Uso comparativo dei diari: Una settimana di lavori conciliari (5-15 novembre 1963)*, in M.T. FATTORI – A. MELLONI (eds.), *L'evento e le decisioni: Studi sulle dinamiche del concilio Vaticano II* (Testi e ricerche di scienze religiose, n.s., 20), Bologna, Il Mulino, 1997, 321-354 (esp. pp. 322-330); M. FAGGIOLI – G. TURBANTI, *Il Concilio inedito: Fonti del Vaticano II* (Testi e ricerche di scienze religiose. Fonti e strumenti di ricerca, 1), Bologna, Il Mulino, 2001, pp. 7-34, esp. p. 19.

14. Thus we will not adopt several of the differences proposed by the authors; e.g. Melloni's distinction between diaries spanning a longer period and thus including a part on the Council; diaries dating from the preparatory period; council diaries.

15. Also diaries written in view of a possible publishing are not oriented towards direct contemporaries – think of Congar's embargo against public use of his journal before 2000. CONGAR, *Mon journal du Concile* (n. 7), vol. I, p. 2.

Basically, this direct contact with the subject applies to the chronological aspect as well: they are produced almost simultaneously with the facts or events described.

Private diaries can then be defined as non-public oriented documents, for personal or private use, in which events are described and commented on, and in which statements as well as ideas, opinions, plans, proposals are written down. The author, at that very moment, finds such statements important for either his own or his allies' information. Because of their private character, they are often 'subjective', direct, confidential, and spontaneous.

An additional internal typology of private diaries can be made on the basis of two properties[16].

Author's Position

The first differentiation of these sources is related to the author, the producer of the text. In order to judge the document's value and proper character, we need to know as many properties as possible about the producer of the text, and as accurately as possible; *in casu*: the author's position, including his function during the Council (pope, Council father, member of a conciliar commission, *peritus*, observer, lay person, diplomat, reporter, etc.), his connections, the networks he is part of, the information at his disposal[17]. But also his personality, his character, his ideas, his style of writing, etc. are important elements allowing a better assessment of the text.

Type of Text

Another difference is related to the type of diary being written. Here, a distinction can be based on the format and the intention of the diary (which are basically intertwined).

In their elementary *form*, diaries may consist of merely notes about all kinds of subjects, written down without much coherence and editing, but they may also be elaborated and structured texts, which are more reflected upon: these are diaries in the stricter sense of the word.

The peculiar format of a diary may be connected to a specific *intention* of the author. Fragmentary notes may be collected as a memorandum

---

16. More or less compliant to the distinction made by FAMERÉE, *Uso comparativo dei diari* (n. 13), pp. 322-330.

17. This matter is not without importance because many things at the Council happened 'secretly': the meetings *in aula*, the meetings of the commissions and several interventions by the pope, which were not even accessible to all members of the commissions. Thus, for example, neither Yves Congar nor Charles Moeller nor Joseph Ratzinger were aware of the tribulations regarding the *Nota explicativa praevia* (see below, pp. 48-51).

on the author's behalf. They may contain merely personal impressions of own experiences or notes intended to inform kindred spirits. But we may also be faced with extensively elaborated diaries, more or less written with the intention of being made available at some time for historical use.

With respect to the latter item, Famerée distinguishes between diaries for historical use and diaries for immediate and private use. The first category is written in a sober and more *ad rem* style, is directly related to the important topics, and pushes through to the core of the matter. The second type is more exhaustive, pays more attention to anecdotic topics, does not hesitate to note down secondary data, and also mentions matters not directly related to the Council.

2. Some Criteria for the Use of Diaries

How can these diaries be used? The two authors mentioned, Melloni and Famerée, make a comparative use of this source. They compare the way in which various authors in their diaries reacted to a certain event: Melloni discusses different impressions of the opening ceremony of the Council on October 11, 1962, while Famerée deals with reactions of people present at some incidents during the general congregation of November 8, 1963. The latter example anticipates the following step: Famerée integrated these data into his survey of the Council's activities in volume III of the *History of Vatican II*[18]. This leads us to another way to use council diaries: they not only include various impressions of council *events*, but they also provide information for reconstructing the editorial genesis of conciliar *texts*. The use of diaries for this purpose obviously presupposes an assessment of their properties, reliability, informative value, etc. This assessment can be made according to the usual methodological rules of historical criticism. As an illustration of how this methodology can be adopted for the interpretation of private conciliar diaries, we will mention two kinds of criteria, related to the above mentioned typology.

Criteria regarding the Author

With regard to the author of the diary, attention should be paid to the position and the character of the person who wrote the text.

18. J. FAMERÉE, *Bishops and Dioceses and the Communications Media (November 5-25, 1963)*, in G. ALBERIGO – J.A. KOMONCHAK (eds.), *History of Vatican II*. Vol. III: *The Mature Council: Second Period and Intersession, September 1963 – September 1964*, Maryknoll, NY, Orbis; Leuven, Peeters, 2000, 117-256, esp. pp. 127-132, 137-138.

First of all, one should take into consideration his *involvement* in the Council: What was his function, e.g. in a conciliar commission? The degree of involvement of church leaders and theologians in these commissions is directly relevant towards their influence in the proceedings. Thus, as a *peritus*, a theologian could play a much greater role in the creation of texts than a possibly more renowned theologian, who was merely present at the Council as an observer (and even here there were differences; e.g. the role of Henri de Lubac was less than that of Yves Congar).

An important question concerns a person's *information sources*: was he the confidant of a good informant? This aspect is of crucial importance for the evaluation of a source. In order to find out if a person was well informed, one should know which personal contacts he had, with which networks he was connected, etc.

One should take into account the *personality* of the author. What kind of character and temperament did he have? Was he 'objectively' reliable or rather naïve? Was he accurate in rendering facts and opinions?

In addition, one should keep in mind the *motives* of an author to keep a diary. Was his primary interest in the importance of facts, or was he rather inclined to write *ad propriam majorem gloriam*, or out of a need to confide?

Criteria Regarding the Type of Diary

Furthermore, questions should be posed concerning aspects of the diaries that were already mentioned in relation to the typology, where diaries were distinguished on the basis of their form and intention. These differences form the basis for an assessment of the value, precision, and reliability of the diary.

The inquiry begins with *formal* aspects, such as the frequency and the time of writing (e.g. every day, or every month, or even years after the facts), and the readability of the text. With regard to the *intention* of the author, we already referred to the difference of a diary that is written 'secretly' and a diary destined for publication. Again, this difference in the intention and motives of the diary is most often only gradual, and even notes of one and the same author can have different intentions, influencing the final result of the text.

The above questions suggest that a thorough knowledge of the background, history and position of the participants and observers at the Council is of the utmost importance if one is to make use of these specific sources. Probably more than for other sources, the explicit evaluation of the informative value and reliability of diaries is extremely important. Moreover, it goes without saying that they always must be used in combination with other sources available. These considerations may be illustrated by the following survey of the major authors of diaries among the Belgians at the Vatican Council.

III. Diaries of Belgian Participants in the Council

Given that this book is focused on "The Belgian Contribution to the Second Vatican Council", we shall present a survey of the Belgian participants in the Council who produced private diaries. This will enable us to have an overview of various protagonists who will be discussed more extensively in this book. Giuseppe Alberigo, in an overall estimate, defined the number of identified and analyzed diaries of Council participants to "almost seventy"[19]. The Belgian contribution may be estimated at about eight. The following is a brief survey of these diaries, a short characterization of the authors and a typification of the sources.

1. Léon-Joseph Suenens

Belgium's archbishop Léon-Joseph Suenens (1904-1996) was one of the key figures at the Second Vatican Council. He was a member of the preparatory commission "De episcopis et de dioeceseos regimine", of the Central Preparatory Commission, of the "Secretariatus de negotiis extra ordinem", of the Coordinatory Commission, and a moderator.

Suenens's Council Fund at the Archdiocesan Archives in Mechelen includes, under the title "Mémoires sur le Concile Vatican II", a 69 page text, which probably dates from the beginning of 1966[20]. It is a tape, recorded and typed with numerous errors, and later corrected by Suenens. The text covers a period from before the Council up until the fourth session, and it contains personal memories and data concerning Suenens' role at the Council[21].

---

19. G. ALBERIGO, *The Sources for the Second Vatican Council*, in G. ALBERIGO – J.A. KOMONCHAK (eds.), *History of Vatican II*. Vol. V: *The Council and the Transition: The Fourth Period and the End of the Council, September 1965 – December 1965*, Maryknoll NY, Orbis; Leuven, Peeters, 2005, 645-652, p. 649.
20. L. DECLERCK – E. LOUCHEZ, *Inventaire des Papiers conciliaires du cardinal L.-J. Suenens* (Cahiers de la Revue théologique de Louvain, 31), Louvain-la-Neuve, Publications de la Faculté de Théologie, 1998 [hereafter: Fund Suenens] nos. 2784-2785.
21. The text clarifies Suenens' involvement in the organization and development of the Council. His judgment on persons (the popes, Felici, cardinals) is subjective but interest-

Next to this, there are, of course, Suenens' 'memoirs', published in 1991 under the title *Souvenirs et espérances*, a part of which are dealing with the Council[22]. These recollections are largely based on the unpublished "Mémoires", and therefore have the same characteristics and deficiencies. Interestingly, several letters and documents are included.

2. André-Marie Charue

André-Marie Charue (1898-1977), the bishop of Namur, an exegete by formation, was a member of and, from December 1963 on, second vice-president of the Doctrinal Commission[23]. His Council diary was published in 2000 by Leo Declerck and Claude Soetens under the title *Carnets conciliaires de l'évêque de Namur, A.-M. Charue*. Charue wrote most of these notes day after day, except during the fourth Council session. There are no notes from the second session and only few from the third. Charue's "Carnets conciliaires" are particularly important because of the many notes he makes regarding the meetings of the Doctrinal Commission[24]. His reports are technically accurate and very reliable and, therefore, valuable for the interpretation of some major Council texts.

3. Joseph Maria Heuschen

Joseph Maria Heuschen (1915-2002), auxiliary bishop of Liège, was appointed a member of the Doctrinal Commission in November 1963. He became a very active and efficient member of the commission, cooperating in the preparation of such important texts as *Lumen gentium*, *Dei verbum* and *Gaudium et spes*. He was an excellent exegete, patrologist and theologian, and was the main collaborator of Gérard Philips. His greatest merit consisted of the classification and processing of thousands

---

ing. Some 'stories' are very authentic. Nevertheless, everything is colored personally. Moreover, Suenens is not accurate concerning dates, chronology, persons present, etc. Also his reports of meetings are often incomplete and selective.

22. L.-J. SUENENS, *Souvenirs et espérances*, Paris, Fayard, 1991, pp. 55-131.

23. For his role at the Council, see the *Introduction* by C. TROISFONTAINES, in L. DECLERCK – C. SOETENS (eds.), *Carnets conciliaires de l'évêque de Namur A.-M. Charue* (Cahiers de la Revue théologique de Louvain, 32), Louvain-la-Neuve, Publications de la Faculté de Théologie, 2000, 5-25.

24. Charue also used these notes as memoranda concerning the discussions during the meetings.

of *Modi* submitted for these three constitutions[25]. During the Council, Heuschen did not keep a diary strictly speaking, but we should mention him here because of his extensive correspondence with his family and the ladies Paula and Maria Verjans[26]. This correspondence is highly informative thanks to the precise dating of many facts; Heuschen wrote every two days. He wrote with great openness, because he knew that his correspondents were discrete[27].

In addition to these letters, we possess "Concilieherinneringen": undated 'memoirs' which Heuschen probably wrote down after his retirement as bishop of Hasselt, after 1989[28]. Heuschen's high age may explain some of the mistakes in the text. These 'Council memories' especially describe episodes in which Heuschen was personally engaged[29].

4. Gérard Philips

Gérard Philips (1899-1972), dogma professor at the University of Louvain, was a member of the "Commissio theologica praeparatoria", a Council *peritus*, and from December 1963 onwards, vice-secretary for the Doctrinal Commission[30]. He was the major editor of *Lumen gentium*, but his role was equally important in the preparation of *Dei verbum* and *Gaudium et spes*. In fact, here, he took over the role of secretary S. Tromp. All this makes Philips a privileged witness for the genesis of the three major constitutions of Vatican II.

From August 8, 1916 to June 20, 1969, Philips wrote down, in Dutch, "personal notes", a kind of diary in two parts. The first part consists of

---

25. Cf. *Note sur les archives conciliaires de Mgr J.M. Heuschen*, in L. DECLERCK, *Inventaires des papiers conciliaires de Monseigneur J.M. Heuschen, évêque auxiliaire de Liège, membre de la Commission doctrinale, et du Professeur V. Heylen* (Instrumenta Theologica, 28), Leuven, Maurits Sabbebibliotheek Faculteit Godgeleerdheid – Peeters, 2005, 3-13.

26. Fund Heuschen, 395-581.

27. The fact that he preserved these letters after the Council, shows the importance he gave to them.

28. In addition to these "Concilieherinneringen", there is a text, "De amendementenslag", including memories of important discussions of *Modi* in which Heuschen was involved. Fund Heuschen, 384-385.

29. The correspondence as well as the "Concilieherinneringen" are interesting for the history and interpretation of some passages of conciliar texts, if the related archivalia in Heuschen's archives are included in the research.

30. For the role of Philips, see the *Introduction* to the publication of his diaries, mentioned in the following note (p. VII, n. 2). See further: L. DECLERCK – W. VERSCHOOTEN, *Inventaire des papiers conciliaires de Monseigneur Gérard Philips, secrétaire adjoint de la commission doctrinale.* Avec une Introduction par J. GROOTAERS (Instrumenta Theologica, 24), Leuven, Bibliotheek van de Faculteit Godgeleerdheid – Peeters, 2001.

seven notebooks, the second of twelve, and the last two of the latter contain notes on his activities at the Vatican Council. These last two notebooks of Philips' diary were recently published with a French translation by Karim Schelkens[31]. Although they include only a limited amount of data and do not cover all of the Council periods[32], they are important for representing discussions in the Doctrinal Commission (especially in the first intersession), as well as for their chronology of the *Nota explicativa praevia* (November 1964) and tribulations concerning *De revelatione* during the fourth session. Philips' representation of theological subjects is always very accurate and precise. This diary also tells us a lot about Philips' spirituality and his personal relationships with some of the major actors at the Council.

In addition, we should not forget the important dossier that Philips composed on the *Nota praevia*. In this dossier, which was published by Jan Grootaers in 1986, various documents are collected around the "Notes pour servir à l'histoire de la Nota Praevia Explicativa (Lumen Gentium, III)", written by Philips in 1969[33].

5. Albert Prignon

Albert Prignon (1919-2000) was rector of the Belgian College in Rome and Council *peritus* from March 1963 onwards. He especially followed the activities of the Doctrinal Commission. Moreover, he was the confidant of Suenens and of most Belgian bishops and *periti* who stayed at the college. His extensive *Journal conciliaire de la 4e session* was published in 2003 by Leo Declerck and André Haquin[34]. It is here that Prignon gives an account of everything he comes to know. He writes for history and

31. K. SCHELKENS (ed.), *Cahiers conciliaires de Mgr Gérard Philips, secrétaire adjoint de la commission doctrinale: Texte néerlandais avec traduction française et commentaires.* Avec une Introduction par L. DECLERCK (Instrumenta Theologica, 29), Leuven, Maurits Sabbebibliotheek Faculteit Godgeleerdheid – Uitgeverij Peeters, 2006. See also Leo DECLERCK, *Brève présentation du "Journal conciliaire" de Mgr Gerard Philips*, in M.T. FATTORI – A. MELLONI (eds.), *Experience, Organisations and Bodies at Vatican II* (Instrumenta Theologica, 21), Leuven, Bibliotheek van de Faculteit Godgeleerdheid, 1999, 219-231.

32. Important periods are lacking: nearly the complete 2nd session; the 2nd and 3rd intersessions are treated sporadically. Moreover, several parts were not written until weeks or months after the fact.

33. J. GROOTAERS, *Primauté et collégialité: Le dossier de Gérard Philips sur la Nota Explicativa Praevia (Lumen gentium, Chap. III)* (BETL, 72), Leuven, University Press – Peeters, 1986, pp. 63-124 (with annexes).

34. L. DECLERCK – A. HAQUIN (eds.), *Mgr. Albert Prignon, Recteur du Pontificio Collegio Belga, Journal conciliaire de la 4e session* (Cahiers de la Revue théologique de Louvain, 35), Louvain-la-Neuve, Publications de la Faculté de Théologie, 2003.

wishes everything to remain confidential. He is extremely well informed, objective and critical in reporting, and very accurate *in theologicis*[35].

Additionally, in his capacity as ecclesiastical adviser to the Belgian embassy to the Holy See, Prignon made reports during the third and fourth Council sessions[36]. A comparison between these reports and Prignon's "Journal conciliaire" is interesting: Prignon does not betray 'secrets' in his reports to the Embassy, but rather adopts another tone and obscures some tensions (e.g. among Belgian bishops). Furthermore, some other notices and transcripts of tapes are preserved in the Prignon Archives[37], along with eight tapes recorded by Prignon himself[38].

6. Charles Moeller

Charles Moeller (1912-1986), professor at Louvain, was a Council *peritus*. Beginning with the first intersession he acted as a secretary and aid for Msgr. Philips. He also participated in the work of the Secretariat for Unity and in some other commissions[39].

From Moeller, numerous "Carnets" are preserved, including about forty-two that deal with the Council[40]. They are handwritten, in a telegram

---

35. However, for the audiences of Suenens with the pope and meetings of the moderators, he is dependent on Suenens' report, which is not always objective and accurate.

36. They are included under the title "Rapports à l'ambassade de Belgique près le Saint-Siège" in the Prignon Archives: J. FAMERÉE, *Concile Vatican II et Église contemporaine (Archives de Louvain-la-Neuve)*. II. *Inventaire des Fonds A. Prignon et H. Wagnon* (Cahiers de la Revue théologique de Louvain, 24), Louvain-la-Neuve, Publications de la Faculté de Théologie, 1991, nos. 1056-1058, 1575-1578. These reports were recently published in Prosper POSWICK, *Un journal du Concile: Vatican II vu par un diplomate belge. Notes personnelles de l'Ambassadeur de Belgique près le Saint-Siège (1957-1968) et Rapports au Ministère des Affaires Étrangères*, ed. R.-F. POSWICK – Y. JUSTE, Paris, François-Xavier de Guibert, 2005, pp. 461-470, 477-492, 512-534, 575-579, 581-586, 587-592, 596-608, 643-657. The Belgian ambassador copied these texts literally into his reports to the Ministry. For the 4th session, there are interesting differences between Prignon's reports to the ambassador and his "Journal conciliaire de la 4e session".

37. Fund Prignon, 512 (2nd session), 823-825 (2nd intersession).

38. The interviews were given from the end of January to the beginning of February 2000. The interviewer was Eric de Beukelaer. The original is preserved by E. de Beukelaer and a copy by L. Declerck. These tapes contain various details on the Council and on the "squadra belga", and also regarding the atmosphere as it was experienced by Prignon. But they include some inaccuracies and errors.

39. He became member of the central sub-commission (of the "Commissio mixta" for Scheme XIII) at the end of November 1964. He also contributed to the chapter "De cultura" in part two of *Gaudium et spes*.

40. See Cl. SOETENS, *Concile Vatican II et Église contemporaine, I. Inventaire des Fonds Ch. Moeller, G. Thils, Fr. Houtart* (Cahiers de la Revue théologique de Louvain, 29), Louvain-la-Neuve, Publications de la Faculté de Théologie, 1989, pp. 73-75.

style, difficult to read, but meticulously kept nearly every day. They contain a wealth of information about events in and around the Council. Contrary to G. Philips and A. Prignon, however, Moeller was seldom involved in 'secret' maneuvers at the Council[41]. His diary is not conceived as a 'technical' report, and since it was not destined for a large public, includes personal, open and free statements.

7. Jacques Dupont

Jacques Dupont (1915-1998), in the days of the Council a monk of the Benedictine Sint-Andries abbey of Zevenkerken (near Bruges), was an exegete and disciple of Lucien Cerfaux. Via Cerfaux, bishop Charue and also by bishop De Smedt, he was consulted especially for *De revelatione* and *De ecclesia*, as well as for the chapter "De Cultura" of *Gaudium et spes*. Dupont was never appointed a *peritus* at the Council, but this did not prevent him from engaging intensively in conciliar work. Eight "cahiers" of his are preserved, covering the period from December 1962 up to 1965. They contain information on numerous subjects and were written as a preparation for informative reports addressed to his abbey[42].

8. Bernard Olivier

Also the Dominican Bernard Olivier (b. 1920) wrote a "chronique conciliaire", dealing with the second and fourth sessions[43]. Olivier was at the service of the Congolese episcopate (since 1958 he was a professor of Moral Theology at Lovanium, the catholic university in Léopoldville). He was a *peritus* from the second session onwards[44]. He did not directly participate in the work of the conciliar commissions, but he made numerous notes for the bishops of the Congo and was present at the meetings of the French language section of the Pan-African episcopate. His chronicle includes personal impressions as well as analyses of the situation,

41. Because he was an emotional person, Moeller sometimes could hardly keep certain secrets. Therefore, these were not communicated to him. Thus, Moeller was not informed about the peripetia of the *Nota praevia*, nor about the changes which G. Philips wished to make in *De revelatione* in October 1965. Also A. Prignon did not confide in him the secret information he knew from Cardinal Suenens.

42. E. LOUCHEZ, *Concile Vatican II et Église contemporaine (Archives de Louvain-la-Neuve). IV. Inventaire des Fonds J. Dupont et B. Olivier* (Cahiers de la Revue théologique de Louvain, 29), Louvain-la-Neuve, Publications de la Faculté de Théologie, 1995, p. 99.

43. Fund Olivier, 169-170.

44. Cf. C. SOETENS (ed.), *Vatican II et la Belgique* (Sillages – Arca), Ottignies – Louvain-la-Neuve, Éditions Quorum SPRL, 1996, p. 183 and LOUCHEZ, *Concile Vatican II et Église contemporaine* (n. 42), pp. 8-9.

and also served as a means of information for his order and for missionary journals.

For the sake of completeness, we recall that excerpts from the diaries
mentioned were included in some publications, such as the dossier on the
birth control discussions in November 1965, published by Jan Grootaers
and Jan Jans in 2002[45], the book on *Vatican II et la Belgique*, published
by Claude Soetens in 1996[46], and the survey already mentioned, by
Joseph Famerée[47].

Finally, in addition to these diaries of participants in the Council, some
other comparable documents were not included in this survey, either
because their extent is very limited or because they consist of notebooks
including only information written down during (sub-)commission meetings. Among those documents can be mentioned: some notes on "Une
journée type du concile" written by the Belgian theologian Philippe Delhaye (1912-1990)[48], fragments of a notebook written down by bishop
Emiel-Joseph De Smedt (1909-1995)[49], and very short 'diaires' written
by the Louvain canonist Henri Wagnon (1906-1983)[50]. Finally, we can
refer to some notices, based on tapes recorded during the Council by
Msgr. Paul C. Schoenmaeckers (1914-1986), auxiliary bishop of the Belgian archdiocese[51], and to the recently published notes and reports made

---

45. J. GROOTAERS – J. JANS (eds.), *La régulation des naissances à Vatican II: Une
semaine de crise. Un dossier en 40 documents* (Annua Nuntia Lovaniensia, 43), Leuven
– Paris – Sterling, VA, Peeters, 2002: contains a report by A. Prignon to the Belgian
embassy (doc. 21) and a part of the "diary" by J.M. Heuschen, for the period Nov. 27-
Dec. 4, 1965 (doc. 38).

46. *Témoignages belges sur le Concile*, in SOETENS (ed.), *Vatican II et la Belgique*
(n. 44), 185-219: excerpts from diaries of Philippe Delhaye (pp. 188-193; see below n.
48), Jacques Dupont (pp. 194-197, 210-219; Fund Dupont, 1726, 1733) and Bernard
Olivier (Fund Olivier, 169-170).

47. FAMERÉE, *Uso comparativo dei diari* (n. 13). Among the diaries used by Famerée,
there are those of the Belgians J. Dupont, Ch. Moeller, B. Olivier, A. Prignon.

48. See J. FAMERÉE – L. HULSBOSCH, *Concile Vatican II et Église contemporaine*
(*Archives de Louvain-la-Neuve*). III. *Inventaire du Fonds Ph. Delhaye* (Cahiers de la Revue
théologique de Louvain, 25), Louvain-la-Neuve, Publications de la Faculté de Théologie,
1993, n. 230.

49. The notes, made *in aula*, only cover three days, Nov. 14, 16, 17, 1962.
Cf. A. GREILER – L. DE SAEGER (eds.), *Emiel-Jozef De Smedt: Papers Vatican II. Inventory* (Instrumenta Theologica, 22), Leuven, Bibliotheek van de Faculteit Godgeleerdheid,
1999, no. 575.

50. Cf. J. FAMERÉE, *Concile Vatican II et Église contemporaine (Archives de Louvain-
la-Neuve)*. II. *Inventaire des Fonds A. Prignon et H. Wagnon*, nos. 185-191, 241.

51. Preserved in the Archdiocesan Archives at Mechelen. The information was destined
for the personnel of the archdiocese; these notes are interesting because they reflect the
atmosphere during the Council. Msgr. Schoenmaeckers was not a member of a conciliar
commission nor a confidant of Cardinal Suenens.

during the Council by Prosper Poswick (1906-1992), Belgium's ambassador to the Holy See and dean of the corps diplomatique[52].

IV. AN EXAMPLE: FROM 'VI COMMUNIONIS' TO 'HIERARCHICA COMMUNIONE' (*LG* 21 §2; 22 §1)

Among the many examples which can illustrate our general considerations on the use of private diaries in council research, we will present one concerning discussions on the schema *De ecclesia*[53]. It is related to the issue of the episcopate as the highest degree of the sacrament of ordination, and more specifically to a modification implemented in the draft of *De ecclesia* at the initiative of Msgr. Heuschen in March 1964. It deals with the sacramentality and collegiality of the episcopate, as it was finally specified in two sentences of *Lumen gentium*:

> LG 21 §2: "Episcopalis autem consecratio, cum munere sanctificandi, munera quoque confert docendi et regendi, quae tamen natura sua nonnisi in hierarchica communione cum Collegii Capite et membris exerceri possunt"[54].

> LG 22 §1: "Membrum Corporis episcopalis aliquis constituitur vi sacramentalis consecrationis et hierarchica communione cum Collegii Capite atque membris"[55].

We will focus on the second sentence, in which membership in the episcopate is defined by a combination of consecration and communion.

Prior to the Council, the issue had been subject to discussions, in which the implications of episcopal consecration were questioned[56]. Opponents

---

52. These documents provide an interesting viewpoint from the part of diplomacy. P. Poswick received much confidential information and could, particularly, make use of the reports provided by A. Prignon (see above, n. 36).

53. This example was elaborated in close collaboration with Leo Declerck. For a similar use of diaries in research of the Council, see, among other studies, L. DECLERCK, *Le rôle joué par les évêques et periti belges au concile Vatican II: Deux exemples*, in *ETL* 76 (2000) 445-464; M. LAMBERIGTS – L. DECLERCK, *Le texte de Hasselt: Une étape méconnue de l'histoire du De Matrimonio (schéma XIII)*, in *ETL* 80 (2004) 485-505.

54. "Episcopal consecration, along with the office of sanctifying, confers also the offices of teaching and governing; these however by their very nature can only be exercised in hierarchical communion with the head of the college and its members". Cf. N.P. TANNER (ed.), *Decrees of the Ecumenical Councils*, London, Sheed & Ward; Washington, DC, Georgetown University Press, 1990, vol. II, p. 865 (in his Latin text, Tanner erroneously writes "docenti" instead of "docendi").

55. "A person is constituted a member of the episcopal body by virtue of sacramental consecration and by hierarchical communion with the head and members of the college". Cf. TANNER (ed.), *Decrees of the Ecumenical Councils* (n. 54), vol. II, p. 866.

56. On this problem, see G. PHILIPS, *Dogmatische Constitutie over de Kerk 'Lumen Gentium': Geschiedenis, tekst, commentaar*, vol. I, Antwerp, Patmos, 1968, pp. 266-269;

argued that the powers proper of the episcopal office, and particularly the governing power, had to be granted primarily by a juridical act by the pope. This opinion implied some dangers for ecumenism, because it would exclude orthodox bishops who were not in communion with the pope from any legal governing power. There was quite some discussion in the Doctrinal Commission, especially with regard to the relative weight of consecration and communion with the pope and the episcopal college. The debate confronted more of a 'sacramental' theology, leaving room for what the orthodox call '*oikonomia*', and more of a juridical-notional theology.

The diaries, memoirs, correspondences and archive materials of some Belgian participants in this debate (Charue, Heuschen, Philips, Thils, Prignon) shed an interesting light on the genesis and significance of the relevant Council texts. We will now discuss the major steps of the discussions, based on these documents.

1. The Debate During the First Intersession

In March 1963, when Gérard Philips had presented the first chapters of his new outline for *De ecclesia* in the Doctrinal Commission, there was a primary skirmish, mentioned by bishop Charue in his diary[57]. When, during the meeting, Charue expressly asked to specify that bishops receive their "potestas propria radicaliter ex consecratione", H. Schauf, M.-R. Gagnebet and S. Tromp responded that this was still a disputed question which should not be discussed. Tromp claimed that, for example, the pope has already received the plenitude of his office since his election.

2. The Debate in Sub-commission V in January 1964

The debate became more concrete early 1964, and a major role was played by Msgr. Heuschen, who was elected member of the Doctrinal

GROOTAERS, *Primauté et Collégialité* (n. 33), pp. 205-207; 211-213 and the commentary by Alois GRILLMEIER, in *Lexikon für Theologie und Kirche: Das Zweite Vatikanische Konzil*, Freiburg – Basel – Vienna, Herder, vol. I, 1966, 217-229. Also C. TROISFONTAINES, *À propos de quelques interventions de Paul VI dans l'élaboration de 'Lumen Gentium'*, in *Paolo VI e i problemi ecclesiologici al Concilio: Colloquio internazionale di studio, Brescia 19-20-21 settembre 1986* (Pubblicazioni dell'Istituto Paolo VI, 7), Brescia, Istituto Paolo VI; Rome, Edizioni Studium, 1989, 97-143, esp. 138-141; and the commentary on *Lumen Gentium* by P. HÜNERMANN in *Herders Theologischer Kommentar zum Zweiten Vatikanischen Konzil*, vol. II, Freiburg – Basel – Vienna, Herder, 2004, 263-582.

57. DECLERCK – SOETENS (eds.), *Carnets conciliaires de l'évêque de Namur, A.-M. Charue* (n. 23), pp. 114-115.

Commission at the end of November 1963. He joined sub-commission V which had been ordered to rewrite the text about the episcopal college, following the debate *in aula* during the second Council session.

On January 12, 1964 Heuschen addressed a letter to Philips including some remarks about the revised text of no. 16 (later no. 22)[58]. In the first remark he discussed the crucial sentence[59]: "aliquis membrum corporis episcopalis constituitur vi sacramentalis consecrationis *et* communionis cum Collegii capite atque membris". Even though this doctrine was correct, Heuschen argued, it could have been be formulated more precisely. Therefore, he proposed to write, instead of the equation "consecrationis et communionis": "membrum corporis episcopalis aliquis constituitur vi sacramentalis consecrationis, *dummodo adsit communio* cum Collegii capite atque membris", hereby indicating that the two elements, consecration and communion, are both required indeed in order to become part of the episcopal college, but that they do not have the same weight.

In his diary, Philips noted that at the meeting of January 20, 1964 it was decided to add Heuschen's notes to the Relator's Report[60]. In his correspondence, Heuschen himself elaborated on the discussion that took place at that meeting[61]. First, he got the opportunity to express his remarks about the exact formulations of the text that had already been approved. On January 21, he explained once again his view with respect to the distinction of the value between both conditions for inclusion into the episcopal college, and eventually he managed to obtain, with both Moeller's and Thils' support, a change which was important for the Eastern churches. It was a difficult discussion, Heuschen concluded, but he learned that, if you do insist, you finally get what you want.

3. The Plenary Meeting of the Doctrinal Commission in March 1964

After this meeting of the sub-commission in January, Heuschen remained dedicated to the issue: he conferred with Thils, who sent him a long text on the effects of episcopal consecration[62]. He wrote about the

---

58. "De quibusdam observationibus in textum n. 16 prout in subcommissione hucusque emendatum", Fund Philips, 1256, 1299; and Fund Heuschen, 134-138.

59. Notice "in l. 18 p. 1 novi textus n. 16" (italics ours).

60. Notice of Jan. 20, 1964: SCHELKENS (ed.), *Cahiers conciliaires de Mgr Gérard Philips* (n. 31), p. 40 (French, p. 117).

61. Fund Heuschen, 526-527.

62. "De consecrationis episcopalis effectibus" (Febr. 16, 1964); Fund Heuschen, 119-120. Thils wrote: "Voici le rapport que j'ai fait – avec l'accord de S. E. Monseigneur Charue – sur un aspect de la collégialité qui est "capital" et qui a été perdu de vue par une distraction incompréhensible! Pas pour tout le monde, cependant, parce que, lorsque Monseigneur Onclin, dans son Projet sur le Schema de Dioecesium Regimine, signalait que

issue to Philips after Charue had called him on the phone[63]. He did research in patristic texts in order to prove that "consecratio episcopalis totalitatem potestatis Ecclesiae confert electo (quidquid sit de usu et exercitio huius potestatis)"[64]. In the meantime, Heuschen's "Observationes" had been multiplied and distributed to the members by the commission's secretariat[65].

At the plenary meeting of March 6 and 7, 1964, the Doctrinal Commission discussed the issues of episcopal collegiality and sacramentality. In his diary, Charue described these discussions extensively[66]. In his view, the second item, the sacramentality of episcopal consecration and its bond with the bishop's triple *munera* or *potestates,* was "le point critique par excellence". The necessity of the bond between consecration and triple power was rejected by Tromp, Schauf, and Gagnebet: they felt that the bishop's powers of governing and teaching depended on the *missio canonica*. There was also some discussion on the preference of using *munera* or *potestates*, whereby Philips proposed to use *munera*. Eventually the draft proposed was approved, including the distinction between consecration and communion as suggested by Heuschen, which was now represented in the text as: "... vi sacramentalis consecrationis et communione..." (the genitive was changed into an ablative).

In a letter commenting on the meeting, Heuschen pointed out that cardinal Ottaviani had tried several times to have the proposed text rejected or to have its significance undermined[67]. However, the text was approved, and hence he considered the previous days "deux journées historiques". The bishops had the Belgians do the work, he wrote. It was a difficult

---

"officium" episcopi pendet a "consecratione", immédiatement Mgr Carli et d'autres lui ont dit: ce n'est pas encore accepté, cela n'est pas dit explicitement etc. [...] Il est inouï de constater combien Mgr Carli et ceux de son groupe sont habiles et intelligents, et savent très bien où se trouve le nœud de tout, et le moyen de "rouler" magistralement, et pour combien d'années, tout l'épiscopat [...] Et que devient le dialogue avec les orthodoxes si cela n'est pas mis au point, et si on leur dit, après le concile, que la consécration épiscopale constitue un collège à moitié vide!!".

63. Charue, in his turn, wrote to Philips on Febr. 21, 1964, drawing his attention to the link between episcopal consecration and "munus regendi". Fund Philips, 1291-1292.

64. Fund Heuschen, 123-124; the same text in Fund Philips, 1294 (a text of two pages with eleven quotations).

65. "De quibusdam Observationibus in textum n. 16 (nunc n. 22) prout in subcommissione hucusque emendatum". Fund Philips, 1349.

66. DECLERCK – SOETENS (ed.), *Carnets conciliaires de l'évêque de Namur A.-M. Charue* (n. 23), pp. 162-164.

67. Letters to his mother and sister, March 7 and 8, 1964, letter to P. and M. Verjans, March 9, 1964. Fund Heuschen, 420-421, 529 (with French translation, pp. 57-58, 91-92).

assignment, but this made it possible to thoroughly correct the text and to make the church's image more human and more real.

More than twenty-five years later, in his "Concilieherinneringen", Heuschen returned to the facts once again and pointed out his contribution and specifically the support by Msgr. Pietro Parente, the Doctrinal Commission's relator on collegiality.

> The text read as follows: "membrum corporis episcopalis aliquis constituitur vi sacramentalis consecrationis et hierarchicae communionis cum collegio Capite atque membris". One becomes a bishop by episcopal consecration, but one can only exercise one's office after the Pope's intervention, who assigns the territory. The jurists of the Curia had a different opinion: it is actually the Pope who appoints the bishop as such. The way in which the text was formulated could lead us to think that the appointment by the Pope is as essential as the consecration to being a bishop. I therefore proposed to read the second membrum: "et hierarchica communione cum...". Msgr. Parente immediately agreed. A real Curia man would not have accepted this[68].

In this reference to the modification of the text, Heuschen, after twenty-five years, made a slight mistake: the adjective "hierarchica" had only been added later, in November 1964, during the last editing stage of De ecclesia.

4. The *Nota explicativa praevia* (November 1964)

The specification "hierarchica" was not just added to the final text of *Lumen gentium*, but was also included in the *Nota explicativa praevia*. It was added more specifically in number 2, which expressly discusses our issue and provides several explanations regarding the notions used (*consecratio, munera, hierarchica communio*). Thus, it states that communion is called hierarchical "not as consisting in some vague *disposition* but as an *organic reality* which requires a juridical form and at the same

---

68. Our translation of the Dutch text: "De tekst luidde: 'membrum corporis episcopalis aliquis constituitur vi sacramentalis consecrationis et hierarchicae communionis cum collegio Capite atque membris'. Men wordt bisschop door zijn bisschopswijding, maar men kan zijn ambt slechts uitoefenen na een tussenkomst van de Paus, die het territorium aanwijst. De juristen van de curie zagen het anders: het is de Paus die de eigenlijke bisschopsbenoeming doet. In de formulering van de tekst kon men de indruk krijgen dat de benoeming door de Paus even essentieel is voor het bisschop-zijn als de wijding. Ik stelde daarom voor het tweede membrum te lezen: 'et hierarchica communione cum...'. Mgr. Parente stemde daar dadelijk mee in. Een echte curie-man zou dat niet aanvaard hebben". Fund Heuschen, 384, p. 4.

time is animated by charity"[69]. The terminology returns in the *Nota bene* added to this, and it reads:

> Without hierarchical communion the sacramental-ontological function, which is to be distinguished from the canonico-juridical aspect, *cannot* be exercised. The commission decided that they should not get into the questions about *liceity* and *validity*; these are left for the discussion of theologians, especially with regard to the power that is in fact exercised among our Eastern separated brothers and sisters and there is a variety of opinions on how this is to be explained[70].

As is well known, the *Nota praevia* caused much agitation, especially among the *periti*, who were completely excluded from its editing and review. Yves Congar was very disturbed, precisely about the *Nota bene*, because he feared that, by postponing a standpoint, it might obstruct the approach to the Eastern churches[71]. However, on November 16, Congar was reassured by Heuschen, who explained that precisely the contrary applied: the *Nota bene* allowed to intentionally prevent a standpoint that would formally exclude the orthodox bishops from any authentic magisterium and governing power.

Heuschen himself has written several letters about this issue. He pointed out that at various occasions he and Philips had to save the openness towards the Orthodox by rejecting impossible proposals. This was also the motive for adding the *Nota bene* to the *Nota praevia*: it was intended to offset a text proposal from the pope, made via A. Cicognani, which would have made dialogue with the Orthodox

---

69. "Non intelligitur autem de vago quodam *affectu*, sed de *realitate organica*, quae iuridicam formam exigit et simul caritate animatur". *Nota explicativa praevia*, n. 2. Cf. TANNER (ed.), *Decrees of the Ecumenical Councils* (n. 54), vol. 2, p. 899. According to Philips, *hierarchica* only means that communion "est structurée d'après les articulations du corps de l'Église". Cf. GROOTAERS, *Primauté et collégialité* (n. 33), p. 207. See also the draft of this part of the *Nota praevia*, typed by Heuschen, in Fund Heuschen, 127 (incorrectly this piece is archived under the 2nd intersession instead of the 3rd session).

70. "Sine communione hierarchica munus sacramentale-ontologicum, quod distinguendum est ab aspectu canonico-iuridico, exerceri *non potest*. Commissio autem censuit non intrandum esse in quaestiones de *liceitate* et *validitate*, quae relinquuntur disceptationi theologorum, in specie quod attinet ad potestatem quae de facto apud orientales seiunctos exercetur, et de cuius explicatione variae exstant sententiae". Cf. TANNER (ed.), *Decrees of the Ecumenical Councils* (n. 54), vol. II, p. 900.

71. On Nov. 11, 1964 Congar wrote: "Maintenant on [cela vient de qui? du Pape? de Colombo? C'est lui qui m'en parle le premier...] ajoute, en tête du chap. III, un NB disant que le concile ne dirime pas la situation de fait des Orthodoxes: on laisse aux théologiens le soin de chercher des explications... Cette note m'a fait beaucoup de mal. Ainsi le concile laisse cela aux théologiens: cela ne l'intéresse pas, LUI!! Mgr Colombo me dit: C'est tout ce qu'on pouvait faire, MAINTENANT [Est-ce sûr?]. – Ce sera pour un prochain concile...!!!". CONGAR, *Mon journal du Concile* (n. 7), vol. II, p. 267.

impossible[72]. Therefore, he concluded, we must try to convince all bishops to vote simply *placet*.

Heuschen recalled that it was precisely in this respect that he got angry at Congar, whom he had to explain why a *placet* for the *Nota bene* did not hamper but rather kept open the approach towards the Eastern churches. Indeed, Congar was not the only one Heuschen had to convince. He also wrote that he had to reassure Cardinal Alfrink, who had been disturbed by Father Schillebeeckx, and that, by mediation of a few German bishops, he had prevented Cardinal Frings, "who had been incited by a German Jesuit, Father Ratzinger"[73], from taking harmful initiatives. Heuschen concluded: "These *periti* can really act like children"[74].

---

72. See the letter to his mother and sister, Nov. 16, 1964; Fund Heuschen, 457 (with French translation, pp. 68-69). See also the remark by G. Philips in his diary on Nov. 14, 1964: "Donderdag werden de laatste vragen van bovenaf in de commissie, mits een lichte wijziging aanvaard. Evenzo geschiedde met de uitbreiding van de *Nota explicativa*. Alleen op één punt heb ik negatief geadviseerd, nl. op de uitleg over de *validitas* en de *liceitas* van de rechts- en leermacht van de afgescheiden bisschoppen. Als we daarop moeten ingaan, en verklaren dat die rechtsmacht ongeldig is, wordt de oekumenische dialoog volstrekt onmogelijk. Op dit punt heeft trouwens niemand aangedrongen", K. SCHELKENS (ed.), *Cahiers conciliaires de Mgr Gérard Philips* (n. 31), p. 57. French transl.: "Jeudi, les dernières questions d'en haut ont été acceptées en commission, sous réserve d'une légère modification. L'amplification de la *Nota explicativa* s'est faite de la même façon. J'ai seulement émis un avis négatif sur un seul point, à savoir l'explication sur la *validitas* et la *liceitas* du pouvoir juridique et dogmatique des évêques séparés. Si nous devrions y consentir et déclarer que ce pouvoir juridique n'est pas valide, le dialogue œcuménique deviendrait absolument impossible. Personne n'a d'ailleurs insisté sur ce point" (*ibid.*, p. 135).

73. "Langs enkele Duitse bisschoppen om heb ik mijn best gedaan om te voorkomen dat Kard. Frings, opgemaakt door een Duitse jezuïet, P. Ratzinger, iets zou ondernemen dat de oppositie zou in het harnas jagen". French transl.: "Par l'intermédiaire de quelques évêques allemands j'ai fait de mon mieux pour empêcher que le card. Frings, excité par un jésuite allemand, le P. Ratzinger, prenne une initiative qui excite l'opposition", letter of Nov. 16, 1964 (see n. 67). Here, of course, Heuschen is mistaken: Ratzinger was not a Jesuit but a diocesan priest. Msgr. Philips equally remarked in his *Notes pour servir à l'histoire de la Nota Praevia Explicativa (Lumen Gentium, III)*: "Le Conseiller du card. Frings, Ratzinger, m'a-t-on dit, a insisté jusqu'à la fin pour faire rejeter le Décret" (GROOTAERS, *Primauté et Collégialité* [n. 33], p. 82). On Nov. 16, 1964, Henri de Lubac wrote in his *Carnets du Concile*: "Le Dr Ratzinger est opposé à la *Nota*, tandis que le chanoine Moeller la défend avec vigueur, comme acceptable en elle-même, et par crainte d'incidents qui compromettent le vote du chapitre 3e. Cette attitude est celle de Mgr Philips (que je ne vois pas directement), du chanoine Thils, du recteur du collège belge, etc. Le milieu belge, et, en général, celui de la Commission théologique, les évêques et experts qui ont travaillé à la correction du texte et obtenu des avantages, défendent leur œuvre, en pensant que le texte leur donne une satisfaction suffisante". Henri DE LUBAC, *Carnets du Concile*, ed. Loïc FIGOUREUX, Paris, Cerf, 2007, vol. II, Nov. 16, 1964, p. 312.

74. "Wat kunnen die periti toch grote kinderen zijn". French transl.: "Comme ces periti peuvent être de grands enfants", letter of Nov. 16, 1964.

V. CONCLUSIONS

1. The Working-method of the Belgians

The struggle for the text modification in *De ecclesia* is typical of the working-method of the Belgians, the so-called "squadra belga", which was characterized in very spirited and appreciative words by Yves Congar in his *Journal du Concile*[75].

First we notice an intense cooperation between Charue, Heuschen, Philips, Thils and also Onclin[76]. They saw to it that the text modification was prepared thoroughly. Thils wrote a complete study and alarmed Charue, Heuschen and Philips. They stayed in touch, even in Belgium[77]. Heuschen carefully prepared his modifications in writing and found the way to have his text discussed, even though the time period for suggesting amendments had already expired[78]. He also prepared the sub-commission's meeting with a few befriended experts on January 20, 1964[79].

This example also shows that the Belgians took a realistic stand and were prepared to compromise. They knew that the text must be approved by at least two-thirds of the Council fathers and that the pope wished a *consensus unanimis*. This was called "la loi de l'assemblée" during the Council: writing beautiful texts was of no use if they were not approved. A well-known adage at the Belgian College, therefore, was: "Le mieux est l'ennemi du bien". This willingness to compromise was a strategy that partially explains the Belgians' success at the Council. But as our example already slightly indicates, this working-method was criticized during and after the Council by like-minded theologians, for example by Edward Schillebeeckx and later on in sharp wording by Hans Küng[80].

---

75. CONGAR, *Mon journal du Concile* (n. 7), vol. II, pp. 53-57.

76. Cf. *ibid.*, vol. II, p. 56: "Nos évêques n'ont pas de technique; ils ne travaillent pas avec les experts. Chez les Belges, les évêques et les experts travaillent *ex aequo,* au plan d'anciens élèves de Louvain".

77. Congar writes: "Ils [the Belgians] se connaissent, souvent sont camarades de cours et se tutoient. Ils sont cohérents et ont les mêmes références; [...] ce qui vient de Louvain est sacré [...] Ils s'alertent entre eux [...] Ils s'organisent, se voient, se revoient" (*ibid.*, vol. II, p. 54).

78. Cf. CONGAR, *Mon journal du Concile* (n. 7): "Les Belges ont une attitude militante, offensive. Ils ne se contentent pas, comme les Français, de proposer timidement des corrections de détail, en prenant le texte tel qu'il est: ILS MODIFIENT LE TEXTE" (vol. II, p. 56).

79. Cf. *ibid.*: "Les Belges ont, pour le travail qu'ils font, des qualités remarquables. Ils sont CONCRETS, ils ont le sens de l'action efficace" (vol. II, p. 56).

80. Philips, experienced as a senator, was very skilled in editing such compromise texts, which gained him Congar's praise; cf. CONGAR, *Mon journal du Concile* (n. 7), vol. II, p. 55. Theologians such as Edward Schillebeeckx and Hans Küng made this working-method responsible for the later recuperation of the Council by 'conservative' forces in the

2. Hermeneutics of Council Texts

A second conclusion to be drawn from our example brings us to our final considerations, whereby we return to the discussion presented at the beginning of this article. Our example illustrated that council texts are often the result of thorough research, vivid discussions, and sometimes complex compromising. These circumstances also often show a high degree of technical precision. The example outlined in this article was about a minor modification of a case: the genitive *communionis* eventually became an ablative *communione*. But this change was the result of a long discussion and introduced an intended difference into its content. Therefore, constructing a detailed editing history of the final text is necessary to understand the correct sense and impact of such words[81]. For this, diaries of participants in this process are very useful, together with other relevant documents, such as working texts, *relationes*, correspondences on the subject matter, and the like[82].

Very often these texts reflect discussions about seemingly little things, details, minuscule word changes, or as Marchetto would put it: "piccola storia". However, they are necessary in order to precisely and correctly understand the composite consensus texts these council documents really are. Specifically at the Second Vatican Council, the final texts were the result of different, sometimes even conflicting opinions, which gives them an inner ambiguity (intended or otherwise). This calls for appropriate, history-oriented hermeneutics; namely, council hermeneutics.

A deliberately 'dogmatic' reading, on the contrary, which seems to be preferred by authors such as Marchetto, considers such hermeneutics redundant or even confusing, and abides by the end text. In doing so,

church. See, e.g., the sharp critique on G. Philips and the Belgians by Hans KÜNG, *Erkämpfte Freiheit: Erinnerungen*, Munich – Zürich, Piper, 2002, pp. 459-471.

81. Sometimes the lack of such background information leads to a failure to notice the nuance. Thus, the distinction is completely absent in the German translation of the sentence in question, in the well-known *Lexikon für Theologie und Kirche* commentary (see n. 51), or in the new *Herders Theologischer Kommentar zum Zweiten Vatikanischen Konzil* (see n. 51): "Als Glied der Körperschaft der Bischöfe wird man kraft der sakramentalen Weihe und der hierarchischen Gemeinschaft mit Haupt und Gliedern des Kollegiums eingesetzt" (p. 111).

82. Heuschen writes in his 'Concilieherinneringen': "Wil men de juiste betekenis van de teksten achterhalen, dan moet men zich niet beperken tot een officiële tekstuitgave, maar ook in de werkdocumenten van de commissies en in de 'relationes' van de tekst de juiste bedoelingen van de eindtekst achterhalen" (Engl. transl.: "If one wishes to retrieve the precise meaning of the text, one should not confine oneself to the official edition of the text, but rather one should discover the precise intentions of the final text in the working documents of the commissions and the "relationes" on the text"). Fund Heuschen, 384, p. 12.

it runs the risk of producing a reading which, if it is not consciously selective and unilateral, might become incorrect and cause misunderstandings. The only alternative is a minute analysis of the texts, based on a detailed reconstruction of their editing history, within the specific context of the Council's decision-making process, and also by using all kinds of relevant sources. Such reading will probably not provide many spectacular new insights. It is never complete and will also have to account for the reception history of the Council and its texts. But it can contribute to a better understanding of the complex significance of Vatican II as a pivotal moment in the confrontation of the Catholic Church with modernity.

Faculty of Theology   Leo KENIS
K.U.Leuven
St.-Michielsstraat 6
B-3000 Leuven
Belgium

SYMPOSIUM SECOND VATICAN COUNCIL

CONTRIBUTION OF THE BELGIANS

This reflection was inspired by the Testament of John Paul II, in which he entrusted the Council's patrimony to "all those who are now and in the future called to realise it" (*Osservatore Romano*, April 4, 2005). I dedicate this reflection, encouraged by the Church in Belgium, to the professors and all others participating in this Symposium. Forty years after Vatican II we remember the contribution of the bishops in the preparatory work and the four sessions of this ecumenical council.

My reflection is an invitation to reread the Council's providential trajectory: the announcement and the final goals, the course followed and the dénouement. All of this, I suggest, is to be read in the framework of official texts and canonically approved documents. My paper is indebted to all the beneficiaries of this historical event, drawn from the preaching of Jesus and his emissaries, and keeps in mind Saint Paul's caution: "I thank God that I speak in tongues more than you all; nevertheless in the gathering of the community I would rather speak five words in understandable language in order to teach others, than ten thousands words in a tongue" (1 Cor 14,18-19).

A witness of this ecclesial season, a labourer in the vineyard of the Lord, I open the shrine of my heart to recall the Church Fathers of yesterday, in accord with Benedict XVI, Vicar of Christ, universal shepherd.

Together with those who lived during this period and who are now stimulated by what history necessitates, we want to put the emphasis on the paths opened by the sixteen signed documents, on the confession of Peter, with an awareness that "the Council is the greatest religious and cultural event of the twentieth century", as John Paul II put it.

It was my good fortune to read to John XXIII a large part of the votes cast by the bishops and the Church organs and institutes, and immediately to recognize that these were valuable theological and practical contributions for drafting the projects and debates. I was impressed by the abundance of material coming from Belgium, especially the writings of Cardinal Léon-Joseph Suenens and Bishop Emile Joseph De Smedt, who from the beginning underlined the serious commitment of the Church, *ad intra* and *ad extra*, and for the '*Ite docete omnes gentes*' of the Divine Master. It is not surprising that serious and urgent questions immediately came to the fore, regarding the conservation and transmission of the *depositum fidei*, the unity of Christians, the salvation of all souls, and everything related to these things. All this was the object of study and discussion that would lead to the pastoral constitution *Gaudium et spes* and to the declarations *Nostra aetate* and *Dignitatis humanae*.

It is not surprising that the Pope was inclined to listen to Cardinal Suenens and trust in him: as a young bishop's secretary he got to know Archbishop Mercier, a close friend of Bishop Giacomo Maria Radini Tedeschi. His classmates had studied in Leuven; the monthly publication of the Curia of Bergamo had taken over from Mechelen the name '*La vie diocésaine*'. During the meeting of 8 June 1961, held in the Vatican, he spoke about decolonisation, about the work of missionaries, about the future of the Congo, about weariness and uncertainty at the heart of the episcopacy. The Pope was pleased to have named Suenens as a Cardinal and successor of Cardinal Joseph Ernest van Roey. He often recalled the contacts with Abbot Dom Lambert Beauduin, apostle of unity, incomparable ascetic in patience and suffering; he talked about his 1925 trip from Rome to Sofia with Dom Constantin Bosschaerts, founder of 'Vita et Pax' in Schotenhof (Antwerp).

All these things awakened in his heart much more than admiration and sympathy. The speech of 8 June 1961, read in the presence of kings and a prominent delegation, is filled with hope, and you get the impression that the Pope could predict the calling and destination of this noble nation.

With confidence he looked toward its future, indeed, because he knew its history. He desired its success in the different initiatives aimed at the well being of all humanity and at the highest good of peace.

Even considering merely the start of the Council, with its slow and difficult beginning, Suenens's contribution was accepted as a favorable 'entry' (even though it was unforeseen), and Pope John appreciated greatly his work because it was indispensable for getting to know persons, situations, and cultures. It was crucial for the establishment of a patient framework, which enabled the progress – albeit difficult – of the Council sessions and which concluded in the spirit of the double term, coined by Pope John and personified by Pope VI: '*Fedeltà e rinnovamento*' (Fidelity and Renewal).

At the end of his life John XXIII had the consolation of witnessing the adoption in the Palace of the United Nations of the encyclical *Pacem in terries*. Cardinal Suenens, as the pope's representative, gave an address worthy of inclusion among the texts of the Greek and Latin patristics.

At that convention Suenens appeared as an extraordinarily dignified envoy, appointed by the Pope, with the collective approval of the Curia.

On 28 October 1963 it was Suenens's turn to celebrate the name and accomplishments of John XXIII on St. Peters Square, in the presence of Paul VI and the Council Fathers, with an address which traces the path of the Blessed Pope: *"Never did he leave (spiritual) childhood; a childhood gradually enlarged by him to the size of his vocation and mission"* (G. Bernanos).

"His life was a grace for the world....

John XXIII was the pope of dialogue, and this has special reference to the men of our times.

It is not easy to make the world of today hear the voice of the Church. It is drowned by too much noise; there is too much static and interference in the air for the message to get through.

In spite of these obstacles, John XXIII managed to make himself heard: he broke through the sound-barrier.

The words of John awakened a response.

Men recognised his voice, a voice speaking to them of God, but also of human brotherhood, of the re-establishment of social justice, of a peace to be established throughout the world.

They heard a challenge addressed to their better selves, and they raised their eyes towards this man whose goodness made them think of God. For men, whether they know or not, are always in search of God, and it is the reflection of God that they sought in the countenance of this old man who loved them with the very love of Christ.

And this is why they wept for him as children for their father, pressing around him to receive his blessing" (L.-J. Suenens, *Ricordi e speranze*, Milano, Paoline, 1993).

At the end of this act of solidarity with my brothers from Belgium, I take the freedom to refer again to the above quoted address which Pope John delivered to the Royal couple. I was moved by the Pope's tribute to the history and traditions of Spain and Belgium:

> ...Quel précieux patrimoine religieux et moral vient ainsi, de vos deux nations, s'unir en vos personnes! Vous avez, Nous le savons, la volonté d'y faire honneur en toute circonstance, dans votre vie privée comme dans votre vie publique, et cette noble résolution constitue, à Nos yeux, le plus beau joyau de votre couronne. A un profond amour pour la Belgique – dont vous partagez tous deux désormais si intimement les joies comme les épreuves – à un sens élevé de vos devoirs royaux et des responsabilités qu'ils comportent, vous savez joindre un attachement inviolable à Dieu et à sa loi et l'humble fierté d'appartenir à la Sainte Eglise: voilà en vérité la plus sûre garantie

d'un règne que Nous souhaitons de tout Notre cœur voir se poursuivre heureux et prospère.

En exprimant ce vœu, Nous aimons à évoquer la belle formule du rite nuptial en usage dans les diocèses de Belgique, et suivant laquelle vous avez vous-mêmes échangé vos serments sous les voûtes nobles et austères de la collégiale de Sainte Gudule: "Je te donne, à toi que je tiens ici par la main, ma foi de mariage" ... La main dans la main: c'est bien l'image de l'engagement sacré des époux, de la communion sans réticence de deux cœurs et de deux âmes. Mais quel symbole suggestif, aussi, de ce que pourrait être la vie des diverses communautés à l'intérieur de chaque nation, et des différentes nations au sein de la grande famille humaine! Ainsi, tandis que Nous élevons vers Dieu Nos prières et Nos vœux à vos intentions, Nous voulons les étendre aussi à toute la Belgique, avec la confiance qu'elle sera toujours, grâce à l'entente unanime de tous ses fils et à la haute qualité de ses gouvernants – dont Nous sommes heureux de saluer ici d'illustres représentants – un facteur d'union, de fraternité et de fructueuse collaboration dans la communauté internationale" (Giovanni XXIII, *Discorsi, messagi, colloqui*, III, pp. 318-321).

I leave the honor to the listeners to agree with these papal accents, a sign for the future of the Church and of Belgium, and, for myself, I add to this the seal of the antique Roman wish: "*Quod bonum, faustum, felix, fortunatumque sit, Deo adiuvante, Virgine Matre intercedente*".

I-24039 Sotto il Monte   Loris Francesco CAPOVILLA
Giovanni XXIII
Bergamo

PART II

CARDINAL SUENENS

THE ROLE OF CARDINAL LÉON-JOSEPH SUENENS AT VATICAN II

I. INTRODUCTION

1. The Influence of Suenens

a. Cardinal Suenens undoubtedly played an important role at Vatican II. His influence was evident from the functions he held during this Council. He was one of the few bishops involved at every turn in important Council organisms from the time of preparation[1] up to and including the post-conciliar period:

- As auxiliary bishop of Malines, he was a member of the Preparatory Commission *De episcopis et de dioeceseon regimine*[2].
- As cardinal and archbishop of Malines-Brussels, he became a member of the *Commissio centralis praeparatoria* on March 3, 1962.
- During the first session he was a member of the *Secretariatus de Concilii negotiis extra ordinem*[3].
- As of December 12, 1962 he served on the Coordinating Commission.
- On September 9, 1963 he was appointed as one of the four moderators of the Council[4].
- On January 4, 1966 he was appointed as member of the *Commissio centralis coordinandis post Concilium laboribus et Concilii decretis interpretandis*[5].

b. In his capacity as Council father and speaker, Suenens was listened to attentively. He was also one who repeatedly intervened (18 times) during

---

1. Interesting is the fact that cardinal Van Roey, archbishop of Malines, was of the opinion that the auxiliary bishops (and as such also Suenens) did not need to be present at the Council. Cf. SUENENS, *Mémoires sur le concile Vatican II*, p. 8 [not published].

2. Suenens became a member of this Commission on July 29, 1960 (cf. G. CAPRILE, *Il Concilio Vaticano II*. Vol. I/1, Roma, Civiltà Cattolica, 1966, p. 220).

3. Suenens expresses his thanks for this appointment to John XXIII on September 29, 1962 (L. DECLERCK – E. LOUCHEZ, *Inventaire des Papiers conciliaires du cardinal L.-J. Suenens* (Cahiers de la Revue théologique de Louvain, 31), Louvain-la-Neuve, Publications de la Faculté de Théologie, 1998, henceforth referred to as Fund Suenens, 444).

4. Fund Suenens, 791: letter of appointment by cardinal Cicognani, September 9, 1963.

5. Letter by Cicognani, January 4, 1966, cf. Fund Suenens, 2729.

the debates: he offered three interventions during the first session, four during the second session, eight during the third session, and three during the fourth session. In total this represents more than 65 pages in the *Acta Synodalia*.

On the level of content, he made a few really remarkable speeches: about *De ecclesia* on December 4, 1962 (actually on his plan for the Council), about the charismas in the Church on October 22, 1963, about the age limit for bishops on October 12, 1963, and about conjugal ethics on October 29, 1964. Also remarkable was his brilliant speech regarding John XXIII's solemn commemoration in St. Peter's on October 28, 1963.

c. Suenens' authority during the Council can be partly ascribed to his non-conciliar activities: he was neither a scientific theologian nor an exegete (as were other members of the 'squadra belga' like Charue or Heuschen). However, thanks to his many popular publications he had become a celebrated writer and speaker whose fame reached beyond the francophone and Italian-speaking milieus and into the Anglo-Saxon world[6]. His familiarity with the milieu of the royal household may also have contributed to his influence[7]. Obviously, these elements need to be taken into account when writing about Suenens' influence on Vatican II.

2. Source Material

We do have a considerable number of sources at our disposal even though, so far, no scientific study has been published dealing with Suenens' influence on Vatican II.

a. Suenens' autobiographical sources are readily available. The fact that he was by far the longest surviving moderator provided him with many opportunities to discuss and comment on the Council. He published *inter alia*:

Cinq ans après Vatican II, in *La Documentation catholique* 1577, January 3 (1971) 35-36.
K.H. FLECKENSTEIN, *Pour l'Église de demain: Conversation avec le cardinal Suenens*, Paris, Nouvelle Cité, 1979, pp. 68-73.
J. GROOTAERS, *Von Johannes XXIII. zu Johannes Paul II.: Ein Gespräch mit Leo Joseph Kardinal Suenens*, in *Herder Korrespondenz* 34 (1980) 176-182.

6. The fact that Suenens was fluent in French, Dutch, English, Italian, and German when combined with his connections to the Legion of Mary (in many countries) may have contributed to this.
7. Cf. his book L.-J. SUENENS, *Le Roi Baudouin, une vie qui nous parle*, Brussels, Fiat, 1995.

Vatican II, vingt ans après, in *L'Osservatore Romano* [éd. française, Novembre 16], 1982, 16-17.

Testimonianze, in *Giovanni Battista Montini, Arcivescovo di Milano e il Concilio Oecumenico Vaticano II: Preparazione e primo periodo, Colloquio internazionale di studio, Milano, 23-24-25 settembre 1983* (Pubblicazioni dell'Istituto Paolo VI, 3), Brescia, Istituto Paolo VI, 1985, 178-187.

L.-J. SUENENS, *Aux origines du concile Vatican II*, in *NRT* 107 (1985) 3-21.

L.-J. SUENENS, *A Plan for the Whole Council*, in A. STACPOOLE, *Vatican II by those who were there*, London, 1986, 88-105 (English translation of the article in the *NRT*).

L.-J. SUENENS, *Souvenirs et espérances*, Paris, Fayard, 1991, mainly pp. 55-131. There is also his intervention at the extraordinary synod of 1985.

And finally, the most important still-unpublished document is his *Mémoires sur le concile Vatican II*, 69 p., which was dictated beginning of 1966 (Fund Suenens, 2784).

b. An inventory of his Council archives was published by L. DECLERCK – E. LOUCHEZ, *Inventaire des Papiers conciliaires du cardinal L.-J. Suenens* (Cahiers de la Revue théologique de Louvain, 31), Louvain-la-Neuve, Publications de la Faculté de Théologie, 1998. The archives are accessible at the Archdiocese of Malines [Fund Suenens].

c. Suenens and the Council have been the subject of a number of publications:

E. HAMILTON, *Suenens: A Portrait*, London, Hodder & Stoughton, 1975.

K. WITTSTADT, *Léon-Joseph Kardinal Suenens und das II. Vatikanische Konzil*, in E. KLINGER – K. WITTSTADT (eds.), *Glaube im Prozess: Christsein nach dem II. Vatikanum*. FS K. Rahner, Freiburg, Herder, 1984, 159-181.

J. GROOTAERS, *Léon-Joseph Suenens*, in ID., *I protagonisti del Concilio*, Milano, San Paolo, 1994, 229-243.

L. DECLERCK, *Le rôle joué par les évêques et periti belges au concile Vatican II: Deux exemples*, in *ETL* 76 (2000) 445-464.

S. MADRIGAL TERRAZAS, *Recuerdos conciliares y esperanzas ecuménicas del Cardenal Suenens*, in *Miscelánea Comillas* 59 (2001) 485-510.

L. DECLERCK, *Das Konzilsarchiv von Kardinal Léon-Joseph Suenens, Erzbischof von Mechelen-Brüssel*, in P. PFISTER (ed.), *Julius Kardinal Döpfner und das Zweite Vatikanische Konzil* (Schriften des Archivs des Erzbistums München und Freising, 4), München, Schnell und Steiner, 2002, 30-40.

d. A number of archives and diaries of important Council participants have become accessible during the last decade.

The documents of important Belgian Council participants allow us to examine which positions Suenens held, his theological preferences, and his strategies. Most important are the archives of Prignon, the confidant of Suenens during the Council, and subsequently those of Charue, De Smedt, Heuschen, Philips, Thils, and Moeller[8].

Also, the archives and diaries of Siri, Congar, Döpfner, de Lubac, Poswick and even of Tromp and C. Colombo[9] shed light – sometimes

8. Cf. C. SOETENS, *Concile Vatican II et Église contemporaine (Archives de Louvain-la-Neuve).* I: *Inventaire des Fonds Ch. Moeller, G. Thils, Fr. Houtart* (Cahiers de la Revue théologique de Louvain, 21), Louvain-la-Neuve, Publications de la Faculté de Théologie, 1989 [henceforth Journal Moeller].

J. FAMERÉE, *Concile Vatican II et Église contemporaine (Archives de Louvain-la-Neuve).* II: *Inventaire des Fonds A. Prignon et H. Wagnon* (Cahiers de la Revue théologique de Louvain, 24), Louvain-la-Neuve, Publications de la Faculté de Théologie, 1991 [henceforth Fund Prignon].

A. GREILER – L. DE SAEGER (eds.), *Emiel-Jozef De Smedt, Papers Vatican II Inventory. With a preface by L. Declerck* (Instrumenta Theologica, 22), Leuven, Bibliotheek van de Faculteit der Godgeleerdheid, 1999 [henceforth Fund De Smedt].

L. DECLERCK, *Inventaire des papiers conciliaires de Monseigneur J.M. Heuschen, évêque auxiliaire de Liège, membre de la Commission doctrinale, et du Professeur V. Heylen* (Instrumenta Theologica, 28), Leuven, Maurits Sabbebibliotheek Faculteit Godgeleerdheid – Peeters, 2005 [henceforth Fund Heuschen and Fund Heylen].

L. DECLERCK – C. SOETENS (eds.), *Carnets conciliaires de l'évêque de Namur A.-M. Charue* (Cahiers de la Revue théologique de Louvain, 32), Louvain-la-Neuve, Publications de la Faculté de Théologie, 2000 [henceforth Journal Charue].

L. DECLERCK – A. HAQUIN (eds.), *Mgr Albert Prignon, Recteur du Pontificio Collegio Belga, Journal conciliaire de la 4e session* (Cahiers de la Revue théologique de Louvain, 35), Louvain-la-Neuve, Publications de la Faculté de Théologie, 2003 [henceforth Journal Prignon].

L. DECLERCK – W. VERSCHOOTEN, *Inventaire des papiers conciliaires de Mgr Gérard Philips, secrétaire adjoint de la Commission doctrinale.* Avec une Introduction par J. GROOTAERS (Instrumenta Theologica, 24), Leuven, Bibliotheek van de Faculteit Godgeleerdheid – Peeters, 2001 [henceforth Fund Philips].

9. Y. CONGAR, *Mon journal du Concile*, présenté et annoté par É. MAHIEU, 2 tomes, Paris, Cerf, 2002.

G. TREFFLER – P. PFISTER (eds.), *Erzbischöfliches Archiv München. Julius Kardinal Döpfner: Archivinventar der Dokumente zum Zweiten Vatikanischen Konzil* (Schriften des Archivs des Erzbistums München und Freising, 6), München, Schnell und Steiner, 2004 [henceforth Fund Döpfner].

G. TREFFLER (ed.), *Julius Kardinal Döpfner: Konzilstagebücher, Briefe und Notizen zum Zweiten Vatikanischen Konzil* (Schriften des Archivs des Erzbistums München und Freising, 9), München, Schnell und Steiner, 2006.

H. DE LUBAC, *Carnets du concile*, introduit et annoté par L. Figoureux, 2 vols., Paris, Cerf, 2007 [henceforth Journal de Lubac].

Diarium Tromp, Archivio Segreto Vaticano, Conc.Vat. II, 789-791, 13 notebooks. Partially published in A. VON TEUFFENBACH, *Konzilstagebuch Sebastian Tromp s.j. Mit Erläuterungen und Akten aus der Arbeit der theologischen Kommission. Vol. I/1-2: 1960-1962*, Rome, Editrice Gregoriana, 2006.

Fund Carlo Colombo, Facoltà Teologica dell'Italia settentrionale, Milano [henceforth Fund Colombo].

P. POSWICK, *Un journal du Concile: Vatican II vu par un diplomate belge. Notes personnelles de l'Ambassadeur de Belgique près le Saint-Siège (1957-1968), et Rapports au Ministère des Affaires Étrangères.* Édités par R.F. POSWICK et Y. JUSTE, Paris, de Guibert, 2005.

B. LAI, *Il papa non eletto: Giuseppe Siri, cardinale di Santa Romana Chiesa* (I Robinson), Rome, Laterza, 1993.

indirectly – on the conciliar activities of Suenens. Careful study of these records is imperative given that (1) Suenens sometimes lacks precision in his autobiographical documents and interviews and that (2) in several cases, he evidenced a fairly selective memory. It is evident that the publication of the *Acta Synodalia* (cf., e.g., Vols. V and VI: reports of the Coordinating Commission and many documents of the General Secretariat) also provides the researcher with essential working tools.

3. Intrinsic Outline

Prignon accurately describes Suenens as: "Il était plutôt un homme d'action qu'un penseur"[10]. Since it will not be possible to describe within the scope of this article all the details of his influence and activities with regard to Vatican II, we will limit ourselves to a number of important topics, in order to subject them to a more thorough historical investigation.

a. The influence of Suenens' plan on the general progress of the Council. Suenens made many attempts to ensure that the Council would proceed smoothly and in a systematic manner. As early as the preparatory period he was working on a plan. Both during and after the first session his key position as a member of the *Secretariatus de negotiis extra ordinem* and of the Coordinating Commission supplied him with the necessary means for submitting proposals in an attempt to try and accelerate the procedures. Even if it is true that Suenens' plan was in fact only a determining factor behind the final form of *Gaudium et spes*, it remains legitimate to conclude that the submission of this plan greatly influenced the rejection of the prepared schemas.

b. Almost from the beginning, the theme *De ecclesia* was a central part of the Council's agenda. By allowing Philips to work, as of October 15, 1962, on a new schema Suenens, as a member of the Coordinating Commission (which was responsible for the schema on the Church), arranged for Philips' schema to be chosen as the new basic text in March of 1963. In July of 1963, he succeeded in getting the chapter *De populo Dei* inserted before the chapter *De hierarchia*. As the driving force behind the

---

10. Bande magnétique III (February of 2000) (eight tapes made during January – February of 2000; Prignon interviewed by E. de Beukelaer, Liège and copied by L. Declerck, Brugge).

five *Propositiones*, approved on October 30, 1963, he made sure that the Council spoke in favour of the sacramental nature of the episcopate, the collegiality of the episcopal *collegium*, and the introduction of the permanent diaconate. At the same time, it is striking that he was hardly involved in the serious difficulties the text faced with regard to the *Nota explicativa praevia* (November of 1964).

The archives now also supply an answer with regard to his influence with respect to the chapter on *De beata*, given that they note that the cardinal sometimes acted as 'cavalier seul'.

c. By means of the speech he gave on December 4, 1962, Suenens contributed in a decisive way to the realisation of a separate schema on the Church in the World. He was also responsible for this document in the meetings of the Coordinating Commission. At the beginning of July 1963, he had the Coordinating Commission reject the preparatory texts. He then asked a group of theologians to write an introductory chapter. This text, known as 'Le texte de Malines' and drawn up under the guidance of Philips, was not retained by the proper commission during the second session. From that moment on, Suenens' influence on schema XIII declined, except for the chapter *De familia* and the issue of birth control. Because of this problem, he wanted a fourth session to be organised. At the same time he was working hard to realise that this schema would become a full fledged constitution, and not just a *Declaratio*, *Litterae Encyclicae* or one of many *Adnexa*. With regard to this topic, he devoted himself to the foundation, the operation, and the re-composition (it would come to include lay persons) of the *Commissio pontificia pro studio populationis, familiae et natalitatis*.

In an Appendix we add a brief summary of the other interventions made by Suenens at Vatican II.

II. Suenens' Plan for the Council
(March of 1962 – January of 1963)

In some of his post-conciliar publications[11] Suenens gives the impression that his plan for the Council was accepted by John XXIII almost *talis qualis*, and that the Council proceeded according to his plan. In reality,

---

11. Cf. L.-J. Suenens, *Souvenirs et espérances*, Paris, Fayard, 1991, pp. 65-80.

matters were more complicated and more nuanced. It is possible to distinguish several different phases.

1. First Phase

On February 7, 1962, Suenens – as a new archbishop – is received in audience by John XXIII[12]. On March 19, 1962 he becomes a cardinal and on this occasion was privately received[13]. The Lent pastoral letter of Suenens[14] is supposed to have been read by the Pope with interest[15]. Suenens expressed his concern about the huge quantity of prepared schemas (more than 70) and the Pope asked him to prepare a note with regard to this subject[16]. According to Suenens' letter to the Pope, he presented the note[17] a few days before May 16, 1962[18]. The notes of John XXIII allow us to be more precise: the presentation took place during the audience on May 10, 1962[19].

Content of his 'Note au sujet du Concile'[20] (five typed pages): From the beginning a distinction is made between the *Ecclesia ad extra* (l'Église face au monde d'aujourd'hui) and the *Ecclesia ad intra* (l'Église en elle-même,

---

12. On February 7, 1962. cf. G. ALBERIGO – A. MELLONI (eds.), *Beatificationis et canonizationis servi Dei Joannis Papae XXIII Summi Pontificis (1881-1963). Biografia documentata*, IVa Pars, Rome, Guerra, 1995, p. 3243.

13. On March 17, 1962, cf. ALBERIGO – MELLONI (eds.), *Beatificationis et canonizationis* (n. 12), p. 3251. During this audience John XXIII mentioned to Suenens his conversation with Adjoubei, son-in-law to Khruschhev, a meeting that took place on March 7, 1962 (Archives personnelles, box 12. Cf. also L.-J. SUENENS, *Mémoires sur le Concile Vatican II* (Fund Suenens, 2784, pp. 15-16).

14. L.-J. SUENENS, *Qu'attendez-vous du Concile?*, Malines, 1962, 24 p. Cf. G. CAPRILE, *Il Concilio Vaticano II*. Vol. I/2, Rome, Civiltà Cattolica, 1966, p. 384.

15. In his *Mémoires sur le Concile Vatican II* (p. 13) Suenens writes: "Il [John XXIII] m'a dit: J'ai lu votre lettre sur le Concile. C'est exactement ce que je voulais dire, vous avez un don d'expression, vous avez un talent de plume, c'est exactement ma pensée".

16. Cf. L.-J. SUENENS, *Aux origines du Concile Vatican II*, in NRT 107 (1985) 3-21, p. 3.

17. Cf. Fund Suenens, 378 and SUENENS, *Aux origines du Concile Vatican II* (n. 16), pp. 6-8.

18. On May 16, 1962 Suenens writes to John XXIII about his "note négative et préliminaire remise il y a peu de jours" (Fund Suenens, 380). But according to *Aux origines* this note appears to have been ready sooner and Suenens' plan for the Council already finished by April of 1962. It appears that this plan became only final after the meeting of the *commissio centralis praeparatoria* (May 3-12, 1962) and after a meeting with Montini on May 11, 1962.

19. Cf. ALBERIGO – MELLONI (eds.), *Beatificationis et canonizationis* (n. 12), p. 3277, May 10, 1962: "Più interessante e preziosa la conversazione sugli affari del Concilio, col nuovo arcivescovo di Malines-Bruxelles, card. Suenens. Vedo che ci intendiamo bene". Although Suenens often mentions his warm friendship with John XXIII, this is the only passage in the diaries of John XXIII indicating anything of this kind.

20. Fund Suenens, 378.

en vue d'ailleurs d'aider celle-ci à mieux répondre à sa mission dans le monde)[21]. He is furthermore of the opinion that 80% of the prepared materials should not be discussed at a Council, but can just as easily be entrusted to post-conciliar commissions. He also feels that many reforms could take place on the level of the bishops' conferences, whose importance should be allowed to increase. He finishes with a plea in favor of an innovative pastoral Council: "Quel bienfait immense ce serait pour l'Église s'il [le concile] pouvait définir dans ses grands traits, comment l'Église tout entière doit être mise en état de mission"[22]. During the audience of May 10, 1962, John XXIII is said to have requested that Suenens draw up a real plan for the Council with the help and advice of a few cardinals.

2. Second Phase

We know that Suenens had a long conversation with Montini at the Collegio Lombardo in Rome on May 11, 1962[23]. Suenens included the project in his letter of May 16, 1962 to John XXIII. There he suggested that the Pope should call together a study group (he proposes four to five members: "quatre serait l'idéal ... comme il y a les quatre évangélistes[24]") and assign to them the task of determining how the different schemas can be fitted into the plan and which schemas should be referred to post-conciliar commissions. In order to make sure that the Pope would be able to understand correctly the proper perspective of his plan, he also enclosed the Italian translation of *L'Église en état de mission*.

The *major features* of this 14-page plan were these[25]:

The Introduction indicated that the central theme should be *De Ecclesiae Christi mysterio* and that this is for several reasons ("continuité avec

21. According to Roger Matthys (Suenens' secretary from 1982 to 1996) this subdivision was designed during a meeting with Veronica O'Brien in the house she was living in at Oppem (Meise).
22. Allusion to the book by L.-J. SUENENS, *L'Église en état de mission*, Bruges, Desclée de Brouwer, 1955.
23. Cf. G. ADORNATO, *Cronologia dell'episcopato di G. B. Montini a Milano, 4 gennaio 1955 – 21 giugno 1963*, Brescia, Istituto Paolo VI, 2002, p. 866.
24. It is probably *not* a coincidence that the four moderators are later also compared to the four evangelists: the three synoptics (Döpfner, Lercaro, Suenens) and Saint John (Agagianian).
25. Cf. Fund Suenens, 381; also SUENENS, *Aux origines du Concile Vatican II* (n. 16), pp. 11-18, where Suenens says on p. 4 that this was his plan 'au stade final'. Suenens will nevertheless send another adaptation of this plan (into which he attempts to insert the existing schemas, cf. infra) to John XXIII on July 4, 1962.

le concile Vatican I, meilleur équilibre doctrinal, un pas vers nos frères séparés, *operari sequitur esse*, l'Église, 'c'est Jésus Christ communiqué et répandu'").

A. *Ecclesia ad intra*, is the first large section. Its four parts can be summed up by the sentence: "Euntes ergo docete omnes gentes, baptizantes eos in nomine Patris et Filii et Spiritus Sancti" (cf. Mt 28,19).

    A.1. Ecclesia evangelizans (vel salvificans) [euntes ergo]
        In this part four topics were to be discussed: (1) The bishops (*inter alia*, the issue of their collegiality); (2) The diocesan and the regular clergy (including the problem of the diaconate); (3)) The male and female religious; (4) The lay persons (with a special plea to enlarge the notion of the Catholic Action[26]).

    A.2. Ecclesia docens [docete omnes gentes]
        One must proclaim the gospel: (1) To every person: problems of religious education, of catechesis, of preaching; (2) With all means available: the modern means of communication.

    A.3. Ecclesia sanctificans [baptizantes eos]
        All the problems connected to the pastoral side of the sacraments.

    A.4. Ecclesia orans [in nomine Patris et Filii et Spiritus Sancti]
        About liturgy and liturgical pastoral work.

B. *Ecclesia ad extra* is the second large section (cf. Mt 28,20: "docentes eos servare quaecumque mandavi vobis") with two subdivisions:

   – Ce que le monde attend: the world is looking for an answer to its problems. What does the Church have to offer?[27].

   – Les réponses: problems concerning the family (the problem of birth control is already mentioned here), economics (the Church has to condemn social injustice and become the Church of the poor), the civil society (with the problem of religious freedom), the international order (with the problems of war and peace)[28].

It *ends* with a *Message au monde*.

---

26. This was a question near to Suenens' heart, since the Legion of Mary was only being tolerated in a number of countries. This was due to its failure to meet the structures of the mandated and specializations of Catholic Action (cf. the speech by Pius XII at the 2nd World conference of the Lay Apostolate in October of 1957, where the Pope, inspired by Suenens, created an opening for the Legion).

27. It is interesting to notice that the first part (11-45) of the Constitution *Gaudium et spes*, Pars I, "De ecclesia et vocatione hominis" corresponds to a large extent to this problem.

28. The second part of *Gaudium et spes* (46-90) will deal with these four subjects and will add a chapter on culture.

A message to Orthodox Christians, to Protestants, to all who believe in God, and, finally, to non-believers. One could then conclude this section by invoking the image of Christ as Pantocrator[29].

3. Third Phase

Suenens' plan is sent to a number of cardinals on May 19, 1962 by Cicognani[30]. On May 22, 1962 Suenens already receives an answer from Cicognani with regard to his letter of May 16, 1962 to the Pope[31]. The Pope wishes Suenens to continue with his 'accennate idee', so that it can be reflected upon during his next visit to Rome. Cicognani also informs Suenens that he will be appointed to one of the commissions (with a limited number of members) to prepare the material that will be directly discussed by the Council fathers[32].

Suenens was received in audience by John XXIII during his visit to Rome for the 12-20 June meeting of the *Commissio centralis praeparatoria*. In this audience on June 15[33] the Pope requested Suenens that he would develop this plan further in cooperation with a number of cardinals.

In June of 1962[34], a select group of cardinals[35] met at the Belgian College in Rome at the invitation of Suenens. The exact date is not known,

29. This concluding message can be attributed to Montini. Suenens notes in his *Mémoires sur le Concile Vatican II*, p. 18: "Lui [Montini] avait une grande idée d'un message à faire, à l'issue du concile, et la partie du plan, qui concerne ce messsage, la dernière page, est en somme le fruit d'une conversation de deux heures avec lui". Montini actually resumes this idea in the letter he sends on October 18, 1962 to Cicognani in which he, in turn, unfolds a plan for the Council in his point 6 (Cf. SUENENS, *Aux origines du Concile Vatican II* [n. 16], p. 20). Paul VI will extend this message to the world at the closing ceremony of the Council on December 8, 1965. Cf. C. SOETENS, *Les messages finaux du Concile*, in J. DORÉ – A. MELLONI (eds.), *Volti di Fine Concilio. Studi di storia e teologia sulla conclusione del Vaticano II* (Testi e ricerche di scienze religiose. Nuova Serie, 27), Bologna, Mulino, 2000, 99-112.
30. To whom is not clear. Probably Siri, Liénart, Montini. Döpfner notes that he received a copy of this letter to Cicognani and of Suenens' plan on October 16, 1962 during a meeting of the *Secretariatus de negotiis concilii extra ordinem* (Fund Döpfner, 3233).
31. Fund Suenens, 385.
32. Suenens becomes indeed a member of the *Pontificia subcommissio de materiis mixtis praeparatoria Concilii Vaticani II* (Suenens answers on June 2, 1962, Fund Suenens, 179). In the same letter Cicognani also says thanks for the receipt of Suenens' book *Amore e padronanza di se* (the Italian translation of L.-J. SUENENS, *Un problème crucial: Amour et maîtrise de soi*, Bruges, Desclée de Brouwer, 1960).
33. Cf. *L'Osservatore Romano*, June 16, 1962.
34. Suenens writes in *Aux origines du Concile Vatican II* (n. 16), p. 4, that this meeting took place at the beginning of July, but he is obviously mistaken. Montini was not in Rome; throughout July he was in Milan (cf. ADORNATO, *Cronologia dell'episcopato di G.B. Montini* [n. 23], p. 880). Döpfner, in his notes on this meeting, dates it to June of 1962 (Fund Döpfner, 2806).
35. According to SUENENS, *Mémoires sur le Concile Vatican II*, p. 17: Liénart, Siri, Döpfner, Montini.

but the Döpfner archives contain some relevant notes[36]. Döpfner was fairly critical of this plan and, *inter alia*, writes (in far from flawless Italian):

> Non si può le materie del concilio ordinare come un articolo scientifico oppure un libro. Nella linea del locus classicus Matth 28,18-20 si svolge una disposizione non adaequata [sic], un pò torta (ad intra/ad extra; E[ccle-sia] evangelizans/docens; E[cclesia] sanctificans/orans). Ma certamente così abbiamo un utile punto da partire.

And Döpfner concludes (in German): "Es wurde beschlossen, die Constitutio De Ecclesia vorzuschlagen. Card. Suenens wollte der Sache an das Staatssekretariat weiter leiten".

After this meeting at the Belgian College, Suenens attempts to fit the 75 prepared schemas into his plan of May 16, 1962. He informs the Pope about the result of his efforts by means of a letter dated July 4, 1962[37].

He first reports on the meeting at the Belgian College: he mentions the initial resistance of Döpfner ("qui se rallia rapidement à l'avis unanime et insistant des cardinaux Montini, Siri, Liénart qui soutinrent très chaudement le plan proposé et qui soulignèrent fortement la nécessité d'un plan architectural à la fois large et cohérent"[38]). He declares that all agreed to start the Council with a doctrinal part (mainly on the mystery of the Church) and that the next session(s) would be devoted to pastoral work. The cardinals present expressed the wish that Suenens would develop a more detailed plan and would fit the prepared schemas into the new general plan. Suenens sends the Pope some thoughts with regard to this overview by means of two enclosed pages[39].

---

36. Fund Döpfner, 2806 (note of two pages). See TREFFLER (ed.), *Julius Kardinal Döpfner. Briefe und Notizen* (n. 9), p. 242. Even Frings had doubts about the plan of Suenens: on August 28, 1962, Döpfner notes: "Frings: Erwähnung der Bestrebungen von Card. Suenens. Nur zu lang für das Konzil" (Cf. TREFFLER [ed.], *Julius Kardinal Döpfner. Briefe und Notizen*, p. 251).

37. Cf. Fund Suenens, 388.

38. Liénart was enthousiastic about this plan (cf. his letter of June 14, 1962 to Suenens; cf. Fund Suenens, 386), but Siri not so much. During a conversation with B. Lai on November 2, 1985, Siri mentions: "Suenens ha sostenuto che solo il cardinale Döpfner si mostrò contrario alla sua proposta, ma che poi accettò l'opinione favorevole di Liénart, Montini e Siri. È una falsità, non accettai proprio nulla. Suenens è uno a cui è sempre piaciuto fare il protagonista"; cf. LAI, *Il papa non eletto* (n. 9), p. 183, note 13.

39. Cf. SUENENS, *Mémoires sur le Concile Vatican II*, p. 17: "J'ai fait alors, pour le Saint-Père, après la note négative [in March] et la note positive [in May] un troisième travail, qui consistait à reprendre ces 70 schémas et à essayer, vaille que vaille, à les faire entrer dans le plan que je le lui proposais. Cette troisième note envoyée à Jean XXIII, constitue un essai pour utiliser au maximum, dans le cadre du plan, les travaux déjà faits. Ce sont les feuilles vertes, qui étaient une tentative un peu désespérée, parce qu'il est difficile de faire entrer, après coup, dans un plan des choses qui n'en aient aucun [sic]. Mais

What is the *content* of this new document, sent by Suenens to the Pope beginning of July?

a. First there is an 'Introduction au plan', a new manual for the plan:

1. The Commission for the new Codex has to be charged with a fair amount of schemas.

2. A general remark about the [existing] schemas:
   Many foreign members of the *Commissio centralis praeparatoria* are of the opinion that the prepared schemas, specially those drawn up by the Theological Commission, are too juridical, and lack inspiration. They show too many 'signs' of having originated in the Holy Office, are too much like theses or warnings, are too negative in tone, and have no 'envergure'. If these schemas are thoroughly amended, taking into account the criticisms expressed by the Central Preparatory Commission, they might become acceptable. But there is reason to fear that nothing much will change. After all, the original authors are still in charge. It is far more desirable that totally new schemas be devised. The *Ordo Concilii* should provide this possibility[40].

3. A remark on the insertion of the schemas.
   3.1. One has taken into account the schemas at hand.
   3.2. Some schemas can be inserted in more than one sector. Choice will clearly have to be made.
   3.3. Since the Theological Commission did not limit itself to texts on the Church, one could consider leaving these together, while grouping the matters as follows:
      – Quaestiones doctrinales 'De Ecclesiae Christi mysterio'.
      – Quaestiones doctrinales particulares.
   3.4. The whole plan is gone over again, and the matching schemas are referred to for each section.
   3.5. The section 'Quaestiones speciales' assembles all the schemas not integrated into other sections of the plan.

b. Suenens then literally resumes his plan of May (15 white pages: actually 14 + one 10bis). To this he adds nine green pages each indicating for

---

c'était une manière de ne pas heurter tous ceux qui avaient déjà fait ces différents schémas".

40. The possibility of submitting totally new schemas keeps causing problems during the first session and the first intersession. Cf. L. DECLERCK, *Le rôle joué par les évêques et periti belges au concile Vatican II: Deux exemples*, in *ETL* 76 (2000) 445-464, p. 449.

a particular chapter of the plan the old corresponding schema. This way he was able to find a home for 42 schemas.

In Appendix I 'Quaestiones speciales' he places eight schemas. And in Appendix II he sends 24 schemas to the Commission for the new Codex.

If the logic of Suenens' plan of May of 1962 may be questioned, it becomes clear that this exercise of 'concordance' could not possibly succeed. It was really the 'quadrature du cercle'; in his *Mémoires* (p. 17), Suenens quite rightly spoke of "une tentative désespérée". The only concordance that did make sense was the chapter *De ecclesia ad extra*, in which Suenens groups:

— De castitate, virginitate, matrimonio, familia.
— De cura animarum et communismo.
— De Relationibus inter Ecclesiam et Statum necnon de tolerantia religiosa (schema from the Quaestiones theologicae).
— De Libertate religiosa (schema drawn up by the Secretariat for the Unity).

Several elements that would be dealt with during *Gaudium et spes* are already present here. Another interesting matter was that 24 schemas were sent to the Commission for the new Codex. For the most part, this was more than justified[41], although all matters with regard to the Eastern Churches were included (*inter alia* the status of the Eastern Patriarchs, the *communicatio in sacris* with the non-catholic Eastern Christians and also the pastoral schema on the religious orders).

In his *Mémoires sur le Concile Vatican II* (p. 20), Suenens mentions another audience at Castelgandolfo in July of 1962[42]. John XXIII was reading the prepared schemas and is reported to have said: "Regardez donc, questi professori, ces professeurs, ils remontent au déluge"[43]. Suenens also signed the letter from cardinal Léger to the Pope, in which the prepared schemas were sharply criticised[44]. On August 23, 1962, John XXIII receives Cicognani and he writes: "La conformità di idee e di

---

41. And the major part of these topics cannot be found in the texts of Vaticanum II.

42. On July 24, 1962. Cf. Poswick, *Un journal du Concile* (n. 9), p. 108: "... à ce sujet il [Suenens] me raconte une anecdote: au cours de l'audience qu'il a eue hier à Castelgandolfo, il avait parlé à Jean XXIII des craintes assez répandues selon lesquelles le Concile serait bâclé, ce qui empêcherait, selon lui, la libre expression de l'Église. 'Rassurez-vous, répondit le pape, et dites-leur que cette fois les Piémontais ne campent pas aux portes de Rome'". Cf. also ALBERIGO – MELLONI (eds.), *Beatificationis et canonizationis* (n. 12), p. 3271.

43. These pages of Suenens' *Mémoires sur le Concile Vatican II* are rather confused and the chronology is often mudled up.

44. Cf. Fund Suenens, 393-397 and *AS* VI/1, pp. 53-62. See also G. ROUTHIER, *Les réactions du cardinal Léger à la préparation de Vatican II*, in *Revue d'Histoire de l'Église de France* 80, n. 205 (1994) 281-302.

buon carattere rende facile e lieto il comune lavoro in vista del Concilio. Accordo perfetto circa la [sua] organizazzione sulla indicazione di un piano ben combinato da un bel gruppo di cardinali". This probably refers to the 'plan of Suenens'[45].

More important was the radio speech of John XXIII[46] on September 11 with regard to the approaching Council, published as *Ecclesia Christi, lumen gentium*[47]. The archives of Suenens contains a copy of that speech as published in *L'Osservatore Romano* and annotated by Suenens[48]. At the top of the document Suenens notes: "Le texte du 12 septembre 1962 est la reprise par le pape du texte du plan proposé".

Clearly a number of passages of this speech refer to Suenens' plan of May of 1962. The text of Mt 28,19-20 appears[49] and the Pope speaks of "vitalità ad intra" and "vitalità ad extra"[50]. And also about: "vivificare, insegnare, pregare", which matches Suenens' suggestion on "Ecclesia salvificans, docens et orans". The Pope also says: "L'uomo cerca l'amore di una famiglia intorno al focolare domestico, il pane quotidiano per sé e per i suoi più intimi, la consorte e i figliuoli; egli aspira e sente di dover vivere in pace così all'interno della sua comunità nazionale, come nei rapporti con il resto del mondo"[51]. This text matches a passage from the plan: "ils cherchent l'amour au sein du foyer, leur pain quotidien pour eux-mêmes et leur famille, la paix tant à l'intérieur de chaque pays que celle entre les nations"[52].

We can conclude that the Pope had obviously read Suenens' plan, found it interesting and quoted from it. However, it does *not* follow from

---

45. Cf. ALBERIGO – MELLONI (eds.), *Beatificationis et canonizationis* (n. 12), p. 3276.

46. Cf. *AAS* 54 (1962) 678-685.

47. This title refers to the passage in the speech: "Ci torna qui opportuno e felice un richiamo al simbolismo del cero Pasquale. Ad un tocco della liturgia, ecco risuona il suo nome: *Lumen Christi*. La chiesa di Gesù da tutti i punti della terra risponde: *Deo gratias, Deo gratias*, come dire: Si: *Lumen Christi: lumen Ecclesiae: lumen gentium*". At the revision of *De ecclesia* in March of 1963, Philips wrote in his diary: "The opening lines state that not the Church, but that Christ is the light of the world: the Church is merely a reflection. Silently I have altered the title proposed by cardinal Suenens" (Cf. K. SCHELKENS [ed.], *Carnets conciliaires de Mgr. Gérard Philips, secrétaire adjoint de la Commission Doctrinale. Texte néerlandais avec traduction française et commentaires* [Instrumenta Theologica, 29], Leuven, Peeters, 2006: Cahier XI, p. 17). Philips is mistaken here: the title had not been proposed by Suenens, but by John XXIII (or even more correctly by *L'Osservatore Romano*).

48. *L'Osservatore Romano* of September 12, 1962. Fund Suenens, 392. This text also contains some notes of Suenens' secretary and vicar-general, R. Ceuppens.

49. *AAS* 54 (1962) 680.

50. *Ibid.*

51. *AAS* 54 (1962) 681.

52. Cf. SUENENS, *Aux origines du Concile Vatican II* [n. 16], pp. 16-17.

this that he had made Suenens' plan his own: that belongs to the category of 'wishful thinking'. The Pope does not mention a plan for the Council; and out of the 230 lines the pope's text contains a maximum of ten can be retraced to Suenens' plan[53]. It remains to be seen whether John XXIII ever intended this or possessed a systematic enough mind to arrange the course of the Council according to a well-considered plan[54].

4. Fourth Phase (First Session)

Suenens' attempts to arrive at a more structured plan for the Council during the first session are to be situated on two different levels: on the one hand are his two interventions on this subject in St. Peter's, next to a draft for an intervention by Frings; on the other hand are his attempts during the meetings of the *Secretariatus de Concilii negotiis extra ordinem*.

a. His attempts in the Secretariatus de Concilii negotiis extra ordinem

In a letter to Veronica O'Brien, Suenens gave an enthusiastic report about the first meeting of this Secretariat in the presence of John XXIII.

> Ce mercredi 16.10[55]: Hier soir à 18h. rendez-vous des six[56] avec H.F.[57]. Durée 1 h. Magnifique accueil, très chaud pour P[58] [lecture probable].

---

53. What Suenens writes in SUENENS, *Souvenirs et espérances* (n. 11), p. 70, seems exaggerated: "Jean XXIII, de son côté, l' [son plan] avait fait sien dans ses traits essentiels. On le devine en interligne, dans le mémorable radio-message qu'il fit le 12 [sic] septembre 1962, annonçant et présentant le concile sous le titre 'Ecclesia Christi, lumen gentium'. Jean XXIII présentait le concile à venir en continuité avec l'ordre du Seigneur: 'Allez, enseignez toutes les nations, baptisez-les au nom du Père, du Fils et du Saint-Esprit; apprenez-leur à garder tout ce que je vous ai prescrit' (Mt 28,19-20). Ces paroles constituaient les thèmes mêmes du plan, et le discours du Saint-Père faisait également sienne la distinction entre l'Église *ad intra* et l'Église *ad extra*, qui constituait la charnière du plan".

54. Cf. also A. RICCARDI, *La tumultuosa apertura dei lavori*, in G. ALBERIGO (ed.), *Storia del concilio Vaticano II*, Leuven, Peeters; Bologna, Il Mulino, 1995-2001, Vol. II, pp. 85-86: "Il papa ha alcune idee ed aspirazioni, ma poi crede di dover lasciar fare al lavoro dei vescovi... Egli [John XXIII] però si confortava, pensando che aveva sempre tenuto fede a questo programma di vita: lasciar fare, dar da fare, far fare".

55. Cf. Fund Suenens, 573. Suenens is mistaken about the date, it should be: "ce mercredi 17.10".

56. Suenens is mistaken: there were 7 members of the Secretariat: Cicognani (Chair), Siri, Montini, Confalonieri, Döpfner, Meyer, Suenens. On October 18, 1962, Wyszynski became the eigth member.

57. Holy Father: John XXIII.

58. Probably P. = Peter: Suenens' code name in those days.

H.F. expose que les '10'[59] sont simplement là pour le normal, qu'il a encadré le 'Felici'[60] pour l'internationaliser [sic] (on sent qu'il n'en est pas ravi mais qu'il le garde par bonté) et qu'il compte sur les 6 pratiquement selon la ligne que j'espérais. Mi[61] en sortant disait: "Jusqu'ici j'avais cru que c'était un groupe *pro forma*; je m'aperçois que c'est sérieux". Le H.F. fait des séries de comparaisons historiques avec le Vat. I, cite de mémoire les 5 – 6 ducs qui étaient là alors pour se réjouir des 80 représentants d'aujourd'hui au plan civil. Il souligne ce qu'il a dit dans ses derniers discours sur esprit positif, pastoral et finit par nous remettre une note Bea[62] qui demande une attention pour les répercussions de nos schémas au plan qui est le sien (excellente note, un peu touffue, qu'il m'avait envoyée déjà ainsi qu'à Munich[63]). Et la conversation commence. Mi demande qu'on tienne compte des Grecs. Accordé. Puis à bâtons rompus, j'ai pu sortir 6-7 mineures suggestions (messe mal réglée, costume à simplifier sur place[64]) mais j'ai commencé par l'important: "Il faudrait tracer une ligne de pensée qui puisse orienter les travaux dans un sens convergent et faire de la note Bea une sorte de vade-mecum parallèle au règlement disciplinaire: un *modus procedendi* qui aille au but pastoral". At once le H.F. déclare qu'il est enchanté de cette idée et Congaf.[65] déclare que je suis tout indiqué pour faire cette note[66]. J'accepte. C'est en somme la reprise de ma note sans le détail du plan, restant dans la procédure mais toute chargée de conséquences. On parle à l'aise de 10 choses à retoucher dans l'organisation. Je constate que le H.F. est toujours de mon avis ou moi du sien, sauf sur la simplification at once du costume pour les séances (on est en costume apparat!). Deux fois il a dit en riant à une suggestion de ma part: "C'est bien mon idée aussi … mais le courage m'a manqué"[67]. En somme c'est l'invitation à l'aider sur la route pratique à réaliser l'idéal général commun. J'étais de loin le Mr qui avait le plus d'idées – et d'idées pratiques!! Voilà ce que c'est quand on est à bonne école, tout arrive! – et je me sentais comme un poisson dans l'eau. À la fin le H.F. a dit – tenez-vous bien – et maintenant Cic.[68] va vous distribuer un texte utile pour guider vos réflexions … et chacun reçut en photocopie avec une note manuscrite photocopiée de Cic. qui résumait ça en italien par lettre … le texte de mon plan! et ma lettre du 16 mai, où l'on

59. The 10 Chairs of the Council.
60. P. Felici, Secretary-General of the Council.
61. Montini.
62. For this note of October 15,1962, cf. Fund Suenens, 610 or *AS* VI/1, pp. 201-204.
63. This refers to Döpfner.
64. Both suggestions made by Suenens (simpler attire and one mass a week to start the meetings – not one a day) were supported by Döpfner and Montini but were rejected by the Pope. This was probably due to Siri's influence. Cf. LAI, *Il papa non eletto* (n. 9), pp. 188 and 364. For the answer of the Pope to Cicognani during the audience of October 19, 1962, cf. *AS* V/1, pp. 28-29.
65. Confalonieri.
66. For this note, cf. Fund Suenens, 564.
67. In SUENENS, *Souvenirs et espérances* (n. 11), p. 60, he writes that the Pope gave this answer in reply to his question: "Pourquoi avez-vous mis à la tête des commissions conciliaires les préfets des congrégations romaines?".
68. Cicognani.

parlait du brain trust et des 4 évangélistes! en tout: 17 pages[69] ... Je viens de passer la matinée à élaborer cette note; j'ai fait travailler Raymond[70] de son côté et puis je lui ai demandé de chercher les textes du H.F. pour étoffer, puis il traduira ... Je compte demain mettre la dernière main à ma note avec Bea qui habite en face[71], puis je la ferai taper et on verra vendredi la réaction des 6, après quoi si cela passe, on enverra cela aux 10 ... pour exécution, soit venant du H.F., soit venant des 6 comme tels, soit venant officiellement des 10. On va voir la meilleure route.

What did Suenens' new note 'De Fine Concilii et de mediis aptis ad hunc finem consequendum'[72] (five typed pages, in French/Latin) contain? *Primo*, the plan of the note was as follows:

I. Orientation fondamentale
    A. Un Concile pastoral
    B. En réponse à une double attente

II. Voies et moyens
    A. Principes d'ordre négatif
        1. Questions mineures
        2. Questions déjà traitées antérieurement
        3. Questions d'école
    B. Principes d'ordre positif
        1. Point de vue pastoral
        2. Point de vue constructif
        3. Point de vue psychologique
        4. Point de vue universel et mondial

Secundo, the first matter of note is the influence of Bea's text. It is obvious that almost all of the Pope's quotes found in Suenens' text (e.g., those from his opening address on October 11, 1962, from the radio message of September 11, 1962, and from the Constitutio Apostolica *Humanae salutis* dated December 25, 1961) were taken from Bea's note.

Tertio, Suenens no longer supplies an intrinsic plan for the Council (as he did on May 16), but limits himself to guidelines for smooth proceedings, a manual for the content of the texts and the spirit in which they

---

69. For this text, dated May 19, 1962, cf. Fund Suenens, 382, 383, 384. The same text can also be found in the Fund Döpfner, 3233, with a note by Döpfner that it was presented to him during a meeting of the *Secretariatus* on October 16, 1962.

70. Probably the code name of René Ceuppens, Suenens' vicar-general, who accompanied him to Rome during the first session.

71. Suenens spent these days in the general house of the Brothers of the Christian Schools, Via Aurelia 476, Roma. Cardinal Bea stayed at the Pontificio Collegio Pio Brasiliano, Via Aurelia 527.

72. Fund Suenens, 564.

should be written. He still mentions *Ecclesia ad intra* and *Ecclesia ad extra*, but he no longer tries to insert the existing schemas into his plan (as he did on July 4). In a way this note reminds us of his *Note au sujet du concile* of April-May of 1962.

Suenens' note was handed out at the meeting of the *Secretariatus* on October 19. Cardinal Siri, however, who had drafted a written reaction with regard to Bea's note[73] and who chaired part of the meeting in the absence of Cicognani, arranged for the group to reject Bea's note, Montini's plan[74], and Suenens' note[75].

At the meeting of the *Secretariatus* on November 5, 1962, Suenens proposes again to limit the number of interveners on a chapter to 50, with preference to Patres who speak in the name of a larger group of bishops[76].

b. Two interventions in St. Peter's by Suenens and an intervention project

1. Suenens' archives[77] contain a text with a handwritten note by Suenens: "Projet de texte d'intervention non prononcée et remplacée par ma 3ᵉ intervention"[78]. This note, which was added by Suenens at a later date, is incorrect. This text, which was drafted during the first week of the Council, has no connection to Suenens' intervention on December 4, 1962. In fact, this note is about a project first described by Suenens on October 13, 1962. In his letter of October 13, 1962[79] to V. O'Brien it reads:

> Nous avons tenu une réunion avec Lille [Liénart], Frings, Vienne [König] et Munich [Döpfner] pour établir aussi le plan de la suite des opérations. J'ai proposé qu'on refasse un 2ᵉ coup de théâtre[80] en vue de remettre sur le

---

73. Cf. *AS* VI/1, pp. 204-206.

74. Cf. Fund Suenens, 613 and *AS* VI/1, pp. 206-210. On October 18, 1962 Montini sent his plan for the Council to Cicognani. It was distributed to the members of the *Secretariatus*. It was centered around the theme of the Church and contains several expressions which can be retraced to Suenens' plan of May 16, 1962: e.g., operari sequitur esse, Ecclesia docens, orans. In a Postscriptum, Montini writes: "Il piano, secondo suggerimento dell'E.mo Card. Suenens, potrebbe essere derivato dalle ultime parole di Cristo di San Matteo 28,18-20: 'Data est mihi omnis potestas ... etc.'". Cf. also RICCARDI, *La tumultuosa apertura* (n. 54), p. 75.

75. Cf. Diario Siri, October 19, 1962 in LAI, *Il papa non eletto* (n. 9), p. 365: "Con buone parole sistemo tutto ed arrivo al punto voluto: nulla di decisivo". Cf. also TREFFLER (ed.), *Julius Kardinal Döpfner. Briefe und Notizen* (n. 9), p. 6 (October 19,1962): "Suenens verliest sein regolamento für labore Concilii".

76. Cf. Fund Döpfner, 3294, handwritten notes by Döpfner.

77. Fund Suenens, 562-563.

78. Those of December 4, 1962.

79. Fund Suenens, 570.

80. The first 'coup de théâtre' was the postponement of the elections of the Council Commissions due to an intervention of Liénart and Frings on October 13, 1962.

métier les schémas établis, de commencer par la liturgie et de partir ensuite par le *De Ecclesia,* la liturgie étant prise pour se donner le temps de préparer le reste. J'ai fait le texte d'une déclaration que Frings mettra aux voix mardi ou jeudi et qui sera décisive pour l'orientation. Il valait mieux que ce soit Frings qui est du conseil de la Présidence car si je pars en flèche il y aura une belle mêlée tandis que pour une fois encore il est normal que cela parte de la table présidentielle ... J'envoie René[81] avec le texte chez Frings...

Suenens' text did not want the request (*propositio negativa*) to start with the four doctrinal schemas[82]; rather, it wanted it to start (*propositio positiva*) with *De ecclesia.* And, since this schema had not yet been handed out, it would be best to start with *De liturgia.* As it turned out, Suenens' text was not necessary: on the evening of October 15, 1962, the Chairs decided to start with liturgy[83]. That same day Suenens wrote to O'Brien[84]:

Lundi soir. Magnifique nouvelle: les présidents ont décidé sans même mettre les choses aux voix que l'on commencerait par la liturgie, ce qui est une manière pratique d'enterrer les 4 premiers schémas qui ne valent rien[85]. Et après cela on peut prendre le *De Ecclesia.* Ce sera donc mon plan qui va triompher. J'avais fait le texte que Frings aurait lu mais il n'a pas été nécessaire puisque (à très faible majorité), les 10 de la présidence ... l'avait décidé [sic]. Pour les 4 schémas de Otto[86] il n'y a qu'à régler l'enterrement: les uns souhaitent une mort lente, les autres une mort rapide ce qui est ma thèse. Je pousse à rejeter les 4 'en bloc' ce qui ferait gagner 3-4 semaines.

2. Intervention of November 14, 1962[87]: At the beginning of the discussion on *De fontibus revelationis,* Suenens took advantage of the opportunity to make some procedural proposals. He had already submitted these proposals to cardinal Döpfner[88] by means of a note. They were no longer concerned with a plan for the Council, but with strictly practical matters:

– Every discussion needs to be followed by an immediate vote to determine whether or not the schema is acceptable for further discussion.

---

81. R. Ceuppens. A proposed handwritten Latin translation by Ceuppens can be found in Fund Suenens, 563.

82. *De fontibus revelationis, De fidei deposito pure custodiendo, De ordine morali, De castitate, virginitate, matrimonio et familia.*

83. G. CAPRILE, *Il Concilio Vaticano II.* Vol. II, 1968, Roma, Civiltà Cattolica, 1968, p. 24; and *AS* V/1, pp. 17-18.

84. Fund Suenens, 571.

85. Suenens' expectation did not prove to be true: after *De liturgia,* the schema *De fontibus revelationis* would be discussed.

86. A. Ottaviani.

87. *AS* I/3, pp. 45-47.

88. Fund Döpfner, 3270, who in a marginal note expressed his agreement with *Propositiones* I and II.

- The *Patres* are, after the oral discussion, with regard to less important matters, limited to the submission of written remarks. The Commission will answer, without delay, the proposed *emendationes* followed by an immediate vote.
- The commissions need to focus on the important elements and the reduction of the schemas ("ne arbores impediant videre silvam!").
- After a vote on a schema, the post-conciliar commissions need to be immediately established in order to examine how the conclusions can be practically implemented.

3. Intervention of December 4, 1962[89]: This was undoubtedly Suenens' most important speech[90] of the first session; it was perhaps his most important of the whole Council. It is worth noting that it was warmly applauded by those present: in fact, it was necessary for the Acting Chair, Cardinal Caggiano, to call them to order. It was a well-prepared intervention, was supported by a number of cardinals, had a real impact on the realisation of the Coordinating Commission, and ultimately led to the reduction of the total number of schemas. It helped pared the original 70 down to 20, then to 17.

In what follows, we will first look at the process of the intervention's preparation. This will then be followed by a discussion of its content and, finally, by a few remarks regarding its influence.

First, the preparation of the intervention: During the first session and in addition to the official meetings of the *Secretariatus*, there were several meetings of cardinals concerned with overcoming the Council's impasse. It is certain that there were meetings on October 13[91], October 25[92], and November 11[93]. Prignon[94] remembers a meeting of a number of

---

89. As always, the comment by G. Caprile (this time he was probably relying on information supplied by the State Secretariat, Dell'Acqua and/or Suenens himself) is worth reading. Cf. CAPRILE, *Il Concilio Vaticano II*. Vol. II (n. 83), p. 264.

90. In his diary (H. FESQUET, *Le Journal du Concile*, Morel, Le Jas par Forcalquier, p. 137) Fesquet mentions "une brillante intervention très vivement applaudie", yet Congar, de Lubac, and Charue make no special mention of it in their diaries.

91. Meeting with Frings, Liénart, König, Döpfner, and Suenens. Cf. Fund Suenens, 570.

92. Cf. LAI, *Il papa non eletto* (n. 9), pp. 367 and 369-370; Meeting with Frings, Siri, Liénart, Montini, König, Döpfner, Suenens, and Alfrink.

93. According to the *Journal conciliaire* of Léger (In P. LAFONTAINE, *Inventaire des archives conciliaires du fonds Paul-Émile Léger*, Outremont, Éditions des Partenaires, 1995. Henceforth referred to as Fund Léger. See Fund Léger, 13): meeting in the Anima, with Frings, Döpfner, Alfrink, Suenens, Liénart, and Léger. At this point we would like to thank G. Routhier, who in a letter dated March 22, 2004 and written to L. Declerck, brought this detail to our attention.

94. Tape III (February of 2000).

cardinals at the Belgian College, the same location where Suenens is said to have prepared his plan for the Council and his intervention. *Inter alia*, he says that Suenens presented his project with the regular interjection: 'if the Pope agrees', even though he was absolutely certain that the Pope would agree. In his *Mémoires* (p. 29) Suenens also mentions that he had dinner with Montini on December 3.

More important is that John XXIII had seen Suenens' text beforehand and had even made some remarks on the text. Suenens recounted this episode in 1966:

> Sachant le pape malade et le croyant même très gravement malade, j'ai pris l'initiative de décider de faire une intervention au Concile en proposant ce plan comme venant de moi-même et sans attendre de directives de plus haut ... j'ai envoyé un dimanche soir, le dimanche qui précède mon intervention qui a été, je crois, le mercredi[95] une petite lettre d'abord de chaude sympathie ... J'ai été la porter le soir, traversant ces immenses corridors du Vatican, un dimanche soir où il n'y avait personne ... J'ai donc remis une lettre pour le Saint-Père et une lettre pour son secrétaire Mgr Capovilla lui disant: "Voilà un texte de l'intervention que je compte faire. Je vous envoie cela pour votre information sans plus".
>
> Une idée qui m'a fait envoyer ce texte à ce moment-là était aussi que je proposais un secrétariat pour ce qui serait plus tard le schéma XIII et que je me disais, tout de même si ça ne convient pas du tout au Saint-Père, c'est un peu ennuyeux de proposer une institution si jamais il ne le souhaitait pas. C'était pour cela que j'avais envoyé à Mgr Capovilla la copie du texte de l'intervention que je me proposais de faire.
>
> À ma très grande surprise, le lendemain lundi matin à 8h., coup de téléphone de Mgr Dell'Acqua pour me demander de venir de toute urgence au Vatican chez lui, avant l'ouverture du concile, qui s'ouvrait à 9h. ... C'était pour m'entendre dire que le Pape avait lu mon texte dans son lit et qu'il l'avait annoté ... Les modifications ne touchaient pas du tout au fond; au contraire, c'étaient des compléments. J'avais donc pour mon intervention le texte original revu et corrigé par Sa Sainteté Jean XXIII, ce qui naturellement, lorsque je me suis levé pour prononcer cette intervention, m'a donné beaucoup plus d'aisance et peut-être même un peu plus d'aplomb que ce que j'aurais dit de mon seul et propre cru[96].

John XXIII[97] made three corrections to Suenens' text: two stylistic and one (small) addendum:

– On page 2[98], the words: "exponatur quomodo ab Ecclesia hodie agendum sit ut quam fidelis remaneat supremo mandato Domini:

---

95. In fact Tuesday, December 4, 1962.
96. *Mémoires sur le Concile Vatican II*, pp. 26-28.
97. Cf. Fund Suenens, 626-627.
98. Pagination of the text Fund Suenens, 629.

'Euntes ergo docete'..." were to be replaced by: "exponatur quomodo Ecclesia hodie *progredi debeat, ut Summorum Pontificum vestigiis insistens, qui viam signaverunt: meminerimus tantum S. Pii X,
cuius voluntas fuit 'instaurare omnia in Christo', et Pii XII,
ejusque fulgentis magisterii, quod a Joanne XXIII continuatur, et ab
ipso definitus est 'quasi fons in aperta platea positus'; ita ut Ecclesia* quam fidelis remaneat supremo mandato Domini: 'Euntes et
docete...'".

- On page 3, to Suenens' phrase: "... sic puto similem Secretariatum
esse creandum in sinu Concilii pro rebus socialibus de quibus supra",
was added: "pro rebus socialibus de quibus supra, *vel saltem specialem
sectionem novae Commissionis*[99]*, cujus munus erit labores ceterarum
Commissionum ordinare et facilioris reddere*"[100].

- And on page 4, instead reading: "Semen quod in lacrymis et contra-
dictionibus magnus ille Ecclesiae episcopus[101] seminavit...", John
XXIII changed it into: "Semen quod *generosa cum prudentia nec sine
quibusdam difficultatibus* magnus ille episcopus...".

It is clear that these changes were minimal and were prompted by a certain *prudentia* and the *stylus curiae* of John XXIII.

Second then, is our discussion of the content of the intervention[102]:
As an introduction, Suenens emphasizes the necessity of arranging the
matters of the Council according to a central theme, as well as the necessity that each commission act as part of the greater whole. The central
theme has to be: *Ecclesia Christi, lumen gentium*. The theme of the
Church should, in turn, be subdivided into two sections:

A. *Ecclesia ad intra*

- in the first place, the nature of the Church "Ecclesia, quid dicis de teipsa?"
- followed by: what is the mission of the Church today ("operatio sequitur
esse") according to the words of Christ "Euntes ergo docete...":
Euntes ergo: Ecclesia evangelizans.
Docete eos: Ecclesia docens.

---

99. Allusion to the Coordinating Commission established on December 5, 1962.

100. In the intervention actually pronounced by Suenens (*AS* I/4, p. 224), this suggestion is not included. It reads: "Ad res sociales quod attinet, optandum sane videtur ut eae
in hoc concilio magis directe et diffuse tractentur, sicut de rebus oecumenicis a proprio sec-
retariatu iam factum est; ac, si opus est, aliquid simile fiat".

101. Désiré Mercier.

102. In addition to his oral intervention, Suenens submitted a written note on the actual
schema *De ecclesia* which was brought up for discussion (*AS* I/4, pp. 225-227). This note
literally copies the text drafted by Philips (Fund Philips, 435).

Baptizantes eos: Ecclesia sanctificans.
In nomine Patris...: Ecclesia orans.

B. *Ecclesia ad extra*

1. On the human person; *inter alia*, the sanctity of life, planned procreation and the problems brought on by the population explosion.
2. On social justice.
3. On the evangelisation of the poor.
4. On peace and war.
   When dealing with these themes, the Church must engage in a three-fold dialogue: (1) With her own believing members; (2) With the "not yet visibly united brothers" (ecumenism); (3) With the modern world. In addition, the establishment of a Secretariat for Social Problems was suggested.

Cardinal Suenens claims that this plan corresponds to the Pope's September 11 speech. In conclusion he demands:

– That the programme for the future evolution of the Council would be determined by the Council in advance.
– That the commissions would immediately review their schemas with this in mind; that they would keep only what was of real importance; and that they would deal with everything from the vantage point of pastoral renewal.
– That the Council would express a desire for the establishment of a Secretariat for the Problems of the Modern World[103]. A Secretariat, which was as productive as the Secretariat for Christian Unity, was one about which he, as the successor of Mercier, the same Mercier who had hosted the 'Conversations of Malines', found particularly gratifying.

Suenens clearly returned to the schema of his plan of May 16. For *Ecclesia ad intra*, he was less specific and no longer referred to the existing prepared schemas. For *Ecclesia ad extra*, he retained only four chapters: the chapter on the family was dropped (in comparison to May 16, 1962), but the problem of birth control was retained and was (ultimately) inserted into the first chapter[104].

---

103. Such a secretariat or commission had been requested by some 14 bishops (among them Himmer, Helder Camara, Ancel, McGrath) in a letter to Cicognani (as chair of the *Secretariatus*) on November 21, 1962 (Fund Suenens, 616).
104. In the end *Gaudium et spes* will follow the plan of 16.05 more closely than that of 04.12.

Third, the intervention's aftermath: Montini[105] (on December 5) and Lercaro[106] (on December 6) supported Suenens publicly during their intervention in St. Peter's. In his *Mémoires*, Suenens attributes Montini's support to John XXIII[107], a fact confirmed by Caprile[108]. Léger's papers[109] contain a document (of December of 1962) which is fairly critical towards this intervention by Suenens[110]. It is, however, a fact that the decisions followed one another in quick succession during the session's last days. On November 23, 1962, the *Secretariatus* issued guidelines to the General Secretariat regarding the order of the schemas to be discussed and requested that an overview for distribution to the *Patres* be drawn up[111]. On November 30, the *Secretariatus* examined and approved an overview, drafted by the General Secretariat[112]. This overview contains a recommendation to the Pope to establish an executive commission, that would coordinate the activities of the Council. A new overview of the schemas

105. "Officii mei esse censeo vos rogare ut peculiari diligentia consideretis ea quae em.mus card. Suenens heri tam perspicue exposuit de fine huic universali Synodo proposito et de ordine logico et congruenti argumentorum in ea tractandorum" (*AS* I/4, p. 291).

106. "Ante omnia insisto in iis de quibus dixerunt em.mi DD. card. Suenens et Montini: de fine huius concilii, de ordine et reductione thematum et praecipue de necessitate enucleandi doctrinam de Ecclesia" (*AS* I/4, p. 327).

107. "Ce fut une surprise générale pour tout le monde de voir que le lendemain le Cardinal Montini s'est levé, sortant de sa réserve ... pour dire combien il se ralliait à cette proposition ... Cette intervention de Montini a été sensationnelle pour cette raison-là. Mgr Capovilla m'a dit que le Pape Jean XXIII lui avait demandé de faire cette intervention. Je n'en savais rien. J'avais soupé la veille au soir chez le cardinal Montini, dans la maison qu'il occupait dans les jardins du Vatican ... Je lui avais dit que j'allais faire cette intervention mais il n'avait pas dit qu'il comptait l'appuyer" (p. 29).

108. CAPRILE, *Il Concilio Vaticano II*. Vol. II, p. 264: "[Suenens] Seppe poi che anche il card. Montini era stato pregato di far noto, nel suo intervento del 5 dicembre, il proprio appoggio alla proposta del collega belga".

109. Fund Léger, 707. The author is not specified; it was perhaps written by one of Léger's advisors.

110. This two-page document reads in part: "Me semble un peu arbitraire aussi la division *De Ecclesia ad intra* et *De Ecclesia ad extra* ... On voit difficilement, cependant, comment tous les travaux des commissions préparatoires pourront rentrer dans ces nouveaux schèmes et cadres ... Il m'apparaît évident que l'utilisation du texte de l'Écriture pour illustrer cette division n'est pas nécessaire. N'est-elle pas un peu forcée ... Il est impossible d'admettre que la famille et le mariage ne laissent plus de problèmes. Cette intervention du Card. Suenens sur le schéma *De ecclesia* ne nous dit rien sur ce que devrait contenir et ce que devrait être le schéma *De ecclesia*". This last remark proves that the author of this criticism had no knowledge of the written text submitted by Suenens together with his intervention of December 4.

111. Report of the meeting on November 23, 1962, Fund Suenens, 596.

112. Report of the meeting on November 30, 1962, Fund Suenens, 597. In Suenens' papers (Fund Suenens, 599) there is a duplicated document "Schema Constitutionum et Decretorum de quibus disceptabitur vel disceptari potest in Concilio". This version still contains 21 Capita.

was distributed on December 5[113], and on December 6 it is publicized that John XXIII will establish a Coordinating Commission. The names of the commission's members – including Suenens – were announced in *L'Osservatore Romano* on December 17-18, 1962.

5. Fifth Phase (first meeting of the Coordinating Commission, January of 1963)

On January 22, 1963, during the first meeting of the Coordinating Commission[114], Suenens made a final attempt[115] to arrange the Council according to *De ecclesia ad intra* and *De ecclesia ad extra* and to insert the 20 schemas into his arrangement[116]. The outline goes as follows:

After an Introduction (*De divina revelatione* [I][117] and *De deposito* [IV]) comes

De ecclesia ad intra

A. De ecclesia in suo esse
   I.   De ecclesia in statu viae: De ecclesia (II)
   II. De ecclesia in statu glorioso: De beata (III)
B. De ecclesia in suis membris
   I.   De episcopis (X)
   II. De clericis (et de sacrorum alumnis formandis) (IX)
   III. De laicis (et de studiis et scholis) (XII)
   IV. De religiosis (XI)
C. De ecclesia in suo operari
   I.   Ecclesia orans: De liturgia (XIV)
   II. Ecclesia salvificans: De missionibus (XVIII)

113. This overview (cf. Fund Suenens, 801) contains only 20 schemas. Schema VII, *De ordine sociali et de communitate gentium*, now contains both the 7th (VII. *De Ordine sociali*) and the 8th chapters (VIII. *De communitate gentium*) of the previous version (cf. Fund Suenens, 599).

114. During these meeting of the Coordinating Commission Suenens had two private audiences with the Pope on January 24 and 29, 1963. Cf. POSWICK, *Un journal du Concile* (n. 9), pp. 225-226.

115. Cf. Fund Döpfner, 3458 (Vorschlag Card. Suenens January 22, 1963) and Fund Suenens, 804 and *AS* V/1, pp. 89-90. On January 22 Suenens also had a conversation with Dossetti, who was in possession of Suenens' new plan for several of the Council's schemas (cf. Fund Dossetti, I.10 and III.225). And on January 22, 1963 at 15.30h. Döpfner had a meeting with Suenens: "Bei Card. Suenens. Besprechung über De Ecclesia, De religiosis" (See TREFFLER (ed.), *Julius Kardinal Döpfner. Briefe und Notizen* [n. 9], p. 11).

116. Lercaro also remains active and requests Suenens in a letter of January 14, 1963 to receive Dossetti regarding the work method and the procedure of the Council (Cf. L. LAZZARETTI, *Inventario dei Fondi G. Lercaro e G. Dossetti*. Introduzione di G. Alberigo [La documentazione bolognese per la storia del Concilio Vaticano II, 2], Bologna, Dehoniane, 1995 [Fund Lercaro, XXV.689]).

117. The Roman numbers refer to the numbers of the overview distributed to the Patres on December 5 (Fund Suenens, 801).

    III. Ecclesia sanctificans: De cura animarum
         (et in adnexo: De matrimonio) (XIII)
D. De ecclesia in sua unitate
    I.   De ecclesiis orientalibus (VIII)
    II. De unione fovenda (XX)

Followed by: *De ecclesia ad extra*

1. De ecclesia et de ordine morali, praesertim quoad respectum vitae perso-
   nalis (V)
2. De ecclesia et de ordine familiali, praesertim sub aspectu matrimoniali (VI)
3. De ecclesia et de ordine communicationum socialium: De instrumentis
   communicationis socialis (XIX)
4. De ecclesia et de ordine sociali oeconomico (VII)
5. De ecclesia et de ordine internationali (VIIbis)

This draft, once more containing all the topics of Suenens' earlier plans, was as artificial as his attempt of July 4, 1962. Ultimately, except for *De ecclesia ad extra*, which (except for the chapter on the social means of communication) prefigures *Gaudium et spes*, it will not be used[118].

The different members' responsibilities had been assigned by December 17, 1962. Suenens was charged with *De ecclesia, De B. M. virgine, De ordine morali, De ordine sociali*. His *Mémoires sur le Concile Vatican II* (p. 31) make it plain that he was well pleased with his assignment:

> Ici encore, ce sera la dernière fois que Jean XXIII me témoignera une sympathie toute spéciale. Il avait donc divisé entre les cardinaux membres de la Commission de Coordination, le plan d'ensemble du concile en nommant chacun de ces membres, 6 ou 7 cardinaux, rapporteur de tel ou tel schéma – nous en avions naturellement plusieurs. Le pape Jean XXIII avait assigné comme lot pour moi, spécialement donc comme rapporteur, le schéma de l'Église *ad intra*, ce qui était le fameux schéma *Lumen Gentium*, qui était la clef doctrinale du concile et puis il m'avait confié le schéma de l'Église *ad extra*, c'est-à-dire le schéma XIII, qui est devenu le schéma XVII par un classement différent et qui est devenu *Gaudium et Spes*. Si bien que j'avais les deux positions-clefs si l'on peut dire, les deux gros morceaux. Il a certainement fait la chose à dessein. Il a confié au cardinal Döpfner les religieux aussi avec le souci de l'innovation dans ces domaines. C'était vraiment le dernier geste de sa confiance et des gestes qui marquaient où lui-même voulait aller dans le concile.

---

118. Cf. *Processus verbalis* of the meeting on January 23, 1963, *AS* V/1, pp. 97-98: "Il *Card. Doepfner*: non dobbiamo necessariamente e ad ogni costo voler creare un piano; altrimenti si finisce per diventare troppo artificiali, e rischiamo di mescolare decreti disciplinari a costituzioni dogmatiche; … Il *Card. Urbani*: Il Card. Suenens ha fatto un piano allo scopo di trovare un posto ai 20 schemi ma non è necessario. Il *Card. Cicognani*: il piano in sé non è del Concilio; e noi non ci dobbiamo legare per forza ad una cornice; al più in un proemio si può dire del piano, ma evitando di essere artificiali".

6. A Few Concluding Remarks

When we consider the influence of the 'plan Suenens' from the historical distance of more than forty years, the following three conclusions become evident:

1. The Council did *not* go according to Suenens' plan. Only *Gaudium et spes* corresponds even remotely well to the section *Ecclesia ad extra*. When it comes to *Ecclesia ad intra*, Suenens' plan had little or no impact. It seems that the plan lacked consistency and was too much centered around a number of 'thematical slogans' (*Euntes docete; operari sequitur esse; ad intra et ad extra*). On the other hand, this was clearly Suenens' strong point: the formulation and presentation of difficult topics in one single sentence. At the same time, it could also be his greatest weakness: the content was sometimes quite superficial and lacking in theological foundation. Since the 75 schemas had already been written out, it was impossible to just discard them. Like Montini's plan of October 18, 1962, Suenens' attempts to insert these schemas into his plan were doomed to failure.

2. Although it appears that Suenens (in his *Mémoires sur le Concile Vatican II* and elsewhere) somewhat overestimated the support of John XXIII for his plan, it remains true that the Pope supported the attempts of Suenens and others to break through the rigidity and artificiality of the prepared schemas. Whether John XXIII was really concerned with the formulation of a systematic and orderly plan for the Council, however, will remain hard to establish until his pontifical archives are opened.

3. The real merit of Suenens' plan is how it significantly contributed to the replacement of the prepared schemas by new texts. It was also his plan that first broached the idea of a 'Coordinating Commission': we know it had been suggested by Suenens as early as May 16. These two facts, when they are combined with the successful election of the Council commissions, constitute the essential contribution of the first session of the Council. Beginning in March-April of 1962, a group of cardinals and bishops (including Suenens, Döpfner, Liénart, Léger, Frings, Montini, König, Alfrink, Hurley) in the *Commissio centralis praeparatoria* were growing more and more concerned with both the large number[119] of prepared schemas (75) and especially with the spirit (they were too 'Holy Office') in which they were being written. Suenens responded by drafting his 'plan', by networking with other cardinals,

---

119. Someone (Tardini?) claimed they acted "de omni re scibili et aliquot aliis".

by organizing two meetings at the Belgian College, by alarming the Pope, and by campaigning in the *Secretariatus*. On the other hand, it is plain that the more conservative wing was making every effort to prevent the rejection of the prepared schemas[120]. Siri made sure that Suenens' and Montini's plans are not retained in the *Secretariatus* even as he objected to any changes being made once the Council had started[121]. In an intervention in the Council on November 17, 1962, Ottaviani resisted the dismissal of the schema *De Fontibus*. He based his resistance on can. 222, §2 and by noting that the Pope had approved the prepared schemas before they were sent to the Patres. Felici attempted to prolong the discussion of this schema even though it had already been rejected by a large majority (1368!) of Patres on November 20, 1962. On December 1, 1962 Ottaviani attacked Philips' new schema *De Ecclesia*. And during the meeting of the Coordinating Commission on January 21, 1963, Cicognani attempted to point out the value of the prepared schemas, which have been approved and adjusted by the *Commissio centralis praeparatoria*[122].

If, simultaneously, there was both substantial support for[123] and stubborn resistance to Suenens' plan, this was because everybody sensed that a new plan for the Council meant the end for the prepared schemas as well as the end of a "certain Roman scholastical theology"[124].

Although Suenens' plan for the Council was not really intended to do so, it nevertheless made a significant contribution to the rejection of the prepared schemas and, along the way, gave a new impetus to the Council during the first intersession. Prof. Grootaers was completely right to characterize this as a 'second preparation'[125].

120. Cf. DECLERCK, *Le rôle joué* (n. 40), p. 449.

121. "Non capisco come non intendano che non si possono fare piani di mutazione a concilio incomminciato" (*Diario Siri* on October 19, 1962, in LAI, *Il papa non eletto* [n. 9], p. 365). And also: "Prima mi aveva raggiunto mons. Vagnozzi, Del. Apostolico agli Stati Uniti e colla faccia alterata mi dice: 'Sa niente?' 'Che?' 'Sta per avvenire un grosso colpo!' 'Quale?'. 'Vogliono buttare a mare tutti gli schemi teologici'. 'Non è vero – dico io...' ". (November 12, 1962) Cf. LAI, *Il papa non eletto* (n. 9), pp. 379-380.

122. Fund Suenens, 811.

123. By Döpfner [in June of 1962 "Ma certamente cosi abbiamo un utile punto da partire" (Fund Döpfner, 2806)], Liénart, Montini, Lercaro etc. Cf. also the applause of the Patres at Suenens' speech on December 4, 1962.

124. When Philip's schema *De ecclesia* is accepted at the end of February as a basic text, it is viewed by Tromp as a diabolical plot against his work and he states: "It is enough to make one weep". Cf. SCHELKENS (ed.), *Carnets conciliaires de Mgr. Gérard Philips* (n. 47), Cahier XI, February 28, 1963.

125. Cf. J. GROOTAERS, *The Drama Continues between the Acts: The 'Second Preparation' and its Opponents*, in G. ALBERIGO – J.A. KOMONCHAK (eds.), *History of Vatican II*.

III. The Influence of Cardinal Suenens upon the Realisation of the Constitution *Lumen gentium*

When Msgr. Garrone refers to *Lumen gentium* as "le schéma belge", he does so with good reason[126]: Philips, Heuschen, Charue, Thils, Moeller and Prignon, as well as Cardinal Suenens were all involved from the very beginning of the new schema on the Church and all contributed to the process of its birth and growth. A correct evaluation of the scale of his influence requires a certain amount of historical research.

1. Anteconcilium

During the preconciliar period we can study Cardinal Suenens' influence from four subsequent angles.

a. Vota antepraeparatoria[127]

The *Vota* Suenens sent on November 10, 1959, are fairly extensive. As far as *De ecclesia* is concerned, the following two are worthy of mention:

Primo, he desires the continuation of the discussion on *munus episcopi*, in order to complement Vatican I; this will also prove important for reconciling the Orthodox.

Secundo, he puts in a request for the introduction of a permanent diaconate. In his view, even married persons should be provided the opportunity to become deacons.

Our Lady is not mentioned in his *vota*.

b. Interventions in the Commissio centralis praeparatoria

During the discussion of the *Schema constitutionis De ecclesia* which occurred between May 3 and May 12, 1962, the following interventions by Suenens are worth mentioning:

- He desired that the "separated brothers" not be hurt needlessly in so far as this can be done without doing violence to the truth. On the other hand, the Church should not lessen her attempts to bring them into the

---

Vol. II: *The Formation of the Council's Identity. First Period and Intersession*, Maryknoll, NY, Orbis; Leuven, Peeters, 1997, p. 359.

126. Cf. A. Prignon, *Évêques et théologiens de Belgique au concile Vatican II*, in C. Soetens, *Vatican II et la Belgique*, Louvain-la-Neuve, ARCA, 1996, p. 164.

127. Cf. *Acta et Documenta Concilio oecumenico apparando* [ADA], I/2, pars 1, 140-148 and Fund Suenens, 418.

light of the full truth. For those who supported a 'broader' theology in this area, this led to the conclusion that no further attempts at conversion should be made[128].

– He wished for more light to be shed on the collegiality of the episcopate at the beginning of the schema and not at the end[129].
– The role of the laity was also important to him. This was at least partially inspired by the 'separated brothers' who, since the Reformation, had been speaking about the 'general priesthood of the faithful' and who had consistently accused the Roman Catholic Church of clericalism. Their dignity in the Church required a clearer emphasis as did their role in the apostolate[130].

Between June 12 and June 20, 1962, he expressed his desire, with regard to *De beata*, to have a clear statement that Our Lady was aware, from the very beginning, i.e., from the Annunciation onward, of the divine character of her Son – not only of his being the Messiah[131].

During the discussion of Caput IX (*De relationibus inter ecclesiam et statum necnon de tolerantia religiosa*) and the Secretariat for Christian Unity's schema *De libertate religiosa*, he makes an appeal for an open discussion of theological matters in Rome in order to free the way for theological progress (and simultaneously hoping to avoid appearing suspect). At the same time, he did not agree with a passage from the schema of the Secretariat which rejected '*improbus proselitismus*' since it supplied arguments to the opponents of the duty of the apostolate[132].

c. Some elements from Suenens' plan for the Council[133]

Although this plan, which was centered around the theme of the Church (*Ecclesia, quid dicis de te ipsa?*), related to the whole of the Council, it still offered some interesting ideas with regard to the specific Church constitution:

– One ought to discuss the college of the apostles and the role of the bishops in the Church in order to complete the unfinished First Vatican Council. This will have ecumenical repercussions with regard to the Eastern brothers "en montrant le lien entre la papauté et le Corps

128. *ADA* II/2, Pars 3, p. 1033.
129. *ADA* II/2, Pars 3, p. 1077.
130. *ADA* II/2, Pars 3, p. 1101.
131. *ADA* II/2, Pars 4, p. 781. Cf. also Fund Suenens, 130.
132. For the intervention by Suenens, cf. *ADA* II/2, Pars 4, pp. 736-737. For the text of *De libertate religiosa*, cf. *ADA* II/2, Pars 4, p. 677.
133. SUENENS, *Aux origines du Concile Vatican II* [n. 16], pp. 11-18.

de l'Église, en montrant la place et le sens du collège épiscopal"
(pp. 12 and 14).
- He suggested the possibility of a permanent diaconate (p. 15).
- He desired that an important statement be made on the role of the lay persons in the Church. This was obviously of great ecumenical importance,
especially with regard to the church's relationship with Protestants, who
had long reproached the Catholics' supposed clericalism and who have
emphasized the "common priesthood of the faithful" (p. 12 and 14).

d. Commission on the bishops

As a member of the Preparatory Commission *De episcopis et de dioeceseon regimine*, Suenens pleaded for the establishment of bishops' conferences[134]. Beyond this, however, he did not intervene regarding the doctrinal themes of *De ecclesia*. His plea for bishops' conferences was
mainly based on practical pastoral motives; it was only secondarily based
upon a theology of collegiality. Because no bishop has authority over
another, it would be desirable for any decision to be validated by a
delegatio of the power of the Holy See to the President of the bishops'
conference. Suenens also pleaded for bishops' conferences on a larger
scale (e.g., continent-wide) such as was the case with the CELAM.

2. Iª Sessio

As early as October 13, 1962 and just after the first plenary gathering
in Saint Peter's, Vatican State Secretary Cicognani is supposed to have
said to Suenens: "Mais pourquoi ne feriez-vous pas un schéma *De ecclesia?*"[135]. On Monday, October 15, Suenens writes to O'Brien: "J'ai
demandé à Philips de se mettre au travail pour un bref *De ecclesiae
natura* qu'ils feront [sic] avec Congar etc."[136]. This is confirmed by
Philips' own diary[137]. A first draft of the new schema was ready at the

---

134. Fund Suenens, 332 (same document, different typography, 398).
135. Letter from Suenens to V. O'Brien, cf. Fund Suenens, 570.
136. Fund Suenens, 571.
137. "The thought of rewriting the schema *De ecclesia* in a more fashionable style
and in a more open spirit takes shape. The bishops deem it necessary to have a text at hand
for immediate presentation when discussing the Church problem. Msgr. Heuschen, and
maybe others also, suggested to the cardinal that I should be asked to draw up such a text.
I will wait and see. After a short while the cardinal did indeed ask me to undertake this
task, i.e., to rewrite the schema in accordance with my own views, on the condition of
consultation with other theologians whose names he mentioned to me. This to prevent
double initiatives. It is the first time that I have spoken with the cardinal in Rome. The
meeting was purely business" (SCHELKENS [ed.], *Carnets conciliaires de Mgr. Gérard*

end of October, followed by a second and improved version at the end of November. Ottaviani publicly attacked this schema on December 1, 1962. This attack was a very painful experience for Philips. It came about despite the fact that Philips had shown Suenens his answer to the letter of Gagnebet[138] and that Suenens had assured Philips that he would protect him from Ottaviani. Either Suenens was too slow or Ottaviani did not heed the former's efforts[139].

The archives show that even during the first session several bishops and theologians sent their remarks on *De Ecclesia* to Suenens or wanted to meet with him: Schillebeeckx[140], Dossetti[141], Hurley[142], Elchinger[143], Degrijse[144] and C. Colombo[145].

On December 4, 1962, during the ecclesiological debate, Suenens spoke, about his 'plan for the Council', and added an important written text with regard to *De ecclesia*. This text had been fully drafted by Philips[146] and represented a justification for and an introduction to the new *De ecclesia* of Philips. It contained four chapters: *De natura ecclesiae*

Philips [n. 47], Cahier XI, p. 3). Heuschen tells the story as follows: "It was decided in the meantime … to prepare a new schema on 'the Church'. At the request of the Western bishops a few people were contacted to work on this: Msgr. Charue, myself, Msgr. Philips and Prof. Thils have all been included. This will keep me busy for 14 days or so". Cf. Letter from Heuschen to Verjans on October 17, 1962 in Fund Heuschen, 512. Y. Congar notes on October 18: "Je reçois différentes visites ce matin, entre autres celle de Mgr Philips. Le cardinal Suenens lui a demandé de reprendre (compléter et amender), avec le P. Rahner et tel ou tel autre, l'ensemble des textes sur l'Église. Je me demande si le travail n'est pas prématuré, puisque ces textes ne doivent venir en discussion qu'à la seconde session". Cf. CONGAR, *Mon journal du Concile* (n. 9), Vol. I, p. 119.

138. On November 23, 1962, Gagnebet wrote to Philips to express his astonishment with regard to this new schema, which was drafted without the approval of the *Commissio theologica praeparatoria*. Philips offered his justification for this on November 26, 1962, but first sent a draft of his answer to Suenens in order to ask for his approval. (Cf. Fund Philips, 429-431).

139. SCHELKENS (ed.), *Carnets conciliaires de Mgr. Gérard Philips* (n. 47), Cahier XI, p. 6.

140. Animadversiones in 'Secundam Seriem'…, cf. Fund Suenens, 639.

141. Dossetti drew Suenens' attention to a text by Gagnebet with regard to the sacramentality of the episcopate (Fund Suenens, 642-643).

142. Animadversiones super schemate Constit. Dogmaticae de Ecclesiae (in genere) (Fund Suenens, 644).

143. Observations et Propositions concernant les chapitres III et IV du Schéma 'De Ecclesia' (Fund Suenens, 645).

144. Fund Suenens, 646-647.

145. C. Colombo wrote to Prignon (November 4, 1962) in order to request a translation of texts by R. Snoeks and P. Anciaux (professors of respectively dogma and sacramentology at the Malines seminary) on the episcopate and for a meeting with Suenens, cf. Fund Suenens, 649.

146. Only one alteration (handwritten) by Philips, on p. 4, was not accepted. Cf. Fund Philips, 435 which notes: "ad usum Card. Suenens, nov. 62", and SCHELKENS (ed.), *Carnets conciliaires de Mgr. Gérard Philips* (n. 47), Cahier XI, p. 7 and AS I/4, pp. 225-227.

(concerning the separated brethren, the Jews and non-Christians), *De epis-copatu* (concerning the sacramental nature of the episcopate and the college of the bishops), *De laicis*, and *De religiosis*. It was explicitly requested that *De ecclesia* end with a text on *De beata*. This was obviously a suggestion that the latter be integrated into *De ecclesia*.

As expected, Suenens was deeply interested in the text on Our Lady. In this regard he received a letter from Laurentin about the integration of this schema in *De ecclesia*[147].

In sum, during the first session Suenens made a major contribution to the rejection of the prepared doctrinal schemata (cf. supra, his action for his "plan") and to focussing the Council's attention on the theme of the Church. His initiative to entrust, from the very beginning, Philips, who was both a moderate and open theologian as well as a highly practical human being, with a new *De ecclesia* proved to be providential during the first intersession.

3. Iᵃ Intersessio

a. On December 17, the competences of the members of the newly established Coordinating Commission were assigned. Suenens was put in charge of *De ecclesia* and *De B. M. virgine*[148]. As soon as this became known, Suenens was regarded as the main party responsible for *De ecclesia*, a role he takes very much to heart. Ancel[149], Silva Henriquez[150], Renard[151] and Helder Camara[152] all wrote to him in this respect. Cardinal Döpfner asked Suenens to send a representative to the Münich meeting of the German episcopate that took place on February 5 and 6, 1963[153]. Suenens soon received the preparatory documents for this meeting[154]. After attending this meeting, Msgr. Musty sends a detailed report to Suenens[155].

---

147. Letter from Laurentin to Suenens, November 28, 1962, with a text "La réinté-gration du schème marial dans le schème *De ecclesia*" (Fund Suenens, 652-653).
148. Fund Suenens, 807.
149. Fund Suenens, 950, letter of December 21, 1962.
150. Fund Suenens, 951, letter of December 26, 1962, in which he communicates that the Chilean episcopate is also preparing a schema with, among others, the cooperation of the Belgians J. Comblin [Cf. Fund Suenens, 995] and F. Hofmans.
151. Fund Suenens, 952: around Christmas Day Renard asks for more attention to be paid to the priests in the new *De ecclesia*.
152. Fund Suenens, 744 (December 16, 1962) and 745 (January 7, 1963).
153. Fund Suenens, 966-967; also TREFFLER (ed.), *Julius Kardinal Döpfner. Briefe und Notizen* (n. 9), pp. 318-319.
154. Fund Suenens, 968-974.
155. Fund Suenens, 975.

With regard to the permanent diaconate, Suenens is approached both by Spellman, who was opposed, and by J. Hornef, an ardent advocate[156].

b. Suenens thoroughly prepares the first meeting of the Coordinating Commission (which took place January 21-27, 1963). His first assistant was Prof. G. Thils, a priest of his diocese and someone with whom Suenens appears to have been very close to[157]. Thils' archives demonstrate that he took this task very seriously:

- On January 5, R. Schutz and M. Thurian send some remarks on *De ecclesia* and *De beata* to Thils[158].
- There is a letter from F. Thijssen, consultor at the Secretariat for the Unity, who asks that section two (of the text Philips) be allowed to begin with *De populo Dei seu de laicis* instead of with *De hierarchia*. And Thijssen remarks: "Please remember that *Populus Dei* also includes the hierarchy". He also asks that he not make a separate chapter of *De religiosis*[159].
- On January 11, 1963, R. Laurentin writes to Thils in order to encourage him to integrate the schema on Mary in *De ecclesia*[160], something he had previously mentioned to Suenens. Later, on January 17, 1963, Laurentin sends Suenens a text proposal which integrates *De beata* in *De ecclesia*[161]. Laurentin sent this text on demand of Thils[162].
- A long note of nine pages by Congar[163], dated January 9, 1963, on *De ecclesia*. This note was probably presented by Congar to Thils during his visit to Louvain on January 12 and 13, 1963.
- On January 13, 1963, Thils organized a meeting at Philips' home together with Msgr. De Smedt and Congar. There they introduce a number of corrections to the schema Philips[164]. On January 14,

---

156. Fund Suenens, 1042-1043.

157. It is clear that Suenens was closer with Thils than he was with, e.g., Philips. It was typical for this privileged relationship with Thils, that Suenens, at least until March of 1963, spoke of the text as 'Philips-Thils' when referring to the new schema *De ecclesia* and that there is also mention in the Fonds Léger of a 'Schéma Suenens' (Fund Léger, 706-711) as distinguished from a schema Philips, although the schema Suenens and the schema Philips were actually one and the same. As of February/March of 1963, Prignon became Suenens' new confidant and 'ghostwriter'.

158. Fund Thils, 313.

159. Fund Thils, 413.

160. Fund Thils, 321.

161. Fund Suenens, 1060-1061.

162. Cf. letter from Thils to Laurentin, 14.1.1963, in Fund Laurentin, 847.

163. Fund Thils, 57.

164. Philips writes: "On Sunday, January 13, I received an unexpected visit – arranged by Prof. Thils – from Msgr. De Smedt, P. Congar and Prof. Thils himself. They came to

1963, Thils already reports in writing on this meeting to Suenens[165].

Thils prepares a text for Suenens that is designed to help him with the relation he must make at the next meeting of the Coordinating Commission[166]. The final text is four (typed) pages in length[167] and consists of three parts:

Primo: What does the Council expect with regard to these matters? The following topics need to be treated:

- The link between Vatican I and II.
- The collegiality of the bishops, something which is also important to the bishops' conferences.
- The importance of the episcopate.
- The link between the episcopate and the college of priests.
- The responsibilities of the lay persons in the Church need to be confirmed.

Secundo: What to think about the schema drafted during the preparatory period?

- The schema was completely rejected (chaotic, a theological tract instead of a Council document, not ecumenical, too juridical, and, not least, it hardly mentioned collegiality).
- Two full pages of criticism are written on the preparatory text with regard to the collegiality of the bishops: the authority of the college is also exercised outside the ecumenical Council, and is not a papal

propose a number of corrections with regard to my first Latin schema-version, a text that had already been somewhat ameliorated in the French version. I do not know who took this initiative, nor if it will have any effect, yet I have meticulously noted the text corrections and have sent them to the cardinal [cf. Fund Suenens, 956-957], who has not responded" (SCHELKENS [ed.], *Carnets conciliaires de Mgr. Gérard Philips* [n. 47], Cahier XI, p. 10).

Congar writes: "Le chanoine Thils m'ayant invité à Louvain, j'ai pensé, connaissant la tâche confiée au cardinal Suenens et voyant bien qu'il s'agissait de travailler finalement pour lui, devoir répondre à cette invitation. Je suis donc allé à Louvain le 12 janvier soir et la journée du 13. En réalité il s'agissait (1) d'arrêter avec Mgr De Smedt la ligne ecclésiologique (le plan) que défendrait le Secrétariat, qui sera appelé tôt ou tard, d'une façon ou d'une autre, à intervenir dans le *De ecclesia*; (2) d'arrêter un plan que le cardinal Suenens défendra; (3) d'indiquer à Mgr Philips un certain nombre d'améliorations souhaitables dans son *De ecclesia* révisé. Le cardinal Suenens est très formellement d'avis de ré-insérer le *De beata virgine* dans le *De ecclesia*" (CONGAR, *Mon journal du Concile* [n. 9], Vol. I, p. 318).

165. Fund Suenens, 955 and 819.
166. Fund Suenens, 819-820.
167. Fund Suenens, 822 and *AS* V/1, pp. 90-96.

delegation[168]; the declaration of Vatican I on the infallibility of the Pope (*ex sese et non ex consensu ecclesiae*) deserves a good explanation.

Tertio: How should the schema be rewritten?
Here the four chapters as developed in the project Philips are presented.

The discussion on *De ecclesia* in the Coordinating Commission took place on January 23, 1963[169]. Cicognani believed that Suenens' criticism of the prepared schemata was exaggerated. He wanted to preserve the material in the prepared schemata as much as possible[170]. In response, Suenens cleverly noted that his proposal used 60% of the material prepared by the *Commissio theologica praeparatoria*.

Cicognani offered a warning regarding the '*episcopalismo*', to which Suenens replied that Christ appointed not only Peter but *all* the apostles to the task of evangelizing the world. Liénart supported Suenens, while Spellman sided with Cicognani. Urbani is in favour of a doctrine on the episcopate, but advocates caution: the emphasis on collegiality should neither be too strong, nor denied altogether. Confalonieri supports Suenens' proposal for the solemn confirmation of collegiality, but insists on precision and a full explication of some of the items. Döpfner also agrees with the project Suenens; for him, the episcopate is the most important and most essential subject of the Council. It is absolutely necessary to distinguish between the "exercitium" of the power of the bishops and the internal structure of the apostolic college.

On January 24, the discussion is briefly continued. Suenens specified that he did not want to go into too much detail, but that the analysis and the solution of the various problems needed to be left to the Doctrinal Commission. Döpfner desired that the religious not be treated in a separate chapter and that *De beata* be integrated into *De ecclesia*. The latter point, however, was disputed by Cicognani. Finally, Suenens was given a mandate to reform the schema according to the suggestions that had been made[171].

---

168. This passage is typical for Thils, who was thoroughly acquainted with the ecclesiological discussions at Vaticanum I.

169. Cf. *Processus verbalis*, AS V/1, pp. 97-100.

170. Even as late as February 21, Cicognani calls Tromp to inform him that the Pope wants things to move along quickly and that consequently no new schema *De ecclesia* is to be drafted, but that the old one should be followed as closely as possible (*Diarium* Tromp, IV, February 21, 1963, Archivio Segreto Vaticano [ASV], Conc.Vat. II, 790).

171. *Processus verbalis*, January 24, 1963, AS V/1, p. 106. Suenens had also a meeting with card. Browne in these days and he writes to Döpfner on January 28, 1963 "qu'il a

c. This meeting of the Coordinating Commission is followed by a period of intense activity in view of the upcoming meeting of the Doctrinal Commission from February 21 till March 13, 1963. On January 30, 1963, Cicognani, as President of the Coordinating Commission, informs the Doctrinal Commission[172] about the document Suenens and requests that the new text should be handed in to the Coordinating Commission on March 10[173]. This announcement confirms the failure of the old schema and the beginning of the battle over a new schema. Ottaviani, aware of the danger, approaches Parente in order to draft a new text[174]. In the meantime Larraín forwards the Chilean schema to Suenens[175] and on January 30 Philips reports to Suenens about a meeting of German theologians in Mainz on January 26 and 27[176].

On February 1, Philips sends Suenens a copy of a letter by Daniélou (Daniélou opposes the German schema of Grillmeier and claims that the French bishops have found inspiration in the schema Philips) with the question what he should reply[177]. On February 8, Cardinal Léger informs Suenens in writing that he will be present at the meeting of the Doctrinal Commission in February and asks him who is his spokesperson in Rome. Suenens refers him to Prignon[178].

On February 9, Prignon advises Suenens against coming to Rome:

> Certains ici, même ou surtout parmi vos confrères, ne voient pas d'un œil toujours égal ni la grande influence que vous avez exercée sur la marche du concile, ni l'importance majorée des charges qui vous ont été confiées, ni les contacts prolongés que vous eûtes avec vous devinez qui [sic][179].

---

eu une excellente entrevue avec le Cardinal Browne qui a très bien accepté nos points de vue" (Cf. TREFFLER [ed.], *Julius Kardinal Döpfner. Briefe und Notizen* [n. 9], p. 357).

172. Fund Suenens, 847 and 850.

173. At that time, the Coordinating Commission still carried a great deal of weight with regard to the Council (although this was possibly due to John XXIII's illness). As of September 1963, this authority is largely taken over by the four moderators. As of the second intersession, Paul VI takes more and more control, assisted by the General Secretariat of the Council and the Secretariat of State.

174. In this respect Prignon writes to Suenens on February 9, 1963: "Tromp et Gagnebet sont tout de même assez désorientés. Ils ne savent pas trop comment rédiger, en conservant l'essentiel de l'ancien schéma, sans s'exposer à un nouveau refus du Concile" (Fund Suenens, 753).

175. Fund Suenens, 958-960.

176. Fund Suenens, 961-962, to which Philips receives no reply; cf. SCHELKENS (ed.), *Carnets conciliaires de Mgr. Gérard Philips* (n. 47), Cahier XI, p. 11.

177. Fund Suenens, 963-964.

178. Fund Suenens, 976-980.

179. Fund Suenens, 753. This probably refers to John XXIII.

And he adds:

> Ne serait-il pas expédient d'avoir alors un schéma de rechange tout préparé (le schéma Philips retouché) et qu'on sera peut-être content d'adopter pour sortir de l'impasse?

From this letter of Prignon it is also evident that Thils and Prignon had met shortly before with Cardinal Browne, whose views on collegiality failed to set their minds at ease. Suenens had already requested to Browne to appoint Prignon to be a *peritus*.

On February 11, both Msgr. Le Cordier and Msgr. Charue sent a text to Suenens concerning *De ecclesia*[180]. This step was also taken by H.M. Féret, Cardinal Doi and Msgr. Mannix[181]. On February 11 and 24, respectively, Msgr. Piérard and Msgr. Guerry send Suenens notes with regard to the issue of collegiality[182]. On February 13, Cardinal Bea sent a draft of chapter I of *De ecclesia* as well as the remarks of the 'Faith and Order' Commission, drawn up by L. Vischer (on January 18, 1963)[183]. On February 15, Suenens sends a letter to Prignon asking him to contact Cardinal Léger about the *De ecclesia* and he adds:

> Je suis prêt à venir à Rome dès que la chose sera utile, mais j'attends une indication précise pour ne pas 'interférer' si ce n'est pas nécessaire[184].

In the meantime, Thils called Philips to inform him that both of them are expected by the cardinal at Malines on February 18. At that meeting, Philips is informed that he is expected to go to Rome in order to attend the proceedings of the Doctrinal Commission, "yet the indications remain vague"[185]. And on February 20, Philips writes to Suenens that he will leave for Rome on February 22 and he adds: "I will gladly receive any of your specifications, and I will keep you informed of the discussions in Rome…"[186]. On February 19, Suenens sends a letter to John XXIII and a '*Note sur les Travaux du Concile*', in which he recommends – regarding *De ecclesia* – a text drafted by a group of Belgian, French and German theologians [in fact this was the schema Philips, which, from the beginning, had been drawn up in cooperation with a group of international theologians].

---

180. Fund Suenens, 763, 981. Charue writes a.o.: "Il me sera précieux de savoir si je suis en parfaite communion d'idées avec vous dans ces pages".
181. Fund Suenens, 984-986, 988-990, 991-993.
182. Fund Suenens, 1035-1037, 1033-1034.
183. Fund Suenens, 1025-1029.
184. Fund Prignon, 284.
185. SCHELKENS (ed.), *Carnets conciliaires de Mgr. Gérard Philips* (n. 47), Cahier XI, p. 11.
186. Fund Suenens, 987.

Also on February 19, Suenens sends a letter to Ottaviani requesting that he appoints Prignon as *peritus*. On February 25, Ottaviani replied that he had forwarded this request with a recommendation to Felici. At the same time he informs Suenens that on February 21 the Doctrinal Commission had appointed a sub-commission of seven bishops to work on *De ecclesia*[187].

d. As early as February 25, Charue informs Suenens in detail about the proceedings of the Doctrinal Commission and of 'the Seven'[188]. He writes:

> Nous allons tâcher de faire admettre le schéma de Mgr Philips ... Il fut décidé hier soir qu'on rappellerait les directives de Votre Éminence pour la succession des chapitres, directives qui correspondent d'ailleurs, au schéma Philips[189].

On Tuesday, February 26, 'the Seven' choose the schema Philips (and Charue informs Suenens[190]). This choice is confirmed by the Doctrinal Commission on March 5, but not without resistance from Ottaviani, something that is made clear by a new letter from Charue[191]. This marks the final start of the new *De ecclesia*.

187. Fund Suenens, 768-770.
188. Cf. DECLERCK, *Le rôle joué* (n. 40), pp. 454-455.
189. Fund Suenens, 995.
190. On February 27, Charue gladly informed Suenens: "Pendant ce temps, nous avons commencé notre travail pour un nouveau schéma *de Ecclesia*. Nous sommes parvenus à faire choisir le texte Philips comme texte de base et à faire mettre Mgr Philips à la tête d'un groupe de *periti* pour faire le travail. Chacun des sept évêques pouvait choisir un *peritus* ... J'avais évidemment choisi Mgr Philips, mais comme Mgr Schröffer se référait aussi au P. Rahner [Rahner had already been selected by König], je lui ai demandé de présenter le chan. Thils, ce qu'il a accepté. Espérons que l'on n'entravera pas leur travail!!!" (Fund Suenens, 996).
191. On March 4, 1963, Charue writes to Suenens: "Pendant ce temps, les *periti* de Mgr Philips, celui-ci en tout premier lieu, travaillent intensément. Le P. Congar étant arrivé, le P. Daniélou lui a cédé la place pour s'occuper quant à lui d'autres commissions. C'est fort heureux. Déjà le premier chapitre a été accepté par la sous-commission des évêques et l'on prépare le chapitre 2. Pourvu qu'il n'y ait pas des manœuvres d'à côté". And he continues on March 5 before the evening meeting of the Doctrinal Commission: "Ce soir, la commission *de Fide* doit aborder l'examen du *de Ecclesia*. Le card. Ottaviani annonçait hier qu'on commencerait par décider quel texte de base on choisirait. Qu'est-ce que cela signifie? La sous-commission du Card. Browne avait eu la mission de faire ce choix. Va-t-on remettre cette décision en question? Il semble bien que le Card. Ottaviani est à tout le moins étonné que l'on n'a pas choisi le texte de Mgr Parente et celui-ci ne vient pas aux réunions de notre sous-commission. Malgré tout, je crois que Mgr Parente accepte sincèrement la préférence donnée au schéma Philips, mais il lui est délicat d'intervenir. Quoi qu'il en soit, nous nous trouvons de nouveau devant une inconnue et un écueil ... Quel accueil va-t-on faire ce soir au texte de Mgr Philips? J'ai déjà noté une parole du Card. Ottaviani. Le Card. Léger l'entendait dire au Card. Ruffini: que c'était de la poésie! Évidemment, ce n'est pas un texte purement juridique et l'auteur s'est efforcé de mettre un peu de souffle dans son exposé. Il n'empêche, d'ailleurs, que l'impression générale est

Prignon keeps Suenens informed in great detail[192]: on March 8-10 he writes him a letter of nine pages. He recounts the course of the debates in the commission on the first and the second chapter of *De ecclesia*. The third chapter (*De laicis*) was drafted by Schauf. *De beata* had not yet been discussed. He also mentions several attempts by Ottaviani to delay matters and a visit by Philips to Cardinal Browne to discuss collegiality ("Le cardinal lui dit avoir reçu les mémoires de Thils mais n'être pas encore convaincu ... Mgr Philips est resté plus d'une heure chez le cardinal Browne et semble l'avoir quelque peu ébranlé"). He received Léger on Thursday evening of March 7. Léger had asked Prignon to keep Suenens informed and Prignon had been able to convince Léger to defer his departure, which had been planned for Sunday. He has also invited him to lunch along with Garrone, McGrath, Schröffer and a number of *periti* on March 11. He continues:

> Le cardinal Léger avait encore téléphoné ce matin pour demander si vous n'alliez pas venir. Sincèrement, Éminence, et ayant pris l'avis des évêques, je crois que, du point de vue tactique, votre venue actuelle serait prématurée. Aucun des autres membres de la commission de coordination n'est venu et l'autre parti vous accuserait de vouloir faire pression. Otto [Ottaviani] ne manquerait pas de dire que vous outrepassez vos pouvoirs en voulant intervenir directement dans la discussion du fond. De toutes façons, je reste attentif et si c'était nécessaire, je vous téléphone ou envoie un télégramme[193].

Suenens apparently keeps a close eye on the goings-on and is ready to commit himself. Even Msgr. Capovilla, secretary to John XXIII, writes to Suenens on March 2 that it does not appear necessary for him to come to Rome early [i.e., before the meeting of the Coordinating Commission on March 25][194].

Finally, on March 14, Charue is able to inform Suenens of the success of this session of the Doctrinal Commission:

> ... tout s'est terminé hier soir d'une façon qu'on peut dire inespérée. On a entendu le Cardinal Ottaviani remercier Mgr Philips et faire de lui, aux applaudissements unanimes, le plus grand éloge. Tout arrive![195]

---

que les membres de la Commission seront en nette majorité pour le schéma de Mgr Philips. Espérons" (Fund Suenens, 1001).

192. The Suenens' archive contains several drafts of chapters I, II and III that date as far back as the end of February/beginning of March and which were probably sent to Suenens by Prignon. Cf. Fund Suenens, 1020-1024, 1031-1032 and 1049. A note by Lucien Cerfaux 'Du Règne de Dieu à l'Église' is also added (Fund Suenens, 1030).

193. Fund Suenens, 754.

194. Fund Suenens, 3024.

195. Fund Suenens, 1002.

Contrary to all expectations, the first two chapters of the new *De eccle-sia* are ready. Chapters III and IV are to be discussed in May. This means that Suenens was able to prepare his report for the Coordinating Commission of March 25-29 in a relatively relaxed state of mind.

e. On March 23, Philips sends Suenens the new official text of chapter I and II of *De ecclesia*. He still has to add the notes and the comments and he needs to work on chapter III *De laicis*. He promises Suenens that he will send him some suggestions in the near future for the discussion [in the Coordinating Commission][196].

On March 28, the text of the new *De ecclesia* is distributed at the meeting of the Coordinating Commission[197]. It is also at this meeting that Suenens presents his *Relatio*[198] drafted by Prignon[199]. He recommends the acceptance of the first two chapters with only one remark regarding chapter II (*De constitutione hierarchica ecclesiae*): the chapter mentions the Pope (at least 24 times!) each time the bishops' college is mentioned. It would be better to state at the beginning: "collegium episcoporum quod semel pro semper intelligitur cum et sub successore Petri"[200]. For chapter III (not yet ready) he expresses the wish that it would be examined not only by the Doctrinal Commission and the Commission on the Lay Apostolate, but also by the Secretariat for the Unity which drafted a document *De sacerdotio fidelium et de officiis laicorum*[201]. For chapter IV on the religious, he expresses the wish that the text be integrated into a broader context, namely *De Sanctitate in ecclesia*[202]. Ottaviani and Tromp are present at the meeting on March 28, and Tromp asks if it would be desirable to decide whether or not to bring together the dogmatic parts of *De religiosis* and *De laicis* with the disciplinary aspect, to which Suenens replies that the dogmatic parts need to be treated separately. Next Spellman noted his objections to the permanent diaconate and was supported in this by Ottaviani. Suenens answered him and was, in turn, supported

---

196. Fund Suenens, 1003-1004.
197. *AS* V/1, pp. 451-462.
198. *AS* V/1, pp. 463-464.
199. Fund Suenens, 880-881, 883.
200. Msgr. De Keyzer, auxiliary bishop of Bruges, with an allusion to the Portiuncula-indulgence, had at the time jokingly remarked, that it would be best to use the formula 'toties quoties'.
201. Drafted by the Subcommissio IV of the Secretariat for Christian Unity, in which Msgr. De Smedt played an important part, cf., *inter alia*, Fund De Smedt, 175, 187, 188.
202. This proposition was defended persistently, but without ultimate success, by Msgr. Charue in the Doctrinal Commission. Cf. C. TROISFONTAINES, *Introduction*, in DECLERCK – SOETENS (eds.), *Carnets conciliaires de l'évêque de Namur A.-M. Charue* (n. 8), pp. 9, 11, 15 and 22.

by Confalonieri and Döpfner. The discussion was not resumed on the next day due to the visit of John XXIII. Felici was commissioned to send chapters I and II to the Council Fathers[203].

Also worth mentioning is a letter from Dossetti to Suenens on March 28 in which he speaks of the problem of '*De membris ecclesiae*' and promises Suenens a text about the involvement of the bishops in universal ecclesiastical jurisdiction[204]. And on April 8, Döpfner writes a letter to Suenens with a suggestion for the chapter, promoted by Larraona, '*De ecclesiae peregrinantis cum ecclesia triumphante relatione ac de cultu sanctorum*'[205].

f. Chapters III and IV are finished at the meeting of the Doctrinal Commission on May 15-31. Suenens receives several text drafts and Thils, who was closely connected with the work on chapter IV *De religiosis*, kept Suenens well informed regarding all the new developments[206].

In the meantime, on April 4, the ever-unquiet Léger warned Suenens about new delays and proposed to replace Tromp with Philips as secretary of the Doctrinal Commission. Suenens replies to Léger that he will warn Philips with regard to these dangers. He is also of the opinion that the sense of the collegiality of the bishops needs be to specified further: the present text is acceptable as a compromise, but needs to be further developed[207].

On May 28, Léger writes a new letter to Suenens in which he reports on the meeting of the Doctrinal Commission which took place on May 15-31 and which he had left prematurely. He mentions the editing of chapter III and IV and praises Philips ("l'un des plus grands théologiens dans l'Église"). He also wants to draw Suenens' attention to the issue of religious freedom[208].

Everything was ready for the meeting of the Coordinating Commission on June 4: due to the death of John XXIII on June 3, however, the meeting was postponed.

203. Cf. *Processus verbalis*, AS V/1, pp. 477-481.
204. Fund Prignon, 292.
205. Cf. TREFFLER (ed.), *Julius Kardinal Döpfner. Briefe und Notizen* (n. 9), p. 404.
206. Fund Suenens, 1056-1057.
207. Fund Suenens, 1005-1006.
208. Fund Suenens, 1007. Léger does not mince words: he describes an inquiry of the Holy Office with regard to the instruction in the Holy Scriptures as: "… des procédés de gestapo qu'il faut dénoncer avant qu'ils ne produisent leurs effets pernicieux". Regarding the atmosphere in Rome he writes: "Je dois vous avouer que l'atmosphère de Rome est très lourde à l'heure actuelle. On a l'impression d'une 'fin de règne'. Les résultats des élections italiennes ont profondément divisé l'Épiscopat. On ne se gêne pas pour souhaiter la disparition de celui qui est, pour plusieurs, considéré comme le grand responsable de cette évolution vers la gauche" [this refers to John XXIII].

g. After the election of Paul VI, the proceedings of the Council are resumed without delay. The Coordinating Commission meets on July 3 and 4 in Rome. Suenens, using a text drafted by Prignon, reports briefly on the status of *De ecclesia*[209]. When Suenens asks him if he has any suggestions for fundamental changes to the text, Prignon suggests the division of chapter III *De populo Dei et de laicis* in two parts: *De populo Dei* and *De laicis*. His main suggestion is to place the chapter *De populo Dei* before chapter II on the hierarchy[210]. Although Suenens, in the meeting on July 4, after a short discussion in the presence of Cardinal Browne and P. Tromp, easily obtained the approval of the Coordinating Commission[211] for this important change (later justifiably referred to as "the Copernican revolution of the schema"[212]), the battle was far from finished. Somewhat surprisingly Döpfner, afterwards, resisted to this change. He had already written to Suenens on July 9[213] in order to indicate that, in principle, he was not against this inversion, but that he felt that it was inopportune given that it might cause a delay in the process of reviewing *De ecclesia* during the second session. Döpfner was fair enough to supply Suenens with a copy of his letter to Cicognani[214], in which he points out that the Coordinating Commission has only recommended this inversion to the Doctrinal Commission without imposing it.

209. For this report cf. Fund Suenens, 898 and *AS* V/1, p. 594. He approves of the new editing of chapter III and IV.

210. Suenens writes: "Praepositi enim Ecclesiae sunt et ipsi membra populi atque a Domino constituuntur ut Populo suo inserviant". And he concludes: "Orientatio pastoralis et oecumenica Concilii commendat hanc modificationem". This idea had indeed been suggested in the circles of the Secretariat for the Unity (cf. e.g. the letter from Thijssen to Thils and the letter from Bea to Döpfner on January 23, 1963: "In Sectio II [of the text Philips, by Bea indicated as the text De Smedt] wäre m.E. nicht an erster Stelle die Hierarchie zu setzen, sondern die 'Fideles', und zwar nicht nur die 'laici', sondern das ganze Kirchenvolk" [Fund Döpfner, 116, or Treffler (ed.) *Julius Kardinal Döpfner. Briefe und Notizen* (n. 9), p. 352]. Still the credit for suggesting this at a crucial moment must go to Prignon.

211. See *AS* V/1, p. 635, *Processus verbalis*: "La seconda parte dello schema *De Ecclesia* viene perciò approvata e dato mandato alla Segreteria di aggiungere una nota al testo indicante la proposta della nuova divisione della materia secondo l'indicazione dell'Em.mo Suenens. Anche l'Em.mo Card. Browne, vice-Presidente della Comm. Teologica, e P. Tromp, Segretario, sono consenzienti, non avanzando alcuna difficoltà alla approvazione del testo ed alla presentazione del medesimo al Concilio con la divisione della materia indicata dall'Em.mo Card. Suenens".

212. Cf. Suenens, *Souvenirs et espérances* (n. 11), pp. 114-115, in which Suenens mistakenly situates the origin of this change during an audience of the moderators with the Pope. It is however true that this change encountered a lot of resistance during the second session and that Suenens defended this 'nova ordinatio capitum' to Paul VI (cf. infra).

213. Fund Suenens, 901.

214. Fund Suenens, 902.

This change became the cause of many discussions during the second session.

Suenens, however, carried on; Prignon was charged with imparting this "decision" to Msgr. Philips. And because Prignon was aware of the enormous amount of work this was going to entail for Philips, he appealed to Msgr. Cerfaux, a faithful friend of Philips, to carry the message[215]. On July 25, from his holiday residence in Trégastel (Brittany), Prignon reported to Suenens regarding his mission. He also asked, yet again, if the Coordinating Commission really 'decided' on this[216]. Thils, always alert, submitted prepared suggestions to Philips on July 29[217]. On August 2, 1963, the Belgian bishops met at Malines along with a few *periti* in order to discuss the Council texts. During that meeting Philips made a number of important remarks on *De ecclesia*[218]. On August 4, 1963, Suenens, in answer to a letter written to him by Döpfner on July 21[219], says:

> Nos théologiens, qui ont élaboré avec le P. Rahner et Congar le *De Ecclesia* ont un projet montrant comment faire le travail [of the new *ordinatio capitum*]: Mgr Musty qui viendra à votre Conférence [meeting of the German-speaking bishops in Fulda on August 26-27, 1963] pourra vous renseigner plus en détail[220].

215. Cf. Bande magnétique Prignon IV.

216. Letter from Prignon to Suenens (Fund Suenens, 755) in which Prignon writes: "Pour le schéma *De Ecclesia*, en vue de la réunion de Malines [meeting of the Belgian bishops on August 2, 1963], nous devons prévoir une petite difficulté, d'ordre psychologique. Après avoir tant travaillé au schéma, Mgr Philips éprouvera peut-être quelque peine à se rallier à un nouveau remaniement. J'ai demandé à Mgr Cerfaux de préparer le terrain et éventuellement de prendre la parole sur ce point à la réunion. Je lui ai demandé aussi un plan détaillé du contenu des chapitres retouchés. Mgr Charue, Mgr Cerfaux et Mr Thils ont accepté d'enthousiasme cette nouvelle présentation. Cependant, nous restons tous incertains sur le mode de présentation au Concile de cette nouvelle rédaction. La Commission de coordination a-t-elle pris une décision à ce sujet?".

217. Fund Philips, 785. The document in Fund Philips, 787 also demonstrates that Thils cooperated with Philips on this new text.

218. Fund Suenens, 685-688.

219. Fund Suenens, 784-786.

220. Fund Döpfner, 689. TREFFLER (ed.), *Julius Kardinal Döpfner. Briefe und Notizen* (n. 9), pp. 492-493. Suenens includes this interesting suggestion in his letter: "Pour ma part, je souhaiterais qu'à une 3ᵉ session on puisse élire à nouveau les membres: on pourrait ainsi dégager des noms plus qualifiés peut-être; cela permettrait au pape de nommer des évêques 'dans sa ligne', et enfin cela permettrait de demander que les présidents et secrétaires de chaque commission puissent être choisis par la commission elle-même. Il est d'usage dans les assemblées internationales que les commissions soient changées chaque année". It is known that at the end of the second session five members were added to the commissions and that the commissions elected a 2d vice-president and a deputy secretary. This document shows that at that time Suenens was still under the impression that the Pope was 'dans sa ligne'.

On September 10, Philips is able to send a '*nova ordinatio capitum*'[221] to Suenens, via R. Ceuppens. This document is forwarded by Suenens to Cardinal Browne on September 16, 1963[222], who has it copied for the members of the Doctrinal Commission on September 28, 1963[223]. As the newly appointed moderator, Suenens has to defend his new '*ordinatio*' during the second session.

Suenens also remains active with regard to the schema *De Beata*. On July 15, he receives a letter from Laurentin with a note on the schema of May of 1963; Balić also sends him notes in this respect[224]. Suenens took the initiative to ask Édouard Dhanis, S.J. for a new text. This was apparently done without the knowledge of Philips, even though Philips had a reputation as a Mariologist[225]. On August 29, Prignon writes to Suenens that Dhanis will work during the next 15 days on this text and that he also desires the integration of *De beata* into the schema *De ecclesia*, since this would allow for a considerable reduction in the length of the text. Prignon suggests that this decision might be put to the Coordinating Commission[226]. On September 18, Dhanis is able to submit his text to Suenens. At the same time, he suggests that the text be reviewed by Laurentin, Philips and Adema[227].

During this first intersession, it is clear that Suenens took his responsibility as *relator* for *De ecclesia* seriously. Many of the episcopates and Council Fathers put their hope in him; he proceeded in very politically-astute manner. He called upon a number of capable collaborators (Philips, Thils, Charue, Prignon, Moeller, Laurentin, Dhanis) and kept close track of all developments[228]. In addition to being personally dedicated to the

---

221. Fund Suenens, 1008-1009.

222. Fund Suenens, 1010.

223. Fund Philips, 792. This official document of the commission (CFM 14/63) is entitled "Nova ordinatio capitum (ab E. Card. Suenens)". This inversion is regarded as a proposal made by Suenens and not as a 'decision' of the Coordinating Commission.

224. Fund Suenens, 1062-1064

225. Cf. Letter from Dhanis to J. Janssens, Praepositus generalis s.j., August 20, 1963: "Le Cardinal Suenens me demande de faire, pour son usage personnel, et à toutes fins utiles un nouveau schème sur la mariologie: plus bref, dépourvu de polémique, clair mais œcuménique par son ton et ses explications. C'est un secret (que dirait le P. Tromp?). Mais je vais me mettre à la besogne pour servir l'Église et la Sainte Vierge. Je me propose de vous envoyer une copie de ce travail, quand il sera achevé" (Arch. Pontificia Universitas Gregoriana, Fund Dhanis, 4).

226. Fund Suenens, 756.

227. Fund Suenens, 1065-1066.

228. This caused irritation in Curial circles. On May 18, 1963, L. Declerck notes: "Tromp is angry with Msgr. Prignon; [he] has already told three people that Prignon phones Suenens every day. He no longer wishes Prignon good day" (Notes L. Declerck, May 18, 1963, Fund Prignon, 512).

task, he was prepared to personally intervene. Moreover, because he was convinced of the Pope's support, he was not afraid of manipulating certain decisions of the commissions without worrying about juridical guarantees. This is also the period in which his prestige was at its zenith in Rome: John XXIII charged him with three important schemata (the Church, the Church in the World, and *De beata*); he visited New York in May of 1963 to present the encyclical *Pacem in terris* to U Thant, the Secretary-General of the UN; his book, *The Nun in the World*, which received a fair amount of media attention, was published simultaneously in several languages; and in the June conclave he was tapped as a possible non-Italian candidate by several newspapers; he appeared at the window of the office of the new Pope during the angelus on June 23, 1963; and, finally, he was appointed moderator in September of 1963.

At the same time it is obvious that his theological interest in a number of the text's crucial points had increased (e.g., collegiality, sacramentality, ecumenical dimension) and had become more specific. Moeller correctly remarks in his diary at the beginning of the second session: "Suenens a évolué. Il commence à comprendre les problèmes théologiques. Il est maintenant un des grands hommes de l'Église au 20e siècle"[229]. Suenens only sticks to his own path with regard to Mariology, away from the '*squadra belga*'.

4. IIᵃ Sessio

The great ecclesiological debate takes place during the second session. Suenens' influence is most obvious in three areas: the battle for the new place of the chapter *De populo Dei*, his role in the posing of the five *Propositiones*, and his influence on the debate via several key speeches.

a. De populo Dei

Although the Coordinating Commission had agreed to the new place of this chapter and although Philips had finished his work, it was still up to the Doctrinal Commission to make these changes official. Given that the Pope himself had hesitated, this could not and, indeed, did not happen without a struggle. On October 2, the matter was discussed at the

229. Journal Moeller, Carnet 16, October 4, 1963. The same day Moeller also notes the following: "Le cardinal Suenens, il y a six mois, se méfiait des dominicains français. Quand Prignon, en janvier, à la commission de coordination a dit à Suenens: 'Incroyable qu'on fasse un schéma sur l'Église, et qu'on ne fasse pas venir Congar', le cardinal répond: 'Pourquoi?' 'Mais', répond Prignon, 'parce qu'il a consacré toute sa vie à ce traité'. Depuis [lors] Suenens a apprécié Congar…".

meeting of the Doctrinal Commission. The discussion was tense; Parente again asked whether the matter had been imposed by the Coordinating Commission or there might still be room for discussion[230]. The meeting ended without a clear decision. Prignon immediately warned Suenens. He prepared a note[231], which Suenens took to the moderators' papal audience on October 10. On October 4, Prignon writes to Suenens that Msgr. Elchinger, at a meeting of French, Dutch, Austrian and German bishops, announced that the new division of the text into five chapters had been more or less decided. Elchinger did not mention his source[232]. On October 6, Moeller was told that Suenens informed Prignon that the Pope did not want to impose the new division, but, instead, wanted the Doctrinal Commission to formulate the request. If it was refused by the Commission the matter would have to be submitted to the Council Fathers[233]. On October 9, a new meeting of the Doctrinal Commission took place. This time a broad majority votes in favor of the new chapter (20 for; 4 against) and in favour of the title *De populo Dei* (15 for)[234]. That same day Prignon writes a 'Note sur les décisions de la Commission De Fide'[235] for Suenens. Moeller also drafts a note for Suenens[236] on October 10.

On that same day, Ottaviani submitted the matter to the moderators[237]. On October 14, Agagianian answered Ottaviani that the majority of the Commission was already sufficient to approve the new *ordinatio* and that all that was needed was the endorsement of the Pope, something which

---

230. CONGAR, *Mon journal du Concile* (n. 9), Vol. I, October 2, 1963, p. 424: "Il semble que le P. Tromp et même le cardinal Ottaviani veulent prendre un long temps et peut-être noyer le projet ... Parente soulève la question préliminaire ... sommes-nous obligés?".

231. Fund Suenens, 1388: "Note à propos de la structure du Schéma *de Ecclesia* à la suite de la réunion de la commission de la foi". Prignon writes a.o. to the cardinal: "Avant le commencement des travaux [of the Doctrinal Commission on October 2, 1963] s'est posée la question préjudicielle: la nouvelle division en 5 chapitres est-elle imposée ou conseillée par la commission de coordination? Mgr Parente, surtout, a insisté pour qu'on ait une réponse avant de continuer les travaux ... Le texte qui a été répandu par le secrétariat [of the Doctrinal Commission] porte la mention du cardinal Suenens. Il y a donc équivoque: d'après cette indication, il semble que ce soit vous qui proposiez *motu proprio* ce texte à la discussion ... Dans l'attitude de plusieurs membres de la commission, italiens et l'un ou l'autre français, il entre une part de mauvaise humeur pour une décision prise *inconsulta commissione theologica*".

232. Fund Suenens, 1375. Moeller confirms this (Journal Moeller, Carnet 16, October 4, 1963).

233. Journal Moeller, Carnet 16, October 6, 1963.

234. CONGAR, *Mon journal du Concile* (n. 9), Vol. I, October 9, 1963, p. 450; Fund Prignon, 512, 10.10.1963.

235. Fund Suenens, 1470.

236. 'Signification pastorale du nouveau chapitre II, De Populo Dei'. Cf. Fund Suenens, 1472-1473.

237. Letter from Ottaviani to Agagianian, October 10, 1963, *AS* VI/2, p. 353.

had already been given[238] (probably at the audience on October 10). But, on October 12, Moeller learns that Tromp, in spite of the vote in the Commission on October 9, still wanted to place *De hierarchia* before *De populo Dei*[239]. Prignon learned the same thing from Philips. Tromp claimed that the pope wished for the hierarchy to be dealt with first and that this would be discussed at the meeting of the Doctrinal Commission on October 15. Prignon immediately warned Suenens, a move which allowed this to be formally denied. On Sunday October 13, Prignon spoke with Suenens by telephone, who, during a beatification that same afternoon, saw Ottaviani and told him that *De populo Dei* will be placed before the hierarchy. In fact, the Moderators met with the pope after Ottaviani's audience[240]. During the meeting of the Doctrinal Commission on October 15, Ottaviani announced that the Pope had approved the new chapter *De populo Dei*, as proposed by the Doctrinal Committee, but that he would prefer to see *De hierarchia* placed before *De populo Dei*. After a discussion, Ottaviani proposed that Philips draw up a note with all the arguments in favor of the order *De populo Dei – De hierarchia*[241]. Philips writes this note immediately[242] and on the copy preserved in the archives Suenens has written by hand: 'Note remise au Saint-Père pour éclairer celui-ci sur l'importance de l'inversion'[243].

In *Souvenirs et espérances* (p. 115), Suenens recalled that the matter did not go smoothly:

> Lors de l'audience hebdomadaire des modérateurs, je fis part au pape de cette suggestion et j'en donnai rapidement les raisons. Le silence du pape,

238. A draft of this letter, dictated October 14, 1963, can be found in Fund Döpfner, 4041. It was written during the meeting of the moderators on October 14, 1963, at 18:45 hrs (Fund Döpfner, 3435). Cf. also *AS* VI/2, pp. 361-363.

239. Journal Moeller, Carnet 16, October 12, 1963.

240. Fund Prignon, 521, 12-13.10.1963.

241. CONGAR, *Mon journal du Concile* (n. 9), Vol. I, p. 475. cf. also Fund Prignon, 512, 17.10.1963: "L'attitude d'Ottaviani était doublement critiquable. Elle remettait en cause la décision des modérateurs, prise, *consulto Sancto Patre*, après la conversation privée que lui-même avait eue avec le pape; et portait ainsi un coup pas très élégant à l'autorité de ceux-ci. 2. Elle le faisait en découvrant la couronne et en faisant peser une opinion privée du Pape sur les discussions de la commission".

242. Fund Philips, 982, dated October 15, 1963 (Cf. also Fund Suenens, 1547).

243. Fund Suenens, 1547. It is in this note that Philips writes: "Ipse Populus eiusque salus est in consilio Dei de ordine finis, dum Hierarchia ut medium ad hunc finem ordinatur". This line may also have been inspired by Prignon, who said: "populus Dei est ultimus in executione, sed primus in intentione", an expression that is said to have convinced the Pope (Cf. C. TROISFONTAINES, *À propos de quelques interventions de Paul VI dans l'élaboration de 'Lumen Gentium'*, in *Paolo VI e i Problemi ecclesiologici al Concilio* (Pubblicazioni dell'Istituto Paolo VI, 7), Rome, Studium, 1989, p. 100, note 7, in fine).

qui ne fit aucune objection, nous fit conclure, à moi comme à mes trois collègues, qu'il se ralliait à la proposition. Rentré au Collège belge, j'annonçai
l'importante nouvelle aux évêques belges. Mgr Charue, membre de la Commission théologique, s'en réjouit. Comme il se rendait ce soir-là à une réunion de la Commission, il advint que le cardinal Ottaviani, président de la
Commission, souligna fortement l'importance du maintien de l'ordre qui
plaçait la hiérarchie avant le peuple de Dieu[244]. Mgr Charue l'informa de ma
conversation avec le pape, affirmant que celui-ci acceptait d'inverser cet
ordre. Le cardinal Ottaviani, avec fougue, réaffirmait que le pape était de
son avis et non du mien. Le lendemain[245], j'allai trouver le cardinal Ottaviani, dans la basilique, pour lui répéter moi-même ce que Mgr Charue lui
avait dit. Il maintint vigoureusement qu'il était sûr que le pape partageait son
avis. Il ne restait plus qu'à attendre l'audience hebdomadaire suivante[246] où,
d'entrée de jeu, je déclarai au Saint-Père que nous avons compris, moi et
mes collègues, qu'il était d'accord sur l'inversion. Réponse: "En fait, mon
opinion privée à moi est celle d'Ottaviani; mais quand vous avez plaidé en
faveur de l'inversion, je n'ai rien dit, laissant la question ouverte à la libre
discussion conciliaire". Et le pape ajouta: "En vérité, je dois dire que je ne
suis pas convaincu du changement souhaité". Je proposai alors que Mgr
Philips lui fasse une note justifiant l'inversion. À la suite de quoi il prit une
attitude de bienveillante neutralité, nous permettant ainsi d'avancer. Je profi-
tai d'un jour où je présidais pour demander aux pères l'inversion des
chapitres. Par un vote immédiat[247], ce fut acquis sans problèmes ni objections de la part de l'assemblée, avec une large majorité des voix[248].

b. The 'Quinque Propositiones'

1. The five orientation questions posed to the Patres by the moderators
on October 30, 1963 as a conclusion of the debate on the chapter *De hierarchia* in *De ecclesia* were extremely important on both an intrinsic and a
tactical level. Not only did they reveal the opinion of the Fathers on a
number of central and frequently discussed issues such as the sacramental nature of the episcopacy, the collegiality of the episcopate, the permanent diaconate, but they also constituted a turning point in the Council: for the first time it was clear that the conciliar commissions (and
especially the Doctrinal Commission) were at the service of the Council

---

244. According to CONGAR, *Mon journal du Concile* (n. 9), Vol. I, p. 475, meeting on
October 15, 1963.

245. According to Prignon's notes, the conversation Suenens-Ottaviani took place on
Sunday October 13. Suenens was mistaken about the dates. And it is at the meeting of the
Doctrinal Commission of October 15 that Charue refers tot the moderators' decision.
Cf. Fund Prignon, 512, 17.10.1963.

246. Audience of November 17, 1963.

247. The date of this vote was not included in the *AS*.

248. Cf. also *Mémoires sur le Concile Vatican II*, pp. 65-66.

and the Patres and not vice versa. This in turn signalled the failure of the plan of certain Curial circles for getting their prepared schemata accepted by the Council. As of that moment, a clear majority of the Council wanted to see the composition of the conciliar commissions modified, which should be realized at the end of November.

The initiative of the moderators was very daring; as expected, it met with a very obstinate resistance. This resistance was intrinsic, i.e., on the doctrinal level, and also organizational and structural.

By presenting their questions the moderators certainly provoked a double conflict[249]: On the one hand there was the question regarding their own power and role: were they only qualified to chair the debates in the Vatican Basilica (as the Presidents had done during the first session) or was it their task to guide the proceedings of the whole Council[250]? And what was their relation to the Council of Presidents, the Coordinating Commission and especially to the General Secretariat[251]? In addition, the moderators asked Dossetti, a confidant of Lercaro, to act as their informal secretary[252], a role Felici claimed for himself. On the other hand there was the conflict with the Doctrinal Commission. Due to the wording of their questions, the moderators had entered the area of doctrine. According to Ottaviani, this area was the exclusive competence of the Doctrinal Commission. He claimed that this commission held a kind of patronage over all the others, much like the way the Holy Office, as *Suprema Congregatio* with the Pope as prefect, was supreme above all other curial congregations.

2. The history of these two crucial weeks is extremely complicated and will not be entirely clear until the archives of Felici, Cicognani, Ottaviani,

---

249. As early as October 17, Prignon notes: "On s'approche de l'éclatement de la crise latente entre les modérateurs et de l'autre côté la secrétairerie du concile, qui s'appuie sur le secrétaire d'État" (Fund Prignon, 512, October 17, 1963).

250. The Suenens' archives contain very interesting documents on this matter, to which mainly Dossetti had applied himself during September and the beginning of October. Cf. Fund Suenens, 792-800. Obviously, the moderators did not succeed in attaining a clear statute.

251. The strong man in this was Felici. He felt he was supported by Cicognani, the Secretary of State, who was also the President of the Coordinating Commission. The conflict with the Council of Presidents was significantly less intense. These Presidents had practically lost all their power due to the establishment of the Coordinating Commission and the appointment of the moderators during the first intersession. Their role became mainly juridical: a kind of Council of State guarding the legality of the proceedings of the Council.

252. On September 27, Prignon notes: "Le matin: réunion des 4 modérateurs. Ils se choisissent Dossetti comme secrétaire" (Fund Prignon, 512).

Paul VI and C. Colombo[253] are open to the public. A. Melloni has already contributed substantially to this history[254]. Cl. Troisfontaines, in a remarkable study, has already examined the doctrinal significance of these *Propositiones* and has situated them in the evolution of the schema *De ecclesia*[255].

3. Suenens' role in this matter was important. This is evident from his *Mémoires sur le Concile* (cf. pp. 40-45) where he makes comments that were largely repeated in *Souvenirs et espérances* (cf. p. 115-118), from the archives of Philips, Suenens, Prignon[256], and from the diaries of Congar and Moeller. In what follows, we will limit ourselves to Suenens' role in this complicated history[257].

It is clear that Dossetti (assisted by Colombo with respect to their precise phrasing) initiated the idea of posing of the various questions[258].

253. It is known that Colombo cooperated with Dossetti on the formulation of the *Propositiones*. Given that the Pope finally approved the moderators' text (subject to some changes), in spite of the enormous amount of pressure applied by Ottaviani, Felici, Siri, Calabria and Cicognani, it then becomes necessary to ask whether Colombo had something to do with this. According to Melloni (A. MELLONI, *L'inizio del secondo periodo e il grande dibattito ecclesiologico*, in G. ALBERIGO [ed.], *Storia del concilio Vaticano II* [n. 54], Vol. III, p. 119) at the end of October Colombo had written a note (Fund Dossetti, III.247) for the Pope in reaction to an article by Staffa, published on October 29, 1963, in *Il Quotidiano*, an article which Cicognani had forbidden Staffa to publish in *L'Osservatore Romano* (letter from Staffa to Cicognani, October 26, 1963, cf. *AS* VI/2, pp. 394-397). This rejection was not mentioned by Melloni.
254. Cf. MELLONI, *L'inizio del secondo periodo* (n. 253), pp. 80-124 and 536-553.
255. TROISFONTAINES, *À propos de quelques interventions* (n. 243), mainly pp. 99-114; 135-137. This is a study that needs augmentation with regard to its historical details. In 1986 the *AS* V and VI had not yet been published, nor were the archives of Suenens (cf. Fund Suenens, 792-800 or Fund Döpfner, 3435, 4040-4041, 4044-4048, 4050, 4053, 4059-4060) Lercaro and Dossetti (for both see: October – beginning of November, 1963), Prignon (Fund Prignon, 459-474, 512-516) and Philips (cf. Fund Philips, 922-929) accessible. The documents of the Archivio Concilio Vaticano II were, of course, also not already available.
256. The documents from Fund Prignon, 459-474 are mostly those Suenens handed over to Prignon. Cf. also the notes by Prignon (Fund Prignon, 512-516).
257. The fact that there are no reports of the many meetings of the moderators during the month of October makes it even more difficult to reconstruct this history. During October, Dossetti acted as informal secretary, but, apparently wrote no reports. To this day we have only some brief and barely legible notes made by Döpfner (Fund Döpfner, 3435).
258. Cf. Fund Döpfner, 3435. TREFFLER (ed.), *Julius Kardinal Döpfner. Briefe und Notizen* (n. 9), p. 23: the matter of the *Propositiones* was already introduced at a meeting of the moderators with Dossetti at 18.00h. on October 11, 1963, after a celebration at Santa Maria Maggiore in honor of the first anniversary of the opening of the Council. Döpfner noted: "Ist hier die Zustimmung des Praesidiums notwendig?", a permission which obviously had not been attained. This makes Felici's reaction on October 15 all the more understandable. On October 14 at 18:45 hrs the moderators also discuss the 'votationes' on the basis of the text by Dossetti (Döpfner notes: "Die Weisen der abschliessende 'votazioni' besprochen (vgl. Entwurf von Dossetti)", cf. Fund Döpfner, 3435. TREFFLER, *Julius Kardinal Döpfner. Briefe und Notizen* (n. 9), p. 25. For the text by Dossetti of October 14, 1963, see Fund Döpfner, 4040 and Fund Dossetti, IV.378a.

On October 7, 1963 the moderators met Ottaviani and Browne and spoke already of the possibility to submit some questions to the Patres[259]. At the audience of the moderators on October 10, this matter was said to have been touched upon with the Pope[260]. On Friday October 11, Suenens has dinner with Philips and Prignon to finalize the text of the five *Propositiones*. On Sunday October 13, Prignon noted that Thils had delivered a draft of the *Propositiones* to Suenens, but that they still needed to be reviewed and submitted to Dossetti[261]. On October 14, Congar writes a note for Prignon, in which he warns that voting on the *Propositiones* immediately after the debate would be catastrophic. According to Congar, the editor of the text [Philips] must, *before* the vote, be able to give a short and clear explanation to the Patres. Prignon noted his intention to relay the message to the cardinal[262]. In their meeting of October 14, 1963, at 18:45 hrs the moderators discussed the *Propositiones*[263]. According to Suenens, it was he, as moderator for October 15, who announced that these four questions would be distributed the next day in the Basilica and put to a vote on Thursday, October 17[264].

Felici's reaction, which led to the postponement of the vote on October 17, is well known. On October 17, he wrote a note of two pages[265] for the Pope and Cicognani which is presented the same day by the Pope to the moderators during their audience[266]. Regarding this audience Suenens writes:

> ... je lui [Paul VI] ai tout de suite posé la question: "Saint-Père il paraît que vous êtes furieux sur ces questions"? Réponse du Saint-Père: "Je ne les ai

259. Cf. Treffler (ed.), *Julius Kardinal Döpfner. Briefe und Notizen* (n. 9), p. 23: "Klärende Abstimmungen?".

260. Cf. Fund Heuschen, 522. Heuschen writes on October 11, 1963: "Le cardinal [Suenens] me disait qu'on pouvait être rassuré pour la suite des débats. Hier soir, il est rentré enthousiaste de son entretien avec le pape: on a obtenu un accord sur la procédure ce qui rendra le débat plus facile et plus expéditif".

261. Fund Prignon, 512, October 13, 1963.

262. Fund Prignon, 512 (with a handwritten note by Congar, October 14, 1963).

263. Cf. Treffler (ed.), *Julius Kardinal Döpfner. Briefe und Notizen* (n. 9), p. 25: "Die Weisen der abschliessende votazioni besprochen (vgl. Entwurf Dossetti)".

264. Cf. AS II/2, pp. 595-597. According to G. Caprile, *Il Concilio Vaticano II*. Vol. III, Roma, Civiltà Cattolica, 1966, pp. 94-97 and 168, Döpfner made this announcement. However, this is unlikely since Suenens was moderator of the day. For this discussion, see Melloni, *L'inizio del secondo periodo* (n. 253), p. 91, note 296.

265. Cf. AS VI/2, pp. 373-374; as well as Fund Döpfner, 4048 (with indication of author and name, but without the title 'Commentarius'); and Fund Prignon, 470 (= the same document). It refers to the document that in Alberigo (ed.), *Storia del Concilio Vaticano II* (n. 54), Vol. III, p. 94, note 309 is still attributed to a 'ignoto autore'.

266. The audience took place on October 17 (cf. Fund Döpfner, 4048 and *L'Osservatore Romano*, October 19, 1963). And not on October 18 or 19 as the note 332, pp. 99 of Alberigo (ed.), *Storia del Concilio Vaticano II* (n. 54), Vol. III, implies.

pas lues". Alors, nous avons poussé tous les quatre un soupir de soulage-
ment ... je l'ai supplié de les lire devant nous, je lui ai un peu forcé la main
pour qu'il les lise et, à notre très grande déception, il a dit: "Mais il faudrait
poser ces questions et en référer à la Commission de coordination"[267].

In preparation for the meeting of the Presidents, the members of the Coordinating Commission and the moderators that was planned for October
23[268], the moderators set to work on a modified text of the *Propositiones*.
The archives contain a note handwritten by Dossetti[269], a new handwritten
draft by Philips[270], and a draft afterwards typed out by Prignon[271]. It is this
text that Döpfner delivers to Felici on October 19, 1963, and which is distributed to the participants of the meeting on October 23[272]. Because Suenens involved Philips, the text grew in theological precision[273] and becomes
acceptable to many (including the Pope). In the meantime Suenens has a
meeting with Tisserant, President of the Council of Presidents, who is willing to declare the matter beyond the competence of the Presidents[274].

On October 20, Moeller notes in his diary:

Par ailleurs on attaque Suenens pour la légalité de la décision: faire voter
sur des textes afin d'orienter la commission [doctrinale]. Il ne sait pas que

267. *Mémoires sur le Concile Vatican II*, p. 42. A confirmation is to be found in Con-
GAR, *Mon journal du Concile* (n. 9), Vol. II, p. 16, February 2, 1964 (and not in 1965, as
quoted in ALBERIGO [ed.], *Storia del Concilio Vaticano II* [n. 54], Vol. III, p. 93): "Alors
que le Secrétaire d'État avait invoqué l'autorité du pape contre les questions, celui-ci a
déclaré de ne les avoir jamais vues. Il les a lues sans faire de réserve sur le fond. Mais il
dit aux Modérateurs: vous auriez dû vous entendre avec la Commission de coordination
et mettre Felici dans le coup". It must be added that here Congar repeats a conversation
with Prignon, and that Suenens is Prignon's source.
268. MELLONI, *L'inizio del secondo periodo* (n. 253), p. 99, note 333, mentions a meeting of the moderators and the Coordinating Commission on Friday, October 18, based on
Congar (CONGAR, *Mon journal du Concile* (n. 9), Vol. II, p. 16). In the AS V/1, there is
no indication of this meeting. Melloni's reference (AS V/1, pp. 18-19) actually refers to a
meeting of the <u>Presidents</u> during the first session on October 18 and 19, 196<u>2</u>.
269. Fund Prignon, 465.
270. Fund Prignon, 461.
271. Fund Prignon, 463A. Prignon has added a note mentioning that this text was
drafted by Philips with the help of Moeller and himself on October 19, 1963.
272. Cf. AS V/1, pp. 699-700.
273. Cf. TROISFONTAINES, *À propos de quelques interventions* (n. 243), p. 102 and
G. PHILIPS, *L'Église et son mystère au IIe Concile du Vatican. Histoire, texte et commentaire de la Constitution Lumen Gentium*, Paris, Cerf, 1967-1968, Vol. I, pp. 29-31.
274. Cf. Journal Moeller, Carnet 16, dimanche Octobre 19, 1963 [but October 20 was
a Sunday]: "Par ailleurs Suenens a vu Tisserant. Celui-ci comme Président des Présidents
a déclaré à être prêt à déclarer [sic] que les présidents sont *incompétents en la matière*".
The support of Tisserant (especially in the meeting on October 23) for these *Propositiones*
is striking (cf. *Processus verbalis*, AS V/1, pp. 701-735). This makes it all the more
surprising that Suenens minimalises Tisserant's role both in his *Mémoires sur le Concile
Vatican II*, p. 43 and in SUENENS, *Souvenirs et espérances* (n. 11), p. 116.

le pape ignore tout de ceci. Suenens a obtenu une audience spéciale pour lundi soir. Que va-t-il en sortir? Une offensive générale contre les modérateurs et aussi contre la collégialité. La curie veut paralyser le concile, c'est évident ... J'apprends par É. Beauduin[275] que l'on veut faire sauter Dossetti, qui est "officieusement" secrétaire des modérateurs.

And Moeller also adds:

D'autre part ceux-ci [les modérateurs] seraient divisés. Döpfner aurait "lâché" ... En tout cas il est mou[276]. Avoir passé le texte [cf. *supra* the text of the *Propositiones*, October 19, 1963] à Felici est étrange[277]. Quant à Agagianian, il est avec Ottaviani etc. Lercaro est brûlé. Suenens est vraiment seul[278].

Suenens is received in audience on the evening of October 21[279]. In February of 1964, Prignon relates the following about this to Congar:

Suenens a vu le pape lundi et lui raconte toutes ces manœuvres. Il a dit lui-même avoir été déchaîné; il a posé au pape la question de l'autorité des modérateurs (qui, dans cette crise, avaient offert leur démission). Suenens a dit: si le Pape cède en ceci, les journaux porteront bientôt en grand titre: Paul VI a trahi Jean XXIII[280].

On October 23, the meeting of the Council of the Presidents, the Coordinating Commission and the moderators took place. In the end, the moderators, after a long debate, obtain the right to present their *Propositiones* to the Patres, on the condition that they make a few changes to the text[281]. Suenens reported on this in his *Mémoires* (p. 43-45) and *Souvenirs et espérances* (p. 117). His report is far from systematic, but two items can be highlighted:

– The approval of one of the *Propositiones* is to be attributed to the absent-mindedness of Spellman during the vote. When Villot, one of the subsecretaries, remarked to Suenens: "Mais ce cardinal se trompe", Suenens replied: "Bien sûr, mais ce n'est pas à nous à le lui faire remarquer"[282].

---

275. Friend of Moeller, nephew of Dom Lambert Beauduin, and a member of the Secretariat for the Unity.

276. It is during this period that Döpfner nicknamed 'der Löwe von München', was unjustly branded by some as 'der Gummi-Löwe'.

277. Indeed, Felici, as early as October 21, 1963, can be seen to have reacted to this text in a note to Cicognani, cf. AS VI/2, pp. 379-380.

278. Journal Moeller, Carnet 16, October 20, 1963.

279. On this same day (October 21, 1963) there was also a meeting of the 'Synoptici' (Suenens, Döpfner, Lercaro). Cf. TREFFLER (ed.), *Julius Kardinal Döpfner. Briefe und Notizen* (n. 9), p. 26.

280. CONGAR, *Mon journal du Concile* (n. 9), Vol. II, p. 17, February 2, 1964.

281. For these *Conclusiones*, see AS V/1, p. 735.

282. *Mémoires sur le Concile Vatican II*, p. 45.

– Another passage sheds light on Suenens' strategy:

> Il y a eu ensuite des interventions de tous les éléments conservateurs, qui, au lieu d'attaquer les questions, attaquaient chaque fois le fond des choses et disaient: "Nous ne sommes pas pour ceci et on ne peut pas défendre ça". À quoi nous [the moderators] répondions: "Mais vous avez parfaitement le droit de répondre non, quand on vous posera la question, nous voulons simplement demander de *poser* la question. Nous ne voulons pas, ici, défendre le fond des choses". Il semblait qu'il y avait là une sorte d'impossibilité, que j'ai remarquée à travers tout le Concile, d'ailleurs. Chaque fois que l'on voulait débattre quelque chose dans les procédures, il n'y avait pas l'ombre de fair play, pas l'ombre de sens de ce que c'est que laisser une question surgir et la débattre selon toutes les lois: on était tout de suite sur le fond et tout était manœuvré pour empêcher les questions de se poser[283].

According to the *Acta Synodalia*, the interventions of Suenens during this meeting were rather limited (29 lines out of approximately 1330 in the *Processus verbalis*[284]). They can be summarised as follows:

– For the first time he defended the *Propositiones* to Ruffini, who claims that the *Propositiones* are in fact a matter for the Doctrinal Commission. Suenens retorts that it was never the moderators' intention to take a position with regard to a theological matter – something that so clearly belonged to the competence of the Doctrinal Commission – but that it was only meant as a kind of opinion poll. He even proposed presenting the different *Propositiones* in the Basilica, allowing each one to be introduced by a *relator,* and then allowing the Patres to express their preference[285].
– Suenens did not desire the universal introduction of the permanent diaconate; but he did wish it to become a theoretical possibility so that the bishops' conferences that were desirous of a permanent diaconate, could proceed '*approbante Sancta Sede*'[286].
– His discussion with Siri was of greater importance. When Siri argues for a different phrasing of *Propositio* III (regarding collegiality), Suenens proposes that Siri put his version to the vote in the Vatican Basilica, next to the text proposed by the moderators. He insists on receiving Siri's text within the next day or two "perché i Padri nell'Aula sono inquieti e domandano che cosa si fa"[287].

283. *Mémoires sur le Concile Vatican II*, p. 44.
284. Cf. *AS* V/1, pp. 701-735. These reports were made by V. Fagiolo and V. Carbone, members of the General Secretariat of the Council.
285. *AS* V/1, p. 710.
286. *AS* V/1., pp. 723 and 728. See also CONGAR, *Mon journal du Concile* (n. 9), Vol. II, p. 16.
287. *AS* V/1, p. 719. As demonstrated by the recently quoted passage from his *Mémoires sur le Concile Vatican II*, Suenens' habit when confronted with difficult

Siri, supported by Calabria, bishop of Benevento, makes the most of this opportunity during the next two days. In his diary entry for October 25, Tromp notes that he was approached by Calabria, President of the Theological Commission of the Italian Bishops' Conference, who, in Siri's name, asked for his advice on the new phrasing of *Propositio* III[288]. Moeller also notices that Schauf speaks to Siri in the Basilica and tells Philips that these *Propositiones* are not to be put to the vote, since the Patres are not aware of what they are voting on and that this will lead to the immobilization of the Commission[289]. The same day Calabria[290] presents a text to Suenens. This text is accompanied by a letter from Siri explaining that he sent Calabria to deliver the text as it was necessary for him to return to his diocese[291]. Siri's text deviates on three essential points from the moderators' text:

1. The *Corpus* or *Collegium Episcoporum* is no longer mentioned.
2. The bishops as a body exercise the supreme power no longer *iure divino*; they are mere *iure divino* successors of the apostles.
3. They exercise this authority only when they assemble [in a Council] or when entrusted by the Pope with a matter which will be decided in a collegial way [The collegiate power is delegated by the Pope].

Siri also added two important *Notes*: (1) This text is the only one which can be presented to the Fathers and is not an alternative text. (2) In the event that another text is to be presented to the Fathers, this must be submitted to and approved by the Doctrinal Commission in advance.

Since Suenens is of the opinion that Siri has not been fair in his treatment of Suenens' proposal to vote on two alternative texts, he decides to eliminate Siri's text from consideration[292].

(theological) issues was to put two or more alternatives to the vote, instead of discussing matters thoroughly. His aim was to gain time and to keep from becoming mired down in difficult theological debates. He was also aware that, in this way, he could usually prevail without too much trouble. It was possibly the Anglo-Saxon influence that led Suenens to pursue this a course of action.

288. *Diarium* Tromp, 7, October 25, 1963.
289. Journal Moeller, Carnet 16, October 25, 1963.
290. Fund Suenens, 1522: Calabria's visiting card for Suenens.
291. Fund Suenens, 1521.
292. In his Nota, published with Siri's text in *AS* V/1, p. 736, Carbone writes: "Huiusmodi textus, redactus ab em.mo Siri (cf. p. 719) et leviter emendatus a P. Tromp, exhibitus fuit die 25 octobris em.mo Suenens sed vim non habuit". He does not mention – and perhaps was not aware – of the reason for this. On a tape, Prignon notes: "... le cardinal Siri a fait parvenir au card. Suenens son texte à lui, que je conserve dans mes archives, et où se trouve la fameuse note dans laquelle le cardinal Siri demandait que l'on publiât ce seul texte. Ce que notre cardinal ne pourrait évidemment pas accepter. Il me fit d'abord préparer un projet de lettre pour expliquer les raisons de son refus au cardinal [Siri]. Puis,

On October 24, the moderators made the final changes to the text during their weekly audience with the Pope[293]. On October 25, during the meeting in the Vatican Basilica, Ottaviani and Suenens are involved in a dispute. Moeller recounts:

> Ce matin, Ottaviani a parlé à Suenens. Lui a dit, avant la messe: "Vous n'avez pas le droit de faire ce que vous faites. C'est un camouflet à la commission de la Foi. Puis vous allez sans cesse chez le pape". Suenens répond: "Mais vous faites de même, d'aller chez le pape. Ensuite, l'assemblée plénière de la Présidence, de la commission de coordination, des modérateurs a décidé de proposer ce vote". Ottaviani, furieux s'en va[294].

Tromp notes that a meeting took place that the same day at 12.30 h. between Ottaviani, Browne, Parente and himself (the *praesidium* of the Doctrinal Commission). Ottaviani discussed his conversation with Suenens and complained that the Doctrinal Commission had not received a copy of the *Propositiones*. Tromp then explained his corrections with regard to Calabria's text. Ottaviani insists on a meeting of the Doctrinal Commission on Monday, October 28[295].

On Sunday, October 27, the moderators had supper with the Pope. The Holy Father is supposed to have said: "Vous avez fait votre chemin de croix, je vous félicite. Je vous ai soutenus, mais soyez plus prudents"[296]. Suenens recounts the following to Prignon: "Le pape lit une dernière fois

---

réflexion faite, il décida de le lui dire oralement dès qu'il le verrait" (Fund Prignon, 512).

293. On Thursday October 24, Prignon writes: "Audience des modérateurs. L'affaire des *vota* semble terminée. Le pape a lu et approuvé le texte qui est fondamentalement celui de Dossetti revu par Mgr Philips, Moeller et moi-même. On a seulement divisé le III en a et b pour que le vote sur le *jure divino* de la collégialité puisse se faire en pleine clarté et sans équivoque. Les questions 2 et 3 du IV, comme décidé hier, ont été supprimées. Le cardinal Siri n'a pas encore remis son texte. S'il ne le remet pas tant pis. On donnera demain l'ordre d'imprimer et de distribuer aux Pères lundi prochain. Le Pape n'a pas fait d'objections au texte. Il est content que l'affaire soit réglée" (Fund Prignon, 512, 24.10.1963). Cf. also TREFFLER (ed.), *Julius Kardinal Döpfner. Briefe und Notizen* (n. 9), p. 26: "24.10.1963: 1. Der definitive Text der votazioni".

294. Journal Moeller, Carnet 16, October 25, 1963.

295. *Diarium* Tromp, 7, October 25, 1963: "Exposuit Praeses [Ottaviani] se habuisse colloquium cum Em.mo Suenens de 4 quaestionibus Concilio proponendis. Dixit moderatorum esse dirigere discussiones non sese ingerere in res quae spectant Comm. doctr. Card. Suenens dixit sic voluisse Pontificem. Commissio theologica ne quidem accepit copiam harum quattuor quaestionum".

296. For this expression, cf. Fund Prignon, 512 (no date) and CONGAR, *Mon journal du Concile* (n. 9), Vol. II, p. 17, February 2, 1964. Cf. Fund Prignon, 512, October 24, 1963: "L'audience [du 24.10.1963] se termine par l'invitation à dîner des 4 modérateurs pour le dimanche suivant à 20h.1/4. Le cardinal Suenens demande si on pourra parler du concile à table et d'autres affaires sérieuses. Oui, dit le pape, mais 'come si fa a tavola'".

le texte préparé et acceptait la demande du cardinal qu'on réintroduisît le *'saltem libere recipiente'*[297]. This, however, did not stop Ottaviani from making a final attempt on October 28 to block the *Propositiones* and have them referred to the Doctrinal Commission.

When Tromp arrived at 08.40h., he was informed that Ottaviani has requested Parente to draw up new *Propositiones*, which, after being approved by the Doctrinal Commission, will be submitted to the Patres. Ottaviani requests the immediate duplication of these texts for submission that same evening to the meeting of the Doctrinal Commission[298]. Ottaviani immediately wrote to Felici to inform him that the Commission would discuss some texts. The note also includes:

> Ne do previo avviso a Vostra Eccellenza affinché, qualora vi fossero altre iniziative del genere, Ella possa far rilevare ai proponenti che su tale argumento sta provvedendo, con sollecitudine, la competente Commissione Dottrinale. Di ciò è stato prevenuto anche il Santo Padre[299].

To this he appends a page with three Vota and one Formula. It was a clear attempt to sabotage the moderators' *Propositiones*. On October 29, Felici replied that he will submit Ottaviani's letter at the next meeting of the Presidents and the moderators[300]. Six *Propositiones*, three Vota and one Formula[301] are indeed put to the Doctrinal Commission at their October 28 meeting[302]. Ottaviani wanted his texts to be discussed and indicates that the moderators should not presume to take the place of the Doctrinal Commission. Charue, however, declared that the moderators will pose their own questions and that they will come from a text approved by the Pope himself[303]. This concluded the matter[304].

---

297. Fund Prignon, 512.
298. *Diarium* Tromp, October 28, 1963.
299. Letter from Ottaviani to Felici, October 28, 1963, *AS* V/1, pp. 738-739 and VI/2, p. 400. Cf. also letter from Ottaviani to Paul VI, October 27, 1963, *AS* VI/2, p. 397.
300. *AS* V/2, p. 13.
301. Cf. Fund Philips, 925-929.
302. MELLONI, *L'inizio del secondo periodo* (n. 253), pp. 114-115, places this discussion on October 29. This is not consistent with the Journal Congar, with the letter from Ottaviani to Felici (October 28, 1963), with the Journal Moeller, nor with the *Diarium* Tromp, 7, October 28, 1963. There was a new meeting of the Doctrinal Commission on October 29, but this was not about the five *Propositiones*.
303. Tromp notes the following in his *Diarium*, 7, October 28, 1963: "*Praeses* [Ottavani]: Quoad ad definienda puncta quaedam gravioris momenti incipiamus a quibusdam conclusionibus praeparatis ab Ecc.mo Parente
Exc. Charue: melius attendere quid hac de re decreverint Cardinales moderatores
Praeses: res non spectat ad eorum competentiam
Exc. Charue: manet in sua opinione
Mgr Philips: notat difficile huiusmodi conclusiones disputari posse ante laborem Subcommissionis particularis de revisione textus.

The moderators' *Propositiones* were distributed in the Basilica on October 29[305]. Even at that stage, Calabria attempted to postpone the vote. He wrote a letter to Felici to propose that the vote, planned for the next day, be preceded by a *relatio*, of which the written text was to be distributed afterwards to the Patres, so that the vote would be an informed one[306]. This letter had no effect.

On October 29, at 17.30, there was a meeting of the Council of Presidents, the Coordinating Commission and the moderators. Lercaro was absent.

The letter from Ottaviani to Felici (October 28, 1963) is discussed. Suenens and Döpfner defend the position that a vote must take place in the Vatican Basilica the next day. After a discussion, this proposal is accepted – albeit with six 'no' votes (Cicognani, Spellman, Ruffini, Wyszynski, Siri, Roberti); there was one abstention (Morcillo)[307]. This is

---

Nil deciditur".

Prignon relates the following: "Le Cardinal Ottaviani nous fit remettre 6 questions comprenant les points essentiels du schéma qu'on pourrait discuter par priorité. Et sur lesquelles on pourrait se mettre d'accord dans un temps assez bref. Comme par hasard les 6 points ... contenaient les 3 premières propositions des modérateurs mais dans un sens Sirianiste extrême. Heureusement Mgr Charue, averti à l'avance par nos soins dans la voiture pendant qu'on le conduisait à la réunion, prit la parole et à trois reprises insista ... demanda s'il ne vaudrait pas mieux d'attendre le vote proposé par les modérateurs, puisqu'il avait été annoncé publiquement. Mgr Parente répartit: *Sed dilatus est*, ce que le card. Ottaviani s'empressa de répéter avec force. Mgr Charue insista pour dire: *scio tamen quod cito veniet*. Ensuite le card. Ottaviani se trouva un peu déconcerté, puis il répliqua: Quelle que soit la révérence des modérateurs, c'est quand-même notre droit à nous commission théologique, à discuter de ces questions comme nous l'entendons. *Vos estis judices*, dit-il, aux évêques. Mais Mgr Charue ne se laissait pas démonter et insista une troisième fois: *cito veniet et fit cum acceptatione Summi Pontificis*. Le card. Ottaviani alors commença une phrase pour dire que même le Souverain Pontife ... puis il s'arrêta" (Fund Prignon, 512).

Congar remarks: "Étrange séance!! Les gens du Saint-Office avaient monté une manœuvre pour torpiller, et même éliminer, les votes préparés par les Modérateurs, et, à travers ces votes l'autorité de ces mêmes Modérateurs. Tout était monté, mais, à la première réaction, tout s'est écroulé; on n'a plus parlé des questions préparées (*dixit* Ottaviani) par Parente". Cf. Congar, *Mon journal du Concile* (n. 9), Vol. I, pp. 504-506.

304. Regarding the next meeting of the Doctrinal Commission on October 29, Moeller notes: "Browne a dit que les questions proposées hier cadunt! 'C'est la première fois que j'ai vu reculer Ottaviani', dit Philips. De fait, mais Martimort dit: 'C'est la victoire, jusqu'à la prochaine escarmouche'". Cf. Journal Moeller, Carnet 16, October 29, 1963. Felici will add that this text by Ottaviani only reached him, after the moderators had presented their papally-approved text to him (*AS* V/1, p. 739, note 1).

305. Cf. *AS* II/3, pp. 573-575.

306. Cf. *AS* VI/2, p. 417. Letter dated October 29, 1963.

307. Cf. *Processus verbalis*, *AS* V/2, pp. 14-17. Regarding this Prignon notes: "Le mardi soir encore il y eut réunion du conseil de présidence et de la commission de coordination et des modérateurs pour accélérer la procédure. En fait au cours de cette réunion, qui eut lieu avant le vote, il y avait une dernière tentative des cardinaux Siri et Ruffini pour empêcher le vote, sous cette forme qu'on demandait de retarder le vote de deux, trois

followed by the vote in the Basilica on Wednesday, October 30. Unexpectedly, a quite substantial majority voted in favour of the *Propositiones*[308]. Suenens noted also:

> Nous avons fait alors vraiment ce que nous avons pu pour réagir. À un moment crucial – ceci n'appartient pas à l'histoire – les modérateurs, c'est-à-dire Lercaro, Döpfner et moi-même avions songé à une lettre de démission. Le Cardinal Lercaro en rédigeait le brouillon lorsqu'il a été appelé chez le Saint-Père à propos de cette question. Il lui a donné alors ce texte, comme étant le reflet de notre pensée, mais sans que ce soit une lettre vraiment signée par nous trois, puisque ce n'était encore qu'une copie, dont nous n'avions pas vu le texte. Mais nous étions pleinement d'accord et il était autorisé à dire que nous étions pleinement d'accord. Ce n'était pas une façon de nous traiter. Le Saint-Père a pris entièrement position *contre* Lercaro et nous étions donc bloqués de ce côté. Il n'a soutenu en rien les modérateurs dans ce moment, qui pour nous était crucial[309].

4. A few concluding remarks on this episode

It is clear from this history of the five *Propositiones*, which were obviously important for the further proceedings of the debate on *De ecclesia* as well as for the whole Council[310], that Suenens played a leading part. He cooperated closely with Dossetti and involved Moeller, Prignon and especially Philips. He defended his case in the 'super commission' and he stood his ground against Ottaviani and even in discussions with the Pope. Nevertheless, he soon came to see that the new Pope was taking command

jours, afin que les Pères aient le temps de réfléchir. Comme le P. Lio m'avait dit ce matin in aula: 'Come possono questi poveri vescovi decidere in una mezza giornata di questioni tanto importanti'. C'est le thème que défendait Siri à cette réunion. Mais il faut croire que les Pères en avaient assez. Le card. Tisserant lui-même fit remarquer qu'il y avait un mois qu'on parlait de la collégialité, que les Pères avaient eu tout le temps de se faire une opinion. Le card. Suenens répondit pour sa part que le texte était ce qu'il était, qu'il était impossible d'en faire un report, que quel que soit le texte qu'on présentât, il y aurait toujours à redire, que la majorité s'était prononcée et qu'on ne pouvait plus reculer. On procéda au vote, on fit même voter les secrétaires. À 3/4 de majorité le vote fut décidé pour le lendemain sans plus de retard" (Fund Prignon, 512).

308. The opposition against this vote will persist. cf. A letter from 5 cardinals, 100 bishops and 50 general superiors to the Pope on November 15, 1963. Cf. AS VI/2, pp. 469-473.

309. SUENENS, *Mémoires sur le Concile Vatican II*, pp. 42-43. Notwithstanding Suenens mentions the audience of Lercaro before the meeting of the Moderators and the Coordination Commission on October 23, it's practically certain that this audience of Lercaro took place on November 15, 1963, when the opposition against the Moderators persisted. Cf. 'Journal A. Nicora' in G. ALBERIGO, *Pour la Jeunesse du Christianisme: Le Concile Vatican II*, Paris, Cerf, 2005, p. 93. And Döpfner notes that there was a meeting of the 'Synoptici' on November 14, 1963 (Cf. TREFFLER [ed.], *Julius Kardinal Döpfner. Briefe und Notizen* [n. 9], p. 28).

310. Cf. TROISFONTAINES, *À propos de quelques interventions* (n. 243), pp. 103-104.

of the Council and was following everything closely (much more so than John XXIII). In addition, Paul VI continued to support Felici (Dossetti was replaced as secretary of the moderators[311]). In this day, it remains a mystery what the Pope truly thought about the issue of collegiality. The fact that at the end of the second session the conciliar commissions were augmented with five additional members and could elect their own 2nd vice-president and deputy secretary was probably an indirect consequence of this episode. During October and November, the leaders of the Doctrinal Commission, who did everything in their power to prevent this vote and, once it was taken, to minimize its impact[312], were increasingly criticised[313] a fact which finally led to this decision of the Pope.

Another surprising aspect is how the various persons who were in charge at the Council – and especially those belonging to Curial circles – did not consider themselves to be at the service of the Council or its organs:

Ottaviani often acted in complete independence of the Doctrinal Commission and took self-willed initiatives without ever considering submitting them to the commission members beforehand. He felt even less restrained by the authority of the moderators[314]. He crossed them at every turn and with every available means. He practically ordered Felici about and addressed himself directly to both the State Secretary and the Pope. He had a low opinion of the theological knowledge of the Council Fathers.

Felici also did not feel subordinate to the moderators. He too turned directly to Cicognani and the Pope in order to counteract them[315]. Felici did not even feel bound by a vote in the Basilica. Staffa did not hesitate to involve *L'Osservatore Romano*. It is obvious that these personalities do not take part in the 'democratic process' of a conciliar meeting. At the same time, it would be unjust to attribute this solely to tyrannical or

311. On Wednesday, October 30, 1963, at 18:30, there was a meeting of the moderators with an agenda (most probably drafted by Felici). It was not a coincidence that the first point on the agenda was: "Definire ed esaminare nei dettagli il compito e l'azione degli Em.mi Cardinali Moderatori riguardo alla procedura della discussione nella Congregazione Generale" (Cf. Fund Suenens, 1391).

312. On November 13, 1963, Ottaviani, in a statement given to the Press Office of the Divine Word, said that he regrets that vote and disputes its value (Cf. CAPRILE, *Il Concilio Vaticano II*, Vol. III [n. 264], p. 170).

313. Cf. a.o. Fund Suenens, 1432-1436.

314. Cf. his intervention in aula on November 8, 1963 (CAPRILE, *Il Concilio Vaticano II*, Vol. III [n. 264], p. 214-215).

315. In a note for the pope 'Osservazioni e proposte sui lavori conciliari' (December 12, 1963) Felici once again attacks the Moderators on the vote of the 5 *Propositiones* and Felici proposes that the Moderators "si astengono dal partecipare ai dibattiti" (Cf. AS VI/2, pp. 551-555).

authoritarian personalities, although this remains a possibility. They were simply accustomed to living under authoritarian popes (Pius XI and Pius XII) and were disconcerted by the relatively *laissez faire* style of John XXIII. They were convinced that all authority in the Church should come uniquely and directly from the Pope and Rome and they felt obliged to perpetuate this attitude.

Suenens, however, was leaning more towards the opinion of the assembly. He believed in the dynamics of the Council and was willing to submit decisions to a more democratic process supposing that the majority would support his proposals. He sometimes took this so much for granted as to want the decisions on dogmatic matters to be resolved by a vote and with a simple majority carrying the day.

5. Some interventions by Suenens during the debate on *De ecclesia*

(1) *De diaconatu permanenti in ecclesia*[316]*:* October 8, 1963. Suenens had already mentioned the diaconate in his *Vota* prior to the Council[317] and in his plan of May 16, 1962[318]. Furthermore, he had requested Philips to include the problem of the diaconate in *De ecclesia* as opposed to, e.g. the text *De presbyteris* since he had doubts about the objectivity of this commission[319].

His intervention was mostly the work of Dossetti[320]. It consisted of three parts: (1) The Church has a sacramental structure, which needs to be experienced fully. (2) The Council need not rule on the introduction of a permanent diaconate but needs only to supply bishops or bishops' conferences desirous of this office with the possibility. (3) Suenens pleaded for the possibility of married deacons and was of the opinion that this would not damage the number of vocations to the celibate priesthood.

---

316. Cf. *AS* II/2, pp. 317-320.
317. *ADA* I/2, Pars I, pp. 143-144.
318. Cf. SUENENS, *Aux origines du Concile Vatican II* [n. 16], p. 14.
319. SUENENS, *Souvenirs et espérances* (n. 11), p.119; SUENENS, *Mémoires sur le Concile Vatican II*, p. 46.
320. Cf. Fund Suenens, 1492 and 1493: Dossetti first wrote a long Italian text (12 p.), followed by a Latin text of five pages. On October 7, Prignon notes: "Ce soir, après la réunion des modérateurs, le cardinal amène Dossetti au collège. Je crois qu'ils vont préparer ensemble l'intervention du cardinal Suenens, le lendemain, sur le problème du diaconat". And on October 8, he writes: "Intervention du cardinal Suenens sur le diaconat. Texte préparé en collaboration avec Dossetti et revu avec moi-même le matin même (pour le rendre plus 'parlant' à l'audition). Il semble que ce texte ait fait impression sur les Pères" (Fund Prignon, 512).

In the end, Suenens proposed that when the debate on chapter II was concluded, a question should be posed to the Patres: "Ubi conferentiis episcoporum opportunum videtur instauratio diaconatus permanentis, libertas eis sit eum introducendi". This was possibly a convenient means for introducing to the last of the five *Propositiones*. This speech by Suenens did not provoke any particular reactions. Congar, however, was quite positive: "Texte très fort, mais trop long"[321], and Dom Egender, prior of Chevetogne, thanked him for this intervention and added some arguments to strengthen his call for the reinstatement of the permanent diaconate[322].

(2) *De Spiritus sancti actione in laicis,* October 22, 1963[323]. Suenens made this intervention during the debate on Caput III (*De laicis*) of *De ecclesia*. In part, it was a reaction against Ruffini[324], who had said that the schema was not supposed to mention special charismas for lay persons[325]. Suenens' archives clearly show that he had initially asked Thils for a text[326] but that, in the end, he went with a text drafted for him by H. Küng[327]. This text was for the most part literally copied[328] but Suenens did add the practical conclusions which attracted so much attention from the world press corps. This text, which had been abundantly interspersed by Küng with biblical quotes, underlined that:

– The hierarchical structure of the Church should not become an administrative organism with no connection to the charismatic gifts of the Holy Spirit.
– The Holy Spirit does not bestow charismas only on the church's pastoral leadership but on all Christians. There is clearly a plethora of gifts. Therefore, the schema on the Church should not limit itself to the apostles and their successors, but should also speak about the role of prophets and doctors in the Church.

321. CONGAR, *Mon journal du Concile* (n. 9), Vol. I, p. 142.
322. Letter of October 22, 1963, Fund Suenens, 1496.
323. *AS* II/3, pp. 175-178.
324. Intervention of October 16, 1963, Cf. *AS* II/2, pp. 627-632.
325. Cf. SUENENS, *Mémoires sur le Concile Vatican II*, pp. 48-50; SUENENS, *Souvenirs et espérances* (n. 11), pp. 120-121.
326. Fund Suenens, 1533 and Fund Thils, 495.
327. FConc. Suenens, 1531. In Suenens' *Mémoires sur le Concile Vatican II* (1966) Küng is still mentioned as author; however, his name does not appear in *Souvenirs et espérances* (n. 11).
328. Except for a few small corrections by Prignon and Msgr. Schoenmaeckers, cf. Fund Suenens, 1532.

– Although the charismas have to be carefully monitored by the pastoral leadership, the various offices in the Church would be sterile and impoverished without them, a fact which needs to be promoted by that same leadership.

After presenting a few theological conclusions, Suenens followed them with his well-known practical suggestions:

– A call to increase the number of lay-auditores at the Council.
– A call to add women as auditors: *mulieres, quae, ni fallor, dimidiam partem humanitatis constituunt*[329].
– A call to add representatives from both male and female religious congregations.

Of course, the intervention was popular with the press, with the religious congregations[330], and within ecumenical circles[331]. Later, *i.e.* in 1972, when Suenens became a protagonist for the charismatic renewal movement, he referred to this intervention 'qui anticipait l'avenir'[332].

c. De beata

Although the debates of the second session did not discuss *De beata* (the text was not ready), his archive makes clear that Suenens followed the matter closely. First there was the vote on October 29, 1963, regarding the integration of *De beata* in *De ecclesia*. Suenens was in favour of this integration, which was narrowly carried. Also certain is that he, possibly because he was in charge of this chapter in the Coordinating Commission, received many letters and was kept informed of all sorts of proposals and drafts concerning it.

– The corrected version of the text by Dhanis (requested by Suenens during the first intersession)[333], Butler's draft[334], and a Chilean schema[335] are still extant.

---

329. This call also earned Suenens a place in the last stanza of the 'Limericks' by Msgr. J. O'Loughlin: "Said Suenens to the Congregatio, I'm fed up with this disceptatio. The bishops are churls; Let's call in the girls. And we'll have a confabulatio (or: Although it may cause admiratio)" cf. Fund Suenens, 1703.

330. Cf. letter from Mother Mary Consolatrice, USA [in September of 1964 appointed to 'auditor' at the Council] to Suenens, October 29, 1963, Fund Suenens, 1536.

331. Cf. the letter from Cullmann to Suenens, February 28, 1964 (Fund Suenens, 1538) as well as V. Borovoj's positive reaction during the meeting of the observers on October 29, 1963, Fund Suenens, 1545.

332. SUENENS, *Souvenirs et espérances* (n. 11), p. 120.

333. Fund Suenens, 1581-1582.

334. Fund Suenens, 1566-1570.

335. Fund Suenens, 1571-1573.

- We also have letters from maximalist Mariologists such as Garcia Garcés, Llamera, Monsegu, Balić, and Montà[336].
- There is a note from Msgr. Hua, presented to Suenens by Congar[337].

Suenens was aware of the fact that Philips was slowly taking on more responsibility with regard to the editing of the schema *De beata*; this allowed him to intervene with Philips during the second intersession.

5. IIa Intersessio

a. The great rewrite of *De ecclesia* took place in January in the subcommissions and in March in the assembled Doctrinal Commission. On January 15, 1964, the cardinal took part in the Coordinating Commission (he missed the December 28, 1963 meeting). Msgr. Charue noted that during the meeting Suenens expressed the desire that all the chapters of *De ecclesia* must be retained[338]. During the January 29, 1964 discussion in the subcommission on the text of the religious, Charue took into account Suenens' wish to mention the duty to the apostolate[339]. It is clear that Prignon, Philips and Thils kept Suenens informed regarding all the developments by sending him copies of the different drafts and *relationes*[340]. On March 10 the Coordinating Commission paid no particular attention to *De ecclesia*. There exists only a brief written report on the proceedings of the Doctrinal Commission[341].

b. On April 16 and 17, Suenens attended the meeting of the Coordinating Commission. On April 18 he was received in audience by the Pope.

c. The meeting on April 16, 1964[342]: Cardinal Agagianian reported on *De ecclesia*[343]. Suenens opposed Agagianian's proposal to limit the

336. Fund Suenens, 1577, 1583-1585, 1586.
337. Fund Suenens, 1578.
338. Msgr. Charue was interested in guaranteeing that the religious did not receive a separate chapter (cf. DECLERCK – SOETENS [eds.], *Carnets conciliaires de l'évêque de Namur A.-M. Charue* [n. 8], pp. 132, 134, 145). This intervention by Suenens is not mentioned in the *Processus verbalis* (cf. *AS* V/2, pp. 119-122).
339. DECLERCK – SOETENS (eds.), *Carnets conciliaires de l'évêque de Namur A.-M. Charue* (n. 8), p. 150.
340. Fund Suenens, 1808-1815; Fund Philips, 1444-1445.
341. Cf. *AS* V/2, pp. 157-158, 163.
342. For a report of this meeting cf. *Processus verbalis, AS* V/2, pp. 289-293. See also the notes by Prignon, Fund Prignon, 823-825.
343. Suenens, fearful that his trip to the U.S. would keep him from attending, had arranged for a replacement. However, since the trip was postponed, he was able to be present.

discussion in the Council to a number of theses taken from the last two chapters (*De indole eschatologica ecclesiae* and *De beata*). It was agreed that the discussion would be identical in form to that held on other chapters. This was followed by a frontal attack by Cicognani regarding collegiality. It was known that Ottaviani, who had approved this text on March 6 in the Doctrinal Commission[344], had changed his mind[345]. Cicognani was of the opinion that such a "dubious" text should not be distributed to the Patres. Suenens defended the idea that the text of the Doctrinal Commission should be sent *talis qualis* to the bishops; according to him, all the other cardinals opposed Cicognani's point of view. Also according to Suenens, it was Döpfner who had proposed that two relators, one from each side, would set forth their views prior to the vote[346].

The *Processus verbalis* mentions that the text *De ecclesia* will be sent to the Patres, but that discussion will still be possible with regard to n. 22 of Caput III[347].

344. Cf. DECLERCK – SOETENS (eds.), *Carnets conciliaires de l'évêque de Namur A.-M. Charue* (n. 8), p. 162.
345. Cf. his letter to Cicognani, April 13, 1964, *AS* V/2, pp. 183-184. On April 17, 1964 Prignon noted: "Le cardinal me dit qu'il a demandé à Felici s'il était bien exact qu'Ottaviani avait envoyé une lettre de rétractation. Felici a répondu qu'il n'avait pas envoyé une lettre mais qu'il l'avait fait *viva voce*. En effet il l'avait vu sortir d'une audience chez le Saint-Père et en sortant du bureau privé du pape, Ottaviani lui avait dit, à lui Felici, qu'il avait signalé au pape le danger, l'insuffisance du chapitre sur la collégialité et qu'il avait dit au Saint-Père qu'il retirait son vote d'approbation. Et comme Felici lui demandait: alors comment il avait pu le donner, il a répondu qu'il s'était laissé entraîner par l'atmosphère de la commission et du fait que tous les Pères s'étaient montrés favorables. Toutefois il semble bien que le cardinal Browne n'ait pas voté" (Fund Prignon, 824). And Döpfner writes in his Diary on April 16, 1964: "Ganz neue Diskussion über n. 22. Cicognani will diese n. stürzen. Ottaviani hat offensichtlich im Hintergrund gearbeitet und das 3. Kapitel an die italienischen Bischöfe geschickt, um die Kollegialität zu stürzen. Ein übles Spiel!" (TREFFLER [ed.], *Julius Kardinal Döpfner. Briefe und Notizen* [n. 9], p. 30).
346. This is what happened *de facto* during the third session. This suggestion is not mentioned in the *Processus verbalis*. Regarding this Prignon notes: "Vu la confusion qui règne toujours à la commission de coordination, le cardinal Suenens nous a répété qu'il ne savait pas ce que finalement les deux secrétaires minutanti [V. Fagiolo en V. Carbone] allaient consigner dans leur rapport et qu'il ne serait pas étonné que ce rapport soit tel qu'il n'apparaisse pas que l'unanimité des cardinaux s'était faite contre le card. Cicognani. On verra bien. Il a l'intention de raconter la chose au Saint-Père et de lui montrer à quel point est arrivé son Secrétaire d'État" (Fund Prignon, 823).
347. Cf. *Processus verbalis*, *AS* V/2, p. 291. This does not mean that the text had already been sent. On May 19, 1964, Felici sends 13 *suggerimenti* on behalf of the pope to the Doctrinal Commission; it was only on July 7, 1964 (cf. *Processus verbalis*, *AS* V/2, pp. 646-647) that the text *De ecclesia* was sent to the Patres (Cf. also *AS* VI/3, p. 151). The 13 *Suggerimenti* were prepared by a small commission, composed by Garrone, Colombo, Ramirez and Bertrams, cf. *Processus verbalis*, *AS* V/2, pp. 166, 184-185.

d. Audience of Suenens on April 18, 1964[348]: According to Suenens, this was an interesting audience. At it he informed the Pope about the incident with Cicognani on April 16 and suggested that it might be time to replace him[349]. He also congratulated the Pope on his speech to the Italian bishops[350]. During the same audience Suenens mentioned the action of the General Superiors for a separate chapter in *De ecclesia* on the religious and asked the Pope if it would not be better if he offered a guarantee that there would be freedom of opinion on this point[351].

e. Suenens did not intervene in the episode of the 13 *suggerimenti* or in the further treatment of *De indole eschatologica ecclesiae* and *De beata*, all of which were discussed in the Doctrinal Commission at the beginning of June of 1964. Nevertheless it is known that Prignon sent him all the documents relevant to the 13 *suggerimenti*[352] and recounted on a tape made at the end of June all details of the Doctrinal Commission's discussions[353]. Charue also kept him informed regarding the compromise that Philips had prepared regarding the *mediatio* in *De beata*[354]. Suenens was not present at the meeting of the Coordinating Commission on June 26, 1964. Agagianian reported on the last two chapters of *De ecclesia* and Felici reported extensively on the discussion of the 13 *suggerimenti*. He mentioned that Msgr. Charue had requested to keep the discussion of these suggestions in the Doctrinal Commission, so that a number of changes was not be accepted by the commission. After a fairly long discussion, it was nevertheless decided to send the text *De ecclesia* to the *Patres*[355].

f. Suenens receives Philips in Malines on August 1, 1964 in order to discuss some ecumenical elements of *De ecclesia* as well as the issue of Mariology[356]. Strong reactions from the Orthodox camp on the issue of collegiality had upset the cardinal. They considered the act of emphasizing this idea to be a worsening of the Roman's 'legalistic'

348. Cf. Fund Suenens, 1705 and Fund Prignon, 825-826.
349. Cicognani, who was born in 1883, remained at this post until April of 1969.
350. This speech was given on April 14, 1964. In it the Pope speaks highly of the Council and requests the full and enthusiastic cooperation of the Italian bishops (cf. CAPRILE, *Il Concilio Vaticano II*. Vol. III [n. 264], pp. 326-328).
351. Fund Prignon, 826.
352. Fund Suenens, 1829-1832.
353. Fund Prignon, 828, June 27, 1964, pp. 5-7.
354. Fund Suenens, 1835-1836.
355. Cf. *Processus verbalis*, AS V/2, pp. 634-638.
356. Cf. SCHELKENS (ed.), *Carnets conciliaires de Mgr. Gérard Philips* (n. 47), Cahier XII, pp. 13-16.

views on the Pope's role and powers. Philips explained that a number of the Orthodox objections were (at least partially) outdated given that *De populo Dei* had been treated before the Hierarchy, by a passage on role of the local churches and the patriarchates, and by the fact that the authority of the primate was balanced by the description of the Bishops' college. At the same time, he also knew that the juridical description of the Pope's authority would never be acceptable to the Orthodox Churches[357].

As far as Mariology is concerned, the cardinal submitted a text[358], "which refers to Mary and the apostolate in very strong terms and which portrayed Mary as source and fundament"[359]. Philips tried to draft a more acceptable version, but acknowledged that it was a hazardous undertaking. In a letter dated August 4, 1964, Philips explained to Suenens the position of the Orthodox. He also sent suggestions for textual changes to *De beata*[360].

g. At the Coordinating Commission of September 11, 1964, the manner of voting on *De ecclesia* was discussed; apparently Suenens did not intervene[361].

h. A few conclusions with regard to the second intersession. Suenens' interventions with regard to *De ecclesia* were drastically reduced

357. Fund Philips, 1172.
358. Fund Suenens, 2898, copied by Philips by hand: Fund Philips, 1174.
359. Cf. SCHELKENS (ed.), *Carnets conciliaires de Mgr. Gérard Philips* (n. 47), Cahier XII, p. 15 where Philips noted: "The Cardinal is usually down to earth, but with regard to mariology, he is a zealot and investigates the matter neither critically nor ecumenically". For this text by Suenens, cf. Fund Suenens, 2898 and Fund Philips, 1174. The archive also contains two handwritten notes by Suenens. One defending the title 'mediatrix' (Fund Suenens, 2897) and another to underlining the role of Our Lady (Fund Suenens, 2899).
360. Cf. Fund Philips, 1173 and Fund Suenens, 2894. Cf. also SUENENS, *Mémoires sur le Concile Vatican II*, pp. 52-53. Suenens had proposed the following text to Philips: "Maria iure dicitur Regina Apostolorum et Mater apostolatus, tum quia in vita sua fuit archetypus omnis apostolatus, tum quia hodie omnis veri nominis apostolatus est participatio Eiusdem maternitatis spritualis, siquidem Christus hodie mystice nascitur et crescit de Spiritu Sancto ex Maria Virgine" (Fund Suenens, 2898 and Fund Philips, 1174). Philips' proposal ran as follows: "Unde etiam in opere suo apostolico [Ecclesia] ad Eam merito respicit, quae genuit Christum, ideo de Spiritu Sancto conceptum et de Virgine natum, ut in cordibus quoque fidelium nascatur et crescat; quae Virgo in sua vita exemplum exstitit materni illius affectus, quo cuncti in missione apostolica Ecclesiae cooperantes ad regenerandos homines animari oportet" (Fund Philips, 1173 and Fund Suenens, 2894). This last text appears almost literally in the final version of *Lumen gentium*, n. 65. Suenens labelled it as "un peu faible encore, mais quand-même c'est plus que ce qui s'y trouvait" (Cf. *Mémoires sur le Concile Vatican II*, p. 53).
361. Cf. *Processus verbalis*, AS V/2, pp. 685-687.

in number, at least when compared to the first intersession and the second session. This was due to factors:

- The new schema had been accepted during the second session (with the guidelines of the five *Propositiones*) and the revision was in good hands. The presence of Charue as vice-president, Philips as deputy secretary, Heuschen, Moeller, Thils, and Prignon as members or *periti* of the Doctrinal Commission, provided a solid guarantee for a well-balanced text and an immediate and direct line of communication to the cardinal.
- The most serious problem, that of collegiality, was treated with decreasing frequency by the Coordinating Commission but evermore directly by Felici, Cicognani and Paul VI[362]. The 13 *suggerimenti* of May 19, 1964 clearly demonstrate this. The *AS*, V-VI, show that Felici was particularly active in this area and had taken several initiatives. They were almost always in defence of the 'minority' view and without the knowledge of the Coordinating Commission or the moderators[363]. Even the Doctrinal Commission (sometimes including Ottaviani, Parente and Tromp) when confronted with some corrections and amendments to the text (for instance the 13 *Suggerimenti*) was not always aware of what was actually taking place nor of the true source of the initiatives. The malaise only increased during the third session, especially with the well-known *Nota explicativa praevia*.
- It is also clear that Cardinal Suenens, although a strong supporter of collegiality and of 'co-responsibility', felt less at ease in this very technical and specialised theological debate[364]. His interest turned more and more toward the schema XIII and especially toward the issue of birth control.

At the same time it is clear that the cardinal was kept well informed of the developments and that he, especially with regard to Mariology, did take some initiatives[365].

---

362. It is striking that the sessions of the Coordinating Commission, which, early on, sometimes lasted for several days, were usually reduced to one meeting of two or three hours during the second intersession. This only served to reinforce the absenteeism of the foreign cardinals.

363. Cf. a.o. *AS* VI/3, pp. 128-129, 136-148, 151, 184-185, 262-263, 357-358.

364. E.g. on January 23, 1964, Suenens writes to Paul VI: "Le Vatican II n'a de sens que dans la continuité du Vatican I et toute opposition entre l'un et l'autre est impensable. Une collégialité qui impliquerait une 'cogestion' quelconque de près ou de loin irait à l'encontre de la pensée du Seigneur et de la Tradition". This sentence clearly lacks precision. Cf. Fund Suenens, 1712.

365. In some, e.g. German circles of the Legion of Mary, Suenens was suspected of having abandoned the maximalistic theses on Mariology, something which was not true

6. IIIᵃ Sessio

The final form of the constitution *Lumen gentium* was approved during the third session. Two of the chapters (VII and VIII) were discussed by the Patres prior to their approval. Suenens made an intervention on both.

a. Suenens' intervention on the canonizations September 16, 1964[366]

Suenens made a number of proposals designed to reduce the time and expense of the canonization process. He even expressed the desire that the process be allowed to take place on the level of the bishops' conferences. He illustrated his text with statistics showing that from the beginning of the 18th century, 85% of the canonizations had been drawn from the ranks of the religious orders and that three European countries had all but monopolized the process by providing 90% of these canonizations [367]. Suenens wrote:

> Mon intention de fond était aussi d'obtenir la canonisation de Jean XXIII par un procédé beaucoup plus rapide. À la dernière minute, je n'ai pas osé donner ce passage, craignant des applaudissements qui auraient pu mettre le pape dans la difficulté et l'embarras et lui forcer la main[368].

The intervention did not make much of an impression. Charue mentions "une intervention guère appréciée"[369]; Congar summarizes the intervention, but refrains from commenting[370]; de Lubac was somewhat critical: "Intervention claire, amusante, simpliste, du genre publicitaire"[371].

b. The intervention on De beata September 17, 1964[372]

In this intervention, the cardinal warned against minimizing the role or status of Our Lady "sub praetextu et specie christocentrismi". Mary was

---

(cf. his intervention during the third session on September 17, 1964). In fact, Hilde Firtel, 'envoy' of the Legion of Mary in Germany wrote to Suenens on January 12, 1964, that she had had to defend the cardinal against accusations that he had made a 180 degree turn with respect to his beliefs regarding Our Lady. She also informs him that F. Duff [founder of the Legion of Mary] did not have a positive word to say about the attitude of the German bishops at the Council (Fund Suenens, 1840).

366. *AS* III/1, pp. 430-432.
367. Suenens used a study made by a Jesuit [H. Midar?] that was based upon statistics from 1800 to 1961. Suenens makes a mistake, when he speaks of "the beginning of the 18th century". Cf. Fund Suenens, 2047.
368. *Mémoires sur le Concile Vatican II*, p. 55.
369. Journal Charue, p. 215.
370. CONGAR, *Mon journal du Concile* (n. 9), Vol. II, p. 137.
371. Journal de Lubac, September 16, 1964, II, p. 118.
372. *AS* III/1, pp. 504-506.

also associated with the redemptive work of Christ: "ne timidi simus: gloria Mariae est gloria Filii sui". Furthermore, he insisted on mentioning the intimate connection between the spiritual motherhood of Mary and the apostolate of evangelization. Marial piety should never be allowed to be separated from apostolic mission. The cardinal's archives provide no information about whether he employed a theologian to help draft this intervention. He wrote:

> Je suis intervenu dans le débat sur la Très Sainte Vierge, sur le texte conciliaire, pour demander qu'il soit renforcé. Je savais que j'allais heurter nos théologiens à nous là-dessus mais j'ai cru de mon devoir de devoir dire que le texte me paraissait minimisant[373].

The reaction to this was fierce. Especially alarming was the passage that claimed that Our Lady had been short-changed "sub praetextu christocentrismi". Msgr. Heuschen, for example, asked: "How can one diminish the role of Mary by elevating her Son?"[374]. It is interesting to note that the cardinal excised this passage from the French translation that was circulated by the press[375]. Charue noted:

> Les interventions du card. Suenens ne furent guère appréciées … l'autre sur le danger de minimalisme dans le De Beata. Le lendemain Bea et Alfrink répliquèrent qu'il faut distinguer entre la dévotion et l'enseignement conciliaire. C'est élémentaire![376].

Philips wrote:

> Today … [there was an] intervention by Cardinal Suenens accusing the schema of minimism and anti-marial christocentrism … The impression is that the cardinal has damaged his prestige. I am sure he had no intention of attacking me personally[377]. The bishops, especially the Belgian ones, are outraged[378]. Several of my friends are concerned that I should not be too depressed but I have no reason to be down. I am not in the service of the cardinal, but in the service of the Church and of the truth. It is now clearer than ever that I am not 'his man'. I never was[379].

---

373. *Mémoires sur le Concile Vatican II*, p. 52.
374. Personal memory.
375. Fund Suenens, 2053.
376. Journal Charue, p. 215.
377. Philips was the primary author of this difficult and controversial chapter.
378. Congar noted: "Mgr Prignon me dit que les Belges (évêques et experts) sont furieux du discours du cardinal Suenens". Cf. CONGAR, *Mon journal du Concile* (n. 9), Vol. II, p. 142.
379. SCHELKENS (ed.), *Carnets conciliaires de Mgr. Gérard Philips* (n. 47), Cahier XII, pp. 22-23.

Moeller was again terribly dismayed:

> Discours du Cardinal. Impression générale est désastreuse ... Les [termes] "christocentrisme antimarial" sont une sorte de monstre théologique. "Peut-on exagérer le christocentrisme" demande un auditeur? ... Philips dit qu'il a été blessé[380].

Even Prignon, always so nuanced in his reports for the embassy, wrote:

> L'intervention du cardinal Suenens, dont la piété mariale est bien connue, n'a pas laissé de surprendre les uns et les autres. Il s'est détaché en effet de sa majorité habituelle. Il semble même avoir employé des termes dans un sens très général, sans se rendre compte séance tenante, que ces mots avaient pris un sens technique cristallisant les oppositions. On dit qu'il a fait une mise au point auprès des instances officielles[381].

As usual, de Lubac was very hard on Suenens:

> intervention digne du chef de la "Légion de Marie": simplisme activiste et mariologique; il contredit Bea: sous prétexte de "christocentrisme". On promeut, dit-il, un dangereux minimisme mariologique[382].

c. Nota praevia

It appears that Suenens did not intervene directly during the intense quarrels on collegiality and on the *Nota praevia* which took place mainly during the first weeks of November. His archives contain a note dated September 18, 1964 that was drafted by Moeller, Lécuyer and Dupuy in defence of collegiality. Suenens eventually gave this note to the Pope[383].

The archive also contains confidential information on the *Nota praevia* but he probably only received this afterwards from Prignon (by way of Philips)[384]. There is no indication that Suenens was actively involved in the compilation of this "top secret" file (Philips and Heuschen both played important roles). On November 12, he supposedly said to Moeller: "Le Pape n'est préparé ni théologiquement ni psychologiquement à la

---

380. Journal Moeller, Carnet 21, p. 7.
381. Fund Prignon, 1056, p. 12.
382. Journal de Lubac, September 17, 1964, II, p. 121. As early as 1946 de Lubac had written a 'Note d'un théologien' in which he warned against the "theology" of the Legion of Mary. Suenens, who was an ardent supporter of the Legion of Mary during the fifties while under V. O'Brien's influence, was very unhappy about the position taken by de Lubac.
383. Cf. Fund Suenens, 2060 and Fund Prignon, 843. On September 17, 1964 Congar wrote: "Mais Lécuyer doit nous quitter très vite: il va à une réunion organisée par Moeller: le Pape, qui continue à recevoir l'assaut des anti-collégiaux, a été, paraît-il, très impressionné par deux rapports en ce sens. Il faut élaborer un rapport qui fasse pièce à ces deux" (CONGAR, *Mon journal du Concile* [n. 9], Vol. II, p. 141).
384. Fund Suenens, 2061-2067.

collégialité"[385]. Of course, this could also be an allusion to the difficulties Suenens had had with regard to his intervention on conjugal ethics on October 29, 1964. It is also clear that neither the moderators nor the Coordinating Commission were involved in this matter: in reality everything had been arranged by the Pope (with his advisors, especially Colombo and Bertrams[386]), the Secretariat of State (Cicognani, Dell'Acqua), Felici, and the Doctrinal Commission.

On December 18, 1964, *i.e.*, after the session, Suenens wrote to the Pope: "qu'il lui sera une joie de vivre la collégialité, désormais fixée dans les textes, en profonde communion avec et sous l'égide du pape"[387].

7. Some final remarks

Suenens played an important role in the formulation and the production of the constitution *Lumen gentium* even if that role was more that of strategist than that of influential theologian.

a. Suenens was an intelligent tactician

– He was partly responsible for the fact that the old *De ecclesia* was rejected and replaced by a new schema.

His 'plan for the Council' contributed, at least indirectly, to the aforementioned rejection and replacement.

He was very farsighted in entrusting Philips (and that as early as October 15, 1962)[388], in cooperation with an international group of theologians, with the editing of a new schema.

As the person in charge of the Coordinating Commission he was able to watch over (and, later, to ultimately secure) the acceptance of Philips' schema by the Doctrinal Commission. This he did with the help of the 'squadra belga': Charue, Philips, Thils, Prignon and Moeller.

– During the second session as moderator, he succeeded in getting the five *Propositiones* approved. At that same time, he engineered the end

385. Journal Moeller, Carnet 23, p. 33.
386. For the role of W. Bertrams s. j. and his relations with C. Colombo, cf. a.o. Fund Colombo, C.XIII-14 ter, C.XVI-21, C.XVI-33, C.XVI-37, C.XVI-40, C.XXI-8.
387. Fund Suenens, 2307.
388. Suenens had known Philips while both were students at the Belgian College (Philips stayed there from 1919 to 1925, Suenens from 1921 to 1929). Nevertheless there was no spiritual or doctrinal connection between them (as Philips witnesses in his Diary): Philips was very critical of some of Suenens' publications. As the leader of the Catholic Action in Flanders, he was dissatisfied with Suenens' commitment to the Legion of Mary. Yet Suenens had the tactical insight to enlist Philips' services for a new *De ecclesia*.

of the obstruction of the conservative leaders of the Doctrinal Commission (Ottaviani, Tromp) not least thanks to the election of a second vice-president and a deputy secretary. To gain an insight into the degree of energy and perseverance he possessed, we only have to consider the fact that Suenens during the last two hectic weeks of October of 1963 made not only an important intervention on the charismas but also (on October 28) gave a splendid commemorative speech in honor of John XXIII.

– The importance of his role – like that of the other moderators – diminished during the second intersession and the third session. This was mainly due to the fact that by then most of the work was being taken care of by the Doctrinal Commission and because Paul VI took over more and more control of the difficult and sensitive collegiality debate.

b. *The following conclusions can be made with regard to Suenens' ideas*

During the course of the Council, Suenens' support for the idea of collegiality grew. This marked a clear evolution in his thinking from pre-Council days. As of the third session there is even evidence of tension between him and the Pope. The conflict between Paul VI and Suenens was over how exactly to implement the Council's statements on collegiality during the post-conciliar period. This conflict reached its climax in 1969-1971.

Suenens also genuinely supported the notion of simplifying the Church[389]. In this respect he made good contacts with Dossetti (Lercaro), Helder Camara[390] and Himmer[391]. Yet it is not possible to claim that he ever became an advocate of "L'Église des pauvres" as propagated by P. Gauthier and well-founded theologically by Congar and Chenu.

As far as Mariology is concerned, Suenens, for the most part, remained very loyal to the traditional ideas of the Legion of Mary.

c. *Ecumenical openness*

The cardinal's ecumenical openness thoroughly evolved during the course of the Council. This occurred mainly under the influence of Thils,

389. Cf. Fund Suenens, 419 where we find a note by Suenens – probably written prior to the Council – regarding 'De Praelaturis, honorificentiis, titulatura ecclesiastica et vestimentariis ornamentis'.
390. Cf. the abundant correspondence of Helder Camara, Fund Suenens, Index onomastique, p. 330.
391. Cf. Fund Suenens, 616, 1251-1253, 1263-1264, 2018.

Prignon and Moeller. He gradually turned from being little receptive to ecumenical thoughts at the beginning of the Council (thanks, *inter alia*, to the activist apostolic ideas he had gleaned from the Legion of Mary) into a defender of religious freedom and the Secretariat for Christian Unity even as he managed to maintain multiple ecumenical contacts.

If Suenens played an important role in the development of the constitution *Lumen gentium*, this is due to his tactical insight, to his ability to appeal to a multitude of capable and diverse collaborators, and, especially, to his courage and perseverance.

IV. THE INFLUENCE OF CARDINAL SUENENS ON THE REALISATION OF THE PASTORAL CONSTITUTION *GAUDIUM ET SPES*[392]

1. Introduction

The *squadra belga* exerted far less influence on the editing process of *Gaudium et spes* than they did upon *Lumen gentium*. *Gaudium et spes* was much more *le schéma français*. Nevertheless, it is clear that several Belgians played a significant role: Msgr. Philips, as deputy secretary of the Doctrinal Commission[393], Msgr. Charue, whose main contribution was to the chapter entitled *De cultura* (he was assisted by the *periti* Moeller, Rigaux, Dondeyne), and Msgr. Heuschen, on the chapter *De matrimonio*, (assisted by Prof. V. Heylen[394]). Msgr. Prignon, Prof. Houtart and L. Dingemans, O.P also contributed.

Cardinal Suenens also played a fairly important role in both the conception and realization of this constitution. In December of 1962, the

---

392. For the history of *Gaudium et spes*, see esp.: R. TUCCI, *Introduction historique et doctrinale à la Constitution pastorale*, in Y. CONGAR – M. PEUCHMARD (eds.), *Vatican II, L'Église dans le monde de ce temps: Constitution pastorale Gaudium et Spes* (Unam Sanctam, 65b), Vol. II, Paris, Cerf, 1967, 33-127. C. MOELLER, *Die Geschichte der Pastoralkonstitution*, in *LTK. Das Zweite Vatikanische Konzil*, Vol. III, Freiburg-Basel-Vienna, Herder, 1968, 242-278; and the standard work by G. TURBANTI, *Un Concilio per il mondo moderno: La redazione della costituzione pastorale 'Gaudium et Spes' del Vaticano II* (Testi e ricerche di scienze religiose. Nuova serie, 24), Bologna, Mulino, 2000.

393. The many records (e.g. during the third intersession: Fund Philips, 2153-2497; fourth session: Fund Philips, 2574-2721) of the Philips Fund bear witness to his enormous influence as editor-in-chief and defender of the text (at least until his illness of October 25, 1965).

394. Cf. M. LAMBERIGTS – L. DECLERCK, *Le texte de Hasselt: Une étape méconnue de l'histoire du De Matrimonio (schéma XIII)*, in *ETL* 80 (2004) 485-505. And also Fund Heuschen.

Coordinating Commission charged him with monitoring this schema's progress. This was natural given that he had been interested in the problem of the Church's relationship to the modern world for some time. Even before the second World War, as philosophy professor at the Saint-Joseph Seminary in Malines, he had been thinking through this issue and its implications. He published several articles in the *Collectanea Mechliniensia* and in *La Revue catholique des idées et des faits*[395]. As vice-rector of the Catholic University in Louvain (1940-1945), he was on good terms with Prof. Franz Grégoire[396], a well-known theology philosopher and specialist in Marxism, and he was involved in the realisation of the Higher Institute of Religious Studies[397]. From his first contacts with the Legion of Mary in 1947, he was, as auxiliary bishop, concerned with how to best invigorate the Church's apostolate to the modern world[398].

He was also Chair of the Belgian section of *Pax Christi* and Chair of the Interdiocesan Commission of the Media[399].

Beginning in 1958, under the influence of Veronica O'Brien, Suenens became interested in the problems surrounding birth control and the moral admissibility of the tools that make birth control possible[400]. Suenens was at the origin of the special 'secret' commission (it was directly dependent of the Secretariat of State and only in second instance from the Holy Office) that John XXIII established in April of 1963 to study this matter. Paradoxically, the existence of this commission was one of the reasons (or pretexts?) behind Paul VI's choice to withdraw this matter from the Council's purview. As of 1964, Suenens' interest increasingly turned to schema XIII's chapter *De matrimonio*. He made many attempts to push the Church toward a more 'open' position. It is impossible to avoid speaking of the issue of birth control in a study of Suenens' influence on *Gaudium et spes* because this was exactly what he was most dedicated to.

---

395. Cf. Fund Suenens, A.P., box 68.

For the *Collectanea Mechliniensia* see esp.: *Individu et Société*, 1934 (offprint, 19 p.); *Aperçus sur la morale phénoménologique de M. E. De Bruyne*, 1935, pp. 524-535; *Pour hiérarchiser nos valeurs religieuses*, 1936 (offprint, 11 p.); *Personne et Société*, 1939, pp. 164-173.

For *La Revue catholique des idées et des faits*, there are several articles in 1938, 1939, and 1940, a.o.: *L'humanisme chrétien*, January 28, 1938, pp. 1-3; *L'art d'arriver au vrai par le détachement*, January 13, 1939, pp. 15-18; *L'unité dans l'Église*, pp. 20-22; *Réflexions sur la morale internationale*, January 12, 1940, pp. 12-15; *Morale et Corps mystique*, pp. 16-18; *La morale de M. E. De Bruyne*, pp. 8-12.

396. Cf. Fund Suenens, A.P., box 1.

397. Cf. SUENENS, *Souvenirs et espérances* (n. 11), pp. 32-34.

398. Cf. a.o. his book SUENENS, *L'Église en état de mission* (n. 22).

399. Cf. *Katholiek Jaarboek voor België*, Brussel, 1960, p. 274, and 288.

400. Cf. DECLERCK, *Le rôle joué* (n. 40), p. 457.

2. Anteconcilium

On June 28, 1958, Suenens held a conference at the '1ère Conférence mondiale de la Santé' (organised in Brussels on the occasion of Expo 1958[401]; H. de Riedmatten[402] was present[403]). It was there that he broached the topic of birth control for the first time. From 1959 until 1974, Suenens was the driving force behind the colloquia on sexuality and sexology organized by and held at the University of Louvain. Thanks to him, Louvain established the "Institut interfacultaire des sciences familiales et sexologiques" in 1961. In 1960, Suenens published *Un problème crucial. Amour et maîtrise de soi*. Although he defended the traditional positions with regard to conjugal ethics, he also inaugurated the discussion about the responsible parenthood[404].

a. Vota Antepraeparatoria[405]

The *Vota* that Suenens sent to Tardini on November 10, 1959 did not contain any social, political, economic or cultural subjects. He did, however, write a small text on *De matrimonio* in which he pled for a more thorough preparation for Christian marriage and requested a more adequate rite for the celebration of marriages by making a direct reference to the profound rite from the Anglican *Prayer Book*. He also believed that it should be possible to involve the religious, both male and female, in the process of preparation for marriage[406].

---

401. "Pour moi, ce problème [du Birth Control] commence par le discours d'ouverture à l'Exposition Internationale de Bruxelles. Lors de l'Exposition, j'ai dû faire le discours d'ouverture au Congrès Mondial de la Santé. Il y avait là 3.000 infirmières, médecins, chercheurs etc. J'en ai profité pour faire un appel pour que tous les chercheurs, tous les hommes compétents en cette matière, mettent leurs efforts ensemble pour essayer d'aider nos familles sur le douloureux problème de la régulation des naissances". Cf. Suenens' text *Mémoire sur le problème du Birth Control tel que je l'ai vécu de 1958 à 1968* (typed text – 18 p. – from a tape made by Suenens, just after the publication of *Humanae Vitae*, Fund Suenens [Birth Control et Humanae Vitae: Henceforth B.C. and H.V.], 1).

402. H. de Riedmatten (1919-1979) o.p., from Switzerland, Permanent Observer of the Holy See at the U.N. in Geneva. Cf. P. CHENAUX, *Le Saint-Siège et les organisations internationals: Le rôle du Père de Riedmatten o.p.*, in *Paul VI et la vie internationale* (Publicazioni dell'Istituto Paolo VI, 12), Rome, Studium, 1992, 106-112.

403. Fund Suenens, B.C. and H.V., 2125.

404. Cf. DECLERCK, *Le rôle joué* (n. 40), pp. 457-458.

405. Cf. ADA I/2, Pars 1, pp. 140-148.

406. Suenens was already concerned with the apostolic task and the formation of the religious (influenced by *inter alia* V. O'Brien and the Legion of Mary). Cf. his book L.-J. SUENENS, *Promotion apostolique de la religieuse*, Bruges, Desclée de Brouwer, published at the end of 1962.

b. Interventions in the Commissio centralis praeparatoria

1. When the schema *De castitate, virginitate, matrimonio, familia*[407] was discussed on May 7, 1962, Suenens held an extensive intervention. He felt that the schema, when discussing sexuality, was too restrictive; it adopted a heavily biological perspective instead of beginning with a broader, human and anthropological approach. Only with the latter approach does it become possible to understand recent discoveries and research and to integrate them into the classical doctrine.

For example:

- the conjugal union must also be seen as a symbol of the union of love between God and his people
- chastity is not to be limited to the "control" of the sexual physical urge; but needs to be situated in the broader perspective of conjugal love
- the traditional doctrine on the *finis primarius et secundarius* of marriage might require a new formulation.

In addition, he believed that it was necessary to provide people with a more positive notion of birth control and of the responsibility of parents when determining the number of children they would produce.

2. On May 11, during the treatment of the schema *De processu matrimoniali*, he noted that it would be better to send this matter to the Commission for the Reformation of the Code of Canon Law[408].

3. On June 16, when dealing with the schema *De praeparatione ad matrimonium*, Suenens launched another proposal on mixed marriages: "Placet iuxta modum i.e. in voto Cardinalium Liénart, König et Ottaviani praesertim quoad instructionem obligatoriam in casu matrimonii mixti et quoad praemium propositum pro iis qui instructionem revera acceperunt nempe eis concedatur maior solemnitas in celebratione matrimonii mixti"[409].

c. Elements from Suenens' 'plan' for the Council[410]

It is well-known that Suenens' presented plan of May 16, 1962 contained two sections: *Ecclesia ad intra* and *Ecclesia ad extra*. In the latter he focused on what both individuals and the world expected from the Church: what are their fundamental aspirations and what does the Church

407. *ADA* II/2, Pars 3, pp. 962-964.
408. *ADA* II/2, Pars 3, p. 1277.
409. *ADA* II/2, Pars 4, p. 400.
410. Cf. SUENENS, *Aux origines du Concile Vatican II* [n. 16], mainly pp. 16-18.

have to offer? He followed this with four areas in which the Church could offer some help and guidance:

- The family community. He desired a new encyclical on conjugal ethics ("Il y aurait lieu de refaire pour l'encyclique *Casti connubii* ce qui a été fait pour *Rerum novarum* revue par *Quadragesimo anno* et remise au point par *Mater et magistra*") which should supply an answer to the crucial problem of birth control.
- The economical community. One expects that the Church will continue to condemn atheistic communism, but one must recognize 'la part de vérité' of communism. It is necessary to strongly condemn social injustice and the unequal distribution of wealth. The goods were created for everyone's use.
- The civil community. In the modern world, there are problems in Church/State relations. For example, the notion of religious freedom is something that the Church claims as its right. What, however, is the Church's attitude toward the religious freedom of others?
- The international community. After two world wars, the world deeply desired peace. The Church has to contribute to the push for peace and has to take a stand against the war, the atom bomb, and address the use of nuclear energy for peaceful ends, etc.

It is striking that, in this plan, Suenens offered a virtual index to what would become *Gaudium et spes*:

Pars I. De ecclesia et vocatione hominis
Pars II. De quibusdam problematibus urgentioribus:
- Caput I. De dignitate matrimonii et familiae fovenda
- Caput II. De culturae condicionibus in mundo hodierno
- Caput III. De vita oeconomico – sociali
- Caput IV. De vita communitatis politicae
- Caput V. De pace fovenda et de communitate gentium promovenda.

Only the chapter on culture was missing from Suenens' plan.

d. John XXIII's radio speech

The radio speech by John XXIII on September 11, 1962, mentions 'la vitalità ad extra' of the Church, an allusion to Suenens' chapter *Ecclesia ad extra* from which he borrowed the following: "ils cherchent l'amour au sein du foyer, leur pain quotidien pour eux-mêmes et leur famille, la paix tant à l'intérieur de chaque pays que celle entre les nations"[411].

---

411. Cf. supra *Suenens' plan for the Council*.

e. Social problems

Suenens' archives also contain a few pages of handwritten notes[412] which he probably used either for interventions in the *Commissio centralis praeparatoria* or for the preparation of his 'plan'. As far as the contents of schema XIII go, two items are recoverable:

– Une prise de conscience familiale. He underlined the fact of the population explosion:

> Si la morale bloque toute solution par le recours aux techniques anticonceptionnelles, il faut chercher la solution à ce problème familial majeur dans une double direction: il faut d'une part que l'homme apprenne à maîtriser son instinct et à le guider lui-même selon les règles de la raison, de la loyauté, de la charité et de la prudence chrétienne. Il faut d'autre part l'aider à acquérir cette indispensable maîtrise de soi par l'éducation progressive mais aussi en favorisant toute recherche scientifique sur le rythme de la fécondité qui peut aider à résoudre un problème crucial de conscience[413].

Suenens believed that this problem should also be dealt with during the process of preparing a couple for marriage.

– Une prise de conscience sociale. "L'explosion démographique pose également avec urgence et acuité le problème non résolu encore de la misère et de la faim dans le monde". The Church must condemn the unequal division of wealth and resources. The concept of private property has its limitations. Before condemning communism, which bases its arguments on the problems this system has generated, one must look for the root of the evil. "Un anticommunisme qui ne proclame pas cette injustice initiale ne peut que nuire gravement à l'Église".

3. Ia Sessio

It is known that Suenens during the first session made several attempts to organize the Council's agenda and subject matter[414]. This was done through his activity in the *Secretariatus pro Concilii negotiis extra ordinem*. Interesting in this connection is the letter written by 14 bishops (including Himmer, McGrath, Larraín, Ancel, and Helder Camara) on

---

412. Cf. Fund Suenens, 417.

413. In the early 1960's, Suenens hoped that scientific research would lead to a more precise understanding of female fertility and thus help the rhythm method become an efficient method of birth control. He travelled as far as the United States looking for support in organizing scientific research for this field (cf. Fund Suenens B.C. and H.V., 146-149, 949-972, 2129-2129bis).

414. Cf. supra: *Suenens' plan for the Council*.

November 21, 1962, and presented by a delegation, headed by Msgr. Him-
mer, to Cicognani, president of this *Secretariatus*[415], on November 28.
In it they requested the establishment of a commission '*de munere Eccle-
siae ad extra*' to deal with the problems of justice, peace, and poverty and
to promote an evangelical revival among both the shepherds and the flock.
This letter was drafted by a number of protagonists of the movement
'Jésus, l'Église et les pauvres'[416]. The fact that they used the terminology
Ecclesia ad extra makes Suenens' influence plain.

In his speech on December 4, 1962, Suenens repeated his desire for a
schema *De ecclesia ad extra* and requested the establishment of a *Secretariatus pro rebus socialibus* and adds "In nuntio nostro initiali [*Le message au monde*, from October 20, 1962] manifesta apparuit coram mundo
voluntas nostra dialogum instituendi. Creatio Secretariatus apparebit ut
expressio practica et concreta huius voluntatis"[417].

Following various maneuvers by the *Secretariatus* and the General
Secretariat, an overview of the 20 schemas to be treated by the Council
was finally distributed to the Patres on December 5, 1962[418]. It included
the following schemas:

    V.   De ordine morali
    VI. De castitate, virginitate, matrimonio et familia
    VII. De ordine sociali et de communitate gentium.

It was important that Suenens was charged with the responsibility for
De ordine morali and *De ordine sociali* (the latter probably included
De communitate gentium, no longer mentioned anywhere else) and Spell-
man with *De castitate, virginitate, matrimonio et familia*.

By the end of the first session, Suenens had successfully brought
together a few chapters of his proposal *De ecclesia ad extra*. During the
first intersession, the chapter *De matrimonio* was added. Also important
is that the idea that these chapters should not only be entrusted to the
Doctrinal Commission, had gradually gained ground. John XXIII had

---

415. Cf. Fund Suenens, 616.

416. Cf. D. PELLETIER, *Une marginalité engagée: Le groupe 'Jésus, l'Église et les pauvres'*, in M. LAMBERIGTS – C. SOETENS – J. GROOTAERS (eds.), *Les Commissions conciliaires à Vatican II* (Instrumenta Theologica, 18), Leuven, Bibliotheek van de Faculteit der
Godgeleerdheid, 1996, pp. 71-72. Rightly D. Pelletier remarks (p. 72): "... le groupe
["Jésus, l'Église et les pauvres"] participe, à une place sans doute modeste et en tout cas
impossible à évaluer avec exactitude, au processus qui va donner naissance au projet de
schéma XVII".

417. Cf. TUCCI, *Introduction historique et doctrinale à la Constitution* (n. 392), pp. 38-
40.

418. Cf. Fund Suenens, 801 and supra: *Suenens' plan for the Council*.

already established a Commissio mixta for *De revelatione,* what was a good omen.

4. Iª Intersessio

a. *Suggestions sent to Suenens*

Even before the first meeting of the Coordinating Commission, Suenens was being contacted regarding *Ecclesia ad extra*:

– Helder Camara wrote letters to Suenens on December 16, 1962, and January 7 and 14, 1963[419].
– On December 25, 1962, Lambruschini, a Roman moral theologian, sent a letter to Suenens in which he informed him that his fifth-year theology course at the Lateranum was using Suenens' book *Un problème crucial. Amour et maîtrise de soi* and in which he offered his help with regard to the Council's work[420].
– On January 15, Henri de Riedmatten wrote to Suenens that, because of the debate being held in the U.N., clear positions are necessary regarding the demographic problem[421].
– On January 17, 1963, Himmer forwarded a copy of a letter by Ancel to Cicognani, in which Ancel repeated the request for a Secretariat ad extra, as requested by Suenens in his intervention of December 4, 1962, and in which he reminded Cicognani of their letter of November 21, 1962[422].
– On January 18, 1963, Houtart sent Suenens a text 'La fonction de l'Église face au monde'[423].

b. *Coordinating Commission of January 21-27, 1963*[424]

1. First is Suenens' final attempt at grouping the 20 schemas around the topics of *De ecclesia ad intra* and *De ecclesia ad extra*[425]. Including among the latter were *De ordine morali, De ordine familiali, De*

---

419. Cf. Fund Suenens, 744-748.
420. Fund Suenens, B.C. and H.V., 2122.
421. Fund Suenens, 1321.
422. Cf. Fund Suenens, 1251-1253. Chenu had written on January 3, 1963 to Ancel to suggest the erection of this secretariate and to contact Suenens in this regard. cf. M.D. CHENU, *Notes quotidiennes au concile*, Paris, Cerf, 1995, p. 51, note 1.
423. Cf. Fund Suenens, 1254-1255.
424. For more details, see TURBANTI, *Un Concilio per il mondo moderno* (n. 392), pp. 181-198.
425. Cf. supra *Suenens' plan for the Council* and Fund Suenens, 804.

ordine communicationum socialium, De ordine sociali-oeconomico, and *De ordine internationali.* To this document Suenens has added by hand: *Ecclesia erga pauperes.* The attempt failed.

2. The meeting of the Coordinating Commission was the first time that schema XVII received a certain amount of both form and consistency. Suenens criticized the current texts very harshly. His archives show that the Cardinal had prepared his reports rather thoroughly and with the help of several theologians.

De ordine morali[426]: In order to critique the existing schema, Suenens sought the advice of L. Janssens, a professor of moral theology at the University of Louvain[427]. On January 4, 1963, R. Ceuppens, Suenens' vicar-general, requested that Janssens send his critical remarks, which he had already noted down for Msgr. De Smedt, to Suenens[428]. On January 7, Ceuppens asked Janssens to come to the archdiocese in Malines. Soon L. Janssens is able to submit four *Animadversiones* on the text and two pages of *Propositiones ad novum schema ordinandum*[429]. These pages, which were loaded with technical details, became, after some retouching by Ceuppens, Suenens' Relatio on this chapter.

The *general* remarks were severe: the text was insufficiently supported by the Scriptures; its doctrine is too polemical; and it takes inadequate notice of recent advances in the psychological sciences. The *particular* remarks contained, *inter alia*, a critique of the use of the 'lex naturae' as a static given and asked for more attention 'pro situatione singulari et personali' of the people. The contents of Chapter VI (*De castitate et de pudicitia christiana*) needed to be addressed in a different context, namely under the rubric of marriage.

De ordine sociali[430]: Suenens himself made critical notes on the text[431]; someone filled eight pages with remarks[432] and, afterwards, the

---

426. Cf. *AS* V/1, pp. 144-147 and Fund Suenens, 825-834.
427. As early as 1939, Suenens had written an extensive review on the magister dissertation of L. JANSSENS, *Personne et société: Théories actuelles et essai doctrinal* (Dissertationes ad gradum magistri in facultate theologica vel in facultate iuris canonici consequendum conscriptae. Series II, 32), Gembloux, Duculot, 1939. Cf. Fund Suenens, A.P., box 68.
428. Cf. Fund De Smedt, 615-617.
429. Fund Suenens, 832-833.
430. Cf. *AS* V/1, pp. 148-152.
431. Fund Suenens, 835.
432. Fund Suenens, 837. The author is not indicated. C. Moeller says that Suenens contacted F. Houtart, Y. Calvez, Lalande and H. de Riedmatten for advice, but does not provide any proof. Cf. MOELLER, *Die Geschichte der Pastoralkonstitution* (n. 392), p. 248.

text was typed out in Malines[433]. The remarks on the existing schema are in French, while the conclusions are in Latin. In the conclusions, Suenens proposed: 'Schema propositum reordinandum mihi videtur' because:

– the text does not take some modern problems into account as indicated in *Mater et magistra* (especially those of socialization, development aid and economic equality)
– the schema was too 'academic' and poorly reflected the contemporary outlook
– the schema, with the exception of chapter V, mainly concentrated on the problems facing Western Europe.

De communitate gentium[434]: H. de Riedmatten drafted the critical analysis of the existing text as well as a plan for the new schema for Suenens[435]. Suenens again concludes: "Schema propositum reordinandum mihi videtur"; this time, he offered the following reasons:

– The literary genre seemed more like a tract on moral law and was not fitting for a Council text. Moreover, its style lacked power and character.
– Several important questions were not dealt with. Others were presented in too juridical and statistical a manner.
– Insufficient attention was paid to the historical progress and the fundamental unity of mankind.
– The text was solely based on the natural law and human reason; no attention was paid to revelation or to faith.

During the meeting the discussion was brief[436]. Suenens proposed that the texts be rewritten by a mixed commission. Cardinal Urbani requested that a single constitution be developed under the title 'De praesentia ecclesiae in mundo moderno'. Indeed, when it was decided to draft one new constitution on January 26, this only became possible because of analogous proposals made by two other relators, Liénart and Urbani. In his Relatio on *De deposito fidei*, Liénart proposed that a doctrinal decree

---

433. Fund Suenens, 838-839.
434. Cf. *AS* V/1, pp. 153-159.
435. Letter from de Riedmatten to Suenens on January 7, 1963, with his added remarks: Fund Suenens, 840-841. Cf. also letter from de Riedmatten to Döpfner on January 15, 1963: "Ich glaube, Kardinal Suenens habe die Absicht, das vorliegende Schema stark zu kritisieren und die Schaffung eines Sekretariats für all diese Problemen vorzuschlagen" (TREFFLER [ed.], *Julius Kardinal Döpfner. Briefe und Notizen* [n. 9], p. 344).
436. Cf. *Processus verbalis*, *AS* V/1, pp. 162-163.

entitled 'De homine' be drafted[437]. In his Propositiones on the Lay Apostolate[438], Urbani proposed that a schema 'De praesentia ecclesiae in mundo hodierno', be drafted by a Commissio mixta (the Doctrinal Commission and the Commission for the Lay Apostolate). This proposal was approved on January 25, 1963[439].

The fate of the schema 'De castitate, virginitate, matrimonio et familia', which had been presented by Spellman in a new text "Schema Constitutionis dogmaticae 'De casta vita Christianorum'"[440], is less clear. In the *Processus verbalis* (of January 23, 1963), we only read:

> Il Card. Urbani: approvo lo schema per quel che contiene, ma suggerisco che sia utilizzato in altri schemi; al più ridurlo alla sola parte 'de familia' con una premessa sul matrimonio, lasciando il resto. Il Card. Confalonieri: lasciare da parte il 'de castitate et virginitate' e ridurre lo schema al 'De matrimonio et familia'. Viene approvato concordamente questa proposta[441].

In fact, this schema disappeared from the agenda and the text *De matrimonio* was deferred to the new schema XVII[442].

Finally, during the last meeting of this session (January 27, 1963), Suenens suggested that the Commissio mixta be presided over by Cardinal Forni[443], while Felici suggested that this matter be left up to the presidents of these two commissions. Cardinal Urbani presented the list of 17 schemata that still needed to be treated, a list that was accepted by the Commission[444]. Although it is not completely clear how the Coordinating Commission came to this decision[445], it is true that on January 30 Cicognani sent a letter to the presidents of the conciliar commissions to which he appended a list of the schemata to be dealt with at the Council. Schema XVII was specifically mentioned: "De ecclesiae principiis et actione ad bonum societatis promovendum". It contained the following elements:

---

437. Cf. *AS* V/1, p. 66.

438. *AS* V/1, p. 117. Cf. also the report made by Glorieux for Urbani, *AS* V/1, pp. 113-114.

439. *Processus verbalis*, *AS* V/1, p. 133, 162-163.

440. For his Relatio and this new text, cf. *AS* V/1, pp. 71-89.

441. *AS* V/1, p. 97.

442. With good reason Spellman protested against this in a letter to Cicognani on February 13, 1963. He also sent a copy to all members of the Coordinating Commission. Cf. *AS* V/1, pp. 516-517 and Fund Suenens, 868-869. He repeats his objections in the beginning of 1964 in a letter to Cicognani, cf. *AS* V/2, pp. 134-135.

443. From 1953 to 1962, E. Forni had been nuncio in Belgium.

444. *AS* V/1, p. 182.

445. The discussions, the decision process and the *Processus verbalis* of the Coordinating Commission are not always perfectly clear.

a) De admirabili vocatione hominis secundum Deum
b) De persona humana in societate
c) De matrimonio, familia et problemate demographico
d) De cultura humana
e) De ordine oeconomico et de iustitia sociali
f) De communitate gentium et pace.

Suenens remained the Coordinating Commission member in charge of Schema XVII. It was also important to him that *De matrimonio* (including the demographic problem) was now also under his competence.

In a project letter, probably dating from February or March and possibly addressed to L. Capovilla, secretary to John XXIII, Suenens claimed to be unaware of whether the Commissio mixta for Schema XVII had already been established and requested that Prignon be appointed *peritus*. He believed that Msgr. Dell'Acqua would make an excellent president of this commission and would be able to safeguard at least some of the commission's independence vis-à-vis the Doctrinal Commission[446].

c. The Coordinating Commission meeting of March 25-29, 1963

According to Cicognani's instructions, a new text needed to be ready before March 10:

1. Suenens' archives prove that he closely followed the preparation of the new text:

– For the Prooemium and Caput I (*De admirabili vocatione hominis secundum Deum*), both a text by Lio from February 18 and a project by Daniélou from February 14 and March 5, 1963 are extant[447].
– For Caput II (*De persona humana in societate*), two text projects are extant[448].
– For Caput III (*De matrimonio, familia et problemate demographico*), projects by L. Janssens and L. Anné are extant[449]. On February 1, 1963, Msgr. M. Lefebvre sent Suenens a few texts on the family[450]. Suenens also contacted P. de Locht in order to ask for his opinion

---

446. Fund Suenens, 790. It is more likely that this letter was addressed to Capovilla than to I. Cardinale [as mentioned by L. Declerck in the inventory].
447. Fund Suenens, 1305-1308.
448. Fund Suenens, 1310-1311.
449. Cf. Fund Suenens, 1316-1317.
450. Fund Suenens, 1322-1326.

on conjugal ethics[451]. On March 4, 1963, Suenens replied to Msgr. Liston, Bishop of Port Louis, that the rhythm method (*i.e.*, periodic abstinence) must be advocated as the acceptable method of birth control. He added that some moralists allow hormones (*i.e.*, the pill), but that several remained hesitant[452]. On March 18, 1963, Msgr. Musty sent Suenens a text by Reuss, (co-written with Hirschmann) in order to Caput III. Reuss presented his text in Rome to Msgr. Charue[453]. On March 19, Msgr. Elchinger sent Suenens a text by Martelet[454]. And on March 21, Reuss himself wrote Suenens: he criticized the text drafted by Lio for Caput III and said that he and Hirschmann had drawn up an alternative text, which he fears will not be accepted. Reuss also noted that he keeps in touch with Elchinger[455].

– For Caput IV (*De cultura humana*), Ch. Moeller sent remarks he noted down for McGrath[456].
– For Caput V (*De ordine economico et de iustitia sociali*), Fr. Houtart sent Suenens lists with names of experts[457].
– For Caput VI (*De communitate gentium et pace*), Suenens received several text projects and he was often in contact with J. Larnaud, F. Russo and Y. Calvez[458].
– McGrath comes to Suenens in Malines on March 19, 1963[459].

2. It took much effort to get a first draft ready for the Coordinating Commission meeting of March 21[460]. It was mainly the work of the Commission for the Lay Apostolate of which Glorieux was secretary. As early as March 2, 1963, Glorieux reported to Suenens on the activities. He also mentioned Spellman's displeasure over the fact that the schema *De castitate*, for which he was responsible, had not been retained by the January Coordinating Commission session[461]. The next day Glorieux sent some

---

451. Letter from de Locht to Suenens, February 27, 1963, Fund Suenens, 1327.
452. Fund Suenens, B.C. and H.V., 6.
453. Fund Suenens, 1328.
454. Text 'Mariage, Amour et Sacrement', 29 pp. Cf. Fund Suenens, 1329-1330.
455. Fund Suenens, 1331.
456. Fund Suenens, 1341.
457. Fund Suenens, 1345. For the 'Schéma des question sociales', Houtart suggested, *inter alia*, Calvez, Heylen, L. Janssens, Lebret. For the 'Schéma des questions internationales', he mentioned de Riedmatten, Dondeyne, Frisque, Vekemans.
458. Fund Suenens, 1350-1353.
459. Fund Suenens, 740.
460. Cf. *AS* V/1, pp. 483-504.
461. Fund Suenens, 1260.

project texts to Suenens[462]. On March 5, Suenens replied to Glorieux and requested that a discussion of the human person, of religious freedom and marriage all be placed within the schema. He advised to consult B. Häring, J. Fuchs and L. Anné for help with this last chapter. For the chapter on the social and international problems, he desired the active involvement of H. de Riedmatten[463].

On March 17, Himmer again forwarded a copy of a letter from Ancel to Cicognani in which Ancel asked that the Council address the issue of the evangelisation of the world and especially that of the evangelisation of the poor[464]. On March 22, Glorieux again reported to Suenens on the activities; he also posed the problem of how and in which capacity lay persons should be consulted[465].

3. At the meeting of March 29, Suenens offered his Relatio on the submitted text. This Relatio had been drafted (for the most part) by Prignon[466] and contained both general and particular remarks[467]. In addition to suggesting a different title, Suenens opined that the editing was simply a first attempt (adumbratio) which needed considerable improvement. The presentation of the doctrine was far too superficial and was still too negative and defensive. A more positive and pastoral approach was desirable. Suenens primarily wished for a clearer treatment of the demographic problem in the chapter on marriage and that the text on religious freedom, as prepared by the Secretariat for Unity, be dealt with in Chapter VI (*De communitate gentium*)[468]. During the discussion in the Coordinating Commission on March 29[469] and in the presence of Cento and Glorieux (but without Ottaviani and Tromp[470]) Suenens noted that the text needed

462. Fund Suenens, 1262.
463. Fund Suenens, 1261.
464. Fund Suenens, 1263-1264.
465. Fund Suenens, 1265.
466. Cf. Fund Suenens, 880-884.
467. *AS* V/1, pp. 505-508.
468. On March 21, Suenens received a letter from Bea and Willebrands with the information that the papally-requested Commissio mixta (after the June 1962 meeting of the Commissio centralis praeparatoria) had been unable to function. The letter also noted that if and when *De libertate* was inserted in *De ordine internationali*, the Secretariat for Unity would request that they be allowed to collaborate on the editing of the text. A reformulated version of the text was added (Cf. Fund Suenens, 1197-1198). Msgr. De Smedt forwarded a final version of *De libertate* to Suenens on March 23 (Fund Suenens, 1199-1200). A handwritten note by Suenens on a draft of this text shows that he desired this insertion in n° 3 of the text *De communitate gentium*, cf. Fund Suenens, 1348.
469. Cf. *Processus verbalis*, AS V/1, pp. 512-516.
470. The president and the secretary of the Doctrinal Commission were not present due to the fact that the text had not yet been formally presented to their commission.

to be edited by the mixed commission; he did not support the idea that a text by the Commission for the Lay Apostolate should be approved by the Doctrinal Commission after the fact[471]. Suenens also said that he would take Spellman's remarks into account. Cicognani remarks on the title, at which Suenens proposes to return to the original title, *i.e.*, 'De praesentia efficaci Ecclesiae in mundo hodierno'. Cicognani also asked that Chapter VI (*De communitate gentium et pace*) take into account the content of John XXIII's encyclical *Pacem in terris*, which was scheduled to appear on April 11. This was followed by Suenens' remark that collaboration with competent lay persons could prove beneficial for the reformulation of the text. Cicognani felt it was more than sufficient to consult lay persons without actually involving them in the commission's activities. Felici proposed to consult the Pope, who, according to him, was in favor of limiting the laity's involvement to consultation. The matter ended there; but following Cicognani's suggestion, it was decided that the lay persons would be given remuneration (*compenso*) for their work.

d. The Issue of Birth Control

It is significant that at the end of April and at the insistence of Suenens upon John XXIII[472], a small working group was established in order to study the problems of birth control and the demographics of overpopulation[473]. The study group was directly dependent on the Secretariat of State, not on the Holy Office (probably so as to give it a bit more doctrinal freedom)[474]. Suenens' influence becomes clear in the correspondence with H. de Riedmatten. On April 30, 1963, de Riedmatten thanked Suenens for his having been instructed by the Secretary of State to put

---

471. Suenens wanted to react against a claim made by some members of the Doctrinal Commission that that commission had the right to control all the Council texts, in so far as they dealt with doctrinal matters. Cf. the fear expressed in a letter on March 11, 1963 from Hengsbach to Döpfner: "Trifft unsere Kommission die Entscheidung über den Text in eigener Verantwortng oder muss sie, was behauptet wurde, das umständliche Placet der gesamten Theologischen Kommission haben?" (TREFFLER [ed.], *Julius Kardinal Döpfner. Briefe und Notizen* [n. 9], p. 390).
472. Cf. Journal Declerck, May 5, 1963 (in Fund Prignon, 512).
473. Initially, the main point of departure for this 'commission' was the problem of overpopulation. Specifically, they wanted to be able to answer the U.N. studies that had concluded in favor of implementing birth control. Cf. correspondence by Suenens in 1962 with Cl. Mertens s.j. [Fund Suenens, 536-539, 543-546, 664-666] and with Prof. J. Mertens de Wilmars [Fund Suenens, 667-669]. Later, under Paul VI, the objectives of this group are broadened and the 'Groupe d'études de la population' was renamed *Commissio pro studio populationis, familiae et natalitatis*.
474. In SUENENS, *Souvenirs et espérances* (n. 11), p. 123, he incorrectly noted that this commission was linked to the Holy Office.

together a 'secret' study group to deal with problems related to childbirth. He added a copy of his letter of appointment from Cicognani – something which Cicognani allowed. It contained guidelines for the composition of the study group. At the same time, he sent a rough draft of an agenda and of the group's purpose statement, which he also submitted to the Secretariat of State. He believed that the doctors collected by Suenens for his *Colloques de Louvain* need representation in this 'secret' study group. In this connection, he mentioned Dr. Marshall, of the University of London. He also gave several suggestions for his presentation of *Pacem in terris* in New York[475]. Suenens' influence in the formation of this group was also made obvious by two other factors:

Primo, the first meeting of the study group took place in October of 1963 in Louvain and de Riedmatten sent Suenens different versions of his report[476].

Secundo, among the six original members[477], three were Belgians (Cl. Mertens, P. van Rossum, J. Mertens de Wilmars). It is very likely that they were proposed by Suenens.

e. *Intermezzo: Suenens' presentation of* Pacem in terris *in New York (May 13, 1963)*[478]

After the publication of the encyclical *Pacem in terris*, the association 'United States Committee for the United Nations'[479] requested that the Holy See send a senior representative to present the encyclical at their meeting taking place in the general assembly hall of the U.N. building in New York. Most likely it was Msgr. I. Cardinale[480] who suggested Suenens' name. It was Cicognani[481] who asked Suenens to carry out this assignment. John XXIII used this opportunity to have the text of the encyclical officially presented (via Suenens) to U Thant, the secretary-general of the U.N.[482]. Suenens comported himself brilliantly both during

---

475. Fund Suenens, B.C. and H.V., 271-273.

476. Fund Suenens, B.C. and H.V., 265-269.

477. H. de Riedmatten (secretary), St. de Lestapis, J. Marshall, Cl. Mertens, P. van Rossum, J. Mertens de Wilmars.

478. Cf. SUENENS, *Souvenirs et espérances* (n. 11), pp. 80-84, and Fund Suenens, A.P., box 20.

479. R. Benjamin was Chair, and Curtis Roosevelt, grandson of the late president Fr. Roosevelt, was treasurer.

480. I. Cardinale, in 1963 head of Protocol of the Secretariat of State, would later become a nuncio in Brussels, a post he held from 1969 until 1983.

481. Letter dated April 22, 1963, Fund Suenens, A.P., box 20.

482. In Suenens' writings, one can get the incorrect impression that he presented the encyclical at a meeting of the whole U.N. General Assembly.

his assignment and at the press conference that followed[483]. It was also during this first visit to the U.S. that Suenens made several other important contacts:

– On the same day, he gave a lecture at the University of Notre Dame. Th. Hesburgh, Notre Dame's rector, was a major figure in American Catholic academia.
– On May 15, he gave a lecture for a large group of sisters (in connection with his book *The Nun in the World*) at the College Mt St Vincent, Riverdale, New York.
– Most important was his contact with the *American Council for the International Promotion of Democracy under God* and the lecture he gave for them on 'Our Collaboration to Peace'. This association was chaired by Peter Grace[484]. And the Belgian Dominican Felix Morlion[485] was one of the directors. Morlion presented Suenens with a complete file on the top secret contacts that had been made between the American N. Cousins, Khruschhev, Kennedy and John XXIII. It is a.o. N. Cousins who spoke first to Khruschhev regarding Slipyi's release[486].

Although the visit to the U.S. was not directly related to the editing of schema XVII, it was important for these reasons:

– This mission offers proof of the degree of trust the Pope had in Suenens; it also contributed to his prestige in both Rome and the U.S.
– The theme of this important encyclical had an enormous influence on the editing of Chapter V (IInd Part) of *Gaudium et spes* (*De pace fovenda et de communitate gentium*; cf. the many footnotes in the text

483. For the text L.-J. SUENENS, 'Le message de l'encyclique Pacem in Terris', cf. *Pastoralia* 9 (1963), and for the press conference, see: '*Questions and Answers after Address by His Eminence the Most Reverend Leon Joseph Suenens*' (Fund Suenens, A.P., box 20).
484. American industrial magnate, married to Margie [Margaret] Grace, who was a member of the Legion of Mary and a collaborator of V. O'Brien. The Grace family gave Suenens ample support during his many travels to the U.S.
485. F. Morlion o.p. (1904-1987) was the founder of the *Pro Deo* 'university' in Rome as well as a conciliar *peritus*. For the role of Morlion during the 1962 Cuban Missile Crisis, cf. G. FOGARTY, *L'avvio dell'assemblea*, in ALBERIGO (ed.), *Storia del Concilio Vaticano II* (n. 54), Vol. II, pp. 115 and 122. For Morlion's links with the text *De Judaeis*, see G. MICCOLI, *Due nodi: La libertà religiosa e le relazioni con gli Ebrei*, in ALBERIGO (ed.), *Storia del Concilio Vaticano II* (n. 54), Vol. IV, p. 174.
486. Slipyi (1892-1984), the Ukrainian archbishop of Lviv, had been held captive by the communist regime in the Soviet Union since 1945. He was released on February 6, 1963, by Khruschhev, thanks to the mediation of John XXIII (via N. Cousins). See N. COUSINS, *The Improbable Triumvirate: J. Fitzgerald Kennedy, Pope John, Nikita Khruschhev*, New York, Norton, 1972. The file, kept in Suenens' achives (Fund Suenens, A.P., box 20), contains interesting additions to what was published by Cousins in 1972.

that reference this encyclical). Because of this trip, Suenens came to be regarded as an 'expert' in this matter by many.
– This visit put Suenens in touch with U Thant as well as with other important U.S. figures[487].

f. The meeting of the Coordinating Commission on July 3-4, 1963

The next meeting of the Coordinating Commission was planned for June 4. Because of the death of John XXIII on June 3, however, it was postponed to July 3-4. At this meeting, Suenens was again supposed to hold a Relatio regarding the status of Schema XVII. Two factors should be highlighted here:

1. Suenens was clearly interested in the evolution of the text. There was a meeting between the Commission for the Lay Apostolate and some 15 lay persons from April 24-27 and a session of the Commissio mixta from May 20-25, 1963:

– On April 2, R. Ceuppens sent, at the request of Suenens, two text drafts (on *De communitate gentium* and on *De ordine sociali*) to Prignon and to Medina[488].
– On April 10, 1963, Cl. Mertens sent an article on birth control to Suenens[489].
– On May 6, Glorieux sent Suenens the texts drafted between April 24 and 27[490].
– On May 17, Msgr. Baudoux sent Suenens seven vota of the Canadian bishops; Suenens replied to it on August 21[491].
– On May 22, Arrighi, in name of the Secretariat for Unity, sent a final draft of *De libertate* and requested that the Coordinating Commission make a decision in this regard[492].
– On May 29, Prignon sent Suenens a "Nota de Schemate XVII ad usum Em.mi Card. Suenens" (May 28, 1963, 6 p.) by Philips, Congar and

---

487. Note, e.g., that Jack Meehan, P. Grace's secretary who assisted Suenens during his stay in the U.S., gave Dr. Mary S. Calderone the advice to submit her file on birth control to Cardinal Suenens instead of to Cardinal Bea. Letter from Meehan to B. Pisani, May 21, 1963, Fund Suenens, B.C. and H.V., 7-8.

488. Fund Suenens, 1266.

489. Fund Suenens, 1332-1333.

490. Fund Suenens, 1267-1269.

491. Fund Suenens, 1270-1272. Msgr. Baudoux says that he sent this vota to the secretariat-general but fears this was useless since it seems that Felici had not taken it into account.

492. Fund Suenens, 1201-1202.

Moeller and a copy of the letter from L. Vischer to Msgr. Guano (April 18, 1963). The latter included the point of view of the World Council of Churches[493].

- On May 30, McGrath sent Suenens a «Votum pro ulteriore emendatione Schematis 'De Ecclesiae munere quoad bonum societatis hodiernae promovendum'» for the Coordinating Commission[494].
- On June 19, Cogels, Suenens' private secretary, thanked J.Y. Calvez for his article 'Rapports de l'Église et de l'État'[495].

2. On July 4, Suenens presented his Relatio on schema XVII to the Coordinating Commission[496]. It had been drafted by Prignon, who had based himself largely on McGrath's votum of May 30, 1963:

- In a preceding note Suenens again underlined the importance of this schema. The expectations of the world, of many bishops, and of lay persons were pointed out and the coronation speech of John XXIII was alluded to.
- The general opinion was that the text, although improved, was not yet ready to be submitted to the Council due to the following reasons:
  It lacked coherence and synthesis
  The subject matter was too profuse
  Some subjects (e.g. birth control and the social function of private property) were insufficiently dealt with.
  Although expressly requested by the Coordinating Commission, the issue of religious freedom was not addressed.
  The text was still 'too European' and had not yet been adapted to include the developing countries.
  Doubts remained regarding the title.
- After a page containing detailed criticisms of the different chapters, Suenens concludes[497]: (1) A special commission is needed to draft a new text on the general principles relevant to the relationship between the Church and the world and on the responsibility of the Church "ad bonum societatis promovendum 'ut omnia instaurentur in Christo'".

---

493. Fund Suenens, 1273-1276. Cf. CONGAR, *Mon journal du Concile* (n. 9), Vol. I, May 28, 1963, p. 381: "Travail avec Mgr Philips et le chanoine Moeller sur le rapport que le cardinal Suenens doit faire sur le schéma XVII".
494. Fund Suenens, 892-893.
495. Fund Suenens, 1353.
496. For the text, see Fund Suenens, 898 (with handwritten notes by Suenens) and *AS* V/1, pp. 630-633.
497. Prignon's archives contain the handwritten note (in French) used by the Cardinal for his proposals; they were possibly translated into Latin by Prignon afterwards. Cf. Fund Prignon, 235.

This could be a kind of 'praefatio theologica vel etiam dogmatica' to the entire schema. (2) The present Caput I 'De admirabili vocatione personae' could be integrated into this doctrinal introduction. (3) For each of the particular topics (marriage, culture, social and economical issues, peace, etc.) a commission could be appointed and asked to work on these matters in collaboration with both lay and religious experts. (4) The Council could 'in forma globali' approve the conclusions of all these commissions without going into the details. These conclusions could be published in the form of 'Instructiones'[498]. (5) The religious freedom must be made the subject of a special study and must be worked on by a mixed commission in cooperation with the Secretariat for Unity.

It is during the discussion[499] and in the presence of Browne (who had been deputized by Ottaviani) and Tromp that Suenens first pointed out the importance of the text on religious freedom. After exchanging ideas (with, *inter alia*, Tromp, Felici, and Cicognani)[500], it was finally decided that the text would be prepared by the Secretariat for Unity and in cooperation with the Doctrinal Commission. After the discussion in the Basilica on the schema *De oecumenismo*, religious freedom could then be inserted in *De oecumenismo* during the rewrite that was to be performed by the Secretariat for Unity. Suenens proposed the establishment of five sub-commissions, one for each chapter, so as to be able to draft a Council decree for the doctrinal part of each while referring the remainder to 'un catechismo sociale'[501]. Liénart asked that the following be discussed clearly in a *prooemium*: "1. La nature des rapports de l'Église avec les sociétés civiles et les états; 2. Le rôle des laïcs chrétiens"[502].

Urbani agreed with Suenens on dividing the matter into two parts: the unchanging principles of the catholic doctrine in a Council decree, and, on

---

498. This matter – the status and authority of *Gaudium et spes* – was repeatedly discussed, even as late as the fourth session. There was a tendancy to divide the text in two parts: (1) A dogmatic part, which was to be solemnly approved by the Council. (2) A more practical part, with a non official approbation.
  In the 4th session, one will opt for 'Constitutio pastoralis', with an explanation in the footnote at the beginning of the text.
  499. Cf. *Processus verbalis*, AS V/1, pp. 636-637.
  500. Tromp noted that the text was taken from the Doctrinal Commission "perchè ritenuto non maturo". Suenens proposed to have the text drafted by the Secretariat for Unity as part of *De oecumenismo*. To the latter, Felici replied that *De oecumenismo* had already been sent to the Fathers.
  501. This came after a critic by Browne that, in the proposed texts, unalterable doctrine was placed next to the discussion of sociological problems.
  502. Cf. Fund Suenens, 905 and 1298. And also in *AS* V/1, pp. 638-639.

the other, 'il catechismo sociale'. Confalonieri suggested that Suenens draft a plan for the conciliar schema (the doctrinal part), which would then be submitted to the Commissio mixta in order to arrive at a final text. It was to be produced in collaboration with experts and divided into subcommissions. Döpfner found Confalonieri's proposal acceptable but noted that there was no rush. Finally, all the members of the Coordinating Commission agreed with Confalonieri's proposal; Suenens accepted the assignment. As early as July 10, 1963, Glorieux informed Suenens that he had made a report (dated July 6, 1963) on this part of the meeting of the Coordinating Commission and that he had explicitly mentioned that Suenens would write the introductory chapter for schema XVII, since Tromp wanted to entrust this task to a few *periti* of the Doctrinal Commission. Fagiolo advised him against giving this report directly to Tromp, but promised to inform Tromp about this matter verbally. Glorieux sent both his report and Liénart's text to Suenens. He suggested to Suenens that most of the bishops and *periti* of the subcommission, who had been working since the previous May on the schema, be retained, but that eventually others could be added. He also requested that Suenens have his text ready before September[503].

g. The 'Text of Malines'[504]

As early as July 5, Suenens wrote an offical letter to Prignon suggesting that he, as his delegate, take the initiative in establishing a study group of theologians in order to draft this introductory doctrinal part. He added: "Je vous donne pleins pouvoirs d'agir en mon nom"[505].

Prignon, who returned to Belgium during the holiday months, went to work immediately. On July 25, he wrote to Suenens from Brittain, where he was vacationing:

> J'ai pu jusqu'à présent alerter Mgr Cerfaux, Mr Thils et Mr Delhaye. N'étant pas arrivé à toucher jusqu'aujourd'hui Mgr Philips (à Lourdes), Mr Moeller (au Canada) et le P. Congar (toujours en route pour diverses sessions, conférences etc.), je n'ai pu leur proposer un jour de réunion commune. Aussi bien, j'ai demandé à chacun de réfléchir au nouveau texte (XVII) et de préparer un écrit. À une réunion postérieure on mettra le tout ensemble et on

503. Cf. Fund Suenens, 903 and 904. Glorieux, although not mentioned as present in the *Processus verbalis*, was present at the Coordinating Commission as secretary for the Commission for the Lay Apostolate (Tromp was also there as secretary of the Doctrinal Commission).
504. Cf. J. GROOTAERS, *Il concilio si gioca nell'intervallo. La 'seconda preparazione' e i suoi avversari*, in ALBERIGO (ed.), *Storia del Concilio Vaticano II* (n. 54), Vol. II, pp. 458-460.
505. Cf. Fund Prignon, 236 and TUCCI, *Introduction historique et doctrinale à la Constitution* (n. 392), p. 50, where 'la personne de confiance' refers to Prignon.

discutera. D'autre part, les gens sont fatigués après une telle année et demandent des délais. Ce sera utile pour la maturation et la décantation des idées. Il serait peut-être préférable de reporter la réunion avec vous après votre retour de vacances[506]. Entre temps, je continuerai à relancer mon monde[507].

At the beginning of August, Prignon (with assistance from R. Ceuppens, vicar-general, J. De Wil and H. Frateur, secretaries of the archdiocese) organized the meeting[508]. All participants received preparatory documents (*inter alia* the Nota by Liénart, with the remarks he presented to the Coordinating Commission on July 4, 1963), a note by Congar, and a note by Suenens[509].

The study group consisted of Philips, Congar, Rahner, Prignon, Tucci, Thils, Moeller, Cerfaux, Delhaye, Dondeyne, Rigaux and Ceuppens, met at the archdiocese in Malines from September 6 through 8; a smaller group met a second time on September 17, in the presence of Suenens[510]. Philips again acted as editor-in-chief. In the meantime Prignon contacted Msgr. Guano, an important member of the Commission for the Lay Apostolate, and asked him to submit the text of this first part (when ready) to Lukas Vischer of the World Council of Churches[511]. In a September 1 letter to Prignon, Guano accepted the proposal and, at the same time, asked for a meeting with Prignon a some point between September 6 and 18[512].

On September 15, Suenens informed the Pope that a 'Document de Malines' is in preparation for schema XVII[513]. On September 22, Philips was able to give the final text to the Cardinal: 'Adumbratio Schematis XVII. De activa praesentia Ecclesiae in mundo aedificando' (12+1 p.)[514]. It consisted of three parts:

I. De ecclesiae propria missione
    A. De evangelizatione mundi
    B. De ecclesiae influxu in ipsum ordinem mundanum
II. De mundo aedificando
    A. De autonomia mundi
    B. De unificatione mundi

506. Suenens spent his August vacation in Scotland. Cf. SUENENS, *Mémoires du Concile Vatican II*, p. 38 and Fund Suenens, 792-793.
507. Fund Suenens, 755.
508. Cf. Fund Suenens, 1281-1293, 1301-1302; Fund Philips, 854-861.
509. Cf. Fund Suenens, 1296-1298.
510. Cf. CONGAR, *Mon journal du Concile* (n. 9), Vol. I, p. 397.
511. Cf. Notes L. Declerck, September 24, 1963, in Fund Prignon, 512.
512. Fund Prignon, 237.
513. Letter to Paul VI, Fund Suenens, 788bis.
514. Cf. Fund Philips, 878 and *AS* VI/2, pp. 407-416, where the list of authors is incomplete (p. 407, footnote) and Mölley stands for Moeller. The same footnote mentions that Cicognani showed the text to the Pope.

III. De officiis ecclesiae erga mundum
    A. De munere testificandi
    B. De servitio caritatis et communione.

For various reasons, this highly theological text was not retained during the second session.

h. Interventions regarding schema XVII in the period of July-September

First, on July 30, A. Pelt, who was secretary-general of the 'Fédération mondiale des Associations pour les Nations Unies' and who had been received by Suenens in Malines on July 13, wrote regarding a statement on disarmement which was to be presented during the next U.N. general assembly[515].

Then, on August 12, Suenens wrote to Willebrands (who had also been received in Malines on August 10) that the Coordinating Commission had decided that *De libertate religiosa* needed to be attached to *De oecumenismo*. On August 17, Suenens specified that the text on religious freedom should not be 'subjected' to the Doctrinal Commission, but that it would be better if it were discussed in a mixed commission[516].

And finally on September 2, de Riedmatten, after meeting Fr. Houtart in Wallis (Switzerland), sent Suenens another 'Note à propos du travail futur sur le Schéma XVII' and he informed him that 'le petit groupe sur la population' would meet in Louvain in mid-October[517].

During the first intersession, Suenens was occupied with the conceptualisation of schema XVII. To a large extent, it corresponded to his *De ecclesia ad extra,* especially given that he had succeeded in adding the chapter *De matrimonio* to it. He also succeeded in keeping the doctrinal parts out of the (exclusive) hands of the Doctrinal Commission and in getting it placed under the control of a Commissio mixta, in which the members of the Commission for the Lay Apostolate had equal representation. And in the Coordinating Commission, he remained in charge of

---

515. Fund Suenens, 2888.

516. Fund Suenens, 1203-1208. The *Processus verbalis* of the Coordinating Commission mentions that Cicognani says: "Il Segretariato della unione dei cristiani può preparare il testo, sentita la Commissione Teologica per l'aspetto dottrinale del problema". Exactly what this signifies is not clear. For more details, see S. SCATENA, *La fatica della libertà: L'elaborazione della Dichiarazione "Dignitatis humanae" sulla libertà religiosa del Vaticano II* (Testi e ricerche di scienze religiose. Nuova Serie, 31), Bologna, Il Mulino, 2003, p. 55, note 101.

517. Fund Suenens, 1277-1278.

the whole. Still another achievement was in the way in which he helped to get the text on religious freedom entrusted to the Secretariat for Unity, even with the involvement of the Doctrinal Commission.

5. IIa Sessio

The second session was mainly dominated by debates on *De ecclesia, De episcopis* and *De oecumenismo*. It was only during the first half of November that it occurred to anyone to convene the Commissio mixta before the end of the session[518].

a. What had happened to the 'Text of Malines'?

First there were problems with the submission of the text to the 'proper authorities'. On October 25, 1963, after Suenens submitted the text to Browne and Cento, which apparently did not suffice, he finally wrote an official letter to Cicognani along with the text. Cicognani then ordered that Felici submit it to Cento and Browne[519]. Suenens recounts this episode as follows:

> J'ai alors remis ce texte aux Cardinaux Browne et Cento, qui étaient chargés de l'élaboration en commun de ce schéma XIII … c'est alors que j'ai fait connaissance avec les subtilités ineffables de la procédure juridique romaine. Je leur avais remis ce texte, puisque j'en avais reçu le mandat devant eux et je croyais que tout était fini. Lorsque, rencontrant Mgr Glorieux quelques semaines plus tard et demandant des nouvelles, il m'a dit: 'Oh, on n'a pas reçu ce texte'. Je dis: 'Mais comment, je l'ai remis aux deux Cardinaux!' – 'Ce n'est pas une manière officielle de le remettre. Il faut que le Président de la Commission de Coordination, à savoir le Cardinal Cicognani, envoie officiellement ce texte à la commission'. J'ai alors été trouver le Cardinal Cicognani pour lui dire que ces deux Cardinaux avaient déjà le texte mais que c'était lui qui devait leur envoyer la copie. Je lui ai remis cette copie et il allait la leur envoyer. Quelque semaines entières se sont passées encore. N'entendant de nouveau plus rien, j'ai encore une fois redemandé. On m'a dit: 'Le texte n'est pas parvenu'. Finalement j'ai abordé un modeste petit minutante de la Secrétairerie d'État, pour lui demander s'il avait des nouvelles de ce texte, s'il traînait quelque part dans les tiroirs

---

518. At the moderators meeting on November 9, 1963, it was requested that the Commission for the Lay Apostolate should intensify the preparation of schema XVII. Suenens submitted a project [the 'Text of Malines'] to the Secretary of State in connection with this (*AS* V/3, p. 710).
519. Letters from October 29, 1963. Cf. *AS* VI/2, pp. 406-407 and 416. TURBANTI, *Un Concilio per il mondo moderno* (n. 392), p. 294, note 8, wrongly claims that Felici had resubmitted this text to Cento on September 29.

de Cicognani. Il m'a dit: 'Je vais arranger cela'. Et le lendemain ce texte était remis officiellement à la commission des Cardinaux Browne et Cento[520].

Second, more problems arose. In the November 29, 1963, Doctrinal Commission meeting Tromp claimed that Suenens had not been granted a mandate to write a new introduction but had only been asked to propose a new schema with the same five chapters. Charue and Philips refused to accept that Suenens might have been mistaken about his assignment. Tromp replied that he was present at the meeting of the Coordinating Commission[521]. In the end, the 'Text of Malines' was not accepted by the *Commissio mixta* for several reasons: it was too "theological"; it did not adequately address questions relevant to modern man, etc.[522]. It was decided to proceed with a completely new editing of this first part of Schema XVII. In addition, a central subcommission (including C. Moeller) was established. Suenens writes:

> Mais à la première réunion de la commission, on a coulé ce texte, en partie je crois, sous l'influence du Père Daniélou qui était très mécontent de n'avoir pas été un de ces théologiens. Je ne l'avais d'ailleurs pas invité, à la demande de tous les autres théologiens. Les évêques français[523] ne semblaient pas très enthousiastes, cela leur paraissait trop lourd et on a purement et simplement enterré ce texte, qui n'a pas eu les honneurs d'être introduit dans le schéma XIII. C'est de nouveau une parenthèse pour la petite histoire[524].

---

520. SUENENS, *Mémoires sur le Concile Vatican II*, pp. 33-34. Suenens recounted an analogous story to Prignon on November 19, 1965 (cf. Journal Prignon, pp. 212-213). See also CONGAR, *Mon journal du Concile* (n. 9), Volume I, November 15, 1963, p. 536.

521. *Diarium* Tromp, IV, November 29, 1963. Congar, who was not present but who had received a report from Labourdette, records the discussion (CONGAR, *Mon journal du Concile* [n. 9], Volume I, p. 574) in which Prignon defended Suenens.

522. For the critiques of the 'Text of Malines', see a.o. MOELLER, *Die Geschichte der Pastoralkonstitution* (n. 392), pp. 254-255. Even Léger was very critical about Suenens and his 'Texte de Malines'. He writes in his Diary about his audience with Paul VI on November 23, 1963: "... [Paul VI] est stupéfait d'apprendre les manœuvres d'Ottaviani et même de celles de Suenens au sujet du schéma XVII" (Fund Léger, 15; with our thanks to G. Routhier).

523. Even Congar noted that the Belgian influence was perhaps becoming too dominant: "C'est un fait que le cardinal Suenens dirige un peu le concile et que le petit groupe belge mène pratiquement les choses..." (CONGAR, *Mon journal du Concile* [n. 9], Vol. I, November 30, 1963, p. 574). Prignon had already written to Suenens on October 4, 1963: "La mauvaise humeur de Mgr Garrone, à propos du Schéma XVII, va s'atténuant. Mgr Philips a eu l'occasion de lui expliquer le caractère international de la rédaction" (Fund Suenens, 1375). This letter by Prignon also contains a handwritten note by Suenens: "Remettre texte Cento-Browne", an indication that he had not yet done this on October 4, 1963.

524. SUENENS, *Mémoires sur le Concile Vatican II*, pp. 35-36.

b. During this session, in which schema XVII was hardly discussed, we see that Suenens receives further information on the problems of Church and world.

- Msgr. J. Gremillion sends him, at the suggestion of Houtart, a note on the population explosion on October 3, 1963[525].
- T. Hesburgh forwards Suenens his report on the Conference of the International Nuclear Agency in Vienna, as well as recommendations on the presence of the Church on an international level on October 16, 1963[526].
- Suenens receives from Glorieux the requested list of the members and the *periti*, who had collaborated on the different chapters of schema XVII[527].
- He received a letter from Helder Camara with a note on the nuclear arms race; there are a number of scientists who desire a meeting with Suenens[528].
- As early as the middle of November, Prignon drafted a note for Suenens in preparation for the presentation of the text to the Pope. It was entitled 'Argomenti per la prolongazione ragionevole del Concilio'[529] (in opposition to the 'plan Döpfner').

c. On October 26, 1963, Felici wrote a letter to Cardinals Ottaviani and Antoniutti (presidents of the Doctrinal Commission and the Commission for the Religious, respectively)[530]. Felici sent a note – a text presented to the Pope by "una altissima Personalità" – that had been given to him by the Pope on October 24, 1963, along with the request that these matters be treated by the authorized conciliar commissions. In these "Observationes clari viri" three problems were formulated: (1) Conjugal ethics: this must be treated by the Council, which should appeal to competent persons in the biological sciences "pour qu'ils trouvent les moyens légitimes et naturels qui aideront les chrétiens à mieux vivre la Loi de Dieu". (2) Social injustice: How much of our wealth and our time should

---

525. Fund Suenens, 1646-1647.
526. Fund Suenens, 1648-1650.
527. Letter of November 9, 1963, Fund Suenens, 1653-1654.
528. Letter of November 18, 1963, Fund Suenens, 1639-1642.
529. Cf. Fund Suenens, 1394bis and Fund Prignon, 547.
530. Cf. *AS* VI/2, pp. 391-392, see also Fund Philips, 1105-1106. The first two parts of this text were distributed at the meeting of the Doctrinal Commission on October 28, 1963. Cf. CONGAR, *Mon journal du Concile* (n. 9), Vol. I, October 28, 1963, p. 504: "Ottaviani fait lire une lettre de Mgr Felici par laquelle il demande, de la part du Saint-Père, l'avis de la commission sur deux points posés en question par une très haute personnalité ... Ottaviani propose d'instituer une sous-commission pour cela". Cf. also the answer of Ottaviani to Felici on October 25, 1963 in *AS* VI/2, pp. 404-405.

we devote to helping the less fortunate? (3) Christian formation of the youth (especially as provided by female religious institutions): Is it not necessary to modernize the rules of the clausura, the religious habit, etc., so that the religious can gain the freedom necessary to take care of their apostolate?

The 'una altissima personalità', who was apparently French-speaking and who mentioned (1) "mon pays à grande majorité catholique", (2) "L'état donne chaque année des subsides très importants à nos écoles catholiques"[531], and (3) "mes tournées à travers le Pays", may possibly have been Baudouin, the king of Belgium[532]. On the other hand, it was well known how important both the problem of birth control and the adaptation of the religious life to the needs of the apostolate[533] were to Suenens and V. O'Brien.

d. An important conference was hosted by Suenens in Florence on November 29, 1963. He had been invited to speak both by Msgr. Florit, archbishop of Florence, and by G. La Pira, the mayor of that city. The 'Federazione Universitaria Cattolica Italiana' also supported that request. Suenens asked G. Dossetti to draw up (most of) the text of the conference 'La Chiesa di oggi di fronte alla pluralità delle culture'. The conference was well received by the press; Ch. Moeller even congratulated Suenens on its success[534].

During the second session, Suenens' energy was largely consumed by his new position as moderator and by the problems of ecclesiology (the five *Propositiones*). Schema XVII was not at all near the center of his thoughts. After the rejection of the 'Text of Malines' by the Commissio mixta, the Belgians' (and Suenens') role decreased during 1964, although it regained importance during 1965. As he had done during the second intersession, Suenens concentrated more and more on the problem of birth control. He campaigned actively for this problem via Schema XVII, the Papal Commission for Natality, and especially via numerous private contacts with the Pope, scientists and theologians.

---

531. In 1959 the 'schoolpact' in Belgium was finalised. This agreement compelled the State to subsidize a large part of the expenses of the free catholic schools.

532. King Baudouin may have given this note to the Pope during his audience on July 1, 1963 (cf. *L'Osservatore Romano*, July 3, 1963) on the occasion of the papal coronation.

533. Cf. SUENENS, *Promotion apostolique de la vie religieuse*, Paris, Desclée de Brouwer, 1962, p. 196, and Fund Suenens, A.P., box 81-83; Archive O'Brien, box 2 and 11.

534. Fund Suenens, 1679-1690.

6. IIa Intersessio[535]

Schema XVII was rewritten during this second intersession (e.g., in Zürich during February of 1964). The text was divided into two large parts: a general part and the *Adnexa*. Due to the rearrangement of the schemas, beginning in April, 1964 and under the influence of the 'plan Döpfner', *De ecclesia in mundo* was called Schema XIII. Suenens, with the help of Prignon, resisted Döpfner's plans to end the Council after the third session[536], since, *inter alia*, this would mean that schema XIII would receive insufficient attention and discussion. Suenens was mainly interested in the chapter on marriage. Suenens' activities during this period were focussed on two areas: Schema XIII and birth control.

a. Schema XIII

– On December 19, 1963, Ancel drafted a project "Projet d'un Schéma sur l'Église en face des problèmes du monde d'aujourd'hui"; Suenens received a copy[537].
– On December 28, from five until seven-thirty in the afternoon, a new meeting of the Coordinating Commission was held[538].

For this meeting, Glorieux sent Suenens a note 'Circa i lavori della Commissione Mista incaricata dello Schema De Praesentia Ecclesiae in mundo hodierno' on December 21[539].

This meeting mainly discussed the 'plan Döpfner'[540]; a number of (tentative) conclusions are drawn. Schema XVII needed to be drafted as quickly as possible and it was decided to (yet again) separate *De Iudaeis* and *De libertate religiosa* from *De oecumenismo* and to place a reduced version of them into Schema XVII[541].

---

535. For this period, cf. DECLERCK, *Le rôle joué* (n. 40), pp. 458-463.
536. Already on July 20, 1963 Döpfner had sent a note to Paul VI with suggestions to ensure smoother proceedings of the Council so that it could end with a 3rd session (cf. Fund Suenens, 784-785). Felici also wanted a quick ending of the Council but for different reasons.
537. Fund Suenens, 1955-1956.
538. Again it is striking to see that several meetings of the Coordinating Commission were very brief. This often resulted in the absence of a large number of foreign members. For example, on December 28, half of the members were absent: Spellman, Urbani, Liénart, Suenens and Roberti.
539. Fund Suenens, 1963-1964.
540. In his Relatio Döpfner proposed that the 5 *Adnexa* of Schema XVII would be reduced at "5 epistulae seu nuntii" [...] "quae in Aula non discutiuntur sed tantum suffragio subiicientur" (cf. *AS* V/2, p. 91).
541. *Processus verbalis*, AS V/2, pp. 95-96. In a letter (January 14, 1964) from Bea to Felici, Bea replied that *De libertate religiosa* must stay with *De oecumenismo*, especially given the text's ecumenical impact. Cf. *AS* V/2, pp. 103-104.

- Häring, the new editorial secretary of the Commissio mixta, offered his Relatio on the December 12, 1963 meeting, where Guano, Blomjous, Sigmond, and Tucci were also present[542].
- On January 4, 1964, Ancel sent Suenens a text project and requested a meeting[543].
- The 12th meeting of the Coordinating Commission took place on January 15, 1964. Again the 'plan Döpfner' was the focus[544]. Prignon had made a note for Suenens in which he argued that it was unrealistic to end the Council after only three sessions[545]. It was requested that the final text of Schema XVII be drafted as soon as possible[546].
- On February 3, 1964, Helder Camara asked that Lebret be appointed as *peritus*[547]; he thanked Suenens for the information on Schema XVII and was of the opinion that the Council could not be terminated after the third session.
- From February 1 to 3, a new version was drafted in Zürich. Suenens was kept informed:
  - On February 5, 1964, Suenens thanked Häring for forwarding the document and asked him for further information after the meeting in Zürich[548].
  - On February 8, Häring reported briefly to Suenens on the meeting in Zürich[549].
  - Msgr. Guano also reported to Suenens on February 10, 1964[550].
- On February 24, Congar forwarded a text from a group in Paris which desired to improve the dialogue between theology and modern science[551]. A. Vanistendael, a Belgian lay 'auditor', also kept Suenens informed regarding his remarks on: 'La participation active des chrétiens à la construction du monde'[552].

---

542. Fund Suenens, 1958.
543. Fund Suenens, 1965.
544. Döpfner was not present due to inclement weather. Cf. the letter from Döpfner to Felici dated January 17, 1964: "Valde dolens quod apparatibus aëreis propter nebulam penitus deficientibus..." (*AS* V/2, p. 122).
545. Fund Suenens, 1739-1740.
546. *Processus verbalis, AS* V/2, p. 121.
547. In fact, Lebret was named *peritus* for the third session.
548. Fund Suenens, 1968-1969.
549. Fund Suenens, 1971.
550. Fund Suenens, 1972.
551. Fund Suenens, 1973-1975.
552. Letter of February 26, 1964. Fund Suenens, 1978-1979.

– Suenens was present at the meeting of the Coordinating Commission on March 10; however, Schema XVII was only mentioned in passing as it was noted that it will be discussed during the third session[553].

– On March 29, 1964, Suenens wrote to Döpfner: "Ce fameux schéma 17 est toujours en gestation pénible: il ne faudrait pas décevoir le monde sur ce sujet"[554].

– At the next meeting of the Coordinating Commission (April 16-17) there is still no mention of Schema XVII. Suenens did, however, get a chance to defend the schema *De ecclesia*[555]. On April 17, Prignon, who had met with Suenens after the meeting, noted:

> On n'a pas parlé du schéma 17 puisque le texte n'est pas encore au point. Et l'opinion assez générale des cardinaux de la commission était que le texte était vraiment bien difficile à accoucher, si on peut dire, qu'on se demandait si on arriverait jamais au bout. Je me suis permis alors de ré-insister auprès du cardinal, de lui répéter l'opinion de beaucoup ici qu'il était impossible d'arriver à mettre un texte au point si on devait finir le concile à la 3ème session … J'en ai profité pour ré-insister sur l'importance de ce schéma aux yeux du monde et l'immense déception qui naîtrait non seulement parmi les chrétiens mais même parmi une grande partie de l'opinion mondiale si le texte voté par le concile n'était pas un texte vraiment sérieux[556].

– During his audience with the Pope on April 18, 1964, Suenens mentioned birth control but only briefly discussed Schema XVII: "Il [Suenens] a parlé aussi du schéma 17 qui était loin d'être en voie d'achèvement. Le Saint-Père a souri, répétant: 'Oui, ce schéma 17, ce schéma 17'"[557].

– On April 25, Suenens thanked Etchegaray for a note on the status of women in the Church[558].

– On May 27, Houtart sent Suenens a 30 page text from the Polish episcopate 'De ecclesia in mundo hodierno'. It was mainly drafted by Wojtyła, with whom he met twice and who had asked him to deliver this schema to Suenens. Houtart felt that this text, at least in some parts, was too apologetic[559].

– On June 3, 1964, Vanistendael sent Suenens a copy of the amendment he sent to Häring on 'De spiritu dialogi'[560].

---

553. *Processus verbalis, AS* V/2, p. 158.
554. Fund Döpfner, 825.
555. *Processus verbalis, AS* V/2, pp. 289-291.
556. Notes by Prignon, to whom the Cardinal reported the same day. Cf. Fund Prignon, 824.
557. Fund Prignon, 825.
558. Fund Suenens, 1982.
559. Fund Suenens, 1983-1984.
560. Fund Suenens, 1985-1987.

- After the June 4-6 meeting of the Commissio mixta, Häring reported to Suenens that the chapter on marriage was finished, even though the last day's discussion was far from smooth[561].
- On June 7, Helder Camara wrote to Suenens: he believed that Adnexum IV was a good text, but feared that there were problems still to come regarding birth control[562].
- The 15th meeting of the Coordinating Commission took place on June 26-27. Suenens was not able to be present since the meeting, which had first been planned for June 16-17, had been postponed to the 26th-27th. He requested that, at a minimum, Schema XVII be printed and sent to the Patres[563]. On June 21, Suenens sent Cicognani a short note. He approved of the new text since several crucial problems had been dealt with in comprehensible and adapted language. This did not mean, however, that he had no further reservations: the theological doctrine was not always accurate (especially in Chapter One) and a number of technical terms remained ambiguous. In spite of these problems, he did consent to have the text presented to the Patres during the following session[564]. On June 17, Suenens informed Lercaro that he had asked Prignon to contact him, since he knew that he would not be present[565]. Prignon contacted Lercaro but mainly to discuss the problems regarding the '13 suggerimenti'[566]. It was Urbani, not Suenens, who drafted the Relatio. He also requested that Schema XIII be sent to the Patres. He very courteously added: "Pregherei tuttavia l'Ecc.mo Segretario di chiedere al Card. Suenens – che del tema è il primo padre e quegli, fra noi, che più di tutti ne ha seguito le non facili vicende – un suo parere scritto"[567]. At the June 26 meeting, it was decided that Schema XIII would be sent to the Patres along with the request that they submit their remarks on it before October 1, 1964[568].

---

561. Fund Suenens, 1989. For the incidents of June 6, cf. Journal Charue, p. 205: "Mgr Franić a eu une intervention de complexé sur la natalité et, de façon maladroite et franchement inadmissible, il a pris à partie le P. Häring pour son enseignement". And CONGAR, *Mon journal du Concile* (n. 9), Vol. II, p. 110: "Cette attaque de Franić a été violente et grossière. Elle lui a plutôt nui, et a plutôt ramené la sympathie vers Häring". There is an extensive report in Journal de Lubac, June 6, 1964, II, p. 100, who writes: "Tout un scénario va alors se dérouler, dont il paraît clair qu'il a été organisé au Saint-Office".
562. Fund Suenens, 1725.
563. *AS* V/2, p. 543.
564. *AS* V/2, pp. 555-556.
565. Fund Suenens, 1781.
566. Transcript of a tape sent by Prignon to Suenens at the end of June of 1964. Fund Prignon, 828.
567. *AS* V/2, p. 631.
568. *Processus verbalis*, AS V/2, pp. 640-641.

b. Birth Control[569]

This issue, which was very dear to Suenens, was simultaneously pursued on two different levels: via the Schema XVII's chapter entitled *De matrimonio*, and via the secret Papal Commission.

1. On December 13, 1963, Cicognani, in the name of the Pope, asked Suenens for advice on the report of the first meeting of the 'Groupe d'études de la population' (which had been under the direction of de Riedmatten) and on the desirability of a statement by the magisterium. On December 24, 1963, Suenens replied with a six-page note to Cicognani; he also forwarded this reply directly to the Pope. *Inter alia*, Suenens wrote that, although the problem was urgent, the Pope should avoid making any rash statements. The Council (via schema XVII) would deal with the main principles; concrete guidelines could be given afterwards in a post-conciliar instruction. He also suggested that the 'groupe de Riedmatten' establish the necessary study groups and, at the same time, collaborate with the conciliar commission[570]. A December 25, 1963 letter from de Riedmatten to Suenens proves the quality of their relationship: according to de Riedmatten Suenens' report was very important, but Schema XVII will only be able to address this matter after a papal intervention[571]. On January 7, 1964, de Riedmatten thanked Suenens for his support and, on February 21, he informed Suenens about the extension of his group and that he had received encouragement from Paul VI during an audience[572].

2. The 'Questionnaire of the Secretariat of State on conjugal ethics': On February 22, 1964, nuncio Oddi sent Suenens the Secretary of State's confidential questionnaire. It had been sent to all the presidents of the bishops' conferences. Suenens (assisted by Prof. P. Anciaux) prepared the advice of the Belgian bishops. He also corresponded with Msgr. De Smedt and with Msgr. Himmer. On March 18, he sent the answer to Cicognani[573]. Suenens

---

569. It is important to note that at the end of 1963 one of the first articles appeared with regard to the moral permissibility of the Pincus' pill (came as contraceptive on the market in 1960): L. JANSSENS, *Morale conjugale et progestogènes*, in *ETL* 49 (1963) 787-826. Suenens had carefully read and annotated this article (Fund Suenens, B.C. and H.V., 771). And on February 16, 1964, S. de Lestapis had submitted his critical remarks on this article to Suenens (Fund Suenens, B.C. and H.V., 13).

570. Fund Suenens, 1959-1962.

571. Fund Prignon, 1035.

572. Fund Suenens, B.C. and H.V., 277-279. The new members include a.o. P. de Locht, priest of the archdiocese Malines-Brussels.

573. Cf. Fund Suenens, B.C. and H.V., 14-16, 18-26.

had also been in contact with other bishops: Silva Henriquez (Chile), Flahiff (Canada), Reuss (auxiliary bishop of Mainz)[574] and Döpfner[575].

3. On January 15, 1964, Helder Camara sent Suenens a text regarding birth control[576]. On March 2, Suenens sent Paul VI a note on the same topic and requested that the Pope read this note before the audience Suenens hoped to schedule for about March 10 (the Coordinating Commission was also scheduled to meet then)[577]. Delhaye also sent Suenens a long note from Montréal in March: 'Recherches et Réflexions concernant l'état actuel du problème moral de la régulation des naissances' (31 p.)[578]. From April 3rd through 5th, the Papal Commission held another meeting. Unfortunately, Suenens' archives lack any documentation regarding it. On April 18, Suenens had another audience with Paul VI. The same day he gave an account of it to Prignon, who, on April 19, 1964, noted the following:

> Parmi les choses importantes il [Suenens] est revenu sur la morale conjugale et il a trouvé cette fois-ci le Saint-Père plus accessible. Il n'a plus eu la réaction crispée des audiences antérieures où il disait: "Mais, si même les moralistes catholiques commencent à douter, il faut que le magistère et que moi surtout réagissent et que je rappelle les principes". Il a admis qu'il y avait de fait des questions difficiles, que tout n'était peut-être pas au point, qu'on devait continuer à étudier. Vu sa bonne disposition, le cardinal lui a passé alors le texte rédigé par un théologien romain ... qui expose au moins la problématique et de façon assez frappante et de nature à ébranler la conviction du Saint-Père. Le cardinal a parlé aussi au pape du contenu des résultats du colloque qui s'est tenu à Rome dans la Secrétairerie d'État pendant la semaine de Pâques par la commission chargée d'étudier les problèmes démographiques dont font partie le chan. de Locht et le P. de Riedmatten. Il me dit que le nom de de Riedmatten suscite toujours un certain hochement de tête d'approbation de la part du pape[579].

– Suenens also asked H. Küng for documentation. In reply, Küng sent him articles by F. Böckle and J. G. Ziegler[580].

---

574. Fund Suenens, B.C. and H.V., 26, 27-28, 29-34.
575. Letter of March 29, 1964. Fund Döpfner, 825.
576. Fund Suenens, 1966-1967.
577. Fund Suenens, B.C. and H.V., 17. The audience took place on March 12, 1964 (Cf. *L'Osservatore Romano*, March 13, 1964).
578. Fund Suenens, 2439-2441. This letter and note were incorrectly filed in the Fund Suenens, for the third intersession. The same text can also be found in Fund Heuschen, 203. There it is dated February 29, 1964. Delhaye mistakenly wrote: "ce texte déjà promis en septembre 196<u>4</u>". It must have been September of 196<u>3</u>.
579. Fund Prignon, 825.
580. Letter of April 21 and answer by Suenens to Küng on April 24, 1964, Fund Suenens, B.C. and H.V., 44-49.

4. At the beginning of May, Suenens traveled to the U.S. to give several lectures[581]. *Inter alia*, he spoke at the University of Chicago Divinity School and for groups of religious in Boston[582]. After a speech in Boston on May 7, he held a press conference at which he claimed that: "… medical research is coming very close to finding a pill which will make it very easy for married couples to plan their families without violating the teachings of the Church"[583]. Suenens had been prepped for the conference by A. McCormack in that McCormack had been able to help him anticipate some of the questions of the journalists[584]. Suenens' statement came in the middle of a controversy among U.S. Catholics regarding an article by L. Janssens, the adoption of a sensationally 'open' position by Msgr. Th. Roberts (the former archbishop of Bombay), and a condemnation of the "new pill" by Msgr. Heenan, the archbishop of Westminster[585].

Suenens' press conference did not go unnoticed in Rome. On May 22, Prignon informed Suenens that his 'interview' had provoked reactions[586]. In fact, Ottaviani had given an interview to *Vita* in which he stated that nobody, not even a bishop or a cardinal, had the right[587] to give his personal opinion on this matter[588]. P. Geenen, a Belgian Dominican teaching at the Angelicum, wrote to Suenens on May 31, 1964. He enclosed a copy of Lambruschini's article in his letter[589]. In his diary for May 30, Msgr. Charue noted:

> Mais il vient d'y avoir l'incident des 'Pilules'. L'hebdomadaire *Vita* vient de publier une interview du cardinal Ottaviani, avec un commentaire, qui prend directement à partie le cardinal Suenens, pour ce qu'il a dit en

---

581. One of the conferences was probably: 'Le Concile et le monde'. The last part of it dealt with 'Église et Birth Control'. Cf. Fund Suenens, B.C. and H.V., 64-65.

582. Cf. *Pastoralia* 112 [May 5] (1964), and Fund Suenens, A.P., box 20.

583. *Catholic Reporter* [May 15] (1964).Cf. *La Documentation catholique* (1964) 895.

584. Fund Suenens, B.C. and H.V., 43. A. McCormack, who was a member of the St Joseph's society for Foreign Missions (Mill Hill Fathers) was active in the Legion of Mary in London. Later, he worked for the Papal Commission *Justitia et Pax* in Rome.

585. For the discussion surrounding Janssens' article, cf. Fund Suenens, B.C. and H.V., 38-42, 56-59 (especially the articles by the Belgian G. De Pauw, who was residing in the U.S. at that time). For the article by Msgr. Roberts, cf. Fund Suenens, B.C. and H.V., 51, 52, 56, 57, 786, 787. For the position of Msgr. Heenan, cf. B. VANDANO, *La Pillola cattolica*, in *Epoca* [May 24] (1964) 22-25.

586. Fund Suenens, 1711. On May 24, Prignon sent Suenens another article by Palazzini [P. PALAZZINI, *Si può e si deve proteggere l'equilibrio della persona*, in *Studi Cattolici* 5/27 (1961) 63-64], that had been provided by L. Anné (Fund Suenens, B.C. and H.V., 63-64).

587. Fund Suenens, B.C. and H.V., 66-67.

588. Cf. L. FURNO, *Benedetta o maledetta la Pillola per le Nascite?*, in *Vita* [June 3] (1964) 10-15, which contains the interview of Ottaviani on p. 13 entitled: *Non creare confusioni*.

589. Fund Suenens, B.C. and H.V., 66-67.

Amérique. Celui-ci nous a d'ailleurs dit hier à Malines qu'on exagère ce qu'il a dit ... À lire entre les lignes et en rapprochant un article de Lambruschini dans *L'Osservatore Romano* tout récent[590], il ressort qu'on reconnaît qu'une nouvelle problématique se présente; mais ce n'est pas à un membre de la hiérarchie, fût-il Cardinal, à risquer une intervention publique dans un domaine aussi délicat[591].

As a result of this controversy, the Secretariat of State informed the bishops via the nuncios that they should refrain from taking sides in this matter and should make sure theologians do not publish articles that deviate from the present course[592]. It is not at all surprising that Suenens (in his letter of June 2 to the Pope) not only informed him about his trip to the U.S. but also explained his press conference[593].

5. The 'Groupe d'études de la population' held a new meeting in Rome between June 13th and 15th. De Riedmatten, de Locht and Prignon kept Suenens well informed:

– On June 8, de Riedmatten wrote to Suenens that he had been asked to assemble his commission as quickly as possible since the Pope was in need of advice on some points. He found Rome stifling. He reported that he had attended the 'Colloque de Louvain'[594] and found it very interesting. Suenens also received a copy of the letter by Cicognani (June 12, 1964) to the members of the commission; in it, he wished them success with their meeting[595].
– Suenens received the report of this meeting[596]. He also received a copy of the Pope's speech to the cardinals on June 23, in which he acknowledged that the issue of birth control was being studied[597]. Prignon wrote to Suenens regarding that speech as follows:

Il [le discours] a sans doute le mérite de souligner que les normes fixées par Pie XII ne sont pas définitives et immuables ... Comme vous le savez, cette

590. Cf. F. LAMBRUSCHINI, *A Proposito dei Progestativi*, in *L'Osservatore della Domenica* [May 31] (1964) 4. Here, Lambruschini spoke about the Janssens article and Suenens' interview in Boston. Beginning in June of 1964, Lambruschini was a member of the Papal Commission.
591. Journal Charue, p. 191.
592. Letter from Oddi to Suenens, June 3, 1964; Fund Suenens, B.C. and H.V., 68.
593. Fund Suenens, 1724.
594. Cf. for the report: 'VIe Colloque de la maîtrise sexuelle', Louvain, May 30-31, 1964, Fund Suenens, B.C. and H.V., 946.
595. Fund Suenens, B.C. and H.V., 287.
596. Rapport sur la Session du Groupe d'études de la population, June 13-15, 1964, 19 p. (Fund Suenens, B.C. and H.V., 286).
597. Cf. *AAS* 56 (1964) 581-589.

déclaration fait suite à la réunion du groupe de la Secrétairerie d'État. Y assistait le chanoine de Locht ... il ne m'a pas dit grand-chose étant tenu par le secret très strict qu'on leur avait recommandé. Mais il m'a tout de même répété, après avoir été assez découragé le premier jour, [qu'] il sortait de cette réunion, assez optimiste, même très optimiste. On était parvenu en effet à rédiger une résolution unanime, même les gens les plus durs, reconnaissant que le problème était difficile et recommandant de ne pas faire de déclaration maintenant, ou, si on jugeait nécessaire d'en faire une à cause de la confusion existante dans les esprits, en tout cas, d'en peser soigneusement les idées et les mots. Il semble évident que cette déclaration a tout de même fait impression sur le Saint-Père[598].

– On July 18, de Riedmatten thanked Suenens for the meeting in Louvain. On July 22, he appealed to him following de Locht's criticism of both the work of the commission and the de Riedmatten report[599].

6. Worried about the rumour that on August 15 the Pope would publish a statement, Reuss wrote to Suenens on July 11 and 16 in order to ask him to use his influence to prevent this. He made the same request to Döpfner[600].

– As de Locht was about to leave for Chile, Suenens wrote to Silva Henriquez on August 1: de Locht would try to meet with him between August 10 and 31. There are rumours that the Pope will publish an encyclical on birth control; Suenens sent a note to Silva Henriquez, which he had also presented to the Pope, explaining why *Casti connubii* must be amended[601].
– On August 3, Suenens wrote to Noonan that his book[602] will be very useful, even if it appeared after the papal encyclical, since the Council still had to debate on this matter in connection with Schema XVII. He asked Noonan to send some of his conclusions to Häring, the Schema's editing secretary, since he was in contact with the Pope[603].
– By August, Suenens was already aware of the initiative of H. and L. Buelens-Gijsen and J. Grootaers to send a document to the Council Fathers[604] in which an international group of intellectuals and scientists pled for change with regard to conjugal ethics[605].

598. Fund Prignon, 828, end of June, 1964.
599. Fund Suenens, B.C. and H.V., 288-293.
600. Fund Suenens, B.C. and H.V., 82-85.
601. Fund Suenens, 1991.
602. J.T. NOONAN, *Contraception: A History of its Treatment by the Catholic Theologians and Canonists*, Cambridge, MA, Harvard University Press, 1965.
603. Fund Suenens, 1992.
604. 'Address to the Second Vatican Council on the Subject of the Problems of the Family' (cf. Fund Suenens, 2271).
605. Fund Suenens, 1993. Philips had also discussed this text with a number of theologians and had submitted his remarks to H. Buelens on August 29, 1964. Cf. Fund Philips, 1779-1781.

During this second intersession Suenens was kept informed concerning schema XIII. He primarily devoted himself to achieving a full-fledged conciliar treatment of the schema, something which added to the necessity of a fourth session. For this reason he would not accept the drastic 'Döpfner plan'. Now that the schema was divided into two major parts: a more dogmatic part and the *Adnexa*, which included the text *De matrimonio*, his chief concern was to achieve a full-fledged statute for these *Adnexa*. This was far from easy, as the third and the fourth session made clear. During the Coordinating Commission meeting of June 26, Felici said:

> Evidentemente bisognerà inviarlo [questo Schema] ai Padri, anche perché si è parlato già troppo di questo schema, vendendo più merce di quella che ha; ma trovo che sarà impossibile esaminare in Concilio tutti i problemi che vi sono trattati. Si potra vedere di ridurli a pochi fondamentali e per altri provvedere con un messaggio in cui si dica che la Chiesa è a conoscenza di essi e chi li studia e ne indicherà quindi le opportune soluzioni[606].

This was not Felici's last attack on the *Adnexa*. Following the failure of the 'texte de Malines', the Belgians were less involved in the final editing of the 'text of Zürich'[607]. Consequently Suenens was less frequently consulted; he focused more and more on the problem of birth control. Gradually he became the 'reference point' for all who wished to see changes on this issue. He had made contacts with Belgians, Americans, Germans, South-Americans, Italians, ... He was able to exert influence through the 'commission' of de Riedmatten, the 'Colloques de Louvain', the Coordinating Commission and, as much as possible, directly upon the Pope.

7. IIIª Sessio

During this session, Schema XIII was discussed from October 20 to November 5 and on November 9 and 10 in the plenary meetings of the Council. Suenens intervened twice, on October 21 and 29. He was also forced to defend the value of the *Adnexa* yet again.

a. The incident with Felici regarding the Adnexa

On September 30, 1964 in the Basilica Felici announced that the *Adnexa* will be distributed while also noting that they do not belong to

---

606. *Processus verbalis*, AS V/2, p. 641.
607. Nevertheless Moeller was present in Zurich, (February 1-3, 1964), Houtart had contacts in Poland and Philips played an important role in the meeting of the central subcommission on September 10 to 12, 1964 (cf. Fund Philips, 1782-1799).

the schema and, as such, will not be part of the debate. They will only serve to illustrate the Schema's content[608]. The next day the secretary-general provided additional clarification. The *Adnexa* were drafted by the Commission for the Lay Apostolate and were sent to the Secretariat to be distributed as a private document, without any official character[609]. During the course of the same morning and after the intervention by Msgr. Compagnone, Felici gave the following specification: At the request of the Coordinating Commission, the text of the *Adnexa* had been drafted by the Commissio mixta, the same commission that had edited Schema XIII. The *Adnexa* are not just a private document, but they will not be debated at the Council and, consequently "non gaudebit valore conciliari"[610]. In a letter to the moderators dated October 10, 1964, Cardinal Cento placed all the blame for this incident on Felici, who had reacted to a question posed by Msgr. M. Lefebvre[611]. At the meeting of the Coordinating Commission and the presidents on October 7, 1964, Felici again emphasized that Schema XIII need not be completed at all costs; but Suenens pled for a fourth session[612]. In Felici's Relatio for this meeting on October 8 (which he made on behalf of the Pope), he repeated his criticism of Schema XIII ("si trattano troppi problemi in forma imprecisa e senza una soluzione adeguata"). Then he proposed to leave this to a '*Messaggio*' or to refer everything to the post-conciliar period along with a written consultation of the bishops. He also added that the majority of the meeting did not think it advisable to extend the Council because of just one schema, especially since it remained doubtful whether it would ever be finished[613].

608. *AS* III/3, p. 59.

609. *AS* III/3, p. 181. Cf. also *AS* V/2, pp. 709-713.

610. *AS* III/3, p. 206. Since the press made mention of manœuvres by the conservatives, *L'Osservatore Romano* published a correction on October 3: the secretary-general never speaks in his own name but always in the name of the moderators or the presidents. Yesterday's intervention took place at Felici's initiative but with the permission of the moderators. Cf. G. CAPRILE, *Il Concilio Vaticano II*. Vol. IV, Roma, Civiltà Cattolica, 1967, p. 118. In a letter addressed to the moderators by Ottaviani and Cento (October 15, 1964), it was again stated that the *Adnexa* will not be discussed in the Basilica, but that the Patres must submit their remarks in writing (*AS* V/2, p. 797).

611. *AS* V/2, pp. 735-736.

612. *Processus verbalis, AS* V/2, p. 760.

613. *Relatio ad Summum Pontificem, AS* V/2, pp. 761-762. In the *Processus verbalis* it is explicitly stated that no concrete decision had been taken with regard to schema XIII (*AS* V/2, p. 760).

On November 11, 1964, Felici, in a Nota to the Pope, wrote: "È difficile prevedere quando lo schema [XIII] potrà essere sufficientemente emendato e se incontrerà il beneplacito dei Padri in tutti i problemi che agita. Secondo alcuni ci vorrebbero ancora almeno due anni. L'eccessiva attesa creata dalla stampa, in seguito particolarmente a indebite e

Suenens commented on this episode as follows:

> Nous avons eu une escarmouche importante à propos de ce schéma XIII dans son avant-dernière forme. Il y avait à ce moment-là un texte avec de longues annexes. Mgr Felici, qui était furieux d'ailleurs et sur le texte et sur les annexes, a voulu donner à ces annexes une allure de documents sans importance, de documents privés. J'ai dû, en pleine séance du concile, l'obliger à rectifier. Je lui ai fait un papier[614] demandant qu'il dise que ces annexes étaient demandées par la Commission de Coordination et que ce plan avait été prévu; que, par conséquent, ça faisait partie de la matière conciliaire. Il l'a fait sans broncher: au moins cette fois-là nous avons été en harmonie[615].

On October 15, 1964 Glorieux sends to Suenens some observations, transmitted by Etchegaray about the discussions of the schema XIII[616].

b. Suenens' intervention in the Basilica on October 21, 1964[617]

On the second day of the general discussion on Schema XIII, Suenens gave his placet to the schema, as both Lercaro and Döpfner had done the previous day. He made four comments:

1. The schema must be more clear on the fact that the Church has answers for the world's problems when viewed from the perspective of her own mission and task (instead of from that of the world).
2. The relation between 'human progress' (*humanizatio*) and evangelization must be better developed. As Pius XI[618] wrote: "Ecclesia civilizat evangelizando et non evangelizat civilizando".
3. The schema must treat atheism more thoroughly; specifically, it must isolate its causes and begin a dialogue.

---

imprudenti conferenze stampa o interviste, ha provocato un'atmosfera di tensione che non ha giovato alla serenità della preparazione e della discussione". And in a footnote Felici adds, possibly still a bit nostalgic: "Si deve però osservare che molti dei temi poi trattati nello schema erano stati sviluppati, forse in forma un po' scolastica, ma con maggiore profondità ed esattezza di dottrina, negli schemi della Commissione teologica [preparatoria]". Cf. *AS* VI/3, pp. 509-510.

614. Suenens preserved this document, cf. Fund Suenens, 2215.

615. SUENENS, *Mémoires sur le Concile Vatican II*, p. 67.

616. Cf. *AS* V/3, pp. 26-27.

617. *AS* III/5, pp. 270-272. The annotations of Poswick on these question are very imprecise and the dates often errroneous, cf. POSWICK, *Un journal du Concile* (n. 9), pp. 492-494 and 498-499.

618. The Latin text (Fund Suenens, 2206) submitted by Suenens incorrectly mentions Pius X. In the French translation he wrote Pius XI (Fund Suenens, 2207), which is correct. For point 2, see also SUENENS, *L'Église en état de mission* (n. 22). Chapter II of this book is entitled: 'Humaniser ou évangéliser?' (pp. 25-51); it is also there that this sentence from Pius XI's message to 'Les Semaines sociales de Versailles' is quoted.

4. It is absolutely essential to carry over a number of topics from the *Adnexa* to the actual schema, e.g., the collaboration of Catholics on an international level and marital love.

Apparently, Suenens did not attach too much import to this intervention. Later he wrote: "[l'intervention] avait tout simplement pour but de défendre la validité ou la valeur du Schéma de peur qu'on ne l'attaque de façon telle qu'il ne fût rejeté"[619].

c. *Intervention on n. 21 of the text (on birth control), October 29, 1964*[620]

It was probably this intervention that provoked the most comment: the subject, the content, the tone, and the reactions of the Pope, the bishops and the public were all factors.

1. On October 28 the discussion of Chapter Four of Schema XIII 'De praecipuis muneribus a christianis nostrae aetatis adimplendis' began. At the beginning, Agagianian, the moderator, proposed that this chapter deal with delicate problems (an obvious allusion to n° 21 on 'Dignitas matrimonii et familiae'). It was therefore deemed improper to have extensive public discussions regarding it. The Patres were invited to submit in all freedom their remarks in writing. It was promised that they would receive all the attention they deserved[621].

In 1968, Suenens supplied the following background information:

> Comme modérateurs nous allions tous les jeudis chez le Saint-Père et à un moment donné, il nous a dit qu'il n'aimerait pas que l'on discute du problème du Birth Control. Mais c'était dit assez vaguement, si bien que je croyais me trouver devant quelque chose qui était certainement un désir très fort mais dans quelle mesure cela était-il un ordre absolu? ... Le jour où l'on s'approche du débat, le Cardinal Agagianian, qui préside la séance ... me fait passer un petit papier, qu'il fait passer d'ailleurs aux trois autres [les 2 autres modérateurs] ... et il avait mis sur ce papier: "Reverendi Patres, il est entendu qu'on ne discutera pas le problème du Birth Control". Les deux autres ne disent rien, laissent passer. Je réponds: "Je refuse mon adhésion à ce papier parce que demain, je compte bien en parler et si vous voulez me couper la parole et m'interrompre et me dire que ... cela fera un beau spectacle de chahut entre deux modérateurs dans l'assemblée"! Je crois qu'Agagianian était un peu troublé. J'ai alors fait une formule de compromis. Je lui ai proposé de dire: "On ne discutera ce problème que par les plus grands principes". Ceci voulant dire: on ne doit pas entrer dans le détail de la pilule,

619. SUENENS, *Mémoires sur le Concile Vatican II*, p. 55.
620. *AS* III/6, pp. 57-59.
621. *AS* III/5, p. 702 – Cf. CAPRILE, *Il Concilio Vaticano II*. Vol. IV (n. 610), p. 291.

mais on entrera dans les grands principes. Les deux autres, Döpfner –
Lercaro, étant d'accord, c'est comme cela qu'il l'a dit, ce qui nous permettait d'aborder le problème[622].

2. Suenens himself called it "la toute grosse intervention"[623]. It was an
intervention which Prignon, who believed it to be too strong and controversial, tried in vain – even in the Basilica itself – to tone down[624]. Suenens had four *desiderata* regarding the crucial problem of the world and
the Church:

– Some doctrinal elements, now mentioned in the *Adnexa*, needed to be
  inserted into the text so that a more biblical and coherent doctrinal synthesis could be produced.
– The conciliar commission needed to work closely with the Papal
  commission.
– This [Papal] commission should conduct a large survey of well-
  known moralists from different countries, of scientists, of university
  faculties from various disciplines, of lay persons (both male and
  female), and of Christian married couples. The names of the members
  of this commission needed to be made public so that they can receive
  feedback from all over the world and, thus, can truly represent the
  people of God.
– A few fundamental guidelines were given for the work to be done by
  this commision:
  A. In keeping with the faith,
     The gospel is unvarying, but the Church must always strive to reach
     a better understanding of the richness of Christ's teachings. In part,
     this means that it is worth asking if all parts of Christian doctrine
     had been evenly preserved. One must pay attention not just to the
     "Crescite et multiplicamini", but also to "Et erunt duo in carne
     una". The commission needs to ask whether or not the reproductive
     duty was not overemphasized to the disadvantage of the equally
     important goal [finis] of marital love. The commisson must also
     strive to address the alarming problems of demographic expansion
     and overpopulation. This was not to be seen as a relaxation of the

---

622. *Mémoire sur le problème du Birth Control*, p. 5. Cf. also (analogue story)
SUENENS, *Mémoires sur le Concile Vatican II*, p. 56.
    623. SUENENS, *Mémoires sur le Concile Vatican II*, p. 56.
    624. Cf. Journal Moeller, Carnet 32, October 4, 1965, p. 3: "Le matin même je l'ai
supplié de ne pas la [son intervention] faire, me dit Prignon. Il [Suenens] a prié longuement à la chapelle le Saint-Esprit, pour être éclairé. Il voulait faire sauter [mot illisible]
qui entourait le pape. Il n'a pas réussi".

Church's moral standards. The problem was not posed because believers selfishly give in to their desires and drives, but because many among them were trying to be faithful to both the teachings of the Church and the obvious demands of marital and parental love.

B. In keeping with natural ethics and scientific truth,

The commission needs to examine whether or not the classical doctrine, especially as formulated in handbooks, sufficiently takes into account the data of modern science. We are constantly gaining insight into the complexity of nature including the interrelatedness of biology and psychology, between body and spirit. A new examination of what 'secundum naturam vel contra naturam' means is needed. We must keep up with scientific developments. Suenens very emotionally added: "Adiuro vos, Fratres. Vitemus novum processum Galilei. Unum enim suffict pro Ecclesia".

The commission's task was to integrate these new elements and to submit the conclusions to the highest doctrinal authority. This is not a collapse into situational ethics. The presentation of the doctrine, which is unvariable in its principles, needs to take into account the contingent factors which have developed over time. The Popes have also done this when writing *Rerum novarum, Quadragesimo anno* and *Mater et magistra*: in each of these, the same principles were more accurately presented as each took into account their own era and context. Suenens concluded with a solemn appeal: Let us keep in mind the words of the Lord: "Veritas – et quidem naturalis et supernaturalis – veritas tota et vitalis – veritas liberabit vos"[625].

3. The reactions to this speech were many and varied

(a) In 1968, Suenens wrote about this with more than a little emotion:

Il n'y a rien de plus ridicule qu'un orateur qui finit en l'air s'il n'est pas soutenu par des applaudissements. Ceci pour essayer de briser cette sorte d'idée que le 'consensus episcoporum' était acquis dans le sens de *Casti connubii*. Je voulais démontrer, face au monde, que cela n'était pas vrai. Les applaudissements très nourris, je crois pouvoir dire de la majorité, en tout cas très nourris, une véritable ovation, ont montré que les Pères étaient loin d'être consentants avec *Casti connubii*. Ceci me paraît un point capital pour l'histoire. Quand, après le discours, je suis allé au bar, il y a des séries de gens, d'évêques, qui m'ont embrassé. J'ai entendu crier quelqu'un: 'Il y a vingt ans que nous attendions cela', des larmes aux

625. In his *Mémoires sur le problème du Birth Control*, p. 6, Suenens writes: "À propos de ce discours, j'ai voulu expressément le terminer sur un ton très pathétique. L'histoire de Galilée je l'ai jetée exprès et aussi 'La vérité vous rendra libres'... un pathos qui obligeait l'assistance à réagir".

yeux ... cela a été pour moi un des moments les plus pathétiques et véritablement, je crois avoir essayé là de rompre publiquement cette sorte de
tabou, cette sorte d'interdiction de quitter le domaine du Saint-Office ...
le Saint-Office est une chose, une Congrégation romaine est une chose,
mais un Concile est au-dessus de tout cela et n'a pas à tenir compte de ces
interventions[626].

All chroniclers focused on the fact that Léger, Maximos IV, and
Suenens, all pleaded for a liberalization in conjugal ethics on the same
day[627]. Suenens also received many positive reactions: from bishops[628],
from priests[629], and from lay persons[630]. Prignon told him: "Vous avez
ouvert l'avenir"[631]. At the English-language press conference for that day,
Charles Davis is reported to have said: "C'est le plus beau jour de ma
vie, comme théologien"[632]. Laurentin also congratulated Suenens on
November 3, 1964. Along with his congratulations, Laurentin sent him
his text ('Témoignages et Données sur le Problème de la limitation des
naissances') with testimonies and another plea for more openness in the
area of conjugal ethics[633].

(b) Negative reactions: According to Moeller, Suenens, by publicly
criticising a decision taken by the Pope, has created a scandal in curial
circles[634]. Ottaviani and Browne both countered Suenens' position in the

626. *Mémoire sur le problème du Birth Control*, p. 6.
627. *Inter alia*, Wiltgen, Fund Suenens, 2261. Congar noted: "Le cardinal Suenens a
même demandé que la Commission réunie par le pape pour étudier les problèmes de la
régulation des naissances devienne publique et travaille avec les organes correspondants
du concile. C'est important. C'est courageux de sa part, parce que le Pape tient à Sa commission et à un travail secret. Mais peut-on garder cette dualité à un moment où le concile étudie ces choses?" (CONGAR, *Mon journal du Concile* [n. 9], Vol. II, p. 232).
De Lubac wrote: "Le P. Gagnebet est mécontent de ce débat public. Nous en causons
quelques instants. C'est un fait que bien des paroles prononcées depuis le début de la discussion du schéma manquent de profondeur humaine et de vigueur chrétienne" (Journal
de Lubac, October 29, 1964, II, p. 261).
628. *Inter alia*, Coderre, Morrow. Fund Suenens, 2246bis, 2256.
629. R. Pleuss (Fund Suenens, 2257); R. Etchegaray who wrote: "Hier matin, in Aula,
ce fut un moment historique quand vous avez – une fois de plus – libéré les esprits avec
un courage et une force convaincante" (Fund Suenens, 2249).
630. *Inter alia*, by G. Zizola, who wrote: "Grazie a Lei ho amato oggi più profondamente la famiglia che Dio mi ha dato; ho amato di più la Chiesa" (Fund Suenens, 2247-
2248). Other reactions came from France (Fund Suenens, 2258) and from the U.S.A. (Fund
Suenens, 2253-2254).
631. See also Prignon's *Rapport à l'Ambassade de Belgique près le Saint-Siège*, in
which he writes: "Bien que la plus modérée dans le fond, l'intervention du cardinal
Suenens, en raison de la personnalité du modérateur et de son influence dans le monde,
eut le plus de retentissement" (Fund Prignon, 1058 et POSWICK, *Un journal du Concile*
[n. 9], p. 513).
632. SUENENS, *Mémoires sur le Concile Vatican II*, p. 58.
633. Fund Suenens, B.C. and H.V., 96-97.
634. Journal Moeller, Carnet 32, October 4, 1965, p. 2.

next day's plenary session[635]. But the most negative reaction came from the Pope himself. Suenens describes it as follows:

> Le matin même ... on a vu Mgr Colombo partir comme une flèche vers le Saint-Père[636] dans un état d'indignation totale. Cela m'a été dit par son voisin dans la loge où il se trouvait et je crois même que c'est à midi qu'il a téléphoné à Mgr Philips pour dire que cela avait fortement déplu en haut lieu ... Je n'ai pas réagi, et comme je ne réagissais pas, le Saint-Père m'a envoyé, deux jours plus tard[637], le Cardinal Agagianian ... Il l'a envoyé pour me dire son très profond mécontentement, et qu'on attendait de moi une rétractation dans la matière. J'ai alors demandé une audience au Saint-Père, et c'est la pire audience de ma vie[638]. Le Saint-Père m'a dit que j'avais perdu tout crédit auprès des évêques du concile. J'avais évidemment sur les lèvres de dire: 'Saint-Père, si vous aviez ouvert votre fenêtre, si Saint-Pierre était ouvert, vous auriez pu entendre jusqu'ici les ovations'. Mais je n'ai rien dit, ce n'était pas le moment. Il était dur, il était cassant, et il n'y avait pas de réplique à donner. Cela s'est terminé en me disant qu'on attendait une rétractation[639].

Indeed, on November 3, Colombo has wrote a letter to the Pope in which he drew the Pope's attention to two of Suenens' "unacceptable" positions: (1) the claim that the Pope must make the names of the commission public in order to make it possible for the bishops to preserve their faith in the Pope and (2) the demand that spouses must also be part of the commission can give the impression that the Magisterium must try to reproduce all the ideas of the "people of God" instead of those of the "Traditio apostolica"[640]. This letter was also written during a period of significant tension regarding collegiality, which, in turn, led to the *Nota explicativa praevia*. It also seems possible that Colombo's letter of November 3 was the

---

635. For the improvised and emotional intervention ["I am the 11th of 12 children and my father was a simple laborer"] by Ottaviani, see *AS* III/6, pp. 85-86. For the intervention by Browne, see *AS* III/9, pp. 86-88.

636. Msgr. Prignon, in his *Rapport à l'Ambassade de Belgique près le Saint-Siège*, wrote: "Déjà au sortir de Saint-Pierre, Mgr Colombo ne cachait pas ses appréhensions concernant les suites possibles de cette suggestion du cardinal" (Fund Prignon, 1059 and POSWICK, *Un journal du Concile* [n. 9], p. 513).

637. Agagianian came to the Belgian College on November 4. Cf. Fund Philips, 1921.

638. Neither in late October nor early November did *L'Osservatore Romano* does not mention a special audience for Suenens. However, the four moderators had an audience on the evenings of October 29 and November 5 (Cf *L'Osservatore Romano*, October 31 and November 7, 1964). Of course, it is always possible that the Pope received Suenens after these audiences or that the audience was not published by *L'Osservatore Romano*.

639. *Mémoire sur le problème du Birth Control*, pp. 7-8. Analogue story in Suenens, *Mémoires sur le Concile Vatican II*, p. 57.

640. "Non entro nel merito del problema cui si riferiva. Mi sembra invece doveroso di far rilevare che esso includeva due posizioni dottrinalmente inaccettabili, e che non dovrebbero diventare mentalità dominante dell'Episcopato:

a) la esigenza che il Romano Pontefice deva far conoscere i nomi delle persone che consulta per l'esercizio del Suo magistero affinche i Vescovi abbiano ad aver fiducia nella

cause of Agagianian's visit to the Belgian College on November 4[641]. On October 30, Aganianian, as moderator, proposed that the Patres conclude the debate on this n° 21. It was accepted without much ado. Some suspected that the Pope exerted pressure in order to achieve this result[642].

4. On November 7, Suenens held a short 'rectification'[643] in the Basilica; the occasion was his intervention on the issue of Missions and missionary activity[644]. He said he wanted to answer some of the public reactions such as that he had said that the teachings and the discipline of the Church regarding conjugal ethics needed to be changed. He claimed merely to have expressed the desire that they needed to be studied and not that this doctrine rejected something that the Church has declared *'authentice et definitive'*. In short, he only wished to offer a synthesis of all the principles germane to these issues. As far as the discipline goes, it is evident that the conclusions of the commission must be submitted to the Pope in order to be judged by his supreme authority. It must also be clear that the method of working used is solely dependent upon his supreme authority.

Suenens recounts this episode as follows:

> Je me suis donc trouvé devant une situation extrêmement difficile. Alors j'ai fait, à la manière de St. Augustin, une re-tractatio, c.-à-d. re-traité une seconde fois du même sujet. J'ai pris le prétexte d'une intervention que je devais faire le lendemain sur les Missions pour raccrocher le wagon à la finale de mon discours, mais comme le Saint-Père est arrivé à cette séance[645], le lendemain, j'ai supprimé immédiatement mon tour de parole

competenza di questo magistero;

b) la esigenza che in una Commissione di studio siano compresi, oltre a teologi et studiosi di varie categorie, anche gli sposi cristiani 'perchè sia veramente rappresentato tutto il popolo di Dio', può suggerire la idea che la funzione del Magistero sia di esprimere il pensiero del 'popolo di Dio' invece che quello della Tradizione trasmessa dagli Apostoli. È opportuno trovar modo di chiarire queste idee, senza polemica?'" (Fund Colombo, LG.03.17).

641. Cf. Fund Philips, 1921.

642. Cf. Journal Moeller, Carnet 22, October 30, 1964, cards added, p. 2: "Prignon, vu ce matin, ne dit rien. Mais quand je lui dis: cette interruption est demandée par le pape, il me répond: 'sapientibus sat'. Il ajoute: 'Je suis tenu par le secret, je ne puis rien dire'".

643. Msgr. Prignon drafted the largest part of this text. In his 'diplomatic' report to the embassy, Prignon writes: "Maints évêques pensèrent que cette mise au point avait bien pu être suggérée par le pape lui-même. On n'en a toutefois aucune preuve. Si l'avenir devait donner crédit à cette hypothèse, il y aurait là un signe de plus que le pape tenait à marquer ses distances vis-à-vis du Concile et affirmer sa primauté comme cela devint très clair dans la suite [allusion to the *Nota explicativa praevia*]" (Fund Prignon, 1059, p. 3).

644. Cf. *AS* III/6, p. 381

645. On November 6, 1964, Paul VI attended part of the meeting to emphasize the importance of the schema *De missionibus*.

pour ne pas faire cela devant lui. Cela aurait été un drame supplémentaire. J'ai donc remis le discours au lendemain – heureusement que, comme modérateur, je pouvais un peu arranger l'ordre des débats – et le lendemain j'ai fait ce discours sur les missions et j'ai terminé en redisant strictement la même chose. Je n'ai pas changé un mot. Un théologien américain a d'ailleurs parfaitement compris. Mais les gens n'ont pas compris. Ils disaient: 'Qu'est-ce que c'est? Il dit que la presse a mal compris?'[646]. Il y avait justement une histoire à une radio italienne qui me donnait le prétexte de dire: 'On comprend de travers, alors je mets au point'"[647].

5. In spite of all of this turmoil, Suenens' intervention was still fruitful[648]. During the same month of November, the Papal commission was extended from 15 to 58 members. Of these 30 were lay persons. The new members included four Belgians: P. Anciaux, Ph. Delhaye[649], J. Férin, G. Lemaître. This brought the total number of Belgian on the commission to eight. And Msgr. J. Margéot[650], also new member, was no stranger to Suenens. He had been the director of the Legion of Mary during the forties when Edel Quinn was the group's 'envoy'. Suenens had corresponded with Margéot when he was working on the biography of Edel Quinn[651]. Suenens tells the following story:

Le Saint-Père était très mécontent de cet appel à l'élargissement, mais quelques mois plus tard, il l'a fait. Il l'a fait, mais pour garder la logique du secret, on n'a jamais publié les noms mais on a donné la photo de tous les

646. Congar was also suspicious: "Le cardinal Suenens, me dit-on, a protesté contre l'interprétation que la Presse a donnée de son discours ... Tel que je le connais, soucieux comme il est de 'faire une brèche' (*mihi dixit*), il ne doit pas être fâché de ces interprétations. Mais il prend ses précautions et peut-être y a-t-il été invité" (CONGAR, *Mon journal du Concile* [n. 9], Vol. II, p. 245). Heuschen writes on November 8, 1964: "Vous aurez lu dans les journaux que notre cardinal a reçu une réprimande du pape à propos de son intervention sur la morale conjugale; ce n'était pas à cause de la doctrine mais parce qu'il avait demandé que la commission pontificale soit élargie ... Cette intervention du pape a fait très mauvaise impression" (Fund Heuschen, 552).

647. *Mémoire sur le problème du Birth Control*, p. 8.

648. During the fourth session, when Döpfner was involved in an incident with Paul VI regarding indulgences, Suenens told him: "qu'il était passé par là l'année dernière et que c'était une *felix culpa* parce que l'expérience lui montrait ... que finalement sa démarche avait porté son fruit" (Journal Prignon, November 14, 1965, p. 200).

649. On December 6, 1964, Delhaye thanked Suenens for his appointment, which had taken place on November 20. Fund Suenens, B.C. and H.V., 282-283.

650. J. Margéot (1916-), priest of the diocese of Port-Louis (island of Mauritius), bishop of Port-Louis from 1969 till 1993, was made cardinal in 1988. During the sixties, the native population of Mauritius participated in an experiment involving the rhythm method. Cf. W.O. MOORE, *Population Limitation in Mauritius*, in Fund Suenens, B.C. and H.V., 80-81.

651. L.-J. SUENENS, *Une héroïne de l'apostolat: Edel Quinn, déléguée de la Légion de Marie en Afrique, 1907-1944*, Bruges, Desclée de Brouwer, 1952. For this correspondence, cf. Fund Suenens, A.P., box 31.

membres dans une audience au Vatican, dans *L'Osservatore*. Il n'y avait qu'à regarder la photo et mettre les noms en-dessous ... Le Saint-Père m'a alors demandé quelques noms. J'ai signalé moi-même 10-12 noms, tous de notre groupe de Louvain[652] et il les a mis dans le groupe[653].

d. Other contacts

Suenens' archives show that the Cardinal remained a point of reference for Schema XIII during the third session:

- On October 15, 1964, Glorieux sent a letter to Suenens containing a number of desiderata and proposals formulated by the delegates of 25 bishops' conferences and in meetings organized by Etchegaray[654].
- The lay-auditors requested that Mrs. Pilar Bellosilo address the Council in their name. The request was refused[655].
- Several periti sent Suenens suggestions and documents: E. Bonet on the planning of the votes[656]; Lebret supplied the documents of the 'Sous-commission française du schéma XIII, Atelier du chapitre IV et des Annexes IV et V'[657] as well as a note requested by Helder Camara[658]; Vanistendael wrote to Suenens about Christian institutions[659] and Houtart wrote about plans for a "Secrétariat Église-Monde"[660]. B. Lambert furnished Suenens with the document 'L'Église dans le monde. Rapport du comité de consultation, composé de clercs et de laïcs'. This commission was presided over by Msgr. Roy, archbishop of Québec[661].

---

652. Participants in the 'Colloques de Louvain'.

653. *Mémoire sur le problème du Birth Control*, p. 10. Here, Suenens was far from precise: new members (e.g., Delhaye) had been appointed as early as November of 1964.

654. AS V/3, pp. 26-27.

655. Letter of October 26, 1964, Fund Suenens, 2213. In SUENENS, *Souvenirs et espérances* (n. 11), p. 120, Suenens writes: "Je ne parvenais pas à obtenir que Barbara Ward – la célèbre et remarquable économiste de l'université Columbia – puisse intervenir dans un débat. Elle rédigea un texte qui fut lu par l'auditeur Nolan". This probably refers to J. Norris. Cf. TURBANTI, *Un Concilio per il mondo moderno* (n. 392), pp. 445-446, note 358: "Tra i laici si era pensato piuttosto di invitare la celebre studiosa americana Barbara Ward, ma questo non fu possibile". J. Norris spoke at the Council on November 5, 1964. The Suenens' archives contain a text by Barbara WARD, *World Poverty and the Christian Conscience* (Fund Suenens, 2231). Cf. J. KOMONCHAK, *L'ecclesiologia di communione*, in ALBERIGO (ed.), *Storia del Concilio Vaticano II* (n. 54), Vol. IV, pp. 46-48. At the meeting of the moderators on October 26, 1965, Suenens made another attempt to have a woman (possibly a religious) address the Council. The result was again unsuccessful. Cf. *Processus verbalis*, AS V/3, p. 741.

656. Fund Suenens, 2218-2220.

657. On October 12, 1964; Fund Suenens, 2222.

658. Fund Suenens, 2226-2227.

659. On October 21, 1964, Fund Suenens, 2229-2230.

660. On November 4, 1964, Fund Suenens, 2236.

661. Fund Suenens, 2224.

– On November 12, 1964, F. Cento sent a letter to the moderators in the name of the central subcommission in order to propose that, much like what had been done with the *Quinque propositiones* on *De ecclesia,* three questions be put to the Patres. It was tabled[662].
– It was probably Moeller who sent Suenens the report on the meetings of the central subcommission that had taken place on November 17, 19, and 20, 1964[663].

Throughout the third session Suenens continued to defend Schema XIII, especially against attacks by Felici[664]. The future of this schema only became safe when the decision was taken to actually have a fourth session[665]. Even then there was a battle with regard to the *Adnexa* and their doctrinal value. During the fourth session this discussion will set off in connection with the title (*Constitutio, Declaratio, Nuntius*) that had been proposed for Schema XIII. It was precisely in connection with the chapter *De matrimonio* that Suenens exerted such great effort in order to ensure that the morality of birth control would be discussed at the Council. He courageously used all his oratorical powers – even going so far as to place his position as moderator at risk. While he gained the approval of the "conciliar majority", his relationship with the Pope was damaged.

8. IIIᵃ Intersessio

The text of Schema XIII was again rewritten during the third intersession. This work took place both in Ariccia and in Rome during February of 1965. The Commissio mixta finished and approved the new text at the end of March/early April. Haubtmann was the new editor-in-chief: but the Belgians' role was once again on the rise. Philips was responsible for both the Latin translation and for conducting the debates in the Commissio mixta. In addition both Charue, as vice-president of the Doctrinal

662. Fund Suenens, 2216-2217 and *AS* V/3, pp. 64-66. At the meeting of the moderators on November 12, 1964, the question received a negative reply. Cf. *AS* V/3, p. 733. During the fourth session a similar procedure was again rejected.

663. Fund Suenens, 2223.

664. Cf. Felici's 'Annotatio ex officio. Appunto sullo schema De Ecclesia in mundo huius temporis', in *AS* VI/3, p. 567 (November 30, 1964).

665. On October 23, 1964, the Patres were informed that the session would conclude on November 21 and that the date of the fourth session would be announced later (CAPRILE, *Il Concilio Vaticano II*. Vol. IV [n. 610], pp. 260-261). Heuschen was able to inform his mother of this fact on October 18 (Fund Heuschen, 443). The scheduled starting date of the fourth session, September 14, 1965, was only determined on January 4, 1965. Cf. *AS* VI/4, p. 12.

Commission, and Moeller, as peritus of the Subcommissio centralis were in positions that allowed them to follow all the developments as they were happening. Msgr. Heuschen and Heylen played a central role in the editing of the chapter *De matrimonio*. Since the Coordinating Commission only held two brief meetings during this period, Suenens turned most of his attention to the problem of birth control.

a. Schema XIII

1. In his Christmas letter to the Pope (December 18, 1964), Suenens once again expressed the hope that Schema XIII will not fail to meet the world's expectations[666]. Suenens was not present at the December 30, 1964 meeting of the Coordinating Commission. He had been unexpectedly summoned to Rome by a telegram from Felici. The meeting was completely devoted to determining of the starting date of the fourth session. Mid-September was proposed since it was hoped that the new version of Schema XIII would be ready to be sent to the Patres by early June[667]. In his December 31, 1964 report to the Pope Felici wrote:

> Si insiste pressi gli eminentissimi Cardinali Cento ed Ottaviani e l'ecc.mo Mons. Guano che lo schema XIII venga ridotto alle linee caratteristiche ed essenziali, evitando di trattare quelle questioni che lo Santo Padre ha già riservato a se stesso o sulle quali non è possibile dire una parola sicura, attesa la contingenza di alcune situazioni[668].

2. In the meantime Msgr. Heuschen had started editing of the chapter *De matrimonio et familia*, a text that had been discussed in February in Ariccia and in Rome. Heylen, one of the co-authors and a priest of the diocese of Malines-Brussels, kept Suenens informed[669]. Heylen was also present at the meetings of the Commissio mixta in April 1965 and he reported to Suenens that Philips had defended the text on marriage with great authority[670].

---

666. Fund Suenens, 2307.

667. *Processus verbalis, AS* V/3, pp. 130-131. Even in this meeting Felici had tried to reduce the Schema XIII to a 'messaggio'. Cf. Letter by Lercaro to Döpfner, January 1, 1965: "Qui il discorso si allargò, indebitamente, entrando nel merito dello Schema e si arrivò a mettere in questione lo Schema stesso per sostituirlo magari con un messaggio (Felici); ma si rientrò poi in argumento" (Treffler [ed.], *Julius Kardinal Döpfner. Briefe und Notizen* [n. 9], p. 623).

668. *Nota pro Summo Pontifice Paulo VI, AS* V/3, p. 132.

669. Letter by Heylen from Rome on February 12, 1965, Fund Suenens, 2446. For the Hasselt text, see LAMBERIGTS – DECLERCK, *Le texte de Hasselt* (n. 394), pp. 485-505.

670. Letter of April 8, 1965, Fund Suenens, 2461.

Houtart also sent Suenens texts on January 12, 1965[671] and on April 13, 1965[672].

3. The most important intervention by Suenens during this intersession was the report he presented at the meeting of the Coordinating Commission on May 11, 1965. As early as March, Haubtmann had sent him a draft of the Relatio with Pars I and II[673]. On April 24, Philips sent Suenens the finished texts and informed the Cardinal that Haubtmann would visit him on April 29[674]. On that day, Haubtmann presented a 'Note sur l'état actuel du texte'[675] to Suenens. On May 3, Philips informed Suenens about a few more elements for the Relatio[676]. On May 5, Suenens replied to Philips: he expressed thanks for everything and noted that he had a good meeting with Haubtmann, who, hopefully, will be present at the meeting of the Coordinating Commission[677]. Suenens then drafted his Relatio for the Coordinating Commission with the help of R. Ceuppens[678]. It was a Relatio written in agreement with Philips' proposals[679]:

– The content of this Relatio[680]: Suenens offered the following remarks on the text after it had been thoroughly rewritten to reflect the Patres' remarks:
  – *First*, regarding the title 'Constitutio pastoralis'. The text, which was mainly pastoral, still contained substantial amounts of doctrine. However, it was no 'Constitutio dogmatica' like *De ecclesia*. Consequently, the text need not be discussed in great detail, as is necessary with a dogmatic constitution. On the other hand, because it contained no practical guidelines it could not be regarded as a decree either. In sum, the title 'Constitutio pastoralis' was appropriate.
  – *Second*, regarding the length of the text and its relatively new character. The new text contains approximately 30.000 words, up from

671. Projet de texte, L'Église dans le monde actuel, Fund Suenens, 2435-2436.
672. It concerns a report by Houtart (April 13, 1965) on a meeting of the World Council of Churches that occurred on March 29-31, 1965. It included his thoughts on the method, the literary genre, and the two main objectives of the schema. Fund Suenens, 2442-2443.
673. Fund Suenens, 2433-2444.
674. Fund Suenens, 2327.
675. Fund Haubtmann, 1628 and Fund Suenens, 2330.
676. Fund Suenens, 2329.
677. Fund Philips, 2471.
678. Fund Suenens, 2331-2333.
679. Fund Philips, 2472.
680. Cf. *AS* V/3, pp. 282-285.

24.000. One must prevent the text from becoming excessively long. The length of the schema was mainly due to the fact that, at the request of several of the Patres, the *Adnexa* had been integrated into the text. Nearly all the ideas of the previous schema had been inserted in the new schema; now, however, they were ordered in accordance with the Patres' comments. The present structure of the chapters also complied with their remarks. This structure was approved by the Subcommissio centralis in Ariccia (during the first week of February) and by the Commissio mixta (March 29 – April 8, 1965). Notwithstanding all of the above, the new text is as long as the previous one, at least if one includes the *Adnexa*. The structure of the text would be seriously damaged if any of its parts were to be omitted without a thorough investigation.

– *Third*, regarding the structure of the Schema. The text was divided into two large parts: the first was largely doctrinal, the second was more practical (just like the *Adnexa*). Because the *Adnexa* were now part of the text, the questions regarding the authority and the necessity of the *Adnexa* had become moot.

– *Fourth*, regarding the work of the commission. The Commissio mixta consisted of 30 members of the Doctrinal Commission and 30 of the Commission for the Lay Apostolate. An additional eight members were co-opted from the third world and from communist countries[681]. The schema was all but unanimously (it lacked one vote) approved. The chapter on marriage, which was accorded a special ballot, also received almost all the possible votes.

– *Fifth*, for whom was the text meant? A great many bishops wished the text to be directed to the entire world.

– *Sixth*, the style of the text. A special style was used. Specifically, it was adapted to the contemporary or modern manner of speaking. In order to do this, one started each time by presenting generally-accepted truths in as biblical a manner as possible and by imbedding them as much as possible in the context of the Christian revelation. And, one frequently used images and examples from daily life. This initially surprised a few members of the Commissio mixta; but, in the end, this manner of speaking was approved by the majority.

– *Seventh*, What about the parts of the text tied to 'current events'? One faced the following dilemma: Either one spoke in an abstract style, which is valid always and everywhere, but fails to draw the

681. K. Wojtyła was one of them.

modern world's attention; or one paid attention to the world's current problems and risked that this part of the text might lose its value whenever the circumstances changed. This must be avoided in a Council text.

Practically the following course of action was chosen: In the introduction (*Expositio introductiva de hominis conditione in mundo hodierno*), one referred in a sober manner to current events. The title of this "expositio" demonstrated the temporary character of this introduction. This way one hoped to meet both of these equally legitimate demands.

This allowed Suenens to formulate the following conclusions:
In order to limit the discussion in the Basilica, only the new paragraphs would be submitted to the Patres for discussion.
It is not necessary to have an oral discussion on the part that deals with the description of the modern world.
From a practical point of view, it was impossible to further reduce the text. The Coordinating Commission could perhaps suggest that the repetitions that do occur in certain areas be dealt with. This schema seemed ready to be sent to the Patres immediately. It was worthy of becoming a conciliar text. The editors deserved every praise and had done a good job for the Council.

Guano was present at the meeting; Haubtmann was not. The discussion of this Relatio took a considerable amount of time[682]. Liénart, Agagianian, Lercaro, Urbani, Confalonieri, Döpfner and Roberti all agreed with Suenens' positive advice. Morcillo and Cicognani criticized the title 'Constitutio pastoralis' claiming that it lent too much weight to the schema. Cicognani proposed to speak of 'Litterae' or 'Declaratio'. This position was not shared by several cardinals; Guano also defended this title. Felici gave a long speech. He, too, felt that such a title gave too much weight to the schema. Moreover, he wished that a number of doctrinal points could be revised (e.g., the passage on the war[683] and conscientious objectors) since they might cause problems for catholic governments. The

---

682. Cf. *Processus verbalis*, AS V/3, pp. 302-304 and also TREFFLER (ed.), *Julius Kardinal Döpfner. Briefe und Notizen* [n. 9], p. 654.

683. Here Felici quotes a passage from n° 98 of the schema: "affirmamus tamen a talibus actionibus bellicis, *cuiuscumque speciei* sint, conscientiam hominum non facile exonerari cum *objective* crimina sint" (italics added by Felici). After the Coordinating Commission, Felici again sent his objections regarding several passages of the schema directly to Paul VI ('Rilievi sullo schema De Ecclesia in mundo huius temporis'). They were all characteristic of his mindset. Cf. AS V/3, pp. 309-310.

schema spoke of complex problems and offered only uncertain solutions. With a certain amount of resignation, Felici concluded: "Evidentemente, noi per il momento non possiamo fare altro che procedere alla stampa del testo, e, se cosi piacerà al Santo Padre, inviarlo ai Padri". On May 28, Paul VI gave his approval to send the text to the Patres.

4. In the months preceding the fourth session Suenens received more documents and amendments regarding the schema. Barbara Ward sent him a memorandum, Etchegaray sent him the French translation, Delmasure provided comments on the political life and G. Hoyois offered some on peace[684].

b. The problem of birth control[685]

1. Contacts with Paul VI:
- At the end of February, 1965, Suenens was in Rome for the consistory and for Cardijn's raise to the cardinalate. On February 22, he had a private audience with the Pope. A tape that was sent to V. O'Brien contains the report[686]. This audience, which lasted about one and a half hours, was, according to Suenens, conducted in an excellent atmosphere. Regarding the issue of birth control, Suenens reported the following:

> J'ai demandé qu'il y ait contact entre la Commission du Schéma XIII et sa Commission qui travaille pour [sic] le Birth Control. J'ai remis la note-réponse à Caffarel[687]. Il [Paulus VI] avait envoyé le même texte de Caffarel à Frings, qui avait répondu en faisant lui aussi des remarques qui doivent être un peu semblables aux miennes et de sorte qu'il était très heureux d'avoir là une mise au point. Il disait d'ailleurs que le texte de Caffarel était d'un traditionalisme très accentué. On sent quelqu'un qui est ouvert, au moins au fait que cela n'est pas clair et qu'il y a donc beaucoup de réflexion à prendre ... Alors il y avait trois professeurs de Malines[688], qui étaient mis

684. Fund Suenens, 2468, 2471-2474, 2476-2477.

685. Only the activities and démarches of Suenens with regard to the Pope, schema XIII and the Papal commission are dealt with here. The 'Colloques de Louvain' and his contacts in the U.S., via, e.g., V. O'Brien and Peter and Margie Grace, are passed over.

686. Fund Suenens, 2306.

687. 'À propos de la *Note sur la régulation des naissances* du chanoine Henri Caffarel', December 11, 1965; Fund Suenens, B.C. and H.V., 682. For this note by H. Caffarel: *Note sur la régulation des naissances*, October 24, 1965, sent by Caffarel to C. Colombo, later published in *Supplément* 123-124, *Anneau d'Or*, août-septembre 1965, cf. Fund Suenens, B.C. and H.V., 683. On December 21, 1964 de Riedmatten writes to C. Colombo: "Je me permets de vous signaler sur le problème du mariage, un travail absolument remarquable du R. P. Martelet, de Lyon" (Fund Colombo, GS.C3.25).

688. This refers to P. Pas, A. D'Hoogh and P. Anciaux, professors at the Seminary in Malines; cf. also Fund Philips, 2085-2086.

en cause pour avoir dit qu'ils défendaient avant tout la morale dynamique. La morale dynamique cela veut tout simplement dire la progressivité en matière de morale; l'application progressive de la loi morale aux gens. Là vraiment, la phrase qu'on leur incrimine est une phrase où je ne vois pas ce qu'on aurait pu leur reprocher. Mais donc il y avait eu une dénonciation contre eux trois ... Donc c'était dit: je [Paulus VI] ne demande pas la réponse, je vous donne cela simplement à titre d'information"[689].

- At this time there was also an interesting letter from an Italian doctor to Suenens[690]. When Dr E. Rosini questioned in 1963 Cardinal Montini regarding birth control, Montini replied by sending him Suenens' *Amour et maîtrise de soi*.
- In the meantime, the rumors began yet again (after the alarm of July/August of 1964) that the Pope would soon make a statement regarding birth control. At the beginning of March, Suenens asked Heylen to draft a text that might eventually be helpful to the Pope in this regard. Heylen came up with several versions; Msgr. Heuschen and P. Anciaux corrected his text[691] and sent a first version to Suenens on March 12[692]. On March 18, he produced a third version of a 'Conclusio pastoralis'[693], and, on March 23, Suenens thanked Heylen but explained that, given the different viewpoints that have been argued for, the Pope should not make a statement but should wait for the activities of the Papal Commission which was meeting that same week[694].
- On March 26, Suenens sent a note by Dondeyne to Paul VI[695]. He also suggested that the Pope have a conversation with Heylen and Dondeyne. On April 1, Cicognani answered that the Pope took note of this study and that the text had been remitted to H. de Riedmatten[696].

---

689. Some sentences on this typed page are less than clear. This could possibly be due to the fact that it was dictated or to mistakes by the typist. It also appears that, here, Suenens gave a less than correct impression regarding some of the Pope's opinions, especially those he issued regarding Caffarel's note.

690. Letter of March 4, 1965, Fund Suenens, B.C. and H.V., 112-115.

691. Fund Heylen, 22-26.

692. Fund Suenens, B.C. and H.V., 307.

693. Fund Heylen, 26.

694. Fund Suenens, 2453, and Fund Heylen, 27. On March 27, Paul VI gave a speech at the fourth meeting of this Papal Commission. In it, he pointed out to the commission the urgency of its task: "La question est trop importante, les incertitudes de certains sont trop douloureuses, pour que vous ne vous sentiez pas pressés par une urgence qui est celle de la charité envers tous ceux auxquels Nous devons une réponse". Cf. *AAS* 57 (1965) 388-390.

695. 'Réflexions sur la crise de la morale conjugale' (17 p.), in which Dondeyne demonstrates that fidelity to the standards of natural law meant that man must follow his 'reason', while arguing against the claim that biological nature in itself constitutes a moral standard (Fund Suenens, 2457).

696. Fund Suenens, 2456-2458.

On June 8, Msgr. Dell'Acqua sent an unsigned censure of the article by Dondeye to Suenens. Suenens passed it on to Dondeyne, who, in turn, replied to Suenens on June 30. This reply was passed on to Dell'Acqua by Suenens on July 1[697].
- In a new letter to the Pope, Suenens sent two more articles and asked the Pope to appeal to Catholic scientists to continue their work on human fertility[698]. On April 10, Cicognani replied to Suenens that the Pope would not be making any statement in the near future and, moreover, would not be appealing to the scientists. He also noted that the proposal had been passed on to the Papal Commission[699].
- On May 13[700] during his audience, Suenens presented a corrected version of the note by Dondeyne (21 p.) as well as a critical note by Dondeyne 'Note sur l'article du R. P. Martelet Morale conjugale et vie chrétienne, in NRT (1965)'[701] to the Pope.
- On June 3, Suenens sent his congratulations to the Pope on the 45th anniversary of his ordination and reported briefly on the "VIIe Colloque de Louvain", one in which de Riedmatten also participated.

2. Other contacts

- Suenens kept in close contact with de Riedmatten. On December 14, 1964, de Riedmatten apologized for not having been able to meet with Suenens and sent him a report on the meeting that had been recently (i.e., December 6-7) convened to prepare the work of the Papal Commission[702]. Suenens also received the report of the fourth meeting of the Papal Commission that took place March 25-28, 1965, in Rome[703]. On April 7, he congratulated de Riedmatten with his work and thanked him for promising to be present at the 'VIIème Colloque de Louvain'.

697. For this critical but anonymous note (by a Roman moralist?), see Fund Suenens, 2487 and Fund Suenens, B.C. and H.V., 133; for the answer by Dondeyne and the correspondence of Suenens, Dondeyne, Dell'Acqua, see Fund Suenens, 2466, 2469-2470 and Fund Suenens, B.C. and H.V., 134.
698. Letter of April 5, 1965. Fund Suenens, 2459. The 'VIIème Colloque de Louvain' of May, 1965 took initiatives on exactly this matter and wanted to establish an International Commission for the centralization of all data on human fertility; cf. Fund Suenens, B.C. and H.V., 947-979, 704-708, 146-155 en 2129, 2129bis. After the Pope passed over his question, Suenens launched a similar appeal during the fourth session in the Council Hall.
699. Fund Suenens, 2459bis.
700. Cf. L'Osservatore Romano, May 14, 1965.
701. Fund Suenens, 2457bis and Fund Prignon, 2075-2076, and Fund Suenens, B.C. and H.V., 127.
702. Fund Suenens, B.C. and H.V., 284-285. At that time, the Papal Commission was still known as: 'Groupe d'études spécial sur la population et la limitation des naissances'.
703. Fund Suenens, B.C. and H.V., 297.

On April 12, de Riedmatten replied that he was of the opinion that the Papal Commission had done a jood job; that he appreciated the work done by de Locht and by van Rossum in the commission; and that he had received Dondeyne's note[704].

– Suenens' advice was again sought by the group, which, after having been inspired by Buelens-Gijsen and J. Grootaers, had delivered the "Address to the Second Vatican Council on the subject of the Problems of the Family" during the third session to the Council fathers. On March 5, H. Buelens wrote to the Cardinal to express his concern with regard to a possible new papal declaration and proposed to draft a memorandum for the Pope. Suenens answered that he is prepared to deliver this memorandum to Rome. On March 8, Buelens sent a draft of the letter to Suenens. Suenens replied that he does not want to influence the phrasing of the text but that he is willing to deliver it. On March 16, Buelens sent Suenens the final draft of the letter[705]. On April 20, Buelens sent Suenens yet another text[706].

During the third intersession it became clear that the end of the Council was near. The roles played by the moderators and the Coordinating Commission became more and more restricted. There was only one planned meeting on May 11 and even it did not last more than a few hours. Suenens performed his not-too-difficult task quite adequately: he had been prepped by Philips and Haubtmann. Still, the objections of Felici and Cicognani indicated that the battle for Schema XIII was not over. One of the biggest problems was that of getting it ready in time. The Commissio mixta succeeded in getting a text ready by May of 1965, a feat mainly due to the tireless work of Haubtmann and Philips. Even then it was only 'ready' because some parts had been drafted quickly and were still unpolished. The chapter *De matrimonio* remained Suenens' main concern. Thanks to Heuschen and Heylen there was a theologically-sound primary text available. Suenens' problem was still the issue of birth control, which, in fact, had been excluded from the Council's discussions. He made many attempts to resolve the issue: via his interventions with the Pope, via calling upon his excellent contacts, via his influence in the Papal Commission, and via his relationships with scientists that had been established at various conferences such as the 'Colloques de Louvain'.

---

704. Fund Suenens, 2460 and 2461bis.
705. Fund Suenens, 2447-2451, 2454-2455; Fund Heylen, 32. During May of 1966, the same group distributed another address, a 'Second Address to the Magisterium of the Church on the subject of Family Problems'. Cf. Fund Suenens, B.C. and H.V., 180-181 and 606-607.
706. Fund Suenens, 2463.

That this matter would lead to a dramatic climax during the last days of the Council was not foreseen. This was because many continued to think that the Pope would support the more 'liberal' point of view.

9. IVa Sessio

a. The Coordinating Commission

At the meetings of the Coordinating Commission (September 13[707], September 20[708], and December 1) and of the moderators (September 16, September 28, October 12, and October 26), Schema XIII was hardly mentioned, except for a few technical matters. It was characteristic of the minor role played by the moderators and the Coordinating Commission during the fourth session that, at their meeting of December 1, 1965[709], not a single word was said about the severe crisis the Council was going through as a result of the four papal modi on De Matrimonio. Instead, the time was spent discussing indulgences[710]. During the meeting of the moderators on October 12, Felici is said to have again voiced his opposition to Schema XIII[711].

b. Suenens' intervention on De Matrimonio, September 29, 1965[712]

1. At the start of the debate on the first chapter of the second part of schema XIII, Suenens took the floor as third speaker[713]. His intent was

---

707. According to the Journal Prignon, p. 266, the report by Suenens was far from enthusiastic: "Une demi-heure! [in reality, it was an hour and a quarter, AS V/3, pp. 347-348] ... Réunion morne...".

708. Another meeting which failed to spark the cardinal's enthusiasm. "Au cours de la conversation à table [at the Belgian College], le cardinal déplore, auprès des évêques, l'absence totale de procédure dans les réunions ... des organes dirigeants ... Sans ordre, chaque cardinal parlant de tout, l'un après l'autre, sans qu'il y ait un président pour diriger les débats, sans qu'aucune règle de procédure ne soit pratiquement respectée" (Journal Prignon, p. 84).

709. Suenens was not present. Cf. Journal Prignon, p. 246.

710. Processus verbalis, AS V/3, pp. 637-641. Even after the moderators final audience with the Pope on December 2, Prignon noted that Suenens told him: "En tout cas, le cardinal avait l'impression que les modérateurs n'avaient plus aucune influence réelle sur le concile, que le pape les recevait parce qu'il fallait bien" (Journal Prignon, p. 251).

711. Journal Prignon, October 12, 1965: "Dans la conversation avec Felici aussi, celui-ci ne cache pas son dédain pour le schéma XIII, et déclare, à plusieurs reprises, qu'il n'était pas encore terminé et qu'on verrait bien s'il arriverait jamais à terme" (p. 155). This is absent from the Processus verbalis (AS V/3, p. 739).

712. AS IV/3, pp. 30-33.

713. Cf. SUENENS, Mémoires sur le Concile Vatican II, p. 59: "Puisque nous ne pouvions pas nous taire lorsque le chapitre sur le mariage arrivait, tout le monde attendant une intervention dans ce domaine".

to draw attention to two wishes (*vota*). Before the session, Suenens had apparently sought the advice of S. Moore, an English Benedictine, who had attended the 'VIIème Colloque de Louvain'[714]. Suenens claims that Heylen also assisted in the work on the phrasing of the 'Primum votum'[715]. Prignon received a first draft on September 16, regarding which he noted: "Il y aura beaucoup à retravailler, le texte me semble devoir être entièrement refait"[716]. On September 28, during the audience of the moderators, Döpfner noted his intention to ask the Pope for instructions regarding the debate on Schema XIII. Suenens advised against this; reflecting upon the difficulties he had in October of 1964, he feared that the Pope might slow down his appeal to scientists who study human fertility. The Cardinal carefully avoided this subject during the moderators audience[717].

2. The content of this intervention. Suenens made two practical and pastoral proposals:

Primo, the Council should take steps to ensure that scientific work in the area of sexuality and marital life would be continued, coordinated and intensified. Especially important was the research regarding female fertility, male psychological control, etc.[718]. Learning from his intervention of the third session, this time Suenens diplomatically added: "votum quod proponimus, in mente nostra nullum iudicium theologicum vel philosophicum implicat de valore morali variarum methodorum quae ad regulandas nativitates adhibentur".

Secundo, just as the Church provides for a regular renewal of the baptismal and religious vows by means of ecclesiastical rites, the liturgy should include a date on which spouses could renew their wedding vows,

---

714. Cf. Fund Suenens, 2674-2675 and Fund Suenens, B.C. and H.V., 948.

715. SUENENS, *Mémoires sur le Concile Vatican II*, p. 60. In these *Mémoires*, Suenens mentions as first suggestion what his speech listed as the "Secundum votum". On September 26, 1965 in a letter to A. Houssiau, V. Heylen wrote: "Le Cardinal [Suenens] a préparé un discours sur la coordination de la recherche scientifique en matière sexuelle et sur deux regrets: dénoncer le danger du sexualisme et mettre une liturgie sur pied pour renouveler le consentement conjugal. Pas sensationnel" (Cf. J. GROOTAERS – J. JANS [eds.], *La régulation des naissances à Vatican II: Une semaine de crise* [Annua Nuntia Lovaniensia, 43], Leuven – Paris – Sterling, VA, Peeters, 2002, p. 260).

716. Journal Prignon, p. 30.

717. *Ibid.*, pp. 89-90.

718. In his *Mémoires*, p. 60 Suenens writes: "La seconde suggestion, très importante dans cette intervention, c'était de souhaiter que le Concile lui-même fasse un appel pour qu'on crée des centres de recherche internationaux, à la recherche de tous les problèmes de moralité conjugale sexologique, engagés dans ce secteur. C'était évidemment avec la pensée de ce Centre de Louvain".

e.g. at the Feast of the Holy Family. Suenens concluded with three brief remarks:

First, the text should contain more warnings against marriages entered into rashly and at too young an age.

Second, the civil authorities should react more strongly to the rise of immorality in contemporary culture (e.g., in books, magazines and movies).

And third, the text should emphasize the value of family prayer; prayer which promotes both the unity with God and familial understanding[719].

3. The reactions to this intervention were rather reserved. It was nowhere near as enthusiastically received as was his October 29, 1964 intervention:

- First there was the complete misinterpretation by the Roman newspaper *Il Messaggero* (September 30, 1965). It interpreted the call for renewing wedding vows as some kind of revolutionary proposal paving the way for the Church's acceptance of divorce. Suenens' answer, which came by telegraph, was published in *L'Osservatore Romano* at Suenens' request[720]. P. Tucci also issued a retraction from the Vatican's press room[721].
- Prignon notes:

> Je dois dire que son [from Suenens] intervention a un peu déçu, parce qu'il se situe sur un plan uniquement pratique et [qu'] il n'y a aucun développement doctrinal. Venant après l'éreintement en règle de Ruffini, on attendait de lui à l'assemblée tout de même une réponse. Et les partisans de la majorité regrettaient qu'il n'ait pas touché de points doctrinaux comme le cardinal Léger[722].

719. This suggestion possibly came from Father Patrick Peyton c.s.c., propagator of the 'Rosary Crusade', whom Suenens had met through the Legion of Mary. On this "Rosary Crusade "organized in the diocese of Bruges in 1959, cf. B. WILLAERT, *Het Rozenkransgebed. Overweging van het christelijk heilsmysterie*, in *Collationes Brugenses et Gandavenses* 5 (1959) 198-210. In fact, P. Peyton approached the Patres to campaign for a modus of Suenens and requesting attention be paid to the issue of family prayer. Cf. Fund Suenens, 2639-2640 and Fund Döpfner, 5045.

720. Cf. SUENENS, *Mémoires sur le Concile Vatican II*, p. 60: "… un journal le *Messaggero* a compris cela tellement de travers qu'il en a fait une proposition pour renouveler le mariage chaque année purement et simplement. J'ai envoyé un télégramme à ce journal pour l'obliger à rectifier. Il a rectifié d'une manière que moi seul pouvais comprendre qu'il y avait une rectification. J'ai envoyé le texte du télégramme de protestation à *L'Osservatore* qui l'a publié in extenso". Cf. Fund Suenens, 2917-2918 and G. CAPRILE, *Il Concilio Vaticano II*. Vol. V, Rome, Civiltà Cattolica, 1969, pp. 127-128, note 4.

721. Journal Prignon, pp. 107-108.

722. *Ibid.*, September 29, 1965, pp. 100-101.

In *Souvenirs et espérances* (p. 124), Suenens is very concise about this intervention: "Enfin, je suis intervenu sur le mariage, formulant des propositions d'ordre pastoral et liturgique".

c. The subsequent evolution of Schema XIII

Suenens retained several contacts concerning Schema XIII, both with regard to the course of the debate over the developed themes and the 'votationes'.

- On September 26, the Cardinal discussed with Prignon the manner in which the debate about the second part should be conducted (*in globo* or chapter by chapter)[723]. On October 14, Philips, at the request of the Cardinal, drew up a schedule for the moderators and planned the end of the Council for December 8[724].
- On September 28, Suenens sent for de Lubac at the Belgian College and spoke with him regarding birth control and Teilhard de Chardin[725].
- When the debate on Schema XIII was near its end, Haubtmann and Garrone conceived the idea, via analogy with the five *Propositiones* on *De ecclesia*, of submitting a few questions to the Patres. As early as October 5, Haubtmann had, via Moeller, asked the Cardinal if he thought it would be useful to ask a few questions. The Cardinal replied that the Commission must make up its own mind and, eventually, that it could direct an official request to the moderators. Suenens was inclined to support this idea, at least if it were limited to a few select questions over the essential points[726]. On October 6, Garrone came to the Belgian College to visit Philips and, later, to meet with both the Cardinal and Philips. This plan was abandoned – not least due to Philip's criticisms of the wording of the questions[727].
- The document's title was still a disputed point. It was not just the conservative voices, such as Felici and Morcillo, who contested the title *Constitutio pastoralis*. Morcillo suggested '*Declaratio*', a term which

---

723. *Ibid.*, p. 42.

724. *Ibid.*, p. 167. For the document by Philips 'De statu laborum in Commissione mixta pro Schemate XIII et de kalendario praeviso', cf. Fund Philips, 2597.

725. Cf. Journal de Lubac, September 28, 1965, II, pp. 418-419, in which de Lubac again speaks very negatively about Suenens.

726. Journal Prignon, pp. 129-130.

727. Cf. *Ibid.*, p.134. For the text of this 'Questionnaire', see Fund Suenens, 2614 and Fund Philips, 2593.

was still too strong for Philips[728]. Philips suggested *Litterae syno-dales*[729], a view shared by Msgr. Dearden[730]. On October 5, Prignon noted that the idea of not using the title constitutio was gaining ground with the bishops and that even Suenens would agree to it now[731]. As late as October 24 the matter remained undecided[732]. On November 18, the central subcommission of Schema XIII was said to have accepted the following Spanish proposal: *Constitutio pastoralis et Declarationes de quibusdam punctis maioris momenti*. Prignon was very critical of this proposal to Heuschen because of the way in which it minimized the value of the second part of the schema, possibly its most interesting part. The same day Msgr. Ancel told Suenens that Garrone would contact him[733]. In the Basilica on November 19, Haubtmann met up with Suenens who made the following suggestion: allow the Patres who object to the title *Constitutio pastoralis* to submit their objections in writing and, after that, take a decision. Suenens asked Haubtmann for a text. It was immediately drafted by Garrone and subsequently read in the Council Hall by Felici[734].

– In addition Suenens, as moderator, received several documents with regard to Schema XIII, even though his contribution to it at that stage was hardly worth mentioning[735].

During this period Suenens' attention was still focussed on the problem of birth control.

d. Suenens' audience of October 18, 1965

The precipitating cause for this audience was possibly the moderators' papal audience of September 28 at which the Pope showed them the Papal

---

728. Msgr. Bengsch, bishop of Berlin, also sent Philips a document with the title *Litterae conciliares* on September 29, 1965, cf. Fund Philips, 2609-2611.

729. Journal Prignon, September 26, 1965, p. 82.

730. *Ibid.*, p. 117.

731. *Ibid.*, p. 127.

732. *Ibid.*, p. 186.

733. *Ibid.*, pp. 210-211.

734. *Ibid.*, p. 242 and CAPRILE, *Il Concilio Vaticano II*. Vol. V (n. 720), p. 424. 541 Patres proposed a different title; during the vote on December 4, the title *Constitutio pastoralis* was approved with 1.873 *placet* against 293 *non placet* (CAPRILE, *Il Concilio Vaticano II*. Vol. V, p. 481).

735. A.o regarding the chapter *De pace fovenda*, on atheism, a modus of Sister Luke (Tobin); cf. Fund Suenens, 2609-2610, 2622-2623, 2608.

commission report[736]. The Pope intended to ask the advice of the chairs of the bishops' conferences regarding this report. In response, Suenens pointed out that the doctrinal part of this report was good but that the pastoral instruction was weak and even bad at points. The Pope replied that that was exactly why he wanted to ask the advice of the chairs. Suenens then concluded that the Pope might possibly give a statement before the end of the Council. He wanted to request an audience for as soon as possible following the Pope's return from the U.N. so that they might be able to discuss this matter thoroughly. He immediately requested that Prignon study the matter with the usual group of theologians (Delhaye, Heylen and Anné)[737].

1. Suenens prepared himself extraordinary well for this audience

– On October 8, Prignon noted that Suenens had asked the theologians of the Belgian College to prepare remarks on the text of the Papal commission. This was in case the Pope decided to ask the chairs of the bishops' conferences for advice[738].
– On October 10, he discussed his forthcoming audience with Prignon. He wanted to know what the Pope was thinking and whether matters are progressing[739].
– At the weekly audience of the moderators on October 12, the Pope informed them of the necessity of a discrete collaboration between the conciliar commission[740] and the Papal commission[741]. The Cardinal interpreted this as 'une petite ouverture' but felt that the Pope was undecided on this matter. During the discussion, he again spoke of a *finis operis* and *finis operantis*. The Cardinal believed that the Pope's personal point of view had not altered at all during the last year and a half[742]. The Cardinal also insisted that the Pope halt further distribution of the Papal commission report. It contained several inaccuracies and was apparently changed by the Holy Office without authorization.

---

736. For the text of the report 'De quaestione regulationis nativitatum' (116 p.), see Fund Suenens, B.C. and H.V., 305.
737. Journal Prignon, pp. 91-92.
738. *Ibid.*, p. 139.
739. *Ibid.*, p. 147.
740. In fact this refers to the subcommission *De matrimonio*.
741. On November 13, de Riedmatten informed Suenens that the Pope told him during a November 12 audience that he agreed with this collaboration (Journal Prignon, November 14, 1965, p. 197). On November 21, there was a meeting at the Belgian College between a few members of the conciliar subcommission *De Matrimonio* and a few members of the Papal commission (cf. Fund Heylen, 83-88).
742. Journal Prignon, p. 155.

The Cardinal's protest is said to have led to the discontinuation of its distribution to the bishops' conferences[743].

— On October 13, Suenens asked Liénart to write to the Pope regarding birth control[744].

— On October 17, Suenens asked Prignon and the theologians who were present to write a note on conjugal ethics that he could present to the Pope the next day. Prignon worked on it with Heylen and Delhaye until the next morning. He then took the text to the Cardinal and discussed it with him for an hour[745].

2. This audience, which lasted an hour and five minutes, inspired Suenens to dictate an extensive report[746]. His version largely corresponds with the notes Prignon made when Suenens called him in order to give a complete account at four in the afternoon that same day[747]:

> Et puis nous sommes glissés alors sur la question Birth Control. Quand j'ai abordé Birth Control, il m'a dit: 'C'est exactement un des points que j'avais noté, dont je devais vous parler'. Et alors il s'est mis d'abord à m'expliquer comment il voyait la situation. Primo, grande conversation pour dire que les médecins lui avaient tous dit – ou en tout cas qu'il en avait consulté des quantités – qui le mettaient en garde contre les mauvais effets pour la santé féminine de la pilule et qu'on ne pouvait pas se prononcer sur la pilule, qui était un médicament tellement dangereux... J'ai essayé d'amener la chose sur le terrain moral. Finalement donc, en interrompant un peu, j'ai dit: "Maintenant je crois effectivement que nous n'avons pas à nous prononcer sur ce terrain médical, mais sur le terrain moral; il y a là vraiment un problème". Il a dit: "Oui, il faut que je parle, il faut cependant qu'il y ait encore ultérieurement un document". Je crois qu'il m'a dit qu'il envisageait une

---

743. *Ibid.*, p. 162. J. Reuss, a member of the Papal commission, thanked the Pope on October 19, 1965, for discontinuing the distribution (Cf. Fund Suenens, 2676). Suenens was informed that some copies were distributed by the Holy Office. Cf. Journal Prignon, October 6, 1965, p. 136 and 138. On September 11, 1965, Felici wrote to Ottaviani regarding the preparation of documents on mixed marriages and birth control. He wanted texts addressing these problems to be submitted by the Pope at the meetings of the Chairs of the Bishops' Conferences during the fourth session. On October 6, 1965, Ottaviani reported to Felici that he is sending 500 copies of the "Relazione sulla 'Regolamentazione delle nascite'" for these meetings (Cf. AS VI/4, p. 470 and pp. 535-536). This never took place: only the laws on fasting, the eating of meat, and indulgences were discussed.

744. Journal Prignon, pp. 166 and 168.

745. *Ibid.*, pp. 173. For these texts by Prignon, Delhaye, and Heylen. Cf. Fund Prignon, 1449-1450.

746. Fund Suenens, 2503. This explains the presence of imprecise and elliptical expressions (attributed to the fact that it was a spoken style and/or to typographical errors) in typed version. The original (if sometimes vague) text is given here.

747. Journal Prignon, pp. 174-176.

encyclique ultérieurement, mais que pour le moment, il y avait une déclaration à faire. Quant à cette déclaration, il a donné son point de vue qui consistait à dire [qu'] il ne faut en rien favoriser l'égoïsme des gens; il ne faut pas compromettre l'esprit de sacrifice, il ne faut rien compromettre de toute la position traditionnelle de l'Église là-dedans. Je durcis peut-être dans les expressions, mais le fond est certainement ce qui se dégageait. Il faut que nous puissions répéter pratiquement la doctrine classique; je n'ai pas vu à un seul endroit une ouverture en quoi que ce soit vers une position nouvelle. Il s'agissait de savoir comment faire une déclaration de ce genre là, tout en laissant évoluer la partie médicale, qui n'était pas le fond des choses.

Alors, il m'a demandé très solennellement en disant: "Vous êtes grand spécialiste de cette question, votre livre *Amour et maîtrise de soi* vous a rendu célèbre et bien je m'adresse à l'auteur de ce livre". Alors il a ajouté: "On m'a dit que vous avez changé". J'ai dit: "Mais, Saint-Père, j'ai écrit ce livre dans l'hypothèse de la doctrine classique de l'Église, par loyauté à ce moment-là. Je me suis naturellement impressionné par les arguments de ce que je dois convenir de dire la grande majorité des moralistes de premier plan…".

Donc il me demande: "Voulez-vous vous mettre à ma place devant Dieu, avec la responsabilité des âmes qui vous entendent et que diriez-vous à ma place? Faites-moi ce texte. J'en ai reçu l'un ou l'autre, je ne vous le cache pas, mais qui ne me satisfont pas. Alors je vous serais très reconnaissant de me préparer un texte où vous exprimeriez ce que vous souhaitez ce que l'Église dise maintenant. Hic et nunc. Sans faire quelque chose qui soit une encyclique. Uniquement la déclaration de ce qu'on avait promis pour passer ultérieurement. Ce n'est donc pas une vérité valable pour quelque temps, mais une vérité de transition dans une certaine mesure".

Alors j'ai essayé de dire: "Est-ce que tout de même le point fondamental n'est pas la déclaration de Pie XI sur le 'intrinsece malum' de l'acte, est-ce qu'on ne pourrait tout de même pas un peu situer cela comme on situe le vol, le meurtre etc., le mensonge, où l'on admet qu'en cas d'extrême nécessité on vole; est-ce qu'on ne peut pas situer cela dans la même ligne, et est-ce qu'on ne pourra pas creuser plus profondément, ne pas voir chaque acte ainsi?". Il n'a pas du tout accepté ce point de vue. Alors j'ai essayé de donner un autre point de vue: est-ce qu'on ne pourrait pas dire que déjà en ayant accepté la méthode Ogino-Knaus, on l'a acceptée en disant que l'acte demeurait "per se aptus ad generationem" ce qui n'est pas [vrai] si vous regardez cela conjugalement et bien il faut vraiment dire que l'acte n'est pas "aptus ad generationem". De nouveau réfutation, réponse. J'aurais peine à résumer quels étaient les arguments parce que je cherchais à établir d'autres terrains en essayant par quel genre d'arguments pourrait-on essayer d'enlever ou de créer là un doute sur la position fondamentale [=classique]. Puis la conversation s'est déroulée ainsi dans un va-et-vient de discussions sur des arguments où le Saint-Père a surtout exposé une nouvelle fois la position classique sur la procréation, la position classique tout en essayant d'intégrer l'amour là-dedans. À ses yeux […] il y a moyen certainement dans sa pensée de faire avancer quelque chose du côté de la place de l'amour. Tout en ne changeant pas la doctrine, il semble qu'il y ait une ouverture du côté de quelque chose, que j'ai peine à préciser, quelque chose côté donc amour à intégrer dans cet ensemble.

De sorte que la conversation s'est donc terminée. Elle a été très longue. Sur Birth Control certainement une demi-heure sur l'heure et cinq minutes ... Il m'a quitté en disant: "Il faut que nous nous aidions fraternellement; c'est l'heure de s'entraider, je compte beaucoup sur vous. Alors vraiment, prions ensemble".

3. After this audience (but still on the same day), Suenens asked Prignon to draft a text for the Pope:

Le cardinal me demande alors de préparer un projet dans le sens suivant, reconnaissant lui-même que c'est à peu près la quadrature du cercle: faire un projet tel que nous souhaiterions que le pape dise [sic], mais compte tenu de l'opinion personnelle du pape, qui est tutioriste et qui sur la plupart des points semble de ne pas avoir bougé. Mais de le faire de telle sorte qu'on laisse tout de même, si possible, une porte ouverte pour l'avenir. D'accompagner ce projet par un second, plus rigide, pour le cas où le pape rejetterait absolument le premier. Il me demande de faire travailler là-dessus le P. Häring, Heylen, Delhaye et moi-même[748].

That same evening Prignon contacted Heylen; the next morning, he paid a visit to Häring. On October 20, Heylen delivered a draft of the text to Prignon[749] which he, in turn, delivered to the Cardinal and Häring. On Thursday, October 21, Heylen and Delhaye drafted a text together. This version was subsequently approved by the Cardinal. The text by Häring, by contrast, was deemed by Prignon to be of little use[750].

On Saturday October 23, there was a meeting of Msgr. Reuss, Martimort, de Locht and (most probably) Prignon and Heylen at the Cardinal's residence[751]. There, final text was drafted. Prignon notes:

Il a fallu rédiger un texte qui, au fond, laisse la situation dans l'état où elle est aujourd'hui: ni ouvrir ni fermer la porte. Un texte aussi qui en fasse

748. *Ibid.*, p. 176.

749. For this text, cf. Fund Prignon, 1461-1462 and Fund Heylen, 73-74; also Journal Prignon, p. 182.

750. For Häring's October 21, 1965 text, cf. Fund Prignon, 1452a, Fund Suenens, 2672, and Journal Prignon, p. 184.

751. Journal Prignon, p. 186. On his copy of the draft Heylen later wrote: "1ᵉʳ projet discuté avec le cardinal Suenens en sa villa" (Fund Heylen, 73). At the time of the fourth session, it was known that the Cardinal usually spent the weekends at the Villa Miani (Via Trionfale, 151) on the Gianicolo, a villa that had been rented for the Cardinal for that Fall by M. Grace. (Cf. for this lease, Fund Suenens, 3048ter). However, this refers to the 'Villa Piccola', an annex of the 'Villa Grande' that was on the same estate. A few of Suenens' collaborators were staying at this 'Villa Piccola' (e.g., V. O'Brien, Y. Dubois, some religious). Several lectures were organized there during the fourth session especially for female religious. B. Häring (on 'The moral formation of sisters to co-responsibility' on November 19) and H. Servotte (on 'John XXIII Seminary, Louvain' on November 24)

prévoir un autre plus développé, qui permet donc de patienter encore et qui, en toute hypothèse, rappelle la générosité nécessaire[752].

On Tuesday, October 26, the moderators had their weekly audience with the Pope. At three in the afternoon, Prignon gave the final text to the Cardinal along with a text by de Locht[753]. The Cardinal himself had to decide which text he would present to the Pope. The Cardinal returned from the audience a satisfied man. After the meeting with the moderators, the Pope had received him separately. It was a most cordial encounter. The Pope had only been able to read the text superficially and promised that he would study it more carefully. Prignon continues:

> Le cardinal lui [the Pope] a fait remarquer les points qui pourraient être interprétés comme un élargissement, tout en lui montrant que le texte était de nature telle qu'il n'ouvrait pas vraiment les portes, mais qu'il ne les fermait pas non plus, qu'il était très équilibré et qu'il montre bien la continuité dans le problème. Et le pape, cette fois-ci s'est montré très ouvert dans la discussion. Il a été impressionné par la liste des questions que le cardinal lui a transmise de la part de Mgr Reuss[754] … Le cardinal a eu l'impression qu'en tout cas son texte sera pris en considération et influencera la rédaction définitive du texte que le Saint-Père publiera à une date qu'il n'a pas précisée mais avant la fin du concile[755].

On November 13, de Riedmatten informed Suenens that the Pope was rather satisfied with the text Suenens had submitted. He also told him that the Holy Father had decided not to issue a statement now but would still prefer to see the Council text become more pastoral. This would enable the Pope to wait until after the Papal commission had completed its work before issuing his encyclical[756]. On Thursday,

---

also lectured there. M. Grace spoke there on October 29 (Cf. Fund Suenens, 2714, 2922-2928, 3047-3048ter). Cf. L.-J. SUENENS, *Les Imprévus de Dieu*, Paris, Fayard, 1993, pp. 201-202.

752. Journal Prignon, p. 187.

753. For this text by de Locht, see Fund Prignon, 1459a.

754. 'Quaestiones adhuc disputatae', October 26, 1965, cf. Fund Prignon, 1458a and Fund Suenens, 2671.

755. Journal Prignon, pp. 191-192. On October 31, Suenens informed Prignon that Msgr. Riberi, who had had dinner with the Pope, had told him how impressed the Pope had been by his responsibility in that matter and that he still had not made a decision (Journal Prignon, p. 193). A. Riberi, the internuncio in China, had written a preface for Suenens' book, *Une héroïne de l'Apostolat* [n. 651], pp. 7-12) from Hong Kong, on February 25, 1952. As nuncio in Ireland, he had corresponded with Suenens regarding the Legion of Mary in 1960 (Fund Suenens, A.P., box 14 and 31).

756. Journal Prignon, November 14, 1965, pp. 197-198. During the same meeting with de Riedmatten, the ever-alert Suenens asked de Riedmatten to make sure that Heylen was made a member of the Papal commission. For whatever reason, this never came about.

November 18, the Cardinal asked Paul VI what he thought of the text. The Pope replied that it was being examined by five persons: he did not specify whether he was satisfied or dissatisfied with it or who these five examiners were[757].

It soon became apparent that the Cardinal's efforts had yielded little: the Pope did not make a statement. On November 23, however, he did send four 'conservative' modi to the conciliar commission.

e. The Papal Modi of November 23, 1965

The history of this last conciliar episode is well known[758]. On November 23, when Cicognani unexpectedly sent (during the last 'expensio modorum') four 'secret' papal modi to Ottaviani, tension was introduced into the Commissio mixta — and especially among the members of the 'majority' party. Finally, largely to help provided by Heuschen and Heylen, the commission succeeded in rendering the modi 'harmless'[759]. This, in turn, meant that birth control was not addressed by the Council.

Suenens' role in this controversy (It is helpful to note that Suenens, due to the death of Queen Elisabeth of Belgium — she had died on November 23 and was buried on November 30 — was absent from Rome from November 28 to December 1):

- On Wednesday evening, November 24, Delhaye came to the Belgian College with the news that the papal modi had been given to the commission. A small meeting was immediately called. Suenens, Delhaye, Heylen and Prignon were all present. During the dinner with the Belgian bishops, Prignon excitedly announced that he thought a campaign should be conducted to try and get the bishops to vote *non placet*. He was interrupted by the Cardinal who told him that this would be impossible due to the scandal. To this Prignon replied that the scandal

757. Journal Prignon, p. 214. On December 2, Suenens repeats the same story to Prignon (*ibid.*, p. 251).

758. See a.o. V. HEYLEN, *La note 14 dans la constitution pastorale 'Gaudium et Spes' Pars II, Caput I, n° 51*, in *ETL* 42 (1966) 555-566; J.M. HEUSCHEN, *Gaudium et Spes. Les modi pontificaux*, in LAMBERIGTS – SOETENS – GROOTAERS (eds.), *Les Commissions conciliaires* (n. 416), pp. 353-358; GROOTAERS – JANS (eds.), *La régulation des naissances* (n. 715); G. ROUTHIER, *Famille, mariage et procréation: Le combat de deux cardinaux canadiens*, in *Cristianesimo nella Storia* 23 (2002) 367-428, mainly pp. 408-422; Journal Prignon, pp. 217-260; Fund Heuschen, 342-364, 503-510, 577-580; Fund Heylen, 104-131.

759. Cf. Fund Heuschen, 577.

would be a lot bigger if the Council were allowed to say things sub-tracted to its authority. The Cardinal made no reply. Later that evening, Prignon privately told him that he was planning to wage a campaign after all[760].
– On Thursday, November 25, Döpfner and Suenens spoke by telephone in order to discuss their strategy[761]. That evening, Prignon phoned Sue-nens in order to report on the meeting of the Commissio mixta. The Cardinal told him that an agreement had been reached that Döpfner would write to the Pope regarding their common function as chair of their respective bishops' conferences and that he had also spoke via telephone with Etchegaray in order to warn the French episcopate that Liénart would take a similar step. He also called Léger to congratulate him[762] and to pledge his continued support[763].
– On Friday, November 26, Prignon again reported to Suenens on the meeting of the commission[764]. The Cardinal immediately tried to con-tact Döpfner by telephone, but Döpfner was unavailable. He was con-cerned whether the Pope would accept the proposed changes. Suenens planned to ask a number of bishops and cardinals to write to the Pope in order to inform him of the morally conflicted[765] situation in which they were finding themselves[766].
– On Saturday, November 27, it remains unsure whether they could mention the Pope's intervention in the report of the commission (drafted by Heuschen and Heylen), and whether the references to Casti

760. Journal Prignon, pp. 219-222.
761. During the afternoon of November 25, Döpfner received a brief handwritten note from de Riedmatten: "Mein lieber, Die Sachen sehen besser aus und man geht einer Entspannung entgegen. Mehr morgen an Telephon" (Fund Döpfner, 1561). It is striking that de Riedmatten was on such friendly terms with Döpfner. He calls him "Mein Lieber" or "Lieber Julius", and he signed the note with his Christian name, "Maurice" (Cf. Fund Döpfner, 1561, 1563). In fact, before entering the Dominican Order, de Riedmatten had studied with Döpfner at the Collegium Germanicum Hungaricum in Rome in 1938-39 (this detail was kindly provided by P. Markus Pillat, s.j., the archivist of the Pontificium Col-legium Germanicum et Hungaricum, in a letter dated June 27, 2005).
762. Léger had intervened at the meeting of the commission (November 24, 1965) and had presented a text (cf. Fund Léger, 1504) prepared by Delhaye and de Locht (Journal Prignon, p. 224).
763. Journal Prignon, p. 227.
764. At this meeting, it was Heuschen and Heylen who succeeded in rendering the papal modi 'harmless'.
765. Both at this stage and at the end of the Council, the bishops had to approve the text either in globo (and de facto, give their approval to the papal modi, something which the Council had had no opportunity to debate) or vote non placet, something which would prohibit the constitution Gaudium et spes from being approved by the Council.
766. Journal Prignon, p. 230.

connubii would be allowed to remain in the footnotes (a move which could give the impression that the Council had simply confirmed *Casti Connubii*). When Prignon pointed out this danger to the Cardinal, he wanted to intervene again. Prignon, however, convinced him to at least wait for the Pope's reaction to the commission proposals that had been submitted by Heuschen. After all, it was only in the case of a negative reaction that it would be necessary to intervene with the Pope. Heuschen stated that, in that case, he would vote *non placet* and ask the other bishops to do the same[767].

– On Sunday, November 28, Prignon and Suenens met. Suenens was impressed by Dondeyne's note 'Réflexions sur la séance du vendredi 27 nov. [sic =26 nov.] de la Commission mixte, consacrée à la discussion des Modi proposés par le Souverain Pontife en vue du texte définitif du chapitre sur le Mariage'[768]. The Cardinal informed Prignon that, after considerable thought and prayer, he had decided to vote *non placet* and that he would conduct a campaign to convince others to do so as well. He also intended to ask cardinals and bishops to send a clear letter to the Pope in which they would formulate their doubts and in which they would point out their responsibility to the Pope: if the Pope wished to uphold traditional teachings, he must do so on his own authority, basing himself on his position as pontiff, and should not ask the Council to support him – especially when no discussion or debate had been permitted. Following this, Döpfner arrived at the college and they lunched together. Suenens later told Prignon that Döpfner was impressed with his point of view, but still wondered if voting *non placet* might create an enormous scandal. Suenens tried to persuade Döpfner but did not know whether he had succeeded. Prignon again asked the Cardinal to wait for the Pope's answer. Suenens had initially said that he would call Heuschen and Heylen before the end of the conversation; in the end, however, he did not. Prignon suspected that the Cardinal feared that Heuschen and Heylen would not have fully supported his radical stance. Prignon also told the Cardinal, that according to Heylen, the text of *Gaudium et Spes* could not be interpreted as a simple confirmation of *Casti Connubii* since the constitution contained so many new elements that *Casti Connubii* lacked. In other words, it was clear that

---

767. *Ibid.*, pp. 233-234.

768. Fund Suenens, 2661 and GROOTAERS – JANS (eds.), *La régulation des naissances* (n. 715), pp. 200-202. Dondeyne was of the opinion that the 'solution' (approved by the commission following the proposal of Heylen and Heuschen) was ambiguous both procedurally and with respect to its content.

the problem has been stated in a new manner. Suenens then left for Belgium[769].

- On Monday, November 29, Dell'Acqua delivered the Pope's positive answer to Heuschen[770]. The Cardinal phoned Prignon from Brussels. Prignon told him about the latest developments and read him the Relatio that Garrone was going to present in the Basilica. Suenens was disturbed by the phrase *continuitati doctrinae catholicae* since he found it ambiguous. Prignon tried to reassure him by noting that the danger has been averted[771]. Later, Prignon wrote:

> Le cardinal me dit alors: "Est-ce que tu donnes ta parole en conscience?" Je réponds: "Oui". Il dit: "Si c'est comme ça, je ne déclenche pas la campagne de voter *non placet*. Mais c'est toi qui en portes la responsabilité". J'ai dit: "J'accepte"[772].

That same day de Riedmatten informed Döpfner of the good tidings as well as that he had been summoned to Dell'Acqua by the Pope to discuss the quotes of *Casti Connubii* that were still so prominent in the text[773].

- When the Cardinal returned to Rome on December 1, he brought Dondeyne's letter and his notes for the Pope and Msgr. Colombo. The atmosphere remained tense: the Cardinal wanted to meet with Lercaro

---

769. Journal Prignon, pp. 235-237.

770. Fund Heuschen, 578.

771. In a letter to Döpfner on November 30, 1965, Häring wrote: "Meines Erachtens zwingt der aktuelle Text des Kapitels über die Ehe weder zu einem NON PLACET noch zu dramatischen Interventionen beim Papst". He also requested that the references to *Casti Connubii* be eliminated from the Council text, a request which was not honored (Fund Döpfner, 5059). Especially problematic was the reference which branded every form of contraception as "facinorosa licentia" (Denzinger-Schönmetzer, [1965] 3716). Häring spoke of "beleidigenden Ausdrücken" (Fund Döpfner, 5059).

772. Journal Prignon, pp. 239-240.

773. The letter of de Riedmatten, who was concerned about the work of his Papal commission, is noteworthy: "Heute liess er [Paul VI] mich wieder von Mgr. Dell'Acqua rufen, um etwas mehr von meiner Stellungnahme über die drei Referenzen an Denzinger mit mir zu sprechen. Ich habe gesagt (und das ist mir heute nachts vom Brief eines ultrakonservativen in der Kommission vollständig bewiesen), die Arbeit werde damit nicht auf dem ganzen Gebiet gehen und einen Kurs nemen sollen, der nach all dem was wir erarbeiteten, einfach zu keiner richtiger Lösung führt. Seine Exz. hat mich gefragt, was ich brauchte, um das zu vermeiden, da das sicher nicht der Gedanke noch die Absicht des Papstes sei. Ich habe gefragt um eine eindeutige Erklärung an die Kommission [the papal commision] über dem Sinn der Referenz und die vollständige Freiheit, die uns bleiben würde. Mgr Dell'Acqua hat mir um eine Note darüber gefragt. Ich habe zuerst Fuchs und Labourdette konsultiert und die ins Vatikan gebracht. Jetzt warte ich mit gutem Vertrauen; ich habe Bischof Reuss gefragt kein "faux-pas" zu tun (dies *intra ambos nos*). Wie sich die Zukunft entwickelt, weiss ich nicht. Für das Konzil ist, glaube ich, die Sache gerettet. Es ist schon viel!" (Fund Döpfner, 1563).

and Döpfner the next day (but before they were received by the Pope) in order to discuss the situation[774].

– On December 2, de Locht submitted yet another note[775] to the Cardinal. The Cardinal, however, was of the opinion that he could not present it to the Pope. That same day, when Cardinal Lercaro and nuncio Oddi came to lunch at the Belgian College, Suenens (no doubt for Oddi's benefit) noted that birth control had still not been addressed. Lercaro supported him completely in this. That day the Cardinal also received two telegrams, one from the 'Boerenbond' and one from the group that drafted the *Address to the Second Vatican Council on the Subject of the Problems of the Family*. When he left for the papal audience, he brought along these telegrams. He was again wondering whether or not he should give Dondeyne's text[776] to the Pope. It was a text Prignon had delivered to the Secretary of State the day before. In the end, he judged it best not to do this so as to avoid arousing a negative reaction from the Pope. In the account given by Suenens after his return, he does not mention birth control specifically (it was probably not even discussed), but he does express his disappointment with the audience[777].

– On December 3, Suenens suggested that Heuschen make an addition to the "famous" note 14, but without the knowledge of the commission members. Heuschen replied that they had always been correct when they protested against such behavior from the 'other side' and that he was unwilling to make the addition[778]. The chapter on *De Matrimonio* was finally approved on December 4, 1965, with 2047 *placet* against 155 *non placet*. (It should be remembered, however, that Paul VI did not publish his encyclical *Humanae Vitae* until July 25, 1968).

774. Journal Prignon, pp. 245-247.

775. For the letter of de Locht to Suenens (December 2, 1965), his note La 'Possessio Iuris' ou la relance des condamnations de 'Casti Connubii' and another text requested by Msgr. Colombo regarding a possible statement by the Pope, see Fund Suenens, 2677-2679.

776. As early as December 3, Dell'Acqua sent remarks to Suenens regarding Dondeyne's Nota: "Osservazioni sulle 'Réflexions' del Prof. Dondeyne circa il problema del Matrimonio". They had been drafted by Colombo (and might have been inspired by Martelet, cf. Journal de Lubac, November 30, 1965, II, p. 472). The Cardinal asked Heuschen and Heylen to draft a reply, but also requested that they refrain from distributing the text – at least for the time being. In reply, Dondeyne later sent a new answer. On December 16, Suenens sent Dondeyne's Nota and Colombo's reply to Léger (Fund Suenens, 2662-2668 and Journal Prignon, p. 259).

777. Journal Prignon, pp. 248-251.

778. Cf. Fund Heuschen, 580 and GROOTAERS – JANS (eds.), *La régulation des naissances* (n. 715), p. 271.

f. The Closing of the Council

At the last regular meeting (held on December 6), Suenens offered a closing word of thanks on behalf of the moderators. In his *Mémoires*, he wrote:

> Je crois que c'était un discours assez amusant, qui en même temps rendait hommage à quelqu'un [Mgr. Felici] qui, pendant 4 ans, avait été implacablement l'adversaire de toutes les idées que nous défendions. Il était 24 heures sur 24 opposé aux tendances du concile. Il s'est véritablement battu avec une habileté consommée, faisant jouer tous les jeux de la procédure contre nous, ne cédant jamais que devant des majorités écrasantes, essayant toujours de faire triompher son point de vue. Il a perdu toutes les grandes batailles au niveau des discussions conciliaires, mais il a certainement été un extraordinaire apport pour l'élément conservateur, qui s'appuyait sur lui et qui s'appuyait aussi sur le Cardinal Cicognani, qui a, à chaque occasion, manifesté la tendance d'extrême conservatisme et qui occupait une position extrêmement importante[779].

Finally, note that at the closing ceremony on December 8 Suenens was charged with the reading the message to the artists. It had only been given to him by the Secretariat of State the night before (December 7). Although it was an honor (the other Cardinals chosen for this were Liénart, Léger, Duval, Zoungrana, Meouchi, Agagianian), Suenens was not particularly enthusiastic about it:

> En tout cas, le texte m'en avait été remis la veille au soir. Je ne l'ai vu que très tard dans la nuit pour le prononcer le lendemain. Je ne sais vraiment pas pourquoi c'était à moi à prononcer le discours pour les artistes et les écrivains. C'est sans doute une allusion aux différents livres écrits. J'aurais préféré d'autre part avoir la parole pour m'adresser aux femmes et aux religieuses...[780]

During the fourth session, Suenens was still involved in a number of difficulties surrounding Schema XIII, even though neither he nor the other moderators played a major role regarding it. The decisive part was played by the Pope, who made sure that the Council approved the schema even in the face of great resistance from several camps. For help he first turned to Msgr. Guano, and, later to Msgr. Garrone. Suenens' commitment was especially intense regarding the matter of conjugal ethics. He surrounded himself with a number of theologians who were experts in this field while also keeping a close eye on the texts' content. By the end of the session (and with more than a little help from others) he had won a limited and temporary victory.

779. SUENENS, *Mémoires sur le Concile Vatican II*, p. 61.
780. *Ibid.*, p. 62.

10. Final Remarks

Suenens was justified in writing at the end of his *Mémoires*: "… ce schéma XIII, dont je suis le père, c.-à-d. l'initiateur"[781]. As early as May of 1962, he had brought together the main chapters of this schema under the title *De ecclesia ad extra* as part of his 'plan for the Council'. In December of 1962, he had been given the responsibility of overseeing a number of texts which later contributed to Schema XVII. Although ultimately not accepted, the 'Text of Malines' played a role. At a later stage (and even after Haubtmann became editoral secretary), Philips became the leading theologian. Without his support and competency, the schema would probably have never reached its final (and approved) form. Despite Felici's opposition, Suenens succeeded in keeping the schema (with its *Adnexa*) on the Council's agenda. And, despite the initial 'plan Döpfner', he made sure that there was a fourth session which, in turn, allowed time for the schema to be thoroughly discussed.

Suenens' great contribution was tactical. Except for birth control, he was not really involved with the various schema topics. He never intervened in the Basilica when atheism, war and peace, culture, politics, or economics were being discussed. This was probably due to the fact that Suenens' interest mainly revolved around the apostolate: How is the message of Christ best carried to the modern world? Many of his earlier publications, especially *Théologie de l'apostolat* and *L'Église en état de mission*, had been concerned with this problem. He realised that the Church must adapt itself to modern civilisation. He therefore became proficient in the use of the modern communication media (press, radio and television) and he called on religious to assume an active and direct apostolate (via, e.g., means of the Legion of Mary), he was confronted with many outdated rules and constitutions within the congregations' hierarchies that he urgently wanted to modernize (Hence his book *Promotion apostolique de la religieuse*). In his opinion, the problem of birth control, which many families were facing, was an obstacle to the enjoyment of the Christian life in this modern day and age. In his work *Amour et Maîtrise de soi*, he continued to deal with that problem according to the traditional morality, even though he soon became convinced that it did not offer an acceptable solution.

The more fundamental issues of *Gaudium et Spes,* e.g., Christian anthropology, atheism, the relationship between the Church and the 'autonomous' and secular world, the possible evolution of the Church via

781. *Ibid.,* p. 67.

what É. Poulat called 'la modernité', were not of immediate interest to Suenens. This may have been the reason why he concluded his *Mémoires* with the claim that: "Je ne suis pas tellement enthousiaste de ce schéma XIII... mais tel qu'il est là, je crois qu'il va faciliter le dialogue avec le monde et qu'il est ouvert à tous les enrichissements futurs"[782].

Faculty of Theology   Mathijs LAMBERIGTS
St.-Michielsstraat 6
B-3000 Leuven
Belgium

Bisdom Brugge   Leo DECLERCK
H. Geeststraat 4
B-8000 Brugge
Belgium

---

782. *Ibid.*, p. 67.

APPENDIX

A Brief Summary of the Other Interventions Made by Suenens at Vaticanum II

Familiarity with the life story of Cardinal Suenens results in an understanding of the importance of his encounter with V. O'Brien and his ensuing commitment to active evangelization according to the methods of the Legion of Mary[783]. It is this commitment which compelled the Cardinal to dedicate himself to a broadening of the concept 'Catholic Action', to modern methods of evangelization, to the reformation of the apostolic religious life, to training seminarians and novices as evangelists, and to the introduction of an age limit for bishops. In short, all of these conciliar interventions, which will be briefly summarized in chronological order in what follows, can be shown to originate from this solicitude.

1. Intervention Regarding De Instrumentis Communicationis socialis (November 24, 1962)[784]

Although he regarded it as excessively long, this schema was substantially approved by Suenens. As it was a pastoral and not a dogmatic text, he did not deem it necessary to closely scrutinize every word. In the pastoral conclusions he emphasized three items:

a. The right to information is to be limited by the right to privacy. This should be provided by legislation or guaranteed by an 'Order of journalists'[785].
b. The faithful and their organizations must be more sensitive to the media including radio, films, and television, in order to be able to influence 'public opinion' both positively and negatively.
c. He pleads for the 'informateurs religieux', who must be aware of their influence and more mindful regarding their duty to evangelize (though not as preachers *per se*).

In his *Mémoires*, Suenens attaches little importance to this Decree and to his own intervention[786]. It seems that Suenens was not directly involved in resisting

---

783. Cf. Suenens, *Les Imprévus de Dieu* (n. 751), mainly pp. 171-188.
784. Cf. *AS* I/3, pp. 462-464 and Fund Suenens, 622.
785. Suenens is clearly thinking of the Belgian 'Order of physicians', an organ which allows member physicians to supervise and control the manner in which physicians practise medicine in that country.
786. Cf. Suenens, *Mémoires sur le Concile Vatican II*, p. 25: "C'est un texte qui ne faisait pas honneur au Concile même tel qu'il a été voté. C'est assez vague. J'ai demandé de réduire ça à quelques propositions fondamentales, d'ordre pastoral, etc. C'est le sens de cette seconde intervention au Concile".

this Decree during the vote of the second session or in the November 25, 1963 incident between Msgr. Reuss, who distributed pamphlets at the Basilica (to vote *non placet*), and Felici, who tried to prevent the distribution. Both Reuss and Felici sent a copy of their respective reports regarding this matter to the moderators, a group which, of course, included Suenens[787].

2. Intervention regarding De pastorali Episcoporum Munere in Ecclesia (November 12, 1963)[788]

Suenens considered this intervention on the age limit of the bishops to be of the utmost importance:

- As an auxiliary bishop he had been confronted with the aging Cardinal Van Roey, who died at age 87[789]. He was convinced that the advanced age of many bishops hindered the pastoral development of their charges.
- As a member of the preparatory *Commissio De Episcopis et de Dioeceseon regimine,* Suenens submitted a text in favor of age limits[790].
- As a member of the *Commissio centralis praeparatoria*, he had intervened on this matter but it failed to gain approval[791].

---

787. For this incident cf. CAPRILE, *Il Concilio Vaticano II*. Vol. III (n. 264), pp. 283-284 and Fund Suenens, 1458-1466.

788. Cf. *AS* II/5, pp. 10-12 and FConc. Suenens, 1597-1603.

789. In SUENENS, *Souvenirs et Espérances* (n. 11), pp. 45-47, the auxiliary bishop Suenens can barely hide his irritation with regard to a certain rigidity that was frequently present in the policies of his aging bishop.

790. Cf. Fund Suenens, 399-400: *Episcopus ut servus, De statuenda limite aetatis.*

791. In SUENENS, *Mémoires sur le Concile Vatican II*, p. 10, he recounts the following colorful anecdote: "L'intervention sur la limite d'âge, intervention où j'ai commencé par un 'Veni Sancte Spiritus' sur place en me disant: maintenant, je coule à pic, faut-il le faire? Je sens qu'il n'y a pas d'ombre d'une chance, mais je crois de mon devoir de le faire. J'ai commencé d'ailleurs en le disant. J'ai plaidé fortement pour cette limite d'âge, avec les arguments qui se trouvent dans la note envoyée un jour à notre Commission [*De Episcopis et de Dioeceseon regimine*]. Cela a été le silence total, l'accueil glacial. On a alors voté, c'est-à-dire que chacun devait donner sa réaction *placet* et *non placet*. Et ce furent les 50 cardinaux, les uns après les autres, tous y compris Montini, tous ont répondu *non placet*. Cela a été un peu mieux quand on est arrivé aux archevêques; je crois qu'il y a une dizaine qui doivent avoir répondu *placet*. Mais c'était l'enterrement pur et simple et à partir de ce moment-là, je ne savais vraiment pas où me mettre. Cela a été un des plus mauvais moments, lorsqu'à l'interruption nous sommes allés prendre une tasse de thé; j'étais un peu le pestiféré de l'endroit et je compromettais tout le monde en faisant une conversation avec qui que ce soit: j'ai bu la tasse de thé comme on boit toute honte incluse et je suis revenu la tête basse, sans regarder ni à droite, ni à gauche, reprendre ma place comme si de rien n'était". According to *ADA* II/2, Pars III, pp. 665 and 671, on May 3, 1962, Suenens pleaded for a recommendation of a voluntary resignation at the age of 70 and a mandatory resignation at the age of 75, while Montini agreed with the idea of voluntary resignation but was unwilling to impose an age limit.

Because of these negative experiences, Suenens prepared his Council speech carefully and thoroughly[792] using all of his considerable oratorical talents to their utmost[793]:

- First he noted that the preparatory commission had, in the end and after many long debates, decided on an age limit.
- In rebuttal to the claim made by some that a bishop is connected to his people by means of an unbreakable marriage-like bond, he observed that the Council Hall was filled with 'episcopi divortiati'[794].
- He emphasized the 'bonum animarum' and 'renovatio pastoralis' two of the primary purposes of the Council.
- He made much of the fact that, in our quickly evolving and thoroughly modern society, economic and political leaders too are forced to resign while still at the peak of their powers.

In anticipation of some of the reactions of his critics, he qualified his position by noting that:

- this measure cannot be applied to the Pope "cuius perpetuitas in munere requiritur ex ipso bono Ecclesiae universalis";
- the Eastern churches probably have their own traditions and regulations;
- the bishop who resigns is entitled to a decent income;
- a *vacatio legis* can be planned so that the measure does not have to be introduced immediately;
- should the Council decide against an age limit, it should at least require the appointment of a bishop coadjutor for all who reach the age of 75.

It will be recalled that the Council did not decide on this matter: in fact, it was Paul VI who decided on a 75-year limit but only after the Council had concluded[795].

---

792. He got Dossetti to make a first project draft and had his own later draft corrected by Dossetti and by Prignon. Cf. Fund Suenens, 1597-1601.

793. In SUENENS, *Mémoires sur le Concile Vatican II* (cf. pp. 47-48), the cardinal writes the following regarding this intervention: "J'ai fait cette intervention-là au concile vraiment avec un peu de crainte et de tremblement, sachant combien l'assemblée allait y être hostile. Effectivement, ce fut un silence glacial, quand j'eus fini, qui accueillit la proposition que je venais de faire. Je l'avais d'ailleurs atténuée pour ce qui concernait les Orientaux. J'avais pris le maximum de précautions; quand-même, malgré cela l'idée ne passait pas: c'était le très grand silence et une espèce de conjuration d'opposition silencieuse à cette idée, que la presse et le public, en dehors, accueillaient naturellement avec plus que de la sympathie".

794. With this Suenens was primarily alluding to the Italian episcopate, where numerous and frequent promotions were the rule not the exception. For example, Italian bishops often moved from a smaller to a larger diocese or from a diocese to a post within the Roman Curia.

795. Cf. Motu proprio *Ecclesiae sanctae*, dated August 6, 1966, in *AAS* 58 (1966) 763.

3. Intervention regarding De Apostolatu Laicorum (October 9, 1964)[796]

Here, Suenens intervened regarding the concept of 'Catholic Action'. During the 1950's, a large number of bishops and priests were reluctant to support the Legion of Mary because it was perceived as competition for the more specialized Catholic Action and which had been given a direct mandate by the episcopate[797]. At the 2nd International Lay Conference held in Rome in 1957, Suenens had succeeded in getting Pius XII to comment on the issue in his speech[798]. Suenens published an article on it in 1958[799].

Suenens also held an intervention in the *Commissio centralis praeparatoria* on this matter[800]. According to him, when the Commission for the Lay Apostolate failed to take his remarks (sufficiently) into account, he sent a letter, dated February 27, 1963, to all the members of this commission together with a copy of his article from the *Nouvelle Revue Théologique*[801]. It is also known that in October of 1962, during the composition of the lists for the election of the conciliar commissions, Suenens did everything possible to ensure that Himmer's name would not be included on the list of the 'Western European' episcopates[802].

During his intervention Suenens gave his well-known plea for liberalizing the concept of 'Catholic Action' in order to break through the existing 'monopoly' so that the Legion of Mary, which he explicitly quotes, can receive full recognition. The problem is that the initial text of the Decree gave preference to a certain, 'historical form' of catholic action and created the impression that other forms are not as conducive to the enhancement of the apostolic goals of the

---

796. Cf. *AS* III/4, pp. 113-118 and Fund Suenens, 2169-2173.

797. The tension was mainly between the J.O.C., founded by Cardijn, and the Legion of Mary, founded by F. Duff. In a 1953 letter to Duff Suenens wrote: "Mgr Cardijn said that the Legion opens the way for communism in India because – he said – the best catholic forces are absorbed by the Legion, so there is no room for his movement. And the J.O.C. is the unique way to obstaculate [sic] the progress of communism since social reforms are the first need in a country where people has [sic] nothing to eat. Do you see the reasoning! In the same way every missionary who is not doing social work is a protagonist of communism!" (Fund Suenens, A.P., box 14). In Belgium, Msgr. Himmer and Msgr. De Smedt were the main advocates of the J.O.C. and the more specialized Catholic Action.

798. Cf. *Les Laïcs dans l'Église: Deuxième Congrès Mondial pour l'Apostolat des Laïcs*, Rome, Comité permanent des congrès internationaux pour l'apostolat des laïcs, 1958, pp. 20-23. See also SUENENS, *Souvenirs et Espérances* (n. 11), pp. 171-175.

799. L.-J. SUENENS, *L'Unité multiforme de l'Action catholique*, in NRT 80 (1958) 1-19.

800. Cf. Fund Suenens, 151-159.

801. Cf. Fund Suenens, 1189-1190.

802. On October 16, 1962, Suenens wrote the following to V. O'Brien: "En tout cas les 65 évêques missionnaires [belges] sont derrière moi – ce qui n'est pas le cas des 7 d'ici [in fact, the six other resident Belgian bishops]... J'ai senti cela aux manœuvres de De Smedt qui voulait mettre Himmer sur la liste des candidats pour la commission Action catholique [the Commission for the Lay Apostolate]. Je lui avais dit en privé que l'idée ne m'agréait pas, mais il est revenu à la charge en public pour qu'on le mette sur notre liste" (Cf. Fund Suenens, 572).

Church. He then added two more pages of written remarks on how best to amend the text to bring it into line with his proposal.

4. Intervention regarding De Activitate missionali Ecclesiae (November 7, 1964)[803]

The archives clearly demonstrate that Suenens took into account the remarks of O. Degrijse, F. Legrand, Msgr. Ogez, and other bishops when he prepared his intervention[804]. Suenens intervened in the name of all African bishops. He emphasized the necessity of missionary activities, which, in his view, belong to the very essence of the Church: 'quidquid sit de possibilitate salutis extra Ecclesiam'. This is followed by a plea for the role of lay persons who have been called to the direct apostolate: they need to receive training for both 'consecratio mundi' and as 'apostoli et duces sociales'. He also pointed out that the 'laici indigenae' need to move toward full responsibility for their countries, even while they are regarded as "mission territories". Because this criticism (as well as that of several other cardinals) was delivered after the Pope had practically approved the schema *De Missionibus*, both by his presence and by his speech of November 6, this intervention had a delicate character[805]. Additionally, at the end of his speech, Suenens delivered his 'retractatio' with regard to the intervention about marriage he had made on October 29[806].

5. Intervention regarding De accommodata Renovatione Vitae religiosae (November 11, 1964)[807]

Because of the influence of V. O'Brien, Suenens was actively laboring for the direct apostolate of the religious even before the start of the Council[808].

---

803. Cf. *AS* III/6, pp. 379-381 and Fund Suenens, 2186-2187.

804. Cf. Fund Suenens, 2188-2195.

805. Cf. SUENENS, *Mémoires sur le Concile Vatican II*, p. 55: "Cela a été un moment très dramatique en ce sens que le Pape avait, en somme, patronné le schéma sur les Missions et nous avons tous, le lendemain de son intervention, démoli ce schéma, je crois à 16 sur 17. C'était le fait que les évêques missionnaires avaient demandé aux évêques de l'Europe, à quelques-uns d'entre eux et aux Cardinaux en général, de vouloir plaider leur cause et c'est au nom de l'épiscopat d'Afrique et d'Asie que je suis intervenu pour souligner certains aspects, certaines déficiences de ce schéma des Missions qui a été coulé à fond". Heuschen wrote the following to his family regarding this intervention by the Pope: "Vendredi, le pape a encore une fois écouté des conseillers mal inspirés en demandant qu'on vote les propositions du schéma sur les Missions. Et ceci quand on savait que les évêques missionnaires étaient opposés au schéma et demandaient que le texte soit renvoyé à la commission. Ceci donnera encore des arguments aux gens de la curie pour dire au pape: 'Vous voyez bien ce que c'est que la collégialité. Vous demandez quelque chose et les évêques n'écoutent plus'" (Fund Heuschen, 453). See also CAPRILE, *Il Concilio Vaticano II*. Vol. IV (n. 610), pp. 381-382.

806. Cf. the intervention on October 29, 1964 *supra*.

807. Cf. *AS* III/7, pp. 439-442 and Fund Suenens, 2097-2104.

808. In several Belgian novitiates (e.g., the Congregatio Immaculati Cordis Mariae [Scheut], the Fratres Scholarum Christianarum, the Sisters of the 'Institut de l'Enfant Jésus'

He believed that numerous adjustments were necessary, especially with regard to the activities of the female religious. This resulted in his book *Promotion apostolique de la religieuse* which was published at the end of 1962. It was instantly translated into several languages[809]. The Cardinal gave conferences based upon this book in the U.S. to religious both in May of 1963 and in May of 1964.

In his intervention Suenens rejected the existing schema because it failed to address the much-needed renewal of religious life – especially with regard to the active apostolic female congregations. He regarded it as imperative that female religious be treated as adults and be provided with the means to develop completely as human beings. They also need to have sufficient freedom at their disposal for their mission. He pled in favor of an adjusted spirituality in which the apostolic assignment would be allowed to acquire a status of its own. The 'evangelical councils' must also be understood in that manner. Suenens ended with a number of practical suggestions with regard to community life, the term of office of the superiors, an adult perception of the vow of obedience and an abandonment of outdated customs (e.g., an adjustment of the religious habit: 'vestis perantiquata tot sororum')[810].

6. Intervention regarding De Institutione sacerdotali (November 14, 1964)[811]

Suenens did not just plan an intense apostolic formation for the religious; he was also deeply concerned for the seminarians. As a new archbishop, he was quick to establish a new diocesan seminary in Louvain. It was named 'John XXIII'[812].

[Nivelles]), Suenens and V. O'Brien had promoted the methods of the Legion of Mary. This actually led to a conflict between V. O'Brien and F. Duff, founder of the Legion of Mary, who was of the opinion that the Legion of Mary should not be promoted to religious congregations lest this should lead to the loss of its "lay" character. Cf. Fund Suenens, A.P., box 80 and 81; Archives O'Brien, box 2. See also SUENENS, *Les Imprévus de Dieu* (n. 751), pp. 177-188.

809. In reference to this Congar remarked: "Le cardinal Suenens donne, en somme, son livre, d'un ton très sûr de soi et assez conquérant" (CONGAR, *Mon journal du Concile* [n. 9], Vol. II, p. 255, November 11, 1964)

810. In his *Mémoires sur le Concile Vatican II*, p. 54, Suenens wrote: "C'était l'intervention qui traduisait le livre 'Promotion apostolique de la Religieuse'... Nous nous sommes réunis toute une nuit avec des experts, pour faire des amendements, qu'on a envoyés aux 2.000 évêques, signés du nom de Döpfner, Huyghe de Arras, et moi-même, le Père Degrijse, je crois, et encore quelques autres et le résultat final de toute cette campagne a été que 14.000 corrections ont été envoyées pour corriger ce texte". For these *modi*, which were signed by 11 of the *Patres* including Cardinal Silva Henriquez, cf. Fund Suenens, 2147-2148.

811. Cf. *AS* III/7, pp. 715-717 and Fund Suenens, 2151-2153. For the background to this debate, cf. A. GREILER, *Das Konzil und die Seminare: Die Ausbildung der Priester in der Dynamik des Zweiten Vatikanums* (Annua Nuntia Lovaniensia, 48), Leuven, Peeters, 2003, pp. 239ff.

812. 1964-1965 was the first academic year for this new seminary. Both Msgr. Ch. Lagasse, Suenens' vicar-general, and Prof. H. Servotte (1929-2004, who was the first president of John XXIII and served in that capacity from 1964 until 1969) gave conferences in Rome on the conceptual basis of this seminary (Lagasse during the third, Servotte during the fourth session). Not all of the Belgian bishops were enthousiastic about this. After

In his intervention Suenens requested the establishment of a commission for the adjustment of the seminaries to the current pastoral needs of the Church. This was followed by a number of specific proposals:

a. In many seminaries, spiritual formation was still too much based upon the established lines of religious life. The diocesan priest is most in need of a spirituality that is based on his apostolic mission.
b. The present division between philosophy and theology needed to be revised with respect to intellectual formation. The Scriptures, liturgy and theology all need to be introduced from the very beginning of the curriculum. The study materials also need to be treated in a more synthetic and psychological manner with a better reference to a 'visio supernaturalis mundi'.
c. Pastoral formation also needed to be valued more highly. Adding a seventh year of pastoral training is not enough: all aspects of the formation must be oriented towards a pastoral dimension and initiation. This pastoral initiation will not harm the more scientific aspects of the curriculum. On the contrary "haec initiatio pastoralis promovebit studia scientifica siquidem non scholae sed vitae discimus"[813].

7. Second intervention regarding De Activitate missionali Ecclesiae (October 12, 1965)[814]

Suenens did not approve of the first draft of the Decree and, although he is a lot happier with the new version, he still wanted the following two changes:

– The preparatory formation for the missionary apostolate needed to be emphasized and structured according to a real 'methodologia'. Future missionaries, especially the native-born among them, need instruction on how to provide for the formation of lay apostles. A genuine and deep initiation into the apostolate is necessary.
– The text did not sufficiently emphasize the 'urgency' of the apostolic mission. The Lord does not send us to confirm everyone in his/her own religion as is done by the movement for the 'Réarmement moral'[815]. He wants us to preach to everyone the truth of the salvation to be found via faith in Christ.

---

a conference by Suenens on the collegiality of and reform for the seminaries, de Lubac noted: "conférence agréable, habile, sans aucun fond, avec de faux raccourcis historiques" (Journal de Lubac, 17 septembre 1964, II, p. 123). On the new John XXIII – seminary, see a.o. Fund Suenens, A. P., box 111.

813. In his SUENENS, *Mémoires sur le Concile Vatican II*, p. 565, Suenens wrote only that: "l'intervention sur le séminaire qui fut un plaidoyer en faveur de l'éducation apostolique et de l'initiation apostolique des séminaires".

814. Cf. *AS* IV/4, pp. 178-187 and Fund Suenens, 2569-2572, 2582-2583, where J. Buckley's appeals to Suenens to include a number of suggestions in his intervention are found.

815. In 1953 Suenens published a book entitled L.-J. SUENENS, *Que faut-il penser du 'Réarmement moral'?*, Paris – Brussels, Éditions universitaires, 1953. In it he attacked this movement for its 'syncretism'. He also wished that Rome would condemn this

Where the Decree mentions the foundation of study centers for theology and of faculties for social and cultural studies, Suenens breaks a lance for the University of Lovanium (in Leopoldville, now known as Kinshasa) and the Eastern Institute in Calcutta[816]. He also added a small, handwritten remarks page in which he primarily pleads for forming seminarians in their native countries.

8. Intervention regarding De Presbyterorum Ministerio et Vita (October 15, 1965)[817]

Suenens criticizes this schema as too abstract and unwordly. It is insufficiently based on the concrete existence and social world of priests. This is an aspect that is necessary given that, nowadays, a priest has difficulties in determining his own position. In the world he is regarded as a 'stranger'; and at the Council he is fallen into oblivion somewhere between the bishops and the lay persons. Suenens believed that the following priestly relationships needed to be explored in the second part of the schema:

– The relationship with the Lord Jesus: the role of the Eucharist, the influence of the Holy Spirit, and the proper mode for venerating the Virgin Mary need to be emphasized.
– The relationship with the college of bishops: the priest is the assistant, the advisor and the friend of the bishop. The requirement of obedience to the bishop should not be perceived by the priest as a renouncement of his own personality.
– The relationship with the laity: the priest should inspire the lay persons; he initiates the apostolate; he acknowledges their different charismata; he is the 'father' of the faithful and their teacher.

To this the cardinal appended three handwritten pages with suggestions for a new division as well as a whole list of detailed remarks[818].

---

movement. Cf. Fund Suenens, A.P., box 32-33 and SUENENS, *Souvenirs et Espérances* (n. 11), pp. 42-43.

816. In his *Mémoires sur le Concile Vatican II*, p. 59, Suenens noted the following with respect to this intervention: "… je suis intervenu trois fois. Une première fois sur le sujet des Missions, pour faire observer que ce schéma était fort bon, mais qu'il ne parlait pas de l'initiation apostolique des missionnaires à la mission, et s'il y avait un endroit au monde où cela devait se trouver, c'était bien là. C'était l'occasion de redire tout le thème du livre SUENENS, *L'Église en état de mission* (n. 22). On en a tenu compte, on y a consacré un paragraphe".

817. Cf. *AS* IV/4, pp. 785-791 and Fund Suenens, 2589-2595.

818. With regard to this intervention, Suenens wrote (cf. SUENENS, *Mémoires sur le Concile Vatican II*, p. 59): "J'ai fait une seconde intervention sur le sacerdoce, pour dire que le schéma était trop abstrait, intemporel, ne répondait pas au problèmes que nos prêtres se posaient et pour encore demander des rectifications. Ce schéma d'ailleurs a été l'objet d'un tir concentré de beaucoup d'évêques et en est ressorti vivifié, corrigé, amélioré etc.".

Almost all of these interventions focused on the theme of the apostolic calling. Although well presented, the majority of these interventions (with the exception of those on the age limit of the bishops) were met with little response in the Council Hall. It is almost certain that the cardinal received help when preparing them (the numerous written suggestions are in all likelihood not from his pen), but very few traces of this assistance can be found in his council archives. Even his confidant Prignon appears to have provided limited assistance to him. It proves that Suenens not only looked for inspiration from well-known Council theologians, but that he could also count on a multitude of collaborators from the ranks of the Legion of Mary, his friends among the religious orders and his own diocesan staff[819].

819. Interestingly, for each session of the Council Suenens arranged it so that he would be accompanied by a different 'secretary': R. Ceuppens (vicar-general) during the first session; A. Van de Ven (inspector catholic education and, later, influential in the charismatic revival movement) during the second session; Ch. Lagasse (vicar-general) during the third session; Y. Nolet de Brauwere and H. Servotte during the fourth session. V. O'Brien was also present in Rome during the third and the fourth sessions.

LÉON-JOSEPH CARDINAL SUENENS
AND JULIUS CARDINAL DÖPFNER

On the occasion of the sixtieth birthday of Julius Cardinal Döpfner, the Archbishop of Munich and Freising, Léon-Joseph Cardinal Suenens wrote an article in the *Münchener Katholische Kirchenzeitung*, dated October 14, 1973[1]. The article's title was *For my dear friend* and ended with the words: "Being his friend I would like to tell him: Don't let your courage fail you on the path that you are following. Real friendship is a virtue rarely to be found in present times. I am grateful for his friendship and will be loyal to him. During the Council, he filled my heart with joy and supported me even when our opinions differed – not as much as to the goals we pursued, but sometimes in the ways and means that had to be chosen to overcome a given obstacle". Three and a half years later Cardinal Suenens returned to these words at a memorial ceremony for Cardinal Döpfner who died on July 24, 1976[2].

This kind of appreciation, however, was not one-sided but mutual. Cardinal Döpfner likewise found very personal words when he held a lecture in Brussels on January 26, 1968. After having expressed to Cardinal Suenens his gratitude for the invitation, he continued, "Two years have passed since we could experience the brotherly attachment of the bishops of the Catholic Church at the Council in Rome in such an impressive way. Our common duty at the moderators' table, even more our accordance on many issues of utmost importance, soon let our hearts bind together in a very special way. It makes my heart fill with joy that the bonds of friendship that were formed at the Council since then became even stronger. With great feelings of thankfulness I think about the kind visit that your Eminence made in the Archdiocese Munich last year. Your directing words about the duty of the Church in the modern world still remain alive in my memory"[3].

Having heard these positive statements do we already have a clear and definite answer to the question about the relationship of our two

---

1. *Münchener Katholische Kirchenzeitung*, October 14, 1973, p. 12.
2. L.-J. SUENENS, *Kirche und Bischofsamt nach dem Konzil*, in *Zur Debatte* 7 (1977) 6-7.
3. J. DÖPFNER, *Die Zukunft des Glaubens: Vortrag in Brüssel am 26. Januar 1968*, Erzbischöfliches Archiv München, Kardinal-Döpfner-Archiv, Ansprachen und Predigten, 1968).

protagonists? Are there really further scientific findings to be expected when analyzing the relationship of these two key figures of the Second Vatican Council? I for myself am convinced that further in-depth research will be a rewarding task because it is the only possible way to determine the real extent of friendship behind the public acknowledgments. Consulting further sources can indeed bring to light the nature of their relationship and the concrete elements it was based upon. Thus, without doubt, it seems fully justified to investigate the relationship and the core of the relationship between the two cardinals. But in my opinion it is even more interesting to put the question how this relationship developed in the course of time and – most of all – what precise consequences derived from it. Following this path one may be able to draw conclusions as to how the relationship between these men, as one determining factor, affected the results of the Council.

Some elements that I am going to look at have already been established. The first part aims to define the results of scientific research as well as to establish the set of sources that can be taken into consideration. In the second part I will focus on the Council Records of Cardinal Döpfner in the Archepiscopal Archives of Munich and Freising. Finally, in the third part I will try to collect evidence from various sources that show examples of agreement or disagreement from which conclusions can be drawn regarding the relationship between the two cardinals.

I. SCIENTIFIC RESEARCH AND SOURCES

The state of the art of historical research with regard to the relationship between the Cardinals Suenens and Döpfner can be summarized in one simple sentence: Up to now – as far as I can see – only Klaus Wittstadt (in his essay *Léon-Joseph Cardinal Suenens and the Second Vatican Council* which was published 1984 in a commemorative publication for Karl Rahner) and Leo Declerck (in his essay about the conciliar archives of Cardinal Suenens) concerned themselves with this topic in brief paragraphs[4]. It is true that one may find further information on

---

4. K. WITTSTADT, *Léon-Joseph Kardinal Suenens und das II. Vatikanische Konzil*, in E. KLINGER – K. WITTSTADT (eds.), *Glaube im Prozeß: Christsein nach dem II. Vatikanum. Festschrift Karl Rahner*, Freiburg – Basel – Vienna, Herder, 1984, 159-181; W. WEISS (ed.), *K. Wittstadt: Aus der Dynamik des Geistes. Aspekte der Kirchen- und Theologiegeschichte des 20. Jahrhunderts*, Würzburg, Echter, 2004, 329-351; L. DECLERCK, *Das Konzilsarchiv von Kardinal Léon-Joseph Suenens, Erzbischof von Mechelen-Brüssel*, in P. PFISTER (ed.), *Julius Kardinal Döpfner und das Zweite Vatikanische Konzil: Vorträge des wissenschaftlichen Kolloquiums anläßlich der Öffnung des*

this issue in various publications on the Council. But these cannot be mentioned at this particular point.

Having this in mind I will try to handle the topic by outlining the sources that are available. Two different perspectives offer a way of coming to terms with the issue. First, the perspective from a third party: newspaper articles give us an idea how journalistic observers assessed church affairs and how the picture of certain persons – in our case the cardinals Suenens and Döpfner – was formed in public. But it is also true that journalists most of the time do not succeed in presenting us with an in-depth view of affairs and therefore published assessments very often remain inadequate[5]. As a consequence I will not take these sources into consideration in the following remarks. Of more importance is the perspective of leading church members who were in contact with both cardinals. One could cite for example Giacomo Cardinal Lercaro who repeatedly made statements about his fellow moderators in the letters to his *ragazzi*[6]; likewise authors of diaries as for example those of Yves Congar[7], Albert Prignon[8], André-Marie Charue[9] and also Klemens Tilmann[10] whose notes have been discovered only a short while ago, and also the memoirs of Hans Küng[11] and Gerhard Gruber[12], Döpfner's council secretary. Of course, when assessing these sources it is important to keep in mind the intention of the author and the situation in which they originated.

The second methodical entrance to the topic can be offered by sources that come from Léon-Joseph Suenens and Julius Döpfner themselves. Different from Döpfner, Cardinal Suenens sometimes published personal

Kardinal-Döpfner-Konzilsarchivs am 16. November 2001 (Schriften des Archivs des Erzbistums München und Freising, 4), Regensburg, Pustet, 2002, 30-40, here pp. 38-40.

5. I come to this conclusion after having done research in the collection of newspaper articles about the cardinals Suenens and Döpfner in the Archives of the Archdiocese of Munich and Freising (*Presseausschnittsammlung*).

6. G. LERCARO – G. ALBERIGO – G. BATTELLI (eds.), *Lettere dal Concilio 1962-1965*, Bologna, Dehoniane, 1980.

7. Y. CONGAR, *Mon Journal du Concile*, présenté et annoté par É. MAHIEU, 2 vols., Paris, Cerf, 2002.

8. L. DECLERCK – A. HAQUIN (eds.), *Mgr Albert Prignon, Recteur du Pontificio Collegio Belga, Journal conciliaire de la 4e session* (Cahiers de la Revue théologique de Louvain, 35), Louvain-la-Neuve, Publications de la Faculté de Théologie, 2003.

9. L. DECLERCK – C. SOETENS (eds.), *Carnets conciliaires de l'évêque de Namur A.-M. Charue* (Cahiers de la Revue théologique de Louvain, 32), Louvain-la-Neuve, Publications de la Faculté de Théologie, 2000.

10. Archiv des Erzbistums München und Freising, NL Klemens Tilmann.

11. H. KÜNG, *Erkämpfte Freiheit: Erinnerungen*, München, Piper, 2002.

12. G. GRUBER, *Kardinal Julius Döpfner – um Gottes und der Menschen willen leben: Erinnerungen eines Begleiters*, in *Beiträge zur altbayerischen Kirchengeschichte* 46 (2001) 257-274.

memories in which he also referred to his relationship with Döpfner[13]. A second comprehensive collection of sources from which conclusions can be drawn about agreement or dissent are the *Acta et Documenta* and *Acta Synodalia* in which interventions of both cardinals are published and the minutes of proceedings for commissions of which both were members. And finally the personal Council Records of both Suenens and Döpfner are open to scientific research with detailed finding aids[14]. In these collections the exchange of letters between both cardinals as well as with other members of the Council and theologians can be found. This is of considerable importance when it comes to the question of circumscribing the network in which both bishops can be localized and the role they possibly played in it. In the following I restricted myself to making only use of the Council Records of Cardinal Döpfner. I will briefly outline the characteristics of this collection.

II. THE COUNCIL RECORDS OF CARDINAL DÖPFNER

Since 1990, when Klaus Wittstadt hinted that German diocese archives keep material profoundly important to the Vatican Council, but that gaining admission to unpublished documents seemed to be difficult[15], the situation has not changed substantially. Again, in 2001, Massimo Faggioli and Giovanni Turbanti had to state that so far entire nations, e.g., Germany, played only a minor role in the research into the Vatican Council[16]. On the one hand this was attributed to the difficulties in gaining access to archival material, and on the other hand to the small number of scholars in these countries interested in the study of the Vatican Council.

13. L.-J. SUENENS, *Souvenirs et espérances*, Paris, Fayard, 1991.
14. L. DECLERCK – E. LOUCHEZ (eds.), *Inventaire des Papiers conciliaires du cardinal L.-J. Suenens* (Cahiers de la Revue théologique de Louvain, 31), Louvain-la-Neuve, Publications de la Faculté de Théologie, 1998; G. TREFFLER – P. PFISTER (eds.), *Erzbischöfliches Archiv München, Julius Kardinal Döpfner. Archivinventar der Dokumente zum Zweiten Vatikanischen Konzil* (Schriften des Archivs des Erzbistums München und Freising, 6), Regensburg, Pustet, 2004.
15. K. WITTSTADT, *Deutsche Quellen zum II. Vatikanum*, in J. GROOTAERS – C. SOETENS (eds.), *Sources locales de Vatican II: Symposium Leuven – Louvain-la-Neuve 23-25-X-1989* (Instrumenta Theologica, 8), Leuven, Bibliotheek van de faculteit der Godgeleerdheid, 1990, 19-32, here p. 31.
16. M. FAGGIOLI – G. TURBANTI (eds.), *Il concilio inedito: Fonti del Vaticano II* (Testi e ricerche di scienze religiose. Fonti e strumenti di ricerca, 1), Bologna, Il Mulino, 2001, p. 34.

Undoubtedly the Council Records of the Munich Archbishop Julius Cardinal Döpfner[17] being a key figure of this most important event in church history in the 20th century are of utmost importance when appraising the procedures and decisions at the Council. For this reason, after Cardinal Friedrich Wetter, now archbishop of Munich, decided to let the Archives of Döpfner be completely inventoried and catalogued, the procedures started with the Council Records.

The so-called "Cardinal Döpfner Archives" are a separate collection within the Archepiscopal Archives of Munich and Freising, comprising the years 1961 to 1976. The records that originated under the administration of Cardinal Döpfner were arranged according to a numerical filing plan which also embodied the Council Records. Apart from the Council Records, other outstanding collections have to be named: Records of the Common Synod of Dioceses in the Federal Republic of Germany, records concerning the Papal Encyclical *Humanae vitae*, records regarding the German and the Bavarian Episcopal Conferences and a collection of sermons and allocutions as well as a collection of photographs. In addition to these sub-collections there are other files concerning the administration of the archdiocese of Munich and Freising and writings that have to be classified as private.

The subgroup Council Records cannot be looked upon merely as registry-documents that were filed after the end of proceedings in its usual way. On the contrary, these records have already been classified and prearranged by Dr. Gerhard Gruber, the council secretary to Cardinal Döpfner at the time. In the course of the prearrangement procedures several separate sections were established: (1) Correspondence; (2) Publicity

17. Literature about Cardinal Döpfner: K. WITTSTADT, *Julius Kardinal Döpfner (1913-1976): Anwalt Gottes und der Menschen*, München, Don Bosco, 2001. See also, *Bibliographie Klaus Wittstadt*, in W. WEISS (ed.), *Zeugnis und Dialog: Die katholische Kirche in der neuzeitlichen Welt und das II. Vatikanische Konzil. Klaus Wittstadt zum 60. Geburtstag*, Würzburg, Echter, 1996, 587-596, and *Bibliographie Klaus Wittstadt (1996-2001)*, in D.M. FEINEIS – E. SODER VON GÜLDENSTUBBE – W. WEISS (eds.), *Kirche und Glaube – Politik und Kultur in Franken. Festgabe für Klaus Wittstadt zum 65. Geburtstag* (Würzburger Diözesangeschichtsblätter, 62/63), Würzburg, Echter, 2001, 17-18. Relating to Döpfner as bishop of Würzburg and Berlin see, H. SCHWILLUS, *Pastorale Praxis und Theologie: Eine Ansprache des Berliner Bischofs Julius Döpfner vom 15. November 1957 im Priesterseminar zu Erfurt*, in FEINEIS – SODER VON GÜLDENSTUBBE – WEISS (eds.), *Kirche und Glaube*, 861-867, and L. BRANDL, *Julius Kardinal Döpfner – Brückenbauer zwischen Ost und West: Bedeutung und Wirkung der Predigt vom 16. Oktober 1960*, in *Ibid.*, 869-887; K. NUSSBAUM, *Klaus Mörsdorf und Michael Schmaus als Konzilsberater des Münchener Erzbischofs Kardinal Julius Döpfner auf dem Zweiten Vatikanischen Konzil: Eine Untersuchung aufgrund des Konzilsnachlasses Kardinal Döpfners*, in *Münchener Theologische Zeitschrift* 55 (2004) 132-150; J. GROOTAERS, *I protagonisti del Vaticano II*, Cinisello Balsamo, San Paolo, 1994, pp. 103-113. For further literature, see also TREFFLER – PFISTER (eds.), *Erzbischöfliches Archiv München* (n. 14), pp. 35-44.

and Public Relations; (3) Proceedings referring to Vatican II; and (4) Official records. All file folders were arranged in chronological order. The important section, *Correspondence records,* is subdivided into nine groups of recipients: among them correspondence with the Vatican, with conciliar fathers and with theologians which will be the basis for a coming publication of original documents of Cardinal Döpfner.

Because of the value of this collection and owing to comparable international standards – e.g., the inventories created for the Council Records of Cardinal Lercaro[18] and Suenens[19] – it was decided to make available the Council Records of Cardinal Döpfner in the form of item listing. This means that every single item has its own index number. The entries in the index list inform about sender, receiver, reference, number of pages, language, dates. The index is subdivided into three categories: Standardized indices of places and names and a large index of topics. The latter lists not only the main subjects that can be seen from an item at first sight but additionally describes other aspects the text refers to. Thus, the inventory will in many ways facilitate access for users and provide an excellent aid for extensive topical research.

Although not yet President of the Fulda Episcopal Conference of Catholic Bishops, but being one of the two German cardinals – at a time when the other cardinal, Josef Frings[20], Archbishop of Cologne, had serious health problems – Döpfner turned out to be the key figure among the German, one may well say all German-speaking and even the Northern European Episcopate during the Council. The regular meetings of these bishops during the council-periods and in the intervals were prepared and led by Döpfner. He pulled the strings when statements of the Bishops' Conference were prepared and brought before the Council. In the light of his correspondence, statements and expertise, the complex system of interrelations that existed between the German-speaking Episcopate, bishops from abroad and theologians can be discerned.

Another important aspect might be Döpfner's relations with various German theologians. They are, to name only the most well known, Klaus Mörsdorf, Klemens Tilmann, Michael Schmaus, Karl Rahner and

---

18. L. LAZZARETTI (ed.), *Inventario dei Fondi G. Lercaro e G. Dossetti,* Bologna, s.n., 1995.

19. DECLERCK – LOUCHEZ, *Inventaire des papiers conciliaires* (n. 14).

20. See N. TRIPPEN, *Josef Kardinal Frings (1887-1978).* Vol. I: *Sein Wirken für das Erzbistum Köln und für die Kirche in Deutschland* (Veröffentlichungen der Kommission für Zeitgeschichte, 94), 2. durchges. Aufl., Paderborn, Schöningh, 2003, and Vol. 2: *Sein Wirken für die Weltkirche und seine letzten Bischofsjahre* (Veröffentlichungen der Kommission für Zeitgeschichte, 104), Paderborn, Schöningh, 2005.

Johannes Hirschmann. There also exist numerous other documents of theologians that cannot be listed here. To assess the contribution of these in respect to Döpfner's own expertises and statements is surely of utmost interest. Döpfner's Council Records are also important in respect to the fact that the whereabouts of some of these theologians' private writings is still unknown.

Further interesting information may be gathered from Döpfner's handwritten notices and council diaries. These notes reflect the immediate state of affairs at the Council without too much distance of time. However, personal statements or characterizations of the other conciliar fathers cannot be expected. Though these notes have to be seen as memory aids, they may provide researchers with a lot of further detailed information.

III. AGREEMENT OR DISAGREEMENT?

In the following some evidence shall be presented from the various types of sources mentioned above that will help in defining the relationship between the cardinals Suenens and Döpfner more precisely. According to their significance some examples have been chosen.

During the Council Cardinal Döpfner worked closely with his Council secretary Dr. Gerhard Gruber who became his vicar-general in 1968. Gruber was responsible for organizational and technical affairs and apart from that regularly called upon by Döpfner when it came to outlining statements on conciliar topics. According to Gruber, Suenens was among those cardinals with whom Döpfner had a close relationship since the period of preparation[21]. Surprisingly then in Gruber's memories the Belgian cardinal doesn't play a significant role. He rather stresses Döpfner's close ties with Cardinal Lercaro whom he visited several times in Bologna[22].

The letters that Cardinal Lercaro wrote from the Council to his *famiglia* in Bologna can be seen as a kind of "conciliar diary". Because Lercaro was one of the four moderators and therefore stood in close contact with Suenens and Döpfner, Lercaro documents have special interest. Together with Suenens and Döpfner he was counted among the so-called "synoptics", whose tight cooperation on all conciliar issues was well known[23].

---

21. GRUBER, *Kardinal Julius Döpfner* (n. 12), p. 265.
22. *Ibid.*, p. 266.
23. LERCARO – ALBERIGO – BATTELLI (eds.), *Lettere* (n. 6), p. 161: "Ci chiamano infatti i quattro grandi (the big fourth), ma anche i quattro evangelisti. E abbiamo trovato che tre siamo allienati perfettamente; e saremmo i tre sinottici; mentre il quarto – Agagianian – pur concordando, come Giovanni concorda con i Sinottici – ha però una linea più sua. Dei tre Sinottici Suenens è Marco, perché di nome è Leo e S. Marco è simboleggiato

Repeatedly Lercaro reports on meetings with the other two moderators[24]. Obviously, these meetings often were aimed to harmonize their proceedings before coming together with the fourth moderator, Cardinal Agagianian, or prior to taking part in a session of the Coordinating Commission. Due to the familiar tone of his letters Lercaro also mentions some amusing anecdotes, e.g., Suenens giving Döpfner the title *"Sua Veemenza"* because of his impulsive temperament[25].

As a last example in this field I would like to cite from the papers of Albert Prignon, Head of the Belgium College, one of the key figures in the *squadra belga* during the Council. Here Prignon describes a dispute between Suenens and Döpfner when Döpfner intended to get direct instructions from the Pope on the schema *De ecclesia in mundo huius temporis* and Suenens wanted to keep room for his own intervention on the topic[26]. Repeatedly Prignon's papers deal with the different positions of the German bishop and the Belgium bishop on this schema, and especially the discontent of the German episcopate[27], which can be found in the numerous corrections suggested by Döpfner[28]. But Prignon's papers also tell us something about the personal relationship between Suenens

dal Leone; io poi sarei Luca, che porto con me l'Appendice degli 'Atti degli Apostoli' rappresentata da D. Dossetti; del resto è nota la mia simpatia per il Vangelo di Luca. Döpfner per necessità è Matteo". But there's also mentioned a different explanation by Levillain in pp. 162-163, n. 2: "Il cardinale Döpfner era Matteo, l'uomo della Legge; il cardinale Suenens, Marco, l'amico di Pietro; il cardinale Lercaro, Luca, l'evangelista dei poveri; il cardinale Agagianian, Giovanni, per un accostamento del tutto negativo: unico curialista, non era sinottico".

24. For example: September 28th 1963: "Ci siamo riuniti stamane qui a Priscilla, alle 9 coi Cardinali Döpfner e Suenens e D. Dossetti. [...] Era una riunione preparatoria a quella di tutti e quattro i *Moderatores*" (LERCARO – ALBERIGO – BATTELLI [eds.], *Lettere* [n. 6], p. 161). October 22nd 1963: "un incontro a tre (Döpfner, Suenens e Lercaro) alle 8" (*Ibid.*, p. 193). November 29th 1964: "Stassera ci siamo riuniti a cena qui a Priscilla i tre 'Sinottici', Döpfner, Suenens ed io per vedere come fronteggiare dal tavolo di Moderatori la situazione e prevenire ogni eventuale infrazione o meglio ogni azione, anche legale, ma tendenziosa" (*Ibid.*, p. 272).

25. LERCARO – ALBERIGO – BATTELLI (eds.), *Lettere* (n. 6), pp. 229-230.

26. DECLERCK – HAQUIN (eds.), *Mgr Albert Prignon* (n. 8), p. 89 (September 28th 1965): "Avant d'entrer chez le pape aussi, Doepfner proposait qu'on lui demande des instructions au sujet du schéma XIII, tout spécialement sur le chapitre de la famille, qui va commencer. Le cardinal Suenens a insisté pour que Doepfner ne demande pas de telles instructions, afin de garder sa liberté de manœuvre pour l'intervention qu'il veut faire sur le vœu à la recherche scientifique".

27. *Ibid.*, p. 109 (September 30th 1965): "Les Allemands continuent à être mécontents du schéma, mais, comme ils ne font pas des propositions très concrètes, il semble que leur opposition n'ira pas beaucoup plus loin, quitte à ce qu'on tienne compte davantage de leurs suggestions dans la rédaction du texte. Il y a tout de même, si j'ai bien compris, une soixantaine de propositions de détail, venant de Doepfner et une centaine de Meouchi, qu'on examinera soigneusement".

28. Erzbischöfliches Archiv München, Fund Cardinal Döpfner, 5041, 5068.

and Döpfner: On November 11, 1965, Cardinal Döpfner requested to speak in the General Congregation about indulgences. His remarks incurred the disapproval of Pope Paul VI and as a consequence Döpfner was told that he had to report to the Secretariat of State. Suenens tried to console Döpfner by saying the same thing had happened to him when he spoke about the marriage issue the year before[29].

After having gathered information that throws some light on the relationship between the two cardinals from an outside perspective, now the two protagonists shall speak for themselves. Presumably the cardinals first met at a session of the Preparatory Central Commission on March 26, 1962[30]. Whereas Döpfner was a member of the Central Commission from the very beginning, Suenens only joined at its fifth meeting soon after Pope John XXIII had made the new Archbishop of Mechelen-Brussels a member of the College of Cardinals[31]. In his memoirs Suenens states that without having arranged this beforehand some cardinals – Döpfner being one of them – usually were of the same opinion and refused certain schemas[32]. According to Suenens' memoirs Cardinal Döpfner was also among those cardinals Pope John XXIII had recommended to him for discussing his conciliar plan[33]. At a meeting at the Belgium College in July 1962 Döpfner at first remained skeptical about the proposal of Suenens. Initially he was of the opinion that the conciliar topics included in this proposal were too academic, too scientific and arranged as in a book. But later he agreed with the common course, which was also supported by the Cardinals Giovanni Montini, Giuseppe Siri and Achille Liénart[34].

Döpfner and Suenens were the only participants at the Council who were members of all major committees from the beginning to the end. In his notes Cardinal Suenens mentioned his first impressions of the other members in the Secretariat for Extraordinary Affairs. Here Döpfner was rated as, "very good, but not brilliant in handling the Italian language"

29. DECLERCK – HAQUIN (eds.), *Mgr Albert Prignon* (n. 8), p. 203 (November 15th 1965).

30. See *AD* II/2.3, p. 13: Processus verbales congregationum (March 26th 1962).

31. Döpfner's membership in the Central Commission dates from December 24th 1960, Suenens' membership from March 21st 1962. See *AD* II/2.1, pp. 13-14 (*Sodales et Consiliarii Commissionis Centralis*).

32. SUENENS, *Souvenirs et espérances* (n. 13), pp. 50-51.

33. *Ibid.*, p. 69.

34. See the letter of Suenens to Pope John XXIII (July 4th 1962), in SUENENS, *Souvenirs et espérances* (n. 13), pp. 69-70. Compare also the handwritten notes of Cardinal Döpfner about the meeting, in Fund Döpfner, 2806.

and Suenens also notes that Montini, Döpfner and he himself would form a triumvirate in this committee, acting in a coordinated way[35].

The correspondence between the two cardinals can be found in the Council Records of Cardinal Döpfner. In the period from January 2, 1963 to July 17, 1964, seven letters addressed to Cardinal Suenens have passed down to us and another seven letters written by the Archbishop of Mechelen-Brussels. Nonetheless, the mere quantity and the limited period of time do not necessarily say anything about the quality of the correspondence. One also has to keep in mind that personal meetings at the Council and phone calls remained undocumented[36]. The first personal letter to be found is dated January 2, 1963[37]. In this letter Döpfner invites a member of the Belgium Episcopate to attend the conference of German speaking conciliar fathers in Munich on February 5 and 6, 1963. Here he should follow the discussions about the revision of the schema *De ecclesia*. It also proposes regularly to exchange information about the working process on the schemata both were responsible for in the Coordinating Commission. Cardinal Suenens accepted this proposal. On January 28 he sent Döpfner a note on the schema *De ecclesia* and informed him about a conversation with Michael Cardinal Browne[38]. That both cardinals were following the same aims can also be seen from a letter of Suenens sent on August 5, 1963, which ends with the words: "Au plaisir de vous retrouver en pleine forme, et de reprendre le travail conciliaire dans le cadre du *idem velle* et du *idem nolle* qui nous unit"[39].

Likewise, Döpfner's diaries can give us an impression about his relationship with Suenens. On October 13, 1962, the day the cardinals Liénart and Frings proposed to postpone the elections for the Council Commissions, Döpfner noted that at four o'clock in the afternoon, cardinals Liénart, Frings, Alfrink, Suenens and Döpfner met in the Anima, the German College in Rome[40]. It was agreed upon to make a Central European list (France, Belgium, Netherlands, Germany, Austria, Switzerland, Poland, Scandinavia) and exchange ideas with other groups. Three days later, on October 16, Döpfner wrote down the most important points that

---

35. SUENENS, *Souvenirs et espérances* (n. 13), p. 61.

36. Albert Prignon gives several hints concerning the contact of the two cardinals by telephone, for example on November 25th 1965: "À 4 h d'ailleurs, Doepfner téléphone au cardinal pour lui parler de la situation. Il avait été mis au courant. Et ils se concertent sur les mesures à prendre" (DECLERCK – HAQUIN [eds.], *Mgr Albert Prignon* [n. 8], p. 227).

37. Fund Döpfner, 423.

38. Fund Döpfner, 477.

39. Fund Döpfner, 689.

40. Fund Döpfner, 3289.

were discussed at a meeting of the Secretariat for Extraordinary Affairs with Pope John XXIII[41]. In this meeting the Pope had presented a letter of Cardinal Augustin Bea, which clearly favoured an open pastoral approach. Bea's demand was supported by Suenens and Döpfner and both cardinals were asked to draw up the guidelines for the working process in the Council Commissions.

The question of accordance can also be answered with the help of the interventions made during the preparation phase and in the General Congregation. In the records to the negotiations in the Preparatory Central Commission repeatedly statements can be found like:

> "*Placet iuxta modum.* [...] *His dictis, adhaeremus schemati in sensu ab Em.mis Döpfner et Alfrink exposito*"[42] or "*Placet iuxta modum: i.e., sto pro sententia Card. Suenens*"[43].

In spite of that, one has to see that quite naturally Döpfner and Suenens also referred to other members in the commission or had their individual priorities when assessing a schema.

In the General Congregations Cardinal Suenens made seventeen oral and five written interventions, Cardinal Döpfner sixteen oral and six written interventions. Looking at the schemas these interventions referred to, it becomes obvious that both cardinals were most concerned with *De ecclesia* and *De ecclesia in mundo huius temporis* without neglecting the other schemas. It can also be noted that Cardinal Döpfner was especially interested in the schemata on the liturgy and on the bishops. With regard to the contents it may well be said that the points both focused and differed at times but not so when it came to the main direction of their intentions. For example, on December 3, 1962, Cardinal Döpfner spoke about the schema on the Church and demanded a complete revision based on the proposals of the conciliar fathers[44]. Only one day later Cardinal Suenens presented his *plan d'ensemble* for the Council and suggested that the Council Commissions should revise their schemas according to the proposals made in this plan with a strong emphasis on pastoral renewal[45].

In very similar statements in October 1963 the two cardinals also argued for the restoration of the diaconate[46]. So far it cannot be seen from

---

41. Fund Döpfner, 3289.
42. *AD* II/2.3, p. 95.
43. *AD* II/2.3, p. 204.
44. *AS* I/4, pp. 183-189.
45. *AS* I/4, pp. 222-227.
46. *AS* I/4, pp. 227-230 (Döpfner), pp. 317-320 (Suenens).

the documents if this was a coordinated motion. It is likely that Döpfner's intervention was partly influenced by Klemens Tilmann who in the 1950s played a prominent role in authoring the German Catechism[47]. In the Council Records of Döpfner we also find a draft of Karl Rahner on this issue[48]. According to Suenens his own intervention was drafted with the help of Giuseppe Dossetti[49].

IV. SUMMARY

What preliminary conclusions can be drawn from the material presented? On the whole the statements made in the secondary literature about the corresponding approach of the two bishops could be confirmed. Indeed, we found numerous examples from the external as well as from the internal perspective. The remark made by Cardinal Suenens, that although they not always agreed on the methods to pursue their goals they usually agreed on the main direction, could also be confirmed. Nevertheless further research is necessary to also examine some disagreements, especially those repeatedly mentioned by the Rector of the Belgian College, Albert Prignon. Here an intensive discussion of the oral and written proposals at the Council could be rewarding as well as a detailed examination of the correspondence with other conciliar fathers and theologians.

Reflecting other sources the initially cited remarks made at two different ceremonies by Cardinal Suenens in Munich and Cardinal Döpfner in Brussels have to be put into perspective. So far, a definitive statement about the real intensity of their personal friendship cannot be made on the basis of the sources available. Therefore, I reckon it more useful to only try to evaluate the relation of both cardinals in their function as conciliar fathers. What conclusions can be drawn from the sources discussed? At first, I think it is important to remember that it would be insufficient merely to focus on these two cardinals alone and consider them the only crucial factors in the decision-making process at the Council. In spite of that, there can be no doubt that both were able to bring their authority and

47. See the diary of Klemens Tilmann (Archiv des Erzbistums München und Freising, NL Klemens Tilmann): "20.10.63. Notizen über die Autofahrt mit Kardinal Döpfner am 5.10. [...] Ich trug ihm, wohl auf Anfrage, meine Ansicht über das Diakonat vor. Tags darauf wurde Gruber beauftragt, für ihn einen Text zu verfassen, im Sinne des Gesprächs im Auto, den er dann in St. Peter vortrug".
48. Fund Döpfner, 4029.
49. SUENENS, Souvenirs et espérances (n. 13), p. 119.

reputation to bear in decisive moments. Most important was their ability to form alliances and gather a sufficient number of conciliar fathers behind them. In my opinion it is also not correct to reduce their role as moderators to a kind of tandem, because with Cardinal Lercaro a third person joined the group. Above all their good relationship with both conciliar popes was of utmost significance.

Methodically it could be useful to consider their general attitude towards episcopal duties. Certainly it can be said that both favored the ideal of a collegial bishop who is working closely together with his brethren without excluding the use of authority when necessary.

There is no doubt that the Council was an extraordinary burden for both cardinals. Pope Benedict XVI passed on to us this nice anecdote: Once during a session at a Bishops' Synod in Rome it was proposed to hold a new Council, whereupon Döpfner lifted both his hands saying in English: "Not in my lifetime![50]".

Erzbischöfliches Archiv München   Guido TREFFLER
Karmeliterstraße 1
80333 München
Germany

50. http://www.br-online.de/alpha/forum/vor9804/19980416_i.shtml: Prof. Dr. Joseph Ratzinger im Gespräch mit August Everding. Sendung in BR-Alpha am 16. April 1998, 20.15 Uhr.

CARDINALS L.-J. SUENENS AND G. LERCARO
AND THE SECOND VATICAN COUNCIL

I. INTRODUCTION

The elaborate contributions of M. Lamberigts, L. Declerck, G. Turbanti and J. Grootaers have made abundantly clear that the cardinals L.-J. Suenens and G. Lercaro exerted considerable influence on the course of the Council. Both cardinals not only had a particular vision on the direction the Council should take, on how the Council should proceed after the preparatory stadium and the first session, both on the practical level, as well as on the intrinsic level of its theological course; they also managed to implement – to a more or less large extent – their vision in the elaboration of two of the most important conciliar documents, *Lumen gentium* and *Gaudium et spes*.

This contribution will expand on Lercaro's and Suenens' pre-conciliar 'biography', since both Suenens' irritation with some of the excrescences of the pre-Vatican II ecclesiastical institutional system, as well as Lercaro's spiritual and pastoral journey in post-War Italy, seem to have determined – or at least heavily influenced – both cardinals' contributions during the Council[1]. Concerning the question of their mutual influence, it is not so much a question of influence – left alone whether it is at all possible to establish such a line of influence, but of compatibility: the utopical point of view of the Bolognese cardinal perfectly connects with Suenens' diplomatic and practical approach.

In terms of the paper's outline, first, Suenens' and Lercaro's pre-conciliar biography will be presented, followed by a selection of elements taken from both cardinals' conciliar history, reflecting their specific backgrounds. With regard to the time span covered, the selection will be limited to the first and second session and the first intersession of the Council[2]. An attempt to compare both cardinals in light of the above made assessments will conclude the article.

---

1. See J. GROOTAERS, *Actes et acteurs à Vatican II* (BETL, 139), Leuven, University Press – Peeters, 1998, p. 315: "… il n'est pas difficile de découvrir une continuité remarquable entre le Suenens préconciliaire et le 'ténor' de Vatican II".
2. This division in time has been chosen because, following the difficulties the *moderatores* had to go through to have the five propositions on *De ecclesia* voted at the very

II. Leon-Joseph Cardinal Suenens, Archbishop of Mechelen

Leon-Joseph Suenens was born on July 16, 1904 in Elsene, a Brussels suburb, as the only child of a master-brewer[3]. At secondary school, the *Institut Sainte-Marie* in Schaarbeek (near Brussels), the young Suenens proved an excellent student. Following his graduation, he expressed the wish to become a priest[4]. At the time, as stated by canon law, suitable candidates for the priesthood who had obtained excellent results in secondary school, were sent directly to Leuven or Rome, to receive their training for the priesthood in an academic setting, and to graduate in philosophy and/or theology[5]. Thus Suenens was sent to Rome in 1921, where he stayed at the Pontifical Belgian College until 1929, and studied philosophy, theology, and canon law at the Gregorian University[6].

beginning of the second session, their direct influence on the Council declined significantly. A second element was the fact that both Suenens and Lercaro differed of opinion on Schema XVII / XIII. Also the role pope Paul VI played, has to be taken into account. Lercaro had a different relationship with Montini than Suenens did, who, to a certain extent, stood closer to John XXIII.

3. At the age of four, Suenens lost his father. See L.-J. Suenens, *Souvenirs et espérances*, Paris, Fayard, 1991, p. 11. It has to be noted that sources for Suenens' biography remain rather scarce. His memoir, *Souvenirs et espérances*, was published in 1991. Suenens describes facts of which some took place more than half a century earlier, interpreting most of these facts from a post-Conciliar point of view, and coloured by his conciliar experiences as well. Therefore the book should be used very carefully, and Suenens' reinterpretation of the past should be taken into account when citing *Souvenirs et espérances*.

4. In Suenens, *Souvenirs et espérances* (n. 3), p. 15, Suenens mentions a proposal made by a niece of his mother. She had married an American businessman, and suggested the young Suenens study economics at university, in order to become the administrator of their fortune, a proposal that Suenens declined.

5. In this matter, the Belgian dioceses acted according the Code of Canon Law, as canon 1380 of the 1917 Code stated that "Optandum ut locorum Ordinarii, pro sua prudentia, clericos, pietate et praestantes, ad scholas mittant alicuius Universitatis aut Facultatis ab Ecclesiae conditae vel approbatae, ut inibi studia praesertim philosophiae, theologiae ac iuris canonici perficiant et academicos gradus consequantur". Apparently, this canonical obligation never became the basic rule in the Church, as becomes clear in the example of the Dutch dioceses. By 1959, the average Dutch bishop had only received the classical philosophical and theological training at his major seminary. Only two out of eight diocesan bishops (Van Dodewaard and cardinal Alfrink) were graduates, in this case of the *Biblicum*. Compared to their Dutch counterparts, all of the Belgian bishops had received doctorates (from Rome and/or Leuven) in either philosophy or theology, and more often in both disciplines.

6. During the Interbellum, students from the Belgian ecclesiastical province in Rome, like Suenens, normally obtained a doctorate in philosophy and theology, in combination with a baccalaureate in canon law. Only a minority among them would specialise in Biblical exegesis (at the *Biblicum*), in canon law, or in Oriental languages. The majority would study at the *Gregoriana*. Most of these elite students were destined for high rank positions in the ecclesiastical administration, or in catholic (higher) education. Cf. the

Many years later, Suenens would remember his academic training as far too scholastic and completely disconnected from real life[7]. Discussions and debate among Belgian College students on all kinds of theological, canonical, and philosophical subjects seem to have had a greater influence on the young student[8]. It was also during his training in Rome that Suenens, like all students, became immersed in the so-called "rich Roman life", the abundant self expression of Roman catholicism, as expressed in all kinds of customs, rituals, and liturgies. Suenens adapted to the system, but seems to have grasped its rather futile nature as well[9].

At the Pontifical Belgian College, Suenens met with fellow students who would form the core of the future conciliar *squadra Belga*. Among them were Philips, a brilliant systematic theologian and future professor at the Leuven theological faculty, and De Smedt, Himmer and Charue, future Belgian diocesan bishops[10].

Even though Suenens might have disliked the nature of his academic training at the Gregorian University, in 1929 he graduated – again – with excellent results, having obtained two doctorates and a baccalaureate. In 1927 he had also been ordained to the priesthood.

On his return to Belgium, summer 1929, Suenens became a teacher at his former secondary school, the *Institut Sainte Marie* in Schaarbeek,

---

1917 Code of Canon Law, canon 1378, where licentiates and doctors are given preference for these functions. See also note 4. For some very general data, see also J. ICKX, *De alumni van het Belgisch Pauselijk College te Rome 1844-1994*, Rome, Pontificio Collegio Belga, 1994.

7. "It was not the academic training that formed or marked me; it clearly was too scholastic and had no connection whatsoever with real life" (my translation), in SUENENS, *Souvenirs et espérances* (n. 3), p. 21.

8. *Ibid.*, p. 21.

9. Hence his proposal together with cardinal Döpfner – to reduce the number of pontifical masses before the meetings *in aula* and to 'simplify' the episcopal attire – during a meeting of the Secretariat for Extraordinary Affairs of October 16, 1962. See A. RICCARDI, *The Tumultuous Opening Days of the Council*, in G. ALBERIGO – J.A. KOMONCHAK (eds.), *History of Vatican II*. Vol. II: *The Formation of the Council's Identity: First Period and Intersession. October 1962-September 1963*, Maryknoll, NY, Orbis; Leuven, Peeters, 1997, 1-67, esp. pp. 63-64. See also SUENENS, *Souvenirs et espérances* (n. 3), p. 60.

10. In his memoir, Suenens mentions meetings with Dom Lambert Beauduin, the Belgian benedictine and founding father of the liturgical and ecumenical movement, at the time teaching at the liturgical institute of Sant'Anselmo, who also acted as Suenens' spiritual director; and with father Lebbe, the famous China-missionary. It is, however, rather difficult to estimate to what extent both persons influenced Suenens, also because in the 1950s Beauduin accused Suenens of betraying the ecumenical cause. SUENENS, *Souvenirs et espérances* (n. 3), p. 25. See also GROOTAERS, *Actes et acteurs* (n. 1), pp. 314-315. The fact that Suenens had met most members of the future *squadra Belga*, did not mean there was a spiritual and/or doctrinal connection with all of them. Suenens, however, became aware of their intrinsic values as theologians, organisers, etc.; and would make good use of this knowledge.

where he taught languages (Dutch and French), and even fine arts to first year students[11]. Within the same year, however, Suenens joined the philosophy department of the major seminary in Mechelen, teaching moral philosophy, epistemology and educational sciences, and providing spiritual guidance to students as well.

Several years later, and although he held this position for almost a decade, Suenens passed a rather severe judgement on the priestly formation as it was perceived and performed in Mechelen: "An artificial, isolated regime ... with its rigid discipline ... It seemed to me this was completely out of line with its initial purpose"[12].

This apparently negative experience, however, was not the only reason for Suenens's judgement. Since the 1950s the average positive attitude towards religion in general and the Catholic Church in particular had begun to change. Though not yet dramatically, this became apparent in a decline in the number of vocations, leeding to calls for adapting the formation for the priesthood to the changing context[13]. Suenens's *animadversiones* and his contributions to the discussion *in aula* of the schema *De sacrorum alumnis formandis* have to be understood in this context[14].

In August 1940, to the surprise of many, cardinal Van Roey announced a new assignement for Suenens: he was to become vice-rector of the university of Leuven[15]. Due to the war, Suenens was thrown in at the deep

---

11. Following the death of cardinal Mercier on January 23, 1926, the archdiocese's vicar-general, J.E. Van Roey had been appointed archbishop of Mechelen and was created cardinal the following consistory. Cardinal Van Roey used to send newly graduated priests to parishes or catholic highschools for a short period of time, usually one year, in order to gain insight and experience in pastoral praxis on different levels. SUENENS, *Souvenirs et espérances* (n. 3), pp. 25-26.

12. SUENENS, *Souvenirs et espérances* (n. 3), pp. 26-28 (my translation). It has to be noted that the young Suenens probably compared the experience of a more or less 'liberal' regime in the Pontifical Belgian College in Rome, as he had experienced under monsignor de 't Serclaes, with the more rigid structures and discipline of a larger major seminary in Mechelen. The negative nature of Suenens' remark can also be traced back to the fact that he stressed the pastoral training (at the expense of the intellectual training) for both seminarians and religious. This training had to be organised according to the methods of the Legion of Mary.

13. For a description of the situation of the priestly formation before Vatican II, see M. LAMBERIGTS, '*Optatam Totius*': *The Decree on the Priestly Formation. A Short Survey of Its History at the Second Vatican Council*, in *Louvain Studies* 30 (2005) 25-48, esp. pp. 26-30. For the situation in Belgium, see J. ART, *De evolutie van het aantal mannelijke roepingen in België tussen 1830 en 1975. Basisgegevens en richtingen voor verder onderzoek*, in *Belgisch Tijdschrift voor Nieuwste Geschiedenis* 10 (1979) 281-336.

14. LAMBERIGTS, '*Optatam Totius*' (n. 13), pp. 34.41, with reference to the *AS* III/7, pp. 715-717.

15. Until the midst of the 1960s, the catholic university of Leuven was administered by the Belgian bishops, the cardinal-archbishop of Mechelen being its chancellor. For the

end[16], but he showed himself a skilfull, eloquent and diplomatic administrator, ready to defend the interests of Church and university if and where necessary[17].

During his stay in Leuven, Suenens became involved in two initiatives that would strongly affect his activity during the Council. In 1942, he supported the idea of two professors of the faculty of theology, Lucien Cerfaux and Albert Dondeyne, to establish a 'Higher Institute for Religious Studies' at the university. Its main purpose was to present lay students with a basic introduction in catholic theology and to improve their often limited knowledge of catholic religion[18].

A second initiative was unknown to the greater public but certainly not less influential, especially with regard to the role Belgian participants

daily administration, however, the bishops appointed a *rector magnificus*, who acted as intermediary between them and the academic community. Suenens's new appointment clearly was a promotion (according to ecclesiastical standards), but by no means, given the circumstances of war, he was to be envied for it.

16. At the opening of the new academic year, October 1940, the university's administration faced several severe difficulties. First of all, the rector and his team had to administer the university in the context of the German occupation. At first this would not create specific problems, but soon the interests of the academic community were at stake and had to be defended against increasing German demands (e.g. to obtain the enrollment listings of students who would qualify for forced labour in Germany), ultimately leading to the arrest and emprisonment of rector Van Waeyenbergh in 1943. Following Van Waeyenbergh's arrest, Suenens *ex officio* became *rector magnificus ad interim*. On the practical level, there was the huge 'collateral damage' university buildings (including once again the library) had suffered from the fighting near and in Leuven, putting an enormous financial and organisational burden on the university's shoulders.

17. Due to his strong personality and his diplomatic but decisive attitude against the occupying forces, many professors would predict "a brilliant career in the diplomatic service". See GROOTAERS, *Actes et acteurs* (n. 1), p. 324. During the war, Suenens was also assigned to the royal household as the private teacher of religion of one of king Leopold III's children, earning him good contacts both in the highest government circles and at the royal court. This fact most certainly played an important role in his nomination as archbishop of Mechelen in 1961.

18. Lucien Cerfaux was a biblical exegete, specialised in New Testament exegesis and Hellenistic culture. Albert Dondeyne, philosopher and dogmatic theologian, was a specialist in the field of philosophy of religion. Suenens almost immediately grasped the potential of the institute, and supported wholeheartedly its establishment. At first not too succesful, the Institute reached great heights in the 1950s and would train numerous laypeople to become teachers of religion and/or catechists. Suenens supported the idea of training laypeople so they could take up their legitimate place and function in the Church. One of the Institute's most succesful teachers was Ch. Moeller (who, at the Council, would become *peritus* of the Canadian cardinal Léger), but also the names of the moral theologian and sociologist Delhaye and systematic theologian Schillebeeckx have to be mentioned here. For an overview (in Dutch) of the Higher Institute's history, see L. GEVERS – M. LAMBERIGTS – B. PATTYN, *Hoger Instituut voor Godsdienstwetenschappen. Faculteit der Godgeleerdheid, K.U.Leuven. 1942-1992. Rondom catechese en godsdienstonderwijs* (Documenta Libraria, 13), Leuven, Library of the Faculty of Theology, 1992.

played at Vatican II. Once a month, Suenens would invite a small group
of professors belonging to the faculty of theology and to the Jesuit *Theologicum* of Egenhoven near Leuven to discuss current, often burning
theological issues[19]. It is interesting to see that again Suenens met with
future (important) participants of the Council and discussed topics that
would be high on the conciliar agenda. Some of these men belonged to
his Roman circle of acquaintances, such as Philips, who had become professor in systematic theology in Leuven in 1942, while others were relatively 'new' to him, such as the biblical exegete Lucien Cerfaux, the jesuit
systematic theologian Édouard Dhanis, and the philosopher and systematic theologian Albert Dondeyne[20].

By the end of 1945, Suenens was appointed auxiliary bishop of cardinal
Van Roey[21]. In his memoir, Suenens mentions the mainly administrative
character of this position: handling current, often canonical, affairs, and
administering the sacrament of confirmation to numerous children throughout the archdiocese. Suenens also mentions – at least as seen from his personal perspective – the lack of a longterm pastoral vision for the archdiocese in particular and the Belgian catholic Church in general[22]. Being an
auxiliary bishop gave Suenens the opportunity to develop some of his ideas
in the field of pastoral care. Again Suenens strongly profiled himself as a
diplomat in the so-called School-conflict, regarding the question of government funding for catholic schools and religious education. The development of a broad pastoral vision also became clear in Suenens's writings[23].

19. The monthly meetings took place in Suenens's house, located in the *Collegium
Veteranorum*, currently belonging to the faculty of theology.
20. The Leuven discussion forum shows an important characteristic of the Belgian
connection on Vatican II: the fact that most of the *periti* were well acquainted with each
other, not only on the personal level, but also as theologians. At the opening of the Council, the Belgian *periti* and bishops more or less knew what they could expect from one and
another. E.g.: Suenens made good use of this knowledge, when defusing the tense situation on the schema *De ecclesia* during the first intersession. See also L. DECLERCK, *Le rôle
joué par les évêques et periti Belges au concile Vatican II*, in *ETL* 76 (2000) 445-464,
esp. 445-457: *L'introduction du nouveau Schéma 'De Ecclesia'*.
21. On December 16, 1945, he received the episcopal ordination. Suenens succeeded
to monsignor E. Carton de Wiart, a former fellow student from the Belgian College
in Rome, who was appointed bishop of the diocese of Tournai. His colleagues auxiliary
bishops were monsignor Emiel-Jozef De Smedt, future bishop of Bruges and monsignor
Constant Schoenmaekers. Suenens was named titular bishop of Isinda.
22. Again, Suenens' words should be interpreted with care. The fact that cardinal Van
Roey took a rather conservative stand (in the sense of immutability of the pastoral praxis)
with regard to the changing pastoral context, made Suenens decide – *post factum* – that
the archdiocese and hence the Belgian ecclesiastical province had no longterm pastoral
vision as well as a consistent and renewing approach tackling the evolving problems.
23. Just to name the most important publications from the 1950s: *Théologie de
l'apostolat de la Légion de Marie* (1957, on the introduction of the specific form of

Within the Belgian ecclesiastical province, Suenens was given the responsibility for the catholic media. During his stay in Rome he had already been a part-time correspondent for two catholic newspapers, covering news from the Vatican. When taking up his new responsibility he soon realised the possibilities the (new) media could have for apostolic purposes and discovered his own talent in dealing with the media as well[24].

To conclude, at the eve of the Council, Suenens was a relatively young auxiliary bishop, who already had shown qualities that would serve him well during the Council: a diplomatic, eloquent 'leader' with a clear pastoral vision for his own diocese and for the universal Church.

III. GIACOMO CARDINAL LERCARO, ARCHBISHOP OF BOLOGNA

Giacomo Lercaro was born in a catholic family of nine children, on October 28, 1891, in Quinto al Mare, a small village on the outskirts of the Italian harbour Genua[25]. He began his ecclesiastical career at the age

---

lay-apostolate through the 'Legion of Mary'); *L'Église en état de mission* (1957, on the revaluation of sacramental meaning of baptism and the task of every christian to act fully and directly as a witness of Christ); *La promotion apostolique de la religieuse*; and *Un problème crucial: amour et maîtrise de soi*. The latter book was the result of the opening lecture Suenens held at the World Health Conference (part of the Brussels World Exhibition, 1958) to representatives of the medical corps. In his speech, Suenens pleaded for further research on the subject of birth-control to allow catholic moral theologians to present more acurate moral orientations on the subjects of marriage, family and sexuality. Suenens's lecture also resulted in a yearly conference held in Leuven (*Colloques de sexologie de Louvain*, from 1959 until 1974), bringing together moral theologians and medical scientists on questions of family and sexuality. In 1961, also on Suenens's instigation, the university of Leuven established an interdisciplinary institute for the study of questions on family and sexuality.

Suenens's writings were quite succesfull and were translated into different languages, among them Italian. On the occasion of presenting a paper at a conference on family (Rome, 1960), monsignor Montini showed interest in Suenens's writings and eventually arranged for two books (*Church is Mission* and *Love and Selfconfinement*) to be translated in Italian. To two of Suenens's works, Montini wrote the prefaces. See also DECLERCK, *Le rôle joué par les évêques et periti Belges* (n. 20), p. 457 and GROOTAERS, *Actes et acteurs* (n. 1), p. 315, n. 7.

24. Monsignor Felici, secretary of the Council, repeatedly objected to the fact that Suenens addressed the press by himself, passing by Felici's conciliar secretariate and its press department (responsible for press-releases and contacts). See e.g. J. GROOTAERS, *Ebb and Flow between Two Seasons*, in ALBERIGO – KOMONCHAK (eds.), *History of Vatican II*. Vol. II (n. 9), pp. 515-564, esp. 555, n. 124.

25. Giacomo Lercaro was the seventh child out of nine. His father was a docker. For more information on Lercaro, see among others: F. OBERKOFLER, *An den Wurzeln des Glaubens: Gott, Sich und die Welt finden. Kardinal Giacomo Lercaro (1891-1976): Leben, Werk, Bedeutung* (Studien zur Theologie und Praxis der Seelsorge, 55), Würzburg, Echter, 2003; G. ALBERIGO – G. BATTELLI – R. CAPILUPPI – A. ALBERIGO (eds.), *Giacomo Lercaro: Vescovo della chiesa di Dio (1891-1976)* (Testi e ricerche di scienze religiose. Nuova

of eleven, by taking the classical road towards the priesthood, i.e. the secondary school at the Chiappeto minor seminary in Genua, where he went on to philosophy and theology at the archdiocesal major seminary. Here, through some of his teachers like father Calcagno and monsignor Moglia, Lercaro came into contact with the ideas of the Liturgical Movement[26]. His ordination to the priesthood followed in 1914.

Following his ordination in 1914, Lercaro was sent to Rome, to study at the *Biblicum*. Though not yet a prerequisite for a teaching position in biblical exegesis in a catholic institution, to local bishops the *Biblicum* guaranteed orthodoxy in matters that at the time were severely poisoned by the raging anti-modernist crisis. After a brief period as prefect of the Genuese minor seminary and as a medic in the Italian army, Lercaro was appointed vice-director and professor at the major seminary of Genua, where he taught Scripture and patristics[27]. He wrote some minor works in the field of biblical homiletics and was also appointed teacher of religion in a local state grammar school, the *Collegio Cristoforo Colombo*[28].

It was in this context that Lercaro introduced to his students the ideas of the Liturgical Movement, as well as a socially orientated apostolate[29]. This emphasis on liturgy combined with a social apostolate, expressed in the notion of *diakonia*, became the hallmark of Lercaro's pastoral action throughout his entire life. Also in the context of this *Azione Cattolica*, Lercaro cooperated with some of his future conciliar colleagues and cardinals like Siri and Montini, as well as future politicians from the *Democrazia Cristiana*, such as A. Moro and G. Andreotti. A first 'National

Serie, 6), Genua, Marietti, 1991; G. LERCARO – G. ALBERIGO (eds.), *Per la forza dello Spirito: Discorsi conciliari del card. Giacomo Lercaro*, Bologna, Dehoniane, 1984; G. LERCARO – G. ALBERIGO – G. BATTELLI (eds.), *Lettere dal Concilio 1962-1965*, Bologna, Dehoniane, 1980. For his archives, kept at the *Istituto per le scienze religiose* in Bologna, see G. LERCARO – G. DOSSETTI – G. ALBERIGO – L. LAZZARETTI (eds.), *Inventario dei Fondi G. Lercaro e G. Dossetti* (La documentazione bolognese per la storia del Concilio Vaticano II, 2), Bologna, s.n., 1995.
    26. OBERKOFLER, *An den Wurzeln* (n. 25), p. 18.
    27. Following his graduation at the *Biblicum*, Lercaro was named prefect of his former highschool. In 1917 he joined the staff of the major seminary as well (as vice-director). When Italy entered World War I as a belligerent party (1917), Lercaro was drafted in the Italian army as a medic. Following his demobilisation in January 1919, he already had received his appointment as professor in the Genova archdiocesean major seminary. See OBERKOFLER, *An den Wurzeln* (n. 25), pp. 21-22.
    28. E.g. G. LERCARO, *La Lettera cattolica di San Giacomo: Commento omiletico*, Brescia, Morcelliana, 1931. Lercaro would also teach philosophy at the *Istituto Vittorino da Feltre*, a grammar school of the Barnabite order located in Genua.
    29. Father Lercaro formed so-called *gruppi liturgici*, groups of students he would celebrate the Sacred Triduum with. Together with this liturgical education, he trained young people to become catechists, the so-called *squadre catechistiche*. See OBERKOFLER, *An den Wurzeln* (n. 25), p. 23.

Conference on Liturgy' held in Genua in 1934 marked the success of this liturgical apostolate[30].

In 1937, Lercaro was appointed parish priest in the *Maria Immaculata*, a large city-parish in the centre of Genua. Here, he began working according to his personal pastoral model: Bible-centered spirituality, combined with liturgy and *diakonia*. Again he engaged laypeople in his pastoral work; he called upon them as adult faithful, to become the living yeast in the parish, both *ad intra*, and *ad extra*, to the outside world as well[31]. To this purpose Lercaro established an institute called the *Didaskaleion*, to train a select group of lay-people in liturgy and theology[32]. Lercaro also paid considerable attention to religious education for children, and especially to the poor in his parish. In 1937, Lercaro also became a commentator for the national broadcasting company RAI, commenting upon liturgical broadcasts and presenting weekly spiritual talks.

January 31, 1947, Pius XII appointed Lercaro archbishop of Ravenna–Cervia. In March 1947, he was ordained bishop by his former co-worker in the liturgical apostolate, archbishop Siri of Genua. At the time, Ravenna was known as a communist stronghold. To the surprise of many, Lercaro did not commence his office and pastoral activities by openly rejecting communism, but by reorganising the pastoral care in his dioceses. His first goal was to restore not only catholic self-esteem, but also to motivate and to train catholics to become responsible and active members of society. He improved the priestly formation significantly by appointing a well-versed professorial corps, as well as by adding courses in liturgy and pastoral theology to the curriculum[33]. Liturgy remained most important as a pastoral tool, and focused on the eucharist, on preaching – with emphasis on Scripture and biblical theology –, and on catechetics. It was in his years in Ravenna, that Lercaro

---

30. From its scholarly surroundings, the liturgical apostolate developed in a specific form of catholic action that spreaded all over Italy. See OBERKOFLER, *An den Wurzeln* (n. 25), pp. 23-24.

31. One must, however, not forget that Lercaro's pastoral action took place in the context of the renewed Catholic Action as instigated at the time by Pius XI; characterised by a growing attention for spiritual life as the main principle grounding catholic presence in society, over direct political action.

32. OBERKOFLER, *An den Wurzeln* (n. 25), pp. 25-26.

33. Like Suenens, for Lercaro, the improvement and/or reform of the priestly formation, was one of the most important issues the Church should tackle in the Council. OBERKOFLER, *An den Wurzeln* (n. 25), pp. 27-28. See for instance his interventions in this regard in the CC. Cf. J. GROOTAERS, *The Drama Continues between the Acts: The 'Second Preparation' and Its Opponents*, in ALBERIGO – KOMONCHAK (eds.), *History of Vatican II*. Vol. II (n. 9), 359-514, esp. pp. 484-485.

made his name in the Liturgical Movement in an Italian as well as a European context.

Again, his successfull pastoral method resulted in a new appointment. April 19, 1952, Lercaro was named archbishop of Bologna, in succession of the late cardinal Nasalli Rocca. Lercaro's appointment clearly was a promotion according to ecclesiastical standings[34], it also expressed an approval by the highest ecclesiastical authorities of his pastoral methodology. Another important reason for Lercaro's nomination, was that, like Ravenna, Bologna was known as a solid communist stronghold too, with the catholic Church remaining in such a deplorable condition, that the diocese was nicknamed 'Bologna, the patient'.

Lercaro began his office by describing and analysing the then present pastoral situation in his archdiocese. To this purpose, he established a sociological institute, the *Ufficio di statistica religiosa della Diocesi* (UdS, 1953), since it was his opinion that the Church should not only "look at the heritage of the Holy Truth, but in the meantime start a dialogue with modern times, ..., with the new forms of life and the new possibilities that become clear for catholic apostolate"[35].

In 1957, the institute became a diocesan centre for socio-religious research, and received extra capacities: it was to set out future lines for pastoral care in line with sociological and statistical analysis.

Liturgy remained in the heart of Lercaro's pastoral action, for it brings people to bear witness to their faith (*Martyria*), to become a living community (*Koinonia*) that takes care of each other's needs (*Diakonia*).

Concerning the latter he showed a remarkable example by housing a number of orphans in his archdiocesal palace, forming what was known as the *famiglia* of the cardinal[36].

In his relations with the communists, he shifted from a policy of direct, and in his eyes unproductive, confrontation towards an attitude focused on careful and critical dialogue, forcing the catholic side to critically evaluate their own position as well.

On the eve of the Council, Lercaro had been archbishop for a considerable time, having achieved major results in his pastoral praxis. In a sense he was an a-typical Italian archbishop with a very clear spiritual and

---

34. *De jure*, the archbishop of Bologna was to be raised to the purple.

35. Cardinal Lercaro, quoted in OBERKOFLER, *An den Wurzeln* (n. 25), p. 38. My translation.

36. Following a flood of the river Po in 1948, Lercaro gave housing to several orphans, victims of the disaster. A temporary measure of *caritas* at first, the initiative was 'institutionalised' as the *famiglia* of the cardinal. See OBERKOFLER, *An den Wurzeln* (n. 25), pp. 74-84.

pastoral vision on how to govern his archdiocese and to enhance spiritual life. This vision was also present in his personal life.

IV. REFLECTING BIOGRAPHIES
SUENENS' AND LERCARO'S CONCILIAR HISTORY

In order to show how the personal biographies of the cardinals Lercaro and Suenens have on the one hand clearly influenced their conciliar activities, and, on the other hand, have determined the level of influence exerted on the Council proceedings, the following elements – taking the limitations as sketched in the introduction into account – will be discussed: Suenens and Lercaro during the first stages of the Council, Suenens efforts to navigate the Council's course in a more Church-centered direction, and Lercaro's interventions in the field of liturgy, as well as his option for the poor as expressed in his intervention in December 1962.

1. Suenens during the First Stages of the Council

Both the announcement of the coming Council (January, 25, 1959) and the request to send *Vota* for the *Commissio Antepraeparatoria*, seemed to have surprised Suenens. The auxiliary bishop sent about ten pages of text to cardinal Tardini's commission, containing an expression of some of his ideas that had matured during his years as a teacher at the major seminary of Mechelen and as auxiliary bishop. Among them were requests for the adaptation of the bishop's role in the life of the Church; the introduction of the permanent diaconate; a reform of the priestly training, especially by improving its pastoral component; the adaptation of the life of the religious to the modern world; some liturgical reforms; more cooperation between laypeople and clergy on every level of the Church; and, a request to stress the Church's missionary responsibility, the so-called *euntes docete*-aspect[37].

At this particular point, Suenens' personal conciliar history might have come to an end[38], were it not for the fact that following the death of cardinal Van Roey (August 6, 1961), Suenens was chosen as his successor

---

37. The *vota* of the Belgian bishops are published in the *Acta et Documenta Concilia Œcumenico Vaticano II apparando, Series I (Antepraeparatoria)*. Vol. II: *Consilia et Vota Episcoporum ac Praelatorum*. Pars I: *Europa*, Vatican City, 1960, pp. 103-156. For Suenens' *vota*, see pp. 141ff.

38. According to Suenens, cardinal Van Roey found it unnecessary for auxiliary bishops to attend the Council: they were to administer the dioceses in absence of the diocesan bishops remaining in Rome.

(november 1961), took possession of the chair of the archdiocese Mechelen, January 24, 1962, and, to the surprise of many, was created cardinal
at the first *consistorium* following his nomination (March 19, 1962). At
the time, being almost fifty-eight years of age, Suenens belonged to the
group of younger cardinals attending the Council[39].

Suenens became involved extensively in the preparatory phase of the
Council. He joined the preparatory commission editing a first draft of the
schema *De episcopis et dioecesium regimine*[40], and was admitted to the
central planning committee, the *Commissio Centralis Praeparatoria*[41].
Suenens also wrote a Lent pastoral letter on the upcoming Council[42].

At the opening of the Council, together with, among others, the cardinals Siri (Genua), Montini (Milan) and Döpfner (Munich), Suenens was
incorporated in the *Secretariatus de Concilii negotiis extra ordinem*, the
secretariate pope John XXIII had established to support the Council of
Presidents in leading the daily discussions and setting out the general
course for the Council[43].

Interventions at the end of the first session by Suenens, Lercaro,
Döpfner and Montini, on the desired Church-centered nature of the Council's future course, had made fathers aware of the need for a controlling
body that should keep up with the reduction of the large number of prepared *schemata*[44], and with the revision of these texts, but also to control
the working of the different commissions during the intersession[45]. To this

39. It remains unclear whether this fast rise of Suenens's ecclesiastical career was due
to the fact that John XXIII felt a certain sympathy for the young archbishop. It is said that
John XXIII had read Suenens' pastoral letter on the coming Council, recognising his own
ideas very adequately expressed in Suenens' text. Therefore, at least according to Suenens
himself, he wanted the Mechelen archbishop to play a more effective role in the conciliar
activities. See SUENENS, *Souvenirs et espérances* (n. 3), pp. 86-87. See also GROOTAERS,
Actes et acteurs (n. 1), p. 316; and the contribution of M. Lamberigts and L. Declerck on
the influence of Suenens at Vatican II in the present volume.

40. *Commissio praeparatoria 'De episcopis et dioecesium regimine'*. Suenens became
a member of this commission on July 29, 1960.

41. Member since March 3, 1962.

42. L.-J. SUENENS, *Qu'attendez-vous du Concile?*, Mechelen, 1962. See also in Dutch:
*Het Tweede Œkumenisch Vatikaans Concilie: Vastenbrief van Z.Em. Leo-Jozef kard. Sue-
nens, aartsbisschop van Mechelen-Brussel*, in *Katholiek Archief* 17 (1962) 253-260.

43. To this list his membership of the post-conciliar coordinating (or 'hermeneutical')
commission (since January 4, 1966), the so-called *Commissio centralis coordinandis post
Concilium laboribus et Concilii Decretis interpretandis*, has to be added.

44. See GROOTAERS, *The Drama Continues* (n. 33), pp. 359-514, esp. 365.

45. The preparatory commissions had presented more than 2000 pages of text, representing about seventy-five documents. Due to the pressure of, among others, cardinal Suenens, their number was reduced to seventeen *schemata*. In fact, the fear some of the fathers
had expressed, was far from being ungrounded, while some members of the minority

purpose, December 6, 1962, the establishment of a so-called *Commissio Princeps*, also known as the 'Coordinating Commission (CC)', was announced. Its members, among them cardinal Suenens, should follow up progress the different conciliar commissions made in preparing final drafts of the different *schemata*, should report to the CC and adjust where necessary[46]. Following the election of cardinal Montini as pope Paul VI, on August 21, 1963, cardinal Lercaro was also added to the CC[47].

As has been made clear by M. Lamberigts and L. Declerck, Suenens clearly showed his intrinsic diplomatic qualities, when making good use of his membership of the CC. At first, in its January session, he had the commission rejecting all remaining preparatory texts, as far as the *schema De ecclesia* was concerned. Second, he managed to have the text of Philips-Thils (*De ecclesia*) accepted as the only *schema* to be discussed by the Doctrinal Commission. Third, Suenens succeeded in changing the internal order for discussion of the document and he managed to push through the vote of the so-called five *propositiones*, concise statements on the direction the debate on *De ecclesia* should take. The vote on October 30, 1963 – two weeks after an initial vote had been denied – showed to be succesful[48].

2. Cardinal Lercaro during the First Stages of the Council

When in 1959 John XXIII announced the coming Council, Lercaro was completely astonished: "How is it possible, that the pope, after

clearly wanted to put an end to the power the fathers exerted when gathered in the aula. On the other hand, most of the commissions were led by members of Curial offices, and the fathers, being no longer present in Rome, would lose control over the commissions and their work.

46. Suenens was named reporter for three documents: the Church (later to become *Lumen gentium*), the Blessed Virgin (later incorporated in *Lumen gentium*) and on the presence of the Church in the Modern World (the so-called *Schema XVII*, later to become *Gaudium et spes*). See GROOTAERS, *Actes et acteurs* (n. 1), p. 202 and ID., *The Drama Continues* (n. 33), p. 365, n. 13, p. 367, n. 20, pp. 369-370, n. 27.

47. Both Montini and Lercaro had not been incorporated in the CC, although this might have been more or less expected, especially because of the latter's prestige in the conciliar aula. One of the possible explanations might have been the fact that the CC was headed by the Secretary of State, cardinal Cicognani. The moment the CC was inaugurated, the fact of John XXIIId's lethal disease was already known to the Council fathers, and in the light of a conclave – to be expected in the near future –, the Italian Curial cardinals clearly did not want to improve the position of what they considered to be 'outsiders', by having them named into what was going to be the Council's most important institution. Montini, and especially Lercaro had been 'outsiders' in the Italian episcopal conference since the beginning of the Council, see e.g. the refusal to elect Lercaro into the Liturgy Commission. See also GROOTAERS, *The Drama Continues* (n. 33), pp. 503-506; ALBERIGO – BATTELLI – CAPILUPPI – ALBERIGO (eds.), *Giacomo Lercaro* (n. 25), p. 230.

48. The *propositiones* meant a shift in the position Suenens held during the following sessions and intersessions of the Council.

hundred years, and only three months following his election, dares to summon a council?... It will ruin his health, and destroy the building of his moral and theological virtues!"[49].

At first, Lercaro remained somewhat sceptic about the pope's initiative, but in time, he increasingly became enthused about the event and the major possibilities it presented both to his local community and to the universal Church. Due to a study tour to the United States as part of his involvement in the Liturgical Movement, Lercaro sent in his *vota* for the coming council with a substantial delay, and, unlike Suenens' more extensive paper, they only covered four pages. Pastoral liturgy makes up for a large part of it, but also a request for more collegiality is present, for improvement of the training for the priesthood, the restauration of the permanent diaconate, as well as a request for the reform of some aspects of ecclesiastical governement[50].

In spite of being an influential cardinal – at least in the context of the Liturgical Movement and outside the Roman Curia, and – as archbishop of Bologna –, having achieved impressive results in the field of pastoral praxis, Lercaro never became involved in the preparatory stadium of the Council. This, however, did not prevent him – in the span separating the *antepraeparatoria* from the opening of the Council – from taking several initiatives to present the coming Council to his faithful as a new Pentecost, an unprecedented opportunity to improve and revitalise the life of the Church. To this purpose, he organised several *Piccoli Sinodi Diocesani* – small diocesan synods – in Bologna, treating different pastoral topics[51] in relation with the coming Council. According to Lercaro, they would not only help to prepare the faithfull and the Bolognese church to the upcoming event of the Council, but also show its major importance for the life of the Church in general.

Once the Council opened, Lercaro, as was to be expected, engaged in full in the debate on liturgy. Due to his somewhat isolated position within

49. Quoted in OBERKOFLER, *An den Wurzeln* (n. 25), p. 88, with reference to O.H. PESCH, *Das Zweite Vatikanische Konzil (1962 bis 1965): Vorgeschichte – Verlauf – Ergebnisse – Nachgeschichte*, Würzburg, Echter, 1993, p. 52. My translation.

50. Lercaro's *vota* can be found in *Acta et Documenta. Series I.* Vol. II: *Consilia et Vota Episcoporum ac Praelatorum, Pars III: Italia*, Vatican City, 1960, pp. 115-118 (accompanying letter on p. 114).

51. January 3-4, 1961, diocesan synod on liturgy and pastoral subjects, and exactly one year later, a diocesan synod on 'pastoral action in confrontation with communism'. Other synods were held during the different conciliar intersessions, and reflect debates and decisions of the ongoing Council: January 2-3, 1963, on Catholic Action and the lay apostolate; January 2-3, 1964 on vocations to the priesthood; and December 29-30, 1964 on the implementation of the constitution on the Sacred Liturgy.

the Italian episcopal conference[52] Lercaro was – at first – denied a place on the list with the names of Italian candidates for the different commissions, including the liturgical. An intervention of Central-European, mainly German bishops, and that of Madagascar, appeared to be necessary to have him elected – with more than a thousand votes – but subsequently, cardinal Larraona, the Spanish Curia cardinal presiding over the commission, unexpectedly appointed two curial officials as vice-presidents, silently passing by cardinal Lercaro, who was considered by many of the fathers as the most suitable candidate for this office[53]. Most of Lercaro's time was spent in what is known as 'the third subcommittee', responsible for the coordination of all conciliar activities and general questions dealing with liturgy[54]. During the debates of the first session on liturgy *in aula*, Lercaro intervened twice, October 22 and October 31, 1961[55].

In the margin of this conciliar activity, in November 1962, Lercaro was invited to join a group of Council fathers and *periti*, gathering in the Pontifical Belgian College at the *Via del Quirinale*. This group was

52. Together with cardinal Montini of Milan, Lercaro was considered to be – to some extent – an outsider within the large group of Italian bishops. Yet his pastoral successes both in Ravenna and Bologna, and the fact that he was known in international catholic circles, had granted him a certain aura of unassailability. Cardinal Siri of Genua, head of the episcopal conference, therefore more or less isolated Lercaro in the debates the group would go through. See for instance J. GROOTAERS, *Von Johannes XXIII zu Johannes Paul II: Ein Gespräch mit Leo Joseph Kardinal Suenens*, in *Herder Korrespondenz* 34 (1980) 179. Suenens notes that: "Als Kardinal Lercaro ... zum vierten Moderator ernannt wurde, geschah das sicher nicht aus Gefälligkeit gegenüber der italienischen Bischofskonferenz. Der Erzbischof von Bologna war ein zu fortschrittlicher Mann, um als Repräsentant der damaligen Bischofskonferenz gelten zu können". See also RICCARDI, *The Tumultuous Opening Days* (n. 9), p. 37.

53. Cf. RICCARDI, *The Tumultuous Opening Days* (n. 9), p. 43. The vice-presidents named by Larraona were cardinal Giobbe and monsignor Jullien. Larraona also replaced the secretary of the Preparatory Commission on Liturgy, being A. Bugnini, by F. Antonelli OFM, member of the Vatican Congregation of Rites. See M. LAMBERIGTS, *The Liturgy Debate*, in ALBERIGO – KOMONCHAK (eds.), *History of Vatican II*. Vol. II (n. 9), 107-166, esp. pp. 107-108; A. BUGNINI, *The Reform of the Liturgy (1948-1970)*, trans. M.J. O'Connell, Collegeville, MN, Liturgical, 1990, p. 30; M. PAIANO, *Les travaux de la commission liturgique conciliaire*, in M. LAMBERIGTS – C. SOETENS – J. GROOTAERS (eds.), *Les commissions conciliaires à Vatican II* (Instrumenta Theologica, 18), Leuven, Library of the Faculty of Theology, 1996, 1-26, esp. pp. 5-8.

54. Some other known members of the commission were monsignor Bekkers of the Dutch diocese of Den Bosch, monsignor Calewaert of the Belgian diocese of Ghent, and monsignor Malula, auxiliary bishop of Léopoldville (later Kinshasa, the capital of Belgian's former colony Congo. For the complete listings, see editions one and two of the handbook *Commissioni Conciliari*, edited by the General Secretariate of the Council. A complete listing of the subcommissions is given in LAMBERIGTS, *The Liturgy Debate* (n. 54), p. 132, n. 183.

55. *Acta Synodalia*, I/1, pp. 311-313, and I/2, pp. 56-58.

named *Jésus, l'Église et les pauvres*, also known as 'The Church of the Poor', and was led by father Gauthier, a former French major seminary professor and worker priest, and was supported, among others, by the Belgian monsignor Himmer, bishop of Tournai. The group wanted to create a sensibility among Council fathers for the relationship between Church, Gospel and poverty: first of all, the Church and the Council should bring a message of hope to the poor in our world. Lercaro had to decline the invitation for practical reasons, but he delegated his personal secretary, father Guiseppe Dossetti. Given his spiritual and pastoral background, it was no surprise to find Lercaro taking interest in the group's program, leading to his famous intervention *in aula* on 'the Church of the Poor', pronounced on December 6, 1962[56]. By the end of the first session, December 1962, the debate had shifted towards the question of the direction the Council should take in the following session or sessions. Lercaro's intervention on the 'Church of the Poor' can be understood in this respect: while cardinals like Suenens and Montini, in their interventions, respectively on December 4 and 5, 1962, already had expressed the need to set for a Church-focused course – the Council should focus on the Church *ad intra* and *ad extra* and revise its program in this respect – [57], Lercaro referred to the essential part evangelical poverty plays in this context. The Church should therefore especially pay attention to the Gospel's message to the poor[58]. One of the indirect and important results of his intervention, was the credit and trust Lercaro gained among fathers from young, missionary, and third world churches[59].

During the first intersession, while Suenens took part in the Coordinating Commission's activities, cardinal Lercaro remained active – as far

---

56. See G. RUGGIERI, *Beyond an Ecclesiology of Polemics: The Debate on the Church*, in ALBERIGO – KOMONCHAK (eds.), *History of Vatican II*. Vol. II (n. 9), 281-357, p. 345, n. 150. Early December 1962, the preparatory text on the Church (*De ecclesia*) was discussed by the fathers. A number of fathers grasped the opportunity not only to discard the presented text (as did monsignor De Smedt of Bruges in very strong wordings), but also to present more elaborate and consistent conciliar programs focused on ecclesiology. Among them the cardinals Montini, Döpfner, and Suenens (for the text of the latter's intervention, see *Acta Synodalia*, I/4, pp. 222-227).

57. GROOTAERS, *The Drama Continues* (n. 33), p. 504.

58. See RUGGIERI, *Beyond an Ecclesiology of Polemics* (n. 56), pp. 281-357, p. 345, n. 147.

59. It was certainly not coincidentally that the majority of the "Church of the Poor" group belonged to these missionary and third world churches, especially from South America. See L. PELLETIER, *Une marginalité engagée: Le groupe 'Jésus, l'Église et les pauvres'*, in LAMBERIGTS – SOETENS – GROOTAERS (eds.), *Les commissions conciliaires* (n. 53), 63-89, and H. RAGUER, *An Initial Profile of the Assembly*, in ALBERIGO – KOMONCHAK (eds.), *History of Vatican II*. Vol. II (n. 9), 167-232, esp. pp. 200-203.

as possible – in his subcommittee of the Commission for liturgy[60]. Following the election of cardinal Montini as pope Paul VI, cardinal Lercaro was added to the Coordinating Commission[61]. It was here he would begin cooperating with cardinal Suenens, and that his direct influence on the Council increased significantly, not in the least because of his longstanding relationship with the former cardinal archbishop of Milan, Montini.

3. Suenens and Lercaro Cooperate: The *Moderatores* and the Secretary

Following his election, pope Paul VI clearly expressed the intention to proceed with the Council[62] and to establish a new institution, an organisational level that would enhance significantly the working of the Council. Paul VI had been thinking of creating two *legati*, who would function as direct intermediaries between the conciliar *aula* and the pope himself, and who would be granted the necessary authority to preside over the debates *in aula*[63]. Two *legati* became four *moderatores*: the cardinals Suenens, Döpfner and Lercaro belonging to the so-called majority, and cardinal Agagianian, head of the *Propaganda fide*, who was considered to belong to the Curial party.

---

60. GROOTAERS, *The Drama Continues* (n. 33), p. 505.
61. *Ibid.*, p. 510. On the election and the relation between Montini and Lercaro in this respect, see A. MELLONI, *The Beginning of the Second Period: The Great Debate on the Church*, in ALBERIGO – KOMONCHAK (eds.), *History of Vatican II*. Vol. III: *The Mature Council: Second Period and Intersession, September 1963-September 1964*, Maryknoll, NY, Orbis; Leuven, Peeters, 2000, 1-115, esp. pp. 1-3.
62. GROOTAERS, *The Drama Continues* (n. 33), pp. 506-507.
63. Initially, Paul VI wanted only one *legatus* in the Conciliar aula. A papal legate would be granted sufficient authority over Curial bodies to act as intermediary between the pope and the fathers. Soon however it seemed impossible to ignore the unofficial division among the Conciliar fathers (minority vs. majority), so Paul VI planned to appoint two *legati*, one of them being cardinal Suenens. Canonists pointed out that according to canon law it was impossible to appoint a papal legate 'inside' Rome – thus referring to their task as high rank papal diplomats outside Rome. Therefore, the idea switched towards an administrative level directly controlling the Conciliar course and working. Derived from the Latin word *moderamen* (person who is steering, controlling), the candidates became *moderatores*. At first Suenens and Agagianian (as a representative of the Curial party) were appointed, but soon Paul VI added the cardinals Döpfner and Lercaro to the list. Their names were no surprise: Suenens, Döpfner and Lercaro had, just like Montini, pronounced a clear vision on the future of the Council. Besides, Lercaro had not only been an old friend inside the Italian episcopal conference, but also one of the most important Italian candidates for the papacy during the 1963 conclave. It was however to a certain extent unfortunately that Paul VI neglected to provide a set of regulations for the *moderatores*. Ultimately, this would lead to severe difficulties for the new body and finally to its unability to establish its own position and authority between the already existing institutions either controlling or setting out the course of the Council. After the second

Concerning Suenens intentions with regard to the *schema De ecclesia*, both Lercaro and Döpfner stood on the same ground, and even Agagian-ian, who was considered to be a conservative, cooperated rather easily with the others. Contacts between Lercaro and Suenens, albeit indirectly, had already been established during the first session. Both cardinals would keep up with current ecclesiastical affairs and events – outside the work-ing of the college of *moderatores* – through the person of father Dos-setti, Lercaro's personal secretary, and his ambassador at the meeting of the so-called 'Church of the Poor' group at the Belgian College. Before being ordained to the priesthood, Dossetti had been a high-ranking mem-ber of the *Democrazia Cristiana*, the Italian Christian-Democratic party. He was trained as a lawyer and a canonist, and had played an important role in the draft of the Italian republic's post-war constitution. Dossetti was a brilliant, independent mind, well versed both in legal matters and in theology. He combined extensive knowledge with a longstanding polit-ical experience[64]. Suenens appealed to Dossetti on a regular basis. Dos-setti's experience and knowledge were invoked for various subjects, of which his propositions for a set of regulations for the *moderatores*, and the so-called *ordo Concilii* were the most important ones[65]. It was also Dossetti who proposed to Suenens a solution to end the stalemate the Council got stuck in by the end of the first session and during the first intersession. Following manoeuvres by the Doctrinal Commission, headed

intersession, the four *moderatores* would therefore loose much of their initial authority among the fathers. See GROOTAERS, *The Drama Continues* (n. 33), pp. 508-513.

64. Giuseppe Dossetti was born in Genua in 1913, in a catholic middle class family. His father was a farmacist. Dossetti studied Law and Canon Law in Bologna and Milan, taught canon law and was active in the resistance during the war. Directly after World War II, he was involved in the drafting process of the new Italian constitution. Dossetti became a highly esteemed member of *Democrazia Cristiana*, for which he seated in Parliament for several years. He also was elected a member of the Bologna city council (as an independent member). In 1956 he expressed the wish to become a priest. In 1959, cardinal Lercaro ordained Dossetti, and named him his personal secretary. In the meantime, Dossetti had shown interest in various forms of monastic life, leading to the foundation of a community in Monteveglio (near Bologna). During the Council, Dossetti first functioned as a private *peritus* of cardinal Lercaro, later he became secretary (unofficially) to the four *modera-tores* but was removed from this office under pressure of monsignor Felici.
See A. MELLONI, *Cronologia e bibliografia di Giuseppe Dossetti*, in A. ALBERIGO – G. ALBERIGO (eds.), *'Con tutte le tue forze': I nodi della fede cristiana oggi. Omaggio a Giuseppe Dossetti*, Genua, Marietti, 1993, 371-389.

65. A number of letters, propositions, drafts of propositions, etc. are kept in Meche-len, in the conciliar archives of Suenens. See for instance: Fund Suenens 607.618, letters by Dossetti on the necessity to establish the CC. Fund Suenens 792-800, letters and notes by Dossetti and Suenens on the need for a set of rules organising the working of the four *moderatores*; and Fund Suenens 929-944: letters and notes of Dossetti, Lercaro and Sue-nens on the so-called *ordo Concilii*.

by cardinal Ottaviani, to delay possible progress concerning the *De eccle-sia*, the *moderatores* looked for a way to overcome Ottaviani's actions. Dossetti proposed to bring forward several concise propositions, presenting the direction the debate on the *De ecclesia* should take. The vote of the fathers would therefore only give an indication, the contents were to be discussed later[66].

It was not only the fact that Lercaro was well acquainted with Montini, that had him named in the CC and one of the *moderatores* on the brink of the second session. Lercaro's conciliar activities also fitted in the original intention for the Council as expressed by John XXIII, as he – and Suenens – had expressed in his intervention on *De ecclesia* by the end of 1962. It comes therefore hardly as a surprise that – in spite of differences on the theological level – both eminencies co-operated rather well during the rest of the Council.

V. Concluding Comparison: On the Influence Exerted

In spite of the fact that every comparison falls short, comparing (some of) the conciliar activities of both cardinals, as well as their respective biographical notes, does reveal information in light of the question of the influence exerted by the Belgian participants, *in casu* cardinal Suenens, at Vatican II, and on their cooperation.

First of all, both cardinals shared some correspondances. Suenens and Lercaro reacted more or less similarly to the announcement of the Council. At first rather sceptic, they soon grasped the special opportunity the event would present for their respective dioceses and for the universal Church. Suenens' Lenten pastoral letter of February 18, 1962, clearly demonstrates this shift: Suenens calls upon the faithful not only to pray, but also to make the Council 'our Council'[67], and to familiarise with it. The same goes for the (pastoral) initiatives Lercaro organised in the archdiocese of Bologna[68].

Once the Council was well on its way, both cardinals were clearly 'present' in the debates as well as in its management, though Lercaro seemed to have taken his time to grow into the Council, or was given time to do

---

66. For a full text of the propositions, see among others G. PHILIPS, *Die Geschichte der dogmatische Konstitution über die Kirche 'Lumen Gentium'*, in *LTK*, Freiburg, Herder, ²1967, p. 144.

67. "An outsider discusses the Council as something happening far away. You won't: because it is our Council, it is yours and it is mine" (my translation). *Het Tweede Œkumenisch Vatikaans Concilie*, c. 259.

68. Cf. note 51.

so. In December 1962, both cardinals pronounced noted interventions on the ecclesiastical course the Council should take following the first session. Suenens became member of the CC, controlling the very conciliar process, Lercaro was soon added to the list. Both Suenens and Lercaro became *moderatores*, which was, at least in its early stages, one of the most influential positions in the conciliar context. Both cardinals were highly respected by a large majority of the Council fathers, and had a good relation with the respective popes, John XXIII (especially Suenens) and Paul VI (especially Lercaro).

But there were differences too. Looking from the angle of 'results', being the input made by both fathers and its impact, there were clear differences between Suenens and Lercaro, and yet in a sense, they can be seen as complementary as well.

When describing the role Suenens played at Vatican II, he almost invariably has been characterised as an 'excellent tactician'[69]. Throughout the entire Council, Suenens managed to implement what he understood to be the essence and most important task of the Council: the ecclesiological debate on the Church *ad intra* and *ad extra*. From his initial activities to steer the conciliar agenda from the preparatory phase onwards to his efforts to have *Schema XIII* thoroughly discussed in a fourth session, every step taken by Suenens can be seen in light of his initial concept of how the Council should proceed. To explain Suenens' success in doing so, one cannot but refer to Suenens' biography, as J. Grootaers mentions in *Actes et acteurs*, while referring to Suenens' war years[70]. Behind his diplomatic attitude and managerial qualities, however, a profoundly pastoral concern was hidden. For Suenens Vatican II essentially treated a pastoral problem: the 're-activation' of so-called christians in name only, so they become an active, responsible and committed community again in the context of our modern world[71].

---

69. See for instance GROOTAERS, *Actes et acteurs* (n. 1), p. 318, analysing Suenens' analytical, intuitive and audacious style: "Les qualités politiques ... qui vont caractériser l'action conciliaire de l'archevêque belge sont déjà bien visibles. Il s'agit de cette aptitude à contribuer à la cristallisation de courants d'idées, à analyser avec lucidité des incidents imprévus et à y réagir rapidement avec sang-froid et avec intuition. ... Suenens à été l'homme de l'audace, qui exprimait avec clarté ce que les autres sentaient confusément et n'osaient pas dire".

70. GROOTAERS, *Actes et acteurs* (n. 1), p. 324: "Ce propos [that Suenens would make an excellent diplomate], ..., révèle en tout cas que le jeune Suenens possédait déjà alors des qualités de souplesse, de 'prudence' ... mais aussi de lucidité et de réalisme. Ce sont précisément ces qualités qui ont fait de lui une des personnalités dirigeantes du dernier concile général".

71. See GROOTAERS, *Von Johannes XXIII zu Johannes Paul II* (n. 52), p. 180. Also quoted in ID., *Actes et acteurs* (n. 1), 324-325.

A comparable pastoral concern marked Lercaro's contributions, perhaps even more outspoken than Suenens', but at the same time, Lercaro saw the Council in a different light. According to Lercaro's secretary and *peritus* Dossetti, he considered the Council to be of a spiritual-charismatic and even liturgical (in its theological sense) nature[72]. This becomes clear when looking at some of Lercaro's major interventions: on the Church of the Poor, and in his unconditional rejection and condemnation of war and his commitment to peace in the discussion on *Schema XIII*. Here also, Lercaro's personal, and especially pastoral biography explains why, on several occasions, driven by his spiritual conception of the Council, he searched for, what G. Alberigo has called, "the most advanced frontier of the majority"[73], often leading to an isolated position, playing the part of "una minoranza nel seno della maggioranza conciliare"[74]. Lercaro's propositions (and through him of Dossetti), managed to emotionally 'hit' the assembled fathers, but the direct result of this attitude was the final rejection of most of his ideas throughout the Council[75].

Yet one can easily imagine the compatibility of both cardinals with regard to the conciliar evolutions, as the second session has made clear. When Lercaro and Suenens were appointed *moderatores*, a more evangelical and even utopical point of view and way of reading the events, joined with a practical orientation of a diplomatic tactician, resulting in a strong but healthy influence exerted on the assembly and the agenda of the Council. In terms of results, however, it was most of all Suenens' who took 'profit' from this cooperation with Lercaro.

Faculty of Theology   Dirk CLAES
St.-Michielsstraat 6
B-3000 Leuven
Belgium

---

72. G. DOSSETTI, *Memoria di Giacomo Lercaro*, in G. ALBERIGO (ed.), *Chiese italiane e Concilio*, Genua, Marietti, 1988, 300-304. Quoted in J. Grootaers' contribution on Philips and Dossetti, paragraph four, *la conception du Concile de Dossetti*.

73. G. ALBERIGO, *Giuseppe Dossetti*, Bologna, s.n., 1998, p. 67. Quoted in J. Grootaers' contribution on Philips and Dossetti, paragraph four, *la conception du Concile de Dossetti*.

74. LERCARO – ALBERIGO (eds.), *Per la forza* (n. 25), p. 59.

75. See the contribution of J. Grootaers on Philips and Dossetti, paragraph four.

L.-J. SUENENS, G. LERCARO E G. DOSSETTI

Nel settembre 1959 mons. Suenens, allora vescovo ausiliare di Malines, fece visita al card. Lercaro per rendersi conto di persona delle sue iniziative pastorali a Bologna, città caratterizzata da una forte presenza operaia ed egemonizzata dai partiti comunista e socialista. Le iniziative di Lercaro per riconquistare la città alla fede erano state in qualche caso clamorose e avevano avuto una certa eco non solo in Italia ma anche all'estero[1].

Di questa visita non sappiamo molto. Probabilmente fu la prima volta che i due vescovi ebbero modo di incontrarsi e conoscersi un po' più a fondo. Non sappiamo se tra di loro abbiano scambiato qualche impressione sull'iniziativa che il nuovo pontefice aveva annunciato qualche mese prima di convocare un concilio ecumenico. Se lo fecero dovette essere comunque in termini assai generali. Il concilio era allora un progetto piuttosto lontano e ancora assai vago. Giovanni XXIII ne aveva avviato la preparazione durante l'estate ma ancora non era ben chiaro a nessuno cosa sarebbe stato. La Commissione antepreparatoria aveva chiesto a tutti i vescovi di mandare a Roma le loro opinioni suggerendo i temi di cui a loro avviso il concilio avrebbe dovuto occuparsi. Né Suenens né Lercaro lo avevano ancora fatto e non si può dire quanto il loro incontro abbia poi influenzato le loro risposte[2]. Certo è che il concilio sarebbe stata l'occasione per conoscersi meglio e per collaborare attivamente al profondo rinnovamento che si stava attuando nella chiesa.

Lercaro era, sotto molti punti di vista, una figura tipica dell'episcopato italiano creato da Pio XII[3]. Era giunto a Bologna nel 1952, dopo essere

---

1. Il "Bollettino dell'Archidiocesi di Bologna" accenna assai rapidamente a questa visita, dicendo che Suenens era stato ospite di Lercaro "per una visita alle opere della Chiesa bolognese" 5 (1959) 481; vedi poi un riferimento in G. BATTELLI (ed.), *Giacomo Lercaro: Lettere dal concilio, 1962-1965*, Bologna, Dehoniane, 1980, 111, n. 3. I ragazzi di Villa San Giacomo, che abitavano con il cardinale bolognese, si ricordavano ancora qualche anno dopo del vescovo belga: "quello che diceva che oggi non ci si muove per vedere dei monumenti, ma per incontrare uomini", *ibid.*, p. 110.

2. Lercaro avrebbe inviato il *votum* antepreparatorio il 10 ottobre, Suenens il 10 novembre 1959: vedi *AD* I/2.3, pp. 114-118 e vol. 2.1, pp. 140-148.

3. Era nato a Genova nel 1891 e aveva ricevuto una formazione ecclesiastica di tipo tradizionale. Era entrato in seminario a undici anni ed era stato ordinato nel 1914. A Genova aveva insegnato filosofia e sacra scrittura in seminario, aveva svolto attività apostolica tra gli studenti, ma aveva dato un contributo importante anche all'apostolato liturgico e all'apostolato del mare. Nel 1947 era stato consacrato vescovo e gli era stata

stato cinque anni nella vicina sede di Ravenna, dove si era messo in luce
per l'energica azione pastorale contro le organizzazioni di sinistra. Alla
morte del vescovo di Bologna, l'anziano card. Nasalli Rocca, Pio XII lo
aveva ritenuto il più adatto a guidare quella diocesi. Si trattava di una diocesi importante, ma molto problematica perché dalla fine della seconda
guerra mondiale la città era dominata dal Partito Comunista. La modernizzazione del tessuto sociale si era accompagnata ad un forte flusso
immigratorio dalle campagne vicine e ad un processo di accelerata secolarizzazione dei costumi. Impiegati per lo più nelle piccole industrie della
periferia urbana i nuovi venuti subivano una inevitabile attrazione nei
confronti delle organizzazioni sindacali e associative di sinistra.

Lercaro era ben consapevole della situazione: i fedeli avevano progressivamente abbandonato la pratica religiosa, gli spazi che la chiesa
ave avuto in città e nelle campagne si erano ristretti, la presenza delle
associazioni cattoliche era diminuita[4]. Per contrastare questi processi
aveva intrapreso da un lato energiche azioni contro l'egemonia della presenza comunista, dall'altra aveva avviato un profondo rinnovamento
pastorale e spirituale della vita religiosa. Strumento privilegiato la liturgia,
che doveva rinnovarsi profondamente nelle sue forme e nei suoi contenuti. Convinto sostenitore sin dagli anni di formazione dell'importanza
dell'apostolato liturgico, Lercaro riteneva che tra le cause dell'allontanamento delle classi popolari dalla chiesa si dovesse considerare anche una
liturgia disincarnata dalla vita degli uomini, per lo più incomprensibile alla
gente semplice con il suo latino e con i suoi riti del passato. Rifacendosi a
quanto andavano sostenendo molti esponenti del movimento liturgico
Lercaro riteneva che una liturgia viva e partecipata avrebbe reso più salda
la vita spirituale dei fedeli e della comunità diocesana, rinforzando anche
l'attività di apostolato[5].

assegnata la diocesi di Ravenna, cinque anni dopo venne trasferito a Bologna: su Lercaro
vedi i saggi raccolti nel volume a cura di A. ALBERIGO, *Giacomo Lercaro: Vescovo della
chiesa di Dio (1891-1976)* (Testi e richerche di scienze religiose. Nuova Serie, 6), Genova,
Marietti, 1991 (in particolare i due saggi biografici di G. BATTELLI, *Da Genova a Ravenna
(1891-1952)* e *Scelte pastorali e linee di governo (1952-1968)*; vedi anche AA.VV.,
L'eredità pastorale di Giacomo Lercaro: Studi e testimonianze, Bologna, Dehoniane,
1992; per il periodo genovese N. BUONASORTE (ed.), *Giacomo Lercaro: Contributo alla
conoscenza del periodo genovese (1891-1947)*, in *Cristianesimo nella Storia* 20 (1991)
91-145.
    4. Cfr. G. ALBERIGO, *Un vescovo e un popolo*, in N. BUONASORTE (ed.), *Araldo del
vangelo: Studi sull'episcopato e sull'archivio di Giacomo Lercaro a Bologna 1952-1968*,
Bologna, Il Mulino, 2004, 103-132; e A. VARNI, *La città e il vescovo*, in BUONASORTE
(ed.), *Araldo del vangelo*, 133-143.
    5. Nel 1955 era uscito il direttorio liturgico *A Messa figlioli!* (Bologna, UTOA 1955),
che aveva incontrato qualche difficoltà di attuazione nella diocesi, ma aveva suscitato un

Questo impegno e queste strategie suscitavano un particolare interesse in mons. Suenens. Questi, più giovane di Lercaro di tredici anni, era giunto all'episcopato un paio d'anni prima di lui, come ausiliare del card. J.E. van Roey nella prestigiosa sede di Malines-Bruxelles. Nel 1961 gli sarebbe successo come ordinario. Gli studi compiuti a Leuven, uno dei centri europei più importanti per le scienze teologiche e religiose, gli avevano consentito una formazione aperta al dibattito teologico internazionale e i suoi frequenti viaggi in tutta Europa lo avevano messo in contatto con esperienze pastorali diverse[6]. Per altro verso l'impegno pastorale nella diocesi gli aveva fatto maturare idee chiare riguardo ai bisogni più urgenti della chiesa e alle sfide che venivano dal mondo moderno. Le esperienze francesi degli anni quaranta e cinquanta lo avevano profondamente colpito, facendogli percepire l'urgenza del problema della secolarizzazione delle masse operaie nelle grandi città e convincendolo della scarsa efficacia dei tradizionali metodi di apostolato. Occorreva un nuovo slancio missionario, capace di portare con rinnovato vigore il vangelo a tutti. Nel suo volume *L'Église en état de mission*, pubblicato nel 1955, si richiamava esplicitamente, anche nel titolo, alle esperienze francesi del card. Suharde del card. Feltin[7]. In epigrafe al volume aveva messo le parole di quest'ultimo secondo cui "c'est l'Église tout entière qui doit se mettre en état de mission". Era un preciso programma di azione: "Ces paroles vont loin. Il faut les prendre au pied de la lettre: elles équivalent a un ordre de marche. À chacun, prêtre, religieux, laïc, de les reprendre a son compte et d'en tirer les conclusions. Elles obligent à reviser notre conception de l'apostolat, à tous les échelons". Imponevano un esame di coscienza sia ai singoli che alle istituzioni e chiedevano di rivedere le vecchie forme di apostolato: "Elles posent un problème d'organisation, de 'mise en état'. Elles nous redisent, sans détour, que l'Église d'ici-bas est, plus que jamais, une Église militante"[8].

---

vivo interesse negli ambienti del movimento liturgico internazionale: Cfr. G. BATTELLI, *La dimensione internazionale dell'episcopato bolognese di G. Lercaro*, in Istrumenti per la storia della chiesa di Bologna, *La chiesa di Bologna e la cultura europea*, Bologna, Barghigiani, 2002, 255-299; e M. PAIANO, *Liturgia e società nel Novecento: Percorsi del movimento liturgico di fronte ai processi di secolarizzazione* (Biblioteca di Storia sociale, 28), Roma, Edizioni di Storia e Letteratura, 2000, 292-303.

6. Vedi in generale il libro di memorie L.-J. SUENENS, *Souvenirs et espérances*, Paris, Fayard, 1991, 11-51.

7. L.-J. SUENENS, *L'Église en état de mission*, Paris, Desclée de Brouwer, 1955. Vedi un accenno autobiografico a questo libro in SUENENS, *Souvenirs et espérances* (n. 6), p. 44.

8. SUENENS, *L'Église en état de mission* (n. 7), p. 9.

La necessità di un rinnovamento dell'apostolato, di una riorganizzazione delle forze e dei metodi costituiva la prospettiva lungo la quale
secondo Suenens il concilio avrebbe dovuto lavorare. Era l'occasione
per quel radicale rinnovamento della chiesa, per metterla "en état de
mission", a partire dall'esame di coscienza dei vescovi rispetto al mandato di evangelizzare. La riforma interna della chiesa era funzionale a
questo rinnovato slancio missionario ed apostolico nei confronti del
mondo.

Questa convinzione era in fondo ciò che accomunava di più Suenens
a Lercaro. Nonostante la diversità della loro formazione spirituale e pastorale, le aspettative finirono per convergere. I loro ruoli in concilio erano
inizialmente diversi, ma i loro progetti si sono incontrati intorno ad alcuni
punti fondamentali per rispondere all'esigenza di rinnovamento della
chiesa e alla sfida che il mondo moderno le proponeva in modo sempre
più urgente.

I. Rappresentazioni del Concilio: il "Piano Suenens"

Nel *votum* che Suenens scrisse prima della preparazione del concilio
non emergeva ancora con chiarezza la linea di rinnovamento della chiesa
che sarebbe poi maturata nelle sue riflessioni[9]. Tra le richieste avanzate a
Roma prevalevano questioni di ordine disciplinare: i poteri e le facoltà
dei vescovi, l'età di somministrazione della cresima, l'obbligo della recita
del breviario o l'introduzione del clergyman per i sacerdoti, la formazione
nei seminari, l'istituzione del diaconato permanente[10]. Era un'immagine
del concilio ancora abbastanza frammentaria, molto condizionata dai temi
della pastorale ordinaria.

Ma al momento di scrivere la prima lettera pastorale come arcivescovo
di Malines, nel marzo 1962, la sua riflessione si nostro più articolata e
teologicamente fondata. Il concilio avrebbe riunito vescovi provenienti da
tutti i continenti per discutere i problemi della chiesa e del mondo e
sarebbe stato certo un evento di portata storica. Non poteva essere para-
gonato ad un organismo internazionale di tipo politico, perché la sua
natura era spirituale e misterica: sarebbe stato un mistero di fede in quanto
incontro con la grazia divina, un mistero di speranza perché tra i suoi

9. Sulla partecipazione di Suenens al concilio vedi l'efficace sintesi di J. GROOTAERS, *I protagonisti del Vaticano II*, Cinisello Balsamo, San Paolo, 1994, pp. 229-243.
10. *AD* I/2.1, pp. 140-148.

scopi c'era quello di avvicinare la salvezza cristiana al mondo, un mistero di carità perché si sarebbe rivolto ai bisogni di tutti gli uomini: "acte de charité aussi envers le monde, le Concile s'efforcera d'aider les hommes a retrouver le sens de la véritable fraternité humaine qui a sa source dans leur commune qualité de fils de Dieu et de frères du Christ"[11]. Era in questo ambito che esso avrebbe affrontato più direttamente i problemi del mondo moderno: le tensioni che a tutti i livelli travolgevano gli uomini, la divisione in classi sociali, la pace, la minaccia delle armi nucleari, la fame, l'ingiusta ripartizione delle ricchezze nel mondo[12]. Soprattutto, il concilio avrebbe dovuto portare direttamente o indirettamente una risposta positiva e costruttiva al comunismo, che dominava un terzo dell'umanità e soffocava l'uomo nella misura in cui era la negazione di Dio. Come aveva detto Giovanni XXIII si trattava di mettere in contatto il mondo moderno con le energie vivificanti del vangelo: "l'enjeu du Concile n'est donc rien moins que l'évangélisation et, par contrecoup, le salut du monde"[13].

Quando, in seguito alla positiva impressione ricevuta da questa lettera, Giovanni XXIII gli chiese di preparare un piano per lo svolgimento del concilio, Suenens ebbe modo di esprimere in termini più precisi cosa a suo avviso esso doveva essere, quali erano i suoi compiti e le sue priorità. L'agenda dei lavori che risultava dagli schemi preparatori gli appariva del tutto inadeguata: se il concilio si fosse fermato alle questioni particolari di disciplina canonica o di rilievo solo locale che dominavano quegli schemi avrebbe fallito il suo scopo fondamentale. Nella prima

11. L.-J. SUENENS, *Qu'attendez-vous du concile?*, Bruxelles, 1962: nella prima parte Suenens sottolineava che il concilio non sarebbe stato paragonabile né ad un parlamento, né ad un congresso internazionale sul modello dell'ONU, che non avrebbe segnato vere rotture rispetto alla tradizione: erano elementi significativi per comprendere a quale ordine di grandezza egli si riferisse pensando al concilio.

12. In particolare nella lettera si diceva: "La mission de l'Église et du Concile sera de souligner tout ce qui unit, par-delà ce qui sépare, et d'aider à résoudre, pour sa part et dans son domaine, les problèmes angoissants que pose la paix internationale, la terrible menace de la bombe atomique qui met le monde à la merci d'une passion humaine incontrôlée, la misère des masses sous-alimentées, misère due à l'inégalité flagrante dans la répartition des richesses et des biens".

13. Suenens ricavava alcuni di questi concetti dalla costituzione apostolica *Humanae salutis* di Giovanni XXIII, dove si diceva tra l'altro: "Il prossimo Concilio dunque si celebra felicemente in un momento in cui la Chiesa avverte più vivo il desiderio di irrobustire la sua fede con forze nuove e di rimirarsi nella stupenda immagine della propria unità; come pure sente più pressantemente di essere vincolata dal dovere non solo di rendere più efficace la sua salutare energia e promuovere la santità dei suoi figli, ma anche di portare incremento alla diffusione della verità cristiana e al miglioramento delle sue strutture". Cf. *AAS* 54 (1962) 5-13.

nota, inviata a Roma nel marzo 1962, Suenens sottolineava la necessità di concentrare il lavoro su alcuni temi più importanti e di prevedere condizioni efficaci di lavoro: occorreva un organo direttivo ristretto capace di dirigere l'assemblea e le commissioni per portare avanti la mole di lavoro previsto. Sarebbe stato utile pensare anche a delle commissioni post-conciliari per attuare concretamente le decisioni prese[14]. La pianificazione del lavoro, l'organizzazione dei temi da trattare, la capacità di prendere decisioni, l'efficacia concreta di quanto stabilito erano preoccupazioni caratteristiche dell'impegno di Suenens e della sua visione del concilio.

Durante l'estate 1962 su invito dello stesso pontefice, si incontrò con alcuni cardinali per mettere a punto il suo progetto. Incontrò anche Lercaro, che tuttavia ebbe un ruolo solo marginale in questa fase[15]. Suenens dovette probabilmente superare qualche scetticismo da parte di Döpfner, secondo il quale sarebbe stato meglio lasciare del tutto liberi i padri conciliari di organizzare l'agenda dei propri lavori, ma incontrò l'appoggio di Montini, anch'egli preoccupato per la dispersione dei temi preconizzata dagli schemi preparatori[16].

Il progetto venne messo a punto nel corso dei mesi successivi. La preoccupazione di sistematicità e di funzionalità si esprimeva con l'articolazione delle materie nelle due sezioni dell'attività 'ad intra' e 'ad extra'[17]. In tutto il progetto dominava la prospettiva di un rinnovamento dell'apostolato e della necessità di un nuovo slancio missionario della chiesa. Il rinnovamento interno doveva ispirarsi al mandato evangelico "Euntes ergo, docete omnes gentes, baptizantes eos, in nomine Patris et Filii et Spiritus Sancti". La seconda parte, quella "ad extra" (riferita alla

---

14. Vedi SUENENS, *Souvenirs et espérances* (n. 6), pp. 66-69. In nome di una istanza di funzionalità Suenens suggeriva anche la possibilità di lavorare in modo decentrato, con commissioni che si riunissero in vari paesi. Sul 'piano Suenens' vedi L.-J. SUENENS, *Aux origines du Concile Vatican II*, in *Nouvelle Revue Théologique* 107 (1985) 3-21; e la *Testimonianza* dello stesso Suenens al colloquio dell'Istituto Paolo VI di Brescia del settembre 1983: *Giovanni Battista Montini, arcivescovo di Milano e il Concilio ecumenico Vaticano II: Preparazione e primo periodo. Colloquio internazionale di Studio a Milano 22-25 settembre 1983* (Pubblicazioni dell'Istituto Paolo VI, 3), Brescia, Istituto Paolo VI, 1985, pp. 178-187. Vedi anche J. KOMONCHAK, *La lotta per il concilio durante la preparazione*, in G. ALBERIGO (ed.), *Storia del concilio Vaticano II*, Leuven, Peeters; Bologna, Il Mulino, 1995-2001, Vol. I, 362-369.

15. Un accenno al coinvolgimento di Lercaro in SUENENS, *Souvenirs et espérances* (n. 6), p. 70, ma non ho trovato altri riscontri.

16. Sugli incontri tra i cardinali SUENENS, *Souvenirs et espérances* (n. 6), pp. 69-71; e KOMONCHAK, *La lotta per il concilio* (n. 14), p. 369.

17. Vedi il "Texte du plan proposé au pape Jean XXIII", in SUENENS, *Souvenirs et espérances* (n. 6), pp. 72-79.

seconda parte del medesimo passo evangelico "Docentes eos servare omnia quaecumque mandavi vobis"), si sarebbe articolata intorno a quattro temi tradizionali nella dottrina sociale, quelli della famiglia, dell'economia, della società civile, della società internazionale. Paradossalmente sarebbe stata questa la parte più dottrinale[18].

Questo progetto ebbe una particolare rilevanza soprattutto nel primo periodo conciliare quando Suenens divenne un punto di riferimento importante per quei vescovi che riconoscevano l'insufficienza degli schemi preparatori e del progetto di concilio che essi esprimevano. In una situazione in cui la procedura stabilita dal Regolamento appariva a tutti inefficace il vero organo direttivo del concilio divenne il "Segretariato per gli affari extra ordinem", all'interno del quale Suenens propose e portò avanti il suo piano per il concilio. Sua fu l'iniziativa di preparare uno schema alternativo al *De ecclesia*, di cui affidò l'elaborazione a G. Philips, accanto agli schemi che si andavano elaborando tra i teologi tedeschi su altri ambiti tematici[19]. Suenens aveva un rapporto privilegiato con Giovanni XXIII. Al momento del suo intervento in aula sul *De ecclesia* fece avere una copia al pontefice, che la annotò di suo pugno. L'intervento proponeva davanti all'assemblea dei vescovi le linee fondamentali del suo piano, conosciute sino ad allora solo in un ambiente ristretto. E le stesse vennero riprese poco dopo dall'intervento del card. Montini, che le avallò con la sua autorità[20].

---

18. Così la 'idée maîtresse' del piano: "Tout naturellement, le Concile pourrait embrasser deux vastes secteurs: celui de l'Église ad intra; celui de l'Église ad extra. Le schéma proposé introduit l'examen de conscience collectif que les évêques veulent faire sur leur mission. La question fondamentale qui se pose à eux et qui pourrait être la question centrale de tout le concile, le carrefour d'où partent ses grandes avenues, pourrait être celle-ci: Comment l'Église du XXème siècle répond-elle à l'ordre ultime du Maître: – Euntes ergo, docete omnes gentes, baptizantes eos, in nomine Patris et Filii et Spiritus Sancti, docentes eos servare omnia quaecumque mandavi vobis. Ce qui conduit tout naturellement au plan suivant: Section A: Ecclesia ad intra: on pourrait prendre comme base de division le texte même de saint Matthieu qui vient d'être cité: – Euntes ergo: Ecclesia evangelizans (vel salvificans); – Docete omnes gentes: Ecclesia docens; – Baptizantes eos: Ecclesia sanctificans; – In nomine Patris et Filii et Spiritus Sancti: Ecclesia orans. Section B: Ecclesia ad extra: ici, on pourra grouper quelques grands problèmes que nous indiquerons plus loin et qui se situent facilement sous ces mots: 'docentes eos servare omnia quaecumque mandavi vobis'". Vedi, SUENENS, *Souvenirs et espérances* (n. 6), pp. 73-74.

19. G. RUGGIERI, *L'abbandono dell'ecclesiologia controversistica*, in ALBERIGO (ed.), *Storia del concilio Vaticano II* (n. 14), Vol. II, pp. 310-312 e le pp. 325-332.

20. Vedi AS I/4, pp. 222-227 (Suenens), pp. 291-294 (Montini). Il piano di Suenens, come è noto, fu molto importante quando alla fine della prima sessione del concilio si giunse ad una effettiva riorganizzazione dell'agenda.

II. RAPPRESENTAZIONI DEL CONCILIO: LE PROPOSTE DI LERCARO

Anche le attese di Lercaro prendevano le mosse dalla sua esperienza pastorale degli anni cinquanta[21]. Tuttavia esse apparivano inizialmente assai più incerte rispetto a quelle di Suenens. Il *votum* inviato a Roma nell'ottobre 1959 rivelava tutti i suoi dubbi. Nella prima parte era evidente la preoccupazione di corrispondere alle intenzioni del pontefice, sottolineando sia lo scopo pastorale che quello ecumenico del concilio: esso non avrebbe dovuto dirimere controversie teologiche o reprimere eresie e non avrebbe dovuto neppure condannare il comunismo perché già era stato condannato dai pontefici precedenti; ma avrebbe comunque affrontato questioni dottrinali importanti come quelle della libertà religiosa, delle relazioni della chiesa con gli stati, della laicità e dei moderni metodi critici nell'interpretazione della s. Scrittura, tutte questioni decisive rispetto allo scopo ecumenico proposto dal pontefice. Nella seconda parte erano proposti quegli argomenti di riforma interna sempre più necessari ad un efficace ministero pastorale, come per esempio la revisione dei benefici, la riforma dell'esenzione dei religiosi, l'abolizione dell'inamovibilità dei parroci, la definizione dei limiti di età per vescovi e clero, la ridistribuzione del clero e delle diocesi, i seminari. Ma i problemi più veri della chiesa derivavano dalla progressiva secolarizzazione della società e dal laicismo sempre più diffuso. Per questo Lercaro si aspettava dal concilio prima di tutto l'affermazione della riforma liturgica per favorire la partecipazione attiva dei fedeli alle celebrazioni eucaristiche, la promozione delle scuole cattoliche, una revisione dei precetti ecclesiastici per contrastare il "lassismo pratico" dei fedeli[22].

Nei mesi successivi divenne più chiara da parte di Lercaro la percezione del rinnovamento che il concilio avrebbe potuto innescare nella chiesa e nel mondo moderno. Il concilio avrebbe davvero potuto avviare l'auspicata riforma liturgica e avrebbe potuto affrontare quei temi che riguardavano le "particolarissime circostanze nelle quali in questo momento eccezionale". Il rinnovamento missionario, la questione sociale, il comunismo, la modernizzazione tecnologica, i problemi della vita interna della chiesa, il rinnovamento dei precetti, i "problemi morali, di

21. Per la partecipazione di Lercaro al concilio vedi G. ALBERIGO, *L'esperienza conciliare di un vescovo*, in G. LERCARO – G. ALBERIGO (eds.), *Per la forza dello Spirito: Discorsi conciliari del card. Giacomo Lercaro*, Bologna, Dehoniane, 1984, 9-62; e il ritratto proposto da GROOTAERS, *I protagonisti* (n. 9), pp. 157-170.
22. Vedi *AD* I/2.1, pp. 140-148. Vedi anche il testo in italiano in LERCARO – ALBERIGO (eds.), *Per la forza* (n. 21), pp. 65-70.

morale individuale, familiare, sociale, di particolare gravità" erano: temi
che avrebbe dovuto affrontare[23]. Sarebbe stato una risposta positiva agli
sviluppi materialistici del pensiero moderno, avrebbe affermato "il pri-
mato dello spirituale", muovendosi sia in favore dell'unità dei cristiani
sia nel senso di una profonda riforma interna della chiesa.

Si trattava solo di poche linee generali di indirizzo, non certo di un
progetto organico e neppure di un'immagine chiara del concilio. Lercaro
non aveva il senso progettuale e la visione sistematica di Suenens, ma
aveva una percezione molto precisa delle situazioni e delle linee di forza
che potevano scaturire dalle circostanze. Più che ad un progetto predefi-
nito da perseguire Lercaro orientò la sua azione ad alcuni obiettivi che di
volta in volta sembravano raggiungibili. Il concilio era l''occasione' concessa dallo Spirito per affermare certi principi e per avviare certe riforme
e doveva svilupparsi nella "docilità allo Spirito". Semmai si poneva il
problema del giusto "discernimento dell'azione dello spirito nelle com-
plesse vicende che vi si svolgevano e che lo determinavano.

Lercaro, a differenza di Suenens, non venne coinvolto nella preparazione e anche durante il primo periodo conciliare rimase ai margini delle
dinamiche decisive che si muovevano dietro le quinte. Occupato intensamente all'interno della commissione sulla liturgia, non ebbe notizie
se non con molto ritardo delle manovre messe in atto dagli episcopati
nord-europei per elaborare degli schemi alternativi. All'oscuro di tutto,
mantenne per tutto il primo periodo una visione piuttosto negativa del
concilio, ritenendo che fosse ancora dominato da forze conservatrici.
Egli aveva una diretta esperienza delle difficoltà procedurali all'interno
della commissione liturgica, il cui presidente, il card. Larraona, faceva
di tutto per ostacolare il rinnovamento proposto dallo schema. Ma difficoltà ancora più gravi erano venute in luce nell'andamento generale del

---

23. "In particolare alla chiesa non può sfuggire la mutata situazione dei continenti, che
fino a non molti anni or sono erano terra di colonizzazione, di missione e ove solo da poco
il clero indigeno, ancora insufficiente ai bisogni, ha preso la direzione delle comunità cattoliche. Come non può sfuggire alla chiesa il vasto anelito a migliori ordinamenti sociali,
non può sfuggire come mai è sfuggito, se già Leone XIII nel 1891 tracciava magistralmente
le vie della Sociologia cristiana. Non sfugge alla chiesa il grave fenomeno del comunismo;
non le può sfuggire, dacché tanta parte dei suoi figli ne risentono penosamente e per tanti
se ne paventa il pericolo. Ma non sfugge neppure alla chiesa, e non è sfuggito – chi non
ricorda i discorsi di Papa Pio XII? – l'importanza degli sviluppi tecnici che danno all'ordi-
namento della via sociale e individuale nuove condizioni, per le quali si stanno aprendo
orizzonti dei quali non si prevede l'estensione": così Lercaro in una lezione sul concilio
che tenne alla "Cittadella di Assisi", poi pubblicata in: G. LERCARO, *Il Concilio ecumenico Vaticano II*, in AA.VV., *Il Simbolo: Credo nella chiesa una*, Assisi, 1961, 242-255,
in particolare le pp. 253-254.

concilio, perché sembrava mancare una linea coerente di guida e anche un'autorità in grado di condurlo verso un obiettivo preciso.

III. RAPPRESENTAZIONI DEL CONCILIO: LE PREOCCUPAZIONI DI DOSSETTI

Alla maturazione di un'idea dinamica del concilio da parte di Lercaro contribuirono da un lato gli studi sulla storia dei concili compiuti dal 'Centro di documentazione' a Bologna, che gli permisero di acquisire una comprensione più approfondita della natura dei concili ecumenici e delle dinamiche che essi potevano mettere in movimento[24], dall'altro la collaborazione diretta di G. Dossetti, anch'egli pronto a cogliere nel concilio la grande occasione che lo Spirito concedeva alla chiesa per rinnovarsi. Dossetti aveva avuto, tra la fine degli anni quaranta e i primi anni cinquanta, significative esperienze politiche come vicesegretario della DC. All'interno dell'Assemblea Costituente era stato investito di importanti responsabilità per la stesura del testo della nuova costituzione italiana. Nel 1952 aveva lasciato l'impegno politico per dedicarsi all'attività di studio e di ricerca nell'ambito delle scienze religiose, convinto che questo fosse uno dei compiti urgenti non solo per la chiesa, ma anche per la società.

Lercaro lo chiamò a Roma come collaboratore nel corso del primo periodo del concilio, per seguire in particolare gli incontri del gruppo della 'chiesa dei poveri' organizzato da P. Gauthier, al quale era stato invitato, ma che non avrebbe potuto frequentare perché già intensamente impegnato nella commissione liturgica[25]. Dossetti visse il suo 'noviziato' al concilio in stretto contatto con Lercaro, rendendosi conto delle difficoltà procedurali che esso stava vivendo anche a causa delle ambiguità del Regolamento adottato per i lavori dell'assemblea. Si trattava infatti di

---

24. Poco prima dell'inizio del concilio era stata pubblicata la raccolta dei *Conciliorum Oecumenicorum Decreta*, a cura dell'Istituto per le Scienze Religiose, con la collaborazione di H. Jedin: cfr. G. ALBERIGO (ed.), *L'Officina Bolognese, 1953-2003*, Bologna, Dehoniane, 2004, pp. 43-48.

25. Per la partecipazione di Dossetti al concilio e per la sua collaborazione con Lercaro, vedi G. ALBERIGO, *Giuseppe Dossetti al concilio Vaticano II*, in G. ALBERIGO – G. RUGGIERI (eds.), *Per una 'chiesa eucaristica'*, Bologna, Il Mulino, 2002, 139-234; in particolare per il primo periodo, pp. 47-163. La collaborazione di Dossetti fu in effetti preziosa per Lercaro e così stretta da porre agli storici il non facile problema della dipendenza e dell'autonomia reciproca tra di loro durante il concilio. È noto che la maggior parte degli interventi conciliari di Lercaro furono preparati da Dossetti che ispirò anche alcune delle sue linee di azione. D'altra parte Dossetti ha sempre riconosciuto di agire su richiesta e indicazione del cardinale, al quale riconosceva un'obbedienza filiale. Certi ambiti di intervento, come quello liturgico, normalmente Lercaro se li riservava a sé.

norme che finivano per rafforzare gli schemi elaborati durante il periodo preparatorio, nonostante essi non avessero incontrato molto favore tra i padri conciliari.

Per questo, il problema più urgente era, a mio avviso, quello di una riforma del Regolamento e durante tutto il primo periodo cercò tenacemente di elaborare e proporre miglioramenti che potessero rendere più efficaci i lavori dell'assemblea, liberandoli dall'ipoteca degli schemi preparatori[26]. Inoltre, per evitare che una deriva conservatrice portasse il concilio su posizioni lontane da quelle enunciate nel discorso di apertura di Giovanni XXIII, occorreva a suo avviso chiarire in via preliminare quale dovesse essere lo spirito e lo scopo del concilio e ridisegnare l'agenda dei lavori sulla base di questi principi di fondo.

Nel *Promemoria per una dichiarazione orientativa*, preparato alla fine di novembre 1962 per il card. Lercaro e per altri cardinali sensibili a questi problemi, il concilio veniva considerato come un evento dello Spirito che si realizzava nel momento in cui i vescovi si riunivano[27]. Puntando il dito sul fallimento dei lavori preparatori Dossetti osservava che essi "in un certo senso *non potevano* riuscire, perché a rigore un *concilio non si prepara*. [...] Il Concilio si prepara quando incomincia la sua celebrazione, cioè quando il Papa e i Vescovi nell'atto della loro riunione *adsunt* allo Spirito, Signore e vivificante". Questo fallimento della preparazione poteva del resto essere considerato come una premessa provvidenziale a una più autentica riuscita del concilio, ma occorreva che il pontefice ne "chiarisse e concretasse" meglio il compito e l'agenda: "non è possibile che la mancanza di un'eresia definita da condannare, possa ancora lasciar credere che allora questo concilio deve occuparsi di tutto, di tutti i capitoli del dogma, di tutti i capitoli della morale, di tutte le istituzioni e di tutta la problematica storica del nostro tempo". Sarebbe stato sufficiente invece scegliere due o tre temi come quello della "chiesa e i poveri" e quello del rapporto tra "la chiesa e le nuove cristianità extra occidentali" e stabilire riguardo ad essi le linee dottrinali e i punti di riforma istituzionale. "Con questo – diceva il *Promemoria* – il concilio avrebbe più che esaurito il suo compito, o almeno la parte urgente e possibile del suo compito"[28].

26. Cfr. gli *Emendamenti urgenti all'Ordo concilii*, in Fondo Dossetti, 195, 414, 536 (presso l'archivio della FSCIRE di Bologna); cfr. G. ALBERIGO, *Dinamiche e procedure nel Vaticano II: Verso la revisione del Regolamento del concilio (1962-1963)*, in *Cristianesimo nella Storia* 13 (1992) 117-119.

27. *Pro-memoria per una dichiarazione orientativa*, in Fondo Alberigo, II/6 (Archivio FSCIRE), e Fondo Dossetti, 198a.

28. Secondo Dossetti si poteva eventualmente proporre di costituire un organo provvisorio post-conciliare di consultazione tra papa ed episcopato "allo scopo di mantenere accesa la fiamma e di insistere per l'effettiva e fedele esecuzione delle norme fissate".

Il presupposto di questa proposta minimalista era la percezione che la
coscienza conciliare non fosse adeguata e la consapevolezza dei rischi
che ci sarebbero stati nell'affrontare problemi troppo impegnativi in
un'aula impreparata. Anche i temi che poi invece sarebbero stati caratte-
ristici del concilio, quelli ecclesiologici o quelli relativi alle nuove ricerche bibliche o teologiche erano a rischio: "tutti questi problemi non sono
maturi. Se affrontati non potrebbero esserlo altro che in modo più capace
di chiudere che di aprire". Per questi problemi era meglio lasciar passare
del tempo e verificare nel concreto la maturazione delle idee e dei fatti[29].

La proposta di una "Dichiarazione orientativa" dei padri al termine
della prima sessione si muoveva in questa stessa prospettiva. Essa avrebbe
dovuto limitarsi a richiamare le indicazioni più significative del discorso
di apertura di Giovanni XXIII "canonizzandole ... come la regola asso-
luta del lavoro futuro, affermando non essere oggi compito del concilio
legiferare in tutti i campi della dottrina, della morale e delle istituzione
ecclesiastiche, ma solo cogliere due o tre aspetti sintetici della problematica cristiana e umana del nostro tempo". Secondo Dossetti il concilio alla ripresa "avrebbe potuto, anche in una sola sessione, pervenire
all'approvazione di due o tre documenti sulla dottrina e l'impegno concreto della evangelizzazione dei poveri, della universalità di fatto della
chiesa e della sua trascendenza rispetto a tutte le culture e civiltà e della
sua pari maternità nei confronti di tutte le genti"[30].

---

29. Così diceva il *Promemoria* (Fondo Alberigo, II/6), p. 3: "A ben riflettere non sembra necessario che [il concilio] faccia altro: non sembra necessario, per esempio, che
affronti problemi teologici come quello della natura della chiesa, o quello dei rapporti tra
papa ed episcopato o quello delle direttive e della ispirazione della nuova ricerca biblica
o teologica. Tutti questi problemi non sono maturi. Se affrontati non potrebbero esserlo
altro che in modo *più capace di chiudere che di aprire*. Mentre non affrontarli non solo
non compromette nulla, ma anzi confermerebbe in modo implicito ma inequivoco che si
vuole l'apertura e non la chiusura. Il resto maturerà a suo tempo. Perché si tratta di una
maturazione che non può avvenire tanto in sede di dottrina, quanto di fatti e di vita.
Per esempio il problema del rapporto tra papa ed episcopato non farà mai tanta strada per
effetto di una Costituzione dogmatica quanta ne potrà fare per l'evento già accaduto del
Concilio e per l'altro evento che potrà accadere di una certa presenza di fatto delle Conferenze Episcopali e di una qualsiasi rappresentanza dell'Episcopato universale presso il
papa: questi fatti ormai, cammineranno da sé per la forza delle cose nel mondo e nel seno
della chiesa".
30. *Promemoria* (Fondo Alberigo, II/6), p. 4. Una proposta di testo per questa dichiarazione orientativa era già pronta, con il riferimento ai compiti che Giovanni XXIII aveva
assegnato al concilio, cioè il rinnovamento della chiesa e l'unione dei cristiani, propo-
nendo però la riduzione dell'agenda a tre punti fondamentali, leggermente rivisti rispetto
al promemoria: la prima era la dottrina sulla chiesa, tenendo conto del compito dell'unità
dei cristiani; poi la questione del rapporto tra collegio episcopale e romano pontefice;
infine alcuni temi più legati al mondo: "evangelizationem pauperum, habitudinem ad reli-
giones non-christianas, officia erga gentes evolutionem suam prosequentes".

L'istituzione della Commissione di coordinamento sembrò tuttavia aprire nuove possibilità e le proposte del gruppo bolognese per lo sviluppo successivo dei suoi lavori si fecero più aperte. Una memoria preparata da Dossetti alla fine del marzo 1963, in vista della seconda riunione della Commissione di Coordinamento metteva ancora in evidenza la necessità di chiarire l'orientamento generale del concilio richiamando le linee indicate più volte da Giovanni XXIII. Inoltre riproponeva la questione delle modifiche del Regolamento, criticando esplicitamente quelle proposte che miravano ad una accelerazione dei lavori col restringere gli spazi di parola dei padri. Dossetti auspicava profonde modifiche regolamentari che investivano sia il lavoro delle commissioni che le congregazioni generali, ma suggeriva anche modifiche parziali a cui eventualmente ci si sarebbe potuti limitare nella ricerca di un compromesso possibile[31].

L'attenzione alle condizioni strutturali imposte dal Regolamento e a quelle contingenti del confronto delle parti evidenziavano una percezione del concilio assai meno definita rispetto alla compatta progettualità espressa da Suenens. Le rappresentazioni del concilio sviluppate dal gruppo bolognese sembravano essere sensibili più alle condizioni concrete e alle dinamiche in atto che al disegno complessivo del concilio. Ma questo non voleva dire mancanza di un orientamento preciso: la rotta da seguire era quella indicata da Giovanni XXIII nell'allocuzione di apertura. Ben presto queste linee divennero il metro di giudizio di tutto il concilio[32].

IV. INSIEME COME MODERATORI: CONVERGENZE SULL'ECCLESIOLOGIA

Le differenze nella rappresentazione del concilio non impedirono a Suenens e Lercaro di saldare un forte legame e di avviare una feconda

---

31. *Ordine dei lavori ed elenco degli schemi aventi ragione di priorità*, Fondo Dossetti, 343. Vedi anche *Provvedimenti in vista dell'intervallo tra la prima e la seconda sessione del concilio*, Fondo Dossetti, 189 bis.

32. A proposito della partecipazione di Dossetti al concilio, Alberigo ha significativamente avanzato la domanda se "Dossetti non abbia intravisto in filigrana oltre al concilio 'reale', al quale ha dato un contributo leale e spesso molto rilevante, anche un altro concilio. Il concilio 'nuova Pentecoste' auspicato da Giovanni XXIII, un concilio capace di un ascolto obbediente allo Spirito sino a una trasfigurazione. Un concilio nel quale l'ascolto della parola di Dio e il confronto con la parola dell'umanità sapessero coniugarsi nel servizio dell'uomo, come aveva 'visto' nel letto di morte papa Giovanni". Vedi ALBERIGO, *Giuseppe Dossetti al concilio* (n. 25), pp. 246-247.

collaborazione. Lercaro aveva cercato dei contatti con Suenens, tramite Dossetti, già durante il primo periodo conciliare[33]. In quella fase Dossetti e Lercaro avevano contatti soprattutto con Döpfner, tramite Jedin, per le proposte di modifica del Regolamento. Tuttavia Dossetti inviò anche a Suenens alcuni documenti con le proposte bolognesi sull'intersessione e sul futuro del concilio[34].

Contatti più stretti furono ricercati da Dossetti dopo il primo periodo, alla vigilia della riunione della Commissione di coordinamento. In effetti l'istituzione del nuovo organo direttivo dette un respiro diverso alle aspettative che si nutrivano a Bologna e in vista della sua imminente convocazione Lercaro spinse Dossetti e il Centro di Documentazione ad avviare un consistente programma di lavoro, che comprendeva non solo l'attività di studio ma anche i contatti con padri conciliari e teologi. Dossetti si recò personalmente a visitare Döpfner, Suenens, Willebrands, Dell'Acqua per cercare di capire meglio quali fossero i loro orientamenti. Incontrò Suenens la sera del 22 gennaio 1963 e da allora i contatti si fecero più diretti.

Dossetti gli comunicò le preoccupazioni di Lercaro e del gruppo bolognese riguardo allo sviluppo del concilio e alla revisione del Regolamento. Per lui il risultato più importante da ottenere in quella fase era ancora la possibilità di presentare schemi alternativi o correzioni organiche agli schemi. Anche la questione della durata del concilio restava decisiva: nell'ipotesi ancora sostenuta da Giovanni XXIII di concludere il concilio entro il 1963 occorreva ridurre sensibilmente l'agenda: "in concreto questo anno: *De ecclesia* (compreso il *De beata*) e *De episcopis*. Non è possibile molto di più". Questa sembrava essere anche la posizione di Suenens che però era più possibilista: "Gli altri schemi o rinviati o praticamente sepolti. [...] Quelli che rimarranno, saranno rinviati oltre il 1963...". "Per le questioni ad extra non mature – annotava ancora Dossetti – piuttosto rinviate che compromesse". Ma sull'ipotesi di rinviare questi argomenti a commissioni o organi post-conciliari Suenens

---

33. Cfr. Dossetti a Suenens (novembre 1962), Fondo Suenens, 590 (in cui si annuncia una visita di Lercaro). Vedi anche la lettera con le osservazioni sulla "Presentazione" dello schema *De Ecclesia* di Gagnebet: Fondo Suenens, 642-643 [Per l'inventario dallo fondo di Suenens, vedi L. DECLERCK – E. LOUCHEZ, *Inventaire des Papiers conciliaires du cardinal L.-J. Suenens* (Cahiers de la Revue théologique de Louvain, 31), Louvain-la-Neuve, Publications de la Faculté de Théologie, 1998].

34. Vedi per esempio la nota "Durante il periodo che va dalla prima alla seconda sessione...", Fondo Suenens, 607, in cui si chiedeva d'istituire una "commissione centrale" durante l'intersessione; Dossetti invia anche i *Provvedimenti in vista dell'intervallo tra la prima e la seconda sessione del concilio*, con lettera del 26 novembre 1962: Fondo Suenens, 618-619.

riconosceva che sarebbe stato possibile farlo solo con un preciso mandato del concilio e che non si poteva affidarli con un delega "in bianco"[35].

In questa occasione, probabilmente, Dossetti presentò a Suenens anche il documento con gli *Emendamenti urgenti* al Regolamento del concilio, insieme ad un altro documento con la proposta "più importante e delicata: quella cioè relativa alla possibilità se non proprio di 'controschemi' almeno di emendamenti organici, che investano non solo qualche punto particolare, ma vaste parti di uno Schema". Egli sapeva che Suenens aveva un canale di contatto diretto con il pontefice al quale forse sarebbe stato opportuno presentare la proposta: "Vedrà vostra eminenza se sia il caso di presentare subito al Santo Padre anche questa proposta. In verità, di tutte essa è proprio quella che più importa: perché solo in questo modo si potranno migliorare sostanzialmente gli schemi; altrimenti non si potranno fare che modifiche secondarie e di minor peso"[36]. Suenens apprezzò i rilievi critici e le proposte di Dossetti e sul Regolamento aprì un particolare ambito di collaborazione con il gruppo bolognese al quale indirizzò mons. Ligutti[37].

La proposta di Dossetti, relativa agli schemi alternativi, presentata a Suenens in questa fase, quando cioè già da molte parti si stava concretamente lavorando a preparare tali schemi, mette in evidenza la marginalità in cui ancora si trovavano Lercato e Dossetti rispetto agli ambiti in cui maturavano le decisioni più significative. Solo a partire dall'intersessione i contatti si intensificarono, anche invitando a Bologna alcuni dei teologi più impegnati in concilio[38].

---

35. Gli appunti di Dossetti sul colloquio con Suenens mostrano bene questa preoccupazione: Fondo Dossetti, II.10.

36. G. Dossetti a [Suenens], 23 gennaio 1963: Fondo Dossetti, 1.12. Il riferimento ad un colloquio del giorno precedente (quindi del 22 gennaio) identifica con sufficiente certezza il destinatario nel card. Suenens. Dossetti promette di inviare nel giro di pochi giorni anche un "appunto relativo ai criteri formali per la redazione degli Schemi (qualificazione teologica delle proposizioni, ecc.)".

37. Le questioni procedurali erano ancora quelle che più interessavano Dossetti. Seguendo l'indicazione di Suenens egli incontrò varie volte nel corso di quel mese mons. Ligutti. Cfr. il resoconto di Dossetti inviato a Suenens il 6 febbraio (Fondo Dossetti, 169) e la lettera di Dossetti a Ligutti (6.02.1963) che programmava un nuovo incontro (Fondo Dossetti, 170). A Bologna si lavorò intensamente intorno ad una proposta di revisione complessiva del Regolamento. Una memoria in questo senso venne inviata a Suenens il 27 marzo 1963: ALBERIGO, *Giuseppe Dossetti al concilio* (n. 25), p. 169. La memoria *'L'Ordo Concilii ha lasciato quasi tutti insoddisfatti...'* in varie redazioni preparatorie: Fondo Dossetti, 176, 23, 557bis. La lettera a Suenens in ALBERIGO, *Giuseppe Dossetti al concilio*, p. 161.

38. Vedi in particolare la visita di Congar a Bologna a metà maggio 1963: Y. CONGAR, *Mon journal du Concile*, présenté et annoté par É. MAHIEU, 2 tomes, Paris, Cerf, 2002, pp. 361-364.

I contatti divennero poi di collaborazione dopo il conclave del 1963, quando Paolo VI nominò sia Suenens che Lercaro Moderatori del concilio, insieme a Döpfner e ad Agagianian. La loro collaborazione divenne istituzionale, con l'avallo del pontefice[39]. Tra di loro si realizzò una sostanziale convergenza di intenti e di strategie in particolare riguardo alle principali questioni ecclesiologiche proposte al concilio, che rappresentavano uno dei due capisaldi su cui si costruiva l'architettura del progetto di Suenens, accanto a quello sull'azione missionaria della chiesa nel mondo moderno. Anche per Lercaro le questioni ecclesiologiche erano fondamentali per dare fondamento a quella riforma il cui primo atto era stata la discussione sulla liturgia. Il suo intervento pronunciato all'inizio della discussione sul *De ecclesia* era stato percepito anch'esso, al pari di quelli di Suenens e di Montini, come programmatico per gli sviluppi del concilio[40].

Certo la prospettiva ecclesiologica su cui si fondava il discorso di Suenens era diversa da quella implicita nell'intervento di Lercaro. Le osservazioni che Dossetti avrebbe fatto nel settembre successivo alla nuova redazione del *De ecclesia*, basata sullo 'schema Philips', non risparmiavano appunti e rilievi critici, rilevavano ciò che ancora mancava e mettendo in luce ciò che si poteva e doveva ancora fare per migliorarlo[41]. Tuttavia c'era una convergenza su alcuni principi di fondo e sulle linee da seguire per affermarli.

Durante la discussione dello schema sulla chiesa i Moderatori ebbero un ruolo fondamentale nel chiarire e approfondire quali fossero i temi più importanti in gioco, in particolare quelli del valore sacramentale dell'episcopato, della collegialità, della comunione, del rapporto con il potere primaziale del pontefice. La proposta di sottoporre all'assemblea alcuni di quesiti orientativi era partita da Dossetti che aveva partecipato

---

39. Sull'istituzione dei quattro Moderatori vedi ALBERIGO, *Dinamiche e procedure* (n. 26), pp. 115-164; e G. ALBERIGO, *Concilio Acefalo? L'evoluzione degli organi direttivi del Vaticano II*, in ID. (ed.), *Il Vaticano II fra attese e celebrazione*, Bologna, Il Mulino, 1995, pp. 212-219, che pubblica in appendice gli appunti di Dossetti alle prime riunioni comuni dei Moderatori.

40. Né Lercaro né Dossetti facevano parte della commissione dottrinale che si occupava dello schema sulle chiese e quando la commissione presentò la nuova redazione del *De ecclesia* elaborato sulla base del progetto di Philips, il giudizio di Dossetti non fu del tutto positivo. Sebbene sottolineasse il progresso decisivo rispetto allo schema preparatorio, egli indicava alcuni difetti importanti, attribuibili per molti aspetti ai condizionamenti di tempo e di strategie conciliari che avevano costretto Philips ad un lavoro inadeguato. La mancanza di una sicura qualificazione teologica delle singole enunciazioni dello schema, la mancata assimilazione dell'ecclesiologia orientale, l'insufficiente rilievo del piano sacramentale erano i difetti principali: ALBERIGO, *Giuseppe Dossetti al concilio* (n. 25), pp. 170-172.

41. ALBERIGO, *Giuseppe Dossetti al concilio* (n. 25), pp. 170-172.

alle prime riunioni dei Moderatori e aveva formulato la prima bozza delle proposizioni sulle quali avrebbero dovuto esprimersi i padri[42]. Esse erano poi state riviste e integrate più volte da Prignon su mandato di Suenens. I quesiti ponevano in luce i punti di contrasto fondamentali emersi dalla discussione in aula e costituivano in un certo senso una piattaforma di principi che qualificava l'ecclesiologia del concilio in una determinata direzione.

L'annuncio della votazione suscitò tuttavia forti opposizioni che costrinsero a rimandare il voto e solo dopo estenuanti passaggi tra gli organi competenti si poté procedere effettivamente alla votazione. I quesiti orientativi del 30 ottobre 1963 rappresentano i principi di base su cui Suenens, Lercaro e Döpfner si trovavano a convergere. In particolare ci fu una salda convergenza di opinioni sulla derivazione dei poteri episcopali direttamente dal sacramento della consacrazione quale ordine supremo de sacerdozio e sull'inserimento dei vescovi, con la consacrazione, nel collegio episcopale quale successore del collegio degli apostoli.

Per certi versi era paradossale che proprio i Moderatori, la cui autorità sul concilio derivava direttamente dal pontefice ed era espressione della sua volontà, sostenessero posizioni che, pur nel fedele rispetto delle prerogative primaziali del vescovo di Roma, intendevano rafforzare l'autorità dei vescovi e la loro responsabilità collegiale nel governo della chiesa. In realtà questa era la linea emersa con sempre maggiore chiarezza in concilio, avallata sia da Giovanni XXIII che da Paolo VI.

I rapporti di fiducia e di collaborazione tra Suenens, Lercaro e Döpfner erano in quel momento assai forti. Una collaborazione che si allargava anche ai rispettivi teologi e gruppi che li sostenevano. Suenens imparò a conoscere il valore della personalità di Dossetti e ricorse a lui in più occasioni sia per gli interventi conciliari che per alcune conferenze al margine del concilio[43].

---

42. Sulla proposta e l'elaborazione dei quesiti sintetici vedi ALBERIGO, *Dinamiche e procedure* (n. 26), pp. 115-164. Dossetti collaborò attivamente con i Moderatori nelle prime settimane della loro attività in quanto perito di Lercaro, ma la sua partecipazione alle riunioni e l'influsso che egli esercitava suscitarono non pochi malumori, tanto che fu costretto a rinunciare all'incarico a partire dalla metà di ottobre.

43. Suenens chiese a Dossetti di preparare un intervento sul diaconato permanente, pronunciato in aula l'8 ottobre 1963: vedi *AS* II/2, pp. 317-320; vedi anche LERCARO – ALBERIGO (eds.), *Per la forza* (n. 21), pp. 313-320. Si trattava di un tema molto sentito da Suenens che sin dal suo voto inviato a Roma nel 1961 aveva affermato l'opportunità di istituire forme di diaconato permanente. Suenens si rivolse a Dossetti anche per la conferenza tenuta a Firenze il 29 novembre 1963 su "La chiesa di oggi di fronte alla pluralità delle culture" che gli avevano chiesto il sindaco di Firenze Giorgio La Pira e il cardinale Florit. Fondo Suenens, 1679-1690. La conferenza fu pubblicata: "La Nazione" del 1 dicembre 1963.

V. DIVERGENZE

Le diverse prospettive sul concilio tra i Moderatori non minavano lo spirito di collaborazione che si era instaurato tra di loro, ma si fecero progressivamente più significative nel corso del terzo e del quarto periodo, quando le rappresentazioni del concilio proprie di ciascuno si manifestarono con maggiore chiarezza e le diverse sensibilità portarono ad una maggiore differenziazione di strategie. Qualcosa era effettivamente cambiato nella stessa percezione del concilio da parte dei Moderatori e anche tra di loro le valutazioni circa ciò che ancora si doveva e si poteva fare tendevano a divergere.

Nell'intersessione successiva al secondo periodo, il progetto preparato da Döpfner per una riduzione sostanziale degli schemi in discussione incontrò probabilmente l'appoggio di Lercaro, ma non quello di Suenens, poco disponibile a concedere che una riduzione dei tempi compromettesse il successo dello schema sulla chiesa nel mondo moderno[44].

Anche l'episodio più critico di tutto il concilio, quello della *Nota praevia*, suscitò qualche tensione e incomprensione. La *Nota* era stata elaborata a partire da un testo che Philips aveva scritto come premessa alla relazione della commissione dottrinale, con il beneplacito di Suenens. Il processo che aveva portato a quel testo mostra le manovre poco limpide che avevano trasformato l'iniziale bozza di Philips in una nota interpretativa preposta al documento stesso, condizionando il voto dei padri[45]. Quando venne presentata in aula suscitò forti malumori anche nell'ambiente bolognese, dove si riteneva che sarebbe stato opportuno votare contro lo schema. Del resto, l'importanza dei moderatori nella direzione del concilio sembrò progressivamente diminuire mano a mano che si fece più

---

44. Vedi gli appunti preparatori, probabilmente di Prignon, per la relazione che Suenens doveva fare alla Commissione di coordinamento il 15 gennaio 1964: Fondo Prignon, 787b (J. FAMERÉE, *Concile Vatican II et Église contemporaine (Archives de Louvain-la-Neuve). II: Inventaire des Fonds A. Prignon et H. Wagnon* (Cahiers de la Revue théologique de Louvain, 24), Louvain-la-Neuve, Publications de la Faculté de Théologie, 1991). Il testo del 'Piano Döpfner' in *AS* V/2, pp. 85-94; per la riunione della Commissione di coordinamento *AS* V/2, pp. 95-96 e 99. Cfr. E. VILANOVA, *L'intersessione (1963-1964)*, in ALBERIGO (ed.), *Storia del concilio Vaticano II* (n. 14), Vol. III, 375-382.

45. J. GROOTAERS, *Primauté et collégialité: Le dossier de Gérard Philips sur la Nota explicativa praevia (Lumen gentium cap. III)* (BETL, 72), Leuven, Peeters, 1986; G. ALBERIGO, *L'episcopato al Vaticano II. A proposito della 'Nota explicativa praevia' e di mgr Philips*, in *Cristianesimo nella Storia* 8 (1978) 147-163. G. CAPRILE, *Contributo alla storia della Nota esplicativa previa*, in AA.VV., *Paolo VI e i problemi ecclesiologici al concilio*, Brescia, Istituto Paolo VI, 1989, 587-697; L.A.G. TAGLE, *La tempesta di novembre: La 'settimana nera'*, in ALBERIGO, *Storia del concilio Vaticano II* (n. 14), Vol. III, 446-475; K. SCHELKENS (ed.), *Carnets conciliaires de mgr. Gérard Philips, secrétaire de la commission doctrinale* (Instrumenta Theologica, 29), Leuven, Peeters, 2006, pp. 23-37.

insistente l'intervento diretto di Paolo VI sui lavori delle commissioni conciliari e anche su quelli delle congregazioni generali.

Nonostante il permanere di un atteggiamento positivo del pontefice nei confronti dei Moderatori, a partire dal terzo periodo il rapporto di fiducia divenne più incerto. Prignon, il fedele collaboratore di Suenens, nel suo diario relativo alla quarta sessione lo rileva più volte: nelle abituali udienze del giovedì Paolo VI sembrava volutamente evitare di affrontare con i Moderatori i problemi più urgenti del concilio parlando a lungo di cose diverse[46]. Suenens attribuiva l'incrinarsi dei suoi rapporti con il pontefice alla reazione sfavorevole che questi aveva avuto dopo il suo intervento in aula sul tema del controllo delle nascite nell'ottobre 1964[47].

Sin dall'ottobre 1963 la posizione di Lercaro si era indebolita tra i Moderatori per l'allontanamento di Dossetti che nelle prime settimane aveva svolto una funzione di segretario. Il rapporto di Paolo VI con Lercaro era stato sino ad allora di piena fiducia, tanto che a lui il pontefice aveva chiesto di esaminare il materiale prodotto dal gruppo della 'chiesa dei poveri' per vedere "cosa potesse entrare nelle costituzioni e nei decreti del concilio". Quando l'anno successivo, dopo una nuova sollecitazione di Paolo VI, Lercaro si incontrò con un gruppo di vescovi, proposti da mons. Ancel, e preparò una relazione sul tema della povertà, essa rimase senza riscontro da parte del papa. Era anche questo il sintomo del progressivo venir meno della fiducia iniziale[48]. Un motivo di frizione venne poi dalla proposta maturata nell'ambiente bolognese tra il 1964 e il 1965 di giungere ad una canonizzazione conciliare di Giovanni XXIII. La conferenza che Lercaro tenne all'"Istituto Sturzo" di Roma nel febbraio 1965 proponeva alcune linee interpretative del concilio che sembravano contrapporre le intenzioni di Giovanni XXIII agli sviluppi del concilio sotto il suo successore. Per evitare questo tipo di interpretazione Paolo VI si oppose a qualsiasi iniziativa in favore della canonizzazione in concilio e decise poi di avviare, attraverso le procedure normali, due processi paralleli di beatificazione per Pio XII e Giovanni XXIII[49].

---

46. L. DECLERCK – A. HAQUIN (eds.), *Mgr Albert Prignon, Recteur du Pontificio Collegio Belga, Journal conciliaire de la 4e session* (Cahiers de la Revue théologique de Louvain, 35), Louvain-la-Neuve, Publications de la Faculté de Théologie, 2003.

47. Cfr. un accenno in SUENENS, *Souvenirs et espérances* (n. 6), p. 123.

48. Il testo della relazione di Lercaro è pubblicato in LERCARO – ALBERIGO (eds.), *Per la forza* (n. 21), pp. 157-170; cfr. anche ALBERIGO, *L'esperienza conciliare* (n. 21), pp. 46-48.

49. Il testo della conferenza era stato preparato da Dossetti e prevedeva in conclusione la proposta di beatificazione. Lercaro preferì non leggere quella parte del testo, ma la proposta venne comunque portata in concilio da mons. Bettazzi, nei suoi interventi in aula durante il terzo e il quarto periodo. Anche il polacco mons. B. Bejze, ausiliare di Lodz

Anche Döpfner ebbe motivi di attrito con il pontefice dopo il suo intervento sulle indulgenze nel novembre 1965, nel quale espresse, a nome della conferenza dei vescovi di lingua tedesca, la sua contrarietà alla "positio" avanzata con il consenso del pontefice dalla Penitenzieria apostolica[50].

La percezione del progressivo aumentare delle pressioni sul pontefice portava i Moderatori ad una maggiore cautela. All'inizio del quarto periodo Prignon ebbe una lunga conversazione con Dossetti sulle prospettive del concilio. Dossetti appariva rassegnato e scoraggiato "me dit qu'il se tiendra passif parce que résigné, de même que son cardinal"[51]. Motivi di pessimismo venivano dall'enciclica *Mysterium fidei* sull'eucarestia, ma anche dal Motu proprio *Apostolica sollicitudo* del 15 settembre 1965, con il quale veniva istituito il sinodo dei vescovi[52]. Inoltre alcuni dei testi ancora in discussione, in particolare quelli sulla libertà religiosa e lo schema XIII, gli apparivano del tutto insoddisfacenti. Questo atteggiamento di sfiducia e di passività aveva preso un po' tutto l'ambiente bolognese e condizionava anche l'azione di Lercaro come Moderatore[53].

Non si trattava solo dell'enciclica, ma della convinzione che il concilio avesse abbandonato l'ispirazione profetica di Giovanni XXIII e avesse perso ormai gran parte delle sue forze vitali. Questa convinzione era maturata progressivamente nel corso dei lavori conciliari, quando si era fatta più chiara la difficoltà di sviluppare quelle premesse ecclesiologiche così faticosamente stabilite con la votazione dell'ottobre 1963. Già nella conferenza su Giovanni XXIII, che avrebbe dovuto concludersi con la proposta di beatificazione conciliare, Lercaro aveva espresso, in modo piuttosto esplicito, un senso di delusione per gli sviluppi che il concilio

propose, con una iniziativa personale, la beatificazione. Per tutto vedi A. MELLONI, *La causa Roncalli: Origini di un processo di canonizzazione*, in *Cristianesimo nella Storia* 18 (1987) 607-636; E. GALAVOTTI, *Processo a Papa Giovanni: La causa di canonizzazione di A.G. Roncalli (1965-2000)*, Bologna, Il Mulino, 2005, pp. 57-77.

50. DECLERCK – HAQUIN (eds.), *Mgr Albert Prignon* (n. 46), p. 210; cfr. P. HÜNERMANN, *Le ultime settimane del concilio*, in ALBERIGO (ed.), *Storia del concilio Vaticano II* (n. 14), Vol. V, 387-394.

51. DECLERCK – HAQUIN (eds.), *Mgr Albert Prignon* (n. 46), pp. 32-33.

52. Lettera enciclica *Mysterium fidei*, in *AAS* 57 (1965), e il Motu Proprio *Apostolica sollicitudo*, in *AAS* 57 (1965) 775-780. Sul Motu Proprio vedi M. FAGGIOLI, *Il vescovo e il concilio: Modello episcopale e aggiornamento al Vaticano II*, Bologna, Il Mulino, 2005, pp. 406-416.

53. Qualche settimana più tardi, l'8 ottobre 1965, quando era in gioco la questione se sottoporre o meno lo schema sulla libertà religiosa ad un voto preliminare di accettazione Suenens confidava a Prignon che era stato "à peu près le seul modérateur qui, sur nos instances [dei belgi], a plaidé vigoureusement en ce sens et aussi pour sauver le principe. Lercaro semble de plus en plus éteint. Il n'intervient plus au concile, il ne fait rien et on dirait que le coup de l'encyclique l'a véritablement découragé". DECLERCK – HAQUIN (eds.), *Mgr Albert Prignon* (n. 46), p. 137.

stava assumendo. Durante l'intersessione e con l'inizio del nuovo periodo conciliare questo senso di disillusione era andato crescendo: il concilio sembrava essere tornato sotto il controllo di tendenze moderate, propense a frenare le proposte più avanzate e a cercare equilibri di compromesso ovunque fosse stato possibile.

L'impegno come presidente del 'Consilium ad exequendam constitutionem de Sacra Liturgia', al quale Paolo VI lo aveva chiamato dopo l'approvazione della costituzione liturgica, proiettava già Lercaro al dopoconcilio e ai problemi della recezione. È come se con l'approvazione delle due costituzioni sulla liturgia e sulla chiesa il concilio avesse già posto le basi di quella riforma che, secondo Lercaro, era il suo compito essenziale. Era da questo rinnovamento ecclesiologico che si poteva infatti fondare un nuovo impulso pastorale ed apostolico nei confronti della società moderna. Gli ulteriori sviluppi del concilio, in particolare riguardo allo 'schema XIII' sulla chiesa nel mondo contemporaneo, non avevano alla base una riflessione teologica sufficientemente approfondita e decisioni troppo impegnative sui temi che lo schema trattava rischiavano di compromettere seriamente la riflessione e l'azione futura.

Suenens non condivideva una posizione così pessimistica. Secondo il cardinale belga lo schema XIII rappresentava un asse fondamentale per tutto il concilio, in un certo senso più importante ancora di quello ecclesiologico perché rispondeva più direttamente al compito di ridare slancio alla dimensione missionaria della chiesa nel mondo moderno con un rinnovato impegno di apostolato. Secondo Suenens "il concilio sarebbe passato alla storia come il concilio della chiesa 'ad extra'": H. Fesquet nelle sue note per "Le Monde" riportava così un'opinione del cardinale belga[54]. Pur espressa in tono giornalistico, questa testimonianza corrispondeva ad una convinzione di fondo di Suenens sin dall'inizio del concilio. La diversa valutazione dello schema XIII tra Suenens da un lato e Lercaro e Dossetti dall'altro era il segno più evidente della loro diversa rappresentazione del concilio.

Già nell'ottobre 1964, quando il testo dello 'schema XIII' era stato presentato la prima volta alla discussione dei padri, Lercaro aveva espresso serie riserve su di esso, rilevando la necessità di un'ampia discussione in aula e di una profonda revisione teologica[55]. Certamente si sarebbe dovuta condurre a termine l'elaborazione dello schema, che

---

54. H. FESQUET, *Le Journal du concile*, Le Jas du Revest-St. Martin (Forcalquier), Morel, 1966, p. 797.

55. L'intervento di Lercaro, preparato da Dossetti, in *AS* III/5, pp. 223-226; vedi anche LERCARO – ALBERIGO (eds.), *Per la forza* (n. 21), pp. 215-223.

rispondeva ad uno dei compiti fondamentali voluti da Giovani XXIII e
alle attese sempre più vive da parte di tutti sia all'interno che al di fuori
della chiesa cattolica, ma sarebbe stato necessario avere a disposizione più
tempo per riflettere e far maturare i principi che esso avrebbe dovuto
esprimere.

Il giudizio di fondo non era molto diverso l'anno successivo, quando
ormai si sapeva che il nuovo periodo conciliare sarebbe stato quello con-
clusivo. Dossetti preparò a nome dei vescovi della regione Emilia Romagna un intervento contro lo schema, pronunciato in aula dal vescovo di
Modena mons. G. Amici il 22 settembre 1965. Pur riconoscendo l'importanza dello schema, Dossetti ne rilevava i limiti fondamentali a cominciare da quelli relativi allo scarso fondamento biblico del testo: gli appariva tutto costruito su categorie di senso comune e poco attento alla
testimonianza scritturistica e alla lettura di fede che la chiesa doveva
farne. Le intenzioni del dialogo con gli uomini del mondo moderno erano
di per sé buone, ma nonne giustificavano l'impostazione complessiva e
la scelta di "procedere pregiudizialmente e principalmente da argomenti
di ragione, esporre, quasi sempre, i vari problemi secondo un linguaggio
e un procedimento umano e tentare soprattutto una sintesi di verità
naturali e tutto a livello di una divulgazione giornalistica e infine aggiungere qualche richiamo alle verità rivelate soltanto come allegazioni di
conferma o di rincalzo di argomenti desunti altrove". Secondo Dossetti,
il procedimento avrebbe dovuto essere esattamente l'opposto: "cioè
partire sempre non dai dogmi ma dai problemi concreti e tuttavia dare
subito e nei termini più diretti e semplici la risposta della rivelazione e
soprattutto dell'evangelo, non nella rielaborazione teologica di scuola,
ma nell'immediatezza e nell'attualità dei suoi enunciati più vigorosi, *sine
glossa*"[56].

Nell'intervento preparato per Lercaro a proposito del capitolo sulla
guerra e la pace, intervento presentato poi solo per scritto, Dossetti rilevava con altrettanta severità questi limiti: era in quel capitolo infatti che
tutto il documento mostrava la sua vera natura[57]. Dossetti riteneva che
questo schema fosse gravemente insufficiente a causa dei suoi assunti
antropologici, proposti sul piano dell'analisi sociologica e filosofica piuttosto che su quello biblico e teologico. Nello sforzo di instaurare un dialogo con il mondo moderno la Commissione mista che lo aveva elaborato

---

56. Il testo dell'intervento in *AS* IV/2, pp. 34-36; il testo in italiano in LERCARO –
ALBERIGO (eds.), *Per la forza* (n. 21), pp. 337-342.
    57. Vedi *AS* IV/3, pp. 761-764; il testo italiano in LERCARO – ALBERIGO (eds.), *Per la
forza* (n. 21), pp. 253-261.

aveva rinunciato a preservare l'originalità del messaggio cristiano e aveva accolto le categorie di giudizio correnti nella cultura moderna, senza un'adeguata prospettiva critica, sino ad accettare argomenti semplicemente fondati sul senso comune. Questo se da un lato non aiutava il dialogo, dall'altro tradiva la funzione critica del messaggio evangelico[58].

Critiche più approfondite sarebbero state espresse da Dossetti in una serie di lezioni tenute a Bologna tra il settembre e l'ottobre 1966: oltre a contestare l'approccio troppo naturalistico del documento e il fatto di fondare il dialogo con l'uomo moderno sulle categorie della cultura di oggi invece che sulla rivelazione e sul vangelo, Dossetti rimproverava allo schema l'incapacità di esprimere la forza dei giudizi evangelici e la debolezza critica verso le categorie antropologiche elaborate dalla storia e dalla cultura umana, che si traducevano nella mancanza di un adeguato fondamento antropologico[59].

Nel preparare l'intervento per Lercaro, Dossetti era tornato a parlare di una 'occasione': come il concilio era stato un'occasione per la chiesa per rinnovarsi alla luce della fede così lo schema sulla chiesa nel mondo contemporaneo era l'occasione propizia per parlare e dire una parola evangelica. Questa volta era un'occasione data a ciascuno come unica e irripetibile: "Ho pregato e faccio pregare per lei e per tutti: – scriveva Dossetti a Lercaro – mi sembra proprio che questa sia per tutti un'occasione 'unica', che per ognuno si dà una sola volta nella vita:

---

58. Argomento di senso comune era affermare che solo l'"equilibrio del terrore" potesse impedire la guerra e accettare il principio della deterrenza come unico mezzo efficace e inevitabile per preservare la pace. L'ottimismo iniziale dello schema riguardo alle capacità positive e buone dell'uomo moderno non reggeva di fronte alla minaccia della guerra nucleare. Ma lo schema non aveva il coraggio di assumere una posizione critica a partire dalla forza del messaggio evangelico: "l'ottimismo insipido che spesso si infiltra nello schema è un ottimismo acritico, di timidità e di conformismo verso le opinioni vulgate, non ha fondamento né soprannaturale né veramente razionale perciò è destinato necessariamente a rovesciarsi [...] in un pessimismo quasi rassegnato di fronte alla più grave minaccia di annientamento che mai abbia sovrastato la civiltà umana". Per dare un contributo concreto alla pace la chiesa e il concilio avrebbero dovuto avere il coraggio di esprimere il giudizio evangelico sul mondo: la chiesa "deve incominciare col giudicare il mondo contemporaneo: nell'umiltà più sincera, nella consapevolezza dei propri errori e delle proprie colpe specialmente nella sua politica temporale del passato, nel disinteresse più puro, nella solidarietà più amante col mondo stesso, la chiesa deve – secondo la parola di Isaia ripresa dal vangelo (Mt 12,18) – 'annunziare il giudizio alle genti'". LERCARO – ALBERIGO (eds.), Per la forza (n. 21), pp. 256-257.

59. G. DOSSETTI, Appunti per un'antropologia critica, pro-manuscripto (lezione tenuta il 14 settembre 1966 all'Istituto per le Scienze Religiose di Bologna); G. DOSSETTI, Per una valutazione globale del magistero del Vaticano II, in ID., Il Vaticano II: Frammenti di una riflessione, Bologna, Il Mulino, 1996, 82-102 (lezione tenuta nel corso di tre giorni presso lo stesso Istituto, 5-8 ottobre 1966).

o diciamo queste cose ora o non le potremo dire mai più"[60]. Un anno dopo, a concilio ormai concluso, il capitolo sulla pace e in generale la costituzione *Gaudium et spes* apparivano a Dossetti come un''occasione mancata', una mancanza comparabile, ma assai più grave, con quella di un approfondimento dell'ecclesiologia della chiesa locale nella *Lumen gentium*[61]. L'aver conservato un testo ambiguo circa gli armamenti, incapace del giudizio evangelico, era anzi un 'peccato', una colpa del concilio "che intorbida il nostro intelletto nell'ambito della riflessione teologica, anche su tutti gli altri problemi, come un ostacolo alla grazia e ai carismi che ci sono necessari per il rinnovamento istituzionale"[62].

La valutazione sull''occasione mancata' dal concilio si contrapponeva alla visione più positiva di Suenens. Certamente anche per il cardinale belga lo schema presentava limiti e superficialità, ma rappresentava comunque un rinnovamento sostanziale rispetto alla tradizionale impostazione della dottrina sociale. Sulla base della costituzione pastorale sarebbe stato possibile innestare quel necessario slancio missionario che era il compito essenziale del concilio stesso. La chiesa poteva chiudere finalmente la stagione della sterile contrapposizione ideologica con il mondo moderno e aprire un dialogo capace di portare con maggiore forza il vangelo a tutti, anche a quelle classi sociali che si erano progressivamente più allontanate dalla fede.

---

60. Biglietto di Dossetti a Lercaro, pubblicato in nota da LERCARO – ALBERIGO (eds.), *Per la forza* (n. 21), p. 254.

61. DOSSETTI, *Per una valutazione* (n. 59), p. 95.

62. "I cattolici, su questo punto, si sono comportati come complici, complici della situazione presente, complici di atteggiamenti che vengono giudicati dalla ragione e ancor più dall'Evangelo. E questo evidentemente non può che intorbidare la nostra riflessione teologica e rendere più debole e più fragile la nostra volontà, di fronte ai problemi dell'autoriforma e della riforma istituzionale. Il problema della pace, eluso soprattutto nelle sue determinazioni concrete, quelle che portano il discorso al grado effettivo di evangelicità oggi richiesto [...] eluso nell'ultimo capitolo della *Gaudium et spes* resta come un peccato che intorbida – per così dire – il nostro intelletto nell'ambito della riflessione teologica, anche su tutti gli altri problemi, come un ostacolo alla grazia e ai carismi che ci sono necessari per il rinnovamento istituzionale. E non è semplicemente una colpa, sia pur grave ma *a latere*, o anche centrale ma isolata; essa si diffonde nel corpo della chiesa e per la sua natura, da incompletezza di uno dei testi del concilio, diventa l'*incompletezza* del concilio, eventualmente insieme ad un'altra, a quella cioè della sanzione, nel significato non solo personale, ma ecclesiale, della santità di papa Giovanni. [...] Certo, i discorsi sono importanti; i principi di luce, per l'uomo che è un animale ragionevole, indubbiamente sono importanti, ma noi sappiamo che certe verità si oscurano nell'intelletto in seguito al peccato, e che anche i principi illuminanti possono poi essere in concreto talmente smentiti dai comportamenti non conformi, da portare a qualche cosa di peggio dell'assenza stessa di quella luce. Ora i problemi che nascono da tutto questo sono gravissimi". Vedi DOSSETTI, *Per una valutazione* (n. 59), pp. 97-98.

VI. LA DIFFICILE RECEZIONE

Occorrerebbe una analisi più distesa dei documenti e delle vicende dei mesi successivi per comprendere come a livello locale convergenze e divergenze nella comprensione del concilio abbiano creato modelli diversi di recezione. Uno studio parallelo dei processi di recezione avviati a Bruxelles e a Bologna potrebbe essere sicuramente ricco di insegnamenti.

Parlare di modelli di recezione non è certo facile, data la complessità di una categoria che presenta molti aspetti teologici e deve essere usata con molta cautela dal punto di vista storiografico[63]. Nella generale attesa di rinnovamento suscitata dal concilio e dalla sua conclusione si intrecciavano molte spinte a favore di una radicalizzazione dei temi conciliari e altre che invece frenavano e tentavano di affermare una lettura riduttiva dei documenti prodotti. In questo contesto Suenens e Lercaro si trovarono uniti nel perseguire un cammino di fedeltà alla loro esperienza conciliare e nel cercare di rendere efficaci le linee dinamiche che ne scaturivano.

I due cardinali erano stati entrambi inseriti nella Commissione centrale post-conciliare istituita da Paolo VI all'inizio del 1966 con il Motu Proprio *Finis Concilio* per studiare e proporre i modi di attuazione delle norme conciliari[64]. La Commissione centrale era composta da membri della Presidenza del concilio e della Commissione di coordinamento. Tenne una prima riunione nel gennaio 1966 per stabilire le linee direttive per le altre commissioni post-conciliari. Quando nel maggio successivo esse avevano terminato il loro lavoro e avevano riportato le loro conclusioni, la Commissione centrale si riunì di nuovo per presentare al pontefice la sintesi del lavoro svolto. Di questa attività non si conosce molto, ma su di essa si è basato il Motu Proprio *Ecclesiae Sanctae*, che recava le *Normae ad quaedam exsequenda Decreta ss. Concilii Vaticani II 'Christus Dominus' et 'Presbyterorum Ordinis'*[65].

Le indicazioni dell'enciclica potevano essere lette come semplici norme attuative da applicare in modo burocratico o come un orizzonte all'interno del quale avviare una riforma più ampia delle diocesi. Il card. Suenens istituì molto presto a Bruxelles un consiglio pastorale di cui facevano parte anche dei laici. A Bologna Lercaro istituì delle commissioni con

---

63. Sulla recezione del concilio Vaticano II vedi G. ROUTHIER (ed.), *Réceptions de Vatican II: Le concile au risque de l'histoire et des espaces humains* (Instrumenta Theologica, 27), Leuven, Peeters, 2004; e più recentemente G. ROUTHIER, *Vatican II: Herméneutique et réception*, Québec, Fides, 2006.

64. PAOLO VI, *Finis Concilio*, in *AAS* 58 (1966) 37-40.

65. PAOLO VI, *Ecclesiae sanctae*, in *AAS* 58 (1966) 757-758; le *Normae*, in *AAS* 58 (1966) 758-787.

larga partecipazione di laici per elaborare un ambizioso progetto di riforma[66]. È significativo che uno dei primi modelli a cui i gruppi guardarono fu proprio quello della diocesi di Malines-Bruxelles, alla quale vennero chiesti documenti e informazioni per conoscere i criteri lì utilizzati nell'elezione e nel lavoro dei consigli[67].

La linea di fondo che accomunava queste prime esperienze di recezione era la forte accentuazione della dimensione locale della chiesa. Le numerose interviste rilasciate da Suenens in quei primi anni dopo il concilio sono tutte concordi nell'indicare questa tendenza. Esse ebbero ampia risonanza e servirono a indicare una direzione di ricerca. Anche all'interno dei gruppi per la riforma della diocesi di Bologna il tema della chiesa locale era centrale, con una forte accentuazione del suo fondamento liturgico ed episcopale. La riscoperta della dimensione misterica della chiesa, della sua natura di Popolo di Dio, si traduceva spesso in una crescente disaffezione per ogni forma di istituzionalizzazione della fede e nella ricerca di piccoli gruppi dove la fede sembrava vivere più intensa e vera.

La parabola postconciliare di Lercaro e di Suenens presenta molti aspetti interessanti se confrontata con la loro esperienza conciliare e la loro diversa rappresentazione del concilio. Dopo aver avviato il processo di riforma della sua diocesi, suscitando numerose inquietudini e critiche tra molti degli altri vescovi italiani, Lercaro non temette di esporsi pubblicamente il 1 gennaio 1968 con una omelia di aperta condanna dei bombardamenti americani in Vietnam. Un discorso che irritò Paolo VI, impegnato in quegli stessi giorni in complessi tentativi diplomatici di mediazione tra le forze in campo. Per quell'omelia Lercaro fu costretto a ritirarsi dal suo ministero episcopale e a lasciare la diocesi al suo coadiutore e successore, mons. A. Poma. Lercaro era consapevole dei rischi che pronunciare quelle parole avrebbe comportato per sé, ma non vi si sottrasse[68]. Non si può non interpretare questo gesto alla luce della riflessione

---

66. Sul lavoro di questi gruppi a Bologna vedi G. GERVASIO, *Diocesi di Bologna: Le dieci commissioni*, relazione tenuta il 14 dicembre 2006 al convegno "L'apporto di Bologna al concilio Vaticano II e la recezione del concilio nelle chiese dell'Emilia Romagna" a cura della facoltà teologica dell'Emilia Romagna, in corso di stampa. G. TURBANTI, *La recezione del concilio a Bologna: Appunti per una ricerca*, in ROUTHIER (ed.), *Réceptions de Vatican II* (n. 63), 175-201.

67. Tra i documenti di lavoro del settimo gruppo, incaricato di progettare la costituzione di un 'Senato presbiterale' e di un 'Consiglio pastorale' e di rivedere la struttura complessiva della diocesi c'era anche il *Vademecum 1966* della diocesi di Malines-Bruxelles: Fondo Lercaro, C.III.2.

68. Sul discorso del 1 gennaio 1968 vedi G. BATTELLI, *Lercaro, Dossetti, la pace e il Vietnam*, in BUONASORTE (ed.), *Araldo del vangelo* (n. 4), 185-304.

di Dossetti sull'occasione perduta in concilio per una parola evangelica sulla pace. Il suo gesto fu quello di recuperare quell'occasione a livello personale ed ecclesiale. Era questa percezione e questa interpretazione che legava con il filo continuo di una medesima riflessione la sua esperienza conciliare e il suo discorso sulla pace.

Da parte sua Suenens, la cui autorità era andata crescendo a livello ecclesiale, sostenne una aperta battaglia contro i tentativi di restringere la portata del rinnovamento conciliare che da più parti ormai si facevano strada. Nel 1969 uscì il suo libro che, sulla base delle decisioni conciliari, richiamava la necessità di allargare la correponsabilità di clero e laici nella chiesa[69]. Il libro suscitò non poca inquietudine in Paolo VI[70], ma ancor più scalpore sollevò l'intervista rilasciata a "Informations Catholiques Internationales" pubblicata il 15 maggio 1969, nella quale riprendeva ad approfondiva alcuni concetti già espressi nel libro[71]. Le sue prese di posizione e favore di una riforma più incisiva delle istituzioni ecclesiali a cominciare dal ministero del pontefice, dalla sua elezione, dal conclave dei cardinali, dalla curia, dal sinodo dei vescovi e dalle conferenze episcopali provocarono non poco imbarazzo a Roma e non poche difficoltà allo stesso cardinale belga. In concilio Suenens non aveva avuto timore ad affrontare apertamente la questione del controllo delle nascite, suscitando il malumore di Paolo VI; ora dopo il concilio non ebbe alcuna remora nell'esprimere le sue opinioni riguardo a temi scottanti all'interno della chiesa, come quello del celibato ecclesiastico o del sacerdozio femminile[72]. Per Suenens queste riforme istituzionali erano improrogabili se la chiesa voleva recuperare quel deficit di credibilità di fronte al mondo moderno che ancora la caratterizzava. Rispetto ad esse, il concilio era stato solo il motore di un rinnovamento che doveva continuare sulla base del carisma da esso espresso più che dai documenti promulgati, che lo rappresentavano solo in parte.

---

69. L.-J. SUENENS, *La coresponsabilité dans l'Église d'aujourd'hui*, Bruges, Desclée de Brouwer, 1969.

70. SUENENS, *Souvenirs et espérances* (n. 6), p. 172. Già l'anno precedente c'era stata un'udienza particolare di Suenens da Paolo VI, assai preoccupato per certe dichiarazioni del primate belga; ne era seguita un lunga lettera di Suenens in cui cercava di chiarire e spiegare le sue posizioni nell'assoluto rispetto delle prerogative papali: SUENENS, *Souvenirs et espérances*, pp. 157-160.

71. Vedi in particolare *L'unité de l'Église dans la logique de Vatican II: Le cardinal Suenens répond aux questions de José de Broucker*, in *Informations Catholiques Internationales* 336-Supplément, 15 maggio 1969.

72. Cfr. J. DE BROUCKER, *Le dossier Suenens: Diagnostic d'une crise*, Paris, Éditions Universitaires 1970; e anche L.-J. SUENENS, *La crisi della chiesa: Dialoghi raccolti da IDOC*, Milano, Mondadori 1971; K.H. FLECKENSTEIN, *Pour l'Église de demain: Conversation avec le cardinal Suenens*, Paris, Nouvelle Cité, 1979.

Questi sviluppi negli anni post-conciliari permettono di cogliere alcuni aspetti della esperienza di Suenens e Lercarto durante il concilio, illuminandola sotto nuovi punti di vista. Se ci fu indubbiamente continuità tra la fase preparatoria, quella conciliare e quella della recezione essa fu nel segno di uno sviluppo e di una profonda maturazione di fede ed ecclesiale. Questo sviluppo si è realizzato attraverso il lavoro comune, la condivisione delle responsabilità, il confronto delle opinioni.

Ripercorrendo in modo sintetico e rapido, come necessariamente è stato fatto in queste pagine, il percorso conciliare di Suenens, Lercaro e Dossetti emergono le loro diverse immagini e rappresentazioni del concilio, dovute in gran parte alle loro esperienze pastorali precedenti e alle attese che sul concilio avevano maturato. Sono elementi importanti per comprendere il diverso atteggiamento e le strategie assunte durante l'assise e hanno rilievo anche come criterio ermeneutico del concilio, nella valutazione circa la sua riuscita, la sua efficacia, il suo significato complessivo. Da questo punto di vista si possono cogliere rilevanti differenze tra Suenens e Lercaro, che hanno continuato ad agire sino alla fine. La divergente valutazione dello "schema XIII" ne è stata la manifestazione più significativa. Tali differenze dipendevano in una certa misura dal diverso temperamento delle due personalità, dalla formazione, dalla sensibilità pastorale propri di ciascuno, ma anche dalle situazioni locali in cui si trovavano ad operare e dalle responsabilità specifiche a cui di volta in volta erano stati chiamati in concilio.

D'altra parte questa diversa percezione del concilio non solo non ha impedito od ostacolato la collaborazione, ma piuttosto ha condotto a convergenze importanti nei contenuti e nelle strategie, in particolare per quanto riguarda l'ecclesiologia e la riforma delle strutture della chiesa. In effetti le loro prospettive non si escludevano e non si contrapponevano. Alcuni elementi in particolare erano comuni: la consapevolezza dell'urgenza di una riforma della chiesa, la percezione dei problemi della pastorale nel mondo moderno di fronte alla rapida diffusione dei processi di secolarizzazione della società, la coscienza che il concilio era un'occasione concessa dallo Spirito per il rinnovamento interiore ed esteriore della chiesa. Su questi elementi c'è stata, tra il cardinale di Bruxelles e quello di Bologna, piena sintonia. Entrambi potevano avvalersi del sostegno di gruppi di lavoro e di ricerca che nei momenti critici delle vicende conciliari hanno permesso un prezioso approfondimento sui significati e sui contenuti dei problemi in gioco. L'apporto della 'squadra belga' è stato importante in numerose commissioni e nell'elaborazione di molti documenti. Quello di Philips in particolare è stato decisivo sia per il *De ecclesia* sia per lo 'schema XIII'. Questa collaborazione, che non è stata esclusiva ma ha coinvolto per altri versi molti altri protagonisti ed équipe di lavoro, ha rappresentato il valore aggiunto che ha permesso di raggiungere i risultati più importanti del concilio.

La dinamica tra le esperienze personali e il lavoro comune rappresenta un nodo ermeneutico importante nello studio del concilio. Gli elementi di differenziazione non devono essere sottovalutati. Le diverse immagini e prospettive erano reali e definivano per ciascuno una particolare esperienza conciliare. Di fatto il concilio è stato inevitabilmente l'incontro di queste differenze, non tanto nel senso di una sintesi raggiunta alla fine, ma come confronto reciproco sino ad una comprensione e all'arricchimento delle ragioni di ciascuno.

Istituto per le scienze religiose   Giovanni TURBANTI
Via san Vitale 114
I-40125 Bologna
Italy

LES RELATIONS ENTRE LE CARDINAL MONTINI / PAUL VI (1897-1978) ET LE CARDINAL SUENENS (1904-1996) PENDANT LE CONCILE VATICAN II

I. INTRODUCTION

Les relations entre Montini et Suenens ont eu une réelle importance pour le déroulement du concile Vatican II[1]. On ne peut oublier que le cardinal Montini fut présent dans le cercle restreint des cardinaux qui à deux reprises se sont réunis, à l'initiative de Suenens, au collège belge en 1962 pour que le concile se déroule selon un plan établi. De plus, le 5 décembre 1962, Montini a appuyé publiquement *in aula* le discours de Suenens du 4 décembre, proposant un nouveau plan du concile, qui aura une influence décisive dans la réduction des schémas préparatoires. Quand Paul VI, devenu pape en juin 1963, voudra donner un nouvel essor aux travaux conciliaires et instituera à cet effet l'organe des modérateurs, on ne sera pas étonné que Suenens soit nommé en septembre 1963 comme un des quatre modérateurs. Dès lors, leurs relations furent intenses jusqu'à la cérémonie de clôture du concile (le 8 décembre 1965), où Suenens fut encore chargé de lire, dans le message au monde, la section adressée aux artistes.

À une certaine période – surtout en 1963 – cette relation était presque devenue une amitié personnelle tandis qu'après le concile elle passera par une crise profonde, surtout en 1969-1971. Aussi, pour mieux comprendre cette relation qui dura de 1952 à 1978, nous traiterons également sommairement des rapports de Suenens avec Montini avant et après le concile.

Pour étudier ces rapports, nous disposons d'une riche documentation dans les archives du cardinal Suenens[2]. Suenens a gardé presque toute

---

1. Comme l'influence du cardinal Suenens sur le travail conciliaire est traitée dans une autre contribution pour ce colloque, nous nous limitons ici surtout aux relations personnelles de Suenens avec Montini.

2. Cf. L. DECLERCK – E. LOUCHEZ, *Inventaire des Papiers conciliaires du cardinal L.-J. Suenens* (Cahiers de la Revue théologique de Louvain, 31), Louvain-la-Neuve, Publications de la Faculté de Théologie, 1998 (archives à l'archevêché de Malines; cité: Fonds Suenens).

sa correspondance avec Montini et il a pris souvent des notes après les audiences avec le pape. De plus, ses livres «autobiographiques» *Souvenirs et espérances* (Fayard, 1991) et *Les imprévus de Dieu* (Fayard, 1993) fourniront quelques repères. Signalons aussi l'interview donnée en 1980 au Prof. J. Grootaers dans le *Herder Korrespondenz*[3], la biographie de E. Hamilton[4] et le livre de K.H. Fleckenstein, *Pour l'Église de demain*[5]. Il faut toutefois noter que Suenens manque souvent de précision historique dans ses notes et que ses livres reflètent son point de vue personnel et témoignent parfois d'une mémoire assez sélective. De ce point de vue il est regrettable qu'on n'ait pas encore accès aux archives de Paul VI. Ceci a comme conséquence que cette brève étude est unilatérale et que le point de vue du cardinal Suenens y est largement privilégié.

Un certain nombre de pièces d'archives de l'Archidiocèse de Milan et l'excellent livre de G. Adornato, *Cronologia dell'episcopato di G.B. Montini a Milano, 4 gennaio 1955 – 21 giugno 1963* (Brescia, 2002) nous ont été un précieux instrument de travail pour la période milanaise de Montini[6]. Signalons également le Fonds Prignon[7] (avec ses Rapports à l'Ambassade et son Journal de la 4e session[8], journal qui nous permet de traiter cette session plus en détail) et les Carnets Moeller[9].

3. Cf. J. GROOTAERS, *Von Johannes XXIII. zu Johannes Paul II.: Ein Gespräch mit Leo Joseph Kardinal Suenens*, dans *Herder Korrespondenz* 34 (1980) 176-182. Cf. aussi J. GROOTAERS, *Léon-Joseph Suenens*, dans ID., *I protagonisti del Vaticano II* (attualità e storia), Milano, San Paolo edizione, 1994, 229-243.

4. E. HAMILTON, *Cardinal Suenens: A Portrait*, London, Hodder and Stoughton, 1975.

5. K.H. FLECKENSTEIN, *Pour l'Église de demain: Conversation avec le cardinal Suenens*, Paris, Nouvelle Cité, 1979, surtout les pp. 68-73.

6. Nous tenons à remercier vivement Mgr B. Bosatra et Mme Dott. G. Adornato des Archives de l'Archidiocèse de Milan (Archivio della Segreteria dell' Arcivescovo Montini, cité ASAM) qui nous ont procuré quelques documents de la période milanaise de Montini.

7. Prignon était l'homme de confiance de Suenens pendant le concile. Pour ses archives, cf. J. FAMERÉE, *Concile Vatican II et Église contemporaine*. II: *Inventaire des Fonds A. Prignon et H. Wagnon*, Louvain-la-Neuve, Publications de la Faculté de théologie, 1991 (cité Fonds Prignon et Fonds Wagnon).

8. L. DECLERCK – A. HAQUIN (éds.), *Mgr Albert Prignon, Recteur du Pontificio Collegio Belga, Journal conciliaire de la 4e session* (Cahiers de la Revue théologique de Louvain, 35), Louvain-la-Neuve, Publications de la Faculté de Théologie, 2003 (cité dorénavant Journal Prignon).

9. C. SOETENS, *Concile Vatican II et Église contemporaine*. I: *Inventaire des Fonds Ch. Moeller, G. Thils, Fr. Houtart* (Cahiers de la Revue théologique de Louvain, 21), Louvain-la-Neuve, Publications de la Faculté de Théologie, 1989, pp. 73-76.

II. PROLOGUE: LES PREMIÈRES RENCONTRES DE MONTINI ET DE SUENENS
AVANT LA PÉRIODE CONCILIAIRE

1. Rencontres avec Montini, substitut de la Secrétairerie d'État et par après pro-secrétaire d'État pour les Affaires Ordinaires de l'Église[10]

On sait qu'après sa rencontre avec V. O'Brien en 1947-48[11], l'évêque auxiliaire de Malines est devenu un partisan enthousiaste de la Légion de Marie. Toutefois la Légion se heurtait à beaucoup de résistance surtout de la part de l'Action catholique spécialisée en France et en Belgique qui défendait son «monopole» et sa «spécialisation»[12], résistance encore intensifiée par une critique sévère des principes théologiques de la Légion, critique faite par le théologien H. de Lubac[13]. Dès lors Suenens cherchait à défendre la Légion de Marie aussi bien par des publications[14] que par des contacts à Rome.

– Le 9 janvier 1952 Suenens obtient une audience avec Pie XII; il fait la louange de la Légion de Marie et met le pape en garde contre le

10. Pro-secrétaire d'État à partir du 29 novembre 1952.
11. Cf. L.-J. SUENENS, *Les imprévus de Dieu*, Paris, Fayard, 1993, pp. 87-96.
12. À titre d'exemple, on peut signaler que, dans les années '50, il y avait eu des tensions entre F. Duff, fondateur de la Légion de Marie, et J. Cardijn, fondateur de la J.O.C. (Jeunesse Ouvrière Chrétienne, mouvement d'action catholique spécialisée). Dans une lettre à Duff (1953), Suenens écrit: «Mgr Cardijn said that the Legion opens the way for communism in India because – he said – the best catholic forces are absorbed by the Legion, so there is no room for his movement. And the J.O.C. is the unique way to obstaculate [sic] the progress of communism since social reforms are the first need in a country where people has [sic] nothing to eat. Do you see the reasoning! In the same way every missionary who is not doing social work is a protagonist of communism!». Et dans une lettre du 24 octobre 1953, Duff écrit à Suenens: «I am much amused at the manner in which Mgr Cardijn reasons that the Legion of Mary leads directly to Communism. So it is because the Legion of Mary absorbs all the best apostolic material! That puts the J.O.C. into a peculiar light as an apostolic instrument. For if an instrument is of apostolic importance and vigour, it should as one of its virtues be capable of attracting membership to itself and that in spite of the competition of other Societies. Unlike Mgr Cardijn, Cardinal Tisserant is never tired of insisting that the Legion of Mary is of all the most efficacious for resisting atheist materialism...». Cf. Correspondance Duff-Suenens, dans Fonds Suenens, Archives personnelles [à l'archevêché de Malines, cité: Fonds Suenens A.P.], b.[boîte] 14.
13. H. DE LUBAC, *Notes d'un théologien*. Cet écrit ronéotypé et non signé avait été envoyé à plusieurs évêques français en 1946. Cf. aussi E. GUYNOT, *Réponse aux 'Notes d'un Théologien'*, 18 avril 1946, 12 p. (Fonds Suenens A.P., b. 79). Mgr P. Flynn, évêque de Nevers, écrit le 1er mai 1946 une lettre aux évêques français pour défendre la Légion de Marie où il dit: «Entre autres moyens de propagande hostile on répand à profusion un tract dactylographié, universellement attribué au R. P. de Lubac s.j. Dans certains diocèses, presque tous les prêtres l'ont reçu personnellement. L'esprit de la Légion y est dénaturé et en des termes qu'on ne peut s'empêcher de qualifier d'injustes et d'injurieux» (Fonds V. O'Brien [Archevêché de Malines], b. 14).
14. Pour ces publications de Suenens, cf. L.-J. SUENENS, *Souvenirs et espérances*, Paris, Fayard, 1991, pp. 40-45.

Réarmement moral; il rend une première visite à Montini, substitut de
la Secrétairerie d'État[15]. Suenens lui parle de son livre *Théologie de
l'Apostolat* et Montini lui dit que le titre ne correspond pas exactement
au contenu.

En effet, Suenens avait publié en 1951 son livre *Théologie de l'Apostolat* (au sujet de la méthode apostolique prônée par la Légion de
Marie) et il cherchait à obtenir une préface du Saint-Père. De là ses
contacts avec Montini. Finalement, c'est Montini[16] qui a écrit cette préface (à partir de la 4e édition), à condition toutefois que le titre soit
changé en *Théologie de l'Apostolat de la Légion de Marie* et qu'un certain nombre de corrections soient introduites[17].

– Suenens, voulant garder de bons contacts, a par après également
envoyé à Montini ses livres *Une héroïne de l'apostolat: Edel Mary
Quinn* (1952) et *Que faut-il penser du Réarmement moral?* (1953)[18].

2. Rencontres avec l'archevêque de Milan

En 1955, Suenens publie son livre *L'Église en état de mission*.
Il annonce la publication à Montini[19] et réussit à obtenir une préface de
Montini[20], archevêque de Milan depuis décembre 1954. Lors d'un voyage

15. Cf. Fonds Suenens A.P., b. 79 et SUENENS, *Les imprévus de Dieu* (n. 11), pp. 142-
145.
16. Dans une lettre du 6 décembre 1952, Montini disait que le pape n'écrivait pratiquement jamais de préface à des livres. Cf. Fonds Suenens A.P., b. 30.
17. Il s'agit de corrections mineures et de vétilles, suggérées par un censeur romain;
par ex. ne pas citer Bergson (auteur dont plusieurs œuvres avaient été mises à l'Index). Ou
encore une critique d'une citation de Newman «Définissez un gentleman, vous avez défini
un saint» (on peut être un gentleman en ne possédant que des vertus naturelles, tandis
qu'un saint doit posséder des vertus surnaturelles…) etc. Aussi V. O'Brien insiste auprès
de Montini pour avoir cette préface du pape dans un entretien de fin mars 1952 (Cf. Lettre
de V. O'Brien à Suenens du 1 avril 1952, Fonds O'Brien, b. 3).
18. Montini a remercié par des lettres respectivement du 9 octobre 1952 et du 14 juillet
1953 (Fonds Suenens A.P., b. 31 et 33).
19. Le 5 février 1955, Suenens, après une conversation à Paris avec Mgr Benelli, écrit
à Montini qu'il aimerait bien avoir une entrevue pour parler des problèmes soulevés dans
ce livre. Le 12 avril 1955, il écrit à «Monseigneur» (probablement Mgr P. Macchi, secrétaire de Montini) pour demander un rendez-vous; il réécrit de Rome au même Monseigneur, le 21 avril 1955, pour confirmer son entrevue avec Montini à Milan, qui aura lieu
le 29 avril 1955. Le 3 mai 1955, Suenens remercie Montini pour son accueil et pour la
visite au grand séminaire de Venegono. Le 22 juillet 1955, Suenens demande à Montini
d'écrire la préface de la traduction italienne de son livre. Le 8 octobre 1955, Suenens
remercie Montini pour cette préface et exprime son désir de parler à Montini au sujet de
la réforme apostolique des couvents et des séminaires (cf. ASAM: Sacerdoti, nn. 5, 4, 6, 10,
7, 8, 11 et 9).
20. Préface (3 pages en italien) fort élogieuse qui débute ainsi: «Stima fortuna la mia,
di presentare questo libro. Altri lo potrebbe fare, assai meglio di me; ma ora, che non
posso lasciarmi sfuggire alcuna occasione per annunciare il regno di Dio, mi par dovere

en Italie, il est reçu le 29 avril 1955 par Montini[21], avec qui il prend le repas de midi. Par après, il correspond encore à ce sujet avec P. Macchi, secrétaire de Montini[22]. Quand en 1956, en pleine «guerre scolaire»[23], Suenens publie un livret *La Question scolaire*[24], il en envoie un exemplaire à Montini «qui exprime ses plus vifs remerciements et les souhaits les plus sincères pour le succès de la lutte scolaire»[25].

– Il est à noter que Suenens a certainement rencontré Montini lors du IIe Congrès mondial pour l'Apostolat des Laïcs à Rome, en octobre 1957. Montini y a tenu une conférence, où il citait le livre de Suenens *L'Église en état de mission*[26]. Et, à l'instigation de Suenens, Pie XII dans son discours fait une ouverture à la Légion de Marie[27].

accogliere l'invito di offrire al pubblico, al Clero e al Laicato cattolico specialmente, questa nuova opera di Sua Ecc. Mons. Suenens, degnissimo Vescovo Ausiliare di Malines. Il nome dell'Autore dispenserebbe, a vero dire, da una prefazione, e per la dignità di cui Egli è rivestito, e per l'ufficio ch'Egli svolge nella più sviluppata diocesi del mondo e per la risonanza che altri suoi scritti gli hanno assicurati» (Fonds Suenens A.P., b. 34).

21. Cf. G. ADORNATO, *Cronologia dell'episcopato di Giovanni Battista Montini a Milano. 4 gennaio 1955 – 21 giugno 1963*, Brescia, Istituto Paolo VI, 2002, p. 80.

22. Lettre de P. Macchi à Suenens, 6 septembre 1955 où il écrit e.a.: «Son Excellence [Montini] a presque terminé la lecture de votre volume… Il en est très content et je pense que sous peu la préface sera faite» (cf. Fonds Suenens A.P., b. 34). Dans une lettre du 10 janvier 1956 (et non de 1955, comme écrit par erreur) à Macchi, Suenens demande encore que la préface de Montini puisse être reproduite dans les autres éditions en diverses langues (cf. ASAM Sacerdoti, n. 1).

23. De 1954 à 1958 le gouvernement belge socialiste – libéral avait pris plusieurs mesures en défaveur de l'enseignement catholique. Les catholiques (et le parti social chrétien CVP-PSC) avaient réagi de façon vigoureuse. Après les élections de 1958 (que le parti social chrétien avait gagnées), cette question fut résolue par le «pacte scolaire».

24. Il est intéressant de voir que Suenens a discuté le contenu de son livre avec le nonce E. Forni, qui avait fait plusieurs remarques, et que L. Collard, ministre socialiste belge de l'enseignement, a réagi de façon très courtoise. Cf. Fonds Suenens A.P., b. 35.

25. Fonds Suenens A.P., b. 35.

26. L.-J. SUENENS, *L'Église en état de mission*, Bruges, Desclée de Brouwer, 1955; G. B. MONTINI, *La Mission dans l'Église*, dans *Les Laïcs dans l'Église: Deuxième Congrès Mondial pour l'Apostolat des Laïcs*, Rome, 1958, p. 79.

27. Pie XII avait notamment déclaré: «L'Action catholique ne peut pas non plus revendiquer le monopole de l'apostolat des laïcs … Il semble nécessaire de faire connaître, au moins dans ses grandes lignes, une suggestion qui nous a été communiquée tout récemment [par Suenens]…», *Discours de Sa Sainteté Pie XII*, dans *Les Laïcs dans l'Église* (n. 26), pp. 20-23.

Pour ce congrès, cf. SUENENS, *Les imprévus de Dieu* (n. 11), pp. 174-175. Dans une lettre du 20 octobre 1957 à V. O'Brien, Mgr Benelli avait dit que pour Mgr Jacques Martin: «[ce congrès] a été un triomphe de Mgr Suenens. Le congrès des Laïcs a été nettement dominé par la personnalité de l'auxiliaire de Malines» (Fonds O'Brien, b. 9).

Mgr Philips cependant était d'une autre opinion et, faisant allusion à l'intervention de Suenens auprès du pape, parlait de «méthodes curieuses» et «d'un certain machiavellisme» (Cahiers G. Philips, 2e série, Cahier IX, 19 octobre 1957).

– Fin 1959, Suenens publie un nouveau livre *Un problème crucial: Amour et maîtrise de soi*[28]. Sujet brûlant qu'il traite entre autres à la demande de V. O'Brien[29]. Il envoie un exemplaire à Montini le 6 janvier 1960[30] et lui en parle à Milan le 22 février 1960[31], lors d'un voyage en Italie pour donner une conférence à ce sujet à Rome. Il est à noter que le cardinal Montini[32] prendra soin que ce livre soit traduit en italien et soit muni d'une préface de Carlo Colombo, son théologien de confiance[33].

Deux documents d'archives manifestent encore l'intérêt de Montini pour ce livre:

– En 1965, le Docteur Ennio Rosini écrit à Suenens qu'en mai 1963 Montini lui avait envoyé ce livre de Suenens pour répondre à des questions qu'il avait posées au cardinal de Milan au sujet du Birth Control[34].
– En août 1968, quelques semaines après la parution de *Humanae vitae*, Paul VI écrit à Suenens que dans cette encyclique il n'a fait que reprendre les thèses défendues par Suenens dans ce livre[35].
– Le 12 septembre 1961, Suenens remercie encore Montini pour les condoléances qu'il a adressées pour la mort du cardinal Van Roey. Et le 23 septembre 1961, Montini répond et redit son estime pour le cardinal défunt[36].

---

28. L.-J. SUENENS, *Un problème crucial: Amour et maîtrise de soi*, Bruges, Desclée de Brouwer, 1960.
29. Cf. SUENENS, *Les imprévus de Dieu* (n. 11), p. 21.
30. Suenens écrit notamment: «Je serais tellement heureux si vous trouviez le temps de le [ce livre] lire et de me faire connaître un jour vos réactions» et il lui envoie en même temps une interview à ce sujet qu'il a donnée à la Radio et à la Télévision belge (ASAM, Sacerdoti, 23 et 24).
31. Cf. ADORNATO, *Cronologia dell'episcopato* (n. 21), p. 652.
32. Suenens dit qu'il a eu d'abord une discussion plutôt difficile à ce sujet avec Montini [créé cardinal par Jean XXIII le 15 décembre 1958], qui n'avait pas encore lu le livre qu'il lui avait envoyé mais que Montini a pris l'initiative de faire traduire ce livre en italien. Cf. SUENENS, *Mémoires sur le Concile Vatican II*, p. 56. (Fonds Suenens, 2784). Ces «Mémoires» non publiés datent du début 1966. Il s'agit d'un texte dicté par Suenens et transcrit avec pas mal de fautes et d'omissions.
33. Cf. lettre de C. Colombo à Suenens du 29 février 1960 à laquelle Suenens répond le 5 mars 1960 (Fonds Suenens A.P., b. 35).
34. Lettre de E. Rosini à Suenens, 4 mars 1965, Fonds Suenens, Birth Control et Humanae Vitae [archives à l'archevêché de Malines, cité: Fonds Suenens B.C. et H.V.], 112-115.
35. Lettre de Paul VI à Suenens, 9 août 1968. Le pape écrit notamment: «... Ma da un lato il ricordo del Suo studio su l' 'amore e maîtrise de soi', dall' altro la voce della nostra coscienza, interrogata lungamente davanti a Dio, ci hanno indotto a rivolgere alla Chiesa e al mondo questa parola» (Fonds Suenens B.C. et H.V., 1397).
36. Cf. ASAM, Sacerdoti, 991, 3 et 4.

– Quand Suenens envoie à Montini en 1961 son recueil de conférences *Vie quotidienne, vie chrétienne* (1961), celui-ci lui répond aimablement le 13 mars 1962, en le félicitant en même temps pour son élévation au cardinalat[37].

Dans cette période, on constate que Suenens a noué à plusieurs reprises des contacts avec Montini; comme substitut de la Secrétairerie d'État, celui-ci était un passage obligé pour accéder au pape; Suenens gardera le contact avec l'archevêque de Milan. Montini appréciait les publications du brillant évêque auxiliaire de Malines; celui-ci cherchait chez l'archevêque un appui pour répandre ses idées au sujet de la Légion de Marie et du Birth Control. Le fait que les idées de Suenens (par ex. au sujet de la mariologie, assez maximaliste; au sujet de l'œcuménisme[38] – voir aussi sa position vis-à-vis du Réarmement moral[39] –; au sujet de sa conception activiste, presque prosélyte, sur l'apostolat[40]) n'étaient à cette époque nullement révolutionnaires (sauf une légère ouverture pour un examen de la licéité des moyens anticonceptionnels) avait sans doute facilité le contact avec Montini, qui, dans certains domaines – p.e. l'œcuménisme –, était plus ouvert que Suenens. Il faut d'ailleurs noter qu'à cette époque, Suenens avait aussi de bons contacts avec plusieurs personnes assez «conservatrices» de la Curie romaine, comme A. Ottaviani et P. Philippe o.p.[41]. Cependant ceci ne l'a pas empêché de jouer plus tard un rôle important à Vatican II dans le sens de l'ouverture.

---

37. Fonds Suenens A.P., b. 35.
38. Tromp note par ex. dans son *Diarium* II, le 4 octobre 1961 (ASV, Conc.Vat. II, 790): «Colloquium cum Mgr Suenens, qui valde timet indifferentismum quo C.M. [Corpus Mysticum] separatur ab Ecclesia, et membra Ecclesiae vocantur etiam heretici et schismatici. Dolet quod Ecclesia catholica non sibi soli vindicat voces christiani, catholici, orthodoxi. Sperat fore ut Comm. Theol. hac in re non accedat ad falsum irenismum: secus post breve tempus inveniemur in medio 'drijfzand' [sables mouvants]».
39. Suenens mettait les catholiques en garde contre le mouvement du *Réarmement moral* à cause de son 'inspiration protestante' et voulait le faire condamner par le Saint-Office. À ce sujet, il est même entré en conflit avec Mgr Charrière, évêque du lieu de Caux, où le *Réarmement moral* avait son centre (lettres de Charrière à Suenens des 14 mars et 7 avril 1953, Cf. Fonds Suenens A.P., b. 33.). Voir le livre de Suenens, *Que faut-il penser du Réarmement moral?*, Paris-Bruxelles, Éditions universitaires, 1953, où il écrit notamment: «Pareils à ces rameurs dont parlait saint François de Sales, qui vont droit au but en lui tournant le dos, nous nous rapprochons en nous séparant, car la vérité seule peut engendrer la vie. L'intransigeance doctrinale de l'Église, si éloignée de notre courte sagesse humaine, est une forme d'amour véritable qui ne heurte que pour libérer la vérité captive dans l'erreur, qui l'étreint, et qui invite au dépassement de soi» (p. 12).
40. Cf. SUENENS, *L'Église en état de mission* (n. 26).
41. Il est significatif que Mgr D. Staffa (pendant le concile un adversaire acharné de la collégialité des évêques), propose, dans une lettre du 1 juillet 1960, Suenens comme candidat-membre pour la Commission théologique préparatoire. Cf. ASV, Conc. Vat. II, 736,

III. LA PÉRIODE CONCILIAIRE

1. Anteconcilium

Comme membre de la commission conciliaire préparatoire *De episco-pis et dioecesium regimine*, Suenens ne semble pas avoir eu de contacts avec Montini. Si on trouve dans les archives Suenens une copie (publiée dans les *ADA*) de la réponse de Montini (9.5.1960) à la lettre de Tardini (qui demandait d'envoyer des suggestions pour le concile)[42], ce document a été copié plus tardivement, probablement en vue de l'article de Suenens *Aux origines du Concile Vatican II*[43].

Quand le nouvel archevêque de Malines-Bruxelles (décembre 1961) est devenu cardinal en mars 1962, il est nommé membre de la commission centrale préparatoire[44] et il rencontre Montini dans les réunions de cette commission. La commission centrale se réunit à Rome du 3 au 12 mai 1962, et on constate que Montini reçoit Suenens au Collegio Lombardo à Rome le 11 mai 1962[45]. Suenens écrit à ce sujet: «J'ai longuement, au Collège Lombard, discuté ce plan [du concile] avec le Cardinal Montini. Lui avait une grande idée d'un message à faire, à l'issue du concile[46], et la partie du plan, qui concerne ce message, la dernière page, est en somme le fruit d'une conversation de deux heures avec lui»[47]. Et, le 16 mai 1962, Suenens envoie son 'plan' à Jean XXIII en disant qu'il le fait après consultation de quelques personnes[48]. Suenens affirme qu'une copie de son plan a été envoyée par le Secrétaire d'État à quelques cardinaux dont Montini. Toutefois, l'accord des cardinaux semble avoir été moins unanime que Suenens ne l'a écrit[49].

Une dernière réunion de la commission centrale a lieu du 12 au 20 juin. À cette occasion Suenens réunit quelques cardinaux au Collège belge à Rome pour discuter de son plan. Parmi les présents il y avait e.a. Montini, Siri, Liénart et Döpfner[50]. Et le 4 juillet 1962, Suenens envoie une

58 (avec nos remerciements à Mlle A. von Teuffenbach qui nous a signalé ce document ainsi que l'extrait du Diarium Tromp de la note 38).
42. Cf. Fonds Suenens, 427.
43. L.-J. SUENENS, *Aux origines du Concile Vatican II*, dans *Nouvelle Revue Théologique* 107 (1985) 3-21.
44. Le 24 mars 1962 (cf. *L'Osservatore Romano*, 25 mars 1962).
45. Cf. ADORNATO, *Cronologia dell'episcopato* (n. 21), p. 866.
46. Il est intéressant de voir que Paul VI a mis cette idée en application lors de la cérémonie de clôture du concile le 8 décembre 1965.
47. Cf. SUENENS, *Mémoires sur le Concile Vatican II* (n. 32), p. 18.
48. Fonds Suenens, 380.
49. Fonds Suenens, 383.
50. En écrivant que cette réunion au Collège belge (cf. SUENENS, *Aux origines du Concile Vatican II* [n. 43], p. 4) eut lieu au début de juillet, Suenens se trompe. En effet,

nouvelle version de son plan à Jean XXIII en mentionnant l'accord de plusieurs cardinaux dont Montini[51]. Dans ses *Mémoires sur le Concile Vatican II*, Suenens note d'une part que Montini était opposé à sa proposition de fixer une limite d'âge pour les évêques mais qu'il a bien reçu son appui pour faire cesser le monopole de l'Action catholique[52].

En août 1962, le cardinal Léger rédige une lettre à Jean XXIII avec des critiques sévères sur les schémas préparatoires et demande la signature de Liénart, Döpfner, Alfrink, König, Suenens et Montini. Suenens a signé cette lettre tandis que Montini a refusé[53]. Suenens note: «Nous [les autres cardinaux concernés] avons été assez mécontents, à ce moment-là, qu'il se soit dérobé, mais il a, sans doute, préféré garder [le silence et] ne pas sortir de sa réserve [sic], comme il l'avait fait d'ailleurs pendant les différentes discussions au cours de la Commission centrale où il n'avait que très rarement pris une position marquée. C'était certainement une grande préoccupation de prudence qui l'animait à ce moment-là»[54]. À ce sujet, Suenens écrira encore le 9 octobre 1962 à V. O'Brien: «Il [Léger] a reçu réponse à la lettre des 7, réponse de Cicognani très aimable mais ne disant rien de précis. Montini n'a pas signé mais les 6 autres. Vous voyez

au début de juillet Montini se trouvait à Milan (ADORNATO, *Cronologia dell'episcopato* [n. 21], p. 880) et, dans les archives Döpfner, il y a des notes au sujet d'une réunion au Collège belge en juin 1962 (Fonds Döpfner, 2806, voir G. TREFFLER – P. PFISTER (éds.), *Erzbischöfliches Archiv München Julius Kardinal Döpfner: Archivinventar der Dokumente zum Zweiten Vatikanischen Konzil* (Schriften des Archivs des Erzbistums München und Freising, 6), München, Schnell und Steiner, 2004.

51. Fonds Suenens, 388-390. Dans ses *Mémoires sur le Concile Vatican II* (n. 32), p. 18, Suenens affirme que tous les cardinaux consultés (donc aussi Döpfner et Siri) étaient complètement d'accord. Cependant, les notes de Döpfner montrent qu'il est assez critique pour le plan Suenens (cf. Fonds Döpfner, 2806: «… Ho questo dubbio: Non si può le materie del Concilio ordinare come un articolo scientifico oppure un libro [sic]. Nella linea del locus classicus Matth. 28,18-20 si svolge una disposizione non adaequata [sic], un pò torta». Notes de Döpfner en italien). De même Siri, probablement invité sur l'insistance de Jean XXIII, n'était guère enthousiaste. Cf. B. LAI, *Il papa non eletto: Giuseppe Siri, cardinale di Santa Romana Chiesa* (I Robinson), Roma, Laterza, 1993, p. 183, note 13: «Suenens ha sostenuto che solo il cardinale Döpfner si mostrò contrario alla sua proposta, ma che poi acettò l'opinione favorevole di Liénart, Montini e Siri … 'È una falsità, non accettai proprio nulla. Suenens è uno a cui è sempre piaciuto fare il protagonista'» (dans une conversation avec B. Lai le 22 novembre 1985). Selon SUENENS, *Mémoires du Concile Vatican II* (n. 32), p. 17, c'est Cicognani qui a dit à Suenens d'inviter Siri.

52. Cf. SUENENS, *Mémoires sur le Concile Vatican II* (n. 32), pp. 10-12, Fonds Suenens, 2784. Le 3 mai 1962, à la réunion de la Commission centrale préparatoire, Montini était d'accord qu'un évêque donne sa démission mais ne voulait pas qu'on fixe un âge-limite. Tandis que Suenens plaidait pour qu'on donne sa démission à 70 ans et qu'à 75 ans elle devait être obligatoire. (cf. *AD* II/2.3, pp. 665 et 671).

53. Cf. Fonds Suenens, 393-397 et Fonds Léger, 128 et 128a.

54. SUENENS, *Mémoires sur le Concile Vatican II* (n. 32), p. 18.

l'homme prudent! Il doit être un as dans cette vertu … cardinale»[55]. Pour cette période préconciliaire, on peut estimer que Suenens considérait Montini comme un cardinal influent et le plus ouvert parmi les Italiens et qu'il croyait important d'avoir son appui.

2. 1ᵉ Session (11 octobre – 8 décembre 1962)

Pendant la 1ᵉ session, on constate que les contacts de Suenens avec Montini s'intensifient[56]. Ceci est dû au fait que les deux cardinaux sont membres du Secrétariat pour les Affaires extraordinaires, où ils se rencontrent pratiquement chaque semaine: 8 réunions pendant cette session. De plus, il y a eu plusieurs réunions «privées» de cardinaux, où et Suenens et Montini étaient présents. Le fait aussi que Montini logeait au Vatican, comme invité de Jean XXIII, montrait son importance et l'influence qu'il exerçait sur le pape. Suenens en était conscient et cherchait à avoir son appui notamment pour son 'plan' du concile, présenté *in aula* le 4 décembre 1962.

– Pour les élections des commissions conciliaires (1ᵉ semaine de la session), Suenens constate avec plaisir que des évêques orientaux ont fait circuler une liste (avec des candidats) pour qu'on vote pour les évêques les plus ouverts à l'Orient et qu'il y figure avec Montini[57]. Et le samedi 13 octobre, il écrit que «Montini lui a montré une liste où figurait même pour la commission théologique le Vagnozzi de Washington… qui n'a rien d'un théologien»[58].
– Au Secrétariat pour les Affaires extraordinaires, Suenens a des contacts réguliers avec Montini. Quand il fait rapport à V. O'Brien sur la 1ᵉ réunion de ce Secrétariat le 16 octobre 1962, en présence du pape,

---

55. Fonds Suenens, 568.
56. Quand l'ambassadeur de Belgique auprès du Saint-Siège Poswick fait remarquer à Suenens, le 9 oct. 1962, que dans le Secrétariat pour les Affaires extraordinaires, les Italiens ont encore la majorité, Suenens réplique: «Cela ne m'inquiète pas car le cardinal Montini sera toujours avec nous». Cf. P. Poswick, *Un journal du Concile: Vatican II vu par un diplomate belge. Notes personnelles de l'Ambassadeur de Belgique près le Saint-Siège (1957-1968), et rapports au Ministère des Affaires Étrangères* (édité par R.-F. Poswick et Y. Juste), Paris, de Guibert, 2005, p. 154. Une autre preuve est fournie par l'invitation que Poswick adresse à Montini pour prendre le déjeuner chez lui le 14 novembre 1962. Poswick écrit: «Son Éminence le Cardinal Suenens m'a demandé d'organiser chez moi une série de déjeuners pour lui permettre de rencontrer à loisir certaines hautes personnalités du Concile. La première d'entre elles qu'il m'a citée est Votre Éminence Révérendissime» (lettre du 10 novembre 1962). Invitation que Montini n'a pu accepter, empêché par d'autres obligations (Cf. ASAM, Enti 1712, 1 et 2).
57. Lettres à V. O'Brien, 12-13-14 octobre 1962, Fonds Suenens, 570, p. 4.
58. *Ibid.* Vagnozzi était délégué apostolique à Washington.

il écrit: «Montini très bien mais sur un plan assez 'ad extra'»[59]. Et aussi que Montini lui a dit en sortant: «Jusqu'ici j'avais cru que c'était un groupe 'pro forma'; je m'aperçois que c'est sérieux»[60]. Le cardinal Siri note aussi que Montini appuie une proposition de Suenens et Döpfner pour ne pas porter les habits de prélat lors des congrégations générales et ne pas commencer chaque session par la messe (pour gagner du temps)[61]. C'est aussi à une réunion de ce Secrétariat – le 19 octobre 1962 – que la lettre de Montini au cardinal Cicognani avec son plan pour le concile a été distribuée à tous les membres[62], lettre que Suenens a bien conservée et publiée par après dans un article de la *Nouvelle Revue Théologique*[63].

– Ce que Suenens a surtout apprécié dans cette session, c'est l'appui que Montini a donné à son 'plan' pour le concile, plan développé par Suenens dans son intervention *in aula* du 4 décembre. Cette intervention de Suenens a été préparée par une réunion au Collège belge (fin novembre – début décembre 1962), réunion où Montini était probablement présent[64]. Suenens mentionne aussi qu'il avait soupé la veille au soir[65] chez le cardinal Montini, dans la maison qu'il occupait près des jardins du Vatican[66]. Suenens avait dit qu'il allait faire son intervention, mais Montini n'avait pas dit qu'il comptait l'appuyer. Cependant, le 5 décembre, Montini commence son intervention importante

59. Suenens fait probablement allusion au caractère réservé de Montini.
60. Lettre à V. O'Brien, 16 octobre 1962, Fonds Suenens, 573, pp. 1-2.
61. Cf. LAI, *Il papa non eletto* (n. 51), pp. 363 et 366. Siri s'oppose à ces propositions. Dans ses *Mémoires sur le Concile Vatican II* (n. 32), Suenens note aussi: «Il [ce Secrétariat] comportait et Montini et Siri, ce qui était une manière de neutraliser les choses» (SUENENS, *Mémoires sur le Concile Vatican II* [n. 32], p. 30).
62. Cf. LAI, *Il papa non eletto* (n. 51), p. 365. Pour le texte de Montini (11 pages), cf. Fonds Suenens, 565.
63. Cf. SUENENS, *Aux origines du Concile Vatican II* [n. 43].
64. On n'a trouvé ni la date exacte de cette réunion ni les noms de tous les participants. Dans une bande magnétique (III), enregistrée le 8 février 2000, Prignon parle de 12 à 15 participants, mais ce chiffre est probablement exagéré et il ne peut pas affirmer avec certitude que Montini était présent. Comme Siri dans son *Diario* (Cf. LAI, *Il papa non eletto* [n. 51], p. 369) parle d'une réunion de cardinaux de l'Europe centrale chez Frings le 25 octobre 1962 et cite comme participants Frings, Liénart, Montini, König, Döpfner, Suenens, Alfrink et lui-même, il est possible qu'il s'agissait d'une réunion du même groupe. D'ailleurs, il faut noter que cet enregistrement de Prignon, déjà octogénaire, réalisé par E. de Beukelaer en 2000, contient beaucoup d'erreurs manifestes (erreurs de chronologie et confusion de certains événements). L'agenda du card. Léger mentionne encore une réunion chez Frings, le 11 novembre 1962, avec Döpfner, Alfrink, Suenens, Liénart et Léger (lettre de G. Routhier à L. Declerck, 22 mars 2004).
65. La veille de son intervention, donc le 3 décembre. Ce qui est confirmé par une carte de visite de Montini avec la date manuscrite du 3 décembre 1962, carte annexée à un document. (Cf. Fonds Suenens, 567 [où il faut corriger la date de 1963 en 1962]).
66. SUENENS, *Mémoires sur le Concile Vatican II* (n. 32), p. 29.

in aula, par un fort appui au plan de Suenens[67]. Selon Suenens, Mgr Capovilla lui a dit que Jean XXIII avait demandé à Montini de faire cette intervention[68].

À la suite de ces interventions et aussi de celles d'Alfrink, Léger et Lercaro, Jean XXIII institua le 5 décembre la Commission de coordination, dont Suenens, mais non Montini, fera partie[69].

3. 1ᵉ Intersession

Jusqu'à la mort de Jean XXIII le 3 juin 1963, on n'a pas trouvé de traces d'un contact entre Montini et Suenens. Et Suenens a observé le secret absolu au sujet du conclave de juin 1963, où Montini a été élu pape le 21 juin 1963[70].

– Mais le dimanche 23 juin, Suenens avait une audience chez le nouveau pape. Lorsqu'à midi le pape devait réciter l'Angelus pour les fidèles qui se trouvaient sur la place Saint-Pierre, il a fait venir Suenens à la fenêtre et l'a présenté à la foule[71]. Ce geste extraordinaire, probablement de pure gentillesse, a été largement commenté dans les milieux romains et dans la presse[72]. Tout en prenant ses distances

---

67. «… officii mei esse censeo vos rogare ut peculiari diligentia consideretis ea quae em.mus card. Suenens heri tam perspicue exposuit de fine huic universali Synodo proposito et de ordine logico et congruenti argumentorum in ea tractandorum» (*AS* I/4, p. 291).

68. Fonds Suenens, 2874, p. 29. Paul VI s'est souvenu de son intervention lorsque, dans une audience, il disait au card. Suenens le 22 décembre 1970: «Avez-vous oublié que c'est moi qui vous ai dit de proposer votre plan au concile et que je l'ai soutenu? J'espérais une collaboration et voilà: l'inverse» (Notes personnelles de Suenens, cf. Fonds Suenens A.P., b. 13). Cette audience se passait pendant la crise dans les relations entre Paul VI et Suenens, cf. *infra.*

69. *L'Osservatore Romano* du 17-18 décembre 1962 publiait les noms des membres: Cicognani, Liénart, Spellman, Urbani, Confalonieri, Döpfner et Suenens.

70. Non seulement dans la presse, mais aussi dans le milieu diplomatique on parlait de Suenens comme *papabile.* L'ambassadeur de France, W. d'Ormesson disait le 15 juin 1963 à Poswick que «les Français (je ne dis pas les cardinaux français, sauf bien entendu le cardinal Tisserant) sont hostiles à la nomination d'un pape étranger parce qu'ils craignaient que ce soit le Cardinal Suenens, ce qui les remplirait de jalousie» (Cf. POSWICK, *Un journal du Concile* [n. 56], p. 285).

71. À deux reprises, *L'Osservatore Romano* (numéros du 24-25 juin et du 29 juin 1963) a publié une photo de cet événement.

72. Par ex. *Il Giorno* (24 juin 1963) publie la photo à la 1ᵉ page et écrit: «Sull'apparizione di Suenens a fianco del Papa, si sono fatti molti commenti. Il cardinale belga veniva considerato pochi giorni fa uno dei pochi papabili stranieri, ed è sicuramente una delle figure intellettualmente più vive della Chiesa cattolica. Membro della commissione di coordinamento per i lavori del Concilio fra le due sessioni, egli ne è stato definito autorevolmente «il motore». È uno dei cardinali più «progressisti» … Il singolare onore concesso a Suenens (che ha un solo precedente: quello di Wyszynski, che Giovanni XXIII

vis-à-vis de ces spéculations, Suenens a interprété ce geste comme un signe d'amitié et peut-être comme un remerciement pour sa franchise à son égard ainsi qu'une manière de souligner son désir de continuer le concile dans la ligne de Jean XXIII[73]. Dans son journal, Moeller raconte: «Suenens a été reçu plus tôt ce jour. Le Pape a fait approcher Suenens de la fenêtre. Suenens ne voulait pas. Le pape l'a forcé. Toute la presse du monde entier en a parlé. Les Romains ne le [lui] ont pas pardonné. On a dit que Suenens deviendrait Secrétaire d'État[74]. Peu de temps après, le Pape a présenté un autre à la fenêtre, puis ne l'a plus fait. Mais le mal était fait»[75]. Même si la presse et certains milieux de la curie ont surestimé ce geste de Paul VI, on ne peut nier que l'autorité morale de Suenens en fut renforcée et que lui-même a fortement apprécié ce geste extraordinaire.

– Le 9 septembre 1963, Suenens est nommé modérateur du concile par Paul VI en même temps que Lercaro, Döpfner et Agagianian[76]. Dans une audience[77] au 'lendemain de sa nomination pontificale', le pape lui aurait dit: «Je songe à nommer deux 'légats pontificaux pour diriger le concile'. S'il y en a deux ce serait vous et le cardinal Agagianian. Si je me décide à en nommer trois, ce serait vous, le Cardinal Agagianian et le Cardinal Döpfner»[78]. Dans une lettre du 15 septembre 1963, Suenens remercie chaleureusement le pape: «Merci pour la confiance, l'estime et l'affection qui sont incluses dans cette nomination dont j'apprécie tout le prix, comme aussi toute la responsabilité»[79]. Il faut toutefois remarquer que déjà fin août commence la discussion

volle accanto di se in identica circostanza) rivela quindi, probabilmente, il desiderio di Paolo VI di continuare a dare grande importanza ai collaboratori di Papa Roncalli: non soltanto quelli del «centro» … ma anche quelli della «periferia» e in particolare di potenziare, come Suenens ha spesso chiesto, il Concilio come strumento del dialogo fra la Chiesa ed il mondo» (Cf. Fonds Suenens A.P., b. 13).

73. Cf. SUENENS, *Souvenirs et espérances* (n. 14), p. 109.

74. Encore le 4 novembre 1963, Poswick fait état de ces rumeurs à Suenens, qui lui répond: «Pour être un bon Secrétaire d'État, il faut un passé de diplomate! En tout cas, ce n'est pas dans mes charismes. Mon 'charisme', c'est la pastorale. Si le Pape me l'offrait, je déclinerais. S'il me l'imposait, à la grâce de Dieu» (Cf. POSWICK, *Un journal du Concile* [n. 56], p. 347).

75. Journal Moeller, Carnet 32, octobre 1965, p. 2. Avec nos remerciements au P. Cesare Antonelli, qui nous a beaucoup aidé dans la transcription de quelques passages de ce Journal.

76. Lettre de Cicognani à Suenens, 9 septembre 1963, Fonds Suenens, 791.

77. Il s'agit probablement de l'audience du 23 juin 1963 puisque *L'Osservatore Romano* ne fait pas mention d'autres audiences de Suenens en juin et juillet 1963.

78. Cf. SUENENS, *Mémoires sur le Concile Vatican II* (n. 32), p. 37. Cf. aussi *Souvenirs et espérances* (n. 14), pp. 110 sv.

79. Fonds Suenens, 788bis et SUENENS, *Souvenirs et espérances* (n. 14), p. 111.

au sujet de la mission et des pouvoirs des modérateurs, discussion qui, comme on le sait, ne s'est pas conclue dans un sens favorable pour les modérateurs.

– Dans le même mois de septembre, le pape prie Suenens de vouloir tenir le discours en mémoire de Jean XXIII pendant la 2e session du concile[80]. Suenens accepte bien volontiers et remercie de cette 'si délicate attention'[81] et déjà le 17 septembre 1963, Cicognani peut lui préciser que le discours peut se tenir en français et qu'il doit durer environ 45 minutes[82].

On peut conclure que, pendant ces premiers mois du pontificat, l'influence de Suenens connaît son apogée, influence attestée par plusieurs gestes de confiance de Paul VI[83]. D'autre part, les contacts entre les deux hommes ne sont pas toujours très faciles ou spontanés[84].

80. Lettre du cardinal Cicognani à Suenens, 7 septembre 1963, qui écrit: «Il a paru à Sa Sainteté que nul plus que Votre Éminence n'était capable d'évoquer devant cette illustre assemblée le Pape Jean XXIII, dans l'enceinte même du Concile pour lequel il a offert ses souffrances et sa vie. C'est le Pape Jean XXIII qui, après vous avoir confié le siège archiépiscopal de Malines-Bruxelles, vous élevait à la pourpre cardinalice, et vous associait aussitôt d'une manière étroite aux travaux du Concile œcuménique du Vatican, dans sa préparation d'abord, puis dans son déroulement. Et c'est vous encore qu'il chargeait de présenter son Encyclique *Pacem in terris*, devant l'auditoire de choix qu'est l'Assemblée des Nations Unies à New York. Aussi le Saint-Père – dont vous savez la profonde estime et la vive affection qu'Il nourrit pour votre personne – m'a-t-il chargé de vous confier en Son nom le soin de tenir en Sa présence le discours commémoratif de Son prédécesseur, qui demeure pour tous le Pape de la paix et le Pape du concile. Il m'est très agréable d'être auprès de Votre Éminence l'intermédiaire de cette nouvelle marque de confiance du Saint-Père…». Cf. Fonds Suenens, 1661.

81. Lettre de Suenens au pape, 15 septembre 1963, Fonds Suenens, 788bis. Dans ses *Mémoires sur le Concile Vatican II* (n. 32), p. 68, Suenens écrit: «Cela a été une marque à laquelle j'ai été particulièrement sensible, d'autant plus qu'il me disait dans la lettre … que j'étais un de ses [de Jean XXIII] plus proches collaborateurs ou peut-être le plus proche de ses collaborateurs en pensée».

82. Fonds Suenens, 1662.

83. Au cours d'une audience donnée à l'ambassadeur Poswick au mois d'août 1963, le pape aurait dit au sujet du cardinal Suenens: «Je l'admire non seulement pour son esprit de synthèse mais pour la faculté qu'il a de faire passer dans les faits les décisions de son esprit» (Cf. POSWICK, *Un journal du Concile* [n. 56], p. 332).

84. Le 19 juin 1963 Suenens aurait dit à l'ambassadeur Poswick: «que le cardinal Montini est devenu, en effet, d'accès difficile. Chaque fois que lui-même est allé le voir à Milan, bien qu'ils se connaissent et s'estiment depuis longtemps, et qu'ils étaient attelés au même travail, l'archevêque est de glace pendant la première demi-heure de conversation; pendant la seconde demi-heure il commence à mollir; pendant la troisième demi-heure il est absolument charmant. 'Mais, ajoute le cardinal Suenens, chaque fois qu'on le revoit, le même travail d'approche est à faire'» (Cf. POSWICK, *Un journal du Concile* [n. 56], p. 287).

4. 2ᵉ Session (29 septembre – 4 décembre 1963)

Encore un peu euphorique du fait des événements de juin-septembre 1963, Suenens est frappé par la connexion étroite entre le discours d'ouverture du pape à la 2ᵉ session et le 'plan' du concile tel qu'il avait été proposé[85].

Le fameux épisode des 5 *Quaestiones*[86] – au sujet du *De ecclesia* – allait cependant pour la première fois mettre à l'épreuve les relations entre Paul VI et Suenens. On sait que Suenens s'est fortement investi dans cette bataille, surtout contre Felici et Ottaviani, pour que les modérateurs obtiennent le droit de poser ces questions interlocutoires et de faire avancer ainsi le travail du concile. Suenens affirme que Lercaro, Döpfner et lui-même avaient songé à une lettre de démission comme modérateur et que Lercaro en avait rédigé un brouillon. Et le pape, dans une audience donnée à Lercaro, a pris position contre celui-ci et il n'aurait soutenu en rien les modérateurs à ce moment[87].

Si les modérateurs ont obtenu finalement gain de cause, ce ne fut pas sans une perte d'influence: leur 'secrétaire' Dossetti (selon beaucoup le 'mauvais génie' de ces questions) a été congédié sur insistance de Felici et les modérateurs avaient expérimenté une première fois que le pape ne marchait pas nécessairement dans la direction de l'aile 'progressiste' du concile.

Huit jours après l'événement, lors d'un déjeuner avec le pape, Suenens aurait dit au pape: «Vous m'avez fait gravir les quatorze stations du chemin de croix». Et Paul VI aurait répondu: «Oui, vous avez gravi ces stations … Je voulais que ce [poser les 5 Questions à l'assemblée du concile] soit fait sous la responsabilité des modérateurs, sans m'engager

---

85. SUENENS, *Mémoires sur le Concile Vatican II* (n. 32), p. 37. Ce sentiment de Suenens est un peu exagéré. Cependant les dernières pages du discours de Paul VI du 29 septembre 1963 (voir les *AAS* 55 [1963] 841-859, surtout pp. 852-859) pourraient être inspirées par le 'plan' de Suenens qui contient en finale un 'Message au monde' (cf. *Nouvelle Revue Théologique* [1985] 17-18). Et Suenens ajoute honnêtement: «Tout ce qui a été dit sur le Christ 'pantocrator', l'hommage au Christ, c'est cela l'idée qu'il [Montini] avait développée lorsque nous avions travaillé ensemble à ce plan».

86. Après le débat *in aula* sur le chapitre II du *De Ecclesia*, les modérateurs voulaient soumettre à l'assemblée 4 et puis 5 Questions destinées à orienter les travaux de la commission doctrinale. Questions qui se rapportaient à la sacramentalité et à la collégialité de l'épiscopat et au diaconat.

87. Cf. *Mémoires sur le Concile Vatican II* (n. 32), p. 42-43. Selon le Journal de A. Nicora, cette audience de Lercaro a eu lieu le 15 novembre 1963 (cf. G. ALBERIGO, *Pour la jeunesse du christianisme: Le Concile Vatican II*, Paris, Cerf, 2005, p. 93). Mgr Prignon mentionne aussi que le cardinal Suenens fut prêt, à un certain moment, à présenter sa démission comme modérateur (Bande magnétique Prignon, IV, 8 février 2000).

personnellement»[88]. À cause du rôle que Suenens a joué dans cet épisode des 5 Questions (avec leur insistance sur la collégialité) il a été dépeint dans certains milieux de droite comme un adversaire de la primauté. C'est ainsi que son ami Benelli, à cette époque auditeur à la nonciature d'Espagne, lui décrit les réactions en Espagne et demande à Suenens de faire, à la fin de cette session, une déclaration pour défendre la primauté[89].

Au milieu de la crise autour des 5 Questions, Suenens a tenu *in aula* son beau discours à la mémoire de Jean XXIII. Il est à noter qu'il a envoyé le projet de son discours au pape en lui demandant des corrections éventuelles. Dans la même lettre, il sollicite du pape la nomination de Frank Duff comme auditeur laïc[90].

Signalons encore que le 22 octobre 1963, dans son intervention *in aula*, Suenens a fait un appel solennel pour que soient nommées des 'auditrices' au Concile («puisque les femmes constituent, si je ne me trompe, la moitié de l'humanité»[91]). Souhait auquel le pape a accédé le 21 septembre 1964[92] en nommant 8 religieuses et 7 'auditrices' laïques au concile[93].

88. Cf. C. TROISFONTAINES, *À propos de quelques interventions de Paul VI*, dans *Paolo VI e i problemi ecclesiologici al Concilio*, Brescia, Istituto Paolo VI, 1989, p. 101. C. Troisfontaines s'est basé sur un entretien avec Suenens du 26 juin 1986. Cette version est reprise par Suenens dans *Souvenirs et espérances* (n. 14), p. 117. Selon le journal de Congar (cf. Y. CONGAR, *Mon Journal du Concile*, présenté et annoté par É. MAHIEU, 2 tomes, Paris, Cerf, 2002, Tome II, p. 17), qui cite Prignon comme source, cet épisode se serait passé le dimanche 27 octobre lors d'un dîner des quatre modérateurs avec le pape.

89. Cf. la lettre de Benelli à Suenens, 15 novembre 1963, Fonds Suenens, 1526. G. Benelli (1921-1982) avait été secrétaire de Montini à la Secrétairerie d'État de 1947 à 1950. Comme auditeur de la nonciature en Irlande, il avait fait la connaissance de Frank Duff et de la Légion de Marie. Comme auditeur de la nonciature à Paris (1953-1960), il avait rencontré V. O'Brien (à ce moment *envoy* de la Légion de Marie en France) et Suenens. Benelli, à situer plus «à droite» que Suenens, a toujours conservé son amitié à Suenens, même lorsque comme substitut de la Secrétairerie d'État (1967-1977) et homme de confiance de Paul VI, sa position n'était pas facile, lors du conflit Paul VI – Suenens dans les années 1969-1971 (cf. infra). Benelli a toujours essayé de «modérer» Suenens, parfois à la demande de Paul VI. Que cette position fût fort délicate pour Benelli, est démontré e.a. par une note de Suenens, écrite après une conversation avec Benelli, le 17 février 1972: «La grande question pour Benelli, c'était que je dise bien au Pape qu'il a fait tout ce qu'il a pu, lui, pour m'amener à prendre une autre position, parce que dans la lettre ils ont dû comprendre, le pape et surtout Villot, que Benelli au fond était de mon côté. Il a très peur de cela et je lui ai soigneusement marqué que ce n'était pas le cas». Et de fait dans le récit de son audience avec le pape, le 18 février 1972, Suenens note: «… j'ai clarifié très fort la fidélité d'Eliot [Benelli] à lui [le pape] contre moi dans le passé» (cf. Fonds Suenens A.P., b. 13).

90. Lettre du 11 novembre 1963, Fonds Suenens, 3033.

91. «Invitentur ut auditores etiam mulieres, quae, ni fallor, dimidiam partem humanitatis constituunt». Cf. Fonds Suenens, 1534.

92. Cf. *AS* VI/3, pp. 367-368.

93. R. Goldie dans *Paolo VI e i problemi ecclesiologici* (n. 88), p. 204, note 4, écrit que Paul VI avait voulu nommer des auditrices dès 1963 en même temps que les auditeurs,

Toutefois, Suenens a dit qu'il a été impossible de faire accepter par le pape qu'une femme parle au concile[94].

5. 2ᵉ Intersession

Pendant la 2ᵉ intersession, les contacts de Suenens avec Paul VI sont évidemment moins intenses que pendant la 2ᵉ session, mais restent imprégnés d'une grande confiance. On constate aussi que le cardinal s'occupe de plus en plus de la question épineuse du Birth Control.

– Le 13 décembre 1963, le card. Cicognani demande au nom du pape, un avis sur le rapport de la Commission pontificale au sujet de la natalité[95] et sur l'éventualité d'un prononcé du magistère[96]. Le 24 décembre 1963, Suenens répond à Cicognani par une note de 6 pages mais quand il présente ses vœux de Noël au pape, il envoie aussi directement sa note à celui-ci[97]. Dans sa note le cardinal disait que la question était urgente mais que la réponse devait être nuancée et mûrie et que la question devait encore être élucidée dans le cadre du schéma XVII et qu'il serait bon de demander un rapport à un groupe international de moralistes et de chercheurs[98].

– Dans une lettre du cardinal à Paul VI, écrite le 23 janvier 1964 à la fin de l'Octave de prières pour l'Unité, Suenens semble vouloir apaiser le

mais que des insistances peu opportunes, au lieu de faciliter ce «geste», l'ont fait remettre d'un an. Il est vrai que Paul VI, homme fin et délicat, n'aimait guère les interventions parfois un peu cavalières de Suenens (cf. son intervention *in aula* de la 3ᵉ session au sujet du Birth Control et plus tard les interviews de 1969, 1970 et 1971). Mais, puisque Paul VI avait déjà nommé des auditeurs laïcs le 14 septembre 1963, il est difficile de penser que R. Goldie fait ici allusion au discours de Suenens, qui ne date que du 22 octobre 1963. D'ailleurs dans une lettre du 3 décembre 2004 à L. Declerck, R. Goldie écrit: «I find it difficult to attribute the origin of the 'insistances' to Cardinal Suenens».

94. Journal Moeller, Carnet 23, 5 novembre 1964, p. 10.

95. Pour ce rapport, cf. Fonds Suenens B.C. et H.V., 266.

96. Cf. Fonds Suenens, 1959. On sait que le P. de Riedmatten a été chargé par le Secrétaire d'État, en avril 1963, d'ériger un groupe d'études sur les problèmes de la natalité. C'est le card. Suenens qui aurait obtenu de Jean XXIII la constitution de cette commission. Parmi les 6 premiers membres (S. de Lestapis s.j., J. Marshall, C. Mertens s.j., H. de Riedmatten o.p., P. van Rossum et J. Mertens de Wilmars), il y avait trois Belges qui étaient nommés grâce à l'influence de Suenens: van Rossum, ami du cardinal; Mertens s.j., qui était en correspondance avec lui à ce sujet [Cf. Fonds Suenens, 536-538, 543, 545, 664, 1332-1334] et J. Mertens de Wilmars, professeur à l'Université catholique de Louvain. On sait que la première réunion de ce groupe s'est tenue à Louvain en octobre 1963. (Cf. L. DECLERCK, *Le rôle joué par les évêques et periti belges au concile Vatican II: Deux exemples*, dans *ETL* 76 [2000] 457-458 et Fonds Suenens B.C. et H.V., 271-273).

97. Cf. Fonds Suenens, 1962.

98. On voit que le cardinal, convaincu qu'une position plus ouverte du magistère n'était pas encore acquise, cherche à gagner du temps. Aussi, pendant la 3ᵉ session, il fera encore un plaidoyer pour une commission plus scientifique et plus internationale.

pape en écrivant: «Il y a trop d'idées imprécises dans un domaine où aucune confusion ne peut régner. Le Vatican II n'a de sens que dans la continuité de Vatican I et toute opposition entre l'un et l'autre est impensable. Une collégialité qui impliquerait une 'cogestion' quelconque de près ou de loin irait à l'encontre de la pensée du Seigneur et de la Tradition»[99].

– Le 2 mars 1964, Suenens fait parvenir à Paul VI une note sur le Birth Control et prie le pape de la lire avant l'audience qu'il demandera aux environs du 10 mars; il écrit également au pape qu'il a été heureux que la Secrétairerie d'État ait envoyé un questionnaire aux conférences épiscopales sur le même sujet[100]. C'est probablement lors de cette audience[101] que le pape aurait dit à Suenens que, «si les moralistes [illisible: hésitaient?] sur la morale conjugale», il devrait intervenir. Le cardinal le supplie d'attendre jusqu'après le concile[102].

– Le samedi 18 avril 1964 à 10h.50, Suenens a une audience d'une demi-heure chez le pape. Mgr Prignon, qui a vu le cardinal immédiatement après son retour du Vatican, en donne un long rapport[103]. Le cardinal a trouvé le Saint-Père plus détendu que dans les deux audiences précédentes de cette année[104]. Il a donné au pape une note d'un théologien romain au sujet de la morale conjugale – note de nature à ébranler la conviction du Saint-Père – et lui a parlé de la 2e session de la commission pontificale pendant la semaine de Pâques[105]. Suenens s'est plaint de l'attitude de Cicognani (à la commission de coordination[106]) au sujet de la collégialité. Et il aurait suggéré au pape que le temps était venu de le remplacer. Suenens a aussi félicité le pape au sujet de son discours aux évêques italiens[107]. Prignon conclut: «Dans l'ensemble il [le cardinal] a trouvé donc le pape toujours aussi affectueux et l'invitant à plusieurs reprises à lui demander tout ce qu'il voulait. Il avait l'impression que le pape désirait vraiment pouvoir lui faire plaisir, même accorder des faveurs. Le cardinal ajouta toutefois: 'Que le vrai problème n'était pas les gentillesses personnelles du Saint-Père mais

---

99. Cf. Fonds Suenens, 1712.
100. Cf. Fonds Suenens, 1981. Pour le questionnaire de la Secrétairerie d'État au sujet du Birth Control et de la morale conjugale, cf. Fonds Suenens, B.C. et H.V., 14-28.
101. Audience du 12 mars 1964 (cf. *L'Osservatore Romano* du 13 mars 1964).
102. Cf. Journal Moeller, Carnet 18, p. 41.
103. Cf. Fonds Prignon, 825-826.
104. Suenens a eu des audiences le 17 janvier et le 12 mars 1964 (Cf. *L'Osservatore Romano* du 18 janvier et du 13 mars 1964).
105. Réunion du 3 au 5 avril 1964. On n'a pas trouvé le rapport de cette réunion.
106. Pour les détails de cette réunion, cf. Fonds Prignon, 824.
107. Discours aux évêques italiens, 14 avril 1964, dans les *AAS* 56 (1964) 378-387.

que le Saint-Père attaque les problèmes essentiels de l'aggiornamento de l'Église'»[108].

- On sait que, pendant son voyage aux États-Unis, le cardinal a donné une conférence de presse à Boston le 7 mai où il a parlé de la question du Birth Control et que cet exposé a suscité des remous à Rome[109]. Prenant les devants, Suenens écrit une lettre franche au pape, le 2 juin 1964, dans laquelle il justifie son interview à Boston et demande une audience[110].

- Dans une bande magnétique envoyée par lui au cardinal en juin[111], Prignon parle à plusieurs reprises des 'hésitations' du pape: le discours aux cardinaux sur le Birth Control[112] qui admet plusieurs interprétations; la question des 13 *suggerimenti* au sujet de la collégialité dans le chap. III de *Lumen gentium*; la question de l'autorité de la Commission post-conciliaire pour la liturgie et les pressions subies par le pape de la part de la Congrégation des Rites; les problèmes de la réforme de la Curie romaine («On dit d'ailleurs de plus en plus dans les milieux romains que le Saint-Père parle fort mais n'agit pas beaucoup»).

- Le 17 juin 1964 le pape donne à Felici des feuilles ronéotypées de Suenens au sujet de la vie religieuse; document que le card. Antoniutti lui avait transmis avec de vives appréhensions[113].

---

108. D'autres problèmes traités à l'audience étaient la nomination de l'évêque de Gand (qui semblait être bloquée par une démarche du premier ministre, Theo Lefevre, à l'instigation de son ami le prof. H. Van den Bussche), les relations Flamands-Wallons, l'Université de Louvain, la grève des médecins en Belgique, le prochain voyage du cardinal aux États-Unis, la politique italienne, le mot d'ordre donné par des supérieurs majeurs pour obtenir un chapitre spécial – sur les religieux – dans *Lumen gentium*.

109. Cf. DECLERCK, *Le rôle joué* (n. 96), pp. 460-461.

110. «Interrogé là-bas [à Boston] par des journalistes sur l'attitude de l'Église au sujet du Birth Control, j'ai fait la plus classique des réponses: il ne faut pas s'attendre à voir l'Église changer de doctrine en la matière, mais l'Église favorise la recherche scientifique qui peut rendre praticable la continence périodique lorsque celle-ci s'impose, à l'exclusion de tout moyen stérilisant. Nul ne peut empêcher les journalistes de déformer la pensée de quelqu'un: le Cardinal König s'est vu attribuer l'idée que la doctrine de l'Église allait changer et a dû démentir à son retour. Et je vois que l'article du 'Tempo' qui introduit une interview très déplaisante pour 'Cardinaux et Évêques' commence par résumer les propos du Cardinal Ottaviani en lui prêtant le contraire de sa vraie pensée. Je ne voudrais pas dramatiser l'incident de cette interview, mais on aimerait que le chef responsable du Saint-Office commence par établir en toute objectivité critique ce qui réellement a été dit avant de se lancer dans une réprimande publique. Ce sont les procédés de ce genre, bien plus que le reste, qui discréditent une institution dont l'Église a besoin. Excusez-moi, Très Saint-Père, de vous avoir parlé avec cette totale franchise qui est pour moi l'expression d'une confiance filiale envers le Père commun des fidèles ... et des Cardinaux». Cf. Fonds Suenens, 1724.

111. Cf. Fonds Prignon, 828.

112. *Allocutio ad Em.mos Patres purpuratos*, 23 juin 1964, dans *AAS* 56 (1964) 581-589, discours où le pape admet qu'un problème se pose.

113. *AS* VI/3, p. 197.

On pourrait conclure que pendant la 2ᵉ intersession les relations personnelles de Suenens avec le pape restent excellentes. Suenens fait confiance au pape, le met au courant de ses projets et voyages, obtient de lui que P. de Locht soit nommé dans la commission pontificale. Toutefois, aussi bien les milieux de la «majorité conciliaire» que Suenens lui-même s'aperçoivent que – contrairement à leur attente – le pape ne leur donne pas toujours son entier appui ou du moins cède aux instances de la 'minorité'[114]. Cette distanciation sur plusieurs sujets importants aura, dans quelques mois, des conséquences pour les relations personnelles entre Paul VI et Suenens[115].

6. 3ᵉ Session (14 septembre – 21 novembre 1964)

On sait que, pendant la 3ᵉ session, plusieurs incidents entre le pape et la 'majorité' du concile ont eu lieu. Incidents qui atteindront leur point culminant pendant la dernière semaine de la session, appelée non sans raison par des journalistes *'settimana nera'*.

Ceci aura certainement une répercussion sur les relations entre Suenens, un des porte-parole importants de la majorité, et Paul VI.

– Le 29 octobre, Suenens fait une intervention retentissante au sujet du problème de la régulation des naissances[116]. Ce discours, qui demandait un élargissement de la Commission pontificale et faisait un plaidoyer pour la recherche scientifique en ce domaine, était courageux et fait pour susciter le mécontentement du pape:

– Le pape ne voulait pas qu'on discute de cette question au concile, puisqu'il avait institué une commission pontificale pour l'étude de ces problèmes. De plus, il était d'avis qu'un concile ne devait pas entrer

---

114. Quand nous parlons de la 'majorité' ou de la 'minorité', il faut savoir que ce sont des concepts 'relatifs' ou 'analogiques' et que des personnes changent parfois de 'camp' selon les sujets traités. Par exemple:
– Si on peut situer Suenens presque toujours dans la majorité, il faut dire que, pour la mariologie, il se trouvait plutôt dans la minorité.
– Le card. Bea, qui lui aussi se situait dans la majorité, va au sujet de la 'veritas salutaris' dans le *De revelatione* rejoindre la minorité.
– Mgr Parente se trouve habituellement dans la minorité (pour le *De beata*, le *De revelatione*). Il se trouve pourtant du côté de la majorité dans la question de la collégialité des évêques.
115. Mentionnons ici les questions de la réforme liturgique (le *Motu Proprio Sacram liturgiam* du 25 janvier 1964), du Birth Control, de la collégialité, de la réforme de la Curie.
116. Pour le texte, cf. Fonds Suenens, 2244 et *AS* III/6, pp. 57-59.

dans le détail de cette problématique. Le cardinal Agagianian, modérateur, avait d'ailleurs explicitement donné cette consigne au début de la congrégation générale du 28 octobre[117].

- Il était inouï qu'un cardinal demande publiquement au pape de rendre publics les noms des membres de cette commission pontificale secrète.
- La fougue oratoire du discours du cardinal (e.a.: «Je vous conjure, mes frères, évitons un nouveau procès de Galilée. Un seul suffit pour l'Église») n'était pas fait pour plaire au caractère discret du pape.

Prignon se rappelle qu'il a fait tout son possible (encore le matin *in aula*) pour que le cardinal change certaines expressions de son discours, mais en vain[118]. On sait le succès de ce grand discours de Suenens et aussi que le pape a déjà fait clore le débat le lendemain 30 octobre par le modérateur Agagianian[119]. Voyons toutefois comment Suenens s'est souvenu de la réaction du pape: «Le matin même Mgr Colombo est parti immédiatement chez le pape … Colombo a téléphoné à Mgr Philips pour dire que le texte avait fortement déplu en haut lieu. Puis, comme sans doute rien ne se produisait de mon côté, j'ai eu la visite du cardinal Agagianian, chargé par le Saint-Père de me dire combien il regrettait pratiquement tout, le ton, la forme, le texte etc. demandant de retraiter le sujet, de revenir etc. J'ai demandé une audience au Saint-Père[120] et au cours de l'audience, qui a été la plus sèche que j'ai jamais eue, la seule d'ailleurs, c'était visiblement le mécontentement. Il demandait une sorte de rétractation tout en disant: 'Je ne vous demande pas une rétractation' mais il la demandait quand même

117. Suenens écrit à ce sujet: «Le Cardinal Agagianian … avait fait un texte pour dire à l'assemblée qu'il priait les évêques de ne pas aborder le sujet. Je lui ai dit que je n'étais pas d'accord avec ce texte et je l'ai modifié en disant: 'Nous traiterons ce sujet, mais uniquement par les premiers principes, sans entrer dans les détails'. Il a accepté cela» (SUENENS, *Mémoires sur le Concile Vatican II* [n. 32], p. 56).
118. Cf. Journal Moeller, Carnet 32, 4 octobre 1965, p. 3: «Le matin même je l'ai supplié de ne pas la [son intervention] faire, me dit Prignon. Il [Suenens] a prié longuement à la chapelle le Saint-Esprit, pour être éclairé. Il voulait faire sauter [illisible] qui entourait le Pape. Il n'a pas réussi».
119. Cf. aussi Journal Moeller, Carnet 22, 30 octobre 1964, fiches ajoutées, p. 2: «Prignon, vu ce matin *in aula*, ne dit rien. Mais quand je lui dis: cette interruption est demandée par le pape. Il me répond: 'sapientibus sat'. Il ajoute: 'Je suis tenu par le secret, je ne puis rien dire'».
120. À la fin du mois d'octobre et au début novembre, *L'Osservatore Romano* ne mentionne pas d'audience spéciale de Suenens. Mais les 4 modérateurs ont eu une audience collective le 29 octobre et le 5 novembre au soir (cf. *L'Osservatore Romano* du 31 octobre et 7 novembre 1964). Il est probable que le pape a retenu Suenens après une de ces audiences. À moins qu'une audience spéciale de Suenens n'ait pas été publiée par *L'Osservatore Romano*, ce qui était parfois le cas (p.e. les audiences de Philips en juillet et en octobre 1964 n'ont pas été mentionnées par ce journal).

et c'était sans rémission, disant qu'on n'attendait pas cela d'un modérateur, que c'était un manque de jugement que d'avoir défendu cette thèse etc.»[121].

Rappelons que C. Colombo, dans une lettre du 3 novembre, attire l'attention du pape sur deux positions doctrinales inacceptables dans le discours de Suenens (l'exigence que le pape rende publics les noms des personnes qu'il consulte, sans quoi les évêques ne pourraient plus garder leur confiance dans ce Magistère; et la demande que des époux fassent partie de cette commission pourrait donner l'impression que le Magistère soit l'expression de la pensée du 'peuple de Dieu' au lieu de la Tradition apostolique[122]) et que c'est le 4 novembre qu'Agagianian s'est rendu au collège belge[123]. Le 7 novembre 1964, Suenens, à l'occasion de son intervention sur les Missions, fait un genre de rétractation en prétextant que l'opinion publique n'avait pas bien compris son intervention. On sait que c'est Prignon surtout qui a rédigé cette déclaration[124]. Que le cardinal ne

121. SUENENS, *Mémoires sur le Concile Vatican II* (n. 32), p. 57. Dans son *Mémoire sur le problème du Birth Control tel que je l'ai vécu de 1958 à 1968* (texte dicté peu après la parution de *Humanae vitae*, Fonds Suenens B.C. et H.V., 1), le cardinal confirme cette version des faits. Il ajoute notamment: «Il [le pape] était dur, il était cassant et il n'y avait pas de réplique à donner ... Alors j'ai fait, à la manière de St Augustin, une *re-tractatio*, c.-à-d. re-traité une seconde fois du [sic] même sujet» (p. 8).

122. Cf. Fonds Colombo, LG-03-17 (Facoltà Teologica dell'Italia settentrionale, Milan), où Colombo écrit: «Non entro nel merito del problema cui si riferiva. Mi sembra invece doveroso di far rilevare che esso includeva due posizioni dottrinalmente inacettabili, e che non dovrebbero diventare mentalità dominante dell'Episcopato:

a) la esigenza che il Romano Pontefice deva far conoscere i nomi delle persone che consulta per l'esercizio del Suo magistero affinché i Vescovi abbiano ad aver fiducia nella competenza di questo magistero;

b) la esigenza che in una Commissione di studio siano compresi, oltre a teologi e studiosi di varie categorie, anche gli sposi cristiani 'perchè sia veramente rappresentato tutto il popolo di Dio' può suggerire la idea che la funzione del Magistero sia di esprimere il pensiero del 'popolo di Dio' invece che quello della Tradizione trasmessa degli Apostoli. È opportuno trovar modo di chiarire queste idee, senza polemica?».

On voit aussi que cette lettre est écrite au milieu du débat sur la collégialité.

123. Cf. Fonds Philips, 1921.

124. Suenens écrit dans ses *Mémoires sur le Concile Vatican II* (n. 32), p. 57: «J'ai repris le sujet, quelques jours plus tard au concile, mais de telle manière que personne ne pouvait y voir une rétractation; j'ai tout simplement répété ce qui avait été dit en soulignant qu'il ne fallait pas comprendre comme ceci et comme cela. Je crois que la comparaison des deux textes montre que le texte est resté identique». *L'Osservatore Romano* (à la p. 2 du 8 novembre 1964), d'habitude assez avare d'informations sur les débats conciliaires, en fait même un sous-titre: «Una precisazione del Card. Suenens per errate deduzioni sull'etica matrimoniale».

Il est encore intéressant de voir comment Prignon rapporte cet épisode dans son Rapport destiné à l'Ambassadeur de Belgique auprès du Saint-Siège (Fonds Prignon, 1058): «Sans rien retirer du fond de son discours, celui-ci [Suenens] en effet affirmait que la décision sur les modalités des travaux – aussi bien que le jugement ultime sur le fond – revenait au pape seul. Maints évêques pensèrent que cette mise au point avait bien pu être

fût pas vraiment repentant est aussi démontré par ce qu'il disait à Döpfner à la 4ᵉ session. Döpfner avait aussi reçu une remarque du pape au sujet de son intervention sur les indulgences. Suenens lui a dit alors: «... qu'il était passé par là l'année dernière et que c'était une *felix culpa* parce que l'expérience lui montrait ... que finalement sa démarche avait porté son fruit»[125]. Prignon affirme encore que quelque temps plus tard le pape se serait excusé chez Suenens pour sa manière un peu brusque d'agir et lui aurait demandé pardon[126]. Il faut aussi remarquer que quelques semaines plus tard, encore au mois de novembre, Paul VI a élargi considérablement la commission pontificale (de 15 à 58 membres, dont 30 laïcs) et que les membres sont apparus sur une photo de leur audience chez le pape, publiée sur *L'Osservatore Romano* (ce qui était une façon de rendre leurs noms publics)[127].

– Un autre facteur d'éloignement, quoique beaucoup moindre, aura été le discours *in aula* de Suenens au sujet des Missions, le 7 novembre 1964. Tandis que le pape par un geste exceptionnel avait, le 6 novembre, donné son appui au schéma *De missionibus*, Suenens et beaucoup d'autres orateurs ont critiqué ce texte avec virulence[128].

---

suggérée par le pape lui-même. On n'en a toutefois aucune preuve [sic]. Si à l'avenir [on] devait donner crédit à cette hypothèse, il y aurait là un signe de plus que le pape tenait à marquer ses distances vis-à-vis du concile et affirmer sa primauté comme cela devint très clair dans la suite».

Et Mgr Heuschen, évêque auxiliaire de Liège et membre de la Commission doctrinale, écrit aux sœurs Verjans le 8 novembre 1964: «Vous aurez lu dans les journaux que notre cardinal a reçu une réprimande du pape à propos de son intervention sur la morale conjugale: ce n'était pas à cause de la doctrine mais parce qu'il avait demandé que la commission pontificale soit élargie ... Cette intervention du pape a fait très mauvaise impression» (Fonds Heuschen, 552).

125. Journal Prignon, 14 novembre 1965, pp. 200 et 203.

126. Dans ses 'Concilieherinneringen', p. 16 (Fonds Heuschen, 384), Heuschen rapporte que le cardinal a dit à Prignon que pendant six semaines, dans la réunion hebdomadaire des modérateurs le pape ne lui a plus adressé la parole mais que finalement le pape s'est agenouillé devant Suenens pour lui demander pardon. Heuschen ajoute toutefois qu'il n'a pas pu contrôler ce récit. En effet, après le discours de Suenens du 29 octobre 1964, la session du concile n'a plus duré que trois semaines. La période de six semaines est donc largement exagérée. L. Declerck se souvient d'un récit analogue que Prignon lui a raconté. Même son de cloche chez Poswick qui écrit en décembre 1964, en relatant des propos de Mgr Prignon: «Malgré les heurts, lors de la dernière entrevue du cardinal Suenens avec Paul VI, avant la fin de la 3ᵉ session, celui-ci l'a embrassé et lui a demandé de l'excuser, s'il avait été parfois un peu vif, excipant de sa grande fatigue nerveuse» (Cf. POSWICK, *Un journal du Concile* [n. 56], p. 504).

127. Cf. *Mémoire sur le problème du Birth Control* (n. 121), p. 10 (Fonds Suenens B.C. et H.V., 1).

128. Dans ses *Mémoires sur le Concile Vatican II* (n. 32), p. 55, Suenens écrit: «Cela a été un moment très dramatique en ce sens que le Pape avait, en somme, patronné le

– Et dans le contexte des tensions au sujet du chapitre III de *Lumen gentium* (1e quinzaine de novembre) il ne faut pas s'étonner que Suenens ait dit à Moeller, le 12 novembre 1964: «Le pape n'est préparé ni théologiquement ni psychologiquement à la collégialité»[129].

– Pendant les derniers jours de la session, lors d'une audience le 19 novembre 1964, Suenens a encore essayé d'obtenir le vote du *De libertate religiosa*, mais le pape a maintenu sa décision, tout en promettant que ce texte serait le premier qui serait discuté à la session suivante[130]. Et Moeller note encore: «L'entretien entre Suenens et le pape a été très cordial. Mais je me méfie de cette cordialité».

À la fin de cette session, on peut voir que les relations entre Paul VI et Suenens se sont rétablies et restent bonnes. Toutefois, lors de cette session, pour la première fois, un désaccord public entre le pape et le cardinal s'est manifesté. Suenens n'a pas hésité à vouloir forcer la main du pape dans la question du Birth Control et de la commission pontificale. Et le pape, qui probablement a été plus blessé par le procédé que par le contenu[131], a exigé une rétractation publique de Suenens. Peut-être que cela a été le début d'un processus d' 'estrangement'.

7. 3e Intersession

Pendant la 3e intersession, on constate que Suenens reste surtout préoccupé de la question du Birth Control (et en conséquence par le schéma XIII et le chapitre sur le mariage). C'est probablement pour cette raison (afin de ne pas compromettre son crédit), qu'il réagit assez fortement contre un article de *Paroisse et Liturgie*[132] et au sujet de quelques autres

schéma sur les Missions et nous avons tous, le lendemain de son intervention, démoli ce schéma, je crois à 16 sur 17».

129. Journal Moeller, Carnet 23, 12 novembre 1964, p. 33. Moeller note aussi qu'Etchegaray lui avait dit que le pape était mal informé et que Suenens avait dit: «J'ai des exemples, dit-il, où le pape a dit: voici comment réagit tel évêque et l'évêque en question réagit exactement à l'envers» (Carnet 23, 12 novembre 1964, p. 36, avec la note 1 au verso de la p. 35).

130. Journal Moeller, Carnet 23, 19 novembre 1964, verso de la p. 54.

131. Moeller écrit dans son Journal: «Ce n'est pas tellement l'allusion à Galilée qui a fait tellement scandale à la curie, mais le fait que Suenens a fait une chose qu'il ne faut jamais faire à Rome: critiquer en public une chose décidée par le pape. Or, il a demandé que l'on publie les noms des membres de la commission pontificale pour 'la pilule'» (Carnet 32, 4 octobre 1965, p. 2).

132. Il s'agissait d'un article publié par le bénédictin belge T. MAERTENS, *De l'obéissance en matière liturgique*, dans *Paroisse et Liturgie*, janvier 1965, qui prônait une assez grande liberté en matière liturgique. À ce sujet M. Lamberigts a donné une conférence intéressante (non encore publiée) au colloque de Klingenthal (1999). Cf. J. DORÉ – A. MELLONI (éds.), *Volti di fine Concilio: Studi di Storia e Teologia sulla conclusione del*

incidents mineurs, qui lui sont signalés par le pape. L'élévation au cardinalat de J. Cardijn, fondateur de la J.O.C., en février 1965, donne lieu
à des festivités et des rencontres de Suenens avec le pape.

Voyons cela plus en détail:

- Dans une lettre du 18 décembre 1964, Suenens envoie ses vœux de
  Noël au pape; il ajoute qu'il espère que le schéma XIII ne déçoive pas
  l'attente du monde [allusion au problème du Birth Control] et puisse
  être le digne couronnement des travaux entrepris. Il souligne enfin qu'il
  se réjouit de pouvoir vivre la collégialité, désormais fixée dans les
  textes, en profonde communion avec et sous l'égide du pape[133].
- Après le consistoire, lors de l'audience du 22 février 1965, Paul VI lui
  parle de l'article de *Paroisse et Liturgie* et des prises de position de
  trois professeurs du séminaire de Malines (P. Pas, F. D'Hoogh et P.
  Anciaux) en morale conjugale[134]. Le cardinal réagit très sèchement[135]
  au sujet de *Paroisse et Liturgie* et écrit une lettre au pape le 17 mars
  1965[136]. Dans cette même lettre, Suenens réagit aussi au fait qu'un
  prêtre de son diocèse a assisté à Berlin-Est à une conférence sur la
  paix, les 17 et 18 novembre 1964[137].
- En mars 1965, Suenens demande à Victor Heylen, professeur de morale
  à l'Université catholique de Louvain, un projet de texte que le pape
  pourrait utiliser en vue d'une déclaration sur le Birth Control. Ce texte
  ne sera pas communiqué au pape parce que, de divers côtés, on plaide
  pour que celui-ci retarde son intervention[138].
- Mais le 26 mars 1965, Suenens envoie au pape une note du Prof.
  A. Dondeyne et lui suggère d'avoir une discussion avec Dondeyne et
  Heylen. Il demande au pape que la question puisse encore mûrir[139].

Vaticano II (Testi e ricerche di scienze religiose. Nuova Serie, 27), Bologna, Il Mulino,
2001, p. 10, note 7.
    133. Cf. Fonds Suenens, 2307.
    134. Fonds Suenens, 2306.
    135. Mgr Charue, pourtant pas un progressiste en matière liturgique, écrit: «J'apprends
que le cardinal Suenens est fort impressionné par la lecture, faite hier soir, de *Paroisse et
Liturgie*. Dès hier soir, il a rédigé un projet de lettre collective [de l'épiscopat belge]. C'est
assez dur, mais il faut une réaction nette» (cf. L. DECLERCK – C. SOETENS (éds.), *Carnets
conciliaires de l'évêque de Namur A.-M. Charue* (Cahiers de la Revue théologique de Louvain, 32), Louvain-la-Neuve, Publications de la Faculté de Théologie, 2000, p. 240).
    136. Fonds Suenens, 2341.
    137. À ce sujet, il y a une lettre (13 février 1965) à Suenens, où le nonce Oddi affirme
que le Saint-Père a été profondément attristé par la présence d'un prêtre de Malines-
Bruxelles à cette conférence (cf. Fonds Suenens A.P., b. 13).
    138. Cf. Fonds Heylen, 22-27 et Fonds Suenens, 2452-2453.
    139. Fonds Suenens, 2456-2457.

Le 1ᵉʳ avril 1965, Cicognani répond en disant que le pape a pris connaissance du texte de Dondeyne et qu'il l'a envoyé à H. de Riedmatten.

– Le 5 avril 1965, Suenens envoie à nouveau une lettre au pape en lui
transmettant deux articles et suggère que le pape demande aux hommes
de science catholiques de poursuivre leurs recherches sur les problèmes
de la fécondité. Cicognani répond le 10 avril 1965 que le pape n'envisage pas de faire une déclaration dans les prochains jours. La proposition du cardinal de faire appel aux hommes de science n'est pas jugée
opportune, mais elle fut transmise à la commission pontificale[140].

– Se trouvant à Rome pour la réunion de la commission de coordination,
Suenens a une audience chez le pape[141] et il lui transmet une nouvelle
version de la note de A. Dondeyne[142]. Le pape fera lire cette note par
un théologien romain, et fera envoyer les remarques de ce théologien
à Suenens par une lettre de Dell'Acqua le 8 juin 1965. Dondeyne
répondra à cette note, réponse qui est transmise par Suenens à
Dell'Acqua le 1ᵉʳ juillet 1965[143].

– Le 14 mai 1965, Suenens écrit encore une lettre à Dell'Acqua au sujet
de modifications apportées au texte sur les Juifs. Il souhaite que la personne du Saint-Père ne soit pas mise en cause[144].

– Le 3 juillet 1965, Suenens envoie au pape ses félicitations pour le
45ᵉᵐᵉ anniversaire de son ordination et ne manque pas l'occasion de
donner un bref rapport sur le VIIᵉᵐᵉ Colloque international de sexologie, qui s'est tenu à Louvain les 29 et 30 mai 1965 et auquel H. de
Riedmatten a assisté[145].

On peut conclure que pendant cette intersession, Suenens poursuit har-
diment son but: une évolution dans la position de l'Église au sujet des
méthodes de contraception. À cet effet, il intervient avec assiduité auprès
du pape. Toutefois en bon stratège il essaie de ne pas perdre son crédit à
cause d'autres questions litigieuses. Cette insistance (*opportune, impor-
tune*) de Suenens trahit en même temps que le cardinal n'a plus la même
confiance filiale dans le pape; il ne se trouve plus sur la même longueur
d'onde que le pape et veut le faire changer d'opinion.

---

140. Fonds Suenens, 2459 et 2459bis. Il faut noter qu'à cette époque, Suenens était fort
actif pour intéresser des hommes de science à des recherches sur des méthodes de régulation de la fécondité. Cf. Fonds Suenens B.C et H.V., 135-161. Cf. aussi le VIIᵉ Colloque
international de sexologie de Louvain du 29-30 mai 1965 (*ibid.*, pp. 947-979).

141. Audience du 13 mai 1965 (Cf. *L'Osservatore Romano* du 14 mai 1965).

142. Cf. Fonds Suenens, 2457bis.

143. Cf. Fonds Suenens, 2466-2467 et 2469-2470.

144. *AS* V/3, p. 321.

145. Cf. Fonds Suenens, B.C. et H.V., 979.

8. 4ᵉ Session (14 septembre – 8 décembre 1965)

Pendant la 4ᵉ session, les relations de Suenens avec le pape restent fréquentes, puisque les modérateurs continuent à avoir leur audience hebdomadaire. Toutefois, le rôle des modérateurs semble se réduire encore. Suenens lui-même obtient à sa demande une longue audience privée le 18 octobre 1965.

Faisons succinctement un survol des contacts de Suenens avec Paul VI, en notant les réactions de Suenens vis-à-vis du pape et de sa politique[146]:

– Le 14 septembre 1965, Suenens est heureux de l'encyclique *Mysterium fidei* au sujet de l'eucharistie, mais il déplore le 'mode': seuls des théologiens du Saint-Office, sans consultation internationale, y ont travaillé. Le cardinal promet à Prignon d'en parler au pape et de lui demander de consulter à l'avenir une véritable équipe internationale[147].

– Le 16 septembre 1965, lors de la première rencontre de la 4ᵉ session du pape avec les modérateurs, le pape donnait l'impression qu'il voulait vraiment faire du synode une expression de la collégialité épiscopale et qu'il en attendait beaucoup. De même il a l'intention de convoquer les présidents des conférences épiscopales et de leur faire soumettre certains points à discuter[148].

– Le 21 septembre 1965, lors de l'audience avec les modérateurs, le pape parle à nouveau très positivement du synode des évêques et aussi de la réforme du Saint-Office. Le cardinal Suenens lui propose de créer une commission internationale de théologiens[149]. De même, le pape est d'accord avec Suenens pour imposer une limite d'âge pour les évêques, mais il rencontre de grandes résistances[150].

– Dans une conversation avec Prignon le 26 septembre 1965, le cardinal confirme qu'il a demandé au pape de nommer Philips cardinal[151].

– Au cours de l'audience des modérateurs le 28 septembre 1965, Suenens fait son possible pour éviter que le pape donne des directives au sujet du débat *in aula* du schéma XIII (et spécialement sur le chapitre du

---

146. À part la transcription d'une bande magnétique de Suenens sur son audience du 18 octobre 1965, notre source principale est le Journal de la 4ᵉ session de Prignon (Prignon note fidèlement ce que le cardinal lui dit, mais les rapports du cardinal ne sont pas toujours précis) à compléter par quelques passages du Journal Moeller (Carnet 32, 19 octobre 1965, pp. 51-52).

147. Journal Prignon, p. 268.

148. *Ibid.*, pp. 29-30.

149. Commission qui sera érigée après le synode de 1967, où Suenens a fortement promu cette idée.

150. Journal Prignon, pp. 62-63.

151. *Ibid.*, p. 79.

mariage). Il veut intervenir à ce sujet et ne pas être gêné, comme l'année précédente, par des directives du pape. Toutefois, à la fin de l'audience, le pape parle lui-même du problème du Birth Control et du rapport de la Commission pontificale[152]. Devant la réaction du cardinal disant que l'instruction pastorale est très faible et même mauvaise, le pape propose de faire réagir les présidents des conférences épiscopales[153]. Le pape est aussi d'avis que l'année précédente [lors de la *settimana nera* à la fin de la 3e session] il n'avait pas eu tort d'intervenir, abstraction faite du *modus* de ses interventions[154].

– Le 5 octobre, Suenens demande à Prignon de lui faire une note au sujet des interventions du pape dans le travail des commissions (e. a. sur le texte *De revelatione*, sur le schéma *De episcopis*) et du danger d'une nouvelle *settimana nera*, note qu'il transmettrait au pape lors de sa prochaine audience privée[155].

– Dans une conversation, Suenens et Helder Camara tombent d'accord pour que Suenens propose au pape de mettre le problème du célibat à l'ordre du jour d'une des réunions des conférences épiscopales, afin d'amorcer au moins la question et de le faire avec toute la discrétion possible[156].

– L'audience des modérateurs du mardi 12 octobre a été agréable mais fut à peu près une cascade de mauvaises nouvelles[157], disait le cardi-

---

152. Pour ce rapport 'De Quaestione regulationis nativitatum', septembre 1965, cf. Fonds Prignon, 1448.

153. Finalement, ce texte de la Commission pontificale ne sera pas soumis aux présidents des conférences épiscopales (e.a. parce que des membres, dont Mgr Reuss, avaient protesté contre le contenu – selon eux incomplet et partiel – de ce rapport). Cependant, Suenens avait déjà demandé à des théologiens de réagir à ce rapport pour le jour où il viendrait en discussion (Journal Prignon, pp. 138-139).

154. Journal Prignon, pp. 89-92 et 99.

155. *Ibid.*, p. 124 et Journal Moeller, Carnet 32, 6 octobre 1965, p. 11 et verso de la p. 10: «Il [Martimort] parle du malaise qui se répand parmi les commissions (Note 1: au point qu'on craint une *settimana nera* plus grave que l'autre, car: dernière session. Plus de possibilité de mises au point) au sujet d'une série d'interventions [du pape]. Il énumère: *De episcopis*, le *De religiosis*, le *De revelatione*, le *De educatione christiana*».

156. Ce qui n'a pas été fait: les conférences épiscopales ont uniquement traité de la discipline pénitentielle dans l'Église et des indulgences. Beaucoup d'évêques, même de la 'majorité', étaient d'avis qu'il ne fallait pas aborder ce problème délicat en session publique du concile, d'autant plus qu'il n'y avait plus que deux ou trois jours de débat. Cf. Journal Prignon, 10 octobre 1965, pp. 144-145.

157. E.a. les sujets à traiter par les évêques (et conférences épiscopales), les critiques du pape au sujet du schéma *De revelatione*, le projet du pape de rendre – à la cérémonie de clôture – un hommage solennel aux reliques 'authentiques' de Saint Pierre [M. Guarducci avait prétendu qu'elle avait découvert ces reliques, mais beaucoup d'historiens, dont Mgr J. Ruysschaert, contestaient cette 'découverte' de Guarducci qu'on appelait 'la romancière archéologique'] etc.

nal. Seule exception: le pape disait qu'il désirait une collaboration entre la Commission pontificale et la [sous] commission conciliaire [pour le *De matrimonio* du schéma XIII]. Suenens avait l'impression que, sur cette question, le pape était fort indécis, mais au cours de la discussion le pape reparlait de la fin primaire et de la fin secondaire du mariage, de la *finis operis* et de la *finis operantis*. Et le cardinal disait à Prignon que le pape, dans sa pensée personnelle, n'avait pas fait un pas en avant depuis un an et demi[158].

– Venons-en à l'audience privée de Suenens du 18 octobre 1965. Cette audience, soigneusement préparée par Suenens, dura une heure et 5 minutes[159]. Elle est rapportée par lui sur bande magnétique[160]; résumons-en les points saillants:

a. Le cardinal remet une note sur la réforme de la curie romaine. Il a beaucoup de peine à développer quoi que ce soit car, dit-il, «[le pape] m'interrompt et se met à expliquer pratiquement le *Corriere della Sera*, son interview sur la curie [sic][161], qu'elle n'est plus du tout comme autrefois, que tous ses abus de jadis ont disparu ... rien dans la conversation ne laisse voir ou entrevoir l'espoir d'une réforme en profondeur de la curie romaine».

b. «J'ai enchaîné sur les commissions post-conciliaires ... Rien dans la conversation n'a pu montrer qu'il [le pape] souhaitait en établir ... J'ai montré aussi que ... [pour] la Congrégation des Séminaires et celle des Religieux combien il était essentiel qu'il y ait là une suite et combien on était bloqué par les personnages présents[162]. Il a répondu que ces personnages n'étaient pas éternels, que la nature était là et rien n'indiquait en quoi que ce soit une innovation quelconque, une nouveauté quelconque».

---

158. Cf. Journal Prignon, pp. 155-158.

159. Il y avait la note au sujet du danger d'une nouvelle *settimana nera* (préparée surtout par Martimort, cf. Fonds Prignon, 144 et Fonds Suenens, 2501) et une note sur le problème du Birth Control faite par Delhaye, Heylen et Prignon (cf. Fonds Prignon, 1449-1450).

160. Cf. Fonds Suenens, 2503. Ce texte, dicté probablement à la hâte par le cardinal, a été dactylographié par une personne qui manifestement ne maniait pas bien le français. D'où les nombreuses tournures curieuses dans le texte, tournures que nous avons parfois corrigées directement. Par ailleurs, ce texte dactylographié correspond fidèlement au rapport oral que le cardinal a fait à Prignon, cf. Journal Prignon, pp. 174-177 et 185.

161. Interview de Paul VI par Alberto Cavallari dans le journal *Corriere della Sera* du 3 octobre 1965.

162. Le préfet de la Congrégation des Religieux était I. Antoniutti. Et à la tête de la Congrégation des Séminaires et Universités se trouvaient G. Pizzardo, préfet, et D. Staffa, secrétaire.

c. Puis vient la discussion sur le Birth Control (une demi-heure).
«Il [le pape] a donné son point de vue, qui consistait à dire qu'il ne
faut en rien favoriser l'égoïsme des gens; qu'il ne faut pas sacrifier
l'esprit de sacrifice; qu'il ne faut rien compromettre de toute la position traditionnelle de l'Église là-dedans. Je [Suenens] durcis peut-
être dans les expressions, mais le fond est certainement ce qui se
dégageait. Il faut que nous puissions répéter pratiquement la doctrine
classique. Je n'ai pas vu à un seul endroit une ouverture en quoi que
ce soit vers une position nouvelle». Puis le pape a dit à Suenens que
l'auteur d'*Amour et maîtrise de soi* avait changé d'opinion, ce que
Suenens a confirmé en disant qu'il s'est conformé à l'évolution de
la majorité des moralistes à ce sujet. Alors le pape a demandé à
Suenens de lui faire un texte où il exprimerait ce qu'il souhaite que
l'Église dise maintenant. *Hic et nunc*. Une déclaration que le pape
pourrait faire maintenant en attendant une encyclique qui serait pour
plus tard.

Suenens a encore essayé de relativiser un peu l'encyclique *Casti
connubii* et de démontrer que les couples qui pratiquent la méthode
Ogino Knaus ne respectent pas eux non plus les 'actus apti ad pro-
creationem'. Mais sans grand succès. En effet il écrit: «... le Saint-
Père a surtout exposé une nouvelle fois la position classique sur la
procréation ... tout en essayant d'intégrer l'amour là-dedans. À ses
yeux, certainement, il y a moyen, certainement [sic] dans sa pensée,
de faire avancer quelque chose du côté de la place de l'amour ...
Tout en ne changeant pas la doctrine, il semble qu'il y ait une ouverture de quelque chose ... côté donc amour à intégrer dans cet
ensemble».

d. Le pape a encore abordé l'érection du diocèse du Limbourg et à la fin
de l'audience il a déclaré: «Je me trouve devant un grave problème
de conscience, devant le *De revelatione* et il a exposé les difficultés
au sujet de la *Traditio constitutiva*, la *veritas salutaris* et l'historicité de l'Écriture sainte. Qu'il savait qu'il s'exposait à une nouvelle *settimana nera* mais que sa conscience était impérieuse là-dedans»[163].
Le cardinal résume ainsi le climat de l'audience: «Voilà, je crois
que [c'est] le résumé fondamental de cette conversation, qui se
déroulait dans le meilleur des climats, avec une impossibilité de se

---

163. Dans son Journal (Carnet 32, 19 octobre 1965, pp. 51-52), Moeller note: «Le
cardinal Suenens est encore allé chez le pape hier. Le pape a dit: en conscience, je dois
intervenir ... Le pape lui-même est du côté de la minorité. Il l'est par crainte, dit Prignon.
Il ne sait pas très bien. On lui dit que la foi est en danger. Il n'est pas théologien. Par tutio-
risme».

faire écouter, parce qu'à la moindre phrase, c'était lui qui parlait, qui exposait et qui donnait ses vues. Il n'y avait à aucun moment cette sorte de position: 'Eh bien, dites-moi ce que vous pensez, même si je ne l'admets pas, mais qu'est-ce que vous pensez', encouragement à expliciter une pensée. J'ai dû la donner par bribes et morceaux, dans des circonstances difficiles, heurtant et presque chaque fois étant impoli, l'interrompant … Je n'ai pas en tête chacun des arguments qu'il m'a objectés, mais je pense que pour qu'on puisse même dialoguer, les longueurs d'ondes étaient tellement différentes que je crois qu'il faut dix préalables pour déblayer et faire le cheminement qu'il faut pour qu'on se rencontre sur le même point. J'ai l'impression que l'on parlait de choses très différentes … Il [ne] me semble donc pas que l'on se trouve devant une ouverture en quoi que ce soit, ni sur le terrain Curie, ni sur le terrain commissions post-conciliaires, ni sur le terrain Birth Control. Il m'a quitté en disant: 'Il faut que nous nous aidions fraternellement. C'est l'heure de s'entraider, je compte beaucoup sur vous. Alors vraiment, prions ensemble'».

– Le 26 octobre, l'audience avec les modérateurs fut excellente. Et le cardinal est revenu rayonnant. La conversation était détendue, familière et très amicale. Le Saint-Père a raconté lui-même comment s'était faite la réhabilitation de Draguet[164] et le cardinal a pu lui parler de la maladie de Mgr J. Leclercq. De plus, le pape semblait de nouveau pencher vers la création de commissions post-conciliaires. Après l'audience collective le cardinal a demandé à voir le pape seul pour pouvoir lui remettre son texte[165]. Il ne l'a pas fait sans appréhension mais, à sa grande surprise, il a été bien accueilli. Cette fois-ci, le pape s'est montré très ouvert dans la discussion. Le cardinal a eu l'impression qu'en tout cas son texte serait pris en considération et influencerait la rédaction définitive du texte que le Saint-Père publierait à une date qu'il n'a pas précisée mais avant la fin du concile[166]. Le cardinal était vraiment content de cet entretien[167].

---

164. R. Draguet (1896-1980), professeur de théologie dogmatique à l'Université catholique de Louvain, avait dû interrompre son enseignement sur ordre de Rome en 1942. Il a été réhabilité en 1965, par une lettre du cardinal Cicognani au cardinal Suenens (2 juillet 1965) à la demande de Mgr Descamps, recteur de l'Université catholique de Louvain (Cf. Fonds Suenens A.P., b. 18).

165. Texte d'une déclaration éventuelle sur le Birth Control demandé par le pape à l'audience du 18 octobre 1965. Pour ce texte, cf. Fonds Prignon, 1460.

166. On sait que le pape, peu après, a renoncé à faire une déclaration concernant ce sujet avant la fin du concile et qu'il a essayé de faire passer ses idées par l'introduction de *modi* dans le texte du schéma XIII. Cf. Journal Prignon, p. 198.

167. *Ibid.*, pp. 189-192.

– À l'occasion de l'audience des modérateurs du 18 novembre, le cardinal demande au pape ce qu'il pensait du texte qu'il lui avait remis le 26 octobre au sujet du Birth Control. Le pape a répondu qu'il le faisait examiner par cinq personnes, mais il n'a pas dit si oui ou non le texte lui plaisait[168].

– Les réactions de Suenens au sujet des *modi* pontificaux dans le *De matrimonio* du schéma XIII sont connues[169]. Notons toutefois que le cardinal est prêt à écrire au pape au nom de la conférence épiscopale belge[170] et, qu'à un certain moment, il se propose de mettre en branle plusieurs cardinaux et évêques pour écrire au pape et porter devant lui tout le drame de conscience devant lequel se débattent les Pères[171]. Le 29 novembre, il est décidé à voter *non placet* et à faire voter *non placet* autour de lui. Mais, après que le pape ait accepté le texte avec le Rapport de l'*expensio modorum*, composé surtout par Heuschen et Heylen, il y renonce sur le conseil de A. Prignon en lui disant: «C'est toi qui en portes la responsabilité»[172].

– Le 2 décembre a lieu la dernière audience des modérateurs. Selon Suenens, elle fut très décevante. Le pape n'a pas parlé une seule fois des grandes questions qui agitent le concile, mais surtout des cérémonies de la fin et des cadeaux qu'il donnerait à différentes catégories de personnes (évêques, chefs d'état etc.). Les modérateurs eux-mêmes n'auraient reçu qu'un merci très rapide et «une clochette d'argent»[173].

Quand le pape parle de la réforme du Code de droit canonique et dit son intention de convoquer les *periti* à Rome une fois tous les 15 jours, le cardinal remarque que les *periti* venant de loin ne pourraient pas venir tous les 15 jours et que c'était pratiquement clore l'internationalisation. Mais le pape lui a coupé la parole en disant qu'on avait pensé à tout cela et que tout serait au point. De même, quand le cardinal fait une suggestion pour le synode des évêques, le pape lui a coupé de nouveau la parole. Le cardinal a l'impression que le pape ne prend pas le synode épiscopal très au sérieux. Qu'il a fait un geste pour satisfaire l'opinion, mais qu'il ne semble pas décidé à jouer selon les règles du jeu et à dialoguer avec les évêques. Et le cardinal ajoute: «Est-ce peut-être parce qu'il [le pape] ne fait plus confiance aux modérateurs, qu'il

---

168. *Ibid.*, p. 214.
169. Cf. *Ibid.*, pp. 219-260 (passim).
170. *Ibid.*, p. 227
171. *Ibid.*, p. 230.
172. *Ibid.*, pp. 235 et 240.
173. En fait, il s'agissait d'une jolie clochette en bronze, avec les symboles des quatre évangélistes, sculptée par Manfrini. Le même cadeau a été offert aux observateurs.

donne sa confiance à d'autres gens? Peut-être à lui, le cardinal, spécialement depuis son discours de l'an passé sur les problèmes du mariage». «En tout cas, le cardinal avait l'impression qu'ils [les modérateurs] jouaient plutôt un rôle décoratif, que les modérateurs n'avaient plus aucune influence réelle sur le concile, que le pape les recevait parce qu'il fallait bien. Le pape est gentil, multiplie les cadeaux, même parfois un peu puérils, mais il fuit le dialogue»[174].

— À la séance de clôture du 8 décembre, des messages furent adressés par plusieurs cardinaux à différentes catégories de personnes. Le cardinal Suenens était chargé par le pape de lire le message aux artistes. C'était certainement une marque de confiance du pape. Toutefois Prignon regrette que ces messages n'aient pas été plus conciliaires, ni dans leur contenu, ni dans la forme dans laquelle ils ont été présentés. C'est la Secrétairerie d'État qui a pourvu à tout. C'est seulement la veille au soir vers 10h.30 qu'on a apporté le texte au cardinal Suenens pour qu'il le lise le lendemain. Il semble que personne au concile n'ait été consulté à ce sujet. «Voilà un signe de plus [montrant] comment la sensibilité du pape est complexe. Il ne cesse de faire appel à la collégialité, mais il agit presque toujours seul. Ses réflexions innées ne sont certainement pas conciliaires»[175]. Suenens fait une réflexion analogue: «... cette 4e session s'est achevée sur la place Saint-Pierre par les messages que nous avons adressés au nom du Saint-Père ... c'était lui-même sans doute qui les a rédigés; en tout cas, le texte m'en avait été remis la veille au soir et je ne l'ai vu que très tard dans la nuit, pour le prononcer le lendemain. Je ne sais vraiment pas pourquoi c'était à moi à prononcer le discours pour les artistes et les écrivains; c'est sans doute une allusion aux différents livres écrits. J'aurais préféré d'autre part avoir la parole pour m'adresser aux femmes et aux religieuses...»[176].

On constate donc que, pendant cette 4e session, les relations personnelles de Suenens avec le pape restent bonnes. Mais, sur plusieurs points, Suenens est déçu par l'attitude du pape: le synode des évêques ne semble pas être un prélude à un gouvernement plus collégial de l'Église, l'hésitation du pape au sujet de l'installation des commissions post-conciliaires, la réforme de la curie romaine qui n'avance guère, et évidemment aussi la question du Birth Control, où le pape reste sur ses positions. Ce sont précisément ces problèmes (ainsi que celui du célibat sacerdotal) qui

---

174. Récit de l'audience par le cardinal à Prignon (cf. Journal Prignon, pp. 249-251).
175. *Ibid.*, p. 264.
176. SUENENS, *Mémoires sur le Concile Vatican II* (n. 32), p. 62.

domineront la période post-conciliaire et qui mèneront à un conflit ouvert
entre Suenens et Paul VI dans les années 1969-1971.

IV. ÉPILOGUE: LES RELATIONS ENTRE PAUL VI ET LE CARDINAL SUENENS
DANS LA PÉRIODE POST-CONCILIAIRE

Il ne nous est pas possible dans le cadre de cet article de traiter de
façon approfondie des relations plutôt tendues entre le pape et le cardinal Suenens dans la période de 1966 à 1971. Signalons rapidement que
les conflits se situent surtout autour de trois problèmes, qui restent
d'ailleurs des questions toujours actuelles …

1. Le problème de la régulation des naissances

Avant la publication de l'encyclique *Humanae vitae* (25 juillet 1968),
Suenens s'engage à fond pour une position plus ouverte de l'Église à ce
sujet:

– Comme membre de la Commission pontificale, il déploie de grands
  efforts dans les réunions de mai et juin 1966 pour atteindre ce but et
  finalement la commission se prononce le 24.6.1966 à une large majorité pour une position plus ouverte[177].
– Dans plusieurs audiences[178], il s'efforce de gagner le pape à son point
  de vue[179].
– Au Symposium des Évêques européens à Noordwijkerhout (juillet
  1967), il fait signer un document[180] par plusieurs évêques pour
  l'envoyer au pape. Et au synode d'octobre 1967, quand il devient clair

---

177. Fonds Suenens B.C et H.V., 547.

178. E.a. dans son audience du 20 avril 1967 où le pape prend la défense de la minorité [de la Commission pontificale sur la natalité] et où il renonce à la suggestion de Suenens de mettre ce problème à l'agenda du Synode avec l'argument: «Il faut trop de préparation pour être compétent». Et, à l'audience du 16 mars 1968, le pape exprime sa
déception que Suenens ne soit pas resté dans la ligne de son livre [SUENENS, *Amour et maîtrise de* soi] qui fut pour lui une lumière. Suenens note à la fin de son mémento: «Comme
position Birth Control, il [le pape] demande de prier, mais les jeux sont faits». Cf. Fonds
Suenens A.P., b. 13.

179. Cf. aussi la lettre adressée au pape le 19 mars 1968, et publiée dans SUENENS, *Souvenirs et espérances* (n. 14), pp. 158-160.

180. Qui avait comme titre: «10 Propositiones quae attinent ad declarationem Summi
Pontificis de licito modo regulandi natalitatem». Cf. Fonds Suenens B.C. et H.V., 214-218.

que le pape ne veut pas soumettre cette question à l'assemblée syno-
dale, il demande à plusieurs évêques d'écrire au pape à ce sujet et il
écrit lui-même une longue lettre (5 pp.) au pape[181].

Après la publication de l'encyclique:

- Le cardinal reçoit une lettre personnelle du pape le 9 août 1968 qui lui
  demande de soutenir son encyclique[182].
- Le cardinal s'engage très fort dans la rédaction de la *Déclaration de
  l'épiscopat belge sur l'encyclique Humanae Vitae* (30 août 1968) et
  garde le contact avec d'autres cardinaux, qui eux aussi ont des problèmes avec l'encyclique. Il participe à une réunion de quelques cardinaux à Essen (9 septembre 1968)[183].
- Le 23 décembre 1968, Paul VI adresse une nouvelle lettre personnelle[184] à Suenens où il dit e. a. que son propre ministère apostolique
  lui réserve des amertumes, surtout quand elles viennent de l'intérieur
  de l'Église (allusion nette à l'opposition au sujet de *Humanae vitae*).

2. Le problème du célibat des prêtres

Ce n'est qu'après la vague de contestation de 1968, également parmi
les prêtres, que le cardinal s'est vraiment intéressé à ce problème[185]. Si,
face à la contestation, il plaide d'abord pour que le problème soit traité
ouvertement, ce n'est que plus tard qu'il prend publiquement position
pour la possibilité d'ordonner des hommes mariés. Il est évident qu'après
la publication par Paul VI de son encyclique *Sacerdotalis caelibatus*

---

181. Fonds Suenens B.C. et H.V., 229-233.
182. Fonds Suenens B.C. et H.V., 1397.
183. Réunion avec Heenan, Döpfner, König, Alfrink et Suenens (Cf. Fonds Suenens
B.C. et H.V., 1410-1436).
184. Fonds Suenens B.C. et H.V., 1405-1406. Le pape écrit notamment: «E diremo al
Fratello ed al Figlio che noi siamo 'in passione socii'; anche il nostro apostolico ufficio
ci riserva non poche amarezze ed è ora gravato da molte difficoltà, tanto più sentite quanto
più direttamente ci vengono dall' interno della Chiesa, da sedi e da persone che per la
stima e l'affezione, di cui sono da noi favorite, le rendono a noi più penose e quasi ines-
plicabili». Suenens a noté qu'une lettre similaire fut envoyée au cardinal Döpfner.
185. En mai-juin 1962, à la Commission centrale préparatoire, Suenens est encore
d'avis que le problème du célibat ne devrait pas être traité par le Concile et qu'une dis-
pense du célibat doit être réservée au Saint-Siège et peut être accordée uniquement en cas
de nullité de l'ordination. Autrement, cela ouvrirait la porte à des demandes de dissolu-
tion du mariage et serait nuisible à sa stabilité. Cf. Fonds Suenens, 167. Pour son intervention à la Commission centrale préparatoire, cf. *AD* II/2.4, p. 429: «Sed Sancta Sedes
misericors sit in diiudicandis casibus *nullitatis* erga ea quae *antecedunt* ordinationem, non
vero post ordinationem».

(24 juin 1967), cette prise de position devait le mettre en conflit avec le pape. Relevons quelques faits:

- Au Symposium des Évêques européens de Coire (juillet 1969), Suenens lit, pendant sa conférence de clôture, une lettre assez dramatique de Hans Küng qui lui était adressée à Coire par express, où celui-ci lançait un appel solennel pour que le célibat des prêtres ne soit plus obligatoire[186].
- Après la prise de position des évêques hollandais, Suenens, qui avait lui-même sollicité une interview avec Fesquet, lance un appel dans le journal *Le Monde* (11-12.5.1970) pour ouvrir le débat sur le célibat des prêtres. Cette fois-ci le pape réagit publiquement et Suenens s'explique dans son homélie de la Pentecôte 1970[187].
- Dans une intervention en son nom propre au Synode d'octobre 1971[188], Suenens relance son appel en disant: «Allons-nous oublier que Jésus a fondé son Église, non sur Jean qu'Il aimait pourtant d'une prédilection spéciale, mais sur un homme marié du nom de Pierre?»[189]. Par après Suenens envoie une note de 8 p. au pape pour expliquer son intervention au Synode[190]. Dans une audience (du 30 octobre 1971) très pénible pour Suenens, le pape lui dit: «Vous créez un esprit mauvais, vous êtes le porte-parole d'une tendance mauvaise; Dieu vous jugera très sévèrement»[191].

3. La mise en application de la collégialité des évêques et les réformes institutionnelles de l'Église

- Après qu'en 1968 le cardinal eut publié son livre *La coresponsabilité dans l'Église d'aujourd'hui*[192], livre qui fut peu apprécié par le pape,

---

186. Il est intéressant de constater que, quelques jours avant la réunion de Coire, Suenens s'est rendu à Sursee (Suisse) chez Küng et que, déjà avant sa conférence de clôture, il avait mis la presse au courant de la lettre de Küng (Cf. Fonds Suenens A.P., b. 115).

187. Fonds Suenens A.P., b. 63.

188. On sait que pour ce Synode Suenens n'a été désigné comme représentant de la conférence épiscopale belge qu'après un deuxième tour de vote. Pour éviter le scandale éventuel d'une non-désignation de l'archevêque de Malines-Bruxelles, Prignon était allé trouver Benelli pour lui demander que le pape suggère aux évêques belges de mandater quand même Suenens. Benelli en a parlé à Paul VI, mais celui-ci aurait répondu: «Judicent episcopi pro conscientia sua» (Fonds Suenens A.P., b. 10).

189. Intervention du 11 octobre 1971: cf. *Pastoralia*, 24, 1 décembre 1971, p. 182 et Fonds Suenens A.P., b. 124-125.

190. Fonds Suenens A.P., b. 124.

191. Fonds Suenens A.P., b. 13.

192. L.-J. SUENENS, *La coresponsabilité dans l'Église d'aujourd'hui*, Bruges, Desclée de Brouwer, 1968.

il donna le 15 mai 1969 une interview retentissante dans les *Informations Catholiques Internationales*[193] (*L'unité de l'Église dans la logique de Vatican II*), où il critiquait ouvertement la curie et, en fait, reprochait au pape la lenteur dans la réforme des institutions de l'Église. Si le pape ne réagit pas en public, plusieurs cardinaux de curie (comme Villot, Garrone, Tisserant[194]) écrivent à Suenens et le cardinal Daniélou publie une interview dans les mêmes *Informations Catholiques Internationales* pour contredire Suenens[195]. En février 1970, le cardinal fait encore publier par J. de Broucker des réactions à son interview, dans un livre intitulé *Le Dossier Suenens*[196].

– Au Synode de 1969, Suenens critique la Constitution apostolique *Sollicitudo omnium ecclesiarum* promulguée par Paul VI le 24 juin 1969 au sujet du statut des nonces apostoliques. Il prend contact avec H. Küng pour faire des propositions en vue d'une réforme du conclave[197]. Lors d'une audience (17 octobre 1969), le pape lui parle de son interview dans les *Informations Catholiques Internationales*[198].

– En 1971, le cardinal donne une autre interview critique dans le *National Catholic News Service* (17 juillet 1971) au sujet du projet de faire précéder le nouveau code de droit canonique par une *Lex ecclesiae fundamentalis*. Malgré le fait que ce projet ait déjà été retiré le 4 juillet 1971 et que tous ses vicaires généraux lui eussent demandé de

193. Voir les *Informations Catholiques Internationales* 336, du 15 mai 1969, *Supplément*, pp. I-XVI. Interview publiée après des incidents à Rome en mars 1969, où le cardinal avait dû se défendre contre des dénonciations du nonce Oddi. Le texte avait été rédigé par Suenens en avril 1969 et publié sous forme d'interview par J. de Broucker (Cf. Fonds Suenens A.P., b. 60).
194. La lettre (28 mai 1968) du card. Tisserant, doyen du Sacré Collège, est particulièrement sévère et se conclut sèchement: «Je termine, non sans tristesse, cette lettre déjà trop longue, en vous invitant à relire le texte de saint Paul: 'Tout est permis, mais tout n'est pas profitable. Tout est permis, mais tout n'édifie pas' (1 Cor. 10, 23). Vous ne m'en voudrez pas, cher Monsieur le Cardinal, de la franchise de mes propos. On peut appartenir à la Curie, et pourtant aimer la vérité et l'Église. Veuillez agréer, l'hommage de mes sentiments respectueux et dévoués en Notre Seigneur». Cf. Fonds Suenens A.P., b. 60.
195. *Informations Catholiques Internationales* 344, du 15 septembre 1969, pp. 16-20.
196. J. DE BROUCKER, *Le Dossier Suenens: Diagnostic d'une crise*, Paris, Éditions universitaires, 1970.
197. Il s'agissait de faire élire le pape non plus seulement par les cardinaux (en dessous de 75 ans et étant toujours en fonction) mais aussi par des délégués des conférences épiscopales (en s'inspirant de la composition du synode). Cf. Fonds Suenens A.P., b. 120.
198. Selon les notes de Suenens, le pape lui aurait dit notamment: «Je vous demande pardon pour ce qui a pu vous heurter ou blesser de ma part ou de la part de mes collaborateurs. J'ajoute que cette interview, je l'ai considérée comme une agression, de nature [à mettre] de l'huile sur le feu … Tournons la page, ne revenons plus sur le passé. Je retrouve le Cardinal Suenens que j'ai toujours connu» et Suenens ajoute: 'Cela voulait dire: je reprends sur le plan de l'amitié'», cf. Fonds Suenens A.P., b. 119.

renoncer à cette publication, Suenens fait quand même publier cette interview[199].

Il est certain que le pape suivait avec inquiétude ces prises de position de Suenens et qu'il n'a pas manqué de le lui dire dans plusieurs audiences. Probablement que Paul VI, homme de cœur, a aussi ressenti de la peine parce que cette amitié était rompue. Toutefois le pape a toujours voulu garder le contact et a même demandé à Mgr Benelli, substitut de la Secrétairerie d'État, de bien vouloir maintenir ses relations avec Suenens parce qu'il savait que Benelli était un ami de longue date de Suenens. Et de fait Benelli a fait plusieurs voyages pour rencontrer Suenens lorsque celui-ci prenait des vacances à Nice (e.a. août 1968, juillet 1970[200]). D'autre part il faut souligner que Suenens n'a agi, ni par esprit de contestation, ni par ambition personnelle[201], mais qu'il considérait comme son devoir d'œuvrer à une réforme de l'Église. Il a même comparé ses critiques sur le pape aux remontrances que l'apôtre Paul a faites à l'apôtre Pierre (cf. Gal 2,11-14).

En 1971, le cardinal fait connaissance avec le renouveau charismatique et avec le mouvement des Focolari. Il décide de laisser dorénavant en repos les problèmes de structures pour donner place à des préoccupations nouvelles, notamment à l'accueil du renouveau charismatique. Dans son audience du 18 février 1972[202], Suenens se réconcilie avec Paul VI,

---

199. Cf. Fonds Suenens A.P., b. 65 et 66.

200. Cf. pour la rencontre d'août 1968, Fonds Suenens B.C. et H.V., 1400; et pour la rencontre du 28-29 juillet 1970, Fonds Suenens A.P., b. 7. Mgr Heuschen, qui avait offert sa démission au pape pour des raisons de santé, témoigne d'une même préoccupation du pape quand en janvier 1970 le pape lui avait demandé de rester évêque résidentiel de Hasselt et ainsi membre de la conférence épiscopale belge, parce qu'il était un des rares évêques qui avait encore l'oreille du card. Suenens. Cf. Fonds Heuschen, 384, *Concilieherinneringen*, page annexe.

201. Certains ont même prétendu que Suenens avait publié son interview dans les *I.C.I.* (15 mai 1969) par dépit, parce qu'il n'avait pas été nommé Secrétaire d'État, mais bien le cardinal Villot (nommé le 30 avril 1969). Or les archives prouvent que cette interview a déjà été écrite en avril 1969, donc avant la nomination de Villot et à cause de quelques incidents de mars 1969. Cf. Fonds Suenens A.P., b. 60.

202. Cf. Fonds Suenens A.P., b. 7. En vue de l'audience du 18 février 1972 [fête de Sainte Bernadette], Suenens notait dans son cahier: «Je dois me souvenir de Bernadette, invitée par la Vierge 'à manger de l'herbe'. C'était vraiment un geste sans élégance et bien peu indiqué à nos yeux. Mais ce que Marie voulait n'était pas cette herbe mais la souplesse, la docilité, l'ouverture d'accueil. Il faut aller à la rencontre 'réconciliatrice' désencombré de soi, de ses plans, de ses vues. Le Seigneur nous demande de laisser à d'autres la réforme 'institutionnelle' toujours indispensable. Mais Il nous oriente vers un autre plan: vers l'animation spirituelle des structures. 'Mes paroles', dit le Seigneur, 'sont esprit et vie'. Il nous demande de donner le meilleur de nous-mêmes à vivifier son Église, à laisser le Christ être voie, vérité, vie. Il nous demande de croire à la parole de Simone Weil

réconciliation confirmée par sa lettre au pape du jeudi saint 1972[203] et par son audience du 6 juillet 1972[204].

À partir de ce moment, les relations redeviennent chaleureuses. Paul VI cite le livre de Suenens *Une nouvelle Pentecôte* (1974) dans l'allocution de l'audience publique le 16 octobre 1974. À la Pentecôte 1975, Suenens dirige un grand pèlerinage (10.000 participants) du mouvement charismatique à Rome, et assiste à la messe pontificale. Le lundi de Pentecôte (19 mai 1975) les pèlerins sont reçus en audience et Paul VI donne la mission à Suenens de veiller à la pleine intégration du mouvement charismatique dans la vie de l'Église catholique.

On peut donc conclure que les bonnes relations se sont rétablies[205], sans que toutefois la vieille amitié n'ait été restaurée. Un détail intéressant encore à noter: quand le postulateur pour le procès de béatification de Paul VI a adressé en 1992, 1993, 1994 de longs questionnaires à Suenens, celui-ci n'a pas répondu[206]. On n'en connaît pas la raison. Était-ce par discrétion ou faut-il attribuer ce silence à son âge déjà très avancé, qui ne lui permettait plus de répondre à des questionnaires détaillés?

Begijnhof 7   Leo DECLERCK
B-8000 Brugge

Herestraat 23   Toon OSAER
B-3000 Leuven

---

lorsqu'elle affirmait: 'Les problèmes humains sont tels que seule la sainteté peut les résoudre'». Cf. Fonds Suenens A.P., b. 10, Cahier I, p. 114. Pour cette audience, voir aussi les notes du Cardinal: 'Séjour à Rome autour du 18 février 1972' (Fonds Suenens A.P., b. 13).

203. Cf. SUENENS, *Souvenirs et Espérances* (n. 14), p. 205.

204. Suenens note à ce sujet: «... c'était l'audience la plus chaleureuse de ma vie; on ne sentait plus aucune espèce de réticence nulle part et c'était détendu à l'extrême. Deo gratias!» (Fonds Suenens A.P., b. 13).

205. Dans le livre de FLECKENSTEIN, *Pour l'Église de demain* (n. 5), pp. 68-73, Suenens esquisse un portrait fort élogieux de Paul VI et justifie quelque peu ses critiques: «On peut critiquer le fonctionnement d'une voiture sans pour autant critiquer le chauffeur».

206. Fonds Suenens A.P., b. 13.

LÉGER ET SUENENS

LES RELATIONS DIFFICILES DE DEUX PRINCES DE L'ÉGLISE

Les cardinaux Léger et Suenens auront été deux coryphées du concile. Ces deux figures, bien que foncièrement différentes, peuvent être rapprochées, non seulement en raison du charisme qui se dégageait de leur forte personnalité, de leur éloquence et de leur rayonnement, mais également parce que les deux avaient des intérêts communs et des positions finalement assez rapprochées sur plusieurs questions débattues au concile. Ces deux faits ne les rapprochent pourtant pas d'emblée. En effet, ce détail est-il indicatif d'une relation difficile, l'index onomastique de l'ouvrage de Suenens où il rapporte ses *Souvenirs* ignore totalement le nom du cardinal Léger[1] alors que celui d'une douzaine d'autres cardinaux leaders de la majorité au concile s'y retrouvent[2]. Est-ce à dire qu'il y aurait peu à dire et encore moins à écrire sur la relation entre les deux hommes à Vatican II? Et c'est bien là le paradoxe, le fait d'avoir souvent épousé les mêmes causes et d'avoir senti les mêmes choses les auront souvent mis en concurrence bien qu'ils aient été fréquemment appelés à collaborer et à s'engager ensemble dans des batailles communes. Sans aller jusqu'à devenir frères ennemis, le concile aura été pour eux une épreuve, les plaçant tour à tour dans une situation d'alliés et de rivaux, de complices et d'adversaires. Ces deux personnalités et leur parcours conciliaire constituent peut-être un cas de figure nous aidant à comprendre la complexité de la majorité conciliaire[3], tantôt capable de donner une orientation au concile et tantôt impuissante à faire aboutir des propositions.

Cet itinéraire commence lors de leur première rencontre à l'occasion de leur participation à la Commission centrale préparatoire, moment fondateur de leur relation. Par la suite, ils seront appelés à exercer des fonctions assez différentes, Léger à la Commission doctrinale alors que Suenens,

---

1. Voir L.-J. SUENENS, *Souvenirs et espérances*, Paris, Fayard, 1991.
2. C'est le cas pour Alfrink, Bea, Döpfner, Frings, König, Liénart, Montini, etc.
3. Sur Suenens et Léger à l'intérieur de la majorité conciliaire, voir C. SOETENS, *La 'Squadra belga' all'interno della maggioranza conciliare*, dans M.T. FATTORI – A. MELLONI (éds.), *L'Evento e le decisioni: Studi sulle dinamiche del Concilio Vaticano II* (Testi e ricerche di scienze religiose. Nuova Serie, 20), Bologne, Il Mulino, 1998, 143-172.

d'abord membre du *Secretariatus pro negotiis extraordinariis*, sera appelé dès la première intersession à siéger à la Commission de coordination avant d'être choisi en septembre 1963 comme modérateur du concile. Cet itinéraire connaîtra des périodes de grande complicité et d'âpre rivalité.

I. UNE RELATION QUI SE CONSTRUIT LENTEMENT

Les premières rencontres entre les deux cardinaux[4] se font dans le cadre des travaux de la Commission centrale préparatoire et les témoignages au sujet de ces premières prises de connaissance sont pratiquement inexistants. Les seules traces dont on dispose sont dans les *Acta et Documenta* et cette source est peu éloquente à propos de l'affinité qui a pu se développer entre les deux hommes. Quoi qu'il en soit, on peut observer que dès la première participation de Suenens à la Commission centrale préparatoire (la cinquième session, 26 mars au 23 avril 1962), à l'occasion de la discussion sur le *De regimine missionum,* Léger fait référence à la position du cardinal Suenens dans son intervention[5]. Ce sera à nouveau le cas, lors de la sixième session (3-12 mai 1962), dans le cadre de la discussion sur le *De episcopis,* alors que Léger donne son appui à la position de Suenens[6]. Les deux se rencontrent, et ce ne sera pas la dernière fois, autour de positions semblables sur le *De castitate, virginitate, matrimonio et familia*[7]. Lors de la même session, le débat sur le chapitre VI du *De ecclesia,* portant sur les laïcs, fournira une nouvelle occasion aux deux cardinaux d'exprimer des positions convergentes[8]. Un même accord semble exister entre les deux hommes lors de la septième et dernière session de la Commission centrale préparatoire (12-19 juin 1962).

---

4. En raison de l'entrée toute récente de Suenens au collège cardinalice (mars 1962), les deux hommes n'avaient pas eu l'occasion de se fréquenter ou de se connaître auparavant lors de consistoires, des plénières des congrégations ou du conclave qui avait élu Jean XXIII. On peut présumer, sans en être tout à fait sûr, que la Commission centrale préparatoire était le premier contact réel entre les deux hommes. Ceci dit, les deux hommes avaient eu l'occasion de prendre contact aupraravant. Ainsi, en 1953, Suenens a envoyé son livre *Une héroïne de l'apostolat: Edel Mary Quinn* à Léger, qui lui a répondu. Il a fait de même en 1955 avec son livre *L'Église en état de mission*, avec réponse de Léger (Fonds Suenens, Archives Personnelles, boîtes 31 et 34).
5. *AD* III, p. 200. On trouve alors cette mention: «J'appuie les déclarations de Suenens».
6. *AD* III, pp. 827-828.
7. *AD* III, pp. 940-944.
8. *AD* III, pp. 1097-1100.

En effet, à nouveau, le *votum* de Léger fera référence à la position prise par Suenens au moment de la discussion sur *De sacrorum alumnis formandis*[9]. La même chose se répète lors de la discussion sur le *De apostolatu laicorum*[10].

Ces quelques traces, trop lacunaires sans doute pour que l'on puisse en tirer beaucoup de choses, indiquent cependant que, déjà avant l'ouverture du concile, les deux hommes ont fait connaissance et ont reconnu leur orientation commune, sans qu'il ne soit démontré par ailleurs une réelle complicité entre les deux hommes. En effet, Léger se réfère davantage aux cardinaux Frings, Döpfner, Alfrink, Bea, Liénart et König qu'à Suenens qu'il n'a connu que tardivement. En fait, Suenens apparaît à l'époque dans un deuxième cercle, où se retrouvent les cardinaux Richaud, Montini[11], Jullien, Silva Henriquez, le Patriarche Maximos IV et Mgr Denis Hurley. On observera aussi que, au cours de cette période, Léger n'est pas associé – du reste aucun cardinal non européen ne le sera – à l'initiative du cardinal Suenens en vue de présenter à Jean XXIII un plan d'ensemble pour le concile[12]. Sur la base des correspondances échangées, du ton de ces correspondances, des visites rendues et du travail en commun, on peut dire que, à cette époque, Léger se sentait plus près de Frings, de Liénart et de Montini que de Suenens, nouvel arrivé au collège cardinalice et que Léger avait peu fréquenté jusque là. Celui-ci ne faisait pas partie des intimes de Léger et l'inverse était sans doute vrai aussi. Ces premières traces, si fragmentaires soient-elles, indiquent cependant une orientation commune et un intérêt pour les mêmes questions: au premier rang, le mariage, le laïcat, l'épiscopat, la formation des prêtres et les missions.

À l'été 1962, au moment où Léger entreprend d'envoyer une Supplique à Jean XXIII, il est significatif d'observer que c'est Frings qui se fera l'intermédiaire entre Léger et Suenens pour obtenir la signature de ce dernier, Léger entreprenant des démarches personnelles auprès de Liénart et de Montini[13]. Par ailleurs, Suenens – pas plus que Montini, Liénart ou

---

9. *AD* III, pp. 65-70.
10. *AD* III, pp. 527-533.
11. Léger avait rendu visite à Montini à Milan, en 1959.
12. L.-J. SUENENS, *Aux origines du Concile Vatican II*, dans *NRT* 107 (1985) 3-21. Ces informations seront reprises, avec quelques nuances, dans SUENENS, *Souvenirs et espérances* (n. 1), pp. 65-71. Certes, il faut toujours être critique avec ces témoignages postérieurs qui reconstruisent le passé.
13. À ce sujet, voir mon article: G. ROUTHIER, *Les réactions du Cardinal Léger à la préparation de Vatican II*, dans *Revue d'histoire de l'Église de France* 80 (1994) 281-302.

Döpfner du reste – ne met Léger au courant de ses propres initiatives qui interviennent au cours de la même période. Cela constitue-t-il une appréciation des qualités du cardinal Léger? Sans doute qu'il ne faut pas conclure trop vite en ce sens. Il n'était probablement pas d'usage encore, à l'époque, de considérer un non-européen lorsqu'il s'agissait de réfléchir aux graves questions concernant le gouvernement de l'Église et du concile. Quoi qu'il en soit, aux dires de Mgr Prignon qui relate des propos de Suenens sur la préparation du concile, il y avait déjà, à cette époque, un «accord, tacite au début, puis plus formel, conclu entre les cardinaux Frings, Liénart, Léger, Döpfner, lui-même et plus ou moins Montini, à la fin des réunions de la commission centrale»[14].

Il faut donc attendre ensuite la veille de l'ouverture du concile avant que les deux hommes se retrouvent à nouveau, alors que les discussions de corridors vont bon train et que les conciliabules en marge de l'ouverture du concile se multiplient. Le 10 octobre 1962, Léger s'entretient avec les Cardinaux Suenens, Döpfner et Bea. Les discussions sont à l'effet que les épiscopats envoient une liste de membres qualifiés en vue des élections de la première session[15]. De ces conversations de coulisses, Pierre Lafortune retiendra ceci: «Le concile [..?] flou – inquiétant. Aucune action concertée ne se dessine. Chacun veut-il faire passer son petit [..?] Le temps presse. On sera pris par surprise. Le cardinal [Léger] est très actif. Le cardinal Suenens veut conclure avec [..?] qui engagerait trop le concile …»[16]. Léger, pour sa part, semble plus optimiste:

> *Mercredi (10 oct.)* je rencontrais le *Cardinal Suenens*[17] et le *Cardinal Döpfner* et j'ai pu causer un instant avec le *Cardinal Bea*. Nous nous entendons alors pour que chaque épiscopat pût présenter une liste de membres qualifiés en vue des élections de la première session, afin que la liste préparée

14. L. DECLERCK – A. HAQUIN (éds.), *Mgr. Albert Prignon: Journal conciliaire de la 4ᵉ Session* (Cahiers de la Revue théologique de Louvain, 35), Louvain-la-Neuve, Publications de la Faculté de Théologie, 2003 (désormais cité Journal Prignon), p. 262.

15. Voir agenda Léger du 10 octobre.

16. P. Lafortune, Notes.

17. Il est intéressant de confronter ce compte-rendu avec une lettre que Suenens adressait à V. O'Brien (L. DECLERCK – E. LOUCHEZ, *Inventaire des Papiers conciliaires du cardinal L.-J. Suenens* [Cahiers de la Revue théologique de Louvain, 31], Louvain-la-Neuve, Publications de la Faculté de Théologie, 1998, désormais cité: Fonds Suenens, 568) et dans laquelle il parlait ainsi de cette rencontre avec Léger: «Ce matin j'ai reçu Léger, un homme émotif et 'traqué'. Il me dit qu'on le met avec Teilhard sur le même rang, que les revues américaines lui en veulent et qu'il n'a personne derrière lui dans son pays, qu'il est épouvanté de l'esprit d'ici etc. Il a reçu réponse à la lettre des 7 [la lettre de Léger à Jean XXIII, signée en fait par 6 cardinaux; cette lettre a été envoyée par Cicognani à Felici le 19 octobre 1962, cf. *AS* VI/1, pp. 52-62], réponse de Cicognani très aimable mais ne disant rien de précis. Montini n'a pas signé mais les 6 autres. Vous voyez l'homme prudent! Il doit être un as dans cette vertu … cardinalice».

par le secrétariat général ne fût pas imposée à cette multitude de Pères qui, ne se connaissant pas entre eux, se seraient ralliés à cette liste 'préfabriquée'. Il fallait donc déjouer la manœuvre et agir en vitesse. Mais comment faire, puisque dès le lendemain c'était la grande cérémonie de l'ouverture du Concile? Cette cérémonie paralysait tous les organismes que nous aurions pu faire agir efficacement.

Puis, c'est apparemment le silence entre les deux hommes, chacun allant son chemin, jusqu'au 24 octobre[18] suivant alors que le cardinal Suenens rend visite au cardinal Léger. À la suite de cette rencontre, Léger notera: «Ai parlé au Cardinal Suenens. Il faut modifier la procédure car l'école du saint-Office peut user le concile. Dans un mois nous serons au même point. Son Ordo du concile déposé dans les mains du pape ne semble pas avoir été adopté par celui-ci. [...] Veut absolument que les schémas sur l'Église soient étudiés après ceux de la liturgie»[19]. Les deux hommes, qui partagent alors des intérêts communs au sujet de l'orientation du concile et de sa direction et qui échangent des informations d'ordre stratégique, ne se reverront pourtant plus avant le 11 novembre[20] alors qu'ils participent tous les deux, avec d'autres cardinaux[21], à une rencontre à l'*Anima*, autour du cardinal Frings. Rien ne transparaît, cependant, d'un lien particulier entre Suenens et Léger à cette occasion, mais il devient apparent que les deux font partie des leaders de la majorité et du groupe restreint de cardinaux qui essaient d'orienter le concile[22]. Leur combat est le même, mais on observe tout de suite

---

18. En date du 20 octobre, on trouve une mention du nom de Suenens au Journal Léger. Lors d'une rencontre avec Achille Glorieux, son nom avait été évoqué: «Entretien avec Mgr Glorieux ... Nous parlons de la commission des laïcs. La thèse du cardinal Suenens passera-t-elle? Conception qui rompt avec la tradition...». Suenens voulait notamment que la Légion de Marie soit reconnue comme mouvement d''Action catholique', ce qui impliquait que le mandat de la hiérarchie n'était pas un caractère spécifique de l'Action catholique et que celle-ci ne devait pas toujours être spécialisée (ouvriers, patrons, agriculteurs, jeunesse ouvrière, jeunesse étudiante etc.).

19. Journal Léger.

20. Dans l'intervalle, Léger avait rencontré Charue, le 8 novembre.

21. Les autres cardinaux sont Frings, Döpfner, König, Alfrink et Liénart. Léger ne participait apparemment pas à une première rencontre de stratégie (25 octobre) qui ne réunissait que des cardinaux européens: Frings, Siri, Liénart, Montini, König, Döpfner, Suenens et Alfrink. Ce soir-là, cependant, il s'était rendu rencontrer Frings à l'Anima et avait pris le repas en sa compagnie. C'est probablement Frings qui l'intègre à ce groupe de cardinaux européens. De même, Léger n'est pas présent à une première concertation (13 octobre) qui réunissait Frings, Liénart, König, Döpfner et Suenens. Ce jour-là, suivant son agenda, Léger rencontrait Montini.

22. Ce matin à 9h30, réunion à l'Anima avec les cardinaux Frings, Döpfner, König, Alfrink, Suenens, Liénart. Présentation d'un schéma préparé par les théologiens du card. Frings et étude de la stratégie à suivre pour faire passer ce document. Le card. Frings

la singularité de Léger dans ce groupe en sa qualité de seul cardinal non-européen du groupe, ce qui constituera toujours pour lui un handicap important.

Autrement, les deux cardinaux vaquent à leurs affaires respectives, les deux ayant des responsabilités différentes, l'un à la Commission doctrinale et l'autre au Secrétariat pour les affaires extraordinaires, ce qui ne leur permet pas de se rencontrer fréquemment ni de collaborer étroitement. Il leur arrive souvent cependant d'intervenir sur les mêmes questions, le même jour parfois, en congrégation générale[23]. Pour l'heure, ce qui semble plus déterminant, c'est la cour entreprise par Moeller auprès de Léger, ce qui conduira Léger à demander que Moeller soit nommé expert au concile[24]. En effet, Moeller qui n'avait pas été invité par un évêque belge à l'accompagner à Rome avait dû rester à Louvain à ronger son frein. Le 8 novembre, Thils l'invite à venir à Rome pour y donner des conférences, ce qu'il fera le 28 novembre[25]. Moeller, qui avait connu Léger à Montréal et lui avait déjà fait parvenir quelques textes[26], se montre plein d'empressement et multiplie les ambassades à son endroit,

me fait songer à un maréchal du Reich (Rommel). Plusieurs voient des objections. Liénart doit rectifier son tir. Il regrette que le schéma soit présenté au nom de l'épiscopat allemand et français! Il fait des dissidents ... Je profite de ces contacts mais je comprends que la prudence est une vertu bien nécessaire pour le moment... (Journal Léger).

23. Léger interviendra beaucoup plus souvent que Suenens dans *l'Aula* conciliaire. Au cours de cette première session, à sept reprises contre trois pour Suenens. Sans qu'il s'agisse d'une action concertée, certaines interventions sont 'synchronisées'.

24. La demande en sera faite le 6 décembre 1962 (P. LAFORTUNE, *Inventaire des archives conciliaires du Fonds Paul Émile Léger*, Outremont, Les éditions des partenaires, 1995, désormais cité: Fonds Léger, 339). Moeller écrira: «Incroyable de voir comment j'ai réussi à rencontrer les gens nécessaires» (F. COLLEYE, *Charles Moeller et l'Arbre de la Croix*, publication à compte d'auteur, p. 265).

25. On verra COLLEYE, *Charles Moeller et l'Arbre de la Croix*.

26. D'abord en date du 14 février 1961, un texte sur la notion d'Église locale (Fonds Léger, 776), ensuite, en mars, trois textes sur la notion de 'Patriarche d'Occident' (Fonds Léger, 777-779), de nouveau, en avril, une note sur la notion d'*Ecclesia particularis* (Fonds Léger, 780), puis une autre intitulée *Triplex distinctio ad regimen Primatus Romani Pontificis clarius exponendum in relatione ad collegium episcoporum Ecclesiae* (Fonds Léger, 781) et enfin, ses conclusions aux Journées oecuméniques de Chevetogne de septembre 1961 sur «Infaillibilité et Vérité» (Fonds Léger, 860). Juste avant l'ouverture de la première session (le 8 octobre), il lui faisait à nouveau parvenir ses remarques sur les deux premiers schémas (Fonds Léger, 614). Ces textes n'avaient pas été écrits pour le cardinal Léger, mais Moeller distribuait largement les textes qu'il rédigeait. On trouve également de nombreux textes de Thils (7 – Fonds Léger, 782-788) dans les archives Léger et qui datent de la période préparatoire. Ils se rapportent essentiellement à l'épiscopat, la collégialité, l'infaillibilité du pape. À cela, il faudrait ajouter l'extrait de son article paru dans les *NRT* sur l'épiscopat (Fonds Léger, 859). C'est dire que les relations étaient également déjà bien tissées entre les deux.

lui rendant visite dès le 29 novembre[27] et lui envoyant des remarques sur les schémas en discussion[28].

Il faut donc attendre les derniers jours de la session avant que le nom de Suenens ne réapparaisse dans le Journal Léger, soit le 4 décembre 1962: «Session des grands jours. Le cardinal Suenens a été magnifique et même ... un peu majestueux. Il eut été déçu, je crois, si l'assemblée n'avait pas applaudi! Mais l'esprit passe aussi, et avec quelle liberté, dans la grande chevelure du chêne». Par ailleurs, les papiers conciliaires du cardinal Léger contiennent une analyse anonyme assez critique de la proposition Suenens[29]. Celle-ci conteste d'abord la division des matières selon le schéma *Ecclesia ad intra* et *Ecclesia ad extra*. Elle critique aussi l'option de regrouper toute la matière sous un *De ecclesia* avant de critiquer la division quadripartite de l'*Ecclesia ad intra*. Il serait difficile aussi, suivant cette analyse, d'aborder la nature de l'Église sans situer l'Église dans le monde. Enfin, observe-t-on, «cette intervention du cardinal Suenens sur le schéma *De Ecclesia* ne nous dit rien sur ce que devrait contenir et ce que devrait être le schéma *De Ecclesia*». Cette note critique n'exprime pas d'emblée le sentiment du cardinal Léger et nous ignorons l'importance qu'il y a attaché, si bien que l'observateur ne peut pas en tirer argument dans un sens ou dans l'autre.

Très significatives aussi, lorsque l'on veut faire une appréciation comparative de la perception qu'a alors Léger de Suenens, les annotations qu'il consigne, les jours suivants (les 5 et 6 décembre 1962[30]) dans son *Journal conciliaire*: «Une autre grande voix s'est élevée ce matin ... Enfin, le cardinal Montini a osé parler. Ton plus sobre que celui de Bruxelles. Plus de nuances ... mais que de richesses dans ce texte, qui je l'espère inspirera les rédacteurs du prochain schéma sur l'Église». Et, le

---

27. Le 2 décembre, il lui envoie ses remarques au sujet du *De ecclesia* (Fonds Léger, 845). Il note: «Le cardinal Léger attend d'urgence mes remarques sur la refonte des 'Deux sources de la Révélation'». Il le fera, le 6 décembre (Fonds Léger, 1104).

28. «Nouvelle invasion d'experts ou d'assistants: Ch. Moeller, Dom O. Rousseau, etc.», écrira Congar le 3 décembre (Y. CONGAR, *Mon Journal du Concile*, présenté et annoté par É. MAHIEU, 2 tomes, Paris, Cerf, 2002, p. 288). En fait, il faudrait écrire comment certains experts belges sont entrés (ou se sont imposés) dans les commissions et comment ils ont été appelés en renfort ou sont devenus experts au concile.

29. Anonyme, sans lieu ni date (Fonds Léger, 707).

30. Lorsque l'on dépasse le cadre strict des rapports entre Léger et Suenens, on observera que les relations avec d'autres Belges sont particulièrement nombreuses au cours de ces journées. En plus de ce que nous avons dit de Moeller, on note que le 5 décembre 1962, Léger prendra le repas du soir avec Philippe Delhaye à la suite d'une réunion de la Commission *De fide*. Le lendemain, 6 décembre, Léger demande la désignation de P. Delhaye comme *peritus* au concile.

lendemain, «[...] Le cardinal Lercaro a parlé ce matin avec les accents sobres mais pathétiques des prophètes de l'A.T. Son regard perçant a découvert la présence de Dieu et de Jésus Christ dans les pauvres. Il nous découvrait ainsi l'une des plus mystérieuses dimensions de l'Église». Ces indications, comme celle des carnets Lafortune du 10 octobre précédent, nous permettent de faire un premier bilan au sujet de la perception de Suenens par les Montréalais: un homme brillant et charismatique, libre et audacieux, avec qui il fallait certainement compter et avec qui il fallait travailler, mais un homme qui manquait peut-être d'un peu de mesure et de profondeur[31]. Sur le fond, Montini et Lercaro avaient davantage touché Léger. Le second, en atteignant une corde sensible du cardinal montréalais, la pauvreté, le premier, par la profondeur, la finesse et la nuance de la pensée. Pour sa part, Léger, dans sa dernière intervention de la session, était revenu sur une idée qui lui tenait à cœur, à savoir la mise sur pied d'une commission de permanence du concile au cours de l'intersession[32]. Aussi, au terme de cette première session, on peut dire que, même si leur collaboration n'était pas toujours étroite, on percevait bien que les deux hommes étaient dans le même camp et faisaient partie, avec Frings, Döpfner, König, Bea, Liénart, Silva Henriquez, Meyer, Montini, Maximos IV et Alfrink, d'un petit groupe de leaders du concile[33].

II. Une complicité d'intérêt

La situation semble tout à fait différente à partir de l'intersession. Certes, les circonstances sont fort différentes: Léger est passé par une

---

31. Une lettre du cardinal Léger à Charles Moeller, en date du 21 décembre 1962, lui annonçant que sa demande en vue de la nomination de celui-ci comme *peritus* conciliaire avait été acceptée, nous fournit un autre indice de la considération de Léger pour Suenens: «Vous savez que votre Cardinal a été nommé membre de la Commission spéciale inter-sessionnelle. J'espère qu'il fera préparer un bon schéma sur l'Église et qu'il interviendra pour obtenir la refonte de toute la partie théologique» (Fonds Moeller, 03036).

32. Déjà, lors de l'audience du 20 novembre, Léger avait recommandé à Jean XXIII de créer un organisme pour gérer l'intersession. Suivant son témoignage, Jean XXIII en aurait parlé sur le champ, au téléphone, avec Mgr Felici et Cicognani. Il revient sur le même sujet, le 30 novembre, dans son Journal et il reprendra cette proposition, lors de son intervention *in aula*, le 3 décembre 1962, alors qu'il suggère la mise sur pied d'une commission permanente du Concile pour surveiller l'élaboration des schémas durant l'absence des Pères (voir le Journal de Léger. Témoignage concordant dans CONGAR, *Mon Journal du Concile* [n. 28], 6 mars 1963, Vol. I, p. 340).

33. Significatif à cet égard l'envoi à Suenens le 22 décembre 1962, par S. Lyonnet, de la réponse de trois professeurs de l'Institut biblique à la lettre des 19 cardinaux, réponse préparée à la demande de Léger et de König (Fonds Suenens, 1154).

rude épreuve à la fin de la première session[34] à la suite de son indiscrétion sur la santé du pape et de son jugement public assez négatif sur la première période du concile[35]. À ce moment, Léger cherche des appuis là où il peut les trouver et il écrit à de nombreux cardinaux pour s'assurer en quelque sorte de leur soutien au moment où il est appelé à se justifier à Rome[36]. Par ailleurs, Suenens a été nommé membre de la Commission de coordination.

Cette nouvelle relation s'étend du mois de février 1963 jusqu'à la mort de Jean XXIII, en juin, et s'exprime à travers une série de sept lettres[37] empreintes d'une grande cordialité et d'un esprit de collaboration remarquable. Elle est inaugurée le 28 décembre 1962 par une correspondance de Léger à Suenens, lettre qui ne trouvera cependant pas d'écho[38]. Quoi qu'il en soit, le 8 février 1963, avant de retourner à Rome, Léger adresse une nouvelle lettre chaleureuse et pleine d'affection à Suenens sur le travail qui les attend à la Commission *De fide*[39]. Après quelques phrases

---

34. Il en parlera souvent comme des jours d'agonie. Cela le conduira à l'hôpital, le lundi 7 janvier, après un malaise cardiaque le 2 janvier et avoir été confiné à sa chambre à l'archevêché pendant quelques jours. Il quittera l'Hôtel Dieu de Montréal le 14 janvier, en soirée.

35. Dans une entrevue à *La Presse* donnée dans le cadre d'une conférence au *Plateau de Montréal* le 17 décembre 1962, le cardinal Léger avait été très explicite sur la faillite du concile au cours de la première session («Tout est à refaire, avait-il dit. Ce qui a été fait a été mal fait…») et sur le très mauvais état de santé du pape (Voir notamment le quotidien montréalais *Le Devoir*, «Jean XXIII est atteint d'une maladie qui serait incurable», 19 décembre 1962, p. 8). Cette déclaration, reprise par *Il Tempo*, avait eu une grande répercussion dans la presse internationale (voir «Un cardinale dichiara che il Papa è affetto da un male inguaribile», *Il Tempo*, 19 décembre 1962) Par la suite, le cardinal est appelé à se justifier auprès de la Secrétairerie d'État (Voir Fonds Léger, 42). Cela s'ajoutait à l'examen auquel le cardinal avait déjà été soumis par la Secrétairerie d'État au cours de la première session (novembre et décembre 1962) à la suite de dénonciations de la Cité catholique (VVV) portant sur l'administration du diocèse de Montréal. À ce sujet, voir l'ensemble du dossier (soustrait à la consultation publique): Fonds Léger, 32-37.

36. Il recevra l'expression du soutien de plusieurs cardinaux, notamment de Urbani, König, Liénart, Meyer (une lettre très touchante), Feltin, Alfrink, Frings, Döpfner, Bea, Silva Henriquez. Seuls Suenens et Montini n'avaient pas répondu à la lettre de Léger (28 décembre 1962) aux cardinaux Suenens, Liénart, Frings, Feltin, Montini, Döpfner, Meyer, Alfrink, Bea et Silva Henriquez (Fonds Léger, 48). Pour l'ensemble du dossier, soustrait à la consultation publique, voir Fonds Léger, 44-67. Montini avait pourtant posé un geste de solidarité important: «Il (Dell'Acqua) m'a confié que dès le lendemain le cardinal Montini faisait paraître dans l'*Italia* un démenti énergique. *Voilà les grandes heures de l'amitié!*» (*Journal*, 20 février 1963).

37. Cinq lettres de Léger et deux de Suenens, auxquelles il faut ajouter une conversation téléphonique.

38. Selon Leo Declerck, Suenens, probablement par négligence, ne répondait pas toujours à ses correspondants (Philips devait s'en plaindre également dans son Journal). Aussi, il ne faut pas en tirer de conclusions trop fermes au sujet de sa relation avec Léger.

39. P. LAFONTAINE, *Inventaire des archives conciliaires du Fonds André Naud* (Cahiers de recherche sur Vatican II, 1), Québec, Université Laval, 1998. Désormais cité: Fonds

introductives où il écrit avoir reçu les documents pour la session du mois de février de la commission, il observe avec plaisir tout le travail de révision des schémas qui a été entrepris et l'espoir que suscite le nouvel agenda du concile proposé par la Commission de coordination. Il souligne à cette occasion l'importante contribution du cardinal Suenens à tout ce travail. C'est alors qu'il revient sur les événements de décembre, se confiant à Suenens comme à un ami:

> C'est dans la fièvre de la préparation de cette réunion que vous avez dû recevoir ma lettre du 28 décembre dernier, et c'est pourquoi je comprends votre silence. J'espère cependant que vous avez bien compris le sens de cette lettre. Je vivais, à ce moment-là, des heures d'agonie qui m'ont d'ailleurs conduit à l'hôpital après avoir éprouvé une légère attaque du cœur. [...]

Après s'être ouvert en toute confiance à son collègue de Malines, il revient aux affaires conciliaires:

> J'aurais bien aimé vous rencontrer avant cette session (de la Commission *de fide*) afin de connaître exactement votre pensée. Auriez-vous la bonté de m'indiquer qui sera, à Rome, votre porte-parole le plus autorisé? Je considère que la rédaction du schéma sur l'Église doit devenir le centre de nos préoccupations. [...] Ce schéma doit faire éclater les frontières juridiques qui ont présenté l'Église comme un ghetto de privilégiés.

L'homme est fragile, blessé. Certes, il a traversé l'orage, s'est relevé, mais on l'a atteint durablement. C'est la première fois qu'il retourne à Rome depuis l'incident de décembre et il craint sans doute ce moment car, à tort ou à raison, il se sait traqué et il prétend que l'on veut le neutraliser, le faire taire. Il a trahi Ottaviani et les autres[40]. Il est devenu dangereux. Dans ces circonstances, il a besoin de conseil, d'appui. Il termine cette lettre sur le ton de la confidence:

> Toutes ces pensées hantent mon esprit et usent mon cœur. Je m'excuse de me livrer ainsi à vous, mais vous avez été pour moi, durant la 1e session conciliaire, un guide prudent et vous avez conquis mon admiration.

Cette fois, dès le 15 février, le cardinal Suenens lui répond[41], lui exprimant d'abord son contentement de le savoir rétabli et d'apprendre qu'il

---

Naud, 112. Fonds Suenens, 976-980. Le mois précédent, il avait adressé deux courriers (14 janvier et 8 février) à Charles Moeller sur les travaux à venir de la même commission, lui donnant en particulier ses avis sur le schéma *De ecclesia* (voir Fonds Moeller, 03037 et 03041).

40. À la suite de la première réunion de la Commission doctrinale, le 13 novembre 1962, réunion au cours de laquelle Léger avait fait une intervention dramatique, il notait: «je perdais une précieuse amitié [Ottaviani] et un puissant protecteur à Rome. – Jusque là, j'étais toujours invité à sa table»: Léger, notes manuscrites et notes dactylographiées (Fonds Léger, 19 et 29).

41. Fonds Naud, 113.

pourra participer aux travaux sur le *De ecclesia* et le *De beata*. De plus, il envoie le rapport complet des travaux de la Commission de coordination de manière à l'éclairer sur les derniers développements et la marche du concile. De plus, il lui indique que Mgr Prignon sera, à Rome, son 'procureur théologique' et que le cardinal Léger pourra le rencontrer pour connaître ses sentiments[42]. Enfin, à titre d'information, il lui indique que Mgr Charue est en contact avec les Allemands[43] et qu'une rencontre est prévue, avec König, à Salvator Mundi, le 20 février. «Ne manquez pas le rendez-vous», ajoute-t-il, avant de conclure au sujet du *De Ecclesia*: «Il me semble que l'essentiel serait d'adopter les grandes lignes du schéma Philips-Thils, de l'améliorer chemin faisant, et d'aller très avant dans la ligne de la collégialité». Puis il lui indique: «Je serai très heureux si vous pouviez me tenir au courant au fur et à mesure, soit directement soit à travers Mgr Prignon».

Rien de particulièrement affectueux dans cette lettre dont le ton demeure celui du traitement des affaires courantes. Cependant, cette fois, le contact est rétabli et les deux hommes s'engagent désormais dans un travail de collaboration qui les unira tout au long de cette intersession. Cette collaboration – stratégique – s'établira sans doute davantage sur la base d'intérêts mutuels que de l'estime véritable. Si les intérêts de Léger à ce moment sont évidents, ceux de Suenens ne le sont pas moins. Il a besoin d'appui à la Commission *De fide* pour que puissent aboutir ce qu'il défend à la Commission de coordination et les schémas élaborés par l'équipe belge.

Suivant les indications du cardinal Suenens, dès qu'il arrive à Rome, Léger s'entretiendra (19 février 1963) avec Mgr Charue et Mgr Prignon qui lui «précisent la pensée du cardinal Suenens».

Le lendemain, Léger recevra le chanoine Moeller, «plein de plans et d'idées», et G. Thils lui adressera ses remarques sur le schéma sur la Révélation. Aussi, tout au long de cette période qui va de la mi-février à la mi-mars, Léger recevra régulièrement des textes du groupe belge[44] et

42. Le même jour, il envoyait une lettre à Prignon lui demandant de prendre contact avec Léger. Voir J. FAMERÉE, *Concile Vatican II et Église contemporaine (Archives de Louvain-la-Neuve). II: Inventaire des Fonds A. Prignon et H. Wagnon* (Cahiers de la Revue théologique de Louvain, 24), Louvain-la-Neuve, Publications de la Faculté de Théologie, 1991 (désormais cité: Fonds Prignon, 284; voir aussi Fonds Suenens 0979).
43. Léger avait par ailleurs reçu directement du cardinal Frings (19 février) des indications sur le *De ecclesia* formulées par les évêques de langue allemande, lors de leur rencontre du 4 et 5 février (Fonds Léger, 209).
44. 28 février, texte de C. Moeller sur des remarques de portée générale sur le 1er chapitre du *De ecclesia*.
1er mars, Projet de Mgr Philips sur le schéma *De ecclesia*. 8 mars, Projet final de Mgr Philips sur le chap II du schéma *De constitutione hierachica ecclesiae*; 16 mars, texte

les contacts sont fréquents[45]. On veut s'assurer surtout de la collaboration de Léger sur le *De ecclesia*[46]. Cela culminera, le 14 mars par une rencontre au Collège belge du cardinal Léger avec Mgr Philips, C. Moeller et Mgr Prignon et, le soir, par une conversation téléphonique avec le cardinal Suenens[47]. Cette période d'étroite collaboration entre Léger et les Belges n'est toutefois pas exempte de tensions, comme en font foi les rapports «quotidiens» (au Cher Edouard) de Charles Moeller[48]. Déjà, au

de C. Moeller sur le schéma sur l'Apostolat des laïcs. Ceci dit, l'agenda Léger indique qu'il prépare ses interventions avec ses deux *periti* montréalais, P. Lafortune et A. Naud.

45. Léger est reçu par Prignon, le 7 mars (ou le 5 mars, suivant l'agenda Léger) de manière à élaborer une stratégie avec le cardinal Suenens. Philips et Moeller participent à la rencontre. Léger lui demande alors de tenir Suenens au courant de l'évolution des travaux et Prignon parvient à convaincre Léger de reporter son départ prévu pour le dimanche. Léger est à nouveau reçu pour le repas du midi le 11 mars en compagnie de Garrone, McGrath, Schröffer et quelques *periti*.

46. Moeller s'assure que Léger optera pour le projet Philips, lui faisant une note à ce sujet, et appuiera les Belges dans leur démarche (voir Propositiones pro elaboratione schematis De Ecclesia, Ch. Moeller, 21.02.1963). On trouve cette note dans le Fonds Philips (L. DECLERCK – W. VERSCHOOTEN, *Inventaire des papiers conciliaires de Mgr Gérard Philips, secrétaire adjoint de la Commission doctrinale. Avec une Introduction par* J. GROOTAERS (Instrumenta Theologica, 24), Leuven, Bibliotheek van de Faculteit Godgeleerdheid – Peeters, 2001 désormais cité: Fonds Philips, 593) avec indication «cette note a été écrite pour le Card. Léger» et dans le Fonds Naud (303), mais elle est absente du Fonds Léger.

47. Un courrier de Léger à Suenens suivra, le 18 mars. Cette lettre restera sans réponse. Voir aussi la bande magnétique que Suenens envoya à V. O'Brien (Fonds Suenens, 0740).

48. «Gros risque hier: un des *periti* de Léger, Naud, dont je t'ai parlé déjà, s'apprête à faire une intervention qui suppose 'deux notions de l'Église, deux communautés', comme je te l'ai dit; je lui avais écrit un mot hier, pour le supplier d'exposer son idée autrement, sous peine de faire tout sauter. Il s'est tu mais il me garde une terrible dent. Situation délicate. Heureusement que j'ai pu aider Léger au moment psychologique: Léger aura saisi que je suis de son côté. Mais comme théologiens Naud et Léger sont nuls». (1er mars 1963; Fonds Moeller, 03042, p. 3; sur ce même événement, voir L. DECLERCK – C. SOETENS [eds.], *Carnets conciliaires de l'évêque de Namur A.-M. Charue* [Cahiers de la Revue théologique de Louvain, 32], Louvain-la-Neuve, Publications de la Faculté de Théologie, 2000, à la p. 92. Désormais cité Journal Charue). Le 5 mars: «Les Canadiens sont saisis de voir comment, dans le milieu actuel, aussi bouché, le schéma Philips est le seul possible; ils comprennent mieux pourquoi j'ai soutenu Philips. Les relations sont de nouveau excellentes. Léger est venu ce soir boire un cognac avec Prignon, moi et ses deux théologiens» (Fonds Moeller, 03043, p. 3). Le 11 mars, alors qu'il situe sur le spectre l'ensemble des membres de la Commission, après avoir situé Lafortune à gauche, il situe à «l'extrême gauche: Monsieur Naud, chez les canadiens, pas dans l'erreur mais s'exprimant mal» (Fonds Moeller, 03046, p. 3). Sur les mêmes événements, la version de Mgr Philips est concordante: «M. Nau (sic) est un missionnaire qui prône une théorie sur la grande distance entre l'Église visible et invisible, théorie qui, dans cette rigueur, est inacceptable et qui met en danger notre point de vue. [...] Au fond il n'y a jamais eu de grandes tensions dans ce groupe de théologiens. Moeller a fait de son mieux pour obtenir que le cardinal Léger et M. Naud ne provoquent pas d'incidents» (K. SCHELKENS [ed.], *Carnets conciliaires de Mgr. Gérard Philips, secrétaire adjoint de la Commission Doctrinale: Texte néerlandais avec traduction française et commentaires* [Instrumenta Theologica, 29], Louvain, Peeters, 2006, pp. 12-13).

cours de cette période, se profile ce qui deviendra manifeste par la suite : la prise de distance de Moeller, qui ressent comme providentiel le fait qu'il ait été là et comme un appel à collaborer avec Philips à la rédaction d'un grand texte[49] et les incompatibilités de tempérament et de vision théologique entre Naud et les Belges[50].

En termes sportifs, on pourrait dire que Léger apparaît sans doute, au cours de cette période cruciale, comme un bon porteur de ballon, un homme capable de porter à la Commission *De fide*, à la Commission mixte sur le *De revelatione* et à la Sous-commission des sept, les positions mises en avant par l'équipe belge ou de défendre les projets de la Commission de coordination. Il est une personne-clé si l'on veut parvenir à imposer le nouveau *De ecclesia 'made in Belgium'* ! Cet échange d'informations entre les deux cardinaux s'avère d'ailleurs fécond et très fructueux. Il permet de démasquer les modifications que l'on apporte aux décisions de la Commission de coordination lorsque celles-ci sont présentées aux membres de la commission doctrinale[51] et de défendre efficacement les orientations données par la Commission de coordination. C'est d'ailleurs ce que fait Léger à diverses reprises, notamment le 27 février, lorsqu'il rencontre Mgr Cavagna, le confesseur du pape :

> Après …, il aborde le sujet du concile. Le pape a été troublé par les nouvelles qu'il a reçues au sujet de la réunion mixte du 25 (lundi[52]). Il veut connaître mon point de vue. J'en profite pour lui parler franchement et ouvertement des problèmes que je considère essentiels.
>
> a) être docile aux directives du St-Père.
> b) Accepter les orientations de la Commission spéciale. […] Ottaviani affirme que Liénart et Suenens n'ont rien à voir dans la confection des schémas.

À nouveau, le 4 avril[53], en préparation à une autre session de la Commission doctrinale qui devait se réunir le 15 mai à Rome, une nouvelle

---

49. Voir notamment – cela ne constitue pas la seule occurrence – son rapport du 9 mars 1963 (Fonds Moeller, 03044, p. 2).

50. Moeller s'interrogera sur cette relation brisée : « Ses deux conseillers théologiques québécois ont peut être eu quelque raison d'en prendre ombrage et de se dire : 'Ce sera lui ou nous'. D'autres nous jugeront : 'Charles s'est servi de Léger pour entrer au Concile, c'est tout' » (COLLEYE, *Charles Moeller et l'Arbre de la Croix* [n. 25], p. 293).

51. Voir « À propos du 'De Ecclesia'. Différences entre le programme reçu de la Commission de théologie et celui reçu directement du cardinal Suenens », Fonds Léger, 711, 19 février 1963.

52. Voir les notes de Léger prises en séance de la Commission mixte où il est intervenu avec vigueur et fermeté (*Journal conciliaire*, 1ᵉ intersession, Fonds Léger, 14).

53. Fonds Naud, 115. Léger avait adressé à Suenens une autre lettre, le 18 mars précédent, lui faisant tenir un « document confidentiel » dont le but « était de vous aider à

correspondance de Léger à Suenens vient ponctuer cette relation d'étroite collaboration qui les unit désormais. «Nous avons reçu, dit-il, cette lettre (de convocation, de Tromp) il y a une semaine, mais les documents qui devaient l'accompagner n'ont pas encore été expédiés. Comment pourrons-nous faire une étude sérieuse de ces schémas avant la réunion de la Commission?». Léger s'inquiète à nouveau sur les retards pris dans l'avancement des travaux, craignant même que ces lenteurs ne viennent compromettre la prochaine session du concile. Il risque ensuite une suggestion qui témoigne de son estime pour Mgr Philips et de la franche confiance qui existe alors entre l'équipe de Malines et celle de Montréal:

> La présentation du schéma de l'Église exigera une participation active de Monseigneur Philips à la rédaction des 'emendationes'. Il faudrait qu'il soit au moins secrétaire adjoint d'une sous-commission active dont le but serait bien déterminé: recevoir les remarques des Pères, les étudier et les intégrer dans le texte, toujours selon l'esprit général du contexte du schéma. Si cette procédure n'est pas adoptée, je crains énormément l'influence plus ou moins consciente du Père Tromp qui tentera, par tous les moyens, de faire entrer dans les textes définitifs l'esprit du vieux schéma. [...] Si vous aviez des directives à me donner au sujet de notre prochaine réunion à Rome, je les recevrais avec joie et reconnaissance. J'espère retrouver Monseigneur Philips à Rome durant cette session de mai, car j'ai l'intention de m'y rendre seul. S'il se retire au Collège belge, il me sera facile de le consulter si jamais nous nous trouvions devant de graves difficultés.

La réponse de Suenens (10 avril[54]) vient sans tarder cette fois. Après avoir remercié son correspondant pour ses deux derniers courriers (18 mars et 4 avril), l'archevêque de Malines lui communique ses dispositions et ses informations: «J'avertis Mgr Philips pour qu'il prenne des dispositions en vue de la réunion de mai. Je vous transmets ci-joint les directives adoptées sur ma proposition en ce qui concerne le chapitre III et IV. Je crois qu'il sera important pour le concile même de bien préciser le sens de la collégialité épiscopale en renforçant encore un texte qui est valable comme compromis mais qui peut encore gagner en précision»[55].

---

préciser le travail de préparation durant la deuxième session de la Commission de coordination». «Vous aurai-je rendu service?», lui demande-t-il dans sa lettre du 4 avril. Les archives montréalaises ne nous renseignent toutefois pas sur cette lettre et sur le document qui y était joint.

54. Fonds Naud, 116; Fonds Suenens, 1005-1006.

55. Quelques jours plus tard, le 12 avril, on trouve une lettre de C. Moeller adressée de Louvain à Léger sur les deux premiers chapitres du *De ecclesia* (Fonds Léger, 849). À nouveau, le 10 mai, le chanoine Moeller communique à Léger un texte de théologiens de Louvain sur le chap III du schéma XVII: *De matrimonio, familia et de problemate demographico* (Fonds Léger, 1524).

À nouveau, sitôt arrivé à Rome, Léger prend contact avec l'équipe belge (14 mai[56]). Peu de temps après, l'activité épistolaire entre Montréal et Malines reprend (20 mai) quand Léger adresse à nouveau une lettre au Cardinal Suenens au sujet de Mgr Philips, d'une rechute du pape et de l'opportunité de mettre sur pied une commission de permanence du Concile[57].

La collaboration est si étroite que, à la suite d'une réunion de la commission de théologie du chap IV du *De ecclesia*, Mgr Charue demande au chanoine Moeller d'en dresser un rapport et de l'envoyer à Montréal pour tenir Léger informé des nouveaux développements[58]. De son côté, sitôt rentré à Montréal (le 28 mai) Léger adresse à nouveau une lettre à son collègue de Malines faisant état des travaux de la Commission doctrinale[59]. Cette lettre témoigne non seulement de la confiance de Léger à l'endroit de l'équipe belge, mais aussi de la collaboration étroite à laquelle on était parvenu:

> L'équipe de Louvain a encore accompli un travail énorme durant cette session de la Commission de théologie. [...] Samedi, Monseigneur Philips a été le Relator du troisième chapitre du schéma sur l'Église 'De populo Dei et in specie de laicis'. J'étais intervenu dès la première réunion pour que la rédaction de ce chapitre lui soit confiée afin d'assurer une certaine unité à travers tout ce schéma. Cela ne fut pas trop facile, car le Père Tromp avait son projet et surtout le fameux Père Lio circulait dans la coulisse.
> Monseigneur Philips s'est surpassé et un peritus qui ne le connaissait pas m'avouait qu'il venait de découvrir l'un des plus grands théologiens dans l'Église. Il faudra maintenant surveiller la rédaction définitive de ce schéma, car derrière les latinistes, se profile le nombre des opposants.
> [...] Le cardinal König, ainsi que Monseigneur Charue dirigeront les débats qui ont lieu en ce moment sur 'De Sanctitate in Ecclesia'. Encore ici, je suis intervenu dès la première séance afin d'obtenir que ce chapitre fût étudié par la Commission théologique. J'ai demandé au Cardinal König que Monseigneur Philips soit le 'relator' et le rédacteur.

56. D'après l'agenda, il ne rencontre que Delhaye (qu'il avait déjà vu à Montréal, le 27 avril) le 14 mai, attendant au lendemain, le 15, avant de rencontrer Moeller et De Smedt et, dans le cadre d'une réunion au Collège français, Charue. Il donnera à nouveau audience à Moeller et Delhaye le 21 mai suivant.
57. Au cours de la session de la Commission doctrinale, C. Moeller communique à Léger ses remarques sur le schéma XVII, le 21 mai, sur le '*Prooemium*' et le chapitre I (Fonds Léger, 1366) et, le 23 mai, sur le chapitre III, «*De matrimonio et familia*» (Fonds Léger, 1525-1526).
58. Lettre de Moeller à P.-É. Léger, Rome, 6.6.1963: Union de prière pour l'élection du prochain pape; reconnaissance pour sa nomination comme *peritus* au Concile, avec annexe, Compte rendu des réunions du 27 – 31 mai 1963 de la Commission doctrinale sur le chap. IV du De ecclesia (Fonds Léger, 850).
59. Fonds Naud, 117; Fonds Suenens, 1007.

Cette lettre à Suenens était aussi accompagnée d'un rapport que Léger voulait remettre au pape lors d'une audience qui était prévue pour le mardi, mais qui avait dû être remise en raison d'une grave rechute du pape dans la nuit de lundi à mardi:

> Dans ce rapport, je demandais au Saint-Père de constituer immédiatement une 'Commission de permanence du Concile' qui aurait accompli, durant la IIe Session (septembre-décembre) et ensuite après le Concile, la mission de la Commission de coordination. Ses pouvoirs auraient été assez étendus et, dans le plan que je proposais au Pape, cette Commission serait devenue le Secrétariat permanent de l'Épiscopat à Rome (aurait représenté la collégialité épiscopale un peu comme le Secrétariat de l'Unité représente nos frères séparés). Cette commission aurait donc pu organiser une sous-commission de rédaction de tous les schémas du Concile afin de mieux marquer l'unité de pensée du Concile. Monseigneur Philips était, pour moi, l'homme tout désigné pour remplir cette mission. [...] Je vous envoie, à titre confidentiel, les notes que j'avais préparées pour l'audience de mardi dernier. Si vous croyez que ces quelques suggestions pourraient intéresser Nosseigneurs les Archevêques de Cologne, Munich et Utrecht, je vous permets de leur en souffler un mot. Il serait peut-être préférable de ne pas indiquer la source de vos informations. Je laisse tout ceci à votre discrétion.

Cette correspondance étroite et suivie entre Malines et Montréal[60] témoigne d'un net réchauffement des relations entre Léger et Suenens, même s'il faut convenir que l'empressement est moindre du côté de Malines, si bien que l'on peut se demander si, de ce côté, on ne trouve pas Léger trop inquiet, anxieux, dramatique, voire importun. Si, à l'été 1962, au moment où Léger lance sa première offensive contre les schémas élaborés au cours de la phase préparatoire, le cardinal Frings est son confident et son intermédiaire auprès de ses collègues cardinaux en Europe, voilà que, une année plus tard, c'est désormais Suenens qui occupe cette position, même si celui-ci est demeuré réservé dans l'expression de ses sentiments et n'a pas toujours payé en retour son correspondant. L'axe Malines-Montréal se développe autour d'un intérêt stratégique au moment de la deuxième préparation du concile: la nécessité

---

60. D'autres témoignages vont exactement dans le même sens. Ainsi la lettre de Delhaye à Lafortune du 30 mai 63: «Je suis d'ailleurs chargé de transmettre à SE les souvenirs de bien des personnes ...: [...] Son excellence Mgr Charue, Mgr Prignon et toute l'équipe...» (P. LAFONTAINE, *Inventaire du Fonds Lafortune* [Cahiers de recherche sur Vatican II, 3], Québec, Université Laval, 2005, désormais cité Fonds Lafortune, 37) ou de Delhaye à Léger, le 1er juin (Fonds Léger, 509). Pour sa part, Mgr Charue notera dans ses cahiers: «Ce sont alors les au-revoir. Plusieurs me disent particulièrement fort leur sympathie: le card. Léger, évidemment [...] Mgr Lafortune me dit son espoir de nous revoir souvent!» (Journal Charue, p. 115, 13 mars 1963).

d'une ligne de conduite commune entre la Commission de coordination et la Commission doctrinale. Le succès de cette seconde préparation était au prix d'une telle cohérence et d'une telle synergie.

On peut d'ailleurs très bien comprendre que Léger construise avec un autre siège européen l'axe Montréal-Europe. Cet axe aurait pourtant pu se construire entre Montréal et Cologne – Léger se retrouvait en compagnie de Frings à la Commission mixte sur le *De revelatione*, comme cela avait été le cas au moment de la Commission centrale préparatoire ou entre Montréal et Lille avec qui les liens ont toujours été réguliers[61]. Certes, malgré ses coups d'éclat lors de la première session, Liénart n'avait sans doute plus l'énergie nécessaire pour s'imposer dans la durée comme leader au concile. Quant à Döpfner, Léger semblait l'avoir en haute estime. N'avait-il pas noté, le 9 décembre 1962, au moment où les noms des membres de la coordination commençaient à être connus:

> Avant la cérémonie (canonisation) j'ai causé un instant avec le cardinal Döpfner. Il est l'un des membres de la nouvelle commission. Il est un espoir. Confalonieri y entrevoit un autre bon signe. Liénart et Spellman ... diplomatie et *ad honorem ut dixit* cardinal Döpfner ... J'espère connaître les autres membres de la commission avant de quitter Rome. La suggestion que je posais au saint-père le 20 novembre dernier, durant l'audience providentielle qu'il m'accordait, a donc été acceptée et devient une réalité. Puisse cette commission sauver le concile!

Sans doute, plusieurs motifs ont dû jouer en faveur de l'axe Montréal-Malines[62]: la langue de communication, mais surtout la cohésion et la force de l'équipe. À la commission mixte, Léger retrouvait De Smedt et Charue. À la doctrinale, Thils, Charue et Philips, en plus de Moeller et Delhaye dont il avait lui-même demandé la nomination comme *periti* au concile, et de Prignon qu'il pouvait rencontrer à Rome. Enfin, la sous-commission des sept qui avait conduit à l'adoption du schéma Philips et où s'étaient retrouvés Léger et Charue, avait scellé cette alliance dès le début de la période. Döpfner, pour sa part, ne pouvait offrir une telle surface de visibilité et ne pouvait pas faire cour auprès de Léger avec une

---

61. Au cours de cette période, en plus des courriers à Suenens, Léger écrit (le 7 mars) aux cardinaux Meyer, Döpfner, Liénart et Montini pour les mettre au courant du déroulement des travaux de la Commission doctrinale. Liénart lui fait réponse le 20 mars 1963 (2 p. – Fonds Naud, 114).

62. Le Journal Charue témoigne éloquemment de la collaboration quotidienne entre Belges et Montréalais, au cours de cette période, comme les rapports de Moeller, du reste. Des 33 occurrences du nom de Léger dans ses cahiers conciliaires, 18 (plus de la moitié) se situent au cours de ces cinq mois (février – juin 1963) où les deux équipes ont collaboré de manière très étroite.

telle assiduité. De plus, la proximité du collège canadien et du collège belge facilitait les rencontres informelles et les visites de courtoisie[63].

Du cercle des cardinaux avec lesquels Léger avait partagé ses espoirs avant l'ouverture du concile, restaient Bea, Suenens, Frings, Döpfner, Liénart, Alfrink et König. Un nom manquait désormais, Montini. Il n'avait pas participé à la rencontre de stratégie à l'Anima au mois de novembre et son nom ne figurait plus non plus sur la liste de Léger lorsque celui-ci confiait ses préoccupations à Suenens à la fin de la période. D'autres noms s'étaient ajoutés au cours de l'éprouvante seconde préparation du concile: Garrone, Charue, Schröffer, McGrath. De nombreuses concertations[64] avaient lieu entre ces hommes au moment où il fallait regrouper les forces et agir de manière concertée[65]. La majorité essayait alors de travailler en équipe.

III. LES RIVAUX

L'été 1963 avait été riche en événements qui avaient modifié sensiblement la donne: le décès de Jean XXIII, le conclave et l'élection de Montini (21 juin) et la décision de poursuivre le concile, le nouveau mandat confié à la Commission de coordination, la nomination des modérateurs (9 septembre). Au plan local, Léger avait passé un été très tendu: sa participation à la rencontre de Foi et Constitution à Montréal, les négociations avec le Gouvernement du Québec sur le système d'éducation dans la Province profondément travaillée par les soubresauts provoqués par la Révolution tranquille[66], les évolutions à l'Université de Montréal[67],

63. On a l'exemple du cognac, en soirée, le 3 mars ou encore le repas du midi au collège canadien, le 28 février (Léger, König, Garrone, Charue, McGrath, etc.) et le 11 mars au Collège Belge (Charue, Léger, Garrone, Schröffer et McGrath). À nouveau, au Collège canadien, le 18 mai (Léger, Bea, Schröffer, McGrath, Garrone, Charue, etc.) Ces rencontres amicales et cordiales facilitaient d'autant le travail en équipe et la collaboration.

64. On en trouve des traces au début de la session de février de la doctrinale (24 février: chez Garrone, Léger, König, Charue, Schröffer, etc.; au collège canadien, le 24 février – voir supra –, puis, à nouveau, à la veille de la session de mai (15): Après une rencontre entre Garrone et Charue, on prend la décision de «téléphone[r] au card. Léger, à Mgr Schröffer et à Mgr van Dodewaard. Nous nous réunirons demain au séminaire français».

65. McGrath avait été «frappé par la force de l'union au Secrétariat pour l'Union». «Il souhaiterait que les membres de la commission de théologie, qui sont de notre tendance (!), se réunissent pour se répartir les interventions, etc.». «Il serait bon que les cardinaux de Vienne et de Montréal nous réunissent encore». Journal Charue, p. 91, 27 février 1963.

66. Léger avait dû rencontrer à deux reprises le premier ministre, au cours de l'été, et à cinq reprises, son ministre de l'éducation.

67. Il s'agit notamment de la nomination de laïcs au Conseil d'administration et dans l'équipe rectorale, décision hautement critiquée à Montréal par ceux qui y voyaient de la faiblesse de la part de Léger et de dangereux précédents. Dans les faits, cela allait

etc. Dans toutes ces affaires, il avait le sentiment de devoir arracher à Rome des permissions car il créait des précédents et s'écartait de la ligne de conduite tenue jusque là[68]. Tout cela l'avait tendu[69] et ne lui avait pas permis de se ménager de repos. Les événements romains, mais aussi les évolutions à Montréal venaient sans doute modifier les équilibres dans les rapports entre les personnes. Malgré tout, la nouvelle session du concile semblait s'ouvrir sous d'heureux auspices pour les relations entre Léger et Suenens. En effet, c'est à son collègue de Malines[70] que Léger réserve une de ses premières visites romaines (après celle à la Secrétairerie d'État), le 27 septembre 1963, deux semaines seulement après la nomination de Suenens comme modérateur. Les notes qu'il consigne dans son Journal à la suite de cette rencontre indiquent pourtant que le climat est désormais totalement différent:

> À 18h00, audience au Collège Belge par Suenens. Cette conversation d'une heure m'a laissé un peu *songeur*. Il est incontestable que cet homme est *puissant*, physiquement et intellectuellement, spirituellement, mais on a l'impression qu'il le sait *trop*. Il était certainement très près de Jean XXIII et il a collaboré avec le cardinal Montini. C'est lui qui a éloigné les anciens schemata et qui a distribué la matière dans les 17 nouveaux schemata. Il a surtout, en collaboration avec le cardinal Montini, orienté les débats du Concile vers le thème de l'Église. Son intervention à la fin de la 1e session fut le point culminant de cette collaboration. Ce serait à la demande de Jean XXIII que le cardinal Montini devait appuyer cette intervention. Tout cela est bien, mais l'homme se sent fort maintenant que le cardinal Montini est devenu Paul VI. Le concile est devenu un peu sa chose. Il a profité de la situation pour éliminer une 'présidence', il faut bien l'avouer, qui n'avait pas été très efficace. Il a mis en place les 'moderatores' et il a bien orienté le choix du Pape! Il a profité de la situation

conduire, quelques années plus tard, à la laïcisation de l'université catholique de Montréal. À l'époque, le bruit a couru que c'étaient les positions de Léger sur la question de l'Université qui lui avaient coûté son siège, Rome lui ayant demandé en secret sa démission. Cette hypothèse ne tient pas cependant, même si les affaires universitaires ont provoqué à Rome une campagne contre la gouvernance de son diocèse par Léger.

68. Il n'est pas étonnant, dans ce contexte, que Moeller, qui avait participé à la rencontre de Faith and Order à Montréal écrive ces lignes à Philips le 29 juillet 1963: «Mgr Léger est comme toujours très inquiet des 'manœuvres romaines'. Il craint un raidissement et que Paul VI ne surveille de très près le concile. Le cardinal Léger vit dans la peur de Rome, peur terrible me disait Mgr Willebrands vu à Montréal» (Fonds Philips, 461).

69. Léger, souffrant toujours d'une certaine insécurité, craignait que ses initiatives soient mal vues ou mal comprises à Rome et qu'elles entraînent à nouveau des dénonciations et des suspicions et que, en finale, on juge qu'il était incapable de tenir son diocèse, cédant à la montée du laïcisme, à l'Université comme dans le système d'éducation.

70. Les deux hommes s'étaient rencontrés une dernière fois, après le conclave, le 1er juillet. Léger s'était également rendu à Bologne, rendre visite à Lercaro, entre l'élection et l'inauguration du pontificat.

pour mettre à l'œuvre l'équipe de Louvain et c'est ainsi que les schemata de Ecclesia XVII ont été modifiés, altérés sans l'agrément des *Commissions* responsables.

Déjà une réaction se fait sentir. Le 'doux' Mgr Garrone a dit au Ch. Delhaye: «on n'a pas échappé à la dictature du Saint-Office pour retomber sous celle de Malines»! Des épiscopats, fiers de leurs traditions et prestige risquent de ne pas «marcher». Les traditionalistes et les «curialistes» pourraient bien se trouver en meilleure position stratégique devant la nouvelle conjoncture … En Belgique, même *l'administration* du cardinal est l'objet de nombreuses critiques (Delhaye[71]). Son livre 'Promotion apostolique de la religieuse' ne reçoit pas un accueil enthousiaste partout. «Ça frise le voltairianisme» (Mgr Géraud) (Autres symptômes: j'écris ces notes une semaine après la rencontre et je n'ai pas encore vu le Ch. Moeller! Gêne? Réserve? Isolement de l'équipe de Louvain? Mgr Philips ne m'a pas salué, mercredi 2 octobre, lors de la réunion de la Commission de théologie…). Il faudra agir avec *prudence* […][72].

À la lecture de cette annotation, trois facteurs semblent à la source de cette nouvelle attitude de prudence: les relations privilégiées entre Suenens et Montini[73], la première place que semble prendre Suenens dans la direction du concile[74] en sa qualité de modérateur et la place importante – sinon envahissante – qu'occupe à ses yeux l'équipe belge qui n'a plus, comme c'était le cas il y a encore quelques mois, le sentiment d'avoir besoin de l'appui des autres, notamment de l'équipe de Montréal. Ces trois facteurs n'ont pas tous la même importance et s'entrecroisent, si bien que les choses sont difficiles à départager. Il faut sans doute les traiter séparément, même s'ils interfèrent constamment.

Il est clair que, malgré la synergie que nous avons observée, les équipes de Louvain et de Montréal n'avaient pas vécu en parfaite harmonie la période de l'intersession. Pour une raison qui n'est pas toujours évidente

---

71. N'ayant pas été nommé professeur à Louvain, Delhaye se montrait assez critique à l'endroit des professeurs de Louvain et des évêques qui les nommaient. Il faut lire dans cette perspective ses remarques à l'égard des évêques belges ou de ses collègues.

72. Cela contraste vivement avec les sentiments que Léger avait pour Moeller, quelques mois auparavant: «Ce sera pour toujours pour moi un souvenir très doux de vous avoir obtenu le titre de 'peritus' du concile. Les liens d'affection qui nous unissent maintenant sont aussi forts que la mort» (Lettre du 14 janvier 1963, Fonds Moeller, 03037). La réserve qu'il sent chez Philips contraste aussi avec toute l'estime qu'il lui vouait quelques mois auparavant.

73. Moeller observera: Léger est «un peu triste, froissé. Il a l'impression que Suenens, maintenant qu'il est bien vu par le Pape, le laisse tomber. C'est un concile de Louvain, dit-il», dans COLLEYE, *Charles Moeller et l'Arbre de la Croix* (n. 24), p. 292.

74. La prévision du 28 juin 1963 de Philippe Delhaye ne semble donc pas se confirmer: «La grande amitié qui vous unit au nouveau Souverain Pontife vous permettra certainement d'avoir encore une influence accrue sur le gouvernement général de l'Église et sur le déroulement du concile» (Fonds Léger, 1431).

à la lecture de la documentation, Moeller apparaît rapidement comme insupportable. Cela transparaît clairement, aussi bien à la lecture des papiers Naud que de ceux de Pierre Lafortune – réputé pourtant d'une grande douceur et d'une grande affabilité – ou même de Delhaye[75]. Dans un premier temps, Moeller semble avoir voulu s'imposer et exclure les autres et, par la suite, avoir simplement lâché l'équipe après s'être servi de Léger pour obtenir une place de *peritus* du concile[76]. Il est vrai également que l'équipe de Montréal était de plus en plus cohérente et l'arrivée de Naud – qui devint *peritus* à ce moment-là – venait modifier les équilibres. Par ailleurs, Philips et Naud, qui ont eu l'occasion de travailler ensemble à la rédaction du chapitre I du *De ecclesia* en février 1963, ne semblent pas avoir d'atomes crochus[77], leur expérience si différente les conduisant à tenir des positions fort différentes sur l'appartenance à l'Église[78]. De plus, Philips semblait beaucoup plus à l'aise de travailler

75. Voir la description qu'il en fait dans une lettre à Lafortune, le 24 mai 63: «Le chanoine Moeller me fait de plus en plus penser au héros de J.K. Jérome, dans 'Trois hommes dans un bateau'». «Je ne puis supporter voir les autres travailler sans les aider, disait-il, c'est plus fort que moi, il faut que je les dirige» (Fonds Lafortune, 27). Dans une autre lettre au chancelier de Montréal, l'ironie est évidente: «Toujours à propos d'amis … Si vous vous languissez du petit Charles (Moeller – il venait de parler de De Gaulle) vous pouvez le trouver à Rome dès le 10, pour une réunion de trois jours consacrée au schéma XVII (= XIII). Tout le monde peut y aller, paraît-il…» (26 août 1964; Fonds Lafortune, 46).

76. Moeller lui-même analyse la situation dans les mêmes termes: Léger doit se dire, «J'ai fait nommer Moeller expert, et cette fois il me lâche», d'où «la résolution prise par Charles d'aller le saluer *in aula*, de lui rendre visite» (COLLEYE, *Charles Moeller et l'Arbre de la Croix* [n. 24], pp. 292-293). Et de s'interroger: «Est-ce parce que j'ai viré du côté de Philips depuis le début octobre? Non, car en mars et mai, j'ai beaucoup travaillé avec lui – mariage, Écriture. Et en fév.-mars, on s'est vu tous les jours…»; «Mais je suis peiné pour Léger. Peut-être ai-je été maladroit» (COLLEYE, *Charles Moeller et l'Arbre de la Croix*, p. 293).

77. On verra en particulier les pages 12, 13 et 27 de son Journal (SCHELKENS [éd.], *Carnets conciliaires de Mgr. Gérard Philips*). Charue aussi – tout comme Moeller – est également assez critique vis-à-vis de Naud.

78. Parmi le petit groupe qui travaillait à la rédaction du chapitre I du *De ecclesia* (Charue, Philips, Léger, Naud, Lafortune, König, Rahner, Browne, Gagnebet, Parente, Balic et ensuite Schauf, Garrone, Daniélou et ensuite Congar, Schroeffer, Thils et ensuite Moeller), tous étaient européens, sauf les trois montréalais et seul Naud (et Léger, les deux ayant été missionnaires au Japon) avaient vécu de manière prolongée en dehors de l'Occident, en milieu où les chrétiens représentaient une infime minorité. Pas surprenant que sa manière d'envisager l'appartenance à l'Église et le salut des non-chrétiens ait été un peu différente de celle des évêques et théologiens vivant en Occident (Voir Journal Charue, p. 92). Pour les textes de Naud et de Léger, voir Fonds Léger, 750 et 754. Naud commentera plus tard ainsi sa participation à cette sous-commission: «Il est peut-être bon de signaler ici un intérêt particulier que j'ai porté pendant le Concile à la question des relations des chrétiens avec les religions non chrétiennes. À la Commission doctrinale, je m'étais inscrit au comité formé pour le chapitre *De populo Dei* précisément parce que c'était dans ce chapitre qu'on traitait cette question à la Commission doctrinale. Ma correspondance avec Congar témoigne

avec Moeller, son concitoyen, «qui fait de son mieux pour obtenir que le cardinal Léger et M. Nau (sic) ne provoquent pas d'incidents», «un collaborateur très précieux et extrêmement serviable» (p. 13), qu'avec ces théologiens issus du nouveau monde. Dans ces circonstances, seul Philippe Delhaye, qui enseignait chaque année à l'institut de sciences religieuses de l'Université de Montréal, restera fidèle à l'équipe montréalaise, contribuant à garder ouvertes les lignes de communication entre Montréal et la Belgique puisqu'il a lui-même le sentiment d'appartenir aux deux mondes[79]. Ces communications sont d'ailleurs utiles pour la poursuite du travail en commission. Ainsi, le 15 octobre, lors de la réunion de la Commission doctrinale, Ottaviani a encore tenté de mêler les cartes. Suivant ses dires:

> Durant la dernière audience que le Saint-Père lui accordait, *incidemment*, la conversation s'orienta vers les affaire du concile et 'il Sanctissimus' lui aurait manifesté ses préférences pour la distribution des chapitres sur le *De ecclesia* selon l'ordre actuel, i.e. Hiérarchie avant *De populo Dei*! Interrogé quelques instants après par Delhaye, Suenens affirmait que le Pape avait sanctionné durant l'audience donnée aux modérateurs, immédiatement après celle d'Ottaviani, la nouvelle distribution des chapitres … À qui se fier![80]

Les liens existent donc encore, mais plus directement comme avant et la majorité n'arrive donc plus à travailler avec la même cohérence. Ces relations difficiles ont certainement contribué à brouiller les relations entre les deux cardinaux, même si on ne sait pas dans quelle mesure. De plus, on peut faire l'hypothèse que l'attitude de Moeller autant que celle de Suenens a contribué à ancrer chez Léger le sentiment d'une dictature de Malines[81].

Par ailleurs, les liens entre Montini et les deux cardinaux sont certainement venus briser les équilibres. L'un et l'autre étaient proches de Jean XXIII, mais cette affection du pape à l'égard des deux archevêques

de mon intérêt pour le traitement donné à cette question cruciale, dont on peut dire qu'elle devient de plus en plus une question d'une extrême importance».

79. Delhaye se plaindra à quelques reprises d'être négligé et de ne pas être intégré à l'équipe belge. Il écrira: «De loin tous les chats sont gris; tous les Belges sont malinois ou louvanistes» (Lettre à Lafortune du 20 juillet 1964; Fonds Lafortune, 43). De fait, au cours de l'intersession 1964, il demandera d'être hébergé au Collège canadien, même si cela ne s'avérera pas possible.

80. Journal Léger, 15 octobre 1963.

81. Léger redoutait certainement que Suenens veuille imposer ses vues au concile. En témoigne CONGAR, *Mon Journal du Concile* (n. 28), en date du 3 octobre 1963 (Vol. I, p. 426). Congar partagera un peu ce point de vue, notant: «C'est un fait que le cardinal Suenens dirige un peu le concile et que le petit groupe belge mène pratiquement les choses…» (30 novembre 1963, p. 574). Voir aussi, sur les relations entre Canadiens et Belges, p. 576.

ne mettaient pas en compétition Léger et Suenens. Désormais, la situation n'est plus la même. L'apparition de Suenens aux côtés de Paul VI lors de l'Angelus du 23 juin, juste après l'élection de Montini, et sa nomination comme modérateur semblent désormais indiquer que la préférence du pape va à Suenens et Léger le ressent durement, d'autant que celui-ci a toujours eu besoin de trouver dans le pape un protecteur et un père. Or, malgré la grande considération que Léger a pour Montini et, sans doute aussi le respect de Montini à l'égard de Léger[82], l'ancien archevêque de Milan n'a pas correspondu toujours aux attentes de Léger qui, étant conscient d'avoir lui aussi joué un rôle déterminant dans la conduite du concile[83], sent soudainement le plancher se dérober sous ses pieds. Un autre semble désormais occuper toute la place et considérer que le concile est sa chose et celle de l'équipe de Louvain qui, elle aussi, tend à occuper toute la place.

Tout au long du premier mois de cette session[84], la figure du cardinal Suenens ne cesse d'occuper les pensées de Léger. Comme en témoigne son *Journal conciliaire*, il en parle pratiquement avec tous ses interlocuteurs. Il tente de se rassurer en collectionnant les témoignages critiques aussi bien au sujet de Suenens que sur l'ascendant que celui-ci peut exercer sur Paul VI. Il n'aura de cesse de se réconforter en consignant dans son Journal des jugements conformes au sien et de tenter d'éroder la confiance que Paul VI met dans le cardinal Suenens.

On en trouve une première manifestation dès le 1er octobre alors que Léger donne audience à Philippe Delhaye. Il en retiendra ce qui suit:

> Il (Delhaye) est lui-même inquiet en constatant la position et les attitudes du cardinal Suenens. Son administration à Malines suscite beaucoup de critiques et quelques-uns de ses gestes risquent de compromettre le Saint-Père. Mgr Charrue a déjà formulé certaines réserves.

---

82. Montini fait très fréquemment référence aux prises de position de Léger lors des travaux de la commission centrale préparatoire. Voir A. RIMOLDI (éd.), *Giovanni Battista Montini, arcivescovo di Milano. Interventi nella commissione centrale preparatoria del concilio ecumenico Vaticano II (gennaio-giugnio 1962)* (Quaderni dell'Istituto, 10), Brescia, Istituto Paolo VI, 1992.

83. Je pense en particulier à sa Supplique à Jean XXIII, à son intervention dramatique lors de la première réunion de la Commission doctrinale le 14 novembre 1962, à son audience avec Jean XXIII, le 20 novembre 1962 alors que le concile était dans une impasse à la suite du vote sur le *De fontibus* et que Léger propose la formation d'une commission mixte et d'une commission de permanence du concile pour l'intersession, et à quelques interventions à la Commission doctrinale au cours de moments clés en février et mars 1963.

84. En particulier du 1er au 29 octobre où les références à Suenens sont vraiment nombreuses. Puis, soudainement (du 30 octobre au 20 novembre), il n'en fait aucune mention.

À la suite d'un dîner avec Gerlier, Feltin et Liénart (6 octobre), il notera: «Lille est toujours alerte et éveillé, attentif mais il ne cache pas sa déception de ne pas avoir été choisi comme moderator. Son amertume est déférente. Ses jugements sur Malines sont assez sévères: les Belges marchent souvent sur les croisées des autres…». Il obtient un avis similaire de son confesseur, Mgr Géraud, lors d'une conversation, le 9 octobre: «Il ne me cache pas ses réserves sur la personne du card. de Malines. Son livre 'La promotion…' manifeste un manque d'expérience pastorale et parfois même de jugement. Certains passages ont le piquant de l'ironie voltairienne … Des supérieurs généraux lui ont exprimé, et avec fermeté, leur désapprobation. Elles reçurent un accusé de réception».

Même chose, le 29 octobre, lors d'un dîner avec Mgr Paul Philippe[85]. «Il n'aime pas Suenens», observe-t-il, ce qui est presque suffisant pour faire de lui «un homme ouvert, qui écoute», même s'«il est religieux et de la curie…», deux qualités qui, normalement, auraient suffi à rendre Léger suspicieux. Il s'ouvre même de cette question (19 octobre) à Mlle Wilmet (présidente AFI) à qui il pose «discrètement la question au sujet de Malines … Il semble que le problème est de notoriété publique en Belgique. Tous désirent, et plusieurs ne dissimulent pas leurs sentiments, que l'intéressé soit promu à un poste 'international' afin qu'il soit remplacé par un 'pasteur' … Situation vraiment bizarre et la convergence des jugements commence à m'inquiéter…».

Sa principale inquiétude est de voir Suenens influencer Montini et jouer un rôle prépondérant au concile et, plus largement dans le nouveau pontificat. De sa conversation avec Mgr Guano (24 octobre), il retiendra de celui qui a bien connu Paul VI: «il croit qu'il aura la tentation de céder à un certain intellectualisme, mais il reconnaît sa loyauté, sa sincérité, son angoisse pastorale. Cependant Montini aura de l'admiration pour un homme comme Suenens. Pas au point, cependant, de se laisser influencer par lui. Il écoute, il réfléchit». Pignedoli lui avait déjà parlé dans le même sens, le 14 octobre après que Léger lui eut exprimé ses «inquiétudes sur la marche du concile et influence de Malines». S'il admet que l'influence de Suenens sur Montini est plausible du fait que cet homme «porté à intellectualiser, doit admirer le brillant de Malines», il croit que cette influence sera de portée limitée.

Léger ne se contente cependant pas de collectionner les réserves au sujet de Suenens. Il lui semble important de prévenir le pape. Aussi, le

---

85. Avant le concile, Suenens avait une grande confiance en Mgr Philippe, mais le concile brouilla ses alliances romaines.

12 octobre, lors de sa rencontre avec «le fin et intelligent archevêque d'Avignon» il lui confie ses appréhensions au sujet de Malines «et il me livre la réflexion d'un évêque belge: 'puisse le pape le nommer à la Secrétairerie d'État afin que nous en soyons débarrassés! C'est un orgueilleux'. Mes intuitions semblent rejoindre la réalité. Pour le bien de la sainte Église il faut que le Pape soit averti. L'unanimité des jugements recueillis en divers milieux ne peuvent être faux. Une collusion avec la Papauté pourrait nuire à l'action de Paul VI. Monseigneur doit voir le cardinal Giobbi, grand ami du Pape et lui confier nos appréhensions...».

Le lendemain, 13 octobre, il revient à la charge:

> Conversation avec le card. Forni. Je lui communique mes impressions sur Malines. Il n'est pas surpris. Durant sa nonciature à Bruxelles il avait constaté que les honneurs, les louanges, lui montaient à la tête. Il admet que son influence au concile pourrait être préjudiciable au Pape. Mais par quel canal faut-il faire passer l'information? Il croit que Confalonieri a l'oreille du Saint-Père.

Cette hostilité, qui semble se porter spécialement sur Suenens, s'étend en fait au groupe des modérateurs. Plus la session avance et plus les modérateurs perdent de leur superbe, plus Léger semble s'apaiser, si bien que l'on peut dire que l'irritation de Léger n'est pas seulement dirigée contre la personne de Suenens, mais se porte sur le groupe des modérateurs qui ont acquis une autorité particulière au concile et qui bénéficient d'une relation spéciale avec le Pape. Il trouvera chez Pavan des appréciations qui correspondent aux siennes. Le professeur du Latran confie au cardinal (20 novembre) que «le déroulement du concile lui cause des inquiétudes. L'autorité des modérateurs est mise en cause. Suenens, Lercaro, sont des personnages discutés. Döpfner a pris des positions que tous n'admettent pas». Cicognani, le 26 novembre, exprime un jugement concordant:

> Il me brosse un bon portrait des modérateurs – Agagianian: debole, Lercaro: mistico, Döpfner: giovane, Suenens: un puo particolare! Ce dernier a manqué de discrétion et le vieux card. me dit que le pape lui-même commence à découvrir les fils blancs. *L'admiration* du début baisse.

La session se poursuit ainsi et l'amour déçu trouve d'autres occasions de s'exprimer. C'est le cas, le 29 novembre, à la suite d'une réunion de la Commission mixte (doctrinale et Apostolat des laïcs):

> L'équipe belge perd un peu la face et Mgr Prignon vole au secours du cardinal Suenens en affirmant que, dans la rédaction nouvelle, il a respecté le mandat que lui avait confié la commission de coordination. Trois heures de discussions et enfin nous obtenons la formation d'une commission *ad hoc*, composée de trois membres de la Commission de l'apostolat des laïcs. Pavan

m'a bien aidé dans l'orientation des débats en affirmant (lui le spécialiste en la matière) qu'il n'avait rien compris à la lecture du document Suenens[86].

Léger note d'ailleurs, à la suite d'un long entretien avec Pavan, qu'il est «heureux d'apprendre que le St-Père met toute sa confiance en lui (Pavan) et qu'il commence à ouvrir les yeux au sujet de Suenens. Il (Pavan) endosse tous les jugements de Cicognani sur les modérateurs». (1er décembre)

Dans cet ensemble un peu aigre-doux, quelques événements se détachent: le 28 octobre, l'éloge de Jean XXIII prononcé *in aula* par le cardinal Suenens. À cette occasion, Léger se fera plus que laconique: «Belle cérémonie à St-Pierre. Le cardinal Suenens a tracé un beau tableau de Jean XXIII. Aura-t-il plu à tout le monde?». Cela est suivi, le 4 novembre, d'une visite du cardinal Léger au cardinal Suenens. Ici encore, Léger demeure discret dans ses notes personnelles: «Entrevue avec le card. Suenens. Homme brillant, intelligent, mais sera-t-il un grand pasteur, un évêque qui se laisse envahir par l'angoisse de l'Évangile?».

Plus important, sans doute, les audiences que lui a accordées Paul VI (30 septembre et 23 novembre). Certes, elles peuvent être à nouveau des occasions de médire un peu au sujet de son rival, ([Paul VI] «est stupéfait d'apprendre les manœuvres d'Ottaviani et même celles de Suenens au sujet du schéma XVII»), mais cela est marginal. Ce sont surtout des occasions de vérifier l'affection, la tendresse et la confiance que Paul VI place en lui. Il en sort toujours comblé, réconforté et les paroles rassurantes qu'il reçoit de Cicognani le 26 novembre le satisfont: «L'impression générale est bonne et en le quittant il me rappelle que le Saint-Père est satisfait de mon travail pastoral et de mes interventions conciliaires». Enfin, cela n'est sans doute pas significatif, jamais les interventions des deux cardinaux au cours de cette session ne touchent des sujets identiques ou n'arrivent lors de la même congrégation générale[87].

On ne peut sans doute pas comprendre ces épisodes étonnants de la deuxième session sans les situer dans un contexte plus large. Les changements de pontificat ont été chaque fois, pour Léger, des passages délicats. Son identification au pape, à la ligne pastorale du pontificat et à

---

86. Il s'agit du 'Texte de Malines' qui devait par la suite être remplacé par le Schéma XVII. Pavan, rédacteur de *Pacem in terris,* qui avait été membre du premier comité de rédaction de ce schéma, avait été en quelque sorte évincé.

87. Léger interviendra à quatre reprises et Suenens, à trois reprises. Pour Léger, voir ses interventions du 7 octobre 1963, sur le chap. 2 du *De ecclesia,* du 30 octobre, sur le chap. 4 du *De ecclesia,* du 19 novembre 1963, sur le chap. 5 du *De oecumenismo* (Liberté religieuse), et du 25 novembre 1963, sur le chap. 1 du *De oecumenismo.* Pour Suenens, voir ses interventions du 8 octobre sur le *De ecclesia* (*De diaconatu permanenti*), du 22 octobre sur *De Spiritus Sancti actione in laicis,* et du 12 novembre sur le *De episcopis* (sur la limité d'âge des évêques).

l'orientation de pensée du pontife conduit à remettre en jeu sa propre existence chaque fois qu'un pape décède. Lui qui avait adopté un style pacellien sous Pie XII, un style roncallien sous Jean XXIII, saurait-il devenir montinien sous Paul VI? Avant de retrouver à nouveau ses marques et de reprendre pied, Léger a cru un instant que tout était fini pour lui. Déjà, il a songé à renoncer à la pourpre, quitter Montréal et se rendre en Afrique, servir humblement les lépreux[88]. Surmené physiquement et psychologiquement à bout, il a vécu une telle épreuve d'abandon au début de cette deuxième session qu'il ne parvenait plus à entrevoir quel pouvait être désormais son rôle au concile et à Montréal. Avait-il seulement la confiance paternelle de Paul VI? Il était prêt à tout abandonner, croyant que l'on n'avait plus besoin de lui. On confiait de nouvelles responsabilités à ses amis d'hier et lui, il demeurait là, sans que l'on fasse appel à lui.

C'est sur cet horizon particulier qu'il faut comprendre ses relations avec Suenens et, plus largement, avec l'équipe belge. Lâché par ses anciens amis de la curie au cours de la première session, apparemment abandonné par le groupe de cardinaux auquel il s'était allié[89], Léger ressentait l'isolement, et l'amour déçu, bien plus que la jalousie peut-être, le faisait parler. Fait significatif, dès que les modérateurs semblent perdre un peu de leur autorité après l'affaire du vote sur les cinq questions, sa passion se calme. Le mauvais sort semble être conjuré.

IV. UN SILENCE RESPECTUEUX

Cette inimitié active de Léger à l'endroit de Suenens, si elle a été vive, fut de courte durée (1 mois). Toutefois, elle laissera des traces durables. Leur relation si suivie à l'hiver et au printemps de 1963 s'est désormais muée en silence respectueux. D'ailleurs, le nom de Moeller, de Thils, voire de Philips et de Charue apparaît de moins en moins dans les papiers Léger. La distance est consommée. Le seul lien qui demeure est avec le Chanoine Delhaye qui, lui aussi, n'arrive pas toujours facilement à être admis dans les cercles belges. Alors qu'il rencontre Léger à la veille de l'ouverture de la troisième session, il lui confiera: «Des nuages s'accumulent sur le concile. Le cardinal Suenens est isolé, son administration à

---

88. C'est à ce moment – et non en 1967 – que se forme le projet de quitter son diocèse pour l'Afrique. À cette époque cependant, Paul VI refusera sa démission, le rassurant en lui confirmant que sa place est à Montréal et que l'on a besoin de lui au Canada.
89. Montini était devenu pape, Suenens et Döpfner modérateurs.

Malines est fort discutée si elle n'est pas discutable». Ce ne sera toutefois que la seule annotation concernant le cardinal Suenens dans le *Journal* Léger au cours de cette session[90], sinon cette phrase bien laconique
en date du 1er octobre: «J'ai échangé un mot avec le card. Suenens ce
matin. Il est content de la marche du concile». Les rencontres sont de plus
en plus rares[91] et les contacts pratiquement inexistants. Les deux poursuivent leur activité conciliaire et, fait paradoxal, c'est au cours de cette
période que les interventions de l'un et l'autre données en congrégation
générale semblent le plus se croiser. Ils interviennent souvent sur les
mêmes sujets, à quelques jours d'intervalle, et adoptant des positions
assez voisines[92]. C'est le cas, le 14 novembre 1964 alors que, dans son
intervention sur la formation des prêtres, le cardinal Suenens se référera
aux propos tenus par son confrère de Montréal.

V. LES FRÈRES RÉCONCILIÉS?

Ce sera le mérite de la dernière bataille du concile de rapprocher
ces deux protagonistes hors série. En effet, la crise provoquée par

---

90. Le *Journal conciliaire* du cardinal Léger s'interrompra subitement le 17 octobre
1964, soit un mois avant la fin de la session.

91. Il y a bien une réunion de stratégie chez Frings, le 11 octobre, pour protester
contre la lettre de Felici qui voulait nommer Marcel Lefebvre au comité de rédaction du
De libertate. On y retrouve Léger, Meyer, Ritter, Silva Henriquez, Lefebvre, Döpfner,
Alfrink, König (Suenens en Belgique et Liénart n'ont pu être atteints). Enfin, le cardinal
Léger ne participait vraisemblablement pas, comme cela était son habitude, à la rencontre
hebdomadaire des évêques canadiens du 9 novembre au cours de laquelle le cardinal Suenens est venu s'entretenir avec eux sur la vie religieuse et sur la formation des futurs
prêtres.

92. C'est le cas, sur le *De beata,* mais en des sens assez différents cependant (respectivement les 16 et 17 septembre), sur la famille, le 29 octobre, les interventions (avec celle
de Maximos IV) les plus retentissantes de tout ce débat, sur les missions, respectivement
les 6 et 7 novembre et sur la formation des clercs, le 14 novembre. Pour une vue
d'ensemble, on verra d'abord les 9 interventions de Léger au cours de cette session et,
ensuite, les 8 interventions de Suenens. Pour Léger, d'abord celle du 28 septembre 1964,
sur le *De Iudaeis et non-christianis,* du 1er octobre sur le *prooemium* et les chapitres 1 et
2 du *De divina revelatione,* du 20 octobre sur le *De ecclesia in mundo huius temporis,* du
26 octobre sur le Chapitre I du *De ecclesia in mundo huius temporis,* du 29 octobre sur le
Chap. IV, No 21 du *De ecclesia in mundo huius temporis,* du 6 novembre 1964 sur le *De
activitate missionaria ecclesiae,* du 14 novembre sur le *De institutione sacerdotali* et du
18 novembre sur le *De educatione christiana.* Pour Suenens: voir son intervention du
16 septembre sur le *De ecclesia* (sur les canonisations), du 17 septembre, sur le *De beata,*
du 9 octobre sur le *De apostolatu laicorum,* du 21 octobre sur le *De ecclesia in mundo
huius temporis (In genere),* du 29 octobre sur le *De matrimonio et familia,* (+ rectification
le 7 novembre dans le cadre de son intervention sur le *De missionibus),* du 11 novembre
sur le *De religiosis* et du 14 novembre sur le *De institutione sacerdotali.*

les *modi* pontificaux sur le mariage et la famille ébranlent à ce point
les états-majors que, du coup, les inimitiés de la deuxième session sont
oubliées. Il est vrai qu'alors, l'axe Montini-Suenens ne présente plus
aucune menace. Il est vrai aussi qu'à ce moment, le désarroi est tel que
l'on a besoin de pouvoir compter sur Léger. Désireux de préparer une
contre-attaque pour le lendemain, Suenens réunit Heylen, Prignon et Delhaye, pour commencer à rédiger des contre-propositions aux *modi* pontificaux[93]. Des contacts sont alors pris avec Léger et son équipe. Le lendemain, en séance, le cardinal Léger intervint avec beaucoup de force[94],
faisant lecture d'une déclaration en six points préparée par une équipe
canadienne et belge où il exposait ses convictions les plus fermes[95].
À nouveau, le soir, Suenens appelle Léger pour le féliciter et lui pro-
mettre de continuer à l'appuyer[96]. Dans l'épreuve, les ponts semblent
rétablis et la collaboration à nouveau possible. Aussi, le 16 décembre
1965, le cardinal Suenens fera parvenir à Léger les réflexions de
Mgr Dondeyne au sujet de la séance du 27 novembre de la Commission
mixte sur le mariage, les accompagnant des remarques de Colombo[97].
Le 7 janvier 1966, Léger adressait sa réponse au Cardinal Suenens[98].

VI. Lorsque les chemins se séparent

La réconciliation n'est pourtant pas complète. Les années d'après
concile présentent à nouveau un contexte fort différent. Les grands ténors
de Vatican II quittent la scène les uns après les autres. Frings et Liénart,
pour raison d'âge, Léger, à la suite de sa démission, Lercaro, mis sur la
touche, etc. Alfrink, toujours actif, est de plus en plus marginalisé et Montini est devenu pape. Des cardinaux qui avaient fait les grands jours de
la commission centrale préparatoire, il ne reste plus que Suenens, Döpfner, König et Bea. Comme on le sait, Suenens est celui qui se montre le
plus actif, multipliant les interventions dans la presse.

---

93. Voir Fonds Prignon, 1618 (24 novembre 65), p. 2.
94. Cela est confirmé par plusieurs autres sources (Butler, Semmelroth). Dupont écrit:
«Léger se lève alors, pour lire un papier, avec beaucoup de force, presque de passion,
dans le plus profond silence» (p. 219).
95. Il s'agit d'un papier préparé la veille au soir par les soins de Naud et Lafortune et
revu par Delhaye et De Locht avant d'être retouché un peu par Léger. Cela représentait
bien sa position sur la question et exprimait parfaitement ses propres convictions. (Fonds
Léger, 1579, 1 p.)
96. Journal Prignon, p. 227.
97. Fonds Suenens, 2668 et Fonds Léger, 1565.
98. Voir Fonds Naud, 120-121.

Après son interview du 15 mai 1969 dans les *ICI*, les réactions furent nombreuses. Déjà en Afrique, Léger s'exprime de manière étonnante au *Corriere della Sera*. En réponse aux propositions de Suenens, il dit souhaiter un pacte de silence d'une année. «Je ne trouve pas équitable qu'un cardinal, comme l'a fait l'archevêque de Malines-Bruxelles, Suenens, répande abondamment dans les journaux et dans les conférences publiques ses opinions sur le gouvernement de l'Église, sur le meilleur moyen de choisir le pape, sur la légitimité de la fonction des nonces. Je trouverais plus respectueux que tout cela soit d'abord discuté avec d'autres évêques et cardinaux pour être, ensuite, présenté conjointement au Souverain Pontife»[99].

Cela peut sembler étonnant à première vue et on se demande si la brouille entre les deux hommes ne finit pas par nuire à la cause qui leur était pourtant commune. Il faut dire que Suenens n'avait apparemment pas fait preuve de beaucoup de délicatesse envers Léger lors de son passage au Canada en 1967. Ses *Souvenirs* le suggèrent, sans le dire explicitement, mais les témoins confirment cette hypothèse:

> Parmi les amitiés nées au concile, je dois mentionner mes rapports chaleureux avec les évêques canadiens anglais. Durant les sessions, il m'arrivait de passer une soirée avec eux pour répondre à leurs questions sur la marche du concile ... et pour raison de sympathie mutuelle. Je suis notamment devenu l'ami d'Alex Carter, l'évêque de Sault-Sainte-Marie (North Bay, Ontario), qui fut le président de la Conférence épiscopale canadienne, et, tout naturellement, l'amitié engloba son frère, le futur cardinal Emmett Carter. Le groupe des Canadiens m'avait demandé de venir les visiter sur place après le concile. [...] Peu après le concile, ils m'invitèrent à prendre part au Congrès théologique national, organisé par les évêques à Toronto en août 1967[100].

Non seulement, au cours de ce voyage, Suenens ne visita pas son confrère montréalais[101], mais il n'inclut pas Léger dans le nombre de ses amis et ne dit mot de leur rencontre à Toronto, Léger intervenant lui aussi à ce colloque.

---

99. *DC*, 1544, p. 681.

100. SUENENS, *Souvenirs et espérances* (n. 1), pp. 151-152. Cela est repris aux pp. 189-190. Il y aurait beaucoup de détails à corriger dans ces deux comptes-rendus. Suenens considère que le cardinal Roy est l'archevêque de Montréal (p. 194), que l'Université Laval est située à Montréal (p. 194), que Alex Carter est «président de la Conférence épiscopale canadienne au concile» (p. 190), ce qui n'est pas exact. Enfin, il donne comme évêques anglophones des évêques considérés comme titulaires de diocèses francophones, même s'ils sont situés hors Québec (pp. 151 et 190). D'autres erreurs de fait dans ces passages mériteraient aussi d'être rectifiées.

101. Cela, même s'il passe par Montréal pour visiter l'exposition universelle et pour y faire d'autres rencontres.

CONCLUSIONS

La présente étude, fondée sur l'état actuel de notre connaissance de la documentation, présente surtout le point de vue du cardinal Léger sur les rapports entre les deux cardinaux, même si plusieurs sources belges ont pu être mises à contribution. En effet, on ne connaît pas vraiment de l'intérieur le jugement que portait le cardinal Suenens sur son confrère de Montréal.

Ces relations sont tributaires certes des psychologies particulières des deux hommes, de leurs positions respectives sur diverses questions, de leur programme conciliaire et, aussi, de leur ambition personnelle. Des facteurs extérieurs sont aussi venus troubler cette relation, notamment la relation privilégiée ou l'amitié particulière que Montini semble avoir accordée à Suenens après son élection et, par-dessus tout, la nomination de ce dernier comme modérateur au concile. Cela semble être la goutte qui a fait déborder le vase, mais cet événement arrivait à un moment où d'autres facteurs intervenaient: la prise de distance de Moeller et l'entrée dans une nouvelle période des travaux conciliaires où l'équipe belge avait moins besoin des appuis extérieurs pour faire valoir ses propres points de vue, le texte du *De ecclesia* étant désormais sur les rails. Dans ces circonstances, Léger devenait inutile dans le cadre d'une relation sans doute fondée davantage sur la base d'un intérêt stratégique de la part de Suenens.

Rétrospectivement, on peut dire que Léger avait davantage besoin de Suenens que l'inverse. Cela tient naturellement à son tempérament (il avait excessivement besoin de reconnaissance), à son état de santé (il a été hospitalisé à trois reprises au cours du concile), aux fortes pressions qu'on a mises sur lui, à l'évolution de ses orientations et de ses amitiés, mais cela tient aussi au handicap permanent que représentait à l'époque le fait de ne pas être européen[102]. En somme, au cours du concile, Léger prit ses distances de ses anciens amis romains de la curie, ceux de qui il

---

102. Cela comporte diverses dimensions: économiques, certes, car les coûts reliés à la participation au concile ne sont pas les mêmes (Léger en fera état dans son *Journal conciliaire*), mais aussi quant aux possibilités réelles de se déplacer fréquemment à Rome. Le Journal Charue revient sans cesse sur un thème après mai 1963: «... manquent le card. Léger...», p. 159; «Léger n'étant pas là...», p. 161; «Le card. König n'étant pas là ... comme d'ailleurs le card. Léger...», p. 163; «Plusieurs ne seront pas présents: Léger...», p. 193; «Sont absents: card. Léger...», p. 227; «Plusieurs manquent, tels Léger...», p. 245; etc.), sans compter le coût physique des décalages lorsque l'on doit traverser l'Atlantique à quatre reprises en huit mois. L'éloignement rend aussi moins facile la possibilité de réunir une équipe à Rome, de faire venir des experts de manière impromptue, etc. Enfin, il faut rappeler que, à l'époque, le collège des cardinaux est encore très majoritairement européen, le reste ne comptant pas encore réellement.

avait été si proche au cours des années Pacelli et qu'il avait fréquentés à Rome au moment où il était recteur du Collège canadien et avec qui il avait entretenu d'étroites relations par la suite. Ses anciens protecteurs et amis lui ont fait payer bien cher cette «infidélité» et ils ont fait tout ce qu'ils ont pu pour le faire trébucher, au cours du concile. Son nouveau cercle d'amis le tint souvent à distance, ne correspondant pas toujours à ses attentes. Il avait le sentiment de ne pas être admis dans le *Brain Trust,* de ne pas être toujours mis au courant des initiatives qui étaient prises – ce qui s'avère exact – et d'être parfois lâché, après avoir été utilisé[103]. Cela le conduira à une certaine démobilisation et à un certain désengagement des travaux du concile[104].

Cette étude nous renseigne également sur les rapports à l'intérieur de la «majorité» qui est tout sauf homogène. Cette «majorité» est efficace en période de crise, où l'on serre les rangs et oublie les différends, elle connaît, à la première session et intersession, une période constructive, mais autrement, chacun mène son programme suivant ses propres idées, son propre programme, voire ses propres ambitions. C'est sans doute au cours de ces périodes qu'elle s'est avérée la plus vulnérable. Ceci dit, au-delà des différends que nous avons identifiés, il ne faut pas négliger les nombreux points d'accord entre les deux hommes: la collégialité, le rétablissement du diaconat, le rôle du laïcat, le mariage, etc.

Il faudrait aussi se demander quelle est la conséquence, lorsqu'une composante de cette majorité occupe une place prépondérante (envahissante, diront certains) dans les travaux des commissions. Indéniablement, cela a d'heureux effets. Cela permet une action cohérente et plus efficace en raison de la concentration verticale et horizontale ainsi obtenue[105].

---

103. On peut faire l'hypothèse que c'est ce qui arriva avec Moeller qui s'est servi de Léger (pour devenir *peritus* au concile, pour entrer dans la Commission doctrinale, y faire valoir quelques-unes de ses idées) avant de le lâcher après avoir bien assis sa position.

104. De Montréal, Philippe Delhaye rédige cette note du 2 avril 1964: «S. Em. le card. Léger reste très nettement anti-conciliaire. Il considère qu'on le rejette du brain-trust et que, par conséquent, il n'a plus rien à faire dans les commissions. D'ailleurs, dit-il, le concile tombe dans le byzantinisme» (J. FAMERÉE – L. HULSBOSCH, *Concile Vatican II et Église contemporaine. 3: Inventaire du Fonds Ph. Delhaye* (Cahiers de la Revue théologique de Louvain, 25), Louvain-la-Neuve, Publications de la Faculté de Théologie, 1993, désormais cité: Fonds Delhaye, 629). Témoignage concordant chez Congar: «Le cardinal Léger ne viendra pas à la session de mai-juin de la Commission. Il est déçu de la façon dont tournent les choses. Il estime avoir été exclu d'un rôle de direction du Concile (il m'avait fait des confidences en ce sens, avec une certaine animosité contre le cardinal Suenens, durant la seconde session)».

105. C'est ce qui arrive à partir de la deuxième session, dans le cas de l'équipe belge. Ainsi, Suenens est à la commission de coordination, Charue et Philips sont à la direction de la Commission doctrinale et d'autres *periti* sont membres des commissions. De cette manière, on contrôle de haut en bas la fabrication d'un schéma, jusque dans la sous-commission

Cela peut cependant provoquer certains ressentiments (on en trouve des expressions éparses), brouiller les relations entre des évêques, ou provoquer un sentiment d'exclusion qui conduit à la démission. La «majorité» a été forte lorsqu'elle a fonctionné comme une coalition de grands archevêques et évêques venant de différents pays. Elle s'est probablement affaiblie lorsque la rédaction des schémas s'est faite entre *periti* d'un même pays, voire d'une même université.

Faculté de théologie et de   Gilles ROUTHIER
sciences religieuses
Pavillon Félix-Antoine-Savard
Université Laval
Québec (Québec)
GIK 7P4 Canada

biblique. «Par le biais d'un contrôle des citations bibliques, cette sous-commission exerce réellement un dernier contrôle sur les textes. À sa faveur, on peut encore modifier ceux-ci après le travail de la sous-commission compétente; on peut réintroduire quelque chose. De toute façon, on a un contrôle sur tout le travail» (CONGAR, *Mon Journal du Concile* [n. 28], Vol. II. p. 56). De plus, en plaçant des *periti* dans les diverses commissions ou sous-commissions, on réussit à obtenir une concentration horizontale. Comme le mentionne à quelques reprises Congar, «Les Belges ne sont que trois ou quatre mais ils ont mis un des leurs partout. Dès qu'un y est, le petit groupe y est et assume le travail» (CONGAR, *Mon Journal du Concile* [n. 28], Vol. II, p. 262) ou encore «Moeller, venu avec la sous-commission des *signa temporum,* bien qu'il soit affecté à la sous-commission *De cultura,* reste avec nous. […] C'est bien la manière des Belges: peu nombreux (…), ils vont partout et se mettent, d'office, là où ils comptent être les plus efficacement influents» (p. 311). Tant et aussi longtemps que l'on n'a pas réussi à mettre en place les éléments de cette concentration verticale et horizontale, des hommes comme Léger sont nécessaires à l'aboutissement des projets de Suenens. Après, on peut s'en passer, un homme comme Léger, qu'on ne pouvait pas diriger et un peu imprévisible, devenait encombrant à ses yeux.

PART III

SQUADRA BELGA

LE RÔLE DU MONASTÈRE DE CHEVETOGNE
AU DEUXIÈME CONCILE DU VATICAN

Le Monastère bénédictin de Chevetogne a été fondé à Amay-sur-Meuse en 1925-1926 par dom Lambert Beauduin. Dom Beauduin a été une des figures les plus marquantes de l'Église de Belgique dans la première moitié du XXᵉ siècle et un précurseur pour un renouveau de la liturgie et de l'ecclésiologie et pour une ouverture au mouvement œcuménique naissant[1]. Voué à la recherche de l'unité des chrétiens, Chevetogne est un monastère international, mais ses liens avec les autorités monastiques et académiques belges ont toujours été très étroits. En raison de sa vocation mais aussi grâce à la variété culturelle de ses membres, dès avant le Concile la communauté avait déjà réfléchi sur des thèmes qui deviendront importants à Vatican II. À Rome, durant Vatican II, aucun moine de Chevetogne n'a fait partie de la célèbre *squadra belga* du Collège belge, mais les contacts ont été continuels avec plusieurs de ceux qui faisaient partie de cette *squadra*. Pour parler du rôle de Chevetogne à Vatican II, il faut d'abord passer en revue un peu longuement plusieurs initiatives liées au Monastère de Chevetogne qui ont préparé de manière efficace les grandes orientations du Concile.

I. LA PRÉPARATION LOINTAINE ET RAPPROCHÉE DU CONCILE DE VATICAN II

1. Dom Lambert Beauduin

Le fondateur, dom Beauduin, exilé pendant près de vingt ans, y était rentré en 1951 et un trait de sa personnalité a marqué la communauté qu'il a fondée pour œuvrer à l'unité des chrétiens: l'importance qu'il attachait à l'étude des anciens conciles en lien avec la doctrine de l'épiscopat. À ses moines il a toujours voulu inculquer cette conviction pour

---

1. Sur dom Lambert Beauduin, voir l'ouvrage de R. LOONBEEK – J. MORTIAU, *Un pionnier: Dom Lambert Beauduin (1873-1960). Liturgie et unité des chrétiens*, Louvain-la-Neuve – Chevetogne, 2001. Et le nouveau livre de J. MORTIAU – R. LOONBEEK, *Dom Lambert Beauduin, visionnaire et précurseur (1873-1960): Un moine au cœur libre*, Paris – Chevetogne, 2005.

ce qu'il appelait «l'œuvre en vue de l'union des Églises». Il estimait que les définitions du premier concile du Vatican devaient être interprétées correctement et complétées. Dès 1927 il entreprenait, dans la nouvelle revue *Irénikon*, la publication d'un article intitulé *L'infaillibilité du pape et l'union*[2]. En finale de la dernière livraison parue il donnait de très larges extraits de la célèbre lettre de l'épiscopat allemand de 1875 qui répliquait à la dépêche de Bismarck affirmant que Vatican I avait conféré au pape «le pouvoir de s'arroger dans chaque diocèse les droits épiscopaux» et de «substituer son pouvoir au pouvoir épiscopal». Dom Lambert en donnait un commentaire qui exposait avec grande clarté la doctrine catholique de l'épiscopat. En raison des difficultés qu'avait dom Beauduin en cette année 1928, la dernière partie de l'article ne fut jamais publiée.

Vingt-huit ans plus tard, en 1956, dom Olivier Rousseau, l'un des premiers disciples de dom Beauduin, reproduisait, toujours dans *Irénikon*, le texte intégral de cette Lettre de l'épiscopat allemand. Il y joignait les approbations officielles que lui avait données le pape Pie IX[3].

Cette publication entendait contrer les articles d'un canoniste, le P. Jean Beyer s.j., qui niaient la nature sacramentelle propre de l'épiscopat[4]. Cela se passait trois ans avant l'annonce du concile par Jean XXIII, en plein dans la fin du règne de Pie XII. Pour préserver l'avenir il était nécessaire de réagir en se démarquant de tendances théologiques en nette opposition avec l'authentique tradition des Églises. Le rôle du collège des évêques devait être réaffirmé avec force contre une ecclésiologie qui réduisait ceux-ci au rôle de préfets dans une monarchie pontificale absolue.

Dans cette riposte aux thèses avancées par le P. Beyer concernant l'épiscopat, le monastère de Chevetogne avait le soutien de son évêque, Mgr André-Marie Charue. Celui-ci, de son côté, publiait, au début de 1957, dans sa revue diocésaine un article sur l'évêque dans l'Église[5]. Cet article fit la joie de dom Beauduin qui rédigea une lettre pour féliciter son

2. L. BEAUDUIN, *L'infaillibilité du pape et l'Union*, dans *Irénikon* 3 (1927) 450-453 et *Irénikon* 5 (1928) 91-98, 231-238.

3. O. ROUSSEAU, *La vraie valeur de l'épiscopat dans l'Église d'après d'importants documents de 1875*, dans *Irénikon* 29 (1956) 122-142. Cf. déjà l'Éditorial d'O. Rousseau, pp. 3-4, qui présente l'article de B. BOTTE, '*Presbyterium*' *et* '*Ordo episcoporum*', pp. 5-27. L'article d'O. Rousseau, «La vraie valeur de l'épiscopat» a été reproduit avec les documents annexes dans le volume collectif, publié par Y. CONGAR – B.-D. DUPUY (éds.), *L'épiscopat et l'Église universelle* (Unam Sanctam, 39), Paris, Cerf, 1962, pp. 709-736.

4. J. BEYER, *Nature et position du sacerdoce*, dans *NRT* 11(1954) 356-373 (et pp. 467-480).

5. A.-M. CHARUE, *L'Évêque dans l'Église*, dans *Revue diocésaine de Namur* (1957) 4-13; et l'éditorial, p. 3.

auteur[6]. Dom Beauduin y disait que Pie XII pourrait convoquer un concile œcuménique pour définir la doctrine de l'épiscopat qui compléterait et rééquilibrerait l'œuvre de Vatican I, restée inachevée. Sur la doctrine de l'épiscopat était née une connivence entre Chevetogne et son évêque, Mgr Charue. Elle allait jouer à Vatican II.

De son côté, dom Beauduin, depuis son retour à Chevetogne en 1951, se plongeait très fréquemment dans l'étude des documents des anciens conciles que lui offraient les volumes de Mansi. Il est significatif qu'il soit mort en laissant tomber son visage sur le volume de l'*Histoire des conciles* d'Hefele-Leclercq qu'il était en train de relire.

On sait que depuis 1923, c'est-à-dire dès avant la fondation d'Amay, dom Beauduin s'était lié d'amitié avec Angelo Roncalli[7]. Au moment de la mort de Pie XII, puis de l'ouverture du conclave, il a dit à plusieurs reprises à des témoins différents: «Vous verrez, ce sera Roncalli; il va réunir un concile».

Le cardinal Suenens, de son côté, a replacé cette prophétie de dom Lambert dans un contexte plus large qu'il est opportun de citer un peu longuement:

> Notre génération avait été marquée par les Conversations de Malines où le cardinal Mercier avait lu le fameux *Mémorandum* de dom Lambert Beauduin, O.S.B. – futur fondateur du monastère œcuménique d'Amay –, sur 'l'Église anglicane unie mais non absorbée'. La thèse collégiale y avait été renforcée par un important 'Mémoire sur l'épiscopat' dû à Mgr Van Roey – à l'époque, vicaire général du cardinal Mercier et membre des Conversations de Malines, et que personne ne pouvait considérer comme un progressiste. En outre, la faculté de théologie de Louvain et les travaux œcuméniques du monastère de Chevetogne avaient préparé nos esprits à soutenir vigoureusement la thèse collégiale. Le rôle de dom Lambert Beauduin dans la décision de convoquer un concile ne peut être négligé. Il nous avait bien souvent parlé de la nécessité de compléter Vatican I et de mieux équilibrer primauté et collégialité. Il avait eu de longues conversations avec Mgr Roncalli, alors délégué apostolique dans les Balkans[8].

Suenens cite alors un passage d'une conférence de Roncalli à Palerme en l'automne 1957, un an donc avant son élection au conclave de 1958, où il fit publiquement et nommément l'éloge de la 'méthode unioniste' de dom Lambert Beauduin[9]. Une fois le concile annoncé, le 25 janvier

---

6. O. ROUSSEAU, *Les journées œcuméniques de Chevetogne*, dans *Au service de la Parole de Dieu. Mélanges offerts à Mgr A.-M. Charue, évêque de Namur*, Gembloux, Duculot, 1968, 451-485 (p. 485, note 45).

7. LOONBEEK – MORTIAU, *Un pionnier Dom Lambert Beauduin* (n. 1), pp. 1064ss.

8. L.-J. SUENENS, *Souvenirs et espérances*, Paris, Fayard, 1991, p. 62.

9. Le texte de la conférence du cardinal Roncalli à Palerme a été publié dans la revue *Oriente cristiano* (Palermo) I (31 marzo 1961), pp. 4-13 (sur dom Beauduin, p. 12).

1959, dom Lambert déclara à ses confrères: «Il faut tout abandonner pour y travailler». Devenu complètement invalide, il continuait à penser sans cesse au Concile. Il dit à Charles Moeller venu lui faire visite: «Tu verras, ce sera une résurrection!»[10].

Dom Lambert s'est éteint le 11 janvier 1960. Il n'a pas vu l'ouverture du Concile mais la communauté des moines de Chevetogne, ses fils, a suivi avec ferveur ses instructions. Dès l'annonce de Vatican II elle a consacré le meilleur de ses forces à s'y préparer.

2. Les Semaines d'études de Chevetogne

Depuis 1942 se tenaient à Chevetogne des colloques de théologiens qui prirent le nom de 'Semaines d'études' puis de 'Journées œcuméniques de Chevetogne'[11]. Elles étaient consacrées à un sujet théologique de l'actualité œcuménique. Après la mort de dom Clément Lialine (†1958), leur fondateur avec Roger Aubert et Charles Moeller, dom Olivier Rousseau avait assumé la charge de les organiser[12].

Ch. Moeller, tant qu'il a pu participer à ces Semaines d'études de Chevetogne, c'est-à-dire jusqu'à son engagement direct dans les travaux du Concile[13], a présenté dans la plupart les conclusions qu'il en tirait pour tous les participants. Dans ses archives déposées à Louvain-La-Neuve, dix-neuf de ses soixante-dix-sept carnets de notes personnelles sont consacrés à ces Semaines d'études[14].

Relevons, en particulier, dès la fin de la II[de] Guerre mondiale les Journées de 1945 où intervinrent Roger Aubert, Charles Moeller, Gustave Thils, Yves Congar, Jérôme Hamer, Jean Daniélou, et qui, centrées sur l'ecclésiologie, soulignèrent, entre autres, l'importance de la notion de 'peuple de Dieu'. Cette notion, mise en lumière en 1942 par L. Cerfaux[15],

---

10. LOONBEEK – MORTIAU, *Un pionnier Dom Lambert Beauduin* (n. 1), p. 1472.

11. ROUSSEAU, *Les journées œcuméniques de Chevetogne* (n. 6), p. 485, note 45.

12. L'article de dom Rousseau, cité à la note 7 et à la note précédente, donne un très bon inventaire de celles qui se sont tenues de 1942 à 1967.

13. En 1963 il n'y eut pas de Semaine d'études à Chevetogne; elle fut remplacée par le Congrès sur le Millénaire du Mont-Athos (cf. *infra*). En 1964, il n'y eut qu'une journée destinée à faire le point sur le Concile. En 1965, Ch. Moeller ne pouvant plus venir, j'ai dû présenter les conclusions de la Semaine avec la collaboration d'Édouard Beauduin et du pasteur J.-J. von Allmen, professeur à la faculté de théologie de Neuchâtel.

14. C. SOETENS, *Concile Vatican II et Église contemporaine (Archives de Louvain-la-Neuve).* I: *Inventaire des Fonds Ch. Moeller, G. Thils, Fr. Houtart* (Cahiers de la Revue théologique de Louvain, 21), Louvain-la-Neuve, Publications de la Faculté de Théologie, 1989, pp. 73, 75. Les carnets contiennent les notes des Semaines d'études depuis 1942 jusqu'à 1962.

15. Dès la première édition de L. CERFAUX, *La théologie de l'Église suivant saint Paul* (Unam Sanctam, 10), Paris, Cerf, 1942, Cerfaux consacre toute la première partie de son travail à la «théologie du peuple de Dieu».

était présentée un an plus tard, mais de manière indépendante, par un autre moine de Chevetogne, mort à la guerre en 1945, dom Nicolas Oehmen[16].

Il est remarquable que certains des thèmes majeurs développés à Vatican II aient été préparés par ces rencontres de Chevetogne. Plusieurs des théologiens qui ont joué un rôle de premier plan au Concile y ont apporté des contributions importantes, voire décisives. Charles Moeller, bien sûr, Gérard Philips, Gustave Thils, Yves Congar, Jérôme Hamer, Jacques Dupont, Jean Daniélou et d'autres encore. Dom Olivier Rousseau rappelle aussi que dans les années 1961-1962, qui précédèrent l'ouverture du Concile, il participa à Louvain à des réunions qui rassemblaient G. Thils, R. Aubert, Ch. Moeller et Édouard Beauduin où fut abordée entre autres la question des patriarcats, qui va occuper une place importante dans les débats de Vatican II.

Avec l'annonce du Concile dom Olivier Rousseau entendit consacrer ces colloques annuels à la préparation de l'événement. Quatre d'entre eux furent conçus à cet effet par dom Rousseau avec le concours de dom Hilaire Marot. Dès l'année même de son annonce par Jean XXIII, la Semaine d'étude de 1959 laissait provisoirement le thème de l'Eucharistie, qu'on était en train d'étudier depuis l'année précédente, pour réfléchir au futur Concile dans le cadre de l'ensemble des conciles.

À cet égard il est significatif de voir la liste de ceux qui ont été invités à présenter un travail dans ce premier colloque préparatoire au Concile[17]. Dom Olivier Rousseau a rédigé la présentation des actes de ce colloque pour la publication. Le sujet traité par les différents orateurs se développe sur le devenir historique des conciles à travers les siècles, depuis l'exposé de dom Bernard Botte sur la collégialité dans le Nouveau Testament et chez les Pères apostoliques, jusqu'à celui du chanoine Aubert sur l'ecclésiologie au concile du Vatican. Il s'agit, bien sûr, de Vatican I.

Parmi les travaux présentés dans ce premier colloque qui prépare le Concile, relevons l'exposé de dom Hilaire Marot, moine de Chevetogne

---

16. N. OEHMEN, *L'ecclésiologie dans la crise: À propos de quelques livres récents parus en Allemagne*, dans *Question sur l'Église et son unité* (= pseudonyme d'*Irénikon*), Chevetogne, 1943, 1-11. La notion de l'Église comme peuple de Dieu y est mise en relief à propos du livre de M.D. KOSTER, *Ekklesiologie im Werden*, Paderborn, Bonifacius, 1940.

17. L'ensemble a été publié l'année suivante, 1960, par les Éditions de Chevetogne en coédition avec celles du Cerf sous le titre *Le concile et les conciles*. On y trouve en plus des noms mentionnés ci-dessus celui de T.P. CAMELOT sur les conciles les IVe et Ve siècles, du professeur H.S. ALIVISATOS, un pionnier grec orthodoxe de l'œcuménisme et aussi historien du droit canon oriental, de G. FRANSEN sur l'ecclésiologie des conciles médiévaux, de Paul DE VOOGHT, spécialiste du conciliarisme, de Joseph GILL, sur le concile de Florence, et d'Alphonse DUPRONT sur le concile de Trente.

et historien de formation. Au cours du déroulement de Vatican II, par la sûreté de ses jugements historiques, il fut un précieux auxiliaire pour dom Olivier Rousseau. Dans ce colloque de 1959 dom Marot traita des conciles anténicéens et des premiers conciles œcuméniques. Il ressortait de son exposé une ecclésiologie de communion fondée sur l'unanimité des évêques des Églises locales[18]. Le P. Congar qui y avait donné un exposé sur 'la primauté des quatre premiers conciles œcuméniques', tira ensuite les conclusions de l'ensemble de cette rencontre.

Cette Semaine d'études sur les conciles mettait l'accent sur la doctrine de la collégialité qui sera l'objet d'un des débats majeurs de Vatican II. Le terme 'collégialité' et le concept qu'il recouvre avaient été lancés par le P. Congar en 1953 dans son ouvrage *Jalons pour une théologie du laïcat*[19]. De ce livre dom Clément Lialine avait donné en 1956 dans *Irénikon* une longue analyse. En finale il y félicitait l'auteur de rendre le terme russe de *sobornost* par celui de 'collégialité'[20]. Ce thème de la collégialité resta dès lors très présent dans la réflexion des moines de Chevetogne. En la même année 1956, dom Rousseau publiait une note non signée où il appuyait le concept de 'collégialité' et attirait l'attention sur quelques publications récentes qui y touchaient[21]. Il est très remarquable que Mgr Charue, dans son article de 1957 sur l'évêque, où il apportait son soutien aux thèses d'*Irénikon*, ait employé dès la première page le terme de collégialité à propos de l'épiscopat.

Après cette Semaine d'études de 1959 où émergeait l'importance du thème de la collégialité, celle de 1960 aborda le sujet de «l'Église locale dans son rapport à l'Église universelle». C'était le pendant ecclésiologique du thème du concile dans la série des conciles. Présidée par Charles Moeller qui en donna les conclusions, les exposés de cette semaine ne furent pas publiés en un volume. Celui de Congar, très significatif, a paru avec compléments dans la collection *Unam Sanctam*; il décrivait la lente évolution qui a mené de l'Église conçue comme communion d'Églises à une conception ecclésiale universaliste[22].

---

18. Hilaire MAROT, *Conciles anténicéens et conciles œcuméniques*, dans *Le concile et les conciles* (n. 17), 9-44. Signalons aussi l'étude de dom MAROT, *Unité de l'Église et diversité géographique aux premiers siècles*, reproduite dans CONGAR – DUPUY (éds.), *L'Épiscopat et l'Église universelle* (n. 3), 565-590.

19. Y. CONGAR, *Jalons pour une théologie du laïcat* (Unam Sanctam, 23), Paris, Cerf, 1953.

20. Recension de CONGAR, *Jalons pour une théologie* par C. LIALINE dans *Irénikon* 29 (1956) 99-101 [101].

21. O. ROUSSEAU, *Propos sur la 'collégialité'*, dans *Irénikon* 29 (1956) 320-329.

22. Y. CONGAR, *De la communion des Églises à une ecclésiologie universelle*, dans DUPUY – CONGAR (éds.), *L'Épiscopat et l'Église universelle* (n. 3), 227-308. Notons que

La contribution que j'ai donnée pour ce colloque trouva place dans la revue *Irénikon*. Elle traitait des Églises locales et des patriarcats à l'époque des sept premiers conciles œcuméniques[23]. Son propos était de mettre en évidence l'évolution homogène qui mena à l'existence des patriarcats anciens, figure ecclésiale intermédiaire entre l'Église locale dont est responsable l'évêque, et l'Église universelle qui s'exprime dans les conciles œcuméniques. Cette vue, grâce à diverses interventions dont on dira un mot ci-dessous, a permis de faire une place, modeste mais réelle, à l'institution patriarcale dans la constitution *Lumen gentium* 23. Elle a donné aussi le cadre d'un paragraphe du futur décret sur l'œcuménisme dans la partie consacrée aux Églises orthodoxes et à leur ecclésiologie, ainsi qu'on va le dire.

Cette question du lien entre l'évêque diocésain, l'Église locale dont il est le pasteur, et les conciles œcuméniques comme représentation de l'Église universelle par l'ensemble de l'épiscopat était au cœur de la réflexion des moines de Chevetogne en vue du Concile.

En lien avec ce colloque de 1960 et en préparation du Concile, dom Théodore Strotmann, moine de Chevetogne, avait écrit des pages importantes sur «L'Évêque dans la tradition orientale». Elles furent publiées quelques mois plus tard dans la même revue *Irénikon*[24]. Leur propos essentiel était de mettre en relief, en se fondant sur la tradition patristique de l'Orient et de l'Occident, l'enracinement de l'évêque dans son Église locale et, en commentant saint Grégoire le Grand, de souligner l'égalité des évêques et des patriarches quant à la dignité de l'épiscopat. Il ne semble pas, hélas! que cette voix ait trouvé véritablement un écho dans la *Lumen gentium*.

L'année suivante, 1961, la Semaine d'études abordait une question théologique destinée elle aussi à rééquilibrer Vatican I. Il s'agissait de l'infaillibilité de l'Église, comme vis-à-vis et comme fondement de

---

comme préface de cet ouvrage Mgr Charue présentait *L'enseignement de S.S. Pie XII et de S.S. Jean XXIII sur l'épiscopat*, 7-16. On sait l'étroite collaboration existant à ce moment entre Chevetogne et son évêque au sujet de la doctrine de l'épiscopat. Dans ce même volume dom ROUSSEAU donnait une étude sur *La doctrine du ministère épiscopal et ses vicissitudes dans l'Église d'Occident*, 279-308.

23. E. LANNE, *Églises locales et patriarcats à l'époque des grands conciles*, dans *Irénikon* 34 (1961) 292-321, repris et mis à jour dans É. LANNE (éd.), *Tradition et communion des Églises* (BETL, 129), Leuven, Leuven University Press, 1997, 387-411; en allemand *Partikularkirchen und Patriarchate zur Zeit der grosse Konzilien*, dans A. DÄNHARDT (éd.), *Theologisches Jahrbuch*, Leipzig, 1965, 459-484.

24. T. STROTMANN, *L'évêque dans la tradition orientale*, dans *Irénikon* 34 (1961) 147-164, repris dans DUPUY – CONGAR (éds.), *L'Épiscopat et l'Église universelle* (n. 3), 309-326.

l'infaillibilité pontificale. Les diverses contributions de ce colloque ont été publiées et elles sont sorties après la première session de Vatican II, en janvier 1963[25]. Dom Olivier Rousseau introduit le volume où il rappelle le propos du colloque: cerner deux conceptions ecclésiologiques qui s'affrontent, d'un côté «une vision totalitaire, monolithique de l'Église, bien qu'elle reconnaisse les misères de l'Église terrestre et cherche à les expliquer; l'autre la conçoit comme essentiellement axée sur une opposition entre l'Église du ciel et l'Église de la terre, soumise au péché». Dans ce colloque les participants non catholiques Jean-Jacques von Allmen, Nicolas Afanassief, Jean Bosc, Henry Balmforth apportèrent des lumières auxquelles la réflexion théologique des catholiques était peu accoutumée.

L'un des exposés les plus importants fut celui du chanoine Gustave Thils qui fit ressortir comment dans la constitution *Pastor aeternus* du Premier Concile du Vatican l'infaillibilité reconnue aux définitions *de fide* du Pontife romain se relie à celle de l'épiscopat dans son ensemble et à l'infaillibilité de l'Église *in credendo*. Cette notion de l'Église infaillible dans son acte de foi était très présente aux Pères qui avaient rédigé la *Pastor aeternus* sans que, peut-être, ces mêmes Pères n'en aient tiré alors toutes les conséquences. C'est ce qu'a fait, par contre, le §12 de la *Lumen gentium* qui traite de la foi et des charismes dans le peuple chrétien, c'est-à-dire au cœur du chapitre II sur le peuple de Dieu, avant le chapitre III sur la structure hiérarchique et sur l'épiscopat, où l'infaillibilité *in docendo* des évêques et du pape n'est traitée qu'après l'apostolicité, la collégialité et la sacramentalité de l'épiscopat. De ce §12 la phrase qui a étonné certains, alors qu'elle appartient au donné le plus traditionnel de la doctrine catholique, est l'affirmation selon laquelle «l'ensemble des fidèles (*universitas fidelium*), ayant l'onction qui vient du Saint, ne peut se tromper dans la foi (*in credendo falli nequit*), et ce don particulier qu'il possède il le manifeste par le moyen du sens surnaturel de la foi qui est celui du peuple tout entier, lorsque 'des évêques jusqu'au dernier des fidèles laïcs, il apporte aux vérités concernant la foi et les mœurs un consentement universel'».

Quinze jours avant l'ouverture de Vatican II eut lieu à Chevetogne un dernier colloque préparatoire au Concile (24 au 28 septembre 1962). Il fut consacré au thème qui allait se trouver en tête du chapitre III de la future Constitution *Lumen gentium*, un des pivots des discussions sur la collégialité: 'les Douze'. Dans la ligne de ce colloque de septembre 1962, la

---

25. O. ROUSSEAU, et al., *L'infaillibilité de l'Église: Journées œcuméniques de Chevetogne, 25-29 Septembre 1961*, Chevetogne, Éditions de Chevetogne, 1963.

dimension collégiale des Douze dans le Nouveau Testament fit l'objet au Concile d'une intervention très remarquée de notre évêque Mgr Charue un an plus tard, le 8 octobre 1963, dont un brouillon se trouve dans les papiers de dom Rousseau.

Parmi les communications présentées à Chevetogne en septembre relevons celles des Pères Théodore Strotmann et Hilaire Marot. Ces deux exposés ont été publiés dans *Irénikon*. La première de dom Strotmann s'intitulait *Les coryphées Pierre et Paul et les autres apôtres*. Il mettait en relief l'importance théologique de la «sainte dyade» dans la tradition liturgique orientale, comme déjà à Rome[26]. L'année suivante, alors que les discussions battaient leur plein au Concile sur la primauté et la collégialité, dom Strotmann combattait ce qu'il appelait la «céphalisation» de l'Église catholique[27]. On voit le jeu de mots.

Dom Hilaire Marot, pour sa part, avait donné un exposé qui allait intéresser très directement les débats de Vatican II sur *La Collégialité et le Vocabulaire épiscopal du Ve au VIIe siècle*[28]. L'exposé était suivi d'une note sur la signification de la titulature du pape comme *Episcopus ecclesiae catholicae*. Cette titulature sera celle utilisée par Paul VI pour la signature de tous les textes promulgués par Vatican II.

En marge de ce travail mais en préparation de Vatican II, dom Marot publia aussi un exposé sur *Unité de l'Église et diversité géographique aux premiers siècles*, où il affirmait la nécessité de maintenir le pluralisme providentiel dans l'unité[29]. Au même moment, pour répondre à une demande venue d'Allemagne, j'ai rédigé une étude destinée à mettre en lumière les caractéristiques propres de l'ecclésiologie des théologiens orthodoxes contemporains quand on la confronte aux positions qui alors avaient cours dans l'Église catholique[30]. Ici encore, certains éléments en seront repris dans la première partie du chapitre III du Décret sur l'œcuménisme.

26. T. STROTMANN, *Les coryphées Pierre et Paul et les autres apôtres*, dans *Irénikon* 36 (1963) 164-176.

27. T. STROTMANN, *Primauté et céphalisation: À propos d'une étude du P. Karl Rahner*, dans *Irénikon* 37 (1964) 187-197.

28. H. MAROT, *La Collégialité et le Vocabulaire épiscopal du Ve au VIIe siècle*, dans *Irénikon* 36 (1963) 41-60 et *Irénikon* 37 (1964) 198-226. Texte reproduit dans Y. CONGAR, *La collégialité épiscopale: Histoire et théologie* (Unam Sanctam, 52), Paris, Cerf, 1965, 59-98.

29. Dans DUPUY – CONGAR (éds.), *L'épiscopat et l'Église universelle* (n. 3), 591-636.

30. É. LANNE, *Le mystère de l'Église dans la perspective de la théologie orthodoxe*, dans *Irénikon* 35 (1962) 171-212 repris et mis à jour dans LANNE, *Tradition et communion des Églises* (n. 23), 413-447. Texte allemand: *Die Kirche als Mysterium und Institution in der orthodoxen Theologie*, dans F. HOLBÖCK – T. SARTORY, *Mysterium Kirche in der Sicht der theologischen Disziplinen*, Tome II, Salzburg, Müller, 1962, 891-925.

Ce rappel de la préparation lointaine, puis proche, de Vatican II à Chevetogne méritait pour trois raisons un développement un peu fourni:

a. Les thèmes abordés dans ces colloques de Chevetogne ont été centraux
   dans les débats du Concile: épiscopat, collégialité, infaillibilité – et
   j'aurais pu ajouter: importance des Églises orientales et relations œcuméniques, voire déjà théologie des réalités terrestres.
b. Plusieurs des participants belges de ces colloques ont eu un rôle décisif au Concile: Mgr Charue, Gérard Philips, Jacques Dupont et surtout,
   bien sûr, Charles Moeller, Gustave Thils; et j'en oublie probablement.
c. Plusieurs des participants non catholiques de ces colloques – orthodoxes, anglicans et surtout protestants – ont pris part, d'une manière
   ou d'une autre, aux travaux de Vatican II, comme observateurs ou
   comme invités spéciaux, et les remarques et suggestions qu'ils ont
   émises, oralement ou par écrit, au cours de ces travaux ont eu leur
   influence.

II. PARTICIPATION AUX TRAVAUX DE VATICAN II

Disons un mot maintenant de la participation active de certains moines
de Chevetogne aux travaux du Concile. Deux d'entre eux furent consulteurs durant la préparation du Concile: dom Thomas Becquet, prieur
conventuel du monastère de Chevetogne, et dans cette communauté le
plus ancien des disciples de dom Lambert Beauduin, nommé consulteur
de la Commission préparatoire pour les Églises orientales le 24 août 1960,
et dom Pierre Dumont, alors recteur du Collège Pontifical Grec, l'un des
premiers moines de la fondation du monastère à Amay, lui aussi disciple
inconditionnel de dom Beauduin, nommé à la même date consulteur du
Secrétariat pour l'Unité des chrétiens.

1. Dom Thomas Becquet (1896-1985)

Prieur conventuel de Chevetogne, dom Thomas Becquet, nommé
consulteur de la Commission orientale préparatoire, ne fut pas renommé
comme *peritus* dans la Commission conciliaire. Sa participation se limite
donc à la phase préparatoire du Concile. De plus, il a démissionné comme
supérieur de Chevetogne au cours de l'année 1963 et dom Nicolas Egender a été élu à sa place dès le mois d'août. Néanmoins il faut faire mention du P. Thomas Becquet à deux titres: (1) Il a rassemblé et transmis
les suggestions de ses moines pour le Concile; (2) Il a été invité à prendre
part aux travaux de la Commission préparatoire des Églises orientales.

a. Les suggestions des moines de Chevetogne ont été transmises et complétées par le P. Thomas Becquet. Le P. Thomas les a envoyées comme un dossier dont l'original de ce que lui ont remis certains moines est conservé dans ses papiers. Ces suggestions m'ont paru modestes, vu l'ampleur de la matière concernant l'unité chrétienne. Le P. Thomas les avait aussi adressées à Mgr J. Willebrands, un des participants assidus des colloques de Chevetogne et le secrétaire du nouveau Secrétariat pour l'Unité des chrétiens. Notons à ce propos que Willebrands avait invité dès le début des moines de Chevetogne à prendre part aux travaux de la Conférence Catholique pour les Questions œcuméniques qu'il avait créée et dont il a confié les archives à notre Monastère. Les suggestions de Chevetogne à la Commission orientale préparatoire portent sur les principaux thèmes traités antérieurement dans les Colloques ou Semaines d'étude dont on vient de faire état: l'épiscopat dans ses rapports avec la papauté et la collégialité; la nécessité de préciser et compléter les définitions de Vatican I et, en particulier, de préciser ce que signifie le célèbre '*ex sese, non autem ex consensu Ecclesiae*'[31]; les patriarcats dans l'Église catholique et la souhaitable abolition du patriarcat latin de Jérusalem; l'invitation au concile de représentants des autres Églises. Dom Becquet ayant fait participer très discrètement certains de ses moines aux travaux qu'il faisait personnellement pour la Commission orientale préparatoire, nous allons y retrouver ci-après les principaux thèmes. Concernant l'opportunité de l'abolition du patriarcat latin de Jérusalem, tous les moines de Chevetogne étaient d'accord, mais le P. Thomas avait une autorité particulière pour en parler du fait que de 1948 à 1950 il avait eu une activité considérable en faveur des réfugiés palestiniens[32].

Je relève ici dans le dossier collectif de Chevetogne remis au P. Becquet par ses moines, certaines des suggestions de dom Grégoire Bainbridge. Il énonce d'abord deux principes pour les travaux du Concile: (1) Celui-ci ne doit pas porter de lois pour les Églises orientales sans le plein consensus des hiérarchies de ces Églises. (2) Il doit distinguer les diverses Églises orientales et ne pas les traiter comme un bloc, alors qu'elles ont chacune leurs usages et traditions propres. Parmi les thèmes que la Commission propose d'étudier, il y a la «réconciliation» des frères séparés. Dom Bainbridge affirme à ce propos trois conditions: (1) Dans la réconciliation des individus exclure le rebaptême et la reconfirmation; (2) Éviter les réconciliations partielles de paroisses ou même de diocèses

---

31. L'exemplaire conservé dans les archives de dom Becquet me paraît avoir été dactylographié avec la machine à écrire dont je me servais. Mais je n'ai aucun souvenir précis à ce sujet.

32. Le P. Thomas avait entrepris un tour du monde avec une grande croix venant de Jérusalem pour intéresser à leur sort les Églises de partout.

et donc ne pas discuter de la formule à employer; (3) La réconciliation des Églises orientales ne peut se faire qu'en convoquant un concile à cette fin. Notons aussi ce qu'écrivait dom Olivier Rousseau dans ses suggestions et observations: «Pour l'Orient Rome reconnaît des institutions et des rites, mais méconnaît l'existence d'un 'monde oriental' capable de conserver sa physionomie patriarcale en dehors du patriarcat de Rome. C'est ce que demandent aujourd'hui les Melkites». Car – on va le dire – les Melkites ont tenu une grande place dans les activités de dom Rousseau au Concile. Relevons enfin à cette occasion que le patriarche melkite Maximos IV avait adressé à dom Becquet la copie des lettres de protestation qu'il avait envoyées à Rome contre un décret de la Congrégation orientale émis juste avant le Concile, qui leur interdisait l'usage de la langue vivante dans la liturgie, alors que chez les Orientaux catholiques de la *diaspora* elle était en usage depuis longtemps. Il lui avait aussi écrit concernant la juridiction du patriarcat melkite. Les propositions des moines de Chevetogne remises à leur supérieur représentent parfaitement l'esprit de la communauté, et déjà celui de dom Beauduin dès la fondation d'Amay. Elles peuvent se traduire en employant les termes qu'il utilisait dès 1926: pas de pêche à la ligne ni même de pêche au filet dans le vivier du voisin. La réconciliation ne peut se faire qu'entre Églises. Parmi le matériel offert au P. Thomas par les membres de sa communauté, signalons une note de cinq pages dactylographiés, mais non signées, sur les relations entre Rome et l'Orient après le Concile de Trente. Cette note courageuse montre l'effet désastreux de la réforme de Trente sur les Églises orientales unies à Rome. Elles ont été latinisées.

b. La nomination de dom Becquet à la Commission préparatoire orientale revêtait une importance particulière du fait que c'était cette Commission, et non le Secrétariat pour l'Unité, qui était chargée de réfléchir sur les relations avec les Églises orthodoxes en vue de faciliter le rapprochement et l'union. C'est devant l'incurie de cette Commission orientale et son incapacité à avoir des contacts avec l'Orthodoxie que cette compétence lui fut retirée par Jean XXIII pour passer au Secrétariat pour l'Unité.

Dom Thomas n'a pas été repris ensuite parmi les experts de la Commission conciliaire pour les Églises orientales. Il y a à cette éviction plusieurs raisons possibles: (1) cette commission dans sa majorité n'était pas favorable aux idées de Chevetogne; (2) elle entendait travailler avec les experts résidant à Rome, en particulier avec les professeurs de l'Institut Pontifical Oriental, dont plusieurs considéraient les questions touchant à l'Orient comme leur monopole; (3) enfin, dom Becquet n'était pas un Romain. Il avait fait ses études en Belgique sans jamais avoir fréquenté aucune institution romaine.

La participation du P. Thomas Becquet aux travaux de la Commission orientale préparatoire a été assidue même si elle a été limitée[33]. La Commission anté-préparatoire avait déjà fait ses jeux et elle laissait peu de place aux nouveaux venus. Parmi les rares annotations personnelles du P. Thomas je relève qu'il se plaint de ce que la Commission préparatoire «traite tout du seul point de vue juridique, canonique, sans véritable attention aux aspects psychologiques ni évangéliques».

Dom Becquet avait d'ailleurs son franc parler au sein de la Commission préparatoire. Il avait été affecté à la section dite 'unionistique'. Au début des travaux de celle-ci, travaux auxquels le P. Thomas prenait part, un des membres de la Commission avait protesté de ce que l'on y parlait toujours des Orthodoxes. Il trouvait cela abusif. Le P. Thomas rédigea une réponse dont il fit des copies au papier carbone pour les distribuer dans la Commission. Au nom de nombreux membres de cette section 'unionistique' il y affirmait: «Notre travail ici serait inutile, parce que contre la nature même du Concile, si nous faisions abstraction des 'frères séparés'».

Par une lettre du 15 septembre 1960 le P. Athanase Welykyj, secrétaire de la Commission orientale préparatoire, avait demandé au P. Thomas Becquet un rapport sur les réactions des Orthodoxes à l'annonce du Concile. Le 6 novembre suivant, le P. Becquet remet à la Commission préparatoire un important dossier sur les réactions des orthodoxes à l'annonce de la réunion du Concile. Il y passe en revue les réactions des hiérarques grecs et russes, mais aussi coptes, celles des professeurs d'Universités, celles de la presse orthodoxe. Le dossier est précédé de huit pages de présentation.

Au sujet des positions assumées par les hiérarques orthodoxes il y relève, entre autres: «On notera l'extrême bienveillance et le respect pour le Souverain Pontife dont toutes ces déclarations témoignent. C'est – dit-il – un fait nouveau et encourageant». Il conclut par une observation finale: «On peut dire que depuis des siècles on n'a plus assisté à une prise de position aussi favorable – ou au moins aussi aimable – des Orthodoxes vis-à-vis de l'Église catholique romaine». Mais il ajoute aussi: «Tous demandent des preuves concrètes préalables, comme le serait la suppression de l'Ounia'», c'est-à-dire la suppression des Églises orientales catholiques et de leur prosélytisme.

---

33. Les citations données ici des interventions de dom Thomas Becquet et des travaux qu'il a fait faire pour le Concile sont prises au dossier qu'il a laissé dans deux cartons déposés aux archives du monastère. Ces pièces demanderaient un classement plus rigoureux.

Cet important dossier de 57 feuillets[34] ne prétendait pas être complet, mais voulait donner un aperçu objectif des réactions de l'Orthodoxie à l'annonce du Concile. Il avait été préparé par dom Becquet en collaboration avec ses moines. Dans l'exemplaire des archives du P. Thomas on reconnaît la main de dom Nicolas Egender dans les sous-titres et références manuscrits ajoutés aux feuillets du dossier. Mais il est évident que ce mémorandum a été préparé principalement par les moines qui rédigeaient la chronique de la revue *Irénikon* et étaient, de ce fait, bien au courant de la manière dont les Orthodoxes – évêques, professeurs de facultés, presse – avaient accueilli l'annonce du Concile: dom Théodore Strotmann, dom Grégoire Bainbridge, dom Olivier Rousseau, dom Hilaire Marot.

Le 30 mai 1961 le P. Thomas Becquet remet à la Commission une note pour l'abolition du patriarcat latin de Jérusalem afin de faciliter l'union avec les Orthodoxes (document 98/1961). Cette note est insérée dans les travaux de la Commission (document 85/1961). Elle prend place avec des considérations historiques et théologiques sur les patriarcats orientaux.

La question des patriarcats a beaucoup occupé la communauté de Chevetogne, en particulier dom Olivier Rousseau, dom Hilaire Marot et le signataire de ces lignes. Ch. Moeller avait rédigé avec dom Rousseau une note destinée au Concile sur cette question des patriarcats et une autre sur les Églises locales.

À la Commission orientale préparatoire dom Becquet a présenté un *votum* dans la section concernant la manière de réconcilier les orientaux dissidents[35]. Ce mémoire de cinq pages porte la date de septembre 1961; il fait l'historique des relations entre les papes et les Églises orientales depuis la rupture de 1054 jusqu'au Concile de Florence. Il est succinct, mais réaliste. Il met en relief les raisons éminemment politiques qui guidaient ces tentatives d'union avec les Grecs. Rome voulait imposer ses vues universalistes. Il souligne les latinisations auxquelles furent soumis les Orientaux. En outre, il fait remarquer que «les masses» n'étaient pas préparées à l'union.

Concernant la '*communicatio in sacris*' les observations des moines de Chevetogne sont ouvertes mais modérées, distinguant entre la '*communicatio sacramentalis*' et celle qui ne l'est pas: prière en commun,

---

34. Certains feuillets ne comportent qu'une citation de quelques lignes tirée de la presse.
35. Pontificia Commissio de Ecclesiis Orientalibus praeparatoria Concilii Vaticani II, 151/1961. De Ecclesiae unitate. De modo reconciliandi orientales dissidentes. Proponens R.P. TH. BECQUET, OSB: «Bref historique des tentatives pontificales depuis 1054 jusqu'à Florence».

prêt des objets liturgiques ou des lieux de culte, etc. Dans le mémoire que dom Becquet remet à la Commission orientale, il estime avant tout que les Orientaux non catholiques doivent être traités comme des frères et que leurs épiscopats, leurs sacrements et leur liturgie doivent être respectés pour ce qu'ils sont, leur valeur n'ayant jamais été mise en doute. Mais il ajoute: '*Sub condicionibus jam statutis* (c'est-à-dire la bonne foi et l'absence de scandale, etc.) *et catholicos ab acatholicis et acatholicos a catholicis fas est et sacramenta accipere*'. Ce '*fas est*', «il est licite», tranche vraiment sur l'opinion commune à l'époque et sur le droit en vigueur. Il anticipe sur la position qui sera celle du Décret sur l'œcuménisme §15.

Plus particulièrement digne d'intérêt est la prise de position catégorique de dom Becquet sur le projet de schéma '*De unitate ecclesiae. Ut unum sint*', préparé par la Commission orientale et qui sera discuté et rejeté à la première session du Concile[36]. Dom Becquet commence par une '*Observatio praevia valde gravis*'. Il y déclare que tel qu'il est, ce schéma nous fait reculer de plus de cinquante ans en arrière. Aussi les observations qu'il propose ne sont pas seulement de forme, mais bien de fond; elles portent sur les idées. Le commentaire du P. Thomas ensuite se divise en '*Observationes generales*' et remarques sur des points particuliers.

Dans ces '*Observationes generales*', la dernière relève ce qu'il appelle sans ambages '*innovatio inaudita et omnino abnormis*', c'est qu'on puisse écrire: «*Unus fiat populus fratrum, communi et visibili Patris et Christi in terris Vicario obsequientium!*»[37]. Il conclut ces remarques générales par ces mots: «*Concludendum diceremus melius esset silere quam loqui*» et il ajoute: «Si vraiment c'était là la voix du Concile, la porte qu'a ouverte avec bonheur notre Souverain Pontife Jean XXIII restera fermée à nouveau pour longtemps». Cette conclusion courageuse était digne d'être signalée. J'ignore dans quelle mesure elle a pu être partagée par l'ensemble des moines, car le P. Thomas était assez scrupuleux sur le secret exigé concernant les documents qui venaient de la Commission préparatoire. Qu'il ait pu écrire cela est remarquable. Moi-même devant me prononcer devant les évêques et abbés bénédictins membres du Concile sur ce *De unitate ecclesiae*, je regrette d'avoir été moins sévère que lui car je pense que c'est lui qui avait vu juste.

---

36. Pontificia Commissio de Ecclesiis Orientalibus praeparatoria Concilii Vaticani II, 192/1961.
37. Les soulignements sont du P. Becquet.

2. Dom Pierre Dumont (1901-1970)

Dom Pierre Dumont – à ne pas confondre avec le P. Christophe Dumont, dominicain, dont on va reparler plus loin – était donc consulteur du Secrétariat pour l'Unité des chrétiens. Malheureusement il ne nous reste pratiquement rien de ses papiers personnels concernant la préparation du Concile[38]. Si mes souvenirs sont bons, il ne prit aucune part au travail du Secrétariat durant la première session de Vatican II et il quitta Rome dès la fin de cette première session. Il n'y revint qu'occasionnellement pour les travaux du Secrétariat et ne nous a pas laissé davantage de documentation.

Je relève cependant une lettre du 19 février 1965 qu'il adressa à dom Olivier Rousseau, son cousin germain. Il y commente l'acceptation contrainte du cardinalat par le patriarche melkite Maximos IV. Il écrit entre autres: «On m'enlèvera difficilement de la tête qu'il y a une volonté de noyer la collégialité»[39] de la part de la Curie romaine, voire du pape lui-même. Il est certain que ce cardinalat, pratiquement imposé à Maximos IV par Paul VI, a créé un climat de désillusion et de méfiance. Le crédit de Maximos IV, un des ténors les plus écoutés au cours des trois premières sessions, s'est effondré et la confiance des œcuménistes à l'égard du pape en a été ébranlée. Le choc s'en est répercuté sur la majorité du Concile.

3. Dom Olivier Rousseau (1898-1984)[40]

Il est temps d'en venir à dom Olivier Rousseau. Jan Grootaers sur la couverture du dossier qu'il m'a remis concernant dom Rousseau à Vatican II, a écrit: «Expert éminent sans avoir été *peritus* officiel». En tant que responsable de la revue *Irénikon* et aussi des Semaines d'études de Chevetogne, il était intéressé au premier chef par la préparation du Concile. Il acceptait toujours de prendre part à des réunions de réflexion où des spécialistes échangeaient sur ce qu'on attendait du Concile. Il y proposait les idées de Chevetogne. Parmi ces rencontres, relevons celle

38. Dom Pierre Dumont ne résidait pas à Chevetogne depuis qu'il avait dû quitter le Collège Grec de Rome à la fin de 1962. Après sa mort, son frère chez lequel il est décédé a retenu tous ses papiers personnels. Chevetogne n'a pu récupérer par la suite que sa correspondance avec dom Lambert Beauduin. Nous ne savons ce qu'est devenu le journal qu'il tenait quotidiennement et que la famille avait conservé pour elle. Durant l'année 1958-1959 il m'en avait fait lire certains cahiers où, au milieu d'annotations concernant sa propre famille (frère, belle-sœur et neveux et nièces), il portait des jugements lucides sur la curie romaine.

39. Fonds Rousseau à Chevetogne.

40. Pour les publications de dom Rousseau relatives à la préparation du Concile et à ses travaux, voir dans la brochure d'E. LANNE, *Dom Olivier Rousseau 1898-1984*, Chevetogne, 1994, la bibliographie établie par dom Lambert Vos à la suite de la notice biographique reprise à *Irénikon* 67 (1994) 163ss.

qui fut promue par les *Informations catholiques internationales* (ICI) dont les rapports furent publiés aux Éditions du Cerf. Sous le titre 'Les espoirs œcuméniques à l'épreuve des réalités', dom Olivier y brosse un historique très compétent et lucide de l'évolution de l'attitude de l'Église catholique à l'égard du mouvement œcuménique. C'est d'abord sous cet angle de la recherche de l'unité entre les chrétiens qu'il envisage le Concile et tout ce qui s'y rapporte[41].

Dom Olivier a pris une part très active au Concile. *Irénikon* annonçant son décès rappelait qu'«à Vatican II il joua un rôle actif en ce qui concerne la liturgie, l'épiscopat et les Églises locales, les Églises orthodoxes, l'œcuménisme»[42]. Dans une visée rigoureusement œcuménique, il a assidûment fréquenté et aidé l'épiscopat melkite qui logeait à la clinique Salvator Mundi. Il y inculquait les idées qu'il défendait. Mgr Nabaa, métropolite melkite de Beyrouth, l'un des quatre sous-secrétaires du Concile, jour après jour donnait au P. Olivier un laissez-passer pour assister dans St-Pierre aux Congrégations générales.

Dom Rousseau avait un don naturel de contact amical; il s'était lié avec d'innombrables évêques et *periti*, comme on a pu le constater en novembre 1963, quand il dut entrer en clinique non loin de la basilique St-Pierre pour subir une opération au moment où commençaient les débats sur le *De oecumenismo*. Des évêques très nombreux et fort divers vinrent lui faire visite et il en profitait pour leur dispenser la bonne parole[43].

En fait, dom Rousseau était venu au Concile en qualité de représentant de notre revue *Irénikon*. Il avait su se mettre dans les meilleurs termes tant avec le monde des journalistes qu'avec les Pères conciliaires et les experts, surtout francophones. Lui-même, d'ailleurs, en plus de ses chroniques dans *Irénikon* qui faisaient le point sur chacune des quatre sessions du Concile, a collaboré occasionnellement ou régulièrement avec d'autres périodiques qui informaient leurs lecteurs sur le Concile. Parmi ces périodiques on a mentionné les ICI[44] qui se distinguaient par leur ouverture catholique et œcuménique. Il y eut aussi la *Revue Nouvelle*, puis l'IDOC

41. O. ROUSSEAU, *Les espoirs œcuméniques à l'épreuve des réalités*, dans J.P. DUBOIS-DUMÉE, et al., *Un concile pour notre temps*. Journées d'études des Informations catholiques internationales (Rencontres, 62), Paris, Cerf, 1961, 190-223.

42. Voir *Irénikon* 57 (1984) 306.

43. Dom Rousseau avait noté jour après jour dans un petit agenda les noms des évêques ou experts qui lui faisaient visite à la clinique. Ce petit agenda est devenu introuvable et il est possible que le P. Olivier l'ait lui-même détruit comme nombre de papiers concernant le Concile.

44. Les *Informations catholiques internationales*, sur ordre supérieur, avaient dû remplacer en 1955 *L'Actualité religieuse dans le monde* au moment de la grande crise qui avait frappé les dominicains en 1954.

et le nouveau périodique œcuménique *Concilium*. Sur le Concile il a donné aussi des chroniques régulières bien documentées dans la revue hebdomadaire bruxelloise *La Relève*.

Pour se faire une idée des centres d'intérêt de dom Rousseau durant le Concile, il est utile de relire les pages qu'il a rédigées en ouverture du volume qui commente la *Lumen gentium* dans la collection Unam Sanctam. Elles s'intitulent 'La Constitution Lumen Gentium dans le cadre des mouvements rénovateurs de la théologie et de la pastorale des dernières décades'. Dom Rousseau y passe en revue les divers chapitres du texte promulgué par le Concile en montrant l'enracinement de chacun dans les divers 'mouvements' de rénovation qui l'ont précédé[45].

Parmi les initiatives de dom Rousseau au cours du Concile il convient de relever la direction qui lui fut confiée du 'Centre de la Presse de Langue française au IIe Concile du Vatican'. Sur les travaux du Concile le Saint-Siège ne diffusait, en effet, que de très laconiques et très secs communiqués de presse. Les journalistes francophones n'avaient pas d'organisme qui leur permette d'échanger des informations. Avec la collaboration de Jan Grootaers et Jean Pélissier, chroniqueur conciliaire du quotidien *La Croix*, dom Rousseau improvisa ce Centre de Presse dans les locaux du Centre Saint-Louis des Français, dirigé alors par Mgr Baron. Par là, non seulement il rendit un service éminent à tous les chroniqueurs francophones, mais lui-même en profita grandement pour ses propres informations concernant le Concile, comme aussi pour faire passer des messages sur les questions discutées dans l'*aula*. Plusieurs fois par semaine, voire chaque jour, il fit appel à des conférenciers bénévoles pris parmi les Pères du Concile, parmi les experts ou parmi les observateurs. Il n'y eut pas que des francophones à fréquenter le Centre mais aussi des étrangers. Dans une lettre du 30 octobre 1962, parlant de ce Centre de presse qu'il venait de lancer, le P. Olivier dit qu' «à beaucoup d'auditeurs et même à des évêques il faut donner des leçons de catéchisme et d'histoire de l'Église»; d'où les conférences d'experts et d'évêques qu'il y organisait.

Je relevais plus haut les étroites relations entre dom Rousseau et l'épiscopat melkite au Concile. Elles ont été constantes dès le début jusqu'à la fin. Le patriarche Maximos IV et ses évêques ont eu en lui un aide d'un dévouement à toute épreuve. Dans ses «Souvenirs du Concile Vatican II», publiés en français, leur langue originale[46], Mgr Edelby (1920-1995)

45. G. BARAUNA – Y. CONGAR (éds.), *L'Église de Vatican II: Études autour de la Constitution conciliaire sur l'Église* (Unam Sanctam, 51b), Tome II, Paris, Cerf, 1966, pp. 35-56.
46. N. EDELBY, *Souvenirs du Concile Vatican II (11 octobre 1962 – 8 décembre 1965)*, Jounieh, 2003, p. 385.

mentionne vingt-quatre fois le P. Rousseau. En novembre 1962 dom Rousseau est avec C.J. Dumont chez les Melkites pour organiser une prise de position négative contre le schéma *De unitate ecclesiae: Ut omnes unum sint*[47]. Toutefois, ce n'est pas avec cet évêque, membre de la Commission orientale, que dom Rousseau a le plus travaillé, mais avec Mgr Elias Zoghby, l'enfant terrible de l'épiscopat melkite[48].

Un autre enfant terrible de l'équipe des melkites était le P. Oreste Kéramé, référendaire du patriarche Maximos IV. Ancien jésuite, le P. Kéramé avait été le mentor œcuménique de trois des évêques melkites de Vatican II: NN.SS. Georges Hakim, futur patriarche Maximos V, Joseph Tawil et Elias Zoghby. Par contre, l'opposition de caractères et d'idées entre Kéramé et Edelby était constante. Kéramé avait un tempérament excessif, alors que Edelby respirait la maîtrise de soi.

Un soir où le P. Olivier m'avait entraîné chez les Melkites pour discuter un texte qu'avec le P. C. Dumont, j'avais préparé pour le Concile, Kéramé est intervenu avec violence contre Edelby qui posait des questions sur ce texte. Il lui répétait avec insistance: «Monseigneur, vous n'êtes qu'un uniate»[49]. Edelby avait quitté la réunion en silence. Nous étions consternés. Depuis cette scène pénible, je n'avais plus guère été à Salvator Mundi pour travailler avec les Melkites. En septembre et octobre 1963, rappelle Edelby, dom Olivier prépare avec les Melkites de Salvator Mundi une note sur les patriarcats qu'il fera signer par des cardinaux et des évêques allemands, français, canadiens, belges, etc.[50]. Parmi les soucis de dom Olivier, en lien avec ses amis melkites, il y avait, en effet, le désir de mettre en valeur en ecclésiologie la figure singulière des patriarcats. Il a raconté lui-même dans les Mélanges Philips l'histoire de l'insertion de leur mention au §23 de la Constitution *Lumen gentium* par l'alinéa qui commence *Divina autem providentia*[51]. Ajoutons tout de suite que si nous-même avons collaboré à la rédaction de cette incise de grande importance dans ce §23, dom Rousseau a aussi

---

47. *Ibid.*, pp. 113-114 et 137.

48. Cf. E. ZOGHBY, *Mémoires: Un évêque peu commode, dit-on*, Jounieh, 1991.

49. Edelby mentionne cette rencontre dans ses souvenirs en date du 21 octobre 1963 (EDELBY, *Souvenirs* [n. 46], p. 206), mais sans faire allusion à la sortie déplaisante du P. Kéramé. Le lendemain, rencontrant Mgr Edelby dans la basilique St-Pierre, celui-ci me raconta avec amusement que durant la nuit Kéramé avait glissé un billet sous sa porte lui redisant: «Je confirme que vous n'êtes qu'un uniate». Kéramé était de père melkite catholique et de mère orthodoxe de Grèce.

50. EDELBY, *Souvenirs* (n. 46), pp. 188ss.

51. O. ROUSSEAU, *«Divina autem Providentia...»: Histoire d'une phrase de Vatican II*, dans *Ecclesia a Spiritu Sancto edocta, Lumen Gentium 53*. Mélanges théologiques. Hommage à Mgr Gérard Philips (BETL, 27), Gembloux, Duculot, 1970, 281-289.

reçu l'aide de dom Marot qui dès la promulgation de *Lumen gentium* a commenté la signification canonique des patriarcats dans l'histoire de l'Église[52].

À l'origine de cette incise dans *Lumen gentium* §23 il y a le père abbé de Scheyern, président de la congrégation bénédictine bavaroise, Johannes Hoeck, membre de la Commission orientale au Concile. C'était un ami de dom Rousseau depuis leurs communes études à Rome au cours des années 20, à l'athénée bénédictin de Sant'Anselmo. En février 1963, Hoeck avait essayé en vain de faire passer dans la partie du schéma de décret sur les Églises orientales qui traitait de la figure du patriarche une phrase qui rappelait leur place traditionnelle dans la structure de l'Église. Les Melkites, de leur côté, regrettaient avec dom Rousseau que le *De ecclesia* ne dise rien des patriarcats. La phrase que Hoeck n'avait pu faire insérer dans le *De ecclesiis orientalibus* allait fournir la trame de ce qui est devenu le célèbre dernier alinéa de *Lumen gentium* §23.

À nouveau durant la deuxième session du Concile, Hoeck avait suggéré à la Commission orientale une nouvelle rédaction de la phrase qu'il proposait, mais celle-ci l'avait à nouveau rejetée. Dom Rousseau eut l'idée de la faire présenter dans l'aula conciliaire dans une intervention de Mgr Zoghby à propos du *De ecclesia*. En janvier 1964 la phrase fut acceptée comme insertion dans la *Lumen gentium*. Elle fut remaniée durant la troisième session du Concile. Hoeck avait pu prendre la parole le 10 octobre pour développer ses vues sur l'importance des patriarcats dans la structure ecclésiale[53]. Sur cette incise le P. Rousseau m'avait consulté. Nous avons suggéré à Hoeck de mentionner les «anciennes Églises patriarcales» comme '*matrices fidei*', selon l'expression de Tertullien (*Praescr. Haer.* 21, 4). La suggestion fut retenue. Elle m'avait été inspirée par ce que nous avions réussi à faire passer dans le schéma de décret sur l'œcuménisme, comme on le dira plus bas. Il semble assez remarquable que ce soit surtout grâce aux relations de dom Olivier tant avec les melkites qu'avec l'abbé Hoeck, avec Gérard Philips et Charles Moeller que cet alinea si important ait pu être inséré.

On est en droit de penser que, grâce aux réflexions préconciliaires des Semaines d'études de Chevetogne et aux travaux concomitants du

---

52. H. MAROT, *Décentralisation structurelle et primauté dans l'Église ancienne*, dans *Concilium* 1 (1965) 19-29.

53. Cf. F.R. GABHAUER (éd.), *Primum Regnum Dei: Die patriarchalstruktur der Kirche als Angelpunkt der Wiedervereinigung. Die Konzilrede von Abt Johannes Hoeck*, Ettal, Benediktinerabtei, 1987. Le texte latin de l'intervention de Hoeck est donné dans ce livre sur un feuillet séparé; la traduction allemande aux pp. 38-43. Voir aussi la revue *Irénikon* 37 (1964) 567ss.

P. Hilaire Marot et de moi-même, l'importance des patriarcats a émergé comme une donnée historique inaliénable de la structure de l'Église. Assurément d'autres en dehors de notre cercle l'avaient perçu, mais les relations de dom Olivier Rousseau avec l'abbé Hoeck, d'une part, et avec les Melkites et surtout avec Charles Moeller et G. Philips, de l'autre, ont permis de la faire aboutir.

Du 10 au 15 septembre 1964 dom Rousseau travailla avec les Melkites à mettre au point des *modi* sur le schéma sur l'Église. Puis sur les schémas sur les Églises orientales et sur l'œcuménisme[54].

Au cours de la dernière session du Concile, dans les discussions sur ce que l'on appelait le 'schéma XIII', a éclaté ce que la presse a nommé la 'bombe Zoghby'. Il s'agit de l'intervention *in aula* de Mgr Zoghby le 29 septembre 1965. Il y prenait la défense du 'conjoint innocent' dans un couple divorcé et souhaitait que l'on envisage d'y appliquer 'l'économie' pratiquée par les Églises orthodoxes[55].

Dom Olivier a aidé Mgr Zoghby à rendre son intervention moins provocante et mieux fondée en histoire de l'Église. Or, Mgr Zoghby, esprit perspicace mais qui aimait le sensationnel pour se mettre en avant, ne mentionne dom Rousseau dans ses Mémoires que pour citer les éloges que celui-ci lui a décernés pour son action au Concile[56]. En fait, dom Rousseau avait constitué un dossier pour Mgr Zoghby en vue de préparer cette intervention *in aula*. Il s'agit d'un texte polycopié, sans date, de vingt-six pages intitulé 'Notes sur la tradition occidentale du IIIe au XIe siècle concernant le remariage durant la vie des époux'[57].

Au moment critique de l'acceptation du cardinalat par Maximos IV, dom Rousseau a écrit le 4 février 1965 une lettre très franche et même dure au patriarche et il a entretenu une correspondance nourrie avec Mgr Zoghby et avec le P. Kéramé. Mais dans ces papiers de dom Rousseau sur Vatican II, on trouve aussi le brouillon dactylographié du communiqué de presse qu'il a rédigé au nom de l'épiscopat melkite pour expliquer l'acceptation de la dignité cardinalice par le patriarche Maximos IV et en atténuer l'effet psychologique catastrophique. Ce cardinalat de Maximos IV a constitué un drame pour ces évêques melkites mais

54. Cf. EDELBY, *Souvenirs* (n. 46), pp. 254ss.
55. Voir ZOGHBY, *Mémoires* (n. 48), pp. 94-104.
56. Voir *Ibid.*, p. 86 et *passim*. L'égocentrisme de cet auteur aux initiatives, souvent excellentes, mais toujours audacieuses, ne surprendra que ceux qui ne le connaissent pas.
57. Ce dossier se trouve dans le Fonds Dupont, 1468 (inventorié dans E. LOUCHEZ, *Concile Vatican II et Église contemporaine (Archives de Louvain-la-Neuve).* IV: *Inventaire des Fonds J. Dupont et B. Olivier* (Cahiers de la Revue théologique de Louvain, 29), Louvain-la-Neuve, Publications de la Faculté de Théologie, 1995, p. 75). Dans le Fonds Dupont le P. O. Rousseau est nommé vingt-deux fois et H. Marot quatre fois.

aussi pour les œcuménistes qui travaillaient avec eux. Rédiger ce communiqué, qui fut publié tel quel, était à la fois de la part de dom Rousseau une marque d'abnégation personnelle et un geste politique opportun.

Mentionnons encore une activité apparemment extraconciliaire, mais qui ne fut pas sans poids pour le Concile: le congrès organisé par dom Olivier à Venise à l'occasion du millénaire de la fondation de la Grande Lavra du Mont Athos en 1963. Cette initiative ressortissait à l'œcuménisme, non sans lien avec le Concile. Elle se proposait, en effet, d'attirer l'attention sur le monachisme de l'Église orthodoxe au moment où l'on allait mettre en forme le décret sur l'œcuménisme et celui sur les Églises orientales catholiques[58].

Après tout ce que l'on vient de rappeler de dom Rousseau avant Vatican II et pendant le Concile, il ne paraît pas exagéré de dire qu'il a eu un rôle déterminant sur certains points clefs des débats et des décisions conciliaires.

4. Dom Emmanuel Lanne

Il est toujours embarrassant de devoir dire un mot de ses propres activités durant le Concile. On risque de se donner trop d'importance alors que la contribution qu'on a pu apporter se révèle assez minime. Plus haut j'ai mentionné le fait que durant la Semaine d'études de Chevetogne de 1960 dom Rousseau m'avait demandé de traiter des Églises locales et des patriarcats à l'époque des sept premiers conciles. Un an après, Mgr Willebrands m'avait proposé de présenter, à la réunion de la Conférence catholique pour les questions œcuméniques qui se tenait cette année-là à Gazzada (Italie), un exposé sur «Les différences compatibles avec l'unité, dans la tradition de l'Église ancienne»[59]. L'une et l'autre de ces contributions ont voulu offrir des suggestions pour le décret sur l'œcuménisme, plus particulièrement dans la partie qui traiterait des Églises de l'Orient chrétien.

Lors de la première session du Concile en automne 1962, le Père Abbé Primat des bénédictins, dom Benno Gut, m'avait demandé de présenter aux assez nombreux bénédictins pères du Concile, évêques missionnaires et abbés présidents de congrégations bénédictines, le schéma préparé par la Commission orientale 'De unitate eclesiae. Ut unum sint'. Je le fis le 26 novembre. Mon exposé critique fut polycopié et distribué à tous ceux

---

58. Le Millénaire du Mont Athos, 963-1963. Études et Mélanges, 2 tomes, Chevetogne, Éditions de Chevetogne, 1963-1964.

59. Texte publié dans Istina 6 (1961-1962) 227-253 et repris dans LANNE, Tradition et Communion des Églises (n. 23), 359-385.

qui étaient concernés[60]. À la Faculté de théologie de Sant'Anselmo, en effet, j'avais depuis quatre ans la chaire de théologie orientale. Ce fut pour moi l'occasion de faire ressortir les faiblesses qui rendaient ce texte inacceptable; mais j'ai déjà noté que dom Thomas Becquet, mon supérieur, était beaucoup plus sévère que moi.

Au début du Concile Mgr Willebrands demanda au P. Pierre Duprey et à moi-même d'être les interprètes latin-français pour les observateurs non catholiques. C'était une occasion merveilleuse de contacts avec ces observateurs le matin dans St-Pierre et souvent l'après-midi dans les réunions organisées pour eux.

Un jour dans St-Pierre, dans les débuts du Concile, à l'issue d'une congrégation générale, le cardinal Suenens me demanda de lui présenter les observateurs dont j'avais la charge. Il aurait voulu s'entretenir avec eux des schémas que l'on discutait. Si mes souvenirs sont exacts, je lui dis devant les observateurs francophones: «Éminence, jeudi prochain nous avons une réunion privée à la faculté de théologie vaudoise pour nous entretenir avec ces observateurs des débats en cours. Si vous croyez pouvoir y prendre part, vous y seriez bienvenu». Dans un premier mouvement le cardinal accepta, mais le lendemain ou deux jours plus tard, il me fit savoir par G. Thils que sa participation était inopportune. Je dus en aviser nos amis réformés qui furent très déçus, mais je comprenais la réaction du cardinal: un cardinal à la faculté de théologie vaudoise, même pour une réunion privée, aurait pu passer pour une provocation. On disait alors couramment à Rome dans les milieux de la Curie que la faculté vaudoise et l'église qui faisait corps avec elle, avaient été construites presque face au Vatican pour le narguer. Au début de janvier 1963 je fus nommé 'membre' du Secrétariat pour l'unité des chrétiens. Je m'attendais à n'être que '*peritus*'; la qualité de membre me donnait droit de vote au sein du Secrétariat pour l'unité et dans les commissions mixtes de celui-ci avec les autres organes conciliaires.

Après la décision ambiguë du 1er décembre 1962 sur le schéma *De unitate ecclesiae* qui devait être refondu en collaboration avec la Commission théologique et le Secrétariat pour l'Unité, le cardinal Bea me demanda à la fin de janvier 1963 de prendre part à la Commission mixte qui réunit avec la Commission orientale les représentants du Secrétariat

---

60. C'était un texte de près de neuf pages grand format qui commençait par mettre en relief ce que le schéma contenait de positif et qui pouvait être repris dans une nouvelle rédaction. Ce sont ces éléments que le P. C. Dumont et moi-même, nous nous sommes efforcés de reprendre dans la tentative de collaboration avec la Commission orientale et qui sont passés, mais très améliorés, dans *Unitatis redintegratio*, 14-17.

pour l'unité et ceux de la Commission théologique. Nous n'eûmes qu'une unique réunion qui se termina par un fiasco[61].

Une petite sous-commission fut désignée pour rédiger un texte commun sur les Églises d'Orient en se basant sur le schéma *De unitate ecclesiae*. Elle comprenait le P. Emile Eid[62], maronite, pour la Commission orientale, et le P. C. Dumont, o.p. – directeur du Centre Istina – et moi-même, pour le Secrétariat pour l'Unité. Après deux réunions, les 1er et 2 février 1963, cette collaboration avorta, la Commission orientale refusant une refonte radicale du schéma *De unitate ecclesiae*, en prétendant qu'il avait été approuvé par un vote du Concile. De notre côté, en effet, nous présentions un texte nouveau, qui s'efforçait néanmoins de reprendre ce qui était recevable dans le schéma oriental présenté au Concile et que j'avais signalé aux évêques et abbés bénédictins[63]. Le P. Dumont et moi-même avions rédigé ce texte en nous inspirant de la perspective présentée dans mes exposés de 1960 et de 1961 sur les Églises locales et les patriarcats et sur les différences compatibles avec l'unité dans la tradition de l'Église ancienne.

Après l'échec de la collaboration avec la Commission orientale, le père C. Dumont et moi nous présentâmes notre projet de texte au cardinal Bea qui l'accepta comme base d'un troisième chapitre du schéma de décret sur l'œcuménisme. Par ailleurs, Mgr Willebrands m'avait demandé de réécrire pour le nouveau schéma sur l'œcuménisme du début de 1963 le paragraphe qui ouvrait le schéma et traitait de l'unité et de l'unicité de l'Église, paragraphe rédigé par Mgr Thils pour le schéma de 1962. Ce que je proposais était une première rédaction du §1 du texte présenté au Concile en novembre 1963. En 1964 on a coiffé le texte du schéma d'un Proemium, en sorte que ce §1 de 1963 est devenu en 1964 le §2 sur l'unité et l'unicité de l'Église.

Durant la révision de février 1964 à Ariccia près de Rome, j'étais le secrétaire du groupe qui s'occupait de ce paragraphe sur l'unité et l'unicité de l'Église. Mgr M. Maccarrone, président du Comité Pontifical pour les Sciences historiques et membre du Secrétariat pour l'Unité des Chrétiens, était membre de ce groupe. Il avait déclaré que dans ce paragraphe il fallait qu'apparaisse clairement que Vatican I avait défini la primauté

61. Alors que le ton montait de façon insupportable, le P. Jérôme Hamer se leva et partit en me disant à mi-voix, mais tous purent l'entendre: «C'est une maison de fous; je m'en vais». À mon tour, en signe de protestation, je me levai pour sortir. Mgr J.F. Arrighi, sous-secrétaire du Secrétariat pour l'Unité, dit alors à haute voix à l'actuaire de la commission mixte: «Prenez note que les PP. Hamer et Lanne ont quitté la réunion».
62. Le P. E. Eid est devenu par la suite évêque titulaire de Sarepta des Maronites, et membre du Tribunal suprême de la Signature apostolique et du Conseil pontifical pour les textes législatifs (*Annuario pontificio* 2004, pp. 1127 et 1151).
63. Voir ci-dessus, note 60.

et l'infaillibilité du pape. Je lui ai objecté qu'aucun des *modi* des évêques ne le demandait. Sur le moment on n'en parla plus. Un jour de très grand froid, Mgr Maccarrone me proposa, pour descendre d'Ariccia à Rome, de l'accompagner en voiture. J'acceptais. Durant le trajet Maccarrone me déclara, avec une insistance qui tenait du 'lavage de cerveau', qu'il fallait absolument introduire les dogmes de Vatican I dans ledit paragraphe parce que le pape le voulait. Je lui ai répliqué que si le pape le voulait, il devait le faire savoir au cardinal Bea; nous verrions alors comment donner satisfaction au pape; mais sans un avis officiel, je ne me sentais pas autorisé à introduire dans le texte une modification qu'aucun des Pères conciliaires n'avait demandée. Les choses en sont restées là. Si mes souvenirs sont bons, un tel changement n'était pas demandé dans les quarante points suggérés par le pape à la veille de la promulgation du Décret, dont on dira un mot plus bas.

Pour le *De revelatione*, en 1963, je fis partie de l'une des petites sous-commissions de la Commission mixte entre la Commission théologique et le Secrétariat pour l'unité qui devait traiter de la relation entre Écriture et Tradition. Parmi les membres désignés par la Commission théologique il y avait le P. Abbé Primat des bénédictins et futur cardinal dom Benno Gut. On passa au vote et je donnais mon suffrage à la proposition qui présentait d'une manière nouvelle la relation entre Écriture et Tradition. Le P. Benno Gut, de position très traditionnelle, aurait voulu que l'on reprenne à la lettre le Concile de Trente. Après le vote il m'apostropha en me disant: «Comment? Vous avez voté contre moi». Il semblait estimer que comme abbé primat de notre ordre et, de plus, ancien professeur d'Écriture sainte à Sant'Anselmo, j'aurais dû me conformer à son opinion. Je lui ai répondu: «Très Révérend Père, j'ai voté en conscience». Il n'était pas content…

J'ai aussi fait partie de la commission très restreinte et assez secrète qui, durant la 'semaine noire' de novembre 1964, examina les quarante *modi* proposés par le pape Paul VI sur le *De œcumenismo*. Nous étions quatre: Willebrands, Duprey, Thils et moi. De ces quarante amendements proposés on sait que nous en avons retenu dix-neuf et nous en avons écarté vingt-et-un. Après la discussion on nous a repris la feuille dactylographiée des quarante propositions de Paul VI, ce qui fait que je ne l'ai pas dans mes archives. Il y a cinq ans, Mgr Duprey pensait avoir retrouvé cette feuille dans ses propres papiers. Par la suite, j'ai cru comprendre qu'il a fait erreur. Nous n'avons pas été autorisé à garder ces *modi* qui étaient couverts par le secret pontifical. À cette époque les photocopieuses n'étaient pas en usage. Peut-être les *Acta Synodalia* les contiennent-ils, mais je ne les y ai pas trouvés et ils ne semblent pas être dans le fonds de Mgr Thils.

En novembre 1964 il s'agissait de faire approuver le schéma sur l'œcuménisme et à cette fin don Giuseppe Dossetti et moi avons convaincu le cardinal Lercaro, l'un des quatre modérateurs du concile, de venir au Collège grec dont j'étais le recteur, pour donner une conférence sur la portée œcuménique du décret en préparation. De cette conférence j'ai entièrement écrit le texte. Don Dossetti, si je me souviens bien, n'a fait que deux suggestions à introduire dans ce projet[64]. Le texte était écrit en français et a été lu dans cette langue par Lercaro devant environ deux cents évêques[65]. C'était le 11 novembre 1964, à la veille des quarante *modi* suggérés par Paul VI pour le décret sur l'œcuménisme.

Durant la session de 1964 fut aussi discuté le nouveau schéma sur les Églises orientales catholiques. Lors d'une réunion avec les Melkites, le 18 octobre, j'avais d'abord pensé que, faute de mieux, il fallait soutenir devant le Concile ce schéma très médiocre[66]. Mais au début de novembre en préparant la conférence qu'allait tenir le cardinal Lercaro et en discutant avec don Dossetti des répercussions œcuméniques de ce schéma sur les Églises orientales catholiques, nous nous sommes persuadés que le Concile ne devait pas voter ce texte, malgré les éléments positifs qu'il contenait. C'est ainsi que j'ai rédigé et distribué un mémorandum expliquant aux Pères du Concile pourquoi il fallait voter '*non placet*'[67].

Il y avait à ce '*non placet*' un motif supplémentaire. Dans les jours où j'écrivais la conférence que devait tenir le cardinal Lercaro, se déroulait depuis le 1er novembre la Troisième Conférence panorthodoxe de Rhodes qui prenait des décisions sur le dialogue avec l'Église catholique[68]. Cette Troisième Conférence des chefs de toutes les Églises orthodoxes confirmait l'état nouveau des relations entre Rome et Constantinople depuis la rencontre entre Paul VI et Athénagoras Ier à Jérusalem au début de cette

64. Dom Rousseau a publié le texte de cette conférence dans *Irénikon* 37(1964) 467-486, sous le titre «*La signification du Décret 'De Œcumenismo' pour le dialogue avec les Églises Orientales non catholiques*» par Giacomo, Cardinal Lercaro, archevêque de Bologne. Le tiré-à-part de 1965 porte le titre: G. LERCARO, *La signification du Décret sur l'Œcuménisme: Dialogue avec les Églises Orientales*. Cette conférence a eu de nombreuses éditions en différentes langues.

65. Lercaro prononça la conférence dans le grand portique du Collegio Greco que j'avais fait transformer en salle de conférence trois mois auparavant, le Collège n'ayant pas d'auditoire capable de contenir réunion aussi nombreuse.

66. Cf. EDELBY, *Souvenirs* (n. 46), p. 287.

67. L'initiative venait trop tard. Elle était d'ailleurs délicate à mettre en œuvre pour le recteur du Pontificio Collegio Greco. Cf. Y. CONGAR, *Mon Journal du Concile*, présenté et annoté par É. MAHIEU, 2 tomes, Paris, Cerf, 2002, p. 222.

68. Cf. O. ROUSSEAU, *La troisième conférence panorthodoxe de Rhodes (1er-15 novembre 1964)*, dans *Irénikon* 37 (1964) 487-507. Voir aussi du même '*Sur la IIIe session du Concile*', dans *Irénikon* 37 (1964) 508-523. La même livraison d'*Irénikon* contient aussi le texte de la conférence de LERCARO, *La signification du Décret* (n. 64).

même année 1964. Soutenir le schéma de décret sur les Églises orientales catholiques revenait à mettre en question la situation nouvelle qui s'était créée et que devait confirmer le décret sur l'œcuménisme.

Voici pour terminer un dernier souvenir. En 1965, la déclaration *Nostra aetate* était approuvée *iuxta modum* et pour le §4 sur les Juifs les *modi* étaient nombreux. Mgr Willebrands chargea Gregory Baum et moi-même d'en faire ce que l'on appelait l'*expensio*, c'est-à-dire d'examiner tous les *modi* proposés pour voir dans quelle mesure ils étaient recevables. Beaucoup de *modi* demandaient que l'on relie la question du judaïsme à celle du mystère de l'Église. Cette requête me semblait tout à fait recevable et même nécessaire. Par contre, Gregory Baum, Berlinois d'origine juive, y était absolument contraire. Comme nous ne pouvions résoudre notre différend et que la question me paraissait grave, j'ai écrit une lettre au cardinal Bea qui exposait notre désaccord. Je voulais que, si la proposition était rejetée, on sache quelle avait été ma position personnelle.

Bea remit la solution du différend à Mgr Willebrands qui, lui-même, nomma Charles Moeller pour nous départager. Celui-ci, qui avait travaillé un an plus tôt au §16 de la *Lumen gentium*, pensait comme moi que la requête des *modi* devait être honorée et il proposa la formule que l'on peut lire en tête de ce §4: «Scrutant le mystère de l'Église, le Concile rappelle le lien qui relie spirituellement le peuple du Nouveau Testament avec la lignée d'Abraham». Cette phrase avalisait les vues que, à la suite de dom Nicolas Oehmen[69], je défendais depuis plus d'une décennie sur «le schisme en Israël»[70].

CONCLUSION

En terminant ces notes on m'accordera, je pense, que si le rôle du monastère de Chevetogne à Vatican II a été assez modeste, il fut, pourtant, loin d'être négligeable. Un dépouillement plus systématique du matériel disponible hors de Chevetogne permettra sûrement de préciser, de compléter, voire de rectifier le contenu de ces pages[71]. Telles quelles, il

---

69. N. OEHMEN, *Le 'Lieu théologique' du schisme et le travail pour l'Union*, dans *Irénikon* 18 (1945) 26-50.

70. Cf. *Irénikon* 26 (1953) 227-236.

71. N'ayant jamais pensé que les papiers du Concile que j'ai conservés pourraient être de quelque utilité hors de mon usage personnel, je ne les ai pas gardés systématiquement et ceux, assez abondants, que j'ai retenus sont, pour la plupart, dispersés dans de nombreuses boîtes, souvent au milieu de bien d'autres choses, sans que j'ai jamais eu le loisir de faire un tri et de les classer.

me semble cependant qu'elles jettent une certaine lumière sur ce qu'a représenté Vatican II pour une communauté vouée par vocation à la quête de l'unité des chrétiens.

Monastère Bénédictin   Emmanuel LANNE, OSB
B-5590 Chevetogne
Belgique

GUSTAVE THILS AND ECUMENISM AT VATICAN II

In the first part of the present contribution, I would like to provide a chronological overview of the work that the Louvain professor Gustave Thils (1909-2000) accomplished as a member of the Secretariat for Christian Unity before and during the Council[1]. The primary goal of this overview is to introduce a number of texts on ecumenical issues that Thils either wrote himself upon the request of the Secretariat or of which he was the main editor[2]. All these texts were produced between July and December 1961. I shall discuss the content of these texts in section two. The main objective of this section will be to show that Thils' views on ecumenical issues actually changed quite significantly during this period. I hope to demonstrate this on the basis of a comparison of the content of the 1961 papers with the 1955 and 1963 edition of his *Histoire doctrinale du mouvement œcuménique*.

I. AN OVERVIEW OF THE WORK OF THILS AS A MEMBER OF THE SECRETARIAT FOR CHRISTIAN UNITY BEFORE AND DURING THE COUNCIL

After Pope John XXIII had taken the decision to create the Secretariat for Christian Unity on June 5, 1960, by means of the motu proprio

---

1. For an introduction to life and work of Gustave Thils I refer the reader to R. AUBERT, *La carrière théologique de Mgr Thils*, in *Voies vers l'unité: Colloque organisé à l'occasion de l'éméritat de Mgr Thils. Louvain-la-Neuve, 27-28 avril 1979* (Cahiers de la Revue théologique de Louvain, 3), Louvain-la-Neuve, Publications de la Faculté de Théologie, 1981, 7-27. The same issue contains the bibliography of Thils from 1936 to 1980. Cf. *ibid.*, 67-102. After Thils' death on April 12, 2000, Joseph Famerée published an overview of his theological œuvre: *L'œuvre théologique de Mgr G. Thils (1909-2000)*, in *Revue théologique de Louvain* 31 (2000) 474-491. The article focuses on the writings of Thils after his retirement, and thus provides a continuation of the assessment given by Roger Aubert of Thils' theological career on the occasion of his retirement in 1979.

2. The idea that it makes sense to pay attention to the specific contribution of Thils to the work of the Secretariat for Christian Unity has already been formulated almost a decade ago by Joseph Famerée. Famereé states: "Deux Belges furent particulièrement actifs au Secrétariat pendant le Concile: Mgr E.-J. De Smedt, évêque de Bruges, et Mgr G. Thils, professeur à l'Université catholique de Louvain". See J. FAMERÉE, *Les décisions conciliaires: Une présentation théologique*, in C. SOETENS (ed.), *Vatican II et la Belgique*, Louvain-la-Neuve, Arca, 1996, 115-140, p. 122.

Superno Dei nutu, the Secretariat gathered for the first time on the occasion of the solemn inauguration of the preparatory phase of the Council. During this meeting on November 14, 1960, eleven sub-commissions were established in order to study the texts prepared by the other conciliar commissions from an ecumenical perspective. Bearing in mind that the Theological Commission was working on a chapter on ecumenism as part of the schema *De ecclesia* and given the fact that the Commission for the Oriental Churches was preparing a schema *De unitate ecclesiae ut omnes unum sint*, it did not seem necessary at first sight for the Secretariat to prepare its own schema on ecumenism[3].

Thils played an important role with regard to two texts that had been discussed during the meeting of August 1961, which took place in Bühl, Germany: *De oecumenismo catholico: Suggestiones practicae* and *De oecumenismo catholico et de opera conversionum*. As far as the former text is concerned, the minutes of this general session indicate that Thils presented 'son rapport' in the morning of August 28[4]. With regard to the latter, however, the minutes are a source of some confusion. Summarising the discussion on *De oecumenismo catholico et de opera conversionum*, the report of the meeting of August 29, speaks about "le rapport du Chanoine Thils"[5]. The report of the session of August 31 introduces Thijssen as the one "qui est avec le Chanoine Thils l'auteur du rapport *De oecumenismo catholico et de opera conversionum*"[6]. We can be sure that Thils is the author of the practical suggestions, because he literally repeated large portions of the text in an article published in 1962 in *Nouvelle Revue Théologique* and in his 1967 book *Syncrétisme ou catholicité?*[7]. We know that Thijssen had been asked to contribute to

3. F. THIJSSEN, *De geschiedenis van het decreet 'de Oecumenismo'*, in *Kerk en oecumene: Decreet over de katholieke deelname aan de oecumenische beweging*, Hilversum – Antwerpen, Paul Brand, 1967, 9-75, p. 18.

4. SECRETARIATUS AD CHRISTIANORUM UNITATEM FOVENDAM, *Sessio Generalis mensis Augusti 1961, 28/8/61, ante meridiem* (Fund Thils, 549). For my selection of the relevant texts from the Fund G. Thils, which is maintained in the library of the Faculty of Theology of Louvain-la-Neuve, I was able to rely on C. SOETENS, *Concile Vatican II et église contemporaine (Archives de Louvain-la-Neuve). 1. Inventaire des Fonds Ch. Moeller, G. Thils, Fr. Houtart* (Cahiers de la Revue théologique de Louvain, 21), Louvain-la-Neuve, Publications de la Faculté de Théologie, 1989 and on the information made available by Professor Soetens himself.

5. SECRETARIATUS AD CHRISTIANORUM UNITATEM FOVENDAM, *Sessio Generalis mensis Augusti*, Feria III (29/8/61) ante meridiem (Fund Thils, 551).

6. SECRETARIATUS AD CHRISTIANORUM UNITATEM FOVENDAM, *Subcommissio III: "De Oecumenismo catholico et de opere conversionum"*, Feria V, 31/8/1961 (Fund Thils, 499).

7. G. THILS, *Pour mieux comprendre les manifestations oecuméniques*, in *Nouvelle Revue Théologique* 84 (1962) 3-16; *Syncrétisme ou catholicité?*, Tournai, Casterman, 1967, esp. pp. 154-163.

the preparation of the document *De oecumenismo catholico et de opera conversionum*. A letter written by Thijssen to Thils indicates that his cooperation consisted at least in sending Thils an article that he had written on 'The ecumenical movement in its relationship to the pastoral care accompanying the personal journey towards the Catholic Church and unification therewith'[8]. Apart from an introduction on the biblical roots of the term ecumenism, however, the said article does not seem to have influenced the text of Thils' presentation to any significant degree. A draft version of *De oecumenismo catholico et de opera conversionum* exists in which both the content and the presence of a few personal notes seem to indicate that Thils was the main or perhaps the only author[9]. I believe this may also be true for the final text that Thils presented on August 29. During the same general session, Cardinal Bea established a new sub-commission entrusted with the task of preparing an ecumenical directory. Thils was again asked to be the relator.

During the session dating from November 27 to December 2, 1961, which took place in Ariccia, Italy, Thils was omnipresent. As Thijssen mentions in his book, "the relator of the sub-commission *De oecumenismo catholico* presented two documents"[10]. The text of both documents is in Latin. A more theoretical report, *Votum de ecclesiae oecumenicitate*, discusses the notion of the ecumenicity of the Church as a particular form of its universality[11]. The first part, a "documentary history" (*historica documenta*) of the terms 'oecumenicitas' and 'catholicitas', is followed by a "theological elaboration" (*elaboratio theologica*). The authorship of Thils is indisputable, however, on account of the evident parallels with his book *Histoire doctrinale du mouvement œcuménique*[12].

---

8. F. THIJSSEN, *De oecumenische beweging in haar verhouding tot de pastorale zorg bij de persoonlijke gang naar – en éénwording met de Katholieke Kerk* (Fund Thils, 510).
   9. *De oecumenismo catholico et de opera conversionum* (Fund Thils, 503-504, 511). Apart from three pages on 'De opera conversionum' the text deals for the most part with 'De oecumenismo catholico'. Under the heading 'secteurs de la rencontre oecuménique', Thils mentions three sectors which also recur in the *Suggestiones practicae* and in the article published in *Nouvelle Revue Théologique* as well as in *Syncrétisme ou catholicité?* (n. 7): 'Activités d'ordre social et humanitaire', 'Activités d'ordre doctrinal' and 'activités de prière et de culte'. This leads me to conclude that Thils was the main author of this document. The section on 'La conversion des communautés' contains some personal remarks: "Voici quelques notes, rapides, écrites le dimanche 16/7 après-midi". He only elaborated '1. Aspect de principe' and added to the title of '2. Aspects prudentiels': "Je n'ai plus de temps: indique le pour et le contre".
   10. THIJSSEN, *De oecumenische beweging* (n. 8), p. 31.
   11. The Thils archives do not contain minutes referring to a public discussion of this text.
   12. G. THILS, *Histoire doctrinale du mouvement œcuménique* (BETL, 8), Louvain, Warny, 1955 and the new edition of 1963 (henceforth *Histoire I* and *II*).

During the same session, Thils also presented a document with suggestions for a doctrinal document *De oecumenismo*, which had been discussed before in the third sub-commission. In the form in which it had been discussed on December 2, 1961[13], it contained *Pro decreto doctrinali elaborando "De oecumenismo" suggestiones*. The minutes of this session mention that Thils began his presentation by explaining "que son intention et celle de ses collaborateurs est de donner une armature pour un travail sur l'oecuménisme". Interestingly enough, this short three page text contains six references to further literature (*Iustificatio et documenta*), including the *Votum de "oecumenicitate"*, but also to Thils' own book *La théologie oecuménique*[14]. We are at liberty to argue, therefore, admittedly with some exaggeration, that it was mainly Thils himself who was the author of draft zero of *Unitatis redintegratio*. The session closes with a request addressed by Cardinal Bea to Canon Thils "de mettre tout cela en lumière et d'élaborer un nouvel exposé qui tienne compte de tout ce qui a été dit"[15]. The revised version now contains six pages of notes, but the references to Thils' book had been dropped[16].

In its "rather thoroughly revised" form, the document *De oecumenismo catholico* was approved during the last plenary session of the Secretariat before the opening of the council, which took place in Rome, from March 6 to 10, 1962. The document acquired its final shape in July 1962, but it did not find its way towards the Council Fathers[17]. This led to negative reactions from members of the Secretariat. Velati mentions a document prepared by Lanne[18] and another prepared by Thils, in cooperation with

13. The text *De oecumenismo catholico* (Fund Thils, 516) seems to be a preliminary version. According to the minutes (Fund Thils, 539), Father Tavard asked for the words 'ubi transitus ille' (IIIb) to be clarified. These words are not to be found in the version found in the Fonds Thils.

14. SECRETARIATUS AD CHRISTIANORUM UNITATEM FOVENDAM, *Pro decreto doctrinali elaborando "De oecumenismo" suggestiones* (Fund Thils, 540), p. 2 (IIIc).

15. Fund Thils, 539, p. 9.

16. SECRETARIATUS AD CHRISTIANORUM UNITATEM FOVENDAM, *De oecumenismo catholico* (Relatio reformata et emendata secundum vota membrorum subcommissionis tertiae atque discussiones in Sessionibus generalibus habitas) (Fund Thils, 415).

17. SECRETARIATUS AD CHRISTIANORUM UNITATEM FOVENDAM, *De oecumenismo catholico (Decretum pastorale)* (Redactio ultima, mense Iulii 1962) (Fund Thils, 519). Cf. C.J. DUMONT, *La genèse du décret sur l'œcuménisme*, in *Istina* 10 (1964) 443-466, p. 462: "Remanié assez profondément, l'embryon de 'schéma' d'un *De oecumenismo* discuté à la session précédente fut adopté. Il reçut sa forme definitive en juillet 1962. Toutefois il ne fut distribué aux Pères, ni avant l'ouverture du Concile, ni durant la première session conciliaire".

18. *Animadversiones in schemate VIII patribus proposito De ecclesiae unitate: "Ut omnes unum sint"* (Fund Moeller, 1978).

Moeller, Beauduin and Onclin[19]. Thils mentions four decisive reasons why the Louvain theologians feel they were unable to agree with the document on ecumenism produced by the Commission for the Oriental Churches. In the first place, it would be better to be careful when speaking about the attitude of the Catholic Church towards ecumenism before the outlook of the Constitution on the Church had become clear. Secondly, the ecclesiology of *De unitate* was too juridical. No reference had been made to the necessity of a healthy exercise of episcopal collegiality. Thirdly, the document also reflected a juridical conception of unity, which did not take into account the theological basis thereof. The latter is situated in the communion of all baptised Christians. Finally, the document spoke almost exclusively about the Orthodox churches and thus appeared to make the distinction between the Orthodox churches and the other separated Christians too sharp[20].

As is mentioned in the minutes[21], Thils also presented a Latin document *Directorii oecumenici prima delineatio* during the same session, which was in fact nothing more than a table of contents for such a directory in 171 points[22]. The schema had been prepared with the cooperation of Thijssen, Davis and Baum. The document had taken into account a few remarks that Mgr. Willebrands had sent to Thils after he and Cardinal Bea had discussed their preliminary French version[23]. Even although Cardinal Bea ended the public debate by encouraging the members of the sub-commission to continue their work, it would appear that other obligations during the Council prevented the Secretariat from doing this[24]. The Thils archives, however, contain a handwritten text of about thirty pages demonstrating that Thils had already begun to elaborate the schema along the lines of a directory[25].

19. *Remarques sur le schema "De ecclesiae unitate"* (Fund Moeller, 1975).
20. I am dependent for this summary upon the account given by M. VELATI, *Le Secrétariat pour l'Unité des Chrétiens et l'origine du décret sur l'oecuménisme (1962-1963)*, in M. LAMBERIGTS, et al. (eds.), *Les commissions conciliaires à Vatican II* (Instrumenta Theologica, 18), Leuven, Bibliotheek van de Faculteit Godgeleerdheid, 1996, 181-204, pp. 186-187.
21. SECRETARIATUS AD CHRISTIANORUM UNITATEM FOVENDAM, *De "Directorio Oecumenico"* (Feria III, die 28a. novembris, horis postmeridianis) (Fund Thils, 926).
22. SECRETARIATUS AD CHRISTIANORUM UNITATEM FOVENDAM, *Directorii oecumenici prima delineatio* (Fund Thils, 925)
23. *Avant-projet de directoire oecuménique (Plan)* (Fund Thils, 933) and the letter from Mgr Willebrands dated October 27, 1961 (Fund Thils, 926).
24. The ecumenical directory was published in two parts in 1967 and 1970. See *Directorium ad ea quae a Concilio Vaticano Secundo de re oecumenica promulgate sunt exsequenda*, in *AAS* 59 (1967) 574-592; 62 (1970) 705-724.
25. An investigatation into the relationship between the final draft of the ecumenical directory and Thils' preparatory work would exceed the confines of this article.

The first debate on ecumenism in the Council hall took place between November 26 and December 1, 1962[26]. We know already that only the document prepared by the Commission for the Oriental Churches was presented to the Council Fathers, according to a decision by the Council's General Secretariat. Many bishops were of the opinion that this document did not pay enough attention to the relationship of the Catholic Church with the churches of the Reformation. A substantial reflection on the unity of the Church was also believed to be lacking in this schema. At the end of the debate, however, the Council fathers did not want to discredit the document entirely. It was decided that a mixed commission would make a synthesis of the three documents prepared by the Commission for the Oriental Churches, the Theological Commission and the Secretariat for Christian Unity.

The redaction of the new schema on ecumenism suffered from the unwillingness of the Oriental Commission to cooperate in a constructive way during the intersession. The secretary of the commission, Athanasius Welykyi, had proposed a new version that was largely based on *De unitate* embellished with a few quotations from the other two documents[27]. When it became clear that the mixed commission was unable to accept this proposal, the representatives from the Oriental Commission withdrew from the activities of this commission and decided to integrate Welykyi's text into the schema *De ecclesiis orientalibus*. The mixed commission decided to follow the structure provided in *De oecumenismo catholico*. A doctrinal chapter would be followed by a chapter on the practice of ecumenism. In order to satisfy the members of the Oriental Commission a third chapter on the Oriental Churches would be added.

A first attempt by Thils to prepare a draft version for the doctrinal chapter *Ut omnes unum sint*, dated February 5, 1963, was unsuccessful[28]. The task of preparing a new draft for this important chapter was entrusted to the Dutch Jesuit Johannes Witte. Witte, a member of the Mixed Commission representing the Theological Commission, completed this task by February 21st[29]. The final version of this chapter, now entitled

---

26. This discussion is described by G. Ruggieri in chapter VII '*Beyond an Ecclesiology of Polemics: The Debate on the Church*' under the heading '*The Melkites' Day*', in G. Alberigo – J.A. Komonchak (eds.), *The History of Vatican II*. Vol. II: *The Formation of the Council's Identity: First Period and Intersession Octobre 1962-September 1963*, Leuven, Peeters, 1997, 317-327.

27. *Schema decreti "Ut omnes unum sint"* (Fund Thils, 522).

28. *Ut omnes unum sint* (Projet III, 05/02/1963) (Fund Thils, 529).

29. Commissio mixta "De Oecumenismo", *De oecumenismo* (caput I), February 21, 1963 (Fund DeSmedt, 685).

De oecumenismi catholici principiis, was dated March 12, 1963[30]. The redaction of the second chapter *De oecumenismi exercitio* had also been entrusted to Thils and was likewise approved on March 12, 1963. Given the fact that so much time had gone in to the discussion of chapter one, however, this present chapter was only approved *substantialiter*. The third chapter, which dealt with the Orthodox Churches and which had been prepared by Dumont and Lanne, was not discussed at all and had simply been forwarded to the Coordinating Commission.

I would like to make bried reference to the results of the assessment by the Coordinating Commission of the two schemata *De ecclesiis orientalibus* and *De oecumenismo*. The members of this commission had no difficulties with the opinions expressed in the former text, which was approved on March 27, 1963. The commission was divided, however, with regard to the latter. Cardinal Cicognani wanted the third chapter to be removed, whereas the same chapter was defended by Cardinals Döpfner, Liénart and Suenens. The debate on *De oecumenismo* took place on March 28, in the presence of the Pope, but not of Cardinals Bea and Willebrands, who had to leave the meeting of the Coordinating Commission earlier because they had been invited to travel to the United States. On the following day, Cicognani withdrew his earlier request. Velati deems it 'not unlikely' that a personal intervention on the part of the Pope had been responsible for this unexpected turn[31]. It was left to the Council Fathers to make a choice between two different accounts of the Orthodox Churches. A new mixed commission was formed to add a second part to chapter three, dealing with the Roman Catholic attitude towards the Protestant Churches. Finally, the document was signed by Pope John XXIII in April 1963. According to Velati, the most important result was "that a text elaborated by the Secretariat could finally arrive in the hands of the fathers of the council"[32].

We encounter the name of Thils once again in studies on Vatican II and ecumenism in the context of the Council's so-called 'black week'. On November 16, 1964, after the Fathers had already voted on each of the chapters of the Decree on Ecumenism and only had to make a final vote on the entire decree, Mgr. Willebrands was informed that the Pope would be unable to promulgate the decree unless a number of revisions were made in the text. According to Duprey, Thils formed part of a small group

30. See *De oecumenismo* (chap. I,2), March 12, 1963 (Fund Moeller, 1982).
31. VELATI, *Le Secrétariat pour l'Unité* (n. 20), p. 201.
32. *Ibid.*, p. 203.

along with Lanne and himself, which studied the proposed revisions in
the afternoon of November 17, together with Mgr. Willebrands. After
Mgr. Willebrands had met Cardinal Bea, Duprey, Thils and Willebrands
finalised a note in which an explanation was given as to why some suggestions could be accepted and others not[33].

Thus far, I have highlighted the work of Thils during the Council as
author or relator of preparatory texts or drafts of *Unitatis redintegratio*.
Apart from preparing texts on ecumenical themes, the Secretariat considered it as another important task "to watch over the work of the other
commissions in order to prevent their texts from being in contradiction
with the ecumenical goals of the Council"[34]. An important example in this
regard was the intervention of Mgr De Smedt during the debate on *De
fontibus*, a schema that completely ignored every ecumenical concern[35].
The bishop made clear that ecumenical dialogue operates according to the
hermeneutical distinction between doctrinal truths on the one hand and
the variety of ways in which these can be expressed on the other. For his
intervention, the bishop had simplified critical reflections made by Thils[36].

During the sessions, the Secretariat also organised regular meetings for
the observers during which they had the freedom to offer their opinion
on the schemata that had been prepared by the commissions. Some of
these meetings were organised in language groups. The Secretariat passed
on their observations to the appropriate commissions. During one such
meeting, which took place on December 3, 1962, Thils introduced
De ecclesia. These meetings took place in a very friendly atmosphere, in
which it became possible for Catholic theologians to criticise some of the
schemata[37].

---

33. Cf. P. DUPRÉ, *Paul VI et le décret sur l'œcuménisme*, in *Paolo VI e I problemi
ecclesiologici al Concilio: Colloquio internazionale di studio, Brescia, 19-20-21 settembre 1986* (Pubblicazioni dell'istituto Paolo VI, 7), Brescia, Istituto Paolo VI, 1989, 225-
258, esp. pp. 241-242. A similar account on the role of Thils during 'black week' is given
in L.A.G. TAGLE, *The 'Black Week' of Vatican II*, in G. ALBERIGO – J.A. KOMONCHAK (eds.),
History of Vatican II. Vol. IV: *Third Period and Intersession, September 1964-September
1965*, Leuven, Peeters, 2003, 409-410. See also J. GROOTAERS, *Le crayon rouge de Paul
VI*, in LAMBERIGTS, et al. (eds.), *Les commissions conciliaires* (n. 20), 317-351.
34. VELATI, *Le Secrétariat pour l'Unité* (n. 20), p. 183 (my translation).
35. *AS* I/3, pp. 184-187.
36. VELATI, *Le Secrétariat pour l'Unité* (n. 20), p. 185: "Le discours est très simpli-
fié même en comparaison d'une première ébauche du texte probablement préparé par
G. Thils pour l'évêque belge". Cf. *De "adspectu oecumenico" doctrinae huius schematis, et ceterorum schematum*, s.d. (Fund Thils, 571).
37. Cf. É. FOUILLOUX, *Des observateurs non Catholiques*, in É. FOUILLOUX (ed.), *Vatican II commence... Approches Francophones* (Instrumenta Theologica, 12), Leuven,
Bibliotheek van de Faculteit der Godgeleerdheid, 1993, 235-261, esp. pp. 250-253.

II. Discussion of the Texts Written or Edited by Thils

As I indicated in the previous section of this paper, Thils was given the task of preparing five documents on behalf of the Secretariat for Christian Unity between July and December 1961. It can be demonstrated that this intensive process of reflection on ecumenism and its significance for the catholicity of the Church contributed to the development of his own theology. This becomes especially clear when one compares the position of Thils *in ecumenicis* before 1961, as it can be observed in the 1955 edition of his *Histoire doctrinale du mouvement œcuménique* with, on the one hand, the revised 1963 edition of the same book, and, on the other hand, the 1962 article *Pour mieux comprendre les manifestations œcuméniques*. Thils even found it necessary to integrate part of the text of *De oecumenismo catholico: Suggestiones practicae* and the *Votum de ecclesiae oecumenicitate* into the said book and article.

1. The Position of Thils in Ecumenicis before 1961

As Camille Focant wrote in his *Hommage à Mgr Thils*, Thils' *Histoire doctrinale du mouvement œcuménique*[38] is not merely an historical overview of the ecumenical movement or a mere description of the theological presuppositions thereof[39]. In the first part of this work, entitled *Les faits et les doctrines*, Thils follows the history of Faith & Order, Life & Work, and the World Council of Churches by introducing their different world assemblies. He focuses, however, on the doctrinal positions of the ecumenical movement, especially those related to ecclesiology[40]. Apart from some minor changes, this first part was almost entirely repeated in the second edition of the book. Thils was able, nevertheless, to add a chapter on the third WCC assembly, which took place in New Delhi in 1961.

This analytical part is followed by a synthetical second part, entitled *Le fait et la doctrine*. In this part of his work he first focuses on the ecclesiology of the ecumenical movement and, as he explains in the introduction to the second edition, on "the problems it implies for the member

38. *Histoire I* (n. 12).
39. C. FOCANT, *Hommage à Mgr Thils*, in *Revue théologique de Louvain* 31 (2000) 467-473, p. 470: "Et par rapport à des histoires événementielles du mouvement œcuménique ou des contributions purement doctrinales, elle garde l'originalité d'être une *histoire doctrinale* du mouvement œcuménique".
40. *Histoire I*, p. 5: "La doctrine des milieux œcuméniques sera l'objet immediate de notre attention, et singulièrement la position ecclésiologique avec les problèmes qui lui sont propres".

Churches and for the Catholic Church"[41]. In both the first and second edition, the second chapter entitled 'La théologie catholique et l'œcuménisme' has been the subject of more extensive development than the third chapter entitled 'Les chrétiens non-romains et le mouvement œcuménique'[42]. It will be this chapter, both in its first and its second edition, that we will look to for the greater part of our information concerning Thils's position *in ecumenicis*.

The fourth chapter entitled 'L'œcuménisme et la théologie', constituted a first attempt to reflect on the necessity of the development of an ecumenical theology. Thils decided a few years later to fully rework this chapter. It appeared as a small book in 1960 entitled *La théologie œcuménique: Notion – formes – démarches*[43]. It remains impossible to say whether Thils changed his opinion on this issue entirely. In 1960, however, he was able to present his convictions on the development of an ecumenical theology within the Catholic theological curriculum in a more systematic way. In the 1960 volume, Thils first treats ecumenical theology as "existential confrontation", given his conviction that the heart of ecumenism, which is the encounter with the other, always implies a certain confrontation. This chapter on ecumenical hermeneutics, as the said endeavour is called nowadays, contains valuable reflections on the difficulty of selecting criteria for ecumenical dialogue and also describes the qualities and conditions necessary for ecumenical dialogue. In the second part, Thils reflects on ecumenical theology as a dimension of theology as a whole. He explains how every theological discipline needs to be enriched by the ecumenical spirit. Finally, the chapter reflects on the theological methodology of an ecumenical theology. In the third and last chapter, he describes the possible point of view of a course on ecumenical theology, a course that he himself had taught in Louvain since the 1950's. I mentioned earlier that the draft of *De oecumenismo catholico*, which had been discussed during the plenary meeting of the Secretariat for Christian Unity on December 2, 1961, contained a reference to *La théologie œcuménique*. I am inclined to doubt, however, whether this book influenced the discussions at the Secretariat for Christian Unity to any significant degree.

---

41. *Histoire II*, p. 5: "Nous nous en tiendrons avant tout à l'histoire *doctrinale* du Conseil œcuménique des Églises et aux problèmes qu'elle soulève pour les Églises membres et pour l'Église catholique".

42. Chapter II comprises 48 pages in the first edition, and 86 pages in the second edition; chapter III was not changed in the second edition and comprises 14 pages.

43. G. THILS, *La théologie œcuménique: Notion – formes – démarches* (BETL, 16), Louvain, Warny, 1960. Whereas the chapter in the previous book comprised 21 pages, the new book has 82 pages.

It is much more interesting to compare the texts of the Secretariat with the views expressed by Thils in the chapter on 'La théologie catholique et l'œcuménisme' of his *Histoire doctrinale*. I will focus in particular on the claims that he abandoned in the second edition.

The chapter starts with a reflection on the term ecumenism. Thils states that ecumenism does not exclusively deal with the return of individual Christians to the Catholic Church, but also with the theological status of "the Churches and separated confessions". Secondly, Thils emphasises, as he will do repeatedly, that "the Churches and separated confessions are bearers of a real and authentic good, be it incomplete and imperfect, which they will never have to deny when they return to the Catholic Church". Finally, "this return will bring to the Catholic Church a true, albeit non-substantial complement"[44]. In the papers that he prepared for the Secretariat on Christian Unity, Thils was to repeat his conviction on the close relationship between ecumenicity and catholicity. Thils probably decided no longer to incorporate his analysis of the conditions that needed to be fulfilled before Catholics could accept the reality of ecumenism in his second edition, because the text focused too much on the ecumenism of return.

The first paragraph of the section on 'The Church of Jesus Christ' opened in the 1955 edition with a description of the Roman Catholic understanding of the Church. The visibly hierarchical nature of the Church forms part of this definition. As a consequence, Thils holds that "it is not possible to give a theological meaning to discussions or movements that would have as their goal to 'construct' or 'reconstruct' the *Una Sancta*"[45]. In his opinion, the Catholic Church cannot accept the

44. *Histoire I*, p. 168: "À prendre l'essentiel de la question, il semble qu'on puisse dire ceci. Il y a 'œcuménisme' en un sens original et acceptable pour un catholique, lorsqu'on reconnaît (a) que la question de la réunion des chrétiens comporte, à côté de celle des 'retours' individuels, un problème théologique concernant les Églises et Confessions séparées comme telles, dont il faut désormais fixer le statut théologique complet; (b) que, en particulier, les Églises ou Confessions séparées sont porteuses d'un bien réel et authentique, quoique incomplet et imparfait, bien qu'elles ne devront nullement renier en revenant à l'Église catholique; (c) que ce retour apportera à l'Église catholique un complément véritable, quoique non-substantiel".

45. *Histoire I*, p. 170: "La théologie catholique est unanime à définir l'Église, face aux chrétiens séparés, de la manière suivante. Le Christ a fondé une Église. Celle-ci est une, sainte, catholique et apostolique. Elle est, sous un certain aspect, une communion visible et historique. Comme le Christ lui a donné l'assurance de son assistance, cette communion historique et visible est indéfectible: elle a existé substantiellement – en ses éléments constitutifs essentiels – depuis sa fondation jusqu'à présent et elle continuera d'exister jusqu'à la fin des siècles. Cette Église est visiblement hiérarchique: elle est dirigée par l'épiscopat et le Souverain Pontife. Par conséquent, il n'est pas possible de donner un sens théologique à des discussions ou des mouvements qui auraient pour but de 'construire' ou de 'reconstruire' l'*Una Sancta*, sous-entendant: ou que celle-ci a cessé d'exister, ou qu'elle

doctrinal position of the World Council of Churches, which holds that "(a) the true Church of Christ does not exist, *quoad substantiam*, in a particular historical community and, (b) the essential unity of this visible historical communion does not exist for the moment: the divided Churches have to "become" the *Una Sancta*, thanks to God's gift and our unanimous action"[46]. Thils repeats the Catholic conviction that "in the event of the return of the dissident Christianities, a complement of unity and catholicity would enter the Church"[47]. All these ideas were to be left out in the second edition.

In 1955 and 1963, Thils speaks about the holiness of the Church in the same words. Protestant reflections on the sinfulness of the Church are difficult to accept for Catholics, unless the distinction Congar had made between the Church as a divine institution and as the congregation of the believers is accepted. We will come back to a small addition to this section, which Thils made in 1963. Thils' perspective with regard to the different opinions on the Kingdom of God evident between Catholic and non-Catholic theologians did not undergo any changes[48].

The section on the participation of the Catholic Church in the World Council of Churches was completely rewritten in 1963. In 1955, Thils was convinced that the Catholic attitude could only be changed if the WCC was willing to recognise the possibility that the true Church could be one of the existing Christian confessions[49].

existe éparpillée dans les diverses Églises et confessions chrétiennes visibles, ou qu'elle se compose de plusieurs communions ou branches, ou qu'elle doit être cherchée au-delà des Églises et confessions chrétiennes historiques".

46. *Histoire I*, p. 173: "Cependant, il semble que l'on peut dire que la plupart des communautés chrétiennes faisant partie du Conseil œcuménique défendent une conception de l'Église selon laquelle: a) la véritable Église du Christ n'existe pas aujourd'hui, *quoad substantiam*, dans une communauté historique déterminée; b) en particulier, l'unité essentielle de cette communion historique visible n'existe point actuellement: les Églises divisées doivent 'devenir' l'*Una Sancta*, grâce au don de Dieu, et à notre action unanime".

47. *Histoire I*, p. 174: "Les théologiens catholiques admettent également que, en cas de retour des chrétientés dissidents, un complément d'unité et de catholicité adviendrait à l'Église, complément authentiquement chrétien bien sûr, mais qu'ils se refusent à dire 'substantiel' quelle qu'en soit l'importance visible ou externe. Car il ne peut être question de compléter la structure essentielle de l'Église véritable".

48. Compare *Histoire I*, pp. 197-205 and *Histoire II*, pp. 231-236. Thils only left out the subsection of 'Royaume de Dieu et espérance chrétienne' entitled "Le Christ, seul espoir du monde" so that the title of this subsection in the second edition now reads 'Le royaume de Dieu'.

49. Compare the opening line of the section 'Participation de l'Église Catholique' in both editions. *Histoire I*, p. 180: "Le grief dogmatique premier et capital que la théologie catholique fait au Conseil œcuménique des Églises, vise la conviction de la plupart des Églises-membres, selon laquelle la vraie Église du Christ n'existe pas actuellement et substantiellement dans une communauté visible et historique". Compare *Histoire II*, p. 260:

Both the first chapter on the ecclesiology of the ecumenical movement and the second chapter on Catholic theology and ecumenism contain a subsection on the elements of the Church. Interestingly, Thils consistently uses the Latin expression *vestigia ecclesiae* in the first edition, which he places between brackets. His summary of the reflections on this theme in the WCC is similar in both editions. Even the section on the elements of the Church as an historical and a dogmatic problem in Catholic ecclesiology has been repeated in the second edition. As I will indicate later, Thils only wrote a few new pages concerning dogmatic reflection on the elements of the Church from a Catholic perspective, which he then added to the second edition.

The final section on *L'œuvre œcuménique* is much shorter in the first edition than in the revised edition, but the two subsections on irenism – making a distinction between false and excellent irenism – and on the instruction *Ecclesia catholica* (1949) and its reception among the other churches have been repeated in the 1963 edition.

There are many new insights to be found both in the papers that Thils wrote or edited in 1961 as part of his work for the Secretariat for Christian Unity and in texts he published in 1962 and 1963. This leads me to believe that Thils's ecumenical views underwent important changes during his most productive period as a member of the Secretariat, between July and December, 1961.

2. Ecumenical Insights Discovered by Thils during the Preparation of the Secretariat Papers which he Integrated in His 1962-1963 Writings

The most innovatory element in Thils' views on ecumenism – in the Secretariat papers he prefers the term ecumenicity/*oecumenicitas* – is that he defines it in terms of the catholicity of the Church[50]. Ecumenicity is only a form of the Church's catholicity, or, as Thils puts it in the revised version of *L'histoire doctrinale*, "actualising the catholicity of the Church is one of the major goals of Catholic ecumenism if not its only major goal"[51].

"À considérer la *Déclaration de Toronto* de manière stricte et formelle, il n'y a, de droit, point d'obstacle à l'entrée de l'Église catholique dans le Conseil œcuménique des Églises".

50. Thils provides more information on the significance of 'Oicumenè et Oicumenicos' in Antiquity, the Bible and the Church Fathers and the significance of the term 'Catholica' in *Votum de ecclesiae oecumenicitate*. The French translation of this text has been added to the second edition of *L'Histoire doctrinale*, pp. 222-227 and 262-265.

51. *Histoire II*, p. 275: "'Actualiser' la catholicité de l'Église est un des propos majeurs, sinon le propos majeur, de l' œcuménisme catholique".

Thils takes his reflection on the catholicity of the Church as his point of departure. Although the Church has sometimes been understood as a 'geographic universality', it also possesses a dimension of 'qualitative universality'. He explains the latter notion as follows, "the Church is not bound to any people, any race, any culture, any social state, in short, any particularism that would, in itself, make it impossible to realise an authentic universality"[52]. When one applies this to the ecclesiastical life, it implies that "the Church is not bound to any particularism of rite, liturgy, theological form, disciplinary custom, etc."[53]. He also formulates it in a positive way: "The Church can perfectly integrate a plurality of rites, liturgies, theological forms and disciplinary traditions"[54]. Referring to Papal statements on the Oriental Churches, Thils finally argues that "the integration of these different values is a quality and a richness, which contributes to the splendour of the Bride of Christ"[55]. These principles characterise the life of the churches in Europe, of the missionary churches[56], but also the relationship between the Catholic Church and the other Christian denominations.

> Catholicity, from this point of view, means concretely: first, that the Church
> is not bound by any particularism or any uniformity in matters of rite,

52. *De oecumenismo catholico et de opere conversionum*, p. 1: "Par universalité, on entend d'abord que l'Église ... doit se répandre jusqu'aux extrémités de la terre (universalité quantitative ou géographique). Mais cette universalité géographique possède dans la révélation un aspect complémentaire, d'ailleurs indispensable, signifiant que l'Église n'est liée à aucun peuple, aucune race, aucune culture, aucun état social bref, à aucun particularisme qui pourrait, de soi, rendre irréalisable une authentique universalité: dans le Christ, il n'y a ni Juif ni Gentil, ni Scythe ni Barbare, ni esclave ni homme libre (Col. 3,11) (universalité qualitative)".

53. *De oecumenismo catholico et de opere conversionum*, p. 2: "Cette même universalité revêt une nuance particulière lorsqu'elle s'applique au domaine proprement ecclésiastique. Elle signifie alors que l'Église n'est liée à aucun particularisme de rite, de liturgie, de forme théologique, de coutumes disciplinaires, etc.".

54. *De oecumenismo catholico et de opere conversionum*: "Au contraire, et de manière très positive, l'Église peut parfaitement – servatis servandis – intégrer une pluralité de rites, de liturgies, de formes théologiques, de traditions disciplinaires". I think it makes sense at this juncture to refer to Thils's 1967 book *Syncrétisme ou catholicité?* (n. 7) in which he makes the important distinction between 'particularism' and 'particularity' in the context of an historical overview of Catholic reflection on catholicity: "Moins la catholicité sera atteinte par les *particularismes* – lesquels sont toujours rétrécissants – plus elle pourra assumer de *particularités* légitimes: ce qui constitue un enrichissement". See THILS, *Syncrétisme ou catholicité?*, p. 80.

55. *De oecumenismo catholico et de opere conversionum*, p. 2: "Bien plus, d'après les déclarations des Souverains Pontifes relatives aux églises orientales, l'intégration de ces différentes valeurs, loin de constituer une faiblesse ou un pis-aller, est un bien et une richesse, qui ajoute à la splendeur de l'Epouse du Christ".

56. *Histoire II*, p. 269: "La diversité et la variété impliquées dans toute véritable catholicité trouvent un point d'application dans la vie de toute l'Église, tant dans celles qu'on appelle les 'Églises-mères' que dans les Jeunes Églises".

spirituality, theological system, religious sensibility, ecclesiastical discipline, except – as is evident – by what is required by the particular exigencies of its authentic unity; furthermore, that the Church can assume, and must integrate in its very unity, the plurality of forms and the diversity of nuances in matters of rite and piety, religious sensibility, theological systems, usages and customs, forms of Christian life and styles of ecclesial existence, which are present in the separated communities, on the condition that they are legitimate[57].

Should typically Protestant doctrinal, liturgical or disciplinary elements be introduced into the Catholic Church as a result of ecumenical dialogue, then this may be "a joyful, even necessary rectification", Thils wrote, even if others may have considered this a corruption of Catholicism[58].

Both catholicity/universality and ecumenicity are a property of the Church of Christ, constitute a gift of Christ to his Church, and are susceptible to growth and progression. Thils also argues that ecumenism is an urgent matter[59]. Its realisation is now easier than before because it is

---

57. *Histoire II*, p. 272: "Enfin, il nous faut dire un mot de cette diversité et de cette variété par rapport aux différentes communions chrétiennes non-romaines. La catholicité, *de ce point de vue*, signifie concrètement: d'abord, que l'Église n'est liée par aucun particularisme ni aucune uniformité en matière de rite, de spiritualité, de système théologique, de sensibilité religieuse, de discipline ecclésiastique, hormis évidemment ce qui est postulé par les exigences certaines de son unité authentique; ensuite, que l'Église peut assumer, et devrait intégrer, dans son unité même, la pluralité des formes et la diversité des nuances en matière de rite et de piété, de sensibilité religieuse, de systèmes théologiques, d'usages et de coutumes, de forme de vie chrétienne et de style d'existence ecclésiale, qui sont présents dans les communautés séparées, à condition qu'elles soient légitimes". In the section on 'Universalité et œcuménicité de l'Église' of Thils' report *De oecumenismo catholico et de opere conversionum* "l'œcuménicité, comme propriété de l'Église" has been defined in more or less the same words. A shorter form is contained in the *Votum de ecclesiae oecumenicitate*, p. 1: "Votum. In Constitutione de Ecclesia declaretur: Oecumenicitas est unicae uniusque ecclesiae Christi catholicitatis super orbem terrarum adimpletio et manifestatio, quae necessario secumfert, negative, et salvi omnibus genuinae unitatis requisitis certis, omnis formae particularismi et uniformitatis remotionem atque, positive, assumptionem et actualisationem, in ipsa ecclesiae unitate, omnis differenciationis et pluralitatis legitimae". After the Council, Thils repeated these lines in his commentary on *Unitatis Redintegratio*, on the occasion of UR 4. See G. THILS, *Le décret sur l'œcuménisme. Commentaire doctrinal*, Paris, Desclée, 1966, p. 86.
58. *Histoire II*, p. 273: "Certaines nouveautés affectant la vie des catholiques, du fait des rencontres 'œcuméniques', peuvent être une mise au point heureuse, une rectification bienfaisante, voire nécessaire". See also *Pour mieux comprendre* (n. 7), p. 11: "Alors, lorsque des catholiques exaltent l'importance de la Parole de Dieu, lorsqu'ils soulignent la place de la Bible dans la spiritualité chrétienne, lorsqu'ils insistent sur la Transcendance de Dieu et la gratuité de la grâce, lorsqu'ils attirent l'attention sur le rôle de la foi dans la vie sacramentelle, etc., etc., comment devons-nous interpréter ces démarches? Est-ce nécessairement introduire des traditions protestantes dans le catholicisme? Non. Ce peut être une œuvre tendant à 'actualiser' plus ou mieux l' œcuménicité la plus authentique de l'Église".
59. *De oecumenismo catholico, suggestiones practicae*, p. 2: "De ce fait, les conditions de l' œcuménisme pratique ont notablement changé. On a écrit jadis, et non sans de bonnes raisons, que les œcuménistes devaient être prudents dans leurs activités, afin de ne point

accepted that the separated communities already possess certain elements
of the Church. In *De oecumenismo catholico et de opere conversionum*,
he gives the example of baptism and eloquently concludes: "Thus it is
clear that a certain fundamental unity – real and sacramental – has been
maintained between the separated churches that has not been destroyed
by the separation and that can be considered as the fruit of virtual ecumenicity, which is always present in the Church of Christ"[60].

As a matter of fact, the papers also show an interesting evolution in the
choice of terminology, which contributes to a better understanding of the
hermeneutics of the Council. Instead of catholicity, one of the first papers,
De oecumenismo catholico et de opere conversionum, prefers to speak
about the universality of the Church. Thils explains this in a note: "We
speak about universality and not about catholicity in order to reserve a
more typical significance to the latter term. Catholicity can refer to a person or a truth, in virtue of their participation in the spiritual and total unity
of the mystery of the Church. For this reason, a believer is said to be
'catholic' (and not universal) and a truth is called 'catholic' (and not universal)"[61]. The minutes of the discussion anticipate the change of vocabulary: "Professor Thils proposes some modifications, in the first instance
with regard to a question of vocabulary. While the term 'universalitas' has
always been used a request has been made to employ the word 'catholicitas'"[62]. The *Votum de ecclesiae oecumenicitate* consequently substitutes

---

scandaliser les fidèles, qui comprendraient mal ces rencontres et ces rapprochements. Mais
aujourd'hui, les meilleurs d'entre les fidèles se scandalisent plutôt de toute forme de particularisme et de petitesse, qui couperait les catholiques et l'Église catholique des grandes initiatives mondiales, non seulement sociales, mais même religieuses. Aux yeux des meilleurs,
de ceux qui sont et font l'avenir, les raisons prudentielles de s'abstenir sont devenues des
raisons prudentielles d'agir. La vraie sagesse chrétienne exige qu'on en tienne compte".
These thoughts have been paraphrased in *Pour mieux comprendre les manifestations œcuméniques* (n. 7), p. 14, and repeated literally in *Syncrétisme ou catholicité?* (n. 7), p. 155.

60. *De oecumenismo catholico et de opere conversionum*, p. 6. Compare *De oecumenismo catholico. Suggestiones practicae*, p. 9: "En effet. L'ensemble de ceux qui participent à ces 'rencontres' sont des baptisés; ils ont entre eux une communauté d'existence ecclésiastique réelle et sacramentelle. De plus, ils possèdent aussi en commun des
valeurs chrétiennes considérables; les Écrits inspirés, une certaine tradition, des éléments
de ministère et de culte hiérarchique, etc. ... tous éléments qui sont peut-être inachevés,
mais non sans consistance chrétienne valable".

61. *De oecumenismo catholico et de opere conversionum*, p. 8: "Nous parlons de
l'universalité et non de la catholicité, pour conserver à ce dernier terme une signification
plus propre. Il y a catholicité, pour une personne ou pour une vérité, en vertu de leur participation à l'unité spirituelle et totale du mystère de l'Église. C'est pour cela qu'un fidèle
est dit 'catholique' (non universel) et qu'une vérité est dite 'catholique' (et non universelle)".

62. SECRETARIATUS AD CHRISTIANORUM UNITATEM FOVENDAM, *Sessio generalis mensis
augusti*, Feria III (August 29, 1961) ante meridiem, p. 1: "Le Professeur Thils propose

'catholicitas' for 'universalitas' and the *Directorii oecumenici prima delineatio* likewise states in n° 22 "de catholicitate Ecclesiae et de eius oecumenicitate". One of the headings employed in the revised edition of *L'histoire* doctrinale is entitled "catholicité et universalité".

Whereas Thils' proposal for a decree *De oecumenismo* (02/12/1961) still contained a definition of ecumenism in terms of catholicity[63], and whereas the final draft of *De oecumenismo catholico* had as its fourth and final paragraph 'Oecumenismi opus tamquam genuinae catholicitatis manifestatio et progressus'[64], the link between ecumenism and catholicity was no longer made in the draft that Thils had prepared for the Mixed Commission (05/02/1962) nor in the final version of this text (12/03/1963). Fortunately, the idea reappeared in the final text of *Unitatis redintegratio*, §4: "All in the church must preserve unity in essentials. But let all, according to the gifts they have received, maintain a proper freedom in their various forms of spiritual life and discipline, in their different liturgical rites, and even in their theological elaborations of revealed truth. In all things let charity prevail. If they are true to this course of action, they will be giving ever better expression to the authentic catholicity and apostolicity of the church".

Thils was also asked to reflect on the relationship between ecumenism and conversion. In *De oecumenismo catholico et de opere conversionum* he believes that Christians who unite themselves to the Catholic Church "represent for her a ferment of incomparable ecumenicity"[65]. By bringing their gifts, they contribute to the accomplishment of the ecumenicity of the Church. In the revised version of *L'histoire doctrinale*, Thils

---

quelques modifications et tout d'abord à propos d'une question de vocabulaire. Le mot 'universalitas' a toujours été employé. On a demandé d'employer le mot 'catholicitas'" (Fund Thils, 0551).

63. SECRETARIATUS AD CHRISTIANORUM UNITATEM FOVENDAM, *Pro decreto doctrinali elaborando "de oecumenismo" suggestiones*, p. 2 (V,b): "Oecumenicitas Ecclesiae forma est eius catholicitatis, qua significatur Ecclesiam quoad ritum, spiritualitatem, sensibilitatem religiosam, systemata theologica, formam vitae christianae, consuetudines ecclesiasticas, nullo particularismo nec ulla uniformitate ligari, immo pluralitatem et diversitatem in sua unitate assumere posse atque integrare debere".

64. SECRETARIATUS AD CHRISTIANORUM UNITATEM FOVENDAM, *De oecumenismo catholico (Decretum pastorale)*, Redactio ultima, mense Iulii 1962, p. 5. The text speaks about the interior renewal of the Church, about the conversion of the heart, but also about 'Oecumenismus ut catholicitatis exercitium', which starts with the following line: "Oecumenismus genuinae catholicitatis exercitium expostulat, immo in eo ipsa catholicitas vere actuatur. Adiuvat enim nos dignoscere et aestimare bona authentica apud fratres separatos, quae de se ad catholicam plenitudinem pertinent. Invitant nos incessanter catholicitatis notam plenius manifestare".

65. SECRETARIATUS AD CHRISTIANORUM UNITATEM FOVENDAM, *De oecumenismo catholico (Decretum pastorale)*, Redactio ultima, mense Iulii 1962, pp. 7-8: "Parmi les chrétiens séparés qui tournent leurs regards vers l'Église catholique, on peut distinguer deux orientations. Ceux à qui l'Esprit inspire de s'unir personnellement à l'Église

also inserted a section on ecumenism and conversions. He starts with a definition:

> One can speak of 'incorporation' or 'conversion' when 1) a Christian (or a group of Christians) passes over to the Catholic Church, 2) because he finds in this passage the concrete solution to a personal religious problem concerning the true way of eternal salvation, 3) without aiming directly nor expressly at the exercise of any form of influence, neither on the community from which he comes, nor on the Catholic Church into which he is incorporated (even if, as is evident, he always necessarily exercises a certain degree of influence de facto)[66].

Thereafter, however, he states that "the term 'conversion' is sometimes used in such an inappropriate way that one can ask whether truth and equity do not require us to proscribe it as a common theological formula"[67].

Another new element, which we find in *De oecumenismo catholico. Suggestiones practicae* in his 1962 article in *Nouvelle Revue Théologique* and in his 1967 book *Syncrétisme ou catholicité?*, is Thils' description of the three sectors of ecumenical encounter. The first sector pertains to social and humanitarian actions, such as the struggle against hunger, illiteracy, disease and economic inequality. The second deals with doctrinal initiatives aimed at conserving and promoting "the spiritualist conception of man and society", "the sense of God and of religion" and "specific and essential values: the Trinity, Christ God and Saviour, the Gospel and its message, the Church and the Last Supper"[68]. Thirdly, Thils speaks

---

catholique, et qui adoptent le type de christianisme qu'elle représente aujourd'hui. Ceux qui, également sous l'inspiration de l'Esprit désirent collaborer avec tous ceux qui œuvrent à épanouir l' œcuménicité de l'Église catholique, afin que celle-ci soit plus manifestement la demeure de tous leurs frères séparés. (…) Lorsque des chrétiens du second groupe s'unissent en fait personnellement à l'Église catholique, ils représentent pour celle-ci un ferment d' œcuménicité incomparable". Cf. also Thils' draft for a decree *De oecumenismo*, IIIb.

66. *Histoire II*, p. 292: "Il y a 'incorporation' ou 'conversion' lorsque (1) un chrétien (ou un groupe de chrétiens) passe à l'Église catholique, (2) parce qu'il trouve en ce passage la solution concrète d'un problème religieux personnel, à savoir concernant la vraie voie du salut éternel, (3) sans qu'il vise directement ni expressément à exercer quelque influence, ou sur la communauté d'où il vient, ou sur l'Église catholique dans laquelle il entre et est incorporé (bien que, évidemment, il exerce toujours en fait une certaine influence, nécessairement)".

67. *Histoire II*, p. 293: "Mais lorsque l'on considère l'ensemble des démarches au terme desquelles un chrétien non-romain entre dans l'Église catholique, le terme 'conversion' est parfois tellement impropre, que l'on peut se demander si la vérité et l'équité n'exigent pas de le proscrire comme formule théologique courante".

68. *De oecumenismo catholico. Suggestiones practicae*, p. 4: "Nous visons ici les initiatives et démarches d'ordre doctrinal visant:
– à conserver et promouvoir la conception spiritualiste de l'homme et de la société …

about activities related to prayer and liturgy. In his opinion, "numerous believers prefer not to wait until certain exceptions are tolerated, but until forms of prayer are maximally encouraged that can help Christians, or certain circles among them, on occasion to realise a prayerful unanimity"[69]. And he adds: "We must also educate believers to understand the true ecumenical and universal significance of common prayer, so that the desires of the 'better part' of believers are not always sacrificed to those of other Christians, certainly great in number, who remain, nevertheless, at a lower level of ecumenical and missionary sensibility"[70]. The document of 1961, though not the article in *Nouvelle Revue Théologique*, also contains a section on missionary activities and activities relating to evangelisation[71]. The three sectors to which he refers are also to be found in the final draft of the text of the Secretariat *De oecumenismo catholico (Decretum pastorale)*, under the headings 'Fratres separatos vere cognoscere oportet', 'Necessitas orationis pro unitate' and 'Cooperatio cum fratribus separatis'[72]. Thils also managed to include these topics in Chapter 2 of *De oecumenismo* as he was commissioned to revise the said chapter on behalf of the Mixed Commission.

3. Ecumenical Insights Formulated by Thils in the Secretariat Papers but no Longer Included in the 1962-1963 Documents

Under the heading 'Conditions of a true ecumenicity', Thils seemed to be aware of the tension between his general principle and Catholic ecclesiology and canon law. "A truly Christian ecumenicity must integrate

---

    – à maintenir et à promouvoir le sens de Dieu et de la 'religion' dans la vie et dans la société ...

    – à maintenir et à promouvoir les valeurs chrétiennes spécifiques et essentielles: la Trinité, le Christ Dieu et Sauveur, l'Évangile et son message, l'Église et la Cène".

69. *Pour mieux comprendre les manifestations œcuméniques* (n. 7), p. 15: "De nombreux fidèles attendent plutôt – compte tenu des réserves que nous signalerons immédiatement – non que soient tolérées certaines exceptions, mais que soient encouragées au maximum les formes de prières qui pourraient aider des chrétiens, ou certains cercles d'entre eux, à réaliser parfois une priante unanimité".

70. *De oecumenismo catholico. Suggestiones practicae*, p. 6: "Encore faudrait-il éduquer les fidèles à la vraie signification 'œcuménique' et 'universaliste' de la prière en commun, pour ne pas toujours sacrifier les vœux de la 'potior pars' des fidèles aux autres chrétiens, nombreux certes, qui en restent cependant à un niveau inférieur de sensibilité œcuménique et missionnaire". These lines have been repeated in Thils's article *Pour mieux comprendre les manifestations œcuméniques* (n. 7), p. 16.

71. Compare *De oecumenismo catholico. Suggestiones practicae*, pp. 8-9 with *Syncrétisme ou catholicité?* (n. 7), pp. 163-166.

72. Cf. Fund Thils, 519, pp. 3-5.

everything that Christ has imposed and given to his Church as constitutive elements *iure divino*, and must reject everything that Christ has considered to be incompatible with his will"[73]. Moreover, "a truly Christian ecumenicity must also integrate what the ecclesiastical authority imposes and determines to be an obligation for all believers *iure ecclesiastico*"[74]. As regards the latter category, however, Thils recognises that norms may be changed in view of new situations. He wonders, therefore, whether "one should not avoid imposing what is not indispensible on the separated Christians and allow them to enter into the house of the Lord with their own traditions, even if they are less perfect and developed under unfortunate circumstances" in order to remain faithful to the spirit of the Apostles[75]. In the revised version of *L'histoire doctrinale* Thils relativises this condition even further:

> Certainly, ecclesiastical organs exist that impose themselves by divine right: such as the episcopal body united and governed by the sovereign Pontiff. But what a diversity is possible in their concrete form! One might imagine the Pope surrounded by a very numerous curia, while the bishops preoccupy themselves only with their particular churches. One might imagine the Pope surrounded by a limited curia and one of a merely administrative order, advised by an episcopal commission that meets in Rome at regular intervals and allows regional episcopal conferences to be convened by each bishop in his particular Church for the benefit of pastoral care. Everything that might be considered 'accidental' can change the concrete 'physiognomy' of the Church considerably[76].

73. *De oecumenismo catholico et de opere conversionum*, p. 5: "L'œcuménicité véritablement chrétienne doit intégrer tout ce que le Christ a imposé et donné à son Église comme éléments constitutifs iure divino, et doit rejeter tout ce que le Christ a considéré comme incompatible avec sa volonté".

74. *De oecumenismo catholico et de opere conversionum*, p. 5: "L' œcuménicité véritablement chrétienne doit aussi intégrer ce que l'autorité ecclésiastique impose et fixe comme obligatoire pour l'ensemble des fidèles iure ecclesiastico".

75. *De oecumenismo catholico et de opere conversionum*, p. 6: "En vertu de cela, et à supposer même que la condition d'existence de l'Église catholique soit plus parfaite, on peut se demander légitimement si, pour être fidèle à l'esprit des Apôtres, on ne devrait pas éviter d'imposer aux chrétiens séparés ce qui n'est pas indispensable, et les laisser entrer dans la demeure du Seigneur, avec toutes leurs traditions propres assumables, fussent-elles moins parfaites et moins heureusement développées".

76. *Histoire II*, pp. 267-268: "Certes, il est des organes ecclésiastiques qui s'imposent de droit divin: tel le corps épiscopal uni et dirigé par le Souverain Pontife. Mais que de diversité possible dans leur condition concrète! On peut imaginer le Pape entouré d'une curie très nombreuse, les évêques étant amenés à se préoccuper seulement de leurs églises particulières. On peut imaginer le Pape, entouré d'une curie restreinte et d'ordre administratif, conseillé par une commission épiscopale siégeant à Rome à intervalles réguliers, et suscitant des conférences épiscopales régionales, pour le grand bien de l'œuvre pastorale à réaliser par chaque évêque dans son église particulière. Tout cela – qui est 'accidentel' – peut changer considérablement la 'physionomie' concrète de l'Église". In 1999, archbishop emeritus John Quinn expressed similar concerns in a book written in response to

Thils' description of ecumenical prayer and liturgy in *De oecumenismo catholico. Suggestiones practicae* contains two practical requests that he did not repeat later. Thils proposes the application of Canon 1258 par. 2 of the Old Code, which allows for "the passive or purely material presence" of Catholic believers in non-Catholic ceremonies for serious reasons to be extended to "all believers who have been invited to participate in ecumenical activities"[77]. Thils also suggests that the possibility of a certain intercommunion between Catholics and Orthodox should be reconsidered[78].

The same document also pays special attention to the role of the laity in the different sectors of the ecumenical movement. On occasion, Thils uses strong words that anticipate *Lumen gentium*: "A balanced ecclesiology demonstrates that the messianic message, the good news of the Gospel, the testimony of personal life and action have also been entrusted to the Christian people. (...) The existence of a magisterium does not exclude the existence of a general mission of the Christian people"[79]. Moreover, when Thils deals with *De iis ad quos opus oecumenicum spectat* in the outline for an ecumenical directory, he first speaks of the 'populus christianus' and only in the second instance of the 'pastores populi'[80].

Finally, the document also demonstrates that Thils was not fully enlightened *in ecumenicis* in the section on the 'abnormal' condition of

---

the invitation formulated by Pope John Paul VI in his encyclical *Ut unum sint* to offer him ideas on how the office of the bishop of Rome could be organised differently. See J.R. QUINN, *The Reform of the Papacy: The Costly Call to Christian Unity*, New York, Herder and Herder, 1999, and especially the concluding chapter on 'The Reform of the Roman Curia'.

77. *De oecumenismo catholico. Suggestiones practicae*, p. 7: "Ne serait-il pas possible d'élargir la portée du canon 1258 par. 2 en faveur de tous les fidèles amenés à participer à des activités œcuméniques, ou du moins à des groupes bien déterminés engagés dans des activités plus limitées?".

78. *De oecumenismo catholico. Suggestiones practicae*, p. 7: "En ce qui concerne les relations particulières entre catholiques et orthodoxes, il faudrait envisager le problème très concret d'améliorer les relations strictement sacramentelles, et notamment la possibilité d'une certaine inter-communion, au sens où l'on emploie ce terme dans les milieux œcuméniques".

79. *De oecumenismo catholico. Suggestiones practicae*, p. 4: "En ce qui concerne la pensée chrétienne comme telle, les laïcs chrétiens ont également une véritable responsabilité. Une ecclésiologie équilibré montre que c'est aussi au peuple chrétien qu'est confié le message messianique, la bonne nouvelle de l'Evangile, le témoignage de la vie personnelle et de l'action. Le rôle important et décisif joué par les pasteurs et chefs spirituels ne peut faire oublier la mission essentielle qui affecte tout ce peuple, comme tel, et donc chacun de ceux qui en font partie. Il y a là, pour chaque fidèle, une mission, une obligation, et donc un droit; l'existence d'un magistère n'exclut pas l'existence d'une mission générale du peuple chrétien".

80. *Directorii oecumenici prima delineatio*, p. 3.

the separated Christian communities. The norm, in his opinion, is that of "unity in unicity"[81].

4. Ecumenical Insights Exclusively Found in the 1962-1963 Documents

In the process of revising his *Histoire doctrinale*, Thils decided to add a comment on the distinction made in official Catholic documents between the Orthodox communities, which are indicated as "churches", and the communions that issued from the Reformation. Thils is aware that the latter communions "are very sensitive to this refusal. They do not understand that their communion, even when it is recognised as a 'means of salvation' may not be called 'Church' in a valid theological sense[82]. The Catholic conviction "that the Church of Christ, which the non-Roman communions already are in an incomplete way, can be nothing else than the Roman Catholic Church", equally sounds strange in the ears of representatives of other Churches. Thils calls this a *crux theologorum*[83].

In the same book, Thils also argues for the first time that the ecumenical task of Catholic theologians consists in the first instance in "cleaning out their own house". They have to take care that their house is not only 'open' for everyone, but 'inhabitable' by all. They have to strive "... to be truly catholic, so that all Christians may find and enjoy all legitimate forms of piety, spirituality, ecclesial existence therein and

81. *De oecumenismo catholico. Suggestiones practicae*, p. 10: "Quelles que soient la consistance et l'authenticité des valeurs chrétiennes présentes et actives – même par la grâce de Dieu, comme dit l'Instruction 'Ecclesia catholica' – dans les communautés chrétiennes séparées, leur statut théologique est toujours celui d'une condition a-normale, au sens de 'extra normam': l'idéal, en effet, est celui de l'unité dans l'unicité". In *Histoire II*, p. 257, Thils is much more careful: "Ces 'éléments d'Église' – on l'aura remarqué – peuvent parfois être dissociés du tout que constitue l'Église catholique. On peut posséder certains d'entre eux, sans posséder les autres. Quelques-uns de ces éléments peuvent être possédés à des degrés divers. Certes, c'est là une situation a-normale; mais la possession partielle peut être réelle et importante".
82. *Histoire II*, p. 230: "Les chrétiens non-romains, membres de ces communions, sont très sensibles à ce refus. Ils ne comprennent pas que leur communion, 'moyen de salut', ne puisse être appelée 'Église' en un sens théologique valable". The same idea is repeated in his commentary on UR 3. See THILS, *Le décret sur l'œcuménisme* (n. 57), p. 56.
83. *Histoire II*, p. 230: "Cette *crux theologorum* se manifeste dans toute son âpreté au moment où les théologiens catholiques, poursuivant leurs réflexions, affirment que cette Église du Christ, que 'sont' déjà les 'communions non-romaines' de manière 'inachevée', ne peut être que l'Église catholique romaine. Il n'y a en effet qu'une seule et unique Église du Christ. Cela sonne étrangement aux oreilles des chrétiens non-romains".

are not obliged to accept one particular form, even if it might be the best form"[84].

I want to conclude my analysis by quoting extensively the conclusion of the newly added section on 'ecumenism and conversions' in the second edition of *L'histoire doctrinale* because it perfectly renders Thils' position *in ecumenicis*, anno 1963:

> Can one say that the final goal of ecumenism is the unity of all Christians in the Catholic Church? *No*, if one understands by this that ecumenism is a tactical means to achieve the conversion of the interlocutor, by feigning encounters and dialogue. (…) The ecumenist accomplishes a specific and valuable task, which is formally distinct from that of "conversion". *Yes*, if one wants to say that the final goal, which Catholics envisage in all ecumenical endeavours, is the acceptance by all Christians of Catholic ecclesiology and, as a consequence, the union of all in the Catholic Church, but a Catholic Church with a new shape, as Vatican II made clear, i.e. with a new vital equilibrium, a new doctrinal equilibrium, a renewed physiognomy, in short: in the spiritual fullness of a catholicity that has been perfectly spread[85].

III. CONCLUSION

If one realises that the beautiful lines on catholicity in LG 13, which speak about the existence of legitimate forms of plurality within the Catholic Church, were only inserted in the final draft of *Lumen gentium* in 1964 as a complement to this paragraph's reflections on the Church's universality, then one cannot but be proud of Louvain theologian Gustave

---

84. *Histoire II*, p. 290: "Certains théologiens catholiques … ont donc constaté que leur tâche œcuménique consiste avant tout à 'balayer leur propre demeure'. (…) Dans quel sens? On peut y répondre en deux mots: pour que la 'maison de tous' soit, non seulement 'ouverte' à tous, mais 'habitable' par tous. En d'autres termes, pour que *tous* les chrétiens puissent y trouver et y épanouir *toutes* les formes légitimes de piété, de spiritualité, d'existence ecclésiale, et ne soient pas astreints à accepter *une* forme déterminée, fût-elle meilleure, pour être véritablement catholiques".

85. *Histoire II*, p. 296: "Cela étant, peut-on dire que le but ultime de l'œcuménisme est l'unité de tous les chrétiens dans l'Église catholique? *Non*, si l'on entend par là que l'œcuménisme serait un moyen tactique visant, sous le couvert de rencontres et de dialogue, la conversion de l'interlocuteur. Il faut être franc et loyal. L'œcuméniste accomplit une tâche *spécifique* et *valable*, qui est formellement distincte de celle de la 'conversion'. *Oui*, si l'on veut dire que l'étape finale envisagée par les catholiques dans toutes les démarches œcuméniques, c'est l'acceptation par tous les chrétiens de l'*ecclésiologie* catholique et, *en conséquence*, l'union de tous dans l'*Église* catholique, mais une Église catholique qu'ils voient déjà au terme de la 'mise au point', dont il a été question à l'occasion du Concile du Vatican II, c'est-à-dire, avec un nouvel équilibre vital, un nouvel équilibre doctrinal, une physionomie renouvelée, bref, dans la plénitude spirituelle d'une catholicité parfaitement épanouie". I find it remarkable that Thils made this reference to Vatican II in 1963, most probably even before the promulgation of the first decrees on December 4.

Thils for the role he played in preparaing such insights. His own attitude towards other Christian churches and the ecumenical movement also changed, as I hope to have made clear by comparing the 1955 and 1963 editions of his *Histoire doctrinale du mouvement œcuménique*. His growing ecumenical openness can be explained by the assignments he received as a member of the Secretariat for Christian Unity.

In the present contribution, I focused almost exclusively on the theological writings of Gustave Thils in the decade before the end of the Council: 1955-1965. I am well aware that Thils started to reflect on catholicity even while writing his dissertation[86]. The Louvain theologian was also dependent in part upon the ideas of other theologians when developing his reflections on catholicity and ecumenicity. One can find references in his work to de Poulpiquet's 1910 book on the notion of catholicity, to Congar's 1937 book on Catholic ecumenism and to an article on catholicity published by the Jesuit theologian Johannes Witte in *Gregorianum* in 1961[87]. A careful comparison of Thils' ideas with the reflections offered by these and other theologians, however, would necessarily exceed the limitations of this contribution.

It would also make sense to study the later writings of Thils in order to investigate the continuity of his reflections in the period immediately prior to the Council and immediately thereafter. I have quoted an important passage in the second edition of *L'histoire doctrinale* in which he assures representatives of other Christian churches that there is fortunately not much by way of divine right in the Catholic Church. It is possible, therefore, that its outlook may change in the future[88]. In 1963, Thils

---

86. Cf. G. THILS, *Les notes de l'Église dans l'apologétique catholique depuis la Réforme*, Gembloux, Duculot, 1937, and the article he published as an excerpt from this dissertation: *La notion de catholicité de l'Église à l'époque moderne*, in *ETL* 13 (1936) 5-73.

87. Cf. A. DE POULPIQUET, *La notion de catholicité*, Paris, 1910; Y. CONGAR, *Chrétiens désunis: Principes d'un œcuménisme catholique*, Paris, Cerf, 1937; J.L. WITTE, *Die Katholizität der Kirche*, in *Gregorianum* 42 (1961) 193-241. Thils was especially charmed by the following line in Witte's conclusion: "Uniformität in allem ist deshalb nicht das Ideal der Katholizität, sondern ihre Karikatur". (WITTE, *Die Katholizität der Kirche*, pp. 239-240) He quotes this line in *Histoire II*, p. 268 and in *Le décret sur l'œcuménisme* (n. 57), p. 80. In his 1967 book *Syncrétisme ou catholicité?* (n. 7) he even says: "Cette déclaration tranchante du R.P. J.L. Witte, professeur à l'Université grégorienne, est caractéristique des travaux récents qui sont consacrés à l'étude de la catholicité". As we have seen (cf. the citation *supra*, n. 84), however, Thils gave a much more nuanced answer to the question whether the final goal of ecumenism is the unity of all Christians in the Catholic Church than Witte, who stated in the same conclusion: "Die Kirche muß sich darstellen als die wirklich universale Kirche, die andere christlichte 'Kirchen' geheimnisvoll einschließt".

88. *Histoire II*, pp. 267-268. Cf. *supra*, n. 76.

still had to dream of a Church in which regional episcopal conferences would play an important role. His 1967 book *Syncrétisme ou catholicité?* contains a passage in which he repeats this dream, while at the same time being aware that church leaders tended to protect uniformity[89]. The elderly Thils was to continue untiringly, often on the occasion of new gatherings of the Synod of Bishops, to reflect on the tension between unity and diversity, and between universality and catholicity in the Church, and thus he tried to keep the memory of Vatican II alive[90].

Faculty of Theology   Peter DE MEY
Sint-Michielsstraat 6
B-3000 Leuven
Belgium

---

89. THILS, *Syncrétisme ou catholicité?* (n. 7), p. 98: "En fait, il faut reconnaître que les responsables de la vie catholique ont souvent protégé plus fermement l'uniformité des institutions et des rites qu'il n'ont garanti leur naturelle et heureuse diversité. Est-ce par crainte des excès? En vertu d'une certaine pédagogie de l'obéissance? Par facilité pratique? Ou peut-être pour toutes ces raisons à la fois? Les interventions conciliaires sur la nécessité de 'décentralisation' et d''internationalisation' des instances supérieures de l'Église catholique montrent qu'on attend quelque diversité. (...) Et les conférences épiscopales de chaque région seront l'instrument d'une meilleure réalisation de la catholicité authentique".

90. Useful titles include: *Unité catholique ou centralisation à outrance?*, Louvain, Église vivante, 1969; *L'Après-Vatican II: Un nouvel âge de l'Église?* (Cahiers de la Revue théologique de Louvain, 13), Louvain-la-Neuve, Publications de la Faculté de Théologie, 1985; *Le prochain Synode extraordinaire des évêques (Rome, 25 nov. – 8 déc. 1985)*, in *Revue théologique de Louvain* 16 (1985) 275-287 and *Le Synode d'évêques: Image de 'l'unité dans l'Église' ou de 'la communion qu'est l'Église'?*, in *Revue théologique de Louvain* 18 (1987) 212-221. Especially since the publication of the Motu proprio *Apostolos suos* (1998), which seems to restrict the application of (effective) episcopal collegiality to decisions of the entire college of bishops, the current generation of ecclesiologists has become more critical about the relationship between unity and diversity, and between universality and catholicity in the Catholic Church. See, for example, my own article *Is Small Always Synodal? The Episcopal Conference in Belgium and the Netherlands*, in A. MELLONI – S. SCATENA (eds.), *Synod and Synodality: Theology, History, Canon Law and Ecumenism in New Contact. International Colloquium Bruges 2003* (Christianity and History. Series of the John XXIII Foundation for Religious Studies in Bologna, 1), Münster, LIT, 2005, 435-460 and *Is 'Affective' Collegiality Sufficient? A Plea for a More 'Effective' Collegiality of Bishops in the Roman Catholic Church and Its Ecumenical Implications*, in *Friendship as an Ecumenical Value: Proceedings of the International Conference Held on the Inauguration of the Institute of Ecumenical Studies (Lviv, 11-15 June 2005)*, Lviv, Ukrainian Catholic University Press, 2006, 132-153.

LUCIEN CERFAUX AND THE PREPARATION
OF THE SCHEMA *DE FONTIBUS REVELATIONIS*

I. INTRODUCTORY REMARKS

On August 6 1960, Henri van Waeyenbergh, theologian and rector of the Catholic University of Leuven[1], wrote these words to Pope John XXIII:

> Nuperrime, maximo gaudeo affecti, in diario *Osservatore Romano*, legimus benigna Sanctitatis Tuae dignitatione quosdam magistros ex nostra S. Theologiae Facultate designatos esse ut sodales aut consultores Pontificiae Commissionis Theologicae II Concilio Oecumenico Vaticano parando[2].

The impetus for his 'enthusiastic' correspondence was that on July 12, official letters of nomination had been sent to the future members and consultors of the preparatory Theological Commission [TC]. No fewer than five Belgians received such a letter[3]. Their names were Arthur Janssen (Leuven emeritus professor of Moral Theology); Gerard Philips (Leuven professor of dogmatics); Édouard Dhanis (study prefect of the Gregorian University); Philippe Delhaye (professor at the University of Lyon) and Lucien Cerfaux (emeritus professor of Biblical exegesis in Leuven)[4]. All

---

1. On rector van Waeyenbergh, see a.o. J. COPPENS – A. DESCAMPS, *Son Excellence Mgr. van Waeyenbergh. In memoriam*, in *ETL* 67 (1971) 553-560, and A. DESCAMPS, *In memoriam H. van Waeyenbergh, Universitatis catholicae lovaniensis Rector magnificus 1891-1871*, Leuven, 1971.

2. Letter kept in the Archivio Segreto Vaticano (ASV), Città del Vaticano: Fund Conc. Vat. II, 371. The official nomination list for the TC was published on the front page of the *Osservatore Romano* on July 18 of 1960 (See *Oss. Rom.* 100/166, 18-19 luglio 1960, p. 1).

3. Transcripts of these letters, as well as files containing biographical background information on the nominees in the list of July 18, are found in the ASV: Conc. Vat. II, 371.

Also on the provenance of the Commission members, see A. INDELICATO, *Formazione e composizione delle commissioni preparatorie*, in G. ALBERIGO – A. MELLONI (eds.), *Verso il Concilio Vaticano II (1960-1962): Passaggi e problemi della preparazione conciliare* (Testi e ricerche de scienze religiose. Nuova serie, 11), Bologna, Il Mulino, 1993, p. 67 distinguishes in his schedules on the basis of birthplace vs. work place.

Cfr. G. CAPRILE, *Il Concilio Vaticano II*, Paoline, Alba, I, p. 210: According to Caprile Dhanis was also nominated in July 1960.

4. A biographical survey of Cerfaux's life can be found in J. COPPENS, *La carrière et l'œuvre scientifique de Monseigneur Lucien Cerfaux*, in *ETL* 65 (1969) 8-44.

were honored with their nominations and without exception they promised
to contribute their best efforts to the Council's preparations[5].

From that point on, many people became increasingly interested in the
activities going on in Rome as to the preparations of Vatican Council II,
and the interest went beyond academic and ecclesiatical circles. One could,
for instance, read the many reports of Baron Poswick – the Belgian Ambassador at the Holy See – informing the Belgian Minister of Foreign Affairs
on any Belgian conciliar activity. On December 15, 1961 Poswick writes:

> La commission théologique, qui est divisée en 5 sous-commissions, est
> l'épine dorsale des autres commissions. Pas moins de quatre Belges sont
> membres de cette commission, et un compatriote figure parmi les consulteurs.

However interesting all of this may be, the scope of our present study
will limit itself strictly to the actions taken by Lucien Cerfaux during this
preparatory period. Attempting to grasp Cerfaux's influence at Vatican II
one is immediately struck by a certain ambiguity. On the one hand, when
historiographical literature on the Council offers lists of influential
Belgians, Cerfaux is omnipresent[6]. Moreover, in exegetical publications,

5. To give an impression, some citations:
Letter from A. Janssen to A. Ottaviani, August 13 1960, in ASV: Conc. Vat. II, 732:
"Eminentissime ac Reverendissime Domine, ex toto corde gratias ago Eminentiae Vestrae
pro congratulationibus mihi missis occasione adnumerationis meae inter Consultores Commissionis Theologicae ad praeparandas Constitutiones doctrinales Patribus futurae Synodi
Vaticanae Secundae proponendas. Pro posse libenter fungar officio sic mihi oblato et col-
laborationem praestabo ad illustrandas et enucleandas quaestiones circa quas Commissio
me interpellare opportunum judicabit".
Letter from P. Delhaye to Ottaviani, August 15, 1960, in ASV: Conc. Vat. II, 732:
"Quomodo dicam quam magnus honor mihi sit ut sim adnumeratus inter Consultores Commissionis Theologicae Concilii Vaticani II. Diu saepe ut 'servus inutilis' laboravi, nixus
fidelitati vocationis et muneris; jam hodie mercedem accipio quam nunquam optare aude-
ram. Certe indignus sum talis electionis et in hac volo praesertim videre signum benig-
nitatis Summi Pontificis et Tuae Eminentiae benevolentiae erga me. Animus meus est
respondendi huic honori ex totis viribus meis ita ut Veritas effulgeat in proximo Concilio
definita ab Ecclesia docente".
Letter from É. Dhanis to A. Ottaviani, August 4, 1960, in ASV: Conc. Vat. II, 732:
"Eminentissime Reverendissime, Ante duos dies, praedicans exercitia spiritualia in Bel-
gio, accepi litteras (Prot., N.4/60) quibus eminentia Vestra me certiorem facit de officiis
quae mihi incumbent ut membro Commissionis theologicae futuri Concilii Oecumenici.
Gratias agens pro congratulationibus Eminentiae Vestrae, libentissime promitto me, pro
viribus meis, muneri meo diligenter operam daturum esse.
Inter quaestiones tractandas eae quibus inde a multis annis in primis studii sunt omnes
illae 'De fontibus revelationis'. Caeteras, quae etiam a Summo Pontifice indicatae sunt, non
ignorari, easque, ut meum officium est, amplius explorabo".
6. See for instance the one in P. Poswick, *Un journal du Concile: Vatican II vu par
un diplomate belge. Notes personelles de l'Ambassadeur de Belgique près le Saint-Siège
(1957-1968), et Rapports au Ministère des Affaires Étrangères*. Edités par R.F. Poswick
et Y. Juste, Paris, de Guibert, 2005, pp. 52-54.

handbooks, etc., one finds multiple references to Cerfaux's excellent work and influence. Yet no one really appears to have studied this theologian and his work at large. It appears that Cerfaux's outstanding reputation (for example, as a 'rare progressive member' of the preparatory Theological Commission) is wider spread than the actual knowledge of his work[7].

Another preliminary observation is that our topic does not simply deal with Cerfaux, but with Cerfaux's contribution to the redaction of the schema *De fontibus revelationis*. This has some consequences regarding the orientation of this study. Sharply contrasting with Cerfaux's writings and career, this schema had a negative reputation, largely due to its conciliar reception in 1962. The discussion of it during the Council's first session – well described under the title, "the first doctrinal clash"[8] – is well known and has had ample impact on later conciliar developments. In a book on the overall Belgian participation to the Council, it is worth noting that perhaps the most important and most influential words of opposition to the Revelation schema were spoken in the St. Peter's Basilica by yet another Belgian: Mgr. De Smedt[9], on November 19, 1962. De Smedt, who, during a meeting only few days before, had been appointed by Cardinal Augustin Bea to present the council Fathers with the opposition of the Secretariate for Christian Unity (SCUF) to the schema[10], made

7. See for instance R. BURIGANA, *La Bibbia nel Concilio: La redazione della costituzione 'Dei Verbum' del Vaticano II* (Testi e ricerca di scienze religiose. Nuova serie, 21), Bologna, Il Mulino, 1998.

8. G. RUGGIERI, *The First Doctrinal Clash*, in G. ALBERIGO – J.A. KOMONCHAK (eds.), *History of Vatican II*. Volume II: *The Formation of the Council's Identity. First Period and Intersession. October 1962-September 1963*, Maryknoll, NY, Orbis; Leuven, Peeters, 1995, 233-266.

9. More information on De Smedt's conciliar activity is found in M. LAMBERIGTS, *Mgr. Emiel-Jozef De Smedt, bisschop van Brugge en het Tweede Vaticaans Concilie*, in *Collationes* 28 (1998) 281-326. See also L. DECLERCK, *Msgr. De Smedt and the Second Vatican Council*, in A. GREILER – L. DE SAEGER (eds.), *Emiel-Jozef De Smedt, Papers Vatican II Inventory. With a preface by L. Declerck* (Instrumenta Theologica, 22), Leuven, Bibliotheek van de Faculteit der Godgeleerdheid, 1999, XV-XXIII.

10. The minutes of the meeting of November 16, 1962, in CSVII: Fund De Smedt, 532, p. 3, state that: "Son Éminence pense que S.E. Mgr. De Smedt pourrait intervenir à ce sujet en Congrégation Générale. S.E. Mgr. De Smedt demande s'il doit parler au nom du Secrétariat. S.E. Mgr. Heenan pense que oui". Interestingly enough, during that same meeting it was suggested to call upon the expertise of Cerfaux in studying de fontibus: See p. 4.: "Chan. Thils demande si l'on peut faire appel à d'autres periti. Mgr Willebrands pense que l'on pourrait demander la collaboration de Mgr. Cerfaux pour la IIe. sous-commission [concerning the chapter De Sacra Scriptura inspiratione, inerrantia, compositione litteraria]".

clear that the TC had refused to cooperate with the SCUF in the preparation of the schemata[11]. In addition – and consequently – Bishop De Smedt's speech[12] (which was itself based largely on a report regarding the ecumenical value of various schemata by Leuven theologian G. Thils[13]) reproached the TC for having written a document that was too unilateral, too Roman in style, and virtually incapable taking into consideration the feelings of non-catholic Christianity. The speech was applauded and immediately drew international press attention[14] leaving De Smedt to

11. It needs to be observed that this was actually only true on an official level, whereas the secretaries of the TC and the SCUF (S. Tromp and J. Willebrands, both Dutchmen) as early as March 1961, had kept an ongoing correspondence throughout the preparatory period, and constantly informed each other on steps taken by their respective bodies, all the while exchanging texts. To illustrate, see for instance A. VON TEUFFENBACH, *Konzils-tagebuch Sebastian Tromp s.j. Mit Erläuterungen und Akten aus der Arbeit der theologischen Kommission.* Vol. I/1-2: *1960-1962*, Rome, Editrice Gregoriana, 2006, on May 1, 1962:
"Die 1 Maii: fer. III in festo S. Josephi.
Vacat. in S. Off. Continuo compositionem relationis Consessus plenarii Martialis. Mane visitatio facta a Secretario pro Unione Christianorum, Mons. J. Willebrands hora 10-11,45. Mihi tradit relationem *'de Traditione et de S. Scriptura factam a subcommissione XIII suae Commissionis.* Dixi me cum n. 6 Voti (pag. 25) consentire non posse. Vespere continuo redactionem relationis". Immediately the next day we find a letter from Willebrands to Tromp, in ASV: Conc. Vat. II, 732, saying: "Reverendissimo Padre, Mi pregio inviare alla Paternità Vostra Reverendissima tre copie, qui unite, della Relazione elaborata da una speciale sottocommissione di questo segretariato sull'argomento: De Traditione et Sacra Scriptura. Le conclusioni di detta relazione sono state accettate unanimiter nella seduta plenaria tenutasi a Roma il giorno 9 marzo scorso". To this Tromp has added a handwritten note, reading: "Resp. 10 maii 62: Doleo relationem ad me missam, gravem in materia gravi non prius ad haec cognitionem pervenum".
12. Text published in *AS* I/3, pp. 184-187, the original notes are found in CSVII: Fund De Smedt, 576.
13. See Gustave Thils', *De 'adspectu oecumenico' doctrinae huius schematis, et ceterorum schematum*, in CSVII: Fund De Smedt, 578. This document bears Thils' handwritten remark: "d'où nécessité de faire appel à des Comm. Mixtes avec le Secrétariat d'Unité".
On the exact relationship between Thils' report and De Smedt's speech, see M. VELATI, *Le Secrétariat pour l'Unité des Chrétiens et l'origine du décret sur l'œcuménisme (1962-1963)*, in M. LAMBERIGTS, et al. (eds.), *Les commissions conciliaires à Vatican II* (Instrumenta Theologica, 18), Leuven, Bibliotheek van de faculteit der Godgeleerdheid, 1996, 181-204, p. 185; and more elaborate [with text comparisons] in K. SCHELKENS, *De Commissio mixta de divina Revelatione. Een bronnenkritisch onderzoek naar de werkzaamheden van de gemengde commissie: November 1962-Maart 1963* [Onuitgegeven Licentiaatsverhandeling. K.U.Leuven], Leuven, 2001.
14. In *Le Figaro* of November 20, R. Millet writes: "L'intervention la plus forte et la plus efficace a été celle de Mgr. De Smedt (Bruges) qui, considéré comme un des évêques 'novateurs' a parlé des chrétiens non catholiques dans les termes les plus émouvants". Equally, *Il Tempo* praised De Smedt's intervention, saying that: "Uno dei Padri conciliari si è espresso in termini di rispetto e comprensione tali verso i fratelli separati da esser largamente applaudito dai Padri conciliari, indipendentemente dall'opinione di ciascuno riguardo la formulazione sulle Fonti della Rivelazione, attualmente all'esame del Concilio". Also the Belgian newspaper *De Standaard* reacted positively and the redaction of

receive letters of felicitation from theologians such as Thomas Becquet[15] and Charles Moeller[16].

One more remark, then: through the study of preparations for *De fontibus* one gets the impression – as did many Council fathers during the first session – that a good deal of contemporary church historiographers were not well acquainted with the redaction history and chronology of the schema on the sources. Accordingly, predicates like 'unilateral', 'roman', 'neo-scholastic', 'void of any sense of history', are easily adopted from the Council's 1962 debate, without any critical survey or study of the schema's background[17].

The Clergy Monthly promptly asked De Smedt's approval to publish his speech in an English translation. See CSVII: Fund De Smedt, 584.

15. CSVII: Fund De Smedt, 581.
16. CSVII: Fund De Smedt, 582.
17. By means of illustration, we quote just a few examples: H. HOPING, *Theologischer Kommentar zur Dogmatischen Konstitution über die göttliche Offenbarung*, in P. HÜNERMANN – B.J. HILBERATH (eds.), *Herders theologischer Kommentar zum Zweiten Vatikanischen Konzil*, Bd. 3, Freiburg – Basel – Wien, Herder, 2005, 695-735, pp. 720-721: "Das Schema De fontibus Revelationis, das insgesamt von einer 'antimodernistischen Geistesart' geprägt ist" [...] "Das Offenbarungsschema ist von einem Begriff der Offenbarung bestimmt, den man als 'instruktionstheoretisch' bezeichnet hat: Offenbarung wird als Mitteilung (instructio) übernatürlicher Glaubenswahrheiten verstanden". – B. VAWTER, *Biblical Inspiration* (Theological Resources), Londen, Hutchinson, 1972, pp. 143-144: "... the commission that prepared it, composed as that was almost exclusively of curial employees and of those who could be presumed to share their outlook on the Church and its orthodoxy. Phrased in the language of textbook scholasticism, it was negative, defensive, anathematizing, having little to say that needed saying anything anew and regarding with unconcealed suspicion most of the serious study that had been devoted to those subjects with which it professed to be concerned". – T.R. CURTIN, *Historical Criticism and the Theological Interpretation of Scripture: The Catholic Discussion of a Biblical Hermeneutic: 1958-1983*, Rome, s.l., 1987, p. 46: "The schema *De fontibus revelationis* took a negative stance towards modern exegetical methods and the study of literary forms. It ignored recent progress in biblical criticism and returned to earlier positions". – B.D. DUPUY, *Historique de la Constitution*, in ID. (ed.), *Vatican II: La Révélation divine* (Unam Sanctam, 70a), Paris, Cerf, 1968, 61-117: "Le schéma sur les sources de la révélation fut préparé sans tenir compte des oppositions, ou même des questions que pourraient soulever à son sujet les autres organismes intéressés par la question de la Révélation et de la Tradition (Commissions conciliaires, Secrétariat pour l'unité, Institut biblique, Facultés de théologie, etc.)". – BURIGANA, *La Bibbia nel Concilio* (n. 7), p. 444: "Nella formazione di un'opposizione al De fontibus e al progetto dogmatica a esso sotteso apparve chiara l'esistenza di una pluralità di opzioni e al tempo stesso l'impossibilità di accetare l'identificazione di una scuola teologica con il pensiero della chiesa universale". – H. SAUER, *Erfahrung und Glaube: Die Begründung des pastoralen Prinzips durch die Offenbarungskonstitution des II. Vatikanischen Konzils* (Würzburger Studien zur Fundamentaltheologie, 12), Frankfurt am Main – Berlin – Bern – New York – Paris – Vienna, Lang, 1993, p. 23: "Im Gesamtkonzept schlägt sich ein deutlicher Positivismus nieder, der sich weniger an Begründungszusammenhängen, sondern vielmehr an einer juridischen eindeutigen Statuierung van Faktizitäten, als Legitimationsgrundlage interessiert zeigt. So fällt sowohl die Frage nach der Offenbarung als solcher aus, als auch die Frage nach der geschichtlichen

Given all of the above, we cannot describe Cerfaux's activities in the redaction process of *De fontibus* without simultaneously offering a renewed reconstruction of the various stages of that process. This will both lead to a better understanding of Cerfaux's place and role in the general framework and allow us to make a more precise and more nuanced judgment more precise and more nuanced concerning the TC's editorial activities.

II. MEMBERSHIP OF THE PREPARATORY THEOLOGICAL COMMISSION

1. Membership Nominations in the TC

The first, and preliminary, question to be addressed when studying Cerfaux's preconciliar contribution is: How and why did Leuven professors like Cerfaux and Philips end up becoming members of the preparatory Theological Commission[18]? In this account, the month of July 1960, mentioned earlier, is already too late as a starting point for our survey. When studying the Theological Commission, and particularily when trying to understand why certain persons became nominated as commission members or consultors, it is necessary to study the prior period. In fact, the election process for the TC members had already begun in the earliest days of June 1960. It is commonly known that on June 5,

---

Herkunft". – RUGGIERI, *The First Doctrinal Clash* (n. 8), p. 233: "especially the week which was devoted to discussion of the schema on the sources of revelation, represented a turning point that was decisive for the future of the Council and therefore for the future of the Catholic Church itself: the turn from the Church of Pius XII, which was still essentially hostile to modernity and in this respect the heir to the nineteenth century restoration, to a Church that is a friend to all human beings, even children of modern society, its culture, its history".

18. Interesting on the account of their nominations is the comment by POSWICK, *Un journal du Concile* (n. 6), p. 53: "La vieille méfiance des Universités pontificales de Rome (et surtout de la Grégorienne) vis-à-vis de Louvain paraît s'être manifestée dans le fait que, comme par hasard, les deux éminents professeurs de Louvain membres de la commission de théologie sont les seuls de notre Université qui ont conquis leurs grades aux Universités pontificales. Mais je ne pense pas que Louvain s'alarmera: le représentant de l'Université Grégorienne à la commission de théologie (préfet d'études de cette université) est belge aussi: c'est le R.P. Dhanis de la compagnie de Jésus. Il est certes intéressant de retrouver ainsi nos compatriotes dans tous les camps, et de constater sur un exemple concret la place nullement négligeable qu'ils occupent autour du Vatican".

Given that the process of electing members and consultors to the preparatory TC has not as yet been studied in detail, this process would in itself require more study. This article however, will limit itself to the details providing background for Cerfaux' story. Nevertheless, it needs to be mentioned that we partly rely on the work done by Mss. Von Teuffenbach on this account.

the *Motu proprio Superno Dei nutu* was promulgated, instigating a series of preparatory commissions, among which the TC[19] figured as the top-ranking one. Less noted is that the day after this promulgation, Cardinal Alfredo Ottaviani was informed of his nomination as Commission president[20]. This early nomination implies that Ottaviani had an entire month left to gather future commission members.

Then on June 18, Dutch Jesuit Father Sebastian Tromp mentions in his diary that he received word of his nomination as TC secretary through Ottaviani (which was rather late, since even prior to his own nomination as president, Ottaviani had sent a letter to General Secretary Felici advising to appoint Tromp as TC secretary, mentioning Rosaire Gagnebet as his second choice[21]). Along with the news Ottaviani informs Tromp of the nomination of seven initial TC members. Since official procedures were lacking at that stage, Ottaviani gathered a working group of theologians all somehow tied to the Holy Office?[22]. These first members were Dino Staffa, Paul Philippe, Antonio Piolanti, Franz Hürth, Rosaire Gagnebet, Salvatore Garofalo and Carlo Balič[23]. The makeup of this group undergoes minor changes throughout the process of the first meetings, yet at stake here is that this team developed its particular election procedure for the future commission members. In brief: on June 24 another meeting was

19. Strikingly, the Theological Commission was the sole commission to already receive a 'task-description': "Commissio theologica, cuius erit quaestiones ad Scripturam Sacram, Sacram Traditionem, fidem moresque spectantes perpendere et pervestigare". See *AD* I/1, p. 95; or *AAS* 52 (1960) 433-437, esp. p. 435.

20. See ASV: Conc. Vat. II, 371: letter from Vatican State Secretary Tardini to General Secretary Felici, on the nomination of Ottaviani as president; and subsequently ASV: Conc. Vat. II, busta 736: letter from Tardini to Ottaviani.

21. See ASV: Conc. Vat. II, 371: letter from Ottaviani to Felici proposing Tromp as Secretary, dated June 3rd 1960. This suggestion may have had as background that Tromp was one of those that had been invited by Pope Pius XI to prepare the re-enactment of the First Vatican Council in G. CAPRILE, *Pio XI e la riprese del Concilio Vaticano*, in ID., *Il Concilio Vaticano II*. Vol. I/1: *L'annunzio e la preparazione*, Rome, Civiltà Cattolica, 1960, 3-35.

22. Tromp's note on this account appears somewhat strange, given that already on June 13, Franz Hürth reports of a first meeting of the TC with Tromp among those present. See APUG: Vat. II, Diary Hürth, 17,12: "13.VI.1960. Finita ordinaria consultatione, invitati per Card. Ottaviani convenerunt: Assessor (Parente) Staffa. Paolo Philippe O.P. (secr. Congr. Relig.), Tromp, Balic, Ciappi, Piolanti – Card. Ottaviani communicavit cum praesentibus: agi de constituenda 'Ia Commiss. Theol.', segretarium huius nominatum esse P. Seb. Tromp S.J. Nunc agendum esse de personis determinandis tq 'membra', tq 'consultores'".

23. See VON TEUFFENBACH (ed.), *Konzilstagebuch Sebastian Tromp* (n. 11), June 18, 1960: "Emus Praeses communicat Secretario eius nominationem. Nominatio membrorum nondum est officialis. Sed pro primis laboribus ut certum supponitur inter membra esse Mgr. Staffa, R.P. Philippe o.p., Mgr. Piolanti, R.P. Hürth, R.P. Gagnebet, Mgr. Garofalo, R.P. Balič (ass. et comm. nolunt interesse)".

held. Based on an initial list compiled by the Holy Office chancellory (in
fact, the list was probably prepared by Balič[24]) – and regarding the fact
that the electors themselves would naturally take part in the commission
– every single member was asked to suggest some new names, and with
their *placet* or *non-placet* make known their approval or veto regarding
the names already listed, at the same time keeping in mind that various
religious orders and schools should have a well balanced representation
on the commission. The resulting lists[25] then served as common ground
for a more general list, on the basis of which later election rounds were
held. Already on June 24, Cerfaux's name was found on the general list,
never to be omitted – unlike the names of compatriots like Charue, Suenens, Belpaire, and others[26]. Then, in the first days of July 1960 a closing election round took place based on new, and more recent short lists
of the TC members who were asked to hand in no more than 9 names[27].
In this phase it will be Piolanti[28] and Verardo who support Cerfaux.
It seems this support was adequate enough to support his candidacy, and
in the list that was sent to Felici for papal approval, Cerfaux is the first
name to appear among the persons categorised under item c.: *dalle università e studiosi di teologia ...*

---

24. It was actually accompanied by document with the title: Memorandum Rev.m. Patris
Carl. Balič pro reunione 24 Junii 1960, which indicated some criteria for its composition,
such as also choosing non-Romans, choosing specialists out of all branches of theology,
choosing only people holding a doctoral degree, persons who are personally known and
therefore guaranteed to be trustworthy, electing some names from the silent churches. See
ASV: Conc. Vat. II, 736.

25. See ASV: Conc. Vat. II, 736, 60.

26. The Belgian names mentioned were: Suenens, Charue, Lottin, Philips, Janssen,
Cerfaux, van den Eynde. The fact that Balic had been involved in the redaction of this list
can partially illumate why these Belgians were inserted, since many of them were known
to him from his study period in Leuven (e.g., Charue), and others through collaboration
in the organisation of colloquia (Philips) or as colleagues (van den Eynde). See CSVII: Acts
of the Leuven Faculty, 1910-1947, pp. 162-170. Balič obtained the STD degree in Leuven,
and was admitted as a candidate for the Magister's title, yet this project was left unfinished.

27. See letter from Tromp to TC-members, June 28, 1960, in ASV: Conc. Vat. II, 736:
"Le invio la lista delle persone prese in considerazione per la scelta dei membri della
Commissione dottrinale e dei Consultori. Poiché è stato stabilito che il numero dei membri della Commissione non debba superare i trenta, e, poiché conviene che gli Arcivescovi
e Vescovi siano membri della Commissione, questa verrà così composta: a) 13 tra i
Arcivescovi e Vescovi; b) 8 attuali membri della Commissione del S. Offizio; c) 9 da
scegliersi tra i nominativi che Le vengono inviati. Pertanto, basterà che Ella indichi quali
sono i Nove da prescegliersi come membri fra tutti i nomi delle varie categorie, inten-
dendosi scelti i restanti come Consultori. Le sarò grato se vorrà inviarmi la riposta non più
tardi del 1 Luglio 1960".

28. See Piolanti's letter to Tromp, dated July 1, 1960, in ASV: Conc. Vat. II, 736:
"Rev.mo Padre, mi onore transmetterLe l'elenco dei teologi, che io ritengo meritevoli di
appartenere alla Commissione per il Concilio Vaticano II".

Verardo's reasons for supporting Cerfaux remain unclear, which is not the case with Piolanti. Antonio Piolanti – rector of the Lateran university[29] – had invited the Leuven exegete to teach classes on Pauline theology at the Lateran University in the academic year of 1960-1961[30]. Both men carried on an ongoing correspondence, and Piolanti was assured of Cerfaux's presence in Rome during the conciliar preparations – a practical argument that can hardly be neglected. It is not surprising, therefore, that Cerfaux, immediately upon reception of his nomination letter, would not only write letters of his gratitude to Ottaviani, Tromp and Felici[31], but also would write the following to the Lateran rector:

> Je dois sans aucun doute vous savoir une grande reconnaissance pour l'honneur qui m'est fait d'être associé de si près à la préparation du Concile œcuménique. J'ai surtout conscience de l'importance de la charge que l'Église nous confie et j'ai la volonté de me donner très sérieusement à la tâche qui sera la nôtre. Selon mes prévisions, j'assisterai régulièrement aux réunions de la commission théologique [...][32].

Beside this, other significant factors made Cerfaux an appropriate candidate. Like Albin van Hoonacker – one of his Leuven predecessors during the Modernist crisis[33] – Cerfaux had been appointed consultor to the Pontifical Biblical Commission. A few years after his appointment in February, 1941, Cerfaux had written a well-read and well-balanced commentary on Pius XII's *Divino afflante Spiritu*[34]. This position offered him

---

29. Which, in fact had only recently – May 17, 1959 – been promoted from Lateran Seminary to the rank of Pontifical University. See S. PACIOLLA, *Nec de nomine tantum hic agitur*, in *Nuntium* 8 (1999) 176-179.

30. Vaguely referred to only by COPPENS, *La carrière et l'œuvre scientifique* (n. 4), p. 9. Cerfaux's correspondence informs us that he was expected to teach in Rome from October 1960 until April 1961.

31. See CLG: Fund Cerfaux, s.n.

32. Letter from Cerfaux to Piolanti, dated July 27, 1960, in CLG: Fund Cerfaux, s.n.

33. See a.o. J. LUST, *Albin Van Hoonacker*, in J.H. HAYES (ed.), *Dictionary of Biblical Interpretation*, Vol. I, Nashville, TN, Abingdon, 1999, 518-519.

34. According to COPPENS, *La carrière et l'œuvre scientifique* (n. 4), p. 15, Cerfaux was nominated in March of that year (yet he refers to the *Osservatore Romano* of 1951), and more recently, D. CLAES, *Theologie in tijden van verandering: De theologische faculteit te Leuven in de twintigste eeuw, 1900-1968*, Leuven, 2004, puts his nomination in the year 1942. Both references are wrong. In the *AAS* 33 (1941) 96, we read: "Con biglietti della Segretaria di Stato, il Santo Padre Pio XII, felicemente regnante, si è degnato di nominare: 13 febbraio 1941 — L'Illmo e Revmo Monsig. Arturo Allgeier, i Revmi Sacerdoti Alberto Clamer e Luciano Cerfaux [...] consultori della Commissione Pontificia per gli Studi Biblici".

See also the short notice in CSVII: Acts of the Leuven Faculty, 1910-1947, p. 397: "Die 7a martii, feria 6a, sessio ordinaria, praesentibus EE. DD. Van Hove, decano, Van der Vorst, Draguet, Coppens, Rijckmans et Grégoire, secretario. Decanus congratulatur E.D. Cerfaux de sua ad munus Consultoris Commissionis pontificiae de re biblica promotione".

some authority as well as some useful contacts in Roman circles. On top of that, his many publications on Pauline literature, and his rather gentle reception of *Humani generis* in 1951[35] had gained Cerfaux a reputation, not only as an outstanding scholar in the field of New Testament studies, but also as an accurate, balanced, and moderate theologian. Also it ought not to be forgotten that Cerfaux, along with his colleague and Old Testament scholar Joseph Coppens, had inaugurated an important series of exegetical conferences[36] culminating in a huge conference precisely on Biblical methodology and theology in August 1958[37], where Pius XII's last official statements on exegetical matters – in a letter to Cardinal van Roey – were read out loud[38]. These conferences originally gave rise to a renewed discussion on the interpretation of Scripture since the 1940s[39]. All of these factors (which had moved the Leuven faculty to call upon an already retired Cerfaux for advice when preparing its conciliar vota[40]), now secured his place on the commission.

Still, Cerfaux was not the only Belgian on the TC. Before dealing with the actual preparations of the *De fontibus* text, we need to mention a TC nomination that will prove crucial to the understanding of Cerfaux's contribution. In fact, during the month of July 1960, not all future commission members received letters of nomination. When reviewing the list of names for the TC in *L'Osservatore Romano*, we see the 5 Belgian names

For the edition of *Divino afflante Spiritu*, see: PIE XII, *Encyclique sur les études bibliques*. Préface de S.E. Monseigneur A.-M. Charue, Évêque de Namur. Introduction et commentaires de L. Cerfaux, Professeur à l'Université de Louvain (Chrétienté nouvelle, 6), Bruxelles, ULB, 1945.

35. E.g. the article L. CERFAUX, *Révélation et histoire*, in *Nouvelle Revue Théologique* 13 (1951) 582-593.

36. For a survey of these conferences and bibliographical references, see F. NEIRYNCK (ed.), *Colloquium Biblicum Lovaniense. Journées Bibliques de Louvain. Bijbelse studiedagen te Leuven, 1949-2001* (Studiorum Novi Testamenti Auxilia, 19), Leuven, Peeters, 2001, pp. 9-11.

37. On the Occasion of the World Expo of 1958 in Brussels, the opening session of the conference was held in the Vatican pavillion 'Civitas Dei'.

38. Letter from Pius XII to J.E. van Roey, of July 28 1958, is found in Archives of the archdiocese of Mechelen-Brussels: Papers Card. J.E. van Roey, II.A.23. This document was published shortly thereafter in the conference acts by J. COPPENS – A. DESCAMPS – É. MASSAUX (eds.), *Sacra Pagina: Miscellanea biblica, congressus internationalis catholici de re biblica*, volumen primum (BETL, 12-13), Gembloux, Duculot, 1959, pp. 14-16.

39. See for instance R.B. ROBINSON, *Roman Catholic Exegesis Since Divino Afflante Spiritu. Hermeneutical Implications* (SBL Dissertation Series, 111), Atlanta, GA, Scholars, 1988. On top, Cerfaux received a doctorate *honoris causa* at the University of Strasbourg in 1957.

40. M. LAMBERIGTS, *The 'Vota Antepraeparatoria' of the Faculties of Theology of Louvain and Lovanium (Zaïre)*, in M. LAMBERIGTS – C. SOETENS (eds.), *À la veille du Concile Vatican II: Vota et réactions en Europe et dans le catholicisme oriental* (Instrumenta Theologica, 9), Leuven, Bibliotheek van de faculteit der Godgeleerdheid, 1992, 169-184.

mentioned above. However, many additional nominations were suggested and added after the publication of the list in *L'Osservatore*, one of them being that of Damien Van den Eynde. This Belgian Franciscan friar, at the time rector of the Antonianum, is often referred to as a 'candidate' for Ottaviani[41], which is fairly incorrect. Van den Eynde's name was mentioned during the election process, yet at the time he did not reach the stage of election. Nevertheless, he is added as TC member in September 1960, upon the request of Franciscan General Superior, Fr. Sepinski. Sepinski had written Ottaviani, complaining about:

> un certo disaggio in cui l'ordine si sente per essere ben poco rappresentato tra I membri facenti parte delle commissioni che nel prossimo Concilio Ecumenico Vaticano dovranno trattare de doctrina [...].

To compensate for this, Sepinski suggested that "almeno venisse nominato il R.P. Damiano Van den Eynde"[42]. The result was that Van den Eynde was nominated without knowing it: Ottaviani simply forwarded Sepinski's request to Tardini, who in turn accepted Van den Eynde's nomination on September 12, 1960[43]. This procedure was not uncommon, but on the other hand, Van den Eynde was among the 'lucky few', for not all requests were accepted this easily. Bishop Joseph Höfer, for instance, had made numerous attempts to have Karl Rahner nominated, and his efforts were rejected time after time, up to the point when Tromp begged him no longer to insist. In any case, like most of his his compatriots, Van den Eynde, too, felt deeply honored and was eager to cooperate in the commission's activities[44].

---

41. Such was suggested by L. CEYSSENS, *Marcel Van den Eynde*, in *Nationaal Biografisch Woordenboek*, 14, col. 187-190.

42. See letter from A. Sepinski to A. Ottaviani, September 3, 1960, in ASV: Conc. Vat. II, 736.

43. See Ottaviani's letter to Tardini, of September 8, 1960 in ASV: Conc. Vat. II, 736, which was very short, formal, and displayed no particular personal preference on van den Eynde's possible nomination whatsoever: "Le sarei grato se volesse proporre al S. Padre la nomina del P. Damiano van den Eijnde [sic] o.f.m., Rettore Magnifico del Pontificio Ateneo Antoniano, a membro della Commissione Teologica per il Concilio Ecumenico Vaticano II". The response came on September 12, through two letters from Tardini to Ottaviani, in ASV, Conc. Vat. II, 736; and to Felici, in ASV, Conc. Vat. II, 371. The nomination was made public in the *Oss. Rom.*, 16 Settembre 1960 (100/216) 1.

See also the official nomination letter from D. Tardini to Van den Eynde, on September 12, 1960; and the letter from Ottaviani and Tromp to Van den Eynde, dated September 16, 1960, in CSVII: Fund van den Eynde, 1.01 and 1.03. The second document was meant to inform the new member regarding the Commission's practical agenda, concerning meetings, the secrecy vow, etc. ...

44. See letter from Van den Eynde to S. Tromp, in ASV: Conc. Vat. II, 732, 32: "Con vivo senso di gratitudine ringrazio l'Em.za V. Rev.ma per il grande onore che si rende al Pontificio Ateneo Antoniano e alla mia persona. Posso assicurarla che non mancherò di

Not being part of the *parva commissio* responsible for the elections, protagonists such as Cerfaux, Philips, and Van den Eynde played no part in the earliest redactions of the *schemata compendiosa*. Nevertheless, our *Schema compendiosum de divina revelatione* will serve as our starting point. Since prior research has left numerous lacunae in the reconstruction of *De fontibus'* redaction chronology – and consequently regarding its theological contents and significance – our chronology is crucial. The various intermediary versions of the schema will serve as chronological anchorpoints, each new version comprising a different number of chapters. We will follow the developments from the initial *schema compendiosum* up to the version of *De fontibus* edited in the summer of 1961.

While the official work of the full Theological Commission would only begin in October 1960, Ottaviani's *piccola commissione* gathered several times during the summer of 1960, drawing up outlines for later schemata. Among them, was a *Schema compendiosum de divina revelatione*, originating from mid-July 1960. Since Msgr. Felici had informed Ottaviani of the Pope's vow for a separate constitution on Scripture and Tradition, the commission inserted this topic. Secretary Tromp drafted a very first document on the sources of Revelation, consisting of eight articles. This handwritten draft was given the title: *Schema de Sacra Scriptura primum tentamen*. Analogous to other drafts, e.g., on the church, on morality, etc., Tromp's text consisted of a series of short propositions and remarks, containing the following ideas:

1. Scripture is not the sole source of *faith*[45], rather Tradition is a necessary second source without which the fulness of the deposit of faith cannot be grasped.
2. Scripture bears the mark of divine inspiration and this implies that it is endowed with complete inerrancy. Any normative judgments on or interpretations of Scripture are reserved to the church's magisterium.
3. Exegetical discussions regarding the authorship of Scripture, regarding its historicity and authenticity, can by no means affect its inspired and inerrant nature.
4. Theological discussion is always subordinate to the norms, limits and definitions offered by the church's magisterium.

---

mettere la mia modesta collaborazione a disposizione della predetta Commissione, della quale V. Em.za ricopre l'altissima carica di Presidente".

45. Italics ours. We wish to stress the fact that – while this became a major issue in the conciliar discussions of 1962 – the distinction between the notion of *'fontes revelationis'* and *'fontes fidei'* was not one present in the mind of the preconciliar subcommission on Revelation.

As the author of Vatican II's very first text on revelation, Fr. Tromp had already written it on July 15[46]. A slightly modified version[47] of the text was then presented to the seven commission members at the *consessus praeliminaris parvus* of July 21. On that occasion Salvatore Garofalo (identified sometimes as co-author of the 'first' schema on July 20[48]) acted as relator for the draft, gave few comments, and introduced it for discussion. Although the commission dealt with all four drafts on that morning, Michael Leclercq's minutes of this meeting prove that a large part of the theological debate circled around topics like: the nature of scriptural inspiration (general or personal), the relationship between Scripture and Tradition (with reference to tridentine discussions), the study of literary genres in Scripture, etc. ... [49]. It should also be noted that the

46. See ASV: Conc. Vat. II, 736: "*Schema De Sacra Scriptura primum tentamen* + 15 Jul 1960: 1. S.Scriptura non est unicus fons deposito fidei. Praeter traditionem S.Scripturam explicans, habetur etiam traditio qua depositum fidei augetur; 2. S. Scriptura, in multis obscura, non a Deo data est singulis fidelibus, sed Magisterio Ecclesiae, ut eam explicat; 3. Licet libri V.T. sint Verbum Dei, tamen religiositas et moralitas ibi exposita, a Christo Domino fuerunt ad altiorem perfectionem evecta. Quare etiam hac de causa lectio totius scripturae non convenit omnibus et singulis fidelibus; 4. S. Scriptura gaudet inerrantia absoluta bene tamen distinguenda ab authenticitate (Aliis verbis: utrum liber S. Scripturae scriptus sit ab A vel B. minime per se afficit inspirationem et inerrantiam absolutam); 5. In S. Scriptura sunt plura genera litteraria, quae omnia perfecte constant cum inerrantia, attamen efficiunt ut sensus litteralis scripturae modo diverso intellegatur; 6. Non omne genus litterarium intactam relinquit inerrantiam S. Scripturae. Explicatio mythica evangeliorum, maxime quod spectat ad enarrata de resurrectione et ascensione Domini destruit historicitatem et inerrantiam eorundem; 7. Licet S. Scriptura prae aliis doceat oeconomiam divinam in historia salutis minime ea finalitas destruit historicitatem librorum sacrorum; 8. Theologia unice nitens S. Scripturae, et negligens S. Traditionem et Magisterium Ecclesiasticum, minatur Ecclesiam periculo protestantismi, et infectio iam adest; 9. Clare explicetur authenticitas Vulgatae editionis latinae".

47. Text found in ISR: Fund Garofalo, 2, dated July 20, and with title: Schema de fontibus revelationis. This text is primarily a reshape of the first outline, in which the only real new elements are: (a) the addition of the danger of rationalism as effected by a merely philological interpretation of Scripture. (b) the addition of an article 11, stating that: "Tractetur problema adaptationis".

The version of this text in the ASV: Conc. Vat. II, 736, bears Tromp's handwritten remark: "Schema factus a secretario de quo relatio fecit Mons. Garofalo feria V in sessione 21 Jul. 1960". This would imply that Garofalo did not take part in the second redaction either.

48. See R. BURIGANA, *Progetto dogmatico del Vaticano II. La commissione teologica preparatoria*, in ALBERIGO – MELLONI (eds.), *Verso il Concilio Vaticano II (1960-1962)* (n. 3), 141-206, see p. 177: "Il primo schema redatto il 20 luglio 1960 da Tromp e Garofalo [...]", and BURIGANA, *La Bibbia nel Concilio* (n. 7), p. 60: "La prima bozza del De fontibus revelationis, redatta da Garofalo [...]".

49. The report of this meeting by Tromp, as secretary M. Leclercq's handwritten notes (Adunanza restricta 21-VII-60) are kept in ASV: Conc. Vat. II, 736, 65. Among other elements, Tromp reports on the following issues:

"– punctum 11: 'tractetur problema adaptionis' erronee intrasse.

– [Garofalo] notat imprimis esse agendum de inspiratione personali contra inspirationem communitatis primitivae.

additional 11th article was again removed from the draft. Finally, the meeting resulted in the redaction of the *schemata compendiosa* which was circulated (by post) among all TC-members in September[50], accompanied by a letter asking for written remarks on the schemata before the planned October meetings.

The one-and-a-half page long *Schema compendiosum* (now counting 13 arts., since issues like personal inspiration and translation of scriptures were added as a result of commission discussion) was still very concise. It was, in fact, a working text, and it hardly did more than sum up some topics and/or major statements regarding inspiration, Scripture and Tradition, historico-critical exegesis and so on ... We will not discuss its contents at length here. Important for our study is the fact that in August 1960, secretary Tromp travelled to Holland to visit his brother, to Germany to visit his good friend Schauf, and to Leuven where he paid a visit to Philips and Cerfaux[51]. On August 29, Tromp wrote in his diary:

> Adeo Lovanium. Mane per tres horas colloquium cum Mgr. Philips, membro Commissionis. Singulis mensibus Romam venire nequit, nisi itineris

- observatur S. Scripturam non datam esse singulis fidelibus, sed addendum esse 'neque doctis'.
- observatur genus litterarium esse determinandum ex indole libri vel partis libri.
- insisterunt Mons. Piolanti et P. Hürth ne fusius ageretur de variis conceptibus traditionis. P. Hürth dixit de variis sententiis Conc. Trid.. Observavit Secretarius a Concilii Tridentini mente abstrahi posse, et simpliciter dicere: 'Sunt veritates, quae non continentur in libris inspiratis'.
- rogatum fuit, ut accuratius describeretur conceptus verus catholicus progressus dogmatici; et ut quid diceretur de LXX.
- P. Gagnebet o.p. expressit votum, ut fieret nova versio officialis totius S. Scripturae".

And, in his usual telegram style Leclercq quotes Ottaviani: "E questi quattro [Garofalo, Tromp, Ciappi, Hürth] incaricati specialmente di prepararsi gli schemi da spedire ai Commissari (verso il 15 sett.)".

50. See for the Schemata and the letter of September 24, 1960 CSVII: Fund Philips, 49-50. The four schemata were presented in the following order and entitled:
- Schema compendiosum constitutionis de ecclesia
- Schema compendiosum constitutionis de fontibus revelationis
- Schema compendiosum constitutionis de deposito fidei
- Schema compendiosum constitutionis de ordine morali, individuali et sociali.

51. This visit was already planned in the beginning of that month, as can be derived from Cerfaux letter to Tromp, dated August 2, in ASV: Conc. Vat. II, 732, 31: "Ce me serait un grand plaisir de vous rencontrer soit à Louvain, soit à Maastricht. Je suis malheureusement absent de Louvain, pour des leçons bibliques que je fais à Lourdes, du 11 au 27 août. Si cette entrevue ne s'arrangeait pas, je nourris en tout cas l'espoir de vous voir au début d'octobre à Rome, ayant le projet d'y passer quelques semaines ou plus au début de l'année". Another letter dated August 9nth can serve to show that Tromp seemed quite insistant on seeing Cerfaux: "Mon Révérend Père, Je rentre de Lourdes le 27 août. Si vous étiez encore à Maastricht au début de la semaine du 29, je vous serais reconnaissant de me fixer le jour et l'heure où je pourrai vous y rencontrer". Tromp's correspondence

pretium restituatur. Prandium apud Mgr. Philips. Vespere per tres horas colloquium habeo cum Mgr. Luc. Cerfaux, exegeta, itemque membro Commissionis. Omnino consentit Schemati de Fontibus. Vult per plures menses
degere Romae, ut collaboret in compositione Constitutionis illius[52].

2. Active Participation

The abovementioned postal distribution of the *schemata compendiosa*
among the TC members as late as the end of September implies that
Cerfaux and Philips would have had prior insight into their content.
This would have been a benefit that allowed them to prepare remarks on
De fontibus even before the TC had set up its respective sub-commissions.
Not only did Cerfaux start out writing a series of commentaries on the TC
drafts, he also set out drafting entirely new documents. Especially in September 1960 and in the period shortly after his arrival in Rome on Octo-
ber 7, the Leuven exegete developed an extraordinary range of activities.
Not only did he keep constant keep track with Gerard Philips (still in
Leuven at the time): Both men exchanged remarks on the TC documents,
and especially on the *Schema de fontibus*[53]. Besides this, Cerfaux under-
took actions in the following areas:

a. For a start, he wrote a five page '*Schema constitutionis praeviae de fide
catholica*'[54]. This is Cerfaux's attempt to offer Vatican II a solid theological basis with perspectives on both creation theology and salvation
history. The draft was designed to serve as a kind of general background
to the entire corpus of texts on revelation, ecclesiology, and morality.
Trying to push his initiative forward, Cerfaux approached Tromp suggesting to alter the order of schemata. His *Constitutio de fide* would
come first, followed by the drafts on Revelation, and on the Church[55].

---

shows that their rendez-vous was fixed only by the end of August. See letter from Philips
to Tromp, in ASV: Conc. Vat. II, 732, 32, dated August 24.
    52. VON TEUFFENBACH (ed.), *Konzilstagebuch Sebastian Tromp* (n. 11), August 29,
1960.
    53. For instance, Cerfaux's colleague Philips had several remarks on the document's
concept of inspiration; on the lack of christological focus; and further comments regard
the question of scriptural inerrancy ... and the lack of clarity concerning the relationship
between exegete and magisterium. See CSVII: Fund Philips, 55: De schemate quattuor constitutionum dogmaticum praeparato pro Concilio Vaticano II, 11 pp., esp. pp. 7-8.
    54. CSVII: Fund Philips, 58.
    55. See CSVII: Fund Philips, 58: L. Cerfaux, Schema constitutionis praeviae de fide
catholica, 5 pp.: "Nous proposerions que le Concile Vatican II commence par une brève
'Constitutio de fide catholica' qui expose les fondements de notre foi catholique. [...] Après
cette constitution fondamentale, nous passerons aux 4 'schemata compendiosa' qui ont été
proposés par la sous-commission. Peut-être serait-il utile d'intervertir les schema I et II".

Tromp did not agree[56] but still he granted Cerfaux permission to distribute his text among the TC-members[57].

b. Second, Cerfaux developed his *animadversiones* regarding the *schemata compendiosa*. We will limit ourselves to his threefold remarks on the *De fontibus* draft: (1) on Tradition: He states that Tradition is (historically) anterior to, synchronical to, and posterior to Scripture, and further: that Scripture is, in fact, a part of Tradition. Therefore, the exegete Cerfaux concludes: *Traditio superior est Scripturae*[58]. (2) on Scripture: here he refers to his Constitution on Sacred Scripture. (3) on the development of doctrine. This has to do with his text on the Catholic faith, where he tries to introduce the idea that doctrine is subject to historical changes and evolution.

c. Third then, Cerfaux prepares a '*Constitutio de Scriptura*'[59] to which he later (toward the end of the year) adds some '*Adnotationes ad constitutionem de Sacra Scriptura*'. We will illustrate the importance of this draft later on. For now we limit ourselves to a short description of it. The contents of this 'constitution' are closely linked with the abovementioned '*Constitutio de fide*', only this time focused on the role of Scripture with regard to revelation theology. A brief survey of its five articles will be most useful:

(1) *Revelatio et traditio.* Cerfaux starts out with a general statement on the relationship between revelation and tradition, clearly indicating that on the one hand Scripture cannot be discussed apart from Tradition, yet on the other hand Tradition is crucial when it comes to gathering insight into divine Revelation. After shortly

56. VON TEUFFENBACH (ed.), *Konzilstagebuch Sebastian Tromp* (n. 11), I, pp. 88-98: "Mane fuerunt in officio Schauf et Cerfaux. Voluit Mgr. Cerfaux in multis transvertere ordinem schematum v.g. ponendo in initio novum Schema quintum: de Deo creante et elevante. Post discussionem reliquunt propositum. Quod ad schema de fontibus spectat, iure putat latius dicendum esse de traditione et de evolutione dogmatum. Non intellego quomodo ultimum punctum omissum sit in Schemate de fontibus. [...] Receptus fuit Mgr. Cerfaux ab Emo Praeside".

57. Diary Schauf, October 15, 1960, on the same meeting: "Auch Cerfaux, einen liebenswürdigen alten Herrn kennen gelernt. Er hatte einen eigenen Vorschlag für Konstitutionen [...]. Tromp gelang es, ihn von der besseren Methode der geplanten Konstitutionen zu überzeugen. Wenn er, Cerfaux, aber wolle, so solle sein Vorschlag vervielfältigt und allen zugesandt werden".

58. See CSVII: Fund Philips, 59: Animadversiones membrorum in schemata, p. 3: "Rev.mus D.nus Cerfaux [...] Praedicatio apostolica continuatur per traditionem subsequentem. Unde traditio Scripturam praecedit, vel simultanea est illi, vel protrahitur post illam: sub quo respectu superior est Scripturae".

59. See ISR: Fund Garofalo, 4: L. Cerfaux, Constitutio de Scriptura, pp. 5 (the original manuscript is kept in CLG: Fund Cerfaux, s.n.).

citing the opening verses of the letter to the Hebrews (indicating that Revelation reaches us through both the Old and the New covenant), Cerfaux offers a foundation for the viewpoints mentioned in his *animadversiones*. Tradition, he claims, is to be founded *christo*-logically, and through it: *theo*-logically. He clarifies the idea with a quotation by Clement of Rome:

> Unde sicut scribit S. Clemens Romanus: "Apostoli nobis evangelii praedicatores facti sunt a Domino Iesu Christo, Iesus Christus missus est a Deo. Christus igitur a Deo et Apostoli a Christo" [... Cerfaux proceeds] Uti iam insinuatur ex emphasi ultimorum verborum Christi in evangelio Matthaei [...] secundum voluntatem Dei, necesse erat Apostolos successores sibi constituere in munere Ecclesiae fundandae, docendae, et sanctificandae. Et ita "per regiones igitur et urbes verbum praedicantes primitias earum Spiritu cum probassent, constituerunt episcopos et diaconos eorum qui credituri erant"[60].

Cerfaux derives the following descending-lineage from this passage:

God

⇩

Christ

⇩

Apostles

⇩

Bishops

The interesting point here is that Cerfaux seeks to combine an essentially theological scheme with an historical development. This is quintessential: The combination of theological and historiographical discourse in one single scheme allows Cerfaux to look at the concept of Tradition as a 'trading process' which plays throughout the history of Christianity, rather than as an immobile concept.

(2) *Scriptura et traditio*: Within the above-sketched framework, Scripture was discussed as imbedded within a Tradition which both precedes and supersedes it. Once again Cerfaux argues as an historian and as a theologian simultaneously. He states that one cannot pretend that the doctrine of the apostles was written in order to stop its being handed on orally. On the contrary, the oral tradition moves on even after the scriptures have been written[61]. As a result,

---

60. ISR: Fund Garofalo, 4: Constitutio de Scriptura, p. 1.

61. ISR: Fund Garofalo, 4: Constitutio de Scriptura, p. 2: "Contra sensum ecclesiae antiquae aliquis aestimaret doctrinam christianam litteris mandatam fuisse ut abrogaretur doctrina oralis. Haec enim quae primum sola existebat, postea semper viva remansit,

Tradition is chronologically both prior and posterior with regard to
Scripture and it has a normative function. Hence, a dogmatic proposition like 'Tradition is larger than Scripture' is acceptable to Cerfaux on both historical *and* theological grounds.

(3) *Libri canonici N.T. eorumque auctores*. This paragraph centers
around the idea that the apostolic origins and the authenticity of the
New Testament writings are grounded in their being part of tradition as a process throughout history. One can state that the gospels
have an apostolic origin, simply because they are a written reflection of the apostolic experience. The concept is further developed
in the fourth paragraph.

(4) *Novum Testamentum et historia*. Cerfaux now treats some difficulties that have marked the preconciliar era. For instance, he highlights the role of the exegetes who, according to the historical and
human character of Scripture, should study Scripture from a scientific viewpoint. Of course, Cerfaux realizes that attempts at reconciling theological and historical-critical approaches of Scripture
have caused many problems in recent church history. That is precisely why he insists on keeping both together, which – he states –
is possible precisely due to the nature of Revelation, since it reaches
us through historical events. Hence, scientific progress and progress
of our knowledge of Revelation should go hand in hand[62]. The
much required concordance between faith and historical reasoning
leads Cerfaux to the issue of the inspiration of Scripture. He states
that a true 'doctrina inspirationis' does not attempt to instrumen-
talize the human authors of scripture: "E vera inspirationis doctrina discimus auctores sacros sub influxu charismatis non amisisse
propriae suae virtutis actionem. Haec enim elevatur a Spiritu, non
comprimitur". This also implies that one should take into account
the fact that the authors did not apply the same modern principles
in dealing with historical narratives. Hence, when it comes to
matters of faith, one should not doubt their veracity, yet one is to
maintain a critical stance wherever difficulties in interpretation

---

consociam habens scripturam. Episcopi semper remanserunt doctores traditionis apostoli-
cae quam a praedecessoribus suis acceperant et succesoribus vicissim tradebant".

62. ISR: Fund Garofalo, 4: Constitutio de Scriptura, p. 2: "Aliunde nos gaudio afficit
progressio omnium scientiarum humanarum, et ante omnia historiae et philologiae, ad quam
alioquin multo contulerunt conatus saepe felices virorum exegesi et theologiae deditorum.
Quae scientiae, si novas quaestiones excitant, solutiones quandoque utiles offerunt ad dog-
mata melius intelligenda. Remanet ergo ut concordiam instituamus inter fidem et scientiam
historicam".

arise. The human imperfection that characterizes the human authors evidently also implies that whatever they write will be imperfect[63].

(5) *Vetus Testamentum*. Given the fact that Christ and his apostles sought a connection with the Old Testament writings in their preaching, and given that they passed these writings on to the Church, it is clear that the Old Testament formed part of the Christian heritage. As a result of this, it is subject to the New Testament, although the latter cannot be interpreted correctly without the first. So far for the Constitution on Scripture.

d. The fourth field of activity concerns 'public relations': in a private meeting with Salvatore Garofalo, the relator of Tromp's text, Cerfaux talks for about an hour and a half on the *schema compendiosum*, improvising a renewed edition of it on the spot. One of the most striking elements of their discussion is:

> J'ai vu Mgr. Garofalo. C'est ce qui m'a le plus éclairé. [...] Nous avons discuté durant une heure et demie, phrase par phrase. Il comprend bien mes remarques qui sont les vôtres, et nous avons improvisé une nouvelle rédaction plus correcte. Les points [...] seraient: antériorité (et donc priorité) de la tradition orale sur les Écritures.

This ever returning standpoint will be crucial when examining Cerfaux's later contribution to the schema. Naturally, Garofalo is not Cerfaux's only contact person. For instance, the diaries of Tromp show that he paid him continual visits to discuss texts[64]. In his correspondence with Philips, Cerfaux mentions having seen the exegetes Benoît and Lyonnet[65]. As mentioned, this Roman activity was possible due to a guest professorship for Cerfaux at the Lateran University, which led to interesting contacts in other circles. For instance, Cerfaux talked with Piolanti and Romeo, and with compatriots such as Dhanis and Devroede[66]. These

---

63. ISR: Fund Garofalo, 4 Constitutio de Scriptura: "homo inspiratus loquitur vel scribit sub motione divina secundum consuetudines quas nos quandoque imperfectas iudicaremus, et tamen aptissimae inveniuntur ad illa exprimenda quae vult Deus. Neque mentitur auctor sacer humano modo loquendo, neque mentitur Deus tale instrumentum assumens".

64. Cerfaux visits Tromp on October 14, 15, 25, and 26.

65. CSVII: Fund Philips, 22: letter to Philips dated November 7, 1960: "J'ai vu le P. Benoît, de Jérusalem; nous avons parlé inspiration, sens plénier, etc. Le P. Lyonnet m'a écrit; il est en pleine polémique avec Mgr. Garofalo du Latran, [...]".

66. CSVII: Fund Philips, 57: letter from Cerfaux to Philips, dated October 12, 1960: "Aujourd'hui j'ai vu Mgr. Piolanti, qui voit les choses de haut ... J'ai insisté pour que nous parlions un peu pour le monde moderne. [...] Vu également Mgr. Romeo, qui continue à fulminer contre le Card. Bea, l'Institut Biblique, etc. Ceci l'intéresse plus que le concile. Il désire que la paix se rétablisse mais à condition d'avoir raison sur tout [...] Vu d'abord

activities could hardly go unnoticed, and at the TC's first plenary meeting on October 26 and 27 (featuring the distribution of members over various subcommissions[67]), there is no surprise in seeing Cerfaux become member of the *Subcommissio de fontibus* (SCDF).

All things considered, when studying Cerfaux's actions, we have an historian speaking who thoroughly realizes that even dogmatical principles and statements put in a classical 'neo-scholastic' discourse are not necessarily void of historical reference. On the contrary, every theological statement in Cerfaux's writings appears to rely on an historical basis. Time and time again the central point of reference is the original and historical experience of the disciples with Jesus of Nazareth. Particularily Cerfaux's *Constitutio de Scriptura* makes clear that any systematic proposition needs to refer to a background of historical experience in order to reach the needed concordance between doctrinal demands and historical-critical research, or in other words, between science and faith. If Cerfaux will appear to have been influential in the redaction of the *De fontibus* schema with his kind of historical theology, it will show the need for a much more nuanced reading of the schema.

3. The Subcommission on the Sources at Work

As we have indicated, during the first plenary TC meeting subcommissions were established after a small discussion on the contents of the TC schemata on October 27, 1960. Garofalo (relator to the schema *De fontibus*, indicating that the document on Revelation was sketched upon 'higher' request) starts out giving some factual information on the subject of Revelation in the preconciliar vota. Then the meeting discusses the order of appearance of the schemata, *i.e.,* the way in which the various theological documents relate to each other. The discussion on this subject was so vehement, that Ottaviani decided to initiate a *Subcommissio de ordine schematum* to reach acceptable solutions[68].

---

le P. Dhanis, qui sera bien d'accord avec nos façons de voir. Je me permettrai de lui passer votre copie également. [...] J'ai vu Mgr. Devroede, de retour à Rome, qui n'est pas dans les secrets des dieux pour l'étape actuelle de la préparation, mais qui a bon espoir dans l'efficacité de notre action".

67. This is done with the use of the letters of response sent in by most members upon their nomination, indicating the field in which they themselves felt confident. These passages were often underlined by Tromp.

68. Tromp and some others argued in favour of a division into two schemata: Relatio Rev.mi Patris Tromp de Quattuor Schematibus, in CSVII: Fund Janssen, 001.03: "Nihil tamen prohibet, quominus quattuor schemata reducantur ad duo: primum 'De Ecclesia et De deposito Ecclesiae tradito'; alterum 'De deposito pure conservando in rebus quae ad

In any case, a subcommission was composed to consider theological topics. The subcomission on Revelation at that time consisted of a very small group of theologians – the smallest in number among the four subcommissions. Its five members were: Salvatore Garofalo (secretary), Maxime Hermaniuk, Lucien Cerfaux, Joseph Schröffer, and Damien Van den Eynde[69], although it appears Piolanti had some reservations on appointing Van den Eynde[70]. Initially the subcommission had only one

fidem et mores spectant'. Proposuit Rev.mus et Ill.mus Dominus Gerardus Philips, ut prius ageretur De fontibus, deinde De ecclesia. Hoc enim postulari ut servetur ordo logicus: Ecclesiam enim suam doctrinam de semetipsa haurire ex fontibus revelationis". Also see Philips's suggestion – in agreement with Dhanis – on the ordo materiae (cfr. CSVII: Fund Philips, 061): "Libenter adhaereo iis quae a R.P. Dhanis dicta sunt. Si bipartita divisio ut magis constructa apparet, quadriptartita pro publico clarior evadet. In omni casu bipartitum duplex schema deinde subdividendum erit [...] Quoad ordinem sequendum inter schema De ecclesia et schema De fontibus, admittere possum quod ab ecclesia exordiatur, dummodo in redactione sedulo vitetur aspectus positivismi ecclesiastici, nempe quasi ecclesia seipsum poneret a priori et postea tantum ad fontes recurreret. [...] Placet omnino propositio Exmi. Eichstattensis, ita intellecta ut in praeambulo generali non proprie definitio de Deo proferatur, sed potius solemnis proclamatio fidei in Deum Dominum omnipotentem ...".

69. Different membership lists for the SCDF are found in the journals of Congar (Y. CONGAR, *Mon Journal du Concile*, présenté et annoté par É. MAHIEU, 2 tomes, Paris, Cerf, 2002, Vol. I, pp. 34-36) and Fenton (CUA: Diary Fenton, 26 oktober 1960), and in Fund Philips, 0025. Burigana's list offers quite a different view than the other sources, simply because he offers the member list of November 1960 instead of the October list (BURIGANA, *La Bibbia nel Concilio* [n. 7], p. 65, n. 71), a list that has been adopted from U. BETTI, *La dottrina del Concilio Vaticano II sulla trasmissione della Rivelazione: Il capitolo II della Costituzione dommatica Dei verbum*, Rome, Antonianum, 1985, p. 25.
On the adding of consultors later on, see Tromps' Verbalia consessuum plenariorum, in ASV: Conc.Vat. II, 791, 6-7: "Consessus I plenarius [...] constituta est subcommissio De fontibus Revelationis: membra nominata sunt Exc.mi Schröffer et Hermaniuk, Ill.mi Domini Garofalo et Cerfaux et Rev. P. van den Eynde". [...] "Statuto principio ad Subcommissionem de Ecclesia additi sunt Mons. Schauf et R.P. Lécuyer Cssp; ad Commissionem De fontibus R.P. Kerrigan o.f.m.".

Burigana	Congar	Tromp	Philips
Garofalo	Garofalo	Garofalo	Garofalo
Hermaniuk	Hermaniuk	Hermaniuk	Hermaniuk
Scherer			
Schröffer	Schröffer	Schröffer	Schröffer
Cerfaux	Cerfaux	Cerfaux	Cerfaux
Schmaus			
Michel			
Van den Eynde	Van den Eynde	Van den Eynde	Van den Eynde
Kerrigan		Kerrigan	Kerrigan
Castellino			
di Fonzo			

70. CUA: Diary Fenton, October 27, 1960: "Piolanti then insisted that another man be appointed for the subcommission on the sources of revelation because, he said, Van den Eynde has peculiar ideas about tradition".

consultor the Irish Franciscan Alexander Kerrigan, professor at the Antonianum, was added to the SCDF, receiving his official nomination letter only a week later (November 3)[71]. The two other SCDF-consultors Lorenzo di Fonzo (November 24) and Giorgio Castellino (November 25), were added toward the end of the month. As for the additional members: Michael Schmaus was nominated on November 21, and Albert Michel on November 19[72]. Also interesting to note is that Garofalo will repeatedly ask for more staff for his commission, suggesting it to be useful to add people from the Biblicum or the École biblique de Jérusalem[73]. This, all together, suggests that the atmosphere in the SCDF was not one of a 'Roman bloc', but rather one of theological discussion open to various viewpoints. With that in mind, and then glancing again through the

71. ASV: Conc. Vat. II, 732, 32: Letter from S. Tromp to A. Kerrigan, dated November 3, 1960: "Praegratum mihi est Te certiorem facere, nomine Eminentissimi Praesidis huius Pontificiae Commissionis, de adlectione Tua in Subcommissionem cui demandatum est agere de Sacra Traditione et de Sacra Scriptura. De iis quae ordinem laborum spectant, consulere poteris Reverendissimum Dominum Salvatorem Garofalo".

72. See ASV: Conc. Vat. II, 731, 20: Puncta pro audientia Sabb. 19 nov.: […] 12) Schmaus in Comm. de Fontibus. Journet, Michel, Audet ep aux Quebec. The nomination letter to Schmaus was written on November 21, 1960 by Tromp (VON TEUFFENBACH (ed.), *Konzilstagebuch Sebastian Tromp* [n. 11], November 21), no date is known to us for the one to Michel.

According to an official TC-document (CSVII: Fund Janssen, Subcommissiones uti stant die 29 XI 1960), on November 29, the SCDF's outlook was the following: Members: Hermaniuk, Scherer, Schröffer, Cerfaux, Garofalo, Schmaus, Michel, Van den Eynde; Consultors: Castellino, di Fonzo, Kerrigan.

73. A first expansion proposal is dated November 19, see Tromp's manuscript 'Puncta pro audientia Sabb. 19 nov.' (ASV: Conc. Vat. II, 731, 20):
"5. Schmaus in Comm. de Fontibus. […]
7. Commissio De fontibus nimis parva. Nullus ex Instituto biblico. Di Fonzo Conv.
Rogavit Mgr. Garofalo secr. Comm. Biblicae ut P.G. Castellino et P. Dhanis pro voto accedere possint ad Archiv. Comm. Bibl. – Respondit Secretarius expedire ut Card. Praeses scribat Card. Tisserant. […]
12. Schmaus in Comm. de Fontibus. Journet, Michel, Audet ep. aux Quebec.
13. Proponitur Benoît O.P. Inst. Bibl. Hier. pro subcommiss. De fontibus".
Zie ook VON TEUFFENBACH (ed.), *Konzilstagebuch Sebastian Tromp* (n. 11): "Die 19 Nov: In commissionem De fontibus assumuntur Schmaus, Michel, Audet. Ut membrum accedet di Fonzo O.M.Conv".
A second proposal is dated november 23:
"Mane habeo colloquium cum Mgr. Garofalo de subcomm. de Fontibus. Expedit ut in illa S.C. non solum studio subiciantur quaestiones difficiliores, sed eodem tempore incoetur redactio provisoria constitutionis dogmaticae. Quia numerus sodalium Romae degentium est parvus, ut membrum additur di Fonzo O.Min.Conv. Proponit Mgr. Garofalo ut nominentur consultores R.P. Vogt rect. Inst. Biblici de Urbe et P. Benoît O.P. Inst. Biblici Hierosolymitani".
See also, ASV: Conc. Vat. II, 731, 20: Puncta pro audientia feria IV 23 Nov:
6) Nominare pro subcommissione De fontibus di Fonzo, Michel
8) Proponuntur a Mons. Garofalo ut consultores nominentur R.P. Vogt s.j. rect. Bibl., R.P. Benoît O.P. Inst. Bibl. Jerusal.

name-list: Cerfaux's key position in the original subcommission's line up is striking, especially when we bear in mind that Hermaniuk[74], Kerrigan[75] and Van den Eynde[76] had, all three of them, either followed his Leuven courses or had studied or lectured with him at his Alma Mater. This, added to the fact that Cerfaux had already been revising the schema with SCDF secretary Garofalo before the respective subcommission was ever composed, puts the Leuven magister in the center of things.

The SCDF's inaugural meeting took place on October 30. The main topic was the distribution of work to be accomplished. Cerfaux was appointed responsible for a text on the New Testament (treating both Pauline literature and the Gospels), and in the period following would be working closely with his apprentice Alexander Kerrigan, who was to develop the draft on the Old Testament. Since both men were consultors to the Pontifical Biblical Commission, they could make good use of the archives of the PBC for their work:

> Nous travaillons chacun de notre côté, à notre sous-commission. Avec le P. Kerrigan, je fouille les archives de la Commission biblique pour savoir comment on a posé en ces temps la question de l'authenticité des livres sacrés. J'ai bien l'impression que pour les évangiles, la première tradition avait un centre d'intérêt historique, nécessaire cependant pour que les évangiles représentent avec fidélité l'enseignement apostolique[77].

The distribution of labour in the commission was such that each member was given one or two articles from the *schema compendiosum* for further development, and each also received a period of private study for their work[78]. Subsequently, only during the first half of 1961 would the schema gradually develop its final structure. Yet, precisely during this

---

74. Maxime Hermaniuk had obtained the degrees of Bachelor, Licentiate, Doctor and of Magister in Theology at the Leuven University, in the 1940's, having written his theses under Cerfaux's direction.

75. Alexander Kerrigan (1911-1986) had obtained the STL degree as a student in Leuven in 1938, and had started to write a doctoral dissertation under Cerfaux's guidance, which – after obtaining permission to submit his work only in 1940 – he left it unfinished due to the break out of World War II. See CSVII: Acts of the Leuven Faculty, 1910-1947, pp. 376, 378-381. See p. 378: "In ordine ad gradum Doctoris in S. Theologia [...] 4. R.P. Alexander Kerrigan, ex Athlone, presb. Ordinis Fratrum Minorum, provinciae Hiberniae, licent. In S. Theologia.

76. Damien Van den Eynde (1902-1969), had obtained the degree of Magister in Theology in Leuven, July 8th, 1933, in a period when Cerfaux was teaching at the Leuven faculty. See J. COPPENS, *In memoriam D. van den Eynde*, in ETL 46 (1970) 208; and CSVII: Acts of the Leuven Faculty, 1910-1947, p. 285.

77. CSVII: Fund Philips, 22: letter to Philips dated November 7, 1960.

78. Manuscript report by Garofalo, dated October 30, 1960, in ISR: Fund Garofalo, 11: "Ad Schema:

period – between the end of 1960 and June 1961 – existing literature offers hardly any valuable indications or reconstructions, and often it calls for readjustment[79]. Yet, archive documentation proves that in January 1961 a new redaction of the *Constitutio de fontibus* was composed, officially printed and distributed among commission members. This new redaction, the first to follow the *schema compendiosum,* counts not five, but only three chapters, all of them written by SCDF consultors:

I.   On Inspiration and Biblical Inerrancy (Lorenzo di Fonzo)
II. On the Books of the Old Testament and their authors (Alexander Kerrigan)
III. On the Literary genres (Giorgio Castellino)

What becomes evident at the outset are the titles assigned to each of these three chapters. The titles indicate that the commission intends to

n. 1: P. Dhanis (defin. di Leone XIII [...]). Archivio PCB – Archivio SO (Introduction à la Bible e Charlier C., Bible et vie chrétienne)
n. 2.: V.S.
n. 3: L'autenticità umana dei Padri
per il V.T. (Pentat.): P. Kerrigan dividere e studio di testo. (Archivio PCB)
vangeli: Cerfaux (Archivio PCB)
Paolo?
n. 4-5: Genera litt. in Tradiz.
ad mentem Pii XII (Archivio PCB)
Castellino? +
n. 6: Cfr. Pio XII v.s. Castellino?
n. 7-8: Voto del biblico – suggerimenti Cerfaux?
n. 9-10: lectio S. Scr.
In ipsa script. (Garofalo)
Ex Patribus (Jouassard)
Ex docum. Eccl. (Garofalo)
n. 11-12: Raccoltà materiali ex magisterio Eccl.? Chi?
n. 13: Importanza della Vg.
Archivio PCB (Div. Affl. Sp.)
Ppi. Benedetto XV (abbazio S. Girolamo)".
79. For instance, the standard historiographical reconstruction of Vatican II's Constitution on Divine Revelation fails to give clear insight in the SCDF activities troughout 1961. It states incorrectly that De Fontibus' final 5-chaptered structure (crucial for later conciliar debate) existed already at the end of 1960. See BURIGANA, *La Bibbia nel Concilio* (n. 7), p. 67: "Fin dalle prime riunioni l'indice dello schema compendiosum venne riformulato secondo una divisione in cinque capitoli: De fontibus revelationis, De inspiratione, De Vetere Testamento, De Novo Testamento e De Scriptura in Ecclesia. Si tratta di un passaggio fondamentale non solo per il De fontibus revelationis, quanto per la stessa costituzione conciliare Dei Verbum, poiché venne determinata la struttura dello schema, rimasta invariata nei suoi 4/5 fino all'approvazione del novembre 1965". The chronology used there is the same as one finds in most literature, and draws on those of F. GIL HELLIN, *Concilii Vaticani II Synopsis in ordinem redigens schemata cum relationibus necnon patrum orationes atque animadversiones: Constitutio dogmatica de divina Revelatione Dei Verbum*, Vatican City, 1993, pp. XXVII-XXIX, and SAUER, *Erfahrung und Glaube* (n. 17), pp. 91-92.

discuss some of the major issues that were at stake in recent exegetical history both from a systematic perspective (matters of inspiration, inerrancy and divine authorship) as well as from a practical perspective (the allowance of historical-critical methodology in the study of Scripture). Also striking is that some items mentioned earlier remain untouched here. This is due to the problematic course of debates within the above-mentioned subcommission *De ordine schematum*. The question as to how the TC should perceive the relationship between its various theological enterprises remained unresolved, and as a result Cardinal Ottaviani decided on November 8, 1960 – awaiting the opinion of some TC consultors on the topic – that "interim subcommissiones istas quaestiones aggrediantur quae sunt independentes ab ordine schematum"[80]. Since Revelation theology was also treated by the TC subcommission *De deposito fidei,* theological debates such as on the relationship between Scripture and Tradition were postponed until further notice. This resulted in the January draft remaining very much a constitution on the Sacred Scriptures, as it had been in Tromp's initial draft.

Subsequently, the threefold constitution was discussed during the second plenary meeting of the TC (February 13-16, 1961) and became the basis for further discussion. The phase we are describing here is quite important for the content development of the schema *De fontibus*, and it is precisely in this period of time that Cerfaux enjoyed an ever-growing authority in the SCDF and in the general TC. Even though Cerfaux's influence on the January-draft is minor, his influence would increase as work on it goes forward. For instance, on February 14th 1961, when Pope John XXIII

---

80. Actually, the commission had finished its job in the beginning of November 1960, but given that it had decided to suggest a split up even within the material on *De ecclesia*, members like Tromp and Dhanis contested the result, and discussion was still open. See VON TEUFFENBACH (ed.), *Konzilstagebuch Sebastian Tromp* (n. 11): "7 Nov. 1960 feria 2. [...] Misit Mons. Carpino acta Subcommissionis de Ordine Schematum. Subcommissio etiam mutavit ordinem internum Schematis de Ecclesia, quod excedit eius competentiam". And later: "8 Nov. 1960 feria 3. [...] vespere colloquium habui cum Patre Dhanis. Dixit subcommissionem De ordine schematum exiisse suam competentiam tractando de rebus ad se non spectantibus. Non dici potest totam subcommissionem pro schemati de Ecclesia, voluisse ordinem proposito a S. Officio. Certe hoc nolunt ipse P. Dhanis, nec P. Gillon, P. Trapè siluit".
As a consequence, Ottaviani distributes the subcommission De ordine report, along with a new proposition by Tromp, some vota of TC members and an elaborate report on the entire debate among the TC members and consultors, and asks them the following: "Quibus omnibus documentis prae oculis habitis, velint igitur Reverendissimi Consultores edicere quid sentiant de systemate, quo ordinanda sunt ea quae fuerunt obiectum Commissionis Theologicae in eius sessione prima plenaria; votumque suum latine conscriptum ante diem 15 Decembris Romam mittant". (CSVII: Fund Janssen, 1.07).

visited the plenary TC meeting, Cerfaux was the one asked to explain the concept of biblical inerrancy. He states (completely in line with his *Constitutio de Scriptura*) that God is infallible, yet that there exists no 'real' infallibility in the scriptures since they are – as any historical document is – human writings[81]. Once more, Cerfaux underlines the importance of an historical approach to scripture. At the time, such an utterance would have sounded much like a firm statement. At least it caused Joseph Fenton to note the following in his diary:

> In the future I must speak out against a statement by Cerfaux. He holds that God is infallible, but that there is no real infallibility in the Bible, because it is written *modo humano*. Of course, every statement that is marked with the charism of infallibility is uttered or written *modo humano*[82].

Still, Cerfaux did more than that at the second plenary TC meeting, beginning already with his preparations for the meeting. As was the usual procedure, all TC members had received the latest drafts of the schemata earlier and were asked to react to them in writing before the meeting in order to be prepared for discussion. As to the schema on the sources of Revelation, only three people responded: Schmaus, Schauf and Cerfaux[83]. Moreover, Schmaus' notes were not used[84] and those of Schauf were positive except for some minor remarks on chapter three which seemed more

---

81. Verbalia consessuum plenariorum, in ASV: Conc. Vat. II, 791, 27: "Consessus plenarius II [...] Invitat Illmus Garofalo Illmum Cerfaux ut exponat quaestionem inerrantiae, de qua in fine n. 6 et n. 7. Illmus Cerfaux dicit distingueri in quaestione infallibilitatis auctorem divinum et auctorem humanum, per quem loquitur auctor divinus. Affirmatio autem divina gaudet infallibilitate absoluta; affirmatio humana quia fit modo humano admittit gradus". And also CSVII: Fund Philips, 72, Relatio de Consessu secundo, pp. 2-3: "hora 11.15 annuntiatur adventus Pontificis, et exit E.mus Card. Praeses ad salutandum Papam, qui mox intrat, conductus a Card. Praeside et a Secretario Commissionis Centralis, Exc. Mo. D. Felici. Postquam Pontifex suggestum sibi praeparatum ascenderat, dictis quibusdam verbis introductoriis a Card. Praeside de materia discussionum, statim, annuente Papa, disputatio de pluralitate auctorum continuatur" [...] "dicente Papa se nunc magis discere velle quam docere. Deinde invitatur Ill.mus Cerfaux, ut exponat nn. 6 et 7 Constitutionis, ubi agitur de inerrantia auctoris sacri, quo facto rogat E.mus Card. Praeses ut cum mente exegetae comparetur mens theologorum. Fine imposito comparationi, Papa praeit in recitanda salutatione angelica cum solitis precibus, quibus devote recitatis E.mus Praeses conatur disputationem de modo citandi Pontifices ad felicem exitum conducere [...]".
82. CSVII: Diary J.C. Fenton, Vol. II, February 14, 1961.
83. Cerfaux's remarks (ISR: Fund Gagnebet, I, 8: Adnotationes ad Constitutionem de fontibus revelationis) are based on handwritten commentaries he had written in the margins of his copy of the new Constitution (CLG: Fund Cerfaux, s.n.).
84. ISR: Fund Gagnebet, I, 19. This text is actually a tardy reaction by M. Schmaus on the Schema compendiosum. Schmaus reacted too late due to health problems, cf. VON TEUFFENBACH (ed.), *Konzilstagebuch Sebastian Tromp* (n. 11): "Die 31 Jan 1961: feria III. [...] Accepi a Prof. Schmaus tria vota spectantia ad quaestionem De fontibus revelationis. Non misit ea prius quia laborat malo pulmoniaco".

appropriate to him as a votum; the demand for a clearer distinction between Scripture's divine *auctor primarius* and its human *cooperatores*; plus some remarks on the personal character of the charism of inspiration[85]. Cerfaux's adnotations are the most elaborate. On Kerrigan's chapter he notes that its closing line on the authorship of Old Testament writings is problematic. Cerfaux critiques Castellino and suggests that genre criticism is not as new as he pretends it to be[86]. Most of Cerfaux's response, however, is devoted to di Fonzo's chapter on divine authorship, inspiration and inerrancy. Again, Cerfaux focusses on the importance of leaving behind abstract notions, and turning things toward lived history. Concerning the first article of the January-draft (in which di Fonzo insinuated that Scripture's word comes immediately from God), Cerfaux rather points out that Christ is the primary and concrete *locus* of the word of God in history. Next he indicates that inspiration should not be thought of merely in terms of vertical communication of revealed truths. Inspiration and revelation should be distinguished in a way that inspiration is seen as an act of service to revelation. The presentation of Leo XIII's inspiration doctrine by di Fonzo should be replaced by his own suggestion, to read:

> Inspiratio non impedit quin auctores sacri modo humano constituant librum scribere, propositumque suum perficiant; sed ea omnia faciunt sub ductu Dei, auctoris principalis, qui "ita eos ad scribendum excitavit et movit, ita scribentibus adstitit.

Clearly, Cerfaux seeks to soften the instrumentalist view of inspiration that is present in the January draft.

Then, on February 13, the TC plenary meeting took place. In the morning, the subcommissions had separate meetings preparing for general discussion. The SCDF used this meeting to prepare Garofalo's relatio of the draft, and already started correcting the January draft according to the

---

85. CSVII: Fund Van den Eynde, 3.10: Animadversiones in Constitutionem de fontibus revelationis: "Quoad n. 4: Quaeri tamen potest an tota quaestio hisce soluta sit. Forsan dici potest illud personale et proprium inspirationis nullo modo excludere collectivitatem auctorem eo sensu ut liber in se unus et indivisus a pluribus confectus sit ut pars una ab illo pars alia ab altero scriptore sit, ita tamen ut redactio unitatis cadat sub assistentia iudicii infallibilis unius vel plurium vel omnium..." [...] "Nota bene: Alicuius momenti esset articulus de quo mihi non constat an a Commissione examinatus sit. Agitur de art. B. BRINK-MANN, *Inspiration und Kanonizität der Heiligen Schrift in ihrem Verhältnis zur Kirche*, in *Scholastik* 33 (1958) 208-233".

86. ISR: Fund Gagnebet, I, 8: Adnotationes (Cerfaux), p. 3: "Adnotatio ad III. De Generibus litterariis. Vellem notare huiusmodi systema vere novum non esse, atque progressui scientiae historicae et philologicae legitime respondere".

remarks of Schauf and Cerfaux. All of Cerfaux's suggestions were accepted at this meeting, and when it came to a discussion on the modalities of inspiration, the SCDF developed a new structure for the future schema on the sources, featuring – at Cerfaux's request – a prologue with particular attention to the *historical process* which binds both sources of revelation[87]. In the afternoon plenary debate was held – once more – on the topics touched by Cerfaux and Schauf. Discussion was held principally on the presentation of Leo XIII's doctrine of inspiration.

4. Background: The Roman Controversy

The '*cantus firmus*' for the work of the SCDF was anything but quiet. Toward the end of 1960 – in a period when Cerfaux was preparing a collection of *adnotationes* to his own *Constitutio de Scriptura* (requested by Garofalo) – one of the Lateran University professors, Francesco Spadafora, strongly attacked some lecturers of the Pontifical Biblical Institute. Roughly stated, one could say that the Lateran accused the Biblicum of Modernism[88]. Spadafora was joined by his colleague Antonino

---

87. CSVII: Fund Van den Eynde, 1.15, Relatio Garofalo, p. 2: "Praemisso prologo in quo de processu historico utriusque fontis revelationis agatur, [...] Postea, per partes, proponentur quae spectant: 1) Divinam inspirationem in specie; 2) Vetus Testamentum in specie; 3) Novum Testamentum in specie; 4) De habitudine theologi et exegetae ad utrumque fontem Revelationis; 5) De S. Scripturae lectione apud fideles, deque usu versionis latinae 'Vulgatae' in Ecclesia".

88. We will consider this topic only briefly. Much more detailed information on the controversy can be found in our K. SCHELKENS – A. DUPONT, *Scopuli vitandi: The Controversy concerning Historico-critical Exegesis between the Lateran University and the Pontifical Biblical Institute*, in *Bijdragen. International Journal of Philosophy and Theology* (2008) forthcoming. See also studies such as: J.A. FITZMYER, *A Recent Roman Scriptural Controversy*, in *Theological Studies* 22 (1961) 426-444; J.A. KOMONCHAK, *The Struggle for the Council During the Preparation of Vatican II (1960-1962)*, in G. ALBERIGO – J.A. KOMONCHAK (eds.), *History of Vatican II*. Vol. I: *Announcing and Preparing Vatican Council II. Toward a New Era in Catholicism*, Maryknoll, NY, Orbis; Leuven, Peeters, 1995, 167-356, esp. pp. 278-283; R. BURIGANA, *Tradizioni inconciliabili? La 'Querelle' tra l'università lateranense e l'istituto biblico nella preparazione del Vaticano II*, in P. CHENAUX (ed.), *La PUL e la preparazione del Concilio* (Studi e documenti sul Concilio Vaticano II, 1), Rome, Pontificia Università Lateranense, 2001; B.W. HARRISON, *The Teaching of Paul VI on Sacred Scripture. With Special Reference to the Historicity of the Gospels*, Rome, Pontificium Athenaeum Sanctae Crucis, 1997, esp. pp. 59-72; B.W. HARRISON, *On Rewriting the Bible: Catholic Biblical Studies in the 60's*, in *Christian Order* 43 (2002) 155-178 and ID., *The Encyclical Spiritus Paraclitus in Its Historical Context*, in *Living Tradition* 60 (1995); M. PESCE, *Il rinnovamento biblico*, in M. GUASCO, et al. (eds.), *Storia della chiesa*. Vol. XXV/2: *La Chiesa del Vaticano II (1958-1978)*, Milan, San Paolo, 1994, 167-216; G.P. FOGARTY, *American Catholic Biblical Scholarship: A History from the Early Republic to Vatican II*, New York, Harper & Row, 1989, pp. 291-296. F. LAPLANCHE, *La crise de l'origine: La science catholique des Évangiles et l'histoire au XXᵉ siècle* (L'évolution de l'humanité), Paris, Albin Michel, 2006, pp. 459-469;

Romeo, who also fiercely attacked the PBI exegetes, and more specifically, the article by Luis-Alonso Schökel, *Dove va l'esegesi cattolica?* On a theological level the issues at stake were the nature of scriptural inspiration in connection with the inerrancy of scripture, and on a methodological level, the acceptance of *Formgeschichte* as a means of scripture study. The controversy between both institutes – discernable in their vota – found a climactic moment in the teaching prohibition of professors Lyonnet and Zerwick and the relegation of Jean Steinman's, *La Vie de Jésus* to the Index[89].

Henri de Lubac, at the time closely connected with people at the Pontifical Biblical Institute, has this entry in his diary:

> Le cardinal Ruffini aurait lu en manuscrit et approuvé l'article de Mgr. Romeo paru dans *Divinitas*, dirigé expressément contre le Père Alonso-Schökel et l'ensemble de l'Institut biblique actuel, et visant également le cardinal Bea et l'encyclique *Divino afflante* de Pie XII. Mgr Piolanti, recteur du Latran, soutient publiquement Romeo; l'un et l'autre, opposés à cette encyclique, ont depuis lors essayé à plusieurs reprises d'obtenir une condamnation des biblistes qui en ont fait leur charte: offensive contre M. Gelin (Lyon), – affaire de l'Introduction à la Bible – critique de la collection biblique italienne patronnée par le P. St. Lyonnet, – attaque dans *Divinitas* contra la doctrine du P. Lyonnet sur le péché originel, etc. – Par son ampleur et sa violence, le nouvel article de Romeo montre que la discussion sera portée au concile. Il faut tenir compte aussi de l'ambition et de la jalousie du Latran qui, devenu Université pontificale, voudrait avoir son Institut biblique; de plus, le milieu Parente-Piolanti-Romeo continue la tradition 'intégriste' de Benigni, Canali, etc., tendance qui trouve encore à Rome plus d'un sympathisant"[90].

K. SCHELKENS, *Perceiving Orthodoxy: A Comparative Analysis on the Roman Controversy in Catholic Exegesis (1960-1961)*, in L. BOEVE – M. LAMBERIGTS – T. MERRIGAN (eds.), *Theology and the Quest for Truth: Historical- and Systematic-Theological Studies* (BETL, 202), Leuven, University Press – Peeters, 2007, 143-164.

89. S. CONGREGATIO S. OFFICII, *Decretum in generali consessu quo opus 'La vie de Jésus' a Ioanne Steinmann scriptum damnatur, 26 iunii 1961*, in AAS 53 (1961) 507-508. See J. MARTINEZ DE BUJANDA (ed.), *Index librorum prohibitorum*, Genève, Droz, 2002, p. 855: "Steinmann, Jean (1911-1963). Né dans le territoire de Belfort. Fra. Prêtre. Vicaire à la Basilique de Notre-Dame de Paris. Auteur de nombreux ouvrages sur la Bible. Le 14 février 1962, le Saint-Office lui interdit toute nouvelle publication en matière biblique. La vie de Jésus, 1959, [...] Decr. S. Off. 26/06/1961. Dernier ouvrage mis à l'Index". TC-member J.C. Fenton was quite delighted upon hearing the news, cfr. Diary Fenton, September 15, 1961.

Actually, it was a letter from Ruffini, dated May 9, 1961, to Ottaviani that had informed the Holy Office on 'problematic issues' in Steinmann's work. See F.M. STABILE, *Il cardinal Ruffini e il Vaticano II: Le lettere di un 'intransigente'*, in *Cristianesimo nella Storia* 11 (1990) 83-113.

90. Diary de Lubac, February 11, 1961 (published as H. DE LUBAC, *Carnets du Concile*. Introduit et annoté par L. FIGOUREUX, Paris, Cerf, 2007).

This contretemps also put Cerfaux, who was living in Rome, in a rather awkward position, since he had ties with both parties in the controversy. On the one side, Cerfaux was teaching exegesis at the Lateran University due to Piolanti's invitation. On the other side, he was a former student of the Biblicum, and had friendly relationships with many of its professors, among them Stanislas Lyonnet, who now came to ask his assistance. At the same time, Cerfaux also owed his TC nomination to Piolanti, and was closely collaborating with Garofalo. Cerfaux attempted to extricate himself from this quagmire by informing both Philips and Mgr. Charue (bishop of Namur) of the matter, and by undertaking a further serious effort to put an end to the controversy.

How so? In February 1961, after his intervention at the TC meeting, Cerfaux wrote a long letter to Cardinal van Roey, archbishop of Mechelen, begging him to intervene by contacting John XXIII[91]. Cerfaux made it clear that the controversy was not merely a minor dispute among experts. In fact, he stated that the entire field of theology was at stake. Van Roey thereupon wrote to John XXIII:

> J'ai été mis au courant, par des prélats et des prêtres qui travaillent à Rome dans des Commissions préparatoires au Concile du Vatican, d'une polémique suscitée par un article de Monseigneur Romeo [...] Je suis frappé par les critiques portées contre l'Institut Biblique Pontifical. Celui-ci a toujours eu la confiance de l'Épiscopat belge, qui y a envoyé plusieurs jeunes prêtres belges, docteurs en théologie de l'Université catholique de Louvain et qui font honneur à cet Institut. Permettez-moi de dire que cette polémique entre deux Instituts Pontificaux nous semble malencontreuse et sans fondement sérieux. Il paraît souhaitable, pour l'honneur de la Curie romaine, qu'elle ne se poursuive pas[92].

Two weeks later Cardinal Tardini replied to Van Roey, stating that the Pope had indeed intervened. It is not entirely clear what was meant by that answer, but it should be noted that on February 2, the Pope made public that Ernest Vogt, rector of the Biblicum, was to join the subcommission *De fontibus* – an indication that he supported the Biblicum. The diaries of Tromp and Schauf clearly indicate that neither Tromp nor

---

91. CLG: Fund Cerfaux, Rapport pour son éminence. Cerfaux explicitly mentions names (Romeo, Piolanti, Pizzardo, and puts a significant: 'non Garofalo'! next to this) of those attacking the Biblicum, yet on the other displays some critique of the Jesuit reaction in general ("les jésuites se sont émus outre mesure, à mon avis"). He ends his letter stating that: "Je pense qu'un mot de Son Éminence au Saint Père aurait une influence bienfaisante. Son Éminence devrait dire que le spectacle d'une congrégation romaine accusant de déviation dans la foi un institut où par ailleurs les futurs professeurs d'Écriture sont obligatoirement formés, est une chose vraiment inouïe et incompréhensible".

92. AAM: Fund Van Roey, letter from Van Roey to John XXIII, February 24, 1961.

Ottaviani had any part in this decision[93]. On the other hand, it should be acknowledged that weeks earlier Tromp had already proposed to Ottaviani to include some people from the Biblicum on the TC, suggesting the names of Benoit and Vogt. In the meantime, Cerfaux had involved himself in the controversy on yet another level – as a consultor to the Pontifical Biblical Commission. The board of consultors to this commission had gathered on March 5 to discuss the ongoing debate, and had decided to show its support to the Biblicum through a letter directed to Vogt. Cerfaux, along with Kerrigan ánd Garofalo (!) were among the ones to subscribe[94]. With this evidence one cannot categorically charge the SCDF with allying itself with the views and actions of the Lateran University at this time. At least three subcommission members, plus Vogt and Tromp, seriously disagreed with the actions undertaken by Lateran professors. Moreover, the subcommission did not have one single member from the Lateran in its ranks (except for Cerfaux, who was a guest professor). In the end, the effect of the controversy upon the SCDF could even be regarded as positive, given the addition of Vogt among its members.

III. APRIL-JUNE 1961: INCREASING INFLUENCE

Against this background, Cerfaux's subcommission continued its work and by the end of May 1961, presented a brand new draft, consisting of

---

93. VON TEUFFENBACH (ed.), *Konzilstagebuch Sebastian Tromp* (n. 11): "Die 1. Mart. 1961. [...] Vespere legi in l'Oss. Rom. nominatum esse membrum commissionis Arch. Quebecensem Roy (quod sciebam); nominati consultores Patres Philippus a Trinitate O.Carm.Disc.; Narc. Garcia Claretanum, et Ern. Voght S.J., rectorem Inst. Biblici (quod ignorabam)"; and "Die 2 Martii 1961. Mane colloquium cum Emo Cardli Praeside qui non erat certior factus de nominatione trium consultorum. R.P. Leclercq adit Secr. Gener. et audit Patrem Vogt fuisse nominatum volente ipso Pontifice". Also in Diary Schauf on March 9, 1961: "Tromp hat von der Ernennung nichts gewusst, erfuhr sie durch den Osservatore und fuhr ins Offiz nicht gerade rosig aufgelegt, auch um den Kardinal Ottaviani zu sagen, dass das doch keine Methode habe. Ottaviani wollte sich bei Tromp beschweren, dass Tromp ihn über die Ernennung nicht informiert habe. Beiden wusste also nichts. Tromp hat dan bei Felici angefragt, wie die Adressen der Ernannten seien und so zu verstehen gegeben, dass man nicht nett gehandelt habe. Vogts Ernennung kommt vom Papst".

94. Archive of the PBC: Letter from Athanasius Miller to Ernst Vogt, March 8, 1961: "Les consulteurs de la Commission Biblique Pontificale réunis en séance générale au Vatican le 5 mars 1961, sentent le devoir d'exprimer au Très Révérend Père Recteur de l'Institut Biblique Pontifical leur vif regret pour les accusations et les attaques lancées contre le sus-dit Institut et ses professeurs par Mgr. A. Romeo dans son écrit: 'L'enciclica Divino afflante Spiritu e le opiniones novae'. Ils profitent de l'occasion pour réaffirmer publiquement leur immuable attachement et leur solidarité avec l'Institut Biblique. Au nom de tous les Consulteurs réunis, le secrétaire, P. A. Miller".

four chapters (the five-chaptered structure presented by Burigana was absent). But what is more important is that the text underwent serious changes with the following new framework:

I.   On the Twofold Source of Revelation (text prepared by Van den Eynde and Cerfaux)
II. On the Inspiration of Scripture, Inerrancy, and Literary Composition (a completely new chapter prepared by di Fonzo and Castellino, integrating both their former texts)
III. On the Old Testament (text by Kerrigan, with minor changes)
IV. On the New Testament (based on Cerfaux's *Constitutio de Scriptura*)

After the three-chaptered January draft, the above outline displays yet another intermediate redaction phase between the *schema compendiosum* and the final five-chaptered constitution, which will be reached by June 1961. What we will do in the following pages is to follow closely the redactory work of the SCDF in the period after the second plenary TC-meeting (discussed above) starting at the end of April 1961. As compared to the previous redaction of *De fontibus*, this is obviously not a case of merely adding a fourth chapter to three existing chapters. The previous schema had been subject to various changes, both in structure and content. Precisely in this process of change Cerfaux's abovementioned activities came fully into play. Two previous chapters had now been integrated into one new text and two new chapters had arrived. The two new chapters (I and IV) bore Cerfaux's particular signature. Because of that, a closer look is in order.

1. The Constitutio de Scriptura Revisited

On April 21-22, 1961, the SCDF had its first meetings after the plenary meeting. From the invitation letter to the members of this gathering, it became clear that Cerfaux would play a certain role in these meetings:

> proxima sessio subcommissionis 'De fontibus' erit feria VI, 21 aprilis, hora 5 postmeridiana (17.00) in Palatio Sancti Officii; et si non finietur hac die, membra rursus vocabuntur die sequenti eadem hora. Ordo agendorum erit ut sequitur:
> 1) Disputabitur de textu parato a Rev.mo D. Cerfaux: 'Constitutio de S.Scriptura' cum relativis adnotationibus, et de textu Rev.mi P. Van den Eynde, 'De fontibus revelationis' (de Traditione).
> 2) Habebitur ratio de votibus [sic] Rev.mi D. Schmaus 'de lectione S.Scripturae privata' et 'de relatione theologi ad S. Scr.'
> 3) Paratur textus emendatus Rev.mi P. di Fonzo 'de inspiratione et inerrantia biblica'".

a. The Scripture and Tradition Debate

The first of these two meetings opened with a welcoming word by Garofalo to new member Vogt, and then immediately proceeded with the discussion of a draft by Van den Eynde[95] on the relationship between Scripture and Tradition. The draft began with the claim that there is one *single* deposit of faith which is being kept *as in* a twofold source – employing thus a terminology that leaned close to the style of Trent. Van den Eynde stated that both the Old and the New Testament had been written under the guidance of the Spirit, and that as such, God is their primordial author (i.e. author of both their content and their 'modus'). Only after that did he speak of two sources, and even then stressed their interdependence. Van den Eynde did not solve the question as to whether the fulness of revelation was found either in Scripture or in Tradition, but merely pointed out that – historically speaking – not everything could be found in Scripture.

The discussion on this draft (on April 21) is surprisingly concise and only touched two minor issues. It would seem that the theological matter

---

95. The original is kept in the ASV: Conc. Vat. II, 739: "D. Van den Eynde, *De Fontibus Revelationis [De Traditione]*;

[1] Eadem sancta mater Ecclesia tenet ac docet depositum fidei in sacra scriptura et divina traditione tamquam in duplici revelationis fonte integrum et sine errore contineri, alio tamen ac alio modo. Nam libri Veteris ac Novi Testamenti ita Spiri-
[5] tu Sancto inspirante conscripti sunt, ut non solum veritates quae in eis continentur verum etiam modus quo ipsae enuntiantur et exprimuntur Deum habeat auctorem. Traditio vero, utpote ipsius Christi ore ab Apostolis accepta aut ab eisdem Spiritu Sancto dictante quasi per manus tradita, sine huiusmo-
[10] di scripto ad nos usque pervenerunt.
Tantum autem abest ut hi duo fontes inter se discrepent, ut mutuam sibi opem ferant. Cum enim apostolica traditio eaque sola via sit qua plures veritates, eae imprimis quae ad inspirationem et canonicitatem sacrorum librorum spectant,
[15] Ecclesiae innotescunt, Sacra Scriptura ad enuntiandas et demonstrandas plerasque veritates traditas instrumentum praebet quo nullum efficacius.
Christus autem Dominum totum depositum fidei, – Sacras nempe Litteras et divinam Traditionem, – et custodiendum et tuendum et authentiae interpretandum non singulis fidelibus utcumque
[20 sic.] eruditis concredidit, sed soli vivo Ecclesiae magisterio. Huius ergo est, tamquam proximae et universalis credendi normae, non modo iudicare de sensu et interpretatione tum Sacrae Scripturae tum documentorum et monumentorum quibus temporis decursu traditio consignata est et manifestata, sed ea quoque
[25] illustrare et enucleare quae in utroque fonte nonnisi obscure ac velut implicite continentur".

at stake was not perceived as troubling. First, the word '*modus*' was problematic in Tromp's view. It was said to be too particular, and the TC secretary proposed a change that would insert a concept of 'verbal inspiration' in the text[96]. This was immediately opposed by Kerrigan, Garofalo ánd Cerfaux, and the case was left open[97]. The second point of discussion revealed how Van den Eynde's draft contained rather balanced theological standpoints. Tromp pointed out again that Tradition does not merely serve as the way to knowledge of things not contained in the Scriptures (*Traditio additiva*) but also serves in order to clarify and explain Scripture (*Traditio explicativa*)[98]. His intention was to install a sharp distinction between these two notions, which is precisely what Van den Eynde was attempting to avoid. The latter had therefore stressed the interconnectedness of Scripture and Tradition as quintessential, and left things quite open. As a representative of an historical theology (much in the footsteps of his Louvain director, Draguet[99]), he refers to the apostolic era, and states that in this period Tradition was never thought of as a monolithic but was always related to Scripture. Ernst Vogt supported, picked up the thread and added to it that Tradition (*i.e.* apostolic preaching)

---

96. See P. HÜNERMANN, *Eine 'kalligrafische Skizze' des Konzils*, in P. HÜNERMANN – J. HILBERATH (eds.), *Die Dokumente des Zweiten Vatikanischen Konzils: Theologische Zusammenschau und Perspektiven* (Herders theologischer Kommentar zum Zweiten Vatikanischen Konzil, 5), Freiburg, Herder, 2006, 447-469, pp. 453ff.

97. See ASV: Conc. Vat. II, 739, 104.10: Handwritten report by M. Leclercq, April 21, 1961: "Garofalo legit textum VdE.

Lin. 6: difficultas de vocabulo 'modus' nimis generico – Tromp proponit: 'verba quibus' VdE notat se loqui de Traditione, oecum. Trid. et Vat. de traditionibus.

Rursus de 'modis' – Non omnes admittunt 'verba' nam nolunt ut intelligatur inspiratio verbalis

Kerrigan – praefero 'modus'

Garofalo – modus facit cogitare de generibus litterariis

Cerfaux – videbimus infra De inspiratione

Tromp – ergo proponeret = 'ennuntiatio' – non admittunt alii.

Garofalo – Relinquamus rem apertam".

98. Tromp's personal copy of Van den Eynde's draft holds a handwritten note where he expands the "Cum enim apostolica traditio eaque sola via sit qua plures veritates, eae imprimis quae ad inspirationem et canonicitatem sacrorum librorum spectant, Ecclesiae innotescunt" with "et multae veritates in S. Scriptura obscure contentae, clare innotescunt". Also see ISR: Fund Garofalo, 10, who has written in the margins of his copy: "traditio non solum additiva sed explicativa".

99. It should not be forgotten that much of Van den Eynde's theological principles (on Tradition, on the Development of Doctrine as a historical process) were influenced by the Leuven professor Draguet, who had been convicted by Rome in the 1940s as a representative of the so-called 'nouvelle théologie'. This sheds a different light on Van den Eynde's current reputation as a 'Roman' theologian ... On Draguet, see a.o. R. GUELLUY, *Les antécédents de l'encyclique 'Humani generis' dans les sanctions romaines de 1942: Chenu, Charlier, Draguet*, in *Revue d'Histoire Ecclésiastique* 81 (1986) 421-497.

is one and integrates Scripture, so there is no way the two could be torn from each other. With this quarrel, the debate was finished, and the SCDF opened discussion on Cerfaux's *Constitutio*.

b. On the New Testament

The *Constitutio de Scriptura* will be studied at length particularily with regard to its implementation in the further preparation process of *De fontibus*, which makes it a key document for the development of a proper hermeneutics of the schema *De fontibus* later on.

Interestingly enough, the subcommission takes its time to read Cerfaux's work in a very detailed manner. They debate every single article, discussing the text line by line (as becomes clear through the detailed meeting reports by Leclercq). As for the first parts of Cerfaux's draft, Garofalo links them to Van den Eynde's draft on Tradition. SCDF secretary Garofalo presents the two opening articles (cf. supra: *Revelatio et traditio*; *Scriptura et traditio*) as a valuable general introduction to the entire schema[100]. The *katabasis* developed by Cerfaux (who relied on Clement of Rome) successfully enabled an integration of his talk on Tradition within a wider framework of salvation history. Thus, at the end of the discussion of these first articles it was decided to combine the draft of Van den Eynde with Cerfaux's insights into a new first part to the schema on the sources[101].

When discussing Cerfaux's article 3 (Libri canonici N.T. eorumque auctores), the *Constitutio* would then be regarded as the basis for a chapter

---

100. An introduction which, as we recall, would stress the historical process underlying any theology of Revelation. Cfr. Garofalo's handwritten remark on his personal copy of the *Constitutio de Scriptura* (next to paragraphs 1 & 2): "Proemio sulla rivelazione come manifestazione d'amore".

101. Report Leclercq, April 21, 1961:
"*Textus Cerfaux*:
Garof – statim transeamus ad Cerfaux, ut videamus utrum coalescat cum VdE.
Num. 1, lin 1-10: Garof – num hic inserenda alia idea introductoria?
Tromp – Forsan ad di Fonzo pertinet
[…] Haec par. 1 maximi momenti pro lectione SS. lin 12-32 = Haec idea optima, et maximi momenti (Gar.). Totum iter salutis describitur. Immo insistendum. Discutit Vde = non ad aliud pertinet? Forsitan de nimia materia in hac parte agitur.
Vogt – Constitutio De Ecclesia melius de via salutis aget.
P. Tromp explicat coordinationem idearum a Revelatione ad SS. Quod aliis placet.
Ergo Cerfaux + VdE simul congruebunt suos textus, et sic habebimus optimum prologum.
Tromp – etiam curanda brevitas".

on the New Testament. Again, apostolicity would become the key concept. Rather than discussing the authenticity of authorship of various New
Testament writings, Cerfaux based their authenticity on their apostolic
origins. This view, which we have already described, was accepted without any opposition. Some discussion was raised on the apostolic origin
of the gospel and on the need to distinguish between items of faith and
issues that pertain to the domain of historiography[102].

The next day the debate went on about the apostolic origins of the New
Testament, with Cerfaux explaining how the Church's faith in the apostolic authenticity of writings depended on their belonging to the Christian, i.e. apostolic tradition. Further on it was agreed to confirm the apostolicity of the NT-writings without any suggestion on the identity of their
(historical) authors. When discussion was raised about article 4 (Novum
Testamentum et Historia) it was decided that this paragraph was too general in character for use, and that it was too close to di Fonzo's work on
inspiration, etc. What mainly raised debate is Cerfaux's statement that
contemporary historians used different principles with regard to reflecting

102. Report Leclercq, April 21, 1961:
"*Unde statim ad N.T.*:
N. 3 – Ab initio Tromp = loquendum de gravissimis erroribus circa N.T., et quidem
latissime diffusis.
Lin. 31-54: Nihil obiiciunt.
Gar – quaerit utrum origo apostolica evangeliorum sit de fide ac non.
Cerf – hoc est traditionalis, sed certitudo potius ad historiam quam ad fidem pertinere
videtur. Proinde, dicit Gar, insistendum in certitudinem historicam. Sed (Tromp) est Eccle-
sia quae docet.
di Fonzo – Origo apostolica est de fide. Talis vel talis auctoris est de certitudine his-
torica. Adhuc maxime disputant de his omnibus.
Tromp – estne quaesitio maximi momenti pro hodie?
Alii consentiunt.
Tromp – sistendum in lin. 37, verbo = retinuit. Rursus disputant de notitiis antiquissimis'
num pertineant ad Traditionem formalem aut non.
Tromp – alio modo respici potest res = sufficit ut per plura saecula, etiam si non
antiquissima. Tenuta sit traditio aliqua!
Vogt – sed in casu non agitur de re stricto sensu revelata!
Castellino – exponit suam conceptionem circa historiam canonis
Insistit Tromp in ideam traditionis non antiquissimae sed recentioris, ex exemplo
assumptionis. Si res historice non potest probari, theologice teneatur.
Kerrigan – agitur non de re De fide sed connexa cum fide. Leo XIII docet rem de
authenticitate librorum SS, V.T. praesertim esse reservatam historicam.
Tromp – origo apostolica est De fide, sed quid de tali et tali apostolo ... ipse putat rem
esse certissimam, sed non dicendum esse de fide vel cum fide connexa". [...]
"Ergo = Ecclesia *credit* originem ab apostolicis viris. – et *semper tenuit* auctores esse
quorum Evangelia gerunt".
[...] "Gar. aliquod votum circa V.T. legit: statum laborum in SSCommissione de V.T.
Res tamen ad essentialia limitentur".

history, than did the biblical authors, implying that one cannot approach both with the same concept of historicity. The latter raises serious debate between Vogt and Tromp but in general, Cerfaux's idea was accepted[103]. Hence, the general ideas were removed from Cerfaux's work, resulting in a text merely contining the application of general ideas upon the New Testament problematic.

At the end of the meeting, the redaction process of the schema concluded with the following agenda:

1. Creating a new Scripture-Tradition draft based on the drafts of both Cerfaux and Van den Eynde
2. Creating a new chapter on inspiration (by di Fonzo), keeping Cerfaux' *Constitutio* in mind and combining elements of Castellino's former and revised chapters.
3. Creating a new chapter on the New Testament based on Cerfaux' notes.
4. Adapting Kerrigan's text to the general ideas as expressed in these meetings.

---

103. See Report M. Leclercq, April 22, 1961:
"di Fonzo – distribuit suum textum in nova redactione
Garofalo – iam paratus etiam textus de V.T.
Tromp – Rogetur quis pro voto utrum M, M, L, et Jo scripserint 4 evangelia, et reincidimus in disputationem hesternae diei.
Resumitur textus Cerfaux
N. 4: lin. 1-15 Tromp – debemusne citare Trident. uti iacet, nam allusio ad 'unanimem consensum Patrum' relinquit apertam
Garofalo – ergo sumatur sensus Trident., quod in calce citatur.
Tromp – etiam hic agitur de rebus quae non tt ad N.T. sed etiam ad V.T. = sicut res ergo quae antea dicenda sunt.
Garofalo – ergo, ad hic tt fit applicatio dicendo de concreta historicitate evangeliorum.
Vde – et de Actibus! Tr = sed hoc tamen minoris momenti.
Vogt – si de historicitate in genere loquimur, etiam aliquo modo alludere debemus ad genus litterarium.
Disputant ergo de formulatione nova illius periodi
Lin 28-37, p. 4, lin 1-55 (totius n. 4) tunc legitur: Explicatio rei, quomodo possibile sit quod secd. modum antiquum nec inspiratio nec historicitas pessumdetur.
Vogt – illa iam ex parte saltem alibi continentur.
Cerf. – forsan remittuntur ad partem generalem, unde aspicitur textus di Fonzo. Ipse tamen di Fonzo putat quod quid specialius dici debet de N.T. [...]
VdE – sed antiqui in genere historico misceant alia! Quod negat Tromp in casu S.S.
Vogt – offert exempla errorum S. Pauli, v.g. ad Corinthios scribentis quod neminem baptizavit, et postea se corrigentis.
Resp. alii – se correxit in ipsa eadem sententia, non est idem ac si se correxisset in eadem epistolam! Longa discussio inter Tr. et Vogt, qui aliquas exceptiones in inerrantia litteraria vult admittere.
VdE: genus historicum antiquorum diversum est a nostro.
[...] Et hic redigitur novus Textus ad mentem
di Fonzo et Cerfaux, IIa redactio
Kerrigan, IIa Redactio
Castellino promittit etiam suam IIa redactionem

2. Further SCDF-meetings. May-June 1961

In the following paragraphs we will give a brief overview of the developments of chapters II-V of the future schema on the sources, and then spend some more time going into detail on Cerfaux's influence on the first chapter. We choose to do so given the fact that scholarly debate on the schema *De fontibus* has focused largely on its chapter on Scripture. Most of the later negative reactions against the schema have to do with precisely this chapter, and at the same time we feel that this is indeed the text that has been least understood in a critical manner, given the lack of information regarding its redactorial background.

a. Chapters II-IV revised

On April 27, 1961, the TC held a meeting among the presidents of its subcommissions reflecting on the work done. Evidently, Garofalo's report reflected the discussion of April 21-22, and his private conversations with abbot Salmon, regarding a text on the Vulgate, to be integrated in the schema on the sources[104]. Finally, Garofalo promised Tromp and Ottaviani to prepare a complete schema for the next plenary TC meeting.

This means that the SCDF members needed all the time they had to work on the revision and creation of the four chapters. Thus, when we look at the SCDF activities throughout the period of May-June, the commission's *modus operandi* changes. We suddenly notice an extraordinary esprit de corps. Whereas in the first phases of *De fontibus*' preparation members played *cavalier seul* writing and preparing documents, now most revisions result from a sense of genuine teamwork. Also striking is the composition of the subcommission. We have discussed this earlier, when reviewing the member lists. Now, when the subcommission is at work it appears that this needs to be nuanced. When making use of M. Leclercq's handwritten reports of SCDF meetings one cannot but notice that the preparation of *De fontibus* was the work of a select core of members and consultors. A. Michel and J. Schröffer, though members, were never present at the meetings. Also Schmaus was absent 90% of the time, leaving the work to a team of four members (Garofalo, Cerfaux, Van den Eynde, Vogt[105]) and three consultors (di Fonzo, Castellino, Kerrigan).

---

104. Garofalo had already, in October 1960, decided to delegate the portion to be written on the Vulgate to the Benedictines of the Roman abbey San Girolamo. See the above quoted report on the first SCDF meeting.

105. Vogt's nomination did not, when looking closely at the preparatory disputes, where he was very active, prove worthless, as was suggested by BURIGANA, *La Bibbia nel*

Reviewing this list, it would be improper to designate this as a 'Roman commission', or at least a commission in which the voice of the *'oltralpi'* was not heard.

It would be appropriate to summarize briefly what happened during and between the series of meetings of May 4, May 18, May 24-25, and finally June 7 in 1961[106]. In general, most chapters were overhauled substantially. A great many existing articles were dismissed and serious efforts were made to put all chapters 'in line'. Again, the preparatory debates of April 21-22 on Cerfaux's *Constitutio* were kept in mind. On some of the new drafts there was a serious "Cerfaux" influence, on others less so. For instance, di Fonzo and Castellino were to write a new chapter on biblical inspiration and inerrancy, making use of their own, and Cerfaux's material. However, in the end – although Castellino's revision of his own work is largely based on Cerfaux – it is mainly di Fonzo's rather intransigent opinion that enters the schema. The opposite is the case with the chapter on the Old Testament, which draws much from Cerfaux's insights on salvation history as the general framework for the schema. As for the chapter on the New Testament, this is clearly a mixture of opinions and the result of debate. The condemnation passages mark a division within the subcommission, and are put in such strong language that one tends to forget their content, which is not that problematic after a close look. They merely tend to put some evident data in a negative fashion, refuting a type of exegesis that dismantles the biblical testimony from its historical grounds. While Cerfaux, Vogt, Kerrigan and Van den Eynde had complained about these statements[107], it is clear that the end of the chapter on the New Testament again contains many references to Cerfaux's "Constitution".

Concilio (n. 7), p. 69: "La sua nomina [Vogt] poteva essere vista come un elemento in grado di mutare l'orientamento della sottocommissione per la recezione delle istanze sull'esegesi delle quali alcuni professori del Biblico si erano fatti portavoci, nel momento in cui proprio il Biblico era sottoposto a un attacco frontale da parte di alcuni teologi, legati al S. Uffizio e all'Università Lateranense. La presenza di Vogt non determinò alcun cambiamento nella formulazione dello schema".

106. A detailed discussion of these meetings is found in my Ph.D. thesis: K. SCHELKENS, *Deus multifariam multisque modis locutus est … De redactie van het preconciliaire schema De fontibus revelationis. Een theologiehistorisch onderzoek met bijzondere aandacht voor de Belgische bijdrage* [unpublished doctoral dissertation, K.U.Leuven], Leuven, 2007.

107. They had even prepared a joint draft replacing the existing one, some fragments of which would eventually be accepted. See CSVII: Fund Janssen, s.n., Cap. De Novo Testamento. Textus Constitutionis cum aliquibus emendationibus propositis d. 24 Maii 1961 a R.D. Cerfaux, RR. PP. Van den Eynde, Kerrigan, Vogt.

b. Once more: Scripture and Tradition

Particularily revealing for a study on Cerfaux and *De fontibus,* then is the revision of the chapter on Scripture and Tradition. Van den Eynde and Cerfaux had finished its redaction on May 9, 1961. It was printed on the 13th and it was discussed at the SCDF meetings of May 18 and May 24-25. The new chapter consists of six articles, and would hardly be changed when compared to the final schema *De fontibus.* Let us have a closer look at it:

Article 1 (*De revelatione Veteris et Novi Testamenti*[108]), copying the Scripture constitution, opens with the first verses from the Hebrews letter, stressing the horizon of salvation history. In this paragraph revelation is generally described as an expression of God's love for humanity, and any comprehension of revelation is connected with the stories of God's salvific action within history in both the Old and the New Testament[109]. Also the second article (*De prima diffusione revelationis Novi Testamenti*) is faithful to Cerfaux's observations, when stating that revelation (as revelation of the Father through Christ) reaches the contemporary person only through the Church's preaching. Reference is made to Christ's preaching mandate to the Apostles and the katabasis-concept derived from Clement of Rome is taken up here[110].

---

108. Titles to the articles are not found in the original print. In ASV: Conc. Vat. II, 739, 114 we find a printed version of Van den Eynde's manuscript, with the following handwritten titles added by M. Leclercq on May 18, 1961 (they will be slightly changed later on:
    1. De revelatione V. et N.T.
    2. De revelatione N.T. per praedicationem Xi et Apostolorum
    3. De transmissione N.T.
    4. De duplici fonte
    5. De habitudine unius fontis ad alterum
    6. De habitudine utriusque fontis ad Magisterium

109. CSVII: Fund Van den Eynde, De duplici fonte revelationis (P. Van den Eynde), p. 1: "1. Revelatio, quam Deus in sapientia et bonitate sua hominibus impertiri dignatus est, duplici quasi gressu nobis advenit, Vetere nempe et Novo Testamento. Et in Vetere quidem Deus multifariam multisque modis patribus in prophetis locutus est (Heb. 1,1); in Novo autem thesauros scientiae et sapientiae toti generi humano per ipsum Filium eiusque Apostolos effudit".

110. CSVII: Fund Van den Eynde, De duplici fonte revelationis (P. Van den Eynde), p. 1: "2. Haec nova revelatio, quae veterem longe transcendit eamque consummavit, Deo ita disponente, potissime per praedicationem ubique terrarum sparsa est et auditu recepta. Christus siquidem Dominus in vita sua filiis Israel arcana regni coelorum viva voce propalavit et post resurrectionem Apostolis suis praecepit ut omni creaturae praedicarent (cf. Mc. 16,15), dicens: 'Data est mihi omnes potestas in caelo et in terra; euntes ergo docete omnes gentes, baptizantes eos in nomine Patris et Filii et Spiritus Sancti, docentes servare omnia quaecumque mandavi vobis' (Mt. 28, 18-20). Unde teste S. Clemente Romano, 'Apostoli nobis evangelii praedicatores facti sunt a Domino Iesu Christo. Iesus Christus missus est a Deo. Christus igitur a Deo et Apostoli a Christo; et factum est utrumque ordinatim ex voluntate Dei. Itaque acceptis mandatis et per resurrectionem

The third paragraph (*De transmissione revelationis Novi Testamenti*) again closely follows the *Constitutio de Scriptura* by explaining how the katabasis-lineage God? Christ? Apostles courses through history under the form of the apostolic succession in the Church? Bishops. We have already pinpointed this argumentation as Cerfaux's way of combining theological and historical reasoning: First there is Christ (as the object of revelation within history), and the experience of the Apostles in meeting him. The apostolic testimony of this experience is then handed on within the Christian community through the episcopate. This time, however, the text focuses on the fact that the testimony (praeconium apostolorum or praedicatio apostolorum) is put in writing. The process of committing the original experience to paper is conceived as a warrant for reliable transmission of this experience on to future generations. By stating things in this manner, the first chapter of *De fontibus* does distinguish between revelation as experienced reality (not as a conglomerate of propositions) and as an a posteriori expression of that reality handed on through Scripture and Tradition[111]. At least this is how Cerfaux conceived of it, and the way he and Van den Eynde intended to adapt their view to the limiting format and discourse of a council text.

Moreover, it is precisely this historico-theological line of thinking, rather than a neo-scholastic manualist discourse, that brings both authors to assert that Tradition is larger than Scripture in articles 4 (*De duplici fonte revelationis*) and 5 (*De habitudine unius fontis ad alterum*). Scripture is a (crucial and normative) moment in the larger historical process of transmitting the apostolic experience[112]. By means of illustration, some

Domini nostri Iesu Christi plena certitudine imbuti verboque Dei confirmati, cum certa Spiritu Sancti fiducia, egressi sunt annuntiantes regni Dei adventum'".

111. csvii: Fund Van den Eynde, De duplici fonte revelationis (P. Van den Eynde), p. 1: "3. Quod autem Christus et Apostoli instauraverunt, hoc volventibus saeculis semper in Ecclesia servatum est. Nam Episcopi, qui in Ecclesiis locum Apostolorum per successionem obtinent, eorum doctrinam semper fideliter tradiderunt et cum auctoritate interpretati sunt. Nec obstat quod quidam ex Apostolis vel apostolicis viris novam revelationem, divino Afflante Spiritu, litteris quoque commendaverunt. Nam tantum abest ut eo vivum ac praesens praeconium Apostolorum abrogatum vel etiam imminutum fuerit, ut posthac, testimonio Novae sicut Veteris Scripturae confirmatum, securius homines in viam salutis dirigat".

112. csvii: Fund Van den Eynde, De duplici fonte revelationis (P. Van den Eynde), pp. 1-2: "4. Christi itaque et Apostolorum mandatis et exemplis instituta, sancta mater Ecclesia semper tenuit ac tenet revelationem non in sola Scriptura sed in Scriptura et Traditione tanquam in duplici fonte integrum contineri, alio tamen ac alio modo. Nam libri Veteris et Novi Testamenti ad hoc quod revelata sine errore continent, insuper Spiritu Sancto inspirante conscripti sunt, ita ut Deum habent auctorem. Traditio vero, utpote Christi ore ab Apostolis accepta aut ab eisdem Spiritu Sancto dictante quasi per manus tradita, sine *huiusmodi* scripto per praedicationem ecclesiasticam ad nos usque pervenit".

doctrinal traditions that necessarily have grown and exist outside of the
Scriptures, are quoted but they nevertheless form part of the Church's
ongoing tradition[113]. In the final part of the chapter, Cerfaux and Van den
Eynde underline the bond between Scripture and Tradition by stating that
only together do they constitute the deposit of faith (to distinguish from
revelation), handed on to the magisterium of the Church[114].

The question now remains as to how the discussions on this new chapter were held within the SCDF. The basic structure laid out in the the first
three articles is generally accepted within the subcommission, implying
that discussion focussed mainly on the fourth and fifth articles of Chapter I[115]. For instance, with regard to article 4, the text is altered. Where it
once read that Revelation is immediately contained in both the Old and
the New Testament, without any errors, this is now reformulated as:

> Nam libri Veteris et Novi Testamenti praeterquam quod revelata continent,
> insuper Spiritu Sancto inspirante conscripti sunt.

The *'praeterquam quod'* establishes – in contrast to the former 'ad
hoc' – a certain distance between the reality of revelation and its reflection in Scripture. Essential here is the omission of *'ad hoc continere'*:
Scripture cannot be said to *be* revelation, rather it bears *witness* to it.
In the same phrase, the 'inerrancy' clause is omitted, and what is most
striking is that there is the adaptation of an explanatory footnote at the
end of the paragraph. Van den Eynde and Cerfaux had thought it sufficient to refer to Vatican I and Trent when discussing the notion of

113. CSVII: Fund Van den Eynde, De duplici fonte revelationis (P. Van den Eynde),
p. 2: "5. Nemo tamen Traditionem exinde minoris facere aut ei fidem derogare audeat.
Licet enim Sacra Scriptura, inspirata cum sit, ad enuntiandas et demonstrandas veritates
traditas instrumentum praebeat divinum, eius nihilominus sensus nonnisi Traditione apostolica certe et plene intelligi vel etiam exponi potest; immo Traditio, eaque sola, via est
qua plures veritates revelatae, eae imprimis quae ad integritatem, inspirationem et canonicitatem omnium et singulorum sacrorum librorum spectat, Ecclesiae innotescunt".
114. CSVII: Fund Van den Eynde, De duplici fonte revelationis (P. Van den Eynde),
p. 2: "6. Ut autem ambo fontes revelationis concorditer et efficacius ad salutem hominum
concurrerent, providus Dominus eos tanquam unum fidei depositum ad custodiendum et
tuendum et authentice interpretandum haud singulis fidelibus utcumque eruditis concredit,
at soli vivo Ecclesiae magisterio. Huius ergo est, qua proximae et universalis credendi
normae, non modo iudicare de sensu et interpretatione cum Scripturae Sacrae tum documentorum et monumentorum quibus temporis decursu Traditio consignata est et manifestata, sed ea quoque illustrare et enucleare quae in utroque fonte nonnisi obscure ac velut
implicite continentur".
115. Report by M. Leclercq, May 24-25, 1961, in ASV: Conc. Vat. II: "Imprimis discussio fit de textu R.P. VdE, nn. 4 et 5".

Tradition. But at this meeting the very notion was discussed seriously and with great interest in the way Chapter I differed from previous council texts. Hence, the new footnote will sum up the three main differences:

1. The word '*Traditio*' is only used in its singular form. The plural '*traditiones*' as used by Trent is no longer referred to.
2. Where once the formula '*sine scripto traditio*' was used, this is now alternatively rendered. Van den Eynde and Cerfaux (historians that they were) had indicated the process of transmission was not merely an oral process. This explains why their article four read: '*sine huiusmodi scripto*'. The '*huiusmodi*' opened up the possibility of accepting various modalities of transmission within the concept of Tradition and illustrates the fact that there are, of course, also writings involved outside of Scripture throughout the history of the Church. The issue is simply that these other writings do not have the same status as Scripture.
3. Here the influence of Cerfaux's constant insistence on Tradition as an historical process of preaching is felt most: The existing definition is enlarged with a reference to the Church's *praedicatio*[116].

One closing remark, concerns the fifth article where there were some minor corrections. In particular the replacement of 'demonstrandas' by the verb 'illustrandas' is noteworthy since it tends to stress that Scripture is not to be reduced to a collection of citations to prove or support theological concepts.

IV. CLOSING TIME ...

At the beginning of June 1961 most of the chapters had reached the end of the process, and on June 14 the SCDF secretary walked into Tromp's office to submit the four chapters[117]. All of the discussions we have mentioned above were taken into account, resulting into four very complex

116. The Latin text of the footnote is found in CSVII: Fund Janssen, 3.01, Constitutio de Fontibus Revelationis, p. 5: "Haec Traditionis descriptio a descriptione Concilii Tridentini et Concilii Vaticani in tribus differt: 1) adhibet vocem Traditio non iam numero plurali sed singulari; 2) pro locutione sine scripto, habet: sine huiusmodi scripto; 3) addit traditionem per praedicationem ecclesiasticam ad nos usque pervenire. Quae modificationes factae sunt, prima, ut textus melius adaptetur actuali modo loquendi magisterii et theologorum; secunda, ut tollatur ambiguitas locutionis 'Traditio sine scripto'; tertia, ut iuxta vota multorum Episcoporum, nexus essentialis Traditionis cum magisterio vivo in ipsa definitione Traditionis indicetur".

117. VON TEUFFENBACH (ed.), *Konzilstagebuch Sebastian Tromp* (n. 11): "Die 14 Junii: fer. IV" [...] "Venit Mgr. Garofalo qui mihi obtulit partem magnam Constit. De Fontibus

chapters. Four? – Thus we have one chapter missing. In order to be able to conclude the redaction of the schema on the sources on deadline, Garofalo had asked his members and consultors in May[118] to develop suggestions for a fifth chapter, *De lectione S. Scripturae in Ecclesia* (Schmaus had delivered a votum on the topic in the month of April). The plan was for four persons to react and hand in a draft: Di Fonzo[119], Kerrigan[120], Cerfaux[121] and Tromp[122]. Again, only those belonging to the SCDF core were involved in the redaction. Only this time there was little teamwork. Since time was short, Garofalo had gathered all drafts only in June and prepared a provisional chapter bearing in mind the various suggestions[123]. This was discussed at the SCDF meeting on June 16 and finally – after some discussion – resulted in a draft[124] for the last chapter. Only at this point was the fivefold structure of the *Constitutio de fontibus* reached. It remained the basis for conciliar debate, and is as follows:

    I.   De duplici fonte revelationis
    II. De S. Scripturae inspiratione, inerrantia et compositione litteraria
    III. De Vetere Testamento
    IV. De Novo Testamento
    V. De Sacra Scriptura in Ecclesia

Finally, on June 23, the *Subcommissio de fontibus revelationis* gathered one last time. The first four chapters, again distributed among those present, were left virtually unchanged, apart from some grammatical remarks by Cerfaux, di Fonzo and Kerrigan[125]. The last chapter was then finalized.

---

in redactione fere definitiva. Opus laudabile". [...] "Die 16 Junii 1961: feria VI. Vespere hora 5-7 sessio SubComm. de Fontibus".

118. See Garofalo's letter to the SCDF-members and consultors, May 8 1961, in ASV, Conc. Vat. II, 739, 114: "Reverendissime Domine, Honori atque pergratum mihi est Tibi mittere textum Cap. III et IV Constitutionis 'de utroque fonte Revelationis' Subcommissioni nostrae concreditae. Exeunte mense Maio mittentur Cap. I (De utroque fonte Revelationis) et Cap. II (De S. Scripturae inspiratione, inerrantia, etc.). Mense Iunio paratum erit etiam ultimum caput V. Te humanissime rogo ut mittere velis animadversiones tuas ad Cap. III et IV, ante finem mensis Iunii, ut inter nos disputari possint antequam sessio generalis Commissionis Theologicae mense septembri habeatur".

119. CSVII: Fund Van den Eynde, 3.23: De lectione S. Script.

120. CSVII: Fund Van den Eynde, 3.22: Ad cap. 5.

121. CSVII: Fund Van den Eynde, 3.21: De interpretatione et lectione S. Scripturae.

122. CSVII: Fund Philips, 0273: De lectione S. Scripturae.

123. ASV: Conc. Vat. II, 740, 128.1: De Sacra Scriptura in Ecclesia (textus propositus a D. Salv. Garofalo). This document in the Archivio segreto displays handwritten notes mentioning the names of those present at the meeting of June 16th: "Gar., Van den Eynde, Cerfaux, Castell., di Fonzo, Tromp, Leclercq. Abest Voght [sic]".

124. ASV: Conc. Vat. II, 800: S. Garofalo, Cap V.: De Sacra Scriptura in Ecclesia (red. 2a), final draft dated June 19, 1961.

125. Report M. Leclercq, dated June 23, 1961, in ASV: Conc. Vat. II, 740: "De fontibus 23 giugno. Garofalo proponit aliquas correctiones parvas (cf. textum correctum,

The subcommission had reached the end of its activities at that point and was the first of the TC subcommissions to do so. A few weeks later TC secretary Tromp noted in his journal: "Mittitur ad typographiam textus Const. De Fontibus". When printed, the document on the sources of Revelation would be 18 pages in length, and on July 29, 1961 it rolled off the presses[126]. Still, the story of its preparations does not end here. The schema will have to pass the examination of another plenary TC meeting, and afterwards be read and throughly discussed by the Central Preparatory Commission. None of these further stages, however, involved the two Belgian architects of the document. Cerfaux[127] will be facing health troubles, and on September 6, 1961 he writes to M. Leclercq:

> Mon Révérendissime Père, Je me vois obligé de vous demander dispense d'assister à la session de septembre de la commission théologique. Une indisposition subite m'a forcé d'entrer en clinique. J'y suis resté huit jours. Il n'y a rien de grave, mais je suis condamné à me reposer encore durant tout ce mois. J'ai l'impression de pouvoir reprendre ensuite mon travail ordinaire. Vous m'excuserez donc avec votre bienveillance habituelle. Je me permettrai de vous envoyer dans quelques jours de brèves remarques concernant les schemata que vous avez bien voulu me communiquer. Je vous suis uni de prière durant ces semaines et je demande au Saint-Esprit de bénir nos travaux[128].

n. 31) – Item Cerfaux – Item di Fonzo – Item Kerrigan. Sic primo pro Cap. I-IV, dein cap. V".

126. VON TEUFFENBACH (ed.), *Konzilstagebuch Sebastian Tromp* (n. 11): "Die 24 Junii 1961: Sabbato. Mane in officio praeparo textum De fontibus, ut typis edi possit". For the further proces of corrections up to the final print see "Die 26 Julii: feria IV ... Corrigo folia typis edita Const. de Fontibus. Vespere eadem folia adeunt typogr. Vatic.: 'si stampi'". [...] "Die 29 Julii: Sabbato: Mane in officio accipio Const. de Fontibus typis editam. Sunt 18 paginae".

127. Letter from R. Laurentin to Lucien Cerfaux, September 5, 1961, in CLG: Fund Cerfaux: "Monseigneur, J'ai admiré votre votum sur le problème des origines humaines – et j'ai deviné votre influence dans le schéma *De fontibus*, qui est un des meilleurs".

128. See also CLG: Fund Cerfaux, letter from Cerfaux to Michael Leclercq, September 6 1961: "Mon Révérend Père et cher ami, Je suis rentré de Rome très fatigué, et j'ai dû me résigner à entrer en clinique. J'en ai eu pour huit fois d'examens. Rien de grave, heureusement, mais je suis condamné à me reposer encore tout ce mois-ci. J'écris par le même courrier au P. Tromp", and VON TEUFFENBACH (ed.), *Konzilstagebuch Sebastian Tromp* (n. 11), on the same day: "Deinde venit P. Dhanis, plura communicat: Impeditus est Mgr. Cerfaux, qui curatus fuit in nosocomio".

Tromp reacts on September 9 (CLG: Fund Cerfaux, Letter from Tromp to Cerfaux): "Iam mihi dixerat R.P. Dhanis te non nimis bene valere, ideoque non interesse posse consessui plenario huius mensis. Valde doleo, et una mecum Emus Praeses, de tua absentia coacta: adsis spiritualiter et nos adiuves tuis precibus, sicut promisisti. Et nos orabimus ut mox salute recuperata Romam adire possis. Praeparatio consessus plenarii non fit sine labore et sudore. Confluunt observationes quae generatim sunt benevolae et criticam continent positivam".

Likewise, Van den Eynde will be absent for the further developments. Exactly one week after Cerfaux, he wrote to Tromp:

> Zeer eerwaarde hooggeleerde Pater Secretaris, Mijn moeder is op 31 augustus laatstleden overleden in de gezegende ouderdom van 85 jaar. Op 4 september werd zij begraven. [...] Pater Generaal heeft mij toegestaan mijn vakantie tot na 15 september te verlengen. Ik weet nog niet precies wanneer ik hier klaar kom, maar het zal in ieder geval niet vóór 23 september zijn. Mag ik u eerbiedig verzoeken mij te willen verontschuldigen bij zijne Eminentie. Ik zal al doen wat ik kan om zo spoedig mogelijk naar Rome weer te keren en ten minste een deel van de vergaderingen van de Commissie bij te wonen[129].

Putting aside all further troubles surrounding this noteworthy document, the schema *De fontibus revelationis* appears to bear a significant 'Belgian' mark. Cerfaux and Van den Eynde have been quite influential in their subcommission. This is something that, up until now, has hardly been noticed. When looking at the way they sought to establish influence, it is striking that Cerfaux's *Constitutio de Scriptura* played a key role in the redaction of the schema. Of course, the schema is, as are all council documents, a composite text. It bears marks of various opinions, various schools of thought. However, with regard to this particular text, this may sound somewhat surprising, given the fact that it is thought to be the bearer of an almost exclusive Roman, manualist, neo-scholastic, etc., theology of Revelation. Only through careful study of its redaction, and through knowledge of the role of actors such as Cerfaux and Van den Eynde can we reach a needed, more equilibrated reading of the schema on the sources. When reading carefully one can find evidence for a theology of Revelation that is purely conceptual and abstract, yet at the same time the attentive reader may be able to detect the trail of an historical theology[130], which is often thought to be absent.

Faculty of Theology   Karim SCHELKENS
Sint-Michielsstraat 6
B-3000 Leuven
Belgium

---

129. ASV: Conc. Vat. II, 732, 32, letter from Van den Eynde to Tromp, September 13, 1961.

130. Our opinion on this behalf is supported by the discourse-analysis on *De fontibus*, made by S. Salati, who points to the constant use of dynamic language as a factor stressing the importance of historical processes in the schema. See S. SALATI, *La chiesa e la sua scrittura: Studio genetico del Capitolo VI della costituzione conciliare Dei Verbum, dalle prime proposte degli anni 1959-1960 all'approvazione finale del 18 X 1965* (Excerpta ex dissertatione ad Doctoratum in Facultate Theologiae Pontificiae Universitatis Gregorianae), Rome, Gregorian University, 2004.

DE REVELATIONE UNDER REVISION
(MARCH-APRIL 1964)

CONTRIBUTIONS OF C. MOELLER AND OTHER BELGIAN THEOLOGIANS[1]

I. THE CONTEXT OF THIS STUDY

This paper represents a further stage in work on the topic, "Theologians at Vatican II: the Moments and Means of their Contribution". My publications of results began in accounts of Piet Smulders's work on *Dei verbum* and expanded recently into a panoramic overview[2]. Provisionally, I find the contributions of theological experts to Vatican Council II falling into ten "moments and means".

The Pre-Preparatory Period, 1959-1960

1. In 1959, for the formulation of pre-preparatory *vota* of future Council members, some theologians made contributions upon request[3].
2. Soon after Pope John XXIII's announcement, and continuing, theologically qualified interpretations began appearing to inform the world,

---

1. The following abbreviations are used in the notes of this paper:
AS: *Acta Synodalia Sacrosancta Concilii Oecumenici Vaticani II*, 6 vols. in 28 parts, Vatican City, Typis Polyglottis Vaticanis, 1970-1999.
DH: H. DENZINGER – P. HÜNERMANN (ed.), *Enchiridion symbolorum, definitionum et declarationum de rebus fidei et morum*, Edizione bilingue, Bologna, Dehoniane, 1996.
I am grateful to the staff of Grasselli Library of John Carroll University for the efficient procurement of books on Vatican II.
2. Five articles on Smulders's theological work have appeared in *Gregorianum*, beginning in 2001 and continuing in 2002, 2003, and 2005. Then, based on a conference at Brescia in February 2004, I brought out *I teologi al Vaticano II: Momenti e modalità del loro contributo al Concilio*, in *Humanitas* 59 (2004) 1012-1038.
3. Reported for some *vota* in M. LAMBERIGTS – C. SOETENS (eds.), *À la veille du Concile Vatican II: Vota et réactions en Europe et dans le catholicisme oriental* (Instrumenta Theologica, 9), Leuven, Bibliotheek van de faculteit der Godgeleerdheid, 1992, e.g. by J. Jacobs on the Willebrands – Thijssen memo on ecumenism adopted by four Dutch Bishops (J.Y.H.A. JACOBS, *Les 'Vota' des évêques néerlandais pour le concile*, pp. 99-110). Also cases of theologians' contribution are reported by J. KOMONCHAK, *U.S. Bishops' Suggestions for Vatican II*, in *Cristianesimo nella storia* 15 (1994) 313-371.

including the future members, of the possible significance and issues of the coming Council[4].

3. Also in 1959-60, the members of fifty-three faculties of theology and related disciplines submitted preparatory "studies" of issues relevant to the Council[5].

The Preparatory Period, June 1960 to June 1962

4. For the Preparatory Commissions and Secretariat for Promoting Christian Unity, experts served in preparing draft schemata[6].

5. In assistance of members of the Central Preparatory Commission, during 1961-62, some experts formulated evaluations of the draft texts coming from the other Commissions[7].

The Conciliar Period, October 1962 - December 1965

6.   Just before and during the First Period of 1962, theologians offered to Council members oral and written presentations in the form of

4. Among the earliest offerings was Y. CONGAR's unsigned essay, *Les conciles dans la vie de l'Église*, in *Informations catholiques internationales* 90 (February 15th, 1959) 17-26. Two early books which circulated widely both in the original and in translation were H. JEDIN's *Kleine Konziliengeschichte: Die zwanzig ökumenischen Konzilien im Rahmen der Kirchengeschichte* (Herder-Bücherei, 51), Freiburg, Herder, 1959 and H. KÜNG, *Konzil und Wiedervereinigung: Erneuerung als Ruf in die Einheit*, Vienna, Herder, 1960. G. Caprile offered regular notes on early publications, some – but not all – theologically weighty, in *La Civiltà cattolica*, reprinted in G. CAPRILE, *Il Concilio Vaticano II*, vol. I/1, Rome, Civiltà Cattolica, 1966, in sections entitled "Rassegna della stampa".

5. *Acta et Documenta Concilio oecumenico Vaticano II apparando*, Series prima (Antepreparatoria), vol. IV [3 parts], *Studia et vota universitatum et facultatum...*, Vatican City, 1960-61. See, for example, M. LAMBERIGTS, *The vota antepreparatoria of the Faculties of Louvain and Lovanium (Zaire)*, in LAMBERIGTS – SOETENS (eds.), *À la veille du Concile* (n. 3), 169-183; and É. FOUILLOUX, *Théologiens romains et Vatican II (1959-1962)*, in *Cristianesimo nella storia* 15 (1994) 373-394.

6. See, for example, the contribution given in this volume by K. SCHELKENS, *Lucien Cerfaux and the Preparation of the Schema De Fontibus Revelationis*. Congar set down his experiences of work for the Preparatory Theological Commission in Y. CONGAR, *Mon Journal du Concile*. Présenté et annoté par Éric MAHIEU. Avant-propos de D. CONGAR, préface de B. DUPUY, Paris, Cerf, 2002, Vol. I, pp. 15-98.

7. For example, Rahner's comments for Cardinal König, *Konzilsgutachten für Kardinal König*, in H. VORGRIMLER – K. RAHNER, *Sehnsucht nach dem geheimnisvollen Gott*, Freiburg, Herder, 1990, 95-149. Another member of the Central Preparatory Commission was Cardinal Frings of Cologne. Hubert Jedin spoke to him about the critical importance of the selection of those who would serve on the Council's Commissions, which may have motivated the Cardinal's call for postponement of elections on the Council's first working day. H. JEDIN – K. REPGEN (eds.), *Lebensbericht*. Mit einem Dokumentanhang (Veröffentlichungen der Kommission für Zeitgeschichte bei der katholischen Akademie in Bayern. Reihe A: Quellen, 35), Mainz, Matthias-Grünewald, 1984, pp. 203-204.

theological updating, explanations and evaluations of the initial draft schemata, and they even at times circulated alternative formulations and texts[8].

7. Beginning in 1962 and continuing, numerous theologian-experts assisted Council members, both individuals and episcopal conferences, in preparing the members' oral and/or written *animadversiones* on Council schemata[9].

8. Such work began in August-September 1962, with evaluations of the first seven draft texts. Some examples: Piet Smulders advising Nuncio Beltrami in The Hague; Yves Congar formulating judgments for Archbishop Weber of Strasbourg; Jean Daniélou helping the Coadjutor Archbishop of Paris, Veuillot; Franz Stegmuller reviewing the drafts and composing an alternative *Schema de Deo* for Bishop Schäufele of Freiburg im Breisgau. Weber, Veuillot, and Schäufele sent on portions of their consultors' work to the Council Secretariat, in texts now in Archivio Segreto Vaticano [hereafter referred to as ASV], *Conc. Vat. II*, 143: *Animadversiones Patrum ante Concilii initium*. Parts have been published in *AS. Appendix*, pp. 69-336. – The best known commentary on the seven initial drafts was by E. Schillebeeckx, a text widely circulated in Rome in the first weeks of the Council in English and Latin, as related by J. BROUWERS, *Vatican II: derniers préparatifs et première session: Activités conciliaires en coulisses*, in É. FOUILLOUX (ed.), *Vatican II commence... Approches francophones* (Instrumenta Theologica, 12), Leuven, Bibliotheek van de faculteit der Godgeleerdheid, 1993, 353-368. – Consultative assistance to groups of Council Fathers expanded into the lectures given by theologian experts, of which an early example was J. Ratzinger's lecture, *Bemerkungen zum Schema De fontibus revelationis*, on October 10, 1962, to the German-speaking bishops. Two weeks later, Ratzinger offered the sketch of an alternative doctrinal text to eight European cardinals, including Siri (cf. B. LAI, *Il papa non-eletto: Giuseppe Siri, cardinale di Santa Romana Chiesa* (I Robinson), Rome, Laterza, 1993, pp. 369-371). The sketch then inspired the Rahner-Ratzinger exposition *De revelatione Dei et hominis in Jesu Christo facta*, distributed in ca. 2000 copies. Elmar Klinger gives evidence for Karl Rahner, assisted by Joseph Ratzinger, being the author of the text that circulated: E. KLINGER, *Der Beitrag Karl Rahners zum Zweiten Vaticanum im Lichte des Karl-Rahner-Archivs Elmar Klinger in Würzburg*, in M.T. FATTORI – A. MELLONI (eds.), *Experience, Organizations and Bodies at Vatican II: Proceedings of the Bologna Conference December 1996* (Instrumenta Theologica, 21), Leuven, Bibliotheek van de faculteit der Godgeleerdheid, 1999, 261-274, on p. 265. The text is given in Latin and French in B. DUPUY (ed.), *La révélation divine* (Unam Sanctam, 70a), Paris, Cerf, 1968, pp. 2 and 577-587, and in Latin and English in B. CAHILL, *The Renewal of Revelation Theology: The Development and Responses to the Fourth Chapter of the Preparatory Schema De Deposito Fidei* (Tesi Gregoriana. Serie teologia, 51), Rome, Editrice Gregoriana, 1999, pp. 300-317. – A special case was the work for the non-Catholic observers by experts of the Secretariat for Promoting Christian Unity. On this: É. FOUILLOUX, *Des observateurs non-catholiques*, in ID. (ed.), *Vatican II commence*, 235-261, especially 250-253, on the weekly presentations by Secretariat theologians such as J. Hamer, Y. Congar, and G. Thils.

9. I treated one theologian's preparation of evaluations taken over by the bishops of Indonesia in articles 2 and 5 of the series, *Pieter Smulders and Dei Verbum*, in *Gregorianum* 82 (2001) 559-593 and 86 (2005) 93-134. Otto Semmelroth's Council *Tagebuch* records his regular preparation of Latin texts for the interventions of Bishop Hermann Volk, who sent to Semmelroth German drafts of what he intended to say. But, late in the Council (Nov. 2, 1965), Congar lamented that some interventions he had prepared for bishops were not delivered nor even submitted in writing, with the result that in

8. As participants in the work of the Council's commissions, during Council sessions and intersessions, experts made essential contributions to revising schemata, as I will show for Charles Moeller and the other Belgians treated in this paper.

9. As schemata neared their final form, experts became active in drafting *modi* for the members, for submission with a view to polishing the Council's documents[10].

10. During the Council's thirty-nine months (October 1962 - December 1965), and in the early post-conciliar period, theologian-experts interpreted the event and the Council documents in hundreds of venues of oral and written commentary[11].

Within this expansive outline, this paper aims to exemplify the eighth type of contribution, that of theologian-experts working with Vatican II commissions. I will present in detail a text by Charles Moeller for the Doctrinal Commission, in the Sub-commission *De revelatione*, during the Council's second intersession of late Winter and Spring 1964. Moeller's work left its mark on the *textus emendatus* on revelation, which proved to be an important positive step toward the Constitution *Dei verbum*. Looking beyond Moeller's work, I will also list a number of other Belgian contributions of Spring 1964 to the successfully revised *Schema de revelatione*. A closing reflection will consider in a constructive vein the truth of the remark of Yves Congar that Vatican II was a Council "largely that of the theologians who ... gave to it enormous labors"[12].

the Commission work of revision, a *peritus* had no basis for introducing a desirable amendment on the basis of a Council member's proposal. CONGAR, *Mon Journal du Concile* (n. 6), Vol. II, p. 460.

10. In August 1964 and after, Congar prepared "our *modi*" for use in the voting on *De Ecclesia* (*Ibid.*, II, p. 120 and 131. But he lamented the severe rules that G. Philips formulated for the *expensio* of doctrinal *modi*, which led to few of the amendments he had drafted being accepted. (CONGAR, *Mon Journal du Concile* [n. 6], Vol. II, p. 187). After distribution of the *textus denuo emendatus* of the draft Constitution on Divine Revelation, in 1965 the professors of the Biblical Institute prepared several *modi* for the Brazilian bishops, which were duly submitted and entered the process of evaluation along with other *modi* on single paragraphs submitted on September 20, 21, and 22, with votes *Placet iuxta modum*.

11. At Münster, late in 1963 and 1964, the author was regularly in the crowds attending the evening lectures on the just concluded Council periods by J. RATZINGER, which then became his *Theological Highlights of Vatican II*, New York, Paulist, 1966.

12. "Ce concile aura été largement celui des théologiens, qui ... y ont fourni un travail énorme". CONGAR, *Mon Journal du Concile* (n. 6), Vol. II, p. 421 (Oct. 5, 1965); in the same vein, II, 81 (May 20, 1964) and II, 465 (November 7, 1965).

II. The Subcommission *De revelatione* March-April 1964

To replace the unsatisfactory schema *De fontibus revelationis* (1962), a draft revision on God's revelation and the communication of God's word in Tradition and Scripture was prepared by the Mixed Commission (Doctrine / Secretariat for Promoting Christian Unity) and sent out to the Council Fathers in May 1963. The text was one product of Vatican II's "second preparation". But in response, during the Summer of 1963 numerous Fathers sent in comments and many proposed changes of this version of *De revelatione*. These were sufficiently critical of the text that the Coordinating Commission concluded on August 31, 1963, that the Mixed Commission's schema was not an adequate basis for discussion during the Council's working period of 1963[13].

But at the end of the second period Pope Paul VI indicated, on December 4, 1963, that the next period of 1964 would include a new round of work on God's revelation, Tradition, and Scripture[14]. After Pope Paul's announcement, several experts and Fathers went to work preparing still further comments on *De revelatione* for submission by January 31, 1964, so they could contribute to the revision that the Doctrinal Commission would have to undertake[15].

---

13. The Commission judged that the Mixed Commission's schema was not viable, because its weaknesses had been brought to light by the "osservazioni abbastanza gravi finora presentate". Letter of Card. Cicognani to Card. Ottaviani, August 31, 1963; *AS* V/1, p. 651.

14. The Coordinating Commission had discussed placing revelation once more on the Council's agenda in late November and on Nov. 29, 1963, the Commission's President, Cardinal Cicognani, told Cardinal Ottaviani that the Doctrinal Commission should prepare to rework the schema on revelation. *AS* V/2, pp. 42, 45-47.

15. After Paul VI's announcement, Umberto Betti began a new study of *De revelatione*. He was with Archbishop Florit in Florence January 9-12, 1964, to prepare 17 pages of comments and proposed amendments, which Florit took over and sent to the Council Secretariat and to the office of the Italian Episcopal Conference for distribution to the bishops of Italy. Betti judged it urgent to have a text more worthy of the Council than the "stunted and spindly" draft on revelation produced by the Mixed Commission the year before (U. Betti, *Diario del Concilio: 11 ottobre 1962-Natale 1978* (Oggi e domani. Serie II, 24), Bologna, Dehoniane, 2003, pp. 26 and 28). Florit's comprehensive text is in *AS* III/3, pp. 831-837; F. Gil Hellin, *Concilii Vaticani II Synopsis in ordinem redigens schemata cum relationibus necnon patrum orationes atque animadvertiones: Constitutio dogmatica de divina Revelatione Dei Verbum*, Vatican City, TPV, 1993, pp. 454-461. Another lengthy comment from early 1964 came from Card. R. Silva Henríquez of Santiago, Chile (*AS* III/3, pp. 794-800; Gil Hellin, *Concilii Vaticani II Synopsis*, pp. 474-480). All the 94 comments, including 16 from groups of Fathers and expressing the views of ca. 340 Council Fathers, are collected in *AS* III/3, pp. 792-919. Gil Hellin, *Concilii Vaticani II Synopsis*, gives on pp. 349-483 the interventions that influenced the revision of March-June 1964.

On March 2, 1964, the members and *periti* of the Doctrinal Commission gathered in Rome for two weeks' work, especially to complete a new draft *De ecclesia*. For revising *De revelatione* Cardinal Ottaviani named, on March 7, a Sub-Commission of seven members, with numerous *periti*, who would first study the Council Fathers' comments, which were on hand in 225 mimeographed pages, and then propose emendations based on desires of the Fathers[16]. The recently elected Vice-President of the Doctrinal Commission, Bp. A.-M. Charue of Namur, was to preside over the revision and he was joined on the new Sub-Commission by Abp. E. Florit of Florence, Bp. G.L. Pelletier of Trois Rivières, Québec, Bp. A.E. van Dodewaard of Haarlem, Netherlands, Bp. F. Barbado y Viejo, O.P., of Salamanca, and the recently elected Commission members, Aux. Bp. J.-M. Heuschen of Liège and Abbot Chr. Butler, O.S.B., of Downside, England.

On March 11, after a mid-afternoon strategy session at the Belgian College, the Sub-Commission met to clarify assignments. Bp. Heuschen became a member of a first group assigned to revise the *Prooemium* on revelation and Chapter One on tradition, with Abp. Florit presiding. The *periti* were assigned to work on particular sections of the *schema*, with Charles Moeller and Albert Prignon assigned to the *Prooemium*, together with P. Smulders and C. Colombo, while U. Betti, Y. Congar, H. Schauf, and K. Rahner were commissioned to prepare a new Chapter One on the controverted issues concerning Tradition, Scripture, and the Magisterium. Bp. Charue will preside over a second group responsible for the biblical chapters II-V, whose members included Bp. van Dodewaard, with Béda Rigaux serving among its *periti*[17].

---

16. CONGAR, *Mon Journal du Concile* (n. 6), Vol. II, p. 33 (March 2: reading of directives from the Coordinating Commission on revising *De revelatione*; distribution of the Fathers' comments); p. 39 (the March 7 appointments). Congar attributes the creation of the Sub-Commission to the recommendation by the Doctrinal Commission's Adjunct Secretary Gerard Philips, but S. Tromp recorded in his Secretary's diary that on March 2 he had suggested the idea to Card. Ottaviani. On this: G. MONTALDI, *'In fide ipsa essentia revelationis completur': Il tema della fede nell'evolversi del Concilio Vaticano II* (Tesi Gregoriani, Serie teologia, 126), Rome, Gregoriana, 2005, p. 333, n. 199.

17. CONGAR, *Mon Journal du Concile* (n. 6), Vol. II, pp. 47-49. Also, on the March 11 meeting, L. DECLERCK – C. SOETENS (eds.), *Carnets conciliaires de l'évêque de Namur A.-M. Charue* (Cahiers de la Revue théologique de Louvain, 32), Louvain-la-Neuve, Publications de la Faculté de Théologie, 2000, pp. 167-169, who adds J. Ratzinger to the *periti* on chapters II and V; and U. BETTI, *La dottrina del Concilio Vaticano II sulla trasmissione della divina rivelazione: Il capitolo II della Costituzione dommatica Dei Verbum* (Spicilegium Pontificii Athenaei Antoniani, 26), Rome, Antonianum, 1985, p. 105, who lists L. Cerfaux among the *periti*. Burigana gives an overview in R. BURIGANA, *La Bibbia nel Concilio: La redazione della costituzione 'Dei Verbum' del Vaticano II* (Testi e ricerche di scienze religiose. Nuova Serie, 21), Bologna, Il Mulino, 1998, pp. 255-258, noting Archbishop Florit's background as one-time professor of the Lateran University.

The *periti* separated on March 14, to begin a month's work of analysis of the Fathers' comments and of drafting revisions of the six sections of the *Textus prior* on revelation, tradition, and Scripture. Their work would be examined by the Sub-Commission with a view to completing an initial *Textus emendatus* in the week of April 20-25, 1964, with further review to follow by the whole Doctrinal Commission in early June.

In what follows, I will review in some detail one Belgian contribution to the redaction of the 1964 revised text on revelation. We will see Prof. Charles Moeller competently carrying out his assignment to analyze the comments by Council Fathers on the presentation of revelation and faith in the *Textus prior* of 1963. Beyond Moeller's work, I will briefly point out other Belgian contributions, such as that of Prof. Lucien Cerfaux – taken up and promoted by Bp. Heuschen – which added a significant element to the notion of tradition in the 1964 draft. Both Moeller and Cerfaux proposed modifications, which entered the *Textus emendatus* of 1964 and are today particularly successful parts of the Constitution *Dei verbum*.

In the interval between sessions in Rome of the Sub-Commission on revelation, Bp. Heuschen convened meetings at Hasselt on April 1 and 15, which brought some of the *periti* together and marked stages in the genesis of the two opening sections of the mid-1964 revision of *De revelatione*[18].

III. CHARLES MOELLER READS, INTERPRETS, AND EVALUATES THE FATHERS' COMMENTS

After returning to Belgium from the March working session in Rome of the Doctrinal Commission, Charles Moeller dedicated a week's study to the 225 pages containing some ninety texts of comments by Council Fathers on the *Textus prior* on revelation. Moeller had to gather from the comments pertinent points on the *Prooemium* of six numbered paragraphs on revelation itself[19]. His study was the first step toward a revised text,

18. Bishop Heuschen also brought together *periti* during the third intersession, on January 11, 1965, for work on a revised text on marriage to present at the Ariccia meeting of the Mixed Commission preparing Schema XIII. See, M. LAMBERIGTS – L. DECLERCK, *'Le texte de Hasselt': Une étape méconnue de l'histoire du De matrimonio (Schema XIII)*, in *ETL* 80 (2004) 485-505.

19. The *Prooemium*, a text of some fifty lines in the *Textus prior* booklet of 1963 gave these headings to its short sections: 1. *Necessitas et obiectum Revelationis*; 2. *Revelatio gradatim peracta*; 3. *Revelatio in Christo ultima et completa*; 4. *Opera Christi signa Revelationis*; 5. *Veritates naturales cum Revelatione connexae*; 6. *Necessitas gratiae ad Revelationem divinam accipiendam*. The *Textus prior* is given in AS III/3, pp. 782-791,

namely identifying and initially evaluating what the Council members had indicated for deletion, addition, or reformulation. Once the Fathers' proposals were clear, the sub-group could begin a revision, with an accompanying *relatio*[20].

We note, parenthetically, that during the April meetings of 1964, the Charue subcommission decided to make what had been the introductory *Prooemium* into Chapter I, leaving only no. 1 as a *Prooemium*. Having a five-paragraph section *De ipsa revelatione* (nos. 2-6) as a chapter made clear that here the Council was *teaching* on revelation and not just introducing its treatment of Tradition and Scripture. But during Ch. Moeller's analysis, and during the redaction of the text after the first Hasselt meeting, the text in question was still the *Prooemium* of six numbered sections.

On March 22, after his week of study, Moeller sent a 6.25 page, single-spaced, analytical report to three of his collaborators on revising the *Prooemium*. These results of Moeller's study went to Bp. Heuschen and to the *periti*, A. Prignon and P. Smulders[21]. The group was scheduled to meet at Hasselt on April 1, Easter Tuesday, but Moeller would be absent because he was going on pilgrimage to the Holy Land. But he contributed in writing the results of his "first *triage*" of the comments and proposals on the *Prooemium*, a work that led him to identify seven general topics and no less than eighty particular proposals of changes in wording, which should be considered. This was Moeller's contribution toward clarifying what should be done to produce a revised text which would agree with the currents of thought and detailed proposals expressed by Council Fathers[22].

---

before the 94 comments of the Fathers; it is also at *AS* III/3, pp. 69-109, parallel with the revision of mid-1964 and the explanatory *relationes* on the revised text.

20. On October 20, 1965, Y. Congar outlined the five steps of such work by *periti* on revising a schema. "Il faut: 1° prendre connaissance sérieusement des remarques; 2° élaborer un texte rénové: parfois assez profondément; 3° soumettre cela à toute la commission de révision; 4° discuter le tout en commission plénière; 5° rédiger une *relatio*…". CONGAR, *Mon Journal du Concile* (n. 6), Vol. II, p. 444. Earlier, on September 24, 1965, Congar formulated the ruling principle of such work of revising schemata: "Tout travail de commission commence par une étude et une analyse précise des interventions faites *in aula* ou remises par écrit. Ce n'est que sur cette base qu'on peut faire le travail" (CONGAR, *Mon Journal du Concile*, Vol. II, p. 407). In March 1964, C. Moeller was carrying out this first step for nos. 1-6 of the 1963 draft, while P. Smulders was doing the same at Maastricht.

21. The text is given below as the Appendix to this paper. It devoted pp. 1-2 to "De Revelatione. Remarques générales sur le Prooemium (n° 1-6)", while pp. 3-7 have the heading, "De Revelatione, remarques de détail". I worked with the copy from the Fund Smulders, KDC Nijmegen, Folder 102. It is also in the Louvain-la-Neuve Fund Charles Moeller, as no. 1816.

22. In his accompanying letter with the mailed copies, mentioning his initial *triage*, Moeller excused himself for typing mistakes on the pages of his report and for the

On April 1, 1964, at the Auxiliary Bishop's residence in Hasselt, four collaborators met to discuss the revision work, that is, Bp. Heuschen and the *periti*, L. Cerfaux, A. Prignon, and P. Smulders[23]. These four had received Ch. Moeller's report of March 22 and so could take it into account as they decided issues about a revised *Prooemium*. After the Hasselt meeting, Smulders prepared a text, with a revised *Prooemium* (3 pp.) and *Relatio* (11 pp.), which he sent on April 12 to U. Betti, for duplication in preparation for the April 20-25 Subcommission meeting. I refer to this later text as the "draft after Hasselt" in the following pages, which indicate some results that followed from Ch. Moeller's study and analysis[24].

1. Principles and Orientations to Guide Revision

Ch. Moeller's report of March 22 first presented to his fellow *periti* the topics on which the Fathers had stated general directions or orientations to be followed in revising the *Prooemium*. On these "general remarks", Moeller added a number of clearly identified "personal reflections" on what should or should not be said in the revised text.

First, the topic of God's revelation needs further development beyond the jejune treatment of the *Textus prior*, whether by defining revelation or by making the account more precise. Three individual Council members want the text to speak of revelation as God's *locutio* to humans, as distinct from the non-verbal deeds and miracles, for the latter give

omission of some references to particular suggestions made for proposed changes in the text – in 9 cases, of the 80. He added that the lost references should be easy to find among the *fiches* then being prepared in Rome by C. Troisfontaines. On the *fiches* prepared at the Belgian College and then used as exact documentation of the Fathers' proposals in revisions of texts of the Doctrinal Commission, see the explanation by Claude Troisfontaines, in his introduction to L. DECLERCK – A. HAQUIN (eds.), *Mgr. Albert Prignon, Recteur du Pontificio Collegio Belga, Journal conciliaire de la 4ᵉ session* (Cahiers de la Revue théologique de Louvain, 35), Louvain-la-Neuve, Publications de la Faculté de Théologie, 2003, p. 14.

23. C. Colombo could not be present, because he was preparing for his episcopal ordination, but he did offer, shortly after, a few comments on the text drafted as the result of the Hasselt meeting. P. Smulders recorded in his *Dagboek* that A. Prignon arrived late in the day of April 1, after Heuschen, Cerfaux, and Smulders had completed their discussion and reached conclusions on revising the *Prooemium* on revelation.

24. In my above mentioned series of studies, "*Pieter Smulders and Dei Verbum*" in *Gregorianum*, the sixth article, still to appear, will follow developments in Smulders's revisions of the *Prooemium*, including his work before and after the Hasselt meeting, and then it will relate how the text was modified as it underwent further review in the Doctrinal Commission. In all of this, the contours of the future *Dei verbum*, nos. 1-6, will be seen gradually emerging from the proposals of many Fathers and *periti*.

validation to the properly revelatory *locutiones*. But a notably larger group of the Fathers wants a different approach, namely stating that, beyond the communication of truths (*veritates*), emphasized in the *Textus prior*, God reveals *Himself*, both in salvation-history and especially in the person of Christ. In such revelation, events or deeds (*facta*) are constitutive moments, not just logically subsequent proofs of validity[25].

To this first general remark about personalizing revelation, Ch. Moeller added a characteristic "Louvanian" reflection that on this issue Canon R. Aubert's approach, in Part III of his book on the act of faith, would be helpful, namely, to follow the lead of the majority in saying that God reveals himself in history, but to do this in a way giving no hint of anti-intellectualism[26]. This was a principle which in fact controlled the composition of the April 12 draft, after the Hasselt meeting, as well as further work leading to the Constitution *Dei verbum*.

Second, some – namely the Belgian bishops – wanted at least one part of the text to state clearly the possibility that humans can come to know God by natural reason. Others, in agreement with this, added a request that the text cite the relevant Pauline text from Romans 1, in combination with the relevant teaching of Vatican I[27]. On this Ch. Moeller reflected that while the revisors have to consider this request, he also wondered about how to implement it. First, would a mere repetition of

---

25. Among the Fathers favoring *locutio* validated by events, Moeller mentioned the Colombian Bp. M. A. Builes, with Bp. L. Carli and Card. G. Siri. Among those desiring emphasis on God's *self*-revelation, also *in* events, were the Belgian Episcopal Conference, Bp. L.-A. Elchinger, the Dutch Conference, a group of central African bishops, Abbot Christopher Butler, and Card. R. Silva Henríquez. Even a group of five conservative French Fathers, including Abbot Jean Prou, O.S.B., and Abp. Marcel Lefebvre, C.S.Sp., agreed that, while deeds and events do support doctrine, they are also part of God's revelation itself.

26. See, in the Appendix below, the example that Moeller gave of such a formulation, in the "Réflexion personnelle" concluding General Remark, no. 1. His reference is to R. AUBERT, *Le problème de l'acte de foi: Données traditionnelles et résultats des controverses récentes* (Dissertationes ad gradum magistri in facultate theologiae vel in facultate iuris canonici consequendum conscriptae. Series 2, 36), Leuven, Warny, ³1958, pp. 689-703, that is, Part III, Ch. II, Introduction and Art. I, "Le foi, attitude de l'âme ou assentiment de l'esprit?" that presents faith as a personal relation to God who comes near, but the relation proves to have a cognitive element or content concerning God and the new life given in Christ.

27. The Belgians were joined by Abp. P. Philippe, O.P., Bp. L. Carli, and the retired Bp. I. A. Russo, O.F.M. This trio urged citing *Rom* 1:20: "Ever since the creation of the world his eternal power and divine nature ... have been understood and seen through the things he has made", in connection with Vatican I's *Dei Filius*, Ch. II, 1, on the possibility of knowing God by reason's natural power. See, N. TANNER – G. ALBERIGO (eds.), *Decrees of the Ecumenical Councils*, Washington, DC, Georgetown University Press, 1990, Vol. II, p. 806; *DH*, 3004.

Vatican I really add to the text? Second, a further explanation of creation's witness to its Creator, already mentioned in the *Textus prior* (no. 2), might well require a longer formulation than is appropriate in this *Prooemium*[28].

A third general point identified by Moeller concerned God's "primaeval revelation" of himself to humans from the beginning, but a problem arises from an opposition found in the comments sent in by the Fathers. Abbot Butler wanted no mention of "revelation" in and through nature, since that is quite different than revelation to Israel and in Christ. One risks equivocation by calling both creation and salvation-history revelatory. But Card. Silva Henríquez furnished a proposed revision in a "Teilhardian" key on God manifested *per Verbum suum* in creation. Moeller, reflecting, found the latter emphasis attractive, since it would connect with Schema XVII on Church and World by speaking to a topic which lay-people find engaging. But, again, the imperative of brevity seems to prohibit such an addition[29].

Fourth, Ch. Moeller noted numerous criticisms of nos. 4, 5, and 6 of the *Textus prior*. No. 4 had presented the life, miracles, and resurrection of Christ as serving to prove the authoritative validity of his oral teaching, which was properly revelatory of his own divinity and of other truths. Moeller had already touched on this in his first general remark and then, below, he mentioned groups of Fathers who had proposed saying that the miracles and life of Christ were themselves revelatory[30]. Here, no personal

---

28. The text produced after the Hasselt meeting of April 1 did include a citation of Rom 1,20 in no. 1, while citing *Dei Filius* on the power of reason in no. 6 at the end of the new *Prooemium*, a placement chosen to make clear that the primary intent of the schema was to treat God's positive revelation in Israel and in Christ. But, with this same motivation, the citation of *Rom* 1 was deleted from no. 1 by the Sub-commission later in April. But no. 6, as it remains in the Constitution *Dei verbum*, contains what the Belgian bishops had requested, that is, a conciliar confession of the power of human reason to reach God, citing *Dei Filius* and adding a parenthetical reference to Rom 1,20.

29. The Cardinal of Santiago, Chile, proposed giving natural revelation a christological basis by saying, "Iam in ipsa creatione mundi Deus per Verbum suum manifestatur, quia haec, cum per Filium et in Filio condita sit (Col 1:16; Heb 1:3; Credo Nicaenum), invisibila Dei nobis conspicere sinit (Rom 1:20)". See *AS* III/3, p. 794; Gɪʟ Hᴇʟʟɪɴ, *Concilii Vaticani II Synopsis* (n. 15), p. 474. But Abbot Butler wanted concentration on historic and positive revelation. By June 1964, the *Textus emendatus*, influenced by Abp. P. Parente, an exponent of "natural revelation", did incorporate Card. Silva's notion, saying, "Deus qui in Verbo suo omnia creavit et in ipsa rerum natura perenne sui testimonium hominibus ostendit," (no. 3) which *Dei verbum* actualizes as, "Deus, per Verbum omnia creans et conservans, in rebus creatis...".

30. On no. 4, Moeller noted the requests to have the text say that Jesus' life and actions, and even all of salvation history, were part of the revelation of God. These came from the Dutch bishops and from five conservative French Fathers, including Abp Lefebvre.

reflection was needed since these comments gave a clear directive, which in fact guided the next and the further redactions of the text.

On *Textus prior*, no. 5, a further general point concerned the statement that revelation conveys truths both supernatural and natural. The Fathers criticize the repetition of the term *veritates*, occurring four times in nine lines, which gave an intellectual tone that this religious text should avoid. Moeller's reflection, in line with his earlier reference to R. Aubert, was that the text should not be dominated by knowledge of supernatural realities and true propositions, but should follow the text offered by Abbot Butler to replace the unfortunate no. 5 of the prior text[31].

The sixth general remark by Ch. Moeller, on *Textus prior* (no. 6), stated a desire of the Fathers, namely, that in treating the response of faith to God's revelation, the schema should be more emphatic on the role of grace. In his points of detail, Moeller singled out six particular reformulations offered by the Fathers to give the revision a properly theological account of faith – which in fact it came to have[32].

The seventh general remark by Ch. Moeller referred to proposed changes given by the Fathers regarding the order of sections of the *Prooemium*. He mentioned one suggestion by Abp. Florit that the two sections on revelation in Christ in the *Textus prior* (nos. 3 and 4) could well be united into a single paragraph. This did occur after the Hasselt meeting and in further texts leading to *Dei verbum*, no. 4.

31. Abbot Butler's reformulation, recommended by Ch. Moeller, became the basis of no. 6 in the text after Hasselt, to overcome what Butler termed "crass conceptualism" of the earlier text. Butler had proposed: "In divina revelatione agitur quidem de eis, quae de seipso ac de aeternae voluntatis suae decretis circa hominum salutem, eorumque intimam divinae vitae participationem, Deus manifestavit. Eidem autem divinae revelationi tribuendum insuper est, ut ea, quae in rebus divinis rationi humanae per se impervia non sunt, in praesenti quoque generis humani conditione ab omnibus expedite, firma certitudine et nullo admixto errore cognosci possint" (*AS* III/3, p. 813; GIL HELLIN, *Concilii Vaticani II Synopsis* [n. 15], p. 463). This followed *Dei Filius*, Ch. II, 1 closely, which P. Smulders's draft *relatio* after the Hasselt meeting stated was an advantage, because with Vatican I's authority behind the formulation, neither *periti* or Fathers would initiate "discussiones infinitae" on it.

32. The proposals came from Bishops A. Tabera Araoz, L. Jaeger, M. Baudoux, and Dom C. Butler. Moeller remarked again that Butler gave the best set of corrections. The text composed after the Hasselt meeting did develop the account of faith beyond the terse and bland *Textus prior*, no. 4. It first spoke of faith as full homage to God of intellect and will by assenting to the truth he reveals (as Aubert would include) and second by calling the grace of faith "prevenient and helping" and "the internal aids of the Spirit", while stating that it gives *suavitas* in embracing the truth. Sub-Commission work later in April led to adding that grace converts one *to God*, while opening the "eyes of the mind". G. Montaldi surveys the whole *iter* of 1964-65 leading to *Dei verbum*, no. 5, on faith, in *In fide ipsa essentia revelationis completur* (as in n. 16, above), pp. 334-383, adding an appreciation of the properly theological aspect on pp. 464-474.

Thus, Ch. Moeller identified major principles which guided the work of revision: (1) God's revelation *of Himself* in a personal vein, but not excluding meaningful formulations; (2) a "holistic" account of how revelation occurs in various complexes of events and speech, of deeds and words; and (3) faith as a human response made possible and animated by the Holy Spirit working to make human beings receptive and believing.

2. Particular Formulations, for Exclusion or Inclusion

Ch. Moeller's contribution of March 1964 to revising *De revelatione* went on from general principles to list eighty points of detail, based for the most part on what the Council Members had submitted on reformulating the *Prooemium* on revelation[33].

Not all of these points were changes that Moeller recommended for introduction into the text. For example, he judged negatively the request by the eighteen bishops of Puglia that an early mention be made about the text's relation to the Councils of Trent and Vatican I, but for Moeller this would add excessively to a text which should be quite concise[34]. Neither, according to Moeller, should mention be made of Pius XII's encyclical *Humani generis* (1950), as requested by Abp. D.L. Capozi, O.F.M., and Bp. L. Carli, for Councils do not receive encyclicals in this way[35]. Thirdly, where the *Textus prior* announced its aim as setting forth "solemnly" Catholic teaching on revelation, Moeller added on his own that "*sollemniter*" should be deleted, to avoid suggesting a dogmatic definition, as had already been done in the Doctrinal Commission when it

33. Recalling the six sections of the *Prooemium* named in n. 19, above, Moeller noted 18 corrections proposed on no. 1, 15 on no. 2, 21 on no. 3, 12 on no. 4, 6 on no. 5, and 8 on no. 6. These drew on 37 of the texts submitted, taking note of 15 points made by Dom Butler, 10 by Abp. L. Jaeger, 9 by Card. R. Silva Henríquez, 9 by Bp. L. Carli, and 7 by Bp. A. Tabera Araoz. Among the Conferences which responded, Moeller mentioned 9 noteworthy points made by the German-speaking Fathers and the bishops of Scandinavia, 4 by the Belgian bishops, and 4 by the Fathers serving in dioceses of Indonesia.

34. The text after Hasselt followed Moeller's judgment against such an inclusion, but this was not taken over by the Charue Sub-Commission later in April. Consequently, in line with the request of the bishops of Puglia, the *Textus emendatus* of mid-1964 did state in no. 1 that on revelation the Council was following (*inhaerens vestigiis*) Vatican I, and *Dei verbum* included the Council on Trent as well, which had gone ahead of Vatican II on how revelation is communicated. The formulation gained notoriety through Karl Barth's chapter, "Conciliorum Tridentini et Vaticani I inhaerens vestigiis?", in K. BARTH, *Ad limina apostolorum: An Appraisal of Vatican II*, Richmond, VA, Knox, 1968, pp. 43-55.

35. This refusal, accepted by those meeting in Hasselt, was noted explicitly in *relatio* of the resulting text and in the next version after the April 20-25 Sub-commission meeting, but it was passed over in silence in the *relatio* on no. 1 of the *Textus emendatus* distributed to the Fathers in July 1964.

lowered the "theological note" of its affirmation of the sacramentality of episcopal ordination, in the draft *De ecclesia*[36].

In no. 2 of the *Textus prior*, on the first stages of revelation, the order of salvation was said to have been restored "soon" (*mox*) after the sin of Adam. And then "later" (*postea*) God chose a people in Abraham, looking to bless all generations. Ch. Moeller reported in a positive vein the request of the German-speaking and Scandinavian bishops that the two temporal adverbs be deleted, so as not to suggest, first, that there was a time when humans did not live in the "order of salvation", or, second, that between Adam and Abraham only a short time elapsed. Also some French bishops criticized *postea* for being open to a view that between Adam and Abraham God was not revealing himself. Both of these adverbs were deleted[37].

Ch. Moeller also acted as a watchdog against the entry into the *Prooemium* on revelation of terms not in harmony with the doctrinal tradition of eastern Christianity. Bp. Carli had proposed amending no. 2 with a reference to God revealing to the human family its "supernatural end", but Moeller said that a Council should not speak of "the supernatural" because it is a technical notion of Western theology, which is unknown to the oriental tradition[38]. Also, an addition recommended by Abbot Butler, to say that in Christ "the Father manifests himself *perfecte*", should in Moeller's judgment not be accepted, because for eastern Christians the theme of the Father's *imcomprehensibilitas* is important. Instead, one could make Butler's point in terms from John's Gospel, "No one has ever

36. Moeller was conscious of giving his own argument here, adding that no bishops had suggested this. But the change did enter the revision after Hasselt and the *Relatio*, both then and in the revised text of July 1964, took over Moeller's point: "Omittitur vero *sollemniter*, sicut factum est etiam in Schemate *De ecclesia*" (*AS* III/3, p. 75; GIL HELLÍN, *Concilii Vaticani II Synopsis* [n. 15], p. 12).

37. Behind the critical intervention of the German-speaking bishops, one can well suppose an influence of Karl Rahner, who remained dissatisfied with the final formulation of this text (*Dei verbum*, no. 3), which he found simplistic in taking no account of the great age of humankind and of "the ways known to God" for offering saving light and grace to human beings outside Israel and Christianity. See K. RAHNER, *Zur 'Offenbarungsgeschichte' nach dem II. Vatikanum*, in *Schriften zur Theologie* 12 (1975) 241-250; ID. *On the 'History of Revelation' according to the Second Vatican Council*, in *Theological Investigations* 16 (1979) 191-198. Rahner repeated the complaint in his 1982 interview given to Hanjo Sauer on his contribution to *Dei verbum*. See H. SAUER, *Erfahrung und Glaube: Die Begründung des pastoralen Prinzips durch die Offenbarungskonstitution des II. Vatikanischen Konzils* (Würzburger Studien zur Fundamentaltheologie, 12), Frankfurt am Main, Lang, 1993, pp. 762-769, at 767-769.

38. The *Relatio* developed after the Hasselt meeting explained that in speaking of God addressing humans *ex abundantia caritatis* and addressing them *tamquam amicos*, the text was in fact indicating the supernatural character of revelation, but it was doing so with language from Scripture and patristic teaching.

seen God. It is God the only Son ... who has made him known" (1,18). But neither of these formulations entered the subsequent texts on revelation.

Among the constructive amendments offered, Moeller singled out for inclusion in no. 1 a proposal of the Indonesian bishops, aiming to over-come the reductive view of revelation solely as *locutio Dei*, namely, that revelation takes place "not only by words but at the same time also by God's mighty deeds in salvation history". This did enter the text and after further polishing remains substantially part of *Dei verbum*, no. 2[39].

For the enrichment of *Textus prior*, no. 2, on revelation in Israel, Moeller singled out the point expressed by the Belgian bishops and by Dom Butler that the text should make mention of God's word to Israel through the prophets, based on Heb 1,1. The role of the prophets in rev-elation to Israel did enter no. 2 of the Hasselt text, on how God formed (*erudivit*) his people in knowledge of himself through Moses and the prophets (no. 2), while Heb 1,1 appeared just after, at the beginning of no. 3 on revelation in Christ.

Affirming the final and complete revelation of God in Christ, the *Tex-tus prior* had in no. 3 linked Christ and the Holy Spirit, for Christ promised the Spirit to the Apostles as the one who would "teach them everything that he had said to them" and so qualify them as unsur-passable witnesses to Christ's revelation. Christ's promise was docu-mented by a reference to John 14,26, which the text had paraphrased. On this, Ch. Moeller called attention Card. Silva Henriquez's critique

---

39. The Indonesian proposal: "Deus autem se ac suum salutis consilium non solum per verba ad homines locuta, sed simul etiam per magnalia in historia sacra facta revelat, ita ut per opera auctoritas verborum confirmetur et per verba mysterium in operibus con-tentum manifestetur" (*AS* III/3, p. 914; GIL HELLIN, *Concilii Vaticani II Synopsis* [n. 15], p. 431). I relate the background of this amendment in J. WICKS, *Pieter Smulders and Dei Verbum. 5. A Critical Reception of the Schema De revelatione of the Mixed Commission (1963)*, in *Gregorianum* 86 (2005) 92-134, at 105-107. The duality of words and events as both revelatory, originated with J. Daniélou and entered Vatican II first in a text sub-mitted by Abp. P. Veuillot (Nov. 21, 1962; *AS* I/3, p. 287) and then, slightly modified, by Abp. G. Garrone in the Mixed Commission (Nov. 27, 1962; *AS* VI/1, p. 320). In both texts of a *Prooemium* on revelation, no. 5 brings out the combination of *locutio/verba* with *opera/actus*, as in "Revelatio Dei in Vetere et Novo Testamento efficitur simul per locu-tionem Dei ad homines et per eius opera in historia salutis". For Christ manifested his divinity by instituting the new law, healing the sick, and declaring himself Lord of the Sab-bath and the Temple. But the tight connection (*simul*) made by the sentence just cited was removed from the *Textus prior*, to make Christ's deeds into subsequent validations of the authority grounding his oral teaching. This has been treated by P. PIZZUTO, *La teologia della rivelazione di Jean Daniélou: Influsso su Dei Verbum e valore attuale* (Tesi Gre-goriana. Serie teologia, 96), Rome, Editrice Gregoriana, 2003, pp. 38-43, with texts given 525-531. Below, this paper will take note of the contribution by G. Philips in April 1964 toward developing the formulation of this aspect of revelation.

of the reference to John 14,26, especially to the words *quaecumque vobis dixero*, which do not convey the more ample Semitic notion of personal communication, but suggest instead teaching offered in concepts and propositions. Moeller agreed that John 14,26 should not figure here, adding that a better text would be John 16,13 (the Spirit "will guide you into all truth" – which Moeller cited in the original Greek), since the latter text had been identified in contributions made at the 1962 Chevetogne ecumenical week as an essential *locus* for the theology of tradition[40].

In the revision after the meeting at Hasselt, the paragraph on revelation in Christ took on a notably changed form, without reference to Christ's promise of the Spirit. But the *Textus emendatus* of July 1964 did include a reference to John 16,13 at the end of no. 8 on the benefits accruing to the Church from the vital influence of apostolic tradition and the Holy Spirit, namely "guiding believers into all truth" (cf. Jn 16,13)[41].

The same no. 3 of the *Textus prior* had concluded that because revelation was definitive and complete (*ultima et integra*) in Christ, therefore no new revelation was awaited, just as no other salvation was expected. Ch. Moeller noted that the Fathers were dissatisfied with this formulation, because it showed no sense of eschatological revelation. In the New Testament the final coming of Christ will be in a sense an event of revelation, as the German-speaking and Scandinavian bishops pointed out, indicating 1 Cor 1,7 and 1 Pt 1,4 and 4,13 as clear testimonies. As a result, the text redacted after the Hasselt meeting pointed to a coming final revelation, saying that no new public revelation was awaited "before the final 'revelation of our Lord Jesus Christ'" (1 Cor 1,7)[42].

Finally, as an example of the refined character of this work by a *peritus* on the Council's texts, Ch. Moeller noted regarding no. 6, on faith, the suggestion by Abbot Butler of inserting the word *idem* to make

---

40. O. ROUSSEAU, et al., *L'infaillibilité de l'Église* (Irenikon), Chevetogne, Éditions de Chevetogne, 1962, in which Ch. Moeller contributed the concluding essay, "Infaillibilité et vérité", pp. 223-255. In the volume, the opening biblical chapter by J.J. von Allmen bore the title, "L'Esprit de vérité vous conduira dans toute la vérité" (pp. 13-25).

41. But later in 1964, Card. Bea criticized the reference to John 16,13, because in its original context it is most evidently addressed, not to all believers, but to the Apostles (*AS* III/3, p. 288; GIL HELLIN, *Concilii Vaticani II Synopsis* [n. 15], p. 649). However the text remained, and is in *Dei verbum*, but without reference to John 16,13.

42. This went into the *Textus emendatus* of July 1964, but it gave way in 1965 to a *modus* that objected to using the term *revelatio* close together in the different senses of revelation in history and at the end of history. Instead, *Dei verbum*, no. 4, speaks of the coming "glorious manifestation" of Christ, with reference to 1 Tim 6,14 and Titus 2,13, which both suggest the difference by using the term *epiphaneia*.

explicit that it was "the same Spirit" who carries out the two works indicated by the text, namely initially making possible faith's acceptance of God's revelation of himself and, then, constantly operating by spiritual gifts to give faith greater depth in its grasp of revelation. The text after Hasselt did add *idem*, with a documentary reference to Abbot Butler's contribution, and the same word stands in *Dei verbum* no. 5, to show the continuity in the Holy Spirit's influence on both the first assent of faith and on subsequent progress in faith.

These examples, from the seven general issues and eighty points of detail noted by Ch. Moeller, show us a *peritus* competently at work for a Vatican II commission. In such work, the theologian had to (1) grasp well the sense of a prior text, (2) read attentively and thoughtfully a mass of critical interventions on that text, (3) identify in the mass the valuable and/or convergent desires and proposals for correcting and modifying passages of the existing text, and (4) point the way judiciously to revisions. The overall aim, of course, was to make the next draft correspond better than the previous one to "the mind of the Council" as this came out in the general and particular comments made by the Council Fathers. Work like this was an important part of what Y. Congar had in mind when he spoke of the "enormous labors" of theologians at Vatican II[43].

IV. Other Belgian Contributions to *De revelatione* in March-June 1964

Here I treat more briefly some products of Belgian expertise which influenced the *Textus emendatus* on revelation which in time was approved by the Doctrinal Commission in early June and then mailed to the Fathers in July 1964[44].

(1) On God's revelation to human beings taking place both by words and deeds or events, the dense formulation of the interrelation of the

---

43. See above, at n. 12.

44. I leave out the examination of the revised text produced in late April 1964 by Bp. E. De Smedt and his *periti* (Sabbe, Willaert, Dupont), for the Secretariat for Christian Unity. R. Burigana indicates some of their comments, along with the conclusion voiced by J. Willebrands that the modifications proposed were not so serious as to justify convening again the Mixed Commission that had produced the *Textus prior* of 1964. See BURIGANA, *La Bibbia nel Concilio* (n. 17), pp. 271-275. Two texts from this review are preserved in U. Betti's archive at La Verna, Italy, as pp. 207-214 in the bound papers, entitled *Conc. Vat. II*, Subcommissio *De divina revelatione*.

two factors which we find in *Dei verbum*, no. 2 goes back to the inter-session of 1964, specifically to a proposal coming out of the Hasselt discussion on revelation and faith in the *Prooemium* (Heuschen, Cerfaux, A. Prignon, and Smulders, on April 1). But Smulders's proposal was further developed in Rome, on April 21-22, by Smulders and G. Philips, especially at an early morning meeting at the Belgian College on April 22. G. Philips's contribution included a thoughtful substitution, replacing "*Quae revelatio fit*", with the more ample, "*Haec revelationis oeconomia fit*", to indicate that comprehensively God's dealings with humankind are marked by the interaction of the two factors, occurring *verbis et gestis*[45].

(2) A recurring theme of the comments by Council members on the *Textus prior* was the call for a further development of the text's "bare bones" account of tradition in Chapter I (nos. 7-10). For the revision of this chapter, the study of the comments by the Fathers was assigned to the *periti* Congar, Rahner, and Schauf. But Bp. Heuschen also became active, asking for a draft revision from Prof. Lucien Cerfaux. At a second meeting at Hasselt, on April 15, 1964, Cerfaux's draft was reviewed by Heuschen, Moeller, and Smulders, leading to a text in three paragraphs *De revelationis transmissione*, which then Bp. Heuschen presented in Rome on April 20 as a revised presentation on (1) the Apostles and their successors as preachers of the Gospel, (2) the presence and interrelation of Scripture and tradition in the Church, and (3) the role of the *Magisterium* in the Church[46].

In revising Ch. I the members and *periti* took a text of U. Betti as the basis of their work on April 22-23, but Betti's no. 7 was fused, in redactional work by G. Philips, with formulations from the Cerfaux-Heuschen text. The particular topic was the way in which the Apostles and their collaborators in composing New Testament books fulfilled Christ's mandate

45. The Smulders-Philips re-formulation on the economy of revelation is as follows: "Haec revelationis oeconomia fit verbis et gestis, intrinsice inter se connexis, ita ut opera, in historia salutis patrata, doctrinam et rem verbis significatam manifestent et corroborent, verba autem opera proclamant et mysterium in eis contentum elucident". The Betti collection preserves G. Philips's handwritten copies of this as pp. 131 and 137.

46. The 7-page Cerfaux draft for the April 15 meeting is in the Funds Moeller, 1830 (Inventory in C. SOETENS, *Concile Vatican II et Église contemporaine (Archives de Louvain-la-Neuve). I: Inventaire des Fonds Ch. Moeller, G. Thils, Fr. Houtart* (Cahiers de la Revue théologique de Louvain, 21), Louvain-la-Neuve, Publications de la Faculté de Théologie, 1989. The resulting text presented by Bp. Heuschen in Rome on April 20 is given in BETTI, *La trasmissione della divina rivelazione* (n. 17), pp. 328-329. S. Tromp's *Diarium Secretarii*, vol. VIII (15 Feb. - 30 Maii 1964), noted the distribution on April 20 of the texts on tradition drafted by Betti, Congar, Heuschen, and Rahner, adding the observation, "Ultima oblata ab Exc. Heuschen mihi videtur optima". See ASV, *Conc. Vat. II*, 791.

to preach the Gospel to every creature as the source of all saving truth and discipline of practice.

What Cerfaux and Heuschen contributed to the 1964 revision of *De revelatione* was a concise account of the two earliest stages of Christian tradition, specifying that Jesus carried out his primordial transmission of revelation to the future Apostles by what he said and taught orally, but also by his *conversatio* (interaction, companionship) with them and by his deeds which they witnessed. Then in the basic transmission to the churches, the Apostles were not solely teachers of doctrine communicated orally as instruction, but as well givers of example by the lives they led and shapers of community life by institutions, that is, by set forms of worship and community service. This enrichment, by only sixteen words, produced a revised account of the early stages of Christian transmission, that by Jesus to his disciples and then by the Apostles to the churches. This is coherent with the doctrinal account in the *Prooemium* (= Ch. I, *De ipsa revelatione*) of revelation as a whole being given by words and deeds. It also fits well with the presentation that follows in the revised no. 8 of tradition-in-the-church as passing on all that contributes to holy living and increasing faith, which is done by doctrine, life, and worship. A narrow doctrinal view of revelation and tradition has been convincingly overcome.

(3) A further Belgian contribution to the 1964 revision of *De revelatione* was made by G. Philips after the April 20-25 sessions of the Charue sub-commission. S. Tromp noted in his Secretary's diary for Saturday April 25 that by noon the sub-commission was agreed on the content of Ch. VI on Scripture in the life of the Church, but still the redaction was not definitive. The members and *periti* could still send comments to Msgr. Philips. This indicates a further preparation of a polished text of the revised schema by G. Philips, who was commissioned to make sure that all the revisions were correctly and concisely entered and that the Latin text was formulated in a manner making for easy reading.

For this work, G. Philips took his notes from the April 20-25 sessions back to Louvain, where he went over mimeographed copies of the draft text and *relatio* of each chapter, making hand-written entries both of the emendations approved at the meetings and of numerous corrections of the Latin, e.g., new placements of verbs and insertions of a more accurate conjunctions. S. Tromp recorded that he received by mail from Louvain the corrected texts of Chapters I-II on May 5 and of Chapters III-VI on May 15. For each chapter, Philips had also edited the respective *relatio*, making them considerably more concise than the texts first drafted by

the *periti*[47]. S. Tromp then had these texts retyped onto stencils for duplication and distribution to all the members of the Doctrinal Commission
for their review in the first week of June 1964. G. Philips's intelligent
editing, along with his accurate and smoothly readable Latin, served
notably to facilitate the next phase of work on this central Vatican II text.

V. A GLANCE FORWARD AT THE ITER OF A SUCCESSFULLY REVISED TEXT

Diary entries by Bp. André-Marie Charue record that at the end of April
1964 a feeling of notable satisfaction swept over the members and *periti*
of the subcommission on revelation. They had completed the basic work
on a *Textus emendatus de divina revelatione* on April 25 and all were
quite contented, "even Fr. Tromp". Cardinal Bea saw parts of the new text
two days later and gave an initial approval. That afternoon Cardinal Ottaviani raised no difficulties when Charue gave him a report on the work
just accomplished. The next day Charue heard that from their different perspectives Frs. Gagnebet and Rahner were both pleased with the new text[48].

In meetings of June 2-6, the full Doctrinal Commission accepted the
Textus emendatus on revelation and Scripture, with the only major difficulty arising from a minority holding out for *latius patet Traditio*
(H. Schauf and F. Franič)[49]. But the Coordinating Commission approved
the text in late June and on July 12 Paul VI authorized it for sending by
mail to the Council members, in a booklet presenting synoptically the

---

47. The six texts are in the ASV, *Conc. Vat. II*, 779 (Fascicle 347). Each is marked on
p. 1, "Textus correctus. G. Ph.".
48. DECLERCK – SOETENS (eds.), *Carnets conciliaires de l'évêque de Namur A.-M. Charue*
(n. 17), pp. 186-189, including what Bp. Charue heard from the young priest of his diocese,
Cl. Troisfontaines, who found the new text quite moving, with its spiritual and pastoral
tone. When he returned to Rome on May 30, Bp. Charue heard that the Secretariat for
Promoting Christian Unity had given a "green light" for the text, obviating any further
meeting of the Mixed Commission (Doctrine/Secretariat) which had produced the *Textus
prior* in 1962-63, which the new draft had extensively revised.
49. On these meetings, DECLERCK – SOETENS (eds.), *Carnets conciliaires de l'évêque
de Namur A.-M. Charue* (n. 17), pp. 191-207, and BURIGANA, *La Bibbia nel Concilio*
(n. 17), pp. 282-293. The debate concerned both (1) the content-issue whether tradition was
or was not a more ample source of revealed truth than Scripture and (2) the procedural
question of speaking so as to leave this debate in its *status quo ante* by carefully avoiding
either position. BETTI, *La trasmissione della divina rivelazione* (n. 17), pp. 105-123, relates
the argument both in the March-April and the June meetings of 1964. I gave background
on this debate in J. WICKS, *Pieter Smulders and Dei Verbum. 4. Assessing the Mixed Commission's 1962 Work on Scripture/Tradition and Biblical Inspiration*, in *Gregorianum* 85
(2004) 242-277, in the midst of which Bp. A. Charue appeared as a clear-sighted participant an otherwise confused Mixed Commission meeting of December 7, 1962 (pp. 254-
255).

Textus prior (1963) and the new *Textus emendatus*, with *relationes* which elucidated the new text and gave justifications for each revision. The justifications rested, essentially, on the comments, critical and constructive, that the Council members had made earlier on the *Textus prior*, which had then been identified in their relevance by *periti* such as Charles Moeller. The revised text of 1964 then proved decisive in the genesis of *Dei verbum*, when it received a positive reception during Vatican II's third period.

In the Council *aula*, September 30 to October 6, 1964, interventions by Council members included clear recognition of the quality of the work done by Bp. Charue's Sub-commission. Sixty-eight Council members commented orally on the text, while forty-eight further comments were submitted only in writing[50]. Of these, a good number omitted general evaluations to go directly to particular points of the text to offer proposed revisions. But thirty-five oral and ten written comments spoke to the text as a whole, and at times to numerous particulars, with quite positive assessments[51]. These *placet* and *valde placet* judgments came in oral interventions by leaders, such as Cardinals Döpfner, Meyer (Chicago), Léger, König, and Bea. Among the approving comments, six oral and four written responses were in the name of conferences or other groups totaling well over three-hundred Council members[52]. In particular, seven interventions in the *aula* commended the Doctrinal Commission for its careful work in reviewing and adopting much of what the Council members had earlier proposed[53]. There were dissenting voices, to be sure, on

---

50. The texts are in *AS* III/3, pp. 142-366 (from the *aula*), pp. 425-511 (written). Burigana reviews them in *La Bibbia nel Concilio* (n. 17), pp. 312-354, adding a treatment of fourteen written comments submitted before the discussion in the *aula* (*AS* III/3, pp. 920-941), on pp. 299-304. H. Sauer reviews only the oral interventions in G. ALBERIGO (ed.), *Storia del Concilio Vaticano II. 4: La chiesa come comunione*, Bologna, Il Mulino, 1999, pp. 229-257 (= Ch. III, Section 3), adding perceptive characterizations of the text and the debate by J. Neuner, L. Vischer, and O. Semmelroth.

51. A succinct review of this discussion, accompanying the further revision, distributed November 20, 1964, stated, "Laudatur Schema a quampluribus, modo sincero et quandoque effuso, in 45 orationibus, quae mentem 297 Patrum, necnon Epp. Poloniae et Neerlandiae referent" (*AS* IV/1, p. 340; GIL HELLÍN, *Concilii Vaticani II Synopsis* [n. 15], p. 7).

52. Among those praising the text orally were three spokesmen (Döpfner, König, and Bp. Schick) for 78 Fathers of the German language area and Scandinavia, as well as Card. Landázurri Rickets for 45 from Peru, Abp. Zoungrana for 54 from Western Africa, Bp. Philbin for 34 Irish and missionary bishops, Bp. Kowalski for the Polish bishops, and Bp. van Dodewaard for the Dutch. In written interventions, Card. Silva Henríquez formulated the *placet* of 25, another approval came from 40 in Brazil, and the 30 bishops of Indonesia declared, "Valde contenti sumus cum hoc novo schemate" (*AS* III/3, p. 511).

53. For example, Abp. G. Ferro (Reggio Calabria) spoke on October 1 of "Hoc schema … ingenti ac diligentissimo studio a commissione confectum, tot … Patrum collatis

topics not formulated in the amended text in a manner to bring the required moral unanimity on doctrine[54]. But the outcome was still a substantive and wide-ranging approval of the amended draft of mid-1964 on divine revelation.

This text was, thus, a significant step bringing the Council well beyond the *malaise* of 1962 over *De fontibus revelationis* and clearly beyond the disappointment over the mediocre text produced by the Mixed Commission in early 1963.

VI. A COUNCIL LARGELY OF THEOLOGIANS?

Yves Congar's Vatican II diary includes striking claims for the contribution of the theological experts to the Second Vatican Council[55].

consiliis, dignum absque dubio videtur quod a nobis laudetur, gratiis exhibitis omnibus commissionis membris" (*AS* III/3, p. 206). Other references to the quality of the Commission's labors: *AS* III/3, p. 147 (Döpfner), p. 202 (Vuccino), p. 210 (Wilczynski), p. 217 (Fares, noting that the Commissione worked with "intelligentia et sagacia peculiari"), and p. 236 (Temiño Saiz).

54. On the option to carefully abstain from taking a position for or against the presence in apostolic oral tradition of revealed truths to which Scripture gives no witness, I find nineteen Council members opposed to the abstinence of the *Textus emendatus*. Such dissent came shortly after reception of the text (Siri, Borromeo, Micara, Mazzoldi), in the *aula* (Ruffini, Browne, Compagnone, Arattukulam, Antipetti, Beras, Nicodemo, and Rubio), and in written submissions (Grotti, De Vito, Maleddu, Periera, Whealon, Pohlschneider, and Cooray). Some of these combined favor for *latius patet Traditio* with praise for other main lines of the text (Nicodemo, Compagnone). L.M. Carli said the revision was "much better" than its predecessor, and he offered two amendments to Ch. II, which did not touch constitutive tradition. He had already made it clear that he wanted the Council to affirm the *latius patet* of tradition over Scripture (*AS* III/3, pp. 817-818, 824-825). But later, and along with others (5, speaking for 35 Fathers), he was more concerned in his intervention with biblical inerrancy and the historicity of the Gospels (*AS* III/3, pp. 923-926). This not negligible group favoring constitutive tradition in autumn 1964 was proportionally consistent with the group defeated, first, in the Mixed Commission in the vote February 23, 1963, on Card. Bea's proposal of observing "abstinence" (29 *placet* / 8 *non placet*), and, second, in the Doctrinal Commission, June 3, 1964, on accepting nos. 8-9 of the amended draft, which neither affirms or denies constitutive tradition (17 *placet* / 7 *non placet*). On the votes see BETTI, *La trasmissione della divina rivelazione* (n. 17), pp. 76-81, 120-122. However, one has to note as well in the Sept.-Oct. discussion several interventions (13, including those for 78 German-speakers, 30 members from Indonesia, and 7 Latin American Fathers), which explicitly commended the text's abstinence on constitutive tradition as a satisfactory treatment of a disputed question.

55. See n. 12, above. When Congar heard of discontented muttering in the Vatican over plans to lauch the journal *Concilium*, he attributed this to fears of a continuation of the theological education of bishops that occurred during the Council. "Ils savent déjà que ce sont les théologiens – et pas les leurs! : les autres – qui ont fait le concile". CONGAR, *Mon Journal du Concile* (n. 6), Vol. II, p. 81 (May 21, 1964).

But Congar could also acknowledge that Vatican II was an event of many-sided cooperation between bishops and theologians[56]. The latter perception is already implicit in Congar's strong sense, shared by Ch. Moeller, of the imperative controlling the work of Commission experts in the revision of a *schema*, namely that changes had to have a documented source in comments by Council members on the prior text being revised[57]. But before proposing an answer to the question posed in our section-heading, we can well recall the theologians' contributions that we have seen in the body of this paper.

Charles Moeller's March 1964 work in studying the Fathers' comments aimed at identifying, by a careful reading, remarks in which the Fathers raised valid points about shortcomings in *Prooemium* of the prior text of *De revelatione* from 1963. Moeller had to understand well the account of God's word and the response of faith set forth in that text, and then perceive when the Fathers had identified weaknesses in the text and were proposing appropriate changes. It was not a question of his own reactions to the earlier text, although his own theological formation at Louvain, as by Prof. R. Aubert, did become helpful. His reading and reflection was, from one perspective, in the service of the Council Fathers who had intervened in order to eventually produce an amended schema far better than the text they had received in mid-1963. Moeller had to bring their well-considered judgments to bear on composing that better text.

In Moeller's work, we see a theologian carrying out an essential part of one of the central processes of the Second Vatican Council. He worked with theological competence to assure that the Fathers' judgments on a prior text became operative in producing a revised text. By Moeller's selection of points for deletion, reformulation, or addition, the revision would be a text better attuned to the aims of the Council, as these had been appropriated by the Council members.

CONCLUSION

Several of the "moments and means" of contributions by theological experts to Vatican Council II are well known, such as their education of the Fathers on Council topics in 1962 and their critical treatment of many *schemata* composed by the Preparatory Commissions. But this paper has

---

56. See his reflections on the post-conciliar commissions, on February 2, 1966, where it is essential "de garder la coopération organique – qui seule a permis et fait le concile – entre évêques et théologiens" (CONGAR, *Mon Journal du Concile* [n. 6], Vol. II, p. 518).

57. See the citations in n. 20, above.

called attention to a lesser known, but no less important, contribution of *periti* at a later moment of Vatican II, in their service of conciliar commissions in revising draft documents.

The theologians serving the Conciliar commissions became engaged in the search, by careful reading of the Fathers' considered opinions, for felicitous proposals of new formulations, as was done by Charles Moeller in March 1964 for the Sub-commission *De revelatione*. In some cases the experts had to make selections out of different proposed revisions, to reach a formulation likely to satisfy numerous respondents. At times, when the Fathers expressed their preferences more generally, the expert had to supply a formulation, as Lucien Cerfaux did in enlarging the account given of the first phases of Christian tradition.

Thus, even without having the authority to make decisions by casting votes on the texts, the theologians serving the Commissions made *essential* contributions to bringing before the Council Fathers the revised documents that in time came to express the results of the Second Vatican Council.

Department of Religious Studies   Prof. Dr. Jared WICKS, SJ
John Carroll University
20700 N. Park Blvd
Cleveland, OH 44118
USA

APPENDIX

Report by Charles Moeller to J. Heuschen, A. Prignon, and Piet Smulders, March 22, 1964, based on Moeller's review of the written comments submitted by Council members on the *Schema Constitutionis dogmaticae De divina revelatione* ("Textus Prior", 1963)[58]. The notes are by the author of this paper, who has adapted the formatting of margins for this publication, while retaining Ch. Moeller's original underlining and quotation marks.

De revelatione. Remarques générales sur le Proemium (n° 1-6)
1.– Beaucoup désirent une définition, au moins une description plus précise de la Révélation.

Il y a deux tendances: une minorité demande que l'on rappelle que la révélation est "locutio", expression de "vérités", même de concepts; la même école demande que l'on maintienne et renforce, dans 4, l'idée que les "miracula", que la "vita" de Jésus-Christ, "comprobant suum testimonium". (Ainsi Builes, p. 156 sv; Carli, Siri, mais qui parlent surtout de la Tradition)[59].
: une majorité d'évêques demande au contraire que l'on souligne que la Révélation est:

- Ipse Deus sese revelans (Ev Belges, 176[60])
- Christus revelans Deum (Ev fr., Elchinger[61])

---

58. In the covering letter with this text, Ch. Moeller explained that he was sending in writing the results of "un premier triage", along with a few personal reflections, since he cannot take part in the meeting at Hasselt scheduled for Easter Tuesday, April 1, 1964.

59. The page-references are to the 225 mimeographed pages of *animadversiones Patrum* on the *De revelatione* draft of 1963. The pages were prepared in the Doctrinal Commission's Secretariat, under Fr. Sebastian Tromp, and were distributed to the members and *periti* of the subcommission on revelation chaired by Bp. A.-M. Charue. This group was formed on March 7, 1964, being commissioned to transform the 1963 draft into a *Textus emendatus,* which could be distributed to the Council Fathers for discussion during the third working period of September-November 1964. The comments by the Fathers are found in *AS* III/3, pp. 792-919, and in GIL HELLIN, *Concilii Vaticani II Synopsis* (n. 15), pp. 349-483, offering the comments that influenced the *Textus emendatus.* The 1963 draft text is given in *AS* III/3, pp. 782-791 and 69-109, synoptically with the 1964 amended text. Gil Hellín gives the two texts as columns I and II of his synopsis, pp. 2-175.

60. The Belgian episcopal conference urged "ut revelatio non exclusive ut 'verbalis' describatur, sed ostendatur etiam eius indoles 'realis', qua Deus 'Seipsum' revelare hominibus decrevit, secundum verba Decreti Vaticani I, Denz. 1785" (*AS* III/3, p. 896; GIL HELLIN, *Concilii Vaticani II Synopsis* [n. 15], p. 453. The reference is to the Constitution *Dei Filius*, Ch. II, 1 (*DH* 3004).

61. Among the comments made on the *Textus prior,* four were by regional conferences of French bishops. From the Western Apostolic Region came this request: "Rogamus quod divina revelatio recte definiatur. Principaliter ostendendum est in tali expositione quod revelatio, non tantum in mysteriorum successione per propositiones et locutiones ex ore Christi et prophetarum collectas consistit, sed ipsa actio Dei vivi est, propositum gratiae

– Facta: vel histora salutis (etiam in VT)
et Vita Christi (ev Hollande, ev. centre Afrique)

En d'autres mots, cette majorité demande que l'on marque que la Révélation ne comporte pas seulement des "veritates", mais des réalités vivantes (Butler, Silva). NB. Certains évêques "conservateurs" demandent cependant que, en ce qui concerne les miracles et la vie du Christ, on montre que ces "faits", s'ils prouvent l'authenticité de la doctrine, font eux-mêmes partie de la Révélation elle-même (De la Chanonie, Prou etc.).

Réflexion personnelle: je crois que, un peu à ma [*sic*, pour "la"] manière dont le chanoine Aubert procède dans sa troisième partie de "Le problème de l'acte de foi", on doit insister dans le sens de la majorité, mais en évitant toute expression qui pourrait faire croire à un anti-intellectualisme[62]. Des formules comme "non tantum veritates manifestat, sed etiam, et amplius et profundius Revelatio est Deus sese revelans, in historia salutis ab electione populi in Abraham, est (vel constituitur) Christus in sua vita…".

2.– Un certain nombre insiste sur la possibilité de la connaissance de Dieu par la raison (Ev belges); certains suggèrent en ce sens de joindre la citation de Rom 1 (qui vient de Sap.) et celle du texte du Vatican I (où du reste Rom 1 est cité) (Philippe, Carli, Russo, p.3, p.8, p.20).

Réflexion: je me demande si cette suggestion n'est pas à reprendre. Du moment qu'on ne dépasse pas le sens de la définition de Vat I (qui ne vise qu'une possibilité au moins de droit). Seulement, cette suggestion, si elle est retenue, entraîne sans doute que l'on maintienne, en n° 2, les lignes 15-17 sur la "revelatio primigenia", car il a un lien entre ces deux thèmes. Or, cette question est si difficile que l'on peut demander si le Concile le peut en parler ainsi "per transennam"? Se borner à ajouter Rom 1, et Vat I, n'est que répéter: est-ce nécessaire? Est-ce utile? En d'autres termes, si l'on insiste sur ce thème de la possibilité de la connaissance de Dieu par la raison, qui, en soi, est utile, il semble nécessaire de le faire en complétant, en expliquant Vat I: or, c'est impossible en deux lignes.

3.– Les uns veulent qu'on ne parle pas de la "revelatio primigenia" (Butler), d'autres veulent au contraire qu'on en parle (Silva).

---

eius revelans et efficiens, novissime etenim in Iesu Christo seipsum manifestans" (*AS* III/3, p. 901; GIL HELLIN, *Concilii Vaticani II Synopsis* [n. 15], pp. 375ff). Bp. Elchinger asserted that revelation "est avant tout le Christ Rédempteur lui-même, en qui Dieu se communique aux hommes pour leur salut, leur manifestant son mystère et son dessein de salut. L'Ecriture dit avec éloquence que le Christ lui-même est, en sa personne, la révélation de Dieu en sa plénitude…" (*AS* III/3, p. 829; GIL HELLIN, *Concilii Vaticani II Synopsis* [n. 15], p. 386).

62. The reference to R. Aubert's work is identified above in n. 26.

<u>Réflexion</u>: Si on en parle, ce qui <u>peut</u> avoir une certaine utilité par rapport au schéma XVII (présence du Verbe créateur dans sa création, qui est "<u>idion plasma</u>", "Hidden Christ", Christ caché dans le monde (comme création) car le Christ est "Seigneur sur l'Eglise et sur le monde"), il faut le faire avec des explications qui sont impossibles ici, me semble-t-il.

J'ai cependant l'impression que d'assez nombreux laïcs, intéressés par les problèmes Teilhard etc., aimeraient qu'on parle de la "revelatio primigenia"; seulement ils l'entendent de la "revelatio" qui est liée à la création elle-même, qui porte, elle aussi, les "vestigia Dei", et les traces de "l'illumination du Verbe-créateur". Est-ce tout à fait en ce sens que l'on parle dans le texte du n° 2 de "testimonium datum generi humano de semetipso et de hominis superni fine"? Je ne le crois pas.

Ainsi qu'on le voit il y a ici, à propos de ces premières lignes du n° 2 (l. 15-17) une série d'ambiguïtés. N'est-il pas mieux, dès lors, de renvoyer le thème du "monde comme création", "révélant" Dieu, au schema XVII, et de s'en tenir ici au sens strict du terme "revelatio", à fin de mieux préparer le chapitre I, sur les relations entre "Traditio et Revelatio".

4.– Les critiques négatives sont très nombreuses sur les n° 4,5,6, dont certains soulignent qu'ils sont très inspirés du "vetus schema"[63] (!)
Particulièrement: n° 4: on critique la mention des "miracula" comme preuve, alors qu'ils sont aussi le contenu de la révélation (cfr. la résurrection, et les remarques <u>supra</u>, n.1).
n° 5: On critique l'emploi excessif du terme "veritates" (4 fois en neuf lignes); on y voit un conceptualisme dangereux.
n° 6: On demande une insistance plus nette sur le rôle de la grâce dans l'acte de foi, en précisant que l'on croit "Deo revelante", et "par la grâce de Dieu, agissante en l'Esprit".

<u>Réflexion</u>: Je crois que toutes ces suggestions sont à retenir, car elles émanent d'une majorité, et elles préparent mieux le problème "Révélation-Tradition".

5.– On suggère des changements dans l'ordre: 2+3 formeraient un seul n° 2
                                                3+4 formeraient un seul n° 3
                                                5 passerait en 2, et formerait un n° 2

---

63. The "old schema" was the draft text *De fontibus revelationis* from the Preparatory Theological Commission, distributed in July 1962 and treated in the Council Aula November 14-21, 1962. Also, some Fathers would have in mind the same Commission's text *De deposito fidei pure custodiendo*, distributed with *De fontibus*, which contained matter pertinent to the present discussion in its Ch. IV, *De revelatione et de fide Catholica*.

6.– NB. Dans les pages qui suivent, remarques de détail, je n'ai repris que les suggestions qui, pour des motifs que je dirai, me paraissent utiles à prendre en considération. L'inventaire est sans doute incomplet, chacun, quand il travaille seul, lisant avec ses propres points de vue. J'ai, manuscrit, le relevé de presque toutes les emendationes demandées, par page et par ligne. Il est inutile de le recopier, des fiches <u>ayant été faites à Rome en ce sens, plus complètes</u>.

7.– Il me semble que tout changement quelque peu sérieux entraîne ipso facto une discussion en Commission mixte Théologie-Secrétariat, soit [erased] plénière, soit en sous-commission mixte (entre le 20 et le 26 avril).

De revelatione, remarques de détail[64]
N° 1
– Ligne 2: barrer "Vaticana secunda": raison: inutile, redondant.
Remarque personnelle: je supprimerais, ligne 3 le terme "<u>sollemniter</u>", tout comme on l'a supprimé dans le numéro sur la sacramentalité de l'épiscopat, et pour la même raison. Mais aucun évêque ne propose cette suppression.

– Ligne 2: mettre "<u>divina</u> revelatione" au lieu de "sacra revelatione", par conformité au titre général du schéma (Carli, 8, Przylek, 20)[65].
On propose d'ajouter la mention du Concile de Trente et du Concile du Vatican I (ev. de Bari, 202), mais ces répétitions sans explications me paraissent inutilement alourdissantes.
On propose d'ajouter la mention de *Humani generis* (Capozi, 2, Carli, 7), mais il faut refuser, un Concile ne citant jamais, comme telle, une Encyclique.

– Ligne 3: au lieu de "proponere" on propose "<u>proponere intendens</u>" (Butler, 195).

– Ligne 5: au lieu de "quae", dans la citation de Ep. Jo., on propose de mettre "quod", qui est dans le texte de la Vulgate. (Nombreuses demandes).

– Ligne 8: ajouter insistance sur la possibilité naturelle de connaître Dieu (ev. Belges, Florit, 180). Je suis d'accord en principe, mais vois mal la possibilité concrète de le faire sans entrer dans d'interminables discussions.

Dans ce sens on propose d'ajouter la citation de Rom 1,20 (Philippe, 3; Carli, 8; Russo, 20). Je renvoie aux remarques générales sub 1.

---

64. In the following points, Ch. Moeller refers to the line numbers in the booklet in which the Mixed Commission's draft text, *De divina revelatione*, was distributed to the Council Fathers by mail in May 1963.
65. The second reference is to the comments of J.B. Przyklenk, M.S.F., bishop of Januária, Brazil.

– Ligne 10: "subsistentiam": de très nombreux évêques demandent la suppression de ce vocable, trop scolastique. On suggère de le remplacer par des termes comme "Deum, Patrem, Filium et Spiritum Sanctum" (Conf. Ep. Allem.-Scand., 112; Lefevre, 124; Ev Indonésie, 143; Tabera, 167; Butler, 195; Silva, 216).

– Ligne 11: ajouter "Incarnationem Verbi per Eius unionem hypostaticam" (Conf. All.-Scand., 113; Tabera, 167). J'ajouterais que les termes "per unionem hypostaticam" sont inutiles; mais la mention du mystère de l'incarnation est importante dans ce contexte, afin de compléter.

Sur ce point il y a cependant une remarque de Saboia (165) disant qu'il ne faut <u>pas</u> mentionner d'exemples de "mysteria prorsus impervia rationi humanae", parce que, par exemple aux Indes, il y a "aliqua adumbratio S[anctis]s[im]ae Trinitatis" dans certains passages des livres sacrés et dans des écrits philosophiques à ce sujet. Il semble cependant que, pris <u>ensemble,</u> les deux grands "mystères", celui de la "théologie" (au sens strict, doctrine sur Dieu en tant que Dieu, donc "un et Trine") et celui de "l'économie" (incarnation, rédemption, qui sont "théologie" au sens large) apparaissent comme totalement inaccessibles à toute raison humaine. Le "mystère" trinitaire n'est du reste connu que dans "l'économie".
J'ajoute une réflexion personnelle: dans quelle mesure n'y-t-il pas une ambiguïté entre le terme "mysteria" (l. 10) dans le sens qu'on lui donne ici et le "mysterium" dont parle Paul dans Eph-Col? Il me semble qu'un évêque propose ici, au lieu de "mysteria", le terme paulinien de "profunda" ("<u>ta bathè tou theou</u>") qui vient de Paul[66], et paraît répondre <u>et</u> à la demande des évêques allemands (mentionner l'Incarnation, mais sous le signe de la "manifestation" qu'elle est des "profunda" de la "théologie" au sens strict) et à la question de Saboia, sur une "adumbratio possibilis Trinitatis" dans la pensée de l'Inde.
En conclusion je propose donc "<u>profunda Dei</u>" avec l'évêque dont je ne parviens plus à retrouver le texte dans mes pages dactylographiées.

– Ligne12: omettre le mot "homines"; "omnes" suffit.

– Lignes 12-14: supprimer, car inutiles, répétant ce qui précède, ou ce qui va être dit sub n° 4 (Butler,195).

Si on garde les lignes 12-14 on propose d'ajouter "de homine <u>eiusque historia salutis</u> (Silva, 216) et "in Christo <u>Salvatori nostro</u>" (Je ne retrouve pas le référence), à la ligne 13.

Je préfère la correction proposée par les ev. d'Indonésie (143), proposant d'ajouter à la fin de la ligne 14: "<u>non solum per verba sed simul etiam per magnalia Dei in historia salutis</u>".

---

66. In his copy of the Moeller-report, P. Smulders wrote in the margin "E 327", identifying this proposal of a phrase from 1 Cor 2,10 as coming from Abp. M. Baudoux of St. Boniface, Canada (*AS* III/3, p. 805; GIL HELLIN, *Concilii Vaticani II Synopsis* [n. 15], p. 391).

N° 2

– Lignes 15-17: on propose de les supprimer, pour lever l'ambiguïté qui en résulte entre "revelatio primigenia" et "Revelatio in Christo preparata et in Christo perfecta" (Butler, 195). Dans le même sens (Raimondi, 87) remarque une ambiguïté possible entre l. 16, où l'on parle de "genus humanum" et l. 17 ou l'on parle de Adam: sont-ce deux choses différentes, ou les mêmes actes de révélation de Dieu à l'homme?

Par ailleurs on demande une insistance plus grande sur la "revelatio naturalis" (Silva, 217).

Réflexion personnelle: cfr. remarques générales, sub 1 et 2.

– Ligne 17: "superno fine": entre les corrections proposées (supernaturali, Carli, 8; ultima ac supernaturali (ev. All.– Scand., 113), je préfère celle de Jaeger (204): "superna vocatione"; il faut éviter l'emploi du terme "supernaturalis" quand la chose est possible, dans un Concile, car, comme tel, il est inconnu de la tradition orientale.

– Ligne 17: au lieu de "promittendo", on propose "praenuntiando" (ev. Gall. merid., 139). Ce dernier terme est plus en place dans un contexte de Révélation.

– Ligne 18: nombreuses demandes en vue de supprimer le "mox" (e.g. Conf. Ev. All.-Scand., 113); on propose la suppression pure et simple, afin de mieux marquer qu'il n'y eut jamais un instant durant lequel l'homme fut dénué de la promesse ou annonce du salut par Dieu; d'autres proposent de mettre "statim" (Tabera, 167), ce qui paraît curieux et inutile.

– Ligne 18: des nombreuses suggestions sur le terme "restauravit", je retiens "restaurandum inchoavit" (ev. Indonésie, 143), ou "instaurata decrevit" (conf. ev. Argent., 135).

– Ligne 19: on propose de supprimer "postea", car il y a bien plus de temps écoulé entre Abraham et Adam qu'entre Abraham et nous (Conf. ev. Allem. Scand., 113); de plus le terme pourrait faire penser qu'il n'y a plus eu de révélation entre Adam et Abraham (ev. Gall. merid., 139).

– Ligne 20: ajouter "et per foedus" (Tabera, 167), afin de marquer l'Alliance.

– Ligne 21: au lieu de "longinquo", on propose "prope" pour les raisons données à propos de "postea" (Conf. ev. Allem. Scand., 113).

– Ligne 21: On propose d'ajouter la "locutio Dei per prophetas" avec mention de Hebr. 1,1 (Ev Belges, 176; Butler, 195).

N° 3

– Ligne 22: On propose d'ajouter à "in Christo", les mots "<u>in quo Pater perfecte</u> <u>Seipsum manifestavit</u>" (Butler, 193). Réflexion personnelle: "perfecte" semble peu heureux, car un thème important de la tradition orientale est, si je ne me trompe, celui de l'*incomprehensibilitas* du Père. On pourrait plutôt exprimer l'idée voulue par Dom Butler en s'inspirant de Jean 1,18: "Nul n'a jamais vu Dieu ... fait connaître".

– Ligne 23: au lieu de "Spiritum Christi" on suggère "Spiritum <u>Paraclitum</u>" ou "<u>Spiritum Sanctum</u>" (Russo, 30).

– Ligne 23: "promissum": on propose d'ajouter: "<u>et datum</u>" (je ne retrouve pas la ref.).

– Ligne 24: "dixerat": question à trancher par la sous-commission Biblique, car on fait remarquer que dans Vulg., il y a "dixero"[67].

– Ligne 24: "dixerat": on critique le terme, en ce lieu, car il ne manifesterait pas assez clairement le sens fort que ce terme revêt dans la pensée sémitique (Silva, 217); on y voit de l'intellectualisme.

– Réflexion personnelle: la manière dont la citation est amenée justifie la remarque de Silva, comme, aussi demande une révision de la sous-commission biblique; mais, par ailleurs, il me semble que, dans ce contexte, il faudrait insinuer, ou même citer le "<u>odègèsei eis tèn alètheian pasan</u>" de Jean 16,13, qui est, je crois, un des lieux théologiques essentiels de "l'infaillibilité" et donc aussi un point d'attaché du thème de la Tradition; c. Rousseaux, Dupuy etc., <u>L'infaillibilité de l'Église</u>, coll. Irénikon, Chevetogne, 1962[68]. Un ev. l'a proposé, mais je ne retrouve pas la référence.

– Ligne 24: on propose de supprimer "publica", mais de préciser à la ligne suivante.

– Lignes 24-26: de nombreux évêques demandent que l'on précise en quel sens la Révélation en Jésus-Christ est "ultima" et qu'il ne faut pas attendre de "nova revelatio". Trois considérations sont faites:

---

67. For the Doctrinal Commission's review of amendments proposed for the draft text *De ecclesia*, a group of Fathers and *periti* with special competence in biblical exegesis formed a sub-commission responsible for deciding all matters concerning biblical citations and references. Ch. Moeller appears to consider, for *De revelatione*, the second group of revisors, under Bp. Charue, which was responsible for amending *Textus prior* chapters II-V on Scripture, to be a body which could decide questions about Scripture citations for the present text.

68. See n. 40, above.

– il faut indiquer que la "Parousie" est, en un sens, elle aussi une "Revelatio" (Jaeger, 203)

– il faut dire plus clairement, si on le veut, en quel sens la "Revelatio" est terminée à l'âge apostolique (je ne retrouve pas la référence)

– il faut préciser en montrant que cette révélation est "ultime" en ce sens qu'il n'y a et n'aura aucun moyen plus profond d'entrer en communication avec Dieu (Jaeger, 204).

Dans ce sens, on propose: ajouter, ligne <u>26</u> "…revelatio <u>publica</u>" (Méouchi, 108; Tabera, 167; Jaeger, 204).

– on propose: ajouter, après "expectanda est": "<u>Ante ultimum adventum</u>" (Conf. év. Allem.– Scand., 114; Silva, 217) ou bien, ce qui me plaît beaucoup plus: "<u>usque ad adventum gloriosum Christi, "ita ut nihil desit in ulla gratia expectantibus revelationem Domini nostri Jesu-Christi</u>" (1 Cor. 1,7).

– on propose d'ajouter, ligne 26: "<u>sed solummodo Revelationis explanatio</u>", lequel semble trop scolaire.

– on propose d'ajouter, ligne 29: "<u>donec dies elucescat et lucifer matutinus oriatur in cordibus vestris</u> (Weber, 101). Proposition qui plaît aussi et peut être jointe à celle de Jaeger.

– Lignes 27-29: nouvelle version, Jaeger, 204. Butler (195) propose de supprimer.

– Ligne 27: le terme "christianismus" est rejeté par de très nombreux évêques, parce que terme d'école, ou trop lié au thème de "l'histoire des religions" (ev. Afr. Centre-Orientale; Ritter, 44; Helmsing, 103). On propose ou "<u>oeconomia christiana</u>" (ev. Prov. Aq. et Mass., 47) ou "<u>aetas christiana</u>" (Conf. Allem.-Scand., 114) qui plaît plus parce que faisant allusion au thème biblique du "<u>kairos</u>".

– Ligne 28: on propose de <u>supprimer</u> "omnino", car redondant (référence perdue).

N° 4
– On propose – de <u>lier</u> 3 et 4 (Florit)
– de <u>supprimer</u> 4, comme inutile (Silva, 217)
– <u>nouvelle version</u> (Baudoux, 78).

– Beaucoup critiquent l'idée centrale du paragraphe: il crée l'impression que la vie et les miracles de Christ "solummodo comprobant doctrinam", alors qu'ils font partie de la révélation elle-même, car "Ipsa vita Christi est Revelatio", "historia salutis est portatrix (sic) revelationis" (Conf. Neerl., 69), "non solum confirmant, sed totum mysterium christianum ostendunt" (de la Chanonie, Prou, etc., 91).

On propose dès lors:
– Lignes 1-2: nova versio dans le sens: "<u>verba Dei loquitur et opera</u> etc." (Conf. ev. Indonésie, 144)

– Ligne 5: mettre "<u>manifestaverint</u>", au lieu de "confirmaverint" (Butler, 195; Jaeger, 204)
– Ligne 8: ajouter "<u>et opus salutis perficitur</u>" (de la Chanonie, 91).

– Ligne 3: à "divinitatem suam", ajouter "<u>et redemptionis gratiam</u>" (Jaeger, 204).

– Lignes 5-8: supprimer, ou remplacer par [une] version nouvelle proposée (Butler, 204).

– Ligne 7: au lieu de "vitam miraculosam" mettre: "<u>per vitam Eius ac miracula</u>", et mentionner la résurrection (Jaeger, 204).

– Ligne 7: après "miraculosam" ajouter "<u>necnon opera Christi in Ecclesia</u>" (référence perdue).

N° 5
– Lignes 9-17: Butler propose de les remplacer par une version nouvelle.

– On critique surtout le mot "veritates, veritates" (l. 10, 12, 13, 14) qui, par sa répétition, oriente vers une vision conceptualiste (Butler, 196). Mais, d'autres, surtout Builes (156 sv.) insistent sur l'idée de "revelatio-locutio", précisant même que la révélation comporte "propositiones, iudicia, conceptus", et l'opposant à la vision de la révélation comme "complexus rerum supernaturalium", connu par "intuitionismum", qui conduit au "relativismus".

Réflexion: le texte doit éviter tant des formules comme "complexus rerum supernaturalium" que des formules comme "propositiones, locutiones etc. …" Il doit s'orienter dans le sens préconisé par Butler.

– Ligne 11: au lieu de "participationis" on propose "<u>consortii</u>" (je ne retrouve pas la référence).

– Ligne 11: après "hominis", ajouter: "<u>in Christo</u>".

– Ligne 18: au lieu de "ad supernaturalem finem assequendum", dire: "<u>ad aeternam vitam assequendam</u>" (ev. Indonésie, 143).

N° 6
– Nouvelle version proposée par Conf. Ev. Allem. Scand. (114), Jaeger (205), Silva (217).

– On demande de souligner plus le rôle de la grâce dans l'acte de foi.
– Pour mieux marquer le rôle de la grâce, on propose:
– ligne 22: ajouter "<u>Ut</u> revelationi…" et supprimer le "sed".

– ligne 22: "Deo divina revelanti" (Tabera, 167; Jaeger, 204).
– ligne 23: "cum fidei actus elicitur, iam ibi operatur Deus" (Baudoux).
– ligne 23: au lieu de "opus est gratia Dei" on propose: "Necessaria est gratia Dei quae, Spiritu Dei operante, sensum…" (Butler, 196).
– ligne 25: ajouter: "idem Spiritus Paraclitus" (Butler, 196).

Réflexion: les corrections [de] Butler sont les meilleures, semble-t-il.

– ligne 26: ajouter: "cf. Jean 6,44; Rom 10,19" (Tabera 167)

Par ailleurs, ligne 23 on propose d'ajouter "fidei actus, qui est assensus intellectus veritati extrinsece prolatae" (référence perdue)[69]. Mais ceci semble trop scolairement énoncé. Cfr. remarques générales, n° 1 et 2.

Charles Moeller
Louvain, 22 mars 1964.

Envoyé à   Mgr. Heuschen
         Mgr. Prignon
         Père Smulders

---

69. In the margin of his copy, P. Smulders wrote "Conway", identifying Bp. William Conway, Auxiliary Bishop of Armagh, Ireland, as the one making this proposal (AS III/3, p. 825; GIL HELLIN, Concilii Vaticani II Synopsis [n. 15], p. 395). The Relatio accompanying the amended draft submitted by Smulders on April 12, 1964, explained that while the text included in its no. 5 on faith the element of intellectual assent to truth, it did not speak of this truth as extrinsecus acceptae, which came from the Oath against Modernism (D 2145/DH 3542) because in the present context it could seem to exclude "internal testimony" from the genesis of faith.

LA CONTRIBUTION DE CHARLES MOELLER
AU CONCILE VATICAN II D'APRÈS SES PAPIERS
CONCILIAIRES

Je me propose de suivre pas à pas l'*iter Concilii* de l'expert belge Charles Moeller[1]. Toutefois, l'abondance et la variété de son activité conciliaire me conduisent à n'examiner ici en détail que son engagement

1. Charles Moeller (Bruxelles, 1912-Bruxelles, 1986), entré à l'abbaye bénédictine du Mont-César (Louvain) en 1928, s'orienta ensuite vers le sacerdoce dans le diocèse de Malines(-Bruxelles). Ordonné en 1937, il obtint en 1942 le doctorat en théologie à Louvain, avec une thèse sur Néphalius d'Alexandrie (néo-chalcédonisme). Éveillé très jeune par son frère aîné au problème de l'unité chrétienne et informé des projets œcuméniques de dom Lambert Beauduin, fondateur du monastère d'Amay-Chevetogne, dont il devint plus tard un disciple fervent, il s'initie, grâce à un autre moine d'Amay, dom Clément Lialine, directeur de la revue *Irénikon*, à la spiritualité et à la théologie orthodoxes. Avec celui-ci et son ami, R. Aubert, il est à l'origine des Semaines œcuméniques annuelles de Chevetogne, dont la première eut lieu en 1942 et dont Moeller fut longtemps l'animateur et le fidèle participant jusqu'en 1965. Les Semaines de 1959 à 1962 apportèrent une importante contribution à l'ecclésiologie développée dans les grandes constitutions du concile Vatican II, surtout *Lumen Gentium*. Titulaire de la classe de Poésie au collège St-Pierre de Jette (Bruxelles) de 1941 à 1954, C. Moeller est aussi maître de conférences à l'Institut des sciences religieuses de l'Université de Louvain à partir de 1949. Il y est nommé professeur en 1954. Attentif au problème de l'athéisme contemporain et soucieux de rendre le message chrétien compréhensible à la culture du 20ème siècle, C.M. scrute la pensée des grands écrivains de son siècle. Ses conférences à Louvain (et plus tard en diverses régions du monde) consacrées à la quête de sens dans la littérature contemporaine le rendirent célèbre; elles furent publiées ensuite sous le titre *Littérature du XXème siècle et christianisme* (6 vol.; la 1ère édition du tome 1 date de 1952). C.M. fut élu en 1970 membre de l'Académie royale de langue et de littérature françaises de Belgique. Il était préparé à jouer un rôle dans le cadre de Vatican II. Nommé expert officiel du Concile le 7 déc. 1962 à l'intervention du card. Léger, archevêque de Montréal, il intervint dans de nombreuses commissions. Il fut par ailleurs un des animateurs au sein de l'équipe des évêques et théologiens belges et entretint des relations suivies avec les observateurs non-catholiques. Il seconda G. Philips dans l'élaboration de la constitution sur l'Église. Il contribua à la rédaction et à l'acceptation par les pères conciliaires de la constitution sur l'Église dans le monde. Nommé, dès avant la fin du Concile, recteur du nouvel Institut œcuménique de recherches théologiques de Tantur, il fut appelé en 1966 à la charge de sous-secrétaire de la Congrégation romaine pour la doctrine de la foi. De 1973 à 1980, il fut secrétaire du Secrétariat pour l'unité des chrétiens. Il sera nommé professeur à la Faculté de théologie de Louvain en 1974 et accédera à l'émérit en 1982. Voir sur lui: J.M. VAN CANGH (éd.), *In memoriam Mgr Charles Moeller*, Louvain-la-Neuve, 1987; J. GROOTAERS, *Charles Moeller, 1912-1986*, dans I. BRIA – D. HELLER (éds.), *Ecumenical Pilgrims*, Genève, 1995, 152-156, et R. LOONBEEK – J. MORTIAU, *Un pionnier: Dom Lambert Beauduin*, 2 tomes, Louvain-la-Neuve – Chevetogne, 2001.

durant la période pré-conciliaire et pendant la première période et la première intersession du Concile. Ces étapes sont déterminantes pour la suite
de son activité. Il y sera principalement question du rôle de Moeller dans
la mise en route du schéma sur l'Église et dans les débuts de ce qui
deviendra la constitution *Gaudium et spes*.

Le P. Congar note dans son journal du Concile à la date du 27 novembre
1965 que, lors d'une réunion tenue alors à Bellagio (lac de Côme) entre
délégués catholiques et non-catholiques pour préparer la fondation de l'Institut œcuménique de Tantur (Jérusalem), la proposition de choisir Moeller comme directeur du futur Institut – ceci en l'absence de l'intéressé –
révéla «une unanimité bouleversante»[2]. Congar ajoute qu'il s'est avéré
que l'expert belge «avait été pour tous et pour chacun comme un ami personnel et qu'il avait été mêlé en profondeur à la vie du Concile et à tout
ce qui s'est fait autour de lui au point de vue œcuménique»[3].

Le même Congar raconte aussi comment, en février 1963, il a été associé, grâce à Moeller, au travail de la commission théologique pour la préparation du nouveau schéma sur l'Église[4]. En cette circonstance débuta
une amitié entre Congar et Moeller, qui se traduisit en collaboration pour
la rédaction de plusieurs textes destinés aux documents conciliaires.

I. LA PÉRIODE PRÉPARATOIRE

Avant d'aborder cette première période-clé, il faut remonter plus haut,
à la phase pré-conciliaire. Dans les premiers mois de la période préparatoire proprement dite, qui commence en juin 1960, des professeurs de
Louvain (G. Philips, L. Cerfaux, G. Thils, A. Janssen) sont nommés dans
les commissions chargées de préparer les textes du futur Concile. Charles
Moeller n'est pas du nombre. Depuis 1949, il est maître de conférences
à l'Institut des sciences religieuses qui a été créé à Louvain en 1942 et
qui organise à partir de 1956 un programme de sciences religieuses à
temps plein à l'intention des laïcs, des religieux-frères et des religieuses.
Moeller y enseigne le dogme et la dogmatique fondamentale. Vis-à-vis
de la Faculté de théologie, sa fonction est subalterne. Il est d'ailleurs rat-
taché à la Faculté de philosophie et lettres. Le considère-t-on uniquement
comme un homme de culture et non comme un théologien? En tout cas,

2. Y. CONGAR, *Mon journal du Concile*, présenté et annoté par É. MAHIEU, 2 tomes,
Paris, 2002, Tome II, p. 493.
    3. *Ibid.*
    4. *Ibid.*, Tome I, p. 335.

comme il a passé son doctorat en théologie à l'insu des autorités diocésaines de Malines[5], il est tenu à l'écart de la Faculté de théologie. Lui-même confiera un jour à son ami Édouard Beauduin: «Je ne serai jamais un inventeur de formules précises»[6].

Toujours est-il que, dès cette année 1960, Moeller manifeste un grand intérêt pour le Concile dans trois domaines: l'ecclésiologie, les relations de l'Église avec la culture moderne et l'œcuménisme. En ecclésiologie d'abord. Il fait parvenir des suggestions sur l'épiscopat et sur la théologie de l'Église locale à Mgr Suenens, alors évêque auxiliaire de Malines[7]. Et il encourage son ami Louis Evely à lui transmettre des textes qu'il compte envoyer à des hautes autorités romaines, sur des problèmes comme l'adaptation de la liturgie, les relations entre le monde moderne et la foi, la centralisation excessive du gouvernement de l'Église[8].

Au début de 1961, Moeller commence à rédiger d'autres Notes à l'intention de Mgr Suenens et d'autres personnalités ecclésiastiques. À la même époque, il fait partie d'un cercle théologique louvaniste animé par G. Philips et aux réunions duquel prennent part notamment G. Thils et des jésuites du collège théologique d'Egenhoven (près de Louvain). Lors de ses réunions en mars-avril 1961, ce cercle examine les deux Notes d'ecclésiologie que Moeller a rédigées sur l'Église particulière et sur le patriarcat d'Occident et qui sont révisées en commun[9].

5. D'après ce que m'a dit le prof. R. Aubert lors d'un entretien le 19 juin 2002.
6. C. Moeller à É. Beauduin, 14 mars 1963, double dans Fonds Moeller, 3049 (C. SOETENS, Concile Vatican II et Église contemporaine (Archives de Louvain-la-Neuve). I: Inventaire des Fonds Ch. Moeller, G. Thils, Fr. Houtart (Cahiers de la Revue théologique de Louvain, 21), Louvain-la-Neuve, Publications de la Faculté de Théologie, 1989). Sur É. Beauduin (1907-1982), neveu de dom Lambert Beauduin, prêtre du diocèse de Liège, directeur de l'Œuvre d'Orient pour la Belgique à partir de 1956, voir ma notice dans la Nouvelle biographie nationale (de Belgique) 9 (2007) 34-36.
7. Lettres des 14 et 26 août 1960, dans Fonds Suenens, 506 et 507 (L. DECLERCK – E. LOUCHEZ, Inventaire des Papiers conciliaires du cardinal L.-J. Suenens [Cahiers de la Revue théologique de Louvain, 31], Louvain-la-Neuve, Publications de la Faculté de Théologie, 1998, pp. 72-73).
8. C. Moeller à L. Evely, 22 décembre 1960, double; Evely à Moeller, 8 janvier 1961, dans Fonds Moeller, 2755-2756. Dans sa réponse, Evely se dit peu capable de rédiger des notes et communique des réflexions «au naturel» (non jointes). Louis Evely (1910-1985) était prêtre du diocèse de Malines et avait été professeur puis directeur du collège Cardinal Mercier à Braine-l'Alleud. En 1960, il s'était retiré dans une trappe de France. Par la suite, il abandonna le ministère et se maria. Il s'était fait connaître comme prédicateur de retraites et par quelques ouvrages de spiritualité destinés aux laïcs, qui furent très appréciés.
9. 'Note sur la notion d'Église particulière', version française datée du 23 mars 1961, 6 p. dactyl., dans Fonds Moeller, 7. On y lit notamment que cette notion est très importante chez S. Paul et que l'ecclésiologie de communion des Églises locales (ou particulières) sera, après le moyen âge, «laissée pratiquement dans l'ombre, pour être remplacée par l'ecclésiologie de l'unus populus sous le signe de la monarchie pontificale». Dans la

C'est, semble-t-il, à la même époque qu'il rédige également des Notes relatives à la nécessaire adaptation de la liturgie et à la récitation privée du bréviaire.

Philips se charge de transmettre les Notes d'ecclésiologie de Moeller, notamment aux cardinaux Ottaviani et Bea et aux jésuites de la Grégorienne Tromp et Dhanis, respectivement secrétaire et membre de la commission théologique préparatoire. À la suggestion de Moeller, le cercle de Louvain aborde aussi, avec A. Dondeyne, la question de l'athéisme. En mai, il traite des 'membres' de l'Église[10]. Et vers la même époque, le chanoine Thils rédige aussi des notes d'ecclésiologie, notamment sur l'infaillibilité pontificale et la collégialité épiscopale, sur lesquelles Moeller s'est du reste basé dans ses écrits.

Si la question de l'ecclésiologie envisagée dans une perspective œcuménique est un des axes principaux des préoccupations de Moeller en vue du Concile, le second domaine prioritaire pour lui est celui de la culture moderne marquée à ses yeux certes par une quête de sens, mais aussi par l'athéisme, comme il le montre depuis de nombreuses années dans ses conférences et ses ouvrages sur la littérature contemporaine. «Comment présenter Dieu à l'homme d'aujourd'hui?». Tel est le titre d'une Note de

«Note sur la notion de 'Patriarcat d'Occident'» (même date, 8 p. dactyl., dans Fonds Moeller, 8), Moeller commence par développer la fonction première du pape comme évêque de Rome, puis montre que la fonction de patriarche d'Occident remonte à la tradition canonique ancienne; et, revenant à la substitution de l'ecclésiologie de communion par celle de la monarchie pontificale – point central de sa première Note –, il illustre les deux niveaux de l'ecclésiologie médiévale occidentale: d'une part celui de la tradition indivise où s'explicite la primauté, d'autre part celui de la *traditio occidentalis*, celle où cette primauté s'exerce en Occident (il en donne trois exemples: celui des liturgies parmi lesquelles s'impose celle de Rome, celui des conciles médiévaux où sont surtout développées les traditions spirituelles, canoniques, liturgiques et théologiques occidentales, celui enfin de la monarchie pontificale développée – à côté de la primauté – dans le sens de l'uniformisation des usages canoniques de Rome). L'auteur propose de reconnaître clairement les traditions du patriarcat d'Occident comme étant valables uniquement pour la chrétienté occidentale, et non dans le cadre de la tradition indivise de l'ensemble des Églises locales.

10. Sur l'envoi des Notes de Moeller et des indications – partielles – sur le cercle louvaniste, cf. Fonds Moeller, 2758 et 2763-2768; Fonds Suenens, 472-473, 478-479; Fonds Philips, 94-104 (L. DECLERCK – W. VERSCHOOTEN, *Inventaire des papiers conciliaires de Mgr Gérard Philips, secrétaire adjoint de la Commission doctrinale. Avec une Introduction par J.* GROOTAERS [Instrumenta Theologica, 24], Leuven, Peeters, 2001). Parmi les autres destinataires des Notes, il faut mentionner Mgr Willebrands, secrétaire du Secrétariat pour l'unité, le cardinal Léger (d'après P. LAFONTAINE, *Inventaire des archives conciliaires du Fonds Paul-Émile Léger*, Montréal, 1995, p. 72 – Fonds Léger) et Mgr De Smedt (Fonds De Smedt, 114-115, voir A. GREILER – L. DE SAEGER [éds.], *Emiel-Jozef De Smedt, Papers Vatican II Inventory*. With a Preface by Leo DECLERCK [Instrumenta Theologica, 22], Leuven, Peeters, 1999, p. 9). En avril 1961, Moeller passe quelques jours à Rome et rencontre notamment le cardinal Bea et Mgr Willebrands (d'après Fonds Moeller, carnet 1).

7 pages, basée surtout sur les écrits de Teilhard de Chardin et sur l'ouvrage de Jean Lacroix, *Le sens de l'athéisme moderne* paru en 1958, Note que Moeller adresse en mai 1962 à Mgr Suenens, devenu entre-temps archevêque de Malines-Bruxelles – et plus tard aussi au cardinal Léger[11] – et qu'il accompagne du commentaire suivant:

> Entre la majorité, très conservatrice, et une petite minorité, très soucieuse des problèmes profanes et théologiques, dans le sens d'un dialogue, va-t-il se dessiner au concile, un *tiers parti*? Question très grave, car cette tendance, si elle se fait jour, permettra d'éviter des définitions, certes qui ne semblent pas prévues, mais des 'constitutions dogmatiques' qui, à en croire les comptes rendus de certaines sessions de la commission centrale, seraient encore en-deçà d'encycliques comme *Divino afflante* par exemple.

Et il ajoute, après s'être dit réconforté par le discours prononcé le 15 mai par le cardinal à propos du Concile:

> Je suis parfois effrayé de voir à quel point à Rome on est peu sensibilisé aux problèmes d'un affrontement et d'un dialogue *réel* avec le monde de l'humanisme moderne, là où il mérite d'être entendu[12].

Sans doute peut-on placer à la même époque – ou alors un an plus tôt – la suggestion de créer une sous-commission sur l'athéisme moderne[13]. Moeller suggérait de faire dépendre cette sous-commission de la 'commission doctrinale', mais s'agissait-il, dans son esprit, de la commission doctrinale du futur concile ou de la commission théologique préparatoire? Il ne le précise pas.

Le troisième secteur auquel Moeller s'intéresse dans la perspective du Concile est celui de l'œcuménisme, dont il s'occupe depuis près de 20 ans. Disciple fervent de dom Lambert Beauduin, il a été, dès 1942, un des initiateurs – sans doute le principal – des Journées théologiques tenues au monastère de Chevetogne. Après l'annonce du Concile en janvier 1959, ces Journées inscrivent à leur programme: en 1959, la notion de 'Concile'; en 1960, le thème de l'Église locale (des idées émises à cette rencontre Moeller tirera une de ses Notes de 1961 et il s'en inspirera dans son travail à la commission doctrinale du Concile pour l'élaboration de *Lumen gentium*); enfin, en 1961, le thème traité à Chevetogne sera «L'infaillibilité dans l'Église». En septembre 1960, Moeller est invité

---

11. D'après Fonds Léger, 1404-1405.
12. C. Moeller à L.-J. Suenens, 30 mai 1962, original dans Fonds Suenens, 462; double dans Fonds Moeller, 2759.
13. Note d'une page dans Fonds Philips, 13. Moeller suggérait comme membres de cette sous-commission H. Urs von Balthasar, A. Dondeyne, J. Lacroix et un certain Rooney.

pour la première fois à la réunion annuelle, tenue cette année-là à Gazzada, de la Conférence catholique pour les questions œcuméniques, qui a été créée huit ans plus tôt par les deux prêtres hollandais J. Willebrands et F. Thijssen. Le thème de cette septième rencontre était «Les différences compatibles avec l'Unité». Moeller avait écrit deux mois plus tôt à Willebrands, futur secrétaire du Secrétariat pour l'unité:

> Tant qu'on ne comprendra pas pratiquement, in actu exercito, que catholicité veut dire aussi multiple splendeur de traditions canoniques, liturgiques, spirituelles, théologiques au sein d'une Révélation une, on n'aura fait que du baratin[14].

En août 1961, Moeller participera encore à la session tenue à Strasbourg, où l'on traita du «Renouveau dans l'Église»[15]. Peu de temps auparavant, il a rencontré le Dr Visser 't Hooft, secrétaire général du Conseil œcuménique des Églises. Celui-ci l'invite à donner en octobre des cours sur l'image de l'homme dans la littérature moderne, à l'Institut d'études œcuméniques de Bossey[16]. Dès lors, l'engagement œcuménique de Moeller en vue du Concile s'intensifie. En janvier 1962, il donne à la demi-heure religieuse de la Radio belge quatre causeries sur des sujets en rapport avec l'unité chrétienne. D'abord sur l'urgence de cette unité; en second lieu sur la troisième Assemblée mondiale du Conseil œcuménique des Églises qui s'est tenue en novembre 1961 à New Delhi et à laquelle son ami Édouard Beauduin a assisté en tant que correspondant de la revue de Chevetogne *Irénikon* (Moeller met en relief les efforts des non-catholiques dans le sens de l'unité); en troisième lieu, il traite de l'appel œcuménique du pape Jean XXIII en vue du Concile; il parle enfin des devoirs des catholiques dans ce domaine[17].

Au cours du Carême suivant, Moeller prononce cinq sermons à la collégiale Ste-Gudule de Bruxelles sur le thème: «Concile et unité des chrétiens», en présentant le Concile dans la perspective d'un ressourcement évangélique, et l'unité sous son aspect d'urgence, bien perçue, selon lui, par les autres Églises lors de l'Assemblée de New Delhi[18].

Cet effort de sensibilisation – dont on pourrait sûrement repérer encore d'autres manifestations – témoigne d'une préoccupation majeure parmi celles qui animeront l'activité conciliaire de Charles Moeller.

---

14. Lettre citée par F. COLLEYE dans son ouvrage non publié: *Charles Moeller et l'Arbre de la Croix* (daté d'août 1998), qui est une chronique détaillée et documentée de la vie de C. Moeller. Citation: p. 225.
15. COLLEYE, *Charles Moeller*, p. 234.
16. *Ibid.*
17. *Ibid.*, p. 236.
18. *Ibid.*, p. 237.

Bien qu'il ait été officiellement inscrit parmi les 10 journalistes belges devant suivre le Concile[19], il ne sera pas présent à Rome, dans le cadre du Concile, avant la fin du mois de novembre 1962. Il y passe cependant, en compagnie d'Édouard Beauduin, la semaine qui précède l'ouverture officielle des assises conciliaires. À cette occasion, il recueille informations et opinions, surtout au Collège belge et au Secrétariat pour l'unité[20]. Il relève notamment que les pères discuteront d'abord du schéma sur la liturgie, puis de ceux sur la Révélation et sur Dieu créateur: ces deux derniers étant, d'après lui, «très mauvais ... refusés en commission centrale, réimposés par Ottaviani»[21]. Mgr Willebrands lui parle de son voyage à Moscou, qu'il considère – même si l'Église orthodoxe russe n'envoyait pas d'observateurs au Concile – comme un fait historique[22]. Le jésuite belge Dhanis, professeur à la Grégorienne et membre de la commission théologique préparatoire, déplore le fait que le pape «se laisse trop faire» et que son confrère Tromp refuse de changer quoi que ce soit aux textes préparés; Dhanis insiste, quant à lui, pour que les évêques refusent d'emblée de discuter ces schémas[23].

Moeller rencontre encore le cardinal Léger, avec qui il est en contact, au moins depuis son voyage au Québec du mois de juillet précédent, peut-être même depuis son premier voyage au Canada en 1959. Si on se réfère à certains propos de Moeller dans ses lettres au cardinal canadien, il semble que celui-ci s'est tout d'abord intéressé aux efforts du professeur louvaniste pour un rapprochement avec le monde de la culture contemporaine vivant éloigné de l'Église[24]. Lors de leur entretien d'octobre 62, Moeller confirme à l'archevêque de Montréal, qui s'était lui-même exprimé clairement à ce sujet à l'adresse du pape[25], la mauvaise qualité des schémas dogmatiques préparatoires. Soit dit en passant, Léger

19. Cf. la liste de 57 journalistes (avec leurs adresses romaines) dressée par J. Grootaers en tant que secrétaire général des Rencontres internationales d'informateurs religieux et datée du 16 octobre 1962 (dans Fonds Thils, Compléments Vatican II, boîte 2). C. Moeller y figure, avec É. Beauduin, comme correspondant de la *Revue Nouvelle*. En fait, seul Éd. Beauduin publiera régulièrement des articles relatifs au Concile dans cette revue.
20. Cf. les carnets personnels de Ch. Moeller, dans Fonds Moeller, Carnets 3 et 4.
21. Carnet 3, pp. 45-46.
22. Carnet 3, pp. 55-57.
23. Carnet 3, p. 50 et Carnet 4, p. 3.
24. Voir notamment la lettre de Moeller à Léger du 10 novembre 1962 (*Fonds Moeller*, n°3031), dans laquelle l'auteur, parlant de conférences qu'il vient de donner en Allemagne du nord et au Danemark, se dit «terriblement frappé de l'ignorance et de l'absence de sens religieux qui marque une partie de la jeunesse de certains pays».
25. Par une supplique d'août 1962. Cf. G. ROUTHIER, *Les réactions du cardinal Léger à la préparation de Vatican II*, dans *Revue d'histoire de l'Église de France* 80 (1994) 281-302.

explique de son côté pourquoi, à la différence de plusieurs autres cardinaux, Montini n'a pas signé la supplique au pape du cardinal canadien: «Après le discours [du pape] du 11 septembre, je crois – écrivait à Léger l'archevêque de Milan – que vous n'avez plus besoin d'approbation»[26].

L'entretien Moeller-Léger témoigne de la relation de confiance existant à ce moment entre les deux hommes. Moeller en tirera bientôt grand profit.

II. LA PREMIÈRE SESSION

De Belgique, Moeller suit la cérémonie d'ouverture du Concile à la télévision. Il note à cette occasion:

> La courte partie orientale [...] concrétise l'œcuménicité de l'Église. Mais il ne faut pas se cacher que les structures sont bien «latinement latines». Les patriarches, par exemple, sont placés après les cardinaux[27].

Et, dans la ligne de sa Note sur le Patriarcat d'Occident, il commente le fait en le qualifiant d'«option grave»[28]. Pendant la majeure partie de la première session, Moeller est à Louvain, où – serait-on tenté de dire – il ronge son frein. Il paraît, de fait, désireux de jouer un rôle plus actif dans la vie du Concile. Il s'occupe surtout de rédiger des analyses critiques des schémas préparatoires au fur et à mesure qu'il les reçoit. Et il cherche visiblement l'occasion de pouvoir se rendre à Rome.

Moeller juge sévèrement les sept schémas qu'il examine à cette époque[29]. Quelques indications d'abord à propos de son analyse du schéma *De fontibus revelationis*[30] et de celui sur la liturgie[31]. Au lieu d'envisager le statut d'une théologie renouvelée au contact de l'Écriture, on présente – écrit-il – une série de mises en garde, par ailleurs bien connues. Il faudrait, par souci des frères séparés, ne pas mettre sur le même pied la théologie puisée à ses sources ecclésiales et des réflexions

26. Carnet 4 de C. Moeller, pp. 9-10.
27. Carnet 4 de Ch. Moeller, p. 17.
28. Des pères conciliaires melkites, tel Mgr Edelby, conseiller du patriarche Maximos IV, réagiront vivement à cette 'option'. Plus tard, on réservera une place spéciale aux patriarches orientaux. Ch. Moeller ajoute dans son carnet quelques indications sur le discours d'ouverture prononcé par Jean XXIII: discours «beau par ces deux idées: plutôt exposer la vérité que condamnation; plutôt voir les bons côtés du monde moderne (contre les oiseaux de mauvaise augure) que les mauvais seulement». Et il qualifie de «très remarquable» le commentaire télévisé de son disciple et ancien élève Fernand Colleye.
29. Dans Fonds Moeller, 2829-2839.
30. Fonds Moeller, 2834. Le texte occupe deux pages dactylographiées.
31. Fonds Moeller, 2832, 2 p. dactyl.

d'école. La partie positive du schéma, où il est question du devoir pour le prêtre de lire l'Écriture et du lien entre théologie et Écriture, est «comme dissimulée par le chapitre 1 où la hardiesse de l'Écriture paraît tempérée par la philosophie de St-Thomas». Les frères séparés y retrouveront «la faute majeure de l'Église catholique: ne plus écouter vraiment l'Écriture». En conclusion de cette partie consacrée à des remarques générales, l'auteur affirme: «parce qu'il ne répond pas aux questions de l'Église, et qu'il répond au contraire à des questions que l'Église ne se pose pas, nous croyons que ce schéma doit être rejeté».

Le schéma sur la liturgie est apprécié, dans son ensemble, de manière beaucoup plus positive. Moeller le juge même «excellent» et «tellement remarquable» que d'autres, par exemple ceux sur Dieu créateur et sur la Révélation, devraient en tenir compte. En effet, il donne la place centrale à l'humanité du Christ et à la résurrection. Il applique de façon heureuse à la liturgie le thème de l'Église comme signe levé parmi les nations, en particulier grâce à l'insistance sur l'Église locale et sur l'évêque en tant que juge des adaptations liturgiques à introduire. Il insiste sur la *mensa verbi Dei* et suggère très heureusement la réintroduction de l'*oratio fidelium*, de la concélébration, de l'usage du calice pour la communion des fidèles et l'élargissement du choix des lectures scripturaires. Viennent ensuite cinq suggestions pratiques et deux questions à propos des langues vernaculaires à utiliser «plus largement», domaine où Moeller estime qu'il y a «une *très grande urgence*». Bref, ce projet de constitution lui paraît «fondamentalement dans la ligne de ce que l'on attend du Concile dans les milieux chrétiens fervents et éclairés, soucieux aussi de présence plus efficace au monde moderne».

Ecclésiologie renouvelée, souci œcuménique, présence au monde contemporain. On retrouve dans ces analyses les domaines dans lesquels Moeller va s'impliquer davantage dans le cadre du Concile. Une question subsiste: à qui destinait-il ces remarques et suggestions qui doivent dater d'octobre ou du début novembre 62? On sait qu'il a envoyé le 10 novembre ses notes sur le *De fontibus* au cardinal Léger, à qui il précise qu'il connaissait le texte du schéma «pour l'essentiel»[32]. Les suggestions concernant le schéma liturgique sont qualifiées de «respectueuses», ce qui donne à penser qu'il les destinait à un ou plusieurs pères conciliaires. D'autre part, Moeller est, à cette époque, en contact épistolaire avec G. Thils, qui se trouve à Rome. Celui-ci a-t-il servi de courroie de transmission? Ce n'est pas impossible. En tout cas, les correspondances conservées de Moeller avec Léger et avec Thils donnent

---

32. Moeller à Léger, 10 novembre 1962, double, dans Fonds Moeller, 3031.

l'impression qu'il n'a pas à cette époque de contact privilégié avec
d'autres pères conciliaires, par exemple avec son évêque, le cardinal
Suenens. Cette impression est confirmée à propos des 14 pages de
remarques sur le *De ecclesia* de la période préparatoire élaborées par des
experts d'Europe centrale et auxquelles Moeller dit, en les transmettant
à Léger[33], avoir «collaboré assez bien» quand il arriva à Rome à la fin
de novembre[34]. En fait, il est difficile de ne pas discerner dans ce texte
très développé une nouvelle expression des préoccupations typiques de
Moeller en ecclésiologie, y compris au point de vue œcuménique, et à
propos de l'attention à accorder au monde qui cherche sa voie en dehors
du contexte traditionnel de la chrétienté.

Le texte de ces remarques à propos de l'Église est divisé en quatre parties. Tout d'abord des généralités, où sont mentionnées successivement
quatre omissions du schéma, à savoir: très peu de développement concernant la réalité eschatologique de l'Église, aucun sur l'Église comme communion des croyants, rien sur le diaconat, ni sur l'Église comme «signe
élevé parmi les peuples» dans la situation concrète du monde moderne.
Ces omissions sont jugées «déplorables au point de vue œcuménique».
La première partie relève encore des incohérences (notamment la façon
de souligner l'institution divine de l'épiscopat à laquelle est jointe l'énumération d'une série de restrictions à l'exercice de la fonction), enfin un
déséquilibre dans le traitement abondant du magistère papal qui n'est pas
mis en harmonie avec le magistère vivant de l'Église dans sa foi, sa liturgie, son corps épiscopal. La seconde partie montre que la relation entre
l'Église et le monde moderne n'est envisagée que dans l'optique des rapports Église-État où l'Église se borne à affirmer ses droits. Rien n'est dit
sur la société civile «constitutivement pluraliste», sur les mentalités, les
réalisations, les recherches du monde contemporain. Dans sa troisième
partie, le texte des 'Remarques' développe la carence du schéma à propos de l'épiscopat, réclamant notamment un exposé sur la coexistence du
pouvoir pontifical et de celui du collège des évêques. Ici aussi, on écarte
une des bases du dialogue possible avec les autres Églises. Dans la quatrième partie, le document taxe encore plus explicitement le schéma d'un
«manque d'esprit et de vraie sollicitude œcuménique». Bref, le schéma
est qualifié globalement de «juridique, centralisateur, négatif, peu
biblique»; il s'en dégage «l'impression d'un appel à l'unité verbal et sté-
rile, et d'un manque total de dynamisme apostolique».

33. Moeller à Léger, 2 décembre 1962, dans Fonds Moeller, 3035, et photocopie de
l'original, dans Fonds Moeller, 3035bis.
34. Voir Fonds Moeller, 34.

À propos de ce texte, je me limite à deux observations. Même si Moeller n'est pas le seul auteur, il me paraît bien exprimer, tout comme d'ailleurs son analyse du *De fontibus*, le caractère fortement critique de la pensée théologique du chanoine. On retrouve cette caractéristique ultérieurement, même quand la collaboration avec Philips et d'autres l'induira à une certaine modération. D'autre part, ce texte me semble un indice assez clair du fait que Moeller, en cette fin de première session, désire ardemment s'engager au maximum dans l'entreprise du Concile.

Parmi les préoccupations de Moeller durant la première session conciliaire, celle relative à l'œcuménisme s'est encore exprimée d'une façon plus spécifique. Il apparaît comme le rédacteur, sinon l'auteur unique, d'une analyse critique du schéma sur l'unité de l'Église qui avait été composé par la commission orientale préparatoire. L'analyse en 6 pages dactylographiées de ce schéma préconciliaire est intitulée «Remarques sur le schéma '*De Ecclesiae unitate*'». Elle est datée de 'Louvain, 25 novembre 1962'[35]. À côté de certaines suggestions du texte jugées excellentes, le rédacteur relève «quatre raisons décisives» qui justifient le rejet pur et simple du schéma. Tout d'abord, celui-ci traite de l'unité avant que le Concile ait élaboré une constitution sur l'Église, sur les évêques et sur la place du laïcat, qui est un des points essentiels du Concile. En second lieu, le schéma s'inspire d'une ecclésiologie juridique et axée sur la «monarchie pontificale», mentionnant à peine les évêques et les anciens patriarcats d'Orient. Troisièmement, la notion d'unité est jugée «étriquée» et, elle aussi, «juridique» au lieu d'être envisagée dans le cadre d'une Église communion fondée sur l'unique baptême, l'unique Trinité, l'unique Écriture. Enfin, «le texte oscille perpétuellement d'un point de vue qui vise tous les dissidents à un autre, de beaucoup dominant, qui vise les seuls orientaux». Or, le véritable œcuménisme doit

---

35. Dans le Fonds Moeller,1974. Une note ms. d'une main étrangère indique que le document a été «élaboré en commun à la fin de la 1ère session pour bloquer le document du St-Office [ceci n'est pas exact] sur l'œcuménisme. É. Beauduin, C. Moeller, G. Thils, W. Onclin». Il est possible que cette indication soit de T. Osborne, le premier à avoir classé les papiers conciliaires de Ch. Moeller; il a pu recueillir l'information de Moeller lui-même. Si l'intervention d'Éd. Beauduin est très vraisemblable (dans une lettre à Léger du 25 novembre 1962, Moeller parle d'Éd. Beauduin «avec qui je partage toutes mes angoisses et espérances sur le Concile»; cf. *infra*), on ne trouve pas trace de copies du document, qui a été dactylographié par Moeller et qui renvoie aux deux Notes de ce dernier sur le patriarcat d'Occident et sur l'Église particulière, dans les papiers conciliaires de G. Thils et de W. Onclin. Il n'en reste pas moins que, si Thils n'a pas participé à la rédaction proprement dite du texte, on peut y déceler, comme dans les deux Notes de Moeller de 1961, l'influence de certaines de ses idées. C'est aussi le cas dans l'article de Moeller paru en novembre 1962 dans la revue diocésaine de Malines. Nous allons y venir.

prendre en compte les divisions entre tous les chrétiens, ainsi que le demande le Conseil œcuménique des Églises. Ensuite, le document expose sept critiques de détail.

Une fois de plus, rien n'indique que ce texte ait été transmis à des pères conciliaires belges, par exemple le cardinal Suenens ou encore Mgr De Smedt, membre du Secrétariat pour l'unité: le document ne figure pas dans les papiers conciliaires de ces deux évêques. Il ne semble pas non plus avoir été envoyé aux autorités du Secrétariat pour l'unité, le cardinal Bea et Mgr Willebrands, alors qu'un article de Moeller sur l'œcuménisme paru dans la revue diocésaine de Malines et daté lui aussi de novembre 1962 a bien, lui, été adressé à ceux-ci[36]. Quant au cardinal Léger, avec qui le chanoine louvaniste entretient à cette époque une correspondance sur les schémas dogmatiques, les deux documents lui ont été envoyés[37].

L'article paru dans le numéro de novembre des *Collectanea mechliniensia* est intitulé «Le sens du dialogue œcuménique»[38]. Son idée centrale est que l'Église romaine est entrée, avec la création du Secrétariat pour l'unité des chrétiens, dans une structure de dialogue. Ce dialogue renouvelle les catholiques dans cinq domaines, que l'auteur développe: une prise de conscience du scandale de la division, une meilleure connaissance mutuelle, un renouveau catholique qui postule un réexamen de la tradition en remettant en avant des vérités négligées (par ex. la notion de Peuple de Dieu ou encore le caractère central du mystère pascal), en équilibrant mieux les vérités (comme l'infaillibilité pontificale par rapport à celle de l'Église), en distinguant plus clairement les vérités de foi et les systématisations spéculatives; quatrième domaine, celui de l'émulation spirituelle entre chrétiens; et enfin, l'auteur estime que le dialogue renouvellera le catholicisme en soulignant la commune espérance de tous les chrétiens, autrement dit «la dimension eschatologique des desseins divins».

Comme dans les deux Notes de Moeller de 1961, on trouve dans les deux textes relatifs à l'œcuménisme dont nous venons de parler l'influence des travaux de G. Thils, lui aussi prêtre diocésain de Malines. Comme membre du Secrétariat pour l'unité, celui-ci est à Rome pendant une bonne partie de la première session conciliaire. Ce n'est pourtant pas pour des questions d'ecclésiologie ou d'œcuménisme qu'il écrit le

36. D'après Moeller à Thils, 15 novembre 1962, double dans Fonds Moeller, 3039.

37. D'après les lettres du 10 novembre et du 25 novembre 1962, doubles dans Fonds Moeller, 3031 et 3034.

38. *Collectanea mechliniensia* 47 (1962) 541-558. Deux exemplaires dactylographiés du texte: dans Fonds Moeller, 1984 et 1993 (l'un avec des remaniements comprenant des ajouts publiés dans l'article et des passages supprimés; l'autre avec les passages rayés dans la publication).

8 novembre à son confrère Moeller[39]. Tout en l'informant sur le déroulement des débats en congrégations générales, il l'invite à venir passer une semaine à Rome pour faire aux conférences épiscopales nationales des causeries sur Dieu, l'athéisme, la culture moderne, en rapport avec les schémas dogmatiques. Thils pensait alors que, comme on allait entamer la discussion sur le *De fontibus*, les schémas *De Deo* et autres seraient abordés ensuite et que le *De ecclesia* serait traité à une autre session. Moeller ne se fait pas prier. Il obtient du recteur de Louvain, Mgr Descamps, la permission d'aller à Rome à chaque 'appel urgent' que lui lancerait Thils. Il s'empresse alors de demander à celui-ci de voir «un peu à arranger ces 'conférences' afin – écrit-il – que je ne sois pas un cheveu sur la soupe»[40]. On ne sait pas si Thils lui a fait parvenir l'appel urgent requis par le recteur. Toujours est-il qu'à la fin novembre, Moeller est à Rome. Et il assiste, en prenant d'abondantes notes, aux quatre dernières congrégations générales de la session en cours[41]. Surtout, il est en contact avec le cardinal Léger, avec lequel il a entretenu une correspondance depuis le début de la session et à qui il a envoyé ses Notes de 1961 et ses remarques sur les schémas préparatoires.

À la demande de l'archevêque[42] et à son intention particulière, il rédige alors «quelques réflexions d'ensemble» sur le *De ecclesia*[43]. Les premières phrases de cette Note de deux pages reprennent quasi textuellement l'appréciation du schéma sur l'Église que l'on trouve dans le texte dit «des experts d'Europe centrale», qui a été rédigé pratiquement au même moment:

> Ce schéma est dépourvu d'unité […], l'esprit en est, pour l'essentiel, négatif, alors que l'on attend une ecclésiologie renouvelée, ouverte au problème œcuménique, ainsi qu'aux aspirations légitimes de l'homme moderne. En particulier trois questions brûlantes, le rôle des évêques dans l'Église, les relations entre Église et monde moderne, enfin l'œcuménisme sont traitées dans un cadre de pensée marqué par l'esprit du XIXe siècle: juridique, centralisateur, négatif, peu biblique.

La suite de la Note détaille les trois 'questions brûlantes'. À propos des évêques, Moeller estime notamment que les textes de Vatican I sur la primauté pontificale sont renforcés, sans qu'aucune précision ne soit apportée sur l'harmonie avec le pouvoir des évêques. Quant à l'infaillibilité, «la part du lion – écrit-il – est donnée au Magistère du Pape» qui absorbe

39. G. Thils à C. Moeller, 8 novembre 1962, dans Fonds Moeller, 3038.
40. Moeller à Thils, 15 novembre 1962, double dans Fonds Moeller, 3039.
41. Celles des 2, 4, 6 et 7 décembre 1962. Ces notes: dans Fonds Moeller, 2840.
42. Dans sa lettre à Moeller du 23 octobre 1962 (dans Fonds Moeller, 3030).
43. Le double de ces réflexions, qui occupent 2 pages dactylographiées, est joint à la lettre de Moeller à Léger du 2 décembre 1962 (dans Fonds Moeller, 3035).

le magistère collégial des évêques et qui néglige l'infaillibilité première, celle de l'Église 'in credendo'. En second lieu, le thème «Église et monde moderne» est envisagé en fonction du 19e siècle. Moeller renvoie le destinataire à une autre Note qu'il a rédigée en songeant – précise-t-il – particulièrement à lui. Enfin, sur la question de l'œcuménisme dans le schéma, il estime que la difficulté majeure consiste dans le fait que, d'une part, on affirme que les autres chrétiens ne sont pas membres de l'Église, et d'autre part on souligne les éléments par lesquels ils participent au Christ et à l'Esprit-Saint. Ici aussi, Moeller renvoie à une Note spéciale faite par lui.

Il conclut en écrivant qu'il faudrait une ecclésiologie fondée sur les images bibliques, qui insiste par ailleurs sur l'élément 'communio' avec les éléments juridique, mais aussi mystique, collégial et celui du 'sensus fidelium'. Enfin, en face du monde moderne, il faudrait insister sur l'image de l'Église comme ferment dans un monde divisé et pluraliste. En finale, il dit croire qu'il faut affirmer sur ce schéma: 'non placet'.

Quant à la réponse de l'archevêque de Montréal, on peut dire qu'elle est résumée dans sa lettre à Moeller du 21 décembre suivant. En annonçant la nomination du cardinal Suenens à la toute nouvelle Commission de coordination, il notait: «j'espère qu'il fera préparer un bon schéma sur l'Église et qu'il interviendra pour obtenir la refonte de toute la partie théologique» (entendant par ceci l'ensemble des schémas doctrinaux préparatoires)[44]. On peut aussi voir une réponse de Léger à Moeller dans le fait que, deux semaines auparavant, il obtenait la nomination de celui-ci comme expert officiel du Concile[45]. Il obtenait en même temps celle d'un autre Belge à la même fonction: Philippe Delhaye, qui enseignait alors la théologie morale notamment au grand séminaire de Montréal. D'autre part, l'archevêque disposait déjà d'un expert canadien dans la personne de Pierre Lafortune, chancelier de son diocèse[46].

III. LA PREMIÈRE INTERSESSION

Au début de février 1963, le cardinal Léger informe Moeller qu'il est convoqué à Rome le 21 de ce mois pour travailler, au sein de la

44. Léger à Moeller, 21 décembre 1962, dans Fonds Moeller, 3036.
45. Diplôme du 7 décembre 1962 signé par le secrétaire d'État Cicognani, dans Fonds Moeller, 3026.
46. Il avait été nommé le 19 octobre 1962. Quand au P. Naud, bien qu'il eût collaboré avec Lafortune à la préparation des dossiers conciliaires du card. Léger, il ne sera nommé expert officiel que le 21 février 1963.

commission doctrinale dont il est membre, aux schémas théologiques que vient de réorganiser la commission de coordination[47]. Léger souhaite que Moeller soit présent: «vous nous rendriez – écrit-il – de grands services». Et il ajoute qu'il y aura beaucoup à faire pour rédiger le schéma sur l'Église qu'il estime être «le plus important parmi ceux qui doivent être présentés à l'approbation du Concile»[48].

Moeller retrouve l'archevêque à Rome vers le 20 février. Il lui communique le lendemain, jour de la première séance de la commission doctrinale, des propositions pour l'élaboration du nouveau De ecclesia[49]. Pour l'essentiel, ces 'propositiones' recommandent à l'archevêque la prise en considération du projet Philips, tout en concédant qu'il faudra y apporter des compléments et des modifications inspirés des projets allemand, français, italien et chilien. Moeller précise ces points, montrant aussi l'importance qu'il y a à mieux exposer l'union entre le chef visible de l'Église et le collège apostolique et le relief à donner à la sacramentalité de l'épiscopat.

C'est le 22 février que, lors d'une réunion privée chez le cardinal König, cinq pères et trois experts de la commission doctrinale, dont Moeller, se mettent d'accord pour proposer le projet Philips comme base du futur schéma sur l'Église[50], proposition entérinée par la Commission le 26. Et, ce même jour, une sous-commission de sept pères, dont Léger, qui sont accompagnés chacun d'un expert, commence son travail sur le texte de Philips. Celui-ci est l'expert de Mgr Charue, l'évêque de Namur, et Thils, sur une suggestion de Charue, est adjoint à Mgr Schröffer, l'évêque d'Eichstätt. Le cardinal Léger y est accompagné du sulpicien canadien André Naud, qui vient tout juste d'être nommé expert. Moeller ne fait pas partie de cette sous-commission dite 'des sept'. Il sera cependant amené à y remplacer parfois Thils auprès de Mgr Schröffer[51]. Mais, en ce même 26 février, ce qu'il trouve 'honteux' c'est que le P. Congar n'est pas

47. Léger à Moeller, 8 février 1963, dans Fonds Moeller, 3041.

48. Ibid.

49. Ces propositions (2 p. en latin): dans Fonds Philips, 593.

50. D'après L. DECLERCK – C. SOETENS (éds.), Carnets conciliaires de l'évêque de Namur A.-M. Charue (Cahiers de la Revue théologique de Louvain, 32), Louvain-la-Neuve, Publications de la Faculté de Théologie, 2000, p. 88 (désormais cité Journal Charue), les 5 pères présents sont, outre König, Garrone, Schröffer, Seper et Charue; les experts: Moeller, Daniélou et Rahner. Une autre réunion privée ayant le même objet a lieu le 24 février chez Mgr Garrone. Y participent, en tant que pères, Léger, Schröffer, van Dodewaard, McGrath et Charue, et six experts, dont Moeller (K. SCHELKENS [éd.], Carnets conciliaires de Mgr Gérard Philips, secrétaire adjoint de la commission doctrinale. Texte néerlandais avec traduction française et commentaires [Instrumenta Theologica, 29], Louvain, Peeters, 2006, p. 29; désormais cité Journal Philips).

51. D'après Journal Philips, p. 30.

appelé à participer à l'élaboration du schéma sur l'Église. Suite à cette remarque, Mgr De Smedt intervient auprès de Mgr Martin, archevêque de Rouen et son collègue au Secrétariat pour l'unité[52], qui en parle au père français de la sous-commission, Mgr Garrone. Celui-ci demande à Congar, présent à Rome depuis peu, de remplacer Daniélou comme expert au sein de la sous-commission[53].

Pendant ce temps, la commission doctrinale réunie en commission mixte avec des membres du Secrétariat pour l'unité discute de la refonte du schéma sur la Révélation. À partir du 5 mars, le nouveau schéma sur l'Église commence à être examiné par la Doctrinale. Moeller participe à ces réunions générales[54]. Et, entre le 1 et le 14 mars, il écrit à son ami Éd. Beauduin huit lettres très développées concernant le travail en cours. Ces lettres, dans lesquelles analyses et impressions s'entremêlent, sont d'un grand intérêt[55].

Il y est d'abord question des réunions de la commission mixte chargée de réviser le schéma sur la Révélation. Le chanoine parle de la «victoire magnifique d'une majorité ouverte qui s'affirme de plus en plus», obtenue grâce aux interventions du cardinal Lefebvre, de Mgr Charue et du cardinal Léger, que Moeller a encouragé à intervenir en lui glissant des billets en cours de séance[56]. La première lettre à Beauduin donne aussi des échos de ce que Moeller apprend au sujet des travaux de la sous-commission du *De ecclesia*. Ici se place un incident qui semble avoir contribué à une certaine prise de distance de Moeller à l'égard, sinon de Léger, en tout cas des deux experts canadiens. Le P. Naud, qui seconde Léger à la sous-commission et qui a été missionnaire au Japon, veut faire passer l'idée qu'il y a «deux notions de l'Église»: l'Église visible et

52. D'après le souvenir du chan. Leo Declerck, alors vice-recteur du Collège belge.

53. Cf. CONGAR, *Mon journal du Concile* (n. 2), Tome I, p. 335. Le 5 mars, Congar s'installait au Collège belge.

54. À noter qu'il intervient, avec Congar, pour proposer une nouvelle rédaction pour le passage du premier chapitre (sur le mystère de l'Église) concernant le corps mystique, en développant également d'autres images de l'Église. Cf. à ce sujet les Notes de Congar et de Moeller (dans Fonds Philips, 618-619); et l'insertion partielle de ces Notes dans l'*adumbratio* du schéma après le débat du 7 mars (dans Fonds Philips, 599).

55. Doubles dans Fonds Moeller, 3042-3049. Ces lettres totalisent 20 pages dactylographiées.

56. Lettre du 1er mars. Moeller dit avoir ainsi poussé Léger à demander un vote immédiat sur la question de savoir si la Tradition l'emporte sur l'Écriture «quant à son amplitude». G. Routhier rapporte d'autre part que le card. Ottaviani a lu une lettre du secrétaire d'État Cicognani qui donnait à penser que le pape serait favorable à cette affirmation et que Léger a lu un billet de Moeller qui mettait en lumière le caractère ambigu de la lettre du secrétaire d'État (ceci d'après G. ROUTHIER, *L'itinéraire d'un Père conciliaire: Le cardinal Léger*, dans *Cristianesimo nella storia* 19 [1998] 121). S'agit-il de deux versions à propos d'un même billet ou de deux billets différents?

institutionnelle d'une part, l'Église plus large, «mystique», formée de membres implicites de l'autre[57]. Moeller écrit à Naud pour lui demander d'exposer son idée autrement «sous peine – écrit-il – de faire tout sauter»[58]. Et il a alerté Léger. Naud n'a pas insisté. Moeller termine son récit de l'incident à É. Beauduin par une appréciation très sévère sur les qualités théologiques des deux Canadiens[59]! Et, tout en se promettant de multiplier les contacts avec l'archevêque, il se demande si sa présence à Rome qu'il dit «toute de conversation, conseils occasionnels, aide à Philips, coups de téléphone» est justifiée. En fait, c'est pourtant bien lors de ces journées de février-mars 63 que se nouent des contacts et se précisent des choix stratégiques qui seront d'un grand poids dans la marche ultérieure du Concile. Un grand rôle est joué à ce moment par le Collège belge, où Moeller commence à trouver sa place.

La deuxième lettre de Moeller à Beauduin, datée du 5 mars, est tout entière consacrée au début de l'examen en commission plénière – qui s'est réunie ce jour-là – du texte Philips pour le *De ecclesia*. Le cardinal Ottaviani, président de la Commission, et le P. Tromp, secrétaire, font tout leur possible pour écarter les deux premiers chapitres déjà prêts du schéma Philips: ceux sur le mystère de l'Église et sur sa constitution hiérarchique. «Ceux qui ont fait échouer – note Moeller – la manœuvre dilatoire sont Charue (magnifique), Léger, Browne (d'une honnêteté parfaite), König»[60]. En fin de séance, Moeller a le «sentiment d'une victoire»: le schéma Philips, révisé avec Thils et Congar, est «sur rail». Le matin même, il avait achevé de dactylographier le deuxième chapitre. Et il commente: «On a bien fait de travailler comme des brutes».

Le soir, Léger, avec ses deux théologiens Lafortune et Naud, est venu au Collège belge boire un cognac avec lui et le recteur Prignon. Si donc, comme l'écrit Moeller, «les relations sont de nouveau excellentes» avec les Canadiens, il précise par ailleurs que lui-même, comme la plupart des membres et experts de la Commission, rentrera quelques jours plus tard, «sauf si Philips reste à Rome et me demande de continuer à l'aider: il l'a

---

57. Naud adresse une Note à Moeller à ce sujet le 28 février 1963 (dans Fonds Moeller, 65).

58. Lettre du 1er mars à É. Beauduin. Dans ses notes du 28 février, Charue résume l'incident et écrit de même: «Parler dans ce sens, c'est faire sauter la poudre» (Journal Charue, p. 92). Philips se montre tout aussi critique envers la thèse de Naud, voir Journal Philips, p. 30.

59. À propos de Léger, G. Routhier relève que, lors des travaux de la commission doctrinale en février-mars 63 sur le *De fontibus* et le *De ecclesia*, l'archevêque s'intéressait surtout aux questions de procédure et de stratégie (dans ROUTHIER, *L'itinéraire d'un Père* [n. 56], p. 120).

60. Lettre du 5 mars à É. Beauduin.

déjà fait à demi-mots ce soir: je crois alors de mon devoir de rester le temps voulu»[61]. C'est ainsi que les choses se passeront, Philips ayant trouvé en Moeller – ce sont ses mots – «un collaborateur très précieux et extrêmement serviable»[62]. Il travaillera jusqu'au 14 mars avec Philips, Congar et Thils à préparer pour la Commission les corrections à apporter aux deux premiers chapitres du *De ecclesia* et à en revoir la rédaction finale[63].

Il n'est pas possible de détailler ici tous les sujets que Moeller traita dans ses huit longues lettres à É. Beauduin. Beaucoup de points des schémas en discussion, notamment, y sont développés; ainsi, ce qu'il appelle «la grande bagarre sur le chapitre II», c'est-à-dire la question du pouvoir des évêques et celle de la collégialité par rapport à la primauté. Lors du débat du 9 mars à ce sujet, Congar lui murmure: «Ils finiront par me faire orthodoxe, si cela continue»[64]! Moeller donne aussi de précieuses indications, glanées auprès du P. Lanne, recteur du Collège grec, sur le schéma *De oecumenismo catholico* et l'état d'esprit au Secrétariat pour l'unité[65].

Dans sa dernière lettre, datée du 14 mars, il annonce qu'il va aider Philips à rédiger les notes des deux chapitres achevés du *De ecclesia*[66], ce qu'il fera en mars-avril avec Thils et Cerfaux, devant pour cela mener «des recherches importantes et précises»[67]. Enfin, il accompagnera Philips, qui ne voulait pas y aller seul, chez le cardinal Suenens pour lui présenter les deux chapitres terminés[68]. À cette première phase importante de sa contribution au Concile, Moeller donne la conclusion suivante:

> Incroyable que les circonstances aient voulu que par Léger je sois mis en liaison avec Philips au moment où celui-ci est appelé à rédiger un des schémas les plus importants de la session prochaine; et que je sois mis au courant de tout [...]. Je suis heureux d'avoir ainsi préparé mes activités au Concile[69].

---

61. Même lettre.

62. D'après Journal Philips, p. 30.

63. Lettres des 9, 10, 11 et 14 mars à Éd. Beauduin. Cf. aussi CONGAR, *Mon journal du Concile* (n. 2), Tome I, pp. 343-345 et 349. Le soir du 13 mars, Congar note: «champagne en l'honneur de la fin heureuse du *De ecclesia*. Moi aussi, j'ai lié ou approfondi une amitié avec Mgr Philips, C. Moeller et Mgr Prignon». Même notation dans la lettre du 13 mars de Moeller à Beauduin.

64. Lettre du 9 mars à É. Beauduin. Sur la collégialité, voir aussi les lettres des 11 et 12 mars.

65. Lettre du 10 mars à Beauduin.

66. Lettre du 14 mars à Beauduin. Voir aussi celle du 13 mars.

67. D'après Journal Philips, p. 38.

68. Lettre du 14 mars et lettre de Moeller à Léger, 12 avril 1963, double dans Fonds Moeller, 3041bis.

69. Lettre du 13 mars à Beauduin.

1. Préparation d'un «chaud» mois de mai romain

La seconde phase 'romaine' importante de la première intersession se déroule au cours du mois de mai 1963. À ce moment viendront en discussion les chapitres 3 et 4 du *De ecclesia* sur les laïcs et les religieux. Par ailleurs se réunira la commission mixte chargée du *De oecumenismo*. Et il sera également question de l'Église dans le monde, traitée dans ce qu'on appelle alors le schéma XVII. Dès le mois de mars, Moeller comptait bien poursuivre ses activités conciliaires en étant présent à Rome, surtout à cause de ce qu'il appelait «la bataille» qu'il prévoyait «terrible» sur l'œcuménisme.

En vue de cette affaire qui lui paraissait de première importance[70], il annote le projet des trois premiers chapitres du *De oecumenismo* du Secrétariat pour l'unité[71]. Pensait-il être invité à intervenir dans le débat sur ce schéma? Ce ne fut pas le cas. Mais il est probable qu'il ait transmis ses notes à É. Beauduin qui participa aux réunions de la commission mixte du mois de mai. Et certaines des modifications suggérées par lui apparaissent dans le décret sur l'œcuménisme adopté par le Concile.

Quant aux chapitres 3 et 4 du *De ecclesia* et au schéma sur l'Église dans le monde, il en traite dans une lettre du mois d'avril adressée au cardinal Léger[72]. Le chapitre 3 (*De populo fideli ac speciatim de laicis*)

---

70. Lettre du 13 mars à Beauduin.

71. Exemplaire annoté du projet des trois premiers chapitres (en 14 p. + 8 p. de notes), dans Fonds Moeller, 1982. Quelques indications: pour le chapitre I (Principes de l'œcuménisme catholique), il ajoute à «l'Église, unique troupeau de Dieu»; «l'Église, communion des Églises locales et...»; dans «les frères séparés ne jouissent pas de la communion parfaite de l'Église», il remplace «parfaite» par «visible»; parmi les éléments constitutifs de l'Église, «quaedam» pouvant exister chez les séparés est remplacé par «plura pretiosa». Au chapitre II (Exercice de l'œcuménisme), il ne fait pas de remarque. Au troisième (sur les Églises orientales), là où il est dit que les Églises d'Orient et d'Occident ont longtemps suivi leur voie tout en restant unies, Rome intervenant lors des différends en matière de foi ou de discipline, Moeller note: «vrai pour la foi, faux pour la discipline». Et là où on dit que la diversité de coutumes, sanctionnée par les Pères, ne nuit pas à l'unité, il précise: par les Pères «et les canons des conciles œcuméniques».

72. Moeller à Léger, 12 avril 1963, double dans Fonds Moeller, 3041bis. Au chapitre III, il souhaite qu'on souligne tant le rôle propre, mais non exclusif (partagé avec la hiérarchie) des laïcs dans l'apostolat et le culte, que leur rôle exclusif dans la «consecratio mundi» (éviter le risque de «vernir tout cela dans une sorte de chape subtilement cléricale»). Pour le chapitre IV sur les religieux, il annonce qu'avec Thils, il a «risqué» de proposer à Suenens, qui s'est dit intéressé, de l'intituler «De sanctitate in Ecclesia», avec un paragraphe sur l'appel à la perfection pour tous, puis la voie des «conseils» présentée non comme ascèse personnelle, mais sous l'angle ecclésiologique, christologique, eschatologique et charismatique. Ainsi toute la constitution sur l'Église aboutirait à la sainteté, ce qui serait mieux compris par les frères séparés et donnerait un meilleur équilibre à l'ensemble du document. Dans cette lettre, Moeller note au sujet du schéma XVII qu'on est toujours dans «le noir»: sauf pour les chapitres sur la vocation de l'homme et sur la

fait l'objet, de sa part le 1ᵉʳ mai, de 'Réflexions' beaucoup plus précises à l'intention du rédacteur Philips[73]. Il souhaite principalement qu'à côté de l'image prédominante de l'Église comme Corps mystique soit mieux développée celle du Peuple de Dieu, qui permet de valoriser le sacerdoce royal de tous les chrétiens, ceci afin d'éviter «l'impression d'un rôle toujours subordonné» des laïcs: «il faut mettre en lumière l'aspect Communauté [...]. Dans le texte on a trop l'impression d'une concession» faite aux laïcs, l'essentiel sur l'Église ayant été dit dans les deux premiers chapitres. Moeller ajoute un second souhait: il faudrait mieux souligner que les laïcs sont envoyés «dans un monde de *Diaspora* (pluralisme) qui cherche son unité». On garde trop l'image sous-jacente de l'Église-chrétienté, qu'il faut défendre et qui doit pénétrer le monde. Loin de faire des laïcs «la masse de manœuvre de la hiérarchie», il faut reconnaître qu'ils accomplissent dans le monde une diaconie «irremplaçable».

Les idées contenues dans les «Réflexions» de Moeller du 1ᵉʳ mai seront développées dans une nouvelle Note datée du lendemain, où – à côté du chapitre sur les laïcs – figurent quelques précisions en vue de restructurer une partie du décret sur l'apostolat des laïcs et des remarques sur le schéma XVII[74]. Moeller s'est fort soucié de réagir également sur le chapitre 4 élaboré en mars en commission mixte (avec la commission pour les religieux) et centré alors sur les états de perfection. J'en parlerai plus loin.

2. Le mois de mai 1963 à Rome

Malgré le souci que se faisait Moeller pour le schéma sur l'œcuménisme, les deux points forts de son activité à Rome en mai 63 furent: 1. les travaux de la commission mixte sur le schéma consacré à l'Église

liberté religieuse, le texte est «très mauvais». Il l'a «dit et redit» au card. Suenens, qui est d'accord. «Je crois qu'il y a là un grand danger auquel il faut veiller. Je ne sais trop comment». Dans cette lettre, il est encore question des positions de Mgr Daem, évêque d'Anvers, au sujet du texte sur les séminaires et universités, de l'avis de H. Wagnon sur la question des mariages mixtes et de rencontres entre W. Onclin, G. Thils et lui-même «pour étudier le statut canonique de la collégialité (conférences épiscopales et représentation à Rome). Point capital et très difficile». Il termine en demandant l'accord de Léger pour aller à Rome en mai: «Thils, Philips, Onclin estiment qu'il *faut* y être, en ce qui me concerne moi aussi».

73. Dans Fonds Philips, 704 (2 pp. mss). Voir aussi ses notes en marge du texte sub n. 703.

74. Cette note du 2 mai 1963 (6 pp. dactyl.), envoyée à Léger, Charue, Garrone, Congar et Thils, fut communiquée également à J. Grootaers, qui avait eu un long entretien avec Moeller la veille à ce sujet. Je remercie J. Grootaers qui m'a aimablement transmis le document.

dans le monde; 2. sa participation aux réunions de la commission doctrinale consacrées au chapitre du *De ecclesia* sur les religieux devenu un chapitre sur la sainteté. Ce second point fit ensuite l'objet d'un rapport au cardinal Léger. Et il intervint dans la rédaction de deux Notes sur le *De ecclesia* et le schéma XVII préparées à l'intention du cardinal Suenens.

3. Le schéma XVII

Le schéma XVII – alors intitulé *'De praesentia efficaci ecclesiae in mundo hodierno'* et composé de six chapitres – est examiné en commission mixte (doctrinale-apostolat des laïcs) à partir du 20 mai 1963.

Moeller a envoyé, peu avant, des remarques générales sur le schéma à Léger, Garrone et Charue, membres de la Commission, ainsi qu'aux experts Thils et Congar, qui lui sont très proches[75]. Ces remarques sont au nombre de cinq. Il demande en premier lieu que le texte commence par une déclaration théologique sur 'le monde': «tout le balancement du schéma en dépend: l'Église est en même temps celle qui lutte contre le mal, celle qui se tourne vers le monde». En second lieu, il reproche au texte son style 'triomphaliste'. Il regrette ensuite l'absence du chapitre annoncé sur la liberté religieuse, qui existe: c'est celui rédigé par le Secrétariat pour l'unité, qu'on a – note-t-il – essayé d'enterrer, alors qu'il est capital pour les frères séparés aussi bien que pour l'homme moderne. Quatrième remarque: le schéma ne semble pas de nature à répondre à l'attente légitime des non-croyants; il révulsera les chrétiens séparés et décevra les catholiques un peu informés. En effet, la philosophie sous-jacente est en-deçà des valeurs acquises de la pensée moderne et le texte manque d'un éclairage biblique, qui est mieux en consonance avec la pensée moderne valable. Enfin, les quatre premiers chapitres doivent être «refondus entièrement», surtout celui sur le mariage qui est «en-deçà des acquisitions légitimes de la phénoménologie et de la théologie du mariage».

Quelques jours plus tard, après la distribution du texte corrigé en sous-commission plénière mixte, l'expert belge rédige des remarques sur l'introduction et le premier chapitre, qui sont plus favorables au document[76]. Il se déclare «pleinement d'accord sur l'orientation d'ensemble du schéma». Il souligne surtout l'importance de l'anthropologie chrétienne de l'image de Dieu en l'homme placée au centre du premier chapitre (*De admirabili vocatione hominis*), car il s'agit, dans ce schéma, de

---

75. Dans Fonds Moeller, 898. Ces remarques figurent déjà dans la Note du 2 mai remise à Jan Grootaers et citée à la note précédente.

76. Fonds Moeller, 912. Ces remarques – générales et de détail – (2 p. dactyl.) sont datées du 21 mai.

rappeler les seules vérités chrétiennes de nature à éclairer les problèmes actuels les plus urgents et car cette doctrine de l'homme-image de Dieu «permet d'intégrer les valeurs authentiques de l'humanisme moderne». Il ne s'agit pas de vouloir présenter une théologie complète sur nature et surnature, ordre des fins, etc., ni, pour l'Église, de se substituer aux lumières qu'apportent, dans leur ordre, les sciences naturelles, humaines et sociales.

Quand, le 23 mai, la commission mixte examine le chapitre 3 (sur le mariage et la famille), Moeller, qui avait jugé le texte 'nataliste' et 'peu équilibré', fait une intervention qui, selon Charue, fut 'remarquée'[77]. Quant au chapitre 4 consacré à la culture, l'expert belge avait noté en mars que le texte pouvait servir «à usage interne» (c'est-à-dire pour justifier l'ouverture à la culture auprès des milieux ecclésiastiques), mais qu'il avait «peu de souffle, et pas de théologie»[78]. Au mois de mai, il participe, avec quatre évêques (dont Léger et Charue) et deux autres experts (Delhaye et Daniélou), au travail de révision au sein de la sous-commission mixte, où le texte, dont Mgr Guano est le principal rédacteur, est «bien accueilli dans l'ensemble»[79]. En commission plénière le 24, Moeller propose un amendement au n°7 traitant de «Ce que l'Église peut apporter à la culture»: à l'affirmation selon laquelle l'Église offre une vision intégrale de l'homme et de l'univers destiné à être transfiguré, il demande d'ajouter qu'elle:

> aide les hommes, auxiliaires de Dieu, dans la tâche de promouvoir le monde à un état qui soit plus conforme à la dignité de la personne humaine et des fils de Dieu, jusqu'à ce qu'il parvienne aux cieux nouveaux et à la nouvelle terre selon les promesses que nous attendons du Seigneur (suivant des références à la Secunda Petri, à l'Apocalypse et à l'épître aux Romains)[80].

La révision du chapitre sur la culture fut effectuée par cinq experts, dont Moeller[81], dont l'amendement fut inséré dans le texte final[82]. Le 28 mai 1963, Philips, Congar et Moeller rédigent à l'intention du

---

77. Journal Charue, p. 124, Mgr Charue accorde la même appréciation aux interventions de Congar et de Ph. Delhaye.

78. Deux pages de remarques, datées du 12 mars, faites à la demande de Mgr McGrath, évêque auxiliaire de Panama, dans Fonds Moeller, 946.

79. Journal Charue, pp. 120 et 124. Texte discuté du 16 au 19 mai: dans Fonds Moeller, 959.

80. Dans Fonds Moeller, 953 et 956.

81. Dans Fonds Moeller, 963-964 et 975.

82. C'était la cinquième rédaction, mise au net le 29 mai et comportant 6 pages dactylographiées: dans Fonds Moeller, 977.

cardinal Suenens une Note de six pages en latin, consacrée à l'état du schéma XVII[83].

Dans le premier point de cette Note, intitulé '*Observatio generalis*', on relève trois questions que Moeller avait abordées au cours des jours précédents. D'abord, on a approuvé un nouveau titre, en partie suggéré par lui: '*De ecclesiae munere quoad bonum societatis hodiernae promovendum*'[84]. Ensuite, la Note à Suenens présente comme possibles deux conceptions quant au but et au contenu du schéma: ou bien on traite de la présence active de l'Église dans le monde actuel sous les aspects de la communion, du témoignage et du service; ou bien on développe les tâches que l'Église peut exercer en éclairant les problèmes majeurs du monde. On se souvient que cette seconde option avait la préférence de Moeller. Congar, quant à lui, inclinait en faveur de la première. La Note évalue les avantages des deux conceptions, tout en annonçant que c'est la seconde qui a été retenue. Le point 1 de la Note se termine par une allusion à la liberté religieuse, matière que les œcuménistes surtout désirent voir traitée, qui a fait l'objet d'un texte préparé par le Secrétariat pour l'unité et qu'il conviendrait d'insérer dans le schéma XVII[85]. Ici aussi, on retrouve le point de vue de Moeller, partagé du reste par Congar[86] et sans doute par Philips.

Dans sa seconde partie, la Note à Suenens contient des observations sur chacun des six chapitres du schéma. Le chapitre premier, sur l'admirable vocation de l'homme, est jugé positivement car il part de la théologie de l'homme comme image de Dieu. Cependant trois réserves sont introduites. La première, dans la ligne des remarques qu'avait formulées Moeller: le chapitre n'harmonise pas assez les considérations de droit naturel avec l'anthropologie chrétienne. Viennent ensuite quatre remarques sur le chapitre II: '*De persona humana in societate*'. Les quatre observations concernant le chapitre sur le mariage et la famille occupent toute une page. Les auteurs relèvent surtout qu'il faudrait insister davantage dans

83. Original dans Fonds Suenens, 1274; copie dans Fonds Philips, 853. Voir aussi CONGAR, *Mon journal du Concile* (n. 2), Tome I, p. 381.
84. La suggestion de Moeller (dans ses Remarques citées du 21 mai) consistait à reprendre le titre donné en janvier 1963 par la commission de coordination: «De Ecclesiae principiis et actione ad bonum societatis promovendum», en préférant toutefois les quatre derniers mots à ceux alors employés («ad ordinem christianum instaurandum»).
85. Moeller reçoit le texte du 'Decretum pastorale de libertate religiosa', élaboré par le Secrétariat pour l'unité, comprenant 6 pages dactyl. et daté du 30 mai 1963 (dans Fonds Moeller, 1999). Il ne note pas ses remarques sur le texte. Un document identique (avec ajout de 4 lignes d'introduction) non daté et présenté comme chapitre V du décret sur l'œcuménisme figure dans Fonds Moeller, 1997.
86. Cf. CONGAR, *Mon journal du Concile* (n. 2), Tome 1, p. 399.

le schéma sur le fait que l'amour fait partie *de iure* du mariage et sur le nécessaire appel aux diverses disciplines concernées pour approfondir l'investigation scientifique. Trois observations suivent sur le chapitre *De cultura et progressu*. Il y est demandé surtout que soit mieux scrutée la fin de la culture et que le lien soit plus explicitement indiqué avec le chapitre premier. Les auteurs estiment qu'il faut approuver notamment ce qu'exprime ce chapitre sur la valeur intrinsèque de l'évangélisation en faveur de la culture humaine et sur l'autonomie de la science dans son champ propre. Quant au chapitre V (*De ordine economico*), il est jugé trop long dans sa partie technique et trop bref sur le caractère humain de l'économie. Il y manque une théologie du travail; et la description du droit de propriété, qui manque de réalisme, devrait être complétée par la considération de l'esprit de pauvreté selon les Béatitudes. Enfin, en trois lignes, le chapitre sur la paix est jugé très bon.

La conclusion générale, en troisième partie, présente quatre suggestions qui sont importantes du fait des conséquences qu'elles auront ultérieurement. Tout d'abord, le schéma devrait être entièrement réécrit selon une perspective théologique explicite et appliquée à la situation actuelle. Deuxièmement, il ne faut pas chercher à donner des solutions définitives à des questions encore discutées et en continuelle évolution. D'où la troisième suggestion: que l'on distingue clairement ce qui relève des principes et les autres parties, qui pourraient être adoptées par le Concile sous la forme 'd'instructions'. Enfin, pour réaliser la révision proposée, il est – affirment les trois auteurs – important de constituer une sous-commission pour poursuivre et mûrir le travail dans une perspective unique. Cette sous-commission pourrait continuer ses activités, en consultant aussi des laïcs, pendant la deuxième session conciliaire.

On peut voir dans les suggestions 1, 3 et 4 l'origine déterminante de l'initiative prise par Suenens – qui s'en est trouvée confortée suite aux décisions de la commission de coordination réunie au début juillet[87] – de réunir à Malines au mois de septembre suivant une équipe d'une dizaine de théologiens chargée d'élaborer la partie 'principes', mais non un nouveau texte intégral du schéma[88].

87. Dans son chapitre sur la première intersession de l'*Histoire du concile Vatican II*, J. Grootaers mentionne une autre intervention, celle du P. Tromp, qui demandait en avril 63 de distinguer dans le schéma une partie consacrée aux principes et une autre aux directives pratiques (voir G. ALBERIGO – É. FOUILLOUX [éds.], *Histoire du Concile Vatican II*, Tome II, Paris, Cerf; Louvain, Peeters, 1998, p. 500, n. 1).

88. À la fin de juillet, Moeller, qui est alors à Montréal, où il rencontre longuement Léger et Willebrands, confirme à Philips que Suenens a fait distinguer les principes et les instructions (lettre du 29 juillet 1963, dans Fonds Philips, 461).

4. Le chapitre du *De ecclesia* sur la sainteté

Moeller a aussi joué un rôle dans les débats de mai 1963 relatifs au chapitre 4 du *De ecclesia* qui était consacré primitivement aux religieux et va devenir un chapitre sur la sainteté dans l'Église. Le changement du titre – et donc du contenu – Moeller et Thils les proposaient en avril au cardinal Suenens, qui se montrait intéressé mais doutait d'une issue favorable[89]. Dans ses remarques destinées à la Doctrinale en mai, Moeller demande que le chapitre primitif soit entièrement révisé. Selon lui, ce travail serait facilité par la rédaction d'une introduction traitant de la vocation de tous les chrétiens à la sainteté. Une telle introduction a été demandée – précise-t-il – par presque tous les membres de la Doctrinale; il cite spécialement Rahner et Congar[90].

Il faudrait développer longuement l'activité de Moeller à propos de ce chapitre: la documentation est abondante sur ses remarques complémentaires et sur le travail de rédaction des notes du texte qu'il effectua par la suite avec Thils en juin[91]. Quant au rapport sur les travaux de la Doctrinale que Moeller rédigea au début de juin à l'intention du cardinal Léger sur la demande de Mgr Charue, il est substantiellement identique à ce que ce dernier a noté dans ses carnets conciliaires[92]. Je signale simplement que l'idée de créer une sous-commission chargée de rédiger une partie introductive sur la vocation de tous à la sainteté et de revoir l'ensemble du texte dans cette optique – idée avancée le 28 mai par le cardinal Browne – avait été lancée par Moeller dès la veille[93] et que celui-ci collabora au travail rédactionnel confié à Philips au sein de cette sous-commission[94]. On peut encore ajouter que le chapitre, réécrit par Philips le 30 mai, fut dactylographié par Moeller et l'expert chilien Medina[95].

Si, pour le schéma XVII, une Note conjointe de Philips, Congar et Moeller avait été adressée au cardinal Suenens, il semble que la Note du même genre concernant les chapitres 3 et 4 du *De ecclesia*, écrite à l'intention du même destinataire, ait été rédigée par Moeller, qui la soumit ensuite à Philips, qui fut probablement le seul co-signataire[96]. Les

---

89. Selon la lettre, citée *supra*, de Moeller à Léger du 12 avril 1963.
90. Remarques faites par Moeller le 28 mai 1963 (4 pp. mss) dans Fonds Philips, 744.
91. Cette documentation occupe les n. 127-144 du Fonds Moeller.
92. Journal Charue, pp. 125-128. Le rapport de Moeller à Léger (qui était encore à Rome, mais ne participa pas aux dernières réunions de la Doctrinale) est daté du 5 juin: original dans Fonds Léger, 850; photocopie dans Fonds Moeller, 3041ter.
93. Note ms. de Moeller, 27 mai 1963, dans Fonds Moeller, 138.
94. D'après Journal Charue, p. 127.
95. D'après Journal Philips, p. 45.
96. Copie de la Note datée du 31 mai 1963, dans Fonds Philips, 773.

indications sur le chapitre *De populo Dei et speciatim de laicis* sont surtout techniques. Il est spécifié cependant que la commission pour l'apostolat des laïcs s'est déclarée «fort satisfaite» du texte. Le chapitre 4, désormais intitulé *De vocatione ad sanctitatem in ecclesia*, fait l'objet d'explications sur l'élargissement de son thème, obtenu avec l'accord du cardinal Browne, vice-président de la Doctrinale. Suivent des précisions sur les deux sections du texte, l'une sur la sainteté à laquelle tous sont appelés, l'autre sur les états de perfection sanctionnés par l'Église. On a veillé à maintenir l'unité entre les deux sections. En finale, Moeller ajoute: «On souhaite que soit plus souligné le caractère *pascal* de la sainteté». Le fait que Suenens a repris ce point dans son rapport à la commission de coordination en juillet suivant tend à prouver que le cardinal a bien reçu cette Note, même si elle n'apparaît pas dans ses papiers conciliaires[97].

5. Au Québec en juillet

Moeller passe le mois de juillet 1963 au Canada. Après avoir donné à Québec des cours et des conférences sur la littérature contemporaine – comme il le fait depuis 1959 –, il séjourne à Montréal où il participe à la quatrième conférence du département Foi et Constitution du Conseil œcuménique des Églises, qui se tient du 12 au 26 juillet. Il voit longuement le cardinal Léger et l'aide – au moins de ses encouragements – à préparer l'allocution que l'archevêque prononce le 21 juillet au cours d'une soirée de fraternité œcuménique sur le thème «Nous sommes un dans le Christ». Malgré les appréhensions du cardinal, cette allocution fut dans l'ensemble appréciée[98]. Cet épisode est considéré comme un moment décisif dans l'ouverture de Léger et des catholiques canadiens à l'œcuménisme[99].

---

97. Pour la *Relatio* de Suenens à la commission de coordination, cf. Fonds Philips, 784.

98. Ch. Moeller traite abondamment de ses contacts québécois dans ses carnets (cf. Fonds Moeller, Carnet 14). En outre, une vaste documentation sur la conférence de Foi et Constitution et sur la soirée œcuménique du 21 juillet est conservée dans le même fonds, sub n. 3580-3647.

99. Cf. R. Burigana – G. Routhier, *La conversion œcuménique d'un évêque et d'une Église: Le parcours œcuménique du cardinal Léger et de l'Église de Montréal au moment de Vatican II*, dans *Science et Esprit* 52 (2000) 171-191 et 293-319. Ces auteurs parlent de l'influence de Moeller sur cette «conversion» et affirment, sans citer de source, que l'expert belge a participé à la rédaction de l'allocution du cardinal du 21 juillet 1963 (p. 303, n. 26).

Le séjour québécois de Charles Moeller, même s'il n'est pas sans intérêt au point de vue du Concile, ne concerne pas directement ce dernier. Je n'en traite pas ici.

6. Les réunions de Malines en septembre

Nous avons vu que, dans leur Note au cardinal Suenens du 28 mai précédent, Philips, Congar et Moeller suggéraient de distinguer, dans la rédaction du schéma sur l'Église dans le monde, des principes généraux et des instructions pratiques. La proposition avait été approuvée par la commission de coordination au début de juillet. C'est ainsi que le cardinal prend l'initiative de réunir à Malines en septembre une équipe internationale de douze théologiens, philosophes et exégètes[100].

Au terme des trois premiers jours d'échanges sur un avant-projet préparé par Philips, il est décidé que chaque membre du groupe rédigera sa proposition sur les quatre chapitres que comptait cet avant-projet, à savoir: 1. la mission de l'Église; 2. le monde; 3. la présence de l'Église au monde; 4. les formes de l'action de l'Église[101]. Il reviendra à Philips de faire une synthèse, à revoir en commun, ce qui aura lieu le 17 septembre. Le texte définitif, daté du 22, ne se compose plus que de trois chapitres[102]: la mission de l'Église; le monde, son autonomie et sa recherche d'unification; enfin les tâches de l'Église à l'égard du monde envisagées selon les trois aspects du témoignage, du service et de la communion, conformément à la proposition du P. Congar[103].

Quelle fut la contribution de Moeller à l'ensemble de l'entreprise? Indépendamment du fait qu'il prit d'abondantes notes (38 pages) – comme souvent presque illisibles – pendant les réunions des trois premiers jours[104], il collabora à la rédaction de la synthèse de Philips préparée pendant l'intervalle entre le 8 et le 17 septembre. On conserve 4 pages dactylographiées de remarques à propos des chapitres 2 sur le

---

100. Sur les réunions de Malines et ses suites, cf. J. GROOTAERS, *Le concile se joue à l'entracte*, dans ALBERIGO – FOUILLOUX (éds.), *Histoire du Concile Vatican II* (n. 87), Tome II, 500-509.

101. À noter que, d'entrée de jeu, Congar, Tucci et Moeller essaient de rédiger un texte commun. Congar note: «mais cela ne va pas [...] on perd du temps, on patine. Finalement, chacun rédige son affaire» (dans CONGAR, *Mon journal du Concile* [n. 2], Tome I, pp. 395-396).

102. «Adumbratio Schematis XVII. De activa praesentia ecclesiae in mundo aedificando», dans Fonds Philips, 878, et dans Fonds Prignon, 243.

103. Cf. GROOTAERS, *Le concile se joue* (n. 100), p. 503. Cet auteur estime que c'est Congar qui a eu sur le texte de Malines «l'influence la plus profonde» (voir la p. 502).

104. C'est-à-dire les 6, 7 et 8 septembre. Cf. Fonds Moeller, 997-999.

monde et 3 sur la présence de l'Église dans ce monde[105]. J'en cite les
points principaux. Là où il est question de la collaboration des chrétiens
à l'édification du monde, Moeller suggère d'ajouter les propositions de
Congar et de Dondeyne sur la consistance de l'ordre créé et sur la «préexistence» de ce monde créé qui est antérieur à la division entre croyants
et non-croyants. Il propose également, en partie d'après le texte de Dondeyne, de développer, toujours dans le chapitre 2, la conscience toute
nouvelle de la condition humaine dans le monde sous le triple aspect
contrasté de l'intersubjectivité, de l'unité possible en même temps que de
la pluralité et de la division entre les hommes; deuxièmement sous
l'aspect des potentialités plus grandes de l'homme mais aussi des menaces
d'un enfermement plus grand dans le Soi; enfin sous celui d'une plus
large liberté, qui est cependant exposée à une négativité mortifère dans
l'athéisme systématique. Quant au chapitre III, Moeller croit utile de se
référer à ce qui a déjà été acquis dans le chapitre du schéma relatif à la
culture concernant le conflit entre Église et culture moderne et la présence de l'Église au monde actuel tant par sa hiérarchie que par le peuple
de Dieu comme ferment et sel de la terre. S'inspirant du 'papier' de
Congar qui propose de centrer tout sur le témoignage, le service et la
communion, il développe les formes de la présence de l'Église au monde,
ce monde que l'Église doit savoir écouter et dont elle doit reconnaître
l'autonomie. Il faudrait, estime-t-il, terminer en parlant de la tension permanente entre Église et monde. Et il dit sa préférence pour une séquence
à quatre termes: témoignage, service, communion, louange.

Quant au chapitre premier consacré à la mission de l'Église, il semble
bien que Moeller ait collaboré à un texte de Cerfaux et Rigaux, qu'il suggère du reste dans la Note précédente de suivre en y insérant des «éléments
de Congar»[106]. Le texte développe la mission de l'Église en trois points:
1. l'envoi des disciples par le Christ inaugure le Royaume et fait croître
son Corps jusqu'à la plénitude du 'tout en tous'; 2. l'espérance et la fin de
toute société humaine est le Christ en qui Dieu a tout réconcilié, libérant
toute créature de la corruption; 3. les chrétiens, citoyens du ciel, sont aussi,
de droit et avec raison, membres de la société humaine, les deux cités
humaine et céleste étant ordonnées l'une à l'autre car elles proviennent
toutes deux du Christ et sont tendues vers lui, de sorte que les chrétiens
sont tenus de collaborer à la paix et à l'unité de la société humaine.

---

105. Dans Fonds Philips, 864.
106. La Note sans titre écrite par L. Cerfaux et longue d'un peu plus de 2 pages manuscrites se trouve dans le Fonds Philips, 870. Philips a inscrit en tête: 'Cerfaux', mais une
autre main ajouta au bas du texte: 'Cerfaux, P. Béda [Rigaux], Moeller'.

Enfin, après la discussion du 17 septembre sur le nouveau texte, Moeller a fait parvenir à Philips trois pages d'annotations proposées par Suenens (concernant la liberté religieuse) et par lui-même, d'une part sur la présence de l'Église dans le monde (au n° 7 du texte – devenu ensuite le n° 6 –, il propose de remplacer 'par son culte à Dieu' par 'par sa constitution'), d'autre part aux n° 20-22 (futur n° 18) sur la triple ambiguïté des biens terrestres (unification du monde, domination de l'homme sur la création, usage de la liberté), il souligne l'utilité de maintenir l'ambiguïté dans toute sa force, mais avec sa signification eschatologique (nous sommes «sauvés en espérance», selon Romains 8,24)[107]. De ces remarques, Philips tiendra compte en partie.

Pour conclure sur la participation de Moeller aux réunions et travaux de Malines en septembre 1963, on peut s'interroger sur la position acquise à ce moment-là par l'expert en fonction du 'projet' conciliaire qui était le sien. Il n'est pas douteux qu'il ait à ce stade obtenu, au sein du groupe des théologiens belges – et aussi de la part du cardinal Suenens – la reconnaissance qu'il recherchait. Il n'a pas, pour autant, négligé de tenir au courant de ses activités le cardinal Léger[108]. Mais surtout – me semble-t-il –, Moeller trouve ici une nouvelle occasion d'évoluer dans le cadre d'une équipe internationale, celle-ci fût-elle formée de gens de la même tendance ouverte que lui[109]. Par la suite, sa capacité à nouer des relations de travail et d'amitié avec des spécialistes de toute origine et sa disponibilité à rendre les services les plus divers ne feront que croître, ce qui lui conférera une position *sui generis*. Plusieurs témoignages de ses proches convergent sur ce point[110]. En mars 1964 par exemple, le P. Congar note dans son journal: «Moeller est partout: Commission théologique,

107. Ces annotations: dans Fonds Moeller, 1003 et dans Fonds Philips, 877.
108. Cf. GROOTAERS, *Le concile se joue* (n. 100), p. 502, n. 3.
109. À propos du groupe réuni à Malines, A. Prignon, qui fut le principal organisateur de ces réunions, parle de «notre groupe habituel de théologiens» (dans sa lettre à Moeller du 30 août 1963, dans Fonds Moeller, 2925). Outre les Belges qui ont travaillé au schéma *De Ecclesia* à partir de février-mars 1963 (Philips, Thils, Prignon, Cerfaux, Moeller), on retrouve à Malines Congar et Rahner, et apparaissent Ph. Delhaye, R. Tucci, A. Dondeyne, B. Rigaux, ainsi que le vicaire général de Suenens, R. Ceuppens.
110. É. Beauduin, son conseiller et confident, lui écrit le 4 mai 1964 (dans Fonds Moeller, 2015): «On t'exploite de tous les côtés: tu t'y précipites et tu as l'air d'y prendre goût […]. Cela m'est pénible de te voir peu à peu la bonne à tout faire du Concile […] tout cela à la longue te fera du tort, surtout chez les gens qui exploitent tes complaisances». Beauduin réagissait surtout à ce moment car Mgr Willebrands demandait à Moeller de rédiger rapidement un texte sur les Juifs. Le 21 septembre 1965, A. Prignon note dans son journal conciliaire, à propos de la première réunion du Secrétariat pour les non-chrétiens: «évidemment, on a demandé au chanoine Moeller d'être présent. Je l'ai un petit peu blagué à ce sujet en lui demandant de quelle commission du concile il n'était pas membre» (dans L. DECLERCK – A. HAQUIN [éds.], *Journal conciliaire de la quatrième session. Albert*

Religieux, Schéma XVII, Secrétariat, etc. Il a été partout aux moments et aux endroits décisifs»[111].

IV. La suite du Concile: Aspects majeurs de l'activité de Moeller

Ce qu'écrivait Congar suggère qu'il faudrait tout un volume pour exposer les nombreux aspects de l'activité de Moeller à partir de la deuxième session du Concile. Je n'évoquerai que quelques traits saillants de cette activité.

Tout d'abord, il a poursuivi sa collaboration à la préparation du *De ecclesia* dès octobre 1963, quand le schéma Philips a été discuté par les pères conciliaires. On relève par exemple sa participation pour corriger, avec G. Thils et L. Cerfaux, l'intervention in aula de Charue sur la collégialité le 8 octobre[112] ou encore pour fournir à Mgr Heuschen, en vue de son intervention du même jour, des références patristiques relatives aux apôtres comme fondements de l'Église[113]. Le 19 octobre, il participe encore, avec Prignon, à la rédaction du texte Philips des Cinq Questions que les modérateurs voulaient poser aux pères[114]. Par la suite, quand il sera question de supprimer, au n. 17 sur le caractère missionnaire de l'Église, la mention des «rites propres» des peuples à conserver et à élever, il obtint que le terme «rites» soit maintenu pour témoigner du souci de l'Église de dépasser définitivement la longue et pénible querelle des rites confucéens en Chine[115].

Quant au schéma sur l'Église dans le monde, auquel Moeller tint particulièrement, on sait que le travail effectué en septembre 63 à Malines a éveillé vis-à-vis des Belges une certaine méfiance. Cela n'empêcha pas Moeller de participer, comme seul Belge, aux travaux de la sous-commission centrale mixte à Zürich (janvier-février 1964), où fut mis en chantier un nouveau schéma. Au mois de novembre suivant, il est membre de la sous-commission centrale qui doit reprendre la rédaction du schéma, et fait partie du comité de rédaction, dirigé par le Français Haubtmann. Et, en avril de la même année, lors du passage de la rédaction F à la

Prignon [Cahiers de la Revue théologique de Louvain, 35], Louvain-la-Neuve, Publications de la Faculté de Théologie, 2003, p. 68).

111. Congar, *Mon journal du Concile* (n. 2), Tome II, p. 54.

112. Texte avec corrections dans Fonds Moeller, 339-340.

113. Cf. L. Declerck, *Inventaire des papiers conciliaires de Monseigneur J.M. Heuschen, évêque auxiliaire de Liège, membre de la Commission doctrinale, et du Professeur V. Heylen* (Instrumenta Theologica, 28), Leuven, Bibliotheek van de Faculteit Godgeleerdheid, 2005, p. 23.

114. Cf. Fonds Prignon, 461.

115. Fonds Moeller, 302.

rédaction G, il semble bien que ce soit lui qui ait proposé de modifier l'ordre des premiers mots du texte: «*Gaudium et luctus, spes et angor*» devenant «*Gaudium et spes, luctus et angor*»[116].

Dès 1964, Moeller s'engage aussi dans le travail du Secrétariat pour l'unité. Il s'agit alors de préparer une déclaration sur les Juifs et les religions non-chrétiennes indépendante du schéma sur l'œcuménisme. À la demande du secrétaire J. Willebrands, Moeller rédige un texte de 3 pages, qui – à propos des Juifs – atténue fortement, suite notamment aux objections des pères conciliaires des pays arabes, celui qui avait d'abord été prévu comme quatrième chapitre du *De oecumenismo*. Le texte de cette déclaration indépendante rédigé par Moeller, peut-être avec l'aide de Congar, se compose de trois parties: le patrimoine commun des chrétiens et des juifs, tous les hommes ont Dieu comme Père, il faut condamner toute discrimination[117]. Il est discuté par le Secrétariat les 25 et 27 avril 1964[118]. Une sous-commission du Secrétariat, à laquelle participa Moeller, retravailla le texte en octobre suivant[119]. Mais des parties du texte d'avril subsistent dans la déclaration définitive *Nostra aetate* approuvée et promulguée en octobre 1965. Il faut ajouter que, dès janvier 1964, Moeller a été invité à une session d'experts chargés d'examiner les remarques envoyées par les pères au sujet du schéma sur l'œcuménisme[120]. Dès lors, sa collaboration avec le Secrétariat et ses contacts avec les observateurs non-catholiques participant au Concile ne s'interrompirent plus jusqu'à la fin de celui-ci. L'activité spécifiquement œcuménique de Moeller pendant Vatican II mériterait une étude spéciale.

Enfin, on observe qu'à partir de mars 1964, notre expert est appelé, avec dix-huit autres, à seconder la sous-commission de sept pères chargée d'élaborer un nouveau schéma (le troisième) sur la Révélation[121]. Sur le début de sa tâche dans ce cadre, je renvoie à l'article du P. Wicks dans ce volume.

V. Comment caractériser l'engagement conciliaire de Charles Moeller?

Par tempérament, Moeller apparaît avant tout comme un homme à la recherche des contacts, un homme de '*public relations*', au surplus

---

116. Fonds Moeller, 1351.
117. Texte daté des 25-26 avril 1964, dans Fonds Moeller, 2016.
118. Notes de Moeller sur ces réunions: dans Fonds Moeller, 2018-2019.
119. Cf. texte de 5 pp. et corrections mss dans Fonds De Smedt,1322.
120. Lettre de J.F. Arrighi à Moeller, 27 janvier 1964, dans Fonds Moeller, 2004.
121. Quelques indications dans le chapitre du père E. VILANOVA dans G. ALBERIGO (éd.), *Storia del concilio Vaticano II*, Tome III, Bologna, 1998, pp. 395-396.

volontiers séducteur. Mais il était aussi vulnérable car il se savait porté au
pessimisme et se croyait toujours inférieur à sa tâche[122]. S'il a éveillé la
sympathie du cardinal Léger, il paraît clair que c'est en bonne partie car le
tempérament des deux hommes était proche. Ce que G. Routhier nous a
montré du caractère émotif et du besoin de se sentir reconnu observés chez
Léger s'applique presque terme à terme à la personnalité de Moeller.

Par ailleurs, celui-ci, tout en sachant saisir intuitivement les courants
de pensée de son temps, était aussi un lanceur d'idées, parfois hardies,
volontiers radicales, même s'il se reconnaissait une difficulté à donner à
ces idées une formulation théologique précise[123].

Il s'engagea tôt, bien qu'à titre privé, dans l'aventure conciliaire, en dif-
fusant ses Notes d'ecclésiologie, en cherchant à échanger avec les théologiens patentés de Louvain, en livrant ses idées à son évêque, en veillant
à «mettre dans le coup» le public catholique belge.

Le rôle de lanceur d'idées, il l'exerce encore par la suite, d'abord au
service du cardinal Léger, et, plus encore, quand, devenu expert conciliaire, il est mêlé aux premières rédactions des futures constitutions *Lumen
gentium* et *Gaudium et spes* et, un peu plus tard, lorsqu'il est sollicité
pour participer aux travaux du Secrétariat pour l'unité.

D'un bout à l'autre du Concile, il a mis toute sa passion (sa capacité
séductrice?) à faire passer dans les textes ses deux préoccupations
majeures. D'abord sa passion pour l'unité des Églises chrétiennes, héri-
tée de dom Lambert Beauduin. À ce propos, il s'est avant tout soucié
d'intégrer le point de vue des frères séparés dans tous les schémas dont
il s'est occupé, et d'abord celui sur l'Église. Une même passion l'animait pour la culture de son temps. Il était spécialement sensible aux difficultés de croire qu'éprouve l'homme d'aujourd'hui. Par là me semblent
s'expliquer son attention soutenue et sa contribution non négligeable à ce
qui deviendrait la constitution *Gaudium et spes*.

Quand, en 1966, Moeller fut nommé sous-secrétaire de la Congrégation pour la doctrine de la foi, le pape Paul VI confia à V. Veronese,
ancien directeur général de l'UNESCO et auditeur au Concile, que cette
nomination «avait pour but de mettre le premier dicastère de l'Église en
contact avec la pensée et la culture contemporaines»[124].

---

122. Lettre citée du 10 mars 1963 à É. Beauduin. Il ajoutait: «Bien sûr, je resterai toujours 'tragique, sombre', comme disait le P. Congar ce soir».
123. «Je ne serai jamais un inventeur de formules précises» (lettre citée du 14 mars
1963 à Édouard Beauduin).
124. D'après P. Poswick, ambassadeur de Belgique près le Saint-Siège, à P.-H. Spaak,
ministre des Affaires étrangères, 21.2.1966, dans Archives du Ministère des Affaires Étrangères (Bruxelles), *Correspondance politique St-Siège*, dossier 14956.

Mais, tout en cherchant à occuper une position reconnue, Moeller ne dédaigna pas, selon son mot, de travailler comme «une brute», en accomplissant du début à la fin des tâches obscures de secrétariat, de tri des *modi* des pères, de correction des textes, de conseil discret, notamment auprès de Philips, et, plus généralement, au sein du groupe du Collège belge, et au-delà à partir de 1964.

Il y a près de vingt ans, l'historien français Étienne Fouilloux a esquissé une typologie des experts conciliaires de l'Europe du nord-ouest[125]. Il proposait trois catégories: d'abord les pessimistes face à la théologie romaine dominante, qui, suspects et exclus, n'attendent rien du Concile (il cite le P. de Lubac); puis les maximalistes, tels plusieurs Allemands et Hollandais, surtout le P. Rahner, qui pensent pouvoir profiter de l'occasion pour faire triompher leurs propres positions; enfin les pragmatiques du noyau belge, avec lesquels s'accorde le P. Congar.

En considérant le cas de Charles Moeller, il semble que la situation de cet expert n'entre pas exactement dans la troisième catégorie. Certes, il s'intégra dans l'équipe belge. Oui, il collabora souvent avec Congar, cherchant ensemble en plusieurs circonstances des solutions acceptables pour une majorité de pères conciliaires.

Mais, à plusieurs égards, la position, le tempérament et les idées de Moeller ne correspondaient pas réellement à cette tendance 'pragmatique': 1. En cherchant à fréquenter les cercles conciliaires les plus divers, peut-être surtout celui des observateurs non-catholiques, il avait à cœur de saisir sans cesse le point de vue des 'autres', qu'ils soient non-catholiques ou éloignés de la religion chrétienne. 2. Est-ce parce qu'il n'était pas théologien de métier – ou pas reconnu comme tel – qu'il osa aborder, avec une certaine naïveté, les questions les plus diverses et les plus complexes en participant aux travaux d'un grand nombre de commissions et sous-commissions? La remarque, faite certes par manière de plaisanterie, que lui adressa Prignon vers la fin du Concile, apparaît un peu comme un reproche vis-à-vis de son manque de modération. 3. Enfin deux autres côtés a-typiques du personnage peuvent encore être relevés.

D'abord sa position marginale comme théologien à Louvain. Je pense que son besoin de reconnaissance s'explique en bonne partie par cette situation. Ensuite, même s'il sut se mettre au service de Philips – le modéré –, surtout pour l'élaboration de *Lumen gentium*, il ne manqua pas

125. É. FOUILLOUX, *Comment devient-on expert à Vatican II? Le cas du Père Yves Congar*, dans *Le deuxième concile du Vatican (1959-1965)* (Coll. de l'École française de Rome, 113), Rome, 1989, 307-331, p. 331.

d'essayer de faire passer ses propres idées – plus audacieuses – déjà en ecclésiologie, mais plus encore en matière œcuménique et en faveur du dialogue de l'Église avec la culture de son temps. En témoignent particulièrement les abondantes remarques personnelles qu'il a laissées sur de nombreux projets de documents conciliaires.

Faculté de Théologie   Claude SOETENS
Grand-Place, 45
B-1348 Louvain-la-Neuve
Belgique

DIVERSITÉ DES TENDANCES
À L'INTÉRIEUR DE LA MAJORITÉ CONCILIAIRE

GÉRARD PHILIPS ET GIUSEPPE DOSSETTI

Notre exposé reste évidemment très schématique en ce sens qu'il indique souvent des pistes à explorer à l'avenir sans pouvoir en faire davantage dans les limites de notre exposé d'aujourd'hui. D'autre part, nous n'allons pas revenir ici sur le rôle spécifique qui, petit à petit, va incomber à Philips dès les premières semaines de Vatican II et que nous avons esquissé ailleurs[1].

I. Une question de terminologie

Une typologie sommaire des tendances à Vatican II reposait, dès le début du Concile, sur une distinction entre *conservateurs* (de la minorité) et *progressistes* (de la majorité). Cependant, il est apparu bientôt que ladite majorité n'était pas un courant homogène. Une 'aile gauche' se manifeste surtout à partir de la seconde lecture du schéma rénové *De ecclesia* (septembre 1964). Ce que l'on pouvait appeler alors une 'nouvelle opposition' regroupait des experts et des évêques qui estimaient que les nouveaux dirigeants de la Commission doctrinale avaient fait trop de concessions à la minorité conservatrice[2]. Cette question touche de près les relations fluctuantes de l'équipe dite belge avec le courant de la majorité.

Déjà en 1992 au colloque de Lyon, le professeur Komonchak concluait son exposé par la constatation suivante: «Les différences et les tensions parmi la majorité dite 'progressiste' au Concile demeure une des questions les moins explorées de l'histoire de Vatican II; mais c'est une étude

---

1. Cf. J. GROOTAERS, *Gérard Philips à Vatican II: Une silhouette exceptionnelle*, dans L. DECLERCK – W. VERSCHOOTEN, *Inventaire des papiers conciliaires de Mgr Gérard Philips, secrétaire adjoint de la Commission doctrinale*. Avec une Introduction par J. GROOTAERS (Instrumenta Theologica, 24), Leuven, Bibliotheek van de Faculteit Godgeleerdheid, 2001, pp. XXIII-XXXVIII.

2. J. GROOTAERS, *La collégialité vue au jour le jour en la IIIème session conciliaire*, dans *Irénikon* 28 (1965) 186-187.

qui est absolument nécessaire non seulement pour comprendre le Concile mais aussi sa réception au cours des décennies suivantes»[3].

Heureusement, depuis lors, nous avons eu une étude approfondie du professeur Claude Soetens au colloque de Bologne de 1996: «La 'squadra belga' all'interno della maggioranza conciliare»[4].

Faisant la synthèse de la méthode de travail des Belges dans le courant majoritaire, Soetens distingue deux données de base de leur action. En premier lieu, il place le leadership du cardinal Suenens, qui s'est engagé à réaliser un plan du Concile dès le printemps 1962. Dès lors les Belges vont en premier lieu s'efforcer de suivre de près les travaux en commission et groupes de travail concernant les projets fondamentaux de Vatican II: pour y parvenir, il y aura une répartition des tâches et une présence constante aux points névralgiques de la procédure. En second lieu, les Belges vont conduire cette action avec discrétion et obstination, mais aussi avec modération et conciliation[5].

Enfin, la réflexion la plus significative sur notre thématique du point de vue théologique provient d'une contribution que le professeur J. Komonchak lui-même a présentée plus récemment au colloque de Klingenthal en 1999 sous le titre 'La valutazione sulla Gaudium et spes: Chenu, Dossetti, Ratzinger'[6]. Nous y reviendrons brièvement en conclusion. Mais, avant d'esquisser l'action de deux acteurs importants du Concile – Gérard Philips et Giuseppe Dossetti – il n'est pas superflu de souligner la difficulté à cerner une terminologie adéquate[7]. L'hypothèse

3. J.A. KOMONCHAK, *The Initial Debate about the Church*, dans É. FOUILLOUX (éd.), *Vatican II commence... Approches francophones* (Instrumenta Theologica, 12), Leuven, Bibliotheek van de Faculteit Godgeleerdheid, 1993, p. 348.

4. Parue dans M.T. FATTORI – A. MELLONI (éds.), *L' evento e le decisioni: Studi sulle dinamiche del Concilio Vaticano II* (Testi e richerche di scienze religiose. Nuova Serie, 20), Bologna, Il Mulino, 1997, pp. 143-172.

5. Dans le même ordre de préoccupations, il conviendrait de consulter aussi l'article du professeur G. ALBERIGO, *Critères herméneutiques pour une histoire de Vatican II*, où se trouvera notamment une interprétation de la pratique de 'compromis' et de la recherche de l'unanimité. Cet exposé a paru en deux endroits différents: dans M. LAMBERIGTS – C. SOETENS (éds.), *À la veille du Concile Vatican II: Vota et réactions en Europe et dans le catholicisme oriental* (Instrumenta Theologica, 9), Leuven, Bibliotheek van de Faculteit Godgeleerdheid, 1992, 12-23; et dans J.P. JOSSUA – N.J. SED (éds.), *Interpréter*. Mélanges offerts à Claude Geffré, Paris, Cerf, 1992, 261-275.

6. Dans J. DORÉ – A. MELLONI (éds.), *Volti di fine concilio: Studi di storia e teologia sulla conclusione del Vaticano II* (Testi e richerche di scienze religiose. Nuova Serie, 27), Bologna, Il Mulino, 2001, 115-153.

7. Depuis plusieurs années, nous avons eu de nombreux échanges de vues à ce sujet avec nos collègues à Bologne et aussi à Würzburg, avec Riccardi (à Rome), mais en premier lieu avec Komonchak (en 1994 à Boston et en 1995 à Brescia) qui nous ont été de la plus grande utilité. Nous en remercions ici nos interlocuteurs.

de travail que je voudrais proposer ici et dont je prends la responsabilité repose sur une double polarité: (1) une *première polarité*, qui se réfère principalement mais pas uniquement à la *stratégie* (ou la tactique) prônée dans le débat conciliaire, oppose des *médiateurs* et des *intransigeants*; (2) une *seconde polarité*, qui généralement traite davantage du *contenu* des documents en discussion, oppose des *possibilistes* et des *radicaux* (ou *maximalistes*).

1. Première polarité: médiateurs — intransigeants

Dès le début de Vatican II, il y eut un courant puissant en faveur de la 'médiation'. Il nous paraît indéniable que l'influence de Jean XXIII a été décisive à cet égard. Après le vote négatif du 20 novembre 1962 concernant le schéma 'des sources de la Révélation', le pape désirait sortir le Concile de l'impasse en instituant immédiatement une commission mixte où les 'novateurs' du Secrétariat pour l'Unité et les traditionalistes de la Commission doctrinale allaient pouvoir dialoguer.

Dans le plan de travail de l'archevêque de Malines-Bruxelles présenté au Concile au début de décembre 1962 – une présentation qui avait au préalable reçu l'aval de Jean XXIII – Suenens stipulait qu'il fallait utiliser au maximum les schémas élaborés pendant la phase préparatoire en leur donnant 'un souffle et un élan' qui leur manquaient actuellement[8].

Par la suite, de nombreuses commissions mixtes furent instituées (pour plusieurs chapitres du *De ecclesia*, pour le *De oecumenismo*, pour le schéma des Églises orientales, pour la Liberté religieuse, pour chacun des dix chapitres du Schéma XIII et même brièvement avec la Commission pontificale pour la régulation des naissances), dans le but évident d'obtenir un rapprochement entre tendances opposées en instaurant un dialogue. Cependant, l'exemple le plus clair de médiation fut le projet de révision du *De ecclesia* qui tiendrait compte du schéma de la phase préparatoire. Lorsque Suenens demande à Philips de réviser le schéma, c'est dans cette perspective[9]. Et lorsque Philips refuse de faire cette révision seul et

---

8. L.-J. SUENENS, *Souvenirs et espérances*, Paris, Fayard, 1991, p. 72; concernant les circonstances de cette intervention importante de Suenens, voir G. CAPRILE, *Il Concilio Vaticano II: Cronache del Concilio Vaticano II.* Vol. III: *Secondo Periodo 1963-1964*, Rome, Civiltà Cattolica, 1966, pp. 247 et 269.

9. À la Commission de coordination, Suenens s'efforce aussi de démontrer que les matières traitées dans le Schéma XVII de 1963 (plus tard Schéma XIII) ont pour une bonne part été puisées dans des textes de la phase préparatoire: e.a. 'De ordine morali', 'De ordine sociali', 'De ordine internationali' et encore trois autres.

s'adresse à un groupe de travail d'origine mixte pour l'assister, il suit les instructions de Suenens: il est le prototype du médiateur.

Plus tard – fin février 1963 – la sous-commission doctrinale *De ecclesia* se trouve devant sept projets différents. Si elle choisit bientôt le texte révisé provenant de l'équipe Philips, c'est parce que c'est le projet le plus 'hétérogène' qui soit présent. Cela signifie qu'il ne s'agit pas d'un texte de *substitution* rédigé à frais nouveaux, mais d'une tentative d'*intégration* des éléments de l'ancien schéma dans une structure nouvelle et une perspective plus large, *et donc* différente.

En ce qui concerne la notion d''intransigeant', il faut prendre ce terme dans son sens premier, donc à la lettre, c'est-à-dire comme désignant «celui qui refuse de transiger, celui qui n'admet aucune concession, celui qui est irréductible»[10]. Il ne s'agit donc pas ici du sens *dérivé* du terme dans les tensions entre idéologies du XIXe siècle dans certains pays d'Europe. Nous avons cité la définition du dictionnaire *Robert*!

Aux yeux des *intransigeants*, ce qui compte, c'est notamment de réaliser le programme radical du renouveau ecclésiologique et de la réforme institutionnelle (notamment de la Curie romaine). Certains parmi eux estiment qu'il faut d'abord renouveler les commissions conciliaires et confier la direction de celles-ci à des figures représentatives de l'assemblée conciliaire.

Les *médiateurs*, par contre, ont conscience des contraintes que le travail en commission impose. Ils tiennent compte de la nécessité d'obtenir un large assentiment de l'assemblée conciliaire, dont les débats se concluent nécessairement par des votes. Le risque des adeptes de la ligne *intransigeante* est de savoir que leurs propositions seront rejetées par la majorité et cependant de les maintenir. Le risque principal de l'attitude de la *médiation*, c'est d'aboutir à des textes non dépourvus d'ambiguïté et de s'y résigner. En plagiant une expression célèbre de Charles Péguy, nous sommes tenté de dire: 'les intransigeants ont les mains pures, mais ils n'ont pas de mains'[11].

La 'pointe' de l'intransigeance se reconnaît lorsque des *periti* refusent toute collaboration à la rédaction d'un texte qu'ils ont critiqué et qu'ils ont l'occasion d'améliorer. À cet égard, le cas de Hans Küng est particulièrement éloquent grâce au récit que le grand théologien suisse y

---

10. Nous citons ici le *Petit Robert* (1984), p. 1026.

11. «Le kantisme a les mains pures, mais il n'a pas de mains», écrivait Charles PÉGUY, *Victor-Marie, comte Hugo*, dans *Œuvres en prose complètes* (Bibliothèque de la Pléiade), Paris, Gallimard, 1992, p. 331. Et Péguy de poursuivre: «Et nous nos mains calleuses, nos mains noueuses, nos mains pécheresses, nous avons quelquefois les mains pleines». Peut-être s'agit-il ici de nos *médiateurs*...

consacre avec verve dans ses mémoires[12]. C'est Karl Rahner qui s'efforce de persuader Hans Küng d'accepter de collaborer à la Commission doctrinale du Concile; celui-ci est d'abord perplexe, mais bientôt il refuse: d'une part il craint de ne plus pouvoir prendre en public des positions aussi critiques s'il a participé activement à la rédaction d'un texte conciliaire, et d'autre part il lui semble qu'il dispose d'autres moyens pour influencer Vatican II, soit par les interventions qu'il prépare pour des évêques et ses exposés aux conférences épiscopales, soit par l'influence qu'il exerce sur la grande presse, et plus tard par ses publications[13].

Un autre exemple est celui de Don Dossetti. Lorsqu'en 1965 celui-ci se plaignit au père Tucci des graves erreurs qui défiguraient le Schéma XIII en discussion au Concile, le rédacteur de la *Civiltà Cattolica* lui proposa aussitôt de rédiger des amendements afin d'améliorer le texte en question. Mais Dossetti semble avoir refusé une telle collaboration[14].

2. Seconde polarité: possibilistes — radicaux

Notre seconde polarité repose sur l'opposition entre les *possibilistes* et les *radicaux* (ou *maximalistes*). Quant au terme de *possibiliste*, on peut le puiser dans l'expérience personnelle du grand théologien conciliaire que fut le père Yves Congar. Celui-ci fut très sensible aux deux termes de cette polarité à l'intérieur du courant majoritaire. Congar nous décrit dans son *Journal* une soirée mémorable avec Hans Küng qui se révèle comme un *radical*. Cela se passe vers mi-octobre 1963 lorsque le schéma sur la Liturgie faisait l'objet de votes et que le *De ecclesia* du groupe Philips était discuté au Concile. Yves Congar décrit alors cette soirée de discussion avec Hans Küng, plein d'intelligence mais extrêmement critique à l'égard du texte sur la Liturgie et à l'égard de A.-G. Martimort, critique aussi devant le *De ecclesia*, selon lui révisé, «plein de naïveté et de banalités».

---

12. Cf. H. KÜNG, *Erkämpfte Freiheit: Erinnerungen*, Tome I, München, Piper, 2002, pp. 465-468: «Kommissionsarbeit – Ja oder nein?».

13. Ayant refusé de collaborer à la Commission doctrinale du Concile et après avoir énuméré les inconvénients d'une discussion conciliaire entre évêques et théologiens qui manquent de compétence, H. Küng conclut qu'il veut suivre un tout autre cheminement: «Je veux en ce qui concerne l'Église proposer mon propre projet, sans concessions et avec précision, sans les pressions des commissions conciliaires et sans les douleurs de compromis théologiques avec la Curie. J'ai pris la résolution d'écrire un livre sur le thème Église. [...] Concrètement, cela signifie qu'au lieu de gaspiller des forces dans la Commission théologique, je vais les investir dans une synthèse ecclésiologique dans l'esprit du Concile». (KÜNG, *Erkämpfte Freiheit* [n. 12], pp. 484-487, notre traduction de l'allemand). Le livre dont le projet est évoqué ici paraîtra en 1967 sous le titre *Die Kirche*.

14. Cf. J. GROOTAERS, *Diarium*, cahier n. 60: entretien avec le père R. Tucci en date du 9 juillet 1967.

Le jeune Küng, remarque Congar, est un fonceur, à l'opposé de Martimort: «Celui-ci est livré au 'possible', à la tactique: c'est un réformiste, un *possibiliste*; Küng est un exigeant, de type révolutionnaire». C'est nous qui soulignons ici le terme de possibiliste, car le même thème et parfois le même terme reviendront sous la plume du grand théologien français, et correspondent bien à un aspect significatif de Vatican II. L'usage qu'un observateur conciliaire aussi averti que Congar en fait nous autorise à nous en servir à notre tour. Au cours de cette rencontre avec Hans Küng, Congar se sent d'abord attiré par ce radicalisme, dont il a une certaine nostalgie, mais ensuite, tiraillé entre les deux 'pôles', il se dit conscient des progrès déjà accomplis par le Concile (par exemple, «on a substitué Philips à Tromp») et surtout «il faut voir aussi ce qui a été possible»[15]. Enfin, lorsque Congar livre sa pensée personnelle, il révèle le fondement de l'attitude possibiliste qui est la sienne à Vatican II: «Moi, je crois profondément aux délais, aux étapes nécessaires. J'ai *vu* que ma conviction était *vraie*. J'ai vu aussi tant de chemin fait en 30 ans. J'ai tellement le sentiment qu'un grand corps comme est l'Église exige un mouvement d'un rythme mesuré»[16].

En plus du 'sens de l'assemblée' évoqué par A.-G. Martimort, Congar nous montre ici un remarquable *sentire cum ecclesia* qui le caractérise. Ces réflexions de Congar ne l'empêchent pas d'être aussi sensible *à ce qui manque* dans le schéma révisé et dans le travail conciliaire. Il note: «Il n'y a pas eu *vraiment* ressourcement». Mais cela aussi fait partie de la perspective possibiliste.

La pensée du professeur Thils au cours du Concile était très proche de cette perspective: il pensait qu'il ne fallait pas forcer la main aux évêques au Concile ni lorsqu'il s'agissait d'œcuménisme ni quand la liberté religieuse était à l'ordre du jour. Si on les entraînait vers des attitudes qui les dépassent encore, une fois rentrés chez eux, ils ne seraient pas capables de réaliser certains engagements pris à Rome[17]. Notre exposé a pour but

---

15. Y. CONGAR, *Mon journal du Concile*, présenté et annoté par É. MAHIEU, 2 tomes, Paris, Cerf, 2002, Tome I, pp. 465-466, en date du 12 octobre 1963. Ailleurs et à un autre niveau, Congar est rempli d'estime pour le *De ecclesia*, schéma alternatif allemand présenté à Mayence (Congar s'y trouve en compagnie de Philips) et élaboré à un haut niveau théologique par le père Grillmeier. Il ajoute: «Mais on ne sait qu'en faire»… Il est obligé de reconnaître que c'est un traité et non un schéma (*ibid.*, pp. 320-321, en date du 26 janvier 1963). À la même époque, ayant reçu des remarques d'un 'excellent théologien' – resté anonyme – concernant les deux premiers chapitres du schéma révisé, Congar écrit à Philips: «Il est clair que c'est à la fois très intéressant et impossible à réaliser». Il termine cette lettre en suggérant à Philips d'assumer quelques idées qui s'y trouvent. Cf. Fonds Philips, 551.

16. *Ibid.*

17. GROOTAERS, *Diarium*, cahier n. 25, le 29 septembre 1964.

de mettre à l'avant-plan la diversification des tensions et des polarités à l'intérieur du courant de la majorité conciliaire. Cette approche pourra, je l'espère, contribuer à démontrer que le rôle des Belges comme médiateurs se situe dans un ensemble plus large et plus nuancé que l'on pourrait croire au premier abord. Nous avons en outre trois aspects à retenir, qui mériteraient des études ultérieures:

a. L'équipe dont le Collège belge est le centre reçoit l'aide d'un certain nombre de non-Belges (parfois une petite dizaine!).

b. Il y avait à Rome au Concile quelques Belges qui tournaient le dos au Collège belge soit parce qu'ils se trouvaient dans le camp de la minorité, soit parce qu'ils appartenaient à la tendance intransigeante ou radicale.

c. L'équipe a connu quelques moments de crise grave lorsqu'il est apparu que les Belges pouvaient être eux-mêmes divisés entre *médiation* et *radicalisme*.

C'est surtout ce dernier phénomène des crises internes de l'équipe belge qui n'a pas été exploré et dont l'étude devrait être approfondie. Ainsi, il serait utile d'étudier la crise qui a entouré l'introduction par Paul VI de la fameuse *Nota praevia* qui, à l'origine, était destinée à accompagner le rapport concernant le chapitre 3 du *De ecclesia*. Mais cette *Nota* fut par la suite majorée par le pape comme interprétation de la Constitution toute entière. Les concessions auxquelles Philips fut alors contraint ont divisé l'équipe qui l'entourait.

Deux autres moments critiques de Vatican II qui ont provoqué des dissensions au sein de la *squadra* eurent lieu au cours de la quatrième période du concile: la crise profonde de fin octobre 1965 autour du schéma *De revelatione* et celle de fin novembre 1965, lorsque Paul VI – en fin de procédure – voulut forcer la Commission du Schéma XIII à introduire quatre amendements dans le chapitre sur le mariage, concernant la régulation des naissances. L'équipe se divisa entre ceux qui acceptèrent une médiation par la rédaction de textes de compromis et ceux qui firent montre d'intransigeance à l'égard des pressions qui venaient du 'sommet'[18].

3. Post-scriptum sur une médiation inversée

À partir du début de la troisième période conciliaire, la 'médiation' va subir une métamorphose et changer de signification: elle aura alors pour

---

18. On trouvera les épisodes de cette dernière «affaire» et la documentation qui s'y réfère dans J. GROOTAERS – J. JANS (éds.), *La régulation des naissances à Vatican II: Une semaine de crise* (Annua Nuntia Lovaniensia, 43), Leuven, Peeters, 2002.

but de tranquilliser la minorité conciliaire. Dans plusieurs cas, c'est à la suite d'une initiative de Paul VI, dans quelques cas c'est en son nom et parfois à son insu.

L'esprit de médiation insufflé par Jean XXIII avait pour but de permettre à la majorité conciliaire de participer au travail rédactionnel du Concile et à l'amendement des schémas. À partir de l'automne 1964, il s'agira d'un autre souffle afin d'introduire des représentants de la minorité dans les commissions dont celle-ci se méfie. Certaines de ces initiatives suscitent un grand émoi au Concile et même l'indignation publique de la majorité: notamment lors d'une nouvelle Commission pour la Liberté religieuse (11 octobre 1964) et par le remaniement de la sous-commission doctrinale chargée de traiter les *modi* du *De ecclesia* (le 21 octobre 1964)[19].

Vers la fin de septembre 1965, il s'agit du Secrétariat pour l'Unité: certains ont le sentiment que la minorité y est sous-représentée et qu'il serait nécessaire 'd'élargir' au Secrétariat le groupe de travail qui rédige le texte du schéma sur la Liberté religieuse en y associant des membres 'd'autres tendances'[20]. Ce ne sont ici que quelques cas mentionnés à titre d'exemples.

4. Quelques milieux typiques

Qu'il nous soit permis d'énumérer en bref quelques 'milieux' qui, à certaines occasions, se sont révélés *radicaux* ou *intransigeants*:

a. Les concertations fréquentes d'un groupe significatif de théologiens allemands et germanophones en contact avec des épiscopats de langue allemande: cette concertation incluait aussi des experts comme Philips, Congar et Schillebeeckx. Il est évident que ce groupe influent n'est pas toujours homogène. Quelques grandes figures épiscopales comme König, Frings, Volk, avaient le souci de garder le contact avec les théologiens allemands, ceux-ci étaient des figures d'avant-plan, mais ils n'appartenaient pas à la même faculté. (Le cas de l'influence de

19. Voir la correspondance de Mgr Heuschen avec des membres de sa famille. Cf. L. DECLERCK, *Inventaire des papiers conciliaires de Monseigneur J.M. Heuschen, évêque auxiliaire de Liège, membre de la Commission doctrinale, et du Professeur V. Heylen* (Instru-menta Theologica, 28), Leuven, Peeters, 2005 [cité désormais Fonds Heuschen], n. 439, du 11 octobre 1964, et n. 404, lettre du 21 octobre 1964.

20. Cf. L. DECLERCK – A. HAQUIN (éds.), *Albert Prignon: Journal conciliaire de la quatrième Session* (Cahiers de la Revue théologique de Louvain, 35), Louvain-la-Neuve, Publications de la Faculté de Théologie, 2003, pp. 50-59, 67-68 et *passim*.

Louvain est à cet égard un cas unique à Vatican II. Autre caractéristique unique: Louvain, étant une université de l'Église locale, donc inter-diocèses.)

b. Le milieu de Bologne: il ne s'agit pas uniquement du cardinal Lercaro, du père Dossetti et du professeur Alberigo, mais aussi d'évêques de proximité comme Bettazzi et Amici et du journaliste R. La Valle.

c. L'Église Melkite avec le Patriarche Maximos IV, grande figure d'avant-garde et aussi quelques Orientaux comme Ghattas et Ziadé. Des experts, dont Dom Rousseau, étaient collaborateurs occasionnels du milieu melkite, dont ils se sentaient très proches.

d. Certains théologiens français du Secrétariat pour l'Unité ont pris à certains moments des initiatives *radicales* (Mgr Willebrands, par contre, fut nettement «médiateur»)[21].

e. L'un ou l'autre théologien de l'Institut Oriental qui travaillait pour des évêques orientaux: par exemple, le père Dejaifve, jésuite belge, refusait la 'médiation' du Collège belge.

f. Quelques figures *maximalistes* quant à la collégialité défendue par eux (principalement en octobre 1964 lorsque la Commission se trouve confrontée *in aula* à de nombreux amendements à cet égard), B. Alfrink (Utrecht), Butler (Londres), Hermaniuk (Winnipeg), Rusch (Innsbrück)[22]. À la même époque, la Commission devait réagir à des amendements de la 'minorité' en faveur d'une papauté 'monarchique' tendant à isoler le successeur de Pierre du collège.

II. LE PROFESSEUR GÉRARD PHILIPS

Il y a un certain paradoxe à vouloir situer les positions conciliaires de deux personnages aussi différents voire même contradictoires que le grand théologien flamand Gérard Philips, artisan conciliaire de Louvain, et le grand spirituel italien Giuseppe Dossetti, qui inspira l'officine de Bologne pendant le Concile[23].

Philips et Dossetti étaient l'un et l'autre d'anciens parlementaires et avaient donc une expérience commune des procédures de la démocratie, expérience qui faisait totalement défaut à la plupart des théologiens de

---

21. Certains de ces théologiens provenaient du Centre Istina (e.a. le père C. Dumont, O.P.), d'autres du Saulchoir (e.a. le père Dupuy, O.P.) et du monastère de Chevetogne (notamment Dom E. Lanne, O.S.B.).

22. Mgr Rusch fit des interventions au Concile – parfois au nom d'un grand nombre d'évêques germanophones – qui causèrent particulièrement l'inquiétude de Paul VI.

23. Voir l'ouvrage documentaire récent de G. ALBERIGO (éd.), *L'officina Bolognese 1953-2003*, Bologna, Centro editoriale Dehoniane, 2004.

métier ainsi qu'aux évêques assemblés à Vatican II. Mais encore cette similitude n'allait-elle pas loin. Dossetti (avant son ordination sacerdotale) fut un homme politique de premier plan, collaborateur de la Constituante et avec un leadership de poids dans la *Démocratie Chrétienne*. Philips, de son côté, était un sénateur coopté pour la province du Limbourg, avec une activité plus morale que politique et sans engagement dans la vie des partis. Nous reviendrons plus loin sur les comparaisons à faire entre ces deux personnalités.

1. La situation de Philips à Louvain

C'est en 1942 que G. Philips fut chargé d'enseigner la théologie dogmatique à Louvain. L'accueil qu'il reçut à la Faculté de théologie ne fut pas particulièrement cordial. Philips avait reçu sa formation à Rome, à la Grégorienne, et ne provenait donc pas du «bercail» louvaniste[24]. En outre, cette nomination suivait de près la condamnation par Rome du professeur Draguet, qui avait dû abandonner la Faculté de théologie. Cette circonstance a pu 'assombrir' l'arrivée de Philips[25].

Malgré les résistances de la Faculté devant la candidature de Philips, c'est le cardinal Van Roey, archevêque de Malines, qui tint bon et imposa la nomination de Philips. Cette circonstance est significative. Le cardinal Van Roey plaidait alors depuis cinq ans pour que la Faculté de théologie se préoccupât davantage des nécessités de l'heure. Il fit un discours important qui, à l'époque, fut mal reçu par les professeurs de théologie[26].

---

24. Il faut remarquer que, plus tard, de nombreux autres évêques et théologiens de la 'squadra belga' provenaient de la Grégorienne!

25. R. Draguet (1896-1980) fut professeur de théologie dogmatique à Louvain. Sur ordre de Rome en 1942 il fut obligé de quitter la Faculté. Il fut réhabilité par une lettre de Cicognani à Suenens le 2 juillet 1965.

26. À l'assemblée annuelle des anciens étudiants de la Faculté en juin 1937, l'archevêque de Malines déclara qu'à l'époque où l'Église était attaquée au plan historique (le modernisme), la Faculté avait fait du très bon travail en se consacrant à la méthode historique. Mais aujourd'hui il fallait se tourner résolument vers les problèmes du jour: une tâche nouvelle s'impose, «l'étude spéculative du message lui-même et l'élaboration rationnelle de son contenu» devant l'émergence des idéologies contemporaines et des courants nouveaux de la pensée religieuse. Ce discours eut plusieurs conséquences, entre autres la création d'une chaire sur «les mystiques contemporaines» (prof. Grégoire), le choix de la thèse de Louis Janssens qui étudia «Personne et Société», l'actualisation du sujet de la maîtrise de R. Aubert sur «l'Acte de foi», et peut-être d'autres encore que nous ne connaissons pas. Quant au discours du cardinal Van Roey du 29 juin 1937, voir B. RIGAUX, *Une importante réunion à la Faculté de théologie à l'Université de Louvain*, dans *Revue catholique des Idées et des Faits* (1937) 10-13. Et, dans le même périodique, le numéro du 22 octobre 1937, le rappel du discours de Van Roey par le recteur Mgr Ladeuze à l'ouverture de l'année académique 1937-1938.

C'est dans ce contexte particulier qu'il faut comprendre la nomination à une chaire complémentaire de dogmatique du chanoine G. Philips, qui avait les qualités nécessaires et l'expérience pastorale qui correspondaient aux vœux du cardinal Van Roey[27].

Suenens et Philips se connaissaient depuis très longtemps: depuis leurs études communes à la Grégorienne à Rome. Ils ne semblent pas avoir été des amis. Bientôt, de vives tensions les ont opposés: il y a l'incompatibilité évidente entre la Légion de Marie, implantée en Belgique par Suenens, et l'Action Catholique, coordonnée en Flandre par Philips à la demande explicite des évêques de Belgique et avec l'appui de ceux-ci: une situation très différente de celle de la Légion de Marie!

Ils se sont opposés notamment au IIe Congrès mondial de l'Apostolat des laïcs (Rome, octobre 1957) au sujet de la position 'privilégiée' de l'Action Catholique, que Pie XII – sous l'influence de Suenens – semblait avoir mise en question dans son discours d'ouverture. Cependant, certaines circonstances les avaient rapprochés à Louvain. Ainsi que nous l'avons indiqué, Philips, nommé à Louvain en 1942, s'y sentait isolé. À la même époque, Suenens, nouveau vice-recteur de l'Université, prit l'initiative peu 'louvaniste' de réunir un groupe de dialogue entre théologiens de l'Université et théologiens de la Faculté jésuite[28]. Bien que nouveau venu, Philips fut alors invité à se joindre à ce groupe informel[29]. Notons que Mgr Suenens était lui aussi, comme Van Roey, préoccupé d'un renouveau doctrinal plus actuel. C'est ainsi qu'il fonda à l'époque un *Institut des Sciences Religieuses* pour la formation religieuse des étudiants laïcs: cette initiative eut à souffrir des critiques sinon de l'opposition de certains professeurs de la Faculté. Le professeur Philips fut lui aussi chargé d'enseignement à ce nouvel Institut.

Plus tard, il paraissait vraisemblable que le rôle éminent que G. Philips a assumé à Vatican II allait contribuer à l'intégrer davantage parmi ses collègues. Son leadership évident à Rome ne pouvait que 'flatter' le milieu louvaniste. Et pourtant, il faut noter que le sentiment de malaise

---

27. Cf. GROOTAERS, *Diarium*, cahier n. 45, entretien avec le prof. R. Aubert, le 11 mars 1966.

28. Il faut rappeler ici qu'une tradition ancienne voulait que la Faculté de théologie n'acceptât en son sein aucun membre d'un ordre religieux: ni dominicain, ni jésuite (à l'exception d'un bénédictin)!

29. Dans un article nécrologique consacré à Philips, le professeur Coppens écrivait: «Philips eut l'occasion de rompre en partie cette situation quand le vice-recteur de l'époque (1940-1945), Léon Suenens, lui aussi *homo novus*, prit l'initiative de réunir mensuellement dans sa maison [...] quelques professeurs pour ce qu'il concevait comme des colloques théologiques. [...] Au départ de Mgr Suenens pour Malines, le professeur Philips continua les réunions chez lui...» (voir les *ETL* [1972] 325, n. 8).

que Philips ressent à l'égard de sa Faculté reste toujours vivace et s'exprime encore dans son *Journal* à la date du 5 mai 1963: «Je ne me sentirai probablement jamais chez moi à la Faculté de théologie de Louvain. Pourtant, avec un certain nombre de collègues, j'ai d'excellentes relations. Mais je ne puis approuver dans mon for intérieur la mentalité propre à l'ensemble. Dois-je 'accepter' cette mentalité? En tout cas, je dois essayer de la 'comprendre' [...] Cela est très difficile»[30]. Le théologien Philips était connu pour une triple spécialisation: 1. le renouveau de l'ecclésiologie; 2. le rôle du laïcat; et 3. la mariologie à laquelle il cherchait à donner une dimension christologique. Il faut y joindre aussi son intérêt, très tôt déjà, pour le mouvement œcuménique et sa participation aux Journées annuelles de Chevetogne. En général ses étudiants estimaient que Philips dans ses leçons orales donnait une théologie très ouverte et très dynamique: une ouverture qui généralement était moins présente dans les ouvrages qu'il publiait.

Enfin, G. Philips fut pendant de longues années (1953-1968) membre coopté du Sénat belge: une activité qu'il a voulu exercer de manière 'œcuménique' au-dessus des partis. Alors que certains collègues de la Faculté jugeaient ce cumul d'un œil très critique, Philips lui-même attachait un grand prix à ses contacts et à sa participation à un milieu aussi 'pluraliste' qu'une assemblée parlementaire[31]. On peut souligner ici que ces centres de réflexion et d'action pastorale de Philips constituaient une excellente préparation à la thématique que Vatican II allait mettre à son ordre du jour.

2. L'évolution d'un 'médiateur' à Vatican II

Lorsque le cardinal Suenens, peu après l'ouverture de Vatican II, demanda à Philips de rédiger une nouvelle version d'un schéma traitant de l'Église, c'est en tenant compte du *De ecclesia* de la période préparatoire, un texte qui, à ce moment-là, n'était pas encore apparu à l'ordre du jour de l'assemblée plénière. Il s'agissait donc de se placer dans une perspective de *médiation*.

---

30. K. SCHELKENS (éd.), *Carnets conciliaires de Mgr Gérard Philips, secrétaire adjoint de la commission doctrinale*. Texte néerlandais avec traduction française et commentaires (Instrumenta Theologica, 29), Louvain, Peeters, 2006, en date du 5 mai 1963 (Désormais cité Journal Philips).

31. Au cours d'une conversation avec Mlle. Rosa Philips, la sœur du professeur, celle-ci tint à nous confier que cette présence au Sénat belge avait pour le prêtre qu'était son frère une signification pastorale. Elle se disait convaincue que la vie parlementaire avait permis à son frère de rester étroitement lié à la «vie réelle». Ses relations amicales concernaient des sénateurs de toutes les tendances. Cf. GROOTAERS, *Diarium*, cahier n. 49, conversation du 10 août 1966.

Le professeur Philips s'efforce donc de prendre deux précautions: il ne veut pas d'un schéma de *substitution* qui viendrait d'un seul auteur ou d'une seule origine nationale (tel le schéma que des amis allemands avaient préparé) et d'autre part il a conscience de l'obligation de tenir compte du schéma préparatoire (de sorte que les minoritaires de bonne volonté puissent s'y retrouver)[32].

D'autres milieux conciliaires, plus tard, se préoccupent de rédiger des schémas de substitution: le cercle réuni à l'initiative des experts germanophones rédige au cours des premiers mois de 1963 un schéma sur la Révélation et un autre sur l'Église. Le groupe de Bologne révèle, lui aussi, une tendance *radicale* comparable. Mais ces milieux tiennent trop peu compte du calendrier d'abord de la Commission de coordination et ensuite de la Commission doctrinale, et ils arrivent trop tard. Cependant, une forte personnalité comme Karl Rahner se montre flexible et a toujours accepté de collaborer avec le groupe Philips-Congar soit pour le *De ecclesia* révisé soit, en septembre 1963, pour un texte introductif à un nouveau Schéma XVII: un groupe qui s'inspire de la perspective de 'médiation' du cardinal Suenens[33]. Cette attitude de médiation est, comme nous l'avons dit, une conséquence directe de la procédure de *conciliation* que Jean XXIII lui-même instaura après le vote négatif du 20 novembre 1962, concernant les sources de la Révélation. Cette initiative typique de Roncalli devient un *modèle* au cours des mois suivants.

Alors qu'au début de la deuxième période du Concile (octobre 1963) des voix critiques s'élevaient à l'égard du *De ecclesia* du groupe Philips, le théologien de Louvain tenait à rappeler que les membres du comité de rédaction avaient accepté à l'époque une responsabilité collective pour l'ensemble d'un *texte-mosaïque* de six auteurs différents et non pas d'un seul auteur! Il régnait alors une atmosphère de confusion et d'incertitude qui pesait sur tout le Concile et aussi sur le groupe rédactionnel de Philips. Cette atmosphère va se résorber avant la fin de la deuxième période de Vatican II.

---

32. À la première réunion de la Commission de coordination du 21 janvier 1963, le cardinal Suenens faisant rapport concernant le schéma ecclésiologique, prend encore la précaution de calmer les esprits alarmés, en démontrant que sept des onze chapitres du *De ecclesia* de la phase préparatoire sont récupérés en tout ou en partie dans le schéma récemment révisé. Cf. *AS* V/1, pp. 94-95. D'ailleurs, Suenens fera de même plus tard pour le Schéma XVII (puis Schéma XIII).

33. Dans une lettre à Philips, datée du 16 janvier 1963, Congar parle des remarques très intéressantes qu'il a reçues d'un excellent théologien, mais «impossibles à réaliser»; le concile ne veut pas donner un *De ecclesia* complet, qui ferait un bon cours. Cf. Fonds Philips, 0551.

Après le vote favorable des cinq questions le 30 octobre 1963 – un véritable tournant du Concile – et la réorganisation de la Commission doctrinale en neuf sous-commissions pour ventiler de nombreux changements de texte, Philips s'est métamorphosé: il retrouvait l'assurance qui lui était nécessaire pour faire progresser la procédure[34], dont les rouages allaient démontrer l'efficacité du Collège belge (même aux adversaires).

À la suite des difficultés du printemps de 1964 – notamment par les 13 suggestions de Paul VI, suggestions de tendance réductrice quant à la collégialité – la troisième période du Concile révélera que le leadership 'dynamique' de Philips a tendance à devenir 'statique'. Philips va devoir mettre en jeu tout le poids de son autorité pour freiner autant que possible le dépôt de *modi* afin de pouvoir 'garantir' l'approbation du texte en cause. Des évêques de la majorité conciliaire cherchaient à introduire des retouches favorables à une collégialité majorée, tandis que des représentants de la minorité tendaient à rouvrir un débat clos pour faire marche arrière. Lorsque l'approche de la *Nota praevia* rend l'atmosphère orageuse, il faut alors que Philips prenne des précautions au risque de mécontenter ses proches amis. Ce fut une crise profonde au sein de l'équipe belge.

L'exemple concret de Congar peut illustrer cette évolution. Au cours de l'intersession de 1962-1963, la stratégie d'un *texte-mosaïque* lui était apparue comme acceptable, mais en fin du parcours de la procédure il en découvre les inconvénients. Congar avait préparé avec soin une série de «modi» importants afin de rendre le *De ecclesia* plus proche de l'ecclésiologie orthodoxe. Il prend soin de diffuser ces propositions parmi les évêques «maximalistes». À deux reprises il découvre que d'abord Philips (fin octobre 1964) et ensuite Philips et Charue (mi-novembre 1964) refusent les *modi* en question. Du découragement Congar passe à l'indignation[35]. L'impatience et l'indignation de Congar sont compréhensibles

---

34. Cf. GROOTAERS, *Diarium*, n. 11 (conversation du 3 octobre 1963) et *Diarium*, n. 16 (conversation du 10 décembre 1963).

35. Cf. CONGAR, *Mon journal du Concile* (n. 15), Tome II, Paris, 2002, le 26 octobre 1964 (p. 227) et le 14 novembre 1964 (p. 267). À la fin du Concile, en date du 3 décembre, Congar, en relisant le chapitre *De populo Dei* de la constitution sur l'Église, prend tout à coup le mors aux dents contre Philips et Thils! Il écrit (p. 583): «Sous-commission *De populo dei*. Nous voyons cruellement, en faisant le travail de près, combien le *De ecclesia* et ce ch. *De populo dei* en particulier, souffrent de n'avoir jamais été CONÇUS. On a pris des morceaux ici et là; un ami de Philips, ayant l'oreille du cardinal Suenens, a introduit ici ou là l'idée qui lui chantait (ainsi le n. *De populo uno et universali*, introduit par Thils, et dont on ne voit ni la raison d'être, ni pourquoi il a été mis là): cela ne fait pas UN TEXTE! Philips a satisfait aux demandes *currente calamo*, avec une facilité déconcertante, ajoutant 'quelque chose' sur l'eucharistie ici, 'quelque chose' sur la mission là, 'quelque chose' sur la diversité des cultures ailleurs. J'ai ses fiches, écrites directement et presque sans rature. Mais c'est sans nerf, sans unité de pensée. Il n'y a pas UNE idée qui

lorsqu'on sait que la préparation de ces *modi* avait été un travail de longue haleine. L'initiative provenait de Congar lui-même dès juin 1964, mais avec l'aide de Dupuy qui lui avait fait part de ses objections contre le schéma *De ecclesia* de 'style belge': ces *modi* sont autant de corrections qui rapprochent le texte des conceptions ecclésiologiques de l'Orthodoxie. Les *modi* de Congar sont répandus à une grande échelle à partir du début de la troisième période du Concile[36].

Cependant, Congar reconnaît que la pression des anti-collégiaux et des «maximalistes en pouvoir papal» a été si forte que c'est surtout vers elle que Philips doit diriger ses efforts[37]. Mgr Philips a acquis une nouvelle autorité en commission à partir de novembre 1963. Cependant, à bref délai, il fera une autre expérience: le rôle de *possibiliste* qu'il assume est un sort peu enviable et particulièrement ingrat[38]. Il ne cesse d'être attaqué par différents milieux de *radicaux* et, d'autre part, son travail fait l'objet d'une vive animosité de la part de la minorité qui souvent fait alliance avec l'aile droite de la Curie contre lui.

3. La conception du Concile de Philips

Au cours d'une retraite que le théologien louvaniste entreprend au début d'août 1964, il désire faire une 'halte' et évaluer ses activités conciliaires. Au cours d'un entretien récent avec le cardinal Suenens, celui-ci l'a incité plusieurs fois à être plus combatif. Malgré son caractère réservé, Philips consacre plusieurs pages de son *Journal* au rôle qu'il a joué personnellement en commission e.a. concernant le schéma sur l'Église.

---

domine et distribue l'exposé». On est loin de la lune de miel d'octobre 1962 et loin de l'appréciation du *texte-mosaïque*.

36. Selon CONGAR, *Mon journal du Concile* (n. 15), Tome II, pp. 131-132, le père Duprey en diffuse 300 exemplaires et, d'autre part, le patriarche Maximos IV diffuse 400 exemplaires de ses «modi» très semblables à ceux de Congar.

37. Une étude systématique du *Journal* conciliaire du père Y. Congar pourrait révéler une bonne trentaine de passages si pas plus où il est question de sa collaboration quasi quotidienne avec l'équipe belge: son appréciation est généralement très positive, sauf dans une demi-douzaine de cas où la critique et un certain agacement prédominent. Le 13 mars 1964, il entreprend un véritable essai de cinq pages (1) sur les structures du groupe belge, et (2) sur l'esprit et l'action qui permettent ces structures. Cet essai élogieux se termine par des regrets de l'auteur, qu'aucune faculté de théologie de France n'ait pu avoir au Concile l'efficacité de Louvain. Cf. CONGAR, *Mon journal du Concile* (n. 15), Tome II, pp. 53-57.

38. Lorsque Suenens en 1987 reçoit un article critique de Bologne concernant Philips et la *Nota praevia*, il fait une annotation sarcastique sur 'l'ultradiplomatie de Mgr Philips', comme si lui-même n'y était pour rien! Cf. L. DECLERCK – E. LOUCHEZ, *Inventaire des Papiers conciliaires du cardinal L.-J. Suenens* (Cahiers de la Revue théologique de Louvain, 31), Louvain-la-Neuve, Publications de la Faculté de Théologie, 1998 [Fonds Suenens], 2831.

Il constate d'abord que tant la *droite* que la *gauche* ont fait appel à son travail et à son influence, surtout parce que ceux-ci étaient pratiquement 'anonymes'. Il poursuit:

> Mon intervention n'a pas été révolutionnaire et il y a très probablement des personnes qui le regrettent. J'ai visé la compréhension de la vérité – aussi large que possible – et l'accord – encore une fois aussi large que possible –, mais je n'ai pas réellement 'lutté'. Je veux dire: je n'ai jamais engagé le combat 'contre' quelqu'un, je me suis même efforcé de mon mieux pour qu'on n'engage pas le combat 'contre' quelqu'un. J'ai essayé de servir la Vérité qui est Notre Seigneur Jésus-Christ, y compris avec mes manquements. Certains de 'gauche' ou de 'droite' ont bien dit que j'étais trop indulgent. En tout cas, j'ai essayé de conserver la paix. Mais non la paix à tout prix. En tout cas, je n'ai rien dit ou défendu que je ne considérais pas comme vrai. Bref, j'ai essayé d'être honnête[39].

À la même page, le 'médiateur' Philips fait la considération suivante: «Quelque chose me frappe toujours chez les théologiens 'romains', à savoir qu'ils écoutent si peu. Ils savent tout et jugent tout à partir de leur conception qui se confond avec la foi. Tout se tient. Tout est absolu au même titre, car si on met quoi que ce soit en question, tout risque de s'effondrer. D'où la théologie de l'angoisse. Cependant, les théologiens de l'autre tendance se laissent aller à plusieurs reprises vers des déviations évidentes. Ce qui fournit alors [aux 'Romains'] un prétexte pour ne plus rien entendre». Quelques jours plus tard, Philips indique la véritable signification du Concile qu'il n'a pas manqué de défendre en de nombreuses circonstances:

> Le Concile ne doit pas effectuer le travail théologique proprement dit, mais indiquer la direction, ne pas couper inutilement les issues, garantir la liberté légitime, et apprendre à chaque croyant à prendre ses responsabilités personnelles devant Dieu. Pour faire valoir ses idées propres, personne ne peut se servir du Concile, ce qui reviendrait à en abuser. Cela ne correspond ni à l'humilité intellectuelle ni à la confiance de la foi. Nous nous trouvons dans la lumière, mais aussi dans l'ombre de la foi. La victoire par la foi provient de Dieu et non pas de notre capacité intellectuelle[40].

---

39. Journal Philips, à la date du 2 août 1964.
40. *Ibid.*, à la date du 10 août 1964. Au même endroit on peut lire: «On répond à une attaque par une contre-attaque, ce qui entraîne un cercle vicieux. Je pense que la largeur d'esprit et la concertation mènent plus loin et demeurent davantage dans la vérité. Est-ce une question de tempérament? Indéniablement, pour une part. Mais cette conduite est aussi fondée sur la certitude que la thèse défendue est exacte et aboutira finalement. Peut-être trop tard? Sans doute! Mais l'autre manière de procéder créera probablement encore plus d'immobilisme, ce qui donnera partiellement raison aux conservateurs».

III. Don Giuseppe Dossetti

Il va de soi que nous ne sommes pas en état ici d'évoquer la grande figure aux nombreuses faces du professeur et plus tard père Dossetti: juriste et canoniste, professeur à l'Université de Modena, membre de la Constituante et ensuite de la Chambre des Députés, vice-secrétaire de la Démocratie Chrétienne, quittant la vie politique en 1952 et universitaire en 1957, inspirateur d'un renouveau religieux dans l'Église d'Italie, fondateur du Centre de documentation à Bologne, proche collaborateur du cardinal Lercaro, un des leaders de Vatican II, et fondateur de communautés religieuses.

Pour les évêques et les experts qui, à l'ouverture de Vatican II, arrivèrent à Rome de l'Europe du Nord – selon l'expression consacrée –, l'archevêque de Bologne et l'*Institut des Sciences religieuses* de son diocèse étaient réputés comme de vrais représentants du renouveau ecclésial en Italie. On peut même dire plus: c'était le seul foyer *progressiste* connu des étrangers qui, peu à peu, au cours du Concile, allaient découvrir d'autres aspects dynamiques de l'Église italienne. C'est dire que, dès l'ouverture du Concile, le prestige de Bologne dans le milieu conciliaire de la 'majorité' fut exceptionnel. Même en nous limitant ici au rôle de Dossetti à Vatican II, nous ne pourrons qu'en tenter une brève esquisse. Heureusement, nous disposons à cet égard de plusieurs études, dont les synthèses du professeur Alberigo, qui sont d'une grande utilité. Ainsi qu'il est connu, Alberigo fut un disciple de Dossetti et devint son successeur à la direction de l'Institut des Sciences religieuses[41].

1. Un point de départ incertain

D'après les témoignages, la convocation d'un concile général par Jean XXIII fut pour le père Dossetti – ordonné prêtre quelques semaines auparavant – un événement significatif qui donna à son action une dynamique nouvelle. Au début de novembre 1962, il est appelé à Rome par le cardinal Lercaro comme *peritus* personnel de l'archevêque de Bologne. En décembre 1963, après avoir été secrétaire des modérateurs, il sera nommé expert officiel du Concile. Au cours de l'intersession 1962-1963, Dossetti

---

41. Cf. G. ALBERIGO, *Giuseppe Dossetti*, dans *Cristianesimo nella storia* 18 (1997) 264-275; ID., *Rinnovamento della Chiesa e partecipazione al concilio*, dans ID. (éd.), *Giuseppe Dossetti: Prime prospettive e ipotesi di ricerca*, Bologna, Il Mulino, 1998, 63-77. Voir aussi G. ALBERIGO, *L'esperienza conciliare di un vescovo*, dans G. LERCARO – G. ALBERIGO (éds.), *Per la forza dello Spirito: Discorsi conciliari del card. Giacomo Lercaro*, Bologna, Dehoniane, 1984, 9-62.

propose une révision du règlement du Concile, dont plusieurs suggestions seront acceptées par Paul VI et intégrées dans un règlement révisé.
La participation active de Dossetti à l'œuvre conciliaire va évidemment
varier selon les circonstances particulières de chacune des quatre périodes
et des 'inter-sessions'.

Les débuts de Vatican II se sont déroulés dans une grande confusion:
il fallait au Concile sortir de l'inertie initiale pour arriver à la formation
d'une véritable conscience conciliaire[42]. Il y avait en outre le chevau-
chement de textes concurrents: la transition des schémas préparatoires
aux schémas officiels révisés n'est pas toujours claire pour les participants du Concile. Certaines correspondances provenant de Bologne illus-
trent l'incertitude du nouveau point de départ. Le 31 janvier 1963, Alberigo adresse une invitation pressante au père Congar afin qu'il accepte de
collaborer à la rédaction d'un nouveau schéma *De ecclesia* sous la direction de Dossetti, en particulier les chapitres sur la nature de l'Église, sur
l'épiscopat et le magistère.

Le théologien français, plutôt embarrassé – car il a déjà collaboré au
projet Philips dès la mi-octobre 1962 –, répond entre autres qu'il connaît
déjà deux tentatives de rédaction d'un nouveau schéma *De ecclesia*:
d'abord celle de Mgr Philips, qui a le 'grand avantage de reproduire à
environ 80% les textes du schéma officiel', mais dans un autre ordre,
plus organique et en ajoutant des passages nouveaux (Congar annonce
qu'il adresse le projet Philips dans sa version du 1er décembre); ensuite
les (théologiens) allemands ont préparé un texte à la demande des évêques
de langue allemande, qui sera discuté par ceux-ci à Munich les 4-6 février
1963: ce texte biblique et très complet a l'inconvénient d'être long et un
peu scolaire, 'pas entièrement conciliaire de ton'[43]. Dans la seconde partie de cette lettre, Congar se déclare prêt à faire tout son possible pour que
les idées du cardinal Lercaro concernant l'Église et les pauvres aboutis-
sent à la deuxième période[44].

Quelques mois, plus tard (en date du 1er avril 1963), Mgr Carlo
Colombo s'excuse auprès de Don Giuseppe (Dossetti) de ne pas lui avoir

42. Voir le titre du tome II de G. ALBERIGO – E. FOUILLOUX (éd.), *Histoire du Concile
Vatican II*: *La formation de la conscience conciliaire (octobre 1962-septembre 1963)*,
Leuven, Peeters; Paris, Cerf, 1998.
43. La lettre de Congar démontre que celui-ci semble être déjà au courant de la liste
des 17 schémas établie le 27 janvier par la Commission de coordination: selon cette liste,
le nouveau *De ecclesia* (de 4 chapitres) relèvera de la compétence du cardinal Suenens.
44. Voir les Archives du Centrum voor Conciliestudie Vaticanum II à Louvain:
«Dossier Y. Congar».

encore rendu visite. Il ne lui a pas non plus envoyé le texte de Parente (il s'agit d'un schéma *De ecclesia*), car il n'était pas autorisé à le faire et, de plus, il savait que ce projet était abandonné. Il est uniquement adopté comme texte de base dans la discussion du texte Philips, mais non dans ses points particuliers[45]. Fin mai 1963, le père Dossetti fait part à Mgr Carlo Colombo de ses objections à l'égard de la nouvelle version du *De ecclesia* (du groupe Philips):

> Il s'agit d'un texte 'trop politique' une mosaïque de manœuvres diplomatiques parfois naïves. Il n'y a plus les 'grands points' du schéma précédent, mais l'inspiration, le cadre mental sont toujours les mêmes. [...] De plus, il reste encore trois points d'étranglement inacceptables: même Mgr Philips, dont la tactique politicienne a tant prévalu, en est bien convaincu. Nous avons parlé longuement et il a dû reconnaître que la présentation que nous proposons n'a rien de maximaliste. [...] *Mieux vaut un silence complet que des phrases équivoques et compromettantes*[46].

2. Critiques d'ordre radical

Lorsque le premier débat du schéma *De ecclesia*, dans sa version révisée, va se déployer en octobre 1963, les critiques du père Dossetti vont être radicales, c'est-à-dire qu'elles exigent un texte qui partirait des *racines* de l'ecclésiologie. On en trouve des échos dans le grand exposé que Lercaro fait in aula le 3 octobre 1963.

Dans une longue note dont les éditeurs des discours conciliaires de Lercaro ont publié des extraits, Dossetti fait d'abord une remarque sévère sur la genèse de la révision:

> Le nouveau schéma *De ecclesia* n'est pas le résultat d'une nouvelle *réflexion radicale* sur le sujet, mais il est en majeure partie le résultat typique du système des ciseaux et de la colle, c'est-à-dire qu'il a été obtenu en opérant d'abord un démantèlement de l'ancien schéma en petits morceaux (souvent une phrase seulement ou même une demi-phrase), en éliminant toute une série de petits morceaux et en emboîtant les autres (parfois d'une manière phraséologiquement discordante). Il en a résulté un ensemble plus acceptable,

---

45. Archives de l'Istituto per le scienze religiose à Bologne, Fonds Dossetti, II.151. Il n'est pas sans intérêt de noter que Colombo et Dossetti étaient liés d'une longue amitié. Déjà pendant la guerre (1940-1945), ils faisaient tous deux partie du 'gruppo di casa Padovani' avec Lazzati, Fanfani et autres précurseurs du renouveau de l'après-guerre. Cf. G. Trotta, *Giuseppe Dossetti – la rivoluzione nello Stato*, Genova, Marietti, 1996, pp. 17-21.

46. Fonds Dossetti, X/1. Voir A. Melloni, *Procedure e coscienza conciliare al Vaticano II*, dans *Cristianesimo nella storia. Saggi in onore di G. Alberigo*, Bologna, Il Mulino, 1996, p. 316, note 6. Voir aussi Congar, *Mon journal du Concile* (n. 15), Tome I, pp. 361-362, conversation avec Don Dossetti en date du 14 mai 1963.

mais non pas plus solide et plus fort du point de vue des concepts: plutôt que d'offrir une vision cohérente et inspirée du mystère de l'Église, il présente en effet une suite d'*équilibres tactiques entre des courants de pensée opposés*. Cette manière de faire n'a rien de modéré [...]; au contraire, ces enchaînements d'équilibres tactiques apparaissent comme un procédé *abusif*, surérogatoire, qui risque de faire considérer ce texte comme déjà dépassé avant même qu'il ne vienne au jour (un texte qui est dépassé et en partie contredit par les autres schémas proposés, par exemple par le schéma *De oecumenismo*).

Dossetti, dans cette note, regrette le manque de relief donné à la dimension sacramentelle en tant que fondement de toute la structure de l'Église[47]. Par la suite, il ne peut accepter le rapport entre l'Église et le corps mystique du Christ tel qu'il se trouve défini dans le schéma révisé:

> Il ne suffit pas de dire que l'Église et le corps mystique sont le même sujet, si l'on n'ajoute pas aussitôt que cela est vrai seulement d'un point de vue essentiel et dans la disposition constituée par son divin fondateur, et que cela ne se vérifie pas pleinement sur terre dans l'ordre existentiel et à travers les différentes situations historiques. L'identité et l'unité plénière sont une identité et une unité de droit destinées à ne s'accomplir pleinement qu'à la fin de l'histoire, alors qu'aujourd'hui sur terre elles subissent encore des tensions et des réalisations imparfaites et seulement partielles[48].

Enfin, si Dossetti reconnaît qu'un progrès évident a été réalisé entre l'ancien schéma et le nouveau, il se dit obligé de signaler de graves omissions qui ont des répercussions sur des aspects essentiels du mystère de l'Église, dont l'omission de l'image de l'Église comme maison (*oikos*) et comme famille de Dieu[49]. En 1964, l'opposition au schéma *De ecclesia* atteint un point culminant lorsque finalement Paul VI impose à la Commission doctrinale une *Nota explicativa praevia* qui répond à la crainte obsessionnelle du pape de voir sa liberté de décision un tant soit peu diminuée.

Le 15 novembre 1964, G. Dossetti adresse une requête aux accents dramatiques à son ami Carlo Colombo, qui, à l'époque, est devenu un des principaux conseillers du pape. Il y exprime d'abord sa profonde amertume à la lecture de la *Relatio* (de la Commission) et de la *Nota praevia*.

---

47. Note de G. Dossetti, Sullo schema *De ecclesia*, dans Fonds Dossetti, 4.422bis (17 pages): parties citées pp. 2 et 3-5: voir ALBERIGO – LERCARO (éds.), *Per la forza dello Spirito* (n. 41), p. 184, note 3 (notre traduction de l'italien).
48. G. Dossetti, Sullo schema *De ecclesia*, dans Fonds Dossetti, 4.422bis, pp. 3-10: voir ALBERIGO – LERCARO (éds.), *Per la forza dello Spirito* (n. 41), p. 185, note 5 (notre traduction de l'italien).
49. Note de G. Dossetti, Sullo schema *De ecclesia*, dans Fonds Dossetti, 4.422bis, pp. 5-7: voir ALBERIGO – LERCARO (éds.), *Per la forza dello Spirito* (n. 41), p. 190, note 18 (notre traduction de l'italien).

L'étude approfondie de ces documents de la dernière heure l'a incité à s'y opposer. Il est indigné de constater que le texte du schéma qui a refusé toutes les améliorations les plus raisonnables suggérées par la majorité, a accueilli uniquement des amendements équivoques[50]. Tout le monde comprendra que c'est là un résultat purement tactique et que ce n'est pas par pareilles voies que l'Église pourra réussir à dire au monde avec clarté qui elle est. Nous ne citerons ici que la finale de ce long message:

> Je crois que – vu la part que vous y avez prise – vous ne pouvez pas ne pas communiquer au Saint-Père quels ont été les sentiments concrets de beaucoup: s'ils sont prêts à reconnaître que le pape doit garder dans certaines occasions la possibilité de faire valoir son avis, ils n'accepteront de le reconnaître que si les voies qui ont été utilisées pour l'exprimer sont les plus claires et les plus responsables, les plus persuasives et surtout les plus aptes à garantir les prérogatives et le prestige de l'Autorité suprême. Cher don Carlo, je vous prie au nom de notre vieille amitié, de ne pas commettre l'erreur qu'ont commise, il y a quelques jours, les conseillers du Saint-Père à propos du schéma sur les Missions: c'est-à-dire de croire que l'embarras d'aujourd'hui soit seulement l'embarras de quelqu'un d'isolé ou d'une minorité. Même si – sous la pression des événements et quasi par crainte du pire – la plupart s'adapteront à un moindre mal, il est certain que beaucoup garderont une impression négative et décourageante. [...] Je n'hésiterais pas à répéter personnellement ces propos au Saint-Père: sans hésitation intérieure, avec un plein respect, mais aussi avec une franchise religieuse.

> J'ai célébré pour lui la Sainte Messe hier et aujourd'hui, et je continuerai à faire de même jusqu'au 21[51].

3. Évaluations post-conciliaires plus nuancées

Au cours de l'évolution conciliaire du schéma rénové *De ecclesia*, l'attitude de Don Dossetti traverse une phase de critiques sévères et parfois radicales. Mais après la clôture de Vatican II, le même auteur prend des positions à certains égards moins intransigeantes et finalement très nuancées. Fort heureusement, plusieurs de ces évaluations qui s'étendent de novembre 1966 à octobre 1994 ont été publiées en un recueil sous le

---

50. On se rappellera ici l'aventure subie par Congar qui avait consacré tant d'énergie et de temps à une série de propositions que Philips et Charue refusèrent de prendre en considération. Dossetti lui-même avait préparé une quinzaine de remarques et propositions qui couvrent 28 pages, et qui, si elles ont été effectivement introduites, ne paraissent pas avoir influencé la rédaction finale. Voir Fonds Dossetti, III.296 (textes datés du 22 avril 1963 à mars 1964).

51. Fonds Dossetti, II.100, 2 pp.: voir G. ALBERIGO, *L'episcopato al Vaticano II*, dans *Cristianesimo nella storia* 8 (1987) 147-163 (notre traduction de l'italien).

titre *Il Vaticano II. Frammenti di una riflessione*, Bologna, Il Mulino, 1996, 237 pp.[52].

Nous nous arrêterons aux deux premiers textes de ce recueil: 1. '*Per una valutazione globale del magistero del Vaticano II*', octobre 1966 (p. 23-102), et 2. '*Alcune linee dinamiche del contributo del Card. G. Lercaro al Concilio ecumenico Vaticano II*', octobre 1991 (pp. 103-190). Pour ce dernier texte, nous disposons aussi de la publication dans *Il Regno*, 21/1991, 1ᵉʳ décembre 1991, pp. 694-706. Dans le premier de ces deux commentaires, le chapitre consacré à *Lumen gentium* débute par des considérations consacrées aux points dynamiques du texte promulgué: l'approche globale de l'Église en tant que 'mystère' et en tant que 'peuple'; le concept du sacerdoce commun est aussi de la plus grande importance. Reste l'interrogation de l'auteur: dans quelle mesure ce texte avec ses qualités et ses défauts sera-t-il capable de stimuler et même de dominer le développement de l'ecclésiologie dans les prochaines décennies? Ceux qui ont dirigé la rédaction du *De ecclesia* ont, selon Dossetti, suivi par ailleurs une *voie minimaliste* à cause de leur erreur de jugement quant aux virtualités que le Concile aurait pu réaliser.

Ce fut donc une 'grande occasion manquée' d'avoir sous-estimé les possibilités d'aller de l'avant. Pareil jugement *post factum* de Don Dossetti n'a pas de base rationnelle. Il nous paraît difficile de 'refaire' l'histoire a posteriori, alors que maintenant le dénouement nous est connu. La position *possibiliste* de personnalités comme Congar, Martimort, Tucci, Philips e.a., ou comme Suenens, Charue, McGrath, Heuschen e.a., devait tenir compte des initiatives incessantes de la minorité, qui d'ailleurs à partir de 1964 se trouva renforcée par la relève d'une génération plus jeune; par ailleurs, il paraissait difficile d'échapper entièrement aux pressions ambiguës et répétées de Paul VI aux moments charnières de la procédure.

Des six points qui, aux yeux de Dossetti, ont affaibli le texte du *De ecclesia*, il y en a trois qui amènent l'auteur à souligner le *minimalisme* de la tendance des médiateurs. Il s'agit de l'absence d'une véritable pneumatologie qui a hypothéqué de nombreux aspects de l'image de l'Église (3ᵉ point). La négligence du rapport entre l'Église visible et l'Église invisible a eu, elle aussi, des répercussions regrettables (4ᵉ point). La faiblesse d'une théologie de l'Église locale a empêché *Lumen gentium* de se développer de manière structurée et a empêché d'éviter la crise de

---

52. On regrettera que ces évaluations n'aient pas été publiées en traduction française ou anglaise. Il faut remarquer qu'en 1987 le prof. Alberigo prend encore appui sur le Dossetti de novembre 1964 et semble ignorer le Dossetti post-conciliaire. Cf. ALBERIGO, *L'episcopato al Vaticano II* (n. 51), pp. 161-162.

l'absence de lien avec la christologie (6ᵉ point). Il est vrai que ce sont là des lacunes regrettables dont les conséquences se sont fait sentir après Vatican II. Le *possibilisme* qui se trouve ici incriminé était, aux yeux des acteurs principaux de l'époque, un moyen d'éviter l'échec de l'entreprise à cause d'une majorité de votes insuffisante.

La suite de ces considérations nous livre des analyses qui apprécient de manière positive les aspects principaux de la constitution comme, par exemple, les développements concernant l'épiscopat[53].

Il va de soi que la seconde évaluation dont nous allons parler maintenant présente un intérêt particulier du fait qu'elle fut entreprise en octobre 1991 et prend en compte une tranche décisive de l'après-concile. De ce fait, elle nous confronte notamment aux 'appropriations réductrices' qui caractérisent le pontificat de Jean Paul II[54]. Le paragraphe de cette évaluation qui traite du schéma *De ecclesia* rappelle le sort de quelques amendements proposés par Lercaro pour le schéma Philips. Dossetti caractérise celui-ci comme étant 'un théologien de Louvain, sénateur coopté du Sénat belge, homme de *médiation* et doté d'un bon talent de diplomate'[55]. Au cours de la discussion conciliaire au sujet de l'incorporation dans l'Église par le baptême et la profession de foi, le cardinal Lercaro proposa de nouveaux arguments pour appuyer la doctrine selon laquelle le baptême seul, reçu de manière valide – comme prévu entre autres par la bulle d''Union avec les Arméniens' au Concile de Florence et lors de la XIVᵉ session du Concile de Trente – confère la pleine communion. Dossetti souligne le fait que les arguments développés sont expressément repris par Philips, cités comme dignes de considération dans son histoire de *Lumen gentium*[56].

Il n'en va pas de même pour un autre amendement de Lercaro dans sa fameuse intervention *in aula* du 3 octobre 1963. L'archevêque de Bologne se déclara alors opposé à l'affirmation simple et absolue de l'*identité* entre le corps mystique du Christ et la réalité visible de l'Église catholique, précisant que pareille affirmation pouvait conduire et avait de fait

53. Cf. *Il Vaticano II. Frammenti di una riflessione*, Bologna, Il Mulino, 1996, pp. 60-65.

54. G. DOSSETTI, *Alcune linee dinamiche del contributo del Card. G. Lercaro al Concilio ecumenico Vaticano II*, dans *Il Vaticano II* (n. 53), pp. 103-190.

55. L'auteur n'évalue pas personnellement la valeur du «schéma Philips», mais se contente de reprendre une description qu'il emprunte aux *Souvenirs* de Suenens: «une ecclésiologie de communion centrée sur le mystère de l'Église considéré dans ses profondeurs trinitaires».

56. G. PHILIPS, *L'Église et son mystère au deuxième Concile du Vatican. Histoire, texte et commentaire de la constitution 'Lumen Gentium'*, 2 Tomes, Paris, Cerf, 1967-1968, Tome I, p. 24.

conduit à des déclarations unilatérales[57]. Cette fois, Dossetti souligne le refus de l'amendement proposé:

> En ce qui concerne l'identification de l'Église catholique avec le corps du Christ, Philips proposa et défendit avec ténacité au Concile une autre formule qui n'affirme plus 'que l'Église du Christ *est* la communauté catholique', mais qui affirme 'que l'Église du Christ *subsistit in*, c'est-à-dire est présente *dans l'Église catholique*'. En d'autres termes, comme l'ajoute Philips dans son commentaire de *Lumen Gentium*, c'est là, dans l'Église catholique, que nous trouvons l'Église du Christ dans toute sa plénitude et dans toute sa force, comme saint Paul dit du Christ ressuscité qu'il est constitué Fils de Dieu *en dunamei* (Rom 1,4)[58].

Dossetti ajoute ici la remarque – qui, selon nous, est erronée – que «le même Philips, quelques années après le Concile, semble moins convaincu à propos de cette formule», car dans son commentaire de *Lumen gentium* il écrit «que la formule *subsistit in* fera couler beaucoup d'encre». Cette dernière expression signifie uniquement que Philips, déjà en 1967, prévoyait que la discussion n'était pas tarie; une prédiction qui s'est réalisée quinze ans plus tard lors de la longue polémique entre le cardinal Ratzinger et le cardinal Willebrands, ce dernier prenant la défense de l'interprétation de Philips en ce qui concerne le '*subsistit in*'.

4. La conception du Concile de Dossetti

Dans un chapitre consacré au cardinal Lercaro, Don Dossetti constate combien la participation au Concile a apporté à l'archevêque «un enrichissement et une dilatation» de sa vie pastorale et a davantage encore favorisé sa vie intérieure, particulièrement au niveau de sa prière personnelle. En approfondissant ainsi la signification du Concile, l'auteur rappelle les différents aspects de cet enrichissement[59]. Mais quant à la conception du Concile lui-même, qui est évoquée comme premier point, Dossetti rappelle que, selon Lercaro, la célébration du Concile est un fait de l'Esprit. Le Concile n'est pas seulement source de créations juridiques mais il constitue une vaste et unique célébration liturgique qui va au-delà

---

57. Voir le commentaire de DOSSETTI, *Alcune linee dinamiche del contributo del Card. G. Lercaro* (n. 54), p. 120.

58. *Ibid.*, p. 122.

59. Cf. G. DOSSETTI, *Memoria di Giacomo Lercaro*, dans G. ALBERIGO (éd.), *Chiese italiane e Concilio*, Genova, Marietti, 1988, 300-304: entre autres, la révision de l'*Ordo Concilii* accepté par Paul VI, la conception de l'ecclésiologie, l'option en faveur d'une théologie autre que celle des documents préparatoires, la collégialité épiscopale et la relation de celle-ci avec la primauté.

des différentes normes promulguées: il est donc une réalité charismatique, un véritable événement de l'Esprit Saint[60].

Cette conception très élevée du Concile impose des exigences et des impératifs de haut niveau. Que ceux-ci ne soient pas facilement acceptés ni même compris par un grand nombre de pères conciliaires entraîne l'équipe de Bologne à des déceptions. À l'occasion de plusieurs grandes interventions *in aula* du cardinal Lercaro – interventions préparées avec l'aide de Don Dossetti –, l'équipe a le sentiment que l'archevêque de Bologne a parfois buté contre un mur d'indifférence ou même d'incompréhension. Il y a notamment trois grands discours qui, aux yeux des Bolognais, n'ont pas reçu l'audience qu'ils méritaient:

a. La proposition du cardinal Lercaro – à la conclusion de la première période conciliaire – de choisir la problématique de l'Église et de la pauvreté comme thème central et perspective générale de l'ecclésiologie;
b. La relation de l'Église et de la culture dans le cadre du Schéma XIII (début novembre 1964);
c. L'intervention en faveur d'une condamnation de la guerre du Schéma XIII et un engagement radical en faveur de la paix (intervention par écrit en novembre 1965).

En ce qui concerne la première proposition de Lercaro (autour de la pauvreté comme thématique centrale du Concile), celle-ci, malgré l'émotion suscitée dans la salle conciliaire, n'a pas eu d'impact sur les travaux et s'est ensablée dans l'inertie des consciences. G. Alberigo, regrettant cet échec, a écrit à ce sujet qu'*une fin de non-recevoir courtoise mais ferme a été opposée par la majorité 'progressiste' du Concile* et a préfiguré le manque d'accueil que d'autres tentatives de Lercaro destinées à élargir l'horizon du Concile allaient subir par la suite[61].

5. Une minorité au sein de la majorité

Selon le même auteur, les deux propositions qui avaient trait au Schéma XIII n'ont pas non plus eu d'influence sur la rédaction finale de la constitution pastorale. Alberigo en a conclu que situer Lercaro dans la

---

60. Dès avant la première réunion du Concile, l'archevêque Lercaro a présenté le Concile à plusieurs occasions – et, en particulier, aux curés de Bologne – comme un ressourcement de l'Église, «de sa vie et de sa finalité, répondant avec un nouvel élan au plan divin tracé par le Seigneur». C'est là une conception qui permet de dépasser la fausse opposition entre une Église une et immuable et d'autre part une Église qui, dans son histoire, a la capacité de répondre également au projet de Dieu dans le Christ. En cela, Lercaro correspondait particulièrement à l'intuition du pape Jean.

61. ALBERIGO, *L'esperienza conciliare* (n. 41), pp. 21-22. C'est nous qui soulignons.

géographie de Vatican II n'est pas chose aisée. Alors qu'il a été un leader du Concile, ses prises de position différentes de celles de la majorité
lui valurent de l'admiration plutôt qu'un consensus. Son rôle semble avoir
été celui d'être *una minoranza nel seno della maggioranza conciliare*,
avec la position d'un out-sider qui guide[62].

Plus tard, le même auteur a décrit comment Dossetti a, pour sa part,
pris contact avec le Concile de manière quasi accidentelle et comme un
«franc-tireur», selon ses propres paroles[63]. Quant à la position de Dossetti, le professeur Alberigo estime que celui-ci a vécu le Concile non
comme un 'projet' mais comme une attitude d'obéissance créative à
l'égard d'une occasion donnée par l'Esprit:

> Avec audace et réalisme, il a, en de nombreuses occasions cruciales, exprimé
> *la 'frontière' la plus avancée de la majorité et en payant souvent le prix de
> l'isolement*, ainsi que lors de la proposition de la pauvreté de l'Église et du
> refus de la guerre[64].

Dans un commentaire – écrit en octobre 1991 – Don Dossetti prend à
nouveau en considération les propositions de Lercaro qui n'ont pas été
reprises dans le texte définitif de *Gaudium et spes*:

> Il y en a qui croient que ces énoncés [de Lercaro] ont été écartés par le
> Concile comme une position de pointe d'un *utopiste inguérissable et isolé*.
> En réalité, ils correspondaient exactement à l'opinion de nombreux pères

---

62. *Ibid.*, p. 59.
63. Cf. ALBERIGO, *Giuseppe Dossetti* (n. 41), p. 67. Cette thématique d'un rôle en
quelque sorte 'marginal' à Vatican II a récemment été analysée par Nikolaus Klein en
conclusion d'un article consacré à l'officine de Bologne. L'auteur remarque que Don Dossetti au Concile était toujours disposé à prendre des initiatives qui le plaçaient en marge
de la majorité comme, par exemple, la proposition de traiter de l'Église de manière radicale comme Église des pauvres. Et aussi le fait d'exiger que le Concile prononce une
condamnation majeure de la guerre comme moyen de la politique. Le père Klein en tire
une conclusion intéressante: 'Que la majorité conciliaire ne l'ait pas suivi à cet égard n'a
pas été compris par lui comme une défaite de son ambition personnelle mais comme une
exigence de reprendre à nouveau des démarches fatigantes afin d'aller à l'encontre des défis
actuels' (N. KLEIN, *Glaube in Geschichte*, dans *Orientierung* 69 [2005] 39). En d'autres
termes, lorsque la majorité ne prend pas en compte une proposition de Dossetti, c'est celui-
ci qui a raison et la majorité qui a tort.
64. ALBERIGO, *Giuseppe Dossetti* (n. 41), p. 76. Notre traduction de l'italien (c'est nous
qui avons souligné). À la fin de septembre 1965, Don Dossetti lui-même s'exprime.
Il adresse au cardinal Lercaro un premier projet de l'intervention que celui-ci va consacrer à 'la paix de l'évangile' (octobre 1965). Il y joint une lettre commentant ce projet:
«Il faut dire un mot qui clarifie toutes les prémisses théologiques et qui évite, me semble-
t-il, des équivoques possibles dans les interprétations de notre attitude entre deux foyers
(les conservateurs et les progressistes). Enfin, pour rendre plus aisée et plus acceptable la
conclusion même du problème de la guerre». Le texte de cette lettre se trouve en note dans
ALBERIGO – LERCARO, *Per forza dello Spirito* (n. 41), pp. 253-254, note 2.

conciliaires et particulièrement de quelques personnalités des plus remarquables de l'assemblée conciliaire et ayant une stature spirituelle, théologique et pastorale majeure. [...] Toutes ces voix furent unanimes pour réclamer de manière catégorique la condamnation de toute guerre, même défensive, et le rejet des armes atomiques[65].

La conception très élevée du Concile comme une vaste célébration qui est le fait de l'Esprit Saint semble apparaître comme une toile de fond du radicalisme qui a inspiré plusieurs propositions de l'équipe de Bologne: c'est ici au moins une hypothèse de travail.

Plusieurs des témoignages que nous venons de citer révèlent que les propositions du cardinal Lercaro et de Don Dossetti ont pu émouvoir l'assemblée conciliaire mais que, finalement et à plusieurs reprises, elles ont reçu «une fin de non-recevoir courtoise mais ferme».

IV. Collaborateurs du cardinal Suenens

Faut-il admettre que les oppositions au sein de la majorité conciliaire peuvent être dépassées par certains dirigeants capables de faire du 'survol' grâce à leur leadership?

Tel semble être le cas du cardinal Suenens qui, dès l'ouverture de Vatican II, est un proche de la tendance des *médiateurs* et en même temps établira une collaboration suivie avec des *intransigeants* notoires.

L'archevêque de Malines-Bruxelles nous présente un aspect du Concile qui n'est pas sans intérêt. Avec Philips, il établit une collaboration durable et efficace. Tous deux appartiennent à la même *squadra*. S'il y a parfois quelques difficultés entre les deux, c'est à cause de tensions entre caractères différents et des dissensions du passé. Les collaborations de G. Dossetti et H. Küng avec Suenens sont évidemment d'un autre ordre.

1. Pas de vies parallèles

Les figures de Gérard Philips et de Giuseppe Dossetti ne se prêtent pas à des 'vies parallèles' à la Plutarque. Cependant, tous les deux ont une vie spirituelle profonde qui est le fondement de leur existence. Les carrières, elles, sont très différentes: celle de Philips témoigne d'une ligne

---

65. DOSSETTI, *Alcune linee dinamiche del contributo del Card. G. Lercaro* (n. 54), pp. 180-181. Parmi les personnalités invoquées par l'auteur se trouvent Alfrink (Utrecht), Léger (Montréal), Liénart (Lille), Duval (Alger) et Bouillon (Verdun), qui parlait au nom de 80 évêques de divers pays. Le cardinal Ottaviani donna également son appui, soulignant qu'aujourd'hui toute guerre est à proscrire absolument.

double – réflexion théologique et engagement pastoral – mais cette ligne est continue, homogène et plus conventionnelle. Celle de Dossetti est évidemment plus brillante mais tissée de nombreux changements de cap et même de brusques ruptures. Don Dossetti a un don personnel qui exerce un pouvoir charismatique évident, tandis que Philips fut l'animateur fidèle de cadres institutionnels. Au Concile apparaît clairement l'opposition entre ces tempéraments différents.

Parlant du *schéma Philips*, Dossetti le qualifie et le disqualifie en soulignant son caractère 'diplomatique' ou 'tactique', ce qui n'est guère flatteur pour un texte théologique. Quant à Philips, apprenant que l'*Avvenire d'Italia* de Bologne publiait un article violent, inspiré par Dossetti, il fait la remarque: «Je n'ai pas lu cette prose de Don Dossetti, qui est un juriste particulièrement dur»[66]. Au cours d'une entrevue Philips-Dossetti chez Congar en mai 1963, celui-ci constate: «Il y a des gens devant qui Philips est braqué»[67]. Tout de suite, au Concile, Philips est considéré comme un excellent *médiateur*: lui-même se veut une figure du *centre*. Dossetti se sent appelé à être à *l'avant-garde*[68]. Sa réputation sera plutôt d'être un intransigeant[69], n'ayant pas toujours conscience des circonstances concrètes dans lesquelles un concile est appelé à fonctionner. Selon les usages de tout bon parlementaire, Philips s'oppose à des *adversaires*, mais ceux-ci ne sont pas des *ennemis*.

Dossetti se trouve souvent *incompris* et parfois même *marginalisé*, mais souvent une telle position paraît le confirmer dans des convictions que les autres n'ont pas pu accepter!

2. G. Philips mis au travail par le cardinal Suenens

À l'inauguration de Vatican II, on ressentit au Collège belge la nécessité de travailler en équipe. Prignon et Heuschen estiment que Suenens devrait mettre Philips au travail sans plus attendre. C'est avec l'accord de l'épiscopat belge que Suenens demande alors à Philips de rédiger une révision du schéma préparatoire sur l'Église sans attendre que celui-ci soit mis à l'ordre du jour du Concile[70].

---

66. Notes pour servir à l'histoire de la *Nota praevia*, p. 83.
67. Congar, *Mon journal du Concile* (n. 15), Tome II, p. 52.
68. Ou «à la *frontière* la plus avancée de la majorité», selon la formule déjà citée de G. Alberigo.
69. Comme nous l'avons indiqué, il ne s'agit pas ici du sens *dérivé* de ce terme dans les tensions idéologiques du XIXᵉ siècle (en France et en Italie). Il s'agit de la signification *première*: «celui qui refuse de transiger» (selon le dictionnaire *Robert*).
70. Le père Congar participe activement aux travaux du groupe rédactionnel de Philips et en suit les étapes dans Congar, *Mon journal du Concile* (n. 15), Tome I, à partir

Mais même dans ces circonstances exceptionnelles les rapports directs de Suenens avec Philips sont parfois difficiles. L'archevêque de Malines-Bruxelles, qui avait besoin de l'aide de théologiens, demandait fréquemment des avis à des 'jeunes' plus proches comme Thils, Moeller ou Prignon. Peut-être était-il mal à l'aise et quelque peu intimidé devant la compétence d'un contemporain comme Philips[71].

Il y eut entre eux quelques incidents au début de Vatican II, mais grâce aux fonctions d'intermédiaire exercées avec beaucoup de doigté par le recteur Prignon – véritable 'agent de liaison' de Suenens et lui-même ami de Philips – on réussit à aplanir des difficultés. Les relations avec Thils comme collègue de Philips et prêtre du diocèse de Malines, proche de Suenens, furent également utiles[72]. Enfin, les rouages du Collège belge n'avaient pas le droit de s'enrayer: aussi bien le cardinal Suenens que le professeur Philips en étaient des pièces irremplaçables car très efficaces.

3. G. Dossetti, secrétaire des modérateurs et expert de Suenens

Les nombreux emprunts que le *De ecclesia* révisé du groupe rédactionnel de Philips avait faits au schéma préparatoire – selon le plan de Suenens et avec l'appui de Jean XXIII – furent et restèrent pendant longtemps l'objet des principaux griefs de la tendance qui refusait de transiger et qui parfois avait l'ambition de proposer un texte de substitution qui serait nouveau[73].

---

du 18 octobre, pp. 119ss. Des groupes parallèles se réunissent entre autres à l'initiative de Mgr Volk: Congar en rend compte également à la même période de son *Journal*.

71. Dans une recension du livre de Suenens sur la Légion de Marie, Philips s'était senti autorisé à remarquer que l'auteur de l'ouvrage n'était apparemment pas théologien!

72. À la clôture de la première période du Concile, Philips rentre chez lui profondément meurtri. Son travail entrepris à la demande de Suenens et de l'épiscopat belge avait été sérieusement attaqué par la «vieille garde» (même en la séance plénière du 1er décembre 1962 par Ottaviani!). Il eût été normal que Suenens prenne sa défense, mais il n'en fit rien ou il le fit trop tard. Il s'en plaint dans Journal Philips, p. 11: «Cet incident a été des plus pénibles pour moi. Le cardinal Ottaviani disait: '*Audiant omnes*' bien avant que le texte *De Ecclesia* fût rendu public, il y avait déjà un autre texte qui était répandu! À ce moment-là il devait normalement avoir connaissance de ma réponse au P. Gagnebet [qui fut écrite avec l'accord explicite du cardinal Suenens]. Il n'en a sûrement pas saisi le contenu. En tout cas il décrit mon travail comme un procédé déloyal et inacceptable. Je ne puis me justifier: nous n'avons ni droit à la parole ni possibilité de parler. On invoque bien la présence de nombreux théologiens étrangers pour faire l'éloge de l'ancien schéma, mais on ne mentionne pas les objections d'un bon nombre de ces mêmes théologiens contre le texte officiel. [...] C'est ainsi que nous sommes prisonniers d'une situation trouble. On fait appel à notre autorité et on tait nos objections». C'est après le retour en Belgique que Prignon fit une démarche auprès de Suenens et que celui-ci chargea Thils de rétablir le contact avec Philips.

73. À l'époque, Y. Congar aussi estime que le projet d'un schéma de substitution est une utopie dans les circonstances présentes. Il y revient à plusieurs reprises dans son

Les relations amicales de Suenens avec Lercaro vont s'affermir dès septembre 1963 lorsque Paul VI instaura un collège de quatre modérateurs – dont l'un et l'autre font partie – pour «diriger les assemblées conciliaires» (lettre de Cicognani du 9 septembre 1963). Dossetti en devient tout naturellement le secrétaire: Suenens et Dossetti partagent la même préoccupation de prévoir un statut reconnu et un règlement pour les modérateurs afin d'établir clairement leurs compétences[74].

Dans le contexte des polarités existantes, on ne s'attendait pas à trouver une collaboration significative entre Suenens et Dossetti. L'importance que le cardinal belge attachait à la perspective pastorale de Vatican II et le souci qu'il montrait à réintroduire de nombreux éléments des schémas préparatoires dans les textes révisés, auraient pu être un obstacle difficile à contourner pour Don Dossetti. Nous ne trouvons cependant aucune trace de pareille difficulté. Il faut réaliser ici combien la personnalité brillante et très forte de Dossetti a dû, dès les débuts des contacts, faire impression sur l'archevêque de Malines-Bruxelles qui par tempérament était sensible à ce genre de rencontres[75].

Quoi qu'il en soit, le mois d'octobre 1963 fut une période conciliaire particulièrement féconde pour Dossetti et Suenens. Ils prirent l'initiative d'importance capitale des 'cinq questions' préjudicielles (notamment concernant la collégialité) soumises aux votes de l'assemblée conciliaire le 30 octobre 1963. Un des buts de cette consultation était de faire sortir la Commission doctrinale de l'inertie que les dirigeants conservateurs lui imposaient. Grâce aux résultats qui firent triompher l'opinion de la majorité du Concile, la Commission fut mise en état d'accélérer ses activités et d'élargir ses cadres de travail par des élections complémentaires[76]. Les projets du statut des modérateurs et d'un règlement pour ceux-ci échouèrent soit à cause de la prudence d'un Paul VI qui resta inerte ou ambigu,

---

Journal: notamment dès le 28 octobre 1962, après une réunion de groupe de Mgr Volk, l'ecclésiologue français écrit: «Mais il me semble pratiquement impossible de si peu tenir compte du travail déjà fait et où il y a du bon et de l'utile. Nous jouons à 'La laitière (Perrette) et le pot au lait'...» (CONGAR, *Mon journal du Concile* [n. 15], Tome I, pp. 156-157).

74. L'échange de correspondance à cet égard entre Dossetti, Suenens et Lercaro commence à partir du 4 septembre 1963 jusqu'à la visite de Dossetti chez Suenens annoncée le 25 septembre 1963, voir Fonds Suenens, 792-800. Voir aussi SUENENS, *Souvenirs et espérances* (n. 8), pp. 110-112.

75. Dès novembre 1962, G. Dossetti est en contact avec le cardinal Suenens. Il lui adresse une lettre avec une note au sujet de la conclusion de la première période conciliaire et par la suite un document plus long avec diverses suggestions pour l'inter-session à venir. Cf. Fonds Suenens, 618 et 619. Voir aussi, au début de 1963, l'échange de correspondance concernant l' 'Ordo Concilii' dans Fonds Suenens, 929-943.

76. Pour l'affaire des 5 questions du 30 octobre 1963, cf. Fonds Suenens 1505-1519; voir aussi SUENENS, *Souvenirs et espérances* (n. 8), pp. 115-119.

soit à la suite de l'opposition de Felici et Cicognani qui préféraient garder les rênes en mains, soit par la conjugaison de ces deux facteurs.

À la suite des retombées du 30 octobre, Dossetti dut abandonner sa fonction de secrétaire des modérateurs. Cette démission fut de fait imposée au pape par Mgr Felici qui considérait que sa fonction de secrétaire général englobait le secrétariat des modérateurs[77].

D'avoir fait passer les principes du schéma *De ecclesia* réécrit, ce «premier cap de la Commission» n'a pas été apprécié par la Curie romaine, écrit Suenens dans ses mémoires:

> Durant les séances conciliaires qui suivirent ce vote, plusieurs orateurs firent le procès des modérateurs, réduits au silence parce que non protégés par un règlement qui aurait défini clairement leur rôle mais qui n'avait jamais pris forme[78].

Malgré la démission de Don Dossetti comme secrétaire des modérateurs, le cardinal Suenens continua à faire appel à lui comme expert[79].

Au cours de cette deuxième période conciliaire de l'automne 1963, Suenens va faire trois interventions significatives: 1. Le diaconat permanent (le 8 octobre); 2. Les charismes des baptisés (le 22 octobre), et 3. La limite d'âge (le 12 novembre). La première et la troisième seront inspirées par Dossetti. (La deuxième est un texte de Hans Küng dont il sera question plus avant)[80]. Le cardinal Suenens attachait depuis longtemps une grande importance à la restauration du diaconat permanent, non pas à cause de la pénurie du clergé mais pour «la valeur intrinsèque de cet ordre sacramentel dans l'Église»[81]. Comme le thème du diaconat permanent avait été rayé du schéma préparatoire sur les prêtres, l'archevêque de Malines-Bruxelles obtint de Philips que celui-ci le mentionne dans le schéma sur l'Église, afin de lui permettre d'intervenir à ce sujet. L'argument théologique, préparé par Dossetti – celui-ci «étant alors son expert»

---

77. Dans ce contexte, il est intéressant de constater qu'un quart de siècle plus tard, l'édition officielle des procès-verbaux des concertations des modérateurs débute par la réunion du 30 octobre 1963: une note au bas de la page indique «qu'à l'occasion des réunions précédentes des modérateurs son Excellence Pericle Felici, secrétaire général du Concile, ne fut pas invité» (*AS* V/3, p. 697). C'est donc là l'explication pour laquelle les procès verbaux des réunions précédentes sont traités comme nuls et non advenus. Quant à Cicognani, selon «des rumeurs de bonne source» à l'époque, le pape aurait eu, à un moment donné, l'intention de le nommer «légat du Concile» (en quel cas il n'y aurait pas eu de modérateur): cf. dans *Le Monde* du 29 juin 1963.

78. SUENENS, *Souvenirs et espérances* (n. 8), pp. 117-118.

79. *Ibid.*, pp. 112-113.

80. Le cardinal Suenens commente ces trois propositions dans SUENENS, *Souvenirs et espérances* (n. 8), pp. 119-121. Il fait mention de Dossetti pour la première proposition mais ne donne pas le nom des inspirateurs des autres propositions.

81. Cf. *Ibid.*, p. 119.

–, faisait valoir que, le diaconat faisant partie de la structure sacramentelle de l'Église, il ne fallait pas le réduire à une simple étape de transition vers le sacerdoce. Selon Suenens, cette intervention fut bien accueillie par les pères conciliaires[82].

L'instauration d'une limite d'âge pour la fonction épiscopale avait déjà été acceptée par la Commission préparatoire (schéma sur l'épiscopat). Au Concile, Suenens proposa un âge précis: soixante-quinze ans. Selon son propre témoignage, l'orateur reçut un accueil glacial. Ce fut le rôle de Paul VI d'introduire cette mesure au début de son pontificat.

Don Dossetti rédigea ce texte concernant la limite d'âge. Suenens a noté de sa main sur ce projet: «texte proposé à moi par Dossetti: je l'ai refait»[83].

4. La collaboration de Hans Küng

Nous avons brièvement rendu compte de la conversation mémorable de Y. Congar avec H. Küng, dialogue entre un *possibiliste* et un *radical*. Nous ne savons pas grand-chose des relations Suenens-Küng, si ce n'est que l'archevêque de Malines-Bruxelles porte grand intérêt aux livres de Küng et lui fait part de son souhait de le rencontrer en Belgique ou à Rome (juillet 1963). Quelques mois plus tard, c'est à Küng que Suenens s'adresse pour lui demander un projet de texte en vue de l'intervention que le cardinal souhaite faire sur les charismes des laïcs[84].

Le discours conciliaire qui repose entièrement sur ce projet de H. Küng sera prononcé le 22 octobre 1963. Il aura une grande répercussion et sera reproduit dans de nombreux périodiques. Hans Küng lui-même raconte que le cardinal Suenens était heureux de disposer ainsi d'un projet de texte avec un fondement biblique reposant entièrement sur la conception paulinienne de l'Église. Selon Küng, cette intervention eut une influence directe sur la dimension charismatique de la constitution sur l'Église[85]. Selon le témoignage du cardinal Suenens, le Concile adopta son point de

---

82. Comme l'inspirateur de cette intervention de Suenens fut Dossetti, ce texte a été repris comme appendice dans le recueil ALBERIGO – LERCARO, *Per la forza dello Spirito* (n. 41), pp. 313-320. Quant au texte de Dossetti utilisé par Suenens, cf. Fonds Suenens, 1492-1493.

83. Fonds Suenens, 1597-1598. Semblable annotation peut être fréquente chez certains évêques qui désirent affirmer qu'ils ont le dernier mot dans la préparation d'une intervention dont le projet a été rédigé par un expert.

84. Fonds Suenens, 787, 1531 et 1540. Il semble que A. Prignon, P. Schoenmaeckers et G. Thils ont été consultés eux aussi concernant ce même thème: cf. les n. 1532-1533.

85. KÜNG, *Erkämpfte Freiheit* (n. 12), pp. 473-474.

vue et la mention des charismes fut intégrée dans le texte sur l'Église «en une formulation sage et nuancée, mais nettement positive»[86].

Il est évident que Suenens par cette intervention à Vatican II a été à l'avant-garde des mouvements charismatiques qui, vingt ans plus tard, vont envahir l'avant-scène de Jean Paul II et devenir une caractéristique déterminante du pontificat wojtylien[87]. Dans son remarquable livre de souvenirs, *Erkämpfte Freiheit*, que nous avons cité, Küng paraît être favorablement impressionné par l'organisation et l'efficacité des théologiens du groupe belge, mais parle avec le plus grand mépris des tentatives de *Vermittlung* – 'médiation'! – de Mgr Philips, qui se font «auf Kosten der Wahrheit», c'est-à-dire «aux dépens de la vérité»[88]. Il faut aussi noter qu'au moment où l'équipe Lercaro-Suenens-Dossetti préparait l'entrée en fonction du collège des modérateurs, un des projets proposés prévoyait la constitution d'une équipe d'experts qui aurait secondé les modérateurs. Ce projet avançait le nom de quatre collaborateurs, dont celui de Hans Küng. Comme on le sait, ce projet n'a pas eu de suite[89].

V. POSTFACE: BACKGROUND THÉOLOGIQUE DES POLARITÉS

Malheureusement, les circonstances ne nous ont pas permis de traiter encore ce dernier aspect essentiel. Je puis simplement rappeler ici que le professeur Komonchak nous a mis en garde contre une distinction trop nette entre l'ecclésiologie (*De ecclesia*), où joueraient des critères de 'stratégie' (entre *médiateurs* et *intransigeants*), et d'autre part le domaine Église et Monde (Schéma XIII), où joueraient des critères de 'contenu' théologique (entre *possibilistes* et *radicaux*).

Un nœud du débat théologique se trouve dans la relation entre l'Église *ad intra* et l'Église *ad extra*. Selon la réflexion de Komonchak, il y a *d'un côté* ceux qui considèrent que les *textes dogmatiques* prennent une place

---

86. SUENENS, *Souvenirs et espérances* (n. 8), p. 120: dans ces mémoires, l'auteur semble avoir jugé superflu de mentionner l'identité de son inspirateur.

87. Selon SUENENS, *Souvenirs et espérances* (n. 8), p. 120, son discours aurait aussi eu un accueil chaleureux auprès du représentant du patriarcat de Moscou car «c'était là un terrain de rencontre pour travailler à l'union des Églises».

88. KÜNG, *Erkämpfte Freiheit* (n. 12), pp. 460-461. Il n'est pas sans intérêt de remarquer que H. Küng, qui est au courant de notre théorie sur la polarité «médiateur» – «intransigeant», a reconnu sa propre position en écrivant lui-même comme dédicace de l'exemplaire de ses *Mémoires* qu'il a bien voulu nous adresser: «À Jan Grootaers avec les meilleures salutations d'un 'intransigeant'. Amicalement, H.K.».

89. Cf. A. MELLONI, *L'inizio del secondo periodo e il grande dibattito ecclesiologico*, dans G. ALBERIGO (éd.), *Storia del concilio Vaticano II*, Leuven, Peeters; Bologna, Il Mulino, 1995-2001, Tome III: *Il Concilio adulto*, pp. 28-29.

centrale dont dépend la thématique de la relation avec le monde et *d'autre part* ceux qui conçoivent les schémas concernant les relations Église-monde comme des textes clés qui influencent les *textes dogmatiques*.

Ainsi on pourrait considérer que les commentaires de Ratzinger et de de Lubac se situent dans la première catégorie (des tendances disons 'augustiniennes' ou 'patristiques') et que Chenu et Congar se trouvent dans la seconde catégorie (des tendances 'thomistes')[90].

Pour les 'patristiques' Ratzinger, de Lubac, Daniélou et Urs von Balthasar, il est possible de proposer une position sur la réalité intérieure de l'Église avant même de prendre en considération les responsabilités de l'Église dans l'histoire et à l'égard du monde.

Ceux qui sont de tendance 'thomiste' – Congar, Chenu, Schillebeeckx, Rahner – ne peuvent pas accepter cette perspective du style Ratzinger et de Lubac. Aux yeux des thomistes, une distinction aussi nette qui se limite aux seules catégories du péché et de la grâce est inadéquate: cette distinction ne prend pas en considération l'*autonomie* et l'*intelligibilité* dans le domaine de la nature, des sciences et de l'histoire[91].

En conclusion: le domaine du 'contenu' de l'orientation théologique et le domaine de la 'tactique' dans l'assemblée conciliaire ne sont pas séparés. Il y a des liens entre les deux, qu'il conviendra d'étudier de manière plus approfondie.

Lieveheersbeestjeslaan, 49   Jan GROOTAERS
B-1170 Brussel
Belgique

---

90. Lettre de J.A. Komonchak à l'auteur en date du 9 janvier 1995.
91. Voir l'article essentiel du professeur Joseph A. KOMONCHAK, *Le valutazioni sulla Gaudium et spes: Chenu, Dossetti, Ratzinger*, dans DORÉ – MELLONI (éds.), *Volti di fine Concilio* (n. 6), 115-159.

GUSTAVE THILS ET LE *DE ECCLESIA*

Un début d'enquête

Pour décrire sommairement l'activité conciliaire de celui qui est encore alors le chanoine Thils, on pourrait reprendre ce qu'un jour Roger Aubert écrivit à ce sujet:

> Mgr Thils prit une part active (à Vatican II) dès la phase préparatoire, comme expert du Secrétariat pour l'Unité, et il joua, tout au long des quatre sessions, un rôle important, souvent dans les coulisses, car c'est un homme discret qui sait que l'efficacité gagne à ne pas s'accompagner de tapage publicitaire.

Et plus précisément, sur sa contribution à l'élaboration du *De ecclesia*:

> Et surtout le spécialiste des prérogatives pontificales à Vatican I a eu plus qu'un mot à dire en vue de réinterpréter et de rééquilibrer les définitions de 1870 dans la perspective nouvelle de la collégialité épiscopale. Enfin, au-delà des passages relatifs à la fonction du pape dans l'Église, Mgr Thils a eu l'occasion d'exercer une heureuse influence sur l'élaboration de la constitution sur l'Église dans son ensemble: il en discutait durant les intersessions avec son collègue de Louvain Mgr Philips; il attirait l'attention de l'un ou l'autre sur le danger de telle expression ou sur l'opportunité de telle restructuration du plan, etc. D'autre part, n'oublions pas que l'action de Mgr Thils, comme de plusieurs autres experts, ne s'est pas seulement exercée dans les commissions officielles, mais comme conseiller de divers évêques qui le consultaient à titre privé[1].

Nous voilà donc prévenus. La contribution de Gustave Thils à la Constitution sur l'Église a été importante et multiple, mais discrète et diffuse. La préciser dans toute son ampleur demandera donc un travail minutieux et même exhaustif de recherche des traces, relativement peu nombreuses, dans les différentes archives disponibles, officielles et privées. Un vrai travail de bénédictin à propos d'un séculier! Nous n'en avons ici ni la prétention ni le temps. À défaut d'une vision d'ensemble complète

---

1. R. Aubert, *La carrière théologique de Mgr Thils*, dans *Voies vers l'unité: Colloque organisé à l'occasion de l'émérit de Mgr G. Thils*. Louvain-la-Neuve, 27-28 avril 1979 (Cahiers de la Revue théologique de Louvain, 3), Louvain-la-Neuve, Publications de la Faculté de Théologie, 1981, 7-27, pp. 23-24.

564   J. FAMERÉE

et plutôt que de nous concentrer seulement sur quelques facettes significatives de cette contribution (les passages relatifs à la sacramentalité de l'épiscopat, à la collégialité épiscopale et aux rapports de celle-ci avec la primauté papale, par exemple), nous voudrions tenter un début, au moins, de reconstitution chronologique de la contribution de Thils au schéma sur l'Église à partir de la première session de Vatican II. Elle sera fragmentaire, car les archives utilisables à cette fin sont lacunaires, comme on pourra s'en rendre compte au cours de cet essai de reconstruction. Pour ne pas nous limiter à des généralités et nous efforcer ainsi de répondre à l'intention spécifique de ce colloque d'approfondissement, nous prenons donc le parti d'exploiter au mieux les sources que nous avons pu consulter et de mettre au jour les différentes informations qui y sont clairsemées. Le travail n'en reste pas moins ardu et risqué: on se trouve devant une espèce de puzzle difficile à recomposer, d'autant plus que certaines pièces font défaut.

Sans ignorer la multitude des activités conciliaires du professeur louvaniste (au Secrétariat pour l'Unité et en lien avec d'autres schémas), nous allons y opérer une espèce de coupe verticale pour nous concentrer sur son apport, direct et indirect, au *De ecclesia*, mais sans chercher à reconstituer l'*iter* comme tel de ce schéma et ses stades successifs de rédaction (ce qui a déjà été étudié par ailleurs[2]). En raison des limites imparties à notre communication, nous avons dû interrompre notre enquête à la fin de la première intersession. À d'autres de continuer la recherche!

En ce qui concerne les fonds privés, nous recourrons notamment aux papiers Thils, Moeller, Prignon, Philips, Suenens, De Smedt et Heuschen[3],

2. Cf., par exemple, G. ALBERIGO – F. MAGISTRETTI (éds.), *Constitutionis Dogmaticae Lumen Gentium Synopsis historica*, Bologne, Istituto per le Scienze religiose, 1975.
3. Cf. C. SOETENS, *Concile Vatican II et Église contemporaine (Archives de Louvain-la-Neuve). I: Inventaire des Fonds Ch. Moeller, G. Thils, Fr. Houtart* (Cahiers de la Revue théologique de Louvain, 21), Louvain-la-Neuve, Publications de la Faculté de Théologie, 1989 (désormais cité: Fonds Moeller; Fonds Thils; Fonds Houtart); J. FAMERÉE, *Concile Vatican II et Église contemporaine (Archives de Louvain-la-Neuve). II: Inventaire des Fonds A. Prignon et H. Wagnon* (Cahiers de la Revue théologique de Louvain, 24), Louvain-la-Neuve, Publications de la Faculté de Théologie, 1991 (désormais cité: Fonds Prignon; Fonds Wagnon); L. DECLERCK – E. LOUCHEZ, *Inventaire des Papiers conciliaires du cardinal L.-J. Suenens* (Cahiers de la Revue théologique de Louvain, 31), Louvain-la-Neuve, Publications de la Faculté de Théologie, 1998 (désormais cité: Fonds Suenens); A. GREILER – L. DE SAEGER (éds.), *Emiel-Jozef De Smedt, Papers Vatican II Inventory*. With a Preface by Leo DECLERCK (Instrumenta Theologica, 22), Leuven, Bibliotheek van de Faculteit Godgeleerdheid, 1999 (désormais cité: Fonds De Smedt); L. DECLERCK – W. VERSCHOOTEN, *Inventaire des papiers conciliaires de Mgr Gérard Philips, secrétaire adjoint de la Commission doctrinale*. Avec une Introduction par J. GROOTAERS (Instrumenta Theologica, 24), Leuven, Bibliotheek van de Faculteit Godgeleerdheid – Peeters, 2001 (désormais cité: Fonds Philips); L. DECLERCK, *Inventaire des papiers conciliaires de*

ainsi qu'aux journaux conciliaires de Mgr Charue, Yves Congar et Jacques Dupont[4]. Il s'agit de plusieurs Pères ou experts avec lesquels Thils a collaboré, à des degrés divers, pour la rédaction de la future constitution *Lumen gentium*. Le journal Charue, généralement bien informé et pondéré tout en représentant nécessairement un point de vue particulier, fournira la trame chronologique de notre parcours, spécialement pour la première intersession. Pour celle-ci, des sources de ce genre, aussi fournies, sont malheureusement assez rares. En outre, la référence à ce journal se recommande particulièrement dans notre cas vu le rôle important exercé, avec beaucoup de sérieux, par son auteur au sein de la Commission doctrinale, dont il était membre et dont il serait élu vice-président à la fin de la deuxième session.

I. LE NOUVEAU SCHÉMA *DE ECCLESIA* (OCTOBRE 1962 – MARS 1963)

Une semaine à peine après l'ouverture solennelle du Concile, Mgr Philips est déjà en train de préparer avec le P. Rahner, le P. Congar et le chanoine Thils un schéma *De episcopis*, qui pourrait devenir un nouveau *De ecclesia*[5].

Monseigneur J.M. Heuschen, évêque auxiliaire de Liège, membre de la Commission doctrinale, et du Professeur V. Heylen (Instrumenta Theologica, 28), Leuven, Maurits Sabbebibliotheek Faculteit Godgeleerdheid – Peeters, 2005 (désormais cité: Fonds Heuschen; Fonds Heylen).

4. Cf. L. DECLERCK – C. SOETENS (éds.), *Carnets conciliaires de l'évêque de Namur A.-M. Charue* (Cahiers de la Revue théologique de Louvain, 32), Louvain-la-Neuve, Publications de la Faculté de Théologie, 2000 [désormais cité: Journal Charue]; Y. CONGAR, *Mon journal du Concile*, présenté et annoté par É. MAHIEU, 2 tomes, Paris, Cerf, 2002; J. DUPONT, *Carnet conciliaire* (8 Cahiers), dans le Fonds Dupont, 1726-1733, voir E. LOUCHEZ, *Concile Vatican II et Église contemporaine (Archives de Louvain-la-Neuve). IV: Inventaire des Fonds J. Dupont et B. Olivier* (Cahiers de la Revue théologique de Louvain, 29), Louvain-la-Neuve, Publications de la Faculté de Théologie, 1995, p. 99.

5. Journal Charue, p. 36 (18 octobre 1962): Philips le dit à Mgr Charue, il lui demande aussi de mettre par écrit les suggestions que celui-ci lui fait pour «introduire» le schéma sur les évêques; le P. Tromp a déclaré à Philips «que 150 évêques environ ont envoyé des critiques importantes contre le premier schéma, mais qu'il n'est pas de leur avis». Nous avons confirmation de la rédaction par Philips d'un nouveau *De ecclesia* dans le journal de Mgr Charue en date des 21 et 27 octobre suivants (cf. *Ibid.*, p. 37 et 41: en date du 27, on apprend que ce schéma bis est approuvé par Congar, Rahner, Thils et Colombo). Sur ce fait déjà bien étudié, nous renvoyons notamment à L. DECLERCK, *Le rôle joué par les évêques et periti belges au Concile Vatican II. Deux exemples*, dans *ETL* 76 (2000) 445-464, pp. 449-457. Cet article, en se basant, entre autres, sur le Fonds conciliaire du cardinal Suenens et le Journal conciliaire de Gérard Philips, apporte de nouveaux éclairages. Le 13 octobre déjà, après le vote reporté sur la composition des commissions conciliaires, le cardinal Cicognani invite le cardinal Suenens à composer «un nouveau schéma sur

Il n'est pas facile de déterminer la contribution exacte de Thils à ce nouveau schéma au cours de la première session. Le professeur louvaniste est membre du Secrétariat pour l'Unité et *peritus* officiel du Concile. À ce titre, il sera amené à suivre de près le *De revelatione*[6], qui n'entre pas ici dans notre champ de recherche. Ceci dit, outre sa participation aux congrégations générales et aux activités du Secrétariat pour l'Unité, Thils participe à de nombreuses réunions ou rencontres avec Philips et d'autres experts (Cerfaux, Congar, Onclin…) autour du *De ecclesia* notamment[7], il prend des contacts pour influer sur l'*iter* de certains textes conciliaires[8], il donne des conférences[9] … À défaut de pouvoir préciser l'apport de Thils au nouveau texte sur l'Église jusqu'au 8 décembre 1962, il est clair, comme il ressort des diaires de Mgr Charue et du P. Congar[10], qu'il est associé par Philips à son élaboration, fût-ce au minimum pour donner son accord au travail réalisé par ce dernier. Par ailleurs, vers la fin de la session, Congar pense à lui pour approfondir, avec Lécuyer, le chapitre sur les évêques au sein du *De ecclesia* officiel, qui sera mis en discussion *in aula* à partir du 1er décembre[11]. C'est au moins un signe de l'implication

l'Église». Le 15 octobre, sur la suggestion de Mgr Heuschen et avec l'accord du cardinal Bea, Suenens demande à Philips «de se mettre au travail pour un bref *De Ecclesiae natura* qu'ils feront avec Congar etc.» (cf. Fonds Suenens, 0573, Archevêché de Malines: lettre du card. Suenens à V. O'Brien, 17 octobre 1962; DECLERCK, *Le rôle joué*, p. 450). Dans une lettre du 17 octobre à P. et M. Verjans, Mgr Heuschen précisément signale qu'il a été décidé de faire un nouveau schéma sur l'Église et qu'à la demande d'un certain nombre d'évêques occidentaux, quelques personnes sont sollicitées d'y collaborer: Mgr Charue et lui-même, Mgr Philips et le Prof. Thils (cf. Fonds Heuschen, 512, Centrum voor Conciliestudie Vaticanum II, Faculteit Godgeleerdheid, Leuven).

6. Journal Charue, pp. 70 (25 novembre, première réunion de la commission mixte sur le *De revelatione* et inquiétude de Thils; voir aussi le 26 novembre) et 81 (commission mixte du 5 décembre et joie de Thils, Cerfaux et Daniélou devant l'acceptation unanime du texte de Mgr Charue pour le 4e chapitre *De Novo Testamento*).

7. Cf. Journal Charue, pp. 39 (23 octobre, au Collège belge), 46 (8 novembre, à l'Institut biblique) et 82 (6 décembre, au Secrétariat pour l'Unité); CONGAR, *Mon journal du Concile* (n. 4), Tome I, pp. 195 (8 novembre, au Biblicum) et 259 (26 novembre, à Saint-Pierre et chez Mgr Garrone); *Carnet conciliaire de J. Dupont*, Cahier 1 (Fonds Dupont, 1726), 5 décembre (à Rome, chez Cerfaux).

8. Cf. *Carnet conciliaire de J. Dupont*, Cahier 1, 5 décembre (avec l'accord de Mgr Jaeger et du *peritus* Eduard Stakemaier, Thils demande au P. Béda Rigaux, o.f.m., et à Dom Jacques Dupont de rédiger un nouveau chapitre I sur Écriture et Tradition pour le *De revelatione*).

9. Journal Charue, p. 42 (en date du 31 octobre, conférence sur l'épiscopat à Sainte-Marthe).

10. Voir les notes précédentes.

11. Le 28 novembre, Congar participe à une réunion restreinte d'archevêques ou évêques français à Saint-Louis. Il y est chargé d'organiser des équipes de travail pour la discussion sur l'actuel *De ecclesia*. Une d'entre elles devrait envisager «la question d'un meilleur *De episcopis*, regroupant tous les éléments qui en parlent et développant des

bien réelle, même si elle est encore potentielle pour une part, du chanoine Thils dans le processus de refonte du schéma présenté au Concile. Le texte latin, suivi d'un commentaire, proposé par lui et un autre *peritus* conciliaire, le dominicain belge J. Hamer, pour remplacer notamment le n° 16 du schéma préparatoire sur le collège des évêques, sera publié dans la première livraison d'*Études et Documents* du Secrétariat Général de l'épiscopat français, datée du 15 janvier 1963, tout entière consacrée à la collégialité de l'épiscopat[12]: (pp. 2-3) I. Fondements historiques de la collégialité (J. Colson, Mgr Dumont); (pp. 3-5) II. Théologie de la collégialité (G. Thils, J. Hamer); (pp. 5-7) III. Collégialité et primat (J. Daniélou). Ce texte, assez différent de celui préparé par Philips, lequel sera d'ailleurs ultérieurement critiqué par Thils sur ce point, manifeste bien les positions de ce dernier en matière de collégialité épiscopale en décembre 1962 – janvier 1963[13], et dans quel sens précisément il s'efforcera de faire évoluer le schéma conciliaire sur l'Église. Il est intéressant de noter qu'en son chapitre II, premier paragraphe (à propos de l'institution des douze Apôtres), le schéma dit français du début de 1963[14], attribué entre autres à Jean Daniélou, reprend presque littéralement la première partie du texte Thils-Hamer[15].

Par ailleurs, si le commentaire critique du *De ecclesia* préparatoire et la note qui l'accompagne concernant l'institution d'une commission épiscopale à réunir régulièrement (au moins tous les deux mois) durant l'intersession, légèrement antérieurs au 8 décembre 1962 et présents dans les

---

aspects qui sont à peine touchés, surtout la collégialité (Lécuyer, Thils)» (CONGAR, *Mon journal du Concile* [n. 4], Tome I, p. 274).

12. Cf. *Études et Documents* 1 (15 janvier 1963) 3-5. Cette nouvelle publication a pour but de répondre à la demande des évêques français réunis à Rome lors du Concile, qui étaient désireux de pouvoir lire des notes préparées par les *periti* à leur intention sur les diverses questions doctrinales traitées au cours des assises vaticanes.

13. La collégialité épiscopale est d'institution divine. Le collège épiscopal, uni à Pierre, dispose d'une pleine souveraineté sur l'Église universelle. C'est du fait de sa consécration que tout évêque est agrégé au collège épiscopal uni à Pierre et participe donc *ipso facto* de la *suprema potestas* sur l'Église universelle. Le pouvoir collégial des évêques ne s'exerce pas seulement dans le concile œcuménique, même si c'est là seulement qu'il s'exerce de façon pleine et suprême: il s'exerce de façon permanente, quoique partielle, dans la vie de l'Église (conciles locaux, Églises nationales, patriarcats, assemblées épiscopales). Le collège épiscopal uni au pape, même dispersé dans les diocèses (en dehors d'un concile œcuménique), est assuré du charisme d'infaillibilité dans son enseignement universel concernant la foi (*sive ordinario et universali magisterio*). Pour l'essentiel (hormis l'exercice permanent, quoique partiel, du pouvoir collégial), ces différentes affirmations de Thils et Hamer seront adoptées dans la constitution dogmatique *Lumen gentium*.

14. Cf. Fonds Naud, 215, p. 1 (texte dactylographié); ALBERIGO – MAGISTRETTI (éds.), *Constitutionis Dogmaticae Lumen Gentium Synopsis* (n. 2), pp. 426-427.

15. Cf. *Études et Documents* 1 (15 janvier 1963) 3-4.

archives de Thils[16], étaient bien de celui-ci, ce qui n'est pas impossible, nous tiendrions alors un témoignage remarquable supplémentaire de son «progressisme» quant à sa vision des rapports Église-monde, du ministère épiscopal et de la mise en œuvre concrète de celui-ci.

Pour l'intersession, les sources sont un peu plus abondantes et attestent l'association active de Thils à l'élaboration du nouveau *De ecclesia*.

Dès le début de janvier 1963, il est chargé par le cardinal Suenens de rédiger le rapport sur le schéma *De ecclesia* que celui-ci devra présenter à la première réunion de la nouvelle commission de coordination[17], du 21 au 27 janvier. À cette fin, Thils invite Congar à une réunion à Louvain le 13 janvier[18]. Y sont présents également Mgr De Smedt et Mgr Philips[19]. Dans son *Journal*, Congar détaille ce qui s'est fait à cette réunion. Il s'agissait d'abord d'arrêter avec Mgr De Smedt la ligne ecclésiologique que défendrait le Secrétariat pour l'Unité quand il serait appelé à intervenir dans le *De ecclesia*. On y fixa ensuite le plan que le cardinal Suenens proposerait. Enfin, on indiqua à Mgr Philips «un certain nombre d'améliorations souhaitables dans son *De ecclesia* révisé»[20]. Il y est aussi question de la réinsertion du *De beata virgine* dans le *De ecclesia*, en faveur de laquelle le cardinal s'est formellement prononcé. Ce nouveau schéma sur l'Église comportera quatre chapitres: (1) *De mysterio ecclesiae* (sur la mission et les membres de l'Église); (2) *De episcopis* (avec développement de la collégialité); (3) *De laicis*; (4) *De beata Maria virgine*. Le dominicain français exprime sa satisfaction à propos de ce voyage «fécond», malgré la fatigue.

Le lendemain, Thils écrit à Suenens pour lui faire part des corrections apportées au texte de Philips lors de cette rencontre[21]; il lui signale aussi qu'il renonce à rédiger son propre schéma puisque celui de Philips a été jugé meilleur. Ces amendements visent, entre autres, à accentuer la collégialité épiscopale[22].

16. Cf. Fonds Thils, 187, Centre Lumen Gentium, Faculté de Théologie, Louvain-la-Neuve.

17. Elle est alors composée comme suit: le card. A.G. Cicognani, président (secrétaire d'État); les card. A. Liénart, Fr. Spellman, G. Urbani, C. Confalonieri, J. Döpfner, L.-J. Suenens; les archevêques ou évêques P. Felici (secrétaire général du Concile), Ph. Nabaa, G.C. Morcillo, J. Villot, J. Krol et W. Kempf (tous les cinq sous-secrétaires du Concile). Cf. *Acta Synodalia* (*AS*) V/1, pp. 36 (14 décembre 1962) et 53 (21 janvier 1963).

18. Cf. CONGAR, *Mon journal du Concile* (n. 4), Tome I, p. 318.

19. Cf. Fonds Suenens, 0955.

20. CONGAR, *Mon journal du Concile* (n. 4), Tome I, p. 318.

21. Cf. Fonds Suenens, 0819-0822 et 0955 (la lettre n'est malheureusement plus accompagnée du texte corrigé); Fonds De Smedt, 704-706.

22. Philips lui-même les enverra à Suenens le 23 janvier suivant, cf. Fonds Suenens, 0956-0957; il les fait parvenir aussi à Thils, cf. Fonds Thils, 30.

À la réunion de la commission de coordination de fin janvier, le cardinal Suenens présente un rapport sur le *De ecclesia*, rédigé partiellement par Thils et à partir des propositions faites à la rencontre de Louvain[23]. C'est ce texte qui deviendra l'*Alligato* 2 envoyé par Mgr Felici le 1er février 1963 aux membres de la Commission de coordination[24]. Le 30 janvier, le cardinal Cicognani vient également de le faire parvenir au président de la Commission doctrinale: ce rapport Suenens constitue, selon la lettre d'accompagnement, les directives de la Commission de coordination pour la rédaction du nouveau schéma sur l'Église. Celui-ci ne devra plus comporter que quatre chapitres[25], au lieu des onze du schéma préparatoire. En outre, le nouveau schéma devra être communiqué à la Commission de coordination avant le 10 mars 1963[26].

Avant de suivre les activités ultérieures de Thils relatives à l'élaboration du *De ecclesia* pendant la première intersession, il est intéressant de consulter sa correspondance disponible pour le mois de janvier 1963[27]. Chaque lettre concerne, entre autres, le schéma ecclésiologique. On y découvre ses relations avec R. Schutz et M. Thurian de Taizé, qu'il associe à son travail conciliaire (sur le *De ecclesia* et le *De beata*), avec Fr. Thijssen, consulteur au Secrétariat pour l'Unité (à propos du rapport entre Peuple de Dieu et laïcat) et avec R. Laurentin, expert comme lui au Concile (concernant l'intégration du schéma marial dans le *De ecclesia*[28], ce dont le théologien français a parlé à L. Suenens, et les observations de Thils sur le schéma Philips). Si l'on ajoute la lettre déjà citée de Philips à Thils pour lui transmettre les corrections faites à la réunion de Louvain, et tout en s'en tenant à ce seul mois de janvier, Thils apparaît

---

23. Cf. Fonds Suenens, 0819-0822.
24. Cf. Fonds Suenens, 0822, 0846 et 0850.
25. Comme c'est déjà le cas du texte Philips amendé à la réunion de Louvain.
26. Cf. Fonds Suenens, 0847 et 0850.
27. Je me limite ici au Fonds Thils. Cf., dans l'ordre chronologique, Fonds Thils, 313 (R. Schutz et M. Thurian à G. Thils, 5 janvier 1963), 413 (Fr. Thijssen à G. Thils, 6 janvier 1963), 321 (R. Laurentin à G. Thils, 11 janvier 1963), 30 (G. Philips à G. Thils, 23 janvier 1963) et 1744 (M. Thurian à G. Thils, 26 janvier 1963).
28. Sur ce point, on peut aussi signaler une lettre antérieure de G. Thils à R. Laurentin, datée du 1 janvier 1963 (cf. Fonds Laurentin, 845). Chargé d'aider le card. Suenens à préparer la commission de coordination de fin janvier, Thils y demande de toute urgence à Laurentin le document que celui-ci a rédigé pour la révision du *De beata* (notes critiques et plan d'un schéma révisé). Le 14 janvier, le jour même où il reçoit la réponse de Laurentin (cf. *supra*, note 27: Fonds Thils, 321), Thils écrit une autre lettre au mariologue français (cf. Fonds Laurentin, 847): il le prie de communiquer directement au card. Suenens, avant le départ de celui-ci pour Rome le 20 janvier, la manière dont «(vous) envisageriez l'orientation générale d'un *De Beata* à l'intérieur du *De Ecclesia* pratiquement comme un ultime chapitre du *De Ecclesia*, les idées que vous développeriez successivement dans l'élaboration de pareil schéma».

comme un interlocuteur significatif, sans être pour autant central. Si l'on ne se limite pas à cette correspondance, on observe même une assez grande proximité et des relations de confiance entre Suenens et le théologien de son diocèse, qui est aussi plus neutre que Philips concernant l'Action catholique, la grande rivale de la Légion de Marie aux yeux du primat de Belgique: c'est Thils qui est chargé en janvier d'écrire sa *relatio* pour la Commission de coordination; jusqu'au début mars, Suenens parle toujours du schéma Philips-Thils[29], alors qu'entre-temps, ce dernier lui a signifié qu'il renonçait à écrire son propre schéma …

Les réunions de la Commission doctrinale ou théologique (en latin *De doctrina fidei et morum* ou en abrégé *De fide*) se tiennent du 21 février au 13 mars. Dès le premier jour, «à mon grand étonnement», écrit Mgr Charue dans son journal[30], «le card. Ottaviani propose pour les sept membres d'une commission centrale de travail les card. Browne, König, Léger, Mgr Parente, Mgr Garrone, Mgr Schröffer et moi-même!». Cette 'commission des sept' (en fait, une sous-commission de la Doctrinale) devra choisir un texte de base pour le nouveau *De ecclesia*. Précisément, le 26 février, celle-ci décide de retenir le schéma Philips, Browne et Parente se rendant finalement à l'avis des cinq autres, qui avaient préparé cette décision lors de deux réunions informelles, l'une chez le cardinal König et l'autre chez Mgr Garrone[31]. En suggérant «qu'on se réfère immédiatement aussi au schéma Parente», Mgr Charue «met de l'huile dans les engrenages». En tout cas, «tous approuvent la raison avancée par Mgr Garrone que le schéma Philips est plus neutre, moins engagé». C'est à cette réunion également que sept *periti*, un par évêque, sont nommés. Charue s'adjoint Philips, qu'il «fait admettre comme président du groupe des experts». König prend Rahner; Garrone, Daniélou[32]; Browne, Gagnebet; Léger, Naud[33]; Parente[34], Balic[35]. Charue précise qu'il a «obtenu de

---

29. Cf. Fonds Suenens, 0977 (Card. Suenens à Card. Léger, 15 février 1963), 0765 (Card. Suenens à Jean XXIII, 19 février 1963) et 0766 (note jointe sur les travaux du Concile), 1000 (Card. Suenens à Mgr M. Baudoux, 4 mars 1963); voir aussi DECLERCK, *Le rôle joué* (n. 5), pp. 455-456.

30. Journal Charue, p. 87 (Jeudi 21 février).

31. Cf. *ibid.*, pp. 88 (Vendredi 22 février) et 89 (Dimanche 24 février).

32. Remplacé par Congar à partir du 2 mars, cf. CONGAR, *Mon journal du Concile* (n. 4), Tome I, p. 332.

33. Remplacé par Lafortune à partir du 2 mars, cf. CONGAR, *Mon journal du Concile* (n. 4), Tome I, p. 332.

34. Remplacé par Mgr Spanedda à partir du 5 mars, cf. Journal Charue, p. 101; CONGAR, *Mon journal du Concile* (n. 4), Tome I, p. 341.

35. Remplacé par Mgr Schauf à partir du 5 mars, cf. Journal Charue, p. 101; CONGAR, *Mon journal du Concile* (n. 4), Tome I, p. 338.

Mgr Schröffer qu'il prenne Thils». C'est donc ainsi que ce dernier se retrouve avec Philips parmi les experts de la commission des sept[36]. La mission de ceux-ci est de fournir un nouveau texte (en fait, les deux premiers chapitres[37]) en prenant pour base celui de Philips, en consultant immédiatement Parente et en puisant dans les autres schémas. En cas de désaccord, ils exposeront les différents points de vue[38].

Au cours de ces journées de réunion de la Commission *De fide* et de sa sous-commission *De ecclesia*, le chanoine Thils est manifestement soucieux d'une affirmation claire de la collégialité épiscopale dans le chapitre II du nouveau schéma[39]. Aux dires de Mgr Charue, en date du 4 mars, «il apprécie beaucoup le travail de Mgr Philips, qui a fait un gros effort et qui est très aidé par Rahner. Cependant il souhaiterait plus de netteté concernant la collégialité et il me demande d'y veiller à la sous-commission». L'évêque ajoute: «le soir, il me dira (...) qu'il a vu (le) nouveau texte (de Mgr Philips), que c'est bien»[40].

36. Appelé par Daniélou à Rome de manière impromptue le 1er mars, Congar, en arrivant sur place, se rend vite compte que «pratiquement, le travail se fait au collège belge, autour de Philips et Thils» (CONGAR, *Mon journal du Concile* [n. 4], Tome I, p. 330). En fait, le travail d'équipe au Collège belge pour la rédaction du nouveau *De ecclesia* est plutôt l'œuvre de Philips, entouré de Moeller, Rahner, Congar et parfois de Lafortune, cf. *ibid.*, pp. 335 (Lundi 4 mars), 344 (Jeudi 7 mars) et 346 (Dimanche 10 mars), par exemple. Thils ne logeait d'ailleurs pas au Collège belge, mais dans un hôtel près de la place d'Espagne (*Carnet conciliaire de J. Dupont*, Cah. 1, 8 décembre), même si bien sûr il est très régulièrement en contact avec le *Collegio belga*, cf. Journal Charue, p. 96 (Lundi 4 mars); CONGAR, *Mon journal du Concile* (n. 4), Tome I, p. 343 (Mercredi 6 mars), par exemple.
37. Les deux autres dépendent en effet des sous-commissions mixtes, cf. Journal Charue, p. 100.
38. Sur cette réunion du 26 février, cf. Journal Charue, pp. 90-91.
39. Le 15 janvier précédent, le texte collectif «La collégialité de l'Épiscopat», déjà évoqué, où son nom figurait aux côtés de Colson, Dumont, Hamer et Daniélou, était paru dans le premier numéro d'*Études et Documents* du Secrétariat Général de l'épiscopat français (cf. Fonds Suenens, 1039); Thils et Hamer ont ensuite élaboré des amendements proposés par Mgr R. Piérard, évêque de Chalons (France), pour les deux chapitres «de Collegialitate episcopatus» et datés du 25 février (cf. *ibid.*, 1034). Vers la même époque, selon toute probabilité, le théologien louvaniste ne ménage pas sa peine pour fournir à Mgr Philips des projets pour des chapitres du *De ecclesia* sur la papauté, le collège épiscopal et les évêques (en deux versions successives), cf. Fonds Philips, 567-580, Centrum voor Conciliestudie Vaticanum II, Faculteit Godgeleerdheid, Leuven.
40. Journal Charue, pp. 96-97; p. 107: suite à la séance de la commission doctrinale plénière du 9 mars, Charue demande à Moeller d'alerter Thils sur la formule adoptée à la fin du *Prooemium* du chapitre II («super Petrum-rupem et super Apostolos aedificavit»), qui évite d'affirmer que les Apôtres aussi sont «fondement» de l'Église; p. 109: le 11 mars, Charue reçoit, par l'entremise de Prignon, des feuilles de Thils (ainsi que de Colson) sur la collégialité. En fait, dès la réunion de la sous-commission des sept experts sur le *De ecclesia* en date du 2 mars, on peut noter que «d'emblée on part du texte Philips», que «d'emblée on parle de la collégialité épiscopale» et même que «l'accrochage majeur a lieu sur la collégialité, dont Balic et Gagnebet voudraient qu'on diminue la part" (CONGAR, *Mon journal du Concile* [n. 4], Tome I, pp. 333-334).

C'est le lendemain que la Commission théologique (*De fide*) plénière, a annoncé son président, le card. Ottaviani, devra décider «quel doit être le schéma de base». «Or, s'étonne Mgr Charue, la sous-commission avait été chargée de le décider. On craint une manœuvre»[41]. Effectivement, pendant la séance du 5 mars, Ottaviani critique le style «peu pastoral» du projet Philips, puis estime qu'on ne peut en examiner utilement le chapitre I «sans avoir le schéma entier»; Tromp aussi fait de l'obstruction à un nouveau schéma. Face aux réponses argumentées, le président se rend. *De facto*, le schéma Philips est ainsi retenu comme texte de base et l'examen de son premier chapitre (le second n'étant pas encore tout à fait terminé) peut commencer[42]. L'étude des deux chapitres se prolongera jusqu'au 13 mars, ultime réunion de la Commission théologique. Au terme de celle-ci, «– qui l'aurait prévu il y a 10 jours?, note Mgr Charue, (le card. Ottaviani) fait un vibrant éloge de Mgr Philips, qui est applaudi par l'assemblée»[43]. La prochaine réunion est prévue pour le 15 mai.

II. Évolution du *De ecclesia* (avril – septembre 1963)

Le schéma de la Constitution dogmatique sur l'Église (première partie[44]) daté du 22 avril 1963, tel qu'il a été amendé par la Commission doctrinale de mars et approuvé par la Commission de coordination du 28 mars[45], est envoyé aux Pères pour appréciation. Entre-temps, les notes de ce texte ont été rédigées à Louvain par Philips avec l'aide de Moeller, Thils et Cerfaux notamment[46]. Dans les papiers Philips, on trouve deux textes dactylographiés porteurs de notes manuscrites, entre autres, de Thils[47].

Ce dernier ne se désintéresse pas non plus du chapitre III sur le Peuple de Dieu et spécialement les laïcs. Aussi, au début mars vraisemblablement, a-t-il rédigé des «Notes» sur ce chapitre dans son état antérieur au

---

41. Journal Charue, p. 98 (Lundi 4 mars).

42. Cf. *ibid.*, pp. 99-101 (Mardi 5 mars) et 102 (Mercredi 6 mars); voir aussi Congar, *Mon journal du Concile* (n. 4), Tome I, pp. 338-341 (Mardi 5 mars).

43. Journal Charue, p. 115; cf. Congar, *Mon journal du Concile* (n. 4), Tome I, p. 356.

44. Ce document latin de 47 p. contient les deux premiers chapitres, respectivement sur le mystère et sur la constitution hiérarchique de l'Église (cf., par exemple, Fonds Suenens, 0948).

45. Cf. J. Grootaers, *Le concile se joue à l'entracte*, dans G. Alberigo – É. Fouilloux (éds.), *Histoire du concile Vatican II (1959-1965)*, Tome II, Paris, Cerf; Louvain, Peeters, 1998, 421-615, pp. 478-479.

46. Voir aussi *ibid.*, pp. 479, note 2, et 481, note 1.

47. Cf. Fonds Philips, 665 (notes mss relatives à 52 p. de Notes pour le chap. I) et 667 (notes mss relatives à 13 p. de Notes «Sacerdotium vero Judaeorum nemo fere...»).

9 mars (date de la fin du travail de la sous-commission mixte de la Doctrinale et de l'Apostolat des laïcs)[48]. Une suggestion de Moeller à Philips, un peu antérieure au 1er mai, relative au texte latin du chapitre III que celui-ci s'apprête à proposer à la Commission doctrinale, manifeste que Thils également est à consulter sur ce point[49]. Le rapport du P. S. Tromp sur les activités de la Commission doctrinale (seule ou avec la Commission de l'apostolat des fidèles) à partir du 15 mai offre quelques informations intéressantes sur le destin de ce *De laicis*[50]. C'est le 25 mai qu'est proposé un nouveau texte datant du 18 mai, selon toute probabilité celui révisé, selon les observations de la réunion du 16 mai, par les rapporteurs Florit, Spanedda et Franic avec l'aide de Philips[51]. Globalement, quelques changements seulement seront demandés[52]. Dans la discussion

48. Cf. Fonds Philips, 696.

49. Cf. Fonds Philips, 704; voir aussi Fonds Prignon, 86 (notes de Thils sur le chap. III, entre mars et mai 1963). Il faut ici relever une conversation des plus éclairantes, en date du 1er mai 1963 à Louvain, entre Gustave Thils et Jan Grootaers, dont ce dernier a consigné la teneur dans son *Diarium 7* (conservé à son domicile), pp. 988-1002. Nous remercions vivement le professeur Grootaers de nous y avoir donné accès. Tout au long de cet échange, le professeur Thils apparaît assez critique, presque impatient, vis-à-vis des travaux en cours relatifs au *De ecclesia*. Dans ses considérations générales à l'égard des «Romains», il inclut aussi son collègue Philips: «Même Mgr Philips reste dans des catégories anciennes; même lui n'est pas capable de se décrocher de l'ancien texte pré-conciliaire» (p. 988). Sur le plan théologique en tout cas, il n'y a donc pas unité de vue entre les experts, même louvanistes, du *Collegio belga*. Cette divergence porte ici plus particulièrement sur le chap. III («De laicis») du schéma sur l'Église. Thils estime que le texte actuel, qui viendra en commission le 15 mai, est beaucoup trop proche du schéma pré-conciliaire: c'est un ensemble incohérent et peu équilibré, qui s'efforce de classer dans un ordre logique les vœux et suggestions des évêques; ce n'est en aucun cas une *grande charte* sur le laïcat. De plus, ce chapitre a été conçu dans un esprit clérical, comme si l'action du laïcat était nécessairement un prolongement de l'action de la hiérarchie ou la liberté du laïcat une liberté concédée d'en haut. De même, on se représente les *charismes* comme quelque chose d'exceptionnel, et non comme quelque chose d'ordinaire pour les simples fidèles aussi, or ceux-ci possèdent une fonction propre qui leur vient directement du Christ et nullement de la hiérarchie. «Ici Thils, note Grootaers, prétend que même Mgr Philips reste attaché aux conceptions de Pie XI et Pie XII et est incapable de voir le point de vue nouveau, nettement évangélique et vécu de l'Église primitive» (p. 996: souligné deux fois). Par ailleurs, pour ce qui est du travail de rédaction et d'amendement du texte, Thils se plaint qu'il faille «se battre pendant plusieurs heures pour que Philips accepte de changer un bout de phrase ou un mot. Méthode qui prend beaucoup de temps et qui décourage» (p. 996). Ce témoignage révèle, de manière un peu inattendue, les tensions doctrinales et psychologiques existant au sein même du *brain-trust*, apparemment si uni, de la *squadra belga*.

50. Cf. *Acta Commissionis de Doctrina Fidei et Morum 13 Mart. – 30 Sept. 1963*. *Relatio Secretarii Commissionis* (cf., par ex., Fonds Prignon, 322, pp. 10-12 [15 mai], 12-13 [16 mai] et 30-32 [25 mai]).

51. Sur cette sous-commission de la Doctrinale, cf. *Acta Commissionis*, p. 13.

52. Le 25 mai, Charue note dans son journal: «j'apprendrai que (le chap. III du *de Ecclesia*) fut adopté haut la main et que le card. Cento félicite Mgr Philips» (Journal Charue, p. 124).

relatée par Tromp, mentionnons deux interventions du chanoine Thils. La première porte sur la distinction entre sacerdoce universel et sacerdoce hiérarchique. Établir une «différence essentielle» entre les deux lui paraît suffisamment précis (*sat acutum*)[53]. Sa remarque vise sans doute à ne pas creuser davantage l'écart entre fidèles et «clergé». À propos du paragraphe sur l'apostolat et les charismes, le théologien de Louvain a le souci aussi d'élargir cette dernière notion, à tous les fidèles en quelque sorte, en observant qu'il y a aussi des charismes mineurs ou modestes[54].

Mais à côté de l'épiscopat et de la collégialité, d'une part, du laïcat, d'autre part, il est un chapitre que l'auteur de *Sainteté chrétienne*[55] suivra avec un intérêt et même une vigilance particulière, c'est le chapitre V *De statibus perfectionis evangelicae adquirendae* du *De ecclesia* préparatoire, surtout à partir du mois de mai. Les 6 et 7 mars, la sous-commission mixte de la Doctrinale et des Religieux avait révisé le premier projet de chapitre concernant les religieux et l'avait intitulé *De iis qui consilia evangelica profitentur*. C'est cette nouvelle version qui accompagne la convocation de la Commission doctrinale par Ottaviani le 3 mai 1963[56].

À son arrivée pour celle-ci, Charue note dans son diaire que le 14 mai, il prend le repas de midi au Collège belge avec Philips, Prignon, Thils et Moeller: «On est d'accord sur les grandes lignes des chap. III et IV du *De Ecclesia*»[57]. Sans vouloir presser cette simple notation, on peut constater cependant qu'il existe alors, une véritable entente, dans l'ensemble du moins, entre les Belges de la Doctrinale, et Thils en est, également pour le chapitre des laïcs et celui des religieux[58].

---

53. Thils «censet statuere 'essentialem differentiam' inter utrumque sacerdotium esse verbum sat acutum», comme Rahner avait estimé que le «*essentialiter* differre» suffisait sans qu'il faille ajouter «non tantum gradu» (*Acta Commissionis*, p. 31).

54. «Notat esse etiam charismata minora» (*Acta Commissionis*, p. 32). À quoi, Tromp lui-même ajoute que les charismes pauliniens ne sont pas tous miraculeux. Le P. Hirschmann renchérit alors, en concluant: «dicendum esse quod charismata miraculosa non sint temere exspectanda» (*ibid.*). On trouvera une confirmation de mon interprétation de l'intervention de Thils sur les charismes dans le *Diarium* 9, p. 1224, de J. Grootaers (conversation avec G. Thils du 1er août 1963), comme d'ailleurs déjà dans le *Diarium* 7, p. 996 (cf. *supra*, note 49).

55. G. THILS, *Sainteté chrétienne: Précis de théologie ascétique*, Tielt, Lannoo, 1958.

56. Cf. GROOTAERS, *Le concile se joue* (n. 45), p. 483.

57. Journal Charue, p. 118.

58. On notera dans le même sens que le 11 mai précédent, d'après l'indication manuscrite de Moeller, celui-ci avait reçu les *Animadvertenda de Capite IV Constitutionis de Ecclesia* de Mgr Charue; dans la carte qui accompagne ces feuilles, l'évêque de Namur l'informe qu'il les a communiquées aussi à Philips, Onclin et Thils (cf. Fonds Moeller, 0142-0143). Sur le plan proprement théologique, on se rappellera cependant les divergences existant, par exemple, entre Thils et Philips.

Trois jours plus tard (la Commission doctrinale et ses sous-commissions se réunissent depuis le 15 mai), nouveau déjeuner de Charue au Collège belge: il a demandé que Thils y soit aussi. Au cours de la conversation, Congar est entièrement de l'avis de Charue et Thils sur le chapitre des états de perfection. Il est convenu que «Thils et Congar vont préparer ensemble un ou deux numéros à mettre en tête du chapitre et qui traiteraient de l'appel universel à la sainteté et des voies diverses pour y tendre»[59]. On voit que Thils, ici avec Congar, est directement mis à contribution en vue d'adapter le schéma soumis à la Doctrinale dans le sens des idées de Charue en la matière, qu'il partage tout à fait[60].

L'examen de ce chapitre IV à la Doctrinale commence le lundi 27 mai[61]. Dès le début, Tromp fait une déclaration au nom d'Ottaviani:

59. Journal Charue, p. 121 (Vendredi 17 mai). On a confirmation de cet engagement de Thils le 18 mai: «je rencontre le chan. Thils, qui va se mettre au travail pour le chap. IV et qui restera pour la discussion» (*ibid.*, p. 122). Pour le 17 mai, Congar signale seulement qu'il déjeune avec «Mgr Charue, Mgr De Smedt, Thils, Delhaye» (CONGAR, *Mon journal du Concile* [n. 4], Tome I, p. 367).

60. À propos de la Commission doctrinale du 16 mai, Charue rapporte qu'il y a obtenu que le chapitre III du *De ecclesia* soit intitulé *De populo Dei, et praesertim de laicis*. Il ajoute qu'il «pense qu'on admettra que le chap. IV soit intitulé: 'De sanctitate in Ecclesia, praesertim apud eos qui consilia...'» (Journal Charue, p. 120). En bon théologien, Charue s'efforce donc chaque fois de replacer ce qui est propre à quelques-uns dans l'ecclésial commun à tous. Notons que Suenens avait exprimé le même souhait lors de la Commission de coordination du 28 mars: le chapitre sur les états de perfection «devrait s'inscrire dans une perspective plus large que celle du schéma préparatoire, une perspective qui serait celle de la vocation à la sainteté de tous les chrétiens» (GROOTAERS, *Le concile se joue* [n. 45], p. 478). Sur ce point, il y a donc convergence entre deux des «têtes de proue» de l'épiscopat belge, de même qu'entre leurs *periti*. Si l'on veut une confirmation de cette convergence d'idées entre Thils et Charue, je renvoie à une note que le premier a rédigée (l'auteur est reconnaissable aux papiers polycopiés à l'encre bleue qu'il utilise) entre mars et fin mai 1963 (après le 7 mars, ultime révision du chapitre IV par la sous-commission mixte, et avant les 27-28 mai, date où un accord est atteint à la Doctrinale pour insérer ce projet de texte dans un cadre plus vaste sur la vocation générale à la sainteté): «Note sur le schéma *De Ecclesia*. Chap. IV: *De statibus perfectionis*» (cf. Fonds Prignon, 93). Thils y propose d'«élargir franchement le chapitre IV et (d')en faire un *de Sanctitate in Ecclesia*, à l'intérieur duquel on traiterait évidemment des deux formes de sainteté, et tout spécialement des états de perfection» (p. 1). Ce n'est donc pas encore acquis quand il écrit cette note.

61. Pour la chronique de cette discussion, nous prenons comme fil conducteur le journal conciliaire de Mgr Charue, membre de la Commission doctrinale et bientôt président de la sous-commission chargée de retravailler le texte (cf. Journal Charue, pp. 125-129 [du lundi 27 au vendredi 31 mai]), ainsi que sa «Note sur la discussion du chap. IV de Ecclesia» (1.6.1963, 3 p. dactyl.), qui complète les carnets sur certains points, mais y introduit sans doute aussi un peu de simplification après coup (cf. Fonds Prignon, 98-99: «Note» et texte de l'intervention de Charue le 28 mai à la Commission). Il est aussi intéressant de comparer ces documents et le rapport des mêmes réunions rédigé par Charles Moeller le 5 juin, à la demande de Mgr Charue (et sans doute pour une part sur la base de son témoignage), pour le card. Léger (cf. Fonds Prignon, 102).

la réunion est anormale; on ne devrait traiter de ce chapitre qu'en commission mixte (plénière) avec les Religieux[62]; il faut donc se limiter à des retouches de détail et les tenir pour de simples propositions[63]. Les réactions ne manquent pas. Le card. Browne, qui préside la réunion en l'absence du card. Ottaviani, conclut qu'il faut maintenir la substance du texte, qu'on peut le modifier dans les détails et qu'on peut aussi l'inscrire dans un contexte plus large à soumettre à la Commission de coordination (prévue pour les premiers jours de juin). La discussion sera vive, mais on constate l'accord des onze membres présents[64], pour insérer le projet de texte dans un contexte plus vaste sur la vocation générale à la sainteté[65].

Le lendemain, l'accord se fait sur une triple décision: revoir le texte proposé et le corriger; l'insérer dans un contexte plus général sur

62. Or les évêques de la Commission des religieux ne sont pas à Rome, cf. Journal Charue, p. 125 (Lundi 27 mai). Signalons que l'évêque de Namur a dû retourner dans son diocèse le 25 mai pour les fêtes mariales du 26; il revient cependant à Rome dès le 27 «pour assister aux réunions concernant le chap. IV *de statibus perfectionis*» et y rester «jusqu'à l'arrivée du card. Suenens le 4 juin» (*ibid.*, p. 125). C'est dire si le sujet lui tient à cœur et il jouera effectivement un rôle essentiel en commission. C'est dire aussi que les évêques belges à des postes clés au cours de l'intersession tiennent à assurer une présence permanente aux moments importants.

63. Congar retient plutôt des éléments doctrinaux de cette déclaration de Tromp: elle va «CONTRE l'idée de faire un exposé plus général sur la sainteté dans l'Église»; le chapitre sur les religieux «doit être mis sous le signe de l'Église, corps organisé, ayant des *ordines*, sous le signe de l'organisation, et aussi sous le signe des services que les religieux rendent à l'Église» (CONGAR, *Mon journal du Concile* [n. 4], Tome I, p. 380).

64. La plupart des Pères conciliaires de la Doctrinale n'avaient pas prévu une session si longue. Sont encore là: les card. Browne et König, NN.SS. Barbado, Charue, Franic, McGrath, Schröffer, Seper, Spanedda, Dom Gut et le P. Fernandez, o.p. Quant aux experts, ils sont encore assez nombreux: Balic, Betti, Bonet, Congar, Delhaye, Gagnebet, Häring, Kerrigan, Labourdette, Laurentin, Lécuyer, Medina, Moeller, Philips, Prignon, Rahner, Rigaux (l'auteur du texte actuel), Salaverri, Sauras, Thils, Van den Eynde, ainsi que Tromp, le secrétaire, et deux *minutanti*, le P. Laberge et Don Molari. Cf. *Acta Commissionis*, pp. 32-37; Journal Charue, p. 126; «Note sur la discussion...» (n. 61), pp. 1-2. Le chiffre de onze membres est confirmé par Congar (CONGAR, *Mon journal du Concile* [n. 4], Tome I, p. 380).

65. Le rapport Tromp, qui ne mentionne pas cet accord sur la vocation générale à la sainteté, noté par Mgr Charue, précise qu'après presque deux heures et demie de discussion, Browne décide que le texte soit examiné maintenant tel qu'il est et qu'ensuite soit nommée une sous-commission pour effectuer la nouvelle rédaction (cf. *Acta Commissionis*, p. 34). Au cours de cette discussion détaillée assez conflictuelle, quand on en vient au n. 2 sur les conseils évangéliques, «Exc.mus Schroeffer rogat ut elementum eschatologicum melius explicetur vel secus tollatur». «Ill.mus Philips putat nec ipsis religiosis placere, si eorum vita dicatur coelestis et Can. Thils rogat num reapse vita religiosa sit vita inchoata superna[e] Ierusalem» (*ibid.*, p. 37). Toujours ce souci, tant de la part de Charue que des Louvanistes et d'autres, de ne pas ériger la vie religieuse en état de perfection supérieur à celui des autres fidèles, tous appelés également à la sainteté (les uns auraient-ils déjà un pied au ciel, alors que tous les autres seraient encore complètement dans la mêlée d'ici-bas?).

la vocation à la sainteté; y parler notamment des prêtres[66]. En raison des occupations des uns et du départ des autres, trois membres seulement restent pour une sous-commission à laquelle le card. Browne veut confier le travail: Mgr McGrath, le P. Fernandez et Mgr Charue, qui présidera[67]. Ceux-ci sont invités à se choisir un ou deux experts: Charue prendra Philips (et non Thils), McGrath, Häring et Fernandez, Gagnebet. À la demande de McGrath, Medina sera le secrétaire. Si Charue prend Philips, c'est selon toute vraisemblance pour qu'il «rédige le chap. IV comme les autres chapitres du *De Ecclesia*», comme ce sera de fait accepté par la sous-commission[68].

Le 29 mai se tient la première réunion de la sous-commission. Vu la situation favorable d'accord entre les participants dès le début, Mgr Charue, sans tarder, propose de prendre comme base le texte de Thils, sans doute celui que le professeur louvaniste, le 17 mai, avait accepté de préparer avec Congar pour le début du chapitre et qui devait traiter de l'appel universel à la sainteté et des voies diverses pour y tendre[69]. Le texte est lu et accepté. On est aussi d'accord, dès lors, pour que Thils assiste aux autres séances de la sous-commission. On demande à Philips de retoucher le texte de Thils avec ce dernier[70], ainsi que le schéma présenté par la sous-commission mixte du mois de mars, portant, lui, spécifiquement sur ceux qui professent les conseils évangéliques. Un titre général est adopté de commun accord: «De vocatione generali ad sanctitatem in Ecclesia»[71].

Le jeudi 30 mai[72], le texte remanié par Philips et Thils pour le «De vocatione generali» est accepté. À la demande de Charue, «là où il est

66. Cf. «Note sur la discussion...» (n. 61), pp. 1-2.
67. «Ironie du sort!», note-t-il (Journal Charue, p. 127).
68. Cf. Journal Charue, p. 127. Il est cependant convenu que Thils, Moeller, Delhaye et Prignon, ainsi que Congar, se tiendraient à la disposition de Philips.
69. Cf. *supra*, note 59 [17 mai].
70. Ils jouirent de la collaboration de Moeller, Delhaye et Prignon, précise la «Note sur la discussion...» (n. 61) datée du 1er juin 1963.
71. Comme Charue l'avait pressenti déjà le 16 mai, cf. *supra*, note 60. Si l'on en croit le Journal Charue, les choses ne se sont pas exactement déroulées, surtout en ce qui concerne la constitution de la sous-commission, telles que les rapporte GROOTAERS, *Le concile se joue* (n. 45), pp. 484-485: Huyghe n'est pas à la Doctrinale le 27 mai et Mgr Seper n'est pas dans la nouvelle sous-commission. Voir, dans le même sens que Charue (à propos de la sous-commission), mais en très bref, CONGAR, *Mon journal du Concile* (n. 4), Tome I, p. 382 (Mardi 28 mai). Selon Tromp (*Acta Commissionis*, pp. 40-41), le nouveau titre du chap. IV annoncé dans une lettre au card. Ottaviani, en tant que président de la Doctrinale, par le card. Browne au terme des trois réunions de la sous-commission est *De sanctitate in ecclesia*.
72. Outre Thils, Labourdette est aussi présent à cette réunion selon le rapport de Tromp (*Acta Commissionis*, p. 40), ainsi que Seper (ce qui est en contradiction formelle avec Charue).

question des prêtres, on parle[ra] aussi des autres clercs et des laïcs qui se dévouent totalement à l'œuvre des évêques»[73]. Accord vite acquis aussi pour l'adaptation proposée de l'ancien texte. Entre autres, on ne parle plus de l'institution divine des conseils évangéliques. Le jour suivant, «à part de légères modifications, tout est accepté»[74]. Ce nouveau texte comprend une introduction (un numéro) et deux sections, dont l'une traite de la vocation universelle à la sainteté pour tous les membres de l'Église (3 numéros) et l'autre des états de perfection dans l'Église (5 numéros). Le card. Browne, invité à la dernière séance de travail, se dit personnellement satisfait, même si le card. Ottaviani, président de la Doctrinale, est «turbatus» et devra être apaisé. Gagnebet a vu Mgr Philippe, membre de la Congrégation des religieux, qui est d'accord avec le nouveau chapitre: ensemble, ils sont décidés à se rendre chez le card. Ottaviani. Quant à Mgr Seper, lui aussi invité à cette ultime réunion, il confiera à Mgr Charue qu'il est «fort content du travail»[75].

En raison de la mort de Jean XXIII le 3 juin au soir, la Commission de coordination, prévue pour le 4 et suspendue juridiquement comme tout le Concile pendant la vacance du Saint-Siège, sera reportée aux 3 et 4 juillet. C'est alors seulement qu'elle examinera les chapitres III et IV du schéma sur l'Église en vue de leur envoi aux Pères.

Entre-temps, bien sûr, les experts poursuivent la finition de ces textes. Thils suit notamment la mise au point du chapitre IV. Ainsi, le 3 juin, fait-il parvenir celui-ci à Philips dans l'état où il a été remis le 1er juin au *minutante* Laberge par Medina, secrétaire de la sous-commission, et l'informe qu'il pourra y découvrir comment ce dernier a exprimé le «moderentur» de Gagnebet[76]. Du 10 au 14 juin, Thils et Moeller préparent à Louvain les notes pour le même chapitre sur la sainteté dans l'Église[77]; le 23 juin, Philips envoie à Moeller les notes mises au point

73. Journal Charue, p. 128.

74. *Ibid.*; «Note sur la discussion...» (n. 61), p. 2.

75. Journal Charue, p. 129.

76. Cf. Fonds Philips, 769 (G. Thils à G. Philips, 3 juin1963: cette lettre accompagne une version du *De vocatione generali ad sanctitatem in ecclesia* – sans doute le *Schema Constitutionis «De ecclesia». Caput IV. De vocatione ad sanctitatem in Ecclesia*, 31 mai 1963, 7 p. et 10 p. de *Notae et commentarius*, cf. Fonds Philips 735 [ce texte deviendra le schéma *De Ecclesia* de la *Tipografia poliglotta Vaticana* daté du 19 juillet 1963, cf. Fonds Philips, 772]). Sur le «bémol» de Gagnebet, cf. Fonds Philips, 768.

77. Cf. Fonds Moeller, 00134 (32 p. dactylographiées, notes mss de Moeller sur la page de garde: «Notes faites à Louvain par Moeller et Thils du 10 au 14 juin 63» et «Notes C. IV De Sanctitate in Ecclesia») et 00135 (même contenu, mais brouillon ms de Moeller et Thils avant la dactylographie).

et son commentaire du nouveau texte pour communication en simple lecture à Congar, tout en signalant à son collègue louvaniste qu'il a fait parvenir les notes au P. Laberge[78]. Il ressort aussi des archives à notre disposition que Thils reçoit une lettre du scheutiste P. Goossens, secrétaire des évêques du Congo-Léopoldville, datée du 20 juillet 1963: il est invité à fournir ses remarques sur les divers schémas; l'épiscopat congolais veut jouer un rôle actif au cours de la seconde session et supprimer le *De missionibus* pour intégrer la mission dans le *De ecclesia*[79]. Le rôle de conseiller théologique, du moins indirect, joué par Thils au profit de cet épiscopat se confirme, comme cela était déjà apparu dans deux lettres du même Goossens adressées en mai 1963 au professeur de Louvain, lui demandant son avis sur trois dossiers préparés pour les évêques du Congo sur le *De revelatione*, le *De missionibus* et le *De ecclesia*[80]. Précisément en août 1963, Goossens envoie aux évêques une circulaire accompagnant des études d'experts, dont Thils, sur ces trois schémas[81]. Parallèlement à cette activité en direction du Congo, une lettre du 17 juillet convoque notre théologien, ainsi que cinq autres *periti* belges (W. Onclin, A. Prignon, G. Philips, L. Cerfaux et Ch. Moeller), à la réunion des évêques belges du 2 août: la concertation entre évêques et experts sur les différents schémas se poursuit donc activement à l'approche de la deuxième session[82]. Le 29 juillet, c'est Thils qui, par lettre, fait à Philips des suggestions pour le futur nouveau chapitre II du *De ecclesia* (*De populo Dei*)[83]. Le 17 août, Mgr Charue écrit à tous les deux pour demander leur

---

78. Cf. Fonds Moeller, 00136 (carte de G. Philips à Ch. Moeller, 23 juin 1963, accompagnant les 23 notes du chapitre IV *De vocatione ad sanctitatem in ecclesia* – 9 p. – et la page et demie de commentaire).

79. Cf. Fonds Thils, 1227 (P. Goossens à G. Thils, 20 juillet 1963).

80. Cf. Fonds Thils, 1224-1225 (P. Goossens à G. Thils, 13 et 11 mai 1963).

81. Cf. Fonds Thils, 1202 (P. Goossens aux évêques du Congo, août 1963).

82. Cf. Fonds Suenens, 0675 (Lettre de convocation de *periti* belges à la réunion des évêques du 2 août 1963, 17 juillet 1963).

83. Cf. Fonds Philips, 785 [ancien n° P.026.04] (G. Thils à G. Philips, 29 juillet 1963). En substance, il lui «semble important de ramener la hiérarchie à l'intérieur du populus Dei, et de traiter des charismata à propos de tous!» On l'avait déjà bien perçu lors des discussions sur le chap. III à la Commission théologique au cours du mois de mai 1963. Plus précisément, il propose que les paragraphes constituant le n. 24 de l'ancien chap. III sur les laïcs soient transférés ici (car ils concernent l'ensemble du Peuple de Dieu, et pas seulement les laïcs) et soient distribués dans le nouveau chap. II comme suit: n° 3, *De sacerdotio universali*; n° 4, *Sanctitas populi in sacramentis nititur*; n° 5, *Populus Dei in Spiritu* (*de sensu fidelium et charismatibus*). Philips enregistre ces modifications dans sa rédaction du nouveau chap. II, mais sans enthousiasme (cf. Fonds Philips, 789-790 [anciens numéros P.026.03 et P.020.07]); en fait, les changements proposés par Thils seront repris dans le chap. II de *Lumen gentium*. Comme en témoigne l'ample conversation de J. Grootaers avec G. Thils le 1er août 1963 à Louvain (*Diarium* 9, pp. 1217-1236), celui-ci mesure toute l'importance dogmatique, œcuménique et pastorale de l'insertion d'un chap. II *De*

avis avant d'envoyer au secrétariat du Concile ses remarques sur le schéma *De ecclesia*[84]: Philips et Thils sont bien les conseillers attitrés du membre de la Commission doctrinale et président de la sous-commission de celle-ci sur la vocation à la sainteté...

Entre-temps, en juillet, a eu lieu la réunion de la Commission de coordination et une décision importante y a été prise. Ainsi, lors de la séance du 4 juillet, la nouvelle rédaction des chapitres III et IV du *De ecclesia* est-elle approuvée; ensuite, le card. Suenens propose un nouvel ordre pour ce schéma, de manière à insérer un nouveau chapitre II intitulé *De populo Dei in genere* après le premier chapitre *De ecclesiae mysterio* et avant l'ancien chapitre II (désormais III) *De constitutione hierarchica Ecclesiae*, lui-même suivi dès lors d'un *De laicis in specie* (chap. IV) et du *De vocatione ad sanctitatem in ecclesia* (chap. V). On sait la signification et l'importance théologiques d'un tel chapitre sur le Peuple de Dieu dans son ensemble avant d'envisager les différentes composantes et fonctions de celui-ci, sans qu'il soit nécessaire de les développer ici; on sait aussi l'origine directe de ce changement souhaité: une suggestion précise de Mgr Prignon au cardinal avant qu'il ne se rende à la Commission de coordination[85]. La proposition ne reçoit pas un appui unanime. Aussi est-il décidé d'entendre les Pères conciliaires sur ce nouvel ordre. Toujours est-il que le secrétariat en avertira tous les Pères à l'occasion de l'envoi des schémas approuvés par la commission[86] ... Toujours est-il aussi que les *periti*, louvanistes notamment, vont se mettre au travail tout de suite pour préparer un projet de nouveau chapitre lors de la réunion de Malines des 6, 7 et 8 septembre suivants, à laquelle Thils participe avec Cerfaux, Philips, Prignon, Mgr Ceuppens, vicaire général représentant le cardinal Suenens, Dondeyne, Delhaye, Moeller, Tucci,

---

populo Dei dans le *De ecclesia*: l'Église, c'est l'ensemble du peuple chrétien, et pas seulement la hiérarchie. D'où vient ce nouveau progrès? Plus on a avancé en mars et en mai, plus on s'est aperçu que «*les résistances étaient facilement vaincues*» et plus on a pu être ambitieux dans les objectifs à atteindre (*ibid.*, p. 1220 bis).

84. Cf. Fonds Philips, 801 (Mgr Charue à G. Philips et G. Thils, 17 août 1963). Voir aussi Fonds Philips 802 (4 p. jointes de remarques de l'évêque namurois sur le *De ecclesia*).

85. La *relatio* du card. Suenens pour cette réunion a d'ailleurs été rédigée pour une très large part par A. Prignon, cf. Fonds Suenens, 0898 (texte de la *relatio* avec notes mss de Suenens).

86. Pour une brève présentation des décisions de la Commission de coordination, cf. TROMP, *Acta Commissionis*, p. 41 (Ottaviani et Tromp ont été invités pour ce qui concerne la Commission doctrinale, mais le président de celle-ci n'a pu y assister). Pour plus de détails, cf. *AS* V/1, pp. 574-594 (texte des deux chapitres et *relatio* du card. Suenens *De ecclesia*) et 635 (procès-verbal de la discussion); voir aussi GROOTAERS, *Le concile se joue* (n. 45), pp. 486-488.

Rahner, Rigaux et Congar[87] ... C'est dans cette perspective qu'il faut situer déjà la lettre de Thils à Philips en date du 29 juillet, citée ci-dessus. Le 18 septembre suivant, C. Colombo écrira à G. Philips pour lui demander le texte du nouveau chapitre *De populo Dei*[88]. Quant au président de la Commission doctrinale, il recevra le 24 septembre le schéma sur l'Église (première partie) transformé par Philips selon le souhait du card. Suenens exprimé le 4 juillet[89]. Entre-temps, celui-ci vient d'être nommé, avec les card. Agagianian, Döpfner et Lercaro, modérateur du Concile pour la deuxième session.

CONCLUSION PROVISOIRE

Sur la base, très partielle, de mon début d'enquête, on peut conclure que le chanoine Thils est un acteur significatif, quoique un peu latéral, de l'élaboration d'un nouveau *De ecclesia* au cours de la première session: il sert un peu de caution à Philips, qui l'associe à la rédaction de son schéma de remplacement.

Au cours de la première intersession, son implication dans la confection du nouveau schéma est beaucoup plus nette. Il sera membre de la sous-commission des sept experts chargée, en février-mars 1963, de fournir un nouveau texte *De ecclesia* (les deux premiers chapitres) en prenant pour base celui de Philips. Il est spécialement attentif à l'expression de la *collégialité épiscopale* et n'hésite pas à exprimer, en privé notamment, son mécontentement vis-à-vis d'un écrit trop peu à son goût. Thils, avec Philips, Moeller et Cerfaux, collaborera à la rédaction des notes du schéma Philips amendé en mars par la Commission doctrinale. Thils participe aux réunions plénières de celle-ci à partir du 15 mai. Au cours de

---

87. À part Thils, je suis l'ordre d'énumération des experts par Congar dans *Mon journal du Concile* (n. 4), Tome I, pp. 394-395 (Samedi 7 septembre 1963). À la p. 395, Congar, arrivé un jour en retard, note: «Le matin, de 10 à 13 h, on achève ce qui a été commencé hier: les remarques sur le *De Ecclesia* et sur la constitution du nouveau chapitre *De populo Dei*».

88. Cf. Fonds Philips, 786 (C. Colombo à G. Philips, 18 septembre 1963).

89. Cf. TROMP, *Acta Commissionis*, p. 42. Le texte dont il est ici question est le *De Ecclesia (Nova ordinatio capitum)*, lat., s.d., 4 p. (Fonds Philips, 791), ronéotypé ensuite par la Commission doctrinale et intitulé *Schema constitutionis dogmaticae de ecclesia. Nova ordinatio capitum (ab E. Card. Suenens)*, lat. 28 septembre 1963, 6 p. (Fonds Philips, 792). Voir aussi Fonds Suenens, 1008 (G. Philips à R. Ceuppens, 10 septembre 1963, envoyant le texte et demandant que le cardinal en fasse parvenir un exemplaire au Secrétariat du Concile), 1009 (texte) et 1010 (Card. Suenens au Card. Browne, 16 septembre 1963, lui envoyant le texte de Philips).

la discussion du 25 mai relative au chapitre III sur le Peuple de Dieu et spécialement les *laïcs*, Thils intervient à deux reprises selon le rapport de Tromp (avec d'ailleurs confirmation partielle par Thils lui-même dans ses conversations avec Grootaers des 1er mai et 1er août 1963), dans la perspective de l'égalité entre tous les baptisés (tous peuvent bénéficier de charismes ordinaires ou modestes) ou du moins en vue de ne pas creuser l'écart entre fidèles et hiérarchie (il est suffisamment précis d'indiquer une «différence essentielle» entre le sacerdoce universel et le sacerdoce hié-rarchique). Mais s'il est un chapitre où l'expert belge joue un rôle mar-quant en mai 1963, c'est le chapitre IV, intitulé «De ceux qui professent les conseils évangéliques». Thils prépare un texte à mettre en tête de ce chapitre et qui traite de l'appel universel à la sainteté ainsi que des voies diverses pour y tendre (l'espoir du professeur louvaniste est de pouvoir élargir le chapitre IV et en faire un véritable *De sanctitate in ecclesia*, à l'intérieur duquel on traiterait des deux formes de sainteté et spéciale-ment des 'états de perfection'). La sous-commission mise sur pied pour examiner le chapitre IV et présidée par Mgr Charue prend comme base le texte de Thils le 29 mai et invite celui-ci à ses réunions. Cet écrit sera retouché par Philips en collaboration avec son auteur et quelques autres, ainsi que le schéma sur ceux qui professent les conseils évangéliques. Le titre global retenu est «De la vocation générale à la sainteté dans l'Église». Les 30 et 31 mai, le texte de Thils et l'ancien schéma, tous deux remaniés (on n'affirme plus l'institution divine des conseils évan-géliques), sont adoptés moyennant de légères modifications. Le nouveau schéma comprend une introduction et deux sections, l'une sur la vocation universelle à la sainteté et l'autre sur les états de perfection. Charue et Thils sont arrivés à leurs fins, au-delà même de leurs ambitions premières, étonnés du peu de résistance[90], … momentanément du moins, car les nombreux religieux de l'assemblée conciliaire (évêques et supérieurs généraux) ne tarderont pas à réagir au cours de la deuxième session.

Par ailleurs, dès qu'il est mis au courant de la *nova ordinatio* des cha-pitres du *De ecclesia*, le théologien belge est enthousiaste et fait des pro-positions, qui s'avéreront judicieuses, à son collègue Philips pour la rédac-tion du nouveau chapitre *De populo Dei in genere*, en y ramenant certains paragraphes de l'ancien *De laicis* sur le sacerdoce universel, la sainteté du peuple chrétien enraciné dans les sacrements ainsi que le *sensus fidei* et les charismes. Ces paragraphes feront effectivement partie du chapitre II de la constitution promulguée.

---

90. Comme le confie le professeur de Louvain à J. Grootaers le 1er août 1963 (cf. le *Diarium* 9 déjà cité, p. 1220 bis; voir *supra*, note 83).

Tels sont quelques faits de la première période jusqu'en septembre 1963 quant à la participation directe de Gustave Thils à la réécriture du schéma sur l'Église. Ceci dit, son activité relative au *De ecclesia* est beaucoup plus large, mais l'efficacité n'en est pas facilement mesurable : outre son appartenance au Secrétariat pour l'Unité et sa présence régulière comme *peritus* aux sessions de la Commission doctrinale, Thils a une activité très diffuse (de nombreuses relations : Suenens, Charue, l'épiscopat belge, le secrétaire de l'épiscopat congolais, Taizé, Laurentin… ; des conférences ; des écrits…), à défaut d'être toujours bien recentrée et efficace. Le professeur louvaniste est certainement moins tacticien et plus effacé ou modeste que d'autres Belges, Gérard Philips notamment.

Du point de vue théologique, le chanoine Thils apparaît comme un «progressiste» et un «maximaliste» à cette époque : dans ses conversations privées surtout, mais aussi dans ses notes ou publications, il ne cache pas son insatisfaction, parfois fort critique, même à l'égard de la rédaction de Philips, qu'il s'agisse de la collégialité épiscopale (trop peu affirmée), des laïcs (trop dépendants de la hiérarchie pour leur apostolat) ou des religieux (monopolisant de manière indue la sainteté dans l'Église). Sa différence, voire sa divergence doctrinale au sein de l'équipe du *Collegio belga*, spécialement par rapport à Philips, en ressort en tout cas nettement. Si, globalement, une bonne collaboration a réuni les deux professeurs de Louvain, on perçoit aussi, en filigrane et parfois explicitement, les tensions de divers ordres qui ont surgi entre eux. Par ailleurs, Thils apparaît au départ comme beaucoup plus proche de Suenens que Philips : il est un prêtre diocésain de Malines-Bruxelles, il a aussi une vue plus souple du laïcat chrétien que son collègue du Limbourg, très attaché à l'Action Catholique et en désaccord sur ce point avec un archevêque promoteur de la Légion de Marie. Thils bénéficie aussi de toute la confiance de Charue pour le *De ecclesia*, en particulier pour le chapitre sur la sainteté dans l'Église. Mais, dès janvier 1963 en tout cas, G. Philips se révèle de fait comme l'homme de la situation, comme le rédacteur principal du nouveau *De ecclesia* en chantier, aux yeux des experts, belges et étrangers, du *Collegio belga*, du card. Suenens et de Mgr Charue, et bientôt de l'ensemble de la Commission doctrinale.

Si le chanoine Thils est moins stratège et manœuvrier que d'autres compatriotes, il est cependant très présent et agit ponctuellement. Il reste avant tout un théologien, plus soucieux de faire passer des idées que d'être un conciliateur réaliste. L'étude minutieuse des deux périodes conciliaires suivantes permettra peut-être de confirmer ces premières conclusions. Elle devrait en tout cas préciser encore et compléter la contribution, non

négligeable, du professeur belge à la future constitution dogmatique
Lumen gentium.

Université catholique de Louvain   Joseph FAMERÉE
Faculté de théologie
Grand-Place, 45
B-1348 Louvain-la-Neuve
Belgique

LA COLLABORATION DE PIERRE HAUBTMANN
AVEC LES EXPERTS BELGES

Le titre de cette communication annonce qu'elle sera consacrée à la rédaction de *Gaudium et spes*, dont le Français Pierre Haubtmann assura la coordination d'ensemble à partir du 17 novembre 1964. Notre domaine de recherche portant sur l'interprétation théologique de Vatican II, nous voudrions examiner en quoi les collaborations entre Haubtmann et les experts belges éclairent la théologie de la Constitution pastorale, particulièrement en regard de la question, très disputée actuellement, de *la contribution de la foi chrétienne aux problèmes éthiques de notre époque*. Nous aurions pu étudier les relations d'Haubtmann avec les évêques belges, dans la mesure où les impulsions de plusieurs d'entre eux, à commencer par le cardinal Suenens, furent décisives pour le schéma XIII. Mais la collaboration des experts nous a paru apporter des éléments plus tangibles et plus facilement exploitables. Nous nous limiterons à trois experts belges: Charles Moeller, Gérard Philips et Albert Dondeyne. Leur rôle est déjà bien connu, mais nous pensons qu'il y a encore à découvrir sur la teneur théologique de leur travail conciliaire, pour ce qui a trait notamment à *la conception des rapports Église-monde*.

L'hypothèse de travail qui sera mise à l'épreuve est la suivante: Pierre Haubtmann, qui était avant tout un spécialiste de pastorale extrêmement impliqué dans les conflits de l'Action catholique en France dans les années 1950, rencontre chez les trois théologiens louvanistes des hommes qui l'aident à asseoir ses intuitions en théologie fondamentale, en théologie dogmatique et en anthropologie. Bien qu'il ne soit pas un théologien de métier, mais un historien de compétence universitaire, Haubtmann n'est pas dépourvu de convictions théologiques. Il ne se laisse pas dicter l'agenda théologique[1]. Il sait ce qu'il fait lorsqu'il intègre tel ou tel accent plutôt qu'un autre, d'autant plus qu'il s'appuie sur de nombreuses lectures personnelles ou sur le soutien actif d'autres théologiens français

---

1. En ce sens, il faut sans doute nuancer l'idée qu'Haubtmann serait «plus sociologue et philosophe que théologien». Voir G. TURBANTI, *Un concilio per il mondo moderno: La redazione della Costituzione pastorale 'Gaudium et spes' del Vaticano II* (Testi e Ricerche di Scienze Religiose. Nuova Serie, 24), Bologna, Il Mulino, 2000, p. 793.

comme Congar et Chenu, sollicités dans la tourmente du début de la quatrième session. Il est clair que, face à l'armada des théologiens universitaires de langue allemande, Haubtmann a terriblement besoin de l'appui
des universitaires belges. Mais cette confiance mutuelle a été gagnée dans
une collaboration de fond qui s'est nouée en quelques mois, dès que le
Français prend sa charge de rédacteur principal. C'est ce que nous voudrions montrer en dépouillant quelques documents historiques, que nous
soumettrons à l'analyse théologique. Il en va de la mise au jour d'un héritage croyant. Les experts conciliaires n'étaient pas seulement des petites
mains, mais de véritables témoins de la foi telle qu'elle s'investit dans
une vie de théologien. Cette foi vécue contribue, le moment venu, à l'élaboration d'un texte conciliaire qui devient ensuite le bien commun de
l'Église et la soutient dans sa mission. Tel sera l'angle d'attaque de notre
investigation.

I. CHARLES MŒLLER ET LE MYSTERE CHRÉTIEN POUR L'HOMME D'AUJOURD'HUI

En décembre 1964 et janvier 1965, Haubtmann multiplie les «contacts
et conversations» à Rome, à Paris, à Bruxelles et à son domicile de Meu-
don, où il reçoit notamment Mgr Ménager avec Mgr Streiff et le P. Hirschmann avec le P. Calvez[2]. À l'exception de Rome, un seul déplacement le
conduit à l'étranger[3], en Belgique où il rencontre à Louvain Mœller, Houtart, puis Philips, le 28 décembre 1964. Peu de temps après, en rentrant
de Rome, Mœller s'arrête à Paris où il consacre la matinée du 12 janvier
1965 à travailler avec Haubtmann. Mœller, expert privé du cardinal
Léger puis expert au concile, fait partie du cercle des très proches. Avec
Tucci et Hirschmann[4], il est désigné par Haubtmann comme l'un des trois

---

2. Fonds Haubtmann, 1481.

3. Dans une lettre du 9 janvier 1965 à Mgr Guano (Fonds Haubtmann, 1448), Haubtmann explique qu'il n'arrivera à Rome que le 28 janvier et non le 15 comme l'aurait souhaité l'évêque de Livourne. Il a besoin de «beaucoup de temps» pour le «travail minutieux» qui consiste à «prendre une connaissance précise de tous les documents en jeu, et
notamment des interventions des Pères». Et pour rédiger le *conspectus generalis mundi
hodierni*, il préfère demeurer à Paris où il «dispose de toute une bibliothèque à laquelle il
est habitué», et où il peut compter sur «l'amicale collaboration du R.P. Calvez, directeur
de l'Action Populaire». Les raisons qu'a Haubtmann de rester à Paris sont donc intellec-
tuelles et pas seulement liées à son manque d'habitudes romaines. Voir TURBANTI, *Un
concilio per il mondo moderno* (n. 1), p. 491.

4. En tant que responsable du Bureau de l'Information Religieuse de l'épiscopat français à Rome, Haubtmann a eu l'occasion de collaborer avec Roberto Tucci, directeur de la
Civiltà Cattolica. Quant au Jésuite Johann Hirschmann, Haubtmann le fréquente par l'intermédiaire de Jean-Yves Calvez. Appréciant ses «grandes orientations» (Fonds Haubtmann,

periti susceptibles de l'épauler lorsque, en novembre 1964, le prêtre français est contacté pour coordonner la rédaction. Évoquant ce trio le 23 décembre dans une lettre à Mœller, Haubtmann écrit: «Je suis persuadé que nous formerons ensemble une équipe soudée, et je crois que le succès du schéma XIII en dépend pour une part»[5].

Durant la séance de travail du 12 janvier, les deux hommes se mettent d'accord sur «la structure» d'ensemble du schéma XIII: elle sera organisée selon un «axe historique», conforme à une approche de l'Église comme «peuple de Dieu» en tension «vers le Royaume»[6]. Mœller évoque aussi deux options rédactionnelles majeures:

(a) la prise en compte de l'aspiration de notre temps à «la dignité, au respect, à la liberté, à l'autonomie et à la participation de tous», y compris dans l'Église où «les chrétiens doivent être traités en adultes»;
(b) la mise à l'écart du vocabulaire de l'ordre naturel et de l'ordre surnaturel, au profit «des expressions bibliques d'alliance, de grâce, de nouvelle création».

Plusieurs documents d'archives permettent d'approfondir les enjeux théologiques de ces choix. Nous disposons premièrement des notes prises par Haubtmann sur un article du jésuite Henri Bouillard mentionné par Mœller à l'appui de leur entente[7]. Comme à son habitude dans les lectures qui soutiennent sa tâche de rédacteur, Haubtmann recopie une vingtaine de paragraphes, ainsi que deux notes de bas de page, l'une sur saint Thomas et le libre arbitre, l'autre sur la divinisation de l'humanité par l'union au Christ chez saint Augustin et chez les Pères grecs[8]. Ce document aide à cerner la cohérence interne des trois options énoncées par Mœller: une perspective historique, la prise en compte de la valeur de la liberté, le recours aux thèmes bibliques. En contrepoint, les annotations sévères portées en marge par Haubtmann sur un texte de Jean Daniélou

---

1427), il lui confie le paragraphe sur les atteintes à la dignité humaine dans la société moderne: «conditionnements psychologiques, expérimentations biologiques, etc.» (Fonds Haubtmann, 1448).

5. Fonds Haubtmann, 1427.

6. C. MŒLLER, *L'élaboration du schéma XIII*, Tournai, Casterman, 1968, pp. 105-106 et p. 111, où Mœller se trompe manifestement lorsqu'il indique le 12 décembre au lieu du 12 janvier.

7. H. BOUILLARD, *L'idée de surnaturel et le mystère chrétien*, dans *L'homme devant Dieu: Mélanges offerts au Père Henri de Lubac*. III: *Perspectives d'aujourd'hui*, Paris, Aubier, 1964, 153-166. MŒLLER, *L'élaboration du schéma XIII* (n. 6), p. 106. Fonds Haubtmann, 1496. Le papier vert, utilisé par Haubtmann, indique qu'il est bien l'auteur de ces notes.

8. Fonds Haubtmann, 1496. La dactylographie est, selon toute vraisemblance, la même que celle du document nr. 1486, rédigé par Haubtmann.

indiquent le type de raisonnement qu'il s'emploie à écarter[9]. Une contribution de Mœller à l'issue de la session d'Ariccia[10] permet encore de constater que leur ligne rédactionnelle commune maintient le cap tout en composant avec d'autres perspectives. On dispose enfin du jugement porté par Lukas Vischer sur le nouveau schéma en réponse à la demande de Mœller[11]: l'observateur du Conseil Œcuménique des Églises se montre sensible à la perspective retenue[12].

1. Annoncer le salut dans l'histoire de la liberté

L'article de Bouillard sur «L'idée de surnaturel et le mystère chrétien» permet à Haubtmann et Mœller d'ancrer la logique du schéma XIII en *théologie fondamentale*. Ils étaient l'un et l'autre assez familiers de la pensée contemporaine pour percevoir l'irrecevabilité de la notion de surnaturel – Mœller l'avait amplement montré chez Sartre[13] – et, partant, l'impossibilité de s'adresser aux hommes de ce temps dans les catégories du naturel et du surnaturel[14]. Mais cette conviction pastorale devait être assumée dans une contre-proposition théologique, que Mœller et Haubtmann empruntent à Bouillard. Ce dernier, ardent promoteur de la prise en compte de l'expérience humaine en théologie fondamentale[15], montre que la critique adressée par le P. de Lubac aux «traités de l'ordre surnaturel» du XIXe siècle a pour heureuse postérité la naissance d'une théologie du «mystère chrétien» qui, grâce au «renouveau des études bibliques et

9. Fonds Haubtmann, 1491.

10. Fonds Haubtmann, 1700.

11. L. Vischer, lettre au Chanoine C. Mœller du 6 avril 1965, Fonds Philips, 2281. C'est au moment de la réunion de Malines que naît l'idée de consulter Vischer sous mode confidentiel, mais Mgr Guano tarde à donner son accord. Voir TURBANTI, *Un concilio per il mondo moderno* (n. 1), p. 277.

12. Il était important de conserver une ouverture œcuménique, sachant que la nouvelle équipe rédactionnelle y était moins portée que celle qui avait conçu le schéma de Malines «selon la trilogie bien connue dans les milieux œcuméniques: *marturia* (témoignage), *diakonia* (service) et *koinonia* (communion)». Voir J. GROOTAERS, *Actes et acteurs à Vatican II* (BETL, 139), Leuven, Peeters, 1998, p. 410.

13. «Qu'en est-il de Sartre? Telle est la question à laquelle je vais essayer de répondre en étudiant la pièce centrale de sa pensée, le refus du surnaturel quel qu'il soit. Sartre est un témoin, un reflet d'une partie de l'âme moderne. Il faut l'écouter». Voir C. MŒLLER, *Littérature du XXe siècle et christianisme*. Tome II: *La foi en Jésus-Christ. Jean-Paul Sartre - Henry James - Roger Martin du Gard - Joseph Malègue*, Tournai – Paris, Casterman, 1953, pp. 37-38.

14. P. HAUBTMANN, *La communauté humaine*, dans Y. CONGAR – M. PEUCHMAURD (éds.), *Vatican II: L'Église dans le monde de ce temps. Constitution pastorale 'Gaudium et Spes'*, Tome II, Paris, Cerf, 1967, 255-277.

15. H. BOUILLARD, *L'expérience humaine et le point de départ de la théologie fondamentale*, dans *Concilium* 6 (1965) 83-92.

patristiques», renoue avec «la densité concrète des notions d'alliance, de grâce, de nouvelle création, de participation à la vie divine»[16]. La thèse de Bouillard est que «le salut de l'humanité par la foi au Christ Jésus» résume «l'essence du christianisme», conformément à «ce qu'annonce le Nouveau testament et [à] ce qu'a répété la tradition chrétienne»[17]. Cette insistance sur l'annonce est centrale. Mœller et Haubtmann veulent partir des thèmes bibliques, mais dans la mesure seulement où ils apparaissent susceptibles de toucher l'homme contemporain, destinataire du message de salut. Caractéristique en ce sens est un texte, intitulé «Comment présenter Dieu à l'homme d'aujourd'hui?»[18], où Mœller s'efforce d'identifier le thème biblique le plus adéquat face à un athéisme légitimement révolté contre «l'infantilisme de certains croyants». Il conclut que «l'idée du Dieu caché qui se révèle comme caché», à ne pas confondre avec le «Dieu inconnaissable», correspond à la fois aux requêtes contemporaines et au paradoxe de la Révélation, très présent dans l'évangile de Jean[19]. À l'inverse, Haubtmann désapprouve cette autre formulation de Daniélou: «Le Concile est fidèle à sa mission quand il enseigne aux laïcs chrétiens leur double devoir de pénétrer de l'esprit du Christ la civilisation contemporaine et de rendre la civilisation contemporaine capable de l'esprit du Christ»[20]. Haubtmann réagit en marge: «Il y a un *tertium quid*!: Révéler le Christ». Daniélou reste à ses yeux tributaire d'une théologie du surnaturel trop peu reliée à l'annonce contemporaine du salut, malgré son ancrage dans l'Écriture et chez les Pères.

Car pour recourir adéquatement aux thèmes bibliques et patristiques, Bouillard fait valoir qu'il faut songer que «c'est à l'homme que sont offertes l'alliance divine, la rédemption, la vie éternelle». C'est donc «en l'homme lui-même» qu'il «faut trouver l'élément qui oblige à distinguer entre le don de la grâce et celui de la nature», et qui n'est autre que «la nécessité de l'option spirituelle». S'appuyant sur saint Augustin et sur saint Thomas, Bouillard souligne que la grâce de la divinisation (ou de la béatitude) ne nous advient «que par la libre conversion de l'homme». En conséquence, «l'intelligence même de l'ordre surnaturel» appelle à «préciser que le sujet de la vie nouvelle est *l'homme en tant que liberté*».

16. Fonds Haubtmann, 1496, p. 2.

17. BOUILLARD, *L'idée de surnaturel et le mystère Chrétien* (n. 7), p. 157. Fonds Haubtmann, 1496, p. 3.

18. Fonds Haubtmann, 1701.

19. «Personne n'a jamais vu Dieu: le Fils unique, qui est dans le sein du Père, lui, l'a révélé» (Jn 1,18).

20. J. DANIÉLOU, *Esquisse d'une anthropologie chrétienne pour le schéma XIII du 23 décembre 1964*, Fonds Haubtmann, 1491.

Haubtmann souligne[21], tant cette insistance sur la liberté lui paraît décisive pour la crédibilité du christianisme à l'époque actuelle. Bouillard la met d'ailleurs en rapport avec *l'historicité du salut chrétien*, puisque c'est «la médiation du Christ» qui «accomplit la liberté humaine». La faille principale de la théologie du «surnaturel» est de masquer «la relation personnelle et historique» entre Dieu et l'homme sauvé.

Dès lors, toute approche du mystère chrétien qui négligerait les paramètres historiques de la liberté humaine semble irrecevable à Haubtmann. Ainsi, lorsque Daniélou mentionne la capacité de l'homme à connaître Dieu et qu'il ajoute: «La dignité de la personne humaine s'exprime aussi en ce que l'homme est libre», Haubtmann vitupère en marge: «Rien sur la conscience!»[22]. Un peu plus loin, il conteste une autre affirmation du jésuite: «L'univers a une valeur religieuse et conduit à lui. La séparation du monde matériel de Dieu, sa désacralisation sont des erreurs». Haubtmann riposte: «Le tout est de s'entendre sur les mots». Pour lui en effet, la désacralisation du monde inhérente à la modernité n'est pas condamnable en soi. C'est aussi l'analyse de Mœller, pour qui «l'homme moderne cherche *un Dieu plus grand*» susceptible de «fonder son *autonomie*» et qui voit dans l'humanisme contemporain «*d'abord* [un] sens de la responsabilité collective des hommes en face de l'univers, plutôt qu'[un] orgueil prométhéen ou faustien»[23].

2. L'annonce du salut contribue à infléchir l'histoire du monde

Le parti pris d'un regard positif sur le monde actuel, fondé dans la foi en la poursuite de l'histoire du salut, méritait toutefois quelques ajustements théologiques, particulièrement bien relevés par Lukas Vischer. Durant la troisième session, ce dernier avait déjà mis en garde contre un usage trop optimiste des signes des temps, alors que le contexte biblique oblige à cultiver un esprit de «conversion», de «pénitence eschatologique» et de renonciation à la «terrible réalité» du «mal», qui se niche dans les signes comme dans leur interprétation[24]. À nouveau sollicité par

---

21. Fonds Haubtmann, 1496. Souligné par Haubtmann.
22. Fonds Haubtmann, 1491.
23. Fonds Haubtmann, 1701. Ce jugement positif sur l'humanisme contemporain subsiste dans le chapitre sur la culture: «Nous sommes donc les témoins de la naissance d'un nouvel humanisme; l'homme s'y définit avant tout par la responsabilité qu'il assume envers ses frères et devant l'histoire» (*GS* 55).
24. Document sur le schéma 13. Travaux. Rome, 3e session, 1964, Fonds Houtart, 27. La contribution de Vischer figure en annexe au rapport de la sous-commission *Signa temporum*.

Mœller au printemps 1965, Vischer se montre satisfait de plusieurs améliorations apportées au schéma. Il cite avant tout la mise en valeur du
«caractère historique de l'Église», dont «l'immutabilité» n'est plus mise
en avant, de telle sorte qu'apparaît mieux «sa vocation à être solidaire
avec le monde»[25]. Ce changement de perspective est une conséquence
directe de la ligne adoptée par les deux experts. Malgré tout, Vischer
regrette que «l'Église et l'histoire restent encore trop à côté l'une de
l'autre». La situation du monde actuel n'est pas assez vue comme une
«conséquence de la prédication», alors que «l'appel à l'obéissance rend
simultanément possible la désobéissance» si bien que «le oui au monde
n'est jamais aussi fort que lorsqu'il s'accompagne d'un non». Pour
Vischer, «la compréhension de l'Évangile s'approfondit dans la confrontation avec le monde». Il aurait aimé que soit développé le caractère dialectique des rapports entre Église et société à travers l'exemple concret
de l'abolition progressive de l'esclavage. Le texte conciliaire n'accède
pas à ce vœu. Mais on peut penser que le quatrième chapitre de la première partie, rédigé à la même époque, bénéficie du correctif apporté par
Vischer dans son approche théologique de l'histoire du salut. Le texte
insiste en effet sur l'aide réciproque que s'apportent l'Église et le monde
(*GS* 41 à 44), ainsi que sur les «avantages» retirés par l'Église «de
l'opposition même de ses adversaires et de ses persécuteurs» (*GS* 44,3).

3. La mise en œuvre rédactionnelle

Terminons cet aperçu sur la collaboration entre Mœller et Haubtman
par l'examen de quelques documents qui attestent à la fois l'influence du
premier sur le texte final et la maîtrise que conserve le second sur les
orientations de fond[26]. Le 15 mars 1965, c'est-à-dire entre la session
d'Ariccia et celle de la commission mixte à Rome, Mœller rédige une version longue et une brève pour un paragraphe à insérer dans le *conspectus generalis*. Recombinant les deux versions, Haubtmann retient trois
phrases qui figurent presque intégralement dans le texte final (*GS* 4,2):
«Le genre humain vit aujourd'hui une période de son histoire caractéri-
sée par des changements profonds et très rapides, qui s'étendent progressivement à l'univers entier. Provoqués par l'homme, [ils] rejaillissent

25. Fonds Philips, 2281. Nous traduisons le texte allemand.
26. Congar, qui perçoit la détermination d'Haubtmann comme une prise de pouvoir,
lui reproche de tout réécrire après la réunion d'Ariccia et de prendre «bien de la liberté à
l'égard d'un texte discuté et admis». Cf. Y. CONGAR, *Mon journal du Concile*. Tome II
(1964-66), Présenté et annoté par É. MAHIEU. Avant-propos de D. CONGAR. Préface de
B. DUPUY, Paris, Cerf, 2002, p. 332.

sur l'homme, sur ses jugements et comportements, individuels et collectifs. [À tel point que] beaucoup n'hésitent pas à parler de mutation sociale et culturelle»[27]. Mgr McGrath rajoute une incise qui subsiste dans le texte final: «Provoqués par l'homme, *par son intelligence et son activité créatrice*, ils rejaillissent sur l'homme…»[28]. On signale ensuite que les effets de la métamorphose sociale et culturelle «se répercutent jusque sur la vie religieuse», pour contenter le binôme Goldie-Fernandez qui voulait que l'on mentionne «l'intensification de l'esprit religieux»[29]. La formulation retenue est minimale, car Haubtmann écarte tout ce qui pourrait ressembler à de la récupération religieuse. Il veut un texte recevable par tous les hommes. C'est sans doute aussi le motif qui le conduit à écarter la version longue de Mœller, dont les termes «dominer la nature» ou «domestiquer les lois et les faire servir à ses desseins» apparaissent trop bibliques pour l'exposé introductif. Haubtmann choisit la sobriété: les changements provoqués par l'homme rejaillissent sur lui. Cela met habilement l'accent sur l'historicité de l'homme lui-même. Mais ces inflexions mineures n'entament pas la convergence de fond entre Haubtmann et Mœller.

Pour Haubtmann, Mœller était l'interlocuteur compétent, sur lequel il pouvait s'appuyer pour concevoir les «axes d'une anthropologie chrétienne adaptée à notre temps»[30]. La communication passait assurément mieux avec lui qu'avec François Houtart, qui fournissait des textes «beaucoup trop longs»[31], et à qui Haubtmann dut rappeler que Mœller était «son co-équipier» – ce qui sous-entendait qu'Houtart ne l'était pas[32]! Mais dégager des axes était une chose, les traduire concrètement dans l'écriture en était une autre. Concernant la première partie du schéma XIII, Haubtmann écrit à Mgr Guano: «Je souhaiterais vivement que cet exposé, bien que lourd de doctrine, soit aussi simple que possible dans son expression et que le bon peuple de notre temps, avec ses activités quotidiennes sans relief spécial, puisse s'y retrouver. Il faudrait aussi que, dans les valeurs humaines et chrétiennes mises en lumière, on retrouve celles du 'cœur', au sens biblique du terme, pour que notre texte soit imprégné d'une certaine chaleur humaine»[33]. Cette tournure pastorale chère à Haubtmann convenait à Mœller, spécialiste de la littérature

---

27. Fonds Haubtmann, 1700. La conjonction «à tel point que» est rajoutée à la main par Haubtmann.
28. Fonds Philips, 2296.
29. Fonds Philips, 2295.
30. Fonds Haubtmann, 1448.
31. Fonds Haubtmann, 1448.
32. Fonds Haubtmann, 1449.
33. Fonds Haubtmann, 1448.

existentialiste. Mais avant que le texte ne soit recevable par l'homme contemporain, il fallait qu'il soit acceptable par les Pères et les experts. C'était le rôle de Philips que d'y veiller. En sa personne, Haubtmann approchait davantage la manière proprement louvaniste, façonnée dans une théologie plus universitaire, celle-là même qui avait conçu le schéma de Malines rejeté par le courant de l'apostolat des laïcs dont Haubtmann était issu.

II. Gérard Philips et la reprise eschatologique de l'anthropologie

Étant donné le rôle majeur du binôme Haubtmann-Philips dans l'avancement de *Gaudium et spes*, nous nous attendions à trouver des documents plus substantiels pour éclairer leur collaboration. Peut-être n'avons-nous pas identifié la bonne filière et n'y avons-nous pas consacré assez de temps. Tout compte fait, il semble aussi qu'il ait manqué à ce binôme les conditions qui leur auraient permis d'outrepasser le cadre d'une association de raison.

1. Une relation complexe

N'oublions pas que, pour le prêtre français propulsé à la tête de l'équipe rédactionnelle, Philips avait des allures de «statue du commandeur». Ses qualités de théologien universitaire, professeur dans l'une des plus prestigieuses facultés européennes, l'autorité qu'il avait acquise au concile[34] en menant à son terme la rédaction de *Lumen gentium*, faisant face avec courage aux oppositions qui pouvaient prendre la forme de manœuvres déstabilisatrices, son expérience du débat institutionnel, dans le cadre parlementaire puis au concile, le prestige d'un homme dont on disait que les évêques belges avaient demandé pour lui la pourpre cardinalice[35]: tout cela ne pouvait qu'impressionner Haubtmann, qui avait certes obtenu de hautes distinctions universitaires en sociologie et en histoire de la philosophie, mais qui était d'abord un pasteur[36]. Engagé dans les difficiles débats de l'Action catholique en France durant l'après-guerre, il avait prouvé sa capacité à tenir une ligne politique dans

---

34. J. Grootaers, *Gérard Philips: La force dans la faiblesse*, dans Id., *Actes et acteurs* (n. 12), 382-419, ici p. 408.

35. A. Prignon, *Évêques et théologiens de Belgique au Concile Vatican II*, dans C. Soetens (éd.), *Vatican II et la Belgique* (Sillages), Ottignies, ARCA – Quorum, 1996, 141-184, spéc. p. 157.

36. P. Bordeyne, *Pierre Haubtmann au Concile Vatican II: Un historien et un théologien de l'inquiétude contemporaine*, dans *ETL* 77 (2001) 356-383.

l'adversité: aumônier national de l'Action catholique ouvrière, il avait
maintenu le cap de la mission comme raison d'être de l'Église, face aux par-
tisans de la sécularisation qui voulaient recentrer les laïcs sur le service du
temporel[37]. Bien qu'il eût peu l'expérience des contacts internationaux, il
avait su s'orienter dans la complexité des débats conciliaires et manifester
un talent de communicateur lors des conférences de presse qu'il organisait
à Rome. C'était aussi un organisateur et un bourreau de travail[38], ce qui fut
bien utile lors du marathon de la quatrième session, où il consacra toutes
ses forces à lever les obstacles sur le chemin de la Constitution pastorale.

Outre les différences de stature internationale et d'enracinement minis-
tériel dans l'Église, certains éléments conjoncturels rendaient les relations entre les deux hommes pour le moins complexes. Premièrement,
Haubtmann n'avait été nommé coordinateur de la rédaction finale qu'à
la suite du refus de Philips, à qui la charge avait été proposée ainsi qu'à
Tucci[39]. Deuxièmement, la situation d'Haubtmann pouvait sembler fragile et inconfortable, dans la mesure où Philips recevait la charge de
«revoir tout le texte du point de vue doctrinal, de la correction de la
rédaction latine, de l'unité technique». Et Philips avait la confiance de
Mgr Guano[40]. Troisièmement, le changement de l'équipe de rédaction
intervenait dans le contexte d'un contentieux non encore apuré entre la
Commission de l'Apostolat des laïcs, qui proposait le nom d'Haubtmann
par la voix de Mgr Ménager, et le groupe de Malines, dont Philips avait
rédigé le schéma écarté. Quatrièmement, le stress du travail sur *Lumen
gentium* et sur *Dei verbum*, qui avait conduit Philips à se récuser pour le
schéma XIII, provoqua l'infarctus et le retour vers la Belgique un mois
et demi avant la fin du concile[41]. Ce contexte de surcharge et de lassitude,

---

37. P. HAUBTMANN, *Simples réflexions sur l'intervention de l'Église dans le temporel*,
dans M.-J. GERLAUD – P. HAUBTMANN – G. MATAGRIN (éds.), *Construire l'homme*, Paris,
Les Éditions Ouvrières, 1961, 9-38.

38. P. DELHAYE, *Histoire des textes de la Constitution pastorale*, dans CONGAR –
PEUCHMAURD (éds.), *Vatican II: L'Église dans le monde de ce temps* (n. 14), Tome I, 213-
277, spéc. p. 225.

39. Mgr Ancel, dans une lettre à Philips du 29 décembre 1964, redoute qu'un manque
d'expérience du travail en commission ne nuise à la qualité du texte. Voir TURBANTI,
Un concilio per il mondo moderno (n. 1), pp. 479-481.

40. R. TUCCI, *Introduction historique et doctrinale à la Constitution pastorale*, dans
CONGAR – PEUCHMAURD (éds.), *Vatican II: L'Église dans le monde de ce temps* (n. 14),
Tome II, 33-127, ici p. 93. À la session d'Ariccia, Congar note que le latin d'Haubtmann
est «médiocre et assez mal prononcé». Voir CONGAR, *Mon journal du Concile* (n. 26),
Tome II, p. 306. Le 15 mars 1965, c'est Philips qui transmet à Haubtmann les insistances
de Guano pour «abréger La Pars III» (Fonds Philips, 1577).

41. À partir de ce moment, c'est le binôme Haubtmann-Tucci qui prend les com-
mandes, sous la supervision de Mgr Garrone. Voir TURBANTI, *Un concilio per il mondo
moderno* (n. 1), p. 720.

accentué par l'immense labeur que représente la traduction en latin des passages rédigés en français[42], rend leur collaboration plus difficile à interpréter, sans compter que la complexité de leurs liens explique en partie la rareté des documents. Les commentateurs situent l'apport de Philips au schéma XIII moins du côté de l'expertise théologique – bien que ce fût là sa charge officielle – et davantage du côté de la tactique institutionnelle ou de la régulation des procédures: la médiation des débats durant la session de la Commission mixte qui commence à Rome le 29 mars 1965[43], la mise au point des règles de traitement des nombreux amendements lors de la quatrième session. Philips et Haubtmann ont cependant eu *des échanges théologiques*, que les documents historiques aident à caractériser.

2. Philips oblige Haubtmann à préciser l'axe théologique du schéma

Commençons par ce qu'Haubtmann pouvait savoir de Philips à partir des archives dont il prend possession à sa prise de fonction. Reportons-nous aux propositions d'amendements formulées par le prêtre belge en septembre 1964, où plusieurs thèmes concernent directement le *conspectus generalis* et l'unité de la première partie autour de la vocation humaine. Philips a réécrit le chapitre 1 (*De integra hominis vocatione*) avec la collaboration d'autres théologiens de Louvain, dont les exégètes Cerfaux et Rigaux qui fournissent deux notes de synthèse en annexe aux amendements proposés[44]. Au plan formel, Haubtmann ne peut que constater la précision du travail linguistique[45], fermement fondé sur des arguments doctrinaux. Le jugement est sans pitié pour ce schéma qu'il a fallu traduire en latin à partir des documents rédigés en français pour la session de Zurich, mais il est évidemment très précieux par sa rigueur. Sur le fond, la critique principale de Philips est qu'il faut *une anthropologie*

---

42. «Espérons que je pourrai terminer en temps voulu», écrit Philips le 25 avril 1965, dans une lettre d'accompagnement où il explique qu'il ne suffit pas de traduire le français en latin: «pratiquement, je dois tout transcrire» (Fonds Haubtmann, 1596). Ce document contient la traduction du n° 20, dont on possède par ailleurs les corrections manuscrites de Philips sur le texte français d'Haubtmann (Fonds Philips, 2319).

43. L. DECLERCK – C. SOETENS (éds.), *Carnets conciliaires de l'évêque de Namur A.-M. Charue* (Cahiers de la Revue théologique de Louvain, 32), Louvain-la-Neuve, Publications de la Faculté de Théologie, 2000, p. 245. Désormais cité: Journal Charue.

44. Fonds Haubtmann, 1252-1253.

45. Dans l'introduction du chapitre concerné, Philips corrige *fines* par *destinatio*, pour éviter qu'on entende «limites», sens possible de *fines*. Ou encore, *coelestibus* est substitué à *supernaturalibus* pour respecter l'opposition avec *terrestribus* – et manifestement pour écarter la référence au surnaturel.

de facture authentiquement biblique, qui explicite la *vocation spécifique* de l'être humain à la lumière de *l'eschatologie chrétienne*[46]. Mais sa théologie biblique est assez intemporelle, bien loin de l'intérêt commun de Mœller et d'Haubtmann pour les thèmes bibliques susceptibles de toucher l'homme d'aujourd'hui. Notamment, l'approche de Béda Rigaux sur l'espérance comme «vertu spécifique du christianisme»[47] ne pouvait que heurter la sympathie qu'avait Haubtmann pour les espérances du mouvement ouvrier et sa soif d'émancipation, dans lesquelles il voyait un point d'impact possible pour la proposition de la foi chrétienne[48].

Notre hypothèse est que le travail réalisé par Philips avec ses collègues louvanistes donne à Haubtmann la mesure de ce qu'attendent les théologiens universitaires et l'aide à anticiper les obstacles à venir. Au moment où il esquisse le nouveau schéma, Haubtmann consulte Dominique Dubarle et Jean Daniélou dont il recueille les écrits[49], tout en multipliant les lectures sur le sens du mot «monde», sur la création et sur l'homme[50]. D'un mot, *Philips le provoque à préciser l'angle d'attaque de l'anthropologie théologique*. Non qu'il y ait divergence majeure entre les deux hommes, mais leurs accents sont différents. À cet égard, il est instructif de comparer l'article dans *Concilium*[51] que Philips communique en primeur à Mœller pour qu'il le transmette à Haubtmann[52] et les notes que ce dernier en extrait[53]. Haubtmann relève qu'il faut «présenter à tous une

---

46. Philips justifie ainsi la nouvelle rédaction: «Il n'est pas seulement question des choses et des activités terrestres, mais aussi de la vocation *de l'homme lui-même* selon la révélation chrétienne. La *res* n'est ici compréhensible que dans sa relation à la personne. De plus, il faut mentionner plus explicitement *le caractère eschatologique* du christianisme, qui ne diminue pas la valeur des choses et des activités terrestres, mais la purifie et la mène à son terme». Voir Fonds Haubtmann, 1252. Nous traduisons du latin.

47. «L'espérance est ainsi la vertu spécifique du christianisme, elle lui donne sa force et son élan. Elle est faite de certitude, de confiance et d'amour. Elle appelle la persévérance et exige la vigilance. Loin de diminuer l'effort de l'homme, son attente eschatologique lui confère de nouvelles vigueurs. Le chrétien ne s'installe pas dans la jouissance et le plaisir, il est tendu et œuvre vers le monde qui vient». Ainsi Béda Rigaux, dans Fonds Haubtmann, 1252, p. 6.

48. Dans le schéma présenté à la session d'Ariccia, Haubtmann écrit: «Bien des désespoirs, bien des ressentiments, de nombreux mouvements sociaux sont avant tout, du moins à l'origine, une revendication de dignité froissée, une protestation contre l'insulte, une révolte de conscience. En définitive, c'est la conscience qui est révolutionnaire» (Fonds Haubtmann, 1501).

49. Fonds Haubtmann, 1495, 1486 et 1490-1491.

50. Fonds Haubtmann, 1489.

51. Voir Gérard PHILIPS, *L'Église dans le monde d'aujourd'hui*, dans le Fonds Mœller, 1220.

52. Fonds Mœller, 1219 du 31 décembre 1964.

53. Fonds Haubtmann,1482 du 12 janvier 1965. Le texte de Philips est probablement remis à Haubtmann par Mœller lors de leur rencontre parisienne de ce même jour. Pour

anthropologie franchement chrétienne, dans laquelle cependant le non-chrétien reconnaîtra des traits fondamentaux qui lui sont chers et qu'il ne voudrait perdre à aucun prix». Mais il passe sous silence l'opposition, deux fois énoncée par Philips, entre «la tâche d'évangélisation», qui serait traitée en *Lumen gentium*, et «l'application à la vie intramondaine des lumières et des normes issues des lumières du Christ», qui serait l'objet du schéma XIII. Pour Haubtmann en effet, cette distinction est ruineuse car l'Église ne cesse pas d'évangéliser lorsqu'elle s'intéresse aux questions temporelles. Haubtmann ne prend guère en note l'idée de Philips selon laquelle l'Église serait, «pour le non-croyant» et «l'athée», «une force spirituelle avec laquelle il peut être utile de s'entendre» face aux grands problèmes de l'humanité, ne serait-ce que pour éviter de «périr ensemble». Et du long passage de Philips sur l'athéisme, Haubtmann retient seulement: «beaucoup se croient athées qui cherchent avec angoisse un absolu». Il pense que si le concile parle de l'athéisme contemporain, ce n'est pas pour se justifier institutionnellement vis-à-vis du bloc des non-croyants, mais pour leur proposer, en tant que sujets responsables, une interprétation de l'expérience humaine qui les pousse à s'engager dans l'action, de telle sorte que soit posée une base existentielle commune pour l'éthique. En tant que spécialiste de l'histoire du mouvement ouvrier, Haubtmann connaît l'ampleur du contentieux des athées avec l'Église institutionnelle et préfère le contourner par un appel à l'expérience intime.

Un tel service de la mission suppose que le concile soit conscient qu'il s'adresse à «un homme nouveau». Haubtmann note soigneusement cette expression, mise par Philips en rapport avec la science et la technique, car il s'intéresse à l'historicité de l'homme. En revanche, il ne relève pas «l'historicité de l'Église», elle aussi mentionnée par Philips. À la différence du Belge, le Français se focalise moins sur «l'interrogation latente que l'Église éveille dans les âmes», mettant ainsi «le monde en défi», qu'à l'inquiétude commune, «qui jette à l'homme un défi et l'oblige à répondre» (*GS* 4,5). En retournant la formule de Philips dans l'exposé préliminaire, Haubtmann change l'approche des rapports Église-monde, qu'il fonde désormais sur une *théologie des conditions de l'accueil de la Révélation chez l'homme s'interrogeant sur son propre agir*. Car il ne s'agit plus tant de désirer le dialogue avec le monde que de le mettre en œuvre avec des êtres de chair, immergés dans l'histoire présente. Tandis que Philips écrivait à Mœller et, par son intermédiaire, à Haubtmann:

la référence de l'article publié: G PHILIPS, *L'Église dans le monde d'aujourd'hui*, dans *Concilium* (1965) 11-25.

«J'insisterais à nouveau pour que l'équipe de rédaction observe la continuité avec le texte discuté au Concile et avec les observations des Pères»,
Mœller porte en marge: «On a fait tout le contraire!»[54]. Haubtmann et
Mœller pensent qu'il faut ancrer le texte dans la problématique contemporaine de la *liberté responsable* pour favoriser le travail de la grâce chez
les destinataires du document conciliaire. C'est pourquoi ils se réfèrent à
l'article de Bouillard qui évoquait «l'urgence de l'option spirituelle».
De sa relecture de la grande tradition chrétienne, les deux hommes retien-
nent que l'aspiration contemporaine à «la dignité, au respect, à la liberté,
à l'autonomie et à la participation de tous» est un paramètre légitime de
l'accueil du salut offert en Jésus-Christ, caractéristique du temps présent.

3. Deux manières d'aborder l'eschatologie chrétienne

Toutefois, l'inspiration d'Haubtmann ne s'alimente pas seulement à la
théologie universitaire. Il recopie plusieurs passages en latin du schéma
sur la Révélation, notamment le début du numéro 2 où il est écrit que
Dieu «donne aux hommes dans les choses créées un témoignage inces-
sant sur lui-même (cf. Rom 1,19-20)»[55], ce qui confirme sa perspective
de *théologie fondamentale*. Dans le même document, le prêtre français a
rassemblé, sur un des collages dont il a le secret, plusieurs faits de vie tirés
du numéro de janvier 1965 de *Témoignage*, revue de l'Action catholique
ouvrière. Puis il note ou recopie en vrac: «Regarder, écouter, réfléchir,
apprendre… et devenir plus homme»[56]; «Quand ils découvrent l'injustice, ils bougent!»; «Une grève intéresse l'Église: à travers ce combat
quotidien, des hommes et des femmes côtoient Dieu»; «Le Christ a
regardé avec respect et amour tous ceux qu'il côtoyait: c'est à partir de
ces réalités familières qu'il évoquera le Royaume de Dieu»[57]. Toujours
dans le même document, figure une citation de Rahner, recopiée dans
une autre revue: «Silencieusement et d'une manière voilée, Dieu est déjà
présent dans l'existence humaine comme le but infini de l'esprit». À travers ces multiples prises de note, on voit bien qu'Haubtmann rejoint
Philips dans la quête d'une *anthropologie chrétienne orientée par l'eschatologie*, mais celle-ci est abordée par lui de manière plus historique et
spirituelle à la fois, à partir des combats pour la justice qui, mettant

---

54. Fonds Mœller, 1219.
55. Fonds Haubtmann, 1497.
56. On reconnaît ici la formule chère à Lebret, cf. P. BORDEYNE, *L'appel à la justice
face au désir d'être plus homme: L'apport de Louis-Joseph Lebret à la rédaction de Gaudium et spes*, dans Oikonomia. *Rivista di etica e scienze sociali – Journal of Ethics and
Social Sciences* 4 (2005) 6-14.
57. Fonds Haubtmann, 1497.

l'homme en mouvement et le rendant acteur de sa propre histoire, l'orientent simultanément vers Dieu. Pour Haubtmann, familier de Proudhon, l'angoisse de la justice est «grosse de Dieu», si bien qu'il omet les passages où Philips estime que l'Église met fin aux angoisses humaines[58]: ce serait briser le ressort existentiel de l'espérance, prise dans un rapport dialectique avec l'angoisse[59]. Réciproquement, les insistances de Philips et son travail rédactionnel permettent une *reprise plus théologique de l'espérance*, pour l'ancrer davantage dans le mystère pascal accompli une fois pour toutes[60]. Dès lors, la tension qui subsiste entre l'histoire du monde et le Royaume annoncé par l'Église est mieux soulignée, conformément aux requêtes de Vischer. Ce faisant, Philips veille à la recevabilité du schéma par «les divers groupes et les tendances opposées au sein même de l'Église»[61], pour qu'il serve le dialogue au lieu de devenir une pomme de discorde théologique.

Ces quelques investigations dans les documents d'archives montrent que de nettes différences subsistent entre Philips et Haubtmann. Ce dernier demeure fondamentalement un pasteur, qui construit sa réflexion théologique à partir d'expressions glanées chez des militants chrétiens ou d'articles théologiques qu'il juge essentiels. Il y a incontestablement un côté laborieux dans cette quête des sources, mais d'un autre côté Haubtmann fait preuve d'une véritable maturité, de telle sorte que ce sont ses propres orientations théologiques qui commandent ses lectures et non l'inverse. Par ailleurs, son œuvre propre consiste à éprouver chaque proposition théologique à l'aune de leur compatibilité avec les questions de l'homme contemporain. Ce n'est pas le moindre effet de la collaboration entre Haubtmann et Philips que d'avoir accentué la teneur eschatologique de *Gaudium et Spes*, les préparant ainsi à mieux accueillir la critique des Allemands, qui exigèrent que «le monde» soit davantage référé à sa restauration eschatologique dans le Christ[62], insistance qui ne figurait pas encore dans l'enquête sémantique de Philips pour l'article de *Concilium*[63].

---

58. La «réponse» reçue par l'Église «de la bouche de Dieu» offrirait «une issue aux angoisses» de l'homme. Ou encore, «le baptisé attend et comprend le message comme la libération d'une situation angoissée». Voir Fonds Mœller, 1220, p. 11.

59. P. BORDEYNE, *L'homme et son angoisse: La théologie morale de 'Gaudium et spes'*. Préface de Mgr. Joseph DORÉ (Cogitatio fidei, 240), Paris, Cerf, 2004.

60. Là où Haubtmann écrivait: «Ce qu'il a fait une fois, [le Christ] le perpétue à travers les siècles par la vertu de son Esprit, jusqu'à ce qu'il revienne», Philips corrige en fin avril 1965: «il en perpétue *l'efficacité*» ou «il en *communique les fruits*». Voir Fonds Philips, 2319.

61. Fonds Mœller, 1220, p. 12. Repris dans le Fonds Haubtmann, 1482.

62. MŒLLER, *L'élaboration du schéma XIII* (n. 6), p. 129.

63. Fonds Mœller, 1220, pp. 5-6.

D'ailleurs, dans les éléments communiqués par Haubtmann à Philips au sujet de la conclusion générale[64], se rejoignent la perspective anthropologique («reprendre l'idée de l'homme qui domine tout le schéma») et son accent eschatologique, focalisé sur l'espérance: on souhaite «une invocation très forte à *l'Esprit Saint*, d'où nous vient *l'espérance*» et l'on envisage de «terminer par *l'espérance eschatologique*». Ces choix sont confirmés dans le texte final (*GS* 91 à 93). La collaboration entre Haubtmann et Philips a contribué à fixer ces orientations. Le premier introduisait une approche plus existentielle et historique de l'espérance, qui enrichissait le discours doctrinal sur la destinée de l'homme et des choses terrestres. Le second donnait à l'espérance une assise plus dogmatique, qui s'appuyait sur la christologie et la pneumatologie pour maintenir la distance entre les espoirs mondains et l'espérance ouverte par la foi chrétienne. Malgré tout, la question de l'incidence de l'eschatologie en morale sociale n'était pas réglée, ainsi que la contribution de Dondeyne va permettre de le constater.

III. Albert Dondeyne et l'historicité de l'homme dans la culture

Dondeyne enseigne la philosophie, ce qui est assez rare chez les experts conciliaires, mais ses intérêts l'orientent vers ce qu'on appelle aujourd'hui la théologie fondamentale. Ce profil atypique est un point de convergence entre Dondeyne et Haubtmann, d'abord sociologue et historien de la philosophie avant qu'il ne soutienne sa thèse de théologie après le concile. Le Français a dix ans de moins que le Belge, mais l'un et l'autre sont représentatifs de la diversification des voies d'entrée en théologie, lorsque le christianisme prend conscience que des cultures se sont constituées et continueront de naître sans lui. On sait que les deux hommes se côtoient à partir de la session d'Ariccia où Dondeyne participe à la rédaction du chapitre sur la culture en tant qu'expert de Mgr Charue et, plus largement, à la révision d'ensemble du schéma XIII[65]. Des pièces d'archives pourront peut-être établir ultérieurement leurs liens de manière plus précise. Dans les limites de notre étude, la figure de Dondeyne *montre sa capacité à engager une médiation intellectuelle entre deux courants* portés à s'opposer après le rejet du projet de Malines, malgré leur accord de fond sur une théologie plus inductive que celle des Allemands: l'aile

---

64. Pierre Haubtmann, Demandé à la Commission plénière mixte, dans le Fonds Philips, 2443.

65. J. Grootaers, *Engagement et contribution du Professeur A. Dondeyne à Vatican II*, dans Id., *Actes et acteurs à Vatican II* (n. 12), 456-484, ici p. 471.

«apostolat des laïcs» et le groupe de Malines, composé surtout de Belges, auxquels s'étaient ajoutés Congar, Tucci et Rahner[66]. Avec ce dernier, Dondeyne avait plaidé pour un schéma qui «s'adresse aussi bien aux non-chrétiens qu'aux chrétiens qui ensemble œuvrent à l'édification du monde»[67], ce qui l'avait conduit à rédiger un «*De mundo aedificando*».

1. Quelle est la théologie la plus pertinente face aux mutations actuelles?

L'introduction de ce texte en annonçait l'argument: «L'appartenance du chrétien à l'Église du Christ et son amour des choses d'en haut (Col 3,2) ne diminuent en rien son appartenance à la cité terrestre et le devoir qui lui incombe d'édifier, en solidarité avec tous les hommes de bonne volonté, un monde toujours plus humain. En effet, le chrétien reste non seulement un homme comme les autres au milieu des autres, mais le grand mandat de l'amour du prochain dont le Christ a dit qu'il n'est pas moins grand que le précepte d'aimer Dieu par-dessus toutes choses, l'incite à considérer et à traiter tous les hommes sans distinction de race, de couleur ou de condition sociale comme ses frères, comme les enfants du seul et unique Père céleste (Mt 5,45). Par conséquent de vouloir *pour les autres* les biens corporels et spirituels qu'il désire pour lui-même – ce qui ne peut se réaliser de manière efficace qu'en *construisant un monde culturel, économique, social et politique* toujours plus digne de l'homme»[68].

Le texte envisage d'abord l'idée de construction du monde, en développant le thème biblique de la terre comme demeure de l'humanité, mise en valeur par le travail et le respect mutuel dans la justice. Puis sont esquissés trois «événements» qui marquent le monde d'aujourd'hui de manière globalement positive: «l'essor prodigieux de la science et de la technique» qui a «libéré des possibilités immenses pour la vie de l'esprit» et constitué «la recherche scientifique pure» comme «valeur spirituelle»; «l'unification de notre planète»; «le réveil des grandes classes laborieuses, des peuples en voie de développement, avec le désir d'un ordre social plus juste». Cette conviction d'assister à une mutation

---

66. PRIGNON, *Évêques et théologiens de Belgique* (n. 35), p. 177.
67. GROOTAERS, *Actes et acteurs* (n. 12), p. 466, d'après les notes de Prignon. Mœller rédige alors un texte qui tient compte de «l'idée de Dondeyne sur la 'préexistence' de ce monde créé antérieurement à la division entre croyants et non-croyants, chrétiens et non chrétiens». Fonds Mœller, 1000, cité par TURBANTI, *Un concilio per il mondo moderno* (n. 1), p. 283.
68. Fonds Philips, 871, Malines, en septembre 1963.

historique et culturelle majeure rejoint la ligne d'Haubtmann et de Mœller. Ce qui diffère, c'est la manière de l'aborder phénoménologiquement et théologiquement.

Un autre document de Dondeyne, plus tardif d'un an[69], permet de cerner les divergences. Le professeur de Louvain y prend position sur un article du P. Joseph Thomas, jésuite engagé dans l'Action catholique[70], proche à la fois d'Haubtmann et de Mgr Ménager[71], membre de la Commission de l'apostolat des laïcs propulsé à la Sous-Commission centrale à la suite de ses critiques contre le projet de Malines. L'article de Thomas contient de vives critiques à l'encontre de la version du schéma XIII remise aux Pères pour la troisième session[72]. Publié par le Secrétariat conciliaire de l'Épiscopat français dirigé par Haubtmann, il est caractéristique de l'offensive de l'aile «apostolat des laïcs», qui aboutit quelques mois plus tard au choix d'Haubtmann pour la rédaction finale. Outre le regret que le schéma se limite à une perspective «européenne» et «atlantique», Thomas y déplore une coupure néfaste entre le traitement des «problèmes temporels» et «la question de l'évangélisation». Celle-ci requiert une prise en compte des espérances collectives de l'homme contemporain, «anxieux de donner un sens à son existence». «Parmi les problèmes essentiels et éternels, l'Église doit répondre au 'à quoi bon?' qui, dans un climat de relativisme, d'existentialisme, se pose aujourd'hui avec plus de netteté que jamais». Face à cette nouvelle donne existentielle, l'anthropologie du schéma demeure «individualiste, statique et spiritualiste», alors qu'elle devrait s'appuyer sur «le lien central entre l'espérance chrétienne et les espoirs de l'homme, chrétien ou non». Thomas est sensible à l'ambivalence du climat contemporain, où l'ampleur de «l'interrogation» sur «les tâches profanes et les luttes de l'humanité» invalide le discours moral basé sur «l'exercice de la charité». Il suggère plusieurs pistes théologiques: «la consommation de toutes choses dans le Corps glorieux du Christ», l'explicitation du «lien entre la construction du monde et l'avènement du Royaume», le recours à la notion de «*Consecratio mundi* pour définir l'essentiel de la mission des laïcs dans le monde».

Dans son manuscrit, Dondeyne avoue qu'il «se sent bien peu en accord avec les critiques de la revue française *Études et documents*» adressées

---

69. Fonds Philips, 1773.

70. Il est à l'époque aumônier national du MICIAC (Mouvement des Ingénieurs et Cadres de l'Industrie – Action Catholique).

71. Haubtmann et Thomas sont les deux interlocuteurs de Ménager lorsqu'il rédige son projet de plan en décembre 1963. Voir Fonds Haubtmann, 845-846, 849-850 et 852.

72. J. Thomas, *Schema De ecclesia in mundo hujus temporis*, dans *Études et documents* 18, le 7 août 1964 (Fonds Philips, 1771).

au schéma issu de la session de Zurich. Il se démarque de la théologie préconisée par Thomas. «Sur la 'consommation de toutes choses dans le Corps glorieux du Christ' et sur le 'rapport entre la construction du monde et l'avènement du royaume' nous en savons encore moins que sur la date du retour du Seigneur (*de die illa nemo scit*). Et pour ce qui concerne la 'consecratio mundi', je trouve que c'est une formule vague et rien de plus qu'une belle mystification»[73]. En l'espèce, Dondeyne se montre du reste plus proche que Thomas du célèbre article publié par Marie-Dominique Chenu dans la *Nouvelle revue théologique* de 1964 et auquel le Jésuite français renvoie pourtant en note. Chenu considère que l'expression «consecratio mundi», employée par Pie XII au congrès mondial de l'apostolat des laïcs de 1957, est trop ambiguë pour être employée avec profit dans le schéma conciliaire. Le sens cultuel de la consécration, évoquant une mise à part et une soustraction aux lois de la nature, même s'il était corrigé par la compréhension chrétienne de la sanctification, risquerait de dévaloriser le monde profane, puisque sa consistance dépendrait de la médiation des baptisés laïcs. Et ceux-ci seraient comme disjoints du corps de l'Église, pourtant tout entière en mission dans le monde[74]. Sur le fond, l'argument de Chenu rejoint donc le souci manifesté par Thomas que l'agir temporel des chrétiens ne soit pas séparé de leur vocation missionnaire. Mais le jésuite de l'Action catholique ne perçoit pas les limites de la notion de *consecratio mundi*. C'est la compétence apportée par Dondeyne, assurément ouvert aux préoccupations pastorales de l'Action catholique[75], mais mieux préparé par le contexte universitaire de Louvain à la rédaction d'un texte conciliaire.

Le désaccord entre Dondeyne et Thomas sur la référence à l'espérance chrétienne est plus subtil. Dans un texte publié après le concile, Dondeyne explique pourquoi le chapitre sur la culture s'abstient de l'argumentaire eschatologique, compte tenu de ce qui est énoncé par ailleurs en *GS* 38 et 39[76]. D'une part, dit-il, la Révélation reste sobre sur le monde à venir, et elle use d'un langage apocalyptique difficile à recevoir à notre époque, soucieuse d'éviter les «fantaisies» médiévales sur «la condition humaine au Paradis terrestre». D'autre part, et plus radicalement, Dondeyne note que la discrétion du texte conciliaire permet de «laisser à la

---

73. Fonds Philips, 1773. Nous traduisons du néerlandais.

74. M.-D. CHENU, *Consecratio mundi*, dans *Nouvelle Revue Théologique* 6 (1964) 608-618.

75. A. DONDEYNE, *La foi écoute le monde*, Paris, Éditions universitaires, 1964.

76. A. DONDEYNE, *Juste promotion de l'essor culturel*, dans K. RAHNER – H. DE RIEDMATTEN – M.-D. CHENU (éds.), *L'Église dans le monde de ce temps: Constitution 'Gaudium et spes'. Commentaires du schéma XIII*, Paris, Mame, 1967, 205-230.

libre recherche des théologiens le domaine entier de l'eschatologie».
Le philosophe louvaniste, proche d'Henri de Lubac, avait réfléchi sur les
rapports entre magistère et théologie. En 1951, il défendait avec courage
face à l'encyclique *Humani generis* la nécessité d'un dialogue en profondeur avec la culture contemporaine, y compris dans ses justes aspirations à l'existentialisme[77].

2. La culture, indice de l'historicité humaine

Par-delà ces divergences théologiques, Dondeyne était en phase avec
l'analyse du monde contemporain développée par l'équipe d'Haubtmann,
sensible à la portée spirituelle de l'inquiétude contemporaine. Dans son
ouvrage de 1951, Dondeyne développait un passage sur «existence et
transcendance» où il se référait au philosophe Heidegger pour établir le
lien entre l'angoisse de la mort et le sens de la responsabilité[78], puis à
Gabriel Marcel pour affirmer que le désespoir de l'homme moderne n'est
pas dénué d'une «puissance tonique et purifiante», «car il est déjà une
manière de *refuser* la situation désespérante». Notre hypothèse est qu'il
faut attendre la session d'Ariccia pour que ce consensus latent se concré-
tise autour d'*une approche phénoménologique* du contexte contemporain,
qui prend corps dans le *conspectus generalis* placé en ouverture du
schéma conciliaire. C'est précisément le domaine où Dondeyne peut faire
médiation, tout comme Mœller du reste, l'un et l'autre étant d'excellents
connaisseurs des courants philosophiques contemporains, ce qui les rap-
proche d'Haubtmann ou de Thomas. Lorsqu'il présente la structure du
chapitre sur la culture, Dondeyne souligne qu'elle est calquée sur celle du
schéma XIII: «description des faits», «section plus doctrinale», «section
plutôt pratique et pastorale» dégageant «quelques devoirs plus urgents
des chrétiens par rapport à la culture». Une solide convergence sur l'interprétation de l'homme d'aujourd'hui permettait de dépasser de légitimes
divergences au plan théologique.

En ce sens, la proximité de l'équipe d'Haubtmann avec le binôme
Charue-Dondeyne[79], qui prit en charge le chapitre sur la culture à partir

77. A. DONDEYNE, *Foi chrétienne et pensée contemporaine: Les problèmes philosophiques soulevés dans l'encyclique 'Humani generis'*, Louvain, Publications universitaires
de Louvain, 1951.
78. «L'approche de la mort possède le pouvoir mystérieux de nous secouer et de susciter en nous le sens du sérieux de la vie», dans DONDEYNE, *Foi chrétienne et pensée
contemporaine* (n. 77), p. 82.
79. Mgr Charue se réjouit de l'aide que lui apporte Dondeyne, qu'il fait inviter à
Ariccia: «Quelle chance d'avoir Dondeyne: il va sympathiser avec le P. Tucci et à eux
deux, ils nous sauveront», dans Journal Charue, pp. 226 et 228. Et durant la quatrième

de janvier 1965, était bien plus grande qu'avec la précédente Commission *De cultura* présidée par Mgr de Provenchères, pourtant issu de la Commission de l'apostolat des laïcs. Car il faut bien se figurer que l'aile «apostolat des laïcs» n'était pas monolithique. Lorsque Mgr Charue prend sa nouvelle charge, Haubtmann sait que sa critique du schéma discuté à la troisième session portait principalement sur *l'absence d'une anthropologie de la culture audible par tous*[80]. Dès lors, Dondeyne devient l'allié idéal. Sa volonté de s'adresser à tous les hommes le démarque du groupe de Malines et notamment de Congar qui continue de penser qu'il convient de s'adresser «d'abord aux chrétiens»[81]. Et ses compétences philosophiques le désignent pour cette tâche, dont on perçoit mieux la difficulté durant la dernière intersession. De fait, l'aide de Dondeyne fut précieuse, notamment pour rédiger l'introduction du chapitre sur la culture.

Comme l'atteste son commentaire lumineux de cette partie du texte conciliaire, Dondeyne a une vive conscience des enjeux contenus dans la rédaction du premier alinéa. «C'est le propre de la personne humaine de n'accéder vraiment et pleinement à l'humanité que par la culture, c'est-à-dire en cultivant les biens et les valeurs de la nature. Toutes les fois qu'il est question de vie humaine, nature et culture sont aussi étroitement liées que possible» (*GS* 53,1). Comme l'avait compris Charue, il fallait réussir à exprimer de manière suffisamment claire «ce qu'est la culture, afin de mettre ensuite plus nettement cette notion en parallèle avec la juste conception de la vie chrétienne»[82]. Mais tout l'art consistait à s'abstenir de parler de la «nature» de la culture, pour échapper à cette conception anhistorique de l'homme qui ne passait plus dans le dialogue entre l'Église et la société. L'astuce consiste à présenter la culture comme le processus nécessaire et habituel par lequel l'homme accède à sa propre humanité. Dondeyne l'exprime de manière lapidaire: «la culture est un événement». Elle «n'est pas une chose, un donné naturel, comme l'eau, l'air, la structure biologique ou la force de l'instinct». Elle est «un événement qui affecte l'homme et tourne à son bénéfice, car l'homme y déploie les virtualités de son être»[83]. Par ailleurs, Dondeyne montre que

---

session: Dondeyne arrive pour traiter les *modi*, heureusement peu nombreux (voir p. 289).

80. «L'Église paraît considérer la culture principalement par rapport à elle-même, et relativement peu par rapport à l'homme lui-même. Il y a là une question d'optique. Certes, c'est l'Église qui parle, mais en pareil domaine, ne s'adresse-t-elle pas à l'humanité entière, et non seulement aux chrétiens? Ne conviendrait-il pas de rappeler cette audience universelle en révisant le projet?» Fonds Haubtmann, 1200.

81. CONGAR, *Mon journal du Concile* (n. 26), Tome II, p. 308.

82. Fonds Haubtmann, 1200.

83. DONDEYNE, *Juste promotion de l'essor culturel* (n. 76), p. 210.

cette compréhension de la culture est elle-même un événement historique, qui rompt avec la conception aristocratique qui prévalait autrefois[84]. Décidément, on ne sort pas de *l'historicité fondamentale de l'être humain*. Dondeyne rejoint le cœur du projet rédactionnel de l'équipe Haubtmann, convaincue que l'historicité appartient à l'auto-compréhension de l'homme contemporain, de telle sorte que la réalisation du dessein de Dieu doit être présentée «à travers l'histoire du monde»[85].

3. L'historicité de la morale est au cœur du dialogue avec les cultures

Cette reconnaissance de l'historicité de la culture est de grande portée pour la conception des *rapports entre le christianisme et les cultures*. Dondeyne résume ainsi la thèse conciliaire: «le message chrétien n'est sans doute lié à aucune culture déterminée, puisqu'il s'enracine dans l'universalité de la Parole de Dieu; pourtant, il a toujours besoin d'une expression culturelle, sans quoi, il cesserait précisément d'être un message, c'est-à-dire une modalité de la parole». De même, de nouvelles normes peuvent être dégagées, en fin de chapitre, sur le droit de tous à la culture (*GS* 60) et le devoir de former l'homme à une culture intégrale (*GS* 61).

On mesure l'inflexion par rapport à la ligne rédactionnelle de la commission de Provenchères. L'opposition nature-culture étant dépassée, on sort du relatif pessimisme envers la culture contemporain qui imprègne encore l'intervention de Mgr de Provenchères prononcée le 4 novembre 1964:

> Le schéma insiste trop exclusivement sur l'aspect positif de la culture moderne; il ne parle pas de l'immense tâche qui reste à accomplir, des abus possibles, des devoirs nouveaux que créent les progrès mêmes de la science. [...] Celle-ci est devenue une puissance: le pouvoir politique est tenté de s'en emparer pour «manipuler» l'homme. Cela crée des exigences nouvelles au plan moral[86].

Un document du dominicain Georges Cottier, théologien de Mgr de Provenchères, fournit l'assise doctrinale de ce constat. Tout comme Dondeyne, Thomas ou Haubtmann, Cottier reconnaît «l'accélération de l'histoire» et la prise de conscience, par l'humanité, d'une unité nouvelle qui «se présente comme l'unité d'une histoire». Mais Cottier en souligne

---

84. «La culture n'est plus le privilège de quelques membres de la société particulièrement favorisés: elle est un caractère essentiel de notre condition d'homme», dans DON-DEYNE, *Juste promotion de l'essor culturel* (n. 76), p. 208.

85. J. THOMAS, *Remarques adressées à Mgr Ménager*, dans le Fonds Haubtmann, 852.

86. Fonds de Provenchères, 1440.

immédiatement les dérives potentielles: «conscient de sa puissance, l'homme est porté à se considérer comme un objet de la nature, tombant comme les autres objets sous l'emprise de sa propre action»[87]. C'est donc dans une opposition entre nature et culture qu'est pensée «la possibilité de manipuler, peut-être de modifier l'homme». Rien de tel chez Dondeyne, pour qui «l'événement» et la nouveauté appartiennent structurellement à la condition humaine.

Dans un document «*sub secreto*» largement distribué dans les cercles rédactionnels par Mgr Heylen, Dondeyne souligne que «l'idée de nature fait problème pour l'homme moderne, tant pour le chrétien que pour le non-chrétien». Elle est d'ailleurs pleine «d'ambiguïté», car elle oscille entre un sens «éthique», un sens «téléologique» et un sens de «légalité causale»[88]. Ce texte est remarquable par l'ampleur de ses vues. Le cardinal Suenens le trouve excellent et l'envoie au pape Paul VI[89]. Dondeyne n'idéalise pas le contexte culturel actuel, mais son optimisme chrétien le porte à croire que, l'histoire du salut se poursuivant dans le temps présent, les questions que se pose l'homme contemporain sont à «prendre au sérieux». Elles obligent à relire les sources historiques de la pensée chrétienne de manière synthétique et critique. Écartant toute acception naturaliste du concept de nature, Dondeyne fait valoir que son sens éthique est *rationnel* chez saint Thomas: il renvoie à la lumière faite pour «la recherche et l'invention du bien […] conforme au dessein de Dieu», qui se manifeste dans l'ordre téléologique du cosmos. Mais Dondeyne observe que «le moyen âge chrétien a fort abusé de l'idée de finalité», alors que l'univers confié à l'homme est «à la fois une *donnée* et une *tâche*». Les changements de mentalité obligent à réviser les conceptions erronées héritées de cette histoire.

> Que Dieu créa les humains homme et femme, pour qu'ils deviennent une seule chair et remplissent la terre, ne veut pas dire qu'ils n'auront qu'à suivre les inclinations de l'instinct sexuel, mais au contraire qu'ils devront humaniser et spiritualiser la sexualité, en la faisant passer par l'institution familiale, constituée par le pacte matrimonial. *Nature et culture sont inséparables*, quand il s'agit de l'homme[90].

Cette formulation synthétique, qui prend finalement place en *GS* 53,1, s'élabore donc dans le contexte de la morale familiale, l'Église cherchant

---

87. Fonds de Provenchères, 1446.

88. A. Dondeyne, Réflexions sur la crise de la morale conjugale, texte du 29 mars 1965, dans Fonds Haubtmann, 1579.

89. Journal Charue, p. 243.

90. Dondeyne rejoint ici l'insistance de Schillebeeckx sur l'historicité du mariage. E. SCHILLEBEECKX, *Le mariage: Réalité terrestre et mystère de salut* [1963], Paris, Cerf, 1966.

à dire comment l'appel évangélique reconfigure la responsabilité conjugale face à la maîtrise biologique de la fécondité. Cette note de Dondeyne donne accès à l'immense culture philosophique et théologique d'un homme qui saisissait avec acuité l'enjeu du *consentement à l'historicité de la morale* pour le dialogue entre le christianisme et le temps. L'enseignement conciliaire sur la culture, très important du point de vue de la théologie fondamentale, doit être attribué à la *squadra belga*. Dans les discussions si âpres sur le mariage, cette ligne doctrinale demeura une boussole pour Mgr Heuschen aidé du professeur Victor Heylen, qui réussirent à éviter des formulations trop restrictives sur la moralité du comportement en matière sexuelle[91].

Au vu des questions qui subsistent, quarante ans plus tard, sur le destin de la loi naturelle en théologie morale catholique[92], comment ne pas regretter que le dialogue entre la ligne Haubtmann-Thomas et celle de Dondeyne-Charue ne se soit pas engagé plus avant? Leur différend sur la référence à l'eschatologie en morale aurait pu éclairer le traitement théologique des questions éthiques complexes, qui nous mettent face à notre ignorance de l'avenir et à nos inscriptions différenciées dans l'héritage biblique. Par ailleurs, le problème de la manipulation de l'homme par lui-même, soulevé mais non suffisamment traité par l'équipe de Provenchères, reste assurément l'un des plus épineux de la théologie morale fondamentale, ainsi que Rahner l'avait vu dès la période conciliaire[93]. Peut-être valait-il mieux, tout compte fait, que le concile laisse cette question au travail ultérieur des théologiens conformément au principe énoncé par Dondeyne, dans la mesure où elle n'avait pas encore été suffisamment élaborée par la recherche théologique.

CONCLUSION

La collaboration entre Pierre Haubtmann et les experts belges permet d'approfondir les enjeux théologiques des rapports entre Église et monde, tels qu'ils sont apparus à la faveur du travail conciliaire et tels qu'ils doivent encore être pensés quarante ans plus tard. Car cette question, on

---

91. «La moralité du comportement doit être déterminée selon des critères objectifs, tirés de la nature même de la personne et de ses actes» (*GS* 51,3). Cf. PRIGNON, *Évêques et théologiens de Belgique* (n. 35), p. 180 et voir aussi M. LAMBERIGTS – L. DECLERCK, *Le texte de Hasselt: Une étape méconnue de l'histoire du De matrimonio (Schéma XIII)*, dans *ETL* 80 (2004) 485-505.

92. J. RATZINGER, *Démocratie, droit et religion*, dans *Esprit*, Juillet 2004, pp. 19-28.

93. K. RAHNER, *La manipulation de l'homme par l'homme* [1965], dans *Écrits théologiques*, Tome XII, Paris, Mame, 123-153.

l'oublie trop souvent, ne ressortit pas seulement à *l'ecclésiologie*, mais aussi à la *théologie fondamentale*: quel est le devenir de la Révélation dans l'histoire et par quelles voies s'adresse-t-elle aux êtres humains confrontés à leur responsabilité morale? Elle concerne aussi la *théologie dogmatique*, puisque les insistances spécifiques dans l'approche organique de la foi chrétienne infléchissent la manière d'envisager les rapports Église-monde. Elle concerne encore *l'anthropologie* puisque, pour s'adresser à des gens qui, non seulement ne partagent pas tous la foi chrétienne mais peuvent aussi avoir un contentieux personnel ou idéologique avec l'Église catholique, il vaut mieux parler de l'homme avant de parler de Dieu – c'est du moins ce que pensèrent les rédacteurs du schéma XIII. Enfin, cette question engage une certaine manière de concevoir *la pastorale*, qui n'est autre que la pratique concrète des rapports entre l'Église et la société qui l'environne, lorsque des baptisés participent, à divers niveaux de responsabilité, à la mission de «proposer le message de salut à tous» (*GS* 1). Or, il n'est pas de théologie qui ne s'enracine dans des pratiques ecclésiales qui nourrissent la foi en tant que prise de position sur l'expérience humaine.

Ce retour sur l'histoire conciliaire doit inciter les théologiens moralistes d'aujourd'hui à s'expliquer sur les options de *théologie fondamentale* qui sous-tendent leur propre recherche. L'intuition qui conduisait à traiter des questions morales dans une constitution *pastorale* propulsait la question des destinataires sur le devant de la scène, pas seulement en tant qu'interlocuteurs d'un texte conciliaire, mais en tant que bénéficiaires d'un «message de salut». Dès lors, le concile nous léguait une question non tranchée, qui avait divisé les experts sans qu'ils en aient toujours pleinement conscience, et qui continue de travailler la morale postconciliaire. Le message de salut a-t-il déjà, de quelque manière, touché ceux à qui l'on s'adresse quand ils répondent à leur «vocation divine» dans un exercice responsable de la liberté, même s'ils se disent athées, de telle sorte que la théologie morale a pour fonction de renouveler et de conduire plus avant une connaissance morale dont les bases sont déjà données à tous? Ou le message de salut est-il tellement nécessaire à l'exercice plénier de la liberté responsable que l'Église se doit de le proposer comme la lumière dont procède le discernement moral, si bien que la théologie morale est l'articulation rationnelle du dépôt vivant de la foi avec la responsabilité morale? On aura reconnu la tension entre «morale autonome» et «morale de la foi».

L'histoire du schéma XIII montre aussi que les options de théologie fondamentale interfèrent avec la conception de *l'eschatologie*, qui influe sur notre interprétation de l'histoire: histoire du salut, historicité de l'homme, historicité de l'Église, représentations de la fin de l'histoire et du monde à venir dans leurs liens avec la vocation terrestre. Là encore, nous avons rencontré des positions sensiblement différentes, entre une approche existentielle de la tension de l'agir responsable vers l'avenir, une reprise théologique de l'espérance, une dialectisation théologique de l'histoire et un appel à la discrétion dans l'argument eschatologique. Des recherches sur la portée eschatologique de l'éthique, aujourd'hui plus nombreuses dans le protestantisme[94], devraient pouvoir déplacer les questions de théologie fondamentale dont nous héritons et les repositionner dans le débat dogmatique.

Faculté de théologie et de   Philippe BORDEYNE
sciences religieuses
Institut Catholique de Paris
Rue d'Assas, 21
F-75006 Paris
France

---

94. J.-L. LEUBA, *Éthique intérimaire et éthique eschatologique*, dans *Fondements de l'éthique chrétienne*, Namur, Artel (Publications de l'Académie Internationale des Sciences Religieuses), 1995, 99-132.

MSGR. CALEWAERT, BISHOP OF GHENT, AND *SACROSANCTUM CONCILIUM*

I. Introductory Remarks

When discussing the Belgians and the Second Vatican Council, Msgr. Karel Calewaert appears as a somewhat isolated contributor. Indeed, only very rarely are any of his letters, proposals or other documents to be discovered in the preserved papers of his Belgian colleagues. The few documents in the Prignon Papers have an "official status", that is, they can also be found in the *Acta Synodalia*. There is no trace of intense contacts between Calewaert and his colleagues as is, for example, the case of Mgr. Jozef-Maria Heuschen and Mgr. Gerard Philips, or of Philips and Léon-Joseph Suenens. Without exaggeration, one can state that Calewaert did not play a prominent role as member of the *squadra belga*. This observation confirms what Leo Declerck in recent articles strongly emphasized about the Belgians: they were not a team, and lacked a clear strategy and/or a central leader(ship)[1].

II. Msgr. Calewaert: A Short Biography[2]

Karel Justinus Calewaert was born in Deinze on October 17, 1893. He studied at the college of Deinze and the Saint Barbara college in Ghent. He was ordained in Ghent on April 23, 1922. To continue his studies, he was sent to the university of Louvain, where he obtained a licentiate degree in theology. He taught moral theology at the military centre for the spiritual stretcher-bearers at Leopoldsburg. In 1927 he became director of the Major Seminary in Ghent, and he would also be its president

---

1. Cf. L. Declerck, *De rol van de Squadra Belga op Vaticanum II*, in *Collationes* 32 (2002) 341-372; Id., *Le rôle joué par les évêques et periti belges au Concile Vatican II*, in *ETL* 76 (2000) 445-464.
2. For a survey of Calewaert's life, see L. Colin, *Calewaert, Charles, Justin, bisschop van Gent*, in *Nationaal Biografisch Woordenboek* 13, Brussels, Paleis der Academiën, 1990, 159-163; A. Rubbens, *Karel Justinus Calewaert (1948-1963)*, in M. Cloet (ed.), *Het bisdom Gent (1559-1991): Vier eeuwen geschiedenis*, Gent, Werkgroep De Geschiedenis van het Bisdom Gent, 1991, 499-509.

from 1931 to 1948. During the Second World War, he continued with the training of the seminarians under quite difficult circumstances. In 1940, his predecessor, Msgr. Coppieters, appointed him vicar general of the diocese, charged with education and religious communities. He was appointed bishop of Ghent on January 28, 1948. His consecration took place on March 8 of the same year. He died in Ghent on December 27, 1963. He has been described as a clever and prudent bishop, just, honest, but also as rather silent and distant.

Calewaert was bishop of a diocese with more than 1300 priests. He knew most of them in his capacity as president of the Major Seminary in Ghent. Others, 477 in total, were ordained by him. At the end of his life, he was, like most other Belgian bishops, confronted with a declining number of vocations to the ordained priesthood. Most of his activities dealt with the organisation of parishes, taking into account the growing urbanization of his diocese. Priests stood at the centre of his pastoral view in diocesan life and organization. He emphasized the importance of traditional priestly work, house and weekly school visits, and he provided guidelines for the priests' behaviour during pilgrimages and youth camps. As bishop, he stressed the importance of decent dress for his priests and even in 1962, when the Belgian bishops allowed priests to wear the clergyman, he asked his priests to continue wearing the soutane. In contrast to the bishop of Bruges, he did not promote the Donum Fidei priests.

With regard to liturgy and sacraments, one can say that he was rather rigorous, if not anxious, and on the subject of the liturgical prescripts, he was rather severe with his priests. Experiments were forbidden. The promoters of the use of the vernacular had no success since the bishop refused to accept changes if they were not explicitly approved by Rome. It took until 1959 before the bishop published a liturgical directory for his diocese, for which he had explicitly asked and received Roman approval. During the preparation of the Council, he warned about exaggerated expectations with regard to renewal.

Calewaert clearly loved the traditional Latin liturgy and was always pleased when people invited him to come to consecrate a church. He often took part in meetings of young people and adults. He regularly went with the faithful of his diocese to Lourdes, was with them in Rome in 1950, and participated in liturgical conferences. In 1954, he received the participants of the liturgical conference held at Leuven in Ghent and met with Father Antonelli, who would become a lifelong friend. It was Antonelli who invited him to the liturgical meetings of Lugano (1955), and Assisi (1956). Calewaert was also present at the Eucharistic Congress of Munich (1960). In other words, Calewaert was seriously interested in the liturgy.

In his yearly fasting letters, he emphasized the importance of abstinence and deplored the decline in faith praxis. He was unhappy with
growing secularisation as revealed in declining Mass attendance. In 1954,
only 20% of the region of Ghent attended Mass! Explanation for this
decline was, according to Calewaert, a changing ethical mentality and
growing leisure activities. In this regard, he was not in favour of mixed
activities of boys and girls in youth movements. Although he appreciated the work of the Christian social organizations, he could hardly be
regarded as a promoter of the lay apostolate. In any case, such apostolate
always needed to be arranged strictly and obediently in agreement with
the hierarchy.

Calewaert, who, for a long time, had suffered from diabetes, died on
December 27, 1963, shortly after the end of the second session of Vatican Council II. His biographers describe him as a protector of tradition
and someone who was hesitant when it came to renewal rejected by the
ecclesiastical authorities. This will also be clearly demonstrated in the
Vota Calewaert submitted during the preparation of Vatican II.

III. What Did Msgr. Calewaert Expect from the Council?

Like many other bishops, Calewaert was surprised by Pope John's
announcement of the Second Vatican Council. By way of introduction,
one may state that many of the wishes of Calewaert were rather traditional, but this could equally be said about many of the proposals made
by other Belgian bishops[3]. Before mentioning these common "desires",
it is well to state that Calewaert first and foremost expected the Council
to repeat once again some fundamental truths of faith, such as the possibility to prove the existence of God by simply referring to creation (the
so-called natural proof of God). In this regard, he deplored that some philosophy professors in seminaries and universities questioned such *demon-
strabilitas*, stating that such proof was impossible without the help of revelation and grace, or allowing that at the very least one could entertain
some doubts about it. Furthermore, he pleaded that the doctrines of original sin, transsubstantiation, and the real presence of Christ in the
Eucharist should be stressed again by the Council. Finally, he asked for
a condemnation of so-called situation ethics[4].

3. For the *Vota antepraeparatoria* of Calewaert, see *ADAP* I,1, pp. 105-106.
4. *ADAP* I,1, p. 105.

Calewaert, not unlike a number of his colleagues, strongly wished that religious should not attempt to withdraw from the Episcopal jurisdiction with regard to the apostolate[5]. He paid attention to the question of celibacy, where he, like Msgr. Jozef-Emiel De Smedt and Msgr. André-Marie Charue, requested that this obligation should remain unchanged[6]. Calewaert further suggested the preservation of Latin as the liturgical language, although he accepted, in line with the Roman instruction of September 3, 1958, that an exception was to be made for the readings. He also deplored that in many seminaries philosophy and theology were no longer taught in Latin and feared that this would result in a less accurate or even incorrect explanation of doctrine. At the very least, he held that the handbooks should be in Latin. With regard to fasting and abstinence, he belonged, with De Smedt and Cardinal Van Roey, to the hardliners: confirmation of the existing precepts. On the matter of the permanent diaconate, Calewaert seemed very hesitant. According to him, allowing married men to the diaconate might be the beginning of the suppression of ecclesiastical celibacy and might result in a gradual decline of the respect the faithful have for their diocesan clergy[7]. In cases where regions suffered from a lack of priests, it would be better to give the laity the possibility to distribute Communion, if necessary; this would be better than allowing deacons to marry. With regard to the dresscode of the priests, Calewaert was less tolerant than colleagues such as Suenens, who suggested the clergyman. As far as Calewaert was concerned, the Council should explicitly forbid lay dressing to clerics, except in special cases[8].

When several other Belgian bishops asked for a clearer definition of the doctrine of the Catholic Action, Calewaert remained silent. In his evaluation of the Vota of the Belgian bishops, Soetens concludes that Calewaert "affiche une grande reserve à l'égard de toute forme de changement"[9]. I think that this evaluation is accurate, but, as mentioned above, in several cases, Calewaert is not alone in his opinions. Other contemporary Belgian bishops were of the same mind-set. Furthermore, if one omits Charue and Suenens, one must simply admit that most of the Belgian bishops were neither yet aware of nor interested in what would

5. See C. SOETENS, *Les 'Vota' des évêques belges en vue du concile*, in M. LAMBERIGTS – C. SOETENS (eds.), *À la veille du Concile Vatican II: Vota et réactions en Europe et dans le catholicisme oriental* (Instrumenta Theologica, 9), Leuven, Bibliotheek van de Faculteit der Godgeleerdheid, 1992, p. 41.

6. *Ibid.*, p. 42.

7. *Ibid.*, p. 44.

8. *Ibid.*, p. 46.

9. *Ibid.*, p. 48.

become the great theological, ecclesiological, and socio-economic challenges of the Council. Like many of their colleagues abroad, several Belgian bishops were not yet ready for renewal, changes, in sum, an *aggiornamento*. In any case, one may conclude that Calewaert's wishes for the Roman-Catholic Church, e.g., with regard to the wearing of the soutane, were very much in line with Calewaert's own diocesan policy.

IV. MSGR. CALEWAERT AND THE PREPARATORY LITURGICAL COMMISSION

On August 22, 1960, Calewaert was appointed to the Preparatory Commission for the Liturgy. At the time, it was suggested that this appointment was the result of a confusion of his name with that of Msgr. C. Callewaert, former president of the Major Seminary of Bruges and a well-known liturgical specialist[10]. However, this supposition is probably not completely correct. As early as 1953, Msgr. Calewaert was invited to the third liturgical conference at Lugano (September 14-18, 1953). At this conference, he presented a paper with regard to the celebration of the Holy Week and Easter in Belgium[11]. People like Cardinal Joseph Frings, Cardinal Ottaviani, Carlo Rossi, dom Bernard Capelle O.S.B. (of Keizersberg, Leuven) were also present at that meeting. And as mentioned before, Msgr. Calewaert was a good friend of the Franciscan Antonelli, whom he had met in Ghent in 1954 and who would become a member of the Congregation of Rites. However, I have to admit that someone like the liturgist Wagner struggled with the name of Calewaert. He speaks of Camillus Callewaert, bishop of Ghent. Only when referring to the meeting in Asissi (1956), does he write the name correctly. I guess that by the time of the preparation of the Council, at least insiders knew that the Calewaert of Ghent was not to be confused with the Callewaert of Bruges.

Thirteen subcommissions were erected in the Preparatory Commission for the Liturgy. Calewaert was member of the fifth one, on sacraments and sacramentalia. Aimé-Georges Martimort stated that Calewaert did not intervene during the work of the Preparatory Commission, because the work was actually done by experts[12]. The inventory of Calewaert's papers

10. Cf. Y. CONGAR, *Mon journal du Concile*, présenté et annoté par É. MAHIEU, Paris, Cerf, 2002, Vol. I, p. 25: "Certains commentent des désignations qui semblent un peu étranges. Il paraît que celle de Mgr. Calewaert à la Commission liturgique est le fruit d'un quiproquo. On a cru que c'était le liturgiste, aujourd'hui défunt".

11. Cf. J. WAGNER, *Mein Weg zur Liturgiereform 1936-1986*, Freiburg – Basel – Vienna, Herder, 1993, pp. 182-185, 195.

12. See A. BUGNINI, *Die Liturgiereform (1948-1975): Zeugnis und Testament*, Freiburg – Basel – Vienna, Herder, 1988, esp. p. 40; C. BRAGA, *La 'Sacrosanctum Concilium' nei*

seems rather to support this claim, for no traces of intense activity can be found. Moreover, it must be said that the Preparatory Commission worked very efficiently[13]. There were only general meetings on November 12 and 15, 1960 (distribution of the work), on April 12-22, 1961 (discussion of the prepared texts and redaction of the schema; only the discussion on the liturgical language seemed to cause problems)[14], and on January 11-14, 1962 (approval of the final version)[15]. The few documents on the preparatory period, preserved in the diocesan archives in Ghent, confirm what has already been said about Calewaert. In his answer to the thirteen questions, prepared by Msgr Annibale Bugnini for the first meeting of the liturgical commission (November, 1960)[16] Calewaert made very clear that he was opposed to any changes. He firmly said no to the renewal of the Eucharist and was against the introduction of the communion under two species. He did not like the idea of con-celebration. In this regard, he referred to the lack of priests. Further, he showed himself to be a convinced promoter of the use of Latin, which he considered as a sign of unity. Here, Calewaert referred to his personal experiences in Rome, Lourdes, and during international Eucharistic meetings. Moreover, he objected to the use of the vernacular during international meetings because participants often did not understand what was said. Further, the use of the vernacular promoted nationalism. The history of the Protestant

lavori della Commissione preparatoria, in Notitiae 20 (1984) 87-134, here p. 101; A.G. MARTIMORT, Les débats liturgiques lors de la première période du concile Vatican II (1962), in É. FOUILLOUX (ed.), Vatican II commence: Approches francophones (Instrumenta Theologica, 12), Leuven, Bibliotheek van de Faculteit der Godgeleerdheid, 1993, p. 310.

13. On the activities of the preparatory commission, see BRAGA, La 'Sacrosanctum Concilium' (n. 12); P. JOUNEL, Genèse et théologie de la Constitution Sacrosanctum Concilium, in La Maison-Dieu 155 (1983) 7-20; BUGNINI, Die Liturgiereform (n. 12), pp. 34-49; A.G. MARTIMORT, La Constitution sur la Liturgie de Vatican II, in Bulletin de Littérature Ecclésiastique 85 (1984) 60-74; ID., L'histoire de la réforme liturgique à travers le témoignage de Mgr. Annibale Bugnini, in La Maison-Dieu 162 (1985) 125-155; M. PAIANO, Il rinnovamento della liturgia: dai movimenti alla chiesa universale, in G. ALBERIGO – A. MELLONI (eds.), Verso il concilio Vaticano II (1960-1962): Passagi e problemi della preparazione conciliare (Testi e ricerche di scienze religiose. Nuova Serie, 11), Genova, Marietti, 1993, 67-140; J.A. KOMONCHAK, The Struggle for the Council during the Preparation of Vatican II (1960-1962), in G. ALBERIGO – J.A. KOMONCHAK (eds.), History of Vatican II. Vol. I.: Announcing and Preparing Vatican Council II. Toward a New Era in Catholicism, Maryknoll NY, Orbis; Leuven, Peeters, 1995, 206-211.

14. BUGNINI, Die Liturgiereform (n. 12), pp. 43-45; H. SCHMIDT, Constitutie over de heilige liturgie, Antwerpen, Patmos, 1964, pp. 69-70.

15. BUGNINI, Die Liturgiereform (n. 12), pp. 38ff. Slightly different dates can be found in SCHMIDT, Constitutie over de heilige liturgie (n. 14), p. 69.

16. Letter of Bugnini, October 13, 1960; Papers Calewaert (Diocesan Archives, Ghent), 5.

communities made clear that such use resulted in splits and divisions. Calewaert stressed that Latin should be the language for philosophical and theological studies. He was opposed to simplification of liturgical vestments. Finally, he emphasized that a fundamental difference exists between priests and the laity. In sum, Calewaert showed himself to be a supporter of the *ne varietur*[17].

On February 17, 1961, Mario Righetti sent Calewaert a letter asking for comments on the chapter dealing with the sacraments and the sacramentalia[18]. In his reply, Calewaert insisted that the Latin language should be used in the form of the sacraments. He agreed that the language used should be known by the faithful, but, at the same time, he was of the opinion that Latin, as a supranational language and symbolic sign of unity, should be preserved. Again, he feared that the exclusive use of the vernacular might endanger the sign of unity, especially with regard to the Eucharist. As in his previous response, he was of the opinion that the use of the vernacular might promote an immoderate nationalism. Also with regard the sacrament of confirmation, Calewaert opted for a status quo: confirmation must be administered by the bishop. Children should be 12 years old and should only receive this sacrament after two years of preparation[19]. This reply also makes clear that Calewaert was not in favor of changes *in liturgicis*. At the same time, it must be said that, with regard to the discussion on the liturgical language, the Preparatory Commission itself would opt for a *via media*[20], partly because there was no unanimity in the commission[21], partly because people like Bugnini wanted to avoid critique from the Curia[22].

V. MSGR. CALEWAERT AT THE COUNCIL

1. Calewaert's Interventions

Calewaert rarely intervened during the general sessions of the Council. However, at least one of his interventions was subject to both criticism and approval.

---

17. Papers Calewaert (Diocesan Archives, Ghent), 6.
18. Papers Calewaert (Diocesan Archives, Ghent), 10a.
19. Papers Calewaert (Diocesan Archives, Ghent), nr. 11.
20. BUGNINI, *Die Liturgiereform* (n. 12), p. 45. For a detailed report on the language problem, see P. BORELLA, *La lingua volgare nella liturgia*, in *Ambrosius* 44 (1968) 71-94; 137-168; 237-266.
21. JOUNEL, *Genèse et théologie de la Constitution Sacrosanctum Concilium* (n. 13), p. 15.
22. MARTIMORT, *L'histoire de la réforme liturgique* (n. 13), p. 132.

On October 26, 1962; Calewaert intervened in the debate on liturgy. In his intervention, he focused on the use of the vernacular. It is a well-known fact that the discussion on the use of Latin and/or the vernacular was one of the key issues during this first period of the first session[23]. At the time, the intervention by Calewaert was not well received by a large number of people, even though his intervention was intended to offer a kind of compromise[24] in a matter fraught with antagonistic positions. In his speech he stressed that people needed a sign or symbol of unity during a time when, due to means of increased communication, people from all over the world meet all over the world. In addition, he was of the opinion that the Latin language, "lingua supranationalis", could serve as an efficient psychological tool to help the promotion of such unity. In order to substantiate his position, he referred to Lourdes and to Rome (the Holy Year of 1950), where people were touched by the singing together in Latin the Creed and Salve Regina, or the Pater and Ave. Nevertheless, he added, in both places people also had the opportunity supplementally, to sing hymns in their own language. He also referred to the Eucharistic Congress in Munich (1960) where a million people were able to sing the Gregorian hymns, but where most of the foreigners did not understand anything of what was said and sung in the German language[25]. A last example he gave was the manner in which bishops from all over the world were able to pray the ordinary of the Mass in one and the same language, again a symbol of unity[26].

Calewaert feared that if everything were prayed in the vernacular, it would lead to a situation where, within a couple of years, simple people would no longer be able to understand what was celebrated outside their own country. This could lead to immoderate nationalism and finally result in national Churches, independent from Rome. According to Calewaert, this was one of the dangers threatening Christian unity. Moreover, the pontifical documents, ancient and recent ones, considered the Gregorian chant as characteristic of the liturgy of the Roman Church. In this regard he mentioned the wishes of the Preparatory Liturgical Commission that had advised a new edition of the Roman Kyriale, in which the tunes

---

23. See M. LAMBERIGTS, *The Liturgy Debate*, in G. ALBERIGO – J.A. KOMONCHAK (eds.), *History of Vatican II*. Vol. II: *The Formation of the Council's Identity. First Period and Intersession (October 1962-September 1963)*, Maryknoll NY, Orbis; Leuven, Peeters, 1997, 117-125.
24. Cf. *AS* I/1, p. 474.
25. It will be clear that Calewaert's arguments are very much in line with his answers to the questions of Bugnini in 1960.
26. See *AS* I/1, p. 474.

should be simplified for small parishes. In other words, simplification but not abandonment was acceptable.

Calewaert continued with the statement that it would be unwise not to use the vernacular for those parts of the liturgy which had a didactical function as well as for the prayers and songs recited by the faithful. Consequently he thought that a widespread use of the vernacular should be allowed for the sacramentals and for those parts of the Divine Office in which people often participated such as Vespers. The same should be done for Baptism, Marriage and the Anointing of the Sick, for these sacraments often have a more personal character[27]. Also those parts in the Eucharist that could be regarded as an expression of a communitarian act, could be prayed in the vernacular. In this regard Calewaert thought of the readings, the common prayers and some canticles.

Latin should be preserved in those parts that could be considered as a sign of unity or that promoted this feeling of unity. The same should also apply to the easy songs, such as the Kyrie, Gloria, Credo, Sanctus, and Agnus Dei, for these can easily be taught to people. For other songs, such as antiphons to the Introitus, Graduale, etc., which will never be learned by people, unfamiliar with Latin, the vernacular should be used[28].

In his *Journal*, Congar, who was not present at the meeting, mentions that he heard that Calewaert was in favour of Latin, and he adds: "Évidemment, en Belgique, l'emploi de la langue populaire poserait des questions momentanément difficiles. Mais la question dépasse les circonstances du flamanguisme"[29].

It seems to me that Congar's informer somewhat exaggerated Calewaert's position. Indeed, Calewaert wanted to offer a moderate solution, taking into account two concerns: Latin as an international language with all its advantages and acceptance was nevertheless a language, difficult to understand by the simple faithful. Further, as member of the Preparatory Commission, he was aware of the problems with regard to the use of Latin as liturgical language. Moreover, the Preparatory Commission was already aware of the need to simplify things, as is explicitly stated in his speech. It should be noted that leading experts of the liturgical commission, such as Martimort, were also fully aware of the fact that the Council would never accept any radical exclusion of

---

27. An exception might be made for the sacramental form and eventually the exorcism; *AS* I/1, p. 475.

28. *AS* I/1, pp. 475-476.

29. CONGAR, *Mon journal du Concile*, Tome I (n. 10), p. 153.

the vernacular, nor the elimination of Latin. This explains why Martimort, in his evaluation of Calewaert's speech, is much more nuanced.
He suggests that Calewaert was misunderstood, "surtout de la part de
collègues les évêques belges"[30]. Msgr. Philips, for his part, remains
rather vague: "Because of this intervention, Calewaert was described as
conservative"[31]. Anyway, in comparison to what Calewaert proposed
in his Vota, I think that one can already speak of a moderate evolution,
for some space is now given to the use of the vernacular. In passing
I might also mention that Calewaert submitted a written text with regard
to communion under two species. This should only be done in case of
con-celebration[32].

During the second session, Calewaert intervened only once. During
the debate on the permanent diaconate (*De ecclesia* II, n. 15), he frankly
stated: "*Dicuntur de diaconatu, nullatenus placent*"[33]. In his introduction he agreed that many positive things were said about the promotion
of the laity and about their apostolate. However, he continued, why must
these lay people be promoted to the diaconate, in other words, why
become members of the clergy? According to him, one could give lay
people the opportunity to preach, baptize, and bring the Eucharist to the
sick in regions where the number of priests was insufficient. Indeed,
this was already a praxis, present from the time of the early Church.
The same had happened during the Spanish Civil War and in the German concentration camps. More vehement in tone was the second part
of his intervention. He could not accept that married people should be
ordained deacons. In the long run, this would lead to a relaxation
of priestly celibacy. Moreover, celibacy of Roman Catholic priests is
highly respected all over the world (by non-Catholics as well as by
Catholics) and it is a clear sign of priests' radical choice for Christ. Calewaert's intervention was also signed by Msgr. De Smedt of Bruges and

30. MARTIMORT, *Les débats liturgiques* (n. 12), p. 311. L. ZANATTA, *Il 'mal di concilio'
della chiesa Argentina: Radiografia di un episcopato al Vaticano II: Prima sessione e
intersessione (ottobre 1962-settembre 1963)*, in M.T. FATTORI – A. MELLONI (eds.), *Experience, Organisations and Bodies at Vatican II* (Instrumenta Theologica, 21), Leuven, Bibliotheek van de Faculteit der Godgeleerdheid, 1999, p. 179, qualifies Calewaert's position
as "tesi conservatrici". For this, he refers to X. RYNNE, *La révolution de Jean XXIII*. Vol. I,
Paris, Fayard, 1963, p 103. However, Rynne does not say this. According to him, Calewaert's intervention was a good example of what probably the majority of the western bishops thought of the use of Latin and/or vernacular.
31. K. SCHELKENS (ed.), *Carnets conciliaires de Mgr. Gérard Philips, secrétaire adjoint
de la Commission doctrinale* (Instrumenta Theologica, 29), Leuven, Peeters, 2006, p. 16.
32. *AS* I/4, p. 504.
33. *AS* II/2, p. 692.

Msgr. Leo-Karel De Kesel, auxiliary bishop of Ghent[34]. At least on this point, his position of 1959 had not been changed. Calewaert's intervention clearly demonstrates that Belgian bishops could indeed differ in opinion, for, it is known that Suenens defended the idea of the permanent diaconate.

Calewaert belonged to the 120 subscribers of an intervention by De Smedt on October 18, 1963. During his intervention on the chapter on the laity in *De ecclesia*, De Smedt first remarked that the text (esp. nrs. 25-26) did not give proper and due consideration to the laity. He contended that a genuinely Christian life among the laity was of great importance. According to him, the laity played an extremely important role in the realization of Christ's kingdom in the world[35]. It is interesting that Calewaert, who never had been a great promoter of the lay apostolate, now supported a text that emphasized the important role of the Christian laity for the development of Christ's kingdom in the world.

2. Calewaert's Activities in the Liturgical Commission

Calewaert was one of the quite large group of members of the Preparatory Commission for the Liturgy who were elected in the conciliar commission for the liturgy. In fact, he received many votes: 1919 out of 2279, only surpassed by Msgr. Zauner, bishop of Linz, and Msgr. Rossi, bishop of Biella.

Within the conciliar commission, Msgr. Calewaert was appointed as president of the 6th sub-commission, which was expected to examine the remarks made by the Fathers on articles 16-32 of the schema. Other members of this sub-commission were Msgr. Fey Schneider, a young missionary bishop from Latin America, Father Martínez de Antoñana, a well-known rubricist, Father Stickler and Martimort. Calewaert seemed to have a high esteem for Martimort since he asked him to act as secretary of this sub-commission[36].

This meant that Calewaert was head of a sub-commission that had to tackle issues that were very much subject to discussion: the authority of the Episcopal conferences and the use of the vernacular.

---

34. *AS* II/2, p. 692.

35. See M. LAMBERIGTS, *Msgr. Emiel-Jozef De Smedt, Bishop of Bruges and the Second Vatican Council*, in FATTORI – MELLONI (eds.), *Experience, Organisations and Bodies* (n. 30), p. 444.

36. The fact that Martimort was also a member of the theological sub-commission might have played a part in the appointment.

a. The Work in the Sub-Commission[37]

The sub-commission first met on November 15, 1962. Martimort had prepared a note in which the nrs. 16-32 were put in a more logical order[38], a response to a request made by several of the Fathers[39]. Instead of the former A (general norms), B (guidelines for adaptation of the liturgy to the particular character and traditions of the people), C (guidelines derived from the didactical and pastoral nature of the liturgy), and D (norms based on the communal and hierarchical nature of the liturgy), the sub-commission opted for the new order A, D, C, B. The introduction remained untouched. Further, no. 28, which dealt with authority in liturgical matters, was given first place among the general norms and was divided into three paragraphs. Finally, although with some hesitation, a passage was added to no. 16 with respect to the setting up of a liturgical codex[40]. The proposal was accepted and extensively motivated. With regard to the matter of the Episcopal Conferences' authority, the advice of the juridical sub-commission[41] was requested.

On November 18, the sub-commission worked on the proposals made by the Fathers, except on those for the nrs. 20-22 (*Normae ex principiis de adaptatione ad ingenium et traditiones populorum*) and no. 24 on the liturgical language. The corrections made by the theological sub-commission were taken into account, except with regard to the word "*communitario*", a neologism rejected by the theological sub-commission – this commission had proposed the word "*communi*" –, but our sub-commission was of the opinion that this word was too vague. For the text on the authority of the Episcopal Conferences[42], the sub-commission had asked the juridical sub-commission to write a proposal. The latter proposed, in its meeting of November 19, to change "*Conferentiae Episcopali*" to "*competenti auctoritati ecclesiasticae territoriali*"[43].

The subcommission worked very efficiently, trying not to change too much and motivating substantially when, after discussion, proposals of the

37. See LAMBERIGTS, *The Liturgy Debate* (n. 23), pp. 154-155.
38. MARTIMORT, *Les débats liturgiques* (n. 12), p. 310.
39. Cf. the report of *Subcommissio VI circa Caput I, Sect. III (art. 16-32)*. Papers Bekkers (Diocesan Archives, Den Bosch), p. 1.
40. Report of *Subcommissio VI*, pp. 2-3.
41. *Subcommissio VI*, p. 2.
42. This text was in the original draft, but was omitted in the text sent to the Fathers.
43. A second proposal of the juridical sub-commission to replace 'Sacra Rituum Congregatio' by 'in illis conficiendis' will result in a dispute in the liturgical commission; for the proposal, see report 8 of the *Subcommissio iuridica*. Papers Bekkers (Diocesan Archives Den Bosch), p. 9.

Fathers were rejected[44]. Indeed, the changes to the remaining numbers were minimal, thus permitting the sub-commission to proceed to a discussion of nrs. 20-22. The sub-commission wanted a more suitable title for this section, for the current one was considered to be an example of "*malae latinitatis*"[45]. Furthermore, it proposed a new order. A phrase had been added which offered the chance to integrate local cultural elements into the liturgy[46]. In addition, no. 21b was changed into a new number which gave the local authorities the opportunity to prescribe adaptations (*adaptationes statuere*).

On November 22, the sub-commission started to discuss the problem of the liturgical language. Much attention was paid to this issue, for the sub-commission was confronted with many opinions, "*quarum aliae pro, aliae contra causam*"[47]. The subcommission opted for the *via media* which had also received much support in aula. In response to requests from the African bishops, among others, the word *occidentali* in the first paragraph had been replaced by *in liturgia latina*. With the addition of "*salvo particulari iure legitime vigente*" respect was shown for those who already celebrated the liturgy in the vernacular with the Holy See's permission[48]. As for the second paragraph, the suggestion that the use of the vernacular should either be clearly limited or permitted without limit was not followed and the text was left unchanged, with the exception of a few minor clarifications[49]. The sub-commission also took into account the proposal, made by Calewaert in his speech mentioned above, and suggested that the subcommission, responsible for Chapter 2, should use this in its text. If the commission would agree, Calewaert's sub-commission was willing to mention in its report to the Fathers that something of the kind would be mentioned in chapter II, in order to reassure the Fathers. The same prudence is to be found with regard to the relation between the local authority and the Holy See *in liturgicis*: a proposal that might offend the rights of one of the two bodies was rejected[50]. The phrase Episcopal Conferences in paragraph three was also replaced with the phrase already mentioned above. It was stipulated that the local bishops could issue stipulations with regard to the use of the vernacular, although such stipulations should be

---

44. *Subcommissio VI*, pp. 5ff.
45. *Subcommissio VI*, p. 13.
46. *Subcommissio VI*, p. 13.
47. *Subcommissio VI*, p. 16.
48. Calewaert's report, pp. 16-17.
49. LAMBERIGTS, *The Liturgy Debate* (n. 23), p. 155.
50. *Subcommissio VI*, pp. 20-21 (esp. with regard to a proposal made by Cardinal Bacci).

reviewed by the Holy See. Finally, it was suggested that a new paragraph was to be inserted which would state that the translation of Latin texts into the vernacular should be approved by the competent local authority[51].

One has the impression that the subcommission really took into account the substantial remarks of the Fathers, but also tried to defend the schema as it was presented in aula. Indeed, some of the proposals, e.g., with regard to liturgical language, were sometimes so entirely incompatible that any substantial change would create new problems. Given the challenging topics that had to be discussed, one can only conclude that this sub-commission worked very efficiency for, in only four meetings, seventeen numbers were taken care of.

b. The Discussion in the Liturgical Commission

During the 13th general meeting of the commission, on November 23, 1962, Calewaert presented the report of his sub-commission. One should realise that at that moment the atmosphere in the commission was far from positive. On that same day, Msgr. Jenny had suggested that the discussion on Chapter 1 should be completed as quickly as possible in order to put it in its entirety to a vote prior to December 8. Otherwise, bishops would have to return home empty handed, a situation which would harm the reputation of the Council and the church[52]. It was quite an eventful meeting. Larraona and Pichler fell foul of each other, since Pichler accused Larraona of not doing his duty[53]. Numerous were the complaints about the fact that the commission did not make any real progress during its meetings. Nonetheless, this meeting and those that followed (November 24, 26, 27, 28, and 30) were dealing with the most sensitive points of the discussion: the power of the Episcopal Conferences and the use of the vernacular.

The new order of the numbers as proposed by the subcommission was accepted[54]. The commission also agreed upon the proposed amendments. However, there was discussion about no. 16. Some were of the opinion that the 'intra paucos annos' was too vague and pleaded for a change in 'quam citissime'. After discussion – two members of the Congregation of the Rites were opposed to this change – the commission decided to use the expression 'quam primum'.

51. Cf. Calewaert's report, pp. 20-23.

52. Papers Jenny, box 8 (CNPL, Paris).

53. T.J. SHELLEY, Paul J. Hallinan: First Archbishop of Atlanta, Wilmington, DE, Glazier, 1989, pp. 173; 321.

54. For the Processus verbalis of this meeting, see N. GIAMPIETRO, Le cardinal Ferdinando Antonelli et les développements de la réforme liturgique de 1948 à 1970, Versailles, Forum, 2004, pp. 153-155.

Criticism was formulated with regard to the idea of adding bishops to the future commission for liturgical reform. Antonelli, the secretary, was of the opinion that adding bishops to the future commission for implementation would only cause difficulties. However, an overwhelming majority of the commission was of the opinion that the bishops could not be overlooked. Finally, the commission opted for the rather vague '*consultis episcopis*' (after consultation of the bishops).

Further, peritus Frutaz, a member of the Congregation of the Rites, was upset by a passage in the report where it stated that the recent reforms were the result of work done outside the Congregation of the Rites. According to him, the Congregation of the Rites was the best instrument for the implementation of the proposed reforms.

The idea of publishing a liturgical code was unanimously rejected, for, indeed, that should be the work of the commission for implementation.

The discussion on the chapters 16 to 31 continued on November 24 (14th meeting), and Calewaert proceeded with the reading of the document, but it appears that little progress was made[55]. In fact, the same could be said of the 15th meeting (November, 26)[56]. During this meeting, a long discussion was held with regard to the numbers 20 and 21. Since no agreement could be found, it was decided to wait for approval until the next meeting on November 27. Especially Chapter 21, dealing with the competences of the Episcopal conferences, was largely debated. Given the fact that this topic had not yet been matter of discussion in the plenary meetings, it was decided to opt for the following expression: "*Coetus episcopales territoriales competentes*"[57]. This expression was rather vague, but had the advantage of being easily adaptable to future decisions on this issue.

As mentioned before, the use of the vernacular had been the object of a heated discussion in the Basilica. For this particular issue, Calewaert's report consisted of approximately eight pages. With regard to the question as to which parts of the liturgy should be translated, the commission finally decided to follow the text proposed by Calewaert's sub-commission. Dante, secretary of the Congregation of Rites, was vehemently opposed to this decision, and Larraona had to remind him "that an Ecumenical Council was superior to the Sacred Congregation of Rites"[58].

---

55. For the report, see GIAMPIETRO, *Antonelli* (n. 54), pp. 155-156.
56. Cf. *ibid.*, p. 156.
57. In the final draft handed to the Fathers, it says: "competentis auctoritatis ecclesiasticae territorialis"; *AS* I,4, p. 274.
58. SHELLEY, *Hallinan* (n. 53), p. 174; cf. also GIAMPIETRO, *Antonelli* (n. 54), p. 159.

The language question was again a point of discussion on November 29. Calewaert c.s. had prepared a corrected text, consisting of four paragraphs. In the first paragraph, it was finally decided to speak of the use of Latin "*in ritibus latinis*" instead of "*in liturgia latina*"[59]. Concerning the authority of the Episcopal conferences, the commission finally followed the proposal of Cardinal Larraona: "*actis ab Apostolica Sede probatis*" instead of "*recognitis*"[60]. Paragraph four dealt with the publication of liturgical books in the vernacular. Calewaert's proposal was rejected[61], probably because the text was both too vague ("*pro quibus isti libri exarantur*") and too concrete ("*exhibeant textum latinum una cum textu juxtaposito rite approbato*"). A new text was written stating that the translation of Latin texts in the vernacular must be approved "*a competenti auctoritate ecclesiastica territoriali*"[62]. This proposal was unanimously approved. Given the many protests of the Fathers during the debate *in aula* against omitting the local bishops in the schema, it was decided to explain this issue in the *Relatio ad Patres*.

Once the text was approved, the sub-commission had to prepare its *Relatio*. This was done at the Belgian College on November 29. All day long, the members worked on their report. Calewaert was exhausted. It was Martimort who in the end finalized the text, I quote, helped by several of the Belgian bishops, "tapant à la machine chaque page dès que j'en avais fini la mise au net"[63].

On November 30, this text was read by Calewaert in the commission. At the demand of Cardinal Larraona, a number of small changes were inserted by Martimort, with the help of the German liturgist, Wagner[64].

Finally, the text was taken to the printer and given to the Fathers on December 4[65]. Although the text was approved, printed and distributed,

59. For the *Processus verbalis* of that day, see GIAMPIETRO, *Antonelli* (n. 54), pp. 159-161; cf. also the handwritten notes of Msgr. Bekkers on the text as proposed by Calewaert. Papers Bekkers (Diocesan Archives Den Bosch).
60. At the meeting of November 30, Msgr. Spülbeck argued that *probatis* was not in accordance with the code of Canon Law and as such suggested to use *confirmatis*. It was then decided to speak of "probatis seu confirmatis"; cf. *Processus verbalis* in GIAMPIETRO, *Antonelli* (n. 54), pp. 161-162.
61. His text runs as follows: "Parentur hunc in finem libri liturgici quia exhibeant textum Latinaum una cum textu juxtapositione rite approbato linguarum vernacularum earum regionum pro quibus isti libri exarantur". Papers Bekkers (Diocesan Archives Den Bosch).
62. *AS* I/4, p. 274.
63. MARTIMORT, *Les débats liturgiques* (n. 12), p. 312.
64. *Ibid.*, p. 312.
65. Bishop Hallinan, who was first furious about the "delay", had to admit that the finished work was impressive and that his suspicions that reactionaries had tried to delay the submission of the text to the fathers, were unfair; cf. SHELLEY, *Hallinan* (n. 53), pp. 175-176.

Msgr. Dante continued to protest against the rights given to the Episcopal conferences, but without result[66]. The report, presented by Msgr. Calewaert to the 34th general assembly on December 5, is extensively discussed in *The History of Vatican II*[67]. Here I will limit myself to a few particular remarks. First Calewaert stated that he spoke on behalf of all the members of the commission, "*qui quasi semper et de omnibus ... unanimes fuerunt*", which was, in light of Dante's obstruction, certainly an exaggeration[68]. He explained why the commission had decided on a new arrangement of the text.

Calewaert then focused on the various individual sections. In his presentation, he time and again stressed the important role of the bishops in the future implementation process. The relocation of no. 28 to no. 22, Calewaert argued, was prompted by the fact that the liturgical renewal had to be realized mainly by the bishops in their different regions and on the basis of a variety of different conditions. With regard to the concept of the 'Episcopal Conferences' – during the debate in aula, it had become clear that not everybody was familiar with it or understood it in an univocal way – the commission's canonists had suggested to write a completely new paragraph to be inserted in this section. In so far as the various Episcopal Conferences had been legally established, they got authority over the ordering of the liturgy with the defined boundaries (no. 22.2)[69]. Further, with regard to the revision of the liturgical books, it was explicitly stated that experts, dealing with this revision, should do this in consultation with the bishops[70]. All these elements make clear that the Liturgical Commission wanted to prove that it would be the bishops' task and responsibility to implement the desired liturgical renewal.

With regard to the liturgical language, strictly speaking a part of section C, a separate section in Calewaert's explanatory remarks was prepared. Calewaert's sub-commission had done the same when presenting its report in the Liturgical Commission. Needless to say, this was and remained a sensitive issue[71], but, and this must be said to Calewaert's

---

66. GIAMPIETRO, *Antonelli* (n. 54), p. 164.

67. See LAMBERIGTS, *The Liturgy Debate* (n. 23), pp. 161-165.

68. *AS* I,4, p. 278.

69. Calewaert added here that since the phrase "Ex potestate a iure concessa" did not imply a juridical or theological statement, there was enough room left for a possible future filling-out of the text; cf. *AS* I/4, p. 280.

70. Cf. *AS* I/4, p. 270; cf. also the commission's motivation on p. 281.

71. Once again ample attention was paid to this point; cf. *AS* I/4, pp. 285-288. No other single item in chapter one received equal attention.

benefit (and his intervention *in aula*), the commission will again choose
a "*via media*", thus respecting the wish of many Fathers. Quite a lot had
been changed in this new no. 36 (formerly 24), as already mentioned
above. This change not only met the desire of, among others, the African
bishops to have the word *occidentalis* dropped, but by using the plural
'rites', recognition was given to the fact that besides the Roman rite, other
rites such as the Ambrosian rite had a right to exist in the Roman Catholic
Church. Since Rome had already permitted liturgical celebrations in the
vernacular in various local churches in the past, the phrase "*salvo particulari iure*" was inserted[72]. The use of the vernacular was also deemed
extremely useful, especially for readings, exhortations and certain prayers
and hymns.

Another proof that the bishops' role in the implementation was recognized could be found in the statement that the bishops have the right
to make decisions concerning the use of the vernacular and the extent of
that use. This proposal met with the desire of a number of the Fathers
to attribute greater competence to the Episcopal Conferences[73]. The
Pope's authority was protected by the fact that all decisions had to be
approved by the Holy See, or in other words, 'confirmed'[74]. The new
choice of phrasing was to give the local authorities greater power to
make decisions and more room for manoeuvring, without infringing on
the rights of the higher authorities[75]. In a completely new fourth paragraph, it was proposed that the translation of the Latin texts into the vernacular for liturgical use should be the responsibility of the territorial
authorities mentioned in no. 36.3, so as to avoid a proliferation of trans-
lations[76]. The report represented not only the position of the Liturgical
Commission at large, but also Calewaert's own view. Indeed, the proposed text, even in its final draft, is less revolutionary than it sometimes
has been suggested.

In any case, the Fathers seemed to be very pleased with the final result.
There was an overwhelming majority for all the numbers[77], and although
the hoped for promulgation did not happen at the end of this first session,
all in all, many regarded the approval of the introduction and the first chapter of the document as proof that *aggiornamento* might be possible in the

---

72. Cf. *AS* I/4, p. 286.
73. Cf. *AS* I/4, p. 288.
74. "de usu et modo linguae vernaculae statuere, actis ab Apostolica Sede probatis seu
confirmatis"; *AS* I/4, p. 273.
75. Cf. *AS* I/4, p. 288.
76. Cf. *AS* I/4, p. 288.
77. For the results, see LAMBERIGTS, *The Liturgy Debate* (n. 23), p. 165.

Church. Whether Calewaert would agree with such interpretation is the subject of academic guesses. In any case, in an *in memoriam* in *La Croix*, it was said that the report of Calewaert was a remarkable one, "qui restera sans doute dans les actes du Concile comme une pièce maîtresse"[78].

In a sense, Calewaert's work was done. Then for the chapters 2-8, other sub-commissions had to do the work – or had already done most of their work before leaving Rome after the first session[79] –, work which was to be presented to the Liturgical Commission during its meeting of April 23 to May 10, 1963[80]. The *Processus verbalis* of these meetings again confirm that Calewaert was rather a silent man. He made few interventions. During one of the meetings of the Liturgical Commission, (May 3, 1963), Calewaert intervened with regard to nr. 80 of the schema. Msgr. Jenny had proposed that the Eucharist, celebrated on Saturday evening, could be considered as a Sunday Mass, such as was already the case for the Paschal Vigil. Martimort and Calewaert protested – it is interesting to see that Calewaert, whenever he intervened, did so in order to support Martimort's position –, Calewaert because he was of opinion that this could damage the value of Sunday. Larraona would reply that such a decision belonged to the ordinary's authority. Moreover, this had already happened in the past and the proposal made by Jenny could be a positive answer to many pastoral needs[81]. Again, it is interesting that Calewaert, who had often complained that the faithful in his diocese did not always celebrate Sunday as the day of the Lord, made such a remark. It reveals the concern of a somewhat anxious bishop, who deplored the decline of spiritual life in his diocese and, by extension, in the Church.

After that meeting in April, most of the work had to be done by Latin specialists. The Liturgical Commission would be kept informed of their work during the meetings of September 27 and 30. Neither the *Processus verbalis* nor Calewaert's papers mention any significant intervention of Calewaert, who, at that time, was no longer in good health. But this would not prevent Calewaert from being a faithful participant in the meetings of the Liturgical Commission during the second session. As far

78. Quoted in MARTIMORT, *Les débats liturgiques* (n. 12), p. 313.
79. This was, e.g., the case with the sub-commission on the Sacraments; cf. SHELLEY, *Hallinan* (n. 53), p. 189.
80. See R. KACZYNSKI, *Toward the Reform of the Liturgy*, in G. ALBERIGO – J. KOMON-CHAK (eds.), *History of Vatican II*. Vol. III: *The Mature Council. Second Period and Intersession (September 1963-September 1964)*, Maryknoll, NY, Orbis; Leuven, Peeters, 2000, 189ff.
81. See the *Processus verbalis* in GIAMPIETRO, *Antonelli* (n. 54), p. 227.

as I can see, his name is never mentioned on the list of the absentees. Calewaert was of the opinion that one should simply do one's duty, which in his case meant, being present at the Liturgical Commission's meetings[82].

During one of these meetings, on October 29, 1963, Calewaert intervened with regard to nr. 54, dealing with the use of the vernacular in Mass, celebrated with the faithful. The sub-commission had proposed to let the Fathers vote on an emendation, in which an extension of the vernacular to the priestly prayers was proposed. Calewaert was opposed to this proposal and received the support from the commission, for such an extension would annihilate what was said in the following sentence: "But steps should be taken so that Christian believers can at the same time also say or sing in Latin the parts of the Mass which are appropriately theirs." It was decided not to put the emendation to the vote in aula[83]. At the same time, Calewaert's intervention is in line with the option as taken by the commission that precisely with regard to this number stressed that it opted for a middle way[84].

No. 54 seems to have intrigued Calewaert. Antonelli read the report on the emendations for Chapter 2 (on the Eucharist) on November 14, 1963, and again, 54 was a much debated number. While some proposed to abandon Latin for the whole first part of the Eucharist, Martimort defended the proposal to preserve the Latin in the praying of the collect. He argued that the Commission tried to find a middle way. Moreover, Larraona added, only 108 Fathers asked for the extension of the vernacular to the collect. When Jungmann proposed to send the question to a post-conciliar commission, Martimort disagreed, stating that such competence belonged to the local authorities. Then Calewaert asked to respect the principle that the faithful must be able to answer in Latin, something which could no longer be validated if one gave up the use of Latin for the first part of the Eucharist. Finally, it was concluded that the text should be vague[85]. I am well aware that these kinds of interventions do not belong to the spectacular acts of a Council, but it is interesting to see that people in the commission took Calewaert's remarks into account.

---

82. I owe this information to Leo Declerck, vice rector of the Belgian College in Rome during that period.

83. See the *Processus verbalis* in GIAMPIETRO, *Antonelli* (n. 54), pp. 245-246.

84. See the report of Msgr. Enciso on behalf of the sub-commission responsible for chapter II (Papers De Clercq, box 2; Archives Centrum voor Conciliestudie Vaticanum II, Faculty of Theology, Leuven).

85. See the *Processus verbalis* in GIAMPIETRO, *Antonelli* (n. 54), pp. 255-256.

VI. CONCLUSIONS

Msgr. Calewaert was, for most of his episcopate, a pre-Vatican II bishop. As such, he must be considered as a good example of a bishop who was obedient to Rome's directives and expected the same obedience from his priests, whom he highly respected and whom he awarded a central place in his diocesan policy. Furthermore, in comparison with some of his colleagues, he was quite reserved, a bit shy, or, to put it another way, not prepared for the role of a 'leader'.

Calewaert's high respect for his priests was strongly related to their celibate life, freely accepted as a sign of God's Kingdom. His opposition to married deacons before and during the Council must be seen in this context. Calewaert accepted and supported that lay people should help in case of need, but this is not the same as making them into lower degree clericals. Here, his position (which is consistent with what he said in his Vota) is supported by De Smedt, while Suenens opts for another solution.

Calewaert was reluctant towards, but not opposed to, renewal. With regard to liturgical language, he developed from a radical yes in favour of the Latin language to a moderate yes in favour of both Latin and the vernacular (mostly because of pastoral concerns). In this regard, it is interesting to see that he really trusted Martimort and was most willing to cooperate with him. He insisted on the advantages of the use of Latin in an international context – his personal (positive) feelings about international liturgical events certainly supported his view on this matter –, a position which in fact fits in very well with what many bishops had pleaded for during the general meetings.

Very dogmatic in some of his Vota, he did not intervene in the debate on the sources of revelation, thus accepting the Council's position(s), including those of the Belgians, in this regard. The fact that, in his conciliar interventions, he quite often brought in elements present in his Vota, reveals that the latter were honest and that Calewaert wanted to support them all the way: Calewaert simply did what he considered to be his job, without striving for success. He preferred honesty over popularity.

As president of his sub-commission – it is hard to trace his specific contribution – he supported, or, at least expected that people went for fair solutions. Furthermore, given the many numbers that had to be examined, he must have been an efficient president, a diplomat with regard to the use of the vernacular, and one of those who accepted if not supported the important role of local bishops. It is also clear that Calewaert took the side of Martimort, whom he trusted and supported. The choice of

Martimort as secretary of his sub-commission is clear proof of this. Finally, little is known about his activities within the Belgian network. The archives keep silent about a silent and distant man.

Faculty of Theology   Mathijs LAMBERIGTS
St.-Michielsstraat 6
B-3000 Leuven
Belgium

EMIEL-JOZEF DE SMEDT, JOHN COURTNEY MURRAY AND RELIGIOUS FREEDOM

The role of the Bishop of Bruges, Emiel-Jozef De Smedt, at the Second Vatican Council is very well known. The inventory of his Council papers, Velati's studies on the Secretariat for Christian Unity, Lamberigts' contribution to the meeting in Bologna in December 1996, Troisfontaines' recent contribution in *Gregorianum*, the volumes of the *History of the Council* and my research on the editorial history of *Dignitatis humanae* – all these studies allow us to track the trajectory of a key bishop of the so-called Belgian team at the council. Additionally, he did not fail to make himself valuable in distant geographical and cultural areas as well[1]. These studies and contributions enable us to scrutinize his commitment in the preparatory period of Vatican II, starting from the moment of his appointment as a member of the Secretariat for the Unity of Christians on October 25, 1960 – particularly in the field of the fourth subcommittee, *De laicatu et de tolerantia* – and subsequently, at the start of the Council, as the reporter of the *De libertate* in its tortuous navigation through the assembly, as an effective orator in assembly, as an "ordinary" Council Father, and more than once involved in the organization of the strategies capable of driving the Vatican II machine that often was difficult to maneuver.

---

1. In a letter of August 1966, addressed by the then second vice-president of the CELAM, McGrath, to the Paraguayan Bogarín Argaña, Bishop De Smedt's style had become a "model"; cf. McGrath to Bogarín, August 11, 1966, Bogarín Fund, Diocesan Archives of San Juan Bautista de las Misiones, Paraguay. For the referred texts, see A. GREILER – L. DE SAEGER (eds.), *Emiel-Jozef De Smedt: Papers Vatican II Inventory*. With a Preface by L. DECLERCK (Instrumenta Theologica, 22), Leuven, Bibliotheek van de Faculteit der Godgeleerdheid [Further referred to as Fund De Smedt], 1999; M. VELATI, *La proposta ecumenica del segretariato per l'unità dei cristiani*, in G. ALBERIGO – A. MELLONI (eds.), *Verso il concilio Vaticano II (1960-1962): Passaggi e problemi della preparazione conciliare* (Testi e ricerche di scienze religiose. Nuova Serie, 11), Genova, Marietti, 1993, 273-350; M. VELATI, *Una difficile transizione: Il cattolicesimo tra unionismo ed ecumenismo (1952-1964)* (Testi e ricerche di scienze religiose. Nuova serie, 16), Bologna, Il Mulino, 1996; M. LAMBERIGTS, *Msgr. Emiel-Jozef de Smedt, Bishop of Bruges, and the Second Vatican Council*, in M.T. FATTORI – A. MELLONI (eds.), *Experience, Organizations and Bodies at Vatican II: Proceedings of the Bologna Conference December 1996* (Instrumenta Theologica, 21), Leuven, Bibliotheek van de Faculteit der Godgeleerdheid, 1999, 431-469; G. ALBERIGO – A. MELLONI (eds.), *Storia del concilio Vaticano II*, 5 vols., Bologna – Leuven, Peeters, 1995-2001; C. TROISFONTAINES, *Mgr De Smedt et la Déclaration 'Dignitatis humanae'*, in *Gregorianum* (2007) 761-779; S. SCATENA, *La fatica della libertà: L'elaborazione della dichiarazione Dignitatis Humanae sulla libertà religiosa del Vaticano II* (Testi e ricerche di scienze religiose. Nuova Serie, 31), Bologna, Il Mulino, 2003.

I do not, therefore, intend in this paper to review the stages of De Smedt's important contribution of sorting out the Council events, particularly those events which led to the promulgation of the *Declaration on Religious Liberty*, considering it as something now to be taken for granted. Rather, I would like to concentrate on only a number of passages – relevant above all to both the intense work of Fall 1964 and the first months of the last intersession – which in my opinion can be useful in scrutinizing the difficulties encountered by a small group of bishops and experts who, in the course of a few years, led the process of calling into question the mentality of large episcopal sectors, which was rooted in centuries of Roman Christianity. In fact, I believe that by "circumscribing" these difficulties, one can more fully appreciate the efforts carried out by the Secretariat, and by De Smedt in particular, in affecting a complex synodal maturation on one of the most decisive bearers of the modern processes of liberty.

De Smedt was one of the few members of the editorial team who followed the events of the elaboration of the text on religious freedom from the beginning to the end. In the preparatory period, after Henri Charrière's initial self-candidacy, De Smedt's leadership was soon felt in the restricted subcommittee which had to look after the tricky matter of religious freedom, in some ways "imposed" by the World Council of Churches on the Secretariat's agenda, as an essential prerequisite for the continuation of the confident relationships established between the Geneva Body and the Catholic Conference for Ecumenical issues[2]. At the subcommittee's first meeting, which was held in Freiburg in December 1960, it was De Smedt, as it is known, who presented the text, *La liberté religieuse*, which then constituted the basis of the Secretariat's work. The Freiburg text, prepared by Louis Janssens, had a decidedly personalist foundation, centered on the concept of the inviolable dignity of the person, which determined the positive substance of tolerance. From this perspective, religious freedom in some ways appeared to be a case of the application of the "freedom of conscience", manifesting itself essentially as an individual's freedom to profess a personal religious faith according to one's own convictions of conscience.

I have recalled the Freiburg text because it seems that De Smedt's subsequent discomfort about the so-called "American framework" is partly attributed to the fact that the Bishop of Bruges never abandoned this original conscience perspective which informed *De libertate*'s first ecumenical versions, reflecting the very concrete manner in which the idea

---

2. For the events in the history of the redaction process to which I will refer from now on see my *La fatica della libertà* (n. 1).

of a schema on religious freedom emerged within the Secretariat. The first, brief confrontation in the assembly hall in November 1963 on the fifth chapter of the *De oecumenismo* clearly offered a glimpse of the risk that the Council debate might come to a standstill because of the interminable *querelle* on the rights of erroneous conscience. Furthermore, the two-track plan on which the *De libertate* moved – specifically, the religious plan as well as the civil and public one – came to be criticized by many. Nevertheless, at the end of January 1964, De Smedt sent the Belgian bishops several predisposed amendment proposals based on the suggestions and observations that Janssens had relayed to him[3]. These observations were partly attuned to the reflections that in the first months of 1964 had occupied the moral theologian from Leuven: in re-framing the substance of the Freiburg text, Janssens specifically underlined in the volume *Liberté de conscience et liberté religieuse* published in the same year how only one perspective, decidedly personalist, would have permitted a positive approach to the entire question.

It is well known that the path sketched by Janssens was not followed by the subcommittee for *De libertate*, which worked intensely on revising the schema between February and March of 1964. Not the least reason for shelving Janssens's draft was the fact that prospects such as his seemed on the whole scarcely beneficial in providing an answer to the need – expressed in the *animadversiones* of many Fathers – of a precise delimitation of the spheres of the right to religious freedom as well as an accurate analysis of the criteria controlling the exercise of it. With regard to the debate within the committee of the preparatory period, the delayed arrival of the Secretariat's schema in the assembly, coupled with the fact of coming into the Council arena, brought about some resistance against *aggiornamento* which, in the field of confrontation with the great questions of the contemporary world, should have provided one of the main test cases. In order to placate the fears expressed by numerous Fathers who felt that the expression of religious freedom may be interpreted as the faculty to define the relationship with God, the Secretariat responded by limiting the lines upon which the still uncertain future schema would have had to move to the sphere of interpersonal relationships and civil liberties.

---

3. Cf. *Decretum pastorale De libertate religiosa*, 2 pg. ds, enclosed in De Smedt's letter to the bishops of Belgium on January 22, 1964, Fund De Smedt, 1021. These amendment proposals were conveyed by Suenens to Bea in February 25, 1965, Fund Suenens, 1916 (Inventory in L. DECLERCK – E. LOUCHEZ, *Inventaire des Papiers conciliaires du cardinal L.-J. Suenens* (Cahiers de la Revue théologique de Louvain, 31), Louvain-la-Neuve, Publications de la Faculté de Théologie, 1998.

In this phase, the collaboration of John Courtney Murray, the theologian from Woodstock College, with the Secretariat had already begun. Murray had been appointed as a *peritus* on April 4, 1963 by the Archbishop of New York. During the summer of that year, Murray had been contacted by Johannes Willebrands who requested from him the *apparatus* for the fifth chapter of the ecumenical schema as well as an invitation to assist De Smedt in drafting the *Relatio* accompanying the text. Willebrands asked his help again on February 10, 1964, that Murray might assist the bishops and experts involved in the study of the observations of the Fathers. However, a serious heart attack at the end of January postponed Murray's full involvement in the redactional work of the schema; in this phase a fundamental role in the attempt to change the direction of *De libertate*'s trajectory was carried out by the writer of *Pacem in terris*, Pietro Pavan, who wanted to bring it closer to the technical-constitutional problem of the *cura religionis* charged to public powers.

De Smedt actively participated in this phase of the redactional work. The result of the effort was a schema which continued to revolve around the moral problem of the rights of conscience. However, it partially distanced itself from the realm of the original ecumenical preoccupations, as it inserted a series of passages and specifications intended to present the right to religious freedom as an interpersonal right pertaining to the sphere of civil liberties. Contextually, this strengthened the move towards rethinking the principles of the restrictions about exercising the right in question. The main foundation of the right to religious freedom was now placed in the nature of the person him/herself, considered through the perspective of the divine vocation: it was in this *vocatio* that the new *Declaratio prior* characterized the maximum dignity of the person, consisting *"in effor-manda sua conscientia"*, in order to examine what *"in concreto suo casu, lege divina exigatur ab ipso"*[4]. De Smedt made more than one reference to the framework of this schema discussed in the assembly in September 1964, in a debate of extremely harsh tones with emotions running high. He referred to it even when – with Murray's entrance into every aspect of the editorial team – the committee was forced to reflect upon the political-legal dimension of the question of religious freedom, thus marking the final abandonment of the conscience perspective of the "ecumenical" versions.

Towards the end of September 1964, it was De Smedt himself who gave Murray, in particular, the responsibility of redrafting the schema, with the charge to provide a new formulation of the text which would

---

4. Cf. the *Relatio* read by De Smedt in the assembly on September 23, 1964, *AS* III/2, pp. 348-353.

reincorporate the content of the *Declaratio prior* as much as possible, but inserting into it some of his own ideas as well. Though De Smedt did not particularly agree with many of the American theologian's positions – positions which incidentally on the eve of the assembly debate were lucidly exhibited in a long article entitled *The Problem of Religious Freedom* and were considered to be the "manifesto" of what from this moment onwards came to be commonly defined as the "American school"[5] – he evidently found in Murray a noteworthy lucidity and clarity in setting forth the problem, apart from the unquestionable experience in discussing with the proponents of the traditional theses. These were essential gifts at a stage when one had to settle accounts concretely with the determination of the opponents of the schema.

Among the many views that confronted and clashed in the assembly hall, Murray actually did not have any doubts on the definitive option to be carried out. In the new project of the schema drafted in the days following the closing of the assembly debate – and which established the actual starting point of the long editorial work at the end of October 1964 that produced the *textus emendatus* in November – Murray's chief concern appeared to be that of linking the problem of religious freedom to the contemporary historical situation. While avoiding the dangers of a new form of "classicism", implying the contraposition between the rights of conscience and the abstract rights of truth, in Murray's opinion the scheme should above all carry out a methodological *aggiornamento*, by way of a more explicit and substantial consideration of the dimension of historicity. The *Declaratio prior*'s residual recall of the requirements of the ecumenical dialogue was therefore definitively abandoned in order to lead the legal and civil institution of religious freedom more explicitly back to the *signa temporum* of the contemporary person's increased personal and political awareness, recognized and established in *Pacem in terris*. Starting from this point of view, in the text revised between October and November 1964 – decisive in molding what would remain the essential physiognomy of *Dignitatis humanae* – the reference to the dignity of the person decidedly went on to shape itself as the fundamental purpose of the scheme, along with the new emphasis placed on the historical and contemporary conscience of religious freedom as an inviolable right of the person and the reality of the

---

5. Written between the spring and summer of 1964, and awaiting publication in "Theological Studies", Murray's extensive article was sent to the Dutch Documentation Centre in Rome, which saw to the translation in various languages for the distribution of the copies to all Fathers at the moment of the assembly works' reopening; cf. Murray to Alter, August 24, 1964, Fund Murray, 18, 986.

role of modern constitutional governments. With the implementation of Murray's leading option, every allusion to the erroneous conscience ultimately vanished from the text. The reference to conscience remained, but notably condensed and drawn closer to other arguments: the integrity of the person, the duty to search for the truth, the nature of the religious act and the limits on public powers (this last one having been already introduced by Pavan in the revised scheme between February and March 1964). The first consequence of this new layout of the problem was the separation between the *ex ratione* and the *ex revelatione* arguments: in other words, the breakage of the unity between the natural order and the supernatural one, upheld in the *Declaratio prior* with the idea of the "divine vocation". The *textus emendatus*, as it is known, considered the development of the biblical argument as well: the entire last section of the schema was dedicated to the *sub luce revelationis* freedom. It was a partial response to the numerous entreaties coming from abroad and from within the Secretariat: a response that nevertheless did not resolve the unanswered problem of a deeper connection between civil liberty in religious matters and evangelical freedom as it is found in the Scriptures.

De Smedt's apprehension towards the new "American" perspective manifested itself during the delicate editorial phases of October 1964. On October 3 he submitted to the editorial staff a project for an alternative draft to Murray's, clearly prompted by the desire to limit the reach of the modifications and innovations made to the text discussed in September by the American Jesuit; after all, it is difficult to discern the scope of his uneasiness was towards "la manière très juridique dont vous traitez la question" – De Smedt wrote to Murray a few months later on January 27, 1965 – and how much the reporter was concerned not to deviate radically from the *Declaratio Prior*'s framework[6]. After the other members of the editorial staff rejected this first project, the following day De Smedt presented yet another one: it essentially represented an attempt to accept in substance Murray's new framework, yet keeping original formulations and passages of the schema just discussed in the assembly in a much more considerable measure compared to the Jesuit theologian's project. The desire to shorten the section containing the rational arguments in favor of religious freedom in particular appeared clearly. The *ratio* was to be explained in the same letter to Murray on January 27 the following year: "Vous savez que je n'ai jamais été un chaud partisan de la manière dont les argumenta ont été presentés [...]. Je continue à penser que cette

6. Cf. De Smedt to Murray, January 27, 1965, Fund Murray, 18, 1006.

façon d'aligner les différents arguments est peu conforme au style conciliaire. Il faudrait en faire une synthèse, tout en conservant les éléments qu'ils contiennent et les termes qui les expriment". At the end of October, the same request to synthesize the *ex ratione* argument had been to a large extent at the origin of De Smedt's subsequent effort to prepare a *textus brevior* which was also receptive to the near unanimous indication that surfaced amongst the five Fathers of the Theological Commission consulted by the Secretariat on October 27. It was said about this that De Smedt convoked a "secret meeting" in order to prepare an alternative draft which would meet the diverse requests that emerged in the debate and re-launched by Parente the day before: a brief text without arguments, limiting itself to affirm only that the Church supports and accepts the right to religious freedom recognized by modern states. De Smedt did not make a secret of his dissatisfaction with the general framework that Murray had given to the text, but his intention seemed to be simply that of abbreviating its rational development. Another aspect of Murray's project which created certain difficulties for the reporter of *De libertate* involved the suppression of the "divine vocation" argument, an element that linked, as previously mentioned, the natural order and the supernatural one: in the project of October 4th De Smedt did not reinstate it but retrieved various expressions which were associated with it in the *Declaratio prior*.

This alternative project remained incomplete because it still lacked the re-elaboration of the theological and biblical section: the lack of a deeper biblical inspiration in fact represented a latent problem for the schema ever since the preparatory debate. With regard to this insufficiency of the *Declaratio*, various Fathers had expressed their views, most of all from the Francophone area, calling for an enlarged and more in-depth scriptural development. Along the same lines, the dissatisfactions of the Protestants were also noted; during the long, difficult days of October 1964, they in fact repeated the request for a more straightforward evangelical foundation of religious freedom. As to a new biblical development and above all the issue of the schema's preamble – should the priority be given to rational arguments or to Revelation? – the Secretariat had animated discussions during the plenary session on October 13-14, 1964. Whereas on the first point it awaited the work of two exegetes of the Biblical Institute, Francis McCool and Stanislas Lyonnet, who had been asked by Murray to elaborate a new biblical *excursus*, on the second point it showed an evident division. Despite the coherence of the new "American" framework, Willebrands himself, in particular, expressed his preference for beginning with the revealed data of the Scriptures, setting aside the second part for the exposition of the arguments of the natural order. On this occasion, De Smedt, while opting for this solution as well, scrupulously played the role of *relator*, restricting himself to stating the main criteria that informed the rewriting of the text.

The frequently schematic juxtaposition of the "American school" and the "Francophone school" has not always helped to grasp the complexity and diversity of reflections in various ways attributed to them. This distinction, officially introduced by Murray himself in a well-known article in 1964, certainly appeared inadequate to account for the wide spectrum of positions that took shape above all in the Francophone circles during the months of the last intersession: positions which were increasingly less open to a *reductio ad unum* of the "French school" generically dissatisfied with the "American" framework of the schema which had "relegated" the *doctrina sub luce revelationis* to the appendix. Of course, there had been various Francophone voices which lamented the absence of evangelical self-criticism and the extrinsicness of the *textus emendatus*'s "hook" between the justifications of a rational kind and the revealed nature of the right to religious freedom: to name a few, I am thinking of Liégé, Dupont, Féret, Pierre Haubtmann, René Laurentin, and Philippe Delhaye, who emphasized that Vatican II should have declared something that was doctrinally more demanding on the primary level of the rights of a conscience in good faith in error. However, the panorama was certainly much more variegated and complex: for instance, positions such as Marie-Joseph Le Guillou's, who found the starting point of the "American scheme" to be excellent for what concerned the presumption that the Church should be open to listen above all to the world and its interrogatives; or the positions of Jacques Maritain, Louis de Broglie, and most of all, Jean Daniélou, who on several occasions wanted to mark their distance from the "chorus" of those who asked to begin with Revelation because in this manner the problem of true religion would have been posed, along with the duties towards it as well as its respective risks.

On the other hand, all of the articulations of Murray's reflection turned out to be much more complex than the "technical" approach that was often implemented as the core of the "American" framework: "Pour vous" – De Smedt wrote in the letter on January 27, 1965 – "la liberté religieuse signifie toujours que l'État n'a pas le droit de s'ingérer dans les affairs religieuses des citoyens". In reality, the simple qualification of "technique" could appear more suitable for defining the declaration's final formulation than for Murray's articulate elaboration: in fact, Paul VI – through an editorial intervention by his trusted theologian Carlo

Colombo – adopted Murray's legal-political line, while disabling its intrinsic dynamism that was derived from that view of historicity of truth itself, which was strictly connected in the American theologian's framework. This perspective found the most significant expression in the text of Fall 1964, which was the one in which the institution of religious freedom was led back to the *segno dei tempi* of the new personal and political awareness of the contemporary person and, in a certain sense, built on the loyalty to the faithfulness to one of his most profound aspirations.

Certainly, the psychological dynamics in the relationship between the Belgian Bishop and the American Jesuit during and following the animated events of the Council's third period had their weight, an observation which is effectively reflected upon in the diary of Yves Congar, who on several occasions, in the months of the last intersession, spoke of De Smedt's disappointment, or rather, in Congar's opinion, of a certain discomfort due to Murray's growing leadership in the editorial group which to some extent overshadowed De Smedt's role as the relator. The evening of February 25, 1965, in commenting the new plan for rewriting the paragraph on the rational foundations of religious freedom prepared by Murray, Pavan, and Congar himself, the French theologian noted in his *Journal* that "Mgr De Smedt n'est pas content de cette dernière mesure. [...] En général, De Smedt n'aime pas beaucoup l'intervention de Murray. Pour lui, Murray est celui qui a transformé le premier texte (De Smedt) dans le textus emendatus; il est aussi, et c'est vrai, l'homme d'un style sec et trop juridique; il voit les choses sous un angle un peu individualiste. Mgr De Smedt aurait voulu, lui, rédiger, sans doute en revenant le plus possible à son premier texte"[7]. Added to this was the disappointment with the behavior of Hamer, who privately declared himself in agreement with De Smedt but sometimes during the meetings he tended to repeat Murray and Pavan's arguments[8]. In particular the day before, on February 24, on the basis of the suggestion made by Congar, Thijssen and Feiner, they returned to vote on whether to give priority to the enunciations drawn from Revelation or to the anthropological and rational argumentation. Hamer, and it seems, Willebrands himself – who a few days before would have expressed himself differently – gave their support to

---

7. Cf. Y. CONGAR, *Mon Journal du Concile*. Présenté et annoté par Éric MAHIEU. Avant-propos de D. CONGAR, préface de B. DUPUY, 2 Vols., Paris, Cerf, 2002. See Vol. II, February 25, pp. 337-338.

8. Cf. Dupont's letter to Sauvage on February 12, 1965, Fund Dupont, 1534 (Inventory in E. LOUCHEZ, *Concile Vatican II et Église contemporaine (Archives de Louvain-la-Neuve). IV: Inventaire des Fonds J. Dupont et B. Olivier* (Cahiers de la Revue théologique de Louvain, 29), Louvain-la-Neuve, Publications de la Faculté de Théologie, 1995).

the approach of Murray and Pavan. A few days later, at the time of the last modifications and corrections to the *textus reemendatus*, Congar once again dwelt on De Smedt's discomfort, who – among other things – was vexed by the acrobatics on the brief reference to the concordats which he preferred to expunge from the text: "J'ai eu nettement l'impression" – Congar wrote – "qu'hier soir il souffrait effectivement. Il est sans doute assez affectif. En fait, il a mis son coeur dans ce texte et surtout dans certains passages. Quand on attaque *objectivement* un texte, on froisse, chez son auteur, des liens vivants, des connexions affectives. J'ai senti nettement hier soir qu'il en avait été ainsi dans une critique faite d'un §, auquel de Smedt tient beaucoup, sur la prière comme premier acte du '*Munus Ecclesiae*'. Mgr De Smedt me dit ce matin: Je n'en peux plus. Je vais partir ce soir"[9].

The pages of Congar's diary are undoubtedly interesting in helping to grasp several aspects of De Smedt's resolute and in some ways emotional personality: a bishop who in the days following the vote adjournment on religious freedom, on November 20, 1964, did not hesitate to express clearly his state of mind and his fears to Paul VI. Beyond these psycho-logical notations, there is another fact which seems interesting above all for the light it throws on his relationship with Murray, who was not any less sincere in revealing his difficulties towards the positions of those who "seem to want a Declaration which will assert that the condition of man in the face of the ultimate questions of human existence is a condi-tion of freedom"[10]: I mean the discomfort expressed by De Smedt towards an "optique américaine, qui nous paraît un peu courte", but he could not nonetheless qualify as an "opportunist" having started as he did from the given situation, the contemporary person's aspiration to reli-gious freedom[11]. Vexed by the numerous criticisms "à notre *doctrina evangelica*", which came to the Secretariat because the biblical references chosen did not demonstrate religious freedom in the legal sense, De Smedt did not have the "recipe" and to Murray he confessed it with a problematic "Que faire?"[12].

Since Murray "imposed" the legal-political dimension of the question of religious freedom to the committee, a different manner of thoroughly understanding the process of *aggiornamento* began to divide the editorial

9. Cf. CONGAR, *Mon Journal du Concile* (n. 7), Vol. II, March 3, 1965, p. 344.
10. Cf. Murray's letter to De Smedt on February 13, 1965, regarding the "French", Fund Murray, 18,1009.
11. Cf. again Dupont's letter to Sauvage on February 12 [Fund Dupont, 1534], in which the Benedictine exegete refers to a long exchange with the Bishop of Bruges.
12. Cf. once again De Smedt to Murray, January 27, 1965.

group as well as numerous theologians and Fathers of the Council majority. A different manner, which manifested itself essentially in choosing a different starting point from which to act in the confrontation initiated by the Council with one of the most salient facts of political modernity: Should they look to the Scriptures, starting from the general concept of Christian freedom and move on to its particular, modern form of "application" – as many, especially in the Francophone area, requested – or should they look to history instead, starting from the contemporary conscience of religious freedom as an inviolable right of the person and thus concentrate on, without a "founding" purpose, the evangelical sense of this self-awareness, as Murray wanted? Behind De Smedt's "Que faire?" it seems that there was awareness of what basically represented the real problem of the schema: the fact that religious freedom, understood above all as the immunity from restrictions in the practice and in the diffusion of one's beliefs, "is not found exactly as such in the Holy Scriptures", as Congar wrote one year after the promulgation of *Dignitatis humanae*[13].

De Smedt predicted this difficulty, and perhaps because of this it was difficult for him to be a convinced proponent of those "Francophone" requests in the editorial group, which he too personally felt close to. From this perspective, the exchange with Dupont in February 1965, immediately preceding the emended text's revision at Monte Mario, was significant. On the eve of his departure to Rome, De Smedt had convened the Benedictine exegete for an exchange of views on the scheme. Once again Dupont emphasized specifically his discomfort in considering the right to religious freedom only within the realm of the relationship between the citizens and the State and for the placement of the passages on the revealed data at the end of the text: the free character of the act of faith was not evidently coextensive with religious freedom, as it was commonly understood by contemporary persons, but nonetheless for Dupont this worked well with his main foundation. To him, a preamble with the revealed data appeared moreover indispensable for avoiding the impression of a text dictated by motives "d'opportunisme diplomatique" [14]: an impression difficult to avoid if one limited oneself to a verification of the universal aspiration to religious freedom without immediately highlighting the profound correspondence with the principles of Revelation.

---

13. Cf. Y. CONGAR, *Avertissement*, in J. HAMER – Y. CONGAR (eds.), *La liberté religieuse: Déclaration dignitatis humanae personae*. Texte latin et traduction française (Unam Sanctam, 60), Paris, Cerf, 1967, 11-14, and his contribution, contained in the same volume, *Que faut-il entendre par "Déclaration"?*, 47-52.

14. Cf. J. DUPONT, *Réflexions sur le schéma De libertate religiosa*, February 11, 1965, in Fund Dupont, 1521.

De Smedt shared many of his interlocutor's perplexities and continued to declare himself "en opposition avec la coalition des juristes (Murray-Pavan) et des conservateurs (Ottaviani-Ruffini), qui sont d'accord pour limiter le problème"[15]. Yet he restricted himself to admitting the difficulty in finding a perfect solution; this was not only due to reasons of Council tactics – after "Black" Thursday "on ne peut plus changer complètement le texte, sous peine de perdre la face; on croirait que le Secrétariat ne sait plus ce qu'on veut" – but also because, as previously mentioned, he had warned that "le point de vue auquel se place le schéma *De libertate* ne peut pas être dit opportuniste. L'Église se place en face d'une realité: elle constate que la liberté religieuse est inscrite dans la charte fondamentale de la plupart des États et que, dans leur immense ensemble, les hommes estiment qu'il doit en être ainsi. [...] Devant cette conviction généralisée, l'Église est interrogée et s'interroge; et elle répond: il est bien qu'il en soit ainsi: cette manière de penser est juste et bonne"[16]. Like Dupont, *De libertate*'s reporter wished to go "beyond" the right to immunity, but he confessed the difficulty in concretely formulating alternatives for resolving several critical obstacles such as the limitation on exercising the right to religious freedom. He recognized that the space reserved for the affirmations drawn from the Revelation was fairly rarefied – and not without "maladresses" – but at the same time he underlined how it would be "bien difficile d'arriver à un exposé biblique solide". "Sur ce terrain les difficultés ne viennent pas seulement de la part de ceux qui voudraient éviter qu'on s'engage sur les principes. Elles viennent aussi de la difficulté qu'on éprouve à trouver des fondations solides", since "le problème tel qu'il se pose est relativement nouveau". "L'Écriture", De Smedt proceeded, "n'envisage évidemment pas ce problème précis", and therefore the only remaining option was to appeal to it "en se plaçant à un point de vue plus général"[17]. Like Dupont, De Smedt remained convinced "que l'Église ne s'engagera vraiment que si elle peut fonder ses affirmations sur la Révélation", yet on the other hand he seemed to be aware that on the exact point of the relationship between Scripture and one of the most characteristic acquisitions of modernity, the maturation of contemporary societies had posed a problem for which the biblical *ressourcement* turned out not to be a path that could be followed as easily as in ecclesiastical or liturgical matter: On the

15. Cf. again Dupont to Sauvage.
16. Cf. Dupont's notes on the interview with De Smedt on February 12, 1965, Fund Dupont, 1540.
17. Fund Dupont, 1540.

subject of religious freedom the return to the authentic tradition of the Church – one of the two poles of the *aggiornamento* dynamics – appeared therefore more problematic than in the other cases, even to those who certainly opted for beginning with the revealed data[18].

It seems to me that in this exchange with Dupont, De Smedt basically gave expression, in a simple and clear manner, to all the difficulties of the Council in its efforts to reinterpret what had been entrusted to the Church in Revelation in the light of several "states of conscience" which by now had become indisputable and irreversible data of historical becoming. In the case in point, he gives expression to the difficulties of a small group of Fathers and experts in confronting the new and crucial problem of the relationship between the free exercise of religion and the notion of Christian freedom, as the participation in the freedom of the Spirit. De Smedt realizes that the document which was taking shape left unanswered the need for a deeper integration between the various liberties it had referred to; he shares the requests of those who asked that the Secretariat's text should assert that the Church accepts the modern religious freedom in loyalty to the Christian faith and Revelation. At the same time, on the other hand, it seems that he also senses, perhaps not with full awareness, that by adopting Murray's "solution", the Church could perform in a certain sense an "act of humility", making itself available to learn and recognize how much it would have gained from the development of both the civilian world and humankind.

Istituto per le scienze religiose   Silvia SCATENA
Via san Vitale 114
I-40125 Bologna
Italy

---

18. De Smedt had asked once again, with hardly any success, to place the entire theological part at the beginning of the scheme on May 10, on the same day that Congar, before somebody else would do it, proposed the elimination of the biblical preface written by him; cf. CONGAR, *Mon Journal du Concile* (n. 7), Vol. II, May 10, p. 378.

ÉVÊQUES MISSIONNAIRES BELGES
AU CONCILE VATICAN II

TYPOLOGIE ET STRATÉGIE

Cet article se découpe en trois segments principaux. D'abord une présentation statistique du groupe des évêques missionnaires originaires de Belgique; ensuite un aperçu de la diversité de leurs activités conciliaires et des méthodes de travail employées, avec un focus particulier sur les évêques d'Afrique centrale, et enfin l'examen de leur apport à la confection du schéma sur les missions.

Quelques présupposés méthodologiques serviront d'introduction. Premièrement, cet exposé ne pourra être qu'une synthèse imparfaite, parce que le temps imparti et les lacunes archivistiques imposent forcément des contraintes. Ensuite, il faut définir précisément ce qu'on entend par évêques missionnaires belges car ce vocable générique recouvre des réalités de terrain assez différentes. En réalité, ce regroupement quelque peu artificiel d'évêques est constitué de trois sous-ensembles: d'abord les plus nombreux, les évêques, vicaires et préfets apostoliques résidentiels toujours en activité à l'aube du Concile, puis les évêques titulaires retraités des missions et enfin les évêques obligés par les événements à quitter leur diocèse, je veux évidemment faire référence ici aux évêques chassés au début des années '50 par le régime communiste de Pékin, deux Belges étant toujours officiellement en poste[1]. J'ajoute que ne seront à l'évidence pas inclus dans cet exposé les Belges supérieurs d'ordres ou de congrégations religieuses[2]. Une troisième remarque méthodologique a trait aux sources employées. Outre les documents officiels du Concile et diverses publications, j'ai également recouru aux archives des Centre Lumen gentium de Louvain-la-Neuve et Centrum voor conciliestudie de Leuven. Le premier conserve notamment les papiers du Père dominicain Bernard

---

1. Il s'agit de Mgr Joseph Julian Oste, évêque de Jehol (28 mars 1893-19 janvier 1971) CICM, ordonné prêtre le 21 novembre 1920, ordonné évêque de Jehol le 28 octobre 1948 et de Mgr Carlo Van Melckebeke, év. de Ningsia. Sur ce dernier, cf. la note 4 *infra*.

2. Soit dans l'ordre alphabétique: Godefroid Dayez (OSB belge), Omer Degrijse (CICM), John Janssens (SJ), Jan Van Kerckhoven (MSC).

Olivier[3], expert pour le Congo-Léo (qui est l'appellation du Congo belge à l'époque), des interviews d'évêques missionnaires, des notes diverses provenant essentiellement des papiers conciliaires de Gustave Thils et une base de données des acteurs conciliaires belges. Le second cité nous a été utile surtout pour les fonds de trois évêques congolais, Jan Van Cauwelaert, Victor Keuppens et André Creemers (y compris leur correspondance), et de façon anecdotique pour celui d'un évêque chinois, Carlo Van Melckebeke[4]. Enfin, une partie des documents employés proviennent d'autres fonds d'archives conciliaires, tels ceux des oblats André Seumois et Amand Reuter à Rome, de Georges Eldarov à Bologne ou du Cardinal Suenens à Malines[5].

3. Bernard Olivier, dominicain belge, occupait au début du Concile le poste de professeur de théologie morale à la Faculté de théologie de Lovanium. Voir pour davantage de détails la note de C. SOETENS dans son article *L'apport du Congo-Léopoldville (Zaïre), du Rwanda et du Burundi au concile Vatican II*, dans É. FOUILLOUX (éd.), *Vatican II commence... Approches francophones* (Instrumenta Theologica, 12), Louvain, Bibliotheek van de Faculteit der Godgeleerdheid, 1993, p. 201. Sur la carrière du Père B. Olivier au Congo et au Concile, le lecteur consultera avec profit ses souvenirs réunis dans B. OLIVIER, *Chroniques congolaises: De Léopoldville à Vatican II 1958-1965*, Paris, Éditions Karthala, 2000. Cf. également ses chroniques de la 2e et de la 4e périodes conciliaires, dans E. LOUCHEZ, *Concile Vatican II et Église contemporaine (Archives de Louvain-la-Neuve). IV: Inventaire des Fonds J. Dupont et B. Olivier* (Cahiers de la Revue théologique de Louvain, 29), Louvain-la-Neuve, Publications de la Faculté de Théologie, 1995, n. 169-170 [désormais cité Fonds Olivier].

4. Jan Van Cauwelaert (Anvers, 12 avril 1914) CICM est ordonné prêtre le 6 août 1939. Arrivé au Congo comme missionnaire en 1940, il est nommé en 1945 professeur de philosophie au séminaire de Kabwé (Kasai). Lors du dédoublement du vicariat apostolique de Léopoldville, est créé un vicariat apostolique d'Inongo dont J. Van Cauwelaert sera le premier vicaire nommé le 6 janvier 1954. Il est élu le 10 novembre 1959 évêque du diocèse d'Inongo et renoncera à sa charge en 1967 au profit d'un évêque africain. Sur l'action pastorale de Mgr Van Cauwelaert, on lira L. MONSENGWO – B. MPOTO, *Mgr Jan Van Cauwelaert: Pasteur et visionnaire*, Bruxelles, Cepess, 1999. Victor Keuppens (15 décembre 1902-11 octobre 1981) OFM, ordonné prêtre le 8 septembre 1928, est désigné évêque de Kamina le 10 novembre 1959. André Creemers (9 mars 1907-23 septembre 1971) OSC, ordonné prêtre le 1 août 1933, est élu le 10 novembre 1959 évêque de Bondo (Congo-Léo). Il renonce à sa charge en 1970. Carlo Van Melckebeke (19 juin 1898-26 août 1980) CICM, ordonné prêtre le 24 septembre 1922, monte le 30 mai 1946 sur le siège épiscopal de Ningxia. Expulsé de la Chine communiste (1952), il prendra une part prépondérante dans l'apostolat auprès des étudiants chinois d'Outre-Mer. Sur cette facette du personnage et sa nomination de visiteur apostolique de la diaspora chinoise (1953), voir M. RUI PING-LI, *Trente ans d'apostolat auprès des Chinois de la diaspora (1953-1980) et Mgr Carlo Van Melckebeke*, dans M. CHEZA – M. COSTERMANS – J. PIROTTE (éds.), *Nouvelles voies de la mission 1950-1980: Actes de la session conjointe du Crédic (XVIIIe session) et du Centre Vincent Lebbe Gentinnes 1997*, Lyon, Crédic, 1999, 161-174.

5. Les fonds Seumois et Reuter, encore non inventoriés, se retrouvent à la Maison générlice OMI de Rome. Le Fonds G. Eldarov (inventaire informatisé) est présent en copie aux archives de l'Istituto per le scienze religiose de Bologne. Sur le fonds conciliaire de L.-J. Suenens, un inventaire détaillé a paru: L. DECLERCK – E. LOUCHEZ, *Inventaire des Papiers conciliaires du cardinal L.-J. Suenens* (Cahiers de la Revue Théologique de Louvain, 31), Louvain-la-Neuve, Publications de la Faculté de Théologie, 1998.

I. Quelques repères statistiques…

D'un point de vue quantitatif, nous nous attacherons en premier à l'examen de la répartition géographique des 57 Pères belges évêques ou ex-évêques de mission dont la moyenne d'âge s'élève à 61 ans (à 57 ans si l'on retire les évêques titulaires), les 3 plus jeunes affichant 42 printemps, le plus âgé 87. Sans réelle surprise, c'est l'Afrique centrale qui fournit le plus fort contingent avec pas moins de 45 pères dont 42 pour le Congo ex-belge – je mentionne pour mémoire que l'indépendance a été accordée par la Belgique en 1960 –, 2 pour le Burundi (la tutelle belge sur le pays et sur le voisin rwandais sera levée en 1962) et enfin un Père blanc, Marcel Daubechies, occupé en Rhodésie du Nord, la future Zambie. L'Asie arrive en seconde position avec 9 évêques: trois ex-Chine communiste, trois en Inde (dont deux retraités, les jésuites Ferdinand Périer, ex-archevêque de Calcutta, et Oscar Sevrin qui s'était retiré en 1957 pour laisser son poste à un évêque autochtone, Mgr Tigga), deux au Pakistan (l'ancien et le nouvel évêque de Lahore) et un vicaire apostolique des Philippines[6]. Il manque trois évêques missionnaires qui sont bien dissimulés puisqu'ils œuvrent en Amérique centrale sur deux îles, l'un, Mgr Jean Collignon à Haïti et les deux autres, Mgr Arnold Boghaert à Roseau, sur l'île antillaise de la Dominique, où réside aussi l'ex-coadjuteur de son diocèse, Antoon Demets[7].

On l'aura deviné, ce sont les évêques ou ex-évêques de l'ancienne colonie belge qui, rien que par leur nombre, interviendront fréquemment dans notre article. Il n'est donc pas inutile de zoomer sur ce grand pays situé

---

6. Marcel Daubechies (23 janvier 1897-23 février 1988) PB, ordonné prêtre le 20 juin 1921, est désigné évêque de Kasama le 25 avril 1959. Pour la Chine, outre NNSS. Oste et Van Melckebeke, il faut ajouter Louis Morel (30 octobre 1880-6 juin 1971) CICM, ordonné prêtre le 16 juillet 1905, et élu archevêque de Suiyüan le 11 avril 1946. Pour l'Inde, outre Oscar Sevrin, Mgr Ferdinand Périer (22 septembre 1875-10 novembre 1968) SJ, ordonné prêtre le 3 octobre 1909, élu archevêque de Calcutta le 23 juin 1924 et Mgr Vincent Dereere (12 février 1880-31 décembre 1973) OCD, ordonné prêtre le 17 juin 1905, élu évêque de Trivandrum le 1 juillet 1937. Au Pakistan, Mgr Hector Catry (27 octobre 1889-18 mars 1972) OFMCap, ordonné prêtre le 6 juin 1914, désigné évêque de Lahore le 28 octobre 1928 et Marcel Roger Buyse (22 août 1892-29 mai 1974) OFMCap, ordonné prêtre le 20 mai 1917, élu évêque de Lahore le 28 octobre 1947. Quant au vicaire apostolique de Mountain Provinces (Philippines), il s'agit de William Brasseur (12 janvier 1903-1 février 1993) CICM, ordonné prêtre le 18 août 1929, élu vicaire apostolique le 10 juin 1948.
7. Jean Collignon (15 août 1904-27 juillet 1966) OMI, ordonné prêtre le 28 juin 1931, élu évêque de Les Cayes le 30 septembre 1942. Arnold Boghaert (21 octobre 1920-27 novembre 1993) CssR, ordonné prêtre le 18 juin 1944, élu évêque de Roseau le 4 juin 1957 et Antoon Demets (19 avril 1905-3 août 2000) CssR, ordonné prêtre le 21 septembre 1931, élu évêque-coadjuteur de Roseau le 13 juin 1946.

au Centre de l'Afrique et sur ses deux petits voisins. En novembre 1959, anticipant quelque peu sur l'indépendance nationale afin de conforter sa position, Rome avait décidé l'érection de la hiérarchie au Congo-Léo de même qu'au Rwanda et au Burundi. De territoire de mission, ces pays se métamorphosaient ainsi en «jeunes Églises», certes fragiles et qui relevaient toujours de la Sacrée Congrégation de la Propagande, un point particulièrement épineux dû principalement à la dépendance financière. Du point de vue de l'épiscopat, la situation diffère sensiblement au Congo-Léo et au Rwanda-Burundi. La majeure partie des évêques en place au Congo-Léo sont d'origine étrangère (Belges évidemment au premier plan mais aussi quelques Hollandais, Allemands, et un Italien[8]). Le pays ne compte au début du Concile que cinq évêques de couleur en fonction et quelques auxiliaires[9]. En cause: la formation de la relève locale qui n'avait pas pu être achevée à temps. Par exemple, la désignation au poste d'archevêque de Mgr Malula, l'évêque auxiliaire de Léopoldville, n'interviendra que le 7 juillet 1964. Alors que la situation au Rwanda et au Burundi se présente autrement puisque les évêques autochtones y sont majoritaires (trois au Rwanda pour un Suisse, André Perraudin, l'archevêque de Kabgayi; égalité parfaite au Burundi, deux Belges et deux Burundais, André Makarakiza et Michel Ntuyahaga)[10].

Ces évêques missionnaires belges d'Afrique centrale sont tous des religieux appartenant à une quinzaine d'ordres et de congrégations, un élément qui ne plaide pas vraiment pour la cohésion de l'ensemble. Les scheutistes, congrégation belge, et les pères blancs à l'Est, soit deux congrégations à l'origine de l'évangélisation de ces contrées à la fin du 19e siècle, fournissent logiquement le plus grand nombre d'évêques.

En reprenant de la hauteur, considérons l'ensemble des évêques missionnaires originaires de Belgique toujours au point de vue de leur famille religieuse; on remarque que les scheutistes (10) et les pères blancs (8) comptent ensemble dix-huit membres soit pratiquement 1/3 du total et qu'ils sont talonnés par la famille franciscaine (7) et les jésuites (6).

8. Mgr Danilo Catarzi, SX, évêque d'Uvira.
9. Les évêques Joseph Busimba (Goma, depuis 1960), Pierre Kimbondo (Kisantu, depuis 1961), Joseph Nkongolo (Kisantu, depuis 1959), Jacques Mbali (Buta, depuis 1961) et Thomas Kuba (Mahagi, depuis 1962).
10. Au Rwanda, Jean-Baptiste Gahamanyi (év. d'Astrida, depuis 1961), Aloïs Bigirumwami (év. de Nyundo, depuis 1952) et Joseph Sibomana (év. de Ruhengeri, depuis 1961). Au Burundi, outre Mgr Antoine Grauls (1 février 1899-26 juillet 1986) PB, ordonné prêtre le 16 juillet 1923, désigné archevêque de Gitega le 10 novembre 1959, et Joseph Martin (29 avril 1903-13 juin 1982), ordonné prêtre le 29 juin 1926, élu évêque de Bururi le 6 juin 1961, on compte deux évêques autochtones: André Makarakiza (év. de Ngozi, depuis 1961) et Michel Ntuyahaga (év. de Usumbura, depuis 1959).

Graphique n. 1: Répartition des évêques par familles religieuses

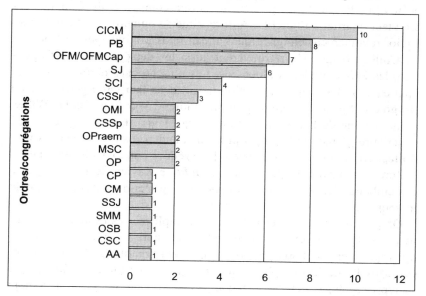

Ensemble, ces quatre familles religieuses totalisent plus de la moitié des évêques missionnaires[11].

Toujours plus haut, avec cette vue satellite de Rome où est indiqué le logement occupé durant la 4e session du Concile par les Pères missionnaires[12]. Ils se répartissent dans pas moins de 21 lieux différents, sur tout le territoire de la cité. Le Collège belge, au 26 de la via del Quirinale, n'est indiqué qu'à titre de référence, aucun évêque missionnaire n'y logeant, et pour rappeler que si la *squadra belga* a pu déployer aussi efficacement ses activités, elle le doit en partie au fait que ses membres y résidèrent tous durant l'entièreté du Concile. De leur côté, nos évêques-missionnaires belges logaient soit dans la maison généralice ou procure de leur ordre, soit à l'hôtel, soit encore dans une maison de religieuses affiliées ou non à leur ordre. Cependant, un groupe d'une bonne vingtaine d'évêques africains, dont les évêques autochtones

11. Cf. le graphique n. 1.
12. Voir la carte *infra*. La mention du logement des évêques belges est reprise à la brochure '*Peregrinatio romana ad Petri Sedem*', Rome, s.d., distribuée avant chaque session aux participants au Concile (présente pour les 3e et 4e périodes dans le Fonds Catry). On trouve également la mention des noms et de l'adresse des évêques d'origine belge dans le document '*Elenchus episcoporum Belgicae originis qui Concilio Vaticano II intersunt*', un document dont Albert Prignon semble être à l'origine (Fonds De Smedt).

et les scheutistes (leur procure romaine n'étant pas assez vaste pour les accueillir, ils ont dû s'adresser au service compétent du Concile) ont tenu leur quartier à l'hôtel Le Anfore, situé au numéro 7 de la viale Tito Livio, relativement éloignée du Vatican mais pratiquement à l'opposé du Collège belge. S'y retrouvèrent aussi les deux experts du Congo-Léo, les Pères Olivier et Goossens. Les plus proches de St-Pierre sont bien entendu les jésuites qui séjournaient dans leur curie généralice au Borgo San Spirito, assurément le plus éloigné Mgr François De Wilde, à une dizaine de km de la basilique (via Mauri). Le lieu de résidence conciliaire n'était évidemment pas sans incidence sur le travail. À titre d'illustration, durant la 3e session, les évêques congolais logeant au Le Anfore ont manqué l'intervention *in aula* de Xavier Geeraerts à cause des embouteillages monstres, un phénomène récurrent dans la capitale italienne[13].

On peut aussi quantifier le travail accompli par les évêques missionnaires belges en relevant l'ensemble de leurs interventions orales, remarques écrites et souscriptions. En ce qui regarde les *locuti* prononcés dans l'aula[14], les évêques missionnaires intervinrent seulement à 12 reprises, chiffre peu élevé en comparaison de leur nombre. On compte quatre interventions durant la 1ère session, un chiffre identique pour la deuxième, une seule au cours de la troisième et enfin trois à la dernière session. Le champion du micro, c'est Mgr Jan Van Cauwelaert, l'évêque d'Inongo au Congo, qui a pris la parole à 4 reprises. Il a sans doute, indique la revue 'La relève', hérité du talent de tribun de son père, Frans Van Cauwelaert, docteur en droit et ministre d'État[15]. Sa seconde intervention, consacrée à la concélébration si désirée par les prêtres et les populations du continent africain, lui valut de chaleureux applaudissements et bien des félicitations de la part des Pères conciliaires[16]. Derrière Jan Van Cauwelaert, Mgr Joseph Guffens, ex-vicaire apostolique du Kwango, aura prononcé deux interventions. Six autres évêques, dont 5 d'Afrique et 1 d'Asie, chacun une. Les Pères missionnaires belges se sont exprimés oralement sur trois schémas conciliaires seulement: celui consacré à l'Église arrivant en tête avec 7 interventions, suivi du schéma sur les missions avec 4 et de la liturgie avec seulement une.

13. Tiré d'une lettre de Jan Van Cauwelaert à ses missionnaires, 15 novembre 1964, dans Fonds Van Cauwelaert, p. 3.
14. Cf. le graphique n. 2 *infra*.
15. *La Relève*, 10 novembre 1962, copie dans Fonds Van Cauwelaert.
16. Ce commentaire provient de son cousin dom Robert Van Cauwelaert qui l'accompagnait à Rome pour servir de secrétaire, dans lettre à la famille, 1 novembre 1962, dans Fonds Van Cauwelaert.

Carte de Rome avec l'indication du logement des évêques missionnaires
belges

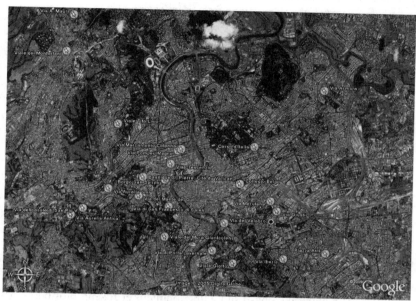

Source: réalisé avec le logiciel *Google Earth*, à partir des données collectées
dans la brochure *Peregrinatio*....

Graphique n. 2: Interventions orales par Père et par sujet

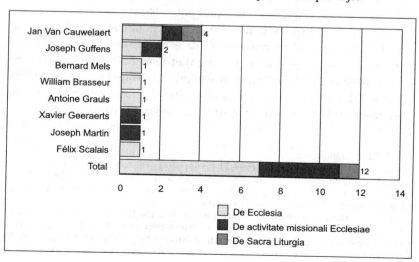

Graphique n. 3: Remarques écrites par Père et par sujet traité

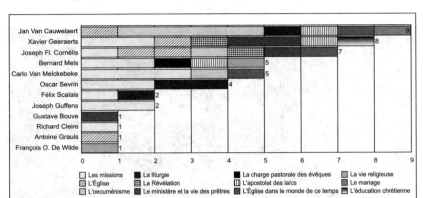

Bien plus nombreuses et variées apparaissent les 46 remarques écrites (*animadversiones* ou *emendationes*) envoyées au secrétariat du Concile[17]. Cette fois, douze Pères ont procédé de la sorte pour faire connaître leurs idées. Derechef, Jan Van Cauwelaert occupe la première place avec 9 remarques scripturaires. Son dauphin, Xavier Geeraerts, ex-vicaire apostolique de Bukavu (au Congo) suit à une longueur et Joseph Floribert Cornélis, l'archevêque d'Elisabethville (Lubumbashi), également à un pas du précédent[18]. Quant aux thématiques abordées, elles s'élargissent aussi: mais cette fois l'activité missionnaire de l'Église devance largement l'Église, l'œcuménisme (avec 14 remarques contre 5 pour chacun des deux autres schémas), la liturgie et le ministère et la vie des prêtres (dont le compteur restera bloqué à 4 remarques pour chacun).

Enfin, la grande majorité des évêques missionnaires belges, hors les malades et à l'exception notable des deux oblats de Marie Immaculée René Toussaint (év. d'Idiofa au Congo) et Jean Collignon (Haïti) ainsi que de Mgr Delaere, un capucin évêque de Molegbe au Congo, ont souscrit à des interventions orales ou écrites de leurs confrères[19]. On ne s'étonnera guère de constater que les schémas sur l'Église et les

17. Cf. le graphique n. 3.
18. Xavier Geeraerts (4 avril 1894-23 février 1971) PB, ordonné prêtre le 15 juillet 1922, est élu le 17 janvier 1952 vicaire apostolique de Bukavu. Joseph Floribert Cornélis (6 octobre 1910-20 décembre 2001) OSB, ordonné prêtre le 28 juillet 1935, est élu le 10 novembre 1959 archevêque d'Elisabethville.
19. Léon Théobald Delaere (1 février 1898-14 juin 1983) OFMCap, ordonné prêtre le 23 septembre 1923, élu évêque de Molegbe le 10 novembre 1959. René Toussaint (5 mars 1920-21 mars 1993) OMI, ordonné prêtre le 8 juillet 1945, est élu évêque d'Ipamu le 10 novembre 1959. Sur la carrière de ce prélat, voir le livre de J.-M. RIBAUCOURT, *Évêque*

Graphique n. 4: Souscriptions des évêques missionnaires belges:
classement thématique

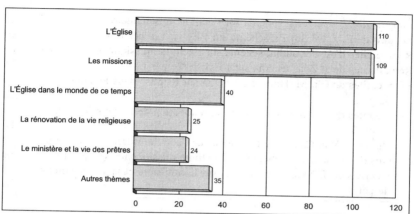

missions mènent largement le classement, tous deux quasiment à égalité parfaite et loin devant le schéma dédié à l'Église dans le monde
d'aujourd'hui[20].

Si l'on examine les interventions ayant suscité le plus de souscriptions
de la part des évêques missionnaires belges, le *locutus* de Xavier Geeraerts consacré au schéma des missions dit «des 14 propositions» (3e session) se situe au premier rang, suivi d'une intervention de Mgr De Smedt
à propos du schéma *De ecclesia* et des remarques écrites d'André Perraudin concernant le schéma sur l'activité missionnaire[21]. Dans ce classement, on retrouve parmi les intervenants 6 évêques d'Afrique (5 du
Congo ou du Rwanda dont un autochtone et un Camerounais, en l'occurrence Mgr Jean Zoa), 2 évêques belges résidentiels (De Smedt et Himmer) et le Supérieur général des scheutistes, le Père Omer Degrijse. Le
plus gros souscripteur (30 au compteur) est le Père blanc Marcel Daubechies (évêque de Kasama) qui signe systématiquement toutes les interventions de son groupe de Pères d'Afrique centro-orientale. Il faut bien
préciser que ceci ne représente pas, loin s'en faut, le signe d'une grande
activité conciliaire. D'ailleurs, Mgr Van Cauwelaert n'a pour sa part souscrit qu'à 13 reprises …

---

d'une transition: René Toussaint (1920-1993). Missionnaire au Congo-Zaïre, Kinshasa,
Éditions Baobab, 1997.
20. Cf. le graphique n. 4 *infra*.
21. Cf. le tableau *infra*.

Tableau: Interventions de Pères ayant suscité le plus grand nombre de
souscriptions de la part d'évêques missionnaires belges

Locutus de X. Geeraerts, schéma sur l'activité missionnaire (3e pér.)	**22**
Locutus de E.-J. De Smedt, schéma sur l'Église (2e pér.)	**19**
Rem. écrites d'A. Perraudin, schéma sur l'activité missionnaire (3e pér.)	**16**
Rem. écrites de J. Zoa, schéma sur l'Église (2e pér.)	**12**
Rem. écrites de Ch.-M. Himmer, schéma sur l'Église dans le monde (3e pér.)	**12**
Rem. écrites de B. Mels, schéma sur la rénovation de la vie religieuse (3e pér.)	**12**
Locutus de J. Van Cauwelaert, schéma sur l'activité missionnaire (4e pér.)	**10**
Locutus de O. Degrijse, schéma sur l'activité missionnaire (4e pér.)	**8**
Rem. écrites de J. Nkongolo, schéma sur le ministère et la vie des prêtres (4e pér.)	**8**

Pour synthétiser le volet «interventions au Concile» de cette partie statistique, on remarque que l'une ou l'autre personnalités se dégagent déjà
du groupe des évêques missionnaires: Jan Van Cauwelaert en premier lieu
mais aussi Xavier Geeraerts, Joseph Guffens, Bernard Mels, Joseph Floribert Cornélis, Oscar Sevrin, Carlo Van Melckebeke, des noms qui reviendront souvent *infra*. Mais aussi émerge déjà la prépondérance du schéma
des missions comme thème ayant le plus mobilisé les Pères missionnaires
belges, surtout si l'on répète qu'une part non négligeable des interventions
consacrées aux autres schémas l'ont été pour mettre en exergue leur dimension missionnaire[22]. Ainsi l'intervention de Bernard Mels sur le *De ecclesia* lors de la première session consistait-elle à réclamer pour ce texte une
accentuation de la mission de l'Église. Et à la seconde, les interventions portant sur ce même schéma comprenaient toutes un arrière-plan missionnaire.

II. TACTIQUES D'INTERVENTION ET ACTIVITÉS

Cette partie évoquera principalement les activités des évêques congolais et du secrétariat de leur Conférence épiscopale. La fameuse Panafricaine épiscopale ne sera pas non plus négligée du fait du rôle moteur joué
en son sein par ces mêmes évêques du Congo-Léo et surtout par leurs
experts. Il faut ajouter qu'au Concile, l'épiscopat du Congo représente

---

22. Par exemple, les interventions des évêques missionnaires ayant trait à la restauration du diaconat permanent sans obligation de célibat ont au minimum un arrière-plan missionnaire.

rien que par ses effectifs le premier groupe africain. Et que la première Faculté de théologie d'Afrique noire est érigée à Lovanium en 1957[23].

Mais entamons nos observations d'abord par les nominations aux commissions conciliaires. Quatre évêques de notre groupe sont directement concernés. Durant la phase préparatoire du Concile, Mgr Alfons Verwimp, jésuite, ex-évêque de Kisantu (Congo-Léo), figure parmi les membres de la Commission centrale préparatoire[24]. Sont nommés par leurs pairs pour figurer dans les commissions conciliaires, Oscar Sevrin à la commission des missions, et Jan Van Cauwelaert à celle sur la discipline des sacrements. Ce dernier raconte dans sa correspondance pourquoi il s'est retrouvé dans cette commission. Il aurait certainement préféré la liturgie – avant le Concile, Van Cauwelaert était déjà réputé pour ses connaissances en matière liturgique des pays de mission parce qu'il présidait depuis 1961 la Commission nationale congolaise pour la liturgie et la catéchèse, qu'il avait écrit plusieurs articles sur ce thème et qu'il avait pris part au Congrès «liturgie et missions» tenu à Nimègue en 1959 – mais un évêque africain, en l'occurrence Mgr Malula, occupait déjà une place dans la commission depuis la phase préparatoire. Un second 'Africain' aurait eu peu de chances de passer et les conférences épiscopales d'Europe de l'Ouest et d'Afrique ont coché son nom pour la commission de la discipline des sacrements[25]. Cette commission n'a tenu aucune réunion durant la 1ère session, hormis une belle réception protocolaire orchestrée par son président le cardinal Paolo Marella[26]. Mais elle tient ses assises durant deux semaines à la fin du mois de mars 1963. Au sein de cette Commission, Mgr Van Cauwelaert sera d'abord désigné avec d'autres membres pour travailler sur la forme valide du mariage, puis sera versé dans la sous-commission chargée du mariage mixte. Il se plaint du poids exercé par la curie via les fonctions de président et surtout de secrétaire, mais il compte bien malgré tout intervenir pour qu'on ne s'en tienne pas qu'à l'ancienne législation avec quelques aménagements pour ménager les susceptibilités protestantes[27]. Enfin le quatrième évêque missionnaire à figurer dans une commission, Bernard Mels, le

23. Sur la fondation de cette université africaine, cf. notamment B. OLIVIER, *Chroniques congolaises* (n. 3), pp. 19-21.

24. Alfons Verwimp (22 mai 1885-11 novembre 1964) SJ, ordonné prêtre le 17 mai 1917, est élu évêque de Kisantu le 10 novembre 1959.

25. Lettre de Jan Van Cauwelaert à ses missionnaires, 25 octobre1962, dans Fonds Van Cauwelaert, p. 3.

26. Lettre de Jan Van Cauwelaert à ses missionnaires, 4 décembre 1962, dans Fonds Van Cauwelaert, p. 7.

27. Lettre de Jan Van Cauwelaert à sa famille, 3 avril 1963, dans Fonds Van Cauwelaert.

'Lion du Kasaï', figurera quant à lui parmi les 5 noms désignés par le pape pour la commission des religieux[28].

Pour tous les évêques missionnaires et les autres, le travail durant le Concile n'a pas manqué et à certains moments, les témoignages directs évoquent carrément la surchauffe. Outre les participations aux congrégations générales d'avant-midi, les après-midi et les soirées sont réservées aux diverses réunions officielles et privées, aux entretiens, aux rendez-vous pris avec les spécialistes de certaines questions, aux conférences et aux réceptions, notamment celles des nonces apostoliques et de l'ambassadeur de Belgique[29].

Le 12 octobre 1962, tous les évêques d'origine belge sont conviés au Collège belge par le cardinal Suenens pour arranger la question des candidatures aux commissions conciliaires[30].

Réunions et conférences s'avèrent particulièrement consommatrices de temps. Trois fois par semaine généralement, entre 17 et 20h, se tiennent les réunions des évêques congolais, parfois avec les Belges et les autres évêques d'Afrique. Mgr Creemers, l'évêque de Bondo, écrit ainsi à son Provincial belge le 12 octobre 1963: «Nous avons aussi depuis lundi presque chaque soir une réunion, parfois les évêques du Congo, parfois les évêques francophones d'Afrique, parfois le Congo, la Belgique et beaucoup des autres pays d'Europe centrale. Nous avons ainsi entendu cette semaine le Père Daniélou, Suenens, Philips, le Père Olivier, Hans Küng et Schillebeeckx. Et pour la semaine suivante, pratiquement chaque jour une conférence est prévue»[31].

Aux réunions classiques de la Conférence épiscopale congolaise, s'ajoutent durant la quatrième session les réunions destinées à traiter de questions particulières pour fournir un avis au pape. Celle du Congo doit ainsi traiter de la discipline pénitentielle et de l'éducation chrétienne[32].

Quelques évêques cumulent même les activités, tel Mgr Van Cauwelaert: outre les réunions de sa commission des sacrements, il doit prendre part à celles de la Panafricaine, de la conférence épiscopale congolaise, et de la commission liturgique de la Panafricaine où il remplit la tâche

28. Bernard Mels (29 novembre 1908-1 janvier 1992) CICM, ordonné prêtre le 15 août 1933, est élu le 10 novembre 1959 archevêque de Luluabourg.
29. La mention de ces réceptions revient fréquemment dans les lettres de Jan Van Cauwelaert à ses missionnaires et de A. Creemers à son Prieur provincial.
30. Lettre de André Creemers au Prieur provincial A. Ramaekers, 12 octobre 1962, dans Fonds Creemers.
31. Lettre de André Creemers à A. Ramaekers, 12.10.1963, dans Fonds Creemers.
32. Id., 18.10.1965, dans Fonds Creemers.

de secrétaire. Et il faut y adjoindre les extras. Trois exemples permettront d'illustrer cela. Un samedi de septembre 1964 (et de nouveau en octobre 1965), il participe à une réunion des responsables de la liturgie pour les pays francophones afin d'envisager le travail de traduction des textes liturgiques entrepris sous la direction de l'épiscopat français. Et quelques semaines plus tard, il assistera à une rencontre de tous les collaborateurs de la revue *Concilium*. Puis encore au mois d'octobre 1965, il prend part avec Mgr Cornélis (tous deux délégués par l'épiscopat du Congo) à un congrès sur le diaconat[33]. De par sa renommée de liturgiste, il est aussi chargé de contacter les autres groupes: français, allemand, hollandais et des évêques ou experts influents. Il rencontre aussi fréquemment les observateurs, les frères de Taizé surtout[34].

Signalons encore une réunion en octobre 1965 pour les évêques africains, cette fois avec le Secrétariat pour les relations avec les religions non-chrétiennes. Une bonne dizaine d'évêques missionnaires belges y prennent part[35].

Toute l'activité des évêques missionnaires se prépare en trois temps au niveau du Secrétariat de l'épiscopat: information par le biais de dossiers préparés par leurs théologiens, discussions, et enfin préparation d'interventions à prononcer ou de remarques écrites à remettre, le tout comprenant les tactiques envisagées pour la plus grande efficacité d'action[36].

Attardons-nous justement un peu sur les tactiques employées par les évêques missionnaires et leurs experts pour imposer leurs conceptions au sein des textes conciliaires.

La distribution de textes via des acteurs majeurs constitua une technique courante et précoce. On peut véritablement parler de 'lobbying'

---

33. La réunion des liturgistes, dans J. Van Cauwelaert à ses missionnaires, 2 octobre 1965, p. 5, dans Fonds Van Cauwelaert; la réunion des collaborateurs de *Concilium*, dans Fonds Van Cauwelaert, le 24 octobre 1964, p. 5. Le congrès sur le diaconat, dans Jan Van Cauwelaert à ses missionnaires, 26 octobre 1965, p. 3, dans Fonds Van Cauwelaert.
34. Lettre de Robert Van Cauwelaert à la famille, 22 octobre 1962, dans Fonds Van Cauwelaert; sur sa rencontre avec les frères de Taizé, voir J. Van Cauwelaert à ses missionnaires, 13 novembre 1962, p. 6, dans Fonds Van Cauwelaert. Sur ses rencontres avec les observateurs, J. Van Cauwelaert à ses missionnaires, 30 novembre 1963, p. 7 dans Fonds Van Cauwelaert.
35. Les évêques Marcel Buyse et Carlo Van Melckebeke pour l'Asie, Jan Van Cauwelaert, Alphonse Van Den Bosch, Joseph Cornelis, Gustave Bouve, François Lehaen, Victor Keuppens, Alain Leroy, Georges Kettel, Bernard Mels et François Van den Bergh pour l'Afrique francophone. Cf. le document '*Réunions des ordinaires intéressés au Secrétariat pour les Non-Chrétiens*', dans Fonds Keuppens.
36. Lettre de P. Goossens aux évêques congolais, 28 avril 1963, 1 p. et G. Mosmans, *Concile. Préparation de la 2ᵉ session*, 15 mars 1963 (avec annexes) dans Fonds Van Kerckhoven.

conciliaire. Des listes d'interlocuteurs ou d'intermédiaires privilégiés furent rapidement établies. Dès avant l'ouverture du Concile, avait circulé un document intitulé *'Memorandum pour les réunions africaines anté-conciliaires'* conçu par les théologiens occidentaux du Congo-Léo et porté par des évêques de ce pays. Il circula assez largement et nous analyserons son contenu par la suite.

Autre tactique, l'intervention directe auprès d'un personnage influent du Concile et, à titre d'exemple, le cardinal Suenens fut sur ce plan sollicité plusieurs fois par des évêques missionnaires belges qui le connaissaient personnellement, mais nous en reparlerons ultérieurement dans la dernière partie consacrée au schéma des missions. Néanmoins mentionnons dès à présent que c'est via le cardinal Suenens que Mgr Scalais a introduit au début de la deuxième session une demande de reconnaissance officielle des deux *periti* du Congo-Léo, démarche qui aboutit d'ailleurs durant cette même seconde session[37]. Et lors de la 1ère intersession, Jan Van Cauwelaert, qui se réunit avec les autres membres de sa commission des sacrements, part trouver le cardinal Suenens, présent lui aussi à Rome, pour se faire 'tuyauter' sur la question du diaconat. Et Suenens lui confie en supplément ses impressions sur la marche du Concile[38].

Troisième stratégie, l'entretien de contacts suivis avec d'autres groupes d'évêques. Le chanoine Gustave Thils jouera ainsi le rôle du mortier cimentant le groupe des évêques belges et leurs homologues congolais, mais aussi africains en général puisqu'il concourt notamment à certaines réunions du groupe des experts de la Panafricaine. Et il se montre, au moins dans les deux premières sessions, actif auprès de la Panafricaine. Il contacte aussi régulièrement les évêques congolais pour des services et est en retour sollicité par les théologiens congolais pour exprimer ses remarques sur les différents schémas[39]. Ajoutons que le chanoine Thils était aussi le directeur de thèse de l'abbé Tarcisse Tshibangu, le premier *peritus* officiel africain[40].

Enfin, dernière technique, durant les 3e et 4e sessions, les évêques congolais s'accordèrent plutôt pour réunir leurs *modi* sous quelques noms représentatifs, le tout afin que les commissions ad hoc les prennent mieux en considération[41].

37. OLIVIER, *Chronique du Concile*, p. 3, dans Fonds Olivier, 169.
38. Jan Van Cauwelaert à sa famille, 3 avril 1963, p. 2, dans Fonds Van Cauwelaert.
39. Lettres de P. Goossens à G. Thils, 13 mai 1963, 1 p.; et 20 juillet 1963, 1 p., dans Fonds Thils, 1224 et 1227. Lettre de J. Van Cauwelaert à ses missionnaires, 3 novembre 1964, p. 1, dans Fonds Van Cauwelaert.
40. Information mentionnée dans le livre de RIBAUCOURT, *Évêque d'une transition* (n. 19), p. 259.
41. J. Van Cauwelaert à ses missionnaires, 26 septembre 1964, p. 5, dans Fonds Van Cauwelaert.

Même pendant les intersessions, les experts programment des réunions des évêques au Congo pour examiner les schémas conciliaires. Afin de pallier le fait que les évêques congolais sont alors de nouveau exclusivement absorbés par les affaires de leur diocèse, une procédure complexe en quatre phases est instaurée afin de continuer le travail durant la 1ère intersession: primo, envoi aux évêques congolais d'un inventaire des questions importantes pour l'Église d'Afrique; secundo, tournée du Père Paul Goossens durant quatre mois dans les pays d'Europe de l'Ouest afin de collecter des avis et des textes doctrinaux sur les schémas à examiner par les Pères pour la seconde session (pour la Belgique, il contacte Suenens, De Smedt, Philips et Thils, et pour la France Congar, Liégé, Henry, Daniélou, Etchegaray); tertio, envoi des dossiers ainsi constitués aux évêques et tenue de réunions locales pour examiner les exposés doctrinaux, mettre au point des applications pratiques concrètes concernant spécialement le Congo et rédiger des notes qui n'auraient pas été prévues. Chaque dossier comprend ainsi un exposé de la question, le contenu du schéma, des critiques générales et des propositions d'amendements. En annexe, figurent les documents justificatifs; quarto, transmission d'une note à Rome et réunion du Comité permanent de l'épiscopat pour déterminer les possibilités d'intervention et finaliser les déclarations à prononcer *in aula*[42].

Quant au cardinal Suenens, il suggère plus simplement que les évêques congolais lui fassent parvenir des textes d'une dizaine de lignes sur les idées qu'ils désirent voir insérer dans les schémas en cours d'élaboration. On pourrait aussi selon lui envoyer quelques évêques congolais devant les commissions[43].

La conférence épiscopale des évêques du Congo qui se réunit le lundi a finalement trouvé son local de réunion à Maria Assunta, près de St-Pierre. Elle installe aussi des sous-commissions d'étude sur certains schémas, celle sur les missions étant mise en place dès la seconde période. Les évêques congolais reçoivent aussi à plusieurs reprises des responsables laïcs d'action catholique[44].

Tout n'est cependant pas parfait dans le petit monde de l'épiscopat congolais. Au fur et à mesure de l'avancée du Concile, des tensions surviennent avec les évêques d'origine africaine. Je cite André Creemers

---

42. Correspondance de Mgr F. Scalais aux évêques congolais, 31 janvier 1963, 3 p. et annexes.

43. G. Mosmans, 'Quelques indications concernant la 2e session du Concile', 10 mars 1963, p. 4, dans Fonds Van Kerckhoven.

44. J. Van Cauwelaert à ses missionnaires, 6 octobre 1963, p. 2 et 13 novembre 1965, p. 3, dans Fonds Van Cauwelaert. Pour des informations complémentaires, voir OLIVIER, *Chroniques congolaises* (n. 3), pp. 206ss.

dans une lettre du 9 octobre 1965: «Nos réunions des évêques congolais sont de moins en moins acceptées, les évêques noirs deviennent exigeants et veulent convenir de tout. Les Blancs commencent à avoir de moins en moins à dire et il y en a qui disent qu'ils ne viendront plus»[45].

La Panafricaine épiscopale s'est mise rapidement sur pied au Concile. Elle a pu obtenir un local pour ses réunions sur la via Traspontina, près de St-Pierre. Le cardinal Rugambwa en assume la présidence, assisté de deux secrétaires, un pour l'aile francophone, Jean Zoa, et un pour l'aile anglophone, Joseph Blomjous[46]. Elle compte un organe de direction composé d'un représentant de chaque conférence épiscopale, 9 grandes régions en tout, Mgr Scalais occupant le poste pour le groupe du Congo-Léo et du Rwanda-Burundi. Après deux réunions communes, le groupe se scinde en deux ailes selon les conférences épiscopales du Congo-Léo d'une part et du Rwanda-Burundi d'autre part. La Panafricaine dispose aussi d'un comité de théologiens. Parmi les plus assidus de ses membres, on compte les théologiens du Congo et du Rwanda-Burundi, Martelet pour le Cameroun, Anselmo pour Madagascar et les jésuites Masson, de Broglie et Gréco. Bref le Congo-Léo se transforme vite en moteur de ce regroupement de conférences épiscopales. Chacune des conférences épiscopales devait nommer un représentant pour les cercles d'études parallèles aux commissions conciliaires.

À la Panafricaine, on s'informe à bonne source. En septembre 1964, c'est le cardinal Suenens en personne qui leur donne un exposé sur les perspectives du Concile[47]. Et plusieurs interventions des évêques missionnaires belges eurent lieu au nom de toute l'Afrique.

Parmi les préoccupations des évêques missionnaires à Rome, figuraient certainement au premier plan les affaires de leur diocèse. Entre les sessions, les Pères, après un bref séjour en Belgique, se hâtaient de rentrer au Congo-Léo afin de visiter les postes de mission, soutenir leurs prêtres et s'occuper de leurs ouailles. La tâche, il est vrai, s'avérait loin d'être une sinécure. L'Afrique centrale vivait, déjà à l'époque, le martyre des

---

45. A. Creemers à A. Ramaekers, 9 octobre 1965, dans Fonds Creemers.

46. Sur la Panafricaine épiscopale, cf. SOETENS, *L'apport du Congo-Léopoldville* (n. 3), pp. 199ss.; G. CONUS, *L'Église d'Afrique au Concile Vatican II*, dans *Neue Zeitschrift für Missionswissenschaft* 30 (1974) 241-255; J.-P. MESSINA, *L'Église d'Afrique au Concile Vatican II: Origines de l'assemblée spéciale du synode des évêques pour l'Afrique*, dans *Mélanges de science religieuse* 51 (1994) 279-295.

47. Lettre de J. Van Cauwelaert à ses missionnaires, 20 septembre 1964, p. 8, dans Fonds Van Cauwelaert.

luttes tribales, des guerres civiles, de la famine et le chômage généra-
lisé[48]. En 1960, à l'occasion de l'indépendance, des troubles sérieux mais
limités avaient éclaté dans le pays causant des dégâts aux missions et
obligeant les Pères à évacuer. Dès 1962, survenaient les épisodes dits de
la sécession katangaise, menée par Moïse Tshombé, et de celle du Kasaï;
des rebelles massacraient à Nkongolo 21 missionnaires dont 18 spiritains.
Mais le grand bouleversement allait survenir deux ans plus tard, en 1964,
lors de la rebellion muléliste. Ce mouvement d'opposition anti-blanc,
d'obédience communiste chinoise, rejetait en bloc toute aide matérielle
ou spirituelle de l'Occident et les missionnaires, hommes et femmes,
représentaient des cibles privilégiées. Plus d'une centaine de missionnaires, de prêtres congolais et de religieuses seront assassinés par les ter-
ribles simbas, et Mgr Wittebols, évêque de Wamba, figurera au nombre
des victimes. Mgr Piérard, un assomptionniste évêque de Beni, devra pour
sa part se réfugier dans l'Ouganda voisin (photo n. 1 *infra*). Mais sa santé
est si ébranlée qu'il démissionera un an après la fin du Concile[49]. Bien
des missions ont été dévastées matériellement et spirituellement. Ces événements dramatiques empêcheront une dizaine d'évêques congolais de
se rendre à la 3e session et pour d'autres retarderont leur arrivée à Rome[50].
Quant aux évêques présents à Rome ou en Europe durant la rébellion, ils
ne pourront plus se rendre avant longtemps dans leur diocèse ravagé, tel
Mgr Creemers l'évêque de Bondo, qui en 1969 finira par rentrer définitivement en Belgique. Des réunions seront tenues à Rome pour engran-
ger les informations et traiter de la situation au pays. On remarque clairement dans la correspondance de plusieurs évêques missionnaires la part
largement prépondérante que prennent les événements congolais par rapport à ceux du Concile. Parmi les décisions, comme les évêques congolais ne peuvent pas compter beaucoup sur la Propagande, ils s'accordent

---

48. Pour un aperçu bref mais éclairant de la situation au Congo et au Rwanda-Burundi
à la période de la décolonisation, cf. M. CHEZA, *La problématique missionnaire dans le
contexte des années 1945-1960*, dans J. PIROTTE – G. ZELIS (éds.), *Pour une histoire du
monde catholique au 20e siècle Wallonie-Bruxelles: Guide du chercheur*, Louvain-la-
Neuve, Arca, 2003, 712-714. On consultera aussi avec profit *Bilan du monde. 1964*,
Tome II, Tournai, Casterman, 1964, aux pp. 179-183 (Burundi), pp. 264-279 (Congo-Léo)
et pp. 767-771 (Rwanda).

49. Mgr Joseph Wittebols (12 avril 1912-26 novembre 1964) SCI, ordonné prêtre le
11 juillet 1937, est désigné évêque de Wamba le 10 novembre 1959. Mgr Henri Piérard
(21 juin 1893-5 mars 1975) AA, ordonné prêtre le 26 juillet 1925, est élu évêque de Beni
le 10 novembre 1959.

50. Ainsi de René Toussaint, empêché de se rendre à Rome pour la 3e période conciliaire et qui n'arrivera à la 4e que le 15 octobre 1965. Repris à RIBAUCOURT, *Évêque d'une
transition* (n. 19), pp. 321 et 334. Sur d'autres évêques empêchés, cf. OLIVIER, *Chroniques
congolaises* (n. 3), p. 270.

Photo n. 1: Mgr Piérard se repose en Ouganda après avoir échappé
à la rébellion muléliste (octobre 1964)

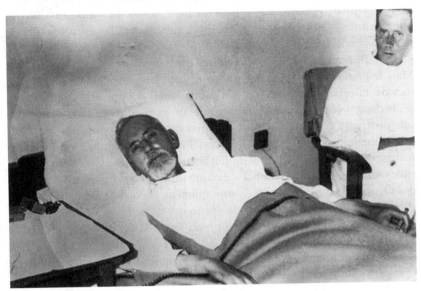

Source: www.fides.org

à demander aux évêques belges que les missionnaires en provenance des diocèses envahis par les rebelles et se trouvant en Belgique puissent parler et récolter des fonds dans les paroisses belges. Mgr Creemers écrit que, dans une telle tension, c'est presque une corvée de s'acquitter du lourd travail conciliaire[51].

Dans ce contexte, plusieurs cérémonies et réceptions se déroulant durant le Concile marqueront sensiblement les esprits des évêques missionnaires congolais et leur apporteront quelque réconfort. Ils sont ainsi reçus une première fois par Paul VI en audience privée le 6 novembre 1963. À cette occasion, le Saint-Père s'informe sur leur travail et sur la situation au Congo[52]. Puis, en groupe compact, ils assisteront au cours de la 3e session à la cérémonie de canonisation des martyrs de l'Ouganda (photo n. 2). Jan Van Cauwelaert écrit à ce propos: «La canonisation

51. Lettres de A. Creemers à A. Ramaekers, 26 septembre 1964, 2 octobre 1964, 4 octobre 1964, 9 octobre 1964 et 25 octobre 1964, dans Fonds Creemers.

52. Pour un compte rendu de cette audience, cf. A. Creemers à A. Ramaekers, 24 novembre 1963, dans Fonds Creemers. Et aussi J. Van Cauwelaert à ses missionnaires, 9 novembre 1963, p. 4, dans Fonds Van Cauwelaert.

Photo n. 2: Cérémonie de canonisation des martyrs de l'Ouganda (1964)

Source: www.fides.org

était vraiment un jour de triomphe pour l'Afrique». Et plus loin dans sa lettre il ajoute: «elle nous a tous remplis d'un grand espoir pour l'avenir de notre Afrique»[53]. Et le 26 février 1965, le pape Paul VI confère à St-Paul-hors-les-Murs les sacrements de baptême et de confirmation à douze néophytes congolais de la région de Stanleyville (photo n. 3). Au cours de la cérémonie, le pontife prononce une allocution dans laquelle il stigmatise solennellement devant le monde entier les crimes commis au Congo-Léo[54]. Enfin, au mois de novembre 1965, Paul VI reçoit les évêques de l'Afrique francophone, par pays. Il réconforte personnellement les évêques congolais touchés par la rébellion et évoque la force spirituelle des martyrs dont le sang apportera dans l'avenir de riches fruits pour le Congo[55].

53. Lettre de J. Van Cauwelaert à ses missionnaires, 20 octobre 1964, p. 3, dans Fonds Van Cauwelaert.
54. Texte intégral de l'allocution de Paul VI dans *Documents pontificaux de Paul VI*, 1965, III, Saint-Maurice, Éditions St-Augustin, 1969, 108-112.
55. Pour plus de détails sur l'audience en question, cf. A. Creemers à A. Ramaekers, 10 novembre 1965, dans Fonds Creemers; Mgr Van Cauwelaert n'en souffle mot dans sa correspondance.

Photo n. 3: Cérémonie de confirmation des catéchumènes congolais
à St-Paul-hors-les-Murs (27 février 1965)

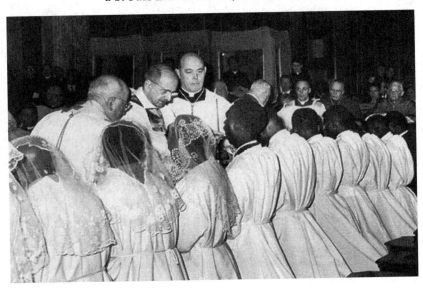

Source: www.fides.org

III. Impact sur le schéma des missions

La troisième partie de cette contribution se consacrera entièrement au schéma des missions. Un bref rappel général s'impose pour resituer le contexte. Durant trois années, le travail au sein de la Commission conciliaire des missions avait été entravé par l'influence de la Propagande. Le schéma des missions devrait se contenter de grandes généralités ou de questions juridiques à régler. Au schéma préparatoire de 1962, succèdent en 1963 deux autres textes, l'un de mars, l'autre de décembre, tous encore fortement marqués par des conceptions missiologiques ou juridiques traditionnelles. De toute façon, le plan Döpfner réduit le texte à 14 propositions qui seront soumises en novembre 1964 à la sagacité des Pères conciliaires. Malgré le soutien inattendu du pape qui intervient dans l'aula le 6 novembre 1964, le texte est rejeté par la majorité des Pères et on décide d'une nouvelle rédaction. Celle-ci est réalisée en janvier 1965 par une équipe de théologiens progressistes (Congar, Seumois, Ratzinger, Neuner) et ce nouveau texte, préfigurant le décret *Ad gentes*, sera soumis

aux Pères au cours de la quatrième session pour ultimes modifications[56].
Posons-nous à présent la question de l'apport spécifique des évêques missionnaires belges à la confection du schéma missionnaire.

Les *vota* des évêques missionnaires belges seront rapidement survolés.
Ils ne contiennent généralement rien de bien révolutionnaire sur la thématique missionnaire ou traitent de problèmes connexes ou juridiques[57].
René Toussaint propose, tout comme son confrère Alfons Verwimp et
le comité permanent des Ordinaires du Congo-Léo et du Rwanda-
Burundi, que l'on associe tous les évêques du monde collégialement à
l'œuvre d'évangélisation. Quant à Ferdinand Périer, il avance l'idée d'une
coordination et d'une coopération entre les différentes congrégations qui
travaillent dans les régions de mission et insiste sur la nécessité de faire
siéger dans les S. Congrégations des consulteurs qui connaissent bien les
modes de vie des peuples sur place. Dans une même unité de pensée,
Carlo Van Melckebeke et Louis Morel en appellent à une internationalisation du personnel de la Curie romaine.

Jan Van Cauwelaert plaide, lui, pour la restauration d'un diaconat sans
célibat. Cette question du diaconat se retrouve d'ailleurs dans pas mal
d'autres *vota*, dont ceux du Comité permanent, quoiqu'avec bien des
nuances. Ainsi pour Louis Van Steene, le diaconat ne peut être admis si
ce n'est avec l'intention formelle d'accéder à l'ordre du presbytérat. La
principale motivation avancée par les pères pour ce rétablissement est de
pouvoir pallier le manque de prêtres ou leur surcharge de travail.

Plus de la moitié des Pères, dont Jan Van Cauwelaert à l'avant-scène,
expriment leur assentiment à une utilisation de la langue vivante pour la
messe, les sacrements et les sacramentaux. A contrario, Mgr Oste prône
la conservation du latin dans la liturgie. Georges Kettel condamne lui les
innovations téméraires en matière de liturgie et demande qu'on réaffirme
que seul le Saint-Siège réglemente la liturgie et approuve les livres

---

56. Pour suivre de façon plus complète les péripéties de la rédaction du schéma, cf.
E. LOUCHEZ, *Les missions au concile Vatican II: Le grand tournant?*, dans CHEZA – COS-
TERMANS – PIROTTE (éds.), *Nouvelles voies de la mission* (n. 4), spéc. pp. 87-101.

57. Les *vota* des évêques missionnaires sont répartis dans différents tomes des *Acta et
Documenta*. Ceux des évêques missionnaires 'retraités', dans *AD* I/2.1, pp. 131-156. Pour
une analyse de leurs *vota*, cf. l'article de C. SOETENS, *Les 'vota' des évêques belges en vue
du concile*, dans M. LAMBERIGTS – C. SOETENS (éds.), *À la veille du concile Vatican II:
Vota et réactions en Europe et dans le catholicisme oriental* (Instrumenta Theologica, 9),
Leuven, Bibliotheek van de Faculteit der Godgeleerdheid, 1992, pp. 38-52. Les vœux des
évêques missionnaires congolais et du Rwanda-Burundi, dans *AD* I/2.5, pp. 138-205. Ceux
des évêques d'Asie, dans *AD* I/2.4, pp. 116-531. Enfin on trouvera ceux des évêques
d'Amérique centrale, dans *AD* I/2.6, pp. 546-571.

liturgiques. Et Mgr Dereere met l'accent sur la préservation de l'unité du
rite latin même dans les pays de mission et sur la limitation de l'usage
de la langue vernaculaire à certaines parties de la messe. X. Geeraerts de
son côté réclame la participation active des fidèles à l'office et une
réforme du jeûne eucharistique. Cette modification des règles du jeûne et
de l'abstinence pour les conformer aux coutumes africaines est de fait
souhaitée par plus d'un. En définitive, c'est une révision du Code de droit
canonique pour l'adapter aux pays de mission qui est portée par plusieurs
évêques (dont Mgr Cleire) et le comité permanent. Bernard Mels, se faisant le porte-parole des évêques de l'archidiocèse de Luluabourg, serait
heureux de voir se généraliser les facultés accordées dans l'emploi des
langues vivantes pour les fonctions liturgiques et se développer l'adaptation aux coutumes locales. Il attire aussi l'attention sur la situation psychologique pénible dans laquelle travaillent actuellement la plupart des
missionnaires, surtout en Afrique. Il faudrait rapidement leur procurer
des encouragements. André Creemers se dit favorable à une adaptation
du bréviaire aux mentalités africaines et à une simplification des empê-
chements de mariage.

En outre, quelques évêques suggèrent que le vêtement des prêtres, des
religieux et des religieuses soit adapté au climat des régions tropicales.
Ainsi Jean Collignon requiert-il la suppression d'ornements ecclésiastiques inconfortables dans les régions trop chaudes.

Pour sa part, Mgr Guffens se prononce pour l'adaptation du message
chrétien à la diversité des cultures, au moins dans la liturgie et la catéchèse.

Alphonse Matthysen cherche la solution aux problèmes de l'Afrique
noire dans trois directions: une christianisation de la culture noire, une
participation plus grande des laïcs, une christianisation de l'économie
moderne, spécialement des loisirs.

Plusieurs évêques désirent qu'on favorise les contacts plus fréquents
avec les autres confessions chrétiennes dans un esprit de compréhension
mutuelle.

Enfin, une série d'évêques n'envoient rien du tout, soit à cause de
leur état de santé ou de leur situation de retraité soit parce qu'ils ne se
sentent pas compétents pour envoyer des souhaits et s'en remettent au
Saint-Siège[58].

---

58. Parmi ceux-ci, R. Lagae (ex vic. ap. de Niangara) âgé de presque 80·ans et C. Stap-
pers (ex vic. ap. de Luala et Katanga) qui meurt en 1964 à l'âge de 79 ans. Mais aussi
Antoon Demets, pourtant bien plus jeune (coadj. Roseau), Marcel Buyse (Lahore),
G. Raeymaeckers (Buta) dont l'état de santé est critique, Jean Fryns (vic. ap. de Kindu),
par modestie. Plusieurs évêques du Congo et du Rwanda-Burundi enfin regroupent leurs

Outre les vœux pré-conciliaires, quelques évêques missionnaires ont adressé leurs suggestions directement au cardinal Suenens. Mgr Van Melckebeke en novembre 1960 pour lui donner des avis sur les problèmes dans les pays de mission. Mgr Verwimp, en avril 1961, sur la formation apostolique dans les séminaires, l'Action catholique et l'apostolat de la religieuse[59].

Le programme de la sixième assemblée plénière de l'épiscopat du Congo se tenant à Léopoldville du 20 novembre au 2 décembre 1961 pourrait utilement compléter ce tableau. Pour une analyse précise de cette assemblée, on renverra à l'article de Claude Soetens sur l'apport du Congo-Léopoldville (Zaïre), du Rwanda et du Burundi au Concile Vatican II[60].

Avant d'envisager le Concile proprement dit, il faut revenir sur la circulation, un peu avant le début de la 1ère session, d'un document d'une vingtaine de pages intitulé *Memorandum pour les réunions africaines antéconciliaires*. Ses auteurs étaient probablement les théologiens du Congo-Léo soutenus par quelques-uns de leurs évêques. On y prônait une décentralisation de l'Église subsaharienne au profit des conférences épiscopales et une internationalisation de la Curie. Une réforme radicale de la Propagande était envisagée: suppression de cette dernière en tant qu'organe du gouvernement pontifical et sa transformation en office d'assistance financière pour administrer les Œuvres Pontificales Missionnaires. Le rapport est accompagné d'un volet statistique et de cartes en couleurs. La Propagande s'en était inquiétée au point d'avoir demandé au Père A. Reuter d'en faire une synthèse et d'avoir fait pression sur certains évêques autochtones pour parvenir à une identification formelle des auteurs du texte[61].

Au cours de la 1ère période, il ne se passe pas grand chose au plan missionnaire, si ce n'est cette organisation rapide de la Panafricaine.

---

vœux ou s'associent à ceux émis par le comité permanent des ordinaires du Congo et du Rwanda-Burundi.

59. C. Van Melckebeke à L.-J. Suenens, 20 novembre 1960, dans Fonds Suenens, 457. Et A. Verwimp à L.-J. Suenens, 12 avril 1961, 1 p., dans Fonds Suenens, 458.

60. SOETENS, *L'apport du Congo-Léopoldville* (n. 3), pp. 195-196.

61. Sur ce *Memorandum*, cf. E. LOUCHEZ, *L'innovation dans le champ missionnaire conciliaire*, dans G. ROUTHIER – F. LAUGRAND (éds.), *L'espace missionnaire: Lieu d'innovations et de rencontres interculturelles. Actes du colloque de l'Association francophone œcuménique de missiologie, du Centre de recherches et d'échanges sur la diffusion et l'inculturation du christianisme et du Centre Vincent Lebbe, Québec, Canada, 23-27 août 2001* (Mémoire d'Églises), Paris, Karthala; Québec, Presses de l'Université Laval, 2002, p. 287. Le document, notamment dans Fonds Catry. Le résumé et la réponse argumentée, dans Fonds Reuter, Maison Généralice des OMI, Rome, 1962, 11 p.

Le 31 octobre, Mgr Van Cauwelaert délivre une intervention sur la concélébration, une pratique qui serait grandement appréciée dans les cultures africaines. Et le 5 décembre, Mgr Mels prononce la sienne, déjà évoquée précédemment, sur la mission de l'Église[62].

Lors de la première intersession, Mgr Oscar Sevrin entame sa participation aux réunions de la Commission conciliaire des missions. Quoique actif et exigeant, il n'y tiendra pourtant pas un rôle de premier plan. Cela était dû à son humilité et à sa volonté de ne froisser personne, selon les mots que son conseiller théologique, le Père Masson, nous a confiés lors d'un entretien[63]. Bien conseillé par Masson, il fait partie des Pères (comme Riobé, le Père Deschâtelets, Mgr Sartre) qui ont voté non placet sur le schéma concocté en mars 1963 par la Commission. Il remet un texte défendant ses conceptions à la Commission et au cardinal Agagianian mais on n'en a pas fait grand cas. Il s'en explique d'ailleurs épistolairement le 25 avril 1963 auprès du cardinal Suenens. «La partie pastorale, écrit-il, devrait former la majeure partie du chapitre sur le régime des missions et être réécrite». Il donne aussi son opinion sur le memorandum: «la Propagande ne doit pas être supprimée, mais réformée dans le sens d'une meilleure connaissance des conditions concrètes des missions et d'une représentation effective des grandes régions missionnaires à Rome»[64].

Dès cette première pause, la mission évangélisatrice de l'Église et le sort du schéma des missions figurent clairement au premier plan des préoccupations de l'Église du Congo. Trois documents en attestent.

D'abord, c'est Bernard Mels et Félix Scalais qui cosignent un texte de 5 pages sobrement titré 'Problème missionnaire de base', qu'ils répandent auprès de personnalités influentes[65]. Ils rappellent l'obligation missionnaire d'annoncer l'Évangile à tous les hommes, surtout dans le chef du corps épiscopal. Ils défendent la nécessité absolue des instituts missionnaires pour, je cite, «faire œuvre profonde et durable». Les deux scheutistes en appellent encore aux organisations catholiques pour qu'elles leur envoient des éléments laïcs de choix. Ils recommandent en plus la suppression du ius commissionis là où le clergé local est

62. Le texte de l'intervention de J. Van Cauwelaert sur le De Sacra liturgia, dans AS I/1, pp. 94-95. Sur les félicitations reçues par J. Van Cauwelaert après son locutus de la part des évêques et des observateurs, cf. R. Van Cauwelaert à la famille, 1 novembre 1962, dans Fonds Van Cauwelaert. L'intervention de B. Mels, dans AS I/4, pp. 312-315.
63. Interview accordée le 26 avril 1996, à Bruxelles.
64. Lettre d'O. Sevrin à L.-J. Suenens, 25 avril 1963, 2 p. Copie de la lettre d'O. Sevrin à G.-P. Agagianian, 6 avril 1963, 3 p. Et texte alternatif 'De vita Ecclesiae in missionibus', s.d., 11 p. Le tout se trouve dans Fonds Suenens, 1221-1223.
65. Notamment le card. Suenens. Le texte, dans Fonds Suenens, 1218.

assez nombreux. Et tout en admettant le caractère utile de la Congrégation de la Propagande, ils réclament un élargissement de son cadre et la transformation de son rôle en centre de planification et de coordination, plus de relations humaines avec les évêques et des contacts réguliers avec les représentants des conférences épiscopales des régions missionnaires.

Durant cette phase du Concile, les évêques du Congo s'interrogent sur la nécessité d'un schéma spécifique sur les missions. Le schéma rédigé étant inacceptable car il se base sur une notion géographique de la mission dépassée et souffre de l'absence d'une théologie valable de la mission, il vaudrait mieux par conséquent un bon texte figurant dans le chap. I du futur schéma sur l'Église. Il faut parler de la Mission et non des missions, concept lié à une situation historique dépassée. Les évêques insistent beaucoup pour qu'on élimine toute trace de mise à part que le terme 'Jeunes Églises' contient encore afin de marquer la solidarité entre vieilles chrétientés et jeunes et pauvres Églises. L'établissement de la hiérarchie entraîne que les Églises anciennement de mission doivent désormais être considérées à l'instar des autres Églises, ce qui met en cause le rôle de la Propagande. De la sorte, la Sacrée Congrégation de la Place d'Espagne serait réduite à un service chargé de ventiler rationnellement et équitablement l'aide financière et les ressources en clergé[66].

On retrouve la même tonalité dans la note *'Concile et problèmes missionnaires. Propositions de l'épiscopat du Congo (Léo)'*[67]. La conférence épiscopale congolaise suggère toujours la rédaction d'un chapitre dédié à la fonction missionnaire de l'Église dans le schéma sur l'Église. Nonobstant, d'autres problèmes pourraient faire l'objet d'un schéma spécial. Et d'énumérer: la supranationalité de l'Église, l'Église n'est pas un empire, l'Église est supra-raciale, l'Église et les gouvernements, l'Église respecte les autres religions.

Du côté asiatique, Mgr Carlo Van Melckebeke s'est quant à lui rallié faute de mieux à un schéma alternatif rédigé par le Père oblat André Seumois, l'un des missiologues les plus réputés à cette époque[68].

---

66. Ce document proposé au Comité permanent des Ordinaires du Congo-Léopoldville, *'Préparation à la deuxième session du Concile: Synthèse des conclusions des conférences provinciales'*, s.d., 6 p., se trouve dans le Fonds Keuppens.

67. Dans Fonds Olivier, 39.

68. Ce ralliement du scheutiste belge au texte concocté par André Seumois ressort clairement dans deux lettres adressées à l'oblat belge le 9 mai 1963 et le 1er août de la même année. Les lettres proviennent des Papiers personnels d'A. Seumois, Maison généralice des OMI. Cf. LOUCHEZ, *L'innovation dans le champ missionnaire conciliaire* (n. 61), p. 281.

Lors de la seconde période conciliaire, en novembre 1963, une critique virulente du schéma officiel est rédigée par les théologiens d'Afrique centrale, au nom de la Panafricaine. Ce texte, qui donne la part belle au rôle propre des jeunes Églises devant se dégager de la tutelle de la Propagande, sera rejeté en commission plénière des missions. Et Mgr Scalais prononce une intervention, inspirée par un papier du Père Xavier Seumois, père blanc et frère de l'oblat, se proposant notamment de mettre en valeur le caractère missionnaire de l'Église[69].

Durant la 2e intersession, Mgr Joseph Guffens avait adressé au Secrétariat du Concile des remarques écrites développées sur le schéma des missions de déc. 1963 (elles couvrent en effet cinq pages des *Acta Synodalia*). Il les avait aussi soumises en mai 1964 au jugement du Cardinal Suenens[70]. D'entrée, il réclame un allégement du texte et une meilleure utilisation des références scripturaires. Il stigmatise le malheureux complexe de supériorité qui engendre des attitudes blessantes pour les populations locales. «Il faut au contraire», écrit-il, «reconnaître les valeurs culturelles de ces peuples et ne pas les traiter comme des enfants ou entamer la litanie de leurs défauts». Il plaide aussi pour qu'on adjoigne une formulation précise de l'objet spécifique de la mission et le jésuite opte pour la théorie de l'implantation de l'Église (*plantatio ecclesiae*). Quant à la formation de cadres laïcs stables, elle doit s'imposer à la pratique du baptême des masses. D'ailleurs, poursuit-il quelques paragraphes plus avant, ce texte ne consacre que bien peu de lignes à l'école. Or, je cite: «Celui-là détient l'avenir, qui forme la jeunesse». Il recommande de veiller à la formation spirituelle, civique, morale et apostolique de tous les étudiants chrétiens, les futures élites de leur pays. Ils pourraient à terme soulager les prêtres des nombreuses tâches dont ils sont surchargés. Enfin, il clôture son texte par un appel à l'établissement de Centres d'instruction (collèges, petits séminaires, écoles normales ou techniques) desservant une vaste région qui déborderait les diocèses. Ce système permettrait des économies d'une part et de l'autre entraînerait un contact prolongé entre étudiants issus d'ethnies et de couches sociales diverses. Il suggère encore l'échange de professeurs et d'étudiants en tant que palliatif aux excès issus de l'esprit clanique.

Nous ajouterons que le 12 août 1964, il se tourne à nouveau vers le cardinal Suenens pour lui soumettre quelques modifications de détail, les

---

69. Le texte de la critique, dans Fonds Olivier, 29. L'intervention de Félix Scalais, prononcée le 3 octobre 1963, dans *AS* II/2, pp. 53-57.
70. Lettre de J. Guffens à L.-J. Suenens, 19 mai 1964, 1 p. et 14 p. de remarques en annexe, dans Fonds Suenens, 1936-1937.

assortissant cette fois de quelques commentaires complémentaires sur l'impréparation manifeste de l'indépendance du Congo[71].

Dans un texte encore plus dense (8 pages des *AS*), son confrère Bernard Mels revient sur la question du problème des rapports entre évêques et religieux dans les régions missionnaires ou les nouvelles Églises[72]. La part des religieux, écrit-il, reste prépondérante dans les œuvres diocésaines. Il faut sortir sur ce point de la dépendance envers la Congrégation de la Propagande. Et il formule les points positifs et négatifs d'une éventuelle suppression de la dépendance à la SCPF. De toute manière, selon lui, faire traiter les problèmes qui se posent dans ces régions par une congrégation romaine risque d'aboutir à des solutions inadéquates. Toutefois, Mgr Mels concède que l'organisation de la vie religieuse en ces régions devrait demeurer sous la supervision de la Propagande. Pour épargner les critiques à cette dernière, il faudrait une internationalisation suffisante de son personnel et un élargissement de son objectif: devenir un centre d'étude et de coordination de tous les efforts missionnaires. Seulement ainsi on parviendrait à atteindre l'aspect de vrai service à rendre aux nouvelles Églises en les soustrayant à l'autorité purement juridique de la SCPF. Ces facultés accordées aujourd'hui par la congrégation romaine seraient transférées aux conférences épiscopales ou aux évêques. Quant aux rapports entre instituts missionnaires et évêques, ils sont toujours régis par le *Ius Commissionis*. Mais quand un évêque séculier est nommé, ce *Ius Commissionis* tombe, le nouveau venu devenant complètement responsable de l'organisation de l'Église. Tout cela serait simple si les nouvelles Églises n'étaient encore largement dépendantes des aides venant de l'étranger. Il faudrait réétudier cette question afin de satisfaire au mieux les desiderata des deux parties. Et B. Mels termine sur cette thématique en disséquant quelques matières concrètes méritant une attention spéciale, spécialement les questions financières.

Quant à Xavier Geeraerts, s'il commence par préciser que ce schéma est recevable car il permet une discussion conciliaire, il ajoute immédiatement qu'il n'expose pas suffisamment clairement les problèmes actuels de la mission et ne propose pas des solutions nouvelles[73]. En plus, il n'est pas ce feu ardent incitant à l'action missionnaire financière. Il revient, comme d'autres, sur l'urgence de l'évangélisation du monde, les classiques arguments statistiques à l'appui. Une action immédiate s'impose dont il balaie quelques pistes:

---

71. Ces trois pages de commentaires sur le schéma *De activitate missionali ecclesiae* et de remarques sur la décolonisation du Congo belge, dans Fonds Suenens, 1938.

72. *AS* III/6, pp. 781-788.

73. *AS* III/6, pp. 748-750.

a. Création près de la Propagande d'un secrétariat des études pour l'évangélisation chargé d'animer et de diriger la stratégie missionnaire.
b. Rédaction d'un compendium des règles et principes destinés à favoriser les vocations missionnaires.
c. Interrogation sur ce qui est fait pour préparer l'évangélisation et mettre tout ceci en relation avec les questions actuelles de la liberté de conscience, l'œcuménisme, le respect pour les valeurs humaines et religieuses.

Selon lui, le Concile devrait aussi profiter de l'occasion pour édicter de nouvelles normes que les jeunes Églises pourraient suivre après l'instauration de la hiérarchie et qui mèneront graduellement à l'application du simple droit commun. Il recommande en ce sens le regroupement des conférences épiscopales des territoires de mission selon les aires des grandes cultures et l'animation par le Saint-Siège des activités des conférences épiscopales aux fins de promouvoir la légitime diversité dans l'unité catholique. Il y adjoint la formulation de nouveaux principes législatifs pour baliser les relations entre les ordinaires et les supérieurs religieux.

Le schéma devrait aussi développer davantage la question de la formation de tous ceux qui œuvrent dans les missions. Mgr Geeraerts clôt ses *animadversiones* par quelques propositions en matière de coopération missionnaire.

Mais l'intervention écrite la plus élaborée provient sans contestation possible de Mgr Richard Cleire puisque son texte occupe en totalité 28 pages et demie des *Acta*[74]. Selon le père blanc, le schéma «ne fait aucune allusion à la conjoncture actuelle des missions qui hypothèque tout leur avenir». L'évangélisation du monde n'a jamais paru aussi urgente et elle doit prendre en compte l'œcuménisme et un respect accru pour les valeurs positives des grandes religions non-chrétiennes. Les jeunes Églises sont une réalité nouvelle, elles doivent être soutenues. De même que le texte ne peut ignorer les appels à l'aide des pays en voie de développement. Il soumet alors chaque article du texte au crible d'une critique détaillée. Pour le premier chapitre, il remarque que les aspects anthropologiques de la mission, bien mis en relief, offrent le danger d'un certain anthropomorphisme. Il faut obvier selon lui en montrant que la

---

74. *AS* III/6, pp. 703-731. Mgr Cleire a également co-signé (il est le seul évêque belge dans ce cas) le *Commentarius in Schema propositionum de activitate missionali ecclesiae* proposé par le groupe dit des évêques missionnaires hollandais le 3 août 1964. Sur ce groupe, cf. LOUCHEZ, *Les missions au concile Vatican II* (n. 56), pp. 108-109.

mission de Dieu et donc de l'Église est tout orientée *à la gloire de Dieu.*
Il voudrait aussi que soit intégré dans ce chapitre un paragraphe montrant comment, dans les services sociaux, l'Église accomplit sa Mission véritable et authentique. Richard Cleire réclame l'insertion du texte de Mt 28,16-20, fondamental à ses yeux pour la théologie de la mission.
Dans le chapitre II, il souhaite qu'on revienne sur l'urgence d'un effort d'évangélisation, en en développant les motifs: pas d'accueil du message chrétien dans les grands ensembles constitués par les grandes religions non-chrétiennes, évolution démographique défavorable aux chrétiens, mutations économiques et sociales des nouvelles nations réalisées sans la présence suffisante du christianisme. Cette évangélisation doit se réaliser dans deux directions: être éclairée par le secours des sciences de l'homme: anthropologie, ethnologie, psychologie, étude des religions; être concertée pour répondre à un plan d'ensemble relatif à chaque grande aire religio-culturelle. Il faut une stratégie missionnaire cohérente. Car les exigences de l'évangélisation ne peuvent trouver de solution vraiment valable ni à l'échelon diocésain ni à celui des conférences épiscopales.
D'où, selon R. Cleire, la nécessité d'un Secrétariat d'études auprès de la SCPF chargé de l'action missionnaire, en vue de l'évangélisation proprement dite. Y travaillera un personnel spécialisé, recruté dans le monde entier parmi les missionnaires spécialisés et possédant en plus d'une science théorique une connaissance directe des situations de terrain et des mentalités. Indispensables aussi une fonction directrice de la SCPF en collaboration avec les conférences épiscopales intéressées et les instituts missionnaires, de même qu'une spécialisation plus développée des congrégations missionnaires suivant les milieux humains. Et de réclamer qu'on leur confère une 'mission canonique' dans le cadre d'une pastorale d'ensemble. Il faudrait aussi veiller à éveiller et entretenir les vocations spécifiquement missionnaires. Toujours pour ce chapitre second, il détaille plusieurs problèmes connexes: évangélisation et liberté de conscience (attitude de tolérance chrétienne), évangélisation et respect pour les valeurs religieuses et humaines des grandes religions non-chrétiennes, évangélisation et œcuménisme, thématique pour laquelle il écrit:

> Au niveau de l'évangélisation, le problème œcuménique est parfois crucial. Dans le passé, il y a eu trop souvent de la concurrence, avec tous les égarements que, suite à la faiblesse humaine, elle peut comporter dans des paroles de dénigrement et des actes déloyaux. [...] La charité devrait imprégner les jugements, et les attitudes des catéchumènes et des néophytes des catholiques vis-à-vis des Frères Séparés et des Églises qui ne sont pas en pleine communion avec Rome, tout en prémunissant contre le relativisme religieux, danger trop réel chez les âmes simples et qui est contraire à tout sain œcuménisme. [...] Au niveau des relations humaines et des services

sociaux, les prêtres catholiques s'efforceront de témoigner de la bienveillance et de la cordialité à leurs Frères en Jésus-Christ qui, bien que séparés, sont Frères. […] Il faudrait aussi s'appliquer à collaborer dans tous les
domaines où, nonobstant les divergences dogmatiques, la collaboration est
possible: notamment dans les Services Sociaux, dans les efforts pour donner une inspiration chrétienne dans le temporel, pour le rehaussement du
niveau humain et spirituel en-dehors du christianisme[75].

Dans ce chapitre II encore, Mgr Cleire aborde une question chère aux
évêques missionnaires, celle des Jeunes Églises. Cette notion n'est, à son
avis, pas assez nette dans le texte soumis. Elle doit être en rapport avec
le Mystère de l'Église et l'institution de la hiérarchie (et non pas tellement avec le fait que l'évêque est autochtone, élément qui, quoique très
important, n'est que secondaire). En somme, pour avoir une Église locale,
il faut 'une communauté de Foi et d'Amour, rassemblée par l'Eucharistie, capable d'assurer sa permanence dans le temps (familles chrétiennes)
et sa croissance (apostolat des laïcs)'. Le père blanc en profite aussi pour
affirmer que le statut de Mission attribué à une Église ne peut venir de
son état de pauvreté en ressources matérielles et en personnel. Selon lui,
dès que la Mission de l'Église s'est réalisée en un endroit, grâce à la
congregatio fidelium, dirigée par un Successeur des Apôtres, l'Église y
est totalement et pleinement présente. L'état de croissance qui marque la
Jeune Église connaît deux conditions: l'assimilation authentique de la
Tradition, âme de l'Église, d'une part et l'expression de cette Tradition
dans des 'traditions' locales faisant corps avec le génie, les dominantes
culturelles et ses modes d'expression d'autre part. Au plan des contin-
gences, cette croissance est limitée par le fait que ces Jeunes Églises ne
disposent pas de la maturité que, seule, confère l'assimilation profonde
de la Tradition authentique, assurée par des institutions stables: centres
de pensée (universités, ordres religieux) et de vie chrétienne ayant un
enracinement solide; par le fait encore qu'elle se heurte au syncrétisme
religieux, à l'indifférentisme, au matérialisme, au marxisme, à la libre
pensée. Pour progresser, ces Églises en croissance doivent recevoir de
l'extérieur une aide en personnel et surtout en ressources. Il faudrait
mettre un terme à la situation actuelle où 'les Évêques des Jeunes Églises
doivent parcourir le monde en mendiants'! Dans ce chapitre II, il poursuit

75. Sur la question de l'œcuménisme dans l'élaboration du décret sur l'activité missionnaire de l'Église, voir E. LOUCHEZ, *L'œcuménisme dans l'élaboration du décret sur
l'activité missionnaire de l'Église*, dans M. CHEZA – M. COSTERMANS – J. PIROTTE (éds.),
*Œcuménisme et pratiques missionnaires. Actes du 21ᵉ colloque du Centre de recherches
et d'échanges sur la diffusion et l'inculturation du christianisme organisé avec la collaboration du Centre Vincent Lebbe (Louvain-la-Neuve, 27-31 août 2000)*, Paris, Karthala,
2002, pp. 63-87.

par des explications sur la structuration des Conférences épiscopales selon les grands ensembles culturels et sur leur contrôle par le Saint-Siège. Il y adjoint la nécessité pour les instituts missionnaires d'une certaine reconversion de leurs activités missionnaires et un développement substantiel sur l'importance des œuvres caritatives, éducatives et sociales et leurs rapports avec les gouvernements locaux. Au plan de l'adaptation, il fait remarquer que la partie sur les applications au culte semble ne considérer que les éléments extérieurs. «Par ces éléments extérieurs, l'Église va paraître chinoise, japonaise, africaine, sans l'être nécessairement. Ce qui importe, c'est l'esprit: s'adapter à la mentalité, aux valeurs d'Église, au génie».

À propos du chapitre III, consacré à la formation missionnaire, Mgr Cleire signale que presque tout ce qu'il en dit se trouve déjà dans les encycliques missionnaires. Or certains problèmes liés à la conjoncture actuelle devraient être envisagés:

a. revalorisation de la vocation missionnaire, mise à mal par la prise de conscience que tout chrétien est missionnaire et par la possibilité pour les prêtres diocésains d'aller travailler dans les Missions; les dernières années accusent une baisse statistique plus qu'inquiétante du nombre d'envois des hérauts de l'Évangile;

b. attention portée à la vocation des Frères missionnaires, vocation spécifique que ne sauraient remplacer les auxiliaires laïcs. Et de même sur le rôle irremplaçable des religieuses spécifiquement missionnaires;

c. examen des nouvelles relations entre les instituts missionnaires et la hiérarchie locale. Un *Debitum adiuvandi* devrait prendre la place du *Ius Commissionis*. En plus de l'aide dans le ministère direct et l'évangélisation, les congrégations missionnaires devraient assumer avant tout la formation des prêtres, les instituts de formation pastorale et les services permanents des Conférences épiscopales;

d. nécessité d'une campagne continue en faveur des vocations presbytérales locales;

e. révision de la formation du clergé autochtone dans les séminaires afin d'éviter d'imposer aux séminaristes des catégories de pensée, des formes culturelles et esthétiques, des habitudes qui ne sont pas de soi liées au Mystère chrétien et les rendent comme étrangers à leur propre peuple;

f. répartition adéquate des effectifs des religieux et religieuses et adaptation des instituts autochtones à leur environnement naturel;

g. valoriser la fonction de catéchiste en intensifiant leur formation humaine et celle plus proprement pastorale.

Reste le chap. IV sur la collaboration des fidèles. Sur ce sujet, R. Cleire réclame un effort particulier de prières, d'information des fidèles sur les problèmes d'évangélisation. Il faudrait instituer selon lui une Octave de prières, avec chaque jour une intention spéciale développée par la prédication. Pour la coopération dans le travail social, il importe que l'on fonde rapidement des Instituts Supérieurs pour la formation de techniciens de plans de développement, dans des perspectives chrétiennes. À la préoccupation des chrétiens de venir en aide aux pays en voie de développement, doit venir s'adjoindre la dimension spirituelle exigée par la Mission spirituelle du chrétien dans le monde, une dimension très importante selon l'auteur. En conclusion, il regrette que ce chapitre soit trop lénitif face à l'urgence de la situation. Il y aurait avantage «à mettre bien en relief la responsabilité conjointe du Collège épiscopal, sa Mission évangélisatrice universelle, son devoir de créer la communion des Églises en vue d'assurer la croissance des Jeunes Églises».

À ces diverses contributions personnelles, il faut ajouter deux textes collectifs. Le premier, émis en janvier 1964, provient encore des théologiens de la conférence épiscopale congolaise et du Rwanda-Burundi et s'intitule 'Schéma de missionibus. Réflexions et suggestions'[76]. On y lit notamment: «Ce schéma ne met pas en relief les vrais problèmes qui apparaissent noyés dans un ensemble plutôt banal si on le compare aux grandes encycliques missionnaires». La question des jeunes Églises devrait être approfondie afin d'aboutir à des conclusions vraiment pastorales et à des directives effectives. Il faudrait aussi envisager les réponses à apporter aux problèmes des pays en voie de développement. La partie sur la formation missionnaire devrait traiter des problèmes spécifiques que posent les agents de la mission: missionnaires, clergé local, congrégations religieuses, auxiliaires laïcs, relancer l'appel *Fidei donum* et revaloriser la fonction de catéchiste. Quant au chapitre sur la coopération, il devrait mettre en lumière le rôle du Saint-Siège, découler davantage de la collégialité épiscopale et en appeler à l'urgence que réclament les situations d'aujourd'hui.

Le second texte sort en mars 1964 et détaille l'opinion de la conférence des ordinaires du Rwanda et du Burundi[77]. Selon eux, ce schéma ne présente pas un visage assez missionnaire, il manque d'actualité et ne mentionne pas toute une série d'éléments importants: l'incidence de la décolonisation sur l'œuvre missionnaire, le manque de protection des

---

76. Le père blanc Xavier Seumois se fait clairement le héraut de ce texte, qui se retrouve notamment dans le Fonds Léger, série 3, 3.10,1863a.

77. *Remarques et suggestions de la Conférence des Ordinaires du Rwanda et du Burundi concernant le schéma 'De missionibus'*, 20 mars 1964, dans Fonds Eldarov, Istituto per le scienze religiose, Bologna.

pays décolonisés contre les influences néfastes venues de l'extérieur, la nécessité d'une coordination plus vaste et d'une collaboration plus ouverte dans le travail apostolique, la désaffection des pays occidentaux vis-à-vis des pays décolonisés, les difficultés économiques des pays décolonisés, l'avance inquiétante de l'Islam et du protestantisme en Afrique, la tendance laïcisante des jeunes États, la tendance à la mainmise des États sur toutes les manifestations de la vie publique, les dérives d'un nationalisme prononcé, etc. Suit une appréciation des différentes parties du schéma et des réponses proposées pour remédier aux lacunes. Ils réclament à titre d'illustration que le Concile décide la création d'une œuvre pontificale en faveur des catéchistes en activité ou en formation. Il faudrait aussi que soient élaborés plus largement le statut et le rôle des catéchistes et qu'on publie une encyclique les concernant.

Au cours de la 3e période, le schéma de 14 propositions subit un feu nourri dans l'aula conciliaire. Mgr Geeraerts, à l'initiative d'Y. Congar et de X. Seumois, prend la parole pour une intervention qui défend le sens anthropologique de la mission au détriment du sens géographique des missions lointaines. Ce schéma, dit-il, doit être basé sur une véritable théologie trinitaire de la mission et associer la collégialité au caractère missionnaire de l'Église. Il faut absolument, conclut-il, que les évêques missionnaires rentrent à la maison avec un document conciliaire apte à donner une nouvelle impulsion aux missions[78].

Quant à Mgr Guffens, il adresse de nouveau des remarques écrites[79]. Mais ce second texte paraît plutôt anodin, puisqu'il se contente de reprendre des remarques qu'il avait déjà émises précédemment. Il réitère l'exigence d'indigénisation des cadres locaux par le biais d'une bonne sélection des enfants doués dans les écoles et met aussi en valeur l'importance du rôle joué par tous ces laïcs imprégnés d'esprit chrétien.

Par contre, d'autres évêques missionnaires belges ont réagi plus substantiellement sur le schéma abrégé.

Carlo Van Melckebeke appelle de ses vœux un nouveau visage de la Congrégation de la Propagande[80]. Il serait hautement souhaitable que cette congrégation tisse toujours davantage des liens étroits avec les diverses missions, et connaisse personnellement chacun des territoires de mission. Il suggère que la SCPF envoie à des moments déterminés des 'missi dominici' modernes, des visiteurs qui conforteront les agents de l'évangélisation, repéreront les nécessités de chaque mission et connaîtront l'usage qui

---

78. *AS* III/6, pp. 431-433.
79. *AS* III/6, pp. 543-544.
80. *AS* III/6, pp. 635-641.

est fait des subsides. Dans un second point, il recommande qu'un nouvel et puissant élan pour l'apostolat dans les terres de mission soit mis en branle auprès de la jeunesse des nations catholiques. Et de pointer une œuvre très urgente qu'il connaît parfaitement, en l'occurrence l'apostolat auprès des étudiants d'Asie et d'Afrique, en Europe, en Amérique du Nord et en Australie. Ceux-ci rentrent souvent chez eux imprégnés de doctrine marxiste et de discipline communautaire qui les transforment en adversaires acharnés des œuvres sociales chrétiennes. Et de plaider pour l'installation d'un Service mondial de coordination chargé de cette tâche, service dont il brosse les axes programmatiques[81]. En troisième lieu, il désire que soit insérée dans le schéma une déclaration en faveur du caractère primordial de l'évangélisation des non-chrétiens (thèse défendue par le scheutiste belge François Legrand, directeur de la revue *Le Christ au monde*). Cette évangélisation est le devoir principal de l'Église et exige des moyens proportionnés. Il la justifie notamment en recourant à de nombreuses citations empruntées aux papes du 20e siècle.

De son côté, Mgr Sevrin envoie surtout des correctifs linguistiques[82]. Le texte, signale-t-il, parle des autres groupes religieux, expression peu claire, alors qu'il suffirait d'évoquer les autres religions. Et, on y perçoit sans doute aucun la griffe de son conseiller théologique Joseph Masson, il suggère de remplacer le vocable 'adaptation' par celui d''acculturation'. Mais cette proposition ne sera pas retenue lors de la rédaction finale du décret *Ad gentes*.

Lors de la 4e session, les évêques missionnaires belges interviendront à trois reprises dans l'*aula*, à chaque fois sur le schéma des missions. Jan Van Cauwelaert se prononce pour un fondement théologique plus solide de l'activité missionnaire basé sur la doctrine du corps mystique et sur la nécessaire collaboration, en terre missionnaire, entre tous les chrétiens dans un esprit œcuménique. On éviterait ainsi ses odieuses rivalités qui scandalisent les non-croyants[83]. Par parenthèse, signalons que cette intervention – et celles d'autres évêques allant dans le même sens – aura été entendue puisque le n°15 du chapitre II d'*Ad gentes* comprend deux ajouts sur l'esprit de la collaboration. Joseph Guffens pour sa part se penche sur l'éducation chrétienne appelée à jouer un rôle fondamental dans les

81. L'action de Mgr Carlo Van Melckebeke en faveur des étudiants chinois d'Outre-Mer a déjà été traitée. Cf. la note 4 *supra*.

82. *AS* III/6, pp. 943-944.

83. Intervention le 13 octobre 1965 lors de la 148e congrégation générale. Le texte se trouve dans *AS* IV/4, pp. 302-305.

pays de mission[84]. Enfin Joseph Martin préconise une répartition équitable des moyens humains entre les champs d'apostolat missionnaire. Cela se fera, dit-il, par la création d'un nouvel organisme et par une bonne coordination entre cet organisme et la Propagande, le synode épiscopal pouvant être l'animateur d'une telle coordination[85].

Cinq autres Pères missionnaires belges remettent des remarques écrites. Mgr Cornélis, l'archevêque d'Elisabethville, défend l'idée qu'il faut nécessairement affirmer dans le schéma sur l'activité missionnaire que l'homme ne peut être sauvé sans le Christ et sans l'Église. Dans sa seconde proposition, il présente l'activité missionnaire comme exercée aussi par les autres Églises et communautés chrétiennes séparées de l'Église catholique. On ne peut l'ignorer, écrit-il, et on doit juger cela plutôt positivement car cette ardeur missionnaire prend sa source sous l'impulsion du Saint-Esprit et par conséquent le fruit de l'opération est reconnu par ce dernier[86].

Mgr X. Geeraerts souligne que toute cette théorie, c'est bien beau, mais que le schéma rate l'occasion unique de montrer clairement au nom de toute l'Église que les théories ne demeurent pas stériles et débouchent sur des solutions pratiques[87]. Dans cet ordre d'idées, il soumet trois additions. 1. Une coordination des conférences épiscopales pour proposer des actions communes au niveau d'une région. 2. Une distinction en ce qui concerne la compétence unique de la SCPF entre l'activité missionnaire des Églises particulières, non dirigée par la Propagande, et l'activité de l'Église universelle, pour laquelle elle constitue le seul dicastère compétent. La SCPF ne peut s'immiscer dans les œuvres telles la Mission de France, la Mission de Paris, etc. 3. Création ou coordination d'instituts scientifiques, parce que l'activité missionnaire, en vue d'une nouvelle impulsion, doit être adaptée aux conditions de notre époque et que des instruments pratiques doivent être dégagés pour promouvoir la culture et la vie économique et sociale en suivant les normes de justice, charité et vérité. La nécessité s'impose de prévoir une investigation scientifique des diverses conditions dans lesquelles l'activité missionnaire est dirigée dans chaque territoire socio-culturel. Pour les universités et les facultés ecclésiastiques fondées dans les Jeunes Églises, les autorités épiscopales devront préparer des statuts et un plan des études.

---

84. Intervention le 12 octobre 1965 lors de la 147e congrégation générale. Le texte du *locutus* de Mgr Guffens dans *AS* IV/4, pp. 186-187.

85. Intervention prononcée le même jour que Mgr Guffens. Le texte de son intervention dans *AS* IV/4, pp. 192-194.

86. *AS* IV/4, p. 473.

87. *AS* IV/4, pp. 513-515.

Quant aux instituts supérieurs de missiologie, pastorale, catéchétique et liturgie, ils collaboreront entre eux étroitement pour le profit des missions. Des institutions identiques devront voir le jour dans les Jeunes Églises.

Dans ses *Animadversiones*, Mgr Félix Scalais demande qu'on lève l'équivoque qui subsiste dans l'introduction entre la mission de l'Église au sens générique et la mission au sens spécifique[88]. Les termes 'missionnaires' et 'mission' peuvent avoir ce double sens. Le sens générique signifie l'annonce de l'Évangile à toute créature, soit auprès des gens de son peuple, soit auprès d'étrangers. Ne pas lever cette équivoque fait courir le risque que les vocations missionnaires au sens spécifique ne diminuent progressivement. Les chapitres I et II manquent de dynamisme, écrit l'archevêque, trop peu de choses sont dites de la nécessité de l'Église et du baptême en vue du salut, comme d'ailleurs de l'exigence de la prédication envers les non-chrétiens. De même, on ne fait que timidement allusion à la grande misère spirituelle dans laquelle se trouvent les non-chrétiens. Le seul témoignage de la charité ne suffira pas s'il n'est pas expliqué par la prédication. Rien ne transpire non plus du caractère urgent de cette prédication aux non-chrétiens. Au plan du catéchuménat, Mgr Scalais pense que le texte se montre trop sévère lorsqu'il indique que les non-chrétiens doivent déjà avoir la foi avant de pouvoir être admis au catéchuménat. Une intention objective et droite est bien suffisante et correspond de fait à la pratique des missionnaires.

O. Sevrin, pour sa part, livre de nombreuses et brèves additions ou modifications textuelles, ainsi que des remarques de détail[89]. Par exemple, il suggère qu'on emploie 'instituts religieux' au lieu de congrégations religieuses qui ne tient pas compte des grandes familles missionnaires issues des ordres religieux. D'un point de vue plus large, il demande que soit amplifiée la partie sur le clergé local autochtone qui apparaît trop comme un objet passif alors que les prêtres locaux sont de véritables missionnaires. Il faudrait en surplus une nouvelle définition du missionnaire qui engloberait tous ceux qui consacrent leur vie à l'extension de l'Église chez les peuplades non chrétiennes: les prêtres et les non-prêtres, les autochtones et les étrangers, les frères, les sœurs et les laïcs ... Il termine en s'associant à la proposition lancée *in aula* par V. McCauley (Ouganda) qui demandait qu'il soit fait mention de la Bienheureuse Vierge Marie dans le schéma sur l'activité missionnaire de l'Église, puisque tous les autres schémas y font référence.

---

88. *AS* IV/4, pp. 617-618.
89. *AS* IV/4, pp. 635-641.

Enfin, Carlo Van Melckebeke, afin que la valeur et l'efficacité du travail accompli par la Sacrée Congrégation de la Propagande soient augmentées, demande, à l'instar de bien d'autres Pères conciliaires, que soient appelés à faire partie de ce dicastère des représentants choisis de tous ceux qui collaborent à l'œuvre missionnaire[90]. Ils pourront se réunir périodiquement et pour un temps déterminé. Ces représentants ne prendront pas la place de la SCPF qui demeurera occupée toute l'année aux travaux missionnaires. Il désire que la SCPF attribue prioritairement aux nouveaux groupements missionnaires des champs d'apostolat dans lesquels l'activité missionnaire est urgente et non pas les missions à la mode, comme le Japon, où l'on déploie beaucoup de moyens pour peu de résultats. Pour conclure, C. Van Melckebeke pense que les subsides aux missions devraient provenir d'autres sources que de la seule SCPF et de citer quelques organes représentatifs comme *Misereor* en Allemagne, le *National Catholic Welfare Committee* aux États-Unis ou encore *Caritas Catholica*.

CONCLUSIONS

Premièrement il faut revenir sur l'influence réelle des évêques missionnaires. Selon le Père Xavier Seumois, l'épiscopat d'Afrique a manqué de poids au Concile car la majorité de ses membres étaient insuffisamment pourvus de bases théologiques et leur nombre proportionnellement insuffisant[91]. Mais tous ces évêques étaient bien encadrés à plusieurs niveaux: conférence épiscopale du Congo et du Rwanda-Burundi, Panafricaine au niveau supérieur; et ils étaient de même bien conseillés par des théologiens formés aux idées nouvelles. Cela a eu pour conséquence que ce groupe s'est orienté majoritairement dans la direction de l'ouverture. En ce qui regarde les évêques d'Asie et d'Amérique centrale, on a pu constater un relatif isolement ou un cadre moins stable. Revers de la médaille, nos évêques missionnaires ont produit peu d'initiatives, seules les personnalités les plus fortes émergeant du système. De fait, la majorité de ces évêques ont peu, voire pas du tout, participé activement aux assises conciliaires. Certains d'entre eux furent même très déçus du Concile, ayant eu l'impression de n'avoir pas eu voix au chapitre.

---

90. *AS* IV/4, pp. 659-660.
91. Entretien de X. Seumois avec C. Soetens, 20 avril 1991, 5 pp. mss, dans la farde interviews, *Centre Lumen gentium*, Faculté de théologie, Louvain-la-Neuve.

Deuxièmement, au plan des résultats, ils ont pu exercer une certaine influence sur la rédaction des textes, à tout le moins celui sur l'activité missionnaire de l'Église, mais il est vrai surtout par l'entremise de leurs théologiens[92].

Troisième et dernière remarque, celle-ci porte sur le fonctionnement du groupe des évêques missionnaires belges. D'abord, ce regroupement ainsi opéré pour l'occasion peut sembler artificiel mais à l'occasion, l'un ou l'autre évêque d'Asie pouvait se rattacher aux vues des Africains. En réalité, ce sont surtout les évêques du Congo-Léo et du Rwanda-Burundi qui ont formé une équipe. Toutefois, il faut nuancer, du fait notamment de leur hétérogénéité congréganiste, et admettre que des divergences de vue ont certainement existé, et pas uniquement entre évêques blancs et de couleur. Leur fonctionnement interne diverge assez sensiblement de celui de la *squadra belga*. L'organisation paraît plutôt rigide, ses membres n'ont pas réellement le sens du compromis dans l'élaboration des textes et ils agissent visiblement en tant que groupe de pression. Pour demeurer dans la métaphore sportive, on pourrait peut-être parler d'un *gruppetto*, terme qui désigne en cyclisme un groupe de coureurs obligés de laisser filer les ténors et qui se rassemblent pour monter à leur rythme les cols aux pourcentages les plus élevés.

Rue Les Fonds, 176   Eddy LOUCHEZ
B-5340 Gesves
Belgique

---

92. On sait que la rédaction de la partie pastorale d'*Ad gentes* doit énormément au père blanc Xavier Seumois. Confirmation du rôle joué par la Panafricaine et l'Afrique centrale dans le développement de la question missionnaire au Concile dans OLIVIER, *Chroniques congolaises* (n. 3), p. 273.

AN ATTEMPT TO SYNTHESIZE THE CONFERENCE "THE CONTRIBUTION OF THE BELGIANS TO VATICAN COUNCIL II"

One might legitimately raise the question: How necessary was this conference on the Belgian contribution to the Second Vatican Council? From one point of view, it could be argued that the topic had already been exhaustively researched. The amount of literature already published on this topic is considerable and insightful. I mention by way of example the specific writings of Leo Declerck[1], Claude Soetens[2], Jan Grootaers[3], Albert Prignon[4], and the various colleagues of Giuseppe Alberigo[5]. In addition to these publications, the *Acta* covering Vatican II during its antepreparatory, preparatory, and actual conciliar stages have published the speeches of the general congregations and many of the intersessions' *modi*, although the minutes and texts of the Commissions have not been published. Likewise, an impressive network of well organized archives are open to scholars not only in Leuven and Louvain-la-Neuve[6], but also at the Archivio segreto vaticano (ASV), under the direction of Dr. Piero Doria, at the Institut catholique de Paris, at the Istituto per le Scienze Religiose in Bologna, and at the Erzbischöfliches Archiv

1. L. DECLERCK, *Le rôle joué par les évêques et periti belges au Concile Vatican II*, in *ETL* 76 (2000) 445-464; see also his *De Rol van de Squadra Belga op Vaticanum II*, in *Collationes* 32 (2002) 341-372.

2. C. SOETENS (ed.), *Vatican II et la Belgique*, Louvain-la-Neuve, Quorum, 1996.

3. J. GROOTAERS, *Actes et acteurs à Vatican II*, Leuven, Peeters, 1998, esp. pp. 340-357, 358-381.

4. A. PRIGNON, *Les évêques belges et le concile Vatican II*, in *Deuxième concile de Vatican (1959-1965)*, Rome, École française de Rome, 1989, 297-305. See also his *Évêques et théologiens de Belgique au concile Vatican II*, in SOETENS (ed.), *Vatican II et la Belgique* (n. 2), 141-184.

5. G. ALBERIGO – J.A. KOMONCHAK (eds.), *History of Vatican II*, Maryknoll NY, Orbis; Leuven, Peeters, Vol. I: *Announcing and Preparing Vatican Council II* (1995); Vol. II: *First Period and Intersession, October 1962-September 1963* (1997); Vol. III: *Second Period and Intersession, September 1963-September 1964* (2000); Vol. IV: *Third Period and Intersession, September 1964-September 1965* (2003); Vol. V: *The Council and the Transition. The Fourth Period and the End of the Council, September 1965-December 1965* (2006).

6. See, Leuven, Faculty of Theology, Centrum voor Conciliestudie Vaticanum II, Faculteit Godgeleerdheid, Katholieke Universiteit te Leuven <www.theo.kuleuven.be/en/centr_vatII.htm>; Louvain-la-Neuve, Faculty of Theology, Centre Lumen Gentium, Faculté

in Munich. In the course of my presentation I mention specific bishops and theologians some of whose journals or diaries are reserved in various archival collections, some of which have been described in this conference by Leo Kenis. A number of congresses that aimed to deepen our understanding of the global achievements of Vatican II have been held in various cities such as Bologna, Leuven and Louvain-la-Neuve, Klingenthal, Quebec City, Houston, Würzburg, and Moscow. Although the postconciliar period in Belgium has received less attention, it has been broached in the third section of Soetens's volume, especially in regard to the Council's impact on the laity and clergy, on the "reception" of the liturgical reforms, on married life, and on church structures in general[7]. What, if anything, has this conference of 2005 added that might be considered new?

I. Already Known, Not Yet Understood

It is true that we have indeed made significant progress in the last several decades and during this week, not only in assembling and amassing a considerable body of very specific factual information, but also in the terms of Bernard Lonergan's eight "functional specialties" (especially "communication") we have, to use Lonergan's terminology, moved beyond *oratio obliqua* (what others have been stating) to the more challenging task of *oratio directa*, our direct discourse (what we judge about the causes, the specificities, the responsibilities of communication). What still remains unfinished is greater synthesis and deeper understanding of the causes and effects of the Belgian impact on the Council and beyond. The presentation at this conference by sociologist John Coleman on the interaction of small groups with larger assemblies raises important methodological issues.

Most of the published analyses of the Belgian contributions have focused by design on (a) bishops from Belgian dioceses and (b) official *periti* based in Belgium who assisted the bishops. This concentration generally does not include bishops of Belgian nationality laboring then as missionaries in foreign countries, especially in the Belgian Congo and Rwanda-Burundi, who were an added and sometimes notable presence at the Council; also excluded were bishops from other countries who were

---

de Théologie, Université Catholique de Louvain, Louvain-la-Neuve <www.hecc.ucl.ac.be/Lumengentium/lgpageentree.html>.
    7. See the third section of Soetens (ed.), *Vatican II et la Belgique* (n. 2), pp. 223-310.

trained in Louvain or Malines. The carefully researched presentation at our conference by Eddy Louchez has shed light on the various categories of Belgian advisers. A distinction has been drawn between Belgian *periti* whose academic base was Belgium, and those Belgian theologians, some *periti*, some unofficial helpers, who, because they were residing in Rome at the time, were often referred to as the "Roman Belgians". (I am thinking, for example, of theologians such as Jérôme Hamer, Edouard Dhanis, Damien van den Eynde, Ignace de la Potterie, etc.) or Belgians who may have come to Rome during the Council and who served unofficially behind the scenes, e.g., Albert Dondeyne, Victor Heylen, Jacques Dupont, etc. Categorization is not always easy. For instance, Dom Emmanuel Lanne, a French Benedictine theologian, resides in a Belgian monastery; the Flemish Dominican theologian Edward Schillebeeckx has long resided in the Netherlands. Some Belgian theologians were, surprisingly, *not* invited to participate in the Council but who *a longe* certainly prepared the way to the Council by their published historical or ethical studies theologians. I am thinking for instance of Roger Aubert and Louis Janssens. Vatican II's *Constitution on the Divine Liturgy* would never have been achieved had it not been for the studies, among others, of the Benedictine liturgical theologians of Mont César: Lambert Beauduin, Bernard Capelle, and Bernard Botte. Another group generally neglected in researching the Council includes even earlier Belgian precursors who in the 1940s and 1950s were preparing for a future *aggiornamento*, scholars such as Emile Mersch, Pierre Charles, Georges Dejaifve, and others.

In the city of Louvain, especially during the era while there was one bilingual university campus, the theology faculty, as is well known, maintained a tradition dating back, it appears, to the fallout from the *de auxiliis* controversy, according to which normally academic posts at the University were restricted to diocesan clergy not members of religious congregations (such as the Benedictines, the Dominicans, the Jesuits, the Franciscans, or the White Fathers). But, as is well known, the contributions of individual theologians from these congregations' theologates and monasteries were notable. Dom Lanne has specifically outlined the contributions of Chevetogne, the first monastery devoted specifically by the Benedictines to overcoming estrangement between Eastern and Western Christianity and founded in Belgium in 1925. A second local Benedictine monastery, Mont César (Keizersberg), was instrumental in the Council's liturgical reform, which is described at some length by Professor Lamberigts. The Jesuit theological faculties at Minderbroederstraat (eventually relocated to Heverlee), as well as its francophone counterpart at the Facultés St. Albert de Louvain in nearby Egenhoven, were the source of notable theological research. Fortunately, in later years, this Berlin-wall separation between diocesan professors and religious congregation professors was eventually dismantled, not to mention the notable increase of lay professors. Another source of theological preparedness emanated from journals such as *Nouvelle revue théologique* and *Questions liturgiques*, which had long been published at Louvain but not under the auspices of the University.

Another methodological decision that has affected the study of Vatican II and Belgium is the choice of a *terminus a quo*. Most studies on the topic of Belgian impact on Vatican II, and this conference has not been an exception, have tended to begin with the 1959 antepreparatory period shortly after the announcement by John XXIII of the proposed Council. (Professor Wicks usefully identifies ten distinctive forms of conciliar activities.) But understanding the potential of Vatican II would not have been possible had it not been for the studies of the anti-maximalists at Vatican I, a group thoroughly researched by Roger Aubert. One could also reach back to the 1920s and the initiatives of Cardinal Mercier at the Malines Conversations, the impact of Gustave Thils's *La théologie des réalités terrestres* (1946-1949) and his *Tendances actuelles en théologie morale* (1940), the volume on the laity by Gérard Philips, *Le rôle du laïcat dans l'Église* (1954) which helpfully complements the similar work of Yves Congar, *Jalons pour une théologie du laïcat* (1954). Why is it that the Belgian Catholic academic community had been able to shake off the disciplinary constraints imposed world-wide by Rome in the wake of Modernism, whereas countries such as the United States and the United Kingdom remained largely constrained especially in their seminaries?

II. So Much by So Few

The well-known quip about Vatican II was that it should have been identified as *Concilium Vaticanum secundum, id est Lovaniense primum*. Participants and journalists, drawing upon an athletic metaphor from the world of soccer, wrote about the Belgian team as a *squadra belga*, highlighting the different talents of both the defense and offense. We need to remember that the Council extended only some thirty-nine months, a short time frame extending from October 1962 to December 1965. According to my calculations (based on the listing in the *Acta synodalia*), there were attending the Second Vatican Council sixteen Belgian bishops, including the former and incumbent *rectores magnifici* of the Catholic University of Louvain raised to the episcopate (Honoraat [Maria] Van Waeyenbergh and Albert Descamps). This number includes Joseph Léon Cardijn, who had attended the second and third sessions of the Council and once he had been created a cardinal, thereby attended the fourth session as a bishop. Bishop Calewaert of Ghent died after the second session on December 28, 1963, and was subsequently replaced by Bishop Van Peteghem. Of the 2500 bishops worldwide who attended Vatican II, this very modest Belgian contingent represents less than one percent. Again, according to my calculations based on the listing in the *Acta synodalia*, there were only nine official *periti* drawn specifically for that purpose from Belgium, plus ten Belgian *periti* living in Rome, and four Belgians invited from the Congo and Rwanda. Several other Belgians, without the official designation of "experts", collaborated unofficially with the bishops on an *ad hoc* basis. (I provide a list of the bishops and the assisting theologians in an appendix.) According to Giovanni Caprile's chart, the Belgian bishops spoke sixty-two times in the aula, a figure that includes the seventeen times that Cardinal Suenens spoke[8].

Albert Prignon – rector of the *Collegio belga* from 1962 to 1972, and right-hand man to Cardinal Suenens during the Council, also described as Suenens's liaison officer and his "indefatible shadow" – characterized the Belgian contingent in the following way: "Un petit groupe d'hommes, ayant chacun une personnalité remarquable, se trouva rassemblé dans une étroite communion au service d'une grande tâche qui exigeait de tous et de chacun un dépassement vers le meilleur d'eux-mêmes"[9].

Why were the Belgians so strongly influential despite their small number? This topic has been treated in some detail by Grootaers[10]. He points to the fact that much long-range work had been done years before in Louvain/Leuven and at Malines/Mechelen. The Belgian theologians had been doing their homework in an atmosphere of relative openness. Unlike academic centers in Great Britain, the Netherlands, Canada, and the U.S.A., countries that lacked a lengthy tradition of Catholic universities, Louvain's university dated back to the 15th century. The year 1958, although not without traces of baroque Catholicism, was an upbeat time for Belgium. Expo, the World's Fair in Brussels (1958), had been a huge success. The long authoritarian episcopate of Cardinal Van Roey who had been bishop since 1926 was beginning to wane.

8. Cited in *Ibid.*, p. 164.
9. Prignon, in *Ibid.*, p. 152.
10. GROOTAERS, *Actes et acteurs à Vatican II* (n. 3), pp. 340-357, 358-381.

The Belgian bishops were well trained theologically. As a group they were far better educated than many of their counterparts from other regions of the world. They had accepted the responsibility (which many other national hierarchies neglected) of responding to Cardinal Tardini's formal request for suggestions about the Council's agenda in advance to the antepreparatory commission established on May 17, 1959, by Pope John XXIII[11]. The Belgian proposals were a mixture of doctrinal, disciplinary, and pastoral suggestions. However, it is interesting to note that no submission from Belgium suggested that the Blessed Virgin Mary should be defined as co-redemptrix. Likewise, no Belgian submission touched on issues of social justice or on the relationship between Church and world.

Given their relatively small number, most of the Belgian bishops were able to be lodged in one location at the *Collegio belga* (26, Via del Quirinale, Rome). Among the periti, Philips resided there as did Moeller (in the building's annex). Even the French *peritus* Yves Congar lived at that Collegio for several months while doing redactional work on the decree on the Church. Other Belgian *periti* visited that residence frequently. This tightly knit venue permitted a form of collaboration that would have been difficult for other national hierarchies spread out as they typically were throughout the city of Rome. The French bishops, for example, were scattered in some fifteen different residences. Most of the Belgian bishops knew one another from their seminary days. They spoke at least one common language. The fact that they spent so much time together meant that they acquired what Soetens describes as a "commensalité quotidienne"[12], a bonding based on the fact that they took their meals and recreation together and shared a common life. Prignon, the Rector, recalls that at first there was only one telephone line for the College which rang in his office. The day after the first general congregation of the Council, some 164 phone calls came to the Belgian College. Hence, rapidly, the rector had installed three incoming lines with fifteen extensions for the Collegio. Other informal, paraconciliar settings besides the Belgian College served as a learning and lobbying location for smaller groups of

---

11. M. LAMBERIGTS – C. SOETENS (eds.), *À la veille du Concile Vatican II: Vota et réactions en Europe et dans le catholicisme oriental* (Instrumenta Theologica, 9), Leuven, Bibliotheek van de Faculteit der Godgeleerdheid, 1992, especially the article therein by SOETENS, *Les 'vota' des évêques belges en vue du Concile*, 38-52. See also the article by J. FAMERÉE, *Les évêques belges: Des 'Vota' à la première période de Vatican II*, in É. FOUILLOUX (ed.), *Vatican II commence… Approches francophones* (Instrumenta Theologica, 12), Leuven, Bibliotheek van de Faculteit der Godgeleerdheid, 1993, 146-162.
12. SOETENS (ed.), *Vatican II et la Belgique* (n. 2), p. 97.

bishops and theologians such as the Foyer Unitas and the Centro pro Unione, the North American College, the Hotel Columbus. But the Belgian College was unique. Of course, not all the Belgian activity took place at their College. Some was accomplished back in Belgium during the intersessions.

The close collaboration among the Belgian bishops and theologians should in no way be interpreted as though there was a sort of isolationism among them that resulted in lack of interest in other national hierarchies or theologians. This present conference has illustrated that in part because of the small size of Belgium, its bishops and theologians reached out to other national episcopacies and theologians. The contacts with non-Belgian bishops such as Giovanni Montini, Giacomo Lercaro, Döpfner, Léger, Carlo Colombo, and theologians such as Yves Congar, Pierre Haubtmann, Aimé Georges Martimort, Roger Etchegaray, Piet Smulders, and Giuseppe Dossetti were notable. How these kinds of contacts and nurtured friendships were important in helping the Belgian agendas become acceptable to others has been discussed by Professor Philippe Bordeyne. These contacts and international exchanges were not always untroubled. Sometimes rivalries, dislikes, antipathies marked the exchanges, as Professor Gilles Routhier has shown in the case of Suenens and Paul-Émile Léger. The tensions between Cardinal Alfredo Ottaviani and many committee members are well known.

The Belgian bishops and experts were disciplined theologians and pastoral care givers, committed to their tasks. Discipline was needed since the committee work included much drudgery and boredom and frustration and not simply exhilaration. For instance, in one of his journal entries, *peritus* Philippe Delhaye alludes to the fact that working for the Council was an arduous task (*une épreuve*): "Dieu m'a fait la grâce (qui fut aussi épreuve d'ailleurs) d'assister au Concile et à sa préparation comme consulteur de la Commission Théologique (1960-1962), comme théologien du cardinal Léger (première session), comme *peritus* officiel (de la deuxième à la fin)"[13]. Another participant noted that the Belgian Gérard Philips, despite the burdensome pressures of the Council, displayed by his demeanor what were "trésors de patience et de finesse"[14].

---

13. P. DELHAYE, *Quelques souvenirs du Concile*, in A.-M. CHARUE (ed.), *Au Service de la Parole de Dieu: Mélanges offerts à Monseigneur André-Marie Charue*, Gembloux, Duculot, 1969, 149-177, p. 149.

14. A. PRIGNON, *Évêques et théologiens de Belgique au concile Vatican II*, in SOETENS (ed.), *Vatican II et la Belgique* (n. 2), p. 169.

III. Bishops at Work

During the preparatory period, Bishop Calewaert, Ghent, served on the Liturgy Commission; Bishop De Smedt, Bruges, was a member of the Secretariat for Unity; Cardinal Suenens served on the crucial Commission for Coordinating the Labors of the Council (seven cardinals) and was appointed to the Commission on Bishops and Diocesan Governance, and later to the Central Commission. Bishop Charue was elected vice president of the Doctrinal Commission of Faith (December 2, 1963) on which Philips served as associate secretary. Among the periti, Cerfaux and Philips were on the Theological Commission as well as the "Roman" Belgians Damien Van Den Eynde, OFM and Edouard Dhanis, SJ (rector at the Gregorian University). Onclin served on the Commission for Training of Clergy and Christian People; and Henri Wagnon, the Louvain canonist, on the Commission for the Discipline of the Sacraments.

All of the Belgian residential bishops except one served on at least one of the conciliar committees, some of them on very influential commissions. Although the Belgian bishops did not bring with them any *periti* to the opening of the Council, by the second period they did arrange to have official *periti* at their side. Grootaers notes that no bishop for the first session of the Council was accompanied by a theologian or a canonist. Those Belgians who were there at the first session were papal appointments[15]. Although there were close ties and sense of solidarity among the Belgians, they did not remain isolated. As we have seen in the course of this congress, there were special ties between Belgium and France, francophone Canada, Italy, and, at least for some topics, with the United States.

Especially after the courageous interventions on October 13, 1962, of Achille Liénart and Josef Frings who argued for the need of the bishops to assume more personal responsibility for the development of the Council by devoting time for choosing competent appointments to various committees, several Belgian Council Fathers emerged as especially influential: Suenens, André-Marie Charue, and De Smedt. It was De Smedt who, during the first session, on December 1, 1962, warned the conciliar participants about the danger of the three "-isms" that continued to thrive and imperil the Catholic Church: triumphalism, clericalism, and legalism.

Cardinal Suenens is credited, among many other accomplishments, with having stressed the need for the Council to proceed according to a

---

15. GROOTAERS, *Actes et acteurs* (n. 3), p. 379.

reasoned outline; it was he also who introduced the distinction of the need for the Council to deal with the Church from two viewpoints: *ecclesia ad intra* and *ecclesia ad extra* (December 4, 1962). Suenens is also credited with having argued successfully with the reordering of the chapters in *Lumen gentium* placing the People of God before the chapter on the hierarchy. By the second session of the Council, now under the leadership of a new pope, Suenens's generally cordial relations with Pope Paul VI during the Council enhanced his influence. No less than six presentations at this 2005 conference (Leo Declerck, Guido Treffler, Dirk Claes, Gievanni Turbanti, Gilles Routhier, and Toon Osaer) were devoted to the impact of Suenens on the Council.

The Belgians had been used to healthy discussions at the diocesan level, at least among the priests. They drew upon the monastic foyer to stress the role of conciliarity; they drew upon the university foyer at Louvain, and the faculty of theology.

One factor that is not often alluded to while bestowing laudatory éloges about the Belgians' contributions to Vatican II has been tactfully noted, however, by Grootaers. Despite the preconciliar activities of various lay groups, Grootaers writes:

> Alors que, dans la Belgique des années préconciliaires, le renouveau religieux et ecclésial est réel, il reste cependant souvent limité à une avant-garde peu nombreuse et sans influence profonde sur la masse des fidèles[16].

The same point about the lack of involvement of the faithful, at least among the Flemish, in the preparation for the Council has been argued by the periodical *Kultuurleven* (1961) where the author claimed, "Il existe une muraille de Chine autour des préparatifs"[17].

Still, despite that, Belgium served as a sort of intermediary between renewal efforts in France and the Catholic centers in the Netherlands. Paradoxically, after the Council, the diffusion of renewal seems to have been faster and more widespread in the Netherlands than in Belgium.

Several of the Belgian participants seemed to understand the temperament and quirks of the Vatican officials; several spoke Italian and other languages and were able to act as go-betweens. They had a realistic sense of strategy and a pragmatic temperament. They understood the constraints of committee procedures. Also they had a tradition of working *en équipe*; they possessed a certain humility and asceticism to accept the necessary

16. *Ibid.*, p. 380.
17. Cited by L. GEVERS in SOETENS (ed.), *Vatican II et la Belgique* (n. 2), p. 229, n. 14.

restrictions in order to achieve the goal. The Belgians generally avoided appearing in the public fora (e.g., press conferences). No Belgian was on the Conference of the 22. These characteristics are expressed in the colorful image of Grootaers: "[Les évêques belges] travaillent dans les 'soutes' du paquebot Vatican II et n'ont ni le loisir ni le souci de se promener sur le 'pont'"[18] – which I would translate a bit freely as: "The Belgian bishops worked in the ship's hold, below deck; they had neither the leisure nor the desire to stroll about on the ship's bridge".

IV. ON-SITE THEOLOGIANS AT WORK

My commentary is not the place to enumerate all the impressive contributions of Belgian *periti* or theologians to specific documents emanating from Vatican II. This work has already been done during this conference by many such as Professors Peter De Mey and Joseph Famerée (on Thils), Professors Jared Wicks and Claude Soetens (on Moeller), Karim Schelkens (on Cerfaux), Professor Grootaers (on Philips). At our congress, however, probably because of time constraints, we have not analyzed the contributions of the other *periti*: Philippe Delhaye, Willy Onclin, Albert Prignon, and Henri Wagnon. I hope that some effort will be made in the future to include at least briefly an account of the specific contributions of those men also. It may not be easy to distinguish what emerged directly from Suenens and what came from the inspiration of Prignon, such as the placing of the chapter "Populus Dei" before the chapter on the hierarchy in *Lumen gentium* or the enhanced references to Pneumatology especially the Holy Spirit's ongoing bestowal of charisms in the Church. (See the 53rd general congregation, October 22, 1963, where Suenens spoke of charisms.) I evoke only briefly the four Belgian theologians whom I consider to have had the most notable impact on the Council, though I could be easily convinced that others may have been just as important.

1. Gérard Philips

Not all *periti* accomplished as much as others. I do not consider it inappropriate to recognize four Belgian theologians whose achievements were

---

18. GROOTAERS, *Actes et acteurs* (n. 2), p. 381.

the most memorable and outstanding. I doubt that many would disagree with my judgment that the *facile princeps* of the Belgian *periti* is clearly Gérard Philips. I will not repeat what Dr. Grootaers has written in the past or newly illustrated in his presentation here on the differences between Philips and Dossetti[19]. Philips's role in drafting a lion's share of *Lumen gentium* remains unchallenged[20]. His theology on the laity is reflected in the conciliar affirmations; his contributions to Schema XVII (eventually *Gaudium et spes*) are notable. He worked closely with Charue and was a calm and skilled parliamentarian. It is said that Philips would have been named cardinal by Paul VI, except that if he were to be so named then the other secretary of the doctrinal commission (Sebastian Tromp) would also have to have been so elevated. The Pope instead presented Philips with a golden chalice as a sign of his appreciation.

2. Gustave Thils

Thils stands, in my judgment, as a close second to Philips as the Belgian *peritus par excellence*. In an uncanny way, he anticipated much of the theology of *Gaudium et spes* in his two volumes on *Théologie des réalités terrestres* published almost twenty years before the Council[21]. He had also anticipated some of the much needed emphases on the theology of the episcopate. In Rome he worked along with Charles Boyer and others on the revelation draft especially the sections that touched upon inspiration, inerrancy, and literary composition. He worked with Charue on the fifth chapter of *Lumen gentium* on "The Call to Holiness in the Church". His seminal study on *Histoire doctrinale du mouvement œcuménique* served as an inspiration for *Unitatis redintegratio*.

---

19. J. GROOTAERS, *Le rôle de Mgr G. Philips à Vatican II*, in A. DESCAMPS (ed.), *Ecclesia a Spiritu Sancto edocta (Lumen Gentium, 53). Mélanges théologiques, hommage à Mgr Gérard Philips* (BETL, 27), Gembloux, Duculot, 1970, 343-380.

20. See G. PHILIPS, *Dogmatic Constitution on the Church: History of the Constitution*, in H. VORGRIMLER (ed.), *Commentaries on the Documents of Vatican II*, Vol. I, New York, Herder and Herder, 1967, 105-137; translated from the supplementary volumes of the *Lexikon für Theologie und Kirche* (1966²). See also Philips's astute article written toward the beginning of the Council: G. PHILIPS, *Deux tendances dans la théologie contemporaine*, in *Nouvelle Revue Théologique* 85 (1963) 225-238.

21. G. THILS, *Théologie des réalités terrestres*, 2 vols., Bruges, Desclée de Brouwer, 1946-1949. See also R. AUBERT, *La carrière théologique de Mgr Thils*, in A. HOUSSIAU, et al., *Voies vers l'unité. Colloque organisé à l'occasion de l'éméritat de Mgr. G. Thils* (Cahiers de la Revue théologique de Louvain, 3), Louvain-la-Neuve, Publications de la Faculté de Théologie, 1981, 7-27, with a bibliography of Thils (J.F. GILMONT – T.P. OSBORNE), 67-102. See also G. PASQUALE, *Gustave Thils: Promotor of a Catholic Historia Salutis*, in *ETL* 78 (2000) 161-178.

3. Philippe Delhaye

Regrettably, during this conference, we have not devoted enough attention to the moral theologian Philippe Delhaye, who merits special commendation for his contributions as a *peritus*. For the preparatory commission on ethics, he wrote, as member of a group which included, at a
distance, Louis Janssens, a draft *De ordine morali* stressing the role of
charity in moral theology. This draft was rejected by the Roman consultors influenced by Professor Franz Hürth who argued that, after all, Jesus
spoke of charity only *per transennam*, or, as we would say, *en passant*[22].
Delhaye also worked with Philips on various sections of *De ecclesia*, and
offered reflections on Schema XVII, chapter one, *de admirabili vocatione hominis*. His description on the genesis of *Gaudium et spes* (he
worked on its sub-commission) contains much useful background information[23]. The presentation of Jan Jans at this conference on the Belgian
contribution to the conciliar theology of marriage further elucidates what
was accomplished in this area of sacramental theology.

4. Charles Moeller

The last theologian I would single out for special commendation is
Charles Moeller, *peritus* and document drafter. Professors Soetens and
Wicks have analyzed his contributions to the Council. Wicks shows that
Moeller, during the period between the second and third sessions from
March to April 1964, meticulously analyzed and summarized the Fathers'
suggested emendations to the first draft of *De revelatione*. (Wicks's text
contains an additional value since he also appeals to the parallel work of
both German and Dutch theologians.) Moeller's specific task was largely
focused on the painstaking study of the numerous remarks formulated by
various Council Fathers in reaction to the initial *De revelatione* draft that
had been judged inadequate. His task was applying theological acumen
not to his personal preferences and emphases, but to the concerned objections or clarifications expressed by those in attendance at the Council.
Moeller's importance for Vatican II would have been substantial indeed
if this were his only contribution. But in fact he contributed to numerous
other drafts and proposals.

---

22. ALBERIGO – KOMONCHAK (eds.), *History of Vatican II* (n. 5), Vol. I, pp. 247, 249,
254.
23. P. DELHAYE, *Histoire des textes de la constitution pastorale*, in Y. CONGAR –
M. PEUCHMAURD (eds.), *L'Église dans le monde de ce temps* (Unam sanctam, 65a), Paris,
Cerf, 1967, Vol. I, 227ff.

By scanning only the first three volumes of the Alberigo – Komonchak *History of Vatican II*, one discovers other Moeller texts. He wrote a paper on the role of the Eastern patriarchs, sent by Philips to Tromp who called it "good history, not theological"[24]; he also wrote a draft, heavily dependent on Batiffol, entitled: "De notione patriarchatus Occidentis" in April 1961 (1.294). He also worked with Cardinal Léger on emphases to include in a text on *ecclesia ad extra*. He was part of a team that worked on the laity section for *Lumen gentium* (2.406). He wrote a note for Léger in favor of Philips's revision of the Church text which helped tip the scales in its favor (2.398). He and Philips together worked on sections of what came to be *Gaudium et spes* (2.423) and participated in the Malines discussions on *Gaudium et spes* (2.424).

What is particularly striking about Moeller, in contradistinction to the other three Belgian *periti* just mentioned, is the impressive variety of his contributions to Vatican II. He even worked with Philips and Prignon on collegiality for *Lumen gentium* (3.84 n. 337) and with Congar on how to express Catholic attitudes toward Jews.

V. Some Doctrinal and Pastoral Questions

Before and during the Council, Catholics prayed fervently: "Veni, Sancte Spiritus". This expressed the hope and longing that the Catholic community would not be left as "orphans" but that the Holy Spirit would assist in the deliberations of the synod. But to what extent did the Holy Spirit assist the Council Fathers? How are we to understand the presence and impact of the Holy Spirit at the Council? While not wishing to assign to documents promulgated by the Council the same kind of "inspiration" that Christians associate with Scripture, still it seems consonant with Catholic belief that the community was convinced that what was promulgated did not embody erroneous teaching and was a reflection of God's will. But does that mean that every important teaching relative to the Church in the modern world would be addressed at the Council? Is it not reasonable to judge that the conciliar documents could reflect, at least here and there, certain gaps not addressed because of failure to be open to promptings of the Spirit? Is it not at least theoretically conceivable that what was published is in some way incomplete, or open to possible misinterpretation because of a lack of clarity? Is it not reasonable to expect that some limitation to divine assistance at the Council might

---

24. ALBERIGO – KOMONCHAK (eds.), *History of Vatican II* (n. 5), Vol. I, p. 203.

be occasioned by human failings, indolence, antipathies between persons and nations, or unwarranted interference by persons in powerful positions? In a recent study that I delivered at a conference sponsored at Bose, Italy, by the Cardinal Suenens Center at John Carroll University, I raised a delicate question about whether, in the long run, it might not be possible to see the presence of the Holy Spirit at work amid those 20th century theologians banned by Rome from teaching and publishing, rather than at work in certain pronouncements of official documents that ultimately, with the passage of time, appear to be flawed or potentially harmful[25]. As we unearth more and more personal opinions about attitudes and conflicts at Vatican II, is it not possible that these limiting prejudices will come to be seen as obfuscating or hindering the movements of the Spirit of God attempting to renew the Church through the *sensus fidelium*?

Does this justify our formulating a cadre of teachings that represents "what the Council could have taught" or perhaps even "what the Council should have taught"?

I am convinced of a conclusion that perhaps Roger Aubert would agree with. Just as was the case of Vatican I, some voting bishops at Vatican II did not comprehend the implications of various constitutions or decrees or declarations for which they voted in the affirmative. But does that possibility minimize the significance of what was promulgated? Can a faulty understanding by a Council Father of a conciliar text affect the meaning intended by those who drafted the statement (a meaning that is crystal clear if one studies the Council's *acta* or the responses to submitted *emendationes*)?

What about the postconciliar "reception" of Vatican II by the faithful, specifically the faithful of Belgium? Did the Belgian bishops and theologians pursue their responsibilities *vis-à-vis* conciliar teaching by effectively communicating what the Council taught? Clearly some conciliar teachings have been "received" more wholeheartedly than others whether they be in Belgium or elsewhere. But were the teachings communicated in a language intelligible to the faithful? Was the task of teaching the clergy and laity seen as a critical responsibility of the pastoral and academic magisterium? The third part of the book edited by Soetens, *Vatican II et la Belgique,* devotes five chapters to the postconciliar era, to the

25. M. FAHEY, *The Ecumenical Movement Inspired by the Holy Spirit*, in D. DONNELLY – A. DENAUX – J. FAMERÉE (eds.), *The Holy Spirit, the Church, and Christian Unity, Proceedings of the Consultation held at the Monastery of Bose, Italy (14-20 October 2002)* (BETL, 181), Leuven, Peeters, 2005, 119-136, p. 124.

fruits of the Council. The chapters written by Lieve Gevers, André Haquin, Pierre de Locht, and François Houtart treat the promotion of reception: among the laity especially in Flanders; the Belgian reception of the liturgical reform; shifts in conjugal morality after *Humanae vitae*; and finally, a synthetic study on the national impact of the Council. This is a good beginning, but it is not complete, especially since to a great extent the "people of God" were not included in the preparation or execution of the Council. The chapter by Houtart provides what I consider to be a reasonable explanation for the decline of certain Catholic practices (including Mass attendance) after the Council when he argues: "For a long time, Catholicism had been able to live within a construction maintained artificially by the strength of the institution. The introduction of new values, those that Western societies had experienced and discovered some two centuries ago, caused this solidarity (which in the last analysis had been more apparent than real) to disintegrate. Faced with this situation, what was needed in the Church were other postconciliar orientations that could respond to the new exigencies of evangelization"[26].

Those charged with special pastoral responsibility in the Catholic Church may explain the changes in Catholic life and practice since Vatican II (e.g., disagreements with official teaching, decline in vocations to the priesthood, falling off of Sunday Mass attendance, impatience with official unwillingness to permit eucharistic hospitality) with a rise of relativism or secularism which promotes a "do-it-yourself" form of Christianity. While this may be a partial accounting for the present situation, it is hardly a complete explanation. Other causes for the incomplete realization of the grand vision of Vatican II's *aggiornamento,* nobly and brilliantly sketched forty years ago by bishops and theologians from Belgium and elsewhere, must be identified and corrected.

Boston College   Michael A. FAHEY, SJ
140 Commonwealth Ave
Chestnut Hill MA 02467-3802
U.S.A.

---

26. See the chapter by F. Houtart in the third section of SOETENS (ed.), *Vatican II et la Belgique* (n. 2). Translation is mine.

APPENDIX

Bishops of Belgium in attendance at Vatican II (see listing in *Acta synodalia, Indices*, pp. 801-926).

	diocese	b.	bishop	d.	session
Calewaert, Karel Justinus	Ghent	1893	1948	1963	1,2
Cardijn, Joseph Léon, Card.		1882	1965	1967	4
Charue, André Marie	Namur	1898	1942	1977	1,2,3,4
Daem, Jules Victor	Antwerp	1902	1962	1993	1,2,3,4
De Kesel, Leo-Karel	Ghent (aux)	1903	1960	2001	1,2,3,4
De Keyzer, Maurits Gerard	Bruges (aux)	1906	1962	1994	1,2,3,4
De Smedt, Emiel-Jozef	Bruges	1909	1952	1995	1,2,3,4
Descamps, Albert	rector UCL	1916	1960	1980	1,2,3,4
Heuschen, Jozef-Maria	Liège (aux)	1915	1962	2002	1,2,3,4
Himmer, Charles-Marie	Tournai	1902	1948	1994	1,2,3,4
Musty, Jean Baptiste	Namur (aux)	1912	1957	1992	1,2,3,4
Schoenmaeckers, Paul Constant	Mechelen (aux)	1914	1952	1986	1,2,3,4
Suenens, Leo Jozef	Mechelen	1904	1945	1996	1,2,3,4
Van Peteghem, Leonce Albert	Ghent	1916	1964	2004	3,4
Van Waeyenbergh, Honoraat	ex-rector UCL	1891	1954	1971	1,2,3,4
van Zuylen, Guillaume Marie	Liège	1910	1951	2004	1,2,3,4

VARIOUS BELGIAN THEOLOGIANS WHO INFLUENCED VATICAN II

(Bold names = official Belgian periti;
++ = Belgian periti resident in Rome;
= Belgian periti from Congo/Rwanda-Burundi)

Vat II	Sessions
Aubert, Roger	
Cardijn, Joseph Léon	2, 3
Cerfaux, Lucien	1, 2, 3, 4
++De Clercq, Charles	1, 2, 3,4
Dejaifve, Georges SJ	
de la Potterie, Ignace SJ	
Delhaye, Philippe	2, 3, 4
++Dhanis, Edouard SJ	1, 2, 3, 4
Dockx, Ignace	2, 3, 4
Dondeyne, Albert	
Dupont, Jacques O.S.B.	
Fransen, Piet SJ	
##Goossens, Paul S.I.C.M.	2, 3, 4
++Hamer, Jérôme O.P.	1, 2. 3, 4
Heylen, Victor.	
Houtart, François	
Janssens, Louis	
Massaux, Édouard	
++Michiels, Gommar OFMCap.	1, 2, 3
Moeller, Charles	2, 3, 4
++Morlion, Felix O.P.	3, 4
##Olivier, Bernard O.P.	2, 3, 4
Onclin, Willy	1, 2, 3, 4
++Peeters, Hermes OFM	1, 2, 3, 4
Philips, Gérard	1, 2, 3, 4
++Prignon, Albert	2, 3, 4
++Raes, Alfonse SJ	1, 2, 3, 4
Rigaux, Béda OFM	2, 3, 4
##Seumois, Andreas O.M.I.	2, 3, 4
Thils, Gustave	1, 2, 3, 4
++Van den Broeck, Gommar O. Praem.	1, 2, 3,4
++Van den Eynde, Damien O.F.M	1, 2, 3, 4
##Vermeersch, Leopold P.A.	1, 2, 3, 4
Wagnon, Henri	1, 2, 3, 4

Not all of the *periti* of Belgian nationality were part of the so-called *squadra belga*. In fact, some of them were unsympathetic to the goals of the core group.

INDEX OF NAMES

BIBLIOTHECA EPHEMERIDUM THEOLOGICARUM LOVANIENSIUM

SERIES III

131. C.M. TUCKETT (ed.), *The Scriptures in the Gospels*, 1997. XXIV-721 p.
60 €

132. J. VAN RUITEN & M. VERVENNE (eds.), *Studies in the Book of Isaiah. Festschrift Willem A.M. Beuken*, 1997. XX-540 p.
75 €

133. M. VERVENNE & J. LUST (eds.), *Deuteronomy and Deuteronomic Literature. Festschrift C.H.W. Brekelmans*, 1997. XI-637 p.
75 €

134. G. VAN BELLE (ed.), *Index Generalis ETL / BETL 1982-1997*, 1999. IX-337 p.
40 €

135. G. DE SCHRIJVER, *Liberation Theologies on Shifting Grounds. A Clash of Socio-Economic and Cultural Paradigms*, 1998. XI-453 p.
53 €

136. A. SCHOORS (ed.), *Qohelet in the Context of Wisdom*, 1998. XI-528 p.
60 €

137. W.A. BIENERT & U. KÜHNEWEG (eds.), *Origeniana Septima. Origenes in den Auseinandersetzungen des 4. Jahrhunderts*, 1999. XXV-848 p.
95 €

138. É. GAZIAUX, *L'autonomie en morale: au croisement de la philosophie et de la théologie*, 1998. XVI-760 p.
75 €

139. J. GROOTAERS, *Actes et acteurs à Vatican II*, 1998. XXIV-602 p.
75 €

140. F. NEIRYNCK, J. VERHEYDEN & R. CORSTJENS, *The Gospel of Matthew and the Sayings Source Q: A Cumulative Bibliography 1950-1995*, 1998.
2 vols., VII-1000-420* p.
95 €

141. E. BRITO, *Heidegger et l'hymne du sacré*, 1999. XV-800 p.
90 €

142. J. VERHEYDEN (ed.), *The Unity of Luke-Acts*, 1999. XXV-828 p.
60 €

143. N. CALDUCH-BENAGES & J. VERMEYLEN (eds.), *Treasures of Wisdom. Studies in Ben Sira and the Book of Wisdom. Festschrift M. Gilbert*, 1999.
XXVII-463 p.
75 €

144. J.-M. AUWERS & A. WÉNIN (eds.), *Lectures et relectures de la Bible. Festschrift P.-M. Bogaert*, 1999. XLII-482 p.
75 €

145. C. BEGG, *Josephus' Story of the Later Monarchy (AJ 9,1–10,185)*, 2000. X-650 p.
75 €

146. J.M. ASGEIRSSON, K. DE TROYER & M.W. MEYER (eds.), *From Quest to Q. Festschrift James M. Robinson*, 2000. XLIV-346 p.
60 €

147. T. RÖMER (ed.), *The Future of the Deuteronomistic History*, 2000. XII-265 p.
75 €

148. F.D. VANSINA, *Paul Ricœur: Bibliographie primaire et secondaire - Primary and Secondary Bibliography 1935-2000*, 2000. XXVI-544 p.
75 €

149. G.J. BROOKE & J.D. KAESTLI (eds.), *Narrativity in Biblical and Related Texts*, 2000. XXI-307 p.
75 €

150. F. NEIRYNCK, *Evangelica III: 1992-2000. Collected Essays*, 2001. XVII-666 p.
60 €

151. B. DOYLE, *The Apocalypse of Isaiah Metaphorically Speaking. A Study of the Use, Function and Significance of Metaphors in Isaiah 24-27*, 2000. XII-453 p.   75 €

152. T. MERRIGAN & J. HAERS (eds.), *The Myriad Christ. Plurality and the Quest for Unity in Contemporary Christology*, 2000. XIV-593 p.   75 €

153. M. SIMON, *Le catéchisme de Jean-Paul II. Genèse et évaluation de son commentaire du Symbole des apôtres*, 2000. XVI-688 p.   75 €

154. J. VERMEYLEN, *La loi du plus fort. Histoire de la rédaction des récits davidiques de 1 Samuel 8 à 1 Rois 2*, 2000. XIII-746 p.   80 €

155. A. WÉNIN (ed.), *Studies in the Book of Genesis. Literature, Redaction and History*, 2001. XXX-643 p.   60 €

156. F. LEDEGANG, *Mysterium Ecclesiae. Images of the Church and its Members in Origen*, 2001. XVII-848 p.   84 €

157. J.S. BOSWELL, F.P. MCHUGH & J. VERSTRAETEN (eds.), *Catholic Social Thought: Twilight of Renaissance*, 2000. XXII-307 p.   60 €

158. A. LINDEMANN (ed.), *The Sayings Source Q and the Historical Jesus*, 2001. XXII-776 p.   60 €

159. C. HEMPEL, A. LANGE & H. LICHTENBERGER (eds.), *The Wisdom Texts from Qumran and the Development of Sapiential Thought*, 2002. XII-502 p.
                                                                         80 €

160. L. BOEVE & L. LEIJSSEN (eds.), *Sacramental Presence in a Postmodern Context*, 2001. XVI-382 p.   60 €

161. A. DENAUX (ed.), *New Testament Textual Criticism and Exegesis. Festschrift J. Delobel*, 2002. XVIII-391 p.   60 €

162. U. BUSSE, *Das Johannesevangelium. Bildlichkeit, Diskurs und Ritual. Mit einer Bibliographie über den Zeitraum 1986-1998*, 2002. XIII-572 p.
                                                                         70 €

163. J.-M. AUWERS & H.J. DE JONGE (eds.), *The Biblical Canons*, 2003. LXXXVIII-718 p.   60 €

164. L. PERRONE (ed.), *Origeniana Octava. Origen and the Alexandrian Tradition*, 2003. XXV-X-1406 p.   180 €

165. R. BIERINGER, V. KOPERSKI & B. LATAIRE (eds.), *Resurrection in the New Testament. Festschrift J. Lambrecht*, 2002. XXXI-551 p.   70 €

166. M. LAMBERIGTS & L. KENIS (eds.), *Vatican II and Its Legacy*, 2002. XII-512 p.   65 €

167. P. DIEUDONNÉ, *La Paix clémentine. Défaite et victoire du premier jansénisme français sous le pontificat de Clément IX (1667-1669)*, 2003. XXXIX-302 p.   70 €

168. F. GARCÍA MARTÍNEZ, *Wisdom and Apocalypticism in the Dead Sea Scrolls and in the Biblical Tradition*, 2003. XXXIV-491 p.   60 €

169. D. OGLIARI, *Gratia et Certamen: The Relationship between Grace and Free Will in the Discussion of Augustine with the So-Called Semipelagians*, 2003. LVII-468 p.   75 €

170. G. COOMAN, M. VAN STIPHOUT & B. WAUTERS (eds.), *Zeger-Bernard Van Espen at the Crossroads of Canon Law, History, Theology and Church-State Relations*, 2003. XX-530 p.   80 €

171. B. BOURGINE, *L'herméneutique théologique de Karl Barth. Exégèse et dogmatique dans le quatrième volume de la Kirchliche Dogmatik*, 2003. XXII-548 p.   75 €

172. J. HAERS & P. DE MEY (eds.), *Theology and Conversation: Towards a Relational Theology*, 2003. XIII-923 p.   90 €

173. M.J.J. MENKEN, *Matthew's Bible: The Old Testament Text of the Evangelist*, 2004. XII-336 p.   60 €
174. J.-P. DELVILLE, *L'Europe de l'exégèse au XVIe siècle. Interprétations de la parabole des ouvriers à la vigne (Matthieu 20,1-16)*, 2004. XLII-775 p.   70 €
175. E. BRITO, *J.G. Fichte et la transformation du Christianisme*, 2004. XVI-808 p.   90 €
176. J. SCHLOSSER (ed.), *The Catholic Epistles and the Tradition*, 2004. XXIV-569 p.   60 €
177. R. FAESEN (ed.), *Albert Deblaere, S.J. (1916-1994): Essays on Mystical Literature – Essais sur la littérature mystique – Saggi sulla letteratura mistica*, 2004. XX-473 p.   70 €
178. J. LUST, *Messianism and the Septuagint: Collected Essays*. Edited by K. HAUSPIE, 2004. XIV-247 p.   60 €
179. H. GIESEN, *Jesu Heilsbotschaft und die Kirche. Studien zur Eschatologie und Ekklesiologie bei den Synoptikern und im ersten Petrusbrief*, 2004. XX-578 p.   70 €
180. H. LOMBAERTS & D. POLLEFEYT (eds.), *Hermeneutics and Religious Education*, 2004. XIII-427 p.   70 €
181. D. DONNELLY, A. DENAUX & J. FAMERÉE (eds.), *The Holy Spirit, the Church, and Christian Unity. Proceedings of the Consultation Held at the Monastery of Bose, Italy (14-20 October 2002)*, 2005. XII-417 p.   70 €
182. R. BIERINGER, G. VAN BELLE & J. VERHEYDEN (eds.), *Luke and His Readers. Festschrift A. Denaux*, 2005. XXVIII-470 p.   65 €
183. D.F. PILARIO, *Back to the Rough Grounds of Praxis: Exploring Theological Method with Pierre Bourdieu*, 2005. XXXII-584 p.   80 €
184. G. VAN BELLE, J.G. VAN DER WATT & P. MARITZ (eds.), *Theology and Christology in the Fourth Gospel: Essays by the Members of the SNTS Johannine Writings Seminar*, 2005. XII-561 p.   70 €
185. D. LUCIANI, *Sainteté et pardon*. Vol. 1: *Structure littéraire du Lévitique*. Vol. 2: *Guide technique*, 2005. XIV-VII-656 p.   120 €
186. R.A. DERRENBACKER, JR., *Ancient Compositional Practices and the Synoptic Problem*, 2005. XXVIII-290 p.   80 €
187. P. VAN HECKE (ed.), *Metaphor in the Hebrew Bible*, 2005. X-308 p.   65 €
188. L. BOEVE, Y. DEMAESENEER & S. VAN DEN BOSSCHE (eds.), *Religious Experience and Contemporary Theological Epistemology*, 2005. X-335 p.   50 €
189. J.M. ROBINSON, *The Sayings Gospel Q. Collected Essays*, 2005. XVIII-888 p.   90 €
190. C.W. STRÜDER, *Paulus und die Gesinnung Christi. Identität und Entscheidungsfindung aus der Mitte von 1Kor 1-4*, 2005. LII-522 p.   80 €
191. C. FOCANT & A. WÉNIN (eds.), *Analyse narrative et Bible. Deuxième colloque international du RRENAB, Louvain-la-Neuve, avril 2004*, 2005. XVI-593 p.   75 €
192. F. GARCÍA MARTÍNEZ & M. VERVENNE (eds.), in collaboration with B. DOYLE, *Interpreting Translation: Studies on the LXX and Ezekiel in Honour of Johan Lust*, 2005. XVI-464 p.   70 €
193. F. MIES, *L'espérance de Job*, 2006. XXIV-653 p.   87 €
194. C. FOCANT, *Marc, un évangile étonnant*, 2006. XV-402 p.   60 €
195. M.A. KNIBB (ed.), *The Septuagint and Messianism*, 2006. XXXI-560 p.   60 €

PRINTED ON PERMANENT PAPER • IMPRIME SUR PAPIER PERMANENT • GEDRUKT OP DUURZAAM PAPIER - ISO 9706

N.V. PEETERS S.A., WAROTSTRAAT 50, B-3020 HERENT